Memorial and
Genealogical

RECORD

OF

SOUTHWEST TEXAS

Containing Biographical Histories and Genealogical Records
of Many Leading Men and Prominent Families.

Illustrated.

Book Publishers

Southern Historical Press
Greenville, South Carolina

Please direct all correspondence and orders to:

www.southernhistoricalpress.com
or
SOUTHERN HISTORICAL PRESS, Inc.
PO BOX 1267
Greenville, SC   29601
southernhistoricalpress@gmail.com

Originally published: Chicago, IL   1894
New Material Copyright 1978 by
The Rev. Silas Emmett Lucas, Jr.
ISBN #0-89308-122-1
All rights Reserved.
Printed in the United States of America

PREFACE.

THE publishers, with much pleasure, present this beautiful and interesting volume to their friends and patrons, for whom it is prepared. It will be found full of thrilling personal and historical reminiscences of the days when Texas was gaining her independence and her proud position among the sisterhood of states. The detailed family records will also be found of great present interest and future value. All sketches, after having been typewritten, were submitted by mail to the subject for correction or revision; still, no doubt, a few mistakes will be found which the publishers, as is their custom, stand ready to correct by special errata sheet to be sent to each purchaser, to be pasted in the book. We are satisfied our work will bear the closest scrutiny and sustain our well-known reputation for accuracy and fidelity.

THE PUBLISHERS.

TABLE OF CONTENTS.

HISTORY OF TEXAS.

8

BIOGRAPHY AND MISCELLANY.

16

TABLE OF CONTENTS.

History of Texas.

THE history of Texas, like the State herself, interests the student and political economist, as it does the ordinary reader. Within its boundaries, the first great explorer of the Gulf region, De Soto,* turned from his westward course toward the Mississippi in 1542, and there also, the chivalrous Robert Cavalier de La Salle, a French traveler, laid down his life March 19, 1687, after having explored the Mississippi to its mouth and the Gulf Coast beyond the mouth of the Trinity.

According to the various authorities, there are several derivations of the name Texas: 1, Spanish, tejas (roof-tiles), because the inhabitants had roofed houses; 2, old Spanish or Celtiberian, denoting a plain; 3, an Indian word signifying friend; 4, another Indian word meaning paradise, or a beautiful land; 5, a common termination of several tribal names in Indian, as Tlaxcaltecas, Chlólutecas, Cuitlachtecas, and Zacatecas.

It is located in the extreme southern part of the United States, between the 26th and 36th parallels of north latitude and the 17th and 32nd meridians of longitude. The distance between the extreme northern and southern points is nearly 740 miles, and about 825 miles from east to west. Custom has divided the State geographically into five parts, namely: Central, northern, southern, eastern and western Texas, though the dividing lines are not well defined. The country lying east of the 19th degree of longitude and north of the 30th parallel of latitude, and known as "East Texas," is characterized by a long range of hills running in an irregular line from northeast to southwest, and containing large deposits of brown hematite iron ore. It is also marked by a heavy growth of timber, consisting principally of forests of pine, oak and hickory.

Texas has an area of 271,856 square miles of land, and 2,510 square miles of water surface, the latter consisting of lakes and bays, making a total of 274,366 square miles, equal to about 8.7 per cent. of the entire area of the United States and Territories. It is much the largest State in the Union, being six times larger than New York, seven times as large as Ohio, and 100,000 square miles larger than all the Eastern and Middle States, including Delaware and Maryland.

The Gulf Coast is thus described by Prof. Loughridge, of the United States Census Bureau: "The coast of Texas presents features different from those of any other State, for while in many other States the mainland coast is greatly cut up into large bays, extending many miles inland, it is here bordered by an almost continuous chain of islands and peninsulas (the latter

---

* In Caddo parish, Louisiana, and in the neighborhood of Marshall, Texas, evidences of De Soto's travels have been unearthed, though history does not state positively that the explorer was ever within her present boundaries.

2   17

having the same trend as the islands). The Gulf border of this chain is a very regular line southwest from the mouth of the Sabine River or lake to near Corpus Christi, which occupies the highest point on the entire coast, and thence turns with a regular curve south and slightly southeast to Mexico."

The territory east of the timber region and north of the Gulf, as above outlined, is a vast open plain composed of gently rolling prairies and gradual elevations. It is covered with a luxuriant growth of native grasses and dotted by an occasional mott of timber, and extends to the Red River on the north and the mountain ranges of the west and northwest. The water-courses and ravines are usually fringed with a growth of hackberry, ash, elm, cottonwood, pecan, walnut and the various oaks. West and northwest lie the hills and mountain ranges of the State, which are continuations of the mountains of Mexico, New Mexico and Colorado. In the extreme northwest, bordering Kansas on the south and New Mexico on the west, is the elevated table land formerly known as the Llano Estacado, or Staked Plains. It is now designated as the Panhandle of Texas, and is destined to be one of the best agricultural and stock-raising sections of the State. On a line north of Austin and San Antonio, and running in a southwesterly direction, there is a low range of hills that marks a change in the topography of the country. Westward it is more broken and the elevations more abrupt. The valleys are broad and the lands very fertile.

The water surface of Texas is estimated at 2,510 square miles. Of this number, 800 square miles are accredited to the rivers and smaller streams which drain the State. The balance consists of bays which lie along the coast of the Gulf of Mexico, and small inland lakes. The principal rivers are the Brazos, which drains 35,000 square miles; the Red River, 29,000 square miles in Texas; the Colorado, 25,000 square miles; the Trinity, 17,000; the Neuces, 16,000; the San Antonio, the Guadalupe, the Rio Grande, the Pecos, the Neches, the Sulphur Fork, the Sabine, San Marcos, Canadian, and Caney, with their feeders.

The figures below denote the elevation above sea level, in feet, of points named:

Galveston 40, Indianola 26, Brownsville 43, Palestine 495, Corsicana 448, Denison 767, Austin 513, San Antonio 676, Fort Ewell 200, Fort Chadbourne 2,120, Jacksboro 1,133, Henrietta 915, Fort Concho 1,888, Fort Stockton 3,050, El Paso 3,370, Fort Davis 4,918, Eagle Pass 800, Fort Elliott 2,500, Silver Falls 3,800, Midland 2,779.

The elevation of the land above the water dates to the middle of the cretaceous time, and is contemporary with the movements that created the Rocky Mountains. The strata, excepting the paleozoic groups, yield easily to disintegration. Eruptive masses are found in the trans-Pecos country and granitic masses in the Central and trans-Pecos paleozoic deposits.

The mineral resources of the State received very little attention until recent years. Silver and lead ores exist in the trans-Pecos region. In Llano and Mason counties silver and gold quartz were mined; copper ores exist in the drift of the gypsum country, and iron in the tertiary formations of Eastern Texas. Wood for fuel abounds in Eastern Texas, but becomes scarcer toward the west, until the mesquite root or Mexican dagger are welcome to the fire-builders. A lignite bed exists from the Sabine River, in Sabine County, west to the Red River, being found in fifty-four counties.

Coke and gas are produced from this deposit. The bituminous coal fields are known as the Brazos or Northern, and the Colorado or Southern. The linear extent of the outcrops of seams No. 1 and No. 7 is 250 miles, and the area 2,500 square miles. Asphaltum is found in Hardin and Liberty counties, as well as throughout the tertiary and cretaceous formations; tar springs are numerous, while oil is found in the Nacogdoches district, associated with natural gas. A phosphate of lime, called apatate, bat guano, gypsum, greensand marl and calcareous marls are counted among the natural fertilizers found throughout the State. Fictile materials, such as glass and porcelain sands, pottery clays, and kaolin are abundant, while granite, porphyry, marble, limestone, sandstone, slate, lithographic stone and cement materials may be quarried in the State. From the Louisiana line, 150 miles southwest, iron ore is found, of various values. The laminated ores are dark brown, ranging to black; the nodular, or geode ores, range from buff to brown in color, and the conglomerate, found in the sand, of a sandy color. Hematite ironstone, hematite and magnetite, abound near the Wolf crossing of the Colorado River; between the Packsaddle and Riley mountains, and in the Iron Mountain belt. Copper ores are found in Hardeman, Archer, Haskell, Throckmorton and other counties in that section of the State. Lead and zinc ores are found in the Riley Mountains, Burnett and adjoining counties. Gold has been panned in the Colorado River, while the quartz of the Quitman Mountains contain the yellow metal. In Presidio County silver ore has been profitably worked. In Burnett and Mason counties tin ore has been mined, as well as mercury, manganese and bismuth. Precious stones, such as the garnet, chalcedony, carnelian, amethyst and agate, as well as the pearls of the Llano, Concha and Colorado rivers show Texas to be rich in these valuable little things. Salt, sulphur, graphite, ochers, alkalies, niter, alum, epsomite and strontia are found in abundance, so that, were the mineral deposits developed, Texas would not only be independent of the outside world for their supply, but might also supply that outside world.

The recorded history of the Caucasian in Texas may be said to begin in 1580, when Catholic missionaries from Mexico City established churches at El Paso and Santa Fé, and ventured eastward toward the Mississippi, preaching to the various Indian tribes and founding missions among them. The early Spanish (Catholic) missions, within the present boundaries of Texas, were established by Franciscan monks, under the auspices of the Spanish government, and were called presidios. They consisted of a chapel for worship, the cells for the monks, the dwellings for the inhabitants, and a fort for defense. The mission was, of course, under the control of the ecclesiastical power, and the military force was under an officer of the army, who, in most matters, was under the control of the priest. A list of the principal missions is as follows: In 1690 the mission of San Francisco was established on the Lavaca River, at Fort St. Louis, by the Spanish fathers, under Captain Alonzo de Leon. In the same year the mission of San Juan Bautista was founded on the Rio Grande River. In 1714 the priests, accompanying Captain Ramon, established the mission of San Bernard, also the mission of Adayes, among the Indians of that name, fifteen miles west of Natchitoches. In 1715 was established the mission of Dolores, west of the Sabine, among the Orquisaco Indians. In the same year, one among the Nacogdoches Indians, near the site of the present town of that name; also another among the Aes

Indians, near the site of the present town of San Augustine. The mission and fortress of San Antonio de Valero was soon after this established on the San Pedro River, near the site of the present city of San Antonio. In 1721 a post and mission were established at the crossing of the Neches, and another on the bay of San Bernard, called Our Lady of the Loretto. In the same year the mission of La Bahia (the bay) was established at the lower crossing of the San Antonio River. In 1730 the church of San Fernando, in the present city of San Antonio, was founded. In 1731 was established, not far from the same place, the mission La Purisima Concepcion de Acuna. All the buildings are yet standing.

Under the old Mexican regime Texas was a province controlled by a "commandant," who resided at Chihuahua, and whose powers in this control were independent of the viceroy. Each province was ruled by a military and political governor, who, by his delegated powers, had cognizance of all causes, being dependent as regards military matters upon the commandant-general. In financial affairs he was subject to the intendant at San Luis Potosi, with recourse to the supreme council of finance at the City of Mexico.

The colonization of Texas by the French was commenced on New Year's Day, 1685, when the merchantmen and frigates of De Beaujeau's fleet anchored near the entrance to Matagorda Bay, Lavaca, and disembarked stores and colonists. Subsequently De Beaujeau acted independently of La Salle and sailed for home on the King's frigate, leaving a ship at the disposal of the colonists to escape from such a dreary land. On that ship La Salle set out for the mouth of the Mississippi, so that he could proceed northward to Fort St. Louis, where Lieutenant Tonti was in command, procure provisions for the colonists and give them hope until the soil would yield its fruits. The vessel was wrecked in the Gulf, but the explorer, escaping, returned to Matagorda to apprise his friends of the wreck and to prepare for an overland expedition to Fort St. Louis. In March, 1687, he with Père Anastace and nineteen men set out on the long journey; but on the 19th of the month, a mutiny took place in which La Salle's nephew, a few of his trusted lieutenants and himself were killed. Shortly after, Spanish troops captured the survivors of the mutiny and the colonists, condemned all the guilty parties to the mines, sent the priests to France, adopted the colonists and summarily closed French designs on Texas until 1817, when St. Denis the commander of Natchitoches in Louisiana attempted to reintroduce French tr..ders beyond the Sabine.

When the purchase of Louisiana was proclaimed in 1803, adventurers and fugitives from justice flocked into Texas, believing that any crimes or conspiracies, against the residents of that part of Mexico, which they might commit, would escape punishment. The great majority of them were unprincipled desperadoes, like Nolan or his Mexican associates—men who would at all times rather rob than earn a livelihood honestly. When Mexico cast off the Spanish viceroys, English-speaking colonists came to cultivate the rich lands. The principal Anglo-Saxon settlements at the beginning of the present century were San Antonio de Bejar, with about 2,000 inhabitants; La Bahia del Espiritu Santo, now Goliad, about 1,400; and Nacogdoches, with 500.

Nacogdoches was first settled by Anglo-Americans in 1822-23, when many of the emigrants who left the United States with the view of joining Austin's colony stopped at this place. The little trade carried on was effected with Mexico, by way of Monterey and Monclova, and with New Orleans through

Natchitoches; the latter, however, was contraband. In 1806 Texas was allowed a port, namely, at Bahia de San Bernardo. The exchange for merchandise consisted in specie, horses and mules.

After the fall of Napoleon, two refugees from France, Generals Lallemand and Rigault, concluded to try Texas as a place of residence, although they received no reply to their request for a permission to do so from the Spanish court. In March, 1818, Lallemand, with 120 settlers, sailed from New Orleans, landed at Galveston Bay and selected a spot on the Trinity River about twelve miles above its mouth, and began to fortify the post. These colonists issued a proclamation that they had settled there to remain, earning their livelihood by the peaceable pursuits of agriculture and the chase, and would defend their settlement, but, after the drought of 1818 and the destruction of the crops, several families left the place, and the Mexicans showed the remaining few that the laws of the territory had to be observed and taxes paid to regularly constituted officers.

The treaty of amity of February 22, 1819, having confirmed her in the possession of Texas, Spain felt herself in a position to remove the exclusion of Anglo-Americans as colonists in her territory, which hitherto had been insisted on in all colonization schemes. Moses Austin saw in this too liberal policy an opportunity to enrich himself. He was a native of Durham, Conn., but in 1797 resided in Missouri, whence he moved to Northern Louisiana in 1799. His son, Stephen Fuller Austin, of New Orleans, received a grant of land on the Brazos from the Mexican authorities, the condition being the settlement thereon of 300 families, who were to receive 640 acres for the father, 320 for the mother, and 100 acres for each child. The price, 12½ cents an acre, to be paid in installments, was levied to pay expenses of transfer and review.

The first immigrants of the Austin colony arrived in December, 1821, settling on the Brazos River at the Bahia crossing, mainly in what is now Austin County; but many difficulties and hardships were encountered. Shipments of supplies from New Orleans failed to reach them, and they had to subsist too much on the products of the chase; and this was dangerous on account of the hostile Indians. During the spring of 1822 Austin went to San Antonio to report progress, and there learned for the first time that under the change in political affairs he would have to obtain from the Mexican congress a confirmation of the grant conceded to his father by the Spanish government, and receive special instructions relative to the distribution of land and other details connected with the grant. This was a sore disappointment. He would have to travel 1,200 miles by land on roads infested by banditti and deserters, and he was ill prepared for such a journey. Nevertheless, in ragged clothes and a blanket, he disguised himself as a poor traveler going to Mexico to petition for compensation for services in the revolution, and unflinchingly started out on the long and perilous journey.

While on his way to the City of Mexico, with but two persons in company, arriving at San Antonio, he (Austin) was told that it was dangerous to proceed without an escort, for a war party of Comanches was abroad. The savages did intercept him and robbed him, but on representations to the chief, his property was restored and permit given to proceed. On April 19, 1822, Austin arrived in Mexico City, but, owing to the delays of the administration, was kept there for about three months. Returning to the Brazos, he found only a few of his colonists there, yet by 1824 he had the 300 families well established and the colony in a prosperous condition. Himself being administrator of civil and military affairs, he ruled like a feudal lord—kind to his friends, hostile to his enemies. Although Austin was exact in his administration of justice and extravagantly benevolent to the needy, there were many in the colony disposed to complain and make trouble. In the United States and Europe the impression began to prevail that Austin's early colonists were in great part fugitives from justice; but he maintained, with every show of fact and reason, that his colony was as moral as any community in the States.

The limits of the county were undefined by the law, and the immigrants were allowed to settle at various distances from the center according to their own free will. In response to Austin's petition, the government allowed him to introduce 500 more families to locate upon the unoccupied lands lying between the tracts already occupied by his colonists. Straggling settlements were made between the Brazos and the Sabine, but not until 1833 was there an appreciable influx of these spirits, who will obtain money or property justly or otherwise.

Two causes seem to have operated to prevent the earlier settlement of the province of Texas and to retard the development of its resources. In the first place the jealous policy of the old Spanish government uniformly discouraged all attempts to penetrate into the country. It was the policy of the government that completely locked up Texas and all the Spanish-American possessions, and excluded even visitors and travelers. It was a favorite saying of the Spanish Captain-general of the internal provinces, Don Nemisio Salcedo, that he would stop the birds from flying over the boundary line between Texas and the United States if it were in his power! This rigid policy prevented any one from attempting to explore the country by land, for perpetual imprisonment was the inevitable result of detection and capture. In the second place, the Carancahua Indians, who inhabited the coast, were represented to be of a character uncommonly ferocious. They were popularly believed to be cannibals; and many tales of most frightful import were told of them—such as, if true, it must be acknowledged, were sufficiently appalling to check the enterprise and damp the ardor of the most eager adventurer. These representations of the character of the Carancahuas, though in a measure true, were greatly exaggerated.

Prior to 1833, fully 20,000 English speaking persons inhabited Texas between the Sabine and Colorado rivers. Though the heads of families had conformed to the articles of citizenship, there is scarcely an instance where the oath was observed in any particular, for every adventurer who preached sedition in secret was safe in the homes of the very people to whom the Mexican Republic gave fertile lands and many rare privileges. The pages devoted to military and political affairs speak very plainly of the relations of the new inhabitants to Mexico, of their wars and of their repeated efforts to establish an independent republic. The last decade brought many advantages to the State. Great numbers of industrious Northern agriculturists settled there; villages were transformed into beautiful cities; railroad lines were constructed in all directions, and Texas became truly a State in population and wealth, as it was in name, organization and area.

From 1801 to 1864, the story of military affairs in this extreme south-western State of the Union is one of romance, full of startling realities and altogether interesting in their number, personnel, desperation, machiavelianism and disregard for human life on the part of ruler and rebel. It was a territory indeed where, when treason succeeded, no one dared to call it treason, until a superior power rose above the ruin of its predecessor. Life was a bagatelle, given to the adventurers to be frittered away in petty insurrections and piracies, or, when opportunities in these directions failed, in attacks upon the Kiowa or Comanche. Beginning with Nolan, in 1801, and ending with Palo Alto, May 13, 1864, the story of Texas in its military bearing is one where gallantry, deviltry, heroism, patriotism and machiavelianism are so mixed that no one can tell where the one begins and the other ends.

Philip Nolan, whose name is associated with the first English speaking adventurers in Texas, was raised in the wild atmosphere of Natchez, by a resident of that town. He it was who made the first map of Texas other than the charts of Spanish and French travelers. He was versed in astronomy, was a student of geography, a surveyor, soldier, horse dealer and stealer and as unprincipled as Aaron Burr, who fashioned his public life after that of Nolan. In July, 1797, he procured a passport to visit Texas for the purpose of buying horses. To do so he swore falsely. At the close of that month he had 1,297 head of horses in the Trinity River pastures, which he drove to Natchez during the fall. In 1800 his plans for the conquest of Texas were matured, and early in 1801 put in practice. On March 21, 1801, Lieutenant Muzquiz, with sixty-eight Spanish regulars and thirty-two volunteers, attacked the entrenched camp of Nolan's army. At nine o'clock Nolan was killed, and his fourteen American, one Creole and seven Mexican followers, with two slaves, made prisoners. Three of them were wounded, one died, one—Ephraim Blackburn—was hanged at Chihuahua, November 11, 1807, and the others were sent to the mines, where all died save Ellis Bean, who returned to Mississippi.

The Louisiana boundary troubles next engaged the attention of the Texan authorities, but the question was settled amicably by making the Sabine River the Western line of United States territory.

The attempt of Aaron Burr to conquer not only Texas but also Mexico, and proclaim himself emperor and successor to the Montezumas, irritated the Mexican authorities. The plans of Burr were so patent that the United States troops had to break up his flotilla and order the arrest of the disturber.

The insurrection of Hidalgo, followed in 1810. This was intensified in January, 1811, when Juan Bautista Casas, captured the governor and officials of Texas. On March 1, following, Zambrano and a *posse* captured Casas and his officers, and restored the vice-regal authority. In 1812, Bernardo Gutierrez de Lara, and Augustus Magee, of Natchitoches, organized the outlaws of Mississippi and the border, and with 800 of those desperadoes entered Texas. On April 1, 1813, Magee's force captured San Antonio, the seat of government, had a council of thirteen members elected, and appointed Gutierrez, governor. The new rulers reveled in blood for a few weeks, butchering their opponents in a wholesale manner, and this continued on a smaller scale until 1814, when the Spaniards restored law and order.

In 1815, shortly after the defeat of the British at New Orleans, an adventurer named Perry really advertised his intention to invade Texas, and, with the connivance of Jose Manuel de Herrera, did establish a State government in 1816, making Matagorda the capital. This adventure ended with the suicide of Perry and the execution of many of his followers; though Commodore Aury continued his piratical doings in the Gulf of Mexico for some time after. Among the troops of Perry, and the marines of Aury, were almost 1,000 of Lafitte's pirates. Indeed, Lafitte, himself, built a residence at Campeachy, near Galveston, where he resided until his second pirate colony was broken up by the United States officers on Mexican territory.

In March, 1818, the Lallemand colonists, 120 in all, came from New Orleans to a point twelve miles above the mouth of the Trinity, and proclaimed their intention of protecting themselves against all comers, while attending to their own affairs. Failure of the first season's crops left the colony in a feeble condition, and the Mexican authorities had little trouble in establishing their authority over it.

The treaty of February 22, 1819, negotiated by the Spanish Minister at Washington, defined the present eastern boundary of Texas; but the Spanish king failed to ratify it, and other disagreements resulted; but on February 28, 1821, the treaty was accepted by the contracting parties. Natchez was then a hotbed of antipathy to French and Spanish authority in North America, as it was from the time that Ellicott and his followers appeared first on the bluff.

In June, 1819 or 1820, James Long and seventy-five men set out for Nacogdoches, Texas, where the old rebel Gutierrez and one Samuel Davenport joined him. Long organized a supreme council, appointed himself President, and on June 23, these self appointed statesmen proclaimed Texas a free and independent Republic.

Long sought the aid of Lafitte at Galveston, but the arch pirate told him it was useless to oppose Mexico without an overwhelming force. *En route* to Lafitte's home, President Long learned that 700 Mexicans, under Colonel Perez, were advancing to destroy his citadel; and sent a dispatch to Cook, his military agent, to drive them back while he himself waited developments at a safe distance. His dupes were killed or captured, while President Long retired to New Orleans. There he met two foolhardy Mexicans—Milam and Trespalacios, and with them organized another expedition early in 1821; entered Texas, were driven off and returned to Orleans to squander their lives away in debauchery. Long was killed there in 1822, and the other leaders died unknown. The doings of Long created tribulations for the legitimate English and French speaking colonists of Eastern Mexico, and brought ruin to the greater number who could in any way be connected with their revolutionary propaganda.

The final revolution may be said to have been born in October, 1825, when Hayden Edwards, returned to Texas to fill his contract with the Texan Governor. It appears that he received a grant of lands, surrounding Nacogdoches, provided he would settle thereon 800 families; but on the date stated found many claimants on such lands and a population unfriendly to his personality and his claims. The election of an alcalde in December, led to the rejection of Chaplin, the son-in-law of Edwards, and to a number of petty acts contrary to the spirit of justice. The annulment of the grant was based on right, as Edwards did not fulfill his part of the contract; so that its subsequent division between David G. Burnett and Joseph Vehlein, was considered equitable, and the action of the new grantees won many immigrants or settlers.

Dewitt, although his first settlers were temporarily driven off by Indians, had laid out the town of Gonzalez in 1825, naming it after Rafael Gonzalez, a temporary governor of the State, and during 1827–'28 he succeeded in introducing considerable numbers of colonists. In De Leon's grant the town of Victoria was founded, and La Bahia del Espiritu Santo had developed into a town of such appreciable dimensions that in 1829 it was raised to the rank of a villa, and the high sounding title of Goliad given to it. Filisola, in an endeavor to wrench an anagram out of Hidalgo's name, spelled the name Golhiad. On the Brazos a flourishing settlement called Brazoria had also sprung up. However, the experience which the Mexican government had with the Fredonians (Edwards' colonists) caused them to be more watchful of the movements of American immigrants. Under the liberal and non-aggressive policy of Guerrero the colonists were left pretty much to themselves, and he even aided them in the abolition of slavery. But when he was overthrown, in December, 1829, and Bustamante seized the helm of government, the sleeping tiger of Mexican suspicion and belligerency arose and showed its teeth.

Lucas Alaman, the Minister of Relations, memorialized Congress, Feb. 8, 1830, showing the carelessness of the State of Coahuila and Texas in carrying out the colonization laws;—that the orders providing that no more than the number of families designated in a contract should settle on the corresponding grant, and that colonies near the boundary line should be composed of settlers, not natives of the United States, had been without effect; and he expatiated on the fact that a large number of intruders had taken possession of lands, especially near the frontier, without any pretension of satisfying the formalities of the colonization laws. To preserve Texas to Mexico, he insisted that the Mexican population in Texas should be increased by making that country a penal settlement, the criminals transported thither to be employed in the cultivation of the soil; that foreign colonists differing from American interests, habits and language should be introduced; that a coasting trade be established between Texas and other parts of the republic, which would tend to nationalize the department; that the colonization law of August, 1824, be suspended as far as concerns Texas, and the settlement of that department be placed under the direction of the general government; and that a commissioner be appointed to examine and report upon the condition of affairs in the Texas colonies, etc. The Congress passed an Act in accordance with the memorial and the exemption from taxes promised hitherto to settlers from the United States was annulled. Also, along with the execution of this odious law the government sent a large military force into Texas, under the command of Manuel Mier y Teran, commandant-general of the eastern provinces, and he was also authorized to establish inland and maritime custom-houses. A military despotism was naturally inaugurated at an early period. The only colonies recognized were those of Austin, Dewitt and Martin de Leon; all other concessions were suspended until their contracts could be examined and their fulfillment verified. Titles were denied to a great number of settlers already domiciled, and new immigrants from the United States were ordered to quit the country immediately upon their arrival. Several large military posts were established, manned by convicts and other bad characters. A series of outrages was directly begun. Military jurisdiction was substituted for that of the local authorities in many places; settlers were dispossessed of their lands and property, many of them were imprisoned, and no redress could be obtained for thefts and robberies committed by the troops.

During the year 1831 the local authorities and also the frequently changing administration were at odds with each other, one party almost constantly colliding with another, and these in so rapid succession that the true interests of the masses were lost sight of. Outrages increased as the military officers were angered by resistance or lack of respect, until even the settlers in the Austin colony began to rise in arms. A spirit of rebellion began to spread like a prairie fire before a wind. One John Austin, not a relative of Stephen F., was an alcalde at Brazoria and a brave and influential citizen. On June 10, 1832, he joined the insurgents, and with about a hundred men demanded the release of certain prisoners at Anahuac, was refused, and some shots were fired. Bradburn, the Mexican officer, agreed to release the men if Austin with his force would retire six miles away. Austin did this, but Bradburn broke faith, opened fire upon the insurgents remaining in Anahuac and drove them from the place. In January, this year (1832), Santa Anna at Vera Cruz pronounced against the government of Bustamante, and the usual war followed, a la Mexican. The colonists, being enraged by the latter's administration, a number of them met at Turtle Bayou, drew up a list of their grievances, June 13, and passed resolutions adopting Santa Anna's plan and pledged their support to the constitution and the leaders who were then fighting in defense of civil liberty.

The first skirmish, June 13, 1832, resulted in the insurgents taking the fort at Velasco from the brave Ugartechea. Meanwhile, John Austin's men around Anahuac successfully cut off supplies and communication. Piedras, commanding at Nacogdoches, hastened hitherward to aid the Mexicans, but before arriving fell into the hands of the insurgents, and was converted to their cause. By his assistance, Travis and other prisoners, were released. Piedras appointed another man to succeed Bradburn at Anahuac, and started back to Nacogdoches; but as soon as he turned his back, the garrison at Anahuac mutinied in favor of Santa Anna. Bradburn was persuaded by some of the officers to re-assume command, but he immediately found so many of the men committed to Santa Anna that he quit in disgust and went to New Orleans.

In the Southern United States the opinion began to prevail that the colonists in Texas were attempting to separate from Mexico and annex themselves to the Union. On this account, Montezuma, commanding at Tampico, and having declared in favor of Santa Anna, sent a force into Texas to reduce the insurgents. His colonel, Mejia, on entering Texas, first had an amicable conference with the leader of the Bustamante party, so as to prevent interruption, and proceeded to the mouth of the Brazos, taking with him Stephen F. Austin, who was on his return from the State Legislature. Consulting John Austin, the latter professed perfect loyalty and said that the insurgents had no intention to separate from Mexico; they were only rebelling against certain tyrannical acts of some of the officers. Mejia went on to Galveston, where he was similarly received, and he returned to Tampico. He actually advocated the cause of the insurgents, and the seed he had sown in Texas, in so doing, bore rapidly. Piedras, at Nacogdoches, being opposed to Santa Anna, was ousted by the Mexicans. By the end of August not a Mexican soldier remained in the Texan colonies, the victory over the Bradburn party was so complete. A troop of about seventy men were stationed at San Antonio, scarcely a sufficient number to keep the Indians in check in that vicinity. Peace was restored. This victory of the Texan colonists would have been far more costly, if not indeed impossible of attainment, had there been no revolution going on beyond the Rio Grande.

The separation of Texas from Coahuila forms an important event in the history of the State. In October, 1832, a convention of delegates from different municipalities was held at San Felipe, and some discussion took place concerning the formation of a State constitution; but as sufficient notice had not been given, and the attendance was slim, the convention adjourned without taking action. Their discussion, however, brought the matter seriously before the public, and when the second convention assembled, April 1, 1833, it was prepared to accomplish the work assigned to it. At this convention were Stephen F. Austin, Branch T. Archer, David G. Burnett, Sam Houston, J. B. Miller and William H. Wharton, the last mentioned being the president of that body. A committee was appointed to draft a form of State constitution, and another committee was appointed to draw up a memorial petitioning the general government to grant a separation of Texas from Coahuila. Sam Houston was appointed chairman of the first, and David G. Burnett of the second. The constitution drafted was thoroughly republican in form, modeled on that of the United States. After much discussion it was concluded that banking should not be provided for by that constitution, and that the document should maintain absolute silence with reference to religious liberty, such was the blighting power of Catholic influence. The commissioners appointed to convey the petition for separation to the City of Mexico were Stephen F. Austin, William H. Wharton and J. B. Miller; but Austin was the only member who actually went there, and on arriving he found that city the scene of virulent party faction and political confusion. Affairs in Mexico had been undergoing the customary vicissitudes and revulsions. No more stability of principle was observable in Santa Anna than in Bustamante. Both used the constitution of 1824 to push themselves into power, and then both cast it to the winds. By the end of 1832, these two generals, after much bloodshed, came to terms, and agreed to unite in support of the said constitution.

On March 30, 1833, Santa Anna was declared duly elected president of the Republic of Mexico, and Gomez Farias, vice president; and from this time on Santa Anna's course was remarkable for subtle intrigue for selfish purposes. He never appeared, however, as the principal actor, but always used other parties as cat's-paws for his own advancement. Dictatorial power was his highest ambition. Farias was the known champion of reform, and Santa Anna absented himself from the capital to intrigue with bishops and religious orders, leaving his colleague at the seat of power to inaugurate his new measures, which he (Santa Anna) knew would foment discord and redound to the discomfiture of the instigator and ultimately to his own advancement. Three weeks later Santa Anna resigned the presidency to lead the army against the rebels of Halpani, while Austin, not understanding the delay in carrying out promises, repaired to Mexico City in October. Austin, seeing the prospective delay, wrote to the city council of San Antonio, recommending that it obtain the concurrence of all other corporations in Texas in a scheme for separation from Coahuila, with the hope that, under the provision of the general law of May 7, 1824, a local government could be successfully organized, even though the general government should refuse its consent.

The result of Austin's visit, after the war had been closed, was a respectful and honest effort to improve the legal facilities of the Texans, but it was believed by the convention assembled for the purpose that the time had not yet arrived for the erection of Texas into an independent State. But Austin, on his return trip to San Antonio, was arrested at Saltillo, by order of Farias, on account of the letter he had written to the San Antonio council, and on account of the hasty language used at the interview at the same time. He was sent back to Mexico, and was in prison eight months, awaiting trial, with no opportunity, much of this time, of communicating with the outside world. He was not finally liberated until the expiration of nineteen months. Much has been said *pro et contra* by Austin's friends and enemies concerning his actions at this period; but the Texans generally believe him to have been sincere and competent, and probably as judicious as any other man they could have commissioned for that errand. Santa Anna seemed to be a friend of Austin and the Texans, but those knowing his character entertained doubts as to his sincerity. The legislature of January, 1834, passed various measures beneficial to Texas. The municipalities of Matagorda and San Augustin were created; Texas was divided into three departments, the new one of Brazos, with San Felipe as its capital, being organized; the English language was permitted to be used in public affairs, and an additional representative at the State congress allowed; the privilege of purchasing vacant lands was granted to foreigners; laws were passed for the protection of the persons and property of all settlers whatever might be their religion, and freedom from molestation for political and religious opinions was guaranteed provided public tranquillity was not disturbed; a supreme court for Texas provided for, and a system of trial by jury.

In 1834, Santa Anna's Centralist party won everywhere, save in Texas, Coahuila and Zacatecas. Hence these States must be punished. Zacatecas was scandalously plundered. Santa Anna, in the meantime, was preparing, under cover of collecting revenue in Texas, for the military occupation of the province. He landed 500 men at Lavaca Bay, and forwarded them under General Ugartechea to San Antonio. The custom-house at Anahuac was taken in charge and enormous dues were demanded. So excessive were they that W. B. Travis raised a company and captured Captain Tenorio and the soldiers at the custom house. They were shortly after released, as the act of Travis was thought by his friends to be too hasty. When Tenorio reported these proceedings to his superior officer, he was sent on a still more uncalled-for errand. A Mexican Republican, Lorenzo de Zavala, had taken refuge in Texas, and Santa Anna, fearing his influence, ordered his arrest; but no one would undertake the task. Another order was sent from headquarters to arrest R. M. Williamson, W. B. Travis, Samuel M. Williams, Moseley Baker, F. W. Johnson and John H. Moore, and a subsequent order included the names of J. M. Carravahal and Juan Zambrano. The two last, being Mexican citizens, were carried off; but the job of arresting the first six persons was considered so dangerous that no officer had the temerity to attempt it. In addition to these Mexican outrages on the Texans, the Indians were becoming troublesome. Merchants and traders were intercepted and killed, and their goods carried off. But these Indian outrages served one important purpose; they gave the Texans an excuse for forming companies, procuring arms and drilling ostensibly for operations against the savages, but really to resist the encroachments of the despotic Mexican government. The companies were called "committees of safety," and their business was to disseminate information, secure arms, ammunition, etc. A central committee was also formed, which met at San Felipe, and an administrative council was organized. The council sent Messrs. Barrett and Gritton to San Antonio on a mission of peace to General Ugartechea, but nothing was accomplished. Stephen F. Austin, in the meantime, was returning, when he was made chairman of the council at San Felipe. He expressed regret at the action of his friends, and stated that he had hoped to find everything peaceful. Santa Anna still professed to have the kindest feelings toward the Texans, and he authorized Austin to tell his people that he was their friend, and that he desired their prosperity; that he would do all he could to promote it, and that in the new constitution he would use his influence to have conditions therein to give Texas a special organization, suited to their education and habits. But Santa Anna could be nothing but treacherous, as the treatment of the people in that portion of the State occupied by his troops but ill accorded with his professions of good will. Citizens were arrested, money forced from those who fell into the hands of the despot's minions, and communities stripped of their arms, the soldiers compelling families to support them, the attempt to disarm all citizens being a principal feature of the plan of subjugation. Captain Castenado was sent to Gonzales to seize a small cannon which had been given to the corporation for protection against Indians. The citizens were unwilling to part with their gun, and prepared to resist the demand of Castenado, who had 150 soldiers to back him. A company was organized, which charged the Mexicans and put them to flight in disorder. The news of this conflict roused a warlike spirit in the Texans. A company was raised to capture the Mexican garrison at Goliad. Captain George Collingsworth led the party, and almost without firing a gun the exultant Texans made prisoners of the whole force, about twenty-five, including Colonel Sandoval, besides obtaining 300 stand of arms and military stores to the amount of $10,000. The Mexican fort at Lipantitlan was also captured shortly after.

Not only had Austin returned, but the noted Benjamin R. Milam had escaped from Monterey and returned and joined the patriot forces. Austin, who was a born commander, was put in immediate command of the Texan forces on his arrival at Gonzales, which was on the 11th of October. The convention met October 16, 1835, but there being only thirty-one members present an adjournment was made until November 1. November 5th a preamble and set of resolutions were adopted, in which the declaration was made that although they repudiated Santa Anna and his despotic government, they yet clung to the Constitution of Mexico of 1824. On November 12th an ordinance was passed for the creation of a provisional government, with an executive council, to be composed of one member from each municipality. Henry Smith was made Governor, and James W. Robinson Lieutenant-Governor. Sam Houston, who, it will be noticed, had figured somewhat in Texas history since 1832, was selected to command the army to be raised.

General Cos, with 500 soldiers, landed at Pass Cavallo, in September, 1835, and marched immediately to San Antonio, when he superseded General

Ugartechea. Austin, after reaching Gonzales, and effecting a reorganization of the volunteers, started for San Antonio. He reached the Mission La Espada, nine miles below the city, on the 20th. On the 27th, after resting his men, he detached the companies of Fannin and Bowie, ninety-two men, to ascend the river and if practicable select a more suitable camping ground. Fannin spent that night in a bend of the San Antonio River, near the Conception Mission. The point was well chosen, but the Mexicans looked upon it as simply a trap to secure their game from, which was all they had to do. It was a natural fortification, but General Cos thought he had a sure thing of it; so he marched out in the morning and made an attack. The Mexicans surrounded their supposed prey, and the battle began. The Texans, with their deadly rifles, plucked off all the gunners from the enemy's battery, as they came within range. A charge was made, or attempted, three separate times, but they were hurled back in confusion by the Texans, who remained masters of the field. Sixteen dead bodies were found near the abandoned cannon, which had been discharged but five times; so true was the aim of the riflemen that the Mexican gunners were shot before they could fire, in most cases. This was the first battle of the Revolution, and the loss of the Texans was one man—Richard Andrews. The Mexican loss was about sixty, as every one of the patriots who fired took aim and usually brought down his man. Austin, in October, moved up about half a mile, on the Alamo ditch, near the old mill, and next day to within one mile east of the city. He had nearly 1,000 men, but they were ill provided with arms and ammunition of war and without cannon. He was poorly prepared to attack a larger force than his own in a strongly fortified city. He, however, sent to Gonzales for the cannon at that place. Then came a number of skirmishes with the enemy and the capture of 300 horses by Bowie. The executive or general council, in view of the lack of funds wherewith to provide the supplies, etc., so much needed at that time, sent Messrs. Austin, Archer and Wharton as Commissioners to the United States, in order to negotiate a loan of $1,000,000 in bonds of $1,000 each, and the commander-in-chief was authorized to accept the services of 5,000 volunteers and 1,200 regulars. Provision was also made for a navy.

The army encamped before San Antonio was under General Edward Burleson. Many of the men had gone home, although others were arriving daily; still, only about half the original force remained. There had been about 1,400 men in the camps at one time; 600 was the number on the 1st of December, while Cos had a much larger force in the city, and was expecting 500 more. Those additional troops arrived in time to take part in the defense of the city. The defenses had been put in order and the old fortress of the Alamo on the east side of the river had been repaired and fortified with cannon. The main plaza had been fortified and the streets barricaded, while the adobe houses in the narrow streets afforded shelter for the Mexican soldiers. Many of Burleson's officers, in consideration of these facts, were in favor of abandoning the siege. On the 2d of December it was decided to make the attack. The force was paraded and a strong address was made by Colonel William H. Jack. A call was then made for volunteers, and 450 men, including the New Orleans Grays, responded, the latter under the command of Major R. C. Norris. It was decided to make the attack next morning, although many considered the project as a hopeless one. But three citizens arrived in camp from the city and gave such encouraging news that the next morning Colonel Milam suggested to Burleson to make the attempt while the enthusiasm was at its height. He agreed, and Milam stepped in front of Burleson's tent and gave a loud and ringing *huzzah,* which, together with his magnetism, aroused the whole camp. He said he was going into San Antonio, and wanted volunteers to follow him. A ready response was made, and the little band, forming into two sections and accompanied by two field pieces, entered the town by different directions. A description of this famous battle has so often been given that its details are almost like household words to all Texans. The result was sufficient almost to place it in the category of one of the "decisive battles of the world," for the *result* of a battle is what makes it great. Hundreds of battles have been fought where thousands on each side have been slain, and yet the result has been *nil.* This siege and capture of the strongly protected city of San Antonio de Bexar was all important to Texas. It gave the Mexicans to understand that not in numbers alone consists the strength of an army. Here was a force of undisciplined frontiersmen, poorly armed and equipped, only a few hundred in number, attacking a well organized army of regular soldiers, advancing into their very midst and forcing them to surrender. The difference in apparent strength of the two forces and the result would appear ridiculous were it not so serious a matter. The spectacle of a general such as Cos seemed to be, surrendering to a few Texans, was a scene to be remembered by those who took part in the siege. But it is the old story of the Anglo-Saxon against the field. He is rarely ever the under dog in the fight at the finish.

During the time the fighting men were doing such splendid work, the politicians were quarreling; nor were they lacking in a more "modern instance" or two, on both sides of Mason and Dixon's line. Governor Smith vetoed some matters that the council had voted, and the council promptly deposed him and placed Lieutenant-Governor Robinson in the executive chair. Smith held the archives and claimed to be Governor still, and there were consequently two governors at once; but that state of affairs is not uncommon in these days. Much other legislative matter of some interest at the time was transacted, but it is not now of supreme importance. The main historic facts are what the compiler wishes to emphasize in these pages. Several declarations of independence were adopted in different sections of the embryo State, but an election was held for delegates to a convention which met on the 1st of March, 1836, and on the second day a committee was appointed to draft a declaration of independence, which was done, and it was unanimously passed, Sam Houston offering the resolution that the report of the committee be adopted. Richard Ellis, for whom Ellis county was named, was president of the convention. A constitution was also framed which was adopted March 17, and a government *ad interim* inaugurated: David G. Burnett, President; Lorenzo de Zavala, Vice-president, and Sam Houston, Commander-in-Chief of the army in the field. Zacatecas, and the district over which Governor Garcia still had nominal sway, the remaining portion of old Mexico wherein the Republicans held out the longest, at last fell, Santa Anna having gained a complete victory over the forces of the Governor. This swept away the last vestige of the Republican party in Mexico. Yet Texas was not only holding her own, but gaining strength with every day; so Santa Anna determined to subjugate this State. He proposed to send two columns into the province, General Urrea being ordered to Matamoras to take one division along the coast to Goliad and Victoria, while the President himself, with the main division, would take the province by way of Presidio, thence to San Antonio and San Felipe.

In January, 1836, Santa Anna reached Saltillo, and Guerrero by the 15th of February. From the latter place he wrote to Señor Tornel, Minister of War, giving that official an outline of his plans in reference to Texas, which were "to drive from the province all who had taken part in the revolution, together with all the foreigners who lived near the sea-coast, or the borders of the United States; to remove far into the interior those who had not taken part in the revolution; to vacate all lands and grants of lands owned by non-residents; to remove from Texas all who had come to the province and were not entered as colonists under Mexican rules; to divide among the officers and soldiers of the army the best lands, provided they would occupy them; to permit no Anglo-American to settle in Texas; to sell the remaining vacant lands at $1 per acre, allowing those speaking the French language to purchase 5,000,000 acres, those speaking English the same, and those speaking Spanish without limit; to satisfy the claims of civilized Indians; to make the Texans pay the expense of the war; and to liberate and to declare free the negroes introduced into the colony." And further, to cut off from Texas the hope of aid from the United States, the Minister of War, Tornel, issued a general order to all commanders to treat all foreigners (volunteers from the United States) as outlaws, to show no quarter, and slay them when taken as prisoners—in short, to take no prisoners alive. Colonel Travis, with 145 men, who was in the vicinity of San Antonio, on the approach of the invading army, retired to the fortress of the Alamo, on the east side of the river. And just here a description of this famous fortress, the Alamo, and its armament, will be in place; and although it has often been described, yet the memories surrounding it, glorious though sad, cannot be kept too fresh in the minds of all who love supreme heroism—the Spartan heroism as shown by Travis and his little band. "The main chapel is 75 x 62 feet, walls of solid masonry, four feet thick and twenty-two and a half feet high, roofless at the time of the siege. It fronts to the west toward the city, one-half mile distant. From the northwest corner a wall extended fifty feet to the convent building. The convent was a two-story building, with a flat roof, 186 x 18 feet. From the northeast corner of the chapel a wall extended 186 feet north, thence 102 feet west to the convent, inclosing the convent yard. From the southwest corner of the chapel a strongly built stockade extended seventy-five feet to a building called the prison. The prison was one-story, 115 x 17 feet, and joined a part of the south wall of the main Alamo plaza, of which the convent formed a part of the east wall; and some low buildings, used as a barracks, formed a part of the west wall. The main plaza, inclosed with walls, was 154 x 54 yards. The different inclosures occupied between two and three acres—ample accommodations for 1,000 men. The outer walls were two and a half feet thick and eight feet high, though as they were planned against the Indians the fortress was destitute of salient and dominant points in case of a bombardment. A ditch, used for irrigation, passed immediately in the rear of the church; another touched the northwest angle of the main square. The armament was as follows: three heavy guns, planted upon the walls of the church—one pointing north, toward the old mill; one west, toward the city;

Gen. Sam Houston.

and one south, toward the village of Lavalleta. Two guns protected the
stockade between the church and the prison; two protected the prison, and an
eighteen-pounder was planted at the southwest angle of the main square; a
twelve-pound cannon protected the center of the west wall, and an eight-
pounder was planted on the northwest angle; two guns were planted on the
north wall of the plaza—in all, fourteen in position. Over the church floated
the flag of the provisional government of Texas, the Mexican tri-color, with
the numerals 1824, in place of the eagle in the white stripe."

The siege began on the 23d of February, and so stubbornly did Travis
and his men resist the furious onslaughts of the Mexicans that not until Sunday, March 6, did the fall of the Alamo occur, an account of which, briefly
told, will here be given: The Mexicans advanced to the attack at about four
o'clock in the morning, but the Texans were ready, and poured upon the
advancing columns a shower of grape and musket and rifle balls. Santa Anna
was watching the operations from behind a building about 500 yards south of
the church. Twice the assailants reeled and fell back in dismay. Rallied
again by the brave Costrellon (who fell at San Jacinto), according to Filisola, the columns of the western and eastern attacks meeting with some difficulty in reaching the tops of the small houses forming the wall of the fort,
did, by a simultaneous movement to the right and to the left, swing northward until the three columns formed one dense mass, which under the guidance of their officers finally succeeded in effecting an entrance into the
inclosed yard. About the same time the column on the south made a breach
in the wall and captured one of the guns. This gun, the eighteen-pounder,
was immediately turned upon the convent, to which some of the Mexicans had
retreated. The cannon on the center of the west wall was still manned by
the Texans, and did fearful execution upon the Mexicans who had ventured
into the yard. But the feeble garrison could not long hold out against such
overwhelming numbers. Travis fell early in the action, shot with a rifle ball
in the head. After being shot he had sufficient strength to kill a Mexican
who attempted to spear him. The bodies of most of the Texans were found
in the buildings, where hand-to-hand fights took place. The body of Crockett,
however, was in the yard, with a number of dead Mexicans lying near
him. Bowie was slain in his bed, and it is said that he killed three Mexicans
with his pistols before they reached him after breaking in the door. The
church was the last place entered by the foe. It had been agreed that when
resistance seemed useless, and suspecting their fate, any surviving Texan
should blow up the magazine. Major Evans, it is said, was performing this
sad duty when he was killed in time to prevent the explosion. Several Texans appealed to their inhuman captors for quarters, but they were cut down
without mercy. The butchery was complete; not a Texan soldier was spared!
Two ladies and a negro servant were the only occupants who remained to tell
the tale of the Alamo. Lieutenant Dickinson attempted to escape with a child
on his back, but their bodies fell, riddled with bullets. 180 bodies of the
Texans were collected and partially buried. The Mexicans lost twice that
number.

Santa Anna, in the meantime, had ordered Urrea to proceed along the
Texan coast, and that general reached San Patricio on the 28th of February,
entirely unknown to the Texans. Some narrow escapes were made by Colonel
F. W. Johnson and others, but a party under Major Morris and Dr. Grant

3

were captured and they fell victims to the Mexican murderers,—for they were nothing less. Colonel Fannin had been ordered to prepare for a descent on Matamoras, but hearing of the advance of Urrea, he re-entered Goliad, where he had been in command some time. Having been requested to send some reinforcements to Captain King, his force was thereby depleted by 112 men. King and his men, after a skirmish or two, by some means got separated from another portion of his force, and were captured and killed. Fannin, in Goliad, on the 16th of March, was reinforced by the Twenty-eighth Cavalry. He then prepared for a retreat; but just at nightfall a large force of the enemy was discovered in the neighborhood, when he remounted his cannon and prepared for defense. The following account of the disastrous battle of Colita, which followed, is copied from an able historian of Texas: "The morning of the 17th was foggy, and as no enemy appeared to be in sight Fannin concluded to make good his retreat. After reaching a point about eight miles away from Goliad, they halted to permit the oxen to graze. They then resumed their march, and were within two miles of Colita Creek when a company of Mexican cavalry was discovered in front of them, issuing from a point of timber. Urrea had taken advantage of the fog to get around and in front of Fannin's force. Horton's cavalry had gone in advance to make arrangements for crossing the stream, and could not get back to their companions. Two charges of Urrea's cavalry were gallantly repulsed by Fannin's artillery, which did great damage to the Mexicans. The fight was kept up till nightfall, when the enemy retired out of range and the Texans prepared for a renewal of the fight in the morning. Their condition was indeed critical. Fourteen of their number had been killed, and sixty others, including Fannin, were wounded. Urrea received during the night heavy reinforcements. With no adequate protection, in an open prairie, without water, surrounded by an enemy five times their number, what could they do but surrender as prisoners of war? A white flag was raised and the following terms of surrender agreed upon: That the Texans should be treated as prisoners of war according to the usages of civilized nations; that private property should be respected and restored, but side arms of the officers should be given up; the men should be sent to Copano, and thence in eight days to the United States, or as soon as vessels could be procured to take them; the officers should be paroled and returned to the United States in like manner.

General Houston had been re-elected commander-in-chief of the army, and had gone to Gonzales, with the intention of reorganizing the forces, in which he had great difficulty, for the fate of Travis and Fannin and their men caused a great panic when the news became known. Besides, thirty-two of the citizen soldiers of Gonzales, who had entered the Alamo the night before the battle, were slain, leaving a dozen or more families of that town without a head. A number of desertions also occurred, and the alarm was, indeed, widespread. Then came some movements on the part of General Houston that caused great criticism of his actions. There was not a very considerable cordiality between the commander and the newly inaugurated president, and in an order to the former from the latter these words were added: "The enemy are laughing you to scorn. You must fight them. You must retreat no further. The country expects you to fight. The salvation of the country depends on your doing so." The affair at San Jacinto followed. The marching of April 18, 19 and 20, 1836, led to the battle of April 21.

According to a report signed by Sam Houston, commander-in-chief, the Texan force numbered 783 men, while the government troops under Santa Anna numbered 1,500 men, including General Cos' division. The First Regiment, commanded by Colonel Burleson, was assigned the center. The Second Regiment, under the command of Sherman, formed the left wing of the army. The artillery, under special command of Colonel George W. Hockley, inspector-general, was placed on the right of the First Regiment; and four companies of infantry, under the command of Lieutenant-Colonel Henry Millard, sustained the artillery upon the right. The cavalry, sixty-one in number, commanded by Colonel Mirabeau B. Lamar, placed on the extreme right, completed the line. The cavalry was dispatched to the front of the enemy's left, for the purpose of attracting their notice, while an extensive island of timber afforded an opportunity of concentrating the forces and deploying from that point, agreeably to the previous design of the troops. Every evolution was performed with alacrity, the whole advancing rapidly in line, and through an open prairie, without any protection. The artillery advanced, took station within 200 yards of the enemy's breastwork, and commenced an effective fire with grape and canister. Colonel Sherman, with his regiment, having commenced the action upon the left wing, the whole line, at the center and on the right, advancing in double-quick time, rung the war cry, 'Remember the Alamo!' received the enemy's fire, and advanced within point-blank shot before a piece was discharged, then advanced without a halt until they were in possession of the woodland and the enemy's breastwork, the right wing of Burleson's and the left of Millard's taking possession of the breastwork, the artillery having gallantly charged up within seventy yards of the enemy's cannon, when it was taken. The conflict lasted about eighteen minutes from the time of close action until the Texans were in possession of the enemy's encampment, taking one piece of cannon (loaded), four stands of colors, all their camp equipage, stores and baggage. The cavalry had charged and routed that of the enemy upon the right, and given pursuit to the fugitives, which did not cease until they arrived at the bridge. Captain Karnes commanded the pursuers. The conflict in the breastwork lasted but a few moments; many of the troops encountered hand to hand, and, not having the advantage of bayonets on the Texan side, riflemen used their pieces as war clubs, breaking many of them off at the breech. The rout commenced at half-past four, and the pursuit by the main army continued until twilight. A guard was then left in charge of the enemy's encampment, and the Texans returned with their killed and wounded — or two killed and twenty-three wounded, six of whom mortally. The enemy's loss was 630 killed, among whom were one general officer, four colonels, two lieutenant-colonels, five captains, twelve lieutenants; wounded, 208, of whom five were colonels, three lieutenant-colonels, two second lieutenant-colonels, seven captains, one cadet; prisoners, 730; President-General Santa Anna, General Cos, four colonels (aids to General Santa Anna), and the colonel of the Guerrero Battalion, are included in the number. General Santa Anna was not taken until the 22, nor General Cos until the 24th, very few having escaped. About 600 muskets, 300 sabers and 200 pistols were collected after the action; several hundred mules and horses were taken, and nearly $12,000 in specie.

During the latter part of 1838 the Nacogdoches rebellion occurred, when a considerable number of Mexican settlers assembled on the banks of the

Angelina, with 300 Indians, under the leadership of Nathaniel Norris, Vicente Cordova, and others. Their numbers soon increased. President Houston, who was then at Nacogdoches, received a communication from these leaders, disclaiming allegiance to Texas. The malcontents then directed their march to the Cherokee Nation. President Houston sent out General Rusk, with the main body of the army, to the headquarters of Bowles, the Cherokee chief, while Major Augustin, with 150 men, followed the trail of the malcontents. Rusk presently discovered that the Mexican leaders had gone to the head-waters of the Trinity River, his followers had dispersed and many of them returned to their homes without any blood being shed. The precise object of this attempt at revolution has never been fully explained.

The rout of the Cherokees from their hunting grounds was the introduction to the massacre of the Comanches. In February, 1840, showing a disposition to enter into a treaty of peace, twelve of their principal chiefs met, March 19, the Texan commissioners at Bejar, where General H. D. McLeod was in command. It was known that the Comanches had thirteen white captives in their power, and the release of these was demanded. The Indians brought forward only one, a little girl. After a brief discussion, in which the Indians exhibited defiance, an order was sent to Captain Howard, to bring his company into the council room; and as soon as the men had taken their position the chiefs were informed that they would be detained as prisoners until the captives were surrendered. A terrible conflict ensued; the twelve chiefs, armed, were all killed in the council room, while the warriors in the yard outside maintained a desperate fight. All were finally slain, thirty-two in number, while seven women and children were made prisoners. Naturally the Comanches in general were resolved on revenge for what they considered treachery, and in return for the destruction of so many of their chiefs. With a band of 600 they raided Linnville and the vicinity of Victoria, which latter place they made two efforts to capture, and carried off to their homes immense numbers of live stock and large amounts of other property. During August (1840) the whites had several skirmishes with them, under command of General Felix Houston, and drove them away, with considerable loss. Furthermore, on October 5th following, Col. John H. Moore, with ninety Texans and twelve Lipan Indians, was sent up the Colorado in pursuit of the escaped Comanches, and on reaching them he destroyed their village and killed many of the escaping Indians. The rout was complete, and Lamar's system of extermination or extinction was for once thoroughly carried out.

A comparatively long interval of peace with Mexico was occasioned by internal strifes in the latter country. The northern "Federalists" failed to establish their "Republic of the Rio Grande," a scheme wholly ignored by the Texans. The latter, however, as has already been remarked, claimed all the territory east of the Rio Grande to its source, which was indeed much farther into the interior than they were warranted in going. Accordingly, in 1841, they sent out an expedition toward Santa Fe, in order more perfectly to establish their possession to that section of the country. This scheme was a wild one, from the fact that the population of Santa Fe was thoroughly Mexican, and separated from the Texas settlements by an Indian country fully 600 miles in width. Indeed it was not sanctioned by the Texan congress, and the scheme was wholly Lamar's. He proclaimed in advance to the authorities at Santa Fe the object of the expedition. If they in that section were unwilling to submit to Texas, said he, then he wished to establish friendly commercial relations with New Mexico. He instructed his commander not to subjugate the country if the people were unwilling to submit; the military organization of the expedition was only for protection against the savages. The expedition, which consisted of 270 soldiers, left Austin June 20, 1841, met with many disasters, and, after some loss of men, was captured before it reached Santa Fe, and most of the men sent to the City of Mexico, where they were kept in prison for a time. Among them was the commissioner, J. A. Navarro, who, after languishing in prison for fourteen months, finally escaped at Vera Cruz, in January, 1845.

As an argument for annexation to the United States, it was stated that Mexico had for six years failed to reconquer Texas or even to send an army within her borders, and that the war therefore might be considered ended, although no formal recognition of the independence of Texas had been made by the mother country. Her prolonged inactivity might be considered an acknowledgment that reconquest was impossible. Mexico, however, in order to make good her claim, prepared at the close of 1841 to invade Texas. On January 9, 1842, General Arista issued a proclamation from his headquarters at Monterey that the Mexican nation would never consent to the separation of the territory, and that it was owing only to the civil wars in Mexico that no effort had recently been made to subjugate Texas. He declared that his country was determined to recover her rights through the only means left her, namely, persuasion or war; that hostilities would be directed against only those who sustained and fought to maintain the Texan nationality; and he called upon the people to reflect and consider their own interests, and return to their allegiance. On March 5, General Rafael Vasquez appeared before San Antonio de Bejar at the head of 500 men. The Texan force there, being small, evacuated when the surrender of the town was demanded. Vasquez entered the place, hoisted the Mexican flag and departed. About the same time small forces of Mexicans occupied Refugio and Goliad, and also soon retired. Aroused, the Texans bristled up for another engagement, and Houston, on the 10th of March, issued a proclamation calling upon all citizens subject to military duty to hold themselves in readiness to repair to the scene of action in the event of a formidable invasion. On the 21st he addressed a letter to Santa Anna, again in power, which was published far and wide. In it were criticisms incited by injudicious correspondence between him (Santa Anna) and Bernard E. Bee and General Hamilton. Santa Anna declared that Mexico would not cease her efforts until she had planted her standard upon the Sabine. Houston replied promptly and boldly, that Texas would never yield, writing a very eloquent letter to the old treacherous Mexican. He declared blockaded all the Mexican ports on the eastern coast from Tobasco, including the mouth of the Rio Grande and the Brazos Santiago. The Texan navy at this time consisted of four vessels, the other vessels that had been purchased by authority of the congress having been wrecked. These vessels were transferred to the United States the next year, upon annexation.

When Vasquez occupied San Antonio much alarm was felt for the safety of Austin and the government archives. The President removed his cabinet to Houston, where Congress held its special session of June 27, 1842, and this aggravated the indignation of the people of Austin. A vigilance committee was formed, the records were packed in boxes and a guard placed over them.

Besides, a force was sent out to guard the roads, to see that no wagon passed with the archives. December 10, 1842, Houston instructed Captain Thomas I. Smith to raise a company secretly and bring the most necessary books and documents to Washington, where Congress was to convene in regular session that month. Smith avoided the regular patrols by a circuitous route, entered Austin December 30, at night, and succeeded in loading three wagons with records. This act was a surprise to the inhabitants of Austin. Smith hastened back, after having been fired upon without effect by Captain Mark B. Lewis, who, having rallied a volunteer company and procured a cannon from the arsenal, fired at the intruders. Smith encamped at Kinney's Fort on Brushy Creek, and on the following morning discovered that Lewis, with his cannon pointed, had taken a position in front. After some parley, Smith agreed to take the wagons back to Austin. This affair has been called the Archive war. No further attempt was made to remove the records. The Austin people retained them until 1845, when, on occasion of the annexation convention being summoned to meet in July, they delivered them over to the administration of Anson Jones, on condition that the convention should assemble at Austin.

This breeze took place during the second administration of President Houston, in 1842. Early in this century the "neutral ground" became the asylum of adventurers and desperate men. Land commissioners, especially in Shelby County, found a profitable business in issuing "headright" certificates. During this year one Charles W. Jackson, an English-speaking resident of Louisiana, and a fugitive from justice, arrived in Shelby County, and offered himself as a candidate for the Texan Congress. Being defeated, he undertook to expose the land frauds, declaring that his defeat was owing to the opposition of the party connected with them. He notified the general land office of the illegal proceedings had there, and a man named Joseph Goodbread intimated that his life was in danger if he did not desist. Jackson shot him dead on the spot. He was called to trial, the court was thronged by armed men, and the judge failed to appear. The Louisianian then organized his party, under the name of "Regulators." Their operations were somewhat irregular, and doubtless many honest men lost their lands, etc., by their work. The "Moderators" were therefore organized in opposition, and a kind of warfare was carried on for three years, when the two factions drew up in actual battle array in front of each other; but the President had General Smith, with a force of about 500 men, put a stop to the threatening strife. However, many a murder was afterward committed in quarrels growing out of the issues.

The Texan Congress authorized war with Mexico, in 1842, but Houston vetoed the Bill, as the Republic had no means to carry on such a war. Independent parties, however, rushed to arms, and under an adventurer named Davis met the Mexicans at Nueces, in July.

In September, the Mexican general—Woll, occupied Antonio, driving out the Anglo-Texan element. Then Matthew Caldwell, with 220 Texans, and Nicholas Dawson, with fifty-three men came forward, met the Mexicans, and were killed, except two who escaped and fifteen who were made prisoners.

In September, 1,200 men answered Houston's call to arms. The expedition may be said to have ended at Mier, where 250 Texans surrendered to Gen. Ampudia. Very few of the members ever returned, for after their escape from the Hacienda del Salado, they suffered untold hardships, many died, others were recaptured, and seventeen of the leaders executed. Of the total, 107 were liberated in 1844 by Santa Anna.

Of course, this act of annexation of Texas to the United States meant war with Mexico on a larger scale than ever. In Texas, at this time, there were probably about 75,000 inhabitants, about 4,000 of whom were Mexicans. The nationality of the new State was very composite. As to the criminal element, there was no more of that, than in any frontier settlement, which generally have a class of ruffians that disappear on the approach of more settled civilization.

When the resolution of Congress in favor of annexation was published, March 7, 1845, General Almonte, the Mexican minister at Washington, demanded his passports. War with Mexico, indeed, the Government had been preparing for, and General Zachary Taylor was ordered to move from the Sabine with a strong force to Corpus Christi, at the mouth of the Nueces, at the end of June, 1845. In the meantime, the Mexicans, too, had been preparing for the contest, establishing their first base at Matamoras. The Texas legislature appointed Governor Henderson to take command of the Texans who might be mustered into the service of the United States. On May 2, 1846, a requisition for two regiments of infantry and two of cavalry was made on Texas. Henderson reached the army of General Taylor at Comargo, after the war had begun. The limited means of transportation, and uncertainty with regard to supplies, induced Taylor, while on his march against Monterey, to leave a large number of volunteers on garrison duty in towns on the Rio Grande, and only the first and second regiments of the Texan division accompanied the main army on that memorable campaign. In the attack upon Monterey, the first regiment of mounted volunteers under Colonel John C. Hays, familiarly known as "Jack," was detached and sent with General Worth west of the town, while Shield's, under Taylor, assaulted the East side, leading to the capitulation on the 24th.

The treaty of Guadalupe Hidalgo, negotiated February 22, 1848, surrendered Texas, New Mexico, Utah, Nevada, Arizona and California to the United States.

In 1857, Texan wagoners committed many acts of violence upon Mexican cartmen in the transportation of goods from San Antonio. The freight rates were so low as to drive the Texan wagoners from the field. The latter, moreover, were not quite so faithful as the Mexicans. Outrages became so numerous and high-handed that General Twiggs, the United States commander at San Antonio, was compelled to furnish a military escort to trains transporting Government supplies. In October, the Mexican minister at Washington addressed the United States Government on the matter, stating that he had been assured that the number of men thus murdered was no less than seventy-five and that many Mexicans had been compelled to fly to Mexico in a state of destitution. In November, Governor Pease addressed special messages to the Legislature on the matter, stating that Mexican citizens engaged in the business of teaming were not safe without a military escort. As the counties in which the deeds of violence were committed did nothing to stop them, he suggested the propriety of legislative interference. The Senate referred the matter to a committee, who reported in favor of inflicting a penalty upon those counties, but introduced no bill to that effect, and so the matter ended. The Legislature, however, approved the action of the Governor in calling out a company of troops, which, by the way, was ineffectual in regulating a large 'section of country with the criminals scattered over it. When the road was abandoned by the Mexican cartmen and booty became scarce, they began to commit depredations on the property of the citizens. The latter, though so indifferent to the rights of the Mexicans previously, were now enraged and resorted to lynching; and in the neighborhood of Goliad, the traveler would see many a corpse suspended from the boughs of the black oaks. The " Cart War," was thus brought to an end.

The Knights of the Golden Circle, organized originally to establish a slave empire in the Antilles, called a convention at Austin for January 28, 1861. That convention, on February 1, 1861 passed the Ordinance of Secession, the vote being 107 pro and 7 contra; which ordinance was to be submitted to a popular vote on February 23. Meantime the delegates elected representatives to the Confederate convention at Montgomery, Ala., and appointed three commissioners to accept the surrender of General Twiggs, with that of the soldiers and property of the United States in Texas. Houston opposed secession in a logical, prophetic speech, but went with the State, "right or wrong." On February 23, there were 39,415 votes cast for secession and 13,841 against it. The revolution of Cortina was an incident of the time, for it caused the devastation of the Rio Grande valley for 120 miles of its length. The civil war was inaugurated at Valverde, February 21, 1862, when the Confederate Sibley with 1,750 men, repulsed the Federal Canby with 3,810 men. Colonel Slough subsequently defeated Sibley, who lost 500 men in the expedition. In May, 1862, the United States vessels appeared before Galveston, but not until October 4, did the United States soldiers retake possession of the town; but the Confederate Magruder ultimately repossessed it.

After the recovery of Galveston Island, no other operation of importance occurred until September, 1863, when the Federals attempted to effect a lodgment at Sabine City, the terminus of a railroad. The blockade of Sabine Pass was temporarily broken by the capture of two United States gunboats, outside the bar. Afterward the Confederates erected a fort at Sabine City, defended by a formidable battery of eight heavy guns, three of which were rifled. A detachment of 4,000 men, with gunboats, from Banks' army, made an attempt in September, 1863, to take Sabine City, but met with ignominious defeat, losing two gunboats, 100 men killed and wounded, and 250 prisoners. The garrison of the fort consisted of only 200 Texans, of whom only forty-two took part in the action. These were presented by President Davis with a silver medal, the only honor of the kind known to have been bestowed by the Confederate government. Late in October, 1863, supported by a naval squadron under Commander Strong, Banks sailed with 6,000 troops from New Orleans for the Rio Grande. The immediate command, however, was given to General Napoleon Dana. By November 2 the force reached Brazos Santiago, and on the 6th took Brownsville, and soon afterward Corpus Christi, Aransas Pass, Cavillo Pass and the mouth of Matagorda Bay. Indianola and the Matagorda peninsula were soon in the hands of the Federals, but early in 1864 all were evacuated, save Brazos Santiago, left in charge of the U. S. Navy, which captured several boats belonging to the Confederacy. Banks' Red River campaign was undertaken with the object of possessing all the country west and south of Red River. The Louisianians and Texans defeated him at all points and drove him ignominiously away.

During the month of September, Brownsville was captured by her old enemy, Cortina, under peculiar circumstances. A French force of about 5,000 took Bagdad, at the mouth of the Rio Grande, with the object of taking possession of Matamoras, where Cortina was then in command. Brownsville was at that time occupied by Colonel Ford with a considerable force of Texan cavalry, and Brazos Santiago was still held by the Federals. On the 6th the French began to move up the right bank of the river, and their advance became engaged with Cortina, who had marched with 3,000 Mexicans and sixteen pieces of artillery from Matamoras to meet them. There seems to have been some understanding between Ford and the French commander, for during the engagement the former appeared on the other side of the Rio Grande with a large herd of cattle for the use of the invading army, and, immediately crossing the river, took part in the conflict by attacking the rear of Cortina's army. The Mexican commander, however, succeeded in repulsing both Ford and the French, who retreated to Bagdad. Cortina next turned his attention to Ford. On the 9th he passed with his whole force and drove the Texans from Brownsville, and took possession of the town for the United States. The tactics of Kirby Smith prolonged the war in Texas until May 26, 1864, when he surrendered to General Canby, the last battle being fought at Palo Alto on May 13—the scene of Austin's defeat in the war with Mexico. The history of the Reconstruction period, would be the reciting of shocking cruelties and injustices, more methodical than during the war, but none the less brutal. Cortina was a mild, just soldier and statesman, compared with the leaders of the conquerors and conquered in Texas, from 1865 to 1871 and, perhaps, until 1879.

Under the rule of Spanish viceroys, Texas was governed by a commandant, who made his headquarters at Chihuahua. Later the commandancy merged into a governorship, which obtained until 1821, when Mexico became a Republic, and Texas with Coahuila became one of her States. In 1830, civil rulers gave place to military government in the joint State, which continued until April 21, 1836, when Santa Anna, the Mexican Republican was defeated at San Jacinto, and the Republic of Texas was master of the situation. The story of the troubles leading up to the formation of the Republic is best told in the pages devoted to military affairs. Here is given a brief sketch of its political life from November, 1835, to February, 1846, when officers were elected to administer Texas as a State of the United States.

By authority of a resolution adopted December 10, 1835, by the provisional government of Texas, which existed from November, 1835, to March, 1836, delegates, clothed with plenary powers, were elected February 1, 1836, to meet in convention at Washington, on the Brazos, March 1. The provisional government was composed of Henry Smith, Governor; James W. Robinson, vice-Governor; and a council. At the period of the meeting of the convention, the council had quarreled with and deposed the Governor, and Mr. Robinson was Acting Governor. A series of resolutions, known as the Declaration of Independence was signed by fifty-eight delegates on March 2, 1836. The executive ordinance was adopted March 16, and the Constitution of the Republic of Texas on the night of March 17, that year. On the 18th of March, the convention assembled for the last time, and elected David G. Burnett President *ad interim* of the Republic, and Lorenzo de Zavala, a patriot Mexican exile, vice-President. They also elected the members of the

Cabinet, namely: Samuel P. Carson, Secretary of State; Bailey Hardeman, Secretary of the Treasury; Thomas J. Rusk, Secretary of War; Robert Potter, Secretary of the Navy; and David Thomas, Attorney General.

In October, 1836, a regular election was held, when Houston was chosen President and Mirabeau B. Lamar, vice-President. Burnett and Zavala retired so as to permit the prompt inauguration of the new president. President Houston appointed as members of his cabinet eminent men from the principal parties. Stephen F. Austin was made Secretary of State; Henry Smith, Secretary of the Treasury; Thomas J. Rusk, of War; S. Rhodes Fisher, of the Navy; Robert Burr, Postmaster General; and J. Pinckney Henderson, Attorney General. General Felix Houston was given command of the Army.

On November 16, Congress empowered the President to appoint a minister to the United States, to negotiate with this government for the recognition of the independence of Texas and her annexation to this Republic. A bond issue for $5,000,000, bearing ten per centum interest was authorized; a twenty-four-gun sloop of war, two armed steamers and two eleven-gun schooners were purchased; the Texas Railroad, Navigation and Banking Company was chartered; the boundaries of the Republic defined and other legislation, just and otherwise, enacted. The recognition of Texas by the United States dates to March 1, 1837. Subsequently Alcee La Branche was appointed United States Chargé d'affaires in Texas, and Mexico lost all hope of ever resuming authority over that great State, which she had so long treated with contempt.

The Congress which assembled May 1, 1837, devoted attention particularly to the intricate land question, to the establishment of county boundaries and the incorporation of towns. The towns of Shelbyville, Brazoria, Richmond, San Felipe de Austin, Lagrange, San Antonio, Victoria, Gonzalez, Matagorda, Mina, Houston, Washington, Crockett, Refugio, Columbia, Clarksville, Lexington, Milam, Goliad, San Patricio and Jonesborough were all incorporated during this session; and the new counties of Montgomery, Fayette, Fannin, Robertson and Fort Bender were created. Some of the above mentioned towns, however, had been incorporated once before.

From the reports of the State officers, it is seen that 10,890 certificates of land title had been issued by the different county boards up to November 1, 1838, representing 26,242,199 acres; that up to October 15, 2,990,000 acres had been distributed to soldiers as land bounties; that the issues of land scrip amounted to 2,193,000 acres, of which scrip to the amount of 870,000 acres had been returned by the agents, and a portion, representing 60,800 acres, had been funded. But financially, the outlook was bad. The public debt had been increased, and the credit of the Republic was nearly exhausted. Considerable legislation was enacted with reference to the public finances, with the prospect that immigration and the increased interest taken in Texan securities by persons in the United States, the way out of their difficulties would be found in due time. By the constitution the term of office of the President was limited to two years, without his being eligible for re-election; succeeding Presidents were to hold their office for three years. Consequently Houston's term expired on the first Monday in December, 1838. The election was held in September, the candidates being Mirabeau B. Lamar, Peter W. Grayson, James Collingsworth and Robert Wilson; but before the election Grayson and Collingsworth both committed suicide. Lamar was chosen President almost unanimously, and David G. Burnett, vice-President. One historian says that during the three years of Lamar's administration the public debt increased from $1,887,526 to $7,300,000, and that the securities decreased from sixty-five and eighty-five to fifteen and twenty cents; but, according to ex-President Houston's subsequent report, matters were not quite as bad as that. It may be said, however, that the officials had as little regard for the purses or property of the people as the carpet baggers of *post-bellum* days had. Legal plundering ruled.

The establishment of the Republic was so well received in the United States that President Jackson sent an agent into Texas to report on the political and military state of the little Republic. This agent found a population of 58,500, and a debt of $1,250,000; reported favorably to President Jackson, and this report led to American recognition in 1837.

During the first presidency of Mr. Houston, General J. P. Henderson was sent to London and Paris to obtain an acknowledgment from those countries of Texan independence, and from the first the British government was favorably disposed, on account of Texas being an agricultural country and the people inclined to free trade, thus opening new channels for English commerce. France, indeed, recognized the independence of Texas in 1839, but this friendly relation was soon interrupted by a ridiculous affair until some time in 1842. Holland and Belgium recognized it in 1840, and England in 1841. But all the efforts made to obtain a like recognition from Mexico failed.

The Texas presidential election of September, 1844, resulted in a victory for the anti-annexationists, being a choice of Anson Jones for President, who was known to be opposed to annexation. Kenneth L. Anderson was chosen vice-President. Edward Burleson was the defeated candidate for the presidency. Houston, in his farewell message, gave a very cheerful view of political affairs. But, being yet weak, Texas was in fact only a shuttlecock for the stronger powers. Houston, by his pacific policy, had brought the Indians to terms of peace, and by his economical administration had improved the financial condition of the Republic, while in agricultural and commercial respects Texas began to thrive. In his inaugural address President Jones said that his policy would be the maintenance of the public credit, the reduction of the expenses of government, the abolishment of paper issues, the revision of the tariff law, the establishment of public schools, the speedy attainment of peace with Mexico and just and friendly relations with the Indians, the introduction of the penitentiary system, and the encouragement of internal improvements. Not a word did he say with reference to annexation. But annexation loomed up so rapidly that Jones' administration was destined to be short. February 28, 1845, only three months after his inauguration, the United States Congress passed a joint resolution in favor of admitting Texas into the Union. May 5th, President Jones proclaimed an election of delegates to a convention to consider the adoption of the proposition of the United States, and, meeting at Austin, July 4, they recommended annexation, and submitted to a popular vote the proposition of the United States Congress, along with a proposed State constitution, which, on October 13, were ratified by a vote almost unanimous. February 19, 1846, President Jones surrendered the executive authority to the newly elected Governor, J. Pinckney Henderson, who was inaugurated February 16, 1846. Thus the lone star of Texas became one of a glorious constellation.

It was once generally believed in Georgia that the Lone Star flag was the workmanship of a Miss Troutman, of Crawford County, that State, who afterward married a Mr. Pope, of Alabama; and that she presented the same to a Georgia battalion commanded by Lieutenant-Colonel Ward. It was of plain white silk, bearing an azure star of five points on either side. On one side was the inscription, "Liberty or Death," and on the other side the appropriate Latin motto, "*Ubi Libertas Habitat, ibi Nostra Patria est.*" This flag was unfurled at Velasco January 8, 1836, and proudly floated on the breeze from the same liberty pole with the first flag of independence, which had just been brought from Goliad by the valiant Captain William Brown, who subsequently did such daring service in the Texas navy. On the meeting of the first Congress the flag of the Lone Star was adopted as the national flag of the young Republic. But another authority denies the Georgian belief, and insists that the first Lone Star flag ever unfurled in Texas was presented by Mrs. Sarah R. Dawson to a company of volunteers raised in Harrisburg, Texas, in 1835, and commanded by Captain Andrew Robinson. The flag was a tri-color of red, white and blue, the star being white, five-pointed and set in a ground of red.

January 14, 1839, Congress appointed five commissioners to select a site for the capital of the Republic. The commissioners were Albert C. Horton, Lewis P. Cook, Isaac W. Burton, William Menifee and J. Campbell, who made choice of the location where Austin now stands. Although at that date the new town, which was immediately laid out, was situated on the extreme frontier of the settlements, the commissioners showed their wisdom in their selection. They aimed at establishing a permanent capital, which would occupy a central position when Texas had become a thickly populated country; and though the government would be near the Indians, Austin as the seat would draw settlers more rapidly westward.

During the month of November, 1840, the Congress assembled there, surrounded by the wilderness. The seat of government for the Republic of Texas, like that of most other new governments, was subject to frequent change. The following is the order, with the dates: San Felipe, November, 1835; Washington, March, 1836; Harrisburg, same month; Galveston, April 16, 1836; Velasco, May, 1836; Columbia, October, 1836; Houston, May, 1837; Austin, October, 1839; Houston, in 1842, a short time; Washington, November, 1842; Austin, 1845 to the present time. The new State capitol has a length of 566 feet 6 inches, inclusive of porticos; width, 288 feet 10 inches at widest point; height, 311 feet from grade line to top of statue on dome.

The chief executives of Texas from 1691 to 1891 are named as follows: The first were the Spanish, who ruled from 1691 to 1822, or for 131 years. The commandants, or governors, being: Domingo Teran, Don Gaspardo de Anaya, Don Martin de Alarconne, Marquis de Aguayo, Fernando de Almazan, Melchoir de Madiavilia, Juan Antonio Bustillos, Manuel de Sandoval, Carlos de Franquis, Prudencia Basterra, Justo Boneo, Jacinto de Barrios, Antonio de Martos, Juan Maria, Baron de Riperda, Domingo Cabello, Rafael Pacheco, Manuel Muñoz, Juan Bautista el Guazabel, Antonio Cordero, Manuel de Salcedo, Christoval Dominguez, Antonio Martinez.

The Mexican governors ruled from 1822 to 1835, or 13 years. Their names and dates of appointment are given as follows: Trespalacios, 1822;

Don Luciana le Garcia, 1823; Rafael Gonzales (Coahuila and Texas), 1825; Victor Blanco, 1826; Jose Maria Viesca, 1828; Jose Maria Letona, 1831; and Francisco Vidauri, 1834.

Under the rule of the Texan—1835 to 1846—or 11 years, were Henry Smith, Provisional Governor, 1835–36; David G. Burnett, President *ad interim*, 1836; Sam Houston, Constitutional President, 1836; Mirabeau B. Lamar, President, 1838; Sam Houston, President, 1841; and Anson Jones, President, 1844–46.

The State government since annexation—1846 to 1894—48 years— has been presided over by the following named governors: J. Pinckney Henderson, 1846; George T. Wood, 1847; P. H. Bell, 1849–51; P. H, Bell, 1851– 53; E. M. Pease, 1853–55; E. M. Pease, 1855–57; H. R. Runnels, 1857–59; Sam Houston, 1859–61; Edward Clark, 1861; F. R. Lubbock, 1861–63; Pendleton Murrah, 1863–65; A. J. Hamilton (Provisional), 1865–66; James W. Throckmorton, 1866–67; E. M. Pease (Provisional), 1867–70; E. J. Davis, 1870–74; Richard Coke, 1874–76; R. B. Hubbard, 1876–79; O. M. Roberts, 1879–83; John Ireland, 1883–87; L. S. Ross, 1887–91; and J. S. Hogg, 1891–94.

In 1868 a new constitution was adopted, and in 1874 the Kiowa and Comanche Indians, who opposed the settlement of the central and plain regions of Texas, were reduced to submission and ultimately driven out. The sale of the original territory of Texas (north and west of her present boundaries), to the United States, for $10,000,000, was a necessary proceeding at that time, and, indeed, a wise one, as was the article which provided for the ownership of all lands within the State boundaries, and the right to divide the territory into five States when such would appear just and profitable. The Legislature consists of thirty-two Senators, elected for four years, and 115 Representatives, chosen for two years, restricted to biennial sessions of ninety days each. There are thirteen congressional and forty judicial districts, embracing 232 counties, of which seventy counties were unorganized in 1880.

As soon as Texas declared her independence of Mexico, she declared in her constitution the necessity of a school system. In 1839 the Congress of the new republic assigned three leagues of land to each organized county, and in the following year an additional league, for the purpose of establishing primary schools. At the same time, fifty leagues were devoted to the establishment of two colleges or universities, to be thereafter created. In February, 1840, a law was passed making the chief justice of each county, with the two associate justices, a board of school commissioners, as an executive body, and under their supervision many schools were organized and conducted.

In 1850 there were 349 public schools, with 360 teachers and 7,746 pupils. By 1860 there were 1,218 schools, with a corresponding increase of teachers and pupils. But even yet the schools were not entirely supported by public tax. Considering the many political revulsions, Indian depredations, etc., to which the State of Texas has been subject, it is remarkable to observe the advance she has made in education, and the refinements of modern civilized life. The last Civil War was, of course, the greatest interruption to her progress in all directions. Under the constitution of 1866, all funds, lands and other property previously set apart for the support of the free-school system were re-dedicated as a perpetual fund.

The constitution of 1868 did not materially alter these provisions, except in one marked particular, namely, the significant omission of the provision appropriating the taxes paid by colored persons for the support of schools for their children. The schools were made free to all. The article in the constitution reads: " It shall be the duty of the legislature of this State to make suitable provisions for the support and maintenance of a system of public free schools, for the gratuitous instruction of all the inhabitants of this State, between the ages of six and eighteen."

Since the adoption of the constitution of 1868, improvements have been constantly made, either by constitutional provision or legislation, until now, when the State has as good a school system as any in the Union.

In seventy-five counties the schools are operated on a peculiar plan called the community system. The community has no geographical boundaries, and enrollment on the community list is a matter of local enterprise. Local taxes can be levied in community counties.

The State endowment of the common schools is large. About $7,427,-808.75 in interest-bearing bonds, more than $14,380,906.37 in interest-bearing land notes, and about 20,000,000 acres of unsold lands constitute the State endowment. Of the unsold school lands a large amount is leased at four cents per acre, and the funds thus derived added to the annual available school fund.

Besides the State endowment fund, each county has been granted by the State four leagues of land, which constitute county endowment. As these lands are sold, the funds received are invested under the authority of the county commissioners' court, and the interest on the investment is annually applied to the support of the schools. A considerable portion of these lands is leased for varying terms of years, and the rental applied as the rental of the State school lands. These lands are under the exclusive control of the county authorities; 3,896,640 acres have been thus granted to counties, and a reservation has been made from the public domain for the unorganized counties.

In 1879 the Normal School was established by the State of Texas, for the purpose of training competent teachers for the public schools. Regarding the Normal School as the heart of the public-school system, it was decided to name the proposed institution the " Sam Houston Normal Institute," in honor of the hero of Texas independence. Houston had spent the evening of his eventful life in Huntsville. Here was his neglected grave. As an everlasting monument to the honored dead the Normal School was located at Huntsville. On the 1st of October, 1879, the institute opened, with Bernard Mallon as principal.

The Prairie View State Normal School is located six miles east of Hempstead, in Waller County. It is a branch of the Agricultural and Mechanical College of Texas, and under the government of the Board of Directors of that school. Originally it was designed for an industrial school, but the lack of education among the colored people of the State, and the pressing need of trained teachers for the colored schools, led to a change of objects, and it was therefore converted into a normal school for training colored teachers. The constant and steadily increasing patronage it has since received, is the best evidence of the wisdom of the change—the session of 1888-1889, having the largest attendance and being the most prosperous in the history of the institution.

The Agricultural and Mechanical College of Texas owes its foundation and endowment to the act of the United States Congress, approved July 2, 1862, amended July 23, 1865, and to a joint resolution of the Legislature of Texas, approved November 1, 1866, and an act of the same body approved April 17, 1871. Under these acts and the special laws of the Legislature growing out of them, the first board of directors met at Austin, July 16, 1875, and proceeded to organize the college. Finally the constitution of 1876, article VII, provided that the Agricultural and Mechanical College of Texas, established by the act of the Legislature passed April 17, 1871, located in the county of Brazos, is "hereby made and constituted a branch of the University of Texas, for the instruction in agriculture, the mechanic arts, and the natural sciences connected therewith." In November, 1866, the Legislature formally accepted from Congress the gift of 180,000 acres of public land for the endowment of an agricultural and mechanical college. This land was sold for $174,000, which sum was invested in 7 per cent. State bonds. As under the act of Congress neither principal nor interest of this money could be used for other purposes than the payment of officers' salaries, at the time of the opening of the college there was an addition to the fund, from accumulated interest, of $35,000. This was invested in 6 per cent. bonds of the State, thus furnishing an annual income of $14,280. The county of Brazos donated to the college 2,416 acres of land lying on each side of the Houston & Texas Central railroad.

The Agricultural Experiment Station of theAgricultural and Mechanical College of Texas, College Station, Texas, authorized by Congress in 1887, was established shortly after.

The University of Texas owes its existence to the wisdom, foresight and statesmanship of the founders of the Republic of Texas, who made the most ample provision for its establishment and maintenance in the legislation of that period. By an act of the Third Congress, fifty leagues of land were offered as an endowment, to which $100,000 were added by the Legislature of February 11, 1858. The constitution of 1876 reappropriated all grants, save the one-tenth section, in lieu of which 1,000,000 acres were set apart of unappropriated lands. In March, 1881, the act for the location and organization of the university was passed, and by vote Austin was selected as the site. On September 15, 1883, the building was open for the reception of students. In that year 1,000,000 acres of the public debt land were added to the permanent university fund, and of all this acreage 2,020,049 acres remained unsold on the last day of December, 1891.

The State Asylum for the Blind was established September 2, 1856, and has for its object the education of blind persons. It is not an asylum where the indigent and helpless are cared for at the public expense, but a school in which the blind receive such general education and training in industrial pursuits as will aid them to become self-supporting as other classes. When the course of study prescribed has been completed the pupils return to their homes, as do the students of other schools, and like them are no longer a charge upon the State.

The State Deaf and Dumb Asylum is situated at the State capital, on a commanding height south of the Colorado River, and is justly regarded as one of the most beautiful and healthful locations in the city.

The Deaf and Dumb and Blind Asylum for colored youth was established by an act of the Twentieth Legislature, which provided for the appointment of a board to select a site near the city of Austin, and appropriated $50,000 for the erection of buildings and the purchase of furniture. An admirable location, about two and a quarter miles northwest of Austin, was selected for the buildings, and the institution first opened for the reception of students October 1, 1887.

The State Lunatic Asylum is situated about two miles north of Austin, on a beautiful plateau of ground adorned and beautified by flowers, plants, summer-houses and forest trees, the latter constituting a splendid park. The estimated value of the buildings and grounds is $505,000.

The North Texas Hospital for the Insane, located at Terrell, in Kaufman County, was opened for the reception of patients July 15, 1885. It was established in obedience to a general demand for increased accommodations for the insane.

The State Orphan Asylum was required to be established by an act of the Twentieth Legislature, approved April 4, 1887. The Governor was required to appoint three commissioners to select a site for the asylum. Competition between the various towns in the State for the location of the institution was invited, which resulted in the selection of Corsicana, in Navarro county. The sum of $5,700 was appropriated out of the available Orphan Asylum fund for the establishment of the institution. Subsequently, at the special session of the Twentieth Legislature, $15,000 and the available fund to the credit of the asylum in the State treasury was appropriated for the erection of the buildings and other improvements. The site on which the asylum is located and the surrounding scenery are unsurpassed by any place in the State for their beauty and adaptability to such an institution. The buildings, which are constructed on the cottage plan, and have a capacity of about 200 inmates, were completed and the institution formally opened July 15, 1889.

Texan benevolence is not solely administered by the State. No less than eight hospitals, with several orphanages and asylums are carried on without State aid.

By act of the Twentieth Legislature, approved March 29, 1887, a State house of correction and reformatory for youthful convicts were authorized, and the Governor required to appoint a commission to locate the same. The institution was located two and one-fourth miles northeast of Gatesville, Coryell county, and the necessary buildings erected there during the summer of 1888. Up to date of the last report of the Superintendent $75,890 had been expended in the purchase of land, erection of buildings, and equipping the institution. The institution has a capacity of about 100, and was opened January 3, 1889.

The law of 1881 for organizing the State penitentiaries provided that the system of labor in the State penitentiaries should be by lease, by contract, by the State, or partly by one system and partly by the other, as shall be in the discretion of the penitentiary board deemed for the best interests of the State. The Eighteenth Legislature in 1883 repealed that portion of the law of 1881 authorizing the lease of the penitentiaries, and consequently the contract and State account systems only are allowed. At Huntsville, Rusk, Harlem and other places the convicts are worked on State and private farms.

Prior to the era of independence about the only efforts, of which there is record, to establish Protestantism in Texas were those of the Baptists, who failed to make their institutions permanent. In 1837 a Baptist church was

STEPHEN F. AUSTIN.

organized at Washington, Z. N. Morrell being chosen pastor, and money was subscribed to build a house of worship. The first Protestant Episcopal church was established in 1838, at Matagorda, by Caleb S. Ives, who collected a congregation, established a school and built a church. During the same year R. M. Chapman organized a parish in Houston. The statistics of religious denominations in Texas is estimated as follows; the actual adult members being only recognized. Methodist Episcopal, South, 151,533; Baptist, 127,377; Episcopal,9,982; Methodist Episcopal(North), 25,739; German Lutheran(1877), 2,270; Presbyterian, 2,414; Southern Presbyterian(1877), 13,555; Cumberland Presbyterian, 24,257; Christian, 55,000; Primitive Baptist, 1,000; Seventh-Day Adventists, 300; Universalists, 95; Brethren (Dunkards), 125; Free Methodists, 100; Catholics, 157,000; Hebrew, 300; Methodist Protestant, 6,300; Colored M. E. Church in America, 12,162; African Methodist Episcopal, 12,900; Colored Baptist, 100,681.

The first printing-press in Texas was put into operation at Nacogdoches in 1819, and was brought to that place by General Long, who established a provisional government and a supreme council, and issued a declaration proclaiming Texas an independent republic. The office was placed under the management of Horatio Bigelow, and was used for the publication of various laws enacted and proclamations issued by that short lived government.

The first regular newspaper, however, made its initial appearance about 1829, at San Felipe, bearing the name, *The Cotton Plant.* Godwin B. Cotten was editor and proprietor. In 1832 its name was changed to the *Texas Republican.*

The second paper was the *Texas Gazette* and *Brazoria Advertiser*, published in Brazoria in 1830. In September, 1832, it was merged into the *Constitutional Advocate* and *Texas Public Advertiser*, with D. W. Anthony as owner and editor, who died in 1833, and the paper ceased.

Next was the *Texas Republican* of Brazoria, by F. C. Gray, in December, 1834. This was printed on the old press brought into the realm by Cotten, before mentioned. In January, 1835, this was the only paper published in Texas, and in August, 1836, it was discontinued.

The fourth newspaper was the *Telegraph*, started in August 1836, at San Felipe, by Gail and Thomas H. Borden and Joseph Baker. A Mexican force seized this in April, 1836, and threw the material of the office into a bayou at Harrisburg, to which place it had been moved after the abandonment of San Felipe by the Americans. In August, that year, the Bordens bought a new press and material and revived the *Telegraph* at Columbia, and subsequently moved to Houston, where the paper was published for many years, under the name of the *Houston Telegraph.*

After the establishment of Texan independence the number of newspapers increased rapidly, until now the State has as many newspapers as any other in proportion to population. The first daily paper established in Texas was the *Morning Star* by Cruger & Moore of the *Telegraph* between 1840 and 1844. The Texas Editorial and Press Association was organized September 10, 1873, and afterward incorporated.

During the last fifteen years railroad systems have been established at a comparatively rapid rate. In 1870 there were less than 300 miles in operation; in 1876, 1,600 miles; in 1885, over 7,000 miles; and in 1890, according to the last census, 8,914.

4

In the time of the Republic numerous charters for railroads were granted, but no road was built. It was not until 1852 that the first road was commenced. That year a preliminary survey was made and some work done on what was then called the Buffalo Bayou, Brazos & Colorado Railroad, starting from Harrisburg and going westerly; and within the same year the first locomotive was set to work at Harrisburg, the first in Texas and the fourth west of the Mississippi. The company was organized June 1, 1850, at Boston, Mass., by General Sidney Sherman, who may be regarded as the father of railroads in Texas. The work progressed slowly, and the Colorado was not reached till 1859, when the line was opened to Eagle Lake, sixty-five miles from the place of beginning. By 1866 the line had reached Columbus, the river being bridged at Alleyton. A change in the charter made in 1870 fixed upon San Antonio as the objective point, and since that time it has been known as the Galveston, Harrisburg & San Antonio Railway, or "Sunset route," but is now incorporated in the great Southern Pacific system. January 15, 1877, the road reached San Antonio, the citizens of Bexar county having voted, in January, 1876, $300,000 in county bonds to secure the speedy completion of the line. In the same month the passenger terminus was changed from Harrisburg to Houston by a line from Pierce Junction. The line has since been extended to El Paso, to connect there with the Southern Pacific, going on to the Pacific coast. At that point it also connects with the Mexican Central. The length of the main line is 848 miles, and no railroad in Texas has had more influence in the settlement and development of the country.

The next railroad commenced in Texas was the Houston & Texas Central. The original charter was granted in 1848, by which the company was incorporated under the title of the Galveston & Red River Railroad Company. Their line was to extend from Galveston to the northern boundary of the State. Work was begun in 1853, at Houston, by the first incorporator, Ebenezer Allen, and at that time the name was changed to its present form. The rivalry between Galveston and Houston was satisfied by a compromise, under which arrangement the two cities were connected by the Galveston, Houston & Henderson Road, which was begun at Virginia Point, and completed in 1865, and a junction was made with the Houston & Texas Central. In 1859 a bridge was constructed across the bay by the city of Galveston.

Construction proceeded slowly, only eighty miles having been made by the time of the breaking out of the Civil War, which completely interrupted further building. In March, 1873, it reached Denison, forming there a junction with the Missouri, Kansas & Texas Road, thus opening rail communication with St. Louis. Houston has become the railroad center of the State, having at least ten trunk lines.

The Gulf, Colorado & Santa Fe line was chartered in May, 1873, as a Galveston enterprise. Construction was commenced at Virginia Point in May, 1875, and the road opened for traffic as far as Richmond in 1878. Other important systems of late introduction are the Missouri, Kansas & Texas, Atchison, Topeka & Santa Fe, San Antonio & Aransas Pass, St. Louis, Arkansas & Texas ("Cotton Belt,"), International & Great Northern, Texas & Pacific, and the recent extension of the Chicago, Rock Island & Pacific from the Red River to Fort Worth by an auxiliary corporation, etc.

All the above mentioned trunk lines have of course several branches, so that it can now be said in familiar parlance that the State of Texas is "gridironed " with railroads, and still construction is going on, and many more lines are projected. The following table shows the number of miles of railroad in the State:

Austin & Northwestern 76, East Line & Red River 121.35, Fort Worth & Denver City 467.34, Fort Worth & New Orleans 40.50, Fort Worth & Rio Grande 112.54, Galveston, Harrisburg & San Antonio 926.30, Galveston, Houston & Henderson 50, Houston & Texas Central 510, Gulf, Colorado & Santa Fe 958.25, Gulf, West Texas & Pacific 111.10, Houston, East & West Texas 191.38, International & Great Northern †647, New York, Texas & Mexican 91, Missouri, Kansas & Texas 389.39, *Sherman, Denison & Dallas 9.53, *Dallas & Greenville 52.43, *East Line & Red River 31.76, *Gainesville, Henrietta & Western 70.57, *Dallas & Wichita 37.62, *Dallas & Waco 65.57, *Trinity & Sabine 66.55, *Taylor, Bastrop & Houston 105.89, San Antonio & Aransas Pass 637.20, St. Louis, Arkansas & Texas 554.05, Southern Kansas & Texas 100.41, Sabine & East Texas 103.47, Texas Central 288.80, Texas Mexican 178.61, Texas, Sabine Valley & Northwestern 38, Texas Trunk 51, Texas & Pacific 1,125.95, Tyler Southeastern 89.08, Texas Western 52.25, Texas & New Orleans 105.10, Weatherford, Mineral Wells & Northwestern 20.05, Central Texas & Northwestern 12, Wichita Valley 51.36. Totals, 8,914.13.

The population of Texas, by decades, is shown as follows—1835—50,000; 1845—150,000; 1850—212,592; 1860—604,215; 1870—818,579; 1880—1,591,749, and 1890—2,235,523. Of the total for 1890, 2,082,567 are natives of the United States and 152,956 of other countries. The number of whites in 1890 was 1,745,935, and the number of Africans, 488,171. There were three Japanese and 704 civilized Indians within its boundaries when the last census was taken. Of the native born white population 1,082,533 are males, and 1,000,034 females; of the foreign born whites, 90,020 are males and 62,936 females, while of the colored population 246,517 are males and 243,071 females. There were 402,422 dwellings in the State in 1800, or 5.56 persons to a dwelling, against 27,988 dwellings in 1850 and 287,562 dwellings in 1880, when there were 5.54 persons to each habitable house. The population by counties (as enumerated in 1890) and the date of organization of each county, are given as follows:

COUNTY.	POP. 1890.	ORGAN-IZED.	COUNTY.	POP. 1890.	ORGAN-IZED.
Anderson	20,923	1846	Bee	3,720	1858
Andrews	24	....	Bell	33,377	1850
Angelina	6,306	1846	Bexar	49,266	1837
Aransas	1,824	1871	Bexar District	....	....
Archer	2,104	1880	Blanco	4,649	1858
Armstrong	944	1890	Borden	222	1877
Atascosa	6,459	1856	Bosque	14,224	1854
Austin	17,859	1837	Bowie	20,267	1841
Bailey	......	....	Brazoria	11,506	1837
Bandera	3,795	1856	Brazos	16,650	1843
Bastrop	20,736	1837	Brewster	710	1887
Baylor	2,595	1879	Briscoe	....	....

†Only 250.80 miles are taxed.
*Operated by the Missouri, Kansas & Texas.

County.	Pop. 1890.	Organ-ized.	County.	Pop. 1890.	Organ-ized.
Brown	11,421	1857	Encinal	2,744	....
Buchel	298	....	Erath	21,594	1856
Burleson	13,001	1846	Falls	20,706	1850
Burnet	10,747	1854	Fannin	38,709	1838
Caldwell	15,769	1848	Fayette	31,481	1838
Calhoun	815	1846	Fisher	2,996	1886
Callahan	5,457	1877	Floyd	529	1890
Cameron	14,424	1848	Foard	......	1891
Camp	6,624	1874	Foley	25	....
Carson	356	1888	Fort Bend	10,586	1838
Cass	22,554	1846	Franklin	6,481	1875
Castro	9	1891	Freestone	15,987	1850
Chambers	2,241	1858	Frio	3,112	1871
Cherokee	22,975	1846	Gaines	68	....
Childress	1,175	1887	Galveston	31,476	1839
Clay	7,503	1873	Garza	14	....
Cochran	......	....	Gillespie	7,056	1848
Coke	2,059	1889	Glasscock	208	1887
Coleman	6,112	1864	Goliad	5,910	1836
Collin	36,736	1846	Gonzales	18,016	1836
Collingsworth	357	1890	Gray	203	....
Colorado	19,512	1837	Grayson	53,211	1846
Comal	6,398	1846	Gregg	9,402	1873
Comanche	15,608	1856	Greer	......	1886
Concho	1,065	1879	Grimes	21,312	1846
Cooke	24,696	1849	Guadalupe	15,217	1846
Coryell	16,873	1854	Hale	721	1888
Cottle	240	....	Hall	703	1890
Crane	15	....	Hamilton	9,313	1858
Crockett	194	1891	Hansford	133	1889
Crosby	346	1886	Hardeman	3,904	1884
Dallam	112	1891	Hardin	3,956	1858
Dallas	67,042	1846	Harris	37,249	1837
Dawson (disap-			Harrison	26,721	1842
peared)	......	....	Hartley	252	1891
Dawson	29	....	Haskell	1,665	1885
Deaf Smith	179	1890	Hays	11,352	1848
Delta	9,117	1870	Hemphill	519	1887
Denton	21,289	1846	Henderson	12,285	1846
Dewitt	14,307	1846	Hidalgo	6,534	1852
Dickens	295	1891	Hill	27,583	1853
Dimmit	1,049	1880	Hockley	......	....
Donley	1,056	1882	Hood	7,614	1866
Duval	7,598	1876	Hopkins	20,572	1846
Eastland	10,373	1873	Houston	19,360	1882
Ector	224	1891	Howard	1,210	1837
Edwards	1,970	1883	Hunt	31,885	1846
Ellis	31,774	1850	Hutchinson	58	....
El Paso	15,678	1871	Irion	870	1889

County.	Pop. 1890.	Organ-ized.	County.	Pop. 1890.	Organ-ized.
Jack	9,740	1857	Morris	6,580	1875
Jackson	3,281	1837	Motley	139	1891
Jasper	5,592	1837	Nacogdoches	15,984	1837
Jeff Davis	1,394	1887	Navarro	26,373	1846
Jefferson	5,857	1837	Newton	4,650	1846
Johnson	22,313	1854	Nolan	1,573	1881
Jones	3,797	1881	Nueces	8,093	1846
Karnes	3,637	1854	Ochiltree	198	1889
Kaufman	21,598	1848	Oldham	270	1891
Kendall	3,826	1862	Orange	4,770	1852
Kent	324	—	Palo Pinto	8,320	1857
Kerr	4,462	1856	Panola	14,328	1846
Kimble	2,243	1876	Parker	21,682	1856
King	173	1891	Parmer	7	—
Kinney	3,781	1874	Pecos	1,326	1872
Knox	1,134	1886	Polk	10,332	1846
Lamar	37,302	1841	Potter	849	1887
Lamb	4	—	Presidio	1,698	1875
Lampasas	7,584	1856	Rains	3,909	1870
La Salle	2,139	1880	Randall	187	1889
Lavaca	21,887	1846	Red River	21,452	1837
Lee	11,952	1874	Reeves	1,247	1884
Leon	18,841	1846	Refugio	1,239	1837
Liberty	4,230	1837	Roberts	326	1889
Limestone	21,678	1846	Robertson	26,506	1838
Lipscomb	632	1887	Rockwall	5,972	1873
Live Oak	2,055	1856	Runnels	3,193	1880
Llano	6,772	1856	Rusk	18,559	1843
Loving	3	—	Sabine	4,969	1837
Lubbock	33	1891	San Augustine	6,688	1837
Lynn	24	—	San Jacinto	7,360	1870
McCulloch	3,217	1876	San Patricio	1,312	1837
McLennan	39,204	1850	San Saba	6,641	1856
McMullen	1,038	1877	Schleicher	155	—
Madison	8,512	1854	Scurry	1,415	1884
Marion	10,862	1860	Shackelford	2,012	1874
Martin	264	1884	Shelby	14,365	1837
Mason	5,180	1856	Sherman	34	1889
Matagorda	3,985	1837	Smith	28,324	1846
Maverick	3,698	1871	Somervell	3,419	1875
Medina	3,730	1848	Starr	10,749	1848
Menard	1,215	1871	Stephens	4,926	1876
Midland	1,033	1885	Sterling	—	1891
Milam	24,773	1837	Stonewall	1,024	1888
Mills	5,493	1887	Sutton	658	1890
Mitchell	2,059	1881	Swisher	100	1890
Montague	18,863	1858	Tarrant	41,142	1850
Montgomery	11,765	1837	Taylor	6,957	1878
Moore	15	—	Terry	21	—

County.	Pop. 1890.	Organized.	County.	Pop. 1890.	Organized.
Throckmorton	902	1879	Washington	29,161	1837
Titus	8,190	1846	Webb	14,842	1848
Tom Green	5,152	1875	Wharton	7,584	1846
Travis	36,322	1843	Wheeler	778	1879
Trinity	7,648	1850	Wichita	4,831	1882
Tyler	10,877	1846	Wilbarger	7,092	1881
Upshur	12,695	1846	Williamson	25,900	1848
Upton	52	—	Wilson	10,655	1860
Uvalde	3,804	1856	Winkler	18	—
Valverde	2,874	1885	Wise	24,134	1856
Van Zandt	16,225	1848	Wood	13,932	1850
Victoria	8,737	1837	Yoakum	4	—
Walker	12,874	1846	Young	5,049	1874
Waller	10,888	1873	Zapata	3,562	1858
Ward	77	—	Zavalla	1,097	1884

The area of the State is 274,366 square miles, or over 70,000 square miles larger than France; about 78,000 larger than Spain; 63,000 larger than the German Empire, in Europe; 73,000 more than the Austro-Hungarian Empire and within 24,000 square miles of Sweden and Norway. In 1890 there were only forty-four inhabitants to every five square miles of its area, while England and Wales, having only an area of 58,320 miles, were credited with 29,001,018 inhabitants in 1891, (of whom 780,457 were registered dependents or paupers) or over 497 inhabitants to each square mile, against eighty-eight in Texas. Were Texas as thickly populated as England, it would contain 136,359,902 inhabitants. With her sea coast, her fertile lands capable of producing cotton and sugar as well as potatoes and wheat, her storehouses of mineral wealth and wealthy neighbors on the West, East and North, Texas to-day holds the key to her destiny. Her development rests in good hands.

BIOGRAPHY.

GEORGE LORD. Cordial in manner, apt in expression and full of the knowledge gathered in many years of intelligent observation, one seldom meets a more interesting man than Mr. George Lord who is now seventy-eight years of age. He was born in County Essex, England, April 21, 1816, and is a son of Felstead and Anna (Siggs) Lord, both natives of England. The father was a bricklayer and by an accident, while repairing a hot brick oven, lost his life. This was when our subject was but an infant. The mother married again and died in London when eighty-two years of age. George Lord was educated in his native country and there continued to make his home until June, 1834, when he took passage for America. Landing in Canada he remained there two years, and then removed to New Orleans where for a few months he ran on the Mississippi River steamers. December 27, 1836, he joined a company of seventy-five men under Capt. Lyons for the war with Mexico, and landed at Galveston February 14, 1837, when there was but one frame building there. On February 14, 1837, he was mustered into service at Camp Independence, on the Lavaca River, in John Holliday's (who escaped from the Fannin Massacre) Company of Second regimental volunteers, under Col. Wiggington. In June, 1837, his company was consolidated with Capt. Jordan's Company and sent to San Antonio in October, 1837. The following year Mr. Lord was discharged. For his services he was granted 1,280 acres of bounty land. The same year he was at the Cibilo, at the ranch of Col. Patton, when about fifty Comanches came to hold a consultation. On their return from the lower country they killed a man named Tolbert. After Col. Burleson's fight with Cordova on the Guadalupe, near Sequin, Mr. Lord joined Capt. Dawson's Company in San Antonio, to intercept those who escaped, and they captured two or three. About September 1, 1839, he joined the forces under Gen. Canalis, on Nueces River, and during the first campaign was at the taking of Guerro, in Mexico, and participated in the following battles: Alcantre, Matamoras and Monterey. During the second campaign he was at the taking of Laredo, and in the battle of Saltillo with Col. Jordon. The men were fighting for the Mexican constitution of 1824, and were led by Molano and Lopez who treacherously bargained to sell their men to the enemy for a doubloon a head, but *failed to deliver the goods.* In June, 1842, Mr. Lord joined Capt. Cameron's Company at Corpus Christi and was with him at the battle of Lipantitlan, July 7, though during that battle he was engaged in scouting duties, at Salado, and was near San Antonio in September of that year and in the battle of and surrender at Mier, which led to the most dramatic incident recorded of any war, the bean drawing. After the surrender Mr. Lord and his comrades made several attempts to escape, first at San Juan River and next at Rinconade, both failures because of treachery in their own ranks. The third attempt was made at Salado, Mexico, where they were imprisoned, and was successful through a piece of marvelous daring. Mr. Lord described it as follows: " When all was ready Capt. Cameron said in a distinct tone, ' Well boys we will go it,' and suiting the action to the word he seized one of the sentinels while S. H. Walker seized the other. It was the work of an instant to disarm the guard and get possession of the outer court where the arms and cartridge boxes were guarded by 150 men. They then charged the enemy outside the building, including the ' Red Caps ' and whipped them in less than two minutes. We had three killed, two mortally and five or six slightly wounded. The enemy lost eight or ten. To sum up: Got up on the 11th inst., ate breakfast, whipped the guard, and traveled sixty-three miles before stopping. A good day's work." After escaping, these brave men retreated towards Texas through a weary, barren land, without the shadow of a great rock to refresh and sustain. They went three days without water and were forced to kill their horses for food. Finally on the eighth day, famished and exhausted, they were easily recaptured by the pursuing Mexicans, and were marched to Salado, where on the 25th of March the bean drawing took place. The following is Mr. Lord's account of it: "Soon after our arrival at Salado we received the melancholy intelligence that we were to be decimated, and every tenth man shot. It was now too late to resist this horrible order. We were closely handcuffed and drawn up in front of our guards who with arms were in readiness to fire. Could we have known it previously we would have again charged the guards and made them dearly pay for this breach of National faith. It was now too late. A manly gloom and proud defiance pervaded all countenances. We had but one alternative, and that was to invoke our country's vengeance upon our murderers, consign our souls to God, and die like men. The decimator, Col. Domingo Huerta, who was especially nominated to do this black deed after Governor Mexier had refused, arrived at Salado ahead of our men. The ' Red Cap ' Company were to be the executioners—those men who had been so humanely spared by us at this place the 11th of February. The decimation took place by the drawing of black and white beans from a small earthen mug, the white beans signifying exemption and the black death. One hundred and fifty-nine white beans were placed in the bottom of the mug and seventeen black ones were placed on top of them. The beans were not stirred, and had so slight a shake that it was perfectly clear that they had not been mixed together, thus showing that they were anxious to catch Capt. Cameron and other officers who had to draw first. Capt. Cameron with his usual coolness said: ' Well boys, we have to draw, let's be at it,' thrust his hand into the mug and drew a white bean. Capt. Eastland was the first to draw a black bean. They all drew their beans with a manly dignity and firmness which showed them superior to their condition. Some of the lighter temper jested over the horrible tragedy. One said, ' Boys, this beats raffling all to pieces;' another said, ' This is the tallest gambling scrape I ever was in.' Those who drew black beans showed no emotion, not even changing color, but on the contrary those who drew white beans seemed completely overcome. They wept and appeared completely unmanned. Poor Robert Beard, who lay upon the ground near by, ill and exhausted from his forced marches, called his brother William, who was bringing him a cup of water, and said: ' Brother, if you get a black bean I'll take your place, I want to die.' The brother with anguish replied: ' No,

I will keep my own place, I am strong and better able to die than you.' These noble youths both drew white beans, but both soon after died, leaving this heroic legacy to their venerable parents in Texas. Several of the Mexican officers who officiated in this cruel violation of their country's faith, expressed much regret thereat, and some wept bitterly. Soon after the fated men were placed in a separate court yard and later executed. Several of us were permitted to visit and receive their dying requests. Poor Cocke, when he drew his fatal bean, held it up between forefinger and thumb, and with a contemptuous smile said: 'Boys, I told you so. I never failed in my life to draw a prize,' and turning to Judge Gibson said: 'Well, Judge, say to my friends that I died in grace.' Cocke further remarked: 'They only rob me of forty years,' and then sat down and wrote a dignified letter of remonstrance to Gen. Waddy Thompson, American Minister to Mexico. Knowing that his remains would be robbed of his clothes, he drew off his pantaloons and handed them to his comrades, dying in his underclothes. Poor Henry Whaling, one of Cameron's best fighters, as he drew his black bean said with as bright a smile as ever brightened a man's face: 'Well, they don't make much off of me, anyhow, for I know I have killed twenty-five of the yellow bellies,' then in a firm voice demanded his dinner, saying: 'They shall not cheat me out of it.' He ate heartily, smoked a cigar, and in twenty minutes was launched into eternity. The Mexicans said he had the largest heart they had ever seen. They shot him fifteen times before he expired. Poor Torrey, quite a youth, but in spirit a giant, said he was perfectly willing to meet his fate; that for the glory of his country he had fought, and for her glory was willing to die, and turning to the officer said: 'After the battle of San Jacinto my family took one of your youths prisoner, raised and educated him, and this is our requital.' Capt. Cameron on taking leave of these brave men, and particularly of Turnbull, a brother Scotchman, with whom he had braved many dangers, wept bitterly, and implored the officers to execute him and spare his men. Just previous to this they were bound with cords, with bandaged eyes, and were seated on logs with their backs to their executioners. They all begged the officer to shoot them in front and at a short distance, and said that they were not afraid to look death in the face. This he refused to do and to make the cruelty as refined as possible, fired at several places, and continued the firing from ten to twelve minutes, lacerating and mangling these heroes in a manner too horrible for description. Such was the effect of the horrible massacre upon their own soldiers who were stationed as guards upon the wall above, that one of them fainted and came near falling over. During the martyrdom of these noble spirits we were separated from them by a stone wall fifteen feet high, and heard their last agonizing groans. J. L. Shepherd, one of the unfortunates, was not killed by the executioners it seems, for the next morning only sixteen bodies were found and we heard afterward that he was recognized on the streets of Saltillo by a Mexican soldier and shot down. When the Mexicans missed him they came to us and demanded another man in his stead. To this we demurred and they finally agreed to let the matter rest. The next morning they marched us out, and halted us before the mangled bodies of our comrades." Their names were as follows: L. L. Cash, of Pennsylvania; J. D. Cocke, of Virginia; Robert Dunham, of Tennessee; Capt. William N. Eastland, Tennessee; Edmond Esta, New Jersey; Robert Harris, Mississippi; Thomas L. Jones, Kentucky; Patrick Mahan, Ireland; James Ogden, Virginia;

Charles Roberts, Tennessee; William Rowan, Georgia; J. L. Shepherd, Ala-
bama; J. M. M. Thompson, Tennessee; J. M. Torrey, Connecticut; James
Turnbull, Scotland; Henry Whaling, Indiana; and M. C. Wing, New York.
An heroic episode touching these martyrs is related by Mr. Lord. "Walter P.
Lane, who during the Mexican War was Major of Hays' regiment of Texas
Rangers under J. E. Wool, was dispatched by the latter with a small body of
men to go South in the direction of San Luis Potosi, to discover all that was
possible in relation to the movements of the Mexican army. There were two
roads to that place, one by Matchuala, a large town, the other by the great
——————of Solada, where the seventeen Mier prisoners drew beans in
1843. The two roads were divided by a range of mountains. Lane took the
left hand or eastern road, and actually penetrated to and entered the city of
Matchuala, with its twenty thousand people and garrison of several hundred
men. He ordered and obtained dinner at a 'meson' (a compromise between
an hotel and a wagon yard), announced that a large American army was near
by, and feasted his men to their satisfaction. Then remounting he retired
across the mountain to the other road, and struck the hacienda of Salado.
Seizing the Alcalde, he ordered the resurrection of the bones of the sixteen
martyrs, and demanded mules, sacks, saddles, and all things necessary to bear
them away. All were furnished and the remains of the dead duly placed on
mules. Lane tipped his beaver to the Alcalde and assembled villagers, and
bore these relics to Gen. Taylor's headquarters. They were taken to La
Grange, on the Colorado River, Texas, by John Dusenberry, of New York,
one of the Mier prisoners, and there, with all solemnity, in the presence of
thousands, interred on Monument Hill, overlooking the country for miles
around. Few know, even to this day, that to Gen. Walter P. Lane Texas is
indebted for the possession of these mementoes of heroism never surpassed."

After the death of these noble men Mr. Lord and his fellow prisoners were
marched to near Huehuetoca, within seven leagues of the City of Mexico.
Capt. Cameron on entering his quarters for the night remarked prophetically,
"Boys we all know who goes in, but God knows who'll come out." About
eight o'clock that night, April 25, orders came from that tyrant, Santa Anna,
to shoot the beloved Capt. Cameron, and after the others had started to march
for the City of Mexico, he was taken to the rear of the village to the place of
execution. A priest was in waiting and asked him if he wished to confess.
He promptly replied, "No, throughout life I believe I have been an honest
man, and if I have to confess, it shall be to my Maker." As the guard
advanced to bandage his eyes he said to his interpreter: "Tell them no, Ewen
Cameron can now, as he has often done before for the liberty of Texas, look
death in the face without winking." So saying he opened the bosom of his
hunting shirt, presented his naked breast, and gave the word "fire." Mr.
Lord was imprisoned in Tacubaya from May 1st, to September 16, 1843, and
was employed in making streets. He was then removed to Perote Castle and
liberated in 1844. Returning to Texas he received a letter patent to 1,280
acres of land which he selected in the beautiful Cheapside country and has
since increased it by purchase to 3,442 acres. His devotion to the Republic
in war and prison covered four years and seven months; to the Mexican
Confederation one year and one month. When Civil War broke out he joined
the home guards and served two years, although he was exempt from service
to his State on account of age.

Previous to this, in 1849, he went to California and dug gold three years, after which he returned to Texas with $7,000 in gold dust which he presented and had coined at the New Orleans mint. This was the basis of his fortune. In politics he is Independent and in religion an Episcopalian. He has served as school trustee and has held other positions. On December 30, 1849, he was married to Miss Kate Myers, who was born in New Orleans, October 15, 1832, and they have had eleven children, nine of whom are still living: Cinthelia Ann, wife of John Johnson; George T., Robert F., Emily Agnes, wife of H. N. Smith; William P., Minnie May (deceased); Sidney Johnston, Henry Lee, Kate A., James E. and Pomona B. (deceased). Mr. and Mrs. Lord have twenty-nine interesting grandchildren.

ABRAHAM LEVI, of Victoria, Texas, was born in the village of Hatte, Alsace, France, on the 24th of June, 1822, his parents being Getchell and Rachel Levi, poor but respected citizens of that country. To these parents four children were born, two sons and two daughters, Abraham being the youngest son and third child. The eldest son, Simon, lives at present in Hochfeld, France, and the two daughters, now Mrs. Melanie Berkowitz and Mrs. M. Haas, live in the city of Paris.

When Abraham was eight years old his father died, and, as the widowed mother was without other means of support, her little children were required to assist her as best they could, and consequently obtained but a limited education. It was while thus engaged in assisting his mother to support the family that Abraham displayed three distinct traits of character which have distinguished him ever since, and have made possible his success in life, both from the standpoints of wealth and honor. He displayed unusual capacity for the abstract calculations of mental arithmetic, remarkable talent for business operations, and a most praiseworthy and commendable conscientiousness, which three qualities have since made both his fame and his fortune. But it may be said that the first two qualities were really one—ability to make shrewd, far-reaching and successful business calculations, all resulting from his boyish capacity for mental arithmetic. Divested of all adornments, his characteristics through life thus far have been remarkable aptitude for business and strict, undeviating integrity. It will be seen in reflecting upon the life of Mr. Levi, that these two qualities embrace many others that are deserving of special consideration, which will be fully shown as this sketch is continued.

As a youth he was not strong or robust, and as a consequence did not learn a trade; but at the early age of thirteen years he began business operations on his own account, his capital being a few francs he had managed to save, and his stock a small line of ribbons and fancy articles, which he undertook to sell in the surrounding country. He followed this venture industriously, and here another good quality, which has since been very valuable to him, exhibited itself—persistence. As long as there was any hope of success he kept steadily at work, nothing daunted by occasional failures to make profitable bargains, watching for the best points of vantage, and making good sales at the various little villages visited on "market days." All his profits were turned over to his mother, who mainly depended upon this slender income, as the eldest son, Simon, had been obliged to enter the army and could afford her no assistance. In about 1841 he also was subjected to the liability of doing military duty for his country, but was fortunate in drawing a lucky number, which thereafter exempted him from such service. In 1843 his mother died, and thus, at the age of twenty-one years, he was free to follow his own inclinations.

He, like all other Frenchmen of his day, had heard with high favor of the United States, and he determined as soon as possible to cross the ocean to the new land. But the funeral expenses of his mother and several debts had first to be met, and he was thus obliged to remain in France about three years longer. He was honest to the last cent, but his meager resources were unequal to meet all the debts; so he determined to go to America and there earn means sufficient to pay the last obligation at Strasburg. He accordingly took passage on a sailing vessel bound for New Orleans, and after a stormy voyage of thirty-eight days reached the famous "Crescent City" of the New World, where so many of his countrymen had preceded him. Here he was in a new land, with scarcely a cent in his pocket, unfamiliar with the current language, obliged to rely solely upon his own exertions. But here it was that another excellent quality manifested itself—never to despair in the face of opportunity. He accepted any honorable labor that offered itself, and by degrees made his way up the river to Natchez, where he secured work for ten dollars and board per month from a butcher. He was required to dig for water in a tank, and managed to save a few dollars. This he invested in merchandise, which he peddled on foot through the country districts, and added not a little to his popularity, and consequent profit, by being the possessor of a very melodious voice, and by the fact that he was a Frenchman, a mark of honor along the river. He steadily added to his capital, but so slowly that he determined to abandon that occupation and try something else. He finally secured a position at Liberty, Miss., with a merchant named A. Schwartz, for fifteen dollars per month and board, and at the end of three months, so faithfully had he served and so thoroughly were his efforts appreciated, his wages were raised to twenty-five dollars, and about three months still later he received another raise to fifty dollars per month, though his employer found it necessary to discharge other help to enable and warrant him in doing this. This was a great lift in the world, and was his real start in the United States. His quick advancement had been merited, for he was active, intelligent, industrious and honest, and was worth the advance to his employer.

He remained with Mr. Schwartz, having his perfect confidence, until 1848, when, having learned of an excellent business opening at Victoria, Texas, he determined to embrace it. So good was his standing with Mr. Schwartz that his credit was excellent with all his acquaintances. Jacob Halfin, brother-in-law of Mr. Schwartz, agreed to advance a credit of $3,000 in the city of New Orleans to his younger brother, Henry Halfin, and Mr. Levi, to enable them to make a business start at Victoria. Mr. Levi started for Victoria to investigate, but missed the steamer at New Orleans, and, coming back, insisted that an investigating tour was useless, and that they should go at once and take the goods with them, which was accordingly done.

Mr. Levi reached Victoria with his goods in 1849, and here, with few interruptions, the business has been continuously conducted down to the present time. At first he had no place to put his goods, but in a few days rented a room of a Mr. Nicholson, and soon the business of the two young men, who were partners, prospered far beyond their expectations. However, in 1854, it suffered seriously in common with all others, owing to the monetary crisis in the country. He lost heavily, but honorably paid his debts, and maintained his credit, and the economical methods thus inculcated saved him from further loss during the greater financial panic of 1857. Before the latter crisis both Jacob Halfin and Moses Schwartz, learning of the excellent business outlook in Texas, sold out their business in Mississippi and joined the young men at Victoria, forming the firm of Halfin, Levi & Co. From this partnership Henry Halfin withdrew in 1859, leaving as partners Jacob Halfin, Moses Schwartz and Abraham Levi. They began a business which increased so rapidly that in 1861 it was the largest in western Texas, and extended all over the Southwest, but on January 1, 1861, the block of buildings in which it was situated, which was mainly owned by them, was burned to the ground, which discontinued the firm of Halfin, Levi & Co. An effort was made to secure the insurance from New York, but before it could be done the war came on and the effort was necessarily abandoned for the time.

Mr. Levi warmly espoused the cause of the South, though he had avoided holding slaves, except the few household servants. Though quite wealthy when the war began, he lost heavily during that sanguinary struggle, and in 1864 went to France, where he hunted up and paid his old creditor at Strasburg in full. The latter had forgotten him, but Mr. Levi had not forgotten the debt, though he had forgotten the name of the debtor. His honesty was fully appreciated by the old man, who treated him with great hospitality.

In 1865 he came back, and stopping at Matamoras, Mexico, engaged in business there, and was soon joined by his family; but when the war in the States ended business in Mexico languished, entailing heavy loss on Mr. Levi. He returned to Victoria to find his home in possession of Federal troops, and, after much trouble and correspondence with the authorities at Washington, he succeeded in obtaining possession of the same. He opened a small store, but his health failing, he started in 1866 for Europe upon the advice of his physician, but on the way, while in New York, managed to collect a percentage of the insurance on the property destroyed by fire January 1, 1861. With this he returned to Victoria, and here the question arose as to how this insurance money should be disposed of. Considerable feeling arose over the matter, but all differences were finally reconciled by paying the entire sum to the creditors of the house, and by Mr. Levi paying out of his own pocket two-thirds of the firm's obligations. Mr. Levi then spent several months traveling in Europe.

During the war between the States he invested extensively and profitably in French securities and returned to America improved in health. In 1867 he purchased a large stock of groceries in New York, and, bringing the same with him to Victoria, began the present wholesale grocery business of A. Levi & Co., in connection with his cousin, Henry Levy. In April, 1879, the latter withdrew from the firm, since which time the members have been A. Levi and his sons, G. A. Levi and C. G. Levi. It is now the largest business house in Victoria and carries a stock worth $25,000, and does an annual business of $150,000, buying all its goods for cash by the car load. The firm owns about 25,000 acres of land, distributed in six counties, and has large cattle interests and other valuable holdings.

In March, 1875, the banking house of A. Levi & Co. was founded, with a capital of $50,000, since increased to $365,000, with a surplus of $25,400.

The present officers are G. A. Levi, President; Charles G. Levi, Vice-president; J. K. Hexter, Cashier. Their fine commercial and office building was erected in 1891. The bank equipment is very modern in all its appliances and furnishings, and is provided with a strong vault filled in with three and a half inches of chrome steel, Diebold make, with a self-acting, automatic time lock. It is one of the safest depositories for the funds of customers in the Southwest.

Abraham Levi deserves high credit for his successful and honorable life. Starting with nothing but good habits and an honest intention, he has crowned his career with wealth and his family name with renown. His qualities would have made him eminent in whatsoever field his lot had been cast. His business career has been characterized by its versatility. If one line of industry could not be made successful, he readily adapted himself to others, and through all the vicissitudes of fortune maintained inviolate his good name.

While a young man in Mississippi Mr. Levi had formed an attachment with Miss Mina Halfin, sister of Henry Halfin, his business partner, which attachment ripened into marriage in 1850. To them were born seven children, six of whom yet survive, the youngest, Elias, dying in 1867, aged three months. The others were named as follows: G. A., born in 1852; Fannie, born in 1854; Leo N., born in 1856; Rosa, born in 1858; Charles G., born in 1860; and Melanie, born in 1861. On the 7th of August, 1867, while her husband was traveling in Europe, Mrs. Levi, beloved by her family and friends for her sweet and lovable character, unfortunately died, to the great loss and sorrow of her bereaved family. Of her children, Fannie is the wife of Soloman Halff, of San Antonio; Leo N. is a prominent lawyer, and a member of the legal firm of Scott, Levi & Smith, of Galveston; Rosa is the wife of Moses Haas, of the firm of Haas & Oppenheimer, of San Antonio, and Melanie is the wife of J. K. Hexter, cashier of the banking house of A. Levi & Co., whom she married December 1, 1886.

G. A. Levi has acquired more than a local reputation as a financier, debater and author. He is an expert on the subject of banking, and has written several able articles on that and other financial topics. He has made himself prominent as a debater in various conventions of bankers in Texas and Louisiana. He is a recognized leader in financial circles, and a rising politician and political economist. He is President of the above-named banking house and managing partner of the mercantile establishment of A. Levi & Co. He was educated in New York City, and was preparing to enter Columbia College when his mother died in 1867. He thereupon completed the commercial course and returned to Victoria in 1869, and at the age of seventeen years joined his father in business. He has since been identified with the growth of Victoria. He has filled many positions of trust in stock companies and in the civil administration of Victoria. In 1882 he was elected Treasurer of the New York, Texas & Mexican Railway, and served two years until a change occurred in the management. In 1884, as a recognition of his conspicuous executive ability, he was chosen by the Democratic party Chairman of the Seventh Congressional District of Texas. He took the stump and distinguished himself by his fervid oratory, and his knowledge of profound public questions. In 1888 he was nominated and elected one of the Cleveland electors from Texas. In all of these positions he has proved his fitness for the uncertain game of politics, and has reflected honor on the name of Levi, so well established and maintained by his illustrious and venerable father. He was one of the organizers and the first President of the Victoria Light, Power & Ice Co., and is Past Grand President of District Grand Lodge No. 7, I. O. B. B. He is also prominent in the circles of the Knights of Pythias. He was married January 11, 1877, to Miss Theresa Gugenheim, of Victoria, whose parents came here from Louisiana in 1854. To this union the following children have been born: Minnie, Marcus C., Leo S. and Rosa. The family live in one of the handsomest residences in Victoria, which was erected in 1884. Mr. G. A. Levi is yet a young man, and no doubt the future has valuable gifts and high honors in store for him.

J. W. BENNETT, one of the large farmers and stock raisers of Lavaca County, Texas, came originally from Alabama, where his birth occurred in 1847. He was the eldest child born to William F. and Amy (Cheschire) Bennett; the father, a native of the Palmetto State and the mother of Alabama. Grandfather, Duke Bennett, was a native of South Carolina, and our subject's maternal grandfather, James Cheschire, was of English descent, a prominent planter, and an early settler of Alabama. William F. Bennett enlisted in the Confederate Army in 1862, and served in General Lee's army until the works were blown up at Petersburg, when he received a wound that resulted in his death. Mrs. Bennett is still living in Alabama. Our subject was reared in Alabama, but received but limited chances for an education. In 1867 he came to Texas, located at Hallettsville, engaged in farming and for the most part has carried this on ever since. He served as Deputy Sheriff from 1870 to 1873, and in the latter year was elected to the office of Sheriff, holding that position and Collector for seven years, after which he declined re-election. This was soon after the war, and the office of Sheriff and Collector was a rather dangerous one to hold, but Mr. Bennett was fearless in the discharge of his duties, and no more efficient and capable official ever held that position. Mr. Bennett is the owner of a stock ranch of 3,000 acres, and two farms near town, with 500 acres under cultivation, mainly improved by himself. He deals principally in stock, buying young steers and raising them for the market, is one of the foremost stockmen of his section, and is President of the Lavaca County National Bank, at Hallettsville. He was married on the 26th of November, 1874, to Miss Fanny Moss, a native of Mississippi, who was reared in Texas by an uncle, Major B. F. Moss, who was an early settler of Lavaca County. Two children have been born to this union—Lydia and Bell. The latter died in infancy. Mr. and Mrs. Bennett are members of the Christian Church, and he is a member of the Knights of Honor.

CHARLES C. HOWERTON. No professional or commercial pursuit affords better opportunities to men of ability and pluck than real estate and insurance; a notable example of advancement in this direction being illustrated in the record of Charles C. Howerton, real estate and insurance, Cuero, Texas. Enterprising methods and progressive ideas were introduced into the management of his affairs from the first, and Mr. Howerton has received a firm footing in commercial circles. He is one of the earliest and most prominent citizens of the above mentioned town, and has held many important positions in the county, being Justice of the Peace and Mayor of Cuero. He is a product of that Grand Old State, Virginia, born in Halifax County, April 5, 1832, and is of English origin on both sides of the house. The Howertons came to Virginia from England as early as in 1665. Charles C., was fifth in order of birth of six children born to James and Susan Independence (Howerton) Howerton, the parents cousins, and natives of the Old Dominion, as were the ancestors for four or five generations. The father's maternal grandmother, a Miss Hayes, was an own cousin of President George Washington. James Howerton went to Kentucky when a young man, remained there a few years, and then returning to his native state entered the army in the War of 1812, as lieutenant. After the war, he married his cousin, as stated, and in 1837 moved to Davidson County, Tennessee, near the Hermitage. Two years later he moved from there to Coahoma County, Mississippi, where he followed farming until 1850. From there he came to Calhoun County, Texas, was Sheriff of that county for nine years, and died at Port Lavaca, September 11, 1868. The mother died at Delta, Mississippi, March 14, 1850. Both were earnest members of the Baptist Church.

Our subject, Charles C. Howerton, had very limited educational advantages, attending school but a few months during his life, and at the early age of ten years was put in charge of a wood yard on an island, No. 68, in the Mississippi River. In three months time he had sold 9,000 cords of wood to passing steamboats, thus showing that even at that early age he had wonderful business ability. When thirteen years of age he engaged in the timber business in the Yazoo Delta, cutting and floating timber out of the swamps to the sawmills on the lower river; was so engaged for about two years, when, in 1850, he came to Texas, locating at Indianola, Calhoun County. There he was engaged in the boating business, buying and shipping wood. In August, 1852, his brother, Philip Washington Howerton, was elected Sheriff of Calhoun County, but died on August 11, before qualifying. Then A. W. Chamberlain was elected, but was unable to fill the office, so our subject and father gave bonds, and took the office off his hands. In 1854 the father was elected, and our subject became deputy and served the constitutional term, four years. Then Charles C. was elected Sheriff, served four years, and then the father was again elected to that position, serving the same length of time. In 1856 Charles C. Howerton was appointed by General Benjamin McCollough, Deputy United States Marshal, and served under him until he was appointed Governor of Utah. Then Mr. McCollough's brother, General Henry E. McCollough, was appointed Marshal in his place, and retained our subject as deputy until the breaking out of the Rebellion. Mr. Howerton was almost immediately appointed Deputy Marshal of the Confederate States by General J. R. Jefferson, of Seguin, for the Western District of Texas, and remained in office during the war. Afterwards he embarked in merchandising at Port Lavaca, but in 1871 moved from there to Victoria, where he was in business until 1873. Then, after the completion of the railroad to Cuero, March 4, 1873, he came to this place on the first mail train, and engaged in business here until 1876. On the 6th of June of that year he was made Mayor, and on the 12th of September, of the same year, he was elected Justice of the Peace of Precinct No. 1, trying a murder case on the same day. On the 19th of that month he was called to try the celebrated Brazell murder case, one branch of which is still pending. He served as Mayor four years and Justice six years. On the 17th of February, 1877, he was appointed Deputy District Clerk by Robert J. Kleburg, and on the next November, 1878, Mr. Howerton was elected District

CAPITOL OF TEXAS.

Clerk, holding that office until 1892, when he declined to serve longer. Since then he has been engaged in the real estate and insurance business, and represents some of the best companies, as follows: Lancaster, Phœnix, North American, North British American, Alamo of San Antonio, Provident of Washington, Commercial Union, &c., &c. Mr. Howerton is an excellent business man, and has been a most efficient official in the many positions he has filled. He owns an excellent farm of 650 acres, well improved, and he also owns town property. On the 5th of October, 1858, he was married at Seguin, Texas, to Miss Theora Petty, a native of Tennessee, and daughter of John H. and J. Petty, who came to Texas in 1854. Her relations were among the earliest settlers of the Lone Star State. Three children have been born to Mr. and Mrs. Howerton: Lelia, wife of Iowa Seligson, of Karnes City; James C., of Dallas, Texas, and Nella Lee, an infant, who died, April 4, 1862. Mr. and Mrs. Howerton are members of the Episcopal Church.

CHARLES A. LEUSCHNER is a native of that country which has given to the United States some of her most honorable, industrious and prominent citizens—Germany—his birth occurring in the Kingdom of Prussia in 1845. He was the elder of two sons born to G. A. and Emily (Keller) Leuschner, the other member of the family being Augustus Frederick. In 1855 the parents decided to seek a home on American soil, and after reaching this country settled in Victoria, Texas, where the father at once engaged in the occupation of carpentering, which he followed successfully until his death, which occurred in 1859. His widow still survives him, and resides in Victoria with her sons. The subject of this sketch laid the foundation of a good education in his native land, and it was fortunate that he did, for after coming to this country he attended the English schools only two months, but being an eager reader he remedied this in a great measure. As a youth he followed farming, or any occupation to which he could profitably turn his attention, and when scarcely sixteen years of age he marched to the war in the ranks of the "old bloody Sixth" Texas Infantry, which regiment proudly bore on its battle scarred flag the names of "Arkansas Post," "Chickamauga," "Resaca," "Mission Ridge," "New Hope Church," "Atlanta," "Franklin" and "Nashville," in all of which, and wherever the indomitable Gen. Pat Cleburne, or dashing Granberry led, no "gray jacket" performed his duty with more bravery than did Mr. Leuschner. He was captured at Arkansas Post and kept a prisoner at Camp Butler, Springfield, Ill., for about three months, when he was exchanged at City Point, Va. Following this he became a member of the Army of the Tennessee under Gen. Bragg, and was a participant in the engagements around Dalton. He was captured at Franklin, Tenn., and was taken to Camp Douglas, Chicago, but was exchanged four months later at Shreveport, La., and was there also discharged. For some time after his return home he was engaged in stock driving and other occupations, and by the exercise of the utmost diligence eventually found himself in possession of a comfortable competency. At the present time he owns 350 acres of fine farming land, and has a very comfortable, commodious and pleasant home. He has always taken an active interest in the political affairs of his section, and it was mainly through his influence that Democratic supremacy was secured in 1869–70, when it gave a Democratic majority of about seven votes. His services in this connection were recognized by all, and he was generally regarded as legitimately standing in the way of the legislative succession as

5

immediate representative of Victoria County, but his sensitive nature led him to distrust his fitness for this position, and he remained in private life. In 1874–75 he served as alderman of Victoria, and in November, 1882, he was elected Treasurer of the county by a handsome majority, though opposed by two of the most popular and worthy business men of the county, and has filled the position very acceptably by re-election ever since. In 1870 he was united in marriage with Miss Sophia Bischoff, a native of Victoria County, and daughter of Anton Bischoff. The latter came to the county in 1844, and now lives on a fine farm fifteen miles from the town, being eighty-two years of age. To Mr. and Mrs. Leuschner nine children have been given: Louisa L., born in 1871; Ida, born in 1873; William C., born in 1875; Adelia S., born in 1877; Leopold A., born in 1879; Victor A., born in 1882; Lizetta, Meta and Regina. The family are members of the Lutheran Church, and Mr. Leuschner is a member of the Sons of Herman. He is a natural musician, and is a member of the city band and orchestra. He is just in the prime of life, and with his robust health, vigorous mind, correct principles, and deserved popularity, can make his future almost anything he elects.

CAPT. JAMES G. STOREY, County Clerk of Hays County, born in 1830 in Georgia, was the sixth of ten children born to John T. and Lucy (McLister) Storey, who were born on the Pedee River in South Carolina. After their marriage Mr. John T. Storey was successfully engaged in tilling the soil in his native State of Georgia, but in the winter of 1845 took up his residence in the Lone Star State in Gonzales County. The following year he, with three of his sons, enlisted in the Mexican War, and was Second Lieutenant in Capt. Henry McCulloch's company, with which he served on the Texas frontier against the Indians. He received his discharge in 1847, and the following year moved to Lockhart, Caldwell County, purchasing him a comfortable home in the town, and a farm in the immediate vicinity. He continued to successfully till the soil until his death, which occurred prior to. the opening of the great Civil War. His was the third family to locate in that place, and its members were always regarded as among its foremost citizens. Both Mr. and Mrs. Storey had been members of the Presbyterian Church from youth, and he was the first elder of the church at Lockhart, and was one of its organizers. He was the first Judge of Caldwell County, and had also been a prominent man in Georgia, having been elected to the State Senate from his district there a number of terms. The paternal grandfather, Edward Storey, was a South Carolinian by birth, and was a soldier of the Revolution. He afterwards moved to Jackson County, Ga., where he spent the rest of his days. He was of Irish-English lineage. The maternal grandfather was of Scotch descent, was an early settler of Georgia from the Old North State, and died in Alabama about 1845. James G. Storey attended school in Georgia up to the age of fifteen years, then came to Texas and finished his education in Gonzales and Lockhart. He began life for himself as a clerk in a store, and in September, 1853, was married to Miss Sarah B. Cheatham, daughter of Judge Henry Cheatham, the first County Judge of Hays County. She was born in Washington, Ark., but came to Texas in the winter of 1846 and settled in what is now Hays County. In 1853 Mr. James G. Storey came to Hays County, and in 1856 was elected to the office of District Clerk, a position he ably filled up to 1861, when he resigned to enlist in the Confederate army. He assisted in organizing a company, was elected its First Lieutenant in February, 1863, of Company A, Wood's regiment of Thirty-second Texas Cavalry, served in Louisiana, and was in several engagements in the Red River expedition against Banks, the engagements of Monet's Ferry and Yellow Bayou. In March, 1862, he was promoted to Captain of his company, served in eastern Louisiana, and at the close of the war was at Houston. He returned home at once and again took upon himself the duties of civil life. He was almost immediately appointed County Judge by Governor A. J. Hamilton, and held that position by appointment and election until removed by Federal authority. He then resumed farming on Blanco River, three miles from San Marcos, and did well in this calling. In 1880 he served as a member of the State Legislature, and while a member of the Seventeenth General Assembly he served on the committees of Internal Improvements and Finance. In 1888 he was elected to the office of County Clerk, and has filled that position with marked ability continuously ever since. His marriage has resulted in the birth of the following children: Arthur B., a lawyer of Lockhart; Horace C., a stockman of this section; James H., a farmer; Mattie, wife of Mark Rogers; Ida, wife of Frank Hensley; Ella, Blanche, Lelia and Ione. Capt. Storey and his wife, and all his children, except one, are members of the Presbyterian Church, and he is an elder in the same. Socially he is a member of the A. F. & A. M. and K. of H.

DR. ROBERT TAGGART KNOX. The profession of the physician and surgeon is one that has drawn to it, the brightest and most honorable of men; for none but an intelligent man, could be a physician at all, and no physician not a man of honor could long retain a profitable practice. Dr. Robert T. Knox is the oldest practitioner of Gonzales, was born at Danville, Ky., in 1832, the second in a family of three children born to Andrew W. and Mary (Daviess) Knox, who were born in Pennsylvania and Kentucky respectively. The paternal grandfather, Abner Knox, was likewise born in the Keystone State and his wife, Miss Elizabeth Taggart, was also of an old Pennsylvania family. At an early day he removed to Kentucky with his family, when his son, Andrew W., was but five years old and in a small way engaged in farming in the vicinity of Danville, his house being built on the block-house plan, to protect himself and family from Indian attacks, and was used by them as a residence for many years, various additions and improvements in the same having been made. The grandfather died in 1790. Andrew W. Knox was reared in Kentucky, and, although a self-educated man, possessed a brilliant intellect. He became a student of law, for his own improvement, but never practiced that profession, and he had a good knowledge of nearly all branches of learning. He devoted his attention to farming and stock-raising, at which he acquired a competency, and in 1863 was called from this life. His widow died in 1870, and both were earnest members of the Presbyterian Church. The maternal grandfather, James Daviess, was a Virginian of Scotch-Irish descent, and the family first became known in this country during colonial times. James Daviess was a minister of the Presbyterian Church and was among the pioneer settlers of Kentucky, to which State he was accompanied by two brothers, Robert and Samuel, who became farmers. Another brother, Joseph (the famed "Joe Daviess"), was killed in the battle of Tippecanoe. Capt. Samuel Daviess became a prominent lawyer of Harrodsburg, Ky., and in the vicinity of that place Robert devoted his attention to tilling the soil. James Daviess was also a farmer, in addition to his ministerial duties, and his wife was Miss Mary Wrisk, a Virginian by birth, who removed with her people to Kentucky and located on Silver Creek, near Richmond.   Her family were greatly troubled by Indians for years, and at one time, in trying to make their escape from them, they ran under a clothes line, which was not seen by the Indians, who were caught by it and thrown to the ground.   One child was captured and nearly killed before it was rescued. Dr. Robert Taggart Knox was reared on Blue Grass soil and was educated in the private school taught by Rev. John L. McKee, who is still a resident preacher at Danville, Ky.   He began the study of medicine in January, 1851, under the tutorship of Dr. J. M. Meyer of Danville, and graduated from the University of Louisville in 1854.   He began the practice of his profession in central Kentucky, but in 1856 came to Gonzales, Texas, of which place he has since been a permanent resident.   He is and has been a member of the Presbyterian Church for many years.   At the beginning of the war he was offered the position of surgeon of various regiments, but in 1862 went out with Terry's Rangers and was with them in camp at Bowling Green, Ky., for some time, but was finally compelled to leave the service on account of ill-health. He returned to Gonzales and was appointed physician, in charge of the hospital there, for the workmen who were erecting a fort in the vicinity of the place.   In 1878 he became a member of the Texas State Medical Association, of which he has since been a very active member, and in 1878 he was elected and served as its first Vice-president.   He is now and has been for the past ten years a member of the "Medical Examining Board" of the 25th Judicial District, most of the time as President.   He has been a frequent contributor to journals on subjects relating to his profession, and as he never writes unless he has something new and original to say, his articles are very interesting. He is of an inventive turn of mind also, and has invented a uterine dilater which is being manufactured by George Tieman & Co., of New York, and is acknowledged by the profession to be the best instrument for this purpose known, and its sales are large and constantly on the increase.   Dr. Knox was a Commissioner to the World's Fair at New Orleans, from this district. The doctor was married in 1860 to Miss Catherine T. Blake, of Chester, S. C., and daughter of Joshua and Martha (Eckles) Blake.   To their union five children were given: Thomas Roger, who graduated in medicine in 1886 from the Ohio Medical College of Cincinnati, took his first course of lectures in the Louisville University, and for one year was a practitioner of Sabina, Mexico, and for the Southern Pacific Railroad.   He afterwards went to Hallettsville, Texas, and is now in partnership with Dr. Ledbetter in a large drug store, and has a large general practice.   He was married to the daughter of Dr. R. H. Harrison of Columbus, Texas, and has three children: May is the wife of Henry Remschel, a merchant of Kerrville, Texas; they have four children: James Atwood is a merchant of Kerrville and is a Knight Templar Mason; Robert Bailey is studying medicine in St. Louis, Mo., and Katie Blake still lives with her parents.   Dr. Knox became a Mason at Gonzales in 1857, and is now a Knight Templar and a member of Gonzales Commandery No. 11.   The doctor is the owner of 200 acres or more of fine farming land, nearly all of which is under cultivation, also a fine family residence in Gonzales, Texas, and he is quite extensively engaged in the raising of Jersey stock.   His home has always been a happy and hospitable one, and, being an amiable and courteous gentleman and an earnest student of his profession, his friends and patrons are legion. He is well and extensively known throughout the vast Empire State, Texas.

WILLIAM B. WALKER is a successful merchant and the popular Mayor of Luling, Caldwell County, Texas, and owes his nativity to the State of Tennessee, where he was born in 1842, the second of six children born to Philip and Sarah (Barbee) Walker, both of whom were born in North Carolina, and at an early day settled in Tennessee. There they made their home until 1854, then came to Texas and made a settlement in Guadalupe County, near Prairie Lea, on quite an extensive tract of land. Here the father died in 1866, and his widow died in 1892, both being worthy and active members of the Baptist Church. They had no child born in Texas. The subject of this sketch and his brother, John P., are the only surviving members of their family.

William B. Walker received his initiatory training in the common schools of Tennessee and Texas, and such progress did he make in the "world of books," that he began teaching school at the age of eighteen years and continued this occupation for some time in Guadalupe County. He then closed his school to enlist in the Confederate Army, becoming a member of Company A, 4th Texas Regiment, of Hood's Brigade. He was at once sent with his command to Virginia, in which State he arrived in August, 1861, and was soon after a participant in an engagement there. He was at Appomattox at the time of Lee's surrender, after which he returned home for the first time since he had entered the service. He was badly wounded at Chickamauga. For two years after the close of the great struggle he was engaged in teaching at Prairie Lea, in Caldwell County, then began milling and farming, and later erected a mill and cotton-gin on the San Marcos. He has become a very extensive planter and is the owner of 700 acres of land in Guadalupe County, of which 400 acres are under cultivation. In 1870 he opened a mercantile establishment at Prairie Lea, but in 1885 came to Luling and has a large gin and mercantile establishment at this place, the name of the firm being W. B. Walker & Co. A stock of goods valued at $35,000 is kept constantly on hand and an annual business of $100,000 is done. This firm has two hardware stores separate from the mercantile house, and they are also large cotton buyers. Mr. Walker is one of the successful merchants of Texas, is interested in all the public affairs of his immediate section and State and has proven himself an able and efficient executive of Luling. He has always been quite active in politics, and prior to being elected Mayor, held the office of City Alderman five years. He was married in 1866 to Miss Mary O. Mooney, a native of Texas and daughter of Thomas Mooney, who came to this State in the '40s. The union of Mr. and Mrs. Walker has resulted in the birth of two daughters: Jessie, wife of W. W. Lipscomb, and Willie A., wife of James A. Prior. Mr. Walker and his family are members of the Methodist Church, and socially he belongs to the A. F. & A. M., in which he has attained to the Chapter of Luling, and to the K. of P. To know Mr. Walker is to respect him, for he is the soul of honor in his business transactions, is high-minded, generous and public spirited; in fact, a model American citizen.

GEORGE W. MONKHOUSE, one of the experienced and influential planters of Gonzales County, Texas, has worked his way up to prominence and the respect and regard of his neighbors by the sheer force of his own character and by his generous and sociable fellowship. He is a native of the Lone Star State, born near Clarksville, Red River County, in 1848, and son of John

Falkner and Harriet (Wyatt) Monkhouse, natives of England. The father was born in London, also married there, and followed butchering in that city until about 1835, when he came to this country. He settled in Red River County, Texas, and there followed planting until his death in 1888. A member of the Baptist Church, and a public spirited and worthy citizen, he allowed no worthy movement to want for support on his side. He never cared for office, but all his life was deeply interested in educational matters. His father and mother preceded him to this country and although the former was in poor circumstances when he came here, by sagacious and energetic trading with the Indians of North Texas and the Territory, he amassed a large fortune. He was one of the earliest traders of that section and wielded considerable influence with the whites and Indians. While engaged in merchandising he also followed cotton planting, and became a large land owner, the finest bottom lands at that time selling as low as fifty cents per acre. He erected a gin and carried this on until his death, which occurred a few years before the war. His wife died when ninety years of age. George W. Monkhouse was educated in Caldwell County, Texas, chiefly in the common schools, and as his father, late in life, met with reverses, George determined to make his own way in life. When sixteen years of age he made his way to Caldwell County with one dollar and fifty cents in money and an Indian pony. The latter he sold for $20 and then spent the fall in picking cotton, though in feeble health. The next year he farmed on rented land and made enough to cover twelve months' schooling. He was fortunate in getting in with an excellent family, the Cardwells, who treated him as a member of the family and refused all pay. Later he engaged in cattle driving for one year, but rough occupation and company proved uncongenial, and he returned to school where he remained two years, working at odd hours to pay his way. Later he rented a farm on shares for two years, and in 1874 was married to Miss Texana V. Sedberry, a native of Marion County, Texas, and the daughter of M. Jones and C. A. (Clark) Sedberry. For about ten months after his marriage Mr. Monkhouse engaged in an unprofitable mercantile business and then farmed for a year. After this he bought a farm of 150 acres on credit, paid for it and fifty acres more within three years. In 1883 he came to Gonzales County, Texas, and is now one of the substantial men of his section. His marriage resulted in the birth of five children: John S., Mary Frances, Charles J., Annie Pearl and Minnie Lane. Mary Frances died at the age of five years. Mrs. Monkhouse's father was born in Montgomery County, N. C., May 4, 1818, and he followed farming for a livelihood. In 1851 he came to Texas, and followed planting in the counties of Marion, Hays, Caldwell and Gonzales, continuing that occupation in the latter county until his death, February 15, 1893, when seventy-five years of age. Although an earnest thinker and voter he never held office. His wife was born in South Arkansas and died a year after reaching Texas. Mr. Sedberry was married in 1854 to Miss Eliza F. Clark, sister of his first wife. She now survives him and is an earnest member of the M. E. Church. The first wife held membership in the Baptist Church.

JAMES W. DICKEY of the *Floresville Chronicle*, which is a newsy, spicy sheet, published in the general interests of the locality, came originally from Choctaw County, Miss., born July 8, 1842. His parents, John Milton and Priscilla Johns (Gillespie) Dickey, were natives of Alabama, where the father followed farming. About 1845 the parents moved to Louisiana and located on Red River, occupying a farm on which the battle of Mansfield was fought during the Rebellion. In 1846 they moved to the Lone Star State and settled in Walker County, remaining there until 1851 when they came to Baxter District, a portion of which now constitutes Wilson County, at that time almost a wilderness, and the father followed stock raising there until his death April 1, 1857. The mother is still living and makes her home at Runge, Karnes County. James W. Dickey had but such educational advantages as were possible at that early day, and his youthful years, when not in the school room, were spent in assisting his father on the farm. In 1861, when the threatening war cloud hung darkly over the nation, young Dickey enlisted in Company E, 3d Regiment, Texas Infantry, and served the first year on the Texas border. Later he was in the trans-Mississippi Department in Louisiana and Arkansas, Walker's Division, and was a brave and faithful soldier. In March, 1865 he came home on a furlough, and on the 9th of April of the same year was married to Miss Martha J. Gillett, daughter of Rev. R. Gillett of West Texas Conference, M. E. Church South. Returning to the army he met the command coming home; reported to the Colonel and was discharged. He then came back to Wilson County and engaged in farming, purchasing land upon which he lived until January 1, 1880, when he came to Floresville. He was appointed County Assessor in 1878 and was elected to that position in 1880, serving four years. Previous to this in 1868, he was elected Justice of the Peace and County Commissioner holding both positions six years, being three times elected to the same. In the month of August, 1882, he bought his paper and has been conducting it since. It is published in the interests of the Democratic party of this county, its crisp and trenchant editorials commanding an ever widening area of circulation, while carrying with them that weight and authority which a calm and intelligent judgment must always secure. Mrs. Dickey died July 1, 1880, leaving six children, one of whom, an infant, died soon after:—Eugene W., Zella A., Marion W., Leonard M, and Clio E. On the 15th of January, 1882, Mr. Dickey was married to Miss Alice Hobbs, a native of Texas and daughter of Job Hobbs, a pioneer from Kentucky. Five children have been born to the second union:—L. Elmore, R. Lilly, Alma B., Maurice and an infant son as yet unnamed. The family hold membership in the M. E. Church South, with which our subject has been connected since the age of fifteen years. When twenty-one years of age he joined the Masonic Order becoming a member of S. G. Newon Lodge, under dispensation attached to the southern army. After hostilities ceased he attached himself to Union Valley Lodge at Union, Wilson County, of which he was Secretary for a time, and is now a member of Floresville Lodge No. 515.

WILLIAM HENRY MORGAN, merchant and farmer at Williamsburg, Texas, is an energetic and business-like man, and one who has won a large circle of friends by the exercise of his many excellent qualities. He is a native of Wales, born December 4, 1840, and the eldest son of William Henry and Mary (Williams) Morgan. When ten years of age our subject began learning the sail makers' trade in his native country, and in 1854 he came with his father to the United States, working at his trade in New Orleans, where he also attended night school in 1854 and 1855. In July of the latter year, on account of cholera in the South, he was sent to his grandparents who had settled in Illinois. There he remained and attended school for one year and a half, after which, in December, 1856, he returned to Louisiana, and for a few weeks was in school there. From there he came to Petersburg and took his brother John William's place as clerk, and was thus employed for two years. Returning to New Orleans, January, 1859, he remained there until July, 1859, when he went up to Illinois and joined his parents with whom he remained until June, 1862, when he enlisted in Company D, 85th Illinois Infantry. He served in the Army of the Tennessee, under Gen. Buell and participated in the battles of Perryville and Murfreesboro. From there he marched to Nashville, Tenn., remained there that winter, and then went to Chattanooga, where he soon after took part in the battle of Chickamauga. He went with Gen. Sherman in the compaign to Atlanta, and then to the sea, and from there went to North Carolina, where he was in the last battle with Gen. Johnston. Mr. Morgan was in the final review at Washington, D. C., was mustered out of service there, and then discharged at Springfield, Ill. He was wounded at Kenesaw Mountain, and his brother Hugh was killed. After the war, Mr. Morgan resided in the Prairie State until the fall of 1869, when he went to New Orleans. From there he subsequently moved to Lavaca County, Texas, where he has since resided, engaged in farming for the most part, but also an active business man. In 1880 he entered into partnership with his brother, J. W., continued with him one year and then returned to his plantation. In 1888 he and his brother again started out in business under the firm name of John Williams & Co., and have since continued the business. On the 13th of February, 1872, he was married to Miss Mary Agnes Clark, whose father, B. F. Clark, Sr., was an early settler of Texas, from Missouri. He was a soldier in the Black Hawk War, and a very prominent citizen of Lavaca County, where he had resided many years and where he died April 26, 1894, at the advanced age of eighty-five years. Mrs. Morgan died June 7, 1873, and left a daughter, Mary Agnes, who was born May 31, 1873. On the 3d of January, 1878, Mr. Morgan married Miss Mary J. T. Patterson, a native of Mississippi, and the daughter of Tennessee Patterson, who settled in Lavaca County at an early date. Mrs. Morgan was born October 13, 1842, and died September 14, 1893. Mr. Morgan owns a fine farm of 300 acres, with eighty acres under cultivation on which he made all the improvements. He joined the Masonic Fraternity in Illinois, in 1867, and is now a member of Murchison Lodge No. 80, of Hallettsville, and has passed through all the chairs except Master, which he declined. Since 1877 he has been a member of the M. E. Church, has held all the offices, and was Superintendent of Sabbath School at Mossy Grove for years.

WILLIAM P. STAFFORD is the efficient Tax Collector of Victoria County and as he has resided here ever since his birth, in 1858, the people have had every opportunity to judge of his character and qualifications as a citizen and man of affairs, and naught has ever been said derogatory to his honor. He was the second of a family of four children born to William J. and Sarah J. (Mulder) Stafford, the former of whom was born in the Lone Star State and the latter in Louisiana. The paternal grandfather, William J. Stafford, was born in Tennessee, moved to Louisiana and thence to Texas, of which State he was one of the early residents. He settled in Fort Bend County, of which section he was among the first of the farmers and blacksmiths, and there he and his wife eventually passed from life. His eldest son, Adam, was in the Texas Revolution and participated in the battle of San Jacinto, but he

afterwards died in Victoria County. William J. Stafford and Sarah J. Mulder
were married in Fort Bend County, and there the father became a very extensive stockman. In 1855 or 1856 he came to Victoria County, and from here
enlisted in the Confederate Army, in which he served throughout the entire
war as a member of Capt. Jones' Company. He died in 1883, but his widow
still survives him. William P. Stafford was educated in the public schools
of Victoria, and upon starting out to fight the battle of life for himself, it
was as a stock dealer, which occupation he successfully followed until recently.
In 1892 he was elected to the office of Tax Assessor of the county, and the
most of his attention is now given to the discharge of his official duties. He
was married in 1879 to Miss Lizzie January, by whom he has four living
children: Joseph January, William Mulder, Belvard January, and Edith
January. Samuel J. died in infancy. Mrs. Stafford is an intelligent and
amiable lady, and is a member of the Episcopal Church. She is a daughter
of the well known Dr. James P. B. January, who was born in Maysville, Ky.,
in 1811, and was educated in Transylvania University. He removed to Mississippi in the winter of 1834, and the following year became a resident of
Texas. He joined the company of Capt. William Graham, in New Orleans,
in April, 1836, which command reached Galveston a few days before the battle
of San Jacinto, but the boat on which he embarked to join the force confront-
ing Gen. Santa Anna, got stuck on Red Fish bar, which prevented his par-
ticipation in the conflict. Dr. January's command eventually reached Victoria, Texas, and there he acted in the capacity of assistant surgeon and later
as surgeon, in which capacity he served until the army was disbanded in
1838. He became a Captain in the regular army of the Republic of Texas
the following year, and was assigned to duty in the First Regulars with which
he remained until its disbandment in 1840. He then practiced the profession
of medicine at Texana, Texas, until April, 1846, when he went to Mexico to
join Gen. Zachary Taylor, but returned to Texas the following year and settled in Victoria. In 1861 he was elected Captain of a company of cavalry,
composed of many of the best young men of Victoria County, and with it he
participated in the battles and campaigns of western Louisiana, and became
noted for his heroism and courage. Although the doctor was somewhat
advanced in years and not of a robust physique, he bore all the hardships and
privations of war well and with the utmost cheerfulness, and in every battle
his martial form towered erect at the head of his company. No braver man
ever trod the crimson turf of a battle field, nor was any man ever more tender or
gentle in the private relations and duties of life than he. He was the
soul of honor, above suspicion, and detraction never assailed his name or
fame. In Dr. January, the poor of Victoria had always an invaluable friend
and the reward for his professional services seems to have constituted with
him a secondary consideration to the good those services could render mankind.
In his younger days he was a splendid specimen of dignified manhood: for he
stood over six feet in height, was straight as an arrow, and although the frosts
of time replaced the raven of his locks, yet even to the last his tread was
martial, his eye undimmed, and every attitude bespoke a resolute will. He
died in the active practice of his profession, and to number those who
mourned his death would be to name the entire population of Victoria. The
names of his children are as follows: John, deceased; Lizzie (Stafford),
Clarke, and Maggie.

DR. JOSEPH M. REUSS. The usefulness of a professional man is not marked merely by his learning and skill, his proficiency in medical practice; but also by his character, both private and professional, his honorable adherence to medical ethics and his personal integrity and prudent benevolence. When a physician combines these characteristics it is with great pleasure that we record his life work, and such a man do we find in Dr. J. M. Reuss. This physician, of Cuero, Texas, one of the oldest in practice here, is a native of Germany, as were also his parents, Stephen and Mary (Muller) Reuss. The father, an hotelkeeper in his native country, died there in 1831, and the mother in 1824. Our subject, whose birth occurred in 1823, was but one year old when his mother died, and he was reared by his elder sister. He received his education in Muennerstadt in Bavaria, and studied medicine at the University of Wuerzburg in 1843-45. Then he began practicing, but seeing a better opening for a physician in America, he crossed the ocean and landed at Galveston in November, 1845. From there he went to Indianola and began practicing, continuing there until after the storm of 1875. In 1876 he came to Cuero. He established the first drug store in Indianola in 1849. In 1861 Dr. Reuss raised a company and was elected Captain of Company B, Shea's Battalion, which was afterwards organized into Hobby's Regiment. He was stationed at Tasslabano and participated in the engagement at Lavaca, but on account of rheumatism he was obliged to resign in the spring of 1864. He had a large practice, and passed through three epidemics of cholera and seven of yellow fever. The doctor was contract surgeon for the United States Custom House at Indianola, both before and after the war, and was contract surgeon for the quartermaster department before that eventful period. Most of the time he was also surgeon of the city hospital at Indianola. He is a member of the State Pharmaceutical Society. In 1873 he established a business in Cuero, mainly on account of his son, Dr. August J. Reuss. Our subject was married in Galveston, Texas, in 1845, to Misa Gesine Stubbeman, a native of Germany. The following children were the fruits of this union: August J., who was educated at Lee University, Lexington, Va., and studied medicine at the Jefferson University, at Charlottesville, Va. Later he entered Tulane University, New Orleans, and graduated in 1870. Following this he entered the Prussian army in the war with France, as assistant surgeon, and after the war studied two years at Wuerzburg and Vienna. Returning to the Lone Star State in the fall of 1872, he practiced medicine at Indianola until the spring of the following year, when he located in Cuero. He was a bright, promising young man, and his death, which occurred in January, 1876, was a sad blow to his parents. The three children following August J. died in infancy. The others are named Oscar J., Bertha, Alfreda and Joseph Henry. Oscar J. is a druggist of Cuero, carrying on the business under the old firm name of J. M. Reuss & Son, and is one of the Board of Pharmaceutical Examiners. Alfreda is the wife of William Frobese, of the firm of H. Runge & Co., and Joseph Henry is a physician in partnership with his father. He was educated in the University of Texas, at Austin, and graduated at the College of Physicians and Surgeons in New York in 1889. He is a member of the State Medical Society, and excels in surgery. The mother of these children died in August, 1893. She was a worthy member of the Lutheran Church. Dr. Reuss was one of the organizers of the cotton mill, and he is interested in the oil mill in the city, and in building and loan associations. He takes a deep interest in educational and religious matters, is a valuable citizen, and is a member of the Board of Medical Examiners of the district. His son, who conducts a drug store, carries a stock of goods valued at $8,000, and does an annual business of $16,000.

JUDGE BASLEY G. NEIGHBORS. The expensive and necessary duty of enacting laws calculated to protect mankind from the doers of evil has always been a serious object of legislation. The office of Judge is one of honor and dignity, and it should, without question, be filled by a man who possesses a thorough knowledge of the law; a keen, analytical mind, and one who can, on short notice, correctly judge of men and motives. These requirements are possessed by Judge Neighbors, who, in his efforts to preserve law and order, has shown much wisdom, good judgment, and has balanced the scales of justice with impartial hand. He is a product of the Blue-Grass State, and there first opened his eyes on the light of day in 1854, being the third of six children born to Henry B. and Louisa F. (Sewell) Neighbors, who were natives of Kentucky and Virginia, respectively. The paternal grandfather, William Neighbors, was a Virginian by birth, and was one of the first settlers of Cumberland County, Ky. The maternal grandfather, James A. Sewell, was born in the Old North State, and at an early day came to Tennessee, later locating in Kentucky, where he was called from life. Henry B. Neighbors devoted his attention to tilling the soil in his native State, and for some time during the great Civil War he was a member of the Federal army. He died in Kentucky, and his wife also passed from life in that State about 1883. Basley G. Neighbors was educated in the common schools, and finished his literary education at Glasgow. He began life for himself as a school teacher, but this occupation was merely a stepping stone to other and better things, and the money thus earned paid his way through college, and he was graduated in 1879. The same year he came to Texas, and located at Lockhart, and during the few terms that he taught school in the vicinity of that place he also pursued the study of law, and in 1881 was admitted to the bar at Lockhart, and entered upon the practice of his profession in that place. In 1882 he was elected to the office of County Attorney, in which capacity he served one term very acceptably. After completing his term he bought out a paper and started the *Lockhart Register*, the first copy of which was issued by him. After publishing this paper for two years he sold out and moved to Kyle, becoming the owner of the *Hays County Times*, but while conducting this paper also practiced his profession. In 1887 he came to San Marcos, was at once appointed City Attorney of the place, and at the expiration of his term was re-elected to the office, but soon resigned. In 1890 he was a popular candidate for County Judge, to which position he was elected, and he was re-elected to the same office in 1892. Judge Neighbors has always been quite active in politics, and has been a delegate to various conventions. He has also been quite active in school work, and by virtue of his office is *ex-officio* Superintendent, and to him belongs the honor of holding the first trustees' convention ever held in the State, at Kyle, in September, 1893. He organized the present Institute of Hays County, and by strenuous exertion has brought it to a high state of perfection. In his office as County Judge he has been laboring to improve the public roads, and owing to his efforts Hays can boast of some of the best highways in the State. He has also called an overseers' convention, which will be the first ever held in the United States. Judge Neighbors is self-made and self-educated, and has made his own way in life from early manhood, and has every reason to be proud of the success which has attended his efforts. He was married September 6, 1888, to Miss Mollie Moore Hubbard, a native of Texas, and a daughter of Miller Hubbard, an early settler of Bastrop County, Texas, from Georgia, and a relative of Governor Hubbard. To Judge and Mrs. Neighbors two daughters have been given: Bessie and Adaline Fairchild. The Neighbors are of Welsh descent, while Mrs. Hubbard's ancestors are of pure English descent. The Judge and his family are attendants of the Baptist Church, and are popular in the social circles of San Marcos.

DAVID S. H. DARST, a pioneer settler of Gonzales, was born in the Territory of Missouri, above St. Louis, in 1821, being the only child born to the marriage of Jacob C. Darst and Margaret C. Hughes, who were born in Kentucky, and on the Holston River in East Tennessee, respectively. The paternal grandfather, David Darst, came from Pennsylvania to Kentucky, thence to Missouri, at an early day, at about the time that the famous hunter and Indian fighter, Daniel Boone, went to that section, and there he made his home until his death. During the early manhood of Jacob C. Darst, he participated in many Indian wars of the Missouri frontier, serving in the capacity of scout, and while out on one of his expeditions ran out of provisions, and not liking to draw attention to himself by firing on game, went for a long time without food. In August, 1830, he started from Missouri for Gonzales, Texas, with his family, but did not reach his destination until January of the following year, for the long journey was made with an ox team. They settled on a farm near the town, but about 1832 moved to a farm about eighteen miles above Gonzales, but Indians were so numerous and hostile that he was compelled to return to Gonzales two years later. In the spring of 1835, when the trouble began with Mexico, he at once began assisting the citizens of Gonzales in their efforts for home protection, and when the Mexicans across the river were charged, Mr. Darst fired the first shot from the only cannon, which was also the cause of contention. He afterwards went with a company to San Antonio, and was in the battles about there, but was honorably discharged and came home before the final surrender of that place. In February, 1836, he made a trip to the coast for a load of salt, being accompanied by his son, David S. H., but as it had not arrived he took a load of ammunition and provisions to Colonel Fannin at Goliad, then returned to the Gulf, got his salt and returned home. At this time, Colonel Travis and his men were besieged in the Alamo, and a messenger had been sent to Gonzales for re-inforcements. A company was at once made up consisting of thirty-two men of which Mr. Darst was one, and they finally reached San Antonio, and entered the Alamo, but all fell in that battle on the 6th of March. On the 12th of March, Mr. Darst's widow and her son, David S. H., started on the "run away," and got as far as the Trinity River, where they were at the time the battle of San Jacinto was fought. They then went to Columbia, where they remained that winter, then lived in Matagorda one year, after which they returned to Gonzales, where the mother died in 1846. Mr. Darst had previously been married, and was accompanied to this State by his daughter Nancy, who was visiting relatives at the time of the bloody battle of the Alamo. She afterwards married Cyrus Crosby, and was living one mile South of Victoria when the Comanche Indians made a raid on that section and burned Linville. She was captured, with one child, by the Indians, and was killed by her captors at the time of the Plum Creek battle, her infant having been previously killed.

David S. H. Darst, was in his tenth year when he came to Texas with his parents, but he only attended school a short time. In 1835 he went as one of a guard to San Antonio, and returned from that place with his father. In July, 1839, he returned to Gonzales, and for some time thereafter was engaged in fighting the Indians. In August, 1840, the Red men swooped down on the outlying towns, and great loss to life and property was the result, and David Darst and 100 other men gave them chase. They followed them to a point on the Clear Fork of Plum Creek, where a bloody battle was fought, and the Indians, numbering over 400, were defeated. This expedition lasted ten days, and Mr. Darst participated in many other engagements prior to the Texas Revolution. In the fall of 1840 he and his mother made a visit to Missouri overland, and returned over the same road that they had traveled ten years previously, in August, 1830. In February, 1842, the country was again aroused by what was known as the Vasques raid, a threatened invasion by the Mexicans. David conducted his mother to a place of safety, and then joined a company, and for a time acted as a scout. Although business was very dull at that time, owing to the unsettled condition of the country, Mr. Darst engaged in merchandising, and this soon grew to extensive proportions, and was continued successfully up to the opening of the Civil War, when business was suspended. In 1862 he was appointed Confederate States Deputy Marshal of his district, and upon the removal of the Confederate Court of Gonzales, his duties were quite arduous. When the war closed he found himself ruined financially, but he worked quietly at what he could find to do for a year or so, then drifted into the hotel business, at which he made money. In 1874, he started a mill and gin, the former being the first put up since 1835. He has ginned twenty crops of cotton. He has a most complete plant fitted up with the latest improved machinery, among which is an eighty horse-power engine. He has two elevators, two cotton presses, with a capacity of fifty bales daily, and in 1874 ran about 240 bales. In 1892–93, he ginned 1,400 bales.

He was married in December, 1845, to Miss Emeline Zumwalt, a daughter of Adam Zumwalt, of Missouri, who was in various battles with the Indians in that State with our subject's father, and in 1828 came to Gonzales, Texas, and here died in 1843. To Mr. and Mrs. Darst three children were born: Imogene, wife of G. W. Betts; John, who was thrown from a horse and killed in 1888, and James D., who is now in Del Rio. In 1860, Mr. Darst erected a handsome residence in Gonzales, which at that time was the largest and finest in the place. He and his wife are members of the Old School Presbyterian Church, and he is a member of the A. F. & A. M., being the first man to join the lodge in Gonzales, after its organization in 1847. He helped to organize the Chapter here, and joined the Commandery at Austin in 1857, and became a charter member of the Commandery at this place. His uncle, Abram Darst, came to Texas in 1828, settled at Damon's Mount, twelve miles above Columbia, and there died, prior to the Texas Revolution, leaving a large family. Five sons were in that revolution, and all participated in the battle of San Jacinto. They are now deceased. Mr. Darst is one of the substantial old residents of Gonzales, and although his career has been a checkered one, he has retained his kind heart and his sympathy for his fellows through all the hardships he has experienced.

JOSEPH VAN GASKEN, M.D., as a druggist and medical practitioner, stands at the head of both professions in Caldwell County, and in the former is known for his accuracy and reliability, and in the latter for his skill, knowledge of his profession, and for the hope and confidence which he inspires in his patients. He was born in Delaware, in 1851, the second of seven children born to John and Harriet (Evaul) Van Gasken, the former of whom was born in Delaware, and the latter in New Jersey. The father was a retired lumber merchant and contractor, a man of upright principles and shrewd intelligence, and has spent the greater part of his life in his native State and is now a resident of Smyrna. He is seventy-four years of age. His wife died quite suddenly in 1862 or 1863. In the public schools of Smyrna, the subject of this sketch, received his literary education, and when old enough to decide for himself, his kindly nature instinctively turned to the profession of medicine for his life work, and in 1869, he began fitting himself for this work. In 1873 he graduated from the Medical Department of the University of Louisville, after mainly working his own way through this institution, succeeding which he spent one year in the city hospital as one of the resident physicians. In the latter part of that year he decided to locate in the Lone Star State, and took up his residence at Luling, when that place was in its infancy; was the first physician to locate here, and is therefore its oldest resident medical practitioner. In 1881 he embarked in the drug business as a member of the firm of T. Cochrehan & Co., but in 1884 the firm name changed and became C. Bellinger & Co. This it continued to remain until 1890, when it became Van Gasken & Francis, and has so continued up to the present time. These gentlemen own the building in which they are doing business, which is now advantageously located in the center of the town, and as their stock of goods is extremely well chosen and complete, and their prices within the reach of all, their house is a very popular one and liberally patronized.

As a medical practitioner, Dr. Van Gasken has been very popular from the start, and in his professional capacity he has entered nearly every home in his section of the country, and wherever he has gone he has made friends. He and Dr. Francis, in addition to their extensive line of drugs, deal in school books, school supplies, paints, oils, etc., which add not a little to their annual income. Dr. Van Gasken is a member of the Caldwell County Medical Society, was one of its organizers, was its second Vice-president, and is now its Vice-president, and he also belongs to the West Texas Medical Association, the State Medical Association, and the American Medical Association.

The doctor was married in 1880, to Miss Annie Power, a native of Galveston, Texas, and a daughter of William Power, who came to Texas during the '50's. He was a merchant, and died in 1880. His brother Charles preceded him to this State, and was married to a sister of General Sam Houston's wife. To the doctor and his wife two children have been given: Lily, who died in 1884 at the age of four and a half years, and Harriet Evaul. Doctor and Mrs. Van Gasken are members of the Episcopal Church, and both are members of the choir. Politically he has always been a Democrat.

RICHARD FRANKLIN NICHOLSON. The family of which Mr. Nicholson is a prominent member is an honored and distinguished one, his father, Isaac R. Nicholson being a lawyer of distinction and Circuit Judge for twenty years.

Judge Nicholson was also an extensive cotton planter, and was appointed on a commission to revise the statutes of Mississippi. Throughout his life he was a Democrat, and his active interests in politics brought about his death. He had just recovered from a spell of fever, and, against the advice of wife and physician, attended a political convention at Clinton. Very warm weather prevailed and, becoming overheated, a relapse ensued which terminated fatally in 1844. For many years he was a Methodist, and socially a Mason, and was buried by Clinton Lodge. His wife, whose maiden name was America Gilmer, was born in St. Stephens, Ala., and died in 1889 at the home of her daughter in St. Louis, Mo., when in her eighty-fourth year. She was a devoted Methodist. Of the twelve children born to this worthy couple, six sons and six daughters, seven are now living. Richard Franklin Nicholson was born in Hines County, Miss., November 15, 1835, and he was partially educated in Clinton, that State. For two years he was under that noted Southern educator, Prof. Tutwiler of Green Springs, Ala., and completed his course at Centenary College, Jackson, La. After this he was an accountant until he came to Texas in 1855, and after settling in Gonzales County he pursued the same vocation until the opening of the war. At that time he enlisted in Wahl's Legion and was appointed Sergeant Major, remaining with this famous legion until after the battle of Vicksburg. The cavalry having been sent out of Vicksburg he thus escaped the capitulation. He was with Gen. Chalmers in North Mississippi in his cavalry raids, and the last year of the war was transferred to Walker's Division, having charge of the quartermaster department. During the surrender he was at Hempstead, Texas, under the immediate command of Gen. Forney. Returning to Gonzales County after the war he kept books for a number of years and later embarked in the fire-insurance business. A life-long Democrat he has ever been. He has been deeply interested in educational matters and was school trustee for some time. In the year 1859 he was wedded to Miss Mary Thomas of Mississippi, and four children were the fruits of this union, all now living:—William I., Rozelle, Anna and Frank G. William Thomas, father of Mrs. Nicholson, was a merchant of Scott County, Miss., and Gonzales, Texas, and died in March, 1876. Her mother's maiden name was Ann E. Rodgers, a native of McMinnville, Tenn. She died in 1865.

Hon. J. B. Polley has been enabled through the successful practice of law to achieve a reputation such as many men might envy. Not only is he among Wilson County's best known members of the bar, but as a soldier and citizen he takes a prominent place. Mr. Polley first saw the light in Brazoria County, Texas, in 1840, and was sixth in order of birth of eleven children born to J. H. and Mary (Bailey) Polley, natives of New York and North Carolina respectively. The father left his native State in 1818 with but a shilling in his pocket, and decided to seek his fortune in the West. He left New York and made his way to St. Louis where he joined Moses Austin, and made a trip to the Lone Star State in 1819. He then returned to St. Louis and joined Stephen F. Austin, going to Texas with the original 300 colonists in 1821. An act of sale granted April 5th, 1825, shows that he made his original settlement on the Western side of Chances' Prairie, on the San Barnard River, in Brazoria County. He was also granted a league of land in Fort Bend County. In the year 1832 Mr. Polley was married to Miss Bailey and subsequently made his home in Brazoria County, where all his children was born except the two youngest. In 1847 he moved to Guadalupe County, now Wilson, and located on the Cibolo Creek, two miles above Sulphur or Sutherland Springs, where the remainder of his days were passed, his death occurring in 1869. The mother passed away in 1888. The original of this notice was born in Brazoria County but came with his parents to Wilson County when seven years of age. In this county he received a fair education and supplemented this by a course in the college at Florence, Ala., which institution he was attending at the breaking out of the Rebellion. Returning home in 1861, just in time to escape the blockade, he enlisted in Company F, 4th Texas Regiment, Hood's Brigade, and was at once detailed in the East, serving during the whole time in Virginia and East Tennessee. He participated in the battles of Ethan's Landing, Gaines' Mill, Second Manassas, Chickamauga, Knoxville, Wilderness, Cold Harbor and Ft. Harrison. Mr. Polley was wounded at Darbytown Road, October 7, 1864, and was in the hospital six weeks. As he had lost a foot he was granted a furlough and came home, arriving April 6, 1865. He had been wounded twice before this. In the year 1866 he was married to Miss Mattie LeGette, a native of North Carolina, and after this engaged in agricultural pursuits and stock-raising. Later he began the study of law and was admitted to the bar in Guadalupe County in 1868, beginning to practice in 1876, when he moved to Floresville when there were but five houses in the place. During 1877 and 1878 he was County Attorney, and in the last named year he was elected to the Sixteenth Legislature, serving one term. Since then he has practiced his profession in Floresville and is one of the best known attorneys of the county, having the respect and confidence of all who know him. To Mr. and Mrs. Polley have been born five children:—Josephine, now the wife of E. M. Goldstein of Floresville; Hortense, wife of L. O. Rudisill of San Antonio; Mattie, Joseph H., Jesse and Imogene who died in infancy. Aside from his practice Mr. Polley is engaged quite extensively in the real estate business.

JAMES J. JONES. Victoria County is noted for its able, trustworthy and faithful officials, and none deserves higher praise for the admirable manner in which he has discharged his various duties than our subject, who is at present filling the responsible position of District Clerk. He is a product of the county, born September 21, 1856, and as a natural consequence has ever had the interest of his natal place warmly at heart, and during his career here naught has ever been said derogatory to his honor, but much to his praise. He was the eldest of five children born to Judge Fielding and Mary (Fulchron) Jones, who were born in Virginia and Louisiana respectively. The paternal grandfather was a Virginian, but in an early day moved to the Blue Grass regions of Kentucky, with his wife and a large family of children, and, while erecting a home for himself and those dear to him, was accidentally killed. Fielding Jones became a resident of Victoria, Texas, in December, 1836, where he engaged in the practice of law, in which profession he afterwards became eminent. He served throughout the Mexican War as First Lieutenant, and in 1848 was elected District Judge, and in September of that year presided over the first term of District Court ever held in that county. He continued to successfully fill this office until his death, which occurred in October, 1862, his widow surviving him until 1880. The early educational training of James J. Jones was received in Victoria, and, after reaching man's estate, he engaged in

· BATTLE OF ·
MURFREESBORO.

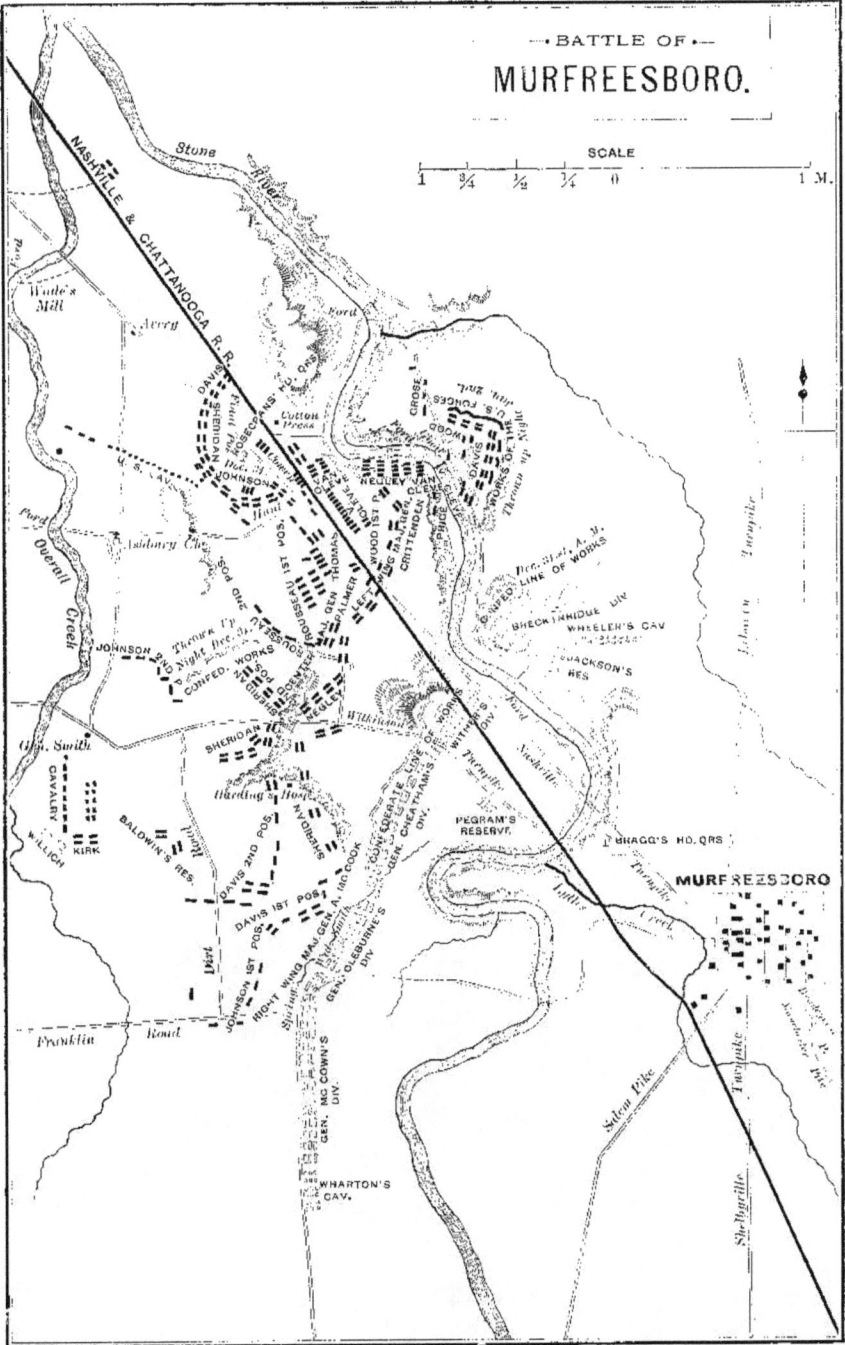

SCALE

1   ¾   ½   ¼   0   1 M.

the raising of stock and through the exercise of shrewd, yet always honorable business methods, he has become the owner of 640 acres of valuable land, three miles from the County Court House, and of which 150 acres are finely improved with good buildings and in an excellent state of cultivation. He served his county for some time as Deputy Sheriff and Collector and in 1893 was appointed District Clerk, which office he still holds. He was married December 6, 1882 to Miss Annie L. Thurmond, a daughter of C. L. Thurmond, better known as "Zip" Thurmond, a sketch of whom appears herein. To the union of Mr. and Mrs. Jones three children have been given: Fletcher, Zip and Maggie. Socially Mr. Jones is a member of the Knights of Honor and the Woodmen of the World.

RICHARD C. WARN. England has many among the best class of citizens in Texas. There is a sterling quality about the nationality that particularly fits them for pioneer life, and we, as Americans, are greatly indebted to settlers of English birth for the rapid advancement made in our civilization. He whose name is at the head of this sketch, and who is a representative pioneer of DeWitt County, was born in Cornwall, England, in 1826. Now, in his sixty-eighth year, the progress that the country has made, and especially that portion in which he lives, is to him as familiar as events in his own daily life. He is the son of Digory and Mariah (Wearing) Warn, both natives of England. In the year 1848 our subject, thinking to better his condition, crossed the ocean to America and settled in Canada, where he remained for two years. From there he went to New Orleans *via* the Mississippi River, and from there to Texas, locating in Matagorda, where he worked at his trade, carpentering, until the breaking out of the Civil War. In the year 1863 he went to Mexico and was engaged in the hardware business until the fall of 1865, when he came to Indianola. Here he carried on business until the storm of 1875, when he lost nearly everything. Mr. Warn has been unlucky in regard to being in the path of storms, for in 1854 he passed through a severe one at Matagorda and lost all of his property. Our subject remained in business at Indianola until 1882, although he had moved his family to Cuero in 1881, and had started a branch store there in 1880. He sold out his business in Indianola in 1884, and in 1890 erected a store in Cuero. Mr. Warn is also interested in the oil mills at Cuero and San Marcos, Texas, and has lumber interests in San Antonio. In the year 1872 he was married to Miss Eliza Bates, a native of England, who died in 1891, leaving six children: Ruth, Richard C., in business in San Marcos; Minnie, in school at Waco; Agnes, Lila, and Fred. Mr. Warn is a member of the Baptist Church, and a member of the Masonic fraternity. He is a stirring, thorough-going business man, and one who has the respect and esteem of all those with whom he has dealings.

MAJOR W. O. HUTCHISON. This gentleman owes his nativity to Loudoun County, Va., where he first saw the light in 1834, being the eldest of ten children born to Beverly and Mary Percell (Hixson) Hutchison, who were also natives of the Old Dominion, in which State the father followed the occupation of farming, and died in 1878, his widow's death occurring there in 1889. Both the Hutchisons and Hixsons settled in Virginia during the colonial days of this country, the first-mentioned family coming thither from Ireland. The paternal grandfather was born in Virginia, and during the war of 1812 held the rank of Captain in the American army. The maternal grandfather, Benjamin Hixson, was of English descent, a Virginian by birth, and in this State his entire life was honorably spent. The subject of this sketch was educated in the schools of his native State, and until he was nineteen years of age his life was spent on a farm. He then commenced the study of law in the old historic town of Charleston, and was admitted to the bar at Richmond in 1859. He at once came to Texas, located in the town of San Marcos, and opened an office for the practice of his profession, and has ever been at the head of the local bar, in fact, is one of the leading lawyers of the State. In January, 1862, he was active in raising a company for the Confederate service, and upon its organization he was elected Second Lieutenant, and when the regiment was organized he was made Major of Col. Wood's brigade, Thirty-second Cavalry, and bore the reputation of being a cool, brave and efficient commander in battle. He served in the trans-Mississippi department in Texas and Louisiana, and was in almost innumerable skirmishes and minor engagements, and in all the battles of the Red River campaign against Gen. Banks, from Blair's Landing to Yellow Bayou. After the battle of Mansura, La., Maj. Hutchison commanded the rear guard of Gen. Bagsby's division, and so ably was this duty performed during that trying time that he was complimented on the field by the General. In 1864 he became Lieutenant-colonel of his regiment, and was in Texas at the close of the war. In 1861 he was united in marriage with Miss Leonora Clifton, a native of Louisiana, by whom he has three sons: Beverly, Oscar, and Louis. The major and his wife are members of the Episcopal Church, and move in the very best social circles of their section. Major Hutchison's views upon the economic and political questions of the day are well known, and in 1893 he was tendered a unanimous nomination by the senatorial convention of the People's Party for State Senator, and was elected by a large majority. His record as a legislator was most honorable and creditable, and he showed great wisdom, prudence and public spirit in looking after the best interests of his section. While a member of this body he served on several committees, among which were Judiciary Nos. 1 and 2. Regardless of the fact that he was the only Populist member of the House, he commanded the respect of his brother Senators, and his influence and strong intellect were felt in that body. From his long and varied business transactions with the people, the major knows their wants, and has always been fearlessly outspoken on all questions that would tend to improve and benefit his section. He is a man who thinks, speaks and acts for himself, regardless of cliques and rings, is honest in his convictions, and is always true to what he believes to be just and right. Personally he is the peer of any man in Texas, for he has the highest sense of personal honor, his habits are exemplary, his executive and business ability of the best, and his views and sympathies are broad and generous. He is a shrewd and well-read lawyer, an excellent student of human nature, and is a thorough scholar and gentleman.

W. V. COLLINS. Some men are known for their upright lives, common sense and moral worth, rather than for their wealth or political standing. Their acquaintances respect them, the young generations heed their example, and when they go to the grave posterity listens with reverence to the story of their quiet and useful lives. Among such men is W. V. Collins, a man of modest and unassuming demeanor, intelligent, a friend to the poor, charitable to the faults of his neighbors, and ready to unite with them in every good word and work, and active in the support of laudable public enterprises. He was born in South Carolina in 1814, the fourth of eight children born to Thomas S. and Annie (Lassiter) Collins, the former of whom was born in South Carolina and the latter in Kentucky. The paternal ancestors came from England in colonial times, and the grandfather and several brothers were soldiers in the Revolutionary War. The maternal grandfather was a South Carolinian of French descent, and was with Gen. Francis Marion in all his noted campaigns during the Revolution. He was a pioneer of Kentucky, and died at the age of ninety-six years. In 1819 Thomas S. Collins moved with his family to Mississippi, and located on the bank of the Pearl River in Marion County, where he followed planting until his death in 1826, his wife's death having preceded his by two years. He was quite active in political matters, and was a stanch Jacksonian Democrat. W. V. Collins was reared, educated and married in Mississippi, the last event occurring in 1837, to Miss Susan H. Tomlingson, a native of Mississippi, and in 1844 he brought his family to the Lone Star State, and for about two years thereafter resided in Sabine County. Since that time he has been a resident of Gonzales, and has been one of the most substantial of its citizens. Here he soon opened an hotel, and in a few years erected a substantial brick building, which, up to within a few years, was occupied as a hostelry. In 1862 he dropped all business to enlist in the Confederate service, and was on duty in Texas until the termination of hostilities. He then returned home and turned his attention to stock-raising, but so serious was the trouble with the Indians at that time that he raised a company to go against them, and was elected its Captain. In 1866 he was elected a Justice of the Peace, an office he held for sixteen years, and during this time he was presiding justice for four years. He was also Mayor of Gonzales for four years. During Cleveland's first term as President Mr. Collins was appointed Postmaster of Gonzales, a position he filled with ability for four years. For two years prior to this he was deputy in the Comptroller's office at Austin. In 1848 he secured the contract to erect the first court house of the county, which was completed in 1849 at a total cost of $3,000, and was in use for some eight years. In 1848 he started a brick-yard, and made the first brick in the place, built the court house of this material, which was the first structure of the kind ever put up in Gonzales. To himself and wife eleven children have been given, five of whom are now living: Medora, widow of Augustus D. Harris, who was killed during the Civil War, has three children; Sydney, died during the war; Wiley, was killed by lightning in 1889; Leonidas, Glenoro, wife of John S. Brown; Emmet is married and resides in Denver, Colo., and John. Mr. Collins and his family are members of the Baptist Church, and for forty years he has been a member of the I. O. O. F., Gonzales Lodge No. 38. He has held every office in this lodge, has been a delegate to many conventions, and as a citizen is highly honored and has numerous friends.

DR. SIDNEY J. FRANCIS. A physician may be well paid for his services, but the cases are numerous where he neither asks nor receives compensation. His profession must ever be regarded as the noblest and most beneficial to mankind. Dr. Francis is an active practitioner, and is also engaged very profitably in another most useful calling, that of the druggist. He was born in Guadalupe County, Texas, in 1867, the eldest child born to Joseph and Miranda (Johnson) Francis, who were natives of Alabama and Texas respect-

ively. The latter died when the subject of this sketch was a small lad, but
the father is still a resident of Guadalupe County, of which section he is a
very prominent citizen. Dr. Sidney J. Francis was educated in the high
school at Prairie Lea, and began life for himself as a school teacher, at the
age of eighteen years. At the same time he began fitting himself for the
practice of medicine by studying during his leisure hours, and after a time
he entered the medical department of Tulane University of New Orleans,
from which noted institution he was graduated in March, 1880, when in his
twenty-second year. He at once began the practice of his profession in
Luling, where he has built up a practice and has made a reputation that is by
no means local. His name is a very familiar one throughout Caldwell County,
especially, and as a medical practitioner he has shown great intelligence,
conscientious effort and painstaking care. His manners are pleasing, and
being of a cheerful disposition, his presence is at once felt in the sick-room
and has a beneficial effect. In the winter of 1893 he took a post graduate
course at his Alma Mater, and he has long been a member of the Caldwell
County Médical Society. He is a member of the drug firm of Van Gasken
& Francis, which establishment is well and attractively appointed; and the
patronage which is accorded these gentlemen is but an index of the high esteem in which they are held, the fine quality of their goods, and the reasonable prices at which they dispose of them.

HARRISON ASKEY, who is one of the wide-awake, enterprising planters of
Gonzales County, Texas, was born in Washington, Hempstead County, Ark.,
December 14, 1824, to the union of Morton and Lucinda (Hill) Askey,
natives of Missouri. The father followed planting both in Missouri and
Arkansas, and a number of years before the Texas Rebellion, came to Nacogdoches County, Texas, where he and wife passed the closing scenes of their
lives, their death occurring prior to that war. Politically the father was a
Whig, and socially a Mason. The mother was a devout Methodist in religious
belief. After his parents' death, which occurred when he was only seven or
eight years of age, he was taken by an uncle, Nicholas Tramwell, and reared
on a farm in Arkansas. He worked for him until twenty years of age, when
he married Miss Catherine Lloyd. Later he moved to Louisiana, bought a
farm, and after two years came to Gonzales County, where he has since
resided. He has always followed planting and is a lover of blooded
horses. Some of the famous race horses of the country were raised on his
farm near Gonzales. The brown stallion, "Joe Murray," holding the fastest
record up to 1884 for seven-eighths of a mile, ever made at Chicago, was
raised on his place; and also the famous mare, "Ella Harper," one-half sister
of "Joe Murphy Murray," came from his ranch, her mile record being 1:40.
He was the owner of "Old Rebel," father of "Joe Murray," one of the
speediest in the annals of racing for three-fourths of a mile. "Little Rebel,"
a great four-mile horse, also came from his ranch. With the approach of
old age Mr. Askey decided to retire from the turf, and sold his stable in 1888.
He is a Democrat, a member of Gonzales Masonic Lodge and has taken the
Chapter degrees. His wife, who is now sixty-six years of age and in the en-
joyment of excellent health, is a worthy member of the Methodist Episcopal
Church. They have had fifteen children, and those living are: Clinton,
Lucinda, wife of John Nixon; John, Elizabeth, wife of Walter Mathews, of
Gonzales County; Otho, and Catherine, wife of Thomas Fussell, of San

Antonio. After seeing his children comfortably settled, Mr. Askey has still a beautiful ranch of 700 acres within five miles of Gonzales, where he is spending his declining years in peace and quiet. He still takes a keen, though inactive interest in all the important issues of the day.

W. C. AGEE. A glance, only, at the vast array of labels and bottles behind the counters and in the prescription department of a well conducted drug shop is necessary to get at the truth of the vast amount of knowledge that a person must possess in order to be able to successfully handle the necessities of a chemist's establishment. A prominent druggist and the original merchant of Floresville, W. C. Agee, is a native of Fayette County, Tenn., born in 1841. He is eighth in order of birth of nine children born to William and Julia (Henderson) Agee, both natives of Alabama. The father, who followed the occupation of a farmer, came to Texas in 1855, locating in Hopkins County, where the closing scenes of his life were passed the same year. The mother, who remained in Hopkins County until after the war, died in Williamson County in 1870. During his infancy our subject was taken to Mississippi by his parents and attended the schools of that State until 1855, when he came with his parents to Texas. Until the breaking out of the Rebellion he remained on the farm, and in 1861 enlisted in the Ninth Texas Infantry, Company F, under Captain Leftwich. He went to Iuka and Corinth and soon participated in the battle of Shiloh. He was in many skirmishes with Gen. Bragg and was in the Kentucky campaign with that General, participating in the battles of Perryville, Chickamauga, etc. He was with Gen. Johnston about Vicksburg, later in the Atlanta campaign, and then was with Gen. Hood in his march north. During this campaign he participated in a pitched battle, where his brother, J. B., of the same company, was killed. Another brother, N. J., also of the same company, was killed at Atlanta. Afterwards our subject was at Nashville and helped to cover the retreat of the army back to Tennessee River. His last engagement was at Bacon Creek. After the war he passed one year in Hopkins County, Texas, and then moved to Williamson County, where he remained until March, 1874. At that date he moved to Floresville, then the recently organized county seat of Wilson County, and started the first store. In 1880 he changed his line of business and started the first drug store, which he has carried on successfully up to the present. He has a neat store, cozy and well stocked with chemicals, drugs, stationery, perfumes and toilet preparations, and has a highly satisfactory business. Mr. Agee was married in 1866 to Miss Carrie Reagan, a native of Mississippi, but who was reared in Texas. Ten children have been the fruits of this union, five of whom are living: John E., Maria, Julia, Walter and Carrie. Harvin died when fourteen years of age, but the others died in infancy. Mr. and Mrs. Agee hold membership in the Methodist Episcopal Church South, and the former is a Mason, being now Worshipful Master of Floresville Lodge No. 575.

WILLIAM GREEN THORNTON, M. D. No profession is so arduous as that of the physician, for it brings into active play all the versatile powers of his being. When the long, cold night rides through wind and rain are taken into consideration as well as the years of careful preparation and constant study, with often little or no compensation received for services given, it is often a fact to be wondered at that the medical man is so conscientious in the discharge of his duties and that he is so universally warm hearted and sympathetic. Of the leading physicans of Victoria County, Texas, none is more prominent than Dr. W. G. Thornton, who has a large, lucrative and constantly increasing practice. He is a product of Illinois, where he was born October 21, 1823, the second child born to David and Susan (Boggus) Thornton, who were natives of Georgia and North Carolina respectively. The paternal grandfather was a South Carolinian, who first left his native State for the wilds of Illinois, and later moved to Arkansas, of which State he was among the pioneers. He was a tiller of the soil, and in this respect his son David followed in his footsteps. The latter left Illinois about 1845 and settled in White County, Ark., where he served in the capacity of Justice of the Peace the most of the remainder of his life, dying during one of the years of the war. His wife had died previously. Dr. Thornton was principally reared and educated in Illinois, but he began the study of medicine in Little Rock, Ark., soon after he located in the State with his parents, and later took a course in the Louisville (Ky.) Medical College, and in the University of Louisiana, at New Orleans, from which he graduated in the spring of 1849. He at once entered upon the practice of his profession at Benton, Saline County, Ark., where he remained one year, and in 1850 he started for California, but stopped and practiced his profession in Mexico for some time, after which he proceeded to California, where he arrived in 1851. He was engaged in mining there one year, after which he returned East and located at Galveston, Texas. In 1854 he was married to Miss Mary Edmunds, a native of Virginia, and a daughter of Pizarro Edmunds, an early settler of the Lone Star State. To the doctor and his worthy wife six children have been given. Annie, wife of Alex. Hamilton; Nellie, Lillian, wife of Lee Josephs of Cuero, Texas; Laura, Mary, and William, who died of yellow fever in 1867. The family are members and attendants of the Presbyterian Church, and socially the doctor is a member of the A. F. & A. M. He is a man of many worthy traits of character and is respected by all who know him.

W. H. GRAHAM is the active, popular and efficient Tax Collector of De Witt County, Texas, and one of the representative business men of the same. The man from Pennsylvania has always been a potential element in the growth and prosperity of the Lone Star State, and Mr. Graham's career is worthy of emulation, for it shows what pluck, perseverance and energy will do. Mr. Graham first saw the light in Erie County, Pennsylvania, in 1844, and was sixth in order of birth of twelve children born to James and Annie Graham, natives of Ireland and New York, respectively. When six years of age our subject was taken by a man named Lee, who lived in Cuba, New York, but one year later this gentleman moved to Iowa, where our subject was reared and educated. In July, 1861, he enlisted in Company G, Fifth Iowa Infantry, and served in the Army of Tennessee. He was at New Madrid, Mo.; Iuka, Miss.; Corinth, Miss., and was with Gen. Grant when he crossed the Mississippi River. He was in all the battles around Jackson, then to Vicksburg, and after the fall of that city went to Chattanooga where he participated in the battle of Lookout Mountain. There he was captured and spent that winter in prison on Belle Island in James River. In the spring he was taken to Andersonville and remained there until November, when he was taken to Florence, S. C., and in December exchanged. He was in prison one year and eleven days. Mr. Graham then made a trip to Iowa, got his discharge, and then went to the Keystone State to see his parents, whom he had not seen since six years of age. Later he re-enlisted in the Ninety-ninth Pennsylvania Regiment, and was sent to Goldsboro, S. C., where he remained until the surrender. He was in the final review at Washington City, May, 1865, and was discharged at Philadelphia in June. A few months later Mr. Graham came to Texas, and as he had enlisted in the regular United States Cavalry, he served three years on the Texas frontier, at various posts. When his time was up he took the money he had saved in the army and went to Eastman's Business College at Poughkeepsie, where he remained for about a year. After that he returned to Texas, and in a few months permanently located in the new town of Cuero, where at first he was stage and express agent. After that he was route agent on the railroad from Cuero to Indianola, and was in the latter place in 1875, during the great storm there. He served as Deputy Sheriff and Collector until 1880, when he was elected Collector of the county, which position he has held since. He possesses many noble traits of character, is entirely self-made, and owes his success in life, and the high estimation in which he is held by all who know him to his upright, manly course through life. He is interested in all good causes, and is one of the public spirited men of the country.

Mr. Graham's happy domestic life began in 1874 when Miss Louisa Demonet, a native of Louisiana, became his wife. Her father, who was a native of France, is now deceased. To our subject and wife have been born three interesting children: Mary Agnes, James Michael and William Henry. He and family hold membership in the Catholic Church. Mr. Graham is president of the Catholic Knights of America, of Cuero, and he has charge of the C. L. & I. Company's land. He also does a general real estate business.

Dr. WILLIAM THOMAS JONES has done much to relieve the pains and ailments to which suffering humanity is heir. He has practiced the "healing art" since 1882, and during this time he has built up a reputation of which he has every reason to be proud, and he is widely patronized by the elite of his section. He was born in Edenton, Ga., in 1853, the second of six children born to William Benjamin and Mary Ann (Rogers) Jones, the former of whom was a Virginian and the latter a native of Georgia. The father was a mechanic by trade, and in the early '40's went to Georgia, where the rest of his days were spent, his death occurring in 1875, and his wife's in 1869. He was one of two sons, and his parents died in Virginia, when he and his brother were children. His wife's people were early settlers of Georgia, from Maryland. In the town of Edenton, the subject of this sketch received a practical education. The first work he did for himself was as a drug clerk in his native town, but after remaining thus employed for one year, he lived successively in Greensboro, Atlanta and Covington, and worked as a drug clerk in each place. In 1872 he married Miss Sallie Williams, of White Plains, Ga., after which he was engaged in farming until 1880, at which time he began the study of medicine under Dr. I. D. Moore, of White Plains, after which he attended the Medical Department of the University of Georgia, and graduated in March, 1884. In 1882 he had come to Texas and practiced for some time in De Witt County, and in the fall of 1884 moved to Hochheim, the same county, where his home continued to be until May, 1893, since which time he has resided at San Marcos, where he has built up a good practice. April, 1893, witnessed the event of his taking a post graduate course at the New Orleans Polyclinic Medical College, and he is now a member of the State Medical Association. To himself and wife, who is a worthy member of the M. E. Church, the following children have been given: Paul William, Annie Ware, Hudnel Marvin, Mary Willie, Campbell Ford, who died in infancy; Harry, who also died in infancy; Eva and Lenon. The doctor is a wideawake gentleman, scholarly and successful in his practice, and he is the owner of a fine farm in De Witt County.

HARBERT SMITH is one of the reliable, substantial and progressive farmers of Gonzales County, who has done much to forward the agricultural interests of this section, for he was reared to the calling of a farmer, and this occupation has received his attention, to a greater or less extent, up to the present time. He is a public spirited citizen, in harmony with advanced ideas, intelligent progress, and active in his support of all worthy enterprises. He is a product of Alabama, born in 1829, the sixth in a family of nine children, born to Isam and Elizabeth (Hodges) Smith, who were Virginians by birth and bringing up, but afterwards became residents of Alabama. They came to Texas in 1841 and settled in Gonzales County, but owing to the trouble with Mexico they were compelled to change their place of abode, and for several years were residents of Fayette County. They sold their possessions there and returned to this county, and became the owners of a very fine farm, which the father was successfully engaged in tilling until his death in 1866, his widow surviving him until 1872. The maternal grandfather, James Hodges, was a Virginian, who resided for a time in Alabama, and in 1835 came to Texas and took up his abode in Gonzales County, and from here took part in numerous fights with the Indians. He died in 1854. Harbert Smith was principally reared and educated in Fayette County, and he began his independent career as a tiller of the soil. In 1857 he was married to Miss Mary S. Laird, a native of Mississippi and a daughter of F. L. Laird, who settled and died in Eastern Texas. In 1861 Mr. Smith entered the State service on the Texas frontier, was later mustered out at Fredericksburg, after which he enlisted in the regular Confederate service in the spring of 1862, becoming a member of Capt. Week's Company, Willis' Cavalry Battalion of Wall's Legion, and was sent to Mississippi. There he was with Gen. Van Dorn at Holly Springs, and was afterwards in numerous engagements in that State, Tennessee and Alabama, the engagement at Jackson, Miss., being one of the most noteworthy. He was at Canton, Miss., when news reached him of Lee's surrender, and from there he returned home on his horse across the State of Louisiana. Nothwithstanding the changed condition of affairs, after the close of the great conflict, Mr. Smith did not sit down and uselessly repine over the days that were passed, but set energetically to work to retrieve his losses, and has since been extensively and successfully engaged in farming, and now has a very fine and valuable farm on the San Marcos River, of which 300 acres are in an excellent state of cultivation and yield abundant harvests. Since 1892 his home has been in the city of Gonzales, where he is very comfortably and pleasantly situated. Four children blessed the union of himself and wife: Tennessee, wife of W. B. Carr, of San Antonio, Texas; Besse B. is the wife of Ellis Danby, of Tennessee; D. H. is married and engaged in farming, and J. B. is unmarried and is still at home. Mr. Smith is a member of the A. F. & A. M., and during his long residence in Gonzales County has made numerous acquaintances, who, in nearly every instance, are his friends.

CAPT. WILLIAM LONDON FOSTER, an early settler of Gonzales County, and now a resident of Luling, Caldwell County, was born in Calloway County, Ky., in 1828, the eldest child born to John E. and Mary (Moore) Foster, who were natives of the State of Alabama. The grandparents on both sides were early settlers of that State, but soon after the birth of the subject of this sketch his parents moved to Tennessee, thence to Alabama, and then to Mississippi. From Monroe County, of the last mentioned State, they came to Texas in 1838, and in June of the following year settled in Gonzales County, where John E. Foster located a headright of 640 acres in the fork of the San Marcos and Guadalupe rivers. He also bought other land, which he improved and resided on. His first wife, the mother of the subject of this sketch, died in Mississippi about 1836, after which he married Mrs. Dilworth (nee Elizabeth Parchman), a sister of the wife of Col. John G. King. John E. Foster died in 1840, while on a trip to Mississippi with a drove of horses and mules, and his property was appropriated by a man who was working for him. His widow resided on the farm in Texas for a number of years, and being a courageous and strong minded woman she improved the farm and managed it successfully. She later married Dr. Hardeman, and eventually passed from life in Guadalupe County. The first wife of John E. Foster bore him two children, and on coming to Texas he was accompanied by them, the three children which his second wife bore him, and the two children born to his third wife by her former husband. From 1840 to 1846 the subject of this sketch assisted on the home farm, but in the last mentioned year enlisted in Capt. Henry McCullough's Company, Jack Hays' Regiment, for the Mexican War, and started for that country, but was recalled to the frontier of Texas, and during that year was Indian scouting. His company was mustered out of service in 1847, after which he joined Capt. Crump's Company, Col. P. H. Bell's Regiment, who afterwards became Governor of Texas, and for some time he was a Texas Ranger. In 1848 he joined another company of the same regiment and was engaged fighting Indians for some time. In 1849 he was out with a surveying company for a German colony; in fact, was a very useful citizen in the early history of the State. In July, 1850, he was married to Mrs. Eliza Ann Rutledge, *nee* King, a daughter of Col. John G. King, after which he located on his farm and ranch on the Guadalupe River, where he made his home for many years. In 1861 he assisted in raising a company for the Confederate army, of which he was made First Lieutenant of Terry's Rangers. He was sent east of the Mississippi River with his regiment, and in December of the same year he withdrew and came home on a leave of absence for sixty days, and at once recruited another company, which was mustered into the Confederate service within thirty days from the time he left Kentucky, and he was made its Captain. It became Company D of Wood's Regiment and operated in the trans-Mississippi Department, participating in the battles in Louisiana in the Banks campaign up the Red River, and was operating on the Brazos River when the war closed. He at once returned home and engaged in farming and stock raising, and lived on his farm above Gonzales until 1889, which consists of about 350 acres under cultivation and 1,000 acres in ranche and pasture. All the improvements on this place were made by himself, and are the result of much thoughtful consideration, for when he became the owner of the place it was totally unimproved. He is a thrifty and painstaking tiller of the soil, and raises, on an average, forty bushels of corn and three-fourths of a bale of cotton to the acre. About 1870 he raised the first crop of wheat in all that section, and at the same time, also, was the first to raise oats. Since that time he has cultivated both crops successfully, and some years the yield has been exceptionally large. Since 1889 Capt. Foster has resided in Luling, and is not actively engaged in any employment. He was left a widower in 1883, his wife having borne him nine children, four of whom passed from life prior to their mother. The names of his children are as follows: Mary, who died in childhood; Elizabeth, who died in childhood also; John King, who is a dentist at Eagle Pass; Thomas Pinckney, who died in childhood; James Chism, who lives on his father's farm; Philip Houston, a dentist of Marion; William Lee, who resides on the old home and manages the farm; Minnie Alice, who is the wife of N. Morrison, of Leesville, and one child that died in infancy. Mr. Foster's second marriage was consummated in August, 1884, and was to Mrs. Martha Ann (Morrison) King, daughter of Wesley Morrison, an early Texan from Mississippi, and an extensive farmer. Mr. Foster is a member of the Baptist Church, while his wife is a Methodist. Out of the kindness and generosity of his heart Mr. Foster has reared eighteen orphans, several of whom were his relatives. He is an honorable man and an excellent citizen, and is universally esteemed.

JAMES SIMMS COOK is among the best known farmers and stock raisers, and well-to-do and influential citizens of Gonzales County, Texas. He was born in Edgecomb County, North Carolina, Sept. 14, 1824. The father, Nathan P. Cook, a native of the Old North State, removed to North Alabama in 1832, and became a prominent cotton planter and the owner of forty or fifty slaves. About 1856 he moved to Arkansas and there died in 1864. His wife, formerly Miss Patience Simms, died in Texas in 1883. Both were members of the Methodist Church, and he was a Democrat in politics. He was Justice of the Peace for many years. Our subject was reared on the plantation in North Alabama, and attended La Grange College, but, owing to failing health while in his junior year, was obliged to give up his studies. After this, for three years he clerked in Decatur, and then was engaged in merchandising three years at Trinity. Returning home, he managed his father's business until he removed to Arkansas, after which he went to Little River County and was engaged in planting until the breaking out of the Civil War. He was then with the Arkansas State troops three months and was then discharged on account of poor health. Mr. Cook then made a visit to his old home in Alabama, and in the fall of 1866 came to Gonzales County, Texas, where he has resided since. He is a leader in planting and stock-raising, and is recognized as authority on all subjects relating to them. He is one of a family of nine children, of whom himself and brother, Nathan Cook, are the only survivors. Fraternally he is a Mason, has taken the Master degree of Gonzales Lodge, and politically a Democrat. A member of the Methodist Church, he has held the office of trustee and class leader at various times, and is prominent in all good work. In the year 1856 he celebrated his nuptials with Miss Mary Francis, daughter of William H. and Elizabeth (Martin) Francis, of Lawrence County, Ala. She is a Methodist also. Nine children have been born to them: Elizabeth, deceased; Hunter, Jane, deceased; Walter, Mary Frances, deceased; J. Earl, Darthula Ellen, wife of Lee Goodlett, of Moulton, Ala.; Nathan and Hibernia V.

Dr. A. D. Evans of Floresville, and now County Judge of Wilson County, came originally from Alabama, where his birth occurred in 1838. He was the eldest of nine children born to his parents, James R. and C. O. (Dorman) Evans, the father a native of North Carolina and the mother of Connecticut. They were married in Alabama, where Mr. Evans carried on the practice of law and served as Probate Judge of Greene County, that State, for many years. About 1865 he came to the Lone Star State, located at Bryan, and served as Mayor of that city. There his death occurred in 1880. The mother is still living and resides in Bryan. Dr. A. D. Evans was educated in his native State and began the study of law in Mobile, in 1854. This he abandoned at the end of eighteen months, and instead took up the study of medicine with Dr. Peterson, of Greensboro, Ala. Later he attended lectures in New Orleans, and graduated in April, 1859. Immediately afterward he came to Texas, settled in Karnes County, near the present town of Kenedy, and practiced his profession successfully until the tocsin of war sounded in 1861. He joined Terry's Regiment in 1861 and went to Bowling Green, Ky. In 1862 he was placed in the medical department, C. S. A. Later he was assigned to duty at Mobile as assistant surgeon, and still later was assigned duty in the Second Alabama Regiment as assistant surgeon, serving in that capacity and as chief surgeon until the close of the war. Returning to Karnes County, he practiced his profession and was County Commissioner there until November, 1883, when he moved to Floresville, where he has remained ever since. As a physician, he has established a first-class reputation throughout the county, and has won the confidence and respect of all. In November, 1890, he was elected County Judge, and re-elected to that responsible position in 1892. The judge was first married in 1859, to Miss Rutledge, of Alabama, who died in 1871, leaving five children. His second marriage occurred in April, 1874, with Miss Ford, a native of Texas and a daughter of H. D. Ford of this county. To this union three children have been born. Dr. Evans and family are members of the Methodist Episcopal Church South. He is very active in fraternity circles, is a member of the Knights of Pythias and the Masonic order, and was one of the organizers of Floresville Chapter No. 160 R. A. Masons and its first High Priest. In 1885 he was made district deputy of the Masonic district in which he resides. He is a leading citizen of the community and one of its substantial men, and is a member of Wilson County Camp No. 215 U. C. Veterans, and is Adjutant of the camp.

Dr. A. A. Ledbetter, probably one of the best known physicians of Lavaca County, Texas, has been unusually successful in the practice of his profession, and throughout this section is considered an authority on medical lore. He was born in Alabama in 1844, and was receiving a preparatory training for college in the State of Mississippi when Civil War broke out. Early in 1862 he enlisted in Company G, Twenty-eighth Mississippi Cavalry, and served in the Departments of Mississippi and Tennessee, under Gen. Van Dorn and Gen. Forest, until the close of the war. He was in all the engagements of the Atlanta campaign, and was twice slightly wounded, once at Adairsville, Ga., and again at Pulaski, Tenn., near the close of the war. Returning home, he again took up his books and began the study of medicine, attending lectures at Tulane University, New Orleans, in 1867 and 1868. After that he commenced practicing in Mississippi, but in the winter of 1868 left that State for Texas, locating in Lavaca County. In 1887 he came to Hallettsville, and in 1891 opened a fine drug store in partnership with Dr. Knok. Previous to this, in 1869 and 1870, he took another course of lectures at Tulane University, New Orleans, and graduated. He was married in October, 1868, in Mississippi to Miss Julia Guitella Denson, daughter of Dr. J. C. Denson, and eleven children were given them, six of whom are now living. Mrs. Ledbetter, who was a worthy member of the Christian Church, died in 1893. The doctor is also a member of that church, and he is also a member of the State Medical Association. He has a fine farm on the Navidad River, and is one of the county's most intelligent physicians and respected citizens. He was sixth in order of birth of ten children born to William and Casandra S. (Black) Ledbetter, both natives of Georgia. The father was a planter until after the war, when he became a merchant. In 1853 he moved his family to Scott County, Miss., and from there to Louisiana in about 1870. His death occurred at Summerfield, La., in 1877, and the mother died in 1883.

COLUMBUS LAFAYETTE THURMOND. Tennessee has given to Texas, some of her most enterprising, and public spirited citizens, and in this connection the name of C. L. Thurmond is eminently worthy of being mentioned. He was born in Lauderdale County, Tenn., November 13, 1833, being the youngest in a family of seven children born to Dr. John G. and Ann Eliza (Sturges) Thurmond, who were natives of the State of Georgia. The subject of this sketch was left fatherless in his early childhood, but he fortunately secured a practical education in the common schools of his native State. An elder brother, Alfred S., went to Texas about 1836 where he participated in the Texas Revolution. He was taken prisoner by the Mexicans and for some time acted as interpreter for them. In 1852 he made a visit to his old home and when he returned to the Lone Star State he was accompanied by the subject of this sketch, who secured a position as clerk and followed that occupation for several years in Victoria. In 1856 he was elected to the position of County Treasurer, which he ably filled for two years. In 1857 he engaged in business for himself and for a long term of years kept a mercantile establishment, being the proprietor of two mercantile houses during the war, one at Goliad and the other at Brownsville. In 1858 Mr. Thurmond was elected County Assessor and Collector and held the office until 1865, when he was removed by Federal authorities. In 1869 he removed to Lavaca County where he tilled the soil and was also engaged in mercantile pursuits for three years, at the end of which time he returned to Victoria. From 1874 until 1880 he held the office of County Sheriff and in 1882 was elected County Clerk. He was re-elected to the office of Sheriff in 1886 and filled this position with marked ability until 1892. In the meantime he held various city offices, and in every sphere of public duty he showed the utmost intelligence and faithfulness, which was, no doubt, the secret of his being kept so constantly in office. He was United States Marshal from 1858 to 1861, was the census taker of Victoria and Goliad counties in 1860 and was bitterly opposed to the Civil War. He was an outspoken Union man, but notwithstanding that fact, the people had so much confidence in his sound sense and in his regard for the people and section in which he lived, that he was in office almost the entire time. He has been quite successful as a farmer and is the owner of a ranch of 2,700 acres, of which 150 acres are in a good state of cultivation, and he has also given considerable attention to the raising of stock. In 1857 he led to the altar Miss Margaret A. McGrew, a native of Mississippi, and to their union eleven children were given, seven of whom survive: Alfred Seymour, a lawyer of Victoria; Columbus L., Jr.; Annie Laurie, wife of James J. Jones (see sketch); Sam Houston, Jessie G., George M. and Mattie. Thomas H. died in infancy; Benton McCulloch at the age of ten years, and two other children died in infancy. Mr. Thurmond, or as he is more familiarly known "Old Zip" Thurmond, is a noted character in Victoria County and served in the capacity of Sheriff when it took a man of cool brain and steady nerve and great determination to fill it acceptably. He discharged his duties in a most exemplary way, and has ever been an honored resident of the county. His brother Alfred organized a company in San Antonio for the Confederate service during the war, of which he was made Captain, and he was with Green's Brigade in all the engagements of the trans-Mississippi Department. He was later a member of the Texas Legislature, and was a man of note. While on board a schooner bound from Rockport to Tucpan, Mexico, he was lost at sea and nothing has ever since been heard of the vessel or people. Rev. John H. Thurmond, another brother, a minister of the Baptist Church, came to Texas in 1854, and died in Victoria of yellow fever in 1867. Dr. Pulaski A. Thurmond, still another brother, became a resident of the Lone Star State in 1854-55 and settled in Lavaca County, his death resulting from the kick of a horse in 1880 at Hallettsville.

JAMES H. MOORE. Few families in Texas have a higher standing for character, and enterprise than the one represented by the name at the head of this paragraph and in its various members it is eminently worthy of the respect which is universally conceded to it. James H. Moore, who was one of the first settlers of the village of Thomaston, Texas, came originally from Mississippi, his birth occurring in Monroe, now Lamar, County in 1844. He is fourth in a family of eight children born to Hon. Thomas C. and Martha (Hollis) Moore, the former a native of South Carolina and the latter of Alabama. The paternal grandfather, James Moore, was born in the Palmetto State and there followed farming for many years. At an early day he moved from there to Mississippi and became a wealthy and extensive planter. There he passed the remainder of his life. The Moore family is of Scotch-Irish origin and the ancestors came to this country in colonial times. They traced their ancestors back to Sir Walter Raleigh. Our subject's maternal grandfather, John Hollis, was born in Alabama where he became a wealthy planter and where he passed his entire life. The mother of our subject with other members of the family moved to Mississippi and in that State she was married to Mr. Moore. The latter, after his marriage, followed planting in Mississippi, and while a resident of that State became quite active in politics, serving in the Legislature of that State and holding other prominent positions. In 1853 he came to the Lone Star State and settled in Bastrop County where he bought land and engaged in farming. His superior abilities were soon recognized and he was solicited to run for the Legislature and for the office of Governor of State. In 1860 he was a member of the secession convention. During the war he continued farming but devoted most of his attention to the Confederate cause, assisting the widows and orphans at home and doing much good. From there he moved to Fayette County where he now resides, engaged in farming. He lost his sight in 1862, but is now one of the best posted men of the State, although having to depend on others to do his reading. In whatever field of action Mr. Moore has been called, he has shown his superior qualities and high character. He and Mrs. Moore are earnest and consistent members of the Methodist Church, and most worthy and esteemed citizens of the county. The original of this notice was but a boy when he was brought by his parents to Texas, and he was reared mainly in Fayette County, where he was attending school when the war broke out. Abandoning his studies he enlisted in Company I, 16th Texas Regiment, and served in Henry E. McCollough's Brigade, participating in the engagements on the Mississippi River, Milligan's Bend, Mansfield and Pleasant Hill. In the last named battle he was wounded and was discharged for disability. Previous to that, however, he was in numerous minor engagements in Arkansas and Louisiana. After returning home he attended school for a time and then branched out as an agriculturist in Fayette County. There he was married to Miss Lou V. Thomas, a native of Fayette County and daughter of Nathan Thomas who was born in Tennessee. At an early day her father came to Texas and first settled in Washington, but afterwards Fayette county. He was a prominent man, served in the Legislature and held other prominent offices. He was thrown from his buggy and died shortly afterward. When he first settled in Texas he bought a tract of 1,190 acres in DeWitt County for thirty-five cents per acre. The railroad passing through DeWitt County crossed this land and a station located on it was named Thomaston in his honor. Soon after our subject's marriage he moved to Mr. Thomas' land in DeWitt County and erected the first house in what soon became Thomaston. The town was laid out in lots by Henry E. McCollough who was surveyor for the railroad. Mr. Thomas donated each alternate lot to the railroad, and the town now has a population of 500, four stores, a gin and mill, two churches, two blacksmith shops, and is surrounded by an excellent farming country. Mr. Moore is the owner of 653 acres of the original tract, with 350 acres under cultivation. His land is rich and productive, often raising fifty bushels of corn and one bale of cotton per acre. Our subject has been somewhat active politically, has been a delegate to Democratic conventions and is now Justice of the Peace of the Seventh Precinct which has been newly created. He is active in church work, organizing a Sunday School here twenty-five years ago and has been its Superintendent constantly since. There is an enrolled school of about 100 scholars. To Mr. and Mrs. Moore have been born seven children: Hattie, wife of M. S. Magee of Thomaston; Sallie, Annie, wife of Dr. W. Shropshire of Houston, Thomas, Susie, Willie, died in infancy; and Hollis—an interesting and most intelligent family. Besides still owning the entire town of Thomaston and his fine farm there, Mr. Moore also owns a most valuable farm in Fayette County. This farm is improved and highly productive, and all his property is rapidly advancing in value. The town of Thomaston is yearly becoming a more active trading and shipping point, and increasing in population. All the surrounding country is fertile and productive. Mr. Moore is a pleasant, courteous and hospitable gentleman and is confident in, and constantly striving for, the advancement of his town and county.

DR. PETER C. WOODS. Before the Good Samaritan dressed the wounds of the man on the Jericho road, the healer of diseases was known for his humanity and kindness. Whatever the skill of the physician and surgeon, he can never be truly great unless he is touched with the spirit of man's infirmities, and moved by a heartfelt purpose to relieve suffering for the sake of the race. In the list of the successful physicians of Hays County, Texas, stands the name of Dr. Peter C. Woods, who has long been a practitioner of San Marcos. He owes his nativity to Tennessee, where he was born in 1820, the second and youngest child born to Peter and Sarah W. (Davidson) Woods, who were natives of Tennessee and North Carolina respectively. The paternal grandfather, Peter Woods, was born in Georgia, and was one of the very first to locate in Tennessee. He eventually died in Missouri, to which State he had removed at an early day. The maternal grandfather, George Davidson, was a North Carolinian by birth and was a soldier in the Revolutionary War, under Gen. William Davidson, an older brother, and saw the most of his service in the Southern States. He in time moved to Tennessee and passed from life in that State. Peter Woods, the father of the subject of this sketch, spent his life in Tennessee, became the Sheriff of Franklin County, and was killed while making an arrest, about 1819, a short time before the birth of the doctor. The latter was reared on Tennessee soil and received the greater part of his literary education at Shelbyville. He then began the study of medicine at Coffeyville, Miss., under Dr. Walker, and graduated at the Louisville (Ky.) Medical Institute in 1842, and at once began the practice of his profession in Water Valley, Miss. In 1853 he came to San Marcos, Texas, and was about the second physician to locate in the place. He continued the practice of his profession up to 1861, then recruited a company here, of which he was made Captain, Company A, Thirty-second Texas Cavalry, and soon after the organization of this regiment he was elected its Colonel. After serving in Texas for a time, his command was attached to De Bray's Brigade and served on the frontier and coast of Texas and in the campaign against Gen. Banks in Louisiana, on the Red River. He was in many engagements, among which was the fight at Yellow Bayou, where he was severely wounded and retired from the service. He has since been a very successful medical practitioner of San Marcos, and is professionally well known in this and surrounding counties. He was first married in Mississippi to Miss Georgia Lawshe in 1846, and she died in Texas leaving seven children. His second marriage occurred in 1874, and was to Miss Ella R. Ogletree, a native of South Carolina, by whom he has five children. The Doctor and his family are members of the Methodist Episcopal Church, and he has been connected with the same for over half a century, and now holds the office of Trustee. He has been a Mason since his twenty-first year and is a member of San Marcos Chapter, has served as Master of his lodge here for twenty years, and held the same position in Mississippi. He is active in his advocacy of Democratic principles, and is a public spirited citizen. In 1866 he served in the constitutional convention convened to frame the present constitution of the State, since which time he has taken little part in politics, though he is still as firm a believer in State's rights as he was at the close of the war. He is the owner of a fine tract of land of 640 acres and is making a specialty of the raising of Poland China swine, and he also has a good grade of Durham cattle. He is no less successful in his farming operations than as a medical practitioner, and his friends are both numerous and devoted. He was a brave and able military officer, lent valuable aid to the Southern cause, and is a thorough Christian gentleman.

Dr. John C. Jones has become widely and favorably known during his long experience as a medical practitioner. His cheerful confidence in the sick room is often almost as effective as his medicines, and throughout a long life devoted to the healing of the sick and afflicted he has been a close student of his profession, and has ever grasped at new truths in science. He was born in Lawrence County, Ala., in 1837, the second of thirteen children born to Tugnal and Susan (King) Jones, who were natives of the Old North State. They were married about 1830 and in 1855 came to Texas, settling near San Antonio, but during the war resided in Jackson County, and in 1865 came to Gonzales County, where Mr. Jones engaged in merchandising for a few years. He then moved back to his former home in Alabama, and there died in 1884, his wife having passed from life in Texas in 1866. The paternal grandfather, Redding Jones, was born in Wake County, N. C., and was of Scotch and Welsh ancestry. He came to America in colonial times. The maternal grandfather, Hartwell King, was of Irish descent, a son of Richard King, who was brought to this country by his parents when six weeks old. The subject of this sketch was educated at La Grange College, from which he graduated in 1856 as an A. B. He came to Texas on a visit to his parents. Very shortly after he began the study of medicine and after a preliminary course of reading, he went to Scotland and entered the University of Edinburgh, where he remained four years, receiving the degree of M. D. in 1860. The university was then in the zenith of its fame, and numbered among its officers Sir William Gladstone and Lord Brougham; in surgery, Sir James Lyme, of whom it was said, "He never spoke an unnecessary word, nor spilled an unnecessary drop of blood;" and Sir James Simpson. From the latter he holds a special diploma in obstetrics, and he also took a special course in surgical pathology and operative surgery under Sir Joseph Lister. After graduating at Edinburgh he went to Dublin and was appointed resident student in the Rotunda Hospitals, one of the most extensive and renowned maternity institutions in Europe. While there he attended the clinics of Stokes and Corrigan, and also the eye clinics of the talented Sir William Wilde, father of the well known æsthete, Oscar Wilde. From Dublin he went to London and took the surgical course of Ferguson, Erickson & Paget, also attended the eye clinics of Bowman & Critchett at the Morefield Eye Hospital. From London he went to Paris and continued his studies in the hospitals under Velpeau, Nelaton, Jobert, Trousseau and Cassaignas. In 1861 he returned to the United States and on the personal recommendation of the late Jefferson Davis was assigned to duty in the Army of Northern Virginia, and served as surgeon in the famous Hood's Brigade until the surrender at Appomattox. He attended the brigade in all its numerous battles and skirmishes, without a day's absence. At the close of the war he returned to Texas and located at Gonzales, where he has continuously resided and practiced medicine up to the present time. He has served on all the examining boards of the judicial district in which he resides, is a member of the Texas State Medical Association, and is an ex-Vice-president of that body; of the American Medical Association and of the Ninth International Medical Congress. The doctor was married in 1867 to Miss Mary Kennon Crisp, daughter of Dr. John H. Crisp, of Columbus, Texas. The doctor and his wife have three sons and two daughters, and he and his family reside in an elegant home, which has become well known for the re-

THE ALAMO.

fined, yet cordial hospitality that is extended to all. The doctor has prospered financially and has amassed a handsome fortune. His time is fully occupied by the demands of his extensive practice, and he has found little time to write, nevertheless he has contributed some valuable papers to the Texas State Medical Association, which have received much notice. Dr. Jones has long been connected with the church and is one of the vestrymen in the Church of the Messiah.

THOMAS WILSON & SONS. Luling may well be proud of the amount of brains and energy possessed by her representative business men. Taken as a whole, there are none brighter, more intelligent, or with more ability and push, than at this date is Thomas Wilson who, with his sons, is engaged in dealing in real estate and owns some of the finest farming land in southwest Texas. The section in which their lands lie is noted for the healthfulness of climate, abundant crop yield, and it is also well improved with good schools, numerous railroads and good home markets for all the chief products of the farm. Besides this they own 100 acres of land within the corporation limits of Luling, which is laid out into 200 lots; make estimates and contract for rock, brick and concrete headraces, stores, wells, cisterns, or other contract work; secure money and make loans on commission; write deeds, mortgages, leases and contracts, in fact, do an extensive general business. They keep in stock for sale Austin pure white lime, Gonzales and Calaveras brick, nine elms and other Portland purest cements, plaster of Paris, paints, white lead, rubber type and inks, molasses barrels and kegs, fence posts and building blocks, seeds of all kinds, are regular price cutters and deal also in the best Sugar-house Louisiana molasses, from twenty-two up to fifty cents per gallon. Their city property is laid out in lots, 150 x 60 feet each, and sell at from twenty-five dollars to thirty-five dollars per lot, according to location. It would be indeed difficult to find more enterprising business men than Thomas Wilson and his sons, and the town of Luling and the County of Caldwell owe much of their prosperity to these intelligent and far-seeing men. The steady ratio of development in that section in the real estate market and the universally high reputation that investments therein have attained, reflect the greatest credit upon these real estate dealers, and are in a great measure due to their persistent and intelligent efforts. Thomas Wilson was born in Yorkshire, England, in 1846, being the youngest of three children born to Joseph and Tamar Wilson, who were also natives of England, the father being a farmer by occupation. He died in his native land in 1886, and his wife in 1884. In the schools of his native shire the subject of this sketch received his early literary training, and after attaining a suitable age served a five years' apprenticeship at cabinet making and building, after which he worked at his trade for three years. He then engaged in the mercantile business at Rosedale Abbey, Yorkshire, and by upright business methods soon secured a large patronage. He soon became the owner of a tract of land which he called "Primrose Villa," and on this piece of property he erected seven houses, which he still owns. He was married in 1866 to Miss Mary Magson, a daughter of Webster Magson, and in December, 1877, he came to the United States, landing at New York City. From that city he came direct to Texas, arriving at Eagle Lake under contract to become emigration agent for the Sunset route on the railroad. Not liking that section he soon came to Luling, being accompanied by thirteen people, and in the spring of 1878 he

7

became emigration agent at this place, and during three and a half years in which he held that office he located about 2,000 people on lands in this vicinity. On retiring from that office, he at once embarked in the land business for himself, and in this business has been universally and deservedly successful. He is the owner of thirteen small farms aggregating about 1,500 acres, owns four dwellings and two store houses in Luling, and a very handsome residence surrounded by twelve acres of land. He is of a speculative turn of mind, but exercises the best of judgment at all times, and since coming thither he has identified himself with the interests of Caldwell County, and has proven one of her most useful and public spirited citizens. He does considerable literary work of a political character and advocates the principles of Free Trade. During the time he was emigration agent, he wrote very extensively as to the resources of Texas, and these articles were largely translated into French and German. In 1893, accompanied by Mrs. Wilson, he made a visit to his old home in England, and in all he has made five trips across the ocean, and two trips to the Pacific Coast. To himself and wife a good old fashioned family of thirteen children have been given: Mary Ellen, wife of J. B. Ure of California; Hannah, wife of James H. Topham; Tamar, wife of John Watson of Gonzales County, Texas; Jane, who died at the age of thirteen years; Thomas, is married and resides in Luling; Joseph, Rosa Lena Primrose, who died at the age of thirteen months; Elizabeth, Annie, John, Eddie, Edwin, and Ernest. Mr. and Mrs. Wilson have had ten grandchildren, but only five are living at the present time. The family are members of the Baptist Church, and Mr. Wilson is a member of the Grange Association and the American Legion of Honor, and every business enterprise in which he has ever been engaged has been a clear and profitable success.

THOMAS JEFFERSON THOMPSON, planter and stock-raiser of Gonzales County, Texas, is a son of the State of Mississippi, born in Pontotoc, January 4, 1851, to the marriage of George and Jane (Dickson) Thompson. George Thompson was a "canny Scot," and came with his parents to the United States when quite a boy. They settled in Mississippi, and engaged in planting and stock raising, young Thompson assisting his parents until starting out in the same occupations for himself. He was educated in Mississippi, and remained there until about middle age when he removed to Arkansas. There he followed planting until his death in 1861. He was a Democrat and could have become prominent in politics had he so desired. Several times he was elected County Judge, but declined to serve. He was a member of the Masonic Fraternity and the Baptist Church. His wife was born in Pontotoc County, Mississippi. Before marriage she was a Methodist, but afterwards joined her husband's church, and continued with the same until her death in 1865. Thomas J. Thompson, sixth in order of birth of ten children born to the above mentioned union, removed with his parents to Arkansas when eight years of age, and there attended the common schools until the death of his father when he was forced to go to work on a farm. In 1872 he came to Navarro County, Texas, farmed one year, and subsequently was on the railroad for four years. Following this he began farming in DeWitt County, continued this ten years, and then came to Gonzales County where he has since resided. In 1875 he married Miss Mollie E. Rankin, of DeWitt County, and daughter of Robert W. Rankin and Irene Rankin. The following children were born to them: Thomas Jesse, Riley Marvin, and Fannie Eula. In politics he is a Populist, and he is a member of the Farmer's Alliance. He has been road overseer and school trustee. He and Mrs. Thompson are Methodists in their religious belief.

ELMORE D. MAYES. Many of the active residents of Wilson County are natives of the same and have here spent the most of their lives. In them we find men of true loyalty to the interests of this part of the State, who understand as it were by intuition the needs, social and industrial, of this vicinity and who have a thorough knowledge of its resources. They are therefore better adapted to succeed here than a stranger could be and are probably without exception warmly devoted to the prosperity of their native place. Prominent in all public movements and a most efficient and capable official is Elmore D. Mayes, County Clerk of Wilson County. His birth occurred in this County in 1855, and of the nine children born to his parents, William D. and Mary Ann (Cotton) Mayes, he was sixth in order of birth. The parents were natives of Tennessee, but as early as 1848 they came to Texas, and located in San Antonio. The following year Mr. Mayes had a bad attack of the gold fever and with a party started overland for the Pacific Coast. This trip was attended by many dangers, trials, and privations, but he reached California in safety. After a short stay there he returned and purchased land near Sutherland Springs, then in Bexar County, where he made his home until after the war. He was exempted from duty on account of his age, but he had one son, Alverado, in the army. In 1866 he moved to San Antonio, where he remained until his death in 1872. The mother died on the old home place in Wilson County in 1879. In addition to a good practical education, received in the schools of San Antonio, our subject spent four years finishing his education in Lebanon, Tenn., after which he returned to the farm. Agricultural pursuits and ranching continued to be his principal occupation for about eight years and in this he met with substantial results. In 1883 he came to the county seat and engaged as Deputy Clerk, holding that position until the fall of 1890, when, the old clerk retiring, Mr. Mayes was elected. He is now serving his second term to the entire satisfaction of all. In the year 1887 he was married to Miss Mary H. Houston, a native of Texas and the daughter of John P. Houston who was one of the early settlers of this State, he and his wife dying at Waco. Mr. and Mrs. Mayes are the parents of two children: Lizzie V., and John H. Mr. Mayes is a member of the M. E. Church South, but his wife is a Baptist in her views. Socially Mr. Mayes is a K. of P., and a Mason, a member of Floresville Lodge No. 515. He is a trustworthy and capable county official and a social, pleasant gentleman.

JOHN FLEMING HOUCHINS is a most popular citizen and official of Lavaca County, Texas, and is the efficient and able Sheriff, whose conduct of the affairs of that office has won him the good will of all, irrespective of party. Mr. Houchins' paternal grandfather, John Houchins, came originally from the Buckeye State to Texas, and was one of the pioneers of the latter State. He settled in Austin County, opened up a fine farm, and became wealthy. This worthy citizen was quite a genius, and was the first man to erect a mill in Austin County. He used to make his own wagons, and became extensively known as a wagon-maker. After the death of his wife he divided his property among his children and then married again, afterwards removing to Bell County, where he died. Our subject's maternal grandfather, Fleming Rees, was born in Tennessee, but when a young man went to Alabama, married there, and later came to the Lone Star State, settling in Austin County. In 1866 he moved to Colorado County, where he died when in his seventieth year. John Fleming Houchins was born in Lavaca County, Texas, in 1837, and was the eldest of twelve children born to G. W. and Sarah F. (Rees) Houchins, natives of Ohio and Alabama respectively. The father came to Texas at an early date, and now resides in this county. In the common schools of Lavaca County our subject received his education, and when it became necessary to choose an occupation he selected agricultural pursuits. He is now the owner of a farm of 500 acres of good land, 200 acres under cultivation, most of which he has improved himself. For several years he has been active in politics. In 1883 he was appointed Deputy Sheriff under Sheriff Smothers, and served for three years. Later he was appointed Constable, served two years, during which time he moved to town, and he was then elected Sheriff, and is serving his third term at the present time. Miss Susan Oliver, who became his wife in 1879, was a native of Austin County, and daughter of D. R. Oliver, one of the early settlers of that county. Six children were born to this marriage: Horace was killed by a horse running away with him in 1888, when eight years of age; Fleming, Warren, Pinkney, Maud who died in infancy, and Oscar. Mr. Houchins has shown his appreciation of secret organizations, and is a thirty-second degree Mason. He is also a member of the I. O. O. F., G. A. R., K. of P., K. of H., and A. O. U. W. He has made an excellent official, and is held in high esteem.

C. A. WERTHEIMER of Victoria County, Texas, owes his nativity to the city of New York, where he first saw the light of day in the year 1836, and from his estimable parents he inherited many of the most worthy characteristics of the German race—among which may be mentioned energy, frugality, intelligence and honesty. Abraham Wertheimer and Barbara Stall were united in marriage in New York, and there the father successfully followed the calling of a jeweler until his death, which occurred about 1864, his widow still surviving him. In the public schools of his natal city the subject of this sketch laid the foundations of a good education. Possessing an adventurous and independent spirit, he started for California in 1852, via the Isthmus of Panama, and after arriving in that State he was engaged in clerking in San Francisco for some time, then followed the same occupation in various portions of the State, and in 1859 he returned to New York. Very shortly after he started for the Lone Star State, landing at Port Lavaca in 1860, and there he at once opened a store with goods he had brought with him from New York, his partner in this business being a Mr. Gross. After continuing there about one year he came to Victoria and formed a partnership in the dry goods business with J. Halfin, the firm taking the name of J. Halfin & Co., which continued as such until Mr. Wertheimer entered the army in the fall of 1862 as a member of Dr. January's company, Waller's Battalion and Green's Brigade. He served in the trans-Mississippi Department, and after participating in many of the battles of east Louisiana, he was taken ill in 1864 and was sent home, and did not again enter the service. In 1865 he was married to Miss Blundine Halfin, a daughter of his former partner, and the following year moved with his young wife to Galveston, where he opened an establishment which was conducted under the firm name of Wertheimer & Halfin. In 1867 Mr. Wertheimer returned to Victoria and did business under his own name until 1886. Since that time he has given his attention to various occupations in the Custom House at Eagle Pass, but in January, 1892, he was appointed Deputy Assessor of Victoria County, in which capacity he served until June of the same year. January 1, 1893, he received the appointment of Deputy County Clerk, and on the 22nd of January, upon the death of E. A. Perrenot, the County Clerk, he was appointed to the position by the Commissioners' Court. He has always been an active Democrat in politics, is an advocate of every enterprise tending to the good of Victoria County, and socially is a member of the I. O. O. F., Victoria Lodge No. 9, the Legion of Honor, and the I. O. B. B., Victoria Lodge No. 205, a Hebrew society. In March, 1894, he was appointed by President Cleveland to the postmastership of Victoria, soon after which he resigned the office of County Clerk, and is now the efficient head of the Victoria postoffice. To him and wife a family of nine children have been given: Jacob, Sophie, Solomon, Isaac, Edward, Celeste, Leah, Marion and Abraham Levi.

DR. C. B. PHILLIPS, of the medical fraternity in DeWitt County enjoys a most extensive practice and is widely known throughout this populous and fertile section of the state. He has built up a large practice by steady devotion to duty and the constant exercise of energy and judgment. Like many of the representative citizens of the county he came from the East, his birth occurring in Hagarstown, Md., in 1842, and he was third in order of birth of seven children born to David and Sarah (Scott) Phillips, natives of that grand old mother of states, Virginia. The paternal grandfather, Samuel Phillips, was born in England and came to Virginia during the Revolutionary war, participating in that war and taking sides with the colonists. He settled in Washington County, Md., where he was a pioneer, and followed farming for many years. His death occurred in Hagarstown. The maternal grandfather, William E. Scott, was also a native of England, and on coming to this country settled in the Old Dominion, where he died. He was a flour-broker and miller. The parents of our subject met and were married in Hagarstown, Md. The father afterwards engaged in milling and farming, and when the Civil War broke out he enlisted in the Confederate army from Augusta County, Va., in the Washington Artillery. He participated in many battles, and was killed in the battle of Gordonsville in 1863. His wife, too, passed away during the war. Two of their sons, David and John, served in the Federal army. The former assisted in raising a company, and became Captain of a company in the Seventh Illinois Regiment. He was captured, and probably died in prison. John was killed in battle. Dr. C. B. Phillips grew to mature years in Maryland, and received his education in Mount St. Mary's College, Maryland. On account of his health he was obliged to leave school, and he began the study of medicine in 1858, with Dr. R. N. Wright of Baltimore. In 1860 he attended Jefferson Medical College, and was graduated from Washington University, Baltimore, Md., 1868. About August 1, 1861, he entered the Confederate army as private, Third Virginia Cavalry, and in October he was called before the medical examining board at Richmond, was passed, and made Assistant Surgeon of the Confederate States Volunteers. He served in various hospitals and camps during the war, and was in the Army of Virginia until the close. In 1865 he went to New Orleans, intending to locate. During the yellow fever epidemic of 1867 he was employed by the Howard Association as surgeon, with which he remained until danger was over. From there he went to Mexico, first to Durango, and then to the City of Mexico, but in the latter part of 1868 he came back to Texas and located in Live Oak County, at Oakville, where he practiced until 1870. He then went to Victoria, Lavaca and DeWitt counties, but finally settled at Burns Station in 1873, and has been practicing in that section since. In January, 1894, he partially withdrew from general practice, and is now treating specially the morphine, liquor and kindred habits by the bi-chloride of gold method. He has an office in Cuero, but is often called in consultation in adjoining counties. Dr. Phillips was married in 1872 to Miss Fannie E. Alkinson, a native of Tennessee, who came to Texas when a child. One son has been born to this union, Calvin B. Phillips.

H. A. McMEANS ably fills the responsible position of County Collector of Hays County, Texas, and is a wideawake pushing and enterprising man of affairs. He was born in Alabama in 1848, the eldest of four children born to DeWitt Clinton and Sarah Jane (Ivey) McMeans, who were Alabamians also. The father followed the calling of a merchant in his native State, and after locating at Palestine, in Anderson County, Texas, in 1854, he engaged in business there also, and did well financially. He was called from life in Palestine, Texas, in 1860, after which his widow and children removed to Louisiana, in which State they resided until 1869, when they returned to Texas, and in 1880 the mother breathed her last in San Marcos. The paternal grandfather, Isaac McMeans, was one of the early settlers of Alabama, and was a member of the first legislature of that State. He was of Irish descent, and in the State of his adoption eventually passed from life. The maternal grandfather, Jesse Ivey, was a South Carolinian, who located in Louisiana, and there passed from life. At the time his parents located in Texas the subject of this sketch was six years of age. He was placed in school at Palestine, and there remained until 1860, at which time he accompanied his mother to Mansfield, La., where he attended school for a short time. In 1865, although scarcely sixteen years of age, he joined the State troops of Louisiana, but saw no active service. From that time up to 1869 he farmed in Louisiana, then returned to San Marcos, where he secured employment as a clerk. In 1874 he was elected to the office of County Treasurer, was re-elected to this position twice, and served in all three terms —six years. In 1875 he embarked on the mercantile sea for himself in San Marcos, and continued to follow this occupation until 1880, when he sold out, and for four years thereafter was a traveling salesman. In 1886 he was appointed Postmaster of San Marcos by President Cleveland, which office he acceptably filled for four years. In 1890, when the census disclosed the fact that the county was entitled to a Tax Collector, Mr. McMeans was elected to that office, and has successfully filled the same ever since. He has always been quite an active worker in the Democratic party, and was a delegate to the State Convention of 1892, and again in 1894. He was married in 1872 to Miss Alice Cocreham, a native of Hays County, Texas, and daughter of D. R. Cocreham, who came to this section in 1854 from Arkansas. He was born in Kentucky, became quite an extensive stockman, and now makes his home with his son-in-law, Mr. McMeans. To the union of Mr. and Mrs. McMeans the following children have been born: Lena Belle, Florence Ivey, Irene K., Alice Estelle, Julia Louise, Jesse Van Zandt, Roland, and Lilla Cocreham, who died at the age of two years. Mr. McMeans and his wife are members of the Methodist Church, and socially he is a member of the A. F. & A. M., the K. of H., San Marcos Lodge No. 119 of the K. of P., the

Woodmen of the World, and the I. O. O. F. He is a genial and intelligent gentleman of social tastes, is an efficient county official, is a shrewd and practical man of business and a public-spirited and useful citizen.

A. W. CLARK. This gentleman is a descendant of Scotch ancestors and was born in Columbia County, Ga., December 23, 1822, the eldest of twelve children born to L. F. and Sophia W. (Sanders) Clark, who were born in North Carolina and Georgia respectively. The paternal grandfather, John Clark, was born in the Old North State, of which section his ancestors became residents during the early history of the country. The maternal grandfather, Reuben Sanders, was a Georgian by birth, and in that State passed from life. His father, Jeremiah Sanders, was a native of the Old Dominion, and was one of the earliest settlers of Georgia, to which State he came with but little means, but prior to his death became wealthy. His wife was a Miss Williams. He was a soldier of the Revolution, and was a participant in many battles in North and South Carolina. In one engagement he was severely wounded, and carried the bullet with him to the grave. L. F. Clark was a farmer by occupation, and died when the subject of this sketch was a boy; his widow dying in 1878 of yellow fever, at the age of seventy-five years. A. W. Clark, the subject of this sketch, was reared to a knowledge of farming in Georgia, and was married there in 1845 to Miss Jane P. Walker, with whom he afterwards removed to Madison County, Miss. There he enlisted, in 1861, in Company C, Eighteenth Mississippi Regiment, and in June, 1861, was sent to Virginia, where he took part in several important battles, and was elected by the officers of his regiment as commissary, a position he held for some time, in what was known as the "Fire Brigade." In 1864, on account of ill health, Mr. Clark was discharged from the service, and upon recovering sufficiently again offered his services to the Confederacy, and was assigned to service in Texas, being in Collins County at the time the war closed. He returned to Mississippi in December, 1865, and at once began tilling the soil, an occupation he continued to follow there until 1867, when he came to Gonzales, Texas. In December, 1869, he went to Rockport, and for some time thereafter was engaged in beef packing, a calling he successfully pursued for eight years. In 1878 he returned to Gonzales, and up to 1882 was engaged in selling drugs and groceries. He then embarked in the lumber business, and as the railroad had just been finished to this place, he sold the first carload of lumber ever brought here, and continued the business with good financial results up to March, 1894, when he retired. He purchased his present home in 1881, besides which he is the owner of a very fine farm of 508 acres, of which 375 acres are under cultivation, all of which is located on the San Marcos River, two miles above Gonzales. On this place are six good tenants' houses, also a handsome cottage, well fenced, and in various other ways is admirably improved, showing that Mr. Clark is a man of energy, thrift and good judgment. Eight children were born to Mr. and Mrs. Clark, three of whom are now living: William L., who entered the Confederate army before he was sixteen years of age, served under General Gano in Missouri, Kansas and the Indian Territory until the war closed, and had the honor of being the first man to scale the walls of Cabin Creek in the Indian Nation. He now resides on his father's farm. Anna E., married and died, leaving one child, Laura O., the wife of J. C. Herring, of Rockport; Mary F., wife of J. R. Rochelle; Guddie, who died in childhood; Charles, who died in infancy; Homer Augustus, who died in Gonzales March 25, 1894, at the age of twenty-eight years; and Harper, who died in early youth. Mr. Clark has been quite active in politics, and from 1889 to 1894 he served as Mayor of Gonzales, and was also city alderman for two years. He and his family are members of the M. E. Church South, and since 1851 he has been a member of the Masonic Fraternity. He is a member of the Chapter and Commandery of Gonzales Lodge, and has held office in each. He has been a church member since 1842, has for years acted in the capacity of steward, and has been Sunday School Superintendent for eight years. He is an active church worker, a man of unblemished reputation and one who has the respect and esteem of many friends.

JAMES KNOX WALKER, (deceased). This gentleman has passed to that bourne whence no traveler returns, yet the memory of his many noble deeds and traits of character will long be cherished in the hearts of those who knew, respected and loved him in life. He was a Tennesseean by birth, born in 1847, a son of Philip and Sarah (Barbee) Walker, who were natives of the Old North State, but removed from that State at an early day to Tennessee. In 1854 they came to Texas, and settled on the San Marcos River in Guadalupe County. (A further history of their career here will be found in the sketch of W. B. Walker.) James Knox Walker received a fair education in youth, and, although quite young in years, he served for a time in the Confederate army during the Civil War. In 1873 he led to the altar Miss Gussie Hamilton, a native of Georgia, and a daughter of John Hamilton, who was born in the Old North State, her mother being Anna Good, a native of Georgia. The family came to Texas in 1850, settling at Lockhart, but soon after moved to Prairie Lea, and there lived until his death in 1871, his widow surviving him until 1886. James Knox Walker began the battle of life for himself as a clerk at Prairie Lea, and after a time engaged in the same line of business for himself at that place, where he built up a good patronage and kept a well chosen stock of goods. In 1875 he came to Luling and was one of the first merchants of this place, and by the exercise of the most honorable business principles, by his desire to please his patrons, and by the fact that his stock of goods was large and well chosen, he was soon doing a very profitable business. He was a wideawake and progressive citizen, and at various times owned a number of mills and cotton gins, and at his death was the owner of a farm of 1,000 acres on the San Marcos River in Gonzales County, which was one of the finest estates in this portion of the State. He was quite active in political matters also, and was always a stanch supporter of Democratic principles. He was one of the most active men in Caldwell County, and his right mode of living won him many friends. Socially he was a member of the Knights of Pythias. He was called from life February 16, 1890, and his widow and six children survive him, the names of the latter being Gertrude, Cecile, James Knox, Ella, Byron, Nicholas, all of whom are honored residents of Luling.

FRANKLIN FRAZIER WOOD is a prominent planter and stock-raiser of Gonzales County, and his fine plantation speaks for itself as to his thrift and successful methods in his chosen calling. His father, Franklin F. Wood, was born in Tennessee, but when young removed to Alabama, when that State was new, and when it was often necessary to barricade the houses at night, to prevent attacks from Indians. He was married in that State to Miss Sarah

Ann Wilson, and in 1858 removed to Texas, where he spent one year in Colorado County. From there he came to Gonzales County and was engaged in planting and stock-raising quite extensively until his death in 1875. He took a deep interest in politics and all other affairs looking to the welfare of his county and its inhabitants. Socially he was a Mason, a member of Gonzales Lodge. For years he was a member of the Baptist Church, and a deacon and active worker in the same, and his wife, who is now living with our subject, is an earnest member of the same. Franklin Frazier Wood, subject of this notice, was born in Talapoosa County, Alabama, May 30, 1842, and was the fourth of eight children born to his parents. He attended Central Institute, Koosa County, Alabama, in 1857, a noted seat of learning in that day, and in 1859 came with his parents to Gonzales. Here he attended Gonzales College until 1861, when he left school to enter the Confederate army, enlisting in Capt. W. H. Kelley's Company, Waul's Legion. He served through Mississippi, Alabama and Tennessee, and was with Van Dorn on his retreat through Mississippi and his famous raid in Gen. Grant's rear. He was wounded at Middleton, Tenn., December 23, 1862, while on this raid. Later on he was with Forrest, and participated in many of that General's daring achievements. Mr. Wood entered the army as third sergeant, was later made Orderly Sergeant, and was eventually breveted Lieutenant. His command was furloughed in April, just prior to the surrender, and he returned to Texas. The trip back was replete with danger. He went to work on a farm with his father and was married in October, 1869, to Miss Carrie Jane Gilmore, daughter of William M. and Caroline (Ingram) Gilmore, of Gonzales County. This union has resulted in the birth of five children: Sarah Jane, wife of Henry C. Barfield; Anna, died in infancy; James Franklin, who married Miss Agnes E. Beaty; Walter Madison, died in infancy; and Mattie Eugenia. Mr. Wood is a Populist in politics and is now the nominee of his party for Treasurer of Gonzales County. Mrs. Wood's father was with Gen. Jackson in the Seminole war in Florida when quite young. He was born in Washington County, Ga., and was engaged as a planter there for fourteen years. In 1858 he came to Texas, where he farmed with marked success until his death, December 16, 1864. He was a Master Mason and a member of Gonzales Lodge. Mrs. Gilmore died September 3, 1870. She was a member of the Baptist Church, as is the subject of this sketch and his wife.

R. R. CREECH, the efficient and reliable Collector of Wilson County, Texas, is among the self-made and practical business men of the same, and has certainly been the architect of his own fortunes, as he began life with little else than a sturdy determination to succeed by industry and thrift. He is a well known official of this county, and owes his success in life, and the high estimation in which he is held by all who know him, to his manly course through life. Mr. Creech was born in Telfair County, Ga., in 1850, and was the youngest but one of eight children born to his parents, D. B. and Judith D. (McLennan) Creech, natives respectively of South and North Carolina. The father was a substantial farmer, and followed that occupation in the East until 1854, when he moved to Alabama. There he received his final summons in 1863. The mother is still living and makes her home in Alabama. Our subject received his scholastic training in the schools of Alabama. In the year 1873 he came to the Lone Star State, followed farming in this county, but subsequently abandoned that occupation and turned his attention to merchandising, which he followed at Union from 1881 to 1892, meeting with substantial results. In 1885 he was appointed Sheriff, and served in that capacity in a very satisfactory manner for one term. In 1888 he was elected Sheriff and Collector, and was again in office one term. Two years later he was elected Collector and has held that position for four terms, thus showing his popularity. His career is an example of industry, perseverance and integrity, rewarded by substantial results, well worthy the imitation of all who start out in life as he did, with very little besides a good constitution and a liberal supply of pluck and energy. He owns several farms, aggregating 450 acres, and is one of the most influential young men of the county. He selected his wife in the person of Miss Emma M. Cocke, a native of Tennessee, and their nuptials were solemnized in December, 1874. She is the daughter of Col. F. B. S. Cocke. Eight children have been born to Mr. and Mrs. Creech. The family holds membership in the Methodist Episcopal Church South and are interested in all worthy movements. Mr. Creech is a member of the Floresville Lodge No. 515, A. F. & A. M. He is a man well qualified for the position he is now holding, and is a genial, intelligent man to meet.

DR. SAM. F. NAVE, one of the best educated and most successful of the younger physicians of Lavaca County, Texas, was born in Colorado County, Texas, in 1857, and of the six children born to his parents, Michael and Rhoda (Rue) Nave, he was the youngest. The father and mother were born and married in Kentucky, and there made their home until 1851, when they came to Texas and settled in Columbus. Later they moved in the country, where the father was engaged in farming and blacksmithing, and then moved to Flatonia where they now reside. In Colorado County Dr. Sam. F. Nave attended the common schools, and later he began the study of medicine. In 1883 he attended lectures at Tulane University, and two years later he attended three courses, graduating in the spring of 1888. Between times he practiced in Fayette County, and afterwards located at Witting, Lavaca County, where he remained until June, 1891, when he came to Shiner. Here he has since practiced his profession and is classed among the leading and successful physicians in this section. In the month of February, 1891, he was married to Miss Emma Dawson, a native of Fayette County, Texas, and the daughter of George Dawson, one of the early pioneers. The Doctor's union has been blessed by the birth of two children, Gordon Fletcher and Mary Love. He is a member of the Masonic Fraternity and the Knights of Pythias, Rathborn Lodge No. 109, and the Knights of Honor.

A. LOWE. It is a fact, which speaks volumes for the high grade of our civilization, that in no land the world over is more care and attention given to all the details of the burial of the dead than in our own favored one. Of the many persons who are engaged in the duties and calling of an undertaker, no more considerate one can be found than A. Lowe. His courteous manners and consideration, together with his careful attention to all the minute details of conducting a funeral in the most desirable manner, have gained him popularity with those in need of his services. He is a native of Knoxville, Tenn., where he was born in 1819, his parents being Elijah and Ann (Hamilton) Lowe, natives of Tennessee also. The father was a farmer and moved to North Alabama during his son's early youth, in which

State the latter was principally reared. The mother died in Alabama about 1837 or 1838, but the father breathed his last in the Lone Star State. The latter had made two trips to this State, the last being in 1843. A. Lowe became a resident of Texas in 1844, and for some time thereafter made his home with his uncle, H. Hamilton, at San Augustine. He then began learning the trade of a wheelwright, at which he worked until May, 1846, then enlisted in Company A, Second Regiment, under Captain O. M. Wheeler and Colonel Woods, respectively, and started for Mexico. He was a participant in the battle of Monterey, and while on his way home passed through Victoria. He took a fancy to the place, and soon after made it his permanent home, locating here in February, 1847. During the Civil War he served in the State Militia for a time, although he was exempt from military duty. For a long time after engaging in business for himself, he was the only undertaker in town, and in the discharge of his business duties he has always been highly regarded. He has been active in civil matters, has been in office for many years, and has long served in the capacity of City Alderman. He was Mayor of the town in 1858, and in 1873 was elected one of the Commissioners of the county, and has served as such for eight years. He was married in 1851 to Miss Josephine Brown, who died in 1858, leaving three children, only one of whom survives. He married his present wife in 1874, she being Miss Catherine Schulz, an orphan girl, reared by Thomas Stern. He and his wife are members of the Presbyterian Church, and are well respected citizens. Mr. Lowe has a comfortable competency, and is the owner of a good river bottom farm.

W. J. McMANUS is among the reputable men of De Witt County, Texas, who, in their conduct of business matters and the duties belonging to the various relations of life, have acquired a worthy name. He is a prominent miller and ginner, as well as Postmaster, at Thomastown. He was born in 1840, in Amite County, Mississippi, to the union of David and Martha (Wright) McManus, products of the Palmetto State and Mississippi, respectively. The father was a planter by vocation, and about 1854 he and family came to Texas and settled in DeWitt County. Now he is living at Yoakus. He served in the Confederate army from Texas, in the reserved corps. He has acted as Justice of the Peace for many years. The mother died in 1883. Our subject received the rudiments of an education in the schools of Mississippi, and after coming to Texas he assisted in tilling the soil until the breaking out of the war. In 1861 he enlisted in Ford's Regiment, Texas Rangers, and was on the Rio Grande River. The following year he enlisted in the Confederate army, in Colonel C. L. Pyron's Regiment, Second Texas Cavalry, and served in Texas and Louisiana, generally on scouting duty, being at San Antonio when the war closed. He was made First Lieutenant in 1862, and in the fall of 1863 he was sent to San Antonio where he served as Post Adjutant, and also for a time was Provost Marshal. After returning home he resumed his farming operations near Terrell, but in 1885 came to Thomaston, where he bought land. Later he purchased the gin at this place, engaged actively in business, and in 1893 erected the present gin and mill. The gin has a capacity of twenty bales per day, and has all the modern machinery. In 1888 Mr. McManus was appointed Postmaster, and has discharged the duties of that office in a most efficient and satisfactory manner since. He is a member of the Presbyterian Church, and a liberal contributor to all worthy enterprises. In the month of January, 1867, he was married to Mrs. Edgar, and five children have been given them: David Brown, Dudley Cullins, Dalton Edward, Mary Ann, and Josephine Charlotte. Fraternally Mr. McManus is a Mason and a Knight of Honor, both of Cuero lodges. He is a valuable resident of this city, and his business is rapidly increasing.

THOMAS J. PEEL. This intelligent gentleman is the District Clerk of Hays County, Texas, and was born in Montgomery County, Alabama, where he first saw the light of day in 1844, the youngest of ten children born to the marriage of David B. Peel and Rebecca Holloway, both of whom were natives of the State of Georgia. The father removed to Alabama at an early day, where he tilled the soil, but died in an adjoining county in Mississippi in 1880. His first wife died in 1848 or 1849, and he afterwards married again, and by his second wife became the father of five children. Thomas J. Peel was reared and educated in his native State, his educational advantages being confined to the common schools. Up to 1863, his attention was given to farming, but he then enlisted in the Confederate army, in Company I, Sixty-First Alabama Regiment, and served in the Army of Northern Virginia, participating in the battles of The Wilderness, Spottsylvania Court House, and others. He was so severely wounded at Cold Harbor in 1864, that he was entirely disabled for further service and was also unfitted for work for several years afterwards. He went home and attended school for some time, then began clerking in a store although he still suffered a good deal from his wound. Later he became a railroad express clerk, and followed this and clerking in different mercantile establishments until 1875, when he came to Robertson County, Texas, and for three years was engaged in farming on the Brazos River, after which he resumed clerking. In 1881 he came to San Marcos, clerked for four years, then became Assistant Postmaster of San Marcos, holding that position two years. In November, 1888, he was elected to his present office, and has been re-elected each expiring term since that time without opposition. Socially Mr. Peel is a member of Hays Lodge of the Knights of Honor, of which he has been Reporter twelve years, and Deputy Grand Dictator; is Secretary of Live Oak Camp of the Woodmen of the World, and is Secretary of Clan Marcos Lodge No. 119 of the Knights of Pythias. He is the oldest in years and in point of membership of the Fire Company of San Marcos, and is Secretary of Elect Hose Company No. 1, which office he has held since the organization of the Company. In 1875 he led to the altar Miss Mattie E., daughter of P. P. Jones, of Hearne, Texas, an early settler of the State, and a brother of Rev. Gifford Jones, of Memphis, Tennessee. To the union of Mr. and Mrs. Peel, the following children were born: Nellie, David, Mary, Coy and Raymond. Mr. Peel and his family are members of the Methodist Church, and are highly esteemed members of the best social circles of San Marcos.

HON. JAMES F. MILLER. The establishment of banks belongs entirely to the modern world. The first bank established in the modern civilized world was the Bank of Venice, which was founded in 1157, according to some authorities. At the settlement of this country the colonists brought with them the financial theories and practices which prevailed at the time in the mother country, and since that time it has been found to be a profitable and most necessary business, and one which, to be successfully conducted, requires intelligence and business acumen of a high order. These requirements are possessed in an eminent degree by Hon. James F. Miller, who is a member of the well known banking house of Miller & Sayers, of Gonzales, Texas. He was born in Tennessee in 1832, the eldest child born to Isaac and Susan (Swan) Miller, who were natives respectively of South Carolina and Tennessee. Isaac Miller was a lawyer by profession, and after reaching manhood removed from the State of his birth to Tennessee, thence to San Antonio, Texas, in December, 1845, and after several years' residence in that city moved to Lockhart, where his attention was devoted to merchandising. Several years later he moved to a farm in Gonzales County, on which he died in 1863, his widow surviving him until 1893. Their son, James F. Miller, was educated in the public schools of Texas, and after finishing his literary education began the study of law in Gonzales in 1855, two years later was admitted to the bar, and immediately thereafter began practicing his profession at this place. His labors were interrupted by the breaking out of the Civil War, and as he was an ardent Southern sympathizer he, in 1861, entered the Confederate Army as a member of Company I, Eighth Texas Cavalry, and was at once sent east of the Mississippi River, and was a participant in all the engagements, hardships and privations of his regiment until the war closed. He was in many bloody battles, was several times captured, but each time managed soon to make his escape. Upon the termination of hostilities he returned home and resumed the practice of his profession, and in 1883 was chosen as a fitting representative of his district to Congress, and so ably did he discharge the duties incumbent on that responsible position that he was re-elected in 1885. At the expiration of his second term he declined a re-election. During his first term he served on the Committee of Banking and Currency, also Mines and Mining, and during his second term he was made Chairman of the Committee on Banking and Currency, and also held a position on Mines and Mining and on Education. He was very active in committee work, and his record for faithfulness to the interests of his constituents, as well as to his district and State, made him very popular with political foes as well as friends. Prior to the war, while associated in the practice of his profession with H. S. Parker, he did considerable exchange business, and upon the resumption of his practice after the war he also re-engaged in that business, and it eventually led to retirement from all law business and to the founding of his present banking house, which was established in 1868. At the same time Mr. Miller formed a partnership with William B. Sayers, which has continued, advantageously to both, up to the present time, first as lawyers and bankers and then as bankers only. Mr. Miller retired permanently from the practice of law upon his election to Congress in 1883, and since that time he has devoted all his energies to his banking and financial interests, theirs being the first institution of the kind established in the place. This bank has had a very prosperous career, and under its able management has steadily increased its business and strengthened itself in the esteem and confidence of the community. Mr. Miller was first married in 1860, to Miss Almira Mathews, a native of Texas and a daughter of William A. Mathews, who was a Tennesseean by birth and was interested with De Witt in colonizing this section. Mrs. Miller died in 1862, leaving one child, James Mathews, who died in infancy. In 1863 Mr. Miller took for his second wife Mrs. Julia A. Batchelor, a native of the Lone

Star State and a daughter of Amasa Turner, an old Texan. Mr. Miller is an enthusiastic Mason, and through all the subordinate branches of that order has advanced to the rank of thirty-second degree in the order of Scottish Rite. He was made a Mason soon after he attained his majority, became a member of the Chapter at Gonzales and was made a Knight Templar at Houston. He was one of the organizers of Gonzales Commandery, and was its first Commander. He is a member of Ben Hur Temple at Austin and of the Chapter of Roise Croix of San Felipe de Austin, at Austin. In 1873 he was elected Grand Master of Masons in Texas, and in 1878 was elected Grand Commander of Knights Templar in Texas. He served for several years as President of the Council of High Priests, and is now President of the Board of Directors of the Masonic Widows and Orphans' Home. He was first President of the Texas Live Stock Association and the first President of the Texas Bankers' Association, of which association he is still an active member.

JAMES MANFORD, a pioneer settler of Texas owes his nativity to Newberryport, Mass., where he first saw the light in 1818, being the youngest of three children born to the marriage of Erasmus Manford and Agnes Sanderhoof, who were natives of Norway and Amsterdam respectively. The father was a ship captain by occupation and was lost at sea in a wreck off the coast of one of the East India Islands in 1818. His widow continued to reside in Massachusetts, and in that State reared her family to honorable maturity, dying in 1863, after a well spent life. The subject of this sketch worked on a farm in his youth, which occupation he followed up to the age of eighteen years, and during this time he learned many useful lessons, and strengthened and improved an already sound constitution. He then entered the service of the United States Government as a soldier, and was a participant in a number of Indian wars in Florida, in which State he remained until 1840. He then emigrated to Texas and engaged in merchandising near Round Top, in Fayette County, where he continued in business about two years, then went to Eaton, Texas, and in 1845 was married to Miss Salina Miller, a daughter of one of the pioneers of that section, and soon engaged in the manufacture of saddles at Round Top, a business he successfully continued for some time. In 1858 he was left a widower with five children, and in 1860 he married Miss Mary Jane Law, a native of Arkansas and a daughter of Thomas Telford Law, who was born in Tennessee, but removed to Arkansas when it was a Territory, thence to Mississippi, and in 1852 came to Texas, settling at Seguin. He was a minister of the Cumberland Presbyterian Church, and while laboring for the good of humanity he established many churches in Guadalupe and surrounding counties. He was also very prominent in Masonic circles, and assisted in organizing many lodges in this section. In 1861 Mr. Manford responded to the call for troops for the Confederacy, became a member of Wood's Company, and for three years served in Texas as a member of the Home Guard. In 1857 he had removed to a farm in Guadalupe County, and this fertile land on the San Marcos River he continued to till very successfully after the close of the war, up to 1880, when he took up his residence in Luling. Throughout his active life Mr. Manford was quite extensively engaged in stock-raising, but since coming to Luling he has lived a somewhat retired life, as he is in quite delicate health. He has a very pleasant home in Luling, has every comfort which could be desired and has the unbounded respect of all and the warm personal friendship of many.

JOHN O'NEALL, has reached the unusual age of eighty-one years, is remarkably well preserved, physically and mentally, and is a typical representative of the energetic and pushing planters of the Lone Star State. He was born in Edgefield District, S. C., December 4, 1813, and is a son of Dr. Charles and Charlotte (Abney) O'Neall. The father was a native Kentuckian, reared there by a cousin, and when he reached mature years began reading medicine with Dr. Moore of South Carolina. He became very noted in his profession, and an exceedingly delicate operation for cancer, performed by him, received widespread mention by the medical journals of that day. His death occurred November 1, 1828, when forty-eight years of age. He was a Master Mason, and he and wife held membership in the Methodist Church. She passed away in 1853, when seventy-two years of age. John O'Neall attended private schools in Edgefield District, and when twenty-one years of age began serving an apprenticeship at the carpenter trade, receiving $50 a year and clothing himself. Two years later he was fully equipped for the trade. Previous to this, when fourteen years of age, our subject was left fatherless, and his brother Charles left home to take part in the Seminole war in Florida. John had joined a volunteer company for the same purpose, but as the family depended on his labor for support he gave up and remained at home, engaged in farming, and later his trade. In 1843, when twenty-seven years of age, he married Miss Mary Rushton, daughter of William and Nancy (Ross) Rushton, of South Carolina, and she died fifteen months later, leaving a child, Sarah, who is the wife of George W. O'Neill, of Live Oak County, Texas. In 1845 Mr. O'Neall married Miss Damaris Rushton, first cousin to the first wife and daughter of Joseph and Nancy Rushton, of South Carolina. The following children have been born to this union: Nancy, wife of Rev. M. A. Black; Belton L., J. Charles, John W., Demaris E., William T., Hugh L., and Mary Ellen, wife of S. V. Billings. Mr. O'Neall and family came to Texas in 1853, and settled in Gonzales County. Later they moved to Bee County, but after a short residence there returned to Gonzales County, where they have resided ever since. Mr. O'Neall owns a good farm and is a most worthy citizen, honored and respected by all acquainted with him. In politics he is a Democrat, and during the war he was a member of the State Militia, guarding the border. He has held the office of Justice of the Peace in this section. He and wife are members of the Methodist Episcopal Church.

L. P. HUGHES. Wilson County is fortunate in having a man of such high character as the subject of this sketch. He was the youngest child born to Jesse and Parcilla (Parker) Hughes. The father was a native of Kentucky and followed agricultural pursuits the most part through life. He died in his native State in 1863. The mother was born in the State of Maryland, and died in Kentucky in 1849. Our subject was born in the Blue Grass region of Kentucky, January 30, 1830. In 1853-54 he came to Texas. He first landed at Galveston, then went from there to Houston, remaining a short time. He next stopped at Bastrop County for a few months, thence to DeWitt County, on the Guadalupe River, where he became interested in a saw and grist mill, and followed this occupation for some three or more years. He afterwards engaged, for several years, in driving stock to adjoining states. He then came to this, Wilson County (then Bexar), and stopped at the villages of Lavernia and Sutherland Springs and continued clerking in these places some three or four years. In July, 1861, he joined Capt. Ed. H. Cunningham, Company F, Fourth Texas Infantry, and went to Richmond Va., where the regiment was organized, with J. B. Hood as Colonel (afterwards Gen. Hood), and was placed in the command of Gen. Whiting, afterwards in Hood's Brigade, Longstreet's command, Army of North Virginia. He participated in the battle of Seven Pines, after which he was ordered to the Valley of Virginia to join Gen. Stonewall Jackson's command, finding him near Staunton. The command was immediately turned back and sent up in the rear of Gen. McClennan before Richmond, where the seven days fight was made. He took part in the battle of Gaines Mill and other notable and minor engagements including Malvern Hill, where the Federals retreated to the cover of their gunboats. He was in the battle of Second Manassas, and next with Gen. Lee's first campaign into Maryland. He was in the engagement at South Mountain and afterwards was in the battle of Sharpsburg, Md. where, while fighting gallantly, he lost his left arm. On the 17th of September, 1862, he resigned as Captain of the company, to which position he had been promoted for conspicuous soldierly qualities and merit, and returned to Texas. He took the office of District Tax Collector under the Confederate government, but afterwards engaged in sheep raising. In 1876 he was elected Tax Assessor of Wilson County, and served two years. In 1878 he was elected County Clerk, and held the office with high credit for twelve years. He has since followed farming and stock raising. In 1876, he was married to Mary B. Peacock, (daughter of Thomas J. Peacock), who was born in Tennessee, and reared in Texas. To Mr. and Mrs. Hughes were born four children, to-wit: Lena, Dora, Elna and Anna.

DR. M. L. EIDSON. The physician is a man who inspires confidence because he is worthy of it. His humanity is expressed in the interest he takes in his patients' welfare as well as for the experience he may gain while pursuing the paths of this arduous profession in order to benefit future sufferers. Dr. M. L. Eidson is a physician of acknowledged ability and, although young in years, has already built up an excellent practice. He was born in Victoria County, Texas, in 1860, and of the eight children born to his parents, Thomas Boyse and Jane (Smith) Eidson, he was the fourth in order of birth. The father was born in Georgia and the mother in Mississippi. About 1851 they came to Victoria County, Texas, where the father followed farming until 1861, when he moved to Lavaca County, buying a farm near the town of Hallettsville. He served four years in the war, and, returning to his home in this county, there passed the remainder of his life, dying in 1874. The mother died in Beeville in 1891. Both were worthy and exemplary members of the Baptist Church for many years. Our subject grew up and received his education in Hallettsville and in St. Louis. Later he began the study of medicine under Dr. East of Hallettsville in 1881, and attended lectures from 1882 to 1884 in the Missouri Medical College, St. Louis, graduating in 1884. He then returned to Lavaca County, practiced in different parts of the same, and then in 1887 came to Shiner, a new town, and is the oldest physician in point of residence here. Dr. Eidson is the local surgeon of the railroad, and examiner of nearly all the life insurance companies here. The doctor was married in December, 1884, to Miss Ida Turner of Hallettsville and

● SANTA ANNA BEFORE GENERAL HOUSTON.

1. Gen. Sam Houston.
2. Gen. Lopez de Santa Anna.
3. Thomas J. Rusk.
4. Mirabeau B. Lamar.
5. Ben McCulloch.
6. —— Chaddock.
7. R. S. McManus.
8. Col. Almonte.

9. Gen. Ed. Burleson.
10. Col. John A. Wharton.
11. Gen. Sidney Sherman
12. Joel W. Robison.
13. Walter P. Lane.
14. J. A. Sylvester.
15. Jesse Billingsby.
16. Tom J. Green.

17. Gen. George G. Alford.
18. Bailey Hardiman.
19. Silas Bostic.
20. —— McFadden.
21. Col. Ed. Burleson.
22. Washington Anderson.
23. James M. Hill.
24. John W. Buntin.

25. M. G. Whitiker.
26. —— Clemens.
27. John Milton Swisher.
28. Deaf Smith.
29. Sterling C. Robertson.
30. Surgeon.
31. Geo. Nall.
32. Dr. S. Perry.

33. —— Hobson.   34. Moses Austin Bryan.

daughter of Col. Louis Turner who was one of the first settlers of Hallettsville. Three children have been born to Dr. and Mrs. Eidson: Louis Boyse, Mamie, and Erna. Dr. Eidson is a Knight of Pythias, Rathbone Lodge No. 9, and was the first member initiated in the same. He is now Past Chancellor. He is also a member of the A. O. U. W. and is examiner of both lodges. The residence he and family now occupy was one of the first erected in Shiner.

REV. FATHER L. WYER is a product of the famous Isle of Erin where he first saw the light of day in 1846, he being the fourth child born to Laurence and Mary Bridget (McAleny) Wyer, and was almost from the time of his birth intended by them for the priesthood. He was given excellent educational advantages and after thorough preparation, was ordained a priest of the Catholic Church in 1868, after which he was made assistant of the parish of Tubbar, which position he retained several years. In 1879 he emigrated to the New World and was assigned to work in the diocese of San Antonio, but gave this up in 1880 and was placed in charge of the Catholic Church at Victoria. He entered heart and soul into his pastoral duties, and almost immediately began the work of reorganizing St. Joseph's College, which had before been founded in Victoria and which had, for various reasons, declined until it had in all things but a name become extinct. No better man could have been found for the work than Father Wyer, for he is the soul of enterprise, energy and determination, and under his capable generalship the present commodious buildings were erected and the school was at once started on its present prosperous course. The furniture and appliances are sufficient for all requirements, and a regular collegiate course is given, comprising eight years. In the lay department there is an attendance of two hundred pupils, over which it has been found necessary to place a corps of eight competent instructors, music lessons being given by an extra teacher. There are twelve pupils in the department of divinity; in fact, the school is established on a sound basis and is already patronized by the best people of the South. He became parish priest of this ward in 1892 and in his priestly labors has been no less active than in his labors for St. Joseph's College. He has built up the Catholic Church of Victoria and as pastor and friend is dearly loved by his flock, as well as those who differ from him in religious faith.

J. F. McCRABB. Much of the enterprise which helps make DeWitt County one of the most prosperous ones of the State belongs, in a considerable degree, to the worthy gentleman whose name is at the head of this sketch. A man's life-work is the measure of his success, and he is truly the most successful man who, turning his powers into the channel of an honorable purpose, accomplishes the object of his endeavor. Mr. J. F. McCrabb, one of the prominent farmers of the county, was born here in 1846, to the marriage of John and Mary (Miller) McCrabb, the former a native of Ireland and the latter of Tennessee. The father grew restive in the old country, bade adieu to friends and scenes long loved, and came to Tennessee, where he married Miss Miller. Previous to this he made a prospecting trip to Texas and located on land in Gonzales District, and then, returning to Tennessee, he was married. Bringing his family back with him, he resided in Victoria, and was there during the Texas Revolution. After taking his wife to Texana, he returned and joined Houston's army, and was in the battle of

8

San Jacinto, remaining in Texas a year and a half. He then brought his wife back and made a permanent settlement on the banks of Guadalupe River. This was an isolated neighborhood and the Indians became so troublesome that Mr. McCrabb soon moved his family near Clinton, where he resided until his death in 1848. He was a very extensive farmer and a very prominent citizen, holding the office of District Clerk of Victoria for some time. He held that position at the only legal execution in that county. At the time of his death he was Assessor and Collector of this district. Mr. McCrabb was a man of education and was very methodical in his work and duty. At the time of his death he owned four tracts of land. The mother's second marriage was with N. J. Ryan, a native of Pennsylvania and an early settler of Texas. He was a soldier in the Mexican War. His death occurred in 1862. In his native county our subject grew to mature years and there received a limited education. He was in the school-room when Civil War broke out and, although but seventeen years of age, he enlisted in the Confederate Army, in S. H. Hudson's Company of Independent Scouts, and served on the Rio Grande River until the close of hostilities. After returning home he engaged in the stock business and became, and still is, a large operator. He has graded his stock and has about 1,200 head of blooded animals. He owns about 7,000 acres, 4,000 acres in a single tract near Thomaston. About 150 acres are under cultivation and is all good bottom land. Mr. McCrabb has one of the handsomest places in the county, and is one of the best stockmen of the locality. In the year 1883 he was married to Miss Cora Augustine, a native of Texas, and daughter of Dave Augustine, a native of this State also, and one of the oldest settlers. Two interesting children have been born to this union, John and Mary.

JUDGE GUSTAVE COOK. Nothing is truer than the broad statement that in this country alone of all the great countries a man's family connections do not assist him to places of honor and trust, either professionally or in the political arena, but he must win his way by his own exertions or by his own honest merit. In the old country the accident of birth determines the preferment of an individual, and if he is not born to a title, or be not the near relative of one who is, his chances are few and far between to ever attain a position of prominence. This government of the people is no discriminator of persons, but opens its doors wide for the entrance for all such as possess the requisite qualifications, and birth is by no means one of these. Judge Gustave Cook, however, comes of an excellent family, and is a product of the State of Alabama, his parents, Nathan and Harriet Anthony (Herbert) Cook, being South Carolinians. The paternal grandfather, John Cook, was born in South Carolina of English parents, and became a successful planter of the State of his birth. His wife was Ellen Hampton. The maternal grandfather, John Herbert, was of English birth, and his wife was Elizabeth Hampton, Ellen being the daughter of Henry Hampton, and Elizabeth the daughter of Edward Hampton. These gentlemen were among five brothers, of whom the well known Wade Hampton was one. The early members of the family came to this country during colonial days and were participants in the Revolutionary War. Nathan Cook was reared and educated in the State of his birth, and in what was then the Territory of Mississippi, but is now a portion of Alabama. He was a soldier in various Indian wars in that section, and was a public spirited and enterprising citizen. He mainly educated himself by study at home, and afterwards began posting himself in the law. He was admitted to the bar in Alabama, after which he served on the bench as Judge for over twenty years. He was a distinguished jurist, and was a particularly able exponent of the common law. He was called upon to pay the last debt of nature in Alabama about 1888, but the mother of our subject died when he was an infant. In 1850 Gustave Cook came to the Lone Star State and took up his abode on the lower Brazos River, where he soon obtained employment requiring him to travel extensively on horseback, which was highly agreeable to his fondness for the horse, which is still a leading passion with him. He was also in the cattle driving business, and for a number of years followed various pursuits. In 1853, at the early age of seventeen years, he married Eliza Jones, a native of Texas, and a daughter of Capt. Randal Jones, well known in early Texas history. He was an officer in the United States Army in the war of 1812, at the close of that war came to Texas, and made several exploring trips to remote interior regions. In 1817 he attempted to settle an American colony, but was prevented from carrying out his designs by Mexicans, after which he became one of Austin's original three hundred settlers. He was an officer in the Texas Rebellion in 1836, and, although not in the charge at the battle of San Jacinto, he was on the east side of Buffalo Bayou with his company, on detached duty, guarding the retreating settlers. He settled on his plantation in the vicinity of Austin, where he resided until after the Civil War. In the latter years of his life he lost his eyesight and thereafter made his home with the subject of this sketch, dying at his residence in Houston, in 1873. He was a skillful and successful Indian fighter and saw some stirring times during the early settlement of the Lone Star State. After his marriage the subject of this sketch made his home in Richmond, Texas, until after the war, having been elected to the office of County Judge prior to that time, and was also appointed to the office of District Clerk, in which capacity he served six months. He began the study of law about the time of his marriage, and was admitted to the bar two years later. In 1861 Judge Cook joined Company H, Eighth Texas Cavalry, known as Terry's Texas Rangers, and soon rose to the rank of Orderly Sergeant, and finally to Captain of that company, and also held the ranks of Major, Lieutenant Colonel and finally Colonel, of his regiment. He practically commanded the regiment for over two years, during which time it was in over 200 engagements, and with the exception of the time that he was confined from wounds received, Judge Cook was in these engagements. He was severely wounded a number of times, but the last and most serious wound that he received was at Bentonville, N. C., the last battle of the war. He was compelled to remain in the vicinity near that battlefield for several months before he was able to be moved, and then he walked to Alabama, where he obtained means with which to return home. He reached home December 1, 1865, where he was reunited with his family, having been home but once during the war. He resumed the practice of law at Richmond, Texas, but in 1869 moved to Houston, where he continued his practice. In 1873 he was elected to the Thirteenth Legislature, which became distinguished in that it formed the transmutation from military to civil government. In 1874 Mr. Cook went on the Criminal Court Bench, by appointment of Governor Coke, which office he held until the last term of Governor Ross, to whom he resigned his commission. This district includes Galveston and Harris counties. Judge Cook has probably tried more criminal cases than any other Judge in America, but becoming tired of exercising power over his fellow man, and for his own relief, he resigned, and has never since held an office, although he has been favorably spoken of for the highest offices in the State. He resumed his practice in Houston and was actively employed up to 1892, when severe hemorrhages, resulting from an old wound in the chest, forced him to seek a home in a higher altitude and he accordingly came to San Marcos and has built up a good practice here. To Judge and Mrs. Cook four children have been given: Ida, now Mrs. E. W. Kyle; Mary Herbert, now Mrs. Owen Ford; Henrietta, now Mrs. John Marrast; Gustave, Jr., all residing in San Marcos and having each children, thirteen in all, who claim the judge and his good wife as grandfather and grandmother, very much to their pride and gratification. Judge Cook is a gentleman of great force of character, self-educated, self-reliant and self-made, and has a well disciplined mind. He is perhaps the best impromptu orator in the State and has always been a strong advocate of the principles of the Democratic party. He has risen by his own ability to his present high place in his profession, and is a courteous and polished gentleman and a useful, law abiding and progressive citizen. His uncle, Col. James R. Cook, was born in the Territory of Alabama, and about 1834 became a resident of Texas. In 1835 he joined the army formed by the Provisional Government, and commanded a company of cavalry as Captain in the battle of San Jacinto in 1836. He died in Washington County about 1844. He was married in the early '40s to Miss Sarah Lott, a member of an old Washington County family. To them were born two sons: John, who resides in Texas, and James, who resides in Louisiana.

W. B. CAVETT. America affords numberless instances of men who have made their way alone in life, having nothing upon which to depend but their own strong arms and a determination to do and to succeed. Such men are always self-reliant, their necessities having taught them that what is to be done must be done through themselves alone. In considering the gentlemen of this class, the name of W. B. Cavett suggests itself, for the reason that he has made his own way in the world, without adventitious aid or circumstances. He was born in Westmoreland County, Pa., April 10, 1828, the fourth of ten children born to Hugh and Priscilla (Beatty) Cavett, who were also born in the Keystone State, as was the paternal grandfather and great-grandfather before him, the latter's birth occurring under a tree while the family were engaged in fighting the savage red man. In his native county W. B. Cavett was reared on a farm and educated in the district schools. In 1845 he bade adieu to home and friends and went to Wheeling, Va., where he learned the tinner's trade, and five years later found him in the city of New Orleans, where he became foreman in a large tin establishment, a position he held until 1853. On account of an epidemic of yellow fever, he then came to Texas and became the first tinner of Gonzales, or, indeed, for a considerable distance round. He soon began doing a profitable wholesale business, but his operations were interrupted by the opening of the Civil War, and he at once enlisted in the Confederate service as a member of Company B, of Wall's Legion, and was sent to Mississippi. After the reorganization of the army at Corinth, he was placed under the command of Gen. Forrest, with whom he served faithfully until the war ended, mostly on detail duty, but he also acted in the capacity of Quartermaster. Upon his return home he at once resumed business, and has been a prosperous merchant of Gonzales ever since, with the exception of four years that he was in business at Austin. In 1890 he erected his present large shop and store room, which is 50 x 70 feet in dimensions, and carries a stock of goods valued at about $6,000, his annual sales reaching the $20,000 mark. He keeps an excellent stock of builders' and shelf hardware, stoves, wooden, glass and tin ware, house-furnishing goods and agricultural implements, in fact he keeps everything that could be desired in his line, and his large and liberal patronage is without doubt due to the fact that his prices are within the reach of all, are of an excellent quality, that he is courteous in his treatment of his patrons, and that he is the soul of honor in his business transactions. He has been quite active in the political affairs of Gonzales County, and in 1880 was elected to the position of City Alderman of Gonzales, has served several times as Mayor, and to this position was again elected in April, 1894, and is now discharging the duties of this office. He wrote the first letter officially to President Pierce, of the Southern Pacific Railroad Company, to induce them to build a branch road to Gonzales, and he again wrote the first letter to President Lott, of the Aransas Pass Railroad to urge them to extend a branch thither, and both roads are now running to or through Gonzales. Mr. Cavett was married in 1860 to Miss Lizzie Polk, a native of Texas and daughter of Dr. Thomas Polk, who came to this State from Tennessee at an early day, and is related to the family of President Polk. He practiced medicine in various towns of Texas, was in the Texas Revolution, and was a participant in the battle of San Jacinto. Later he moved to Gonzales, gave his attention to farming, and died here. To Mr. and Mrs. Cavett two children have been born: Cora Willie, who died at the age of nineteen years, and Milam Edward, who is associated in business with his father, the firm being known as W. B. Cavett & Son. The family are members of the Presbyterian Church, and are leaders in church society and in the social and business circles of Gonzales.

HON. THOMAS CALHOUN GREENWOOD. It is a pleasure to review the career of a man whose efforts have been crowned with distinction, and whose life has been honorable and praiseworthy. We all have strivings after a high ideal, but an ideal alone is of little value if not reinforced by the example of those who, like ourselves, have human frailties, yet have been enabled to so overcome them as to lead lives of usefulness and honor. Thomas C. Greenwood was born in Monroe County, Miss., April 14, 1823, the sixth of eight children born to Thomas Greenwood and Lydia (Moore) Greenwood, who were natives of Virginia and North Carolina respectively. The former was a planter by occupation, and died in 1854, his wife's death occurring two years later, both of whom had been members of the Baptist Church for about sixty years. The subject of this sketch was reared in the northeast part of Mississippi, and was educated at LaGrange College, Alabama, from which well-known institution he graduated in 1843. Soon after leaving this institution he began the study of law, was admitted to practice in 1844, and soon after opened an office at Greensborough, Choctaw County, Miss. He was the valedictorian of his class, and the following extract therefrom is quoted from the *North Alabamian* of June 9, 1843:

Mr. Greenwood's address was characterized by sound reasoning, and bore the impress of a strong mind, habituated to deep thought, and well versed in the history of the day and country.

It was not long before his intelligence, native ability and knowledge of his profession began to be recognized, and his faithfulness to the interests of his clients, whose cases he usually won, was soon the means of winning him a very large practice. In 1848 he moved to Chickasaw County, Miss., where, for a time, he edited a Democratic paper—*The Patriot*—in partnership with Judge T. N. Martin. After locating in this section he again soon found himself in the midst of a successful practice, and there he remained and became widely and favorably known until 1852. Declining health then compelled him to make a change. He removed to Seguin, Texas, and during the most of the four years that he resided there he was in partnership with the distinguished Judge, John Ireland. Following his usual habits of faithfulness, industry and attention to his profession, he was very successful in his practice. In a few years his health again failed, and, quitting the law, he went to the country and settled on his farm in Caldwell County, where his home has since continued to be. His estate comprises 800 acres of excellent land, of which 200 acres are under cultivation, and all the improvements instituted thereon have been made by himself, and are of a character to add greatly to the value of the property. On this farm he has made his home for forty years, and during this time his walk through life has been characterized by prudence and circumspection, by many deeds of benevolence and kindness, and by his desire to live an upright and useful life. He is held in high esteem by the citizens of the county, and has prospered financially in the conduct of his affairs. During the war, although ill health debarred him from entering the service, he served the county as Commissioner, and did much to assist those families whose fathers, husbands and brothers were fighting their battles at the front. Without doubt, had his health permitted, he would have risen to a high place in his profession and in the offices of the State. In 1844 he was married to Miss Juliet Crocker, a native of South Carolina, and he attributes much of his success in life to her unfailing good judgment and helpful spirit. To their union eight children were born: Thomas, who was drowned in the San Marcos River, in 1879, was a noble man and highly respected. He entered the Confederate army when seventeen years of age, and served with distinguished ability in Gen. Green's Brigade. Calphurnia became the wife of W. J. Grubbs; James is County Judge of Guadalupe County; Carrie is the wife of A. M. Benner, and resides in Gillespie County; Emmett yet resides with his parents on the farm; Paul Jones is a lawyer at Luling, and Eugenia graduated from Waco University, and died three days afterwards, in 1881. One child died in infancy. Mr. Greenwood was ordained a minister of the Baptist Church in 1858, and has served as pastor of several churches in his vicinity, mainly at Prairie Lea and Seguin. He and his faithful wife are now in their seventy-second year. They hope to celebrate the fiftieth anniversary of their marriage during this year, 1894. He ascribes his length of days to temperate habits, and a cheerful, abiding faith in God, who "watches the sparrow's fall and feeds the young ravens when they cry."

GEORGE, AARON AND THOMAS WATSON. The push, energy and enterprise necessary for a successful career are plainly discernible in the lives of these gentlemen, and is but another evidence of what can be accomplished by those of foreign birth who seek home and fortune on the free soil of America. Their parents, William and Loise Watson, are natives of County Durham, England, as were also their grandparents, Aaron and Mary Watson. The grandfather was an active, industrious citizen in his native country, and for many years was engaged in mining. In connection he also followed farming. William Watson was born December 15, 1834, and remained in his native country until 1878, when he recognized the advantages to be derived from a residence in the United States. He came with his family to America and first settled on a farm near Luling, Texas, where he remained until 1889. From there he moved to Gonzales County, bought land and has since devoted much attention to stock raising, principally cattle. To his marriage, which occurred in 1856, were born these children: Hannah, wife of Thomas Urwin; Elizabeth, wife of Joseph Peadon, came to Texas and died within one month of getting here, August 2, 1878; she left two children, one of which, a son, died August 29, 1878, and the other, also a son, George Peadon, was reared by his grandparents and is now a young man; George, Aaron, Thomas, and Maggie, wife of George Brown, of England. In politics the father of these children is a Democrat and in religion a Methodist. George Watson, the eldest son, first saw the light in County Durham, England, December 9, 1860, and he there received his education. When eighteen years of age he crossed the ocean with his parents, and for a number of years resided at Luling, Texas, with them. After that he was engaged in railroad work for five years, principally bridge building, then planting for two years, and then made his advent into Gonzales County. In 1892 he joined his brother Thomas in erecting a public gin and mill, and this has since averaged 700 bales of cotton and 2,000 bushels of corn per year. Mr. Watson is well liked in his neighborhood, and has held the office of School Trustee for some time. In the year 1892 he married Miss Tamar Wilson, daughter of Thomas and Mary Wilson, of Luling, Texas, and one child has been given them, Thomas William. Aaron Watson, the second son born to William Watson, was also a native of County Durham, England, his birth occurring April 6, 1863. He was partially educated in England, and was fifteen years of age when he crossed the ocean. He assisted on the farm near Luling and then, with his father and brothers, came to Gonzales County, Texas, where he joined them in the purchase of land. He has paid much attention to the breeding of Holstein cattle, and has a fine herd of thirty head now in pasture. He is a public spirited young man and has held the office of road overseer. Thomas Watson, the youngest son, was born in Yorkshire, England, January 19, 1871, and he attended school for two years in the old country. When but a lad of seven years he accompanied his parents to this country and attended the public schools of Luling until fourteen years of age, after which he went to work on the farm. He takes a lively interest in the welfare of his section and has held the position of road-overseer. When his father and brothers invested in land in Gonzales County he invested with them, and is now in business with his brother George in the gin and grist mill, something very badly needed in this section. Like his father and brothers he is an ardent Democrat in politics.

DR. J. T. BURROWS has been a close student of his profession, and in his mission of "healing the sick" his generous treatment of his patients, his liberality and kindness of heart, have won for him not the respect alone, but the earnest regard of the large clientele which he has gathered around him. While engaged in the cares of his laborious profession, he has not forgotten to fulfill all the demands of good citizenship, and no enterprise of a worthy public nature has appealed to him in vain for support. Born in Mississippi, in November, 1843, he was the eighth in order of birth of nine children born to James and Millie (Wilkinson) Burrows, the former a native of Tennessee, and the latter of Kentucky. During the winter of 1849 and '50 the family moved to Texas and located in Gonzales County, where the father engaged very extensively in farming and stock raising. He also operated a gin, and cotton was brought to it from long distances. Mr. Burrows died on his farm in 1855, and his wife in 1880. In the schools of Gonzales County our subject received his education, and in 1861 he enlisted in Company D, Thirty-second Regiment Texas Cavalry, under Capt. W. L. Foster and Col. D. C. Woods. For the most part he served in Texas and Louisiana, and was in the Red River campaign against Banks. When the war closed he returned to Gonzales County and engaged in farming and stock raising, which continued to be his chosen occupation until 1869, when he began the study of medicine. In 1872 he graduated at the Texas Medical College and at once began practicing in Guadalupe County, remaining there three years. Then returning to Gonzales County he remained there for five years, after which he went to Wilson County and practiced in the eastern part of the same for ten years. In 1891 he came to Floresville, where he has since had a good practice. He was married in 1867 to Miss Ameta B. Cone, a native of Georgia, and the daughter of Dr. Archibald Cone, who came to Texas in the winter of 1851, settled in Guadalupe County and followed farming and stock raising until 1857. He then moved to Wilson County and resided here until his death in 1870. He and his sons were merchants, farmers and large stock men. To Dr. and Mrs. Burrows have been born six children: Georgie, Myrtie, Bruce, Jacob T., Jr.; Edgar and Ameta. The Doctor is a Mason, a member of Floresville Lodge No. 515. He has devoted much of his life to his profession, in the practice of which he has been eminently successful. He has a pleasant home in Floresville, and will probably make his permanent residence here.

C. L. WILLIAMS. There are few men in business circles who show as much fitness for their avocation, in that they are wideawake, experienced, reliable and energetic, as C. L. Williams, and there are none who have a more thorough knowledge of lumber than he. Mr. Williams, the prominent lumber merchant of Shiner, was about the first settler in that town. He was born in Tennessee in 1848, and was the only child born to William and Dorcas (Creswell) Williams, both of whom were natives of Tennessee. The father was a farmer, and died when our subject was an infant, in 1849, while on the way with his family to the Lone Star State. He died of cholera, in Arkansas, where many more of the party died at the same time from the same disease. Mrs. Williams and her young child then remained in Arkansas about four years, after which she proceeded to Texas and settled at Fort Gates, Coryell County, where she remained two years. For ten years after this she was at Lampasas, and then moved to Fort Worth. She now makes her home with her son, our subject. C. L. Williams was educated in Lampasas and Fort Worth, and learned the carpenter trade in the latter city. From there he came to Flatonia and began his career as a carpenter and builder. Being trusty and a thorough workman he soon had all the work he could attend to, and many buildings he erected were worth $20,000. In 1887, at the time of the location of the town of Shiner, in Lavaca County, Mr. Williams moved there November 15, and opened the first business of the place, a lumber yard, and drove the first nail to erect a building there, his office being the first building erected. Within two weeks he had twelve buildings under contract, and has erected three-fourths of all the buildings here. He carries a stock of lumber valued at $20,000, all builders' material, hardware, paints, wire, buggies and farm wagons, etc., and does an annual business of $50,000. Mr. Williams is agent for H. B. Shiner in the sale of city property, also of other interests, besides extensive duties of his own. He owns a good farm of 200 acres, well improved, near Flatonia, all fenced, with good buildings, orchard, etc., and has 100 acres under cultivation. Politically he is a Democrat, is chairman of the Democratic party of this precinct, and attends the State conventions. He was a member of the first Board of City Aldermen and was appointed Mayor to fill a vacancy. Mr. Williams is a Mason, a member of the Chapter, and he is also a member of the Knights of Pythias. In February, 1892, he married Mrs. Jury, a native of Lavaca County, and daughter of " Buck " Harris, who was one of the early settlers of Lavaca County. He is a self-made man, and one who is well respected by all who know him.

JUDGE R. H. COLEMAN. It is a real pleasure to review the career of a man whose efforts have been crowned with success, and whose life has been honorable in every particular as has that of Judge R. H. Coleman. He was a member of one of the F. F. V.'s. and first saw the light in the Old Dominion in 1820, being the eldest child born to John J. and Catherine (Hawes) Coleman, who were of English descent, but Virginians by birth. The father was an extensive planter, and followed this occupation during the five years that the family resided in Kentucky. At the end of that time they returned to Virginia, and there the parents spent the rest of their lives. Judge Coleman received a better education than the majority of youths of his day and was an attendant of Virginia College. When starting out in life for himself, he took up the occupation to which he had been reared, and with which he was most familiar, and for some time gave his attention to farming. At the age of twenty years he was appointed Sheriff of Nelson County and filled the office very acceptably for two years. In 1858 he came to Texas and upon locating in Victoria engaged in various speculative enterprises, such as dealing in stock, land, etc. During the Civil War he was principally engaged in furnishing supplies for the Confederate Government, but was for a time a member of the State Militia. At the close of the great conflict between the North and South, Judge Coleman began carrying the United States mail under Government contract, and as he, at this time, was the proprietor of a large livery stable in Victoria, he did an immense business, carrying passengers to all adjoining counties. With shrewd forethought he caused a position bridge to be erected across the river at Victoria and this brought him in a large revenue. He has at all times shown the best of judgment in his business ventures, and, as a result, is the owner of much valuable city property and good ranch property. During all these years he has also been engaged in mercantile pursuits in Victoria, his partner in this branch of human endeavor being William Shrieve. In 1878 he was elected County Judge of Victoria County and for twelve years was elected successively, which speaks for itself as to his popularity as a citizen and politician.

J. D. ANDERSON. Few men have lived more quietly and unostentatiously than J. D. Anderson, and yet few have exerted a more salutary influence upon the immediate society in which they move, or impressed a community with a more profound reliance on their honor and ability of sterling worth. His life has not been illustrious with startling or striking contrasts; but it has shown how a laudable ambition may be gratified when accompanied by pure motives, perseverance, industry and steadfastness of purpose. Mr. Anderson is now the owner of a large and excellent farm, and as a stock raiser stands second to none in the county. He is a native of the Palmetto State, as were also his parents, James and Margaret (Dorrah) Anderson. The paternal grandfather, D. Anderson, was a native of Virginia, while the maternal grandfather, James Dorrah, was born in Scotland or Ireland. William Anderson and wife, who was a Miss Denny, with two sons, David and John, came from Ireland and settled in Pennsylvania, but afterwards moved to Charleston, S. C. and thence to Laurens County, S. C., just below the court house. After they had moved to Laurens County, they had four more children: Rebecca, Sallie, one name unknown, and Denny. They afterwards moved to Spartanburg County, on Enoree River, and thence to Tiger River, where William Anderson, at an advanced age, was killed by the Tories and Indians. John Anderson married and settled in York County. David married a Miss Mason and settled on Tiger River, in Spartanburg County. Rebecca never married. Sallie married a man by the name of Brakin, in Charleston, S. C., where they lived. She had one son who moved to Missouri. Denny married a Miss Elizabeth Massey and settled on Enoree River, S. C., Spartanburg County. They raised a family of eleven children: Rebecca, William, David, John, Denny, Mary, James, Samuel, Martha, Henry and Elizabeth. Elizabeth Massey Anderson, wife of Denny Anderson on the maternal side, was descended from the Smiths, of Halifax County, N. C. The father of our subject was a successful agriculturist and tilled the soil in his native State until his death in 1883. The mother passed away in 1851. Both belonged to the Presbyterian Church, and were active workers in the same. Our subject was born in the year 1832, educated in the old field schools and was prevented from entering college by the death of the mother and the subsequent illness of the father. For some time he managed his father's estate, and, when twenty-eight years of age, was married to Miss Ianthe J. Wallace, a daughter of Hon. Alexander Wallace, a well known South Carolinian, who was prominent in State and National affairs, and who was a member of Congress for some time. In 1859 our subject came to the Loan Star State, located in DeWitt County, and in 1862, he enlisted in Company B, Twentieth Texas Regiment, infantry, serving on the coast in Texas principally and holding the rank of Lieutenant. He was in service until the close of hostilities. In 1865, Mr. Anderson bought a portion of his present farm located near the village of Thomaston, 489 acres in the river track, highly improved and 200 acres under cultivation. He also owns other tracts, containing 3,000 acres with 200 acres under cultivation, and he has one of the handsomest homes in the whole section. His fine residence is on a natural building site, a ridge overlooking the beautiful Guadalupe valley, and he is surrounded by all the comforts of life. His marriage has been blessed by the birth of nine children, three being deceased. They are named as follows: Robert W., N. Bertie, wife of C. E. Kaapke; George S., Mary Ianthe, wife of Rev. A. H. P. McCurdy, William Irvin and three died in childhood. The family holds membership in the Presbyterian Church.

MAJOR SAMUEL B. BALES. Few have lived as quietly as Major Samuel B. Bales, and few have exerted a more salutary influence upon the immediate society in which they move, or impressed a community with a more profound reliance on their honor, ability or sterling worth. His life has not been illustrious with startling incidents or striking contrasts, but it has shown how a laudable ambition may be gratified when accompanied by pure motives, persevering industry and steadfastness of purpose. He was born in South Carolina in 1817, the eldest of seven children born to John and Mary (Blue) Bales, who were also natives of the Palmetto State, where the father followed farming and blacksmithing throughout life, and eventually passed from life. The paternal grandfather, John Bales, was born in the Isle of Erin, and just before the opening of the Revolutionary War in this country had emigrated thither, located in South Carolina, and from that State enlisted in the Colonial Army. The maternal grandfather was also a Revolutionary soldier from South Carolina. In the State of his birth the subject of this sketch was reared and he began life for himself as a tiller of the soil. In 1849 he came to Austin, Texas, with a colony of nine families, and he very soon after became superintendent of the erection of the Capitol building in Austin, which occupied his time and attention for about one year. Following this he was engaged in building mills and gins until 1856, when he married, and until 1859 was engaged in farming in Travis County, since which time he has been a resident of Hays County, and for many years devoted his attention to agriculture. His wife was Elizabeth Henry, a native of Tennessee, and a daughter of John Henry, who became a resident of Texas in 1851, and took up his abode at Austin. In 1863, Mr. Bales entered the Confederate Army, soon became attached to Green's Brigade as Ordnance Officer, and was in the battle of Mansfield, where Gen. Green was killed. He was detailed to return to Austin with the General's remains, and after that sad duty had been performed was detailed for post duty in that city, where he served until the war closed. For about eighteen months following he was in the service of the United States, in charge of stock and forage, then returned to his farm and once more began tilling the soil. In the fall of 1868 he moved to San Marcos and established the first livery stable of this place, and after conducting it very successfully for a long time he sold out and now owns and conducts a grain and feed store and boarding stable. His farm, which comprises 360 acres, is an exceptionally fertile and valuable one, and seventy-five acres are in an excellent state of cultivation. Major Bales was elected Alderman of San Marcos in 1890, was re-elected at the end of his first term, and is now President of the Board of Aldermen. During this time many improvements in the town have been made, and there are now over seven miles of macadamized roads. The Major is a Mason of long standing, and he and his wife are members of the Cumberland Presbyterian Church, in which he is one of the Elders. They have two living children. John H., and Mary, wife of John Cape. Another child died in infancy, unnamed. Major Bales saw much of early Texas life in the rough, and was on several expeditions against the Indians, and was thoroughly familiar with life on the frontier.

GILFORD RAMSAY. In the discharge of his duties as a servant of the public, the subject of this sketch has been faithful, efficient and trustworthy. He has long been a resident of the Lone Star State, but was born in Macon County, Ala., in 1843, the fourth of seven children, born to Daniel and

Welthy (Collingsworth) Ramsay, who were North Carolinians by birth, but who removed to Alabama about 1835. The father was a participant in the Indian wars of 1836-37, and in Alabama he continued to make his home until after the close of the Civil War, when he came to Texas, and, after residing two years in Fayette County, made a permanent settlement in Gonzales County, on Sandy's Creek, where he lived until death closed his career in 1880, his widow surviving him until 1890. Both parents were members of the Missionary Baptist Church, and he was for many years a member of the Masonic fraternity. In Alabama the subject of this sketch was reared and educated. On the 12th of May, 1862, he enlisted in Company H, Thirty-third Alabama Infantry, and served principally in Lowery's Brigade in Mississippi, Tennessee, and Kentucky, and was a participant in the battle of Murfreesboro, in which engagement he lost his arm from a fragment of shell. He was at one time captured and taken to Springfield, Ill., at Camp Butler, was afterwards taken to City Point, Va., and was there exchanged April 15, after which he returned to his old home. He then attended school for two years, at the end of which time he came to Texas with his parents and finally located in Gonzales County, purchasing with his father a tract of land containing 200 acres, and soon after 200 acres more, on which they made some valuable improvements, and now has ninety acres in a good state of cultivation, but a considerable portion of which is in pasture land. He raises a good grade of horses and mules, and has also given considerable attention to the raising of cattle, an occupation that he has found to be quite profitable. Since 1876 Mr. Ramsay has been quite an active politician, in which year he was elected to the position of County Assessor, being the first to hold that office after its creation. In 1880 he was again elected to the office, and in 1886 was elected to his present office, that of County Collector, the duties of which he has discharged ever since. December 2, 1874, he was married to Miss Josephine Williams, a native of Gonzales County, and daughter of David Williams, who is one of the pioneers of the county, and to them a family of nine children have been given: Della, wife of R. J. Shelby, now of Seguin; Lenna, Daniel, Whitson, Richard, Edgar, Lunnette, Sue and Hue, the last two mentioned being twins. Mr. Ramsay, Mrs. Ramsay and her daughter, Della, are members of the Missionary Baptist Church. Socially Mr. Ramsay is a member of the Knights of Honor, and since being elected to his present official position has been a resident of Gonzales, where he has gathered about him many friends.

EDWARD MALLOCH. He whose name heads this sketch was until recently engaged in the important business of merchandizing, and seemed well fitted for the calling ; for he is enterprising, honest and industrious, and held in good esteem by those who were his patrons, and by the people generally, most of whom are well acquainted with him.

He is a native of Perth, Scotland, born in 1816, and possesses many of the sterling traits characteristic of the Scotch people. He was the youngest child born to John and Margaret (Robertson) Malloch, natives of Scotland, the former of whom was a carpenter by trade, and died in 1840, his wife's death occurring ten years prior to his own. In his youth, the subject of this sketch learned the trade of a cabinet maker, and worked at his trade for some time in his native land. He came to the United States in 1840, and for one year thereafter resided in Charleston, S. C. He then came to Texas, and for twelve years resided at Gonzales, most of which time he followed merchandising. He was appointed Assessor and Collector of Taxes for Gonzales County, and afterwards was elected to the office for a term of two years. In 1853 he came to Prairie Lea, Caldwell County, and here he opened a mercantile establishment with J. C. McKean and T. M. Hardeman. He continued thus associated for about two years, when the firm became McKean & Malloch. And this continued until the opening of the great conflict between the North and South. During the war Mr. Malloch served as County Commissioner, and after the war was elected to the same position, and since that time has served four years in the same office. He owns as fine a tract of land as there is in Coleman County, and owns, in the vicinity of Prairie Lea, two farms, some other lands and a number of lots in town. The cultivated portion of his land yields about thirty-five bushels of corn to the acre, and of cotton from one-half to two-thirds of a bale. In 1853 Mrs. Lucy Ellen Blackburn (nee McKean) became his wife. Her father, J. C. McKean, was born in Pennsylvania, was an early settler in Texas, when it was a part of Mexico, and after the death of Green DeWitt, brought a large number of families to Texas, who settled in De Witt's colony, and located many leagues of land. In this he was associated with William A. Matthews, and the company of Matthews & McKean, acquired many tracts of lands. J. C. McKean, in 1850, settled in Caldwell County, and died at Prairie Lea in 1880, at the age of eighty-three years.

To the union of Mr. and Mrs. Malloch; the following children were born: Margaret, wife of B. H. Pittman, of Coleman County; Lucy Ellen, wife of W. O. Read, of Coleman; Carrie, Edward, Jean, and John, who died at Prairie Lea in 1888, aged twenty years, and an infant son, deceased. Mr. Malloch was a soldier in the army of the Texas Republic, before annexation to the United States, and is a member of the Texas Veteran Association, and the only one of them now living in Caldwell County. He is a member of Prairie Lea Lodge A. F. & A. M. No. 116, and has been Treasurer of said lodge for over twenty successive years.

He was at Gonzales when Gen. Woll of the Mexican army captured San Antonio in 1842, and the battle of Salado occurred. Col. Matthew Caldwell commanding the Texans, sent word by express to Gonzales, that fifty Mexican cavalry, under the command of an officer well known in Texas, would, on the following night, be in Gonzales to destroy the town. The Mexicans came as far as the forty-mile water hole; that distance from San Antonio, and thirty-five miles from Gonzales. The advance guard having killed three sick men, who were found at this place, the commander deemed it prudent to advance no farther, and returned to San Antonio. Ezekiel Williams, who had in his charge two cannon and fifty muskets, which had been brought from San Antonio, after the raid made on that city, under Gen. Vasquez, in the spring of the same year, placed the arms in charge of Mr. Malloch, who loaded the guns, so as to give the enemy a warm reception. There were plenty of arms and ammunition, but only five men, as all the others who could find horses to ride, were in the battle with Col. Caldwell. This retreat of the Mexicans no doubt saved old Gonzales from a second destruction, as the town was burned in the war of 1836.

ROBERT H. CARSON. Like many of the representative men of the county Mr. Carson has spent the principal part of his days tilling the soil, and is a man highly esteemed for his many estimable qualities.   He came originally from York District, South Carolina, his birth occurring January 28, 1822, and is a son of William and Jane (Wallace) Carson, both natives of the Palmetto State.   The parents met and married in their native State, and there passed the remainder of their days.   The father was Irish and the mother of Scotch descent, and both were most worthy Christians.   In politics the father was against John C. Calhoun and nullification.   In the schools of South Carolina, Robert H. Carson received a good, practical education, and later learned the trade of coachmaker and ginwright.   In 1850, when Gonzales County, Texas, was but sparsely settled, Mr. Carson made his way here and worked as gin-house builder until the breaking out of the war.   He was then drawn to serve in the State Militia for six months, but at the expiration of that time he was released at Victoria, his trade exempting him from further service.   Since that time he has followed his trade to some extent, but for the most part has been engaged in planting, at which he has been fairly successful. Although not an extensive land owner, he owns a fine tract, and has it under a good state of cultivation.   In 1840 he was married to Miss Mary A. Abernethy, daughter of John J. and Eliza (Gray) Abernethy, of South Carolina, and five children are the fruits of this union, four sons and one daughter: Hazel Albert, Jesse Claudius, John William, Sarah Jane, wife of Charles S. Power; and Robert.   Mr. Abernethy was a planter, a nullifier, and a member of the Masonic Fraternity.   In his political views Mr. Carson is a stanch supporter of Democratic principles, and socially he is a Third Degree Mason.

JACK SUTHERLAND.   This prominent citizen is a descendant of one of the pioneer families of Wharton County, Texas, where he was born in January, 1838, and he inherits many of the worthy and sterling traits of his Scottish ancestors.   His grandfather, John Sutherland, or Sutherlin, as the name was originally spelled, came to this country from Scotland in the early half of the eighteenth century, and settled on Dan River, where he began the cultivation of tobacco.   In 1800 he moved to Clinch River, Tennessee, and engaged in farming, residing there until his children had all married.   He then went to Alabama, and made his home with his son John, until his death.   He was a pioneer in every sense of the word, and a man whose upright, honorable career endeared him to all.   John Sutherland, father of our subject, was born in Virginia in 1792, on the site of the present city of Danville, and began life as a merchant at Knoxville, Tennessee.   While a resident of Knoxville he was married to Diana Kennedy, of that city, by whom he had three children, David, Sarah Agnes, and James.   About 1825 he moved to Decatur, and thence to Tuscumbia, Alabama.   While residing in Decatur he was President of a bank, and while in Tuscumbia, a merchant. His first wife, having died, he selected his second wife in the person of Miss Ann Bryan Lane, a native of Alabama, and our subject was one of the younger children born to this union.   In 1835 John Sutherland came to Texas prospecting and looking for a location, and was in San Antonio in 1836, when the Mexicans besieged the Alamo.   He was within the walls of that place and was sent out by General Travis with dispatches to Gonzales.   By the time he returned the Alamo had fallen and the force had been slain.   Returning to Gonzales, he joined the forces of General Houston, who had arrived at that place, and was sent by that officer with dispatches to President Burnet—with whom he served as Aid-de-camp and Private Secretary until the close of hostilities. Returning to Alabama he moved his family to Texas in 1838, settling on the west side of the Colorado River, where he established a ferry which goes by the name of Sutherland's ferry to this day. In the year 1840 his second wife died, having borne him three sons: George Q., Levin L., and Jack. In 1841 he married a third wife, Ann M. Dickson, widow of Abisha Dickson, killed with Fannin at Goliad. In March, 1849, he moved to a place on the Cibolo Creek, where a small town was laid out and named Sutherland Springs, and a postoffice established, of which he was the first postmaster. This county was mainly organized by his influence, and Sutherland Springs became the first county seat. There his death occurred in May, 1867, at the age of seventy-four years and eleven months. In this county our subject was mainly reared, but his education was received in Knoxville, Tennessee. In the year 1861, he enlisted in Company F, Fourth Texas Infantry, a part of Hood's Texas Brigade. It will be remembered that this regiment was the first to break General Porter's line at Gaines' Mill, June 27, 1862, and turn the tide of battle in favor of the Confederates. Mr. Sutherland is quite proud of his honorable record as a member of Hood's Immortal Brigade—is well posted on the history of the war, and though a good loyal citizen of "Our Own Common Government," as Uncle Abe would put it, says he is as *unreconstructed* as ever. He went to Virginia, and was organized at Richmond. Mr. Sutherland participated in all the campaigns, and in all the battles of that section, missing but a few engagements. He was severely wounded at Darbytown Road in October, 1864, and was retired on account of disability. He came home just as the war ended. He was promoted from the ranks to Lieutenant and Adjutant. After the war Mr. Sutherland engaged in surveying and farming for some time, and after the death of the father was administrator of the estate. Until 1885 he lived at Sutherland Springs, when he moved to Floresville to educate his children. He is the owner of 500 acres near the Springs, and is one of the ranchers of the county. Upon the organization of Wilson County in 1860, he was elected District Clerk, holding that office when he went to the war, and leaving his father as deputy. In the year 1870 he was married to Miss Mary E. Sutherland, of Victoria, daughter of Dr. William Sutherland, a native of Kentucky. Her father came to Texas in 1852, was an early physician of this section, and died in Victoria in 1891. To our subject and wife eleven children were born, ten of whom are now living: Mamie, Annie, Jack, Jr., Agnes, Winnifred, Walter, Frederick, John, Levin, Lucy, and Lizzie who died in infancy. Mrs. Sutherland is a worthy member of the Baptist Church.

DR. R. L. SMITH, an early settler of DeWitt County, Texas, was born in Rankin County, Mississippi, on the 8th of January, 1833, and of the family of seven children born to his parents, Merrill J. and Susan (Lusk) Smith, he was the third in order of birth. The father and mother were natives of South Carolina, but at an early day moved to Mississippi, and from there to Texas in 1847, settling in DeWitt County. There the father followed farming until 1859, when he came to Lavaca County, and died near Hallettsville the following year. He was a prominent man in political affairs, but no office-holder. The mother died in Luling in 1879. Both were earnest and steadfast members of the Baptist Church. The last words spoken by the father when on his death bed were, " It is nothing to die when one is prepared." Our subject was reared in the Lone Star State, and educated at Milton College, Mississippi. He began the study of medicine in DeWitt County, Texas, in 1855, under Dr. Hodge, and attended his first course of lectures in New Orleans. Later he was in the Texas Medical College and Hospital at Galveston, from which institution he graduated in 1874. In 1861 he enlisted in Company A, Eighth Texas Infantry, as private, and was in the barracks at Hearnsted, where he was made post surgeon and soon after surgeon of the regiment. He was in service eighteen months, and then resigned, on account of ill health, at Little Rock, Arkansas. Returning home he was made examining surgeon of the district, and served in that capacity, with office at Hallettsville, until the close of the war. In 1865 he went to Comal County, and engaged in the sheep business for one year, after which he resumed practice in Caldwell County, and remained there fourteen years. He then bought out Caldwell's Mineral Springs, near Luling, and was proprietor of that establishment for three years. From there he came to Lavaca County, practiced his profession for three years, and then went to Albany, Shackelford County, where he engaged in the sheep business, but also carried on his practice for three years. Coming back to Lavaca County, he settled on the present site of Shiner, and has since been actively engaged in the practice of his profession. He was made Postmaster there in 1893. The doctor was married in 1657 to Miss Theressa Smith, a native of Iowa, and daughter of Paris Smith, who came from Virginia to Texas in 1840. Dr. and Mrs. Smith's union was blessed by the birth of eight children: Guy M., residing at Clinton, this State; Ida T., wife of T. A. Logan, of San Antonio; R. C., a physician of Clifton, Bosque County; Carrie, wife of Stuart Johnson, of Eastland County; Paris, Druggist, of Comanche County; French, Assistant Postmaster at Shiner; Emmit, editor of the *Bosque County Banner;* and Virgie. Dr. Smith is a Mason, and a Knight of Honor. He is a pleasant, social, genial gentleman, and one who has many friends.

CAPT. H. S. CUNNINGHAM. The business enterprises of Victoria, Texas, are of an important character, are ably and successfully carried on, and have secured for this town a reputation of which any place of its size might well be proud. Prominent among the successful business men of the town is Capt. H. S. Cunningham, who possesses more than ordinary acumen and foresight. He is a product of the State of Alabama, where he was born in 1831, the third child of John A. and F. C. (Wallace) Cunningham, natives respectively of Tennessee and South Carolina. The father was a successful merchant of Greenville, Butler County, Ala., until 1836, at which time he removed to Texas, and until 1840 was a resident of Shelby County. He then removed to Washington County, and after a residence of four years there he came to Victoria County, and made a permanent settlement in the town of Victoria, January 1, 1845. While residing in these different localities in the Lone Star State he was engaged in farming, and continued that occupation until his death, July 29, 1888. He became a prominent character in the affairs of the county, served in the capacity of Alderman and Mayor of Victoria and also as County Judge, the duties of which he discharged in a manner calculated to win him the highest respect of his fellows. Prior to the Civil War he was a strong Union man and a thoroughly loyal citizen, but after the Southern States had seceded he became a strong adherent of the Confederacy. He and his wife, who died in 1850, were members of the

MISSIONS.

Presbyterian Church, in which he was for many years an elder. H. S. Cunningham was reared and educated in Victoria, and when starting out in life for himself he became a clerk in a mercantile establishment, but soon embarked in business for himself. This he soon discontinued to enter the Confederate service, and in 1861 he assisted in raising Company B of the First Regiment of Texas Cavalry, and was mustered in on the Square in Victoria in September, 1861, as First Lieutenant. At the battle of Pleasant Hill he was promoted to the rank of Captain, and held the same until the war closed His company was first sent to the Texas frontier, and from there was ordered East in 1863 to Louisiana, in which State he participated in the battles of Mansfield, Pleasant Hill and Yellow Bayou. After being in the east part of the State for a time he was ordered back to Texas, and was in the northeastern part of this State when the war terminated. Captain Cunningham immediately returned to Victoria, and once more engaged in business, and since that time has conducted a well-appointed grocery store with marked success. He now occupies the largest store building on the Square, a two-story building, erected in 1882, and carries a stock of goods valued at $8,000, his annual sales amounting to about $50,000. The Captain is an elder in the Presbyterian Church, and socially is a member of the Blue Lodge and Chapter of the A. F. & A. M. His brother, Capt. A. P. Cunningham, well known as the kindest of the kindly and the bravest of the brave, commanded a company of the Sixth Texas Infantry, Granbury's Brigade, and fought at Arkansas Post, Chickamauga, Resaca, Mission Ridge, Kenesaw Mountain, New Hope Church, Atlanta, Franklin, Nashville and other places of less note, and died in Victoria of yellow fever in 1867. Another brother, James, was Sheriff of Victoria County, and died some years before the war. John L. and Lee, also brothers, reside in Victoria. Capt. H. S. Cunningham was married in 1869 to Miss Emma Goodwin, the accomplished daughter of Dr. Sherman Hould Goodwin, who was born in Burton, Ohio, November 21, 1814. In 1834 and 1835 he studied medicine in Lake Erie College, of Willoughby, Ohio, and in 1837 graduated from the Jefferson Medical College of Philadelphia, Penn. In 1848 he became a resident of Victoria, Texas, and was here called from life January 8, 1884, having for seventeen years been a ruling elder in the Presbyterian Church of Victoria. He was married on the 25th of April, 1838, to Miss Lydia Cook, who was born in Burton, Ohio, August 3, 1816, and she was also called from life in Victoria on the 14th of August, 1880. To the union of Captain and Mrs. Cunningham the following children were given: Marion G., Ethel Ida, and Lydia Emma. The mother of these children died in 1885.

JAMES MOONEY is one of the early settlers of Cuero, Texas, and one of the most prominent citizens of this thriving village. He is one of those liberal, public-spirited, enterprising and executive men who have done so much to develop the resources of a new country and build up the interests of his adopted home. He was born in Ireland in 1820, and his parents, Thomas and Margaret (Morgan) Mooney, were natives of the same country. About 1836 the parents grew restive, bade adieu to friends and scenes long loved, and pitched the household tent in the metropolis of the United States. From the age of sixteen until 1844 our subject resided in New York City, and he there learned the machinist's trade. From there he went to Pennsylvania, and worked at his trade on railroad engines for some time. In the year 1856

9

he went to New Orleans and engaged with the Morgan Line of steamships, and was with the same for many years, being foreman of the ships in Algiers. In 1873 he came to Texas, where he had charge of the Gulf, Western & Texas Pacific Railroad, as Chief Engineer, for twenty-one years. When he came to Cuero only a few houses were in the place, and he has witnessed the wonderful changes that have taken place from that time to the present. He is now retired from the active duties of life, and has a pleasant home in that town. Mr. Mooney was married in 1838 to Miss Julia Garland, who died in 1894. Five children were born to this union: Margaret M., wife of John McCluskey, who resides in New Orleans; Thomas, Helen (deceased), Julia Ann, widow of G. W. Smith, and ———. Mr. Mooney and children are members of the Catholic Church. Cuero has been Mr. Mooney's home since the storm that destroyed Indianola in 1875. He was in the latter town at that time, and lost nearly all his possessions, barely escaping with his clothes. The railroad shops, which were then located there, were also swept away, and rebuilt at Cuero, where our subject soon located and where he has since resided. He is universally respected and esteemed, and has a host of warm friends. For his reliability, industry and other excellent qualities Mr. Mooney was well liked by the steamship company, and on retiring was given a pension. He has accumulated a comfortable competency, and although approaching toward the close of a long, active, industrious and useful life, he has the satisfaction of knowing that he is highly esteemed by all his fellow citizens and that his character is without reproach.

DR. WILLIAM DYCHE FINNEY. Prominent in the ranks of the foremost of the brilliant circle of physicians of Gonzales County, Texas, stands the name of Dr. William D. Finney, who has a most thorough and practical knowledge of his profession. He was born March 6, 1845, in Aberdeen, Miss., son of Michael and Eliza (Dyche) Finney, natives, respectively, of Tennessee and Georgia. The father came to Mississippi in his youth, and died at Independence, Mo., of cholera, on the overland route to California, in 1849, when our subject was but four years old. His wife now finds a comfortable home with our subject, and is eighty-four years of age. The father was a Cumberland Presbyterian and the mother a Presbyterian in their religious views. In the schools near Aberdeen, Miss., Dr. William D. Finney received his education, and when twenty-two years of age removed to Gonzales County. When the Civil War broke out he enlisted in Company G, Forty-third Mississippi Regiment, under Captain Walton, and was in the Army of Tennessee. He was in the siege and surrender of Vicksburg, and after two weeks was paroled. Later he was in the retreat of the army to Resaca, Ga., and was in Johnston's entire retreat. At the time of the surrender he was in Greensboro, N. C. After the war, having a mother and sister to support, he came to Texas and drove stock and farmed for two years, by which means he accumulated sufficient means to take a course of lectures, in 1870–71, at Galveston Medical College. From that institution he graduated in 1872, and practiced his profession in Leesville, Texas, until 1881. After this he attended Bellevue Hospital Medical College, in New York, during the session of 1881–82, and received the degree of M. D. from that institution, and returning to Wrightsboro entered actively upon his career as a practitioner of the healing art. He has steadily risen in the channels of medical life, and is a physician of established reputation, standing second to none in the county. Of a cheerful disposition himself, he has the faculty of imparting courage to those who are despondent from illness, and his skill in the diagnosis and treatment of diseases is the cause of the success he has won in his profession. On the 3d of December, 1882, Dr. Finney was married to Miss Florence L. West, daughter of Larkin N. and Rebecca (Conn) West, of Leesville. The father was born in Louisiana, and was an old Texas veteran. He was a Royal Arch Mason and was a member of the Blue Lodge of Leesburg, No. 334, and was a Baptist in his religious views. Merchandising was his principal occupation, and he followed that until his death in 1890. His wife, died in 1885. The marriage of our subject has been blessed by the birth of five children: Lilian Rebecca, Willie Florence, Vida West, William Larkin (deceased) and Eugene Lamar. In politics the doctor is a Democrat, and socially a Third Degree Mason—a member of Shuler Lodge No. 317.

JUDGE ED. R. KONE. One of the well-known attorneys of Hays County, Texas, who commands the respect as well as the admiration of his brother practitioners, is Judge Ed. R. Kone, who is an experienced, shrewd and keen-witted lawyer, whose labors for his clients are herculean, and whose efforts to bring the guilty to justice and to right the wrongs of his fellow-citizens have done much to bring about law and order in Hays County. He is a product of Montgomery County, Texas, born in 1848, the eldest of ten children born to Samuel R. and Rebecca S. (Pitts) Kone, natives respectively of South Carolina and Georgia. In 1839 the former came to Texas at the age of fourteen years, and at once engaged in farm work in Grimes County, and for some time had charge of a force of negroes belonging to his uncle, Louis Depree. He remained in Grimes County until 1850, then bought a farm in Montgomery County, on which he located and which he greatly improved. He came to Hays County in 1851, bought a tract of land at "Stringtown," and was very successful in tilling the soil and in raising stock. After serving in the Confederate army for about one year, he was discharged on account of ill health, returned home and resumed farming, which he continued up to the time of his death, in 1873. He was an active Methodist, and a steward in that church. His father, Samuel Kone, was a carpenter and builder by occupation, and did some important State work in South Carolina. The maternal grandfather of the subject of this sketch, Gen. John D. Pitts, was born in either Virginia or Georgia, which is not definitely known. He was married in Georgia, followed planting there, and represented the section in which he lived in the Georgia State Legislature, serving twice in that capacity. He came to Grimes County, Texas, in 1846, engaged in planting and stock raising, but his vigorous intellect and many acquirements soon brought him into prominent notice, and he was elected Clerk of the Lower House of the State Legislature, in which capacity he served several sessions, and he was then elected State Comptroller, a position he ably filled for one or two terms. He had taken up his residence in Austin in 1848, but in 1849 or 1850 he came to Hays County, and was the first settler of what is now locally called "Stringtown." After a remarkably well-spent life, he breathed his last in 1861 at that place. The immediate subject of this sketch was educated in the schools of San Marcos and at Bastrop, under Col. R. P. Allen. He began life for himself as a clerk at San Marcos, but at the end of one year began the study of law under Major W. O. Hutchinson, and upon attaining his majority was admitted to the bar. He then formed a partnership with the major, and after remaining thus associated for three years, was appointed to fill a vacancy in the Sheriff's office, and held that position for eight months. After practicing his profession one year the next general election came around, and he was elected Presiding Justice of this county, and held the office until it was made vacant by the present constitution. He then declined to run for County Judge, although strongly urged to do so, and soon after formed a partnership with Capt. H. B. Coffield, which he held about one and one-half years, at the end of which time he was elected County Judge, and ably discharged the duties of this office for twelve years in succession. During this time he was instrumental in building the present courthouse and jail. At the time he was elected Presiding Justice the county was in debt about $30,000, and script was so low that the county was being greatly injured. He went to Austin and was instrumental in having a special act passed, authorizing the funding of the floating debt at 8 per cent. This act enabled the county to proceed on a cash basis, so that in three years the total debt was canceled. He, as ex-officio School Superintendent, built up the schools of this county greatly, for when he entered the office there were but thirteen schools in operation, and when he left the office fifty were in fine working order, which admirable state of affairs had been brought about through his own good management and persistent efforts. After twelve years of service he declined further election to the Judgeship, and once more resumed the practice of his profession, and after a time formed a partnership with L. H. Browne, which continued for two years, but since that time he has practiced alone. He has always been active in political matters, and is now a member of the State Democratic Executive Committee, in which capacity he also served several years ago. He has been a delegate to the State conventions every year since he attained his majority, with one exception, and for years has been at the head of the county Democratic organization. His official life was characterized by a desire to benefit his section, and he labored faithfully with that object in view, and success crowned his efforts in almost every instance. He is familiar with all branches of his profession, is a thoroughly posted, keen and far-seeing lawyer, and those who place their interests in his hands may rest assured that they will be carefully guarded. Judge Kone was married in November, 1872, to Miss Lula H. Martin, a native of Texas, and a daughter of Archie Martin, who was killed during the Civil War while serving in the Confederate army, and she also was left motherless when an infant. Her union with Judge Kone has resulted in the birth of four children: Julia R., Carrie, Eula Lee and Edna Woods. The Judge and his wife are members of the Methodist Church, and socially he is a member of the A. F. & A. M., the I. O. O. F., the K. of P. and the K. of H.

HENRY L. QUALLS. This gentleman who has so ably and efficiently officiated as Treasurer of Gonzales County, Texas, during the past four years, was born in Charleston District, S. C., May 13, 1826, being the only child born to the marriage of Jesse and Mary (Lawrence) Qualls, the former of whom was born in the Old North State, and the latter in South Carolina. The mother's earthly career was closed when the subject of this sketch was about seven months old, after which the father married again, and about 1832 removed with his family to Lowndes County, Miss., settled in the vicinity of Columbus, where he followed farming until his removal to Texas in 1854. They located in Austin (now Waller) County, where they made their home until after the war, then came to Gonzales County, and here Jesse Qualls made his home with his children until his death, which occurred at the age of eighty-nine years. He had long been a member of the Methodist Episcopal Church, and was a man of noble principles, kind heart and charitable disposition. Up to the opening of the Civil War he had accumulated, through his own efforts, a large amount of worldly goods, the most of which was swept away during the great struggle between the North and South, with the exception of his land. His early life had been a rather hard one, for he was left an orphan in his youth, and was compelled through necessity to begin the hard battle of life when quite young, his first services being compensated with the munificent salary of $4 per month. Henry L. Qualls was principally reared in the State of Mississippi, but unfortunately in his youth received but limited educational advantages. Upon attaining his majority he became a clerk in a country store, a position he held for about one year, then returned home and was engaged in farming for a like length of time. In 1849 he came to Texas, and for some time thereafter was engaged in clerking in a small place known as Cincinnati, on the Trinity River, where he remained six months. He then went to Swartout and obtained a position as clerk at a salary of $25 per month and his board, and there remained for two years. After spending a short time in Galveston, he came to Gonzales, and after two years spent in farming he became a clerk for Benjamin B. Peck & Co., with whom he remained from 1855 to 1858, then became a partner in a branch business started at Old Moulton, the firm being known as Peck & Qualls. The business was very successfully carried on until the opening of the great Civil War, when it was given up. In the spring of 1862 he enlisted in Company D, Willis' Battallion, Wall's Legion, and was sent at once to Mississippi. When the army was reorganized Mr. Qualls was detached from his command and placed in the Post Commissary Department, where he was actively employed until the war terminated. In the winter of 1864 he returned home, and was in Texas at the time of Lee's surrender. For one year thereafter he was engaged in the stock business, after which he moved to Gonzales and was in business for himself for about ten years. Following this he purchased a farm on Peach Creek, which he owned for some ten years and which he farmed for a short time, then sold out and purchased a farm near the town, but disposed of it five years later and purchased the farm which he now owns, consisting of 200 acres five miles from town. All the improvements that have been made on this place have been made by him, and thirty-five acres of the same are under a good state of cultivation. On the 15th of February, 1859, he was married to Miss Mary E. Stansell, a native of Texas, and daughter of Benjamin B. Stansell, who came to Texas from North Carolina in 1836, and died in Fayette County in 1866. To the union of Mr. and Mrs. Qualls seven children have been given: Anna Cora, wife of A. S. Lowe, of this county; Minnie Ella, wife of Walter Cook; Mary Elizabeth, Julia, who died at the age of seven years; Henry L., who died at the age of three and a half years; Eddie (a daughter), and Peck. Mr. and Mrs. Qualls are members of the Methodist Church, and Mr. Qualls is one of the church trustees. He was made a Mason in Belmont, Texas, in 1853, and is now a member of the Chapter.

W. N. McKINNEY. The mercantile business occupies a very important position in the commerce of every large city, every town and every hamlet, because this department of business includes nearly every necessary article of wearing apparel of foreign and home manufacture.   Mr. McKinney is a reliable and enterprising man of business, and since locating in Prairie Lea has done much to build up the business interests of the place.   He is a member of the firm of Blanks, McKinney & Co., which has become widely known throughout Caldwell County, and is one of the most pushing and enterprising members of the firm.   He was born in Sabine County, Texas, in 1839, the eldest child born to Henry and Permelia (Foy) McKinney, natives of Tennessee and Monroe, La., respectively.   The maternal grandfather, Frederick Foy, was a South Carolinian by birth, and came to Texas from Louisiana in 1828, and until 1851 resided in Sabine County.   He then came to Caldwell County and engaged in farming in the vicinity of Prairie Lea, becoming quite prominent.   He died in 1854.   He had held the position of Judge of Sabine County.   In 1838 Henry C. McKinney came to Texas, and was married the same year.   He was a carpenter by trade, and made his home in Sabine County until 1851, when he came to Prairie Lea and purchased an interest in and built the first mill on the San Marcos River at that place.   During the war, however, he resided on a farm in Guadalupe County, but afterwards he returned to Caldwell County, and here breathed his last in 1868.   The mother died in 1873.   W. N. McKinney was mainly reared in Prairie Lea, and began life for himself as a teacher in the schools in which he obtained his own education.   In February, 1862, he entered the Confederate army as a member of Company K, of the Thirty-second Texas Cavalry, and served with Debray's Brigade in the State of Texas, was a participant in the Red River campaign, and afterwards served in Louisiana and Texas until the close of hostilities. He then returned to his old home in the Lone Star State, and for two years thereafter was engaged in farming, then became a clerk and book-keeper for Blanks & Walker, with whom he remained for several years.   He then again took up the occupation of agriculture, which he followed successfully until January, 1892, when he formed his present partnership.   Their stock of goods is valued at about $4,000, and an annual business is being done of about $20,000.   Their establishment is well supplied with all necessary articles, and as their patronage is among the best people of the section it speaks well for their upright dealing.   Mr. McKinney is the owner of a fine farm of about 200 acres, and has over 100 acres under cultivation.   He was married in 1869 to Miss Mary Harris, a native of Texas, and a daughter of Abner Harris, who was a pioneer of this State, became a very prominent citizen of Guadalupe County, and in that county was called from this life.   To the union of Mr. and Mrs. McKinney the following family was born: Henry, Frederick, Clarence, Lee, Thomas and Hattie.   The mother of these children died July 9, 1890.   Mr. McKinney is a member of the Baptist Church, and belongs to Prairie Lea Lodge No. 114, of the A. F. & A. M.

JOSEPH DILLARD GATES.   Many of the best known farmers and stockraisers of Gonzales County, Texas, have been born in this State and are keenly alive to its interests.   They are prosperous, industrious and law abiding.   Joseph Dillard Gates, whose birth occurred in Washington County, August 9, 1839, was the second of a family of five children born to Samuel Hardin and Eliza (Dillard) Gates.   Samuel Hardin Gates was born in Arkansas and was brought to Texas when but six years of age.   He attended school in Washington County six months, but being a bright, ambitious boy, and under the influence of an intelligent and cultivated mother, he became a man of rare accomplishments. Especially was he gifted in mathematics. During his younger days he followed farming, but in the year 1849 he was seized with a violent attack of gold fever, which gave him no rest until he visited the Pacific coast. There he spent a year and a half in the gold mines. Returning to Texas he engaged in the gunsmith business and continued this in connection with other enterprises until his death in 1864. He took part in the Texas war for independence, was at Gonzales during the skirmish there, and would have been in the battle of San Jacinto, but at that time was on detached service. During the Civil War he was too old for active service, but was appointed Captain of State Militia in Gonzales County. Mrs. Gates died in 1872. Both were members of the Methodist Church and he was a Democrat in politics. Joseph D. Gates was seventeen years of age when he came with his parents to this county, and in Washington County and this he received his education. At the present time he is living on the headright league granted by the Republic of Texas to his father. When Civil War broke out he joined Company I, First Texas Regiment, and was mustered into service at San Antonio March 1, 1861. This was the first company mustered into the Confederate service, and he was appointed Second Sergeant. As it was the Sergeant's duty to call the roll, he in the order of precedence answered first, and it was an accident that his company was called I, instead of A. Mr. Gates served on the upper Red River twelve months in the Indian service, and after being mustered out came home. After reorganization he went out as Waul's Legion, and was directly under Gen. Forrest skirting around Vicksburg and avoiding the siege. Later he was at Holly Springs and was wounded in the arm at Moscow, Tenn., and captured near Oxford, being imprisoned at Memphis for two months. He was there when Forrest made his famous raid on Memphis, trying to liberate Confederate prisoners. Mr. Gates almost effected the escape of himself and companions by bending the rods of the window down, but when everything was about ready the guard came and drove them back. Later he was exchanged and sent to Mobile. He was home on a sixty days' furlough, when the surrender took place. The plan was to draw lots for furloughs, but Mr. Gates received his purely for merit, not having lost a day from sickness through his entire service. On the 25th of July, 1865, he was married to Miss Adeline Duren, daughter of Wiley and Bernettie (Bird) Duren. Mr. Duren was a planter of Gonzales County and he there held the office of County Commissioner. He and wife were Methodists, and she died in 1859 and he in 1891. Mr. Gates is a Democrat in his political ideas, and has been Inspector of Animals for the county. Although often urged to run for the Legislature, he has always declined, preferring to give his undivided attention to farming and stockraising. He owns about 800 acres of land and is one of the stirring, enterprising men of the county. His marriage resulted in the birth of twelve children, ten of whom are living: Annie Jane, widow of James Ferguson; Samuel Dillard and Wiley Bird (twins); Daniel Alexander and Bernettie (twins); Ida and Ada (twins); Thomas Duren, Mabel and Amos Hardin. Mr. Gates' paternal grandfather was a member of Austin's 300, and his grandmother was the second white woman to cross the Brazos River. So rare was corn in those days that Grandfather Gates paid $25 for twenty-five quarts for seed, and lived without bread until this was planted and matured. The Gates family date their ancestors as patriots of the American Revolution.

WILLIAM GREEN. There is no more important industry in a growing city than that carried on by the lumber merchant, and he may at once be designated as one of the foremost and useful developers of a vicinity. William Green, a member of the firm of Flate & Green, lumber merchants at Shiner, is a man who is thoroughly trustworthy and reliable. Aside from his interests in the lumber business, he is one of the most extensive farmers in the county, owning 4,000 acres, about three and a-half miles from town. Mr. Green is a product of this State, born in Gonzales County in 1855, and was the eldest child born to William and India (Griffith) Green, the former a native of North Carolina and the latter of Alabama. About the year 1850 the parents came to Texas and settled in Gonzales County, where the father cultivated the soil until his death, in 1877. Mrs. Green died in 1894. Their son William was reared in Gonzales County, and after growing up, branched out for himself as a farmer and stock-raiser. He also started a store at Winton, and was made Postmaster at that place. Possessed of an unlimited amount of energy and perseverance—the secret of his success, young Green came to Shiner in 1889 and bought out a lumber business. Here he has since been engaged in that business, and, as in all other ventures he has made, has met with the best of success. He is doing an extensive business and deserves the success to which he has attained. This firm is also engaged extensively in buying, shipping and raising cattle, and does the largest business in this section. Of the 4,000 acres of good land that he owns, Mr. Green has 1,000 acres under cultivation, and has made all improvements. He also owns considerable town property. He is the most extensive farmer in all the section; a self-made man with rare executive ability to further increase his possessions, and a "hustler" for Shiner. Mr. Green was married in 1882 to Miss Julia Dickson, a native of Lavaca County and daughter of W. P. Dickson, one of the first settlers of Texas. Mr. Green is a member of the K. of P.

JOSEPH SCHWAB. Place the native German where you will and he will make a living for himself and those depending on him, for in him are ingrained those qualities which go to make the successful man, chief among which may be mentioned energy, perseverance and undoubted honesty. Although he was born in Germany in 1833, and there made his home until 1849, he is in every essential a loyal American citizen, and has identified himself with the interests of his adopted country as far as it has been possible for him to do so. Like the great majority of German youths, he was given the advantages of the common schools of Germany, and as he was apt and ready and willing to apply himself, he acquired a good practical education, amply sufficient to fit him for the ordinary duties of life. He was a youth of considerable pluck and ambition, and he early came to the conclusion that America afforded for him opportunities for rising in the world, which his native land could not do, and thither he emigrated in 1849, coming almost immediately to the Lone Star State. He joined some friends who had proceeded him, in De Witt County, and at once turned his attention to the occupation of farming, but was engaged in tilling rented land until about 1860, at which time he was married to Martha Hock, a native of Germany, who came to Texas in 1845, and soon after made his first purchase of land on the Guadalupe River. This land he successfully tilled until 1862, when his sympathies became so thoroughly enlisted in the Southern cause, that he abandoned the plow to become a votary of Mars, becoming a member of

Waul's Legion, C. S. A., and served in Mississippi. After the fall of Vicksburg he returned to Texas and once more began tilling the soil on the Gaudalupe River farm, where his home continued to be until his removal to Yoakum in 1893. In 1880 he became the proprietor of cotton gin which he took with him to Yoakum and which he has since operated with success and reasonable financial results. He is the owner of an excellent farm of 200 acres, of which 150 acres are under cultivation. In 1883 Mr. Schwab was called upon to mourn the death of his first wife, after she had borne him twelve children, and in 1888 he was married a second time, to Miss Mary Ann Jacobs, who is an earnest and devoted member of the Baptist Church. Mr. Schwab's parents were Valentine and Mary (Sanger) Schwab, natives of the Fatherland and farmers by occupation.

JOHN L. CONNALLY. He whose name heads this sketch has been a potential element in the civilization and development of Texas, and has identified himself heart and soul with the interests of this section and has always been one of its most substantial, law abiding and progressive citizens.

He was born in Alabama, in December, 1819, the son of John Connally, who was a Virginian by birth and one of the early settlers of Northern Alabama. He opened an hotel there which became known as the Green Bottom Inn, and which became a favorite resort of travelers of that day. Gen. Jackson often stopped there, and he was a personal friend of Mr. Connally's, and he would often run his own horses on the fine race track owned by the latter. Mr. Connally was extensively engaged in the raising of race horses, and bred many famous horses, among them being the world renowned "John Bascomb," named by consent after Rev. Henry Bascomb; "Bill Austin," "Red Mariah," "Longfellow," "Mollie Long," and many others. Throughout his entire life Mr. Connally was a great admirer of Gen. Jackson, and he was always a stanch Democrat of the Jacksonian type. He was also a personal and warm friend of President Polk. He died in 1844. In the State of his birth the subject of this sketch was reared and educated, and he assisted his father on the farm and in attending to the stock, during which time his inherited love for the noble animal, the horse, was intensified and he came to thoroughly understand its management.

In 1847 he made a trip to Texas, crossing over much of the State, and passing by the San Marcos Springs he became impressed with the country and accordingly purchased 250 acres of land on the San Marcos River. He then returned to Alabama, but was taken with the "gold fever," and accordingly started for California, via the Isthmus of Panama and the Pacific Ocean. He at once went to the mines and after successfully following that occupation for about four years, he, in 1853, returned to his home by way of the Isthmus. After spending a few months in Alabama he came to Texas and settled near the town of San Marcos, but sold his first purchase of land and bought a large tract three miles southwest of town, locally known as "Stringtown." He brought with him a number of blooded horses from his father's place in Alabama, and from these animals he raised some of the best horses west of the Mississippi River. He raised "Rebel," whose sire was "Socks" from Tennessee. He became the best known horse in Texas and became the sire of a long line of running horses. Another one of his animals was "Last Chance," who was never beaten although he ran against some of the best horses; "Moonstone," another horse, became famous; "Grindstone," was sired by "Tar River," "Miss Socks," sired by "Socks" became a famous breeder, and he owned many other horses that became noted on the race course. He was very successful in his management of his race horses, which were without doubt the best blooded horses of Texas, trained them intelligently and won nearly all the races and carried off the first premiums at fairs. He introduced stock that is now represented by their posterity throughout the entire State of Texas, and his horses always sold for a high price, almost invariably for $1,000, and many times for much more. Mr. Connally was married in 1856 to Miss Joyce Rucker, a native of Tennessee, and a daughter of James Rucker, who died in Tennessee, after which his widow and children came to Texas, in 1854. The mother had formerly been married to a Mr. Johnn, by whom she became the mother of four sons, one of whom, Major Johnn, is a noted State official. She died in 1868. To Mr. and Mrs. Connally the following children were born: William, a school teacher; Lucy Bedford, wife of Tom Johnson; Edward Glover, Robert Burns, and Mary Nash, who died in infancy. Mrs. Connally is a member of the Methodist Church. During the Civil War Mr. Connally served in the Confederate army, wholly in Texas on scouting duty until the close. He then returned to his farm and built a cotton gin, and was engaged in farming, ginning and stock breeding for many years, or until his removal to San Marcos, May 15, 1889. He is a most pleasant and agreeable gentleman to meet, is social in disposition, and the many friends whom he has gathered about him, attest to his many sterling qualities and his upright and honorable mode of living.

DR. FORT P. VERSER. The noble profession of medicine affords to the student in that science a never ending source of investigation and experiment. New remedies are constantly being discovered, steady progress is being made in surgery and new diseases are presenting themselves under varying forms of civilization. Whatever may be said of the discoveries in the other fields of knowledge, and certainly they are astonishing, it can be truthfully said of this science that not one can equal it in the great strides it is making toward a comprehensive grasp of the whole subject of man, in relation to health and disease, and the prevention and cure of ills that flesh is heir to. In the noble army of workers in this great field may be found the name of Dr. Fort P. Verser, who is classed among the prominent physicians of his section. *He was born in Madison County, Tenn., the sixth of eleven children born to Daniel and Lautha (Fort) Verser, natives of the Old North State. The paternal grandfather, Nathan Verser, was also a North Carolinian, of French extraction, whose early ancestors settled in Virginia upon coming to this country. The maternal grandfather, William Fort, is supposed to have been born in North Carolina also. Daniel Verser was engaged in tilling the soil throughout life, and from 1827 until the time of his death was a resident of Madison County, Tenn. He died in 1875, at the age of eighty-three years, his wife's death occurring about 1873. Both were worthy members of the Baptist Church and active workers in the same. The paternal grandfather was a soldier of the Revolution, and bravely fought his country's battles on many fields. Dr. Fort P. Verser was reared in Madison County, Tenn., there obtained a practical education, and in 1854 began studying medicine privately, graduating in 1856 from the Eclectic Medical School at Cincinnati. Immediately thereafter he began practicing his profession in his native State, but in 1857 removed to Prairie County, Ark., where he remained successfully engaged in practice for many years. In 1861 he entered the Confederate Army, McCoy's Company, Turnbull's Regiment, in which he was offered the position of Assistant Surgeon, but on account of poor health was compelled to decline, and in a few months was discharged on account of disability, at Corinth, Miss. He had three brothers in the service: John L., who enlisted from Memphis; Calvin C., was first in Stevens' Regiment and later with Gen. Forrest, and Daniel Judgson, who was with Stevens' Regiment from Jackson, Tenn. He was killed at the battle of Shiloh, at which time he had his discharge for ill health in his pocket. He was feeling much better at the time that bloody struggle opened, and at the beginning of the battle went in as a volunteer, his death resulting from the explosion of a shell. Until January 1, 1876, Dr. Verser practiced the healing art in Arkansas, then started for Texas and located at Prairie Lea, where he has been since in the enjoyment of a good practice. He is the owner of a fine farm on the San Marcos River, on which there has been erected a handsome residence; the place is admirably improved, and seventy acres are in a fine state of cultivation. He was first married in 1861 to Miss Emma P. Murrell, a native of Tennessee, and it was owing to the fact that her health was very delicate that the family came to Texas. She, however, died in December, 1883, leaving three children: Ida, a finely educated young lady, graduated from Baylor College at Independence, after which she went to Arkansas on a visit in the spring of 1885, and died there in the fall of that year; Arthur, who is married and settled in life, and Huron Judson. The Doctor's second marriage was celebrated in May, 1885, to Mrs. Irene Lowery (*nee* Smith), a native of Louisiana and daughter of Joseph Smith, who came to Texas and settled in the vicinity of Prairie Lea. He died soon after the close of the war, and his widow survived him until October, 1893, when she passed away at the age of eighty-three years. Dr. Verser has been a member of the Baptist Church forty-eight years, joining when he was eighteen years of age. He is now a Deacon of the Church at Prairie Lea, and has been an earnest worker in the same. He is a worthy man, an able physician, and a law abiding and useful citizen.

JOHN STEEN. Pioneer and representative Texas planters, like the old landmarks, are yearly becoming scarcer, and it is a pleasure to run across one whose career runs back to 1846, the year when Mr. John Steen came to the Lone Star State. He was born in Rankin County, Miss., October 30, 1825, son of William and Mary (Enoch) Steen, and the ninth in order of birth of fourteen children. The father was a product of Mulberry District, S. C., and died near Nacogdoches in 1846, whilst on his way to southwest Texas. He was a member of the Baptist Church, as was also his wife, who died in Mississippi in 1846. In politics the father espoused the principles of the Democratic party. Grandfather Steen was in the Revolutionary War and in the battle of King's Mountain, where he was wounded. His wife, hearing of his trouble, drove an ox cart eighty miles entirely alone and carried him home for nursing. He narrowly escaped hanging by Gen. Ferguson, but a charge of the patriots at the right moment saved him and badly routed the British. After the war he removed to Tennessee, and there the close of his life was passed. His heroic wife, after his death, removed to Mississippi with her family and died there at the advanced age of eighty-eight years. John Steen, our subject, was educated in Rankin County, Miss., and when twenty-one years of age came with his father to the Lone Star State. For one year he resided in

De Witt County, and another year near Gonzales, and in 1849 bought a part of his present beautiful plantation. On that he has since resided. Mr. Steen's plantation is probably the most beautiful one in Texas. His residence, a handsome and commodious one, is located on a range of hills overlooking the valley of the Guadalupe River, where he owns 3,000 acres of arable land, ranking in fertility with the alluvial soil of the Mississippi delta. At the commencement of the war Mr. Steen was drafted, but the commander gave him an unlimited furlough. When the conscript act was passed he put in a substitute, but when this act was revoked (last year of the war), he entered the service, but did not leave the State. Eleven years previous to the war, April, 14, 1850, Mr. Steen was married to Mrs. Mahala Manning, widow of Hilliard Manning, and daughter of David and Mary Burkett, of Gonzales. Mr. and Mrs. Burkett were colonists from Missouri, and settled in Gonzales, Texas, in 1830. Both died in that county. Mrs. Steen died November 25, 1881. She was the mother of these children: James Polk, Mary Virginia, married Dr. C. Campion, of Georgia; Martha Adaline, wife of Home Haynes; Margaret Ann, wife of Hiram Brown; Sarah B., married Berry Brown; William D., John, Mahala Ophelia, wife of Sidney Johnson; Robert E., Narcissa Campion, Josephine Antoinette, wife of James North; Bartholomew and Walter E.

JOHN HALLET, (deceased.) It is a pleasure to speak of those worthy citizens whose active lives have ceased on earth, but whose influence extends still, and will continue to extend among all who knew them. This truth is doubly true when such a man has established for himself and children a reputation for integrity, character and ability. Such is the case with John Hallet, the original settler of Lavaca County, Texas. He was born in Worcestershire, England, and was the younger son of an English nobleman. When but a lad he was commissioned in the British navy, but served only a short time. Being threatened with punishment by one of the officers of the ship he climbed overboard in the night time, and swam to an American vessel in the harbor. The captain of this vessel brought him to the United States and adopted him. He was then in his twelfth year. He followed the sea with his adopted father for years, and was a volunteer in an engagement in Chesapeake Bay against the British. Later he sailed as Captain from both the ports of New York and Baltimore for several years. About the year 1808 he married, in Virginia, Miss Margaret P. Leatherbury, a native of the Old Dominion and of an old and prominent family of that State. While sailing on the ocean he lost a ship at Key West, Florida, and with the insurance money he started in business at Goliad, Texas. Soon after the Mexican government confiscated his stock, and later he retired from that business. In 1833 he became a member of the Austin colony and came to Texas, securing his league of land, on which the present town bearing his name was built. He made but few improvements, erecting but a small cabin, and died at Old Goliad in October of the same year. Three children were born to this marriage: John, was killed by the Indians in San Antonio in 1837. He was a soldier in the Texas army and was in the battle of San Jacinto. He had settled near San Antonio and was about twenty-three years of age at the time of his death; William Henry was reared in Matamoras, Mexico, from his eleventh to his twenty-first year, and then came here to his mother. Later he was sent by Gen. Johnson and Felix Houston to buy land claims in Matamoras, was arrested as a spy and confined for some time, but was finally paroled. After that nothing further was heard of him by his family; Benjamin, died in 1836, when ten years of age; and Mary Jane, the only daughter. Mrs. Hallet resided on her farm until her death in 1863, when seventy-six years of age. In 1836 a town was laid out on her place, she donating one-half the land for a town site, and it was named in her honor Hallettsville. During these early days she had the genuine pioneer spirit, and deserved great credit for her fortitude and energy. She was justly called the mother of Hallettsville. A most intelligent lady, a great reader and well posted, though in a measure self-educated. She retained her property until death and it then went to her grandchildren. Mary Jane, her youngest child, was educated at home, and when in her fifteenth year was married to Collatinus Ballard, who was born in Virginia, and who came to Texas in 1840. He started a store in Mrs. Hallet's house, and this was the first store in the whole country. In 1843 he married Miss Hallet, as stated, and became an extensive merchant. He also followed farming and stock raising to some extent. This worthy citizen was a member of the Baptist Church and died in 1867. To his marriage were born twelve children, eight of whom grew up and five are now living: James, Mary A., died when seventeen years of age; Margaret P., married W. P. Ballard, and died leaving seven children; Fredonia Jane, now the wife of Mr. Roue; Frances B., wife of M. B. Woodall; Collatinus, John L., Ezbell, died when in her twentieth year, and two others died in infancy. Mrs. Ballard now resides with her children and has forty-five grandchildren and six great-grandchildren. She has lived in Texas under the Mexican rule, through all the career of the Lone Star Republic, and has seen it become one of the most properous States of the Union. She has heard the Indian war whoops, the cry of the panther about her door, but has survived all, and now resides, respected and esteemed, in a city that has grown on her ancestors' estates. Her eldest son, James Ballard, was born in Lavaca County, in 1844, and was educated at Baylor University, Independence, and later at Waco. When the war broke out he left school and entered the Confederate army, at first in Shay's Battalion, when he served on the coast, and later in Company K, Thirty-third Texas Cavalry, when he served mainly on the coast. On his twenty-first birthday he was married to Miss Alice Ione Russell, a native of Louisiana, and a daughter of Robert C. Russell, who was an early settler in this part of the Lone Star State. Soon after marriage he began teaching, followed that for about fourteen years, mainly in Hallettsville, and then served as County Surveyor from 1888 to 1892. For some time now he has been engaged in surveying. Mr. Ballard has a fine place, partly in the town, and on it he has laid out an addition to the town. He is a member of I. O. O. F. and the A. F. & A. M. His wife is a member of the Baptist Church. To their marriage were born ten children, six of whom are living: Susan A., wife of Rev. J. W. Daniels; Beulah, wife of W. C. Baird; Mary E., Addison, Schiller, Eunice H., and four died in infancy.

DR. MARSHAL B. BENNETT. This gentleman has been a close student of his profession, and in his mission of "healing the sick" his generous treatment of his patients, his liberality and kindness of heart, have won for him not the respect alone, but the earnest regard of the large clientele which he has gathered around him. The family physician, he becomes also in scores of cases the family adviser in matters of business and affairs other than of a professional nature. He was born in Tuscola, Ala., in 1820, a son of Stephen and Mary (Breazeal) Bennett, natives of the Palmetto State, who removed to Alabama in 1818, the paternal ancestors being of Irish, and the maternal ancestors of Scotch descent. Stephen Bennett removed to Texas in 1840, and for three years was a resident of Washington County, after which he moved to Gonzales County and bought the Whitson League at 25 cents per acre, which place he cleared, improved and made of it a very valuable farm. He resided there until 1877. His wife, who was born in 1800, died in 1880, and he himself lived to be nearly ninety-five years of age. He was an old line Whig politically, and was one of the pioneers of Alabama and also of Texas. The subject of this sketch was educated in Tuscaloosa University, Alabama, from which institution he was graduated in 1839, after which he at once began the study of medicine, attending his first course of lectures in Louisville, Ky., from which place he came to Texas in 1840. In 1841 he went before the Board of Medical Censors—Asa Hoxice of Independence, W.P. Miller of Fort Bond, J.P. Henderson of Marshal—and by them was given a permit to practice medicine, which he at once proceeded to do at Mount Vernon, then the county seat of Washington County, Texas. In 1842 he went with Capt. Sam Beauregard on the Vasques campaign, during which the Mexicans retreated, and in the fall of the same year was in the Woll campaign. After returning from this campaign, Dr. Bennett settled at Gonzales and practiced there till May, 1846, when he volunteered in Ben McCollouch's Company at Matamoras, and was appointed Assistant Surgeon of Hays' Regiment. He served throughout this war, and was in the battles of the Northern campaign in Taylor's Army. Upon his return, he located in Lavaca County, and was instrumental in securing the county seat at Hallettsville, where he erected the second house in the place and made his home for thirty years. He opened a drug store at that point, and consequently was the first merchant of the place. During the time that he resided there he was the leading physician of the county, having thoroughly fitted himself for the profession by graduating from a well known medical institution of New Orleans in 1858. He was strongly opposed to secession and the Civil War, but did not take sides during the struggle. He has been a Mason since 1843, at which time he joined the lodge at La Grange, Texas, having now attained to the Royal Arch degree. He is the owner of a farm of 228 acres, of which 100 acres are under cultivation, and has always given considerable attention to stock raising, which he has found both an agreeable occupation and one profitable financially. He moved to Yoakum in 1892 and is now engaged in a lucrative practice, his long experience adding much to his popularity. In 1859 he married Mrs. Mattie Harmon, of Hallettsville, who died in 1861, leaving one son, William H. He was married in August, 1863, to Miss Carrie West, daughter of Dr. Isaac West, of Washington County, by whom he has two children, Steve Lee and Sallie, of San Antonio, Texas. The doctor is a gentleman of the old school, agreeable, sociable and exceptionally well informed.

MAJOR CLEMENT READ JOHNS (deceased). In the death of this gentleman, which occurred July 30, 1886, Texas lost one of the most striking types of her early citizens. The profound sorrow which was expressed from every corner of his own State, as well as from all parts of the Union, from business men whose confidence he enjoyed, indicated the high esteem in which he was held. He was born in Rutherford County, Tenn., in 1816, of Welsh-English parentage, and upon arriving at a suitable age entered Jackson College, where he took a complete course in particular branches. Soon after his graduation, in 1836, he became attracted by the reports from Texas, and being fired with praiseworthy ambition, he left his home for new fields of enterprise, and opened up a farm on Red River. In the fall of the same year he assisted in the work of extending the jurisdiction of Texas (then a Republic) over a portion of the territory that had been a part of Arkansas. He soon enlisted in the border warfare of the Lone Star State, was appointed Brigade Inspector, with the rank of Major, and held the position from 1837 to 1845, and did effective service in expelling the hostile Indians from that field. In 1840 he became a member of the Fifth Congress of the Republic, and was the author of several very important bills. In 1846 he settled on a farm in Hays County, and his bachelor home became noted for its hospitality. In 1852 he wedded Amanda F. Durham, of San Marcos, and their life together was an exceptionally happy one and was blessed with healthy, intelligent and handsome children. The latch-string of his hospitable home was always on the outside, and friend or stranger, rich or poor, received a cheerful and hearty welcome. In 1858 he was elected to the office of Comptroller of Public Accounts of the State, which office he held three successive terms, and discharged his duties with marked ability and distinction. In 1861 he was sent, by special act of the Legislature, to collect a sum due the State by the United States, but owing to the fact that several States had seceded from the Union the claim was not allowed. While holding the position of Comptroller under Governor Houston some wordy duels were exchanged between them in regard to the duties of Mr. Johns, in which the latter almost invariably proved himself to be in the right, the result being that these gentlemen were estranged for several years, but they eventually became reconciled. In 1861 Major Johns became a member of the Military Board, and at once began the work of securing military supplies of all kinds for the defense of the State, and the sound and practical judgment which he displayed during this crisis was fully appreciated. In 1865 he retired from the office of Comptroller and returned to his home, for the fresh breezes and blue waters of which he had sighed while faithfully performing his professional duties; but as the war had left him broken in fortune, and with a growing family to be educated, he leased his farm to his former slaves and moved to Austin. He established a real estate and collecting agency business, and after a time added banking and exchange, and his business was eventually carried on under the name of the well known firm of C. R. Johns & Co. In 1876, owing to financial depression, the firm was compelled to make an assignment, and from that time up to the day of his death he was engaged in various occupations, the latest association being with the corporation of C. R. Johns & Sons in the Texas State Agency, established May 12, 1884. While not a member of any church, he loved to listen to broad, liberal views of tolerant and enlightened men that he heard from the pulpit, and his own views, while not orthodox with strict church creeds, embraced all the necessary principles for correct living. His reverence for the Deity was a part of his nature, and his love for his wife, who came to him in her girlhood, never wavered. As a father, his kindness and solicitude for the success and honor of his children, while not without parallel, was perfect. Strict justice and liberality characterized his dealings with his fellow-man; he was the soul of honor in his business transactions, and his clients' interests were faithfully and carefully guarded. He disliked ostentation, and many of his numerous acts of charity remained unnoticed and unknown save by their recipients. He was a noble character, and it may be summed up in a few words that he was a good, generous, pure, just and great man. Texas losing him, sustained a great loss, and his many noble deeds and traits of character will never be forgotten by those among whom he lived so long.

CAPT. JONATHAN NIX. Intelligence, integrity and system are qualities which will advance the interests of any man or profession and will tend to the prosperity to which all aspire. The life of Jonathan Nix, in the professional arena, has been characterized by intelligence, sound judgment and persevering industry. He is one of Caldwell County's most popular and capable attorneys, who has acquired prominence on the wings of that section's prosperity. He was born in Mississippi in 1824, to Solomon and Elinor (Johnson) Nix, both of whom were natives of South Carolina, the former being of English descent. They were early residents of Mississippi, and from there moved to West Tennessee, Henry County, and about 1842, the father came to Texas and made his home in Lamar County until his death which occurred about 1845. His widow died in Williamson County in 1855. Jonathan Nix was about eighteen years old when the family moved to Texas, and in the private schools of his native State, Tennessee, and in Texas, he received a practical education. He came to this State about 1840, with an elder brother Benjamin, and after a short residence in Lamar, he moved to Grayson County, and in 1845 came to the western part of the State. He joined Capt. Cady's company of Rangers, at the city of Austin, Texas, and in July, 1846, was attached to the troops for the Mexican War, advanced to the Rio Grande River and took the town of Presidio, a few miles inland from Eagle Pass. The Regiment was then ordered back to San Antonio, and in the fall of 1846 the men were discharged. Mr. Nix then spent one year in Grayson County and in December, 1847, came to Lockhart, then known as Lockhart Springs. Very soon afterwards he engaged in merchandising, and in 1851 was appointed Clerk of the District Court, was soon after elected Justice of the Peace and filled both offices until the fall of 1853. He was then admitted to the bar and began his long career as a legal practitioner. In 1861 he assisted in organizing a company, which became a portion of Sibley's Brigade, and he was elected First Lieutenant. He was in the New Mexico Campaign and took part in the battle of Val Verde and Glorietta, and in July, 1862, returned to San Antonio. He was elected Captain while on that campaign and was afterwards in Texas until after the battle of Galveston, after which he went to Louisiana. After skirmishing around in that State, he returned to Texas and left the service on account of poor health. He was soon after elected District Attorney, an office he held until the war closed, after which he resumed the practice of his profession. In 1859 he formed a law partnership with L. J. Story, which was interrupted by the war, but which was resumed after the close of hostilities and continued until 1887. In 1871, Capt. Nix also engaged in merchandising once more, under the firm name of Blanks, Nix & Story, and afterwards under other firm names, and in 1880, it became J. Nix & Co., and although Mr. Story retired in 1890 the firm name still continues. In 1872 or '73 he also started a banking house, which was conducted for several years.

BATTLE OF
SHILOH,
April 6, 1862.

One Mile

N
W E
S

Road to Crump's Landing
Impassible
Snake Cr.
W. H. L. Wallace's Division
Brier Cr.
Field
Pittsburg Landing
TENNESSEE RIVER
Lexington
Purdy Road
Mill
McClernand's Division
Sherman's Division
Hurlbut's Division
Oak Cr.
Shiloh Ch.
The Hornet's Nest
Prentiss' Division
Upper Landing
Polk's Corps
Hospital
Corinth Road
Hospital
Stuart's Brigade
Bragg's Corps
Cotton Press
Breckenridge's Reserve
Hardee's Corps
Lick Cr.

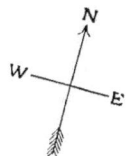

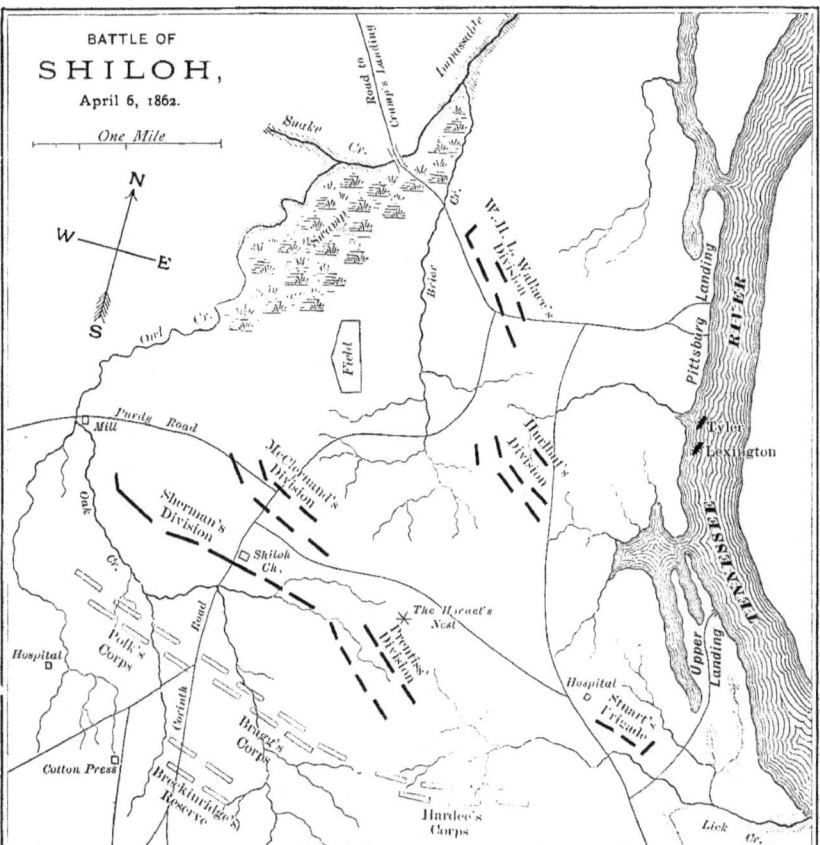

POSITIONS
LATE ON THE EVENING
OF THE 6TH.

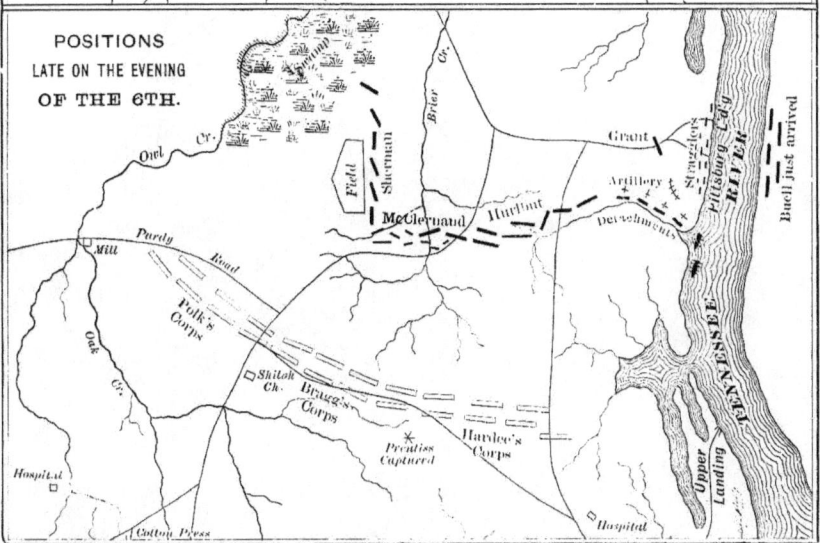

Owl Cr.
Sherman
Brier Cr.
Field
Grant
Artillery
Stragglers
Pittsburg Ldg.
Buell just arrived
TENNESSEE RIVER
McClernand
Hurlbut
Detachments
Purdy Road
Mill
Polk's Corps
Oak Cr.
Shiloh Ch.
Bragg's Corps
Prentiss Captured
Hardee's Corps
Upper Landing
Hospital
Cotton Press
Hospital

He has been a very enterprising and public spirited man all his life, and has been an active worker for the Democratic party and a delegate to various State conventions. He has been quite extensively engaged in stock raising and owns a ranch and a large drove of graded stock in this county. July 1, 1849, he was married to Miss Mary L. Witter, a native of Tennessee and a daughter of Dr. Witter, who located in Gonzales at an early day, and was killed by Indians in a raid on that place. To Captain and Mrs. Nix four children have been born: Warren, Austin, Julia, wife of John T. Story, and John L. who died in infancy. Being one of the earliest settlers of Lockhart, Capt. Nix has always worked for the good of his section, and has made his way from limited circumstances and obscurity, to a prominent and substantial position in life. He was a brave and fearless soldier, is a shrewd, practical and successful lawyer, and is one of the substantial citizens of Caldwell County. Socially he is a member of the A. F. & A. M., and his wife is a worthy member of the Christian Church.

JOHN JOHNSON. The exhaustless pages of history fail to disclose an older or more honorable calling than that of the agriculturist, and few, if any, among those engaged in this calling at the present time, maintain a higher reputation for integrity and reliability than Mr. John Johnson. He is a native Virginian, born in Fauquier County, November 17, 1837, to the union of Thomas Y. and Fannie (Petty) Johnson, both natives of Virginia, and the father of Welsh and mother of Scotch descent. All his life the father followed planting and died in his native State when seventy-two years of age. The mother died in 1868. Their son, John Johnson, was educated in the Old Dominion, attending the Clifton High School, in the class with Robert E. Lee, jr., but was prevented from taking a collegiate course owing to the breaking out of war. He left his books and enlisted in the Fourth Virginia Cavalry, his company acting as body guard to Stonewall Jackson, and served as a private throughout the war. He served as courier to Jackson at the battle of Antietam, and, at the battle of Chancellorsville, carried a dispatch to Gen. Lee telling that the enemy was flanking. At Antietam he was wounded. Stonewall Jackson had very few staff officers, and private soldiers frequently performed the duties usually done by officers. At Antietam Mr. Johnson was with him during the whole day and carried verbal messages to the different Generals under his command. The flank movement was at the bloody battle of Chancellorsville. Gen. Hooker and Gen. Lee were on opposite sides of the Rappahannock River. Mr. Johnson, with several of his company, was scouting behind the Federal lines, and, discovering Hooker's Army marching up the river to attack Lee's left flank, immediately notified Gen. Lee, who marched up the River on the other side, and the battle of Chancellorsville followed. While the army was in Fauquier County young Johnson acted as guide to Gen. Jackson. He participated in all the important battles in Virginia, except the Battle of The Wilderness, and was captured near Warrenton, but imprisoned at Fort Delaware, where he was held until three months after the surrender. When twenty-eight years of age he came to Texas, and after a short stay in Fort Bend, located in Gonzales County, where he has remained up to the present time. As an agriculturist and stock raiser, he has met with success, and as a citizen and neighbor has the respect and esteem of all. Mr. Johnson's happy domestic relations began in 1869, when he married Miss Cinthelia Lord, daughter of George and Kate Lord, (see

10

sketch). This union has resulted in the birth of nine children: Cora A., Thomas W., Charles R., Zetta M., John H., Fannie E., Bessie L., Everett S., Mona B., George H. and Kate. The last two are deceased.

HON. M. S. TOWNSEND. A great deal of very desirable and most advantageously located property is to be found on the books of the gentleman whose name heads this sketch, who is now not only the popular Mayor of Hallettsville, Texas, but a very successful and reliable real estate dealer. Moses Solon Townsend was born in Colorado County, Texas, April 29th, 1864, and his parents, Moses S. and Annie E. (Harvey) Townsend, were natives of Georgia and Tennessee respectively. His grandfather, Asa Townsend, came to Texas from Georgia in 1836. In this family there were eight brothers, who settled in Colorado and Fayette Counties, and they all married and reared families. Many of their descendants now reside in this section. When our subject was three years old his father died; the mother married again in 1874. She died in 1879. Moses S. grew up in his native county, received his education there and at A. & M. College, Bryan, where he attended the sessions of 1881-2-3, and in 1884 he attended the Capital Business College at Austin, from which he subsequently graduated. Following that he taught two months in the school and then became telegraph operator for the Southern Pacific Railroad Company for two years. In August, 1887, he went to Yoakum as agent of the S. A. & A. P. R. R., and was in charge of this office until February, 1888, after which he was transferred to Hallettsville. This office he had charge of until May, 1890, when he resigned. In April of the same year he was elected Alderman and served until December 15 when, having been elected Mayor to fill the vacancy occasioned by the death of Mayor Jesse Green, he entered that office. In April of the following year he was re-elected for the full term and again elected in 1893, without opposition. He is now holding his third term. Since Mr. Townsend has held this position the water works system and the electric light plant were put in, and a general spirit of advancement prevails. A system of sewerage is now being put in. Mr. Townsend is the right man in the right place and as such is looked upon by all. He studied law for some time and was admitted to the bar in 1891. Socially he is a K. P., is Past Chancellor, and during the last year, and is now, Deputy Grand Chancellor. In April, 1889, he was married to Miss Mary A. Fink, born in LaGrange, Fayette County, Texas, March 30th, 1868, and daughter of Casper and Louise Fink, who came to this State about 1848. Mr. and Mrs. Townsend have two children: August Emmett, born January 11th, 1891, and Moses Solon, Jr., born August 9th, 1893. Early in 1890 Mr. Townsend erected his residence in the West End, and has one of the pleasantest homes in the city. He was one of the first organizers and one of the first board of directors of the Arctic Ice Company, of Hallettsville. He was also one of the organizers of the Lavaca Oil Mill Company. Mr. Townsend is now engaged in the real estate business and has several desirable tracts of land in and around town. He has sixty acres near town, part in pasture, and on this he has some blooded Jersey cattle. This prominent citizen was also one of the original stockholders in the Citizens' Building and Loan Association. He is active in all things necessary for the good of the town, is popular with the people, and well deserves the success that has rewarded his efforts. He is a brother of State Senator M. H. Townsend, of Columbus, Texas, and is a member of the State Democratic Executive

Committee, elected for two years commencing August, 1894. He has three brothers: M. H., H. L. and E. L. Townsend, and a half sister, Rebecca Grace Waller.

DR. ADAM J. BEALL. There are always in the medical profession some individuals who become eminent and command a large patronage, and among those deserving special recognition is Dr. Adam J. Beall, whose face is a familiar one in the home of the sick and afflicted. He was born in Georgia September 15, 1827, the tenth of thirteen children born to Thaddeus and Mary W. (Jones) Beall, who were natives of the Old North State and Georgia respectively. The father was engaged in merchandising during the early part of his life, but afterwards gave his attention to farming. He removed to Alabama in 1836, and in that State made his home until 1865. The paternal grandfather, Thaddeus Beall, is supposed to have been born in England of Scotch-Welsh parents, and upon coming to this country resided in Georgetown, Md., for some time, but prior to the revolution moved to North Carolina, and from that State served as an officer in the struggle with the mother country. In private life he was a farmer and a man of good repute. The maternal grandfather, Adam Jones, was a Virginian, but removed to South Carolina prior to the opening of the Revolutionary War and participated throughout that entire struggle of seven years. He afterwards moved to Georgia, where he tilled the soil until his death. In Alabama Dr. Adam J. Beall was reared, and in Lafayette he secured a good classical education. In 1848 he removed to Louisiana, and there began the study of medicine, and the following year took a medical course in the University of New Orleans. Following this he returned to Georgia, and for some time studied with his cousin, Dr. J. Beall, and in 1850-51 he pursued his medical investigations in the University of Pennsylvania at Philadelphia, from which institution he graduated in the last mentioned year. Until the fall of that year he practiced his profession with his cousin in Georgia, then went to De Soto Parish, La., and was in practice there some thirty-five years or more. He was one of the pioneer physicians of that section and built up a practice there that extended over a wide territory. He was the only physician left in that section during the war; consequently his work was arduous. The war left him greatly crippled financially, but he once more commenced at the bottom of the ladder, and has retrieved his fallen fortunes. He was at the battle of Pleasant Hill, and attended to many of the wounded thereafter. In 1887 he came to San Marcos, and is now the second oldest physician in practice here, and is popular and well liked. He is a close student of his profession, is able, experienced and conscientious in his work, and therefore deserves the success with which his efforts have been rewarded. He inherits the liberal stature, fine physique, commanding presence and robust constitution for which the Beall family are noted, and is a genial, whole-souled gentleman, charitable and kindly-hearted, and is a favorite in social circles. Although he has passed through many epidemics of contagious diseases he never contracted any, his fine constitution and wise precautions being his safeguards. He was first married in 1851, to Miss Annie E. Sanders, a niece of Rev. Billington Sanders, of Georgia, founder of Penfield College, and daughter of D. Sanders, of Macon, Ga. She died in 1869, leaving five children: Kate, wife of S. B. Lee, of Louisiana; Billington S., who died in early youth in Louisiana; Joseph A., studied medicine with his father, graduated from the University of Louisville, Ky., in 1889 or 1890, and is now associated with his father in San Marcos; Edwin F., studied medicine also, graduated from an institution of New Orleans in 1890 and subsequently took a post-graduate course in New York City, after which he practiced his profession at Coushatta, Red River Parish, La., but is now associated with his father at San Marcos; and Nettie. Br. Beall's second marriage was celebrated June 5, 1870, Miss Emma H. Durham becoming his wife. She was born in South Carolina, and is the granddaughter of an officer of the Revolutionary War, lost two brothers in the Mexican War and one in the late Civil War, he being a member of the Confederate Army. Mrs. Beall is a member of the Baptist Church. The Bealls are a family of physicians, and Dr. E. J. Beall, of Fort Worth, Texas, is a cousin of the subject of this sketch, and a son of the latter's early preceptor. He is a physician of National reputation, is one of the most skillful in the United States, is a deep and earnest student and possesses fine literary tastes. He is especially skilled in surgery, and has successfully performed many dangerous and difficult operations.

HON. M. R. STRINGFELLOW. He whose name heads this sketch has become prominent in the legal profession and is well known as one of the most talented legal lights in his section of the State. He comes of good old Virginia stock and first saw the light of day in the Old Dominion in 1840, being the third of four children born to Robert and Eliza (Martin) Stringfellow, and a grandson of James Stringfellow and William Martin, all of whom were Virginians by birth. The last mentioned was a soldier of the War of 1812, and was of English-Scotch and Irish descent. Robert Stringfellow was a worthy tiller of the soil and his entire life was spent in the State of his birth, where he filled the position of Justice of the Peace for many years. The immediate subject of this sketch was educated by private tutors until 1860, when he entered the University of Virginia, where he remained one year, then dropped his books to become a votary of Mars, joining, as a private, a company of students commanded by Capt. J. Parron Crane, which became a part of Wise's Brigade in West Virginia. This company was disbanded in the month of December, 1861, and in the spring of 1862 he enlisted in a company belonging to the Eleventh Virginia Infantry, Company I, and during part of the time was Orderly Sergeant. He was with Gen. Lee at the time of the surrender. He was, participant in the battles of Williamsburg, Seven Pines and Frazier Farm, and was there captured and taken to Fort Delaware, where he was kept a prisoner for six weeks and then paroled, and soon after exchanged. During the latter part of the war he was on clerical duty at headquarters. After his return home he worked with his father on the farm for some time, then taught school for a year or two, and in 1867 came to Texas, and during 1867, 1868 and 1870 was engaged in teaching school in Caldwell County, during which time he also pursued the study of law, and in 1869 was admitted to the bar at Lockhart and to the Supreme Court bar in 1872. In 1880 he was elected to the Seventeenth General Assembly from Caldwell County, and while filling this responsible position he was on the Committee on Internal Improvements, the Judiciary Committee and also the Committees on Roads, Bridges, Elections, etc. During this session, a bill regulating railroad traffic was introduced by him, but did not become a law. In 1872 he was married to Miss Texie Early, who died in 1885, leaving three children: Early, Emma, and Bruce, wife of R. R. Salter, a resident of Colorado. Mr. Stringfellow's second marriage occurred in 1886, and was to Mrs. Emma Wiley, a sister of his first wife. One son has been born of this union: Robert. Mr. Stringfellow is a member of the Episcopal Church and is a Royal Arch Mason. The cause of education has always found him to be a hearty supporter, and he has been a member of the School Board, and in 1874 and 1875 Superintendent of Schools in this county, and he was the first to grade teachers' certificates. In 1878 he, with several others purchased a couple of carloads of thoroughbred shorthorn cattle, which was about the first improved stock ever introduced into the county. Mr. Stringfellow has been very successful in the practice of his profession, is a genial, public spirited and enterprising gentleman and is a most excellent and useful citizen. His career has been characterized by the most honorable principles and by a desire to do what was right at all times.

THOMAS CARTER. In him is found a man whose career through life is a decidedly interesting one, showing the shrewdness, business ability and competency which can be attained by the natives of other countries. Thomas Carter is a prominent capitalist of Gonzales County, Texas, and a man who wields considerable influence in his section. He is a typical representative of the English race, honest and upright, energetic and progressive, and of a decidedly practical turn of mind. Mr. Carter was born in Leicestershire, England, April 27, 1822, just the day on which Gen. Grant was born, and his parents, Thomas and Jane (Jacques) Carter, were both natives of that shire. The father's principal occupation in life was farming, and he carried it on in his native country until his death. There the mother received her final summons, too. They were upright, honest people, and both were charmingly genial and cordial in their home. In his native country Thomas Carter received a good practical education, and subsequently became a commercial traveler, following the road for a number of years. The advantages to be derived from a residence in the States caused him to leave the land of his birth in about 1852 and cross the ocean. He settled on a farm near La Grange, Texas, and there made his home for a period of thirty-eight years, meeting with success in his chosen calling and winning the regard and respect of all. In 1890 he removed to Gonzales County, where two of his sons had preceded him, and there he resides at the present time. Wherever he makes his home Mr. Carter is well liked for his many qualities of mind and heart, and he has already won many friends in this section. In his political views he adheres to the principles of the Democratic party. He has been school trustee. In the year 1848 he was married to Miss Mary Garrett, who died in 1852. In 1857 Mr. Carter married Miss Mary Arnold, who has borne him seven children, as follows: Mary, wife of Robert Allert, and Eliza (twins); Joseph, Arthur, Anna, wife of Sam. Dickens; Lancelot A. and Sarah Jane.

DR. H. S. CLARK. This early settler and physician of Lavaca County, Texas, was born in Tennessee, in 1834, and was second of seven children born to Isaac C. and Mary A. (McCleary) Clark, natives of North Carolina and Tennessee, respectively. The paternal grandfather, Robert Clark, was a native of the Old North State and a pioneer of Tennessee, where he was one of the first settlers of Tipton County. He was a planter and in that county spent the balance of his days. Isaac E. Clark was but a boy when he came with his father to Tennessee, and he has lived in Tipton County ever since. He was quite prominent in county affairs, held county offices for about thirty years, and now resides on the old homestead. He is almost ninety years of age. The mother died during the war. Her father, James A. McCleary, was a native of Georgia, and of Scotch descent. He came to Tennessee at a very early day, settled in Tipton County, and there spent the remainder of his life. Dr. H. S. Clark received his scholastic training in Covington, Tenn., under James Byars, a noted educator of that State, who is now teaching a select class of young men of that city. In 1848 our subject began reading medicine and later graduated at Jefferson College, Philadelphia, in the spring of 1854. He then came to Texas, located at Fairfield, and there practiced his profession for four years. For five years after that he resided in Polk County, and in 1862 he entered the Confederate Army as surgeon of Ford's Brigade, and served with him in Texas, on the coast and on the Rio Grande. He was in the last battle of the war, near Brownsville. After the war he located in Lavaca County, on his present place, seven miles North of Hallettsville. He at first bought 300 acres, but year by year he increased his possessions until he became the owner of the 1,000 acres, 600 of which is under cultivation. He has erected a handsome residence and has made all the improvements Dr. Clark is now extensively engaged in rearing trotting horses, and has, on the authority of S. D. Bruce, author of the "American Stud Book," one of the best bred stallions in America—the stallion Depew, by Almont Jr., a brother to Bell Hamlin, with a record of 2:12. Dr. Clark has five standard bred mares registered, and has colts in training. Dr. Clark was first married in the fall of 1854 to Miss Cleopatra A. Robinson, a native of Tennessee. She died in 1866, leaving three children: Minnie Willie, wife of W. E. Myers, of Floresville; Isaac E., a physician of Schulenburg; was educated by Prof. Byers of Covington, Ky., his father's old instructor, and Marietta, wife of M. W. Punell, of Gonzales. The doctor was married again in 1867 to Miss Mary Edds, a native of Alabama. He is a member of the State Medical Association and his son is Vice-president of the same. Our subject has practically retired from practice and now devotes most of his time to the management of his fine estate. There are few handsomer places in the county.

DR. JAMES HENRY COMBS. The dentist when well up in his profession is a most valuable man in any community, and in Hays County, Texas, there are none who rank higher than Dr. James H. Combs. He commands a thorough knowledge of his profession, and his ability and insight into his calling have won him a large and constantly increasing practice. He is a product of the State of Missouri, and there first saw the light in 1841, being the youngest of five children born to David B. and Rebecca (Burras) Combs, who were natives of the Blue Grass State. They removed to Missouri in 1834, settling in Johnson County, where the father followed the occupation of farming and was also engaged in the manufacture of tobacco. He died in 1841, after which his widow married D. R. Cocreham, with whom she came to San Marcos, Texas, in 1845, and soon after purchased land in the vicinity of Stringtown where Mr. Combs engaged in tilling the soil and stock raising for many years, but now resides in San Marcos. The mother died, December 31, 1891. The paternal grandfather, David Combs, was an early settler of Kentucky, and was a Captain in the Indian wars of that

State at an early day. He came originally from Virginia, as did also David Burras, of Kentucky, the maternal grandfather of the subject of this sketch. In the public schools of Texas, James Henry Combs obtained a practical education, but his school days were cut short by the opening of the Civil War, for he at once dropped his books to enter the Confederate service, becoming a member of Company E, Sixth Texas Infantry, and after the capture of Arkansas Post, being assigned to Company H, Seventeenth Consolidated Texas Regiment, served in the trans-Mississippi Department. He was in the battle of Harrisburg, La., also in other engagements of considerable note, and took part in numerous skirmishes till the battle of Mansfield, when he was severely wounded and left on the field of battle. This wound incapacitated him from further duty in the infantry, and he was detailed to the Commissary Department in which he served until the close. He had four brothers in the service: John Wesley was wounded at Port Hudson and later assigned to duty in the Commissary Department in Texas, with the rank of Captain; David S. was a member of Terry's Rangers until the war closed; John William and Sylvester Cocreham were in the Fifteenth Texas Cavalry, and the former died at Little Rock, Ark. in 1862. Sylvester was taken prisoner at Arkansas Post, was exchanged at City Point, Va., and was soon after killed in the battle of Chicamauga. After returning from the war, James H. Combs was engaged in farming for a few years, then began the study of dentistry and entered upon the practice of Dentistry at San Marcos in 1868, and has since done remarkably well in following this calling. He was married in November, 1864, to Miss Fannie Dailey, a native of Georgia and a daughter of David Dailey, who came to this State in 1855 and followed the occupation of farming, practicing medicine and preaching the gospel, being a minister of the Methodist Church. He died in 1873, a well known and highly esteemed citizen. His wife was Mary E. Lamar, a member of the well known Lamar family of Georgia. To the union of Dr. and Mrs. Combs twelve children have been given, three of whom are deceased: John William studied dentistry with his father and graduated at Vanderbilt University, and is now practicing his profession at San Marcos; David A. also graduated in dentistry at that institution, and is at present associated with his father and brother in San Marcos. Their offices are fitted up in excellent taste, are beautiful and comfortable, and they have also an office in New Braunfels; Henry B. graduated in medicine from the Medical Department of Vanderbilt University, and is now practicing at Bastrop, Texas; Robert Lee was educated at the Philadelphia Dental College, and is now located at Seguin, Texas, engaged in the practice of his profession; James F. is a student in the schools of San Marcos; Kay died at the age of two years; Marvin and Lizzie are students at Coronal Institute, San Marcos; Mary E., wife of O. E. DuBose, of Marlin, Texas; and two children who died unnamed. In 1893 Dr. Combs erected a fine business building, two stories in height, on the Public Square, in which they have their offices, besides which he owns other buildings and residence property, and has a comfortable, commodious and handsome home. He and his family are members of the Methodist Church and since 1872 he has been an officer in the church, and has been a member of the annual and general conferences. He has been Sunday School Superintendent since 1883, and has been active in all church work. In 1884 he was elected to the State Legislature; was an active member of that body, and served on the committees of Education, Public Health, and other special committees. Dr. Combs has always been interested in educational matters, and upon the organization of Coronal Institute he was elected trustee, and has served in that capacity ever since. He is one of the most enterprising citizens of the county, is a courteous and agreeable gentleman, is a skillful and successful dentist, and was one of the organizers of the "San Marcos Chautauqua," the first institution of the kind in Texas, and for a number of years he has been one of the Board of Directors.

DR. GEORGE CASE MILNER, physician and surgeon, has been a resident of the Lone Star State since 1883. He came originally from Georgia, his birth occurring in Madison County, of that State, June 2, 1859, and of the ten children born to his parents, Robert W. and Sarah (Lane) Milner, he was fourth in order of birth. The father was a minister of the Old School Presbyterian Church, and a North Carolinian by birth. When a child he came with his parents to Georgia, and attended Oglethorpe Seminary, at Milledgeville, Georgia. His death occurred in Clinton, South Carolina, in 1889. The mother is alive at this writing. Dr. George C. Milner received a good, practical education in Athens, and later attended the University of Georgia, the Medical Department of the University of Georgia, at Augusta, Ga., where he received his diploma in 1882. He practiced in different points in Georgia and the South, and came to Texas in 1883, as before stated. For three years he practiced in Concrete, and then moved to Cheapside, where he has since practiced. In his political views he affiliates with the Democratic party, and is deeply interested in the welfare of the same. In the year 1884 he married Miss Rosalie Miller, daughter of Michael and Mildred (Webb) Miller, of DeWitt County. Mr. Miller was one of the first settlers of the lower Guadalupe, and a prominent planter and stock raiser. His death occurred in 1885. His wife is still living. To Dr. and Mrs. Milner were born two interesting children, Robert M. and Chauncey.

COL. WILLIAM LINDSEY, (deceased). There is little need to portray the virtues or defend the memory of this gentleman, for he lives in the affection of his family and friends as a kind husband and father, an accommodating neighbor, and a public spirited and useful citizen. During the many years of his residence in Texas, he was to the people all that is required in good citizenship, public enterprise and sympathetic friendship. In the love of his family he found his cares lightened, and in the respect of his fellow-citizens he received the reward of his faithfulness.

He was born in Georgia, May 17, 1801, and was married in that State to Mary Chandler, after which he devoted his attention to tilling the soil, and also worked in the gold mines to some extent. In 1837 he came to Texas on a prospecting tour, and began surveying land on Galveston Island, and also inland to San Antonio, and being pleased with the appearance of the country, he, in 1839, brought his family thither and located them at San Antonio. In 1848 he came to San Marcos, in the vicinity of which place he owned a large body of land. He assisted in laying out the town of San Marcos, and until death in November, 1852, he resided in this place, and identified himself with its interests. His wife died while they were residing in San Antonio, after having borne him six children, of whom the following grew to maturity: Louisiana., William F., Andrew M., Mary E., and Queene E., now a resident of San Marcos. William, Andrew and Mary are dead. The two sons served in the Confederate Army during the war, and Andrew died about the close of that period. William died in the early '70's. Louisiana was married in 1842 to U. N. Blair, a native of Alabama, who was engaged in tilling the soil until his death, in 1843. To this union one child was given, Mary S., who died in infancy. Mrs. Blair afterwards married again, becoming the wife of Harbert S. Harvey, a native of Alabama, who came to Texas in the fall of 1839. He first settled in Washington County; in 1845 removed to Fayette County, and was married there in 1846 to Mrs. Blair. After coming to San Marcos he engaged in farming, or rather continued that occupation, and accumulated a comfortable competency. He did his full share in the settlement and improvement of this section, and his death, which occurred January 2, 1894, was a source of much regret to all who knew him. He served in the Texas Rebellion; socially, was a member of the I. O. O. F., and had long been connected with the Presbyterian Church. His union with Mrs. Blair resulted in the birth of the following children: Mary Elizabeth, who died at the age of five years; William Duncan, who died at the age of six years; Andrew F., who died when twenty-four years old, and Alice. While living in San Antonio, in 1840, Mrs. Harvey witnessed the entire Indian battle in the Court House there, in which eight white men and thirty-three Indians were killed. This was one of the most tragic events in the history of that time, or that ever occurred in that historic city. Mrs. Harvey and her sister, Miss Queene Lindsey, are the only living members of their father's family, and both reside in San Marcos.

BENJAMIN FRANKLIN BAKER, one of the representative farmers and stock raisers of Gonzales County, Texas, is a native of this county, and has here spent the most of his days. In him the county has found one of its most earnest, industrious citizens, ever ready with his means to further all worthy movements. Mr. Baker was born December 4, 1858, and was fourth in a family of five children born to Thomas and Eliza (Winn) Baker. The father was a native of Alabama, and when but an infant was brought to Mississippi by his parents. There he was reared and apprenticed to learn the carpenter trade, serving seven years in Natchez, Miss. He then engaged in carpentering, and continued this until twenty-nine years of age, when, in partnership with P. G. Fulcher, he started for California. Reaching Gonzales, Texas, he fell in love with the country, and concluded to locate in this section. He sent back for his wife, and boarded with W. V. Collins for several years in Gonzales. He and Mr. Fulcher, his partner, put up the first frame building in Gonzales. In 1857 Mr. Baker bought property in the picturesque Cheapside country, and there passed the remainder of his life. When the Civil War opened he was placed in the Home Guards, with the important duty of looking after the families of soldiers. To provide food and raiment for his charges it was necessary to make several trips to the Rio Grande, where he made exchanges with the Mexican merchants, our ports being blockaded. These trips were exceedingly dangerous. On one of them a friend, Mr. Nichols, went across from Brownsville to Matamoras, when the latter town was in the hands of the Union soldiers. Failing to return, Mr. Baker became uneasy, and went across to look him up. While thus engaged he was captured, and, with his friend, was given sticks to kill ants by way of punishment. Through the intercession of an unexpected friend Mr. Baker was released in a short time. In politics he was ever a stanch Democrat, and socially a Royal Arch Mason, a member of Gonzales Lodge. His death occurred in 1884, when sixty-three years of age. The mother is still living, and is now seventy-three years of age. Our subject attended school in Cheapside neighborhood, and when twenty-one years of age commenced working on his own account. Two years later he married Miss Elizabeth W. Peterson, daughter of William C. and Lucy (Wright) Peterson, both now living in Kerrville. Mr. Baker is a member of the Masonic Fraternity, and in politics is a Democrat. He has held the office of School Trustee. Mrs. Baker is a member of the Missionary Baptist Church. Their children, six in number, were named as follows: Lucy E., Thomas O., William C., Mollie O., Ira W., and one unnamed.

HON. GEORGE T. McGEHEE. It cannot be expected in a work of this kind, where but brief biographical sketches of prominent citizens of the county are given, that justice can be done to this much esteemed and honored citizen, and yet he has long been identified with the county's interests; his name is very familiar to all and he has also been prominent in the political arena. He is a product of Bastrop County, Texas, was born February 5, 1836, and was the second white child born in the town of Bastrop, and the second child born to his parents, Thomas G. and Minerva (Hunt) McGehee, who were natives of the State of Alabama. In the State of his birth Thomas G. McGehee followed the calling of a merchant, but after his removal to Texas, in 1835, he devoted his attention to tilling the soil in Bastrop County until 1843, afterwards in Fayette County, and again in Bastrop County in the winter of 1845. In the fall of 1846 he came to San Marcos, in the vicinity of which place he had located a league of land in July, 1835, and in December, 1846, he erected the first building for a residence in what is now Hays County, and during the years that he resided here he cleared and improved a considerable portion of his land. He entered the Texas army in 1835, and fought for Texas independence until the war closed. On the day of the famous battle of San Jacinto he was serving on detached duty, consequently did not participate in that engagement. He was on a number of Indian expeditions and in several battles, the principal one being at Brushy Creek, in Williamson County, in 1837. He died at the home of the subject of this sketch, in San Marcos, on November 13, 1891, at the age of eighty-one years. He and his wife were worthy Methodists, and assisted in the organization of that church at San Marcos. He was a charter member of Cushney Lodge No. 28, of the A. F. & A. M., at San Marcos, and being a man of great public spirit, intelligence and push, he made many friends, who remained faithful to him until death closed his career. The paternal grandfather of the subject of this sketch, Thomas McGehee, was born in the Palmetto State, and was descended from Scotch-Irish parents, who, on coming to this country, first settled in Virginia, and afterwards in South Carolina, where they reared a large family of sons. The maternal grandfather was George Hunt, whose father settled on the present site of Huntsville, Ala., and his name was eventually given to the town. When the McGehees came to San Marcos the subject of this sketch was eleven years of age. He had attended school in Ruddersville, and in 1852-53 pursued his studies at Seguin, but in 1862 cast aside all personal considerations to take up arms in defense of the loved South, and became a member of Company D, Thirty-eighth Texas Cavalry (Terry's Rangers), served in all the engagements of that regiment, and was wounded at Farmersville, Tenn., and very severely at Aiken, S. C. At the close of hostilities he returned to San Marcos and after some years spent in trading he, in 1870, bought a farm on the San Marcos River, and engaged in tilling the soil. He still owns several fine and valuable tracts of land and is well fixed as regards worldly possessions. He has resided in San Marcos since 1883, and is one of the most highly honored citizens of that place. He has been active in political matters, and has been delegate to numerous State conventions. In 1887 he was elected to the State Legislature, and while a member of that body served on the committees of Revenue and Taxation, Finance, Penitentiaries and State Asylums. He was re-elected to this position, served on the same committees, and was made Chairman of the Committee on Penitentiaries. He was the author of several bills which became laws. He was elected to the Twenty-third General Assembly as a Clarke Democrat, and served on the committees of Finance, Penitentiaries, and Revenue and Finance. He was specially active in securing legislation to ameliorate the condition of the State insane, and did much to secure the establishment of the Southwest Asylum at San Antonio, also the State Reform School at Galesville. He did noble work on the Penitentiary Committee, and made a reputation for himself as one who favored reforms, and was anxious to promote the interests of his section and State. He was one of the organizers of the oil mill at San Marcos and also of the Glover National Bank. He was married in 1870 to Miss Sarah Woods, a daughter of Dr. P. C. Woods, a sketch of whom appears in this work, and he and his wife are worthy members of the Methodist Church, and socially he is a member of the A. F. & A. M. Mr. McGehee's brothers and sisters are as follows: John, a sketch of whom appears in this work; Charles, a member of Terry's Rangers during the war, was taken sick at Nashville, Tenn., in 1861, was discharged and came home, and upon recovering joined Wood's Regiment. He now resides at Weatherford; Alexander, William, who was a physician of this county, and who is now dead; Edward resides in the northern part of the State; Palmira is the widow of Dr. J. D. Oliver; Sarah is the wife of T. A. Hill, a banker of Weymer, and Ann is the deceased wife of Milton Watkins.

SANFORD VANDEVER PUTNAM, farmer and stock-raiser of Gonzales County, Texas, is a native of the Palmetto State, born in Lawrence District to the marriage of Reuben and Mary Putnam, cousins, and both natives of South Carolina. The father followed farming in his native State until the winter of 1837, when he emigrated to Texas and resided in Gonzales County one year. At that time he joined the stampede created by the approach of the Mexicans from the battle of the Salado, and went to Washington County with the idea of returning to South Carolina. However, he was persuaded to stop one year and was so well pleased that he remained there the balance of his days, his death occurring in 1839. Mrs. Putnam died in Gonzales County about two years prior to the Civil War, while on a visit to her son. Both father and mother were members of the Baptist Church. Our subject received a fair education in his native State and Washington County, Texas, and when seventeen years of age, being of an adventurous disposition, ran away from home and returned to Gonzales County where he traded all his possessions for a Spanish pony. For several years he had a "good time," giving very little thought to the future, and as the woods were filled with nearly all kinds of big game he spent much time in hunting.   Mr. Putnam asserts that he has often stood upon a hill near his home and seen deer feeding as thick as cattle can now be seen.   Realizing at last that he must put his time to better use he went to work, and in time accumulated considerable means and 1,500 acres of land.   He was married at the age of twenty-four to Miss Martha A. Mitchell, daughter of Moses and Elizabeth (Switchler) Mitchell.   Mr. Mitchell was born in England and at an early age came to America, locating in Missouri, where he followed the blacksmith trade.   After marriage he came to Texas, and farmed until the breaking out of the Mexican War, but he took no part in that trouble.   He lived in Lavaca County, but died in 1840 in Louisiana, to which State he had retreated in the general stampede caused by the war.   He was an Episcopolian in religion.   His eldest brother also died in Louisiana, Claiborne parish.   Mrs. Mitchell was a Baptist in belief and died in Gonzales County in 1859.   During the Mexican War Mr. Putnam enlisted in Company H, Capt. Ketchings, and served as heavy artilleryman on Galveston Island where he was kept two years.

D. H. REGAN.   It has been said, and truly said, that "some men are born great, some have greatness thrust upon them and some achieve greatness," and to the last most important class belongs the subject of this sketch, D. H. Regan, who is noted as a practical, shrewd, honorable and successful business man, who has made the most of his advantages, and has always grasped at opportunities for bettering his financial, moral and social conditions.   He was born in the Isle of Erin in 1842, in which country his parents, John and Margaret (Regan) Regan, were also born.   In 1852 the family emigrated to America and after a short stay in the city of New York they removed to New Orleans, La., where they resided until their respective deaths, which occurred during the progress of the great Civil War.   Soon after the location of the family in this country the subject of this sketch was taken into the family of an uncle, who located in Chicago, Ill., and in that city D. H. Regan was reared and educated.   After reaching a suitable age he engaged in the railroad business, and in 1862 enlisted in a regiment raised by the various railroad companies of the country, which was attached to the Army of the Cumberland, and participated in the battles of Perryville, Murfreesboro, Mission Ridge, all the engagements of the Atlanta Campaign and the battles of Franklin and Nashville.   He was captured once by Terry's Texas Regiment while on a train going to Nashville, but was almost immediately paroled.   He was mustered out of the service at Nashville, in June, 1865, and was paid off in Chicago.   All of the immediate members of his family had taken up their abode in the South, and one brother, John Regan, was a soldier in the Confederate Army, being in the Washington Artillery of Louisiana, but his death occurred soon after the termination of the war. In 1865 D. H. Regan made a visit to the South to see his people, but found that his parents had died.   From New Orleans he came to Texas in 1865, and at once embarked in a dry goods, boots, shoes, clothing, etc., business at Indianola, Calhoun County, but in 1875 a cyclone swept away his store and stock, his loss amounting to about $15,000.   Nothing daunted, Mr. Regan at once rebuilt his place of business and began business on a larger scale than before, but in 1886 Old Boreas once more swooped down upon him, and this time, not only his store building, his stock of goods and his books with all his accounts were swept away, but also the house in which he and his family lived, but fortunately the latter was carried into some trees near by and the family escaped uninjured. The loss which Mr. Regan sustained this time by wind and fire, amounted to over $20,000, but as prior to this time he had established branch stores at Cuero and Victoria, he was not left absolutely destitute. He and his family at once made their headquarters at the store in the latter place, and here he has conducted his business with such marked ability that he is now doing an annual business of $75,000, and carries a stock of goods amounting to $40,000. This business has from the start been markedly large and is constantly increasing, for Mr. Regan does all in his power to please his patrons, and has an exceptionally well selected stock of, goods, consisting of dry goods, clothing, boots and shoes. He is advantageously located in a large two-story brick block on Main street, and his patrons are among the elite of the city. In past years his annual business exceeded $100,000. He was one of the organizers of the electric light and the street railway of Victoria, in both of which he sustained heavy losses, but he is now in good circumstances and has acquired considerable wealth through his shrewd and original, yet always honorable, business methods. In 1868 he was united in marriage with Miss Mary V. Hogan, a native of Houston, Texas, and a daughter of William Hogan, a native of Ireland. The latter was a merchant of Houston for some time, but later became a resident of Victoria. Mr. and Mrs. Regan have twelve children: Charles, Grace, Agnes, William, Effie, May Louise, Eleanor, Angela, Edward, John, Arthur and Kathleen. The family are members of the Catholic Church.

PERLEY PORTER PUTNAM, one of the substantial and prominent farmers of Jackson County, Texas, now resides on his fine farm three miles west of Edna, on the Lavaca River. Mr. Putnam was born in Covington, Tioga County, Penn., September 30, 1835, and was fourth of six children born to Thomas and Zilpha (Porter) Putnam. The father was born in Massachusetts in 1790, and at the age of three years moved with his father to New Hampshire, and in 1810 to Pennsylvania, and the mother was born in Vermont in 1799, and at the age of six years moved with her father to New York State, and in 1813 to Pennsylvania. The paternal grandfather, Elijah Putnam, was born in Massachusetts, was engaged in the battle of Bunker Hill, Saratoga, and others of the Revolutionary War, and was a cousin of General Israel Putnam. Grandfather Porter, after living in Vermont and New York States, moved to Pennsylvania in 1813. The parents lived in Pennsylvania from 1810 to 1813, and there passed the remainder of their days; the father dying in the year 1874, and mother dying in the year 1876. The father was an officer in the State militia and was known as Gen. Putnam in that locality. In the schools of Tioga County, Pennsylvania, Perley Porter Putnam was educated, and when about eighteen years of age he started out as a surveyor, an occupation his father and brother had followed. When twenty years of age, Mr. Putnam and his brother, Samuel M. Putnam, went to Minnesota, and located on land on the Mississippi River, at Little Falls, Morrison County, 108 miles above St. Paul. They were county surveyors, also had a Government contract surveying off public land into townships. There the brother died in 1857, when about twenty-four years of age. After his death Mr. Putnam returned to Pennsylvania, and was married there to Miss Ellen Marvin, daughter of Tilly Marvin, an old settler of the Keystone State. Our subject followed merchandising and farming, and held various county offices. In

1866, at the request of Dr. Royal A. Porter, uncle of our subject, the latter came to Texas, to take charge of the uncle's stock and ranch in Jackson County. After managing it for him one year, he then bought the estate, and almost immediately afterward was made Clerk of the Board of Registration, and later its President. In 1867, he was appointed District Clerk, held that office about a year, and then was elected Justice of the Peace and County Commissioner of Precinct 5, and held that position about ten years. At the present time he is County Surveyor, and has held the position four terms. Mr. Putnam now has 400 acres of good land with about seventy acres under cultivation. This will make one bale of cotton to the acre. Though not an office seeker, by any means, he has been in office nearly all the years since his majority. His marriage resulted in the birth of thirteen children, eight of whom are now living: Perley Porter, Jr., resides at Portersville, Cal.; James Ajax, Royal Augustus, of Portersville, Cal.; Samuel Morris, is with his father; Tilly Thomas, at home; Hallie A., wife of B. F. Ward, in Portersville, Cal.; Reward Ellen; Zilpha Eliza, at home, and those deceased are: Fluella Ionia, died when twenty-two years of age; Minnie I., died when ten years of age, and the remainder died in infancy. Mr. Putnam has succeeded fairly well with fruit, and claims that this is a good country for such varieties as are adapted to this climate. He is a self-made man and what he has accumulated is the result of hard work on his part. He secured his education in the rough school of experience, and has been a pupil in the same all his life.

DR. T. J. McFARLAND. This prominent physician of Port Lavaca, Texas, owes his nativity to Alabama, born in the year 1837, and third in a family of five children born to Gazaway Davis and Mary (Poe) McFarland, natives respectively of Georgia and Alabama. The maternal grandfather and grandmother, Thomas and Mary Poe, were among the early settlers of Greene County, Alabama. The McFarlands were early settlers of Georgia. The father of our subject followed farming all his life, and died in Copiah County, in 1881. The mother passed away in 1876. Dr. T. J. McFarland was educated in Jonesborough, Ala., and at Fannin, Miss. He began the study of medicine in 1858, with Surgeon M. S. Craft, of Jackson, Miss. After remaining with him for some time Mr. McFarland entered Tulane University, New Orleans, and graduated at the School of Medicine in 1861. He was commissioned a surgeon by Governor Moore of Louisiana, and assigned to post duty at Holly Springs, Miss., in the hospital for Louisiana troops. After remaining there for about three months, he was then transferred to Tupelo, Miss., where he was ordered before a board appointed by the Secretary of War for the examination of all medical officers. The board was composed of Prof. D. W. Yandell, of Louisville, Ky., Dr. L. T. Pinn, of St. Louis, Mo., and Dr. J. H. Hustes, of Mobile, Ala. He was then commissioned by the Secretary of War as surgeon in the Confederate Army, and was placed on detached service at different posts. In 1862 he was made a member of the operating board of the Army of Tennessee, and was placed on post duty to attend at all battles. This service he continued until the close of the war, when he was at Columbus, Ga. Returning to Mississippi, he began practicing medicine, and remained there until February, 1867, when he went to Texas, and located on Oyster Creek, where he practiced his profession until 1870. From there he moved to Fannin county, practiced there for four years, and then returned to the coast, settling in Jackson County, and practiced along the coast of Jackson, Wharton and Victoria Counties, becoming well known as a most eminent and successful member of the healing art. He had a large practice, and remained there until 1881, when he moved to Indianola, Calhoun County, where for twelve years he was the only physician. He was also surgeon of the United States Marine Hospital Service at Indianola, and continued in that service until the storm of 1886, when the post was transferred to Eagle Pass. For a few months he was at Edna, but afterwards was permanently located at Port Lavaca, where he was appointed State Quarantine Officer at Pass Cavallo, holding that position four years. He had the present quarantine station built. Since then he has been Health Officer of Calhoun County, and has a very large practice besides. The doctor is local railroad surgeon of the Southern Pacific, is a renowned physician and surgeon in Texas, and his clearness of perception, accuracy of diagnosis and boldness of operation, have won for him many admirers. He led to the hymeneal altar Miss Carrie Jayne, youngest daughter of Judge Brewster H. Jayne, who came to Texas in 1841, and was killed by Indians in the suburbs of Austin in the following year. Judge Jayne was a native of Long Island, New York, and a prominent politician. He moved from New York to Mississippi, and thence to Texas. Mrs. McFarland was born in Austin, Texas, 1842, and by her marriage became the mother of these children: Marion M., business manager of the *Victoria Daily Times;* Thomas Carlisle, editor of the *Victoria Daily Times;* Van Earle, of the *Port Lavacian*; Paulina, widow of Joseph Sheldon; Juliette, Jessie, and Bell. The family hold membership in the Baptist Church, and the doctor is a member of the Masonic Fraternity, W. P. Milby Lodge. At present the doctor is in the quarantine service, commissioned by Governor Hogg of Texas, as State Quarantine Inspector.

DR. J. Q. A. DAUGHTRY. This successful physician and farmer of Karnes County, Texas, was born in 1826, in Georgia, of which State his parents, Bryant and Nancy (Neal) Daughtry were also natives. In tracing the genealogy of both families, we find that the ancestors came originally from Ireland, and were settlers of Georgia. The father of our subject was a farmer, and passed his entire life in his native State. The original of this notice received his scholastic training in Georgia, and as he had been early trained to the duties of the farm, it was but natural that when starting out for himself, he should select agricultural pursuits as his chosen occupation. When the war broke out he enlisted in Company B, Eleventh Georgia Infantry, served three years, and was in all the engagements of his regiments: battle of The Wilderness, the Petersburg siege, when the mine exploded in that city, and was at Appomattox with General Lee when he surrendered. After returning home Dr. Daughtry engaged in farming. In early manhood he became convinced that there was certain work Providence had ordained that he should do —curing diseases, and immediately after the war he engaged in it. He soon built up an excellent practice, and met with the best results. In 1878 he came to Texas, and located in Houston County, where he at once entered upon his career as a physician. Since then his practice has extended over a large portion of the eastern and southern part of the State, and he is considered a first class practitioner of the "healing art." In the year 1891 he moved to Karnes County, and located two and a half miles south of Karnes City where he has a fine farm of 150 acres, all well improved and well cultivated. His pleasant home is presided over by his wife, formerly Miss Narcissa Hancock, a native of Georgia, and seventeen children were the fruits of this union. Thirteen children grew to mature age, and eleven are now living. Dr. Daughtry and family are members of the Baptist Church, and he is a prominent member of the Masonic Fraternity. Aside from his fine farm, Dr. Daughtry is the owner of some valuable lots in Karnes City, and is a practical, wideawake citizen.

WILLIAM ALEXANDER THOMPSON. The force of well directed energy, steadfast purpose, and never ceasing effort is strikingly illustrated in the life of our subject, who is now one of the prominent farmers and millers of Hays County, Texas. His birth occurred in Carroll County, Mississippi, March 31, 1836, and of the four children born to his parents, William and Mary Ann (Gilbert) Thompson, he is second in order of birth. He had one brother die in Georgia during the war. A sister, Mrs. John W. Lane, resides in Dallas, Texas. The other sister, Mrs. H. C. Withers, resides in Austin. The father was born in Georgia, but when a young man removed to Louisiana, and thence in 1850 to Texas, settling in Caldwell County, on the San Marcos River. He was at one time a Whig in politics, but later became identified with the Democratic party, and socially he was a Royal Arch Mason. For many years he was a member of the Old School Presbyterian Church. His wife, who was a native of Alabama, died in the Lone Star State, and there Mr. Thompson passed the remainder of his days. William Alexander Thompson spent the greater part of his boyhood in Caldwell and Hays counties, and attended the neighborhood schools. The war began when he was twenty-two years old, and he went out in Captain Mayer's company, which afterwards, and for the greater part of the way, was commanded by Captain J. L. Lane. He served in the trans-Mississippi Department, and was at Marsfield, Pleasant Hill and Yellow Bayou. His brother was a member of Colonel John B. Hood's immortal Fourth Texas Regiment, and during the march through Georgia, took sick and died. Returning home William A. began farming on a few acres left him by his father, and as luck smiled upon him, he is now the owner of a handsome competency. In addition to 800 acres of land, 500 acres of which are under cultivation, he is running a public gin (1,000 bales ginned each year), and a grist mill. In politics he is a Democrat, but has never held office. In the year 1875 he married Miss Elizabeth Polk Hardeman, of the famous Tennessee Polk family on one side, and the famous Texas Hardemans on the other, Major Monroe Hardeman being her father. To this marriage have been born four children: William Hardeman, James Fentress, Frank Withers, and Monroe Jones. Mrs. Thompson was born at Prairie Lea, in Caldwell County, Texas, and was reared there and lived there until her marriage. Major Monroe Hardeman was educated at Nashville, Tenn., and in 1836, while yet a young man, came to Texas, and became identified with the State in its struggle for independence. He and his two younger brothers fought at the battle of San Jacinto, and he commanded a company of volunteers at the battle of Plum Creek, in Caldwell County, against the Indians. During the Civil War he was a member of Colonel Hood's Regiment of Texans, and as such participated in many important engagements and campaigns. While thus serving he died in Tennessee.

HON. LOUIS FRANKE, (deceased). He whose name heads this sketch passed to that bourne whence no traveler returns in 1874, having been one of the early settlers and for many years a resident of Black Jack Springs,

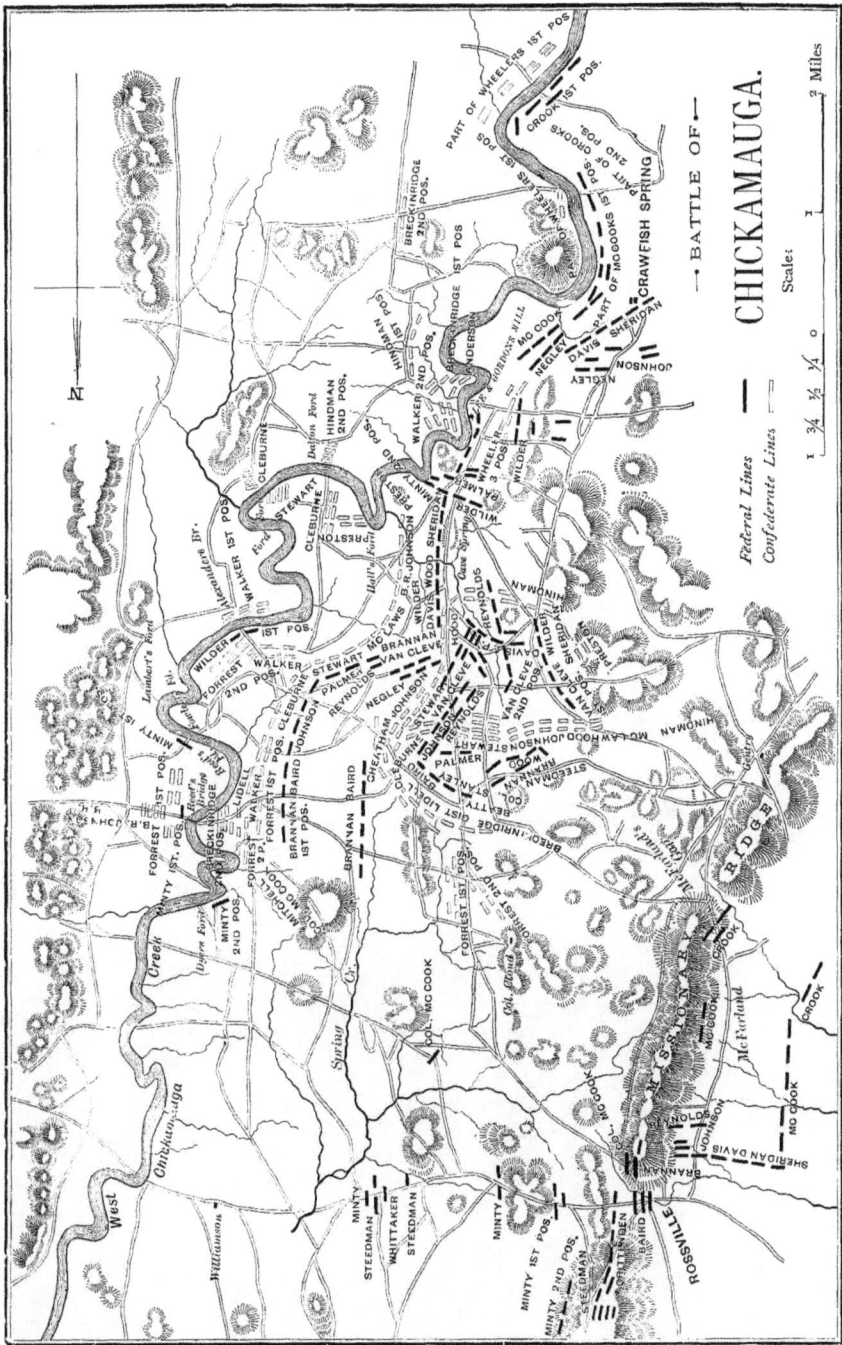

→ BATTLE OF ←

CHICKAMAUGA.

Scale:

Federal Lines
Confederate Lines

Fayette County, Texas. He was born in Germany, and in that country was educated, and graduated from Jana University, completing the classical course. In 1847, while still in his early manhood, he came to Texas and fitted himself for the bar, but never followed that profession. In 1855 he was married to Miss Bernadina Romberg, also a native of Germany, who emigrated to Texas with her parents in 1846. Her father, John Romberg, was a poet of unquestioned ability and genius, and left in manuscript many valuable articles, which his widow and descendants are desirous of having published. His ability as a poet was recognized at his old home in Mecklenburg, Germany, and he was constantly being called upon to prepare and read at public gatherings some appropriate poem. The hard life of a frontiersman on the Texas plains turned his attention to other occupations to some extent, yet he always wrote more or less all his life. He became a very extensive farmer at Black Jack Springs, and upon his death, in 1890, left considerable property and many descendants. Mr. Franke was for some time Professor of Music, in Baylor University, at Independence, Texas, and after giving up his position, he settled on his farm in the vicinity of Black Jack Springs, where his home continued to be until death closed his career. He was a popular citizen of Fayette County, which he represented in the State Legislature during the administration of Governor Daviess. During a session of the Legislative body, just after Mr. Franke had received his pay and was walking down the steps of the old Capitol building, he was assassinated by some persons unknown, it is supposed for his money. He was a practical and progressive farmer, always endeavored to keep out of old ruts, and in every respect was thoroughly up with the times. The children born to himself and wife were as follows: Henry, a jeweler of Yoakum; Paul, a farmer of Wharton County; Anna, wife of a Mr. Schueddamagen; Mary, wife of Dr. Fouts of Gonzales; Benoni A., graduated from an educational institution of Huntsville in 1884, then took a year's course at the University of Lexington, Ky., is a teacher of considerable prominence; Louis is a Master of Musical Notes, Rudolph is a Professor of Brenham College, and Herman. Mrs. Franke and her husband were strict members of the Lutheran Church, and he was quite active in church work, a liberal contributor to all religious enterprises and educational work, and was a fluent and interesting conversationalist. One of his brothers, who resides in Germany, is quite a celebrated writer, is a noted water-cure physician, and has written several interesting works on that subject, which are standard and an authority. His nom de plume is "Rausse."

JAMES AUSTIN BURKE, (deceased). There is no inheritance so rich as the records of the worthy lives of those who have departed this life and who had human frailties, yet were so enabled to overcome them as to lead lives of usefulness, integrity and true godliness. Such a man was James Austin Burke, a very prominent and popular citizen of Goliad County. He was born in Johnston, New York, August 28, 1824, and was the son of Peter and Bridget (Kelly) Burke, natives of County Mayo, Ireland. Peter Burke received a thorough classical training, being educated for the ministry, and left his native country for this at an early date. He settled in Canada, and began life as a teacher. Later he came to the Empire State, still continued to teach, and was so engaged at Johnston when our subject was born. A few years later, he moved with his family to Louisiana, and located at Minden, where he was Professor of a college for some

11

time. From there he went to Natchitoches, La., and was residing there when the trumpet call to arms roused all men to action. In 1876, he came to the Lone Star State and made his home with his son, our subject, until his death in 1882. Teaching was his life work, and he always followed this wherever he resided. Prior to the Civil War, he came to Goliad and taught in the old Aranama College for a time. Mr. Burke married against the wishes of his parents who had intended him for a Catholic priest, and on that account he was disinherited. His parents were very wealthy and of the aristocracy of Ireland. His wife died in 1870. To this worthy couple were born three sons and two daughters: Mary, now the wife of Judge McGowan; Josephine, wife of Judge Wiley; James A. (subject), Peter and Ross E. James Austin Burke was educated by his father, and received a thorough classical training. He made his home in Louisiana until the outbreak of the Mexican War in 1846, and was there married to Miss Elizabeth Fulcrod. Immediately afterwards he started for the war, having previously enlisted. He participated in the battle of Monterey on the anniversary of his wedding day, and was in all the engagements of Taylor's Army. He was twice wounded, once in the ankle, and this troubled him more or less through life. After the war he located with his young wife at Goliad, in 1848, and entered upon his career as a farmer. The following year he was elected County Clerk, the first in that office in Goliad County, and filled that position in a very satisfactory manner until the breaking out of the Civil War. He then resigned and enlisted in the Confederate Army. He assisted in recruiting a company, of which he was elected Lieutenant, and it became Company A, Third Texas Mounted Artillery, Green's Brigade. At first they operated in Arizona, but were subsequently moved East, and became attached to the trans-Mississippi Department, serving through the war under Generals Taylor and Kirby Smith. He and the company were in nearly all the engagements of these armies and he served with distinction until cessation of hostilities, thus being the hero of two wars. This ended his military career. Following this, he engaged in farming for some time, but in a few years he was elected Sheriff of Goliad County, serving a few terms, and then was made County Clerk, holding that office until his death, July 3, 1892. He was an excellent business man, a most efficient official and a citizen respected and esteemed by all. A strong and active worker for the Democratic party, he served in most all conventions, was Chairman of County and Congressional committees, and in all ways was a prominent and popular man. His first wife died in 1851, leaving two children: Josephine, wife of John Cosgrove of Vernon and Alzenith, wife of R. T. Davis (see sketch). Mr. Burke's second marriage occurred in 1868, with Miss Joan E. Welsh, and she now survives him. Ten children were the fruits of this union, nine sons and one daughter: James A., Ross E., Robert E., J. Guss, Mary E., died when thirteen years of age; Colby, died in infancy, Shilby, William H., Thomas B. and John F. Socially Mr. Burke was a Knight Templar in the Masonic Fraternity, and passed through all the chairs at Goliad, serving in nearly all as Secretary. He was also a prominent Odd Fellow. Mr. Burke's eldest son, James B. Burke, succeeded his father as County Clerk at the next election. He was born October 7, 1869, and received a good practical education at Goliad and Austin, graduating at the latter place in 1888. He then became Deputy in his father's office, filled that position until 1891, when on the organization of the First National Bank, he became Assistant Cashier. That position he held until elected to the office of County Clerk. He is a member of the Knights of Pythias, Goliad Lodge No. 163, and is Keeper of Records and Seals. He is a stock holder in the First National Bank and the Goliad Oil Mill, Gin and Manufacturing Co., and is one of the rising young men of the county.

ELDER JAMES MILTON BAKER. In addition to looking after the spiritual welfare of his fellows, James Milton Baker has also devoted much of his attention to tilling the soil, and in both these occupations has met with a more than ordinary degree of success. He is a product of Fayette County, Ala., where he first saw the light of day November 13, 1831, being the second in a family of twelve children born to William and Vashti (White) Baker, the former of whom was born in Wilkinson County, Ga. When quite a lad he was taken by his father, John Baker, to Alabama, and was reared and educated in Tuscaloosa County. After his marriage he removed to Fayette County, Ala., where he was engaged in planting until his removal to DeWitt County, Texas, in 1852, in which section he made one crop, after which he moved to Guadalupe County and bought land near the present town of Luling the place now owned and occupied by the subject of this sketch. He had organized a regiment in Alabama for readiness for service for the Mexican war, but it was never called into service. He was always prominent in military matters, and was appointed Colonel of a militia regiment, and was always afterwards known as Colonel. He was twice a candidate for the Alabama State Legislature on the Democratic ticket, and for many years was a very worthy and active member of the Primitive Baptist Church. He was called from life in November, 1870, and his wife, who was a native of Georgia, died in June, 1861. The subject of this sketch received a limited education in Fayette County, his entire schooling not exceeding over a year, but by reading and study at odd times he has in a great measure remedied this defect. He was always a steady, industrious boy, and, as it is with truth said "that the child is father of the man," he has always been a moral, energetic man. He was never known to use an oath in his life, was never seen under the influence of intoxicating drink, but has habitually kept himself pure and unspotted from the world. He has devoted himself to business on his father's and his own farms, and has been successful in the conduct of his affairs. In February, 1857, he was licensed to preach by the members of the San Marcos Church, and in June, 1857, was regularly ordained by the ministers of the Primitive Baptist Church. For years he attended and administered to churches fifty miles away, when he would leave his plow standing in the field, mount his horse on Friday and return on Monday. For thirty-five years he has filled the pulpit of the San Marcos Church, and throughout his ministry has never charged one dollar for his services. His labors have been bestowed as freely and as willingly as the dews from heaven, blessing the receiver and the giver. In addition he has given thousands of dollars in the way of help to the needy. For years he has been a contributor to his church papers, and was for years Moderator of Providence Association. He has prospered as a planter, and is now the owner of 560 acres of San Marcos Valley land, 300 acres of which are under cultivation, yielding on an average of one-half bale of cotton to the acre and thirty bushels of corn. When the Civil War opened he enlisted in the Confederate service as a member of Eugene Millet's Company, and was in the Louisiana campaign, participating in some of the engagements of that movement. He served three years altogether. He could have started out in command of a company, but never coveted military honors. He was married January 9, 1851, in Fayette County, Ala., to Elizabeth, daughter of Rev. Robert Guttrey, a prominent man of that section. Nine of the twelve children born to him are still living: Robert W., died September 14, 1888; Sarah Vashti is the wife of L. C. Allen; Martha Ann is the wife of J. D. Anderson; Franklin Pearce died October 27, 1867; Joseph R., Andrew Jackson, Mary Elizabeth, wife of William West; Jane, wife of John Allen; Eveline, wife of J. Burke Moore, died October 27, 1889; William, Abel, and Arminta, wife of F. M. Burns.

ANDREW JACKSON CONLEY, President of the Luling Oil and Cotton Company, came originally from Tennessee, his birth occurring in Rutherford County August 11, 1840. His parents, Hardy S. and Elizabeth (Reed) Conley, were both natives of Tennessee, and the father continued to reside in that State until the breaking out of war, when he moved to Williamson County, Ill., and died there in 1884. He was a mechanic by trade, and in connection also carried on farming. The mother died in 1843. Our subject received a partial education in Illinois, and served an apprenticeship to the cabinet maker's trade, working in the shop for wages after finishing his apprenticeship. In 1865 he opened a shop of his own at Marion, Ill., but three years later moved to Carbondale, that State, where he made his home until 1871. He then came to the Lone Star State, where he conducted his former business with good success. While in Illinois sickness in his family had reduced his finances so low that when he came to Texas he was without a dollar. He settled near Luling, in Guadalupe County, rented a farm, and in connection with his trade carried this on. Later he engaged in the mill and gin business at Luling, and was the only resident of that place when the townsite was surveyed. He built the first house in the town. In 1890, having met with good success in milling and ginning, he erected a cotton mill with modern attachments in Luling, and late in that year added an oil mill. Baumgarten's press is used, Callahan's attachments, and the capacity is ten tons daily. He is using Hall gins, five stands, with a capacity of forty bales, and has the Thomas steam press. The whole is run by Wiggins & Simpson's 100-horse power engine. A grist mill is attached, with a capacity of twenty bushels to the hour. Associated with him in this mammoth enterprise is his son, C. W. Conley, R. L. Heflin and C. Baumgarten, and the capital stock is $20,000. Politically Mr. Conley is a Democrat, and he was elected to the office of County Commissioner without notification, after the county had been canvassed for two months by other parties. He has been offered nearly every office in the county, but has steadily declined, preferring to devote his time to his growing business. He is a member of the Knights of Pythias, Luling Grange, and has been a member of the Methodist Church since 1871, in which he has been Steward or Trustee all the time. In 1861 he was married in Illinois to Miss Eliza Newton, daughter of James Newton, who was a native of Tennessee, but who subsequently moved to Illinois. He is now deceased. To Mr. and Mrs. Conley were born eight children, six now living: Charles W., Martha E., wife of Hugh Milligan; Dovey J., Georgia, Thomas M. and Minnie. Two children died in infancy. Mr. and Mrs. Conley have a comfortable home in Luling.

WILLIAM DUNN. Although a native of the Palmetto State, born in the year 1820, much of Mr. Dunn's recollections are of the Lone Star State, in which he settled in the year 1846. Since the year 1847 he has resided in Seguin, Guadalupe County, Texas, and all his interests are centered in this section. He understands, as it were by instinct, the needs, social and industrial, of this vicinity, and has a thorough knowledge of its resources. His parents, John and Elizabeth Dunn, were natives of Ireland, and died when William was but a small boy. The latter began working at the printer's trade when seven years old, but subsequently engaged in other pursuits. In 1846 he came to Texas, and the following year settled in Seguin, where he began carpentering and wagon making. In a few years he was elected Sheriff, and was the third Sheriff of that county, holding that position until the breaking out of the Civil War. In 1831 he was a soldier of the Florida War, and in 1861 he volunteered in Company D, Fourth Texas Regiment under Colonel Hood, who soon became commander of the brigade. Mr. Dunn served in all the engagements of his army corps until the close of the war, when he returned home, and was elected Justice of the Peace. A short time afterwards he was again elected Sheriff, and was the first Democratic one to hold that position after the Reconstruction, serving six years in succession. Later he was elected Justice, and served in that capacity until 1892. In the year 1839 he was married in his native State, and his excellent wife died in 1892, after bearing him five children, three of whom survive: Middleton, the eldest now living, was born in South Carolina, and now resides in Austin. He was a private in Company D, Fourth Texas Regiment, and was elected Representative from Guadalupe County in 1866; Mary, a native of South Carolina, is the wife of William Coleman of Edna, Texas; Emma, born in Seguin, is the wife of Mr. J. A. Woods; and Sallie Dunn, married. Martha, died in infancy. This family holds membership in the Methodist Church, of which our subject is a trustee. Mr. Dunn was made an Odd Fellow in early manhood, in Palmetto Lodge No. 9, of Columbia, South Carolina. He is now a member of Amity Lodge No. 60, Seguin, in which he has held every office in the Lodge, and is a member of the Grand Lodge of Texas. In 1894 he was given a handsome medal for having been a member of that order for twenty-five consecutive years. He is a man of unquestioned integrity, and has been one of the county's most able officials. Ever since his residence here he has been one of the most public spirited men, and has fought with Texas in all her struggles for growth and material advancement. He was a good soldier, and is a highly esteemed citizen. Now, retired from the active duties of life, he has a comfortable and pleasant home in Seguin.

HON. FREDERICK HERMANN SEELE. The success of men in general depends upon character as well as upon knowledge, it being a self-evident proposition that honesty is the best policy. Mr. Frederick Herman Seele, the most efficient Postmaster of New Braunfels, Texas, is a man whose character is above reproach and whose education has been most thorough and complete. He was born in Hildesheim, Kingdom of Hanover, Germany, April 14, 1823. His parents were J. C. and Annie (Runge) Seele, natives of Germany, in which country they passed their entire lives. Young Seele became well grounded in the rudiments of an education in the public schools of Hildesheim, and later took a course in the Gymnasium Andreanum, mastering the modern and classic languages, and the scientific branches taught at that admirable institution. He was of a bold and enterprising spirit, and early in life decided that America offered the finest field for the exercise of his versatile talent, hence he embarked for the young Republic of Texas, and on December 12, 1843, landed in Galveston. In that county and in Brazoria County he remained for two years, and in 1845 removed to New Braunfels with the first colonists of the German Emigration Society who came over. Here he became at once a leading spirit in all things making for the upbuilding of his section, and to his intelligent interest and energetic endeavor is largely due the symmetrical growth of the colony. He studied law after reaching these shores, with the purpose of making it his life's work, and was admitted to the bar April 27, 1855. While in the Fatherland, as far back as 1837, he had become a member of the Protestant Evangelical Church, and in his new home he set about founding a church of the order. In 1845, soon after his coming, he aided in the organization of the German Protestant Community, of which he has continuously been an active member and leader. In that year, August 11, also, he opened the first German-English school west of the Colorado River, and engaged in teaching. At that day the endeavor to advance civilization in the wilderness was attended with hardship and danger enough to daunt any save the boldest heart. It is stated that this organization at its inception held its services beneath the boughs of a beautiful grove, one of God's first temples. It was Mr. Seele who first advocated that each community should have the right to tax itself for the support of education, for the good of the great majority of the people who were not able to pay for it, and at an early day he secured the co-operation of the late Hon. Jacob Walder, of San Antonio, who was instrumental in having embodied in the constitution of Texas that clause authorizing it. The Legislature passed laws relative to it, and to-day it is a proud reflection that, under the beneficent system of free schools, 100,000 of the scholastic population of Texas have received, and are receiving, free education; the system first adopted by the little city of New Braunfels as early as 1852. Mr. Seele is the author of the "History of New Braunfels," "History of German Emigration in Texas," "Sketches of Prominent German Citizens and Statesmen of Texas—Living and Dead," "Sketches of the Early Life of the German Colonists," etc., and these messages from his facile pen wrought mightily towards inducing emigration from Germany to this favored land, and to them may be largely ascribed the honor and distinction Comal County now enjoys of being a county filled with a patriotic, God-fearing, debt-paying, law-abiding people. Previous to the Civil War he was a Democrat, and made several canvasses in Comal and adjoining counties in the interests of the party, and served several times as delegate to the State Democratic Convention. He was a strong Union man until the State seceded. Then, like thousands of others, natives of Texas by adoption, when the alternative was presented of taking up arms for or against Texas, his love for his adopted State prevailed, and he entered in her service at once, and from 1861 to 1865 served as Adjutant and Inspector General of the Thirty-first Brigade, Texas Militia, with the rank of Major. When the war was over he joined the Republican party and has affiliated with it ever since. At the last Presidential election in 1890, he was a candidate for Elector of the Republican ticket, and received the largest vote cast for any man on the ticket. In addition to his long and efficient services as an educator in New Braunfels, he has filled many responsible offices. As Principal of the Protestant Sunday School he was efficient and beloved. For eight years he filled the office of Clerk of the District Court with distinguished ability. A part of the time during the war he served as Major. He has been Justice of the Peace and Mayor of the city, and is now Postmaster of New Braunfels. He once represented his people in the State Legislature, serving in the memorable eleventh session. He is a zealous Mason, a member of the Knights of Honor, and a member and officer of the New Braunfels Mutual Aid Association and Krankenhaus Verein. While serving as Alderman his action and advocacy gave the city its splendid system of water works, and he was organizer and promoter of the Texas "Saengerbund," as early as 1853. Having been a correspondent for various newspapers in Texas and elsewhere, he acquired a fondness for journalism, and was early instrumental in the establishment of a good paper in his town. In 1852, with the aid of others, he established the *Zeitung*, and contributed to its columns for a long while. For a time he had editorial control of the paper. At a time when land titles were clouded, and owners of land were assailed by other claimants and threatened with irritating and expensive suits, the citizens organized a committee who pledged themselves to aid each other in defense of their rights of property. He was a member of the committee, and exerted himself faithfully in carrying out the objects of the organization. After a litigation of thirty years in the District and Supreme courts of the State, a suit was decided by the Circuit Court of the United States, April 24, 1879, which settled the question, and it is claimed that to-day hundreds of families are in great part indebted to Mr. Seele's unceasing activity for the quiet possession of their homesteads, and the quieting of their title to the same. January 25, 1862, Mr. Seele was married to Miss Matilda Blum. They have four living children: Harry, Hulda, Emily and Fritz. All four are married. Harry and Fritz reside at San Antonio, and Hulda is the wife of Mr. George Eiband, and Emily that of John Faust, both successful merchants of New Braunfels. Mr. Seele is now one year beyond the scriptural allotment of three score and ten years, and is still in harness, whose burden he does not feel. A clear-eyed, open-browed, ruddy-cheeked, stalwart man of seventy-one, he is a striking example of what a man without hereditary taint, by clean and wholesome living, may attain to. A man of pious mind and poetic temperament, benevolent instinct and habit, and pleasant, agreeable ways, he seems to carry perpetual summer in his heart.

W. O. McCURDY. Among the newspaper men of this part of Texas who are planning so wisely to help forward the interests of their section in the future we are pleased to mention W. O. McCurdy, publisher and editor of the *Beeville Bee*, an independent Democratic paper. He inherits his push and energy from his Scotch ancestors, his grandfather, Darius McCurdy, having been born on the Island of Skye, near Scotland. The latter came to America at an early date and settled in Mississippi. This was prior to 1834, for during that year he was in the Creek Indian war. He resided for a short time in North Carolina, then Kentucky, afterwards Alabama, and finally Mississippi, where he spent the balance of his days. Our subject's maternal grandfather, John McDonald, was born on board a vessel bound from Scotland to America. He grew to manhood in Mississippi, and became an extensive cotton planter. The parents of our subject, William and Mary (McDonald) McCurdy, were natives of Mississippi, and the father was an extensive cotton planter. During the war he enlisted in the Confederate Army, Company K, Thirty-seventh Mississippi Regiment, and was made Captain. He served during the whole time and surrendered at Greensboro, N. C. He is now residing at his old home in Jasper County, Miss. W. O. McCurdy, the second in order of birth of four children, was born in Claiborne, Jasper County, Miss., in 1866, and there received his education. When sixteen years of age he left school and became part owner of the *Heidelberg Review*, and soon after assumed the entire management, conducting the paper for two years. In 1885 he came to Texas and worked on a paper in Victoria for six months. However he soon moved to Beeville and established the *Beeville Bee.* This was in 1886 and it was the first paper in the county. He is very successful as a newspaper man, and although but recently started, his paper commands an ever widening area of circulation. Fraternally Mr. McCurdy is a Mason, a member of Beeville Lodge No. 161. He is also a Knight of Pythias, Queen Bee Lodge No. 121, and a member of the Uniformed Rank, Division No. 30, of the same lodge.

JACOB FOX. The patrons of agriculture in Victoria County, Texas, have a worthy representative in the person of Jacob Fox, who is also extensively engaged in ginning and milling. He is a product of Alsace, France, where he first saw the light November 9, 1844, his parents being Jacob and Mariana Fox, both natives of Alsace also. In 1845 the Fox family left the land of their birth to seek a home in the fertile Mississippi Valley, landed at the city of Galveston, and soon after came to Victoria where they permanently located, the father becoming the purchaser of a considerable amount of land in the vicinity of the town, which he began energetically to till. Although he at first experienced many vicissitudes and hardships, he continued to pursue his labors faithfully and earnestly, in time bent the force of circumstances to his will, and eventually gained a competency which he was enjoying when he paid the last debt of nature in 1891, at the age of eighty-five years. His wife survived him but one year. The subject of this sketch was reared in Victoria, and in 1860 began the battle of life for himself. When the great and lamentable Civil War came up, he, in 1861, enlisted in the Confederate army as a member of Company B, Sixth Texas Infantry, which was camped near Victoria until the spring of 1862, after which it was sent to Arkansas, and was in the engagement at Arkansas Post. At that place Mr. Fox was captured, and after being kept a captive for three months was exchanged at City Point, Va. He was then detailed to go to Vicksburg, but upon his arrival at Knoxville, Tenn., the order was countermanded and he was ordered to join the Army of the Cumberland. He then took part in the battles of Chickamauga, Missionary Ridge, and all the engagements of the Atlanta campaign, and then back to Franklin, where he was wounded very badly in the hand. He was also wounded by a fragment of a shell at Atlanta, July 22, 1863. On account of his wounds he was granted a furlough, and came home early in 1865. The war was then nearing its close, and Mr. Fox turned his attention to farming, and for eight years tilled the soil of rented land, at the end of which time he had accumulated sufficient means to purchase the place. After a time Mr. Fox put up a horse-power gin on his place, which had a capacity of two bales a day, but it burned down, and in 1880 he put up another gin, which is operated by steam power. This he replaced in 1890 by some new and finely improved machinery, which cost about $5,000, and his gin now has a capacity of about twenty-five bales per day. He has four gin stands, two elevators, and, in fact, is finely equipped to do an extensive business in this line. His grist mill is also a well-equipped establishment, and occupies about one-fourth of a block. In 1893 Mr. Fox erected his present residence, which is one of the handsomest homes of the city. He is the owner of 210 acres of good bottom land, of which 110 acres are under cultivation and well improved. He was first married to Miss Minia Schrader, who died in 1867 of yellow fever, leaving one child, who died five years later. His second marriage was to Mrs. Clara Fremuth, a daughter of Henry Noble, who was a native of Tennessee and one of the early settlers of Texas, coming to this State with his father, Thomas Noble. Henry was the second son of a large family of children, and eventually became an extensive stock raiser. He was murdered on account of a stock feud in 1853, the year of the birth of his daughter Clara. His widow married again in 1856, becoming the wife of James S. Bennett, and is once more a widow, being now sixty years of age. She is an intelligent and entertaining conversationalist, and resides alternately with her daughters in San Antonio, or with Mrs. Fox in Victoria. Her mother, Mrs. Margaret Wright, was born in Louisiana, and first married a Mr. Hayes, by whom she had two children. After his death she married M. de Treudeau-Toudor Pronounce, the Governor of the Province of Louisiana. Upon his death she removed to Texas in 1821, and settled near where the town of Victoria now stands, and as she was a colonist of Martin de Leon she received a league of land five miles above town, and after her marriage with John D. Wright, who came to Texas in 1827, they settled on her headright. By Mr. Wright she had two daughters, Amy Ann, who married Gen. Ramirez, of Mexico, and Tennessee, the widow of James Bennett. The former was murdered at her ranche on the Rio Grande River by a Mexican in 1877, for money, and the mother, after a life of toil, was called from life in October, 1879, in the ninetieth year of her age. To the union of Mr. and Mrs. Fox nine children have been given: Jacob Henry, Mamie, Emma, Willie, Clara, Marguerite, Benjamin F., Charles L. and Lawrence. By her first husband Mrs. Fox became the mother of one daughter, Rosalie.

L. F. WELLS, County and District Clerk of Jackson County, was born in Jackson County, Texas, May 18, 1846, to the union of F. F. and Martha (McNutt) Wells, natives of Virginia and Louisiana respectively. When two years of age F. F. Wells was left an orphan, and he was reared by his uncle, Matthew Flournoy, of Georgetown, Ky., and educated there. Later he studied medicine, graduated at Louisville Medical College, and subsequently moved to La Rapids Parish, La., where he began practicing his profession. He then married Miss McNutt and subsequently made a visit to Texas, where he secured a grant of land in Jackson County, dated July 21, 1824, in the colony of Stephen F. Austin. Dr. Wells moved his family to the Lone Star State in 1828 or 1829, and first settled in Brazoria County. He afterwards moved to Jackson County, settling on the Lavaca River, where, in 1836, the Mexicans burned his house. After this he resided in the town of Texana, practicing his profession until 1856 or 1857, when he retired from the active duties of life until his death in 1867. The mother died in 1863. One daughter is now living, Flora A., wife of George F. Simons. Our subject was educated in Texana, the county-seat of Jackson County, and when sixteen years of age he enlisted in the Confederate army, Company K, Second Texas Infantry, under Capt. C. L. Owen and Col. John C. More. He was in the battle of Shiloh, and served until July or August, 1862, when he came home on account of youth. In the fall of 1863 Mr. Wells re-enlisted in the same company, and served in Texas until the close of the war. After this he was engaged in driving cattle until 1871, when he engaged in merchandising in Texana for a time. After that he studied law, and was admitted to the bar in 1873. In 1876 he was elected County Judge, served four terms, and was then elected County and District Clerk, which office he has held since. Mr. Wells has discharged the duties incumbent upon the various positions he has held in a very able manner, and is classed among the representative men. In the year 1873 he was married to Miss Frances M. Sutherland, daughter of Thomas S. and Mary Sutherland. Her grandparents were pioneer settlers of Texas, coming here in 1830 and settling in Jackson. To Mr. and Mrs. Wells were born these children: Robert W., Thomas J. and Flora S., and Elizabeth M. Wells, adopted. Mrs. Wells is a member of the Episcopal Church. Mr. Wells is a member of the A. F. & A. M. Lodge, Texana No. 123, the K. of H. and the K. of P.

EDWARD EDGAR, Sheriff of Calhoun County, Texas, is a native of the Emerald Isle, born in 1844, and fifth in order of birth of eight children born to Edward and Letitia (McMahon) Edgar, natives also of Ireland. After coming to America this family settled in St. Louis for a short time and then went to Steubenville, Ohio, and still later returned to the old country. A short time afterwards they returned to this country, and located in New Orleans, where the father was engaged in the mercantile business as book-keeper for some time. He then engaged in the commission business with Emerson, but later was taken ill and retired from the active duties of life. His death occurred in 1856. The mother had died of yellow fever in 1853. In the schools of New Orleans, Edward Edgar secured a good education, and in 1856, the same year his father died, came to Texas, where he joined a cousin in Calhoun County, in the month of August. Here he learned the tinner's trade, and followed it until 1859, when he went to Indianola, and remained there until 1861, when he enlisted in Company D, Sixth Texas Infantry, and went to Victoria with the company, where the regiment was formed. From there he was sent to Arkansas Post, Arkansas, where he remained until its fall. He was then sent to Springfield, Ill., as a prisoner of war, and subsequently was exchanged at City Point, Va. After that he joined Gen. Bragg's army and was in the battle of Chickamauga, Missionary Ridge, New Hope Church, Dug Gap, and all the battles of the Atlanta campaign. Later he was sent back to Tennessee with Gen. Hood, and was in the battles of Spring Hill, Franklin and Nashville. He joined Gen. Johnston in North Carolina, and was with him until he surrendered at Bentonville, N. C., in April, 1865. Mr. Edgar remained in Mobile until some time in May, 1867, and then returned to Port Lavaca, Texas. For several years after this he was in the printing business, and worked in Corpus Christi for a short time. He then drove cattle to Kansas, and remained in that State until 1873, engaged in the cattle and hay business. For four years after this he was in Corpus Christi, remained there until 1884, and then returned to Port Lavaca, where in 1886 he became deputy under Sheriff O'Neil for two years, during which time he did most of the business. In 1888 he was elected to the office of Sheriff and has been re-elected each successive time up to the present. The county has never known a more able or efficient officer than Mr. Edgar, who is fearless in the discharge of his duty, and who has won the good opinion of all by his uprightness. Mr. Edgar was married on January 28th, 1877, to Miss Annie B. O'Neil, a native of Port Lavaca, Texas, and daughter of Thomas O'Neil. They have two children, John E., and Ethel E. Mr. Edgar is a member of the Masonic Fraternity, W. P. Milby Lodge No. 84, also the Knights of Honor, and Woodmen of the World, Victoria Lodge. The father of Mr. Edgar was born in Buncrana, Ireland, and the mother in Carrick Fergus. On the 30th of December, 1834, they came to America, and these children were born here: Edward Sproule Edgar, born October 11, 1835, at St. Louis, Mo., and died in that city, March 16, 1838; Letitia Moore, born in St. Louis, December 16, 1837, and Mary, born at Stubenville, Ohio, August 15, 1841. About this time the family returned to Ireland, and in that country these children were born: Robert Moore, born July 5, 1843, at Buncrana, Ireland, and died in New Orleans, La., September 10, 1856; Edward Edgar (subject), born at Buncrana, Ireland, October 20, 1844; John, born February 1, 1846, at Buncrana, Ireland, is now a banker at Steubenville, Ohio; Annie, born, February 2, 1848, also at the same place in Ireland, and then after the parents returned to this country another child was born, Helen (McClintock), born November 9, 1849, resides in New Orleans. Members of the Edgar family settled in South Carolina as early as 1780.

PERRY THEODORE BOST. Hays County ranks deservedly high as a great agricultural center, and prominent among those who have helped to bring it to its present state of prosperity stands the name of Perry Theodore Bost. Born in Catawaba County, North Carolina, August 23, 1850, to the marriage Marcus S. and Levisa (Bolick) Bost, he was second in order of birth of three children. The father and mother were also natives of North Carolina, and although a tiller of the soil and a man of intelligence, Fortune was chary of her smiles with Mr. Bost, and he accumulated very little of this world's goods. His son, our subject, grew to sturdy manhood on the home place, and then decided to start out for himself. With a small sum of money, derived from the sale of two pigs, he paid his way to Kansas, and after remaining in that State for five months, met a Mr. Mitchell, whose home was in Texas, and who was there with a drove of cattle. He paid young Bost's way to San Marcos, and the latter worked for him for eight years. At the end of that time, having accumulated some little means, he purchased the farm on which he is now living. Although he came to the Lone Star State without a dollar, and with the cost of transportation from Kansas to pay back, he has since then (1870), become one of the most successful of the many successful men of this part of the State. His plantation, which lies within four miles of San Marcos, contains 1,500 acres of land; 700 acres under a good state of cultivation. The improvements are modern and complete, and his public gin contains two stands—one Pratt and one Smith—sixty saws each; capacity, eighteen bales a day, and on an average of 700 bales a year. His farm is well stocked with Jersey and Durham cattle, and he is also raising mules and horses. Although an ardent supporter of Democratic principles he has never aspired to office, but prefers to give his undivided attention to his farming interests. He is a Blue Lodge Mason, a Knight of Honor, a United Workman, and he is a member of the Methodist Church. Miss Alice A. Scott, whom he married in 1874, was a native of Alabama, as was also her father, James T. Scott, who is now a resident of San Marcos. Of the nine children born to this union, all are living and doing well. They are: Lula, Julia, Meda, Daisy, Berry T., Jr.; Mitchell, Thomas, Alice A. and Mary. Mr. Bost is an example of what can be accomplished by push and energy. Starting out in life with very little education and no means worth speaking about, he is now one of the substantial men of this section and his sound, good sense and honesty and uprightness are well known.

GEORGE WASHINGTON ALLEN, M.D. One of the noblest professions, one of the most beneficial to mankind, is that of medicine, and while it is prosecuted for gain it is in its very nature nearest to beneficient charity, and is very exacting upon its devotees. One of the most prominent physicians of Fayette County, Texas, is Dr. G. W. Allen, of Flatonia. He is a native of Walton County, Ga., born in 1849, the seventh of nine children born to John William Barkley, and Martha (Camp) Allen, also Georgians by birth, in which State both the Allens and Camps settled many years ago. John W. B. Allen was a Minister of the Methodist Church, and in 1851 removed to Texas and located in Fayette County. The most of his work as a Minister of the Gospel was done in this county, and he was one of the early circuit riders. He became Presiding Elder of the Columbus District about 1869–70, and while filling that honored position did noble and effective work for the Master. His career of usefulness was closed by death, August 16, 1890, but his widow still survives and makes her home with the subject of this sketch, and her other children. Dr. G. W. Allen was reared and educated in Fayette County, and completed his literary education in Bastrop Collegiate Institute. He began the study of medicine in 1866, took a course of lectures at Galveston, and then began practicing. In the spring of 1872, he graduated from the Medical Department of the State University of Kentucky and Louisville. In 1893 he took a post graduate course at the New York Polyclinic, then returned home once more. He has been an active practitioner since 1868, and his first work as a medical practitioner was done on Sandy Fork Creek, in Gonzales County, during which time he boarded with a Mr. Gentry. October 21, 1868, he was married to Miss Amanda Louisa Evans, daughter of Dr. Isaiah Evans, who came to this State from Missouri, and was a successful and well known medical practitioner of the section in which he lived. After his marriage Dr. Allen moved to Fayette County, and there spent the most of his time until the fall of 1871. In 1872 he located at Old Flatonia, but at the end of one year moved to Fort Worth, and there made his home for two years. At the end of that time he came to Flatonia, and after practicing here for three or four years took up his residence in Brown County, where his home continued to be for some ten years. In 1889 he returned to Flatonia, where he is now permanently located, and where he has built up a prosperous and continually increasing practice. To himself and wife nine children were born, seven boys and two girls, three of the male children died in infancy. Beverly Lemme, John Elijah Matterson and Emmett Russell died, while the other six still survive, consisting of two girls and four boys, Martha Louisa, wife of Dr. G. W. Cross, and Emily Elizabeth, are the two girls; George W., Jr., Theophalus Parvin, William Isaiah, and Theodore Litton, are the four living boys. The Doctor and his family are Methodists, and socially he is a member of the A. F. & A. M. and the A. O. U. W.

H. C. Thompson. The family of which H. C. Thompson is a distinguished member is of Irish origin, and the first member to settle in the United States was Henry Thompson, the paternal grandfather of our subject. He was a native of the Emerald Isle, and subsequently moved to England, where he resided until 1804, when he came to the " land of the free and the home of the brave." He followed agricultural pursuits in Georgia until the breaking out of the War of 1812, when he enlisted and fought with General Jackson in the battle of New Orleans. After the war he removed to Lauderdale County, Ala., and thence to Tuscumbia, Colbert County, that State, where the remainder of his days were passed. His son, T. W. Thompson, was born in England, and came with his parents to America. He was reared to mature years in Alabama, and there passed his entire life. He married Miss Mary D. W. Wilder, a native of Kentucky, and eighteen children were the fruits of this union, our subject being sixth in order of birth. The father was a prominent man in his county, holding the office of Probate Judge, Collector of Taxes, County Commissioner, Justice and other positions. H. C. Thompson, our subject, was born in Franklin County, Ala., in 1843, obtained the rudiments of an education in the schools of the county and then attended the Academy of Cornersville, Tenn. He then branched out as a teacher, following the same in the northern counties of Mississippi until 1879, when he moved to Texas, locating at Prairie Lea, Caldwell County, where he tilled the soil. From there he moved to San Marcos, Hays County, and was engaged in agricultural pursuits until 1887, when he moved to Goliad County. In 1893 he moved to the town of Goliad and was elected to his present office, District Clerk of Goliad County, in November of that year. In 1880 he was married to Miss Samantha Norman, a native of Mississippi, and two children have been given them: Rose Wilder, died in infancy, and Della A. The family holds membership in the Baptist Church, and Mr. Thompson is a member of the Knights of Pythias and Independent Order of Red Men. He is honored and respected, and has made a name for himself as a public-spirited citizen and a promotor of new enterprises.

Daniel Franklin Smith. This thrifty and successful farmer and stockman, of Guadalupe County, Texas, is a native of Fayette County, Ala., born October 23, 1844, the fifth of eleven children born to Moses Howell and Cynthia E. (Jones) Smith, the former of whom was born in Georgia, and when a young man removed to Alabama, where he married and engaged in farming. He emigrated to Guadalupe County, Texas, in 1854, purchased a tract of land on which he lived until January 8, 1871, when death called him home. He was a man of retiring and quiet habits, fond of his home and family, but during his entire life took no active interest in politics. His wife was born in Alabama, and died a few years after coming to Texas, in 1859. The subject of this sketch was reared in Guadalupe County, and went to school but ten months in his life. When the great Civil War opened he ran away from home, being but seventeen years of age, and enlisted in Captain White's company, Churchill's Division, and was in service in Arkansas. He was captured at Arkansas Post, was taken prisoner to St. Louis, was there exchanged and came home on furlough. After a time he re-enlisted in Captain Georgis' company, at Houston, was sent to Galveston, and was on duty there until the close of the war. In 1865 he returned to his old home, at which time his sole possessions consisted of a pony, and with this modest beginning he has accumulated one fine plantation and one not so good, his home place containing 235 acres and his place on " Bushy " 435 acres. About 200 acres are under cultivation, and are devoted to the raising of cotton and corn, one-half bale of the former and twenty-five bushels of the latter, being the average per acre. Much attention is given also to the raising of horses and mules, and he now has five fine brood mares and a very fine jack. He is a member of the Primitive Baptist Church. His wife, whom he married February 15, 1866, was Mrs. Jennie Hoke, widow of B. H. Hoke and daughter of Thomas Hubbard. The latter lived in Caldwell County, Texas, and while moving to northern Texas was taken sick and died in Hamilton Valley. His family then returned to Caldwell County, Texas. To Mr. and Mrs. Smith eight children have been given: William M., Maston, Mary, wife of John Jones; Fannie, wife of Rufus Cordray; Thomas, Abner, Minnie and Guy.

WILLIAM LACKEY is an honorable and progressive farmer, and as such no name in the memorial department of this work is more worthy of mention. He is a product of Tennessee, born near Winchester, Franklin County, October 4, 1807, and is the second in order of birth of four children, two sons and two daughters, born to William and Elizabeth (Parks) Lackey. The father was a native Virginian, and entered the Revolutionary War when but sixteen years of age, and fought until peace was proclaimed. Afterwards he was a pioneer of Alabama, but subsequently moved to Tennessee, when that State was full of Indians. Our subject relates that when he was a very little fellow he remembers seeing them dancing in his father's yard after night. The father met with an accident near Huntsville, Ala., in 1812, and this terminated in his death. The mother was a member of the famous Parks family of that region, and two of her brothers were officers in the battle of Lundy's Lane, and were men of great physical vigor. " Devil Bill Parks," as he was generally called, was one of the most powerful men of his day, and his match was not to be found in the section. After the death of Mr. Lackey his widow went to the home of relatives near Winchester, Tenn., and there her children were reared. Educational advantages were poor in those days, and her children received very little instruction. William Lackey was apprenticed to a carpenter, and seeing that a knowledge of drawing would aid him very materially he picked up that study himself. When twenty-four years of age he removed to the neighborhood of Americus, Ga., where he carried on his trade and collecting for fourteen years. He there was married to Miss Amanda Ball, of Houston County, Texas, January 22, 1836, and then entered into partnership with a Mr. Shields to manufacture gins. Their plant was erected in Minden, La., and they met with fair success. Later Mr. Lackey bought land and negroes and farmed in that State for nineteen years. He then sold his plantation for Confederate money, which became utterly worthless, and he then came to Texas, where he had to start over again, and although over fifty years of age, has since that time amassed another competency. This is an example of perseverance and industry that might well be copied. When he first came to this State he stopped for a month in Bosque County, and then removed to Washington County, where he rented a farm for one year. On that he cleared about $1,500, and with this bought a place on the Colorado River in Colorado County, which he soon afterwards sold for $4,000. After that he bought a place of 300 acres in Caldwell County, on

Plum Creek, which is now well improved and stocked. He rents this out, and for the past seven or eight years has resided in Luling, where he has a large and comfortable home. He has ever been a man of exemplary habits, and is very neat in person and dress. Though eighty-seven years of age he is well preserved, and has the appearance of a man of sixty. For nearly seventy years he has been an active member of the Methodist Church. To himself and wife sixteen children have been born, twelve of whom grew to mature years and eight are now living: Sarah, widow of Dr. Laidley; Balsora, wife of V. D. Letulle; Anna, wife of L. E. Letulle; Janie, single; George G.; Mahala, wife of A. J. Shaw; Belle, Emma, wife of Jesse Humphries, died July 2, 1894, in Luling, and Fannie, wife of W. C. Sewell. The mother of these children died in 1886. She was also an earnest and consistent member of the Methodist Church.

Dr. James W. Fennell. This gentleman, the oldest practicing physician in Seguin, Texas, is a native of Alabama, born in the year 1832, and of the nine children resulting from the marriage of his parents, I. H. and Margaret (Fennell) Fennell, he was second in order of birth. The parents were natives of North Carolina and Virginia, respectively, but were married in Alabama, whither their parents had moved at an early date. Mr. Fennell followed agricultural pursuits in Alabama until 1854, when he made a visit to Texas and chose a location near Seguin. Two years later he moved with his family to this (Guadalupe) county and bought an improved farm three miles from Seguin. His wife had died in Alabama in 1845, and he survived her until 1882. Both were members of the Methodist Church. In the schools of Alabama James W. Fennell received a fair education, and in 1856 he came to Texas with his father. In the year 1851, while a resident of Alabama, he began the study of medicine, and later attended college. To further perfect himself in medicine he went to Jefferson Medical College, Philadelphia, and left that institution with his diploma in 1854. After that he began practicing in Alabama and continued practicing there until he came to Texas as stated. For one year after reaching the Lone Star State he followed farming, but in 1857 he came to Seguin, where he has had a successful practice since. In the year 1854 he was married in Alabama to Miss Caroline Beard, a native of Kentucky, and four children blessed this union, all now living: Florence, widow of Mr. Collins; Margaret, wife of Mr. Ewing; Mollie, wife of Joseph Dibrell, and Jefferson Davis, physician of Seguin, and a graduate of Bellevue Hospital College, New York. In the year 1862 Dr. Fennell enlisted in the Fourth Texas Regiment, a member of the medical department, and aided in establishing camp hospitals. He served in the Army of Virginia, was in many of the hardest battles of the war, and during his four years' service only made one visit home and that was on army duty. After the war he immediately resumed practice in Seguin and is one of the prominent physicians of that section. He is a member of the Southwestern and the Texas State Medical Association, has held offices in both, and has been an earnest worker in both. He and wife and children are members of the Methodist Church, and he is a Mason of the Royal Arch degree, and has been very active in Masonic matters.

Alexander Louis Kessler. Since the tide of immigration first set toward America, perhaps no class of people who have found homes upon her shores has done more to build up her interests or contribute more to her commercial importance and national prosperity than the sturdy, honest-hearted and industrious Germans, who have come here to enjoy the freedom of thought and independence of action denied them in the Fatherland. Alexander Louis Kessler was born December 5, 1837, in the Province of Nassau, on the Westerwald, Germany, and his parents, Ludwig and Christina Kessler, were natives of that country. The father was a man of moderate means and followed the occupation of a carpenter and farmer. In 1845 he left Germany for the United States, and brought with him his wife, sons, A. L. and Ludolph (the latter of whom died soon after his arrival in this country), and his wife's father, who also died soon after reaching the States. He landed in Indianola in due time, and remained in that place six months, waiting to secure some kind of overland conveyance. At last he engaged an ox team and removed with his family to New Braunfels, where he accumulated a competency, and, until recently, with his beloved wife, spent in ease and comfort the pleasant evening time of their lives. He died in his eighty-first year, leaving his beloved wife, who has very recently passed away (spring of 1894). In 1857 Mr. A. L. Kessler was a member of a surveying party that located and established the boundary line between Texas and New Mexico, and in the latter part of that year drove a stage between St. Louis and Santa Fé. During the war, owing to the fact that he spoke the Mexican language fluently, he was detached by Gen. Magruder to do business with Mexican trading parties. After the war Mr. Kessler became a government contractor, furnishing horses and supplies, and made money. From 1868 to 1873 he engaged in merchandising, and was also successful in that line. In 1866 he married Miss Hermina Floege, a native of New Braunfels, and the daughter of Charles and Augusta (Weinert) Floege, who were born in Germany, but who came to this country and here died. Mr. and Mrs. Kessler's only child, a son, Alexander L. A., aged seventeen years, contracted a fatal illness at Austin, and died in April, 1884. This was a sad blow to the devoted parents, who saw in the unfolding talent of their beloved son the promise of many years of usefulness. Mr. Kessler has several times served as Mayor of New Braunfels, and was a member of the House of Representatives of the Texas Legislature in 1874, '75 and '76. As a member of the Legislature he ranked among the leading men of that body, and made a record of which he may well be proud. He was a member of many important committees: Internal Improvements, Finance, and Claims and Accounts; introduced amongst others a bill to exempt woolen and cotton mills from taxation, for the term of ten years, from State, county and municipal taxes, which was, however, defeated after considerable debate. He was favorably mentioned as a candidate for Congress this year, and, although not consenting to run, expressed his views, to-wit:

" NEW BRAUNFELS, July 1st, '94.

"Editor, New Braunfels Zeitung:

"In your last issue you say that there is no want for Congressional candidates in the coming election; that among others the undersigned name has been mentioned; that I was not a partisan, and that if I had any such aspirations that the people should know on what platform I would run. In answer to this I will say that I have not seriously considered the matter; however, should I conclude to make the race, the following is an outline of my position:

" TARIFF.—I am and always have been in favor of a protective tariff, or for revenue, which is about the same as in the past. Tariff has been about equal

John W. Slayton,

to the expenses of the government. I favor protection for other reasons. First, it gives employment to our labor, creates consumers for our produce, leaves our money at home, and will in the near future develop the South, as manufacturers will go near raw material and a milder climate, and, further, it is the easiest and most satisfactory way of raising taxes. I am unalterably opposed to any system of taxation which is inquisitorial in character, communistic in principle, and a rewarder for perjury.

"Coinage of Silver.—I am in favor of the coinage of silver, but only such as is produced by our mines in the United States, at the ratio of sixteen to one, to be legal tender for all debts, private and public; to be paid for pensions, salaries and wages by the Government in pro ratio so as to keep in circulation.

"Our Patent Laws.—I am opposed to our present patent laws for the following reasons:

"1st. Not more than thirty out of a hundred of the inventors are benefited, but are forced to sell out to some speculator, who reaps the benefit.

"2d. It gives the patentee the right to extort from the people ad libitum, without limitation, for seventeen years, and at the end of this period he has only to make oath that he has not made money enough out of the invention, for which he gets an extension of seven years more, making twenty-four years in all.

"3d. It takes labor from our people and artisans, and makes them part and parcel of the machine. In fact, I am not convinced that labor-saving machinery to the extent that it has developed in the last quarter of our century is a blessing to mankind.

"4th. I believe all applications for a patent should be made to a commission of the Government, and, if found practical, the inventor should be paid a fair price for it, and the manufacturing of the same should be left for competition.

"Government Ownership of Railroads.—I am in favor of Government ownership of railroads. The ownership to be acquired in a fair and business-like way, by no means in a spirit of confiscation; to be appraised by a competent authority, and with the consent of the owners be bought at their actual value: to be paid for in United States bonds bearing a low rate of interest and convertible into United States Treasury notes at pleasure of owner. But in case of refusal of the owners of said railroads to sell, then the Government should build its own. I believe that the Government ownership is the only remedy for the strikes now so frequent. Besides, the private capital now invested in them would seek other investments, principally in manufactories, of which we in the South would get our fair proportion. It would stop the immense avenues to concentrated wealth which are a menace to our free Constitution.

"All of the employes of the Government to run such roads should be appointed by a competent board, after a rigid examination as to their qualifications for their respective positions, but afterwards not removable except for cause, with prospects for promotion and to be pensioned after a certain period of service. In case of death of a married man, his widow to receive the pension; but not allowed to vote, or in any way to participate in politics, the same as our soldiers.

"Strikes and Unemployed Labor—Is a matter most alarming and of the gravest importance. Steps should be taken at once to ascertain the cause thereof. Honest and willing labor should be able to find employment, for a hungry stomach and the cry of children for bread knows no law except that of nature. A remedy should be found without delay for the relief of such persons. On the other hand, a strict law should be enacted against vagrants and professional tramps; in fact, no man able bodied and in health should be allowed to beg. We should be just and strict."   "A. L. KESSLER."

He was elected as a Democrat, but has since severed his connection with all parties. Socially he is a Mason, a Knight of Honor, member of the Independent Order of Odd Fellows and Ancient Order of United Workmen. He resides one mile from New Braunfels, and owns 1,000 acres of the finest farming land in Comal County, having a river front of two miles, and two water-powers, one of 1,100 and the other of 350 horse-power. He has all of his land under fence and about 450 acres under cultivation. Annually he raises graded cattle and horses, and has accumulated a fortune. His success in life is due to his own exertions, for he started without capital or influence, and has fought his way to an honorable position and acquired a handsome competency. Possessing superior attainments and charming social qualities, to know is to like and admire him. He is a clear and forcible writer on public questions, and often contributes to the newspapers.

HENRY WILLIAM WILSON. Admired no less for his modest, gentle disposition and entire freedom from affectation than for his intellectual force, which raised him into prominence at once, Mr. Wilson has taken with him into his retirement the esteem, respect and admiration of the people. He was born in Southampton, England, January 17, 1819, where, at the age of fourteen, he was apprenticed to the printer's trade. After having served seven years, in 1840 he went to London, where he worked at his trade for one year. In 1841 he determined to travel, and went to the Cape of Good Hope, where he remained for eighteen months, and from thence took passage to Calcutta, where he remained for fifteen months; from thence he went to New Zealand, South Australia, Australia Felix and New South Wales, and thence crossed Bass' Straits to Tasmania. In 1849 the gold fever for California became epidemic, and he determined on visiting the gold fields. He was among the first in the Sacramento Valley, in the Yurba and Feather River country. There were no buildings in San Francisco, Sacramento or Marysville at that time. After traveling over the territories of Washington, Oregon, and the entire Pacific coast of the United States he went to Mazatlan, San Blas, Acapulco, and crossed the mountain range of Guerrero to the City of Mexico, where he remained thirteen years. From the City of Mexico he went to Vera Cruz, from whence he sailed to New Orleans, thence to Rockport, in Texas, and Beeville, in Bee County, which he made his home. Here he has held a number of local positions. He has been appointed and elected to various offices in the county, and has the confidence and esteem of everyone, and few hold higher place in the regard of the people. He was elected County Superintendent of Public Instruction for four years. In 1874 he was appointed by Judge D. D. Claiborne District and County Clerk for two years, and was subsequently elected to the same position for four years more, serving three terms in succession. In the Masonic order he was preeminently prominent, having been elected Worshipful Master of Beeville Lodge No. 261, A. F. & A. M. for seven consecutive terms, from 1874 to 1880, inclusive, during which time he entered, passed and raised every man that was made a Mason in the county, and performed the last sad rites and offices paid to the dead, depositing their remains with the usual formalities. Mr. Wilson is a member of the Protestant Episcopal Church. On his arrival in Beeville he bought 2,200 acres of land adjoining the town, a portion of which he has laid out into an addition of Beeville, of which he gave the San Antonio and Aransas Pass Railway six blocks, each 100 yards square, with a sixty-feet-wide street between each block, as a bonus. He also gave to the Protestant Episcopal Church a town block of the same dimensions. All these blocks are now the most desirable portion for residence property. His own house, inclosed in its evergreen park of thirty acres, with its hundreds of arbor vitæs and red cedars, glistening in the sun and bending to the prevailing summer southeast winds, erected on a large and generous scale, is an almost perfect type of a home. Modern improvements, bath-rooms, never-failing cisterns of rain and well water, with its Eclipse wind engine, and an extensive library, everything about the place speaks of a refined and literary taste. In this ideal home, surrounded by all that makes life enjoyable, Mr. Wilson, who is now in his seventy-sixth year, expects to pass the remainder of his days.

COL. NEWTON CANNON GULLETT. The name of Gullett is one of the most influential and widely known in Texas, and is one of the most respected in the community in which Mr. Gullett resides. This gentleman is possessed of that independent spirit, that enterprise, push and energy necessary for a successful business career, and his life has been a useful and prosperous one, in direct refutation of the saying that "a rolling stone gathers no moss." He inherits the French and English blood of his parents, Samuel and Rebecca (Thompson) Gullett, he being one of their ten children, born in Maury County, Tenn., in 1822. The father was born in Maryland and the mother in North Carolina, and in the latter State they were united in marriage about 1798. Immediately thereafter they removed to Tennessee and settled in what is now Maury County, being the first settlers of that region, where the father followed tilling the soil, and resided on the farm on which he first located until his death in 1829, his widow surviving him until 1856. On the old homestead in Tennessee the subject of this sketch was reared, his education being acquired in Columbia. At about the age of nineteen years he began merchandising at Lynnville, Giles County, Tenn., but a few years later went to Mississippi. He only remained there a short time, however, when he returned to his native State. In 1850 he went to New Orleans, and the next year came to Texas and started in business in San Antonio, where he was engaged in speculating. In 1856 he once more returned to New Orleans, and there in 1857 engaged in the grocery business, which he continued successfully until 1860, when he engaged in the commission business. He left New Orleans, under the order of Gen. Ben Butler, as an enemy to the Federal Government, and in 1864 attached himself to the staff of Gen. Richardson of the Confederate Army, with the rank of Captain, being in the ordnance department of Gen. Forrest at the close of the war. He at that time returned to New Orleans with very little means but re-engaged in the commission business, and being the only merchant in the cotton seed trade his profits were enormous, and in two years' time made $100,000. He continued in this business until 1876, and did an extensive and profitable trade. In 1875, however, he came to

Texas, and decided to make this State his permanent home, and the next year made a settlement in Refugio County, where he at once engaged extensively in the raising of cattle. In the fall of 1876 he went to New York and bought a shipment of wire to fence in his ranche, and in November of that year built the first wire stock fence in the State of Texas, this being before the day of barbed wire. Col. Gullett now has a fine ranche of 25,000 acres at the mouth of the San Antonio River and on Hines Bay, which comprises a fine lot of land, with nearly all of it suitable for profitable farming operations. Much of the bottom land is capable of producing the best sugarcane, and all of it is admirably adapted for the successful raising of corn and cotton. This land lies on a high bluff along the bay, is very healthfully located and is a grand site for an open port or a city, which the village of Tivoli will eventually become. Although most of the large stockraisers are averse to dividing their large pastures, Col. Gullett sees the great benefit to be derived if the country is filled with a desirable class of settlers, and he has concluded to sell off portions of his estate to thrifty and respectable applicants, and will do so on terms to suit the purchaser. There is no better climate, no more healthy locality or more fertile lands in Texas, and at the village of Tivoli a postoffice has been secured by Col. Gullett, which promises to become a flourishing place. He also owns land in half a dozen other counties, some of which is the best in the State, aggregating over 10,000 acres. Besides the Colonel there are two other members of his family living, a brother and a sister. The brother, Samuel, was born in 1818, and still lives on the old estate on which his father settled in Maury County, Tenn, while the other member is his sister Angeline, now the Widow Leftwich, who resides with her brother in Tennessee. A brother John lived in Missouri, and served as State Senator for some twenty years. He died about 1883, leaving a large family. The father had three brothers: Wakeman went to Illinois, and died in that State about 1836, leaving a large family; Dr. William went to Alabama, where he passed from life; and James went to Georgia, where he reared a family. Col. Gullett is a pleasant, courteous and genial gentleman, who has been an extensive traveler and has been a close and keen observer. He traveled over much of the United States before there were railroads, and can recount many interesting reminiscences of the early days of the Lone Star State. He has been a shrewd and practical man of business, is thoroughly conversant with the affairs of his State, of which he is one of the leading financiers.

HENRY T. CHIVERS. This representative citizen and prominent attorney of Edna, Texas, first saw the light in Wilcox County, Ala., in 1852. He was the seventh son born to Algernon Sidney and Jane (Plunkett) Chivers, natives of Georgia, in which State they were married. From there the parents moved to Alabama, and thence a short time afterward to Mississippi, and finally to Texas in 1855, on the line between Lavaca and Jackson Counties. Later they moved to Lavaca, bought land two miles Southwest of the present site of Edna, and there the father cultivated the soil until the breaking out of the Civil War. From there he moved to the Caranahua River, and managed a large farm for his brother until his death in 1862. The mother died November 24, 1892. Both were members of the Baptist Church, and he was a deacon in that church for twenty years, and an active worker. He was very successful as a farmer, and his brother, James Madison Chivers, was at the outbreak of the war perhaps the largest farmer in the county. The latter came to this State about 1859 with about seventy-five negroes, from Alabama, and later entered the army as Lieutenant of Boden's Company. He was discharged on account of ill health in 1863, and he was also over age. After returning home Mr. Chivers engaged in cotton speculating, and ran extensive wagon trains to the Rio Grande River and into Mexico. He often had forty wagons on the road, and made an immense fortune, nearly all of which he lost at Matamoras, Mexico. He died in Jackson County, Texas, in 1886. The original of this notice was reared in Jackson County, and had limited educational advantages. He made two trips with his uncle to Mexico with the wagon train, and was with him in Brownsville and Matamoras one year. After this he spent three years driving cattle, and in the spring of 1869 went to Mississippi with a herd of cattle for Gen. Wade Hampton. He remained in that State two years and then returned in 1871, and for one year was working with stock. After that he made a trip to Kansas. In the fall of 1871 he took charge of the Sheriff's office for E. A. Matthews, as deputy, and in 1874 ran for that office. For two years after this he followed farming, and in 1877 was married to Miss Emma Blewett, a native of Texas and the daughter of Capt. William Blewett of Jasper County. Capt. Blewett died in Little Rock, Ark., in 1862, while Captain of a company. In 1875 Mr. Chivers began the study of law, continued this for a short time, and then resumed again in 1879, being admitted to the bar in 1881. In the fall of 1884 he was elected to the office of County Attorney, held that position four years, and, after being out two years, was again elected to that position, holding it one term. He is quite an active politician, and has served in many conventions, being a member of the one at Victoria in 1875, when William H. Crain was nominated for State Senator. He was a candidate for the Legislature, but was withdrawn on the morning of the day of convention. Since that time Mr. Chivers has been engaged in the practice of law and the real estate business. His wife died November 30, 1888, leaving three children: William Blewett, aged thirteen; Jib and Emma. Mr. Chiver's second marriage was with Miss Rosa Dupy, a native of Jackson County, and the daughter of Bartholomew Dupy who for many years was a County official and at the time of his death, which occurred in 1890, was Tax Assessor. One child has been born to this union, an infant, unnamed. Mr. Chivers is a member of the Masonic Fraternity.

WILLIAM B. GEORGE, County Tax Assessor of Calhoun County, Texas, is a man thoroughly qualified in every respect for his present position and one who has won a large circle of friends by his upright, honorable career through life. He is a native of this county, born in Port Lavaca, in 1849, and the site of this city is on the league formerly belonging to his parents, Wiley and Annie (Bernson) George. The father was a native of Alabama, and the mother of Ohio. The latter was the widow of Thomas McConnell at the time of her marriage to Mr. George. Wiley George came to the Lone Star State about 1840, and located in San Antonio, where he engaged in business for Mr. Moore for a few years. Later he moved to Victoria County, married Mrs. McConnell, and subsequently engaged in the stock business very extensively, speculating in horses. These he bought in Mexico and took North to sell. His death occurred in 1863. Mr. George was a soldier in the War of 1812, and was with Gen. Jackson in the battle of New Orleans. Mrs. George died at Dallas, Texas, in March, 1884. They were honorable, straightforward and well respected citizens. William B. George, our subject, was reared in Port Lavaca, whither his parents had moved in 1845, and he secured a fair education there. For a short time after growing up he clerked, but later he engaged in the cattle business, continuing this until 1874, when he moved to Goliad County, where he engaged in farming and sheep raising. Five years later he went to Dallas and remained there for one year, engaged in buying hides. In 1880 he returned to Goliad County, but later went to Hamilton County and thence back to Jackson County, where he remained three years, engaged in farming. In 1888 he returned to Calhoun County, engaged in clerking, and soon after was appointed Assessor, which position he now holds. He selected his wife in the person of Miss Susan E. Crain, of Goliad County, and their nuptials were celebrated in 1874. Mrs. George died in 1879, leaving two children: Susan A. and James B. Mr. George was married again in 1880, to Miss McNulan, a native of Texas and a daughter of Henry B., who was an early settler of Lavaca. Four children have been born to this union: Gussie Lu., Julia Mabel, Virginia and Harvey G. In his social relations Mr. George is a member of the A. F. & A. M., the K. of P., Lodge No. 164, and he has been Secretary of the Masonic Lodge. He and wife hold membership in the Baptist Church.

ROBERT KYLE. No name is justly entitled to a more enviable place in the history of Hays County, Texas, than the one that heads this sketch, for it is borne by a man who, though young in years, has yet been usefully and honorably identified with the interests of this county and with its advancement in every worthy particular. Like many prominent men of the county Mr. Kyle is a farmer, stock raiser and ginner, and has met with substantial results in these occupations. His parents, Felix and Grace (Burleson) Kyle, were natives of Mississippi, and they came to Texas in 1849, settling on a place in Hays County, given Mr. Kyle by his father-in-law, Gen. Edward Burleson, who was of the distinguished Burleson family. There he followed farming and stock raising for some time, but subsequently moved to the mountains of Hays County where he continued his former occupation. During the Civil War he enlisted in Capt. Carrington's Company, and served on the border. This worthy citizen is still living and makes his home near Martindale, Caldwell County. The mother is deceased. On the 27th of February, 1851, a son was born to their union whom they named Robert. He grew to sturdy manhood on the farm in Hays County and here he has spent his entire life, receiving his education in the common schools. After reaching mature years he clerked for about two years in San Marcos, and then, with the means he had accumulated, bought one hundred acres of land on which he immediately began farming. All he has made has been the result of his own industry, for he received very little assistance from his father, and he is now the owner of 1,000 acres of land with 625 acres under cultivation. He annually raises many hogs and cattle and has a well equipped steam gin, two Pratt gins, sixty saws each sixteen bales daily, and 1,200 annually. In politics he espouses the principles of the Democratic party, but is not an office seeker. He is public spirited and gives his hearty support to all worthy measures. In the year 1873 he married Miss Anna Randle, daughter of Wilson and Sarah Randle. Mr. Randle was born in Tennessee, and is now deceased. The mother is living at the present time (1894). Mr. and Mrs. Kyle's union was blessed by the birth of seven children, all of whom are now living, except one: Zante, Emma, Bessie, Felix, Mattie and Addie. Exum is deceased.

RICHARD O. FAIRES. A man's life work is the measure of his success, and he is truly the most successful man who, turning his powers in the channel of an honorable purpose, accomplishes the object of his endeavor. Such a man is Richard O. Faires, who was born in Fayette County, Texas, in 1841, the fourth of eight children born to William A. and Ada (McClure) Faires, who were born in Alabama and Tennessee respectively, their marriage taking place in the latter State. In 1883, they came to Texas and settled in what is now Fayette County, on the Colorado River. In that early day, the Indians were quite troublesome, and while he was engaged in tilling his land and looking after stock, he was obliged to carry a rifle with him. He served in the Texas Revolution, and died on his farm, on which he first settled in 1885, his wife having crossed the river in 1874. They were worthy and consistent members of the Baptist Church. The subject of this sketch was reared and educated in the county of his birth, and upon the bursting of the war cloud which had so long hovered over the country, he, in 1861, enlisted in the Confederate service and was in the campaign in New Mexico, and a participant in the battle of Val Verde. He was a member of Company I, a private, Regimental Commissary Sergeant, Orderly Sergeant of the company, and Lieutenant of the company under Capt. Killough, Green's Regiment, Sibley's Brigade, and took part in every principal engagement in which his regiment participated, except the retaking of Galveston. He was in the battles of the Red River Campaign and at the time of Lee's surrender was with his command in Texas. He at once returned home and turned his sword into a plowshare, and set energetically about tilling the soil with the consciousness of having been a faithful soldier during the war. In 1869 he was elected to the position of County Sheriff, and discharged his duties faithfully and well at the time when it demanded a more than ordinary degree of personal courage and determination. He entered upon his duties in May, 1870, and served one term of four years, declining to become a candidate for re-election on account of bad health. He has twice been elected Mayor of Flatonia, in which capacity he is now serving (1894). He was married in 1877 to Miss Eliza Killough, a daughter of his former Captain and a granddaughter of Col. John H. Moore, an early Indian fighter of the State of Texas and the founder of La Grange, capital of the county. Mrs. Faires was born in the Lone Star State, and has borne her husband three children: Ira G. and Fairie (daughter) and Richard O. Jr. In 1878, Mr. Faires came with his family to Flatonia, which is located on his father's headright, where he has since made his home. He has been somewhat active in politics, is a stanch Democrat, and is a member of the A. F. & A. M., I. O. O. F. and other secret societies. He is an agreeable and genial gentleman to meet, has a hospitable and comfortable home, and by his correct mode of living, has gathered about him numerous friends.

JUDGE DANIEL D. CLAIBORNE. To the citizens of southwest Texas, the names of very few prominent officials are better known than that of Judge Daniel D. Claiborne. He was born in Smith County, Tennessee, May 21, 1820, to the union of John and Catherine (Ferguson) Claiborne, the former a native of Virginia and the latter of Scotland. The Claiborne family came originally from England, the first member, William Claiborne, touching the American coast in 1632. (See Frost's History of the United States). He became Secretary to the Governor of Virginia, and held that office until his death. Our subject's paternal grandfather, Daniel Brown Claiborne, emigrated to Tennessee in 1800, and was among the early settlers. He was a Methodist preacher and followed his ministerial duties until his death in 1865. His son, John Claiborne, father of our subject, was born in Virginia, in 1796 and died in Tennessee in 1878. He followed the occupation of a farmer and miller and was an industrious, hard-working citizen. He was in the War of 1812, and was in the battle of New Orleans. On the maternal side our subject is descended from King Fergus I. of Scotland, his ancestors first coming to the United States in 1790 and settling in North Carolina. About 1804, they moved to Tennessee. Judge Daniel D. Claiborne was reared and educated in Tennessee, taking two courses in Clinton College, that State. In 1841, he began the study of law and was admitted to the bar at Jacksonville, Ala., in 1843. Immediately afterwards he began practicing, and in 1845 returned to his old home, where he continued his legal duties. He was Clerk and Master of the Chancery Court for some time and was very prosperous. About 1858 he came to Texas and settled at Brenham, bringing with him fifty-one negro slaves, all of whom became free in 1865. When the war closed, our subject was at Columbus under medical treatment, but soon afterwards he resumed his practice at the bar following if for five years. He was then appointed District Judge by Governor Davis and confirmed by the Senate, with headquarters at Goliad. That office he held for six years and then retired from the bench, and has practiced his profession since. During the last few years, he has confined his business to the higher courts. No judge in this part of the State is better known than Judge Claiborne, whose sound sense, legal knowledge and personal honor have won for him an enviable reputation. True merit never fails to win. In whatever field of action the judge has been called, he has shown his superior qualities and high character. Judge Claiborne was first married in August, 1849, to Miss Elizabeth R. Hogg, a native of Tennessee, who died in 1853. Three children were born to this union, all of whom passed away before her. On the 27th of June, 1855, he married Miss Hanna A. Traver of Wilson County, Tennessee, and four children were the fruits of this union. All are deceased except one daughter, Kate Denham, who resides in Goliad. The Judge is a member of the M. E. Church South, and is the oldest Mason and Odd Fellow in his section of the country. He is one of the first members of the Sons of Temperance of Tennessee. He have passed all the chairs of these orders and is prominently identified with the same. For years he has been a prominent figure in this section, and his mental capacity and penetration are well known among the people. He is also a writer of ability, having furnished a history of Fannin's massacre, also a history of Goliad heretofore published in the *Galveston News*, of which paper he has been correspondent for many years. He is also the author of many articles published in said paper, giving the best account of the life of Gen. Sam Houston in Tennessee, all of which are preserved in the archives of the State at Austin, Texas.

WILLIAM PLEASANT BLAIR. In tilling the soil and raising stock a more than average degree of success has been acccorded to William Pleasant Blair, whose thrifty ways and laudable ambition have met with a just reward. He was brought up to a thorough knowledge of agriculture on his father's plantation in Alabama, and when commencing the serious work of life for himself, it is not to be wondered at that he chose the occupation to which he had been reared and has met with success in it. He was born in Cherokee County, Ala., September 2, 1850, a son of Ezekiel Stone and Jane (Henry) Blair, both of whom were born in the State of Tennessee. After their marriage they removed to Alabama and settled in Cherokee County, at a time when Indians were very numerous. The father pre-empted land there, became prominent, and being long an active worker for the Democrat party might have held any office within the gift of the people had he so desired, but his tastes ran in other channels than that of the political. When the great Civil War opened, old age prevented him from entering active service, but his sympathies were with the South, and he served for some time in the Home Guards. He was a sagacious and successful man, and never incurred an obligation which he could not discharge. He was much given to acts of benevolence and brotherly kindness, and as a result everyone was his friend. He died in Alabama in 1882, and his wife also passed from life in that State in 1866, both being worthy members of the Baptist Church, in which the father had long been a Deacon. In the county in which he was born, the subject of this sketch was reared and educated, and for some time he was an attendant of the school at Center. He remained in Cherokee County until 1877, when he came to Texas, after having clerked and farmed for some years in his native county. He settled in the vicinity of Palestine, where he tilled the soil successfully for about a year, then moved to Robinson County, where he made one crop, and from thence to Guadalupe County and here, in 1880, he purchased the farm on which he is now residing, which contains 250 acres of fine farming land. Mr. Blair is very much in love with his place and would not sell it at any price, although he was recently offered fifty dollars per acre for it. He has made numerous improvements since becoming its owner, and has been quite successfully and profitably engaged in the raising of Jersey cattle and has done considerable marketing of the dairy product. Mr. Blair started from his old home in Alabama with ninety dollars in his pocket, and by the time he had reached Texas, all this had been spent and he was compelled to commence at the bottom round of the ladder. He met with success in his business ventures and is deserving of much praise for the energy and push which he has always displayed. He was married in Alabama at the age of twenty-two years to Miss Fannie Andrews, a daughter of James M. and Mary Andrews, of Calhoun County, Alabama, to which union six children have been given: Charles M., John D., Homer H., Martin S., Irene and Frederick. Mr. Blair and his wife are members of the Missionary Baptist Church and he has always been a Democrat politically. Mr. Blair's attention has not alone been confined to farming, for he was engaged in merchandising at Martindale for some years.

ADDISON PLEASANT TOWNS, whose success as a thorough-going and progressive farmer is well known, has been a resident of the Lone Star State since 1849, and during all these years his career has been above reproach. His birth occurred in Jasper County, Ga., December 14, 1817, and of the four children born to his parents, John G. and Cynthia (Walker) Towns, he was second in order of birth. The parents were natives of Georgia, and the father was a successful and prosperous planter, and left a good property to his children. He died when our subject was but a boy, but the mother lived to the advanced age of eighty-four years. Mr. Towns was a brother of George W. B. Towns, and first cousin to Governor Humphries, of Georgia. Addison

P. Towns went to school two years to Richard Walker, in Pike County, and in his fifteenth year went to Macon, where he clerked for Gen. Griffin two years. Governor Griffin was the promoter of the Monroe & Macon Railroad, the second road built in Georgia, and found it necessary to deposit $10,000 in the State Bank at Milledgeville. Placing young Towns on horseback, he gave him the money to carry to that city and deposit. About this time a little pamphlet had just been issued telling of Murrill's depredations in Tennessee, and the other clerks in the general's employ endeavored to scare him by reading these to him, and predicting that he would be held up. He reached the city all right, deposited the money, and returned with the receipt to his employer. He says the relief was great after he had disposed of the money. In 1836 he went to Mississippi and clerked for his brother, J. M. Towns, at Madisonville, for three years. In 1849 he left that State. While in that State he clerked most of the time, and during one session of the Legislature served as Enrolling Clerk under Gen. Price, Chief Clerk. In 1849 he came to Gonzales County, Texas, was soon married, and has since made his home there and in Luling. He has ever been an active politician, and was once a candidate for the Legislature. He has held the office of Justice of the Peace, Notary Public, etc., and has ever been a strong Democrat and a great admirer of Governor Hogg. Mr. Towns knew the great Sergeant S. Prentiss personally, and often played whist with him in Jackson, Miss. For forty years now he has aided in the upbuilding of this part of Texas, and is now residing in Luling, enjoying the comforts obtained by his many years of labor. The 16th day of June, 1860, he married Miss Sarah Adeline Coe, daughter of Capt. P. H. Coe, of Gonzales County, a large land owner and a native of Georgia. Capt. Coe came to Texas in the '20's, and took part in all the Mexican trouble. At one time he owned 20,000 acres of land. He was a great Sam Houston man, and was in the battle of San Jacinto. He paid great attention to fine stock, and he and Sam Houston were partners in fine horse breeding, importing stock from Tennessee. He died December 14, 1852. Mrs. Towns' mother, Elizabeth (Parker) Coe, was a native of Louisiana, and died March 16, 1866. To Mr. and Mrs. Towns were born six children: Mary Elizabeth, wife of John W. Foster; James P., Liola, widow of John Robertson; Leanora, wife of William T. Price; John G., and Jennie Augusta, wife of M. T. Davis.

CAPT. FRANCIS ASBERY VAUGHAN. The lives of our prominent men should be written for the sake of the lessons, that men everywhere may place themselves in contact with facts and affairs, and build themselves up and into a life of excellence, not in any sphere but in their own rightful place, where they may keep and augment their individuality. To record in some respects the details of such a life is purposed in the following history: Capt. Francis A. Vaughan, who is now one of the most prominent citizens of Seguin, Texas, is a native of the State of Tennessee, from which have come so many of this county's prominent men. He was born in the year 1831, and was thirteenth in order of birth of fourteen children born to George and Catherine (Roberts) Vaughan, natives respectively of South Carolina and Virginia. The paternal grandfather, James Vaughan, was a native of South Carolina, and of Welsh origin. He served in the Revolutionary War. The maternal grandfather was a native of Pennsylvania, and came of old colonial stock. George Vaughan remained in his native State until grown, and then moved with his father to

Tennessee. He was married to Miss Roberts in 1808, and his family was born in Tennessee. In 1833 he moved to Lowndes County, Miss., where he was engaged in farming. In 1840 he, with others, formed the Columbus Tombigbee Transportation Banking Company, with headquarters at Columbus, and was elected President. In connection with this was a large mercantile business. He held offices in both Tennessee and Mississippi. In 1853 he came to Texas and located on the San Marcos River, in Caldwell County, near Prairie Lea, where he died soon after his arrival. The mother passed away in 1870. Francis A. Vaughan was educated in good schools in Mississippi, and was in his twenty-third year when he came to Texas with his parents. After the death of his father he took charge of the estate and conducted the farm until the war. In 1855 he was married to Miss Adeline McKenzie. Her father, Joseph M. McKenzie, came to Texas in 1840 and located at Linnville, on Matagorda Bay. He had just completed a fine home when the place was besieged and burned by the Indians. The family escaped by taking a boat and going on the bay. After a few years the family moved to Gonzales County, where the father died. To Capt. and Mrs. Vaughan were born nine children: Frances Adeline, wife of Thomas D. Terrell; Sam Houston, died when eight years old; George Wesley and Thomas Milton, (twins); Dora Isabel, Nettie Louise, wife of William T. Vickers; Lizzie Ella, Guy Edgar, and Daniel Glenn. In 1862 he entered the United States Army as Lieutenant of Company A, First Texas Cavalry, and served in the Department of the Gulf. In 1864 he became Captain of Company F, same regiment, and was at Baton Rouge at the close of the war. He was ordered to Texas and mustered out at San Antonio in November, 1865. The same year he was appointed Deputy Collector of Internal Revenue for the Third Division of the Third District of Texas, including Bexar, Guadalupe and Caldwell counties, serving four years. He was a member of the constitutional convention under which the State of Texas was readmitted to the Union, and on the adoption of the constitution he was elected District and County Clerk of Guadalupe County, holding this position four years. In 1875 he engaged in merchandising in Seguin, continued this until 1880, and was then appointed Supervisor of Census for the Sixth District of Texas, doing the work to the great satisfaction of Gen. Walker, who was the Census Superintendent. In 1882 he was appointed Collector of Customs for the District of Saluria, Texas, with headquarters at Indianola, and held that position until 1885. In 1890 he was again appointed to the same office, with headquarters now removed to Eagle Pass, and held that office until the spring of 1894, greatly increasing the receipts of the office. In 1868 he bought his handsome residence in Seguin, with thirty acres of land, and an excellent farm of 150 acres on the Guadalupe River. He lost his wife in 1880, and two years later married Miss Carrie Woolfley, a native of New Orleans. He lost two brothers with Col. Fannin's army, who were taken prisoners and massacred at Goliad, Texas, in 1836. Capt. Vaughan is a member of the Masonic order. He is a Republican, and a leader in the politics of his party in this part of the State.

CARL A. JAHN. Among those who have achieved eminence solely by excellence of character, without any of the modern appliances by which unworthy persons seek to gain undeserved and transient popularity, the subject of this sketch occupies a conspicuous place. He is a manufacturer and dealer in furniture and mattresses, and he is also a real estate dealer of considerable prominence.   Born in New Braunfels, Comal County, Texas, August 12, 1851, he is a son of John and Anna (Klein) Jahn, and is now living on the lot where he was born.   The father was a native of Stralsund, Germany, and was a cabinet maker by trade.   In 1844 he emigrated to America, settling in New Braunfels, where he remained for a short time, and then went to New Orleans, thinking that a better field, but after a few months returned to New Braunfels, Texas.   There he followed cabinet making and dealing in furniture.   In 1866 he imported his first furniture from New York.   In politics he was always a Democrat, but had no political aspirations.   He was a man whose manly creed was: "Do right, and fear not," and he held to this to the last moment.   When a very young lad he entered as an apprentice to a cabinet maker, and after serving five years, started out on his own resources, and afterwards made his way unaided.   For six years before coming to America, he had resided in Switzerland.   At the time of his return from New Orleans his worldly wealth consisted of ten cents, and with this small sum he amassed a comfortable independence, educating and providing for his two children, Emma and Carl A.   On the 9th of January, 1883, his death occurred, and his wife survived him a little over ten years, her death occurring January 18, 1893.   Carl A. Jahn was reared in New Braunfels, and during the war, when money was difficult to obtain, his father not only kept him continually at the New Braunfels Academy, but gave him the benefit of private tutors, so we may well conceive he is well grounded.   Upon reaching his majority, he entered his father's store as a clerk and general assistant, and at his father's death he assumed charge of the business, and is still conducting it under the old firm name.   A Democrat in politics, and for eight years a member of the City Council, he was instrumental in securing the I. & G. N. Railroad for New Braunfels in 1880, and has always been a man of enterprise and intelligence.   He is one of the charter members of the I. O. O. F., and is one of the organizers of the New Braunfels "Maennerchor," and, with the exception of two years, has been its President since it was organized twenty years ago.   In the year 1886 he was married to Miss Emma Holtz, daughter of C. H. and Georgina (Conring) Holtz, natives of Germany, but who are now residents of the United States.   Mr. Holtz was Postmaster at New Braunfels fifteen years, and is now teaching school in the vicinity.   His wife is also living.   Mr. and Mrs. Jahn are the parents of two daughters and two sons, and their names are: Anna, Rudolph, Nellie and Paul.

JOHN W. FLOURNOY.   The legal profession is one of the most highly honored as well as one of the most exacting.   It requires an abundance of legal lore to gain the plane of success, but when that plane is once reached, the reward of patient study and work is a goodly and honorable one.   It is interesting to note the progress of such promising young men as John W. Flournoy in this direction.   He is a member of the well known law firm of Beasley & Flournoy, and if his success continues, as it doubtless will, he has every reason to hope for a future of honor and distinction.   He is already classed among the prominent legal lights of Bee County, and although his career as a professional man has been a short one, it has already been marked with bright success and fidelity to his clients' best interests in every case.   Mr. Flournoy was born in Guadalupe, Texas, in 1854, and was the eldest child born to the marriage of Francis and Elizabeth (Netherland) Flournoy, parents natives of Virginia and Kentucky, respectively.   Mr. and Mrs. Flournoy were married in Lexington, Ky., in 1849, and the father at once started for California, overland. On reaching the Pacific coast he engaged in mining, and remained there until 1852 or '53, when he returned to Texas and joined his wife who had located with her parents in that State in 1851. He made a permanent settlement in the State, locating in Hays County, but subsequently moved to Guadalupe County, where he followed agricultural pursuits. There he made his home until 1890, when he moved to Taylor, Williamson County, and makes his home there at the present time. The mother is also living. Our subject supplemented a good, practical education received in the common schools by attending Emery & Henry College, Virginia, and graduated from that institution in 1879, being valedictorian. In 1885 he began the study of law, and three years later was admitted to the bar. He at once began practicing here, and the present partnership was formed in 1890. They practice in all the courts and do a large business. After graduating, Mr. Flournoy taught the school at Beeville, being principal of the same for seven years, and was a very successful educator. He was married in the year 1881 to Miss Gussie Hitchings, a native of Texas, and daughter of Caleb Hitchings. Mr. and Mrs. Flournoy are members of the Presbyterian Church, and socially he is a Mason. Mrs. Flournoy is a lady of more than ordinary attainments, and has taught in the Beeville schools since 1881, being considered one of the most successful instructors.

NIRAN WHIPS. The gentleman whose name heads this sketch comes of an excellent family and is, himself, one of the substantial men of Victoria County. His career presents an example of industry, perseverance and good management, rewarded by substantial results well worthy the imitation of all who start out in life as he did, with no capital except a good constitution and a liberal supply of pluck and energy. He was born in Quincy, Ill., on December 12, 1847, and was the third of five children born to John Newton and Elizabeth (Rudy) Whips, who were born and reared near each other in Kentucky, and were married in the city of Louisville. During an exceptionally happy married life, they were never separated for more than a week or so at a time, although the father followed the calling of a civil engineer to some extent. The main part of his attention, however, was given to farming, and this occupation he followed during the short time that he resided in Illinois and continued to pursue after taking up his residence in Missouri in 1857. They made their home in Saline County, until a few years prior to their deaths, when they moved, on account of the mother's health, and because two daughters had married and located there, to Shell City, Mo., where they both were called from life, the father in 1880 and the mother in 1879. In Saline County, Mo., the subject of this sketch was reared and educated and in 1870 he first started out for himself as a raiser of osage orange hedge fences, in the pursuit of which enterprise he was successful. At the end of four years he engaged in farming and feeding stock in Montgomery County, but this venture proved disastrous and he lost all that he had previously made. In 1878 he came to Waco, Texas, and worked for a time on a ranche, but soon became an employe of the Texas Express Company as messenger, and when that company was bought out by Wells Fargo Company, he still remained with them and ran as messenger on the various lines in Texas. He was night clerk in Galveston for some time, but soon after, in 1884, was sent to Victoria, where he has since been located. In September, 1887, he was appointed to fill an unexpired term as City Assessor and Collector, and at the expiration of each term has been re-elected ever since, which fact is a sufficient guarantee as to his ability, efficiency and popularity. Mr. Whips is a member of the Christian Church and socially belongs to the A. F. & A. M., in which he has taken the Royal Arch degree, and the Knights of Pythias. In 1881 he was married to Miss Georgia Watson, a native of the Lone Star State, and a daughter of George Watson, a member of an early family of Texas. The union of Mr. and Mrs. Whips has resulted in the birth of five children: Walter, Birdie, Livie, Virgie and Mary.

JUDGE JOHN O'NEIL, ex-Judge of Calhoun County, Texas, and one of the sound, substantial and popular men of the county, has fully borne out the reputation of that class of energetic and far-seeing men of Irish origin who have risen to prominence in different portions of this country. Mr. O'Neil is a native of Calhoun County, Texas, and the fourth of seven children born to Thomas and Mary (Gallagher) O'Neil, natives of the green Isle of Erin. The parents were married in their native country, and seeing a prospect for bettering their condition in the "land of the free," emigrated to the States in 1845, and first settled in the city of New York. From there they went to Philadelphia, resided there for several years, and then went to Alabama, where they resided in Montgomery and Mobile for several years. They then came to the Lone Star State and the father engaged in stock-raising, which he continued until his death in 1858. He became quite wealthy and owned large stock interests. His wife followed him to the grave in 1867. In the town of Port Lavaca our subject was reared and educated, and on the 12th of July, 1863, he enlisted in Company E, Waller's Battalion, Green's Brigade, and was in all the battles of Banks' campaign on Red River. After that he served in Arkansas on scout duty, but subsequently returned to Texas, where his regiment was disbanded early in 1865. Following this he at once engaged in the cattle business and soon had a large herd of stock on hand. About 1876 he bought land around Port Lavaca and soon became the owner of a fine ranch there. In 1888 he erected the Seaside Hotel, a fine house. Judge O'Neil has ever been alive to matters of public importance, is an active politician, and in 1887 he was elected Sheriff, serving one term. After that he was elected County Judge and served in a very satisfactory manner for two terms. He has often served as delegate to conventions and has always been an active worker for his party. In 1890 he sold his ranch business. Judge O'Neil's happy domestic life began in 1872, when he led to the altar Miss Janie Robinson, a native of Louisiana, and the daughter of William Robinson, who died when a comparatively young man. Eight children, all of whom are living, were born to this marriage: James D., Estella, Annie, Edgar, Jueldine, Louie, John and Florine. Judge and Mrs. O'Neil are members of the Catholic Church, and he is a Mason. Both are highly esteemed in the section.

MAJOR ISRAEL B. DONALSON. The oldest citizen of Hays County, Texas, and whose career is of the greatest historical interest, is Major Israel B. Donalson, who, at this writing, resides in San Marcos, and although ninety-eight years of age is well preserved, physically and mentally. Full of the knowledge of men and events, gathered in many years of intelligent observation, one seldom meets a more interesting gentleman, and it is not often, certainly, that one has the privilege of chronicling the life of a man of that age. In 1892 quite a full memoir of Major Donalson was prepared and published by

Isaac H. Julian, the veteran journalist of San Marcos and now the editor of
The People's Era and Free Press. Its unusual historic interest was recognized by the Kansas Historical Society, which solicited from Mr. Julian a
copy of the memoir and a photograph of the major, to be embodied in their
publications. And that eminent and excellent lady, Mrs. John A. Logan,
with whom, and her father and husband, he was associated during his service
in the Mexican war, and to whom the author sent a copy, responded in the
following handsome terms:

" WASHINGTON, D. C., July 25, 1892.

"My Dear Mr. Julian:

"I thank you most sincerly for the copy of the sketch of dear old Major
Donalson. I remember him as if I had seen him only yesterday, and know
so well how fond my husband and my father were of him. He is one of nature's noblemen, and in his long and useful life has done much for mankind.
I was so glad to hear from him once more, though father and the general
have both preceded him to the unknown land, where we hope we shall meet
by and by. I shall write Major Donalson, and will take great pleasure in giving notice of your article, and of him. Very sincerely yours,

"MRS. JOHN A. LOGAN."

Mrs. Logan is editor of the *Home Magazine* at Washington. It will thus
be seen that the major is verifying to a considerable extent the Scripture,
which declares that "A prophet is not without honor save in his own country."
So much by way of preface. Now to a biographical outline compiled from
the memoir: Major Donalson is a native of Bourbon County, Ky., born January 12, 1797. He was baptized by Elder Barton W. Stone, the famous
apostle, who at that time was an old school Presbyterian, afterwards of the
old Christian or Newlight movement. His father was of English and his
mother of Irish ancestry. His father, John Donalson, served under Washington, as Lieutenant, through the Revolutionary war. He was a pioneer to
Kentucky, and his first wife was a sister of the celebrated Tom Ewing, Senator
from Ohio. She became the mother of five children. His second wife,
Elizabeth Donnell, was the mother of our subject, who came upon the scene
when people were living in block houses. The latter was about five years of
age when his father died, and not many years older when his mother passed
away. When sixteen years old he began building boats and for some time
was engaged in boating on the Mississippi River to New Orleans. In the
year 1819 he married Miss Lucy Lee Calvert, of Kentucky, and five children
were born to them. After her death, or in 1821, the major married Miss
Lucy Ann Lee, a remote cousin of Robert E. Lee, and eleven children were
the result of this union, seven of whom are now living: Lucy, wife of A. B.
Cherewith; Benjamin Franklin, contractor; Chauncey B., a farmer at Blanco;
George W., banker; Elizabeth, wife of Edward Northcraft; Laura, wife of Dr.
Price, of Blanco City; and Vernetha, widow of Dr. McGee. In 1835 Major
Donalson was tendered the Democratic nomination for the Legislature and
elected, serving with Tom Marshall, Cassius M. Clay and other noted men.
In 1839 Mr. Donalson removed to Pike County, Ills., where he was elected
Probate Judge, and had a brief service in the Mormon war. In 1847 he
raised a company of volunteers for the Mexican war. He was elected Major
and placed in command of five companies. He served through the war in
New Mexico. Later he was voted a handsome sword by the Illinois Legisla-

ture for his services. He next joined the '49-ers in their overland march to California, where he engaged in mining and store-keeping. After an absence of two years and four months and the accumulation of about $15,000, he returned home. In 1854 he was tendered by President Pierce the position of United States Marshal for Kansas Territory, and accepted. His term ran through the terrible period of civil commotion in that Territory, and was a most trying experience. He got out by resignation, not removal, which was the fate of so many other officials in Kansas at that time. Having business at Washington he was present at the execution of John Brown, of which his recollections are among the most interesting which have appeared. He remained in retirement during the war at his home in Canton, Mo. In 1865 he removed by wagon, there being no railroads, to Hays County, Texas, where he has ever since resided. The above is the merest outline of the career of Major Donalson of what is set forth with considerable detail in the memoir prepared and published by Mr. Julian, of which we copy below the three closing paragraphs: Not the least remarkable of his characteristics has been his protracted physical force. At the age of seventy-two he did the work of a vigorous man in the harvest-field, and ten years later he showed no decline of body or mind, walking erect, alert and vigorous. He attributes his lengthened years to his practice of "temperance in all things," his disinclination to "worry" and his disposition to look on the bright side of life. Major Donalson was born under the administration of President Washington and has voted at every Presidential election from Monroe down. In his birth he was contemporary with a host of other Americans of note, who passed away so long since that the remembrance of their names has become dim. James K. Polk, only two years his senior, has been dead over forty years; William Cullen Bryant, whose venerable head and his face are so familiar through his portraits, born three years before Major Donalson, died fourteen years ago, at the age of eighty-four, while our more aged fellow-citizen still lives. At the birth of Jefferson Davis he was eleven, and at the birth of Abraham Lincoln, twelve years old. Robert Burns died only the year before he was born. At his birth Sir Walter Scott was a young man unknown to fame, Lord Byron a lad of nine years, and Napoleon Bonaparte had just entered upon his career of transcendent military renown at the head of the French army in Italy. These facts, which might be largely extended, may cause us to realize more vividly what a veteran we have yet lingering in our midst. In him we are permitted to behold one whose life is coincident with that of our great Republic, almost from its beginning. Such a man should be greeted with affectionate reverence by all, more especially by the rising generation, as a link binding them to all the past of their native land.

BANK OF GOLIAD. Closely identified with the financial interests and commercial progress of this community is the Bank of Goliad. It is one of the solid institutions of the State, enjoying a reputation for reliability and safety that extends far beyond the limits of the county. This bank was organized May 1, 1891, by L. A. Maetze & Bro., W. A. Pettus and A. Levi & Co., and is one of the oldest banking firms in the town. For some time it was engaged in an exchange business. The incorporators are among the leading men of the town, and from the above mentioned date until the present time it has been the principal bank of the county. This bank is well equipped and furnished, and it has an individual responsibility of $1,000,000. L. A.

GEORGE LORD.

Maetze, President of this bank, is widely known as a leading financier and merchant, and a man whose high sense of honor commands the respect and confidence of all with whom he has business relations. He was born in Germany in 1839, and was the eldest of three sons now living born to Gottlieb and Amelia (Haase) Maetze, also of Germany. About 1855 the family came to the United States, and settled in Yorktown, Texas, where the father followed the tailor's trade until his death in 1885. The mother passed away in 1856. L. A. Maetze received a thorough scholastic training in his native country, and when seventeen years of age came to the Lone Star State with his parents, working with his father at his trade for some time. In 1858 he engaged with Koehler, of Cuero, as clerk, and remained with him until 1870, with the exception of the time he was in the army. In 1861 he enlisted in the Confederate army, Hubby's Battalion, Capt. McCampbell's Company, but on account of illness was soon after discharged. Again he enlisted, and served in the Quartermaster Department until the close. In 1872 he started a mercantile business at Goliad under the firm name of L. A. Maetze & Bro., and this has since become the largest enterprise of the kind in the town. They carry a stock of goods valued at $15,000, and do an annual business of about $30,000. On the first of May, 1891, our subject started the Bank of Goliad. He and his brother own a fine tract of land of 5,000 acres one mile from town, and much of it is improved. It is valuable property. They each own fine homes in the town, and are surrounded by every comfort. Both are good Democrats in politics.

JOHN DOUGLAS STAPLES. Of all the farmers and stockmen of Guadalupe County, Texas, not one is more deserving of honorable mention than John D. Staples, for he began at the very lowest round of the ladder and by dint of perseverance and energy has built up a comfortable competence. He first opened his eyes on the light of day in White County, Tenn., January 9, 1829, a son of John and Stacey (Waller) Staples, the fifth of a family of six children. The father was born in Virginia, and when a young man removed to Tennessee, and thereafter devoted his time and attention to merchandising up to the time of his death. His wife died at the age of seventy-seven years. In the State of his birth the subject of this sketch resided until he was fifteen years of age, then removed to Livingstone, Sumter County, Ala., and, with two of his brothers, carried on a harness and saddle manufacturing business, in which they succeeded remarkably well and made money. In 1855 Mr. Staples came to Texas and bought the place on which he has now been living for nearly forty years. When the Civil War opened he went out as a member of Company A, Thirty-second Texas Cavalry, commanded by Col. Woods, of which Maj. W. O. Hutcheson and Capt. Story were also members, and all of whom now live in San Marcos. Mr. Staples was in the Louisiana campaign, participating in the engagements at Mansfield, Pleasant Hill and Yellow Bayou, and numerous skirmishes. When the war closed he was at San Antonio, having been detailed to service there by Gen. Kirby Smith, and after the war had closed he returned to his home at Staples, and in 1870 opened a store, which he conducted with reasonable success for ten years, and then sold out that he might give closer attention to his farming interests. He had not a dollar with which to commence life for himself, and after he had, by hard work and strict attention to business, accumulated a comfortable property, it was all swept away during the war and he was once more left penniless. He did not sit down and uselessly repine over this state of affairs, but began laboring earnestly to recover his fallen fortunes, and his efforts have been rewarded with success and he is now well fixed financially. Mr. Staples has filled various positions of trust of a minor nature, but has had no political aspirations. He is a Master Mason of Prairie Lea Lodge, and has been a worthy member of this order for over thirty years. He was married in 1856 to Miss Cordelia Appling, of Guadalupe County, by whom he became the father of six children: Frank F., William A., Eugenia, wife of M. M. Hargis, of Llano, who is a banker and County Clerk of that place; Douglas, George and Cordelia. The mother of these children died in 1870, and two years later Mr. Staples wedded Mrs. Amanda Jeffrey, widow of Rufus Jeffrey, who was killed in the Confederate service, and daughter of Rody and Elizabeth (Spruell) Allen. To Mr. Staples' second union six children were also given: Leona, wife of R. F. Holmes; Andrew J., Maggie, Elizabeth, Robert Lee and James L.

CARNOT BELLINGER, of Luling, Texas. Edmund Bellinger, the father of Carnot Bellinger, of Luling, was born in Beaufort, S. C., March 4, 1802, received a classical education and completed a full collegiate course of study at Columbia College, South Carolina. He was prevented from graduating, but received a certificate of high standing in all his classes by the faculty. In 1826 he married Miss Ann Le Gare Roach, a native of Charleston, S. C., a daughter of William Roach, of Bristol, England. Through her mother she was a descendant of the "Huguenots" through the Le Gare family, and through her grandfather her family reaches back to the McGregor clan, in Scotland, to the year 700 A. D. Hugh Swinton Le Gare, her first cousin, was Attorney General of the United States. By marriage she was connected with William Gilmore Simms. Mr. Bellinger was directly descended from the "Landgraves" of South Carolina, a title hereditary conferred by one of the Georges of England on Edmund Bellinger of Westmorland County, England, who married Elizabeth Cartwright, and emigrated to America about the year 1688, at which time he was created first Landgrave. His son Edmund was second Landgrave. He married Elizabeth Butler; their son Edmund became third Landgrave. He in turn married Mary Lucia Bull; their son Edmund was fourth Landgrave. William Bellinger, the youngest brother of the fourth Landgrave, was the father of this Edmund Bellinger, who, with his wife, soon after his marriage, moved to Illinois. He remained there six years, and came to Texas in 1839, and assisted in the early development of this country, then "The Republic of Texas." He took part in the Indian troubles, and participated in the battle of Plum Creek and others. The hardest of these struggles fell upon his wife, a woman reared amongst all the luxury and refinement of the most aristocratic society of Charleston, S. C. It is a wonder she passed through those perilous times and lived to enter and almost complete her four-score years. A few of her perils will give an idea of the life she endured in those days. One night she was left alone in her little cabin, with her babe and two small children. Mr. Bellinger had gone as an express on horseback to warn some settlers, fifty miles distant, of their danger from an invading party of Indians, estimated to consist of 500 warriors. He was to collect what men and boys he could to pursue the enemy. At midnight came a gentle tapping on the door, with these words: "Mrs. Bellinger, get up very quietly; we are in great danger. Don't speak or

strike a light. Fifty Indian warriors are within 100 yards of this house."
To use her own words, she came out in a few moments "more dead than
alive," with her baby wrapped in her cloak, the two small children in their
night clothes. They made their way, with the neighbor who came to warn
them, to a house where all the women and children were assembled, under
the protection of four men who were left to guard them. Every other man
and boy who was able to handle a gun had gone in pursuit of the Indians
under Captain Caldwell (better known in Texas history as Old Paint). The
names of those four men who stood guard that night will always be remembered by the descendants of those women who sat up all night to hush and
keep their babies quiet—Pleasant Barnet, Adam Zumwalt, Ezekiel Williams
and John Patrick. That terrible night of suspense passed with no further
alarm. The next day it was considered safe for all to go to their homes.
That night Mrs. Bellinger was again aroused with the whispered words:
"The Indians are burning and killing as they go; come quick, we are going
to the woods (or river bottom) for safety." The news of the burning and
massacre at Linnville reached town that night. Whilst they were crouched in
the thicket, the mothers keeping watch over their little children, the well-
known voice of Capt. (afterwards General) Ben McCollough, was heard,
hallooing at the house he was accustomed to stop at, as saying, "All is well;
come, get us something to eat." All emerged from their hiding places. The
balance of the night was employed by the women in baking corn bread and
molding bullets, the men in getting their saddles, bridles and guns in order
for the next day's battle with the Comanches, which took place at Plum
Creek, near where the town of Lockhart now stands. Edmund Bellinger
owned a ranch in Gonzales County, paid much attention to raising horses and
cattle, for many years was County Judge, and was a man of established
reputation. During the Civil War he was a Union man and opposed to the
war, as were Sam Houston and others. However, three of his sons were in the
Confederate service, and one of them gave his life to the cause. While residing near Springfield, Ill., he came to know and admire Abraham Lincoln,
and at a time when it was almost treason to speak his name in kindness Mr.
Bellinger had the courage to express his admiration for that great man.
Mr. Edmund Bellinger died in Luling in 1878, at the residence of his son,
our subject. His wife died in San Antonio in 1885. Carnot Bellinger was
born in Gonzales, Texas, June 23, 1850, the youngest of ten children born to
the above mentioned couple. He was reared in that town. The war coming
on interrupted his education to some extent. This he has greatly remedied
by reading and contact with the world. When eighteen years of age he
entered a drug store, and after clerking for a number of years became a
thorough pharmacist. He opened a drug store in Prairie Lea in 1869. In
1874 he removed to Luling, was appointed its first Postmaster and held the
office for twelve years. In 1889 he associated himself with the Luling Lumber Company. Later he purchased a dairy farm, and has now a herd of fifty
Jersey cows. About the same time he bought a controlling interest in the
Luling Water Works, which he still holds. In 1894 he engaged in the
grocery business with Mr. W. G. Weaver, under the firm name of Bellinger
& Weaver, and is doing a good business. He is a Democrat, and a member
of the K. of P. In the year 1878 he married Miss Mary E. Keith, at Beaumont, Texas, daughter of Cortez and Sarah (Le Port) Keith, residents of

eastern Texas. Six children have blessed their union: William, Franklin, Bessie, May, Addie and Marguerite.

RICHARD J. BURGES, who is the able and most efficient County Collector of Guadalupe County, Texas, was born in Jackson, Tenn., in 1840. While a man of no great wealth he is the possessor of that which is far more valuable —an honorable name and the confidence and friendship of those who know him best. His great-grandfather, Rev. Henry John Burges, was a native of Devonshire, England, and came to Virginia in colonial times. He was rector of an Episcopal church, and was one of the first professors in William and Mary College at Williamsburg, Va. When the Revolutionary War broke out he sided with the colonists, and on many occasions preached to the troops. He was arrested by Colonel Tarlton, who threatened to hang him. Col. William Washington learned this, and sent word to the Royalist leader that if he hanged his prisoner he would hang an English officer for every hair on his head. This secured Mr. Burges' release. After the war he continued in the ministry until his death. Our subject's grandfather, Dr. A. S. H. Burges, was born in the Old Dominion, and was quite a prominent man there, being a member of one of the constitutional conventions. He died full of years, and since the Civil War. The maternal grandfather of our subject, Dr. Richard Fenner, was born in North Carolina, and is of Irish origin. His father, Capt. Richard Fenner, was one of twenty sons and one daughter, he the youngest and only one born in America, the family coming to this country and settling in North Carolina in colonial times. He was a Captain in the colonial army during the Revolutionary War, and afterwards resided in North Carolina and Tennessee, dying in the latter State when quite aged. He was a member of the Order of Cincinnatus, which was started by Washington for the officers of his army. One of the early members of this family fought with Drake against the Spanish Armada. W. H. Burges, the father of our subject, was born in North Carolina, began life as a midshipman in the United States navy, and served on the old seventy-four frigate Guerrier from twelve to nineteen years of age. He then resigned and married Miss Eugenia A. Fenner, with whom he moved to west Tennessee about 1837. There he resided until his death in 1851. He was a man of much intelligence and was well read and well posted on all public affairs, but could not be induced to enter public life. His wife is still living, and finds a pleasant home with her son, Richard J., in Seguin. He was and she is a member of the Episcopal Church. Socially he was a Royal Arch Mason, and was greatly devoted to that order. Richard J. Burges was reared and mainly educated in Tennessee. When he was fifteen years of age the family moved to Texas and spent one year in Navarro County. On the first of January, 1856, they came to Seguin, and there our subject attended school for over a year. From there he went to New Orleans, engaged in business there, and was there at the outbreak of the war. In the month of August, 1861, he enlisted in the Confederate army, joining Company D of the Fourth Texas Infantry, Hood's Brigade, and served one year in Virginia. He was in five engagements, and at the battle of Manassas was shot through the body. After this he was in the hospital for a long time and was a cripple for four years. In 1864 he was elected County Clerk, served a short time and was removed by Federal authority in 1865. The following year he went back to New Orleans, was engaged in business there until 1872, and then returned to Seguin, where he

9

carried on business enterprises for three years. In 1878 he was appointed Deputy Sheriff, and placed in charge of the tax collections in this office for two years. In 1880 the office of Tax Collector was separated from the Sheriff's office, and Mr. Burges was elected its first Collector, and has been re-elected at the expiration of each term since. He was married in 1874 to Miss Gray Smith, a native of this county, and daughter of George P. Smith, who was one of the early settlers to Texas from Missouri. Seven children were born to this union: Richard J., Jr., William H., Ellis G., Mary G., Bettie M., Eugenia F. and George P., who died in infancy. Mr. Burges is a member of the Episcopal Church and his wife a member of the Baptist Church. He is a Mason—a member of Guadalupe Lodge No. 109, and has held nearly all the offices from Master down. He is also a member of the Alamo Lodge, San Antonio, A. O. U. W. He has served as Mayor of Seguin four terms, having been elected each time unanimously.

JUDGE FELIX J. HART, the present Judge of Bee County, is justly recognized as a man of superior ability, force of character and determination. He is a native of this county, his birth occurring in December, 1862, and the fourth child born to the union of Luke and Ann (Hart) Hart, natives respectively of New York and Texas. The maternal grandfather, Felix J. Hart, came to Texas at a period antedating the Revolutionary War and engaged in stock-raising. He was murdered in San Patricio County by the Mexicans. The paternal grandfather, John Hart, was born in Ireland and came to Texas with the McGlowan and McMullen colony. He was also murdered in San Patricio County by the Mexicans at about the same time. Luke Hart, father of our subject, followed in the footsteps of his ancestors and engaged in the stock business principally. During the Civil War he served in Col. Hobby's Regiment and served in Texas. While a resident of San Patricio County he held a number of local positions and was County and District Clerk for a long time prior to the war. In 1861 he moved to Bee County and was County Commissioner and Justice of the Peace for about fifteen years. A few years prior to his death, which occurred in Papalote, Bee County, in 1883, he resigned the above mentioned positions. Mr. Hart was a man of unquestioned ability, a deep thinker and a close reasoner. The original of this notice was educated in the public schools of Bee County, and after his father's death he took charge of the ranch, conducting it successfully until 1890, when he came to Beeville and engaged in merchandising. He has filled a number of local offices, having been a member of the second Board of Aldermen, and in November, 1892, he was elected to his present position. He is a man of straightforward character and genial disposition. These, coupled with indomitable energy, formed the keystone to his success in life. In the year 1892 he was married to Miss Edith Mussett, of Corpus Christi, and a native of Texas. Her father, Elias T. Mussett, came to Corpus Christi when a child, and became one of the most prominent residents. He was Marshal of the city, and was murdered there on the night of May 5, 1892, by John Parker. Our subject is a member of the Catholic, and Mrs. Hart of the Baptist Church. Socially he is a Knight of Honor. While his father was Commissioner our subject did much of the work, and in 1886 he was appointed to fill that position, serving until 1888. The Judge's brothers and sisters were named as follows: Mary J., Catherine (deceased), was the wife of Joseph Ryan; John, Bridget, wife of O. F. West; Luke, Timothy and Maggie, wife of H. F. Otto, and Albert Hart.

FRANK R. PRIDHAM. In the whole range of commercial enterprise no interest is of more importance than that respecting the sale of hardware, and among the most notable dealers in this line of goods is Frank R. Pridham, who was born in the town in which he is now doing business, in 1841, a son of the marriage of P. U. and Malinda (Roberts) Pridham, the former of whom was born on the Isle of Guernsey in 1812. He was taken to the vicinity of London, England, when quite young, married there before attaining his majority, and immigrated to Montreal, Canada, in 1832. From this place he moved to Texas with his wife and one child, a son, and settled near Lynchburgh, in 1834, near where the battle of San Jacinto was afterwards fought, in which engagement he took an active part in the ranks of the Texan Volunteers. He continued to reside in that section until he lost his wife and a little daughter by malarial fever, then moved with his surviving son to Victoria in 1839. During the terrible Indian raid of 1840 Mr. Pridham volunteered to make the perilous journey to Gonzales for assistance, and, keeping near the timber along the river, he succeeded in passing the Comanche camp on Spring Creek, and reached his destination in safety. After his return home he assisted in an attack on the Indians at Placido Creek, and later engaged them in battle on Peach Creek, where the savages were defeated. In 1841 Mr. Pridham was married to Miss Malinda Roberts, by whom he became the father of one son, Frank R., the subject of this sketch. Mr. Pridham held the office of Chief Justice for some time, and soon after became Assessor and Collector of the county, an office which he efficiently and successfully filled until 1853, at the same time discharging the duties of a merchant. In 1848 he moved to the country, about five miles from Victoria, to the now well known fishing resort, Pridham Lake, and about this time, with a man by the name of Wm. Gamble, started the first cotton gin in this section of the country. He was a worthy member of the A. F. & A. M., and was buried by that order. In 1858 Frank R. Pridham, after receiving a thorough education, went to San Antonio and engaged in newspaper work on the *San Antonio Herald,* having charge of the office from the time of entering it until 1861. He lost both his parents while he was still a mere child, and was cared for by his uncle, Judge G. W. Palmer, proprietor of the *Advocate,* and it was while under his care that he learned the printer's trade. When his uncle became associated with Col. Logan in the proprietorship of the *Herald,* at the Alamo City, he remained with him until the opening of the Civil War. He became a Knight of the Golden Circle and was active in advancing the cause of the impending Confederate Government, and assisted in securing the Federal arms at San Antonio. With other chivalrous and brave young men of Victoria he joined G. J. Hampton's Company, Sibley's Brigade, later known as Green's Brigade, and was in the severe campaign in New Mexico, taking part in the battles of Val Verde and Glorietta. Upon the reorganization of the Southern forces he was sent to Louisiana, and was in several engagements there, and almost daily skirmishes. He was in Galveston when that city was recaptured, then returned to Louisiana and was in all the engagements of Banks' expedition on the Red River, from Mansfield to Yellow Bayou. He was then for some time engaged in scouting duty in Arkansas, and in May, 1865, was mustered out of the service in Burleson County, Texas. After leaving the service he became a salesman in the large mercantile establishment of R. Owens, and subsequently became associated with Victor M. Rose in the management of the *Victoria Advocate*. Mr. Pridham soon became its sole proprietor, and continued its publication until the year 1874. Two years later he was elected Assessor of Taxes for the county, which position he held continuously for twelve years, a fact which speaks eloquently as to his efficiency and popularity. In 1883 he was appointed receiver of the Texas Continental Meat Company, under bonds of $400,000, and in 1888 was in the Custom House service at Eagle Pass, in each and every one of which capacities he acquitted himself very creditably. In 1891 he started in his present business with Mr. L. G. Kreisle, the firm being known as Pridham & Kreisle, and they carry a stock of general hardware valued at $10,000, and do an annual business of some $20,000 or more. These gentlemen are shrewd and practical business men, and Mr. Pridham is well known for his high sense of honor. He is a most worthy citizen in every respect, and is a decided addition to the business circles of Victoria. In 1881 he was married to Miss Minnie, the accomplished daughter of R. Owens, and to their union one son has been given, who has been named Richard Owens, in honor of his maternal grandfather. Mr. Pridham and his wife are members and attendants of the Catholic Church.

JOSEPH M. BICKFORD. As has often been quoted, the finger of time is one of the most satisfactory and reliable endorsers of a man's business career. Many people may, with justification, halt and refuse to listen to the solicitation of a beginner, but the voice of the old, established house always carries with it attention and respect. Joseph M. Bickford, an old time merchant and the oldest citizen of Port Lavaca, Texas, was born in the Granite State in 1827. His parents, Thomas and Ammis (Morse) Bickford, were natives of that State also, and both were of English origin. The ancestors on both sides came to America in colonial days. Joseph M. Bickford received his education at several preparatory schools at Newbury, and in 1851 entered Dartsmouth College, from which institution he graduated four years later, taking a full classical course. After this he taught an Academy for over a year in Lisbon, New Hampshire, and then began the study of law. On account of his health he was advised by his physicians to come South and he first settled in Jackson, Miss., where he remained about six months. From there he went to the Lone Star State, and settled in Calhoun County, where, notwithstanding his poor health, he started to school on Matagorda Island. He met with the best of success and was a very prominent and popular educator. When the war broke out he intended entering the army, but was prostrated with a severe fever, and was in bed for six months. Afterwards he was in feeble health for some time. From there he came to Port Lavaca and started the Lavaca Institute, which soon became one of the most promising schools in southwest Texas. This continued until 1869, pupils coming from quite distant points, and most of the time he had an attendance of 125. In 1869 Mr. Bickford engaged in merchandising and has continued in business since that time. He carries a large stock of general merchandise, groceries, notions, glass and crockery ware, boots and shoes, &c., in the same house that he has occupied since 1886. Aside from this he has also been engaged to some extent in the stock business, but has sold much of his ranch property, although he still owns 600 acres of excellent land near the town. In the year 1867 he was married to Miss Mary Hensley, a native of Port Lavaca, and daughter of William R. and Mary P. Hensley, natives of Kentucky, and among the earliest settlers here. Mr. Hensley was a merchant and surveyor, and surveyed much of this and adjoining counties. He was a prominent man, and died in 1849. His wife died in 1872. To the marriage of Mr. and Mrs. Bickford were born four children, all living: Mabel A., Mary L., Florence O. and Joseph Harry. Mr. Bickford is a prominent Mason, a member of Port Lavaca Lodge, the chapter that was located at Indianola, and the San Felipe De Austin Commandery at Galveston. He has held all the offices in the Blue Lodge and the Chapter, and has been an active worker. For years Mr. Bickford has been school examiner, and he has also served a term and a half as County Treasurer.

J. GUS PATTON. Success in professional life is a guerdon that is very cautiously bestowed upon a person by the goddess, who, in a measure guides, and invariably decorates, man's efforts. And this same success is far more apt to come because of the pursuer's genius or adaptability for his calling, than from any mere luck, ambition, push or demand. This is particularly the case in the law, a profession which J. Gus Patton's talents caused him to adopt in 1878. After graduating he set out with the determination to win for himself a high place in legal circles and with the goodly store of reading that he had treasured up and the earnest worth of honest friends, he at once gained a substantial foothold in his profession. He is now the oldest lawyer in practice in Goliad. Mr. Patton was born in Williamson County, Tenn., in 1842, and his parents, Dr. John W. and Malinda (Pickens) Patton, were natives of that State, too. The paternal grandfather, Isaac Patton, was a soldier in the Revolutionary War. He came to Texas at an early date, but not to locate, and returned and died in Tennessee. The maternal grandfather was of the South Carolina Pickens. The father of our subject was a successful physician of Tennessee, but in 1846 he came to Texas, and settled in Washington County, where he remained one year. From there he went to Victoria County, remained there until 1855, and then came to Goliad, where he practiced until 1873. His death occurred in 1885, when seventy-seven years of age, and his wife followed him to the grave in 1887, when seventy-four years of age. He was a popular and successful physician. J. Gus Patton was educated in Goliad, and in 1861 joined the army, and served on the Rio Grande until 1862, when he came home on sick furlough. While at home he had the yellow fever, and when he had recovered was commissioned to raise a company. This he did and was made Captain of Company B, Anderson's Regiment, serving in North Texas and the frontier until the close of the war. There were 120 men in his company, and he was quite a young officer. After the war he came to Goliad and engaged in merchandising, and also read law. Later he sold out and embarked in the cattle business, owning a large ranch and many sheep, horses and cattle. In 1878–79 he was admitted to the bar, and began practicing. Almost immediately afterwards he was elected County Attorney and held that office for eight or ten years, doing a general business. In 1893 he formed a partnership with his son-in-law, Ross E. Burke, under the firm name of Patton & Burke, and they are doing a good business. Mr. Patton celebrated his nuptials with Miss Sue Peck, daughter of Capt. Barton Peck (see sketch), on the 26th of March, 1867. To this union have been born five children: Mary, now married ; Lonnie Willie, wife of Ross E. Burke ; Fannie, wife of John Van Bohlen; J. Gus, Jr., and Barton Peck. Fraternally Mr. Patton, is a member of the Knights of Honor, the Masonic Fraternity, Ancient Order United Workmen, and in politics is an active Democrat. He and family hold membership in the Methodist Episcopal Church South. Mr. Patton has three farms, aggregating 180 acres under cultivation, and has 640 acres under fence and in pasture.

JAMES BENTON MANNING. The calling of the farmer and stock raiser has found in Mr. Manning a worthy follower, for he is an intelligent man, well posted in his calling, honest, thrifty and industrious, and the success with which his efforts have been attended is well merited. He first opened his eyes on the light of day in Benton County, Alabama, October 1, 1837, a son of Edward and Nancy (Warnock) Manning, the former of whom was born in the State of New York, and was apprenticed at the age of sixteen years to a silversmith, who took him to South Carolina. Becoming dissatisfied Mr. Manning left his employer and went to Georgia, where he remained for some time, thence to Alabama, out of which State he helped to drive the Indians. In 1869 he emigrated to Texas, in which State he was called from life in 1890 at the age of eighty-seven years. His wife was born in the Palmetto State and died in 1867. The subject of this sketch was reared and educated in Benton County, Alabama, and when the great struggle between the North and South commenced, he enlisted in Company H, Tenth Alabama, and on the 18th of June, 1861, was sent with his command to Virginia in time to take part in the battle of Drainsville. He was in all the engagements around Richmond, Fredericksburg, etc., and at the battle of Sharpsburg was wounded quite severely, and on this account was given a thirty days' furlough, which was the only time he lost from active service after his enlistment. At Petersburg he was slightly wounded, and stacked arms on that historic field, after Lee's surrender at Spottsylvania Court House. He held the rank of Sergeant, but was a non-commissioned officer in charge of his company at the surrender. After hostilities had ceased he returned to his old home in Alabama, and was actively engaged in farming there until 1870, when he removed to the Lone Star State and settled on the San Marcos River, and about fourteen years ago became the owner of the farm on which he is now residing, which makes him a comfortable living, and his home is a pleasant and well appointed one. He is a Master Mason of Prairie Lea Lodge, was a charter member of Martindale Lodge, and is a worthy member of the Methodist Church, in which he has been a steward and trustee for a number of years. He was married to Miss Victoria Isabella Miller, a native of Calhoun County (formerly Benton County), Alabama, and to their union ten children were born: Thomas E., Nannie A., John L., Lizzie S., James V., Oscar L., Effie L., Ira L., Mark I. and J. B., Jr.

CAPT. JOHN LAFAYETTE LANE. Among the men of Caldwell County, Texas, who have been active and efficient in the work of building up the agricultural and stock-raising interests of this section, Capt. John LaFayette Lane takes a prominent position. Born in Jefferson County, Tenn., January 3, 1830, he was fourth in order of birth of nine children born to Pleasant W. and Mary (Colthorpe) Lane. On the paternal side he comes of a prominent old Virginia family, who trace their lineage directly back to the Capt. Lane who was left in charge of the first English settlement on the James River. This man turned his attention largely to mining, and the authorities censured him for not devoting every energy to agriculture. Our subject's paternal grandmother was a Fitzgerald and a member of the famous family of that name that came to America in an early day. Pleasant W. Lane was born in Tennessee, and was a physician and farmer. In 1847 he emigrated to Caldwell County, Texas, and the following year settled near Lockhart, and until 1868 practiced over a wide scope of country. While he was on his way to Texas he lingered behind his family and friends to attend to some business, and while riding horseback near the present city of Waco was surrounded by Indians. They examined his saddle bags, pulled the stoppers out of his bottles, inhaled their contents, and then neatly rearranging everything, bade him "go." Their reverence for "medicine men" probably saved the doctor's life. Mrs. Lane died in Arkansas in 1844 while on the way to Texas, and the family lingered for two years in that State after her death. Capt. LaFayette Lane was partially reared in Tennessee, and was in his seventeenth year when he accompanied his parents to Texas. He had received but a limited education, and in 1852 he went to California and mined for gold six years, being quite successful. Returning to Texas in 1858, he engaged in the stock business, and was in Arizona gold mining when the war opened. Again he returned to Texas, and enlisted as First Lieutenant in Capt. Meyers' company. He was in the trans-Mississippi Department, and served through the entire Louisiana campaign, taking part in the battles of Mansfield, Pleasant Hill, Yellow Bayou, etc. He was in the cavalry, and while at Galveston, Meyers was promoted, and our subject became Captain of his old company, serving as such the remainder of the war. The last charge at Mansfield was made by the cavalry commanded by Capt. Lane, and all the men were armed with six-shooters. 'Twas known as the "Peach Orchard Charge." After cessation of hostilities Capt. Lane returned to Lockhart, and with the exception of four years spent in the Sheriff's office has devoted all his time to farming and stock-raising. He owns a valuable ranch of 600 acres, which averages one-half bale of cotton and forty bushels of corn to the acre. In his political views he has always affiliated with the Democratic party, and fraternally he is a Royal Arch Mason. In the year 1872 he was married to Miss Laura Jane Ferris, who died within ten months without issue. In 1873 the captain married Miss Minerva Ann McMahan, a native of Alabama, whose parents were John and Rebecca McMahan. The mother died in Alabama, but the father came to Caldwell County, Texas, in 1855, and is still living. Capt. Lane's second union resulted in the birth of five children: Annie Laurie, John LaFayette, Queen, George Franklin and Samuel Tipton.

DR. THOMAS W. MOORE. It would indeed be hard to find a man better posted in everything pertaining to medicine than Dr. Thomas W. Moore, who is now County Physician of Guadalupe County. There is no man in the community more highly esteemed than this family medical practitioner; and there is not among all the physicians of Guadalupe County one who is held higher in the public favor than this much esteemed pioneer. He is a product of Mississippi, born in Aberdeen in 1848, and is the fourth son and sixth child of nine children born to Col. T. C. and Martha (Hollis) Moore, natives of Tennessee and South Carolina respectively. The Moore family is of Scotch origin, and our subject's paternal grandfather, James Field Moore, was born in North Carolina. The grandmother, whose maiden name was Woods, was a descendant of Scotch ancestors who came to America in early days. The name was originally Wallace, but on coming to the States it was changed to Woods. Grandfather Moore was an especial friend of Henry Clay. He was a surveyor of what was known as the military route from Mississippi to New Orleans, and held the office of Major under General Jackson. Early in life he served in the Legislature of his native State, in both the Lower House and the Senate, but aspired to no higher office, preferring to give the most of his attention to his large plantations. He was very wealthy at the outbreak of war. His death occurred in Aberdeen, Miss., in 1865. The Doctor's maternal grandfather, James Hollis, was a native of North Carolina, but subsequently moved to Alabama, where he became a large planter near Mormon Springs, Marion County, where the first Mormons organized the first church. He was a lineal descendant of the Hollis who signed the anti-Stuart constitution of Scotland. The Hollis family came to America in colonial times through France as one of the Huguenots. Hon. John H. Bankhead, the Congressman from Birmingham District, Ala., is James Hollis' grandson. Col. T. C. Moore, father of our subject, removed to Alabama with his parents in childhood, was well educated at LaGrange, Ky., where he was a classmate of Jefferson Davis, whose life-long friend he was, and in later days, Davis, knowing his ability, offered him a Brigadier-General's commission in the Confederate army. After serving in the Creek Indian or Florida war, he moved to Mississippi and became a planter, although immediately after his majority he was elected to the Legislature of his State. He was one of the members to vote for permission to two young ladies, sisters, to develop the first silk culture of Alabama. Later he moved to Mississippi, and served in both the House and the Senate, but about 1851 he decided to move to Texas. In this State he followed farming for a few months, but subsequently embarked in merchandising at Bastrop, where he remained until 1857. From there he moved to Fayette County, and resides there at the present time. In 1860 he was elected a member of the Secession Convention, and voted for secession, but was fair enough to continue a life-long friend and confidant of Sam Houston. During the war he and Gen. William Webb were the General and Lieutenant-General of militia for this part of Texas, but in a few months he became blind from an accident, which of course closed in a great measure his usefulness to his State and the Nation. He now resides at West Point with his estimable wife, and although but eighteen years of age at the time of his marriage his domestic life has been a happy one. Thomas W. Moore, his son and our subject, was educated in the schools of Texas, and when seventeen years of age he began the study of medicine at the University of Louisiana, and continued there during 1867 and 1868. In the latter year and 1869 he attended the medical department of the University of Pennsylvania, at Philadelphia, and graduated in 1869, before reaching his majority, receiving one of the three prizes offered by Prof. Geo. B. Wood. He was admitted to practice in Texas, and began his duties at LaGrange, but subsequently went to Victoria, where he was appointed Assistant Superintendent of the Austin Lunatic Asylum. After leaving that office he traveled a few months in Mexico, and then settled in Seguin, where he has since worked up a large practice. He is now County Physician, President of the Board of Public Schools, and Chairman of the Board of Stewards of the Methodist Episcopal Church South. He is also at the present time an Alderman of the city. In 1876 he went to Philadelphia and took a post-graduate course, studying especially female surgery. In the year 1871 he was married to Miss Ellen Thomas, daughter of Col. N. Thomas, of Fayette County, who was a member of the old Texas Congress, and a relative of Gen. Thomas of the United States army. She died in 1874, leaving two children, both of whom afterwards died. In 1876 Dr. Moore wedded Miss Pearl, daughter of Lock McAuley, who was born in Scotland. She died in Austin, Texas, in 1881, leaving two daughters, Ethel Elise and Maud Ellen. Mrs. Moore was a cousin of Gen. Robert E. Lee. Her grandfather was a Captain in the Mexican War, and participated in the battle of Monterey, where he was killed while leading his company in an assault. In the year 1884 Dr. Moore was married to his present wife, who is the only daughter of J. B. Dibrell, and sister of Hon. J. B. Dibrell, Jr. She is also a cousin of Hon. Barret Gibbs, of Dallas, Hon. John H. Reagan, and Hon. George B. Dibrell, of Tennessee, who represented his State in Congress for twenty years. She is descended from the Dibrells who came over in the "Mayflower." Mrs. Moore is a member of the Methodist Episcopal Church, and an ardent worker in the same. At present she is State Treasurer of the Woman's Home Parsonage and Missionary Society of Texas.

D. A. T. WALTON. One of the foremost of Bee County's citizens, as well as one of her best known, is D. A. T. Walton, who has been Sheriff of the county for nearly twenty years. He is a product of Alabama, born in 1837, and the only child resulting from the union of John L. and Nancy A. (Sealey) Walton, the father a native of Mississippi and the mother of Alabama. The former died in our subject's infancy, and Mrs. Walton subsequently married Isaac Allen, with whom she moved to Texas in 1847, settling in Guadalupe County. There the mother died in Pleasanton, Atascosa County, Texas, in 1859 and Mr. Allen at Seguin, Guadalupe County in 1851. The principal part of our subject's education was receive at Seguin, Guadalupe County, and in 1855 he joined a Texas ranging company, a campaign of three months, and was stationed on the headwaters of Guadalupe River. This company had several engagements with the Indians and ranged to the Rio Grande River. Later it crossed into Mexico, won a battle there, and put a stop to all further depredations for a number of years. This company had a most exciting time, and was besieged by the Mexicans in a town opposite Eagle Pass. After a short visit home he went to Mexico prospecting, and when he returned home he located in Bandera County for two years, following farming there. In 1857 he was elected Assessor of that county, but at that time he was away after Indians and did not qualify for the office or fill it. From there he went to Atascosa County, and in 1859 was married there to Mrs. A. M. Lee. Immediately afterwards he moved to Bee County, and, locating in the North part of the same, engaged in stock raising. The town there, Walton, is named in his honor. In 1861 he enlisted in Company K, Twenty-first Texas Cavalry, known as Parson's Brigade Confederate Army, and upon organization, was elected Lieutenant, serving in the trans-Mississippi Department throughout the war. He was in many skirmishes, but for the most part, the company was on scouting expeditions throughout Arkansas and Louisiana. He served until cessation of hostilities and then returned to his home in Bee County, where he engaged in stock raising, both horses and cattle. In 1875 he was appointed Sheriff and has been re-elected each term since, serving longer in that capacity than any other man in the State. He has been a member of the Sheriff's Association and is now Vice-President of that organization. Mr. Walton is an entertaining conversationalist and relates some interesting experiences, for he held the office of Sheriff when there were many tough characters in that section. He had many "close calls," but never flinched from duty, and his services are appreciated by the people of Bee County. For some time now he has been living in Beeville, but he still owns a fine ranch. To his marriage have been born eight children: Paloma, wife of I. S. Malone; J. David jr.; Ella, wife of J. P. Wilson; Nannie, wife of A. R. Dugat; Lula, wife of Lee Kilgore; Norina, Baylor and Allen. Mr. Walton and family are members of the Baptist Church. Mr. Walton is a Mason, a member of Goliad Commandery, and is deeply interested in the affairs of his lodge. He joined the Masons in Beeville before the war. Mr. Walton is a man of pleasant address, hair and beard tinged with gray, but his carriage is erect and soldierly. He is well and favorably known all over this section, and no man in the county has more admirers.

Hugh P. Jordan. There is no greater pleasure for the hand and pen of the biographer or historian to perform than in recording the life and achievements of a man who has begun life's battles under adverse circumstances, and through his own unaided efforts has secured the general acknowledgment of being an honest man, a gentleman, and one who has acquired wealth by his own good fighting qualities. He owes his nativity to Allegheny County, Virginia, where he was born in 1830, the second in family of thirteen children born to Edwin and Mary Jane (Paxton) Jordan, also Virginians, in which State they were among the F. F. V's. The paternal grandfather, Col. John Jordan, was a Virginian and an officer of the War of 1812, but was an Englishman by descent, although a thorough American in principles. He was a pioneer in the iron industry in Virginia and the maternal grandfather, Hugh Paxton, was a pioneer farmer on the James River in the Old Dominion. Edwin Jordan was an iron manufacturer and farmer by occupation, and died on his homestead in 1864, his wife having passed from life in 1858. In his native county the subject of this sketch was reared and business life began in the iron mills of that county. He fortunately received a practical education, sufficient to fit him for the ordinary duties of life, and in 1852, anticipating the advice of Horace Greeley, he decided to "go West" and located in Victoria County, Texas, six miles from the town of Victoria, where he, in 1857, purchased 640 acres of land. To this he has since added sufficent land to make 12,000 acres, on which he herds large droves of cattle annually, and at the present time he is fattening 1,200 head of steers for the market. All the real estate of which he is the owner is fertile and well adapted to raising in abundance the products of the region. He is one of the most extensive and successful stock raisers of the county, is thoroughly familiar with all its details, and is considered an authority on all matters pertaining to that line of human industry. During the Civil War he enlisted in Company B, First Texas Cavalry, Col. Buschell's Regiment, and the first year served on the frontier of the Rio Grande River. When the regiment was sent to Louisiana, Mr. Jordan was detailed to escort a wagon train out of danger and was later detailed to build iron works for the Confederacy, for which purpose he removed to Marion County, Texas, to erect a forge, and was made General Superintendent of the iron works, and at this place was made the first bar iron south of the Red River. He remained at this place until the close of the war, then returned home and re-engaged in the pursuits of civil life, which had been interrupted by the turbulent and unsettled times of war.

He was first married in 1849 to Mrs. Judith A. Shirkey, a native of Virginia and a daughter of Col. John Shirky, an officer of the War of 1812 and a member of one of the oldest families of Virginia, that was of Scotch-Irish lineage and came to Virginia in colonial times. Mr. Jordan was left a widower in 1887, after having become the father of two sons: Edwin and William, both of whom own ranches adjoining their father's and are also engaged in business in Victoria. Mr. Jordan was married a second time, to Mary Bell Shirkey, a Virginian by birth and a daughter of Maj. Charlton Shirkey of the State Militia of Virginia. Mr. Jordan and family are members of the Presbyterian Church, of which he has been a member since his youth, and for some time past has been an elder.

JUDGE WILLIAM MOORE. Among the early settlers of Calhoun County, Texas, it is but just to say that Judge William Moore takes a prominent place, for he has resided here for a number of years and always occupies a conspicuous and honorable position. He came originally from the State of Maine, his birth occurring in 1839, and his parents, Daniel and Kate Moore were probably natives of Ireland and Scotland respectively. Our subject started out to hoe his own row in life at a very early age, and engaged in different occupations until he had seen his twelfth birthday, after which he went to sea. For several years he followed that and then came to Mobile, thence to Indianola, and was wrecked on the Bass Cavala Bar December 12, 1857. Following this Mr. Moore engaged in trade along the coast in vessels of his own, and also as Captain for others, until the breaking out of the Civil War. On the 5th of October, 1861, he enlisted in Company B, under Capt. Rice of Shea's Battalion, which was afterwards consolidated with other regiments, and he served all the time in the Lone Star State. In 1863 he was transferred to the Marine Department and served on the gunboat John F. Carr until cessation of hostilities. At one time he engaged in boating, and in 1867 he became Master of one of the mail boats from Indianola to Rockport and Corpus Christi. In 1875 he became a sub-contractor, carrying mail on the same route until 1881, when the route was discontinued. Mr. Moore continued boating until about 1884 when he was appointed County Judge to fill a vacancy and gave all his time to the office. After this he was elected to two full terms and during this time the county seat was changed from Indianola to Port Lavaca and under his supervision the court house was erected. Prior to holding the office of County Judge, Mr. Moore was County Commissioner for four years. He served as Chairman of the Democratic County Executive Committee for about fourteen years and then declined further service. He attended the State convention to elect delegates to the National Convention that nominated Gen. Hancock, and was in the State Convention when Ireland was nominated for Governor the first term, in 1882. He was in the Congressional Convention at Victoria which nominated W. H. Crane for Congress in 1884, has been in several State Senatorial conventions, and to all the County conventions for years. The judge served as pilot for a year or more from 1882 and in 1889 he was appointed Chief Boatman and Guard of the quarantine station at Pass Cavallo, a position he has since held. Judge Moore was married in May, 1863, to Miss Frances Weisenburg, a native of Germany, who came to Texas with her parents in childhood. Six children have been born to this union, five sons and one daughter: W. A., George O., Frank R., Kate L., Charles R. and Henry D. Judge Moore is a Royal Arch Mason, and Mrs. Moore is a member of the Presbyterian Church.

Dr. Thomas H. Nott is a medical practitioner of more than local renown, which fact may be, in a measure, attributed to his love for his profession, and to him the arduous duties of his calling are a "labor of love." Whatever the social or financial condition of the patient who seeks his service, no effort is spared in the treatment of his case, for he believes it is the highest duty of the physician to cure the ills to which mankind is heir if it lies within his power to do so. He devotes himself to his work with conscientious zeal, and gives little regard to the rewards or emoluments that are to follow. He believes in a progressive system of medicine, and notes with eager interest every progressive step taken by his profession. The doctor is a product of Arkansas, born in Fayette County, in 1843, and is a son of Dr. R. A. and S. W. (Whitaker) Nott, both natives of Columbia, S. C. About 1841 they went to Arkansas, where the father practiced medicine and tilled the soil until 1849, and then moved to Louisiana, where he remained until 1855. At that date he moved to Colorado County, Texas, and practiced medicine there until the breaking out of the war. He enlisted in the Confederate army, Twenty-seventh Louisiana, as Surgeon, and soon after was made Brigade Surgeon, and still later Post Surgeon at Vicksburg, under Gen. M. L. Smith. After the fall of Vicksburg he was paroled and remained in Louisiana until cessation of hostilities. He was with the army at the battles of Mansfield and Pleasant Hill, and fought bravely for the lost cause. Returning to Texas after the war he practiced his profession until the close of his life, his death occurring at Goliad in 1887, when in his seventy-fifth year. He was a Chapter Mason. The mother is still living. Her people were prosperous farmers and now reside in and about Columbus, S. C. Our subject's paternal grandfather, Judge Abraham Nott, was a member of the Supreme Court of South Carolina for thirty years. The family is of Scotch-Irish origin. The first member of the same family to come to this country was Sargent John Nott, who left Nottinghamshire, England, in 1634, and settled in Connecticut. He had two sons, Josiah and Clark, and after both, our subject's uncle, Dr. J. C. Nott, was named. Judge Abraham Nott was born in Connecticut, and went to Camden, S. C., where he married, studied law, and became an eminent man. He was Judge of the Supreme Bench of South Carolina at the time of his death. He had six sons, all of whom became prominent physicians. The youngest, G. A. Nott, was for twenty-four years professor in Louisiana Medical College, New Orleans, and another son, J. C., of Mobile, Ala., is one of the foremost physicians and surgeons in the United States. He is an author and inventor of many surgical instruments. During the entire war he was Gen. Pragg's Medical Director. All the six sons were classical scholars, graduates of South Carolina College, and they also graduated in medicine at Charleston and Philadelphia. Three of the sons, G. A., J. C., and our subject's father, spent three years in Paris, in the hospitals of that city, under the instruction of Ricord, Velpeau and other old masters. James H. Nott, an uncle, went to California in 1842, amassed a fortune, and was lost at sea when on his way home in 1859. Henry J., another uncle, and Professor of Languages at South Carolina College for many years, married a French lady in Paris, and he and wife were lost on the ship "Home," when on their way to visit her parents in Paris. The second oldest son, Wm. Blackstone Nott, moved to Missouri, where he married a Miss Naylor, and practiced his profession a few years, after which he returned to South Carolina and did an extensive county practice at Limestone Springs until his death, which occurred during the war. He has two sons and two grandsons practicing medicine. All the sons and grandsons of the Notts are doctors. The original of this notice, Dr. Thomas H. Nott, was attending school in South Carolina when Civil War broke out, but he threw aside his books and enlisted at Shreveport, La., in Company G, Twenty-seventh Louisiana Regiment. From there he went to Vicksburg and remained until the fall, then, with the help of a negro servant, he rode across the State to Shreveport, La. Later he joined the army again, and was in the battles of Mansfield and Pleasant Hill. For some time he was guard in a prison camp at Tyler, Texas. Later he joined Green's Texas Brigade and was with it until the close of the war. Immediately afterward he secured a professorship at Baylor University, Independence, Texas, chair of ancient languages, and remained there one session. He then engaged in the drug business at Independence and continued in this one year, after which he formed a partnership with his brother-in-law, W. A. Williamson, son of Judge R. M. Williamson, known as "three-legged Willie," of Texas fame. Soon after our subject and his partner removed their business to Brenham, and here their goods were destroyed by fire after one day's sales of $127. From there Dr. Nott went to Louisiana and farmed for two years, after which, in 1870, he came to Texas. He selected his wife in the person of Miss Julia Robertson, daughter of Gen. J. B. Robertson, of Independence, and sister of Gen. Felix H. Robertson, now of Waco. In 1871 the doctor went to Rockport and took charge of his father's drug store, but a year later went from there to New York with his wife and took two courses of lectures in Bellevue Medical College. In 1874 he graduated at Long Island Medical College in Brooklyn. Returning to Rockport he practiced medicine two years, and in 1876, was made a member of the Medical Examining Board, when the first law regulating the practice of medicine was passed, and he has been a member of the board since. In the fall of 1876 he came to Goliad, where he has since made his home. In 1879 he went to New York and took a course in the College of Physicians and Surgeons, graduating from that institution in 1880. He was made First Vice-president of the State Medical Association at Tyler in 1883, and President of the same at Dallas in 1886. He has been a member since 1876, and is now an honorary member of the West Texas Medical Association of San Antonio. The Doctor is also a member of the Central Texas Medical Association at Waco, and a member of the North Texas Medical Association. He owns two good river farms of 300 acres, in cultivation, and he has stock in and was one of the organizers of the oil mill and the First National Bank of Goliad. His first wife died in 1885, leaving no children. He was married in 1887 to Miss Mary Ray, daughter of Elijah Ray, an old pioneer of Goliad, Texas, settling here in 1852. He was born in Fayette County, Ala., and was an extensive stock-raiser. At the present time he owns a large ranch of 25,000 acres in Goliad County. During the war he served in the militia on the frontier of Texas. Of this family there were two sons and four daughters, all now residing in this county except James F. Ray, of Bee County. George A. Ray owns a large ranch in this county. To Dr. and Mrs. Nott was born one daughter, Julia May. All are members of the Episcopal Church. The doctor is a member of Masonic Lodge Goliad No. 94, Goliad Chapter No. 54, Fannin Commandery No. 17, and was Eminent Commander of the Commandery. He has been through all the chairs of the

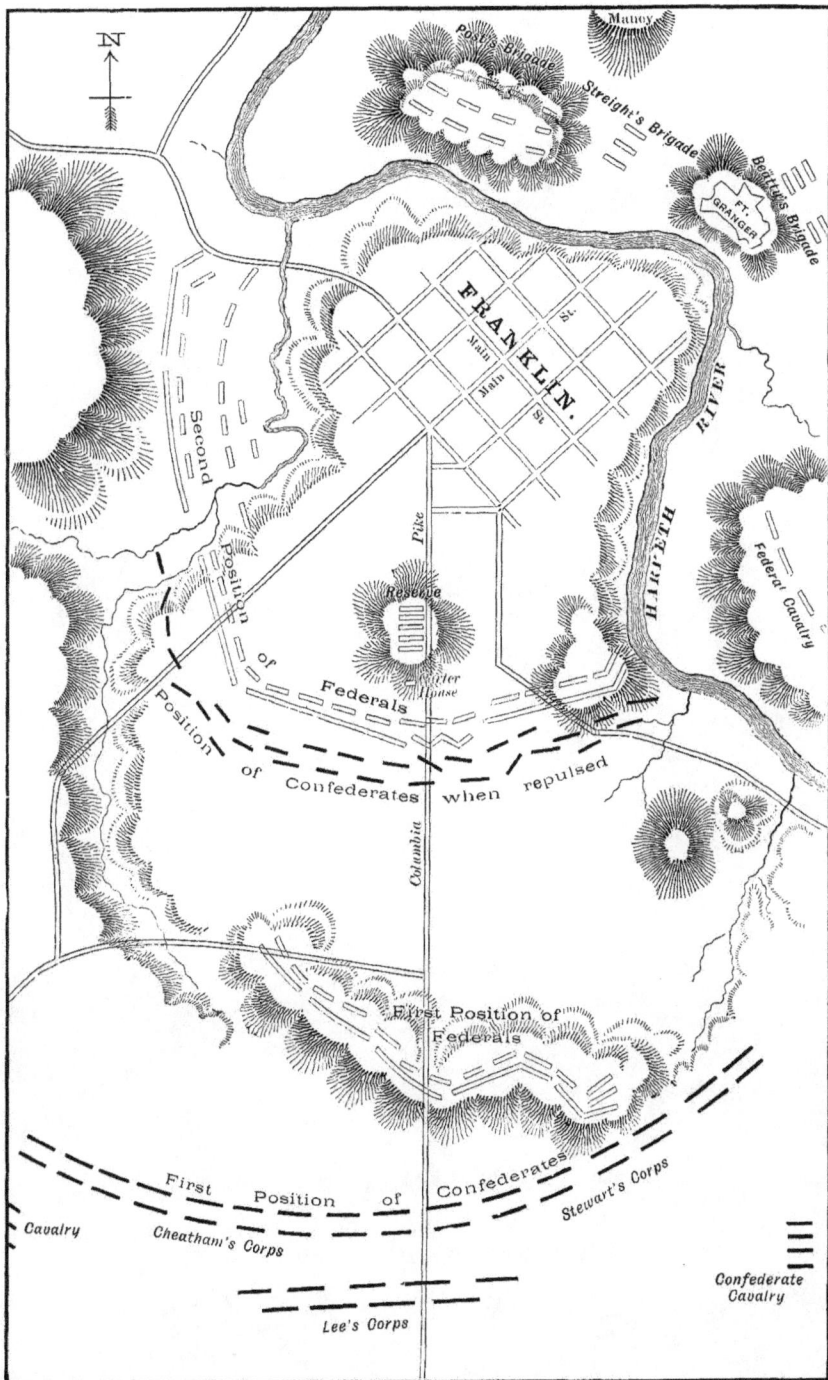

N

FRANKLIN.

Main St.

Main St.

Post's Brigade

Maney

Streight's Brigade

Bellius's Brigade

FT. GRANGER

HARPETH RIVER

Second Position

Federal Cavalry

of

Position

of

Federals

Reserve

Carter House

Pike

Position of Confederates when repulsed

Columbia

First Position of Federals

First Position of Confederates

Stewart's Corps

Cavalry

Cheatham's Corps

Confederate Cavalry

Lee's Corps

orders. He received the Knights Templar degree at Morton Commandery No. 1, New York City, in 1880, and on his return to Goliad he organized the Commandery of that place. For two terms he has served as District Deputy.

HARMON LUTHER LOWMAN. Farming has long constituted one of the leading industries of the United States, and among its followers who has made a complete success of this occupation stands the name of Harmon Luther Lowman, a prominent agriculturist of Guadalupe County, Texas. He came originally from the Palmetto State, where he remained until twenty-two years old, and where he received his education. He then decided to move to Alabama, and upon reaching that State, settled in Crenshaw County. There in connection with farming he wielded the birch in the school room until forty-four years of age, and in 1878 came to Caldwell County, and two years later settled in Guadalupe, Texas. His wife, whose maiden name was Rebecca Wise, and who was also a native of South Carolina, became the mother of eight children: Quincy Joseph, Thaddeus T., a farmer of Guadalupe County; Roston Pollard, John H., deceased; Joel Abner, now a resident of Caldwell County; Julia A., wife of B. F. Griffin; Emma J., wife of R. E. Burkett, and George L. Both parents of these children are now living and are honored and esteemed citizens. These children came to Texas with the father and two of them, Quincy Joseph and Roston Pollard, formed a co-partnership in 1889, under the firm name of Lowman Bros., public ginners, farmers and stock-raisers. They started out with very little besides an unlimited amount of pluck and determination and have since been notably prosperous. They own a fine water power on the San Marcos, and are using Munger system partially—elevator, distributor-case, turbine wheel, four gins, two of Catham, seventy saws each, two Eagles, sixty saws each—daily capacity of twenty-five bales. They will average 1,500 bales a year. Bright, enterprising and progressive, they are classed among the most successful men of this section. Quincy Joseph is but thirty-seven years of age, his birth occurring in Crenshaw County, Alabama, May 27, 1857, and his brother, Roston Pollard, is about three years younger, having been born in the same county July 21, 1860. Quincy Joseph was educated in his native county, and was twenty-one years of age when he came to Texas, with his father, whom he aided on the home place for several years. He was married January 10, 1894, to Miss Mellie Scott, of Guadalupe County. Roston Pollard was also educated in Crenshaw County. He selected his wife in the person of Miss Nunoly Francis of Harris County, and their nuptials were celebrated in December, 1891. They have one child, Manetta. In their ranch the Lowman brothers have 600 acres, 325 acres under cultivation, and with their brother, Abner, also own 915 acres in Caldwell County, which is managed by the latter. They are engaged quite extensively in raising horses and mules. Both brothers are Democrats in politics, and Quincy Joseph is a member of the Knights of Honor.

FELIX KYLE. Tennessee has contributed many of her representative citizens to swell the population of Texas, but she has contributed few who are more industrious, persevering and progressive than Felix Kyle, who was born in Hawkins County, that State, April 18, 1829. This worthy citizen was fourth in order of birth of ten children born to Wiley and Catherine (Creed) Kyle, both natives of Tennessee. Wiley Kyle spent the greater part of his days in that State, but late in life removed to Franklin

County, Ala., where he bought a farm and resided until his death, when fifty-five years of age. After her husband's death Mrs. Kyle removed to Monroe County, Miss., where a half-brother of her husband's was living, and there died when sixty-five years of age. Felix Kyle was partially reared in Tennessee and Alabama, but spent the greater part of his youth in Monroe County, Miss. His educational advantages were limited, on account of his father's death, and in 1849 he came to San Marcos, Texas, where he raised and dealt in horses. When the war started he enlisted in Capt. Carington's Company, Confederate Service, and was at Sabine Pass, Galveston, and on the border. When the war ceased he was at Brownsville. Returning home, he invested about $10,000, which he had made in the stock business, in a ranche at Stringtown neighborhood, but sold that five years ago and bought the ranche on which he now resides. He was married in the year 1851 to Miss Grace Burleson, daughter of Gen. Edward Burleson, and they have had five children, two of whom are living: Robert and Edward Wiley. Mrs. Kyle died in 1860, and the following year Mr. Kyle married Miss Martha Kyser, who has borne him nine children, seven now living, as follows: Joseph, died December 25, 1893; William, Houston, Polk, Felix; Mattie, who died December 12, 1879; Walter, Lola and Rodger. The three children born to the first union were named as follows: Emma, married Joseph Carter, of Austin, and died April 23, 1877; Claiborne, died July 12, 1859, and Jefferson, died March 3, 1883. All his life Mr. Kyle has been a Democrat, but he has never aspired to office.

JOHN DONEGAN, the present Tax Assessor of Guadalupe County, Texas, is worthy and well qualified for the position he now occupies, and, being a most agreeable and social gentleman, is deservedly popular with the public. He inherits much of his energy and perseverance from his Irish ancestors, no doubt, and his sterling integrity and sound judgment have given him a reputation of which he may well be proud. He is a native of Alabama, born in the year 1842, and of the seven children born to his parents, Joshua and Sarah (White) Donegan, he was the youngest. The mother was a native of Alabama, and after the death of her husband, which occurred when our subject was but an infant, she came, with her family, to Texas, in 1854, and located in Guadalupe County. There she died in 1885, when eighty-three years of age. Young Donegan received his education in the Lone Star State, and followed farm labor until the opening of the war. In 1861 he enlisted in Company E, Sixth Texas Infantry, and went to Arkansas, where he was in the siege and fall of Arkansas Post. After this he was a prisoner in Camp Butler, near Springfield, Ill., was exchanged at City Point, Va., and served thereafter in the Army of Tennessee. During the battle of Chickamauga he received a wound and was out of service until the next May. He participated in all the fighting about Atlanta until the fall of that city, and then marched to Tennessee with Gen. Hood. During the bloody battle of Franklin he lost his left arm and was in the hospital for a short time, and then started to the rear, marching much of the way to Georgia. From there he went to Alabama, and remained in that State until the cessation of hostilities. Upon his return to Texas he went to school for about one year, and then engaged in teaching, and continued this for several years, being interested in stock raising in a limited way at the same time. In 1875 he was married to Miss Hattie Benton, a native of Texas, and daughter of Nat. Benton, formerly of Tennessee, and one of the early settlers of Seguin. After his marriage Mr. Donegan followed farming until 1888, when he was elected County Assessor. So well did he discharge the duties of that office that he has been re-elected to that position each term since. His marriage resulted in the birth of six children, as follows: Hugh and Howard (twins), the latter died in infancy; Henry, Hattie May, Alva and Cora Lee. Mr. Donegan is a member of the Primitive Baptist Church, and an able and capable official.

DR. O. L. ABNEY. The value to any community of a citizen is not marked merely by his learning or the success which has attended him in his business or professional undertakings, but also by his character in public and private life, his honorable adherence to all that is good and pure, by his personal integrity, and by the interest he has taken in the welfare of the section in which he has made his home. An honorable and public spirited citizen of Victoria, Texas, is Dr. O. L. Abney, who has been a prominent resident of the place since 1887. He was born in the Palmetto State in 1853, the second of three children born to Zack and Elizabeth (Davenport) Abney, who were also born in South Carolina, the former a planter. He became a resident of Louisiana during the '50's, and was killed in that State during the war, the mother's death occurring in 1862. After the death of his parents Dr. Abney was placed in school at the University of Virginia, and later in a well known institution of New York City, and in 1879 he began the study of medicine in the city of Cincinnati, and later pursued his investigations in Louisville and New York, graduating from medical colleges in the two last mentioned cities. He began the practice of his profession in Louisiana, where he remained one year, but in 1882 came to Texas, and in 1887 came to Victoria from Fayette County, and this place has since been his home. In 1888 he married Miss Mary Welder, daughter of Mr. John Welder, the head of one of the oldest families of this section. In 1890 he began breeding trotting horses and graded Jersey cattle, and now has a herd of ten registered Jerseys, which are by far the finest herd of the kind in the county. He has a small stud of eleven horses, embracing some of the descendants of some of the leading trotting horses of the world, to wit: Electioneer, Dictator, Wilkes and Sultan. On his breeding farm, which is one mile from the town, and consists of 120 acres, he keeps a professional trainer to handle his stock, and in order to still further insure his success he has applied himself to the study of veterinary surgery. The head of his stud is a son of Baron Wilkes, his dam having been a producing daughter of Nutwood. The farm is fitted up with all necessary buildings and all appliances to carry on the work successfully, among which is a fine training track. Dr. Abney is perhaps the first man to make a success of breeding thoroughbred trotting stock or full blooded Jersey cattle, and his fine herd and handsome stud show the care he has taken in the selection of his propagating animals. He has practically retired from the practice of the medical profession and is now devoting his time to the study and advancement of his stock interests. He is a member of the State Medical Society, and is President of the District Medical Examining Board.

WINN TRAYLOR (deceased). When the measure of human life has reached its almost ultimate limit of years, as well as its perfection in fulfillment of duty, a title to distinction is earned that men are naturally impelled to recog-

nize and honor. The lifework has been completed, its fruits have been gar-
nered and the record of its incidents remains to tell the story of worthy success
in living. Such was the life of him whose honored memory claims the tribute
of these lines. Through an active career, extending considerably over three
score years and ten, the life of Winn Traylor presents an example of usefulness and worthiness the contemplation of which serves as an inspiration to
those who seek to deserve respect and love while living, and veneration after
death. Born in Oglethorpe County, Ga., March 17, 1807, he was soon after
removed by his parents to Dallas County, Ala., where he grew to manhood.
In May, 1831, he was married to Miss Martha Chapman. He came to Texas
in 1840, and in February of that year settled on the place so long familiarly known as "Old Man Traylor's," about twelve miles southeast of town.
Although a poor man, Mr. Traylor was industrious and economical; and
slowly and steadily his fortune increased until, at his death in November,
1883, it comprised a principality in extent, and was estimated to be worth
$250,000. For many years he was a communicant of the Presbyterian
Church. To his marriage were born the following children: Thomas, the
eldest son, died about the year 1868; William T., married Miss Orie Terry
in 1865, and lost his wife about the year 1880. He was the father of two
daughters and a son. William T. served through the war with credit, and
has accumulated an estate valued at $100,000; Pascal, familiarly called
"Pack," was a member of the Sixth Texas Infantry in Georgia, and was killed
in battle; Henry, the youngest son, married Miss Sue Spencer, of Mississippi,
and resides at the old homestead; Alabama, the eldest daughter, is the wife
of John Hunt, and Eliza married Capt. Pat. Hughes about the year 1865, but
unfortunately did not live long. She left one daughter, who is now Mrs.
Eliza Hughes Welder. The youngest son, Henry C. Traylor, was born June
5, 1853, and was reared and educated in Texas. On the 22d of December,
1875, he was married to Miss Sue Spencer, as above stated. She was
born in Mississippi, and is a daughter of William Spencer, who was a native of England. After his marriage Mr. Traylor resided on his ranch for
the most part, but spent his summers at Port Lavaca. Since 1893, however,
he has resided in Port Lavaca. He owns a ranch of 9,000 acres at the old
homestead, all good land, and he owns two other good farms. He is in
partnership with H. G. Austin in the cattle shipping business, and is a
thrifty, practical man. Mr. Traylor has one of the pleasantest places in Port
Lavaca, and is wideawake and progressive. Mrs. Winn Traylor died December 10, 1888. Winn Traylor was a brick mason and brick maker by trade
and manufactured the first brick in Victoria, and assisted in building many
houses in that town. Mrs. W. Traylor's father died in 1827 at Montgomery,
Ala. After some time he engaged in farming, and moved to and from Calhoun County, and in 1844 made a permanent settlement on the river, twelve
miles below Victoria, where he passed the remainder of his days. H. C.
Traylor has one son living. He is fourteen years old and bears his grandfather's name, Winn Traylor.

HENRY LEVY. The worthy gentleman whose name is here mentioned is
now living, retired from the active duties of life and in the enjoyment of a
liberal income, the result of his own good fighting qualities, and the respect
and friendship of all who know him, whom he has gathered about him by his
correct mode of living. He was born in sunny France, February 22, 1825,

the second of four children born to Benjamin and Louisa (Bloch) Levy, the death of the latter occurring while he was an infant. The father followed the occupation of a tanner, and when the subject of this sketch was but a lad of thirteen years he was left fatherless to fight life's battles as best he could. He had no opportunities for acquiring an education, for under the rule of Charles XI. of France public schools were unknown, and even if there had been any he, in all probability, could not have taken advantage of them, owing to the fact that he had to make his own way in the world. He was apprenticed to a shoemaker for three years in Alsace, and after completing his apprenticeship, remained there as a workman for one year. When in his eighteenth year, he went to Paris and worked in that city until he became subject to military duty and was then drafted into the French army, with which he served for seven years in the Marines under King Louis Philip and Napoleon II. During this time he participated in the expedition to Madagascar. He was honorably discharged from the service in 1852, and after spending a short time in Paris went to Montasche, where he became an employe in the India Rubber Works of Goodyear & Co., with whom he remained for eleven months as a workman, then was promoted to the position of foreman, and filled this position with marked ability for nineteen months, when he was taken ill and compelled to give up the work. He was then given a letter of recommendation to the firm in America, and started for a seaport town. Upon reaching Havre he met a friend and was advised to go to New Orleans, and in this city he eventually arrived June 9, 1855. Here he visited a sister for a short time, and, following her advice, came to Victoria, Texas, and joined his cousin, Abraham Levi, who was a successful merchant of the place. He worked for him, or rather for the firm of Halfin & Levi, for several months, then started out as a peddler, and traveled throughout the country on horseback. After a time he purchased a wagon and another horse, after which he pursued his calling through this and adjoining counties, and was hourly in danger of his life from Indians and Mexicans, for the country was at that time very thinly inhabited. After a time he was taken ill with chills and fever, and in 1859 was compelled to return to New Orleans and there remained about seven months. During this time he accumulated a stock of goods and upon his return to Texas, opened a store at Refugio in 1859, where he continued to conduct a reasonably successful business until 1862, when he was drafted into the Confederate army and sold his stock of goods, and as the most of his money was out in accounts, it was nearly all lost. He entered Gen. Crosling's Brigade, but on account of being a shoemaker, he was allowed to remain in Victoria, where he followed his trade for the benefit of the Confederate Government. In 1864 he went to Brownsville, where he was engaged in clerking in a mercantile establishment for a short time, then went to Matamoras, where he acted in the capacity of city salesman for importing houses on commission, and in a few months made several thousand dollars. With this money he saw that he could make a new start, so he purchased a stock of goods, a part of which he sold in Galveston and brought the remainder to Refugio, which he disposed of at a good profit. From that time until 1867 he made his home in Victoria, but the yellow fever breaking out, he went to New York, where he met A. Levi, who was returning from Europe, and together they laid in a stock of goods, which they later brought to Victoria, and Henry Levy became a partner in the firm of A. Levi & Co., with which he continued until 1876, then retired with a comfortable fortune. He then invested $16,000 in cattle, and after following the stock business for several years, sold out and is now the owner of a 2,140 acre ranch near the city of Victoria. He also owns six houses in the town, which he rents, and one of the handsomest residences in the place, which he erected in 1879, and in which he is passing a serene old age. He was married in 1868 to Miss Barbara Deutsch, by whom he has one son and one daughter: Justine, wife of S. Lewin, of San Antonio, and Benjamin, who is a bookkeeper in Levi's bank. Mr. Levy is a member of the A. F. & A. M., with which he has been connected for many years, and he is President of the Hebrew Benevolent Association, and on many occasions has contributed liberally to charitable enterprises. No better citizen can be found in the town of Victoria than Mr. Levy, for he possesses the most sterling characteristics, and he stands at the head of the substantial self-made men of the place.

CAPT. WILLIAM M. RUST. This prominent lawyer of Guadalupe County, Texas, is a native of that grand old State, Virginia, and comes of an old and prominent family of that State, his father and grandfather having been born there. The first members of the Rust family to settle in America were three brothers, who came from England to New York in colonial times, and their descendants finally drifted to Virginia. Capt. William M. Rust's birth occurred in Frederick County in 1825, and he was the elder of two children born to Marshall and Jane M. A. (Redmon) Rust, the mother also a native of Virginia. Marshall Rust was a physician by profession, but in connection was also engaged in farming. His death occurred when he was but twenty-eight years of age. His wife subsequently moved to Tennessee, thence to Kentucky, where she married, and later, while on a visit to Virginia, died there in 1854. Her father, John Redmon, was a native of Scotland, and came to this country in command of a merchant ship about 1800. He married Miss Pamelia Thomas, of Westmoreland County, Va., and spent the balance of his days there. Our subject's paternal grandfather, John Rust, followed farming for a livelihood, but held many offices in his county, being Justice of the Peace and High Sheriff for years. Until fifteen years of age Capt. William M. Rust was reared by his mother, and then went to live with his paternal grandfather, who was his guardian. After remaining with him for several years he went to Kentucky, and there taught school for some time. Later he attended Centre College at Danville, Ky. In 1850 he and a friend, Ab. Hunter, started overland for California, but reaching Portland, Ore., remained there until the following spring, when they proceeded to California. They spent the summer in the mines, near the present city of Shasta, and in the fall came home by way of the Isthmus. After spending a short time in Virginia and Kentucky, Mr. Rust came to Texas and located at Seguin, where he began surveying for the Texas Immigration and Land Company, remaining with the same about one year. He then became Deputy County Clerk of Guadalupe County, filled this position for one year, and then became Deputy District Clerk for some time, filling that position in a very satisfactory manner. In the year 1860 Mr. Rust married Miss Sallie McDowell Shelby, of Kentucky, and then moved to Burnet County, where he engaged in farming and stock-raising. In 1862 he enlisted in the Twenty-first Texas Cavalry, and was at once made Captain of Company B. The regiment started for Virginia, but at the Red River was sent to Arkansas. Capt. Rust's regiment was in several engagements in southeast Missouri, and participated in the battles on Red River, in Louisiana, against Gen. Banks. Afterwards he was in the campaign on Saline River, but on account of sickness came home in the winter of 1864, and was there when the war closed. Soon after he came to Seguin, was admitted to the bar, and began practicing. In politics he is an active Democrat, and in 1876 was elected by that party to the State Legislature, being Chairman of the Committee on State Affairs, member of Judiciary No. 1, Penitentiary and Education. This was the first Legislature after the new constitution of 1876, and Capt. Rust was active in many important measures. He practices in the Supreme and other courts of the State, and is a close reasoner and profound thinker. His wife died in 1874, leaving one daughter, Marie Augusta, wife of Frank L. Baker. Capt. Rust was married again in 1879 to Miss Arrabelle Campbell, a native of Kentucky, who died in 1886, leaving one child, William M., Jr. The captain is a member of the Masonic order, Guadalupe Lodge No. 108, and is also a member of the Chapter and Commandery at Gonzales.

DR. THOMAS SEWELL PETTEY, physician and farmer of Martindale, Caldwell County, Texas, is a native Virginian, born in Norfolk, November 3, 1836, and one of two children living of a family of nine children born to John and Mary (Norris) Pettey. The father was interested in a fishery, but also carried on farming. He was also a native of Virginia, and died there in 1842. In tracing back the genealogy of this family we find that three brothers emigrated from England to this country prior to the Revolutionary War, and two of them served under King George, and the third under Gen. George Washington. One of them was in the navy and was killed, and the other returned to County Kent, England, where his descendants are living at the present time. John Pettey, who fought under Washington, and who was the grandfather of our subject, married in Virginia, reared his family there, and there passed the remainder of his days, dying in Princess Ann County. The mother of our subject was born in Princess Ann County, Va., and died in Brenham, Texas, in 1861. She was of Welsh descent. The boyhood and youth of our subject were spent in Virginia, Alabama, Georgia and other States, and during 1853 and 1855 he attended school in LaGrange, Ga. In 1855 he followed his mother to Texas and took a scientific course at Baylor University, then at Independence, Texas. He attended lectures at the University of Louisiana in New Orleans, medical department, and received his diploma in 1859. His first practice was at Brenham. Dr. Pettey enlisted in the Confederate service, and with eight or ten others went to Virginia and independently tended the wounded on the battlefield of Manassas. In 1862 he was appointed Surgeon of the cavalry. Previous to this, in 1861, he was sent by the Surgeon-in-chief to Nashville, and established the first Confederate hospital there. Later he was Senior Surgeon of Gen. Walter P. Lane's brigade, and when the war ceased he was at Eagle Pass, where he had released another physician in charge of a hospital. This trip was made in the way of a furlough and rest. After the war Dr. Pettey joined Gen. Walker's expedition to Mexico, but after six months returned to Martindale, where he has since been engaged in his practice and farming. He is a Royal Arch Mason. On the 13th of December, 1866, he was married to Miss Emma T. Norris, a cousin and daughter of William and Ann Norris, pioneers of Texas and natives of Virginia. Only one child, a son, has been born to Dr. and Mrs. Pettey. This son is now in the drug business at Martindale and is a wideawake, progressive young man, is married and has one son.

HENRY CLAY KOONTZ. Among the most esteemed and respected citizens of Victoria County, Texas, there is not one who has been a more public spirited citizen, a more pleasant or agreeable member of society, or a more thorough or sagacious business man than the gentleman whose name is mentioned above. His life of industry and usefulness from the time of his early boyhood, and his record for honesty and uprightness have given him a hold upon the community which all might well share. He is a native of Matagorda, Texas, born April 12, 1847, a son of Henry and Dorothy Koontz, who were born in the Republic of Switzerland. The father came to America when a young man, and in 1832 took out naturalization papers in Selma, Ala. He became an early resident of Texas and secured a headright for services rendered the Republic of Texas. He was married to the mother of the subject of this sketch in Texas, and died in Indianola, this State, in 1852, his wife and daughter dying about the same time, in the epidemic of that year. After being left an orphan at the tender age of five years he was taken into the family of a man by the name of Varnell, and was brought by him to Victoria County in 1859, and reared and assisted him on the farm on which he located. Upon starting out to make his own way in the world he became a cattle driver at $15 per month and later received $30 per month for his services. At the end of five years he began merchandising in partnership with C. Letts in Victoria County, but at the end of three years sold out to his partner, after which he was engaged in the buying and selling of horses for four years. On the 1st of May, 1879, he was united in marriage with Miss Mary Finnigan, a native of Alabama, who came to Texas in 1870. In October, 1879, Mr. Koontz once more began merchandising, in the vicinity of his former place of business, where he continued until about 1885, when he removed his stock to Inez, a town which had just been established, and opened the first mercantile house of that place. He soon after purchased a cotton gin, which he has equipped with all modern machinery, and now has two stands with a capacity of about fourteen bales per day. About nine years ago he was made the Postmaster of Inez, and has held this office up to the present time. His stock of goods is valued at about $3,000, and his annual sales amount to about $8,000, while his cotton gins bring in some $10,000 more. He is the owner of a ranch of about 800 acres, and has about 125 acres under cultivation, but gives considerable attention to the buying and selling of cattle. His residence, store, and nearly all the buildings about his gin in the town of Inez have been erected by him. The gin was purchased by him, and he has added new buildings since its purchase. He has at all times shown himself to be a man of great enterprise, push and public spirit. He is a thorough type of the self-made man, and is the mainstay and ruling element of his town, doing almost all the business of that place. He is hale, hearty, cordial, and has an interesting and intelligent family of children whose names are as follows: Nannie Bell, a pupil at the Convent in Victoria; Mamie Nell, Beatrice, John Henry, Henry Clay, Jr., Jasper and Vivian.

FRANK NUSOM. This enlightened and energetic farmer of Charco, Goliad County, Texas, has a ranch of about 7,000 acres pasture, and 300 acres under a good state of cultivation. He is eminently the type of the progressive American citizen, has pushed his undertakings to a satisfactory issue, and success has crowned his efforts. He was born in Mississippi in 1844, and is a son of Thomas A. and Margaret L. (Simmons) Nusom, natives respectively of North Carolina and Mississippi. The parents were married in the latter State and came to Texas in 1852, spending the first winter in Victoria. The following spring they moved to the Northern part of Goliad County and there the father engaged in the stock business until his death soon after. The family resided there for some time afterward, and the mother married Dr. Lipscomb. From about his eighth year our subject was reared in Goliad County, and attended school until the breaking out of the Civil War. In the spring of 1861 he enlisted in Company A, Seventh Texas Cavalry, and served in New Mexico and Louisiana until the war was over. He was in all the engagements of Louisiana, and was on scout duty most of the time, pariticipating in many skirmishes. In November, 1863, he was sent to New Orleans as a prisoner, but one month later came home, and soon after again joined the army, remaining in service until the war was over. Returning to his home he entered actively upon his career as rancher. In 1866 he married Miss Mildred E. Box, a native of Alabama, and daughter of Rev. A. M. Box, and soon after engaged in driving cattle to Kansas, continuing this for about eight years. In 1875 he began working cattle on the range, and in 1880 he began pasturing. He now has about 1,000 head of cattle, all improved, and a small herd of full-blooded Durhams. To Mr. Nusom's marriage have been born five children: Henry L., Nannie, wife of W. J. Porter, Jr., of Karnes County; Maggie, Lonnie L., and Allen C. This family holds membership in the M. E. Church South. Mr. Nusom was made a Mason in Alamito Lodge at Helena, Texas, and was made a Royal Arch Mason at Goliad. He is now a member of the committee on work. In December, 1893, he was elected Grand High Priest, and is a prominent man in Masonic circles, has always been an industrious and upright citizen, and is regarded as one of the county's most substantial residents.

JOHN H. WOOD. The philosophy of success in life is an interesting study. In whatever pursuit individual study is directed, it should be entered with a theoretical knowledge and not blindly. In choosing a pursuit in life, taste, mental gifts, opportunity and disposition of labor should be considered, as every young man, who has any ambition to become a respectable and useful citizen, desires to succeed therein. A narrative of success in life affords a lesson from which others can profit, therefore, a sketch of the life of John H. Wood will be proper in this connection. He was born September 6, 1816, near Poughkeepsie, N. Y., his parents being Humphrey and Maria Wood, the latter of whom died when the subject of this sketch was about eleven years old. She was a daughter of Richard De Cantillion, and was connected with some of the oldest and most aristocratic families of the Empire State. Humphrey Wood came of Puritan stock, and like his ancestors before him followed the sea for some time, becoming the Captain of a vessel. Later he abandoned the sea and engaged in farming, establishing a pleasant home for himself and family on the banks of the Hudson, between Poughkeepsie and Hyde Park. He died in Genoa, N. Y., in 1873, at the extreme old age of 103 years. John H. Wood received a common school education, and after the death of his mother he attended school in the city of New York for a short time. Three years were then spent as a clerk in a dry goods store, after which he was in a grocery establishment for some time. Upon leaving this house, he bound himself to learn the painter's trade, and it was while serving his apprenticeship that news of the troubles of the Texans spread throughout the Northern States, and met a response from many true hearts, among which was that of John H. Wood. Stanley and Morehouse, emissaries of the Provisional Government of Texas, were in New York recruiting, and Mr. Wood, procuring permission from the painter to whom he was apprenticed, called on these men and enrolled his name. One hundred and eighty-four men whom the agents represented as emigrants, sailed on a chartered vessel—the Matawomkey—on the night of November 25, 1835, and the first night out they encountered a severe storm. They reached the island of Eleuthera, one of the Bahamas, and anchored for a few days, the passengers and crew going ashore. Many of the volunteers were from the low districts of the city of New York and stole many things while at that place, and were guilty of other acts that brought them into *bar depure*. The captain of the vessel compelled them to return all the stolen articles when possible, and paid all persons who made complaint. He then sailed for Balize. A fisherman of low character, named Knowles, who lived near where the ship had anchored, went to Nassau, on the island of New Providence, and notified the British authorities that a pirate was hovering in those seas, had ravished women and been guilty of pillage. He said he was one who had suffered from the incursion, his object being to put in a claim for damages. The British ship at once gave chase to the Matawomkey, captured the ship and took her to Nassau, where all were confined for sixty days, the guards being mainly negroes, with whom the men had much sport. The Grand Jury on examining Knowles were convinced that the charge of piracy was false, but indicted some for theft, but these men were also soon acquitted. The Americans had often been insulted by British seamen, and just before sailing joined in a melee with some of the citizens of the place, and on shore gave them a thrashing they well merited. No lives were lost in this riot, and the Americans were allowed to depart. After a narrow escape from shipwreck on the coast of Cuba, they reached the mouth of the Mississippi, where the vessel waited for supplies. The ship, accompanied by the Texas man-of-war Brutus, proceeded to Pass Caballo, where the volunteers disembarked March 1, 1836, and marched to Matagorda. Many men of high ability and brilliant talents were also of this party, and were mustered into the Texas service at Matagorda. At this time the Alamo had fallen, the horrible massacre of Fannin and his command at Goliad had taken place, and Santa Anna was sweeping eastward with his victorious columns. Morehouse and his companions pushed forward, intending to join Gen. Houston's retreating army, but at Casey's Ferry, on the Colorado, he was met by a cousin who delivered orders from headquarters, commanding him to gather together his men to protect the families west of the Brazos River, and assist them in their efforts to leave the country. A few days before the battle of San Jacinto Morehouse and his men, numbering about 175, were encamped at the head of Oyster Creek, on the east side of the Brazos, but after that noted engagement Maj. Wood served as one of the soldiers in the mounted force that, under Gen. Rush, followed the retreating army of Gen. Fisisola as far as Goliad. At this place Maj. Wood assisted in the burial of the charred remains of Fannin's men, a sad but necessary duty. After the war Maj. Wood went to Victoria, and took charge of the houses of the Quartermaster's Department, a position he held for about six months. By law the property of Mexicans was confiscated, and Maj. Wood was given as pay for his services by Quartermaster Colonel Caldwell an order for some cattle, and thus his present large stock was founded. For a time he continued this business in the vicinity of Victoria, then on the Lavaca River, near the present town of Edna. In the fall of 1845 he went to Corpus Christi and had a conference with Gen. Taylor, who was then preparing to occupy the Rio Grande frontier, in which he stated that it was his desire to remove his cattle to Neuces River, if Gen. Taylor would promise to furnish, as far as in his power, protection from Indians and Mexicans. The promise was given, and early in 1846 Maj. Wood moved to that section. In August, 1849, he moved to Refugio County and established a home at St. Marys, where he has since resided. In that early day Southwestern Texas was infested with hostile Indians, and Maj. Wood had the opportunity of witnessing many of their savage acts, and was often one of a party to drive them back or to wreak vengeance for murders and other crimes committed. During the war between Mexico and the United States, Maj. Wood made frequent trips to Brownsville for supplies, and more than once witnessed the robbing of wagon trains by the highwaymen who infested the roads. He often came in contact with these bands, and had numerous experiences more interesting than amusing, but was never seriously molested. During the Civil War he entered the Confederate army, and served in Texas as a soldier and Major of the coast guards. He has always been a Democrat in politics but has never been a politician in any sense of the word, although he was for fifteen or twenty years a Commissioner of Refugio County, in which capacity he served with efficiency and faithfulness. A few years since he became a member of the Catholic Church and has donated to Nazareth Convent of Victoria 900 acres of valuable land, adjoining that town. He was married in Victoria February 1, 1842, to Miss Nancy Clark, a noble Christian lady, who was for nearly half a century his loved counselor, friend, companion and devoted wife, making his home the abode of domestic happiness and love, lightening his cares and filling his years with sunshine. She died in March, 1892, of heart failure, at the residence of her daughter, Mrs. Maria Carroll, of Victoria, her death being deeply deplored by her husband and children. Her memory is enshrined in the heart of him whose every thought during their life's journey was to render her happy, and it will live and glow with fire supreme as long as the spark of life lingers in his breast, and until the golden links of the severed chain are re-united in eternity. To their union twelve children were given: Maria, wife of W. C. Carroll, of Victoria; Catherine, wife of Henry Sullivan, of San Patricio, died in New Jersey, whither she had gone in search of health, in July, 1867; Richard H., married Miss Cannie Howard, of St. Marys, and now lives at Rockport; Agnes, is the wife of Albert J. Kennedy, of Beeville; James, died at Goliad, March 15, 1875, leaving a widow (*nee* Miss Mary Wilder), and one child; Cora, is the wife of Peter Mahon, of Victoria; Tobias D., married Miss Mary Mahon and resides in Victoria; Ida, is a nun of the order of the Incarnate Word in the Convent at Victoria; Willie, married Miss Nellie Borland, and resides in Victoria; Julia, is the wife of William C. George, of Beeville; Marian, who is a nun of the order of the Incarnate Word in the Convent at Victoria, died in February, 1890; and John, who married Miss Millie Sullivan, of San Patricio, and who died in February, 1891, is a resident of Beeville. Maj. Wood has made an immense fortune, the most of which he has divided among his children, but he is still the owner of 35,000 acres of fine land in Southwest Texas, has 7,000 cattle and 600 or 700 head of horses, besides a large number of mules. He also owns valuable real estate in other parts of Texas. His elegant home fronts on Copano Bay, affording a view of unsurpassed beauty, and is situated about a mile from the quaint little fishing village of St. Marys. His home is fitted up with every modern convenience and luxury, and here, with an excellent library, he spends the greater part of his time during the fall and winter, and in summer usually has many visitors. He often visits the homes of his children, where a place of honor is always reserved for him, and greatly enjoys the society of his grandchildren. He is a man of great intellectual force, a gentleman of the old school, a warm friend and a devoted father. He is a man who started the hard battle of life without adventitious aid and has succeeded in the attainment of all things worthy the ambition of an honorable man, has manfully and successfully run life's race, and now surrounded by loving children and grandchildren and hosts of friends he peacefully waits for the final summons. Of him it may be said "Well done thou good and faithful servant."

William A. Wood, son of above, is a prominent ranchman of Victoria, was born at St. Marys in 1861, and was educated in Victoria and in Georgetown, D. C. After attaining his majority he began working for his father, and in 1886 became the owner of his present ranche of 11,000 acres, nine miles East of Victoria. He has some 3,000 head of cattle, and at the same time buys and sells stock also, and is one of the most extensive dealers in hides in Victoria. He was married in 1890 to Miss Nellie Borland, a native of Victoria County, and a daughter of Alexander J. Borland, who came to Texas in 1857 or 1858. Her mother's people came to this State from New York, but her grandfather, with his party, were murdered by the Indians on or near the present site of Beeville, her mother escaping this fate by having remained in Victoria. Mr. Wood is one of the enterprising and progressive men of Texas, and being a native of the State, he is thoroughly loyal to its interests, and is a living illustration that the native Texan can be a gentleman in the fullest sense of the word and a man of culture and refinement. He has a beautiful home, a wife of taste and culture and two promising children—Jessie and Margaret.

G. M. AUTRY. A number of years passed in a sincere and earnest endeavor to thoroughly discharge every duty incumbent upon the office of Sheriff has served to place Mr. Autry among the leading and influential men of the county. His long residence here and his intimate association with the various material and official affairs of the county have gained for him an extensive acquaintance. Born in Mississippi in 1842, he was the eldest child born to Jacob B. and Tempy (Embry) Autry, both natives of the Palmetto State. The father and mother were married in Mississippi, whither their parents had moved at an early day, and there passed the remainder of their days, the mother dying in 1848 and the father in 1856. Surrounded by healthy country air, on a farm, our subject reached the age of fifteen years and eleven months, and was then married to Miss Angelina Wilson, who was one month his junior. After this rather unusual marriage Mr. and Mrs. Autry continued on the farm until the Civil War broke out, when, in 1861, Mr. Autry enlisted in Company K, Thirty-fourth Mississippi Regiment. He was in the battles of Shiloh, Perryville, Murfreesboro, Chickamauga and Lookout Mountain. At the latter place he was captured November 24, 1863, and taken to Rock Island, Ills., where he was kept a prisoner until the war closed. Returning to his home he found that his house had been destroyed and his possessions swept away. Although this was rather a severe blow, he went actively to build up his fallen fortune in the same place and remained there until 1869. He then came to Texas, located in Harris County for four years, and then moved to Guadalupe County, where he bought a farm on the San Marcos River. This he has improved in every way and has a handsome place, all the result of his own exertions. All his life he has adhered to the principles of the Democratic party and has been an active worker for the same. In 1888 he was elected Sheriff of the county and has been re-elected each term since. He is a man of unquestioned integrity and has many warm friends in this section. To Mr. Autry and wife have been given ten children: J. B., John W., died when thirteen years old; Gustave A., William J., died when fifteen years of age; Bettie, George, James D., Mary, Rosa, and Lena. Mr. Autry is a member of the A. F. & A. M. (at Martindale) and the K. of P. at Seguin. He is a self-made man and an upright, honorable one. Mrs. Autry is a worthy member of the Christian Church.

ROBERT MONROE MARTINDALE. There is no volume which, if published, would make more interesting reading than a history of pioneer times. The civilization of our day, the enlightenment of the age, and the duty that men of the present time owe to their ancestors, to themselves, and to their posterity, demand that a record of the lives of the early settlers be made. Among the representative pioneers of Caldwell County, Texas, stands the name of George Martindale, the father of our subject, who came to this county as early as 1851. He was a Hoosier by birth and bringing up, and a farmer by occupation. During Jackson's administration he came to Mississippi, before the Indians had been removed to their reservation, and there he resided until 1851, when he came to Caldwell County. Here his death occurred three years later. He was married to Miss Nancy Martin, a native of South Carolina, who lived to be eighty-four years of age, dying in 1890. Of the eleven children born to this estimable couple our subject was seventh in order of birth. He was born in De Seto County, Miss., May 15, 1839, but spent the most of his boyhood days in Caldwell County, Texas, whither his father moved when he was twelve years of age. After reaching mature years he embarked in the stock business, but had followed this but a short time when the Civil War broke out. He enlisted in the Confederate service, Calhoun's Company, Donnell's Regiment, and served in Arkansas, but was in the hospital when the battle of Arkansas Post occurred. He was afterwards transferred to Company K, Thirty-second Texas Cavalry, and in the Banks campaign through Louisiana participated in the battles of Mansfield, Pleasant Hill and Yellow Bayou. He was Orderly Sergeant throughout, and had fever and chills through the entire war, but never came home on account of it. For three years after the war he dealt in stock, and in 1869, having accumulated about $2,000, he embarked in merchandising at Martindale. He kept the first store and postoffice there and the town was named in honor of his family. After following merchandising for ten years, Mr. Martindale began farming and stock raising, crossing with Durham cattle. At present he raises horses and mules too, but owes the greater part of his success to cattle raising. In 1883 he sold 700 head at $19 each, netting him the snug sum of $13,300.

He pays tax on 7,000 acres of land, all paid for, and he bought 4,605 acres of this in 1877, at $1.25 per acre. Some of his land, however, he paid as high as $20 for. He is stirring and enterprising, and considered by many as the wealthiest man in Caldwell County. In politics he is a stanch advocate of the Democratic party, and but recently has been brought out for the Legislature with the idea of cementing factions in his party. He has been school trustee for some time, and is an active member of the Missionary Baptist Church. He selected his wife in the person of Miss Roxie M. Harper, daughter of B. F. Harper, an old citizen of this section, and their nuptials were celebrated in 1875. Three children have been born to this union, two sons and a daughter: Frederick, Norman and Lucy. Mr. Martindale is charitable and public spirited, and gives liberally of his means to support all worthy movements.

RICHARD T. DAVIS is a public spirited citizen, in harmony with advanced ideas, intelligent, progressive, and has at heart the good of his country generally. He is now a prominent rancher and real estate man of Goliad County, and he is respected by all for his honorable and upright career through life. Mr. Davis is a native of the Lone Star State, born at Ft. Houston, Anderson County, in 1848. He is fourth in order of birth of nine children born to Richard Wayne and Harriet E. (Mitchell) Davis, both natives of Kentucky. About 1840 the parents came to Texas and settled in Anderson County, where the father engaged in farming. The Indians were so plentiful and so dangerous that much of his time was spent in fighting them. This continued until 1851, when Mr. Davis moved his family to Rio Grande City, Star County, then Davis' Ranch, which was settled by his brother, Henry Clay Davis, who came to Texas in 1832; served in the Mexican and the Confedrate wars with distinction as an officer; fought Indians in an early day, killing an Indian chief in single combat; represented the people in the Texas Legislature [see "Following the Drum," by Mrs. Vealey, for part of his very interesting personal record]. In 1854 Mr. Davis came to Goliad County and settled in town on account of the school advantages. He bought considerable land around the town and engaged in farming. The various offices of the county were tendered him. First he was a Justice, then District Clerk, Treasurer, etc., and Mayor of Goliad. He also served as United States Marshal in the sixties. In 1867 he bought the county paper, *The Intelligencer*, and changed its name to *Goliad Guard*, which he conducted for several years, after which he turned it over to his son, our subject. After this he retired to his farm, where he died March 5, 1885, after a long and useful career. The mother passed away on the 12th of July, 1893. This worthy couple celebrated their golden wedding in 1883. Socially Mr. Davis was a Royal Arch Mason and a prominent man in his day. He was a Republican in his political views, but always won the votes of Democrats wherever known. Richard T. Davis received his education in the schools of Goliad, Palestine, etc., until the breaking out of war. When his father started the *Guard*, our subject entered the office and learned the trade. In 1871 he assumed charge of the paper, conducted it until 1892, and then sold out to N. M. Vogelsong, who now has charge of the paper. Our subject had a good office for his paper, but in August, 1880, it was totally destroyed by a cyclone, everything gone but his press, and that was badly damaged. Mr. Davis has 500 acres of good river bottom land, all under cultivation, and considered as good land as there is to be found in the county. He was married January 27, 1880, to Miss Alzenith Burke, a native of this county and daughter of Capt. James A. Burke (see sketch). Six children have been given this union: Katie C., Fleda Ray, Hattie E., Wayne Burke, Flora A. and one deceased. Mr. Davis is a Royal Arch Mason, an Odd Fellow, a member of the A. O. U. W., and is quite active in all. He was one of the organizers of the oil mill and the First National Bank, being a stock holder in both. He bought his pleasant home in 1882 and is surrounded by all the comforts of life. For fifteen years he was County Treasurer and he is now City Councilman. Mr. Davis' brothers and sisters were named as follows: Celicia, wife of W. J. Redding (see sketch); Flora C., wife of A. W. Appleby; Mary B., wife of D. H. Hardeman, and Kate, Amos, G. C. and G. W.; the last three named are dead.

JUDGE JAMES GREENWOOD. Although the weight and responsibility of many of the leading positions of Guadalupe County, Texas, have been assigned to Judge James Greenwood because of his peculiar fitness as a man of ability and rare judgment, age has not laid his dignifying hand upon him, for he was only born September 21, 1851. His birth occurred in Chickasaw County, Miss., and of the eight children born to his parents, T. C. and Juliet (Crocker) Greenwood, he was fourth in order of birth. (For further remarks on parent see sketch of T. C. Greenwood). From Mississippi our subject came with his parents to Texas, and in the schools of Guadalupe County he received the rudiments of an education. When twelve years of age he began attending school in Caldwell County, but on account of the breaking out of the Civil War his advantages were limited. Like many others of the best citizens of the county he grew to sturdy manhood on a farm on the banks of the San Marcos River, a few miles from Seguin, and when about twenty years of age he became desirous of studying law. After studying with his father and Mr. Goodrich, in 1873 he was admitted to the bar at Lockhart, Caldwell County. Since then he has been licensed to practice in all the State and Federal courts. He began practicing, but in 1876 he was elected to the office of County Attorney, serving in that capacity six years. In 1888 he was elected County Judge, and this office he now holds. Since being elected to this position many improvements have been made in the county. The county jail was erected, a large bridge was placed across Guadalupe River and a general improvement in the roads throughout the county has been made. Judge Greenwood is not a single man. On the 5th of October, 1876, he was married to Miss Corrinne Henderson, a native of Tennessee. Her grandfather Turney was Judge of the Supreme Court of Tennessee for many years. Her father, Alexander Henderson, and her mother, Maria (Turney) Henderson, came to Texas in the fifties and located at Seguin, where the father died in 1883. The mother is still living. Judge Greenwood's marriage resulted in the birth of four children: James, Jr., Alexander H., Thomas B. and Eugenia. Judge Greenwood has been active in politics, is a stanch Democrat, and has been a delegate to nearly all the State conventions since his majority. He has a handsome home, and has a great taste for all that is pleasant and beautiful in life. He is a great admirer of Jersey cattle, and is the owner of several fine animals. He is a Mason, a Knight of Honor and an Odd Fellow, has filled all the chairs in the latter order and represented his lodge in the Grand Lodge of the State.

James Stampley Reed possesses the push, energy and enterprise characteristic of the Reed family, and as a natural consequence he has been
successful in the accumulation of means and has won a reputation for honesty
and fair dealing that is in every respect justly merited.   He is a prominent
merchant and planter of Reedville, Caldwell County, and was born in Winston
County, Miss., May 4, 1855, son of Absolom W. and Martha Elizabeth (Ellison)
Reed, natives of Madison County, Miss., and Alabama, respectively.   The
father was a merchant in his native State, and when the war opened he
organized an infantry company.   Twelve months later he was furloughed
home on account of ill health, but soon went out again in the Fifth Mississippi, of which he was elected Major.   He participated in the numerous battles,
and was a brave officer and faithful soldier.   After the war he followed merchandising and farming until 1876, when he emigrated to Texas in December
of that year and located on a plantation of his purchase.   He located the
town of Reedville, named in his honor, and conducted his farm until his
death, the result of an accident, September 12, 1891.   The mother is still
living.   James Stampley Reed and his brothers were reared in Winston
County, Miss., and our subject was about twenty-one years of age when the
father came to Texas.   Until 1890 young Reed followed farming, and then
engaged in merchandising, having become familiar with that business while
his father was living.   His brothers are in business as follows: John C. and
Robert S. are merchandising under the firm name of R. S. Reed & Co.;
William J. is farming near Reedville; Absolom is farming in Mississippi,
and Forrest is clerking in the store at Reedville.   Our subject is a Master
Mason—a member of Sonora Lodge No. 462, and in politics is a Democrat.
His father was County Commissioner at the time of his death, and James
was appointed his successor.   The latter is now Justice of the Peace.   In
1878 Mr. Reed married Miss Nancy Pauline Harper, daughter of B. F. and
Sarah Ann (Martindale) Harper, who came from Mississippi to this county
prior to the Civil War.   Mrs. Harper is a sister to Robert M. Martindale, of
this county (see sketch).   Seven children have been born to Mr. and Mrs.
Reed, and all are living: James E., Myrtle A., Thomas P., Ada L., Sarah E.,
Franklin A. and Mary R.

W. J. Redding.   Among Goliad's younger business men are many whose
interest in the city is going to make it twenty years hence what it is to-day
compared with that of a generation ago.   Many of these have already made
their mark, but few have attained the distinction and prominence that W. J.
Redding can justly claim and be proud of.   Mr. Redding is a Mississippian,
born in Atala County, in 1840, to the marriage of William and Martha
Whiten (Beall) Redding, the former a native of North Caroliana and the
latter of Georgia.   The father came to Texas in the spring of 1849, bought
land in Harrison County and put in a crop.   That summer he sickened and
died.   In the fall of the same year the family came to the State with an
uncle, the mother's brother, and located in Marshall.   There the family
resided until November, 1854, and then moved to Seguin.   In the meantime
the mother's people had come to Texas and located near Seguin.   In 1859
Mrs. Redding moved to Goliad County and bought land on the Manahuilla
Creek.   Our subject was now nineteen years of age, and his brother was
seventeen years of age, and as the mother had a small herd of cattle they
branched out in the cattle business.   In 1861 W. J. enlisted in Company B,

WESLEY OGDEN.

Yeager's Battalion Cavalry (organized in October), and after six months in camp was ordered to Brownsville, where our subject was discharged on account of illness. He came home and subsequently re-enlisted in J. Gus Patton's Company, Fulcrod's Battalion, cavalry, which was afterwards organized in Col. Scott Anderson's Regiment, and served in the trans-Mississippi Department until the close. Returning to Goliad County he resumed the stock business and continued this until 1868. After this he bought a farm on the San Antonio River, fifteen miles below town, and engaged in both farming and stock raising until 1880. From there he came to Goliad, and bought a mill and gin, but was burned out September 10, 1891, losing all he had. On the 17th of October he again engaged in the ginning business, and at that time formed a partnership with T. J. Bell, the firm name being Redding & Bell. The present gin is now located near the depot, and has a daily capacity of thirty bales. They have the Jumbo Thomas revolving steam press, Thomas elevator and cleaner, Winship gins, Straub grist mill and Atlas boiler and engine of forty horse power. They have a large building. In 1893 and '94 they ginned 1,300 bales. This is a large and thoroughly equipped establishment. On the 28th of January, 1862, Mr. Redding was married to Miss Cilicia C. Davis, daughter of R. W. Davis (see sketch). Mrs. Redding is a member of the Christian Church, and Mr. Redding is a member of the A. O. U. W. and the K. of H.

JOHN HENRY SCHNEIDER. No better citizens have come to Victoria County, Texas, than those who have emigrated from the Republic of Switzerland and who brought as their inheritance from Swiss ancestors the traits of character and life that have ever characterized them. Mr. Schneider was born in that country in May, 1822, a son of Rudolf and Elizabeth (Schaffner) Schneider, and with his father came to the United States in 1851, the father's death occurring the next year at the age of seventy-two years. The mother was called from life in Switzerland. The subject of this sketch was married in his native land to Elizabeth Schneider, who died in 1852 in Victoria, Texas, leaving one child, Arnold, who died at the untimely age of fifteen years. Upon his arrival here Mr. Schneider at first engaged in hauling freight from the Gulf ports to different inland towns and made many long and dangerous trips. After personally superintending this work for a few years he hired a man to take his place, and they continued to run these wagons for twenty-five years. Soon after coming here Mr. Schneider engaged in the occupation of farming on land which he purchased in 1856 or 1857, and to this occupation a considerable portion of his time and attention has been given ever since. He now has about fifty-five acres of land under cultivation, the most of which he cleared and improved himself, and in addition to this occupation he has devoted much attention to its kindred pursuit—stock raising. He has held the position of Alderman of Victoria for eight or ten years, has been a reputable, law-abiding and public-spirited citizen, and as he came to this section in his early manhood he has been an observer of all the stages of its development, and is now quietly and unostentatiously enjoying the fruits of his early industry. His second marriage took place in 1853 to Wilhelmina Maronde, who died in 1893, having become the mother of thirteen children, only four of whom are living at the present time: Albert, now in Fort Worth, Texas; Charles Frederick, John Henry, and Emma, wife of Adolph Wilson. Mr. Schneider is a member of the Methodist Church, and is a man

15

whose correct principles throughout life and honorable business methods have won him a host of friends. Charles Frederick Schneider is a furniture dealer of Victoria and is a wideawake, shrewd and successful man of business. He was born in the town in which he is now doing business in 1858, and in his early youth was given the advantage of a good private school in Victoria. At about the age of fifteen years he began learning the cabinet maker's trade, at which he worked for about eight years. He then, on account of ill health, made a trip to the coast where he later secured work in the car shops of Corpus Christi. He only remained there but a short time when he went on the road as a bridge builder, which work occupied his time and attention for about one year. He then returned to Victoria, but shortly after went to Gonzales where he was engaged in carpenter work with a brother for about three months, then both began working as railroad bridge builders. Three months later they entered the employ of the Texas Continental Meat Company, for whom they assisted in erecting several large buildings in Victoria, and with this company they continued to remain until they closed their business at this place. In August, 1885, he started in business for himself in a small way, but under his able management the business has expanded until it has reached its present admirable proportions. He carries a stock of goods valued at between $3,000 and $4,000, his annual sales reaching a large figure, and in addition to his building on Santa Roas street, he has a warehouse for the storage of other stock. He was married in 1889 to Miss Emily Klein, a native of Germany, but a resident of Victoria from childhood, and to their union three children have been given: Charles F., Georgia L., and an infant son, Earl H. Mr. Schneider is a member of the I. O. O. F. and the Woodmen of the World. John Henry Schneider, Jr., merchant of Victoria, and like his brother, a progressive man of affairs, is also a native of the town in which he is doing business, his birth having occurred in 1860. He received a practical education in Victoria and began life for himself as a clerk in a lumber yard and office of B. F. Williams, with whom he remained eight years. July 1, 1892, with A. D. Wilson, he bought out the stock of D. H. Regan's branch store and commenced mercantile life under the firm name of Wilson & Schneider, continuing thus until May 15, 1893, when Mr. Schneider became the sole proprietor, and has since been a successful dry goods merchant. He is now occupying a fine store on Main street, and carries a stock of goods amounting to about $10,000, his annual sales reaching a satisfactory figure. He keeps a well selected line of dry goods, clothing, boots and shoes, notions, etc., and his store is exceedingly well arranged and admirably conducted. He was married November 23, 1893, to Miss Henrietta Winkleman, a native of Texas.

THOMAS MENEFEE. To keep green the memory of the departed whose lives were worthy and filled with good deeds is an object deserving much effort. Not only do the children of those who have passed on to the other world desire to perpetuate their memory, but their neighbors and friends may well feel that they are benefited by rehearsing the incidents of the life that has closed. He, of whom we write, was born in Virginia in 1779, and came of English-German stock, his ancestors settling in America during colonial times. John Menefee, our subject's father, was a soldier in the Revolutionary War. He moved to East Tennessee in about 1785, and followed farming there until about 1820, when he moved to Alabama, settling in Morgan

County. There were passed the remainder of his days, his death occurring about 1823 from a fall from a horse. He was the father of nine children, and our subject, Thomas Menefee, was second in order of birth. He was reared in Knox County, Tennessee, and chose as his occupation in life farming and milling. In the year 1812 he was married to Mrs. (Sutherland) Paine, a widow with one child, Mariah H., and afterwards resided in Tennessee until 1823, when he moved to Morgan County, Alabama, settling near Decatur. There he followed farming until 1830, when he came with thirteen other families to Austin Colony, Texas, what is now Jackson County, and made his home there for twenty-eight years, dying in 1858. The latter part of his days were passed with one or the other of his children, as his wife had died in 1829. Both were members of the Methodist Episcopal Church. Mr. Menefee became the owner of a very fine tract of land, raised sugar, cotton, etc., and became very wealthy, leaving enough to give his children all a good start in life. Of the nine children born to his marriage, two died in Alabama and one in Tennessee. Mariah H., died in Tennessee; John S., George, Susanna L., Frances O.; Thomas, died in Alabama; Agnes Shelton, William and Thomas Nelson. All these are now deceased except Frances, now the Widow Peck, and William, who reside in Goliad. John S. and George were in the war or Texas Revolution in 1836, and the latter was in the battle of San Antonio. John S. was in the battle of San Jacinto and both served until the close. William was in the Mexican War, enlisting June 14, 1846, at Port Isabel, and was in the battle of Monterey. He returned in October, 1846. He was also in the Civil War, as was his brother Thomas, Company M, Whitfield's Legion. The former was discharged in 1862 and came home. Later he was with the militia, and in an engagement on Mustang Island he was captured and taken a prisoner to New Orleans. Three months later he made his escape and joined the army in Texas, going to Galveston, where he remained until the war closed. He was twice married and both wives are deceased. His four children died during the years of the war. Thomas was taken ill and died in Arkansas in 1862. He left one son, Thomas N. John S., married twice, first Miss Angeline Clark, and after her death Miss Frances E. Dover, who died leaving two children, Steve Austin and Lucy. Their father died November 4, 1884. George married Miss Laticia D. Mercer, and died in 1891, leaving one child, George. Susan L. married J. W. Hodges, who died in the spring of 1858. She followed him to the grave March 16, 1893, leaving five children, four having died previously. Agnes Shelton was twice married, first to Rev. R. H. Hill, who died in 1857, leaving five children, and again to Newton Lander by whom she had two children. He died in the army, and she in 1873. William resides with Mrs. Peck in the fine old rock house erected by Mr. Peck many years ago. This house is located on the highest ground in Goliad, in an oak grove which gives shade from the sun in summer, and protects them from such winter winds as visit this sunny land. It is a beautiful spot. Both these worthy people have seen the country grow from a wilderness infested by hostile Indians to a region of peace and plenty, and no worthier people have lived in the county. Mrs. Peck is surrounded by many descendants, children and grandchildren, who are a comfort and a blessing to her in her declining years. Mr. Menefee's family have all passed over the river before him, but he, hale and hearty, a hero of two wars, is more active than many a younger man to-day.

WILLIAM SYLVESTER SMITH, ginner, farmer and lumber dealer, of Reedville, Caldwell County, Texas, is a pushing, stirring, business man, and one who has met with fair success in the different occupations in which he has engaged. Born in Hawkins County, Tennessee, December 26, 1849, he is a son of Calvin M. and Nancy (Spears) Smith, both natives of Tennessee. The father was a farmer and merchant, and in connection followed boating on the Holston River. During his younger days he taught school, and was a man possessed of varied accomplishments. When Civil War broke out he enlisted in the Confederate army, was Lieutenant of Bradford's Thirty-First Tennessee, and was killed at Morristown while commanding Company D. He was also a soldier in the Mexican War, under General W. S. Scott, and was a a man of unusual literary attainments, and kept a diary of his life. During the Mexican War he floated down the Holston River on a flatboat to New Orleans, enlisted for the war, and embarked at that point for Vera Cruz. The mother is still living, and makes her home with her son, George R. Smith, at Waelder. William S. Smith was reared and educated in Tennessee, and when twenty-three years of age came to the Lone Star State, where he followed his trade of carpentering. Later he purchased a farm and mill, and in 1892 came to Hays County, on the San Marcos River. One year later he removed to Reedville, and erected a public gin which has a capacity of forty bales per day. He will probably gin about 2,000 bales this year. Mr. Smith has been a Democrat, with a coloring of Prohibition, and is one of the county's progressive, thrifty citizens. He thoroughly understands every detail of his various enterprises, and has accummulated a fair share of this world's goods by his energy and foresight. In the year 1876 he was married to Miss Savannah Howell Bond, a native of Georgia, of which her mother was also a native. The father was born in Tennessee, and they were old settlers of Gonzales County, and much esteemed citizens. Both are now living, and in the enjoyment of good health. The seven children born to Mr. and Mrs. Smith are named, as follows: Arthur H., and Oscar C., twins, born on Christmas day, 1876; Fred B., Carl S., Olivia Grace, Maggie L., and Vannie C., all pictures of perfect health.

ALEXANDER ERWIN WILSON. The subject of our sketch, Alexander Erwin Wilson, is County Clerk of Guadalupe County, and a widely known and popular citizen. He is a native of Iredell County, North Carolina, born in the year 1843, and fourth in a family of nine children born to Rev. J. M. and Philadelphia Herndon (Fox) Wilson. He inherits sturdy Scotch blood from his paternal ancestors and English from the other side of the house. His grandfather, John McKarmie Wilson, was born in the land of "thistles and oatmeal," but came to America in colonial times, and was a signer of the Mechlinburg Declaration of Independence. He also served in the Revolutionary War. The Foxes came from a prominent old Virginia family. Rev. J. M. Wilson was a Presbyterian Minister, but he also carried on agricultural pursuits to some extent. In 1856 he came to Texas, located near Seguin, and entered actively upon his duties as an agriculturist. For many years he preached at Seguin and Lavernia, and he also owned and taught the famous Guadalupe Female College for a number of years after the war. The family came to Texas by way of Missouri, where they resided for five years. Mr. Wilson died in 1873, but his wife is still living, and finds a pleasant home with her son, our subject. The latter attended Westminister College at Fulton for five years and came to the Lone Star State with his parents in 1856, afterwards attending the school at Seguin for the most part until the opening of war. In 1861 he enlisted in Company D, Fourth Texas Regiment, Hood's Brigade, Longstreet's corps of Gen. Lee's Army, and went at once to Virginia, where he was in nearly all the battles of that army. He was wounded on two occasions, but served until the close, surrendering with Gen. Lee, April 9, 1865. Afterwards Mr. Wilson remained with relatives in North Carolina for several months, and then, in the month of August, 1865, he returned to Texas, where he was at once engaged in farming. In February, 1868, he was married to Miss Julia M. Fenner, a native of Tennessee, and the daughter of Richard and Marianna (Johnson) Fenner who came to Texas in 1856. To Mr. and Mrs. Wilson have been born three children, Alexander Erwin, Julia Adelaide, and Richard Fenner. The parents and children hold membership in the Presbyterian Church. Mr. Wilson is a Master Mason and an Odd Fellow, and holds the office of Past Grand. He still owns a part of his father's old farm, 100 acres, all under cultivation and lying about one mile from town. He was elected to the office of County Clerk in 1886, and filled that position in such an able and satisfactory manner that he has been re-elected each term since. He was a brave soldier, is a pleasant, sociable gentleman, and an excellent official.

JAMES CALHOUN JONES. In every community there are to be found men whose lives have been enterprising, upright and useful, and of this class in Caldwell County the name of James Calhoun Jones in prominent. He was born in Giles County, Virginia, August 22, 1847, a son of Willis and Sarah (Bogle) Jones, the former of whom was a native of Amherst County, Virginia, and followed planting throughout life. He was active politically, but was never desirous of holding office, although he spent much time and money in advancing the interests of the Whig party. He was a member of the A. F. & A. M., and died in 1863. His father was a native of Scotland, and came to the United States soon after the close of the Revolutionary War. His wife, like himself, was a native of Virginia, was of Irish-English descent, and died in Virginia, in 1878, at the old family homestead. James Calhoun Jones was reared and educated in Virginia, and after he had attended Emory & Henry College of that State for one year, he with about forty other students, took French leave of the college, and hied them away to the wars. He enlisted in Company H, Forty-seventh Virginia Cavalry, which was afterwards consolidated with the Forty-sixth Virginia, and became known as the Twenty-sixth Virginia Cavalry, and was under command of Col. John B. Lady. Mr. Jones became Post Sergeant, and was a participant in the battle of Newmarket, under Gen. Breckinridge, against Gen. Sigel; was at Lynchburg at the time of Hunter's raid, and pursued him into Maryland. He was under Gen. Jubal Early at Monocacy, and was with him also at Winchester and Cedar Creek. He was then east of the Blue Ridge at Orange Court House, and at Cedar Creek had his horse killed under him. While holding his horse at Liberty Mill, it was killed, but he escaped unscathed. He was at home on a thirty days' detail to get another mount, and Lee surrendered before the expiration of his detail. After the war he was engaged in farming and teaching school for two years, and during this time took up the study of medicine under Dr. John C. Blackburn, but after a short time decided to turn his attention to other pursuits. He removed to Ohio, and for some time thereafter was engaged in cutting cord wood, at which he saved some money. He then went to Truckee, but was discouraged by the heavy snows and returned to West Virginia, and clerked in a commissary store on the Chesapeake & Ohio Railroad. He finally became foreman of two sections, and later served in the same capacity on a section of the Baltimore & Ohio. In 1876 he came to Texas, and after prospecting the State thoroughly, settled in Caldwell County, where he established, by means of a dam, a fine water power on the San Marcos, and also built a gin and grist mill. He now has three gin stands, and uses the Munger system, Pratt gins. He gins on an average of 1,200 bales annually, and two of his gins are of sixty saws and the other of seventy. He was married in 1878 to Miss Z. J. Fuller, a daughter of Ralph and Nancy (Dunn) Fuller, natives of Virginia, the former of whom died in Caldwell County in 1891, and the mother is still living (1894). To the union of Mr. and Mrs. Jones, the following children have been given: William B., James E., Clint, Walter C., Louisa and Della.

JOSEPH DANIEL MITCHELL, a native of Calhoun County, Texas, born in 1848, and a prominent citizen of Victoria, that State, is a son of I. N. and Mary Augusta (Kerr) Mitchell, natives respectively of South Carolina and Missouri. The father came to the Lone Star State in the '30s, and located in Lavaca County, of which he was one of the organizers. As a farmer and stock-raiser he gained a wide reputation, and he became the owner of an immense amount of land in this county, as well as a large ranche in Calhoun County. He commanded a company during the Somerville expedition. His death occurred in Calhoun County in 1853, when in the prime of life. Our subject's maternal grandfather, Dr. James Kerr, was a native of Missouri, and came to Texas in 1824 as a member of Austin's first colony of 300 souls settling at Brazoria. He was a well educated man. Later he became a surveyor, and he was the first one west of the Colorado River, surveying for the early colonies. In 1836 he was elected a member of the convention for independence, but did not arrive in time to vote for independence. Later he moved his family to Sabine River, and on his return to join the army he heard of the battle of San Jacinto. He lost his wife and two sons at Brazoria, and then came further West. There his death occurred. The mother of our subject came to Texas with her parents when a small child, and was mainly educated by her father. She inherited from him a rare taste for the study of natural history, and from her our subject has inherited the same taste. She was a brilliant woman for that day and time, and saw the changes that grew over the country as the years passed by. She accompanied her father on many of his expeditions, going horseback with him when a child, and at one time they were chased by Indians, on Skull Creek, and had a close call. When but seven years of age she rode a horse across Port Lavaca Bay from Cox's Point to Noble's Point, near Linnville. During her childhood she spent much of her time among the Tonkaway Indians, they occupying lands near her father's headright. About 1842 she was married to Mr. Mitchell, and her death occurred in 1882, at Hallettsville, Lavaca County. She was an earnest member of the Catholic Church. The early life of our subject was spent in Calhoun and Lavaca counties, and he attended school at Galveston, Bay St. Louis, Miss., and San Antonio, Texas. Apart from the schools, which he attended at an early age, and but for a short time, he is self-educated, and began life for himself as a cowboy when sixteen years of age. Soon after he took charge of their estate, stock, etc., and later became a large stock-raiser himself and the prosperous owner of a good ranche. He was the first to introduce blooded stock in this county, he put up the first windmill for stock purposes west of the Colorado River, and erected the first wire fence for stock purposes perhaps in Texas. Mr. Mitchell had fine graded cattle; his first Durham bull was perhaps the first blooded animal brought to this section after the war. In 1892 he sold 13,500 acres in Calhoun County to a party of Swedish settlers, and there are now over fifty families in the colony. After that Mr. Mitchell practically retired from the stock business, and is now devoting his time to the study of natural history, giving much of his attention to the branch of conchology; has already collected a large number of marine and fresh-water shells, which he is adding to constantly. At the present time he is working under the direction of Prof. Dall of the United States National Museum. Mr. Mitchell has discovered two shells new to science, which have been given names in his honor. His collection of Indian relics, mineral specimens, bird eggs, reptiles peculiar to Texas, particular shells, both salt and fresh water, is arranged with painstaking care, showing both knowledge and a love for the work. Being a man of leisure and means, he is not hampered in his investigations, and it may be expected that much good will be the result of such study. His is an inherited taste for several generations on his mother's side, and with his means he can gratify it. Mr. Mitchell made his home in Victoria several years ago, and in 1892 he erected his present handsome residence, which was designed mainly by his wife, who was formerly Miss Agnes Ward, a native of Jackson County, Texas, and daughter of Capt. Lafayette Ward, who was born in Missouri, and who was one of the early settlers of Jackson County. Mrs. Mitchell was educated in Texas, and is a lady of refined accomplishments, sympathizing with Mr. Mitchell in his studies and pursuits. To this union ten children were born, seven of whom survive: Mary Agnes, Rudolph Ward, Susie Maud, Chapin Maxwell, Rebecca Wilson, Helen Densmore and Joseph Daniel. This family holds membership in the Catholic Church.

CAPT. BARTON PECK (deceased). The name which we now give was for many years counted as among the prominent farmers of Goliad County, and although Capt. Barton Peck has now passed from earth's activities, it is but just and satisfactory that we recount his life narrative among those who have done such excellent service in subduing the wilderness and bringing it into its present splendid condition, physically, socially and morally. He was born in the Old Bay State, but was reared in New York, where he remained for some time. From there he went to Indiana, and in that State raised a company of patriots to come to Texas and assist those people in the struggle for independence. This company started in the fall of 1836, but did not arrive until after the battle of San Jacinto. Capt. Peck was in the military service for about eighteen months. After arriving in the Lone Star State he was stationed on the Lavaca River, Jackson County, where he met Miss Frances O. Menefee, daughter of Thomas Menefee (see sketch), and their nuptials were celebrated in 1838. The following year, 1839, he returned to the Hoosier State, and resided there until 1841, when he came to Texas. Shortly afterwards he went back to New York and engaged in business, but, on account of poor health, returned to Texas in 1845. The following year he located in

Goliad County, about twenty miles above the town, and there passed the closing scenes of his life, dying in Goliad in 1861. He was a worthy member of
the Methodist Episcopal Church. He was an extensive farmer, ranger and
stock-raiser, and became a wealthy citizen. His widow still lives and resides
with her brother, William, in Goliad. To his marriage were born ten children,
five of whom are now living: Sue M., wife of J. Gus Patton; Frances A.,
widow of Geo. W. Meriwether; Barton, Alonzo, Mary L., wife of Dr. A. W.
Gray, of Edna; Lucy married D. F. Meriwether, and died in 1880, leaving
two children; Fannie, now Mrs. Brown, and Frank T.; Viola E. married
T. B. Word, and died in 1869, leaving one child, Viola Peck, wife of L. H.
Woodsworth; Samuel W., was struck by lightning and killed in 1881;
Thomas M., died December, 1883. The eldest of all these children, William
Barton, died in infancy.

ISAAC H. JULIAN. Among the earlier western poets the name of Isaac H.
Julian was once familiar and is still remembered. He began writing in boyhood, and his productions appeared in various publications, notably the
Ladies' Repository, Cincinnati, and the *National Era*, Washington, D. C.
Of the latter John G. Whittier was corresponding editor, and in it Mrs.
Stowe's " Uncle Tom's Cabin " first appeared as a serial. Other contributors were the Cary sisters, "Grace Greenwood," etc., with whose names that
of the subject of this sketch was honorably associated. The Julian family is
of French extraction in the paternal line, and dates 200 years in America.
Prior to the Revolution, the progenitors resided in Maryland, Virginia and
North Carolina. Isaac Julian, father of the poet and the third of that name
in regular succession, was a native of the State last named, and removed in
1808 to that part of Indiana Territory known as Wayne County. The
year following he was married to Rebecca, a daughter of Andrew Hoover, a
member of the Society of Friends, also from North Carolina. Isaac and
Rebecca Julian settled on a farm near Centerville, the county seat, and endured all the privations of pioneer life during the War of 1812, when Indians
and wild beasts were among their frequent visitors. In 1822 Mr. Julian was
a member of the Indiana Legislature, which then convened at Corydon. The
subject of this sketch was born June 19, 1823. In the fall of that year the
father removed his family to what is now the county of Tippecanoe, where he
died in the December following, and his widow and young family returned to
their relatives in Wayne County. In consequence of this disaster, their subsequent lot was a hard one. The opportunities for obtaining an education
were limited to the log school houses, and a few sessions in these comprised
the school attendance of Isaac Julian, Jr. But this was fairly supplemented
by self education. In the intervals from farm labor he early accomplished
quite an extensive course of reading in the departments of history and general
literature. Mr. Julian resided in Iowa from the spring of 1846 to the fall of
1850. Heretofore his poetic effusions had been casual and desultory. But
in 1848 he became deeply interested in the political and social upheavals of
that period, more especially in the anti-slavery cause. These gave inspiration to many of his subsequent poems. Later he studied law and in 1851
was admitted to the bar, but found the practice so distasteful that he did not
long engage in it. In 1854 he went to Fort Wayne, and for a short time
edited the *Standard* of that city. In 1857 he prepared and published an interesting pamphlet on the " Early History of the Whitewater Valley." In

1858 he bought the *True Republican,* newspaper, at Centerville, and removed it to Richmond in 1865, afterward changing the name to the *Radical,* and continuing its publication to the fall of 1872. He was Postmaster at Centerville during Lincoln's first term, and at Richmond from May, 1869, to July, 1871. He was married in 1859 to Miss Virginia M. Spillard, of College Hill, Ohio, by whom he had five children, three of whom survive. Because of his wife's failing health, he removed in the summer of 1873 to San Marcos, Texas, and began the publication of the *Free Press* from which he retired in August, 1890. His wife died a few months after their arrival in Texas, leaving a family of young children to his care. Thus engrossed with an exacting business and severe domestic cares and trials, Mr. Julian for many years had very small opportunity for the gratification of his literary taste.

The above biographical sketch appeared in the *Magazine of Poetry* of Buffalo, N. Y., for January, 1892, in connection with selections from the poems of Mr. Julian. To render it more complete, it should be added that in 1872 he allied himself with the Liberal movement for National reconciliation, led by Horace Greeley as its candidate for President, and thereafter acted with the Democratic party down to 1892, when he identified himself with the People's party, the leading principles of which had received his life-long advocacy, and began the publication at San Marcos of the *People's Era,* in which he is still engaged. In 1893 he was again married, the lady of his choice being Mrs. Belle McCoy Harvey, of Minnesota. A sample of Mr. Julian's poetic effusions is appended. It has a Western flavor befitting these pages, and the antecedents of the author:

TO THE GENIUS OF THE WEST.

O Genius of "my own, my native land,"
    Majestic, glorious presence of my dreams!
I own the impulse of thy guiding hand,
    I hail the light upon thy brow that gleams,
    Dear and familiar as the sun's bright beams!
For thou didst smile upon my life's first dawn,
    A child, lone-wandering by thy woodland streams,
Far from the vain and noisy crowd withdrawn,
Thy favoring glance didst mark and seal me as thine own.

Thou had'st me tune with joy my rustic reed,
    While smiling Love and Fancy led the strain;
And first my willing voice, as thou decreed,
    Essayed to sing the glories of thy reign.
    Since, wandering wide, out o'er thy broad domain,
Thy presence still has cheered me in the way;
    And 'mid those vaster scenes, didst thou again
Inspire a higher and a sadder lay
Than that of sportive love, to crown my manhood's day—

A lay of Truth, inscribed unto my kind,
    Their joys and griefs, their liberties and wrongs;
The spirit that would every chain unbind,
    By thee invoked, inspired my later songs
    With stern rebuke of lying pens and tongues.
O still be with me, Genius of the West!
    And grant the boon for which my spirit longs—
To weave the verse which *thou* shalt deem the best,
Ere 'neath my natal soil I peaceful pass to rest!

RICHARD M. GLOVER. The official position which Mr. Glover is filling at the present time is one which he well merits and one which he is eminently capable of filling, for he is not only energetic, determined and courageous, but he is also a believer in law and order, and has the best interests of Gonzales County warmly at heart. He was born and reared here, is public spirited in a high degree, and although the citizens have had every opportunity to judge of his character and qualifications, no disparaging word has ever been truthfully said of him. He first saw the light of day in 1862, and he was the only child of his parents, Richard M. and Delilah (Bundick) Glover, who were natives of Mississippi and Louisiana respectively. H. B. Glover, the paternal grandfather, was an old Mississippian, a member of one of the prominent families of the State, and by occupation was a planter. During the war he had several sons in the Confederate service, and while visiting them at Vicksburg, that place became besieged and he was killed. The maternal grandfather, William Bundick, was of Irish descent and a native of Lousiana. About 1854 he became a resident of Gonzales County, Texas, and here spent the rest of his days. He was quite prominent in the political affairs of the county, and was a public spirited and law abiding citizen. Richard M. Glover, the father of the subject of this sketch, was principally reared in the Lone Star State, and from this State entered the Confederate service in 1861, as a member of Wall's Legion, and died at Holly Springs, Miss., in 1862. The subject of this sketch was reared by his mother on the farm, and in addition to attending the public schools of the county he was for three years an attendant of the schools at Goliad. He began life as a farmer and stock-raiser and is now the owner of a fine farm of 350 acres, of which 130 acres are under cultivation, and well improved with buildings, fences, etc. It lies in the western part of the county, is a valuable tract of land, and susceptible of the highest cultivation. Like his father before him, Mr. Glover has been quite active in the political affairs of the county, has been a member of various conventions, and in November, 1890, was elected to the office of Sheriff, being at that time the youngest man to hold the position in the State. He is a resident of Gonzales at the present time, but expects to return to his farm when his term of office expires, and is now erecting a commodious and substantial residence there for his occupancy. Although he is still young in years he has shown that he is possessed of business and official ability in a more than ordinary degree, and the admirable way in which he has discharged all his duties has won him the esteem and respect of his fellows. He was married in the fall of 1887 to Miss M. A. Colley, a native of Georgia and a daughter of G. W. Colley, who came from that State to Texas in 1879. They have four bright and promising children: Florence, Georgia and Dixie (twins), and an infant daughter unnamed.

JOHN MCGEHEE. This gentleman is one of the substantial and highly honored residents of San Marcos, of which place he has been a resident since 1892, and where he has a beautiful and comfortable home. He was born near Bastrop, Texas, in 1838, the third child born to Thomas D. and Minerva (Hunt) McGehee, for the history of whom see the sketch of George T. McGehee. In 1861, when the first guns were fired on Fort Sumter, Mr. McGehee's southern blood was roused, and being in warm sympathy with the South he at once joined Company B, 4th Texas Regiment, under Col. Hood, and was sent at once to Richmond, Va., where his regiment was organized. He then participated in the battles of Elthan's Landing, the second battle of Manassas, Antietam, and was in the seven days' fight around Richmond, where his regiment did effective work, and Sharpsburg where he was wounded, after which he returned home on furlough. After his recovery he was assigned to Col. Wood's regiment, 32d Texas Cavalry, and was in the many skirmishes in Gen. Banks' retreat down the Red River, also in the severe engagement at Yellow Bayou. He was then ordered back to Virginia, but the war closed before he could start, and he returned home. He was engaged in trading for a time, then purchased a farm near San Marcos, and in 1878-79 kept extensive outfits on the "Staked Plains" hunting buffalo, and the first year over 1,200 were captured. He was married in 1863 to Miss Mary Davis, a native of Georgia, and a daughter of H. W. Davis, and to their union nine children have been born, eight of whom are living at the present time: John Hood, who is the Postmaster at San Marcos; Kate, wife of E. L. Thomas; Tulula, wife of Dr. J. Beall; Sally M. and Polly, Albert Scott, Maud and Mary. Mr. and Mrs. McGehee are members of the M. E. Church, and socially he is a member of the K. of H. and Woodmen of the World.

LEROY CLAY WRIGHT. Although now over seventy-four years of age, this venerable citizen of Gonzales County, Texas, is well preserved both in mind and body, and is a splendid type of the enterprise, industry and self-reliance of the early Texas pioneer. Over forty years ago he braved the dangers, trials and privations of pioneer life in order to establish a home and competency, and where are now productive fields of grain, all was a wilderness. Mr. Wright is a product of Alabama, born in Perry County, Nov. 20, 1820, and a son of James and Lucy (Waters) Wright, natives of Georgia and Virginia respectively. James Wright's mother, Miriam Clay, was first cousin to Henry Clay. Mr. Wright followed planting in his native State for many years and then moved to Panola County, Mississippi, where his death occurred in 1854. His wife died there in 1866. Both were members of the Baptist church, and he was a Whig in politics. Leroy C. Wright secured his education in Alabama, and when twenty-one years of age went to Mississippi, whither his father came later. He followed planting there until 1851, and then moved to Texas, settling in Gonzales County. After working several years for other people, driving stock, etc., he had saved enough money to buy the ranch on which he is now living, close by the village named in his honor, Wrightsboro. When he first settled there there were but three families south of the Guadalupe in the county, and the Indians were troublesome, the Comanches and Mexicans making life almost a burden to the pioneers. Mr. Wright's horses were stolen on one occasion by the Indians and carried over to the Cibalo and Devil's rivers. Gathering a few of his neighbors, Mr. Wright went in pursuit and came up with them on the Cibalo. After a fight in which one white man and several Indians were killed, the horses were again in Mr. Wright's possession. These troublesome days existed until the breaking out of the Civil War, when the presence of troops in southwestern Texas brought about order. So inured were men to danger and so prepared to meet it that marksmanship was reduced to a science. Mr. Wright states that he has often ridden at full speed, firing at trees no larger than a man's body and seldom missed them. When the war broke out he enlisted in Capt. Kelly's company, Home Militia, but subsequently entered the regular army under Capt. Watson, whose Lieutenant he became. After the death of the latter, he assumed command of the company and remained so until cessation of hostilities. For the most part he was guarding the border of the Rio Grande, and was probably in the last fight of the war, the same occurring on

that river.   The next day a courier brought tidings of the surrender.
Returning home, Mr. Wright entered actively upon his career as a stock-
raiser, and continued this business for a number of years.   For ten years he
held the office of County Commissioner.   Mr. Wright was married in Panola
County, Mississippi, June 20, 1844, to Miss Margaret M. Rayburn, daughter of
John and Elizabeth Rayburn, natives of Tennessee.   Mr. Rayburn was a
surveyor and located much of the land of the State.   He represented the
county in the legislature several terms, and died here some years before the
war.   His wife also died before the war.   To Mr. and Mrs. Wright were
born nine children, all living: Jane G. widow of Balaam Anderson;
William J., Samuel G., James P., Michael B., Margaret L., wife of Joseph
Hoket; Ella C., wife of A. G. Henry; Lucy Waters, wife of Henry
Trammel, and Elizabeth.   Just after the war Mr. Wright and his son,
William J., had the difficulty with the noted desperado, Tom Dodd.   The
latter had the first shot and touched Mr. Wright's hat-band.   Then Mr.
Wright and his son tried their hands and Dodd is now sleeping 'neath the
sod, near the scene of the trouble.   First Mr. Wright was a Whig in
politics, but after the war he became a Democrat, with which party he has
remained up to the present.   Although well advanced in years, Mr. Wright
has never had a decayed tooth in his head and attributes it to this fact: When
a boy a Frenchman told him that if he would kill a rattlesnake and bite it,
he would never lose a tooth.   He was once bitten by a rattlesnake when a boy.

BENJAMIN T. PALMER.   If elections to positions of trust and honor are a
criterion by which a man's popularity is gauged, then Benjamin T. Palmer
enjoys to an unusual degree the esteem of his fellow men.   A native of Pickens County, Ala., he was born July 17, 1832, the eldest of five children born
to Joseph D. and Mary (Beckwith) Palmer, who were natives of the Palmetto
State, but who were married in Alabama and moved to Lafayette County in
1836, to Oxford, Miss., in 1840, and in January, 1850, to Chickasaw County,
of the same State.   He became remarkably well known as a successful medical practitioner, and on the 19th of June, 1869, was called from life.   His
widow survives him at the age of eighty-two years, and makes her home with
the subject of this sketch.   The early educational advantages of Benjamin T.
Palmer were limited, and his earliest pursuit was that of a clerk in Mississippi.   In March, 1862, he entered the Confederate army, Company H, 31st
Mississippi Regiment, but owing to ill-health was at once discharged.   He
soon after re-enlisted and became a clerk in the Quartermaster's Department
under Capt. Owen, who was the Post Quartermaster at Lauderdale Springs,
Miss.   He was then transferred to Capt. Kennedy's department, Post Commissary at West Point, and here he acted as purchasing agent for a division
until the war closed.   Upon returning home he engaged in merchandising
and farming, and became part owner in a good steam mill.   After a time he
became book-keeper for a firm in West Point and filled the position ably and
acceptably up to 1873, when he came to San Marcos, Texas, moved to Travis
County a short time after, and at the end of one year to Caldwell County, and
began farming in the vicinity of Lytton Springs.   In November, 1880, he
was elected Clerk of the District Court of Caldwell County and has been
successively re-elected to this position ever since, a fact which speaks eloquently as to his popularity and efficiency.   In 1893 he erected and opened
the Palmer Hotel, one of the best hostelries in the place, and it has already

become popular with the traveling public, and also has a large home patronage. He was first married Oct. 7, 1856, to Miss Fannie Fliett, a native of Alabama, who died April 2, 1884, leaving nine children, all of whom are still living. His second union was consummated Oct. 21, 1884, and was to Mrs. F. C. (Pullian) Rhodes, a native of Missouri, by whom he has one child. Mr. Palmer is a Deacon in the Baptist Church, has been quite active in the same, and was elected Clerk of the San Marcos Baptist Association in 1880. In 1884 he was elected Moderator of the Association, and has since held that office, with the exception of one year. He is a Royal Arch Mason, of Lockhart Lodge No. 690, Luling Royal Arch Chapter No. 196, has been King of the Chapter and Master of his lodge for years. He was made a Mason in Mississippi, in 1856, became a member of the Chapter in that State soon after, was Master of the lodge there, and was High Priest of the West Point Chapter.

JOHN WILLIAMS. It is ever a grateful task to the biographer to answer the call to give the life story of a man who has served on the field of battle, and has also done his duty as a private citizen in the ordinary walks of life. This double career exhibits virtues of various scope, but they are after all in union, as they are based upon integrity, conscientiousness and devotion to duty. Such a life do we find in the gentlemen whose name we here give. This former member of the Confederate army came originally from Tennessee, where his birth occurred on the 1st of June, 1831, and he is now one of the prominent and substantial farmers of Lavaca County. His parents, William D. and Mary A. (Phillips) Williams, were natives of North Carolina and Tennessee respectively, and his maternal grandfather, Massy Phillips, was one of the first settlers of Middle Tennessee, and a pioneer in every sense of the word. He died in Bedford County, that State. The paternal grandfather spent his life in North Carolina. The father of our subject moved to Tennessee when a young man, was married there to Miss Phillips, and there passed the remainder of his days, engaged in farming. John Williams remained in his native State until twenty years of age, and then came to Texas with his brother and family. He first stopped in Titus County, where he married Miss Catherine Coffee, who came from Alabama to Texas with her father in 1844. The father moved to Lavaca County in 1856 and died in his son-in-law's house a few years later. After his marriage, or in 1854, Mr. Williams came to Lavaca County and bought 100 acres, ten miles North of Hallettsville, to which he has added from time to time until he now owns 800 acres, with nearly 400 acres under cultivation. He has made nearly all the improvements and has a fine place. In 1862 he enlisted in the Confederate army, Company M, of Whitfield's Legion under Gen. Ross, and afterwards crossed the Mississippi River to Corinth where the company was reorganized. In a battle at Davis' Bridge on Hatchie River in the fall of 1862 Mr. Williams was captured and taken to Boliver, Tenn., where he was paroled. Returning home he was exchanged and subsequently joined his command in Middle Tennessee. He was in all the battles of the Atlanta campaign and returned with Gen. Hood to Nashville. After the retreat from Nashville he went to Mississippi and from there was furloughed and came to Texas. While in this State the war ended. Since then he has made all his property and is now one of the influential and wealthy men of this section. To his marriage were born four children, only one, James, now living. Mr. Williams and his wife are consistent church members.

CRAWFORD BURNETT. This gentlemen has been a resident of Gonzales County, Texas, for the past forty-one years, and during that time he has identified himself with the interests of his section, has won numerous friends, and has built up a reputation for honesty, enterprise and fair dealing that is in every way merited. Gonzales County is an Eden of fine farms and agricultural tracts, and there are comparatively few small places. Mr. Burnett is one of the most extensive agriculturists of the county, is the owner of a fine ranch of 10,000 acres, of which 1,000 are under cultivation, and nearly all the rest is susceptible of cultivation. He raises a good grade of stock, his cattle being part Durham, and much attention is also given to raising horses. He has one of the finest horses in the State, registered on both sides, and is a thoroughbred Hambletonian named "Al. S." Mr. Burnett has done much to improve the grade of stock in the county, and this excellent example has been followed by others. Although he has always been keenly alive to his own interests, yet he is noted for his fair and honorable business methods, and for his ready adoption of new and improved methods connected with his calling. He is a native of Harris County, Texas, where he was born April 10, 1835, the youngest of four children born to Crawford and Anna (Simons) Burnett, who were born in the blue grass regions of Kentucky, from which State they moved to Illinois, thence to Missouri, from there to Louisiana, and finally came to Texas in 1827, locating on Spring Creek, thirty miles north of the present city of Houston, coming thither as members of Austin's colony. Mr. Burnett took his headright in Brazos County. He was accompanied to this State by two brothers, Matthew and William, both of whom participated in the Texas Revolution. William was a participant in the battle of San Jacinto, and afterwards became prominent in public affairs. He was in the Confederate Army during the Civil War, although quite well along in years, and was in the battles of the Red River Campaign under Gen. Banks. He died soon after the war closed. Matthew died in 1843 or 1844. Crawford Burnett's father died before he was born, and he was also left motherless before he was old enough to realize his loss or remember her. He was reared by his Uncle Matthew and wife, and was engaged in the stock business in Harris County until 1853, when he came to Gonzales County and purchased a farm about nineteen miles east of the town of Gonzales. Here he continued to raise stock, but his operations were for a time interrupted by the opening of the war, for he at once joined a company for the Confederate service. Very soon after joining he was detailed to return home and raise stock for the Confederacy, and this he successfully did until the war closed. He is one of the most substantial men of which the county can boast, is a practical and extensive farmer and stockman, and was one of the most influential and active promoters of the San Antonio & Velasco Railroad, which runs through over ten miles of his estate. In 1857 he led to the altar Miss Sarah E. Dillard, who was born in Washington County, Texas, in 1838, to Abraham Dillard, a Missourian who came to Texas in an early day and was a participant in the battle of San Jacinto. Her maternal grandfather, Andrew J. Kent, was a Pennsylvanian, was an early settler of the Lone Star State, and was killed in the bloody engagement at the Alamo. Nine children have been born to Mr. and Mrs. Burnett, eight of whom survive: Elizabeth, wife of a Mr. Robinson; Sarah Ann, wife of a Mr. Livingston; Frances, who was married and is now deceased; Henrietta is the widow of John A. Clark; James C.,

Otho, Lone, Sam Houston and Jesse. Mr. Burnett has long been a member of the A. F. & A. M., and although he has always been active in the political affairs of his section, he has by no means been an office seeker, as his time has been fully occupied in looking after his extensive agricultural and farming interests.

D. M. CROSTHWAIT. This wideawake man of affairs is the able manager of the Kyle Oil Co., of Kyle, Hays County, Texas, and it may with truth be said that no more fitting man for the position could be found, for besides being intelligent and energetic, he is thoroughly reliable and efficient. He owes his nativity to the State of Alabama, where he was born in 1847, the fifth of six children born to Asa B. and Eliza M. (Miller) Crosthwait, who were natives of Virginia and South Carolina respectively, but became early residents of Alabama. The mother's brother, Hon. W. D. Miller, came to Texas about 1834, and settled in Gonzales district, where he was in command and there had command of a company during the Revolution of 1835–36. He was a member of Congress of the Texas Republic from Gonzales County, and after the annexation of Texas to the Union he became Secretary of State under Governor Wood. He was the private secretary of Gen. Sam Houston during the latter's term as Governor, and at the time of the opening of the great Civil War, in 1861, he was in the census bureau at Washington, D. C. He immediately resigned this position and came South with Hon. John H. Reagan, and was appointed Chief Clerk in the Postal Department of the Confederacy. In the latter part of the war he was transferred to the trans-Mississippi Department, and he had complete charge of postal matters in this section until the war ended. He then located in Galveston and associated himself with a banking firm, and while thus employed was called from life in 1867. His record was a remarkable one—an officer in the army during the Texas Rebellion; in official life during the entire time that Texas was a Republic; an officer of trust under the State Governors; in the service of the United States Government until the organization of the Confederate States, in which he held a prominent position in the postal service until the downfall of the cause, and afterwards a prosperous banker until his death. He was widely known throughout Texas, and highly honored by all. Asa B. Crosthwait became the owner of 1,700 acres of land in what is now Travis County, Texas, during the '40's, and the celebrated Manchaca Springs are on this place. He had the place improved somewhat under the direction of his brother-in-law, Mr. Miller, but he died in Alabama about 1849, before he could complete his arrangements to come to Texas and take charge of the place for himself. In 1852 Mrs. Crosthwait and her family came thither by water, but the vessel on which they embarked, the James L. Day, was wrecked in crossing the Gulf of Mexico. The passengers, however, succeeded in reaching a small island, and after some repairs had been made and there was a calm in the weather, they proceeded on their journey, and from Port Lavaca traveled inland to Austin, where Mrs. Crosthwait made her home until 1869. In the city of Austin D. M. Crosthwait was educated, and in youth he learned the trade of a machinist at Galveston. He helped to build the Galveston bridge, and afterwards ran a mill and cotton gin at Austin and in several other places in Texas. In 1889 he came to Kyle and bought the cotton gin at this place, which he wholly replaced with new machinery and mostly new buildings, until it is now one of the best equipped gins in the State. He now runs four 80-

horse power daw gin stands, with Thomas press, elevators, etc., and is now doing a very prosperous business in this line. Believing that Kyle could and should sustain an oil mill he, in 1892, organized the Kyle Oil Co. with H. Hillman, President; H. C. Wallace, Treasurer; Fred Schlemmer, Secretary, and Mr. Crosthwait as General Manager and Superintendent. With an organized capacity of $20,000 this company bought land and began the work of erecting their plant. The first season their capacity was crowded and in 1894 the capital was increased to $40,000, and their present complete works finished. The ground and buildings occupy ten acres in the city limits, and the mill is fitted up with Caldwell presses, and has a capacity of about twenty-five tons of seed per day, their oil being rated among the best. Mr. Crosthwait was married in 1879 to Miss Mary May Oatman, a native of Texas and daughter of Dr. W. A. Oatman, of Bastrop County. To this union seven children have been given. Mr. Crosthwait is a Mason, and he is an extremely public spirited citizen and what may be termed a "hustler." He has a fine herd of cattle which he feeds from an ensilage and cotton-seed hulls. His sill holds 800 tons, and is one of three in southern Texas, and is without doubt the largest in the State. It is erected in the style of those in Illinois, which he visited and examined.

ALPHEUS ALEXANDER TALLEY. For the man who is by natural bent and training a farmer to adopt any other calling is a rare occurrence, but when he does so he invariably rises to success in it, because his whole life has been based upon the principle of integrity, with the firm conviction that in all the avenues of trade, honesty should be the ruling spur. Mr. Talley, a popular merchant of Wrightboro, Texas, was born on his father's farm in Hickory Flat, Tippah County, Miss., April 17, 1850, son of William and Martha (Barnett) Talley. The father was a native Virginian, and in that State made his home until twenty-five years of age, when he moved to Mississippi, and there followed planting. When Civil War broke out he enlisted from Ripley, Miss., in Col. Faulkner's regiment and was wounded in the battle of Payton Mills. This disabled him from further service. Mr. Talley came to Gonzales County, Texas, in 1885, and died there three years later. He was a Methodist in his religious belief, and in social circles a Master Mason, a member of C. T. Bond Lodge of Hickory Flat. The mother, who is still living, and in the enjoyment of comparatively good health, was born in Alabama. Our subject attended the schools of Mississippi, but like many boys of that day, his education was interrupted by the war. He came to the Lone Star State in 1870, and for two years was engaged in farming near Austin. In 1874 he removed to Luling, clerked there for a year, and then went to Kingsbury, which was then the terminus of the Southern Pacific Railroad. Being troubled with rheumatism, he went to Caldwell Springs, Caldwell County, and in 1877 came to Gonzales County and engaged in farming and stock raising, eight miles from Gonzales. In 1891 he removed to Wrightsboro, where he has since been engaged in merchandising. He has met with fair success in this occupation and possesses a true appreciation of all the requirements of his line of business. Mr. Talley is a Populist in politics, and while a resident of Gonzales held the office of Public Weigher for two years. He is a third degree Mason, a member of Gonzales Lodge No. 30. On the 15th of October, 1879, he was married to Miss Mary Bell Cardwell, daughter of William and Mary Cardwell, now resident of Gonzales County. Five children have blessed this union: Edna,

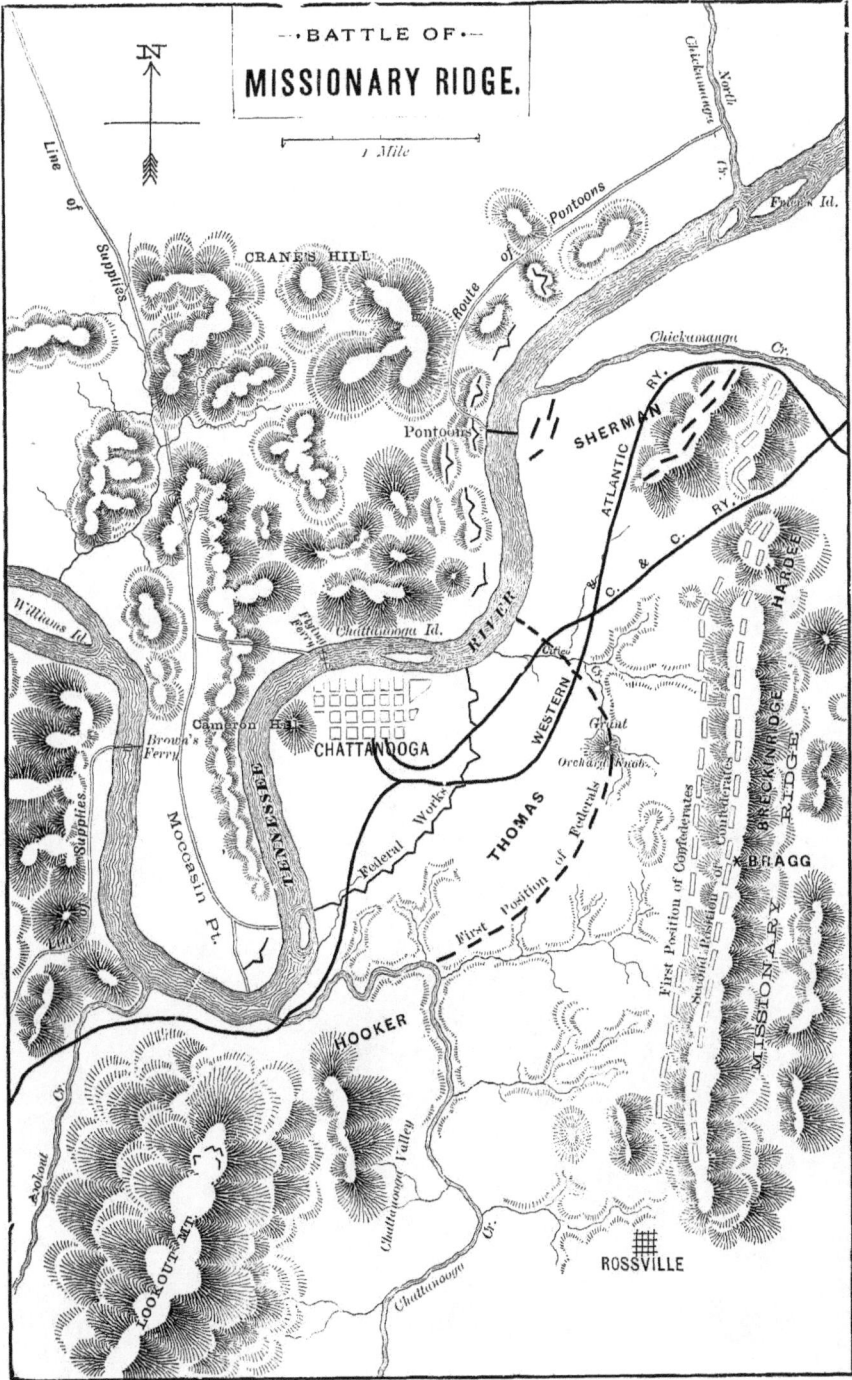

- BATTLE OF -
MISSIONARY RIDGE.

N

1 Mile

Line of Supplies

CRANE'S HILL

Route of Pontoons

Chickamauga Cr.

North

Foster's Id.

Pontoons

Pontoons

SHERMAN

Chickamauga Cr.

ATLANTIC RY.

W. & C. & C. RY.

HARDEE

Williams Id.

Citico

Chattanooga Id.

Friars Ferry

RIVER

WESTERN

Grant

Orchard Knob

Second Position of Confederates

BRECKINRIDGE RIDGE

Brown's Ferry

Cameron Hill

CHATTANOOGA

TENNESSEE

Federal Works

THOMAS

First Position of Federals

BRAGG

MISSIONARY

of Supplies

Moccasin Pt.

First Position of Confederates

HOOKER

Chattanooga Valley

Chattanooga Cr.

LOOKOUT MT.

ROSSVILLE

Willie Ida, Monnie I., Mary Bell and Alpha Alma. Mrs. Talley is an earnest member of the Methodist Church.

ZACHARY TAYLOR CLIETT (deceased). The name which is here given was for many years counted as among the leading and successful farmers and stock-raisers of Caldwell County, Texas, and although he has now passed from earth's activities it is but just and satisfactory that his life's narrative be recounted among those who have done excellent service in making Caldwell County among the most prosperous in the commonwealth of the State. Born in Sumter County, Ala., September 5, 1847, he accompanied his parents, while yet a child, to Chickasaw County, Miss., then to Caldwell County, Texas, in the fall of 1859, and settled on the San Marcos River near Martindale, where he resided up to the time of his death. He was an ardent Democrat and took an active part in the councils of his party—from which he is sadly missed—and for years he attended the State and County conventions as a delegate. He was often sought to run for office, but his large business interests absorbed his attention, and he always respectfully declined. He was a member of the Methodist Church and was most zealous in all acts of brotherly kindness. When he married he was the owner of fifteen acres of land, and with this trifling beginning he amassed one of the handsomest properties in Caldwell County. He was a symmetrically rounded man, of broad sympathies, and his loss was very deeply deplored. He had been weighing cotton on September 9, 1892, and at about dusk, as he was starting for his home, he and his horse were instantly killed by a stroke of lightning. He was married January 17, 1872, to Mrs. Jennie Caldwell, widow of J. W. Caldwell, who died in Jacksonville, Fla., and daughter of B. W. and Lottie (Compton) Smith, the former of whom is still living in San Marcos. The mother died in 1875. Mrs. Cliett was born in southwest Georgia, and she and her three children are residing in their pretty and comfortable home near Martindale. The children she bore Mr. Cliett are the following: Leila and V. T., two attractive and accomplished daughters, and Oran, an intelligent and promising boy. Mr. Cliett was often selected Chairman of the conventions he attended and made an excellent presiding officer, well versed in parliamentary law, cool and collected. He was a Knight of Honor, and was a man of unblemished reputation.

NATHAN AVANT. Industry, enterprise and perseverance are characteristics which will advance the interests of any man and will tend to the prosperity to which all aspire. Such are some of the traits of Nathan Avant, an early settler of Lavaca County, and one of the influential farmers and stockmen of this locality. Mr. Avant owes his nativity to Tennessee, his birth occurring in DeKalb County in 1835, and of the old fashioned family of eleven children born to his parents, Benjamin and Margaret (Fite) Avant, he was sixth in order of birth. His maternal grandfather, Leonard Fite, was a native of Pennsylvania, and at a very early period came to Tennessee, where he was among the first settlers. He located in DeKalb County in 1800 and some of his descendants were and are among the prominent people of that State. The paternal grandfather moved to Tennessee about the same time. The parents of our subject were born in North Carolina and Tennessee respectively, and they were married in the latter State about 1820. At the last birthday celebration of our subject's grandmother, in 1866 or '67, when she was 105 years of age, there were present 360 descendants. The father of our subject

16

came to Texas in 1857 and bought land in Gonzales County, where he died in 1874, when seventy-four years of age. The mother died in 1891, when eighty-six years of age. Of their large family of children all grew to maturity and nine are now living. Until the age of eighteen Nathan Avant remained in his native country and received his education, after which, in 1855, he came to Texas. First he located in Gonzales County and engaged for a time in teaming, following this for about four years. He then sold his team and went to McMillan County, where he engaged in the stock business till 1865, after which he came to Lavaca County, locating on the river below the town. He now owns 1,700 acres of land and has 250 acres under cultivation. He has some graded cattle, Jerseys and Holsteins. In the month of February, 1860, Mr. Avant was married to Miss Marietta Heath, a native of Texas, and daughter of Richard Heath, who came from Tennessee to Texas in the '30s. Mr. and Mrs. Avant have had six children, as follows: Ella C., deceased; Ada Dora, wife of John Daly; Marietta, wife of L. B. Avant, of Tennessee; Benjamin, Theodore, and Carrie, who died when five years of age. Mr. Avant is quite active in politics, is a worker in the People's party, and has served two terms as County Commissioner. He and Mrs. Avant are members of the Methodist Episcopal Church.

REV. ALLEN H. WALKER. In addition to looking after the spiritual welfare of his fellows, Rev. Allen H. Walker has devoted much of his attention also to tilling the soil and raising stock, and in both occupations has met with well deserved success. A product of Tennessee, he was born June 13, 1818, the eldest child born to Elijah and Mary (Wade) Walker, who were natives respectively of Tennessee and Georgia. The paternal grandfather, Allen Walker, was born in one of the eastern States, but was one of the early settlers of Tennessee, and was there killed by the Indians on the site of the present city of Nashville, when that section was a wilderness of cane brake and the majority of its inhabitants the redman and the no less savage wild animals of the region. The maternal grandfather, Thomas Wade, moved from Georgia to Tennessee in the early part of the nineteenth century and settled on Duck River, in Hickman County. He was of Welsh descent, and his wife was an Englishwoman, but the paternal grandfather was of German extraction. Elijah Walker, his father, was born, reared and followed the occupation of farming in Tennessee until his death in 1845. Although Rev. Allen H. Walker was born in Hickman County, Tenn., he was reared in the western part of the State, and owing to the scarcity of schools, received but a limited education. In early manhood he procured a license to preach the doctrines of the Cumberland Presbyterian Church, and began his ministerial duties as a circuit rider before he had attained his twentieth year. During this time he also did some farming, and realizing the need of a better education he attended a small private school for a short time, apart from which he is wholly self-educated. In 1847 he came to Texas and located in Grimes County, which at that time had no county seat, although a small settlement, then called Fantops (now Anderson, the county seat) had been established. Mr. Walker located in the timber, five miles away, near the present site of Navasota, where he lived two years, then moved to La Grange, Fayette County, and was a resident of that town or county until 1853. He then came with a large herd of cattle to Gonzales County and located on a ranch twenty miles south of town, and for years was a very extensive dealer in cattle. In

1859 he sold out his interests for $45,000 and moved to Gonzales for the purpose of educating his children, on the outskirts of which place he bought a farm, on which he has ever since resided. Ever since locating in Texas he has preached the Gospel to his fellows, and has done this as a labor of love, for he found it wholly inadequate to provide the wants of his family, and for this reason much of his attention was given to agriculture and stock raising. He continued to preach up to 1887, when he retired and is now enjoying the fruits of a well spent life. He has married more couples in Texas than per- haps any other preacher in the State, and has also officiated at hundreds of funerals. He is a sterling old citizen and highly honored by his fellows. He was made a Mason in Grimes County, Texas, and was a charter member of the lodge at Helena, Karnes County. In 1839 he married Miss Lucinda Ramer, a native of Alabama, but who was reared in the western part of Ten- nessee, and to their union nine children were given: Mary Elizabeth, widow of Jurian Hopkins, who was killed in the battle of Chickamauga, Tenn.; Car- oline, died in early girlhood; Robert M., served in Capt. Robert Davis' Company during the war, and is now a resident of Wyoming; Fannie, mar- ried Thomas Matthews, and is a resident of Dakota; Thomas McFarland, is a farmer of this county; Amanda, is the wife of Rev. John Hodges; Kate, is the wife of William Hodges; Frederick Chandler, died in boyhood; Adaline, died in childhood, and Henry C. was drowned in boyhood during a large overflow on the Guadalupe River. Mr. Walker has ever been regarded as an honest and industrious man, and one of the most successful farmers in his section of the country.

DR. FRANK R. MARTIN. The profession of the physician is one that demands the undivided attention of its devotees and he who follows this call- ing must possess a hardy and vigorous constitution to stand the wearing loss of sleep, the exposure to the inclemency of the weather, and the contact with many forms of dread disease. Dr. Frank R. Martin has been a successful practitioner of the "healing art" for the past twenty-one years, and in pursu- ing this calling has made both fame and fortune for himself. He was born in Copiah County, Mississippi, in 1845, the fourth of ten children born to William W. and Mary (Miller) Martin, who were born in the Palmetto State and Mississippi respectively, the former being a planter by occupation. He was taken to Mississippi when young, was there reared to manhood and educated, and was there also united in marriage. He became prominent in public life, was a member of the Mississippi State Legislature, and for years was custodian of the poor fund for Copiah County. He died in 1858 at the age of forty- five years, and his wife in August, 1890, a worthy member of the Baptist Church. The father was a member of the A. F. & A. M. In the schools of his native county the subject of this sketch was given a practical education, and took an academic course at the Richland Academy in Rankin County, but at the early age of sixteen years dropped his books to become a votary of Mars. In the fall of 1861 he joined the Seven Stars Artillery, which was soon after attached to Miles' Brigade, and after a service of fifteen months was discharged. Six months later he re-enlisted in Company C, Morman's Battalion of Cavalry, and served principally in the northern part of the State under Gen. Wirt Adams, and was a participant in a number of important engagements. He served for a time as Quartermaster on the Big Black River, and, although he was but a stripling, he gave the South his best energies and they were of no mean order. When the war terminated he returned home and resumed his studies for three years, after which he was engaged in teaching for a number of years, during which time he began the study of law under the direction of Wiley P. Harris. After one year devoted to this science he abandoned it and began reading medicine under Drs. Rowan and Rea, of Wesson, Miss. He afterwards attended lectures in the Medical Department of the University of Louisiana, and graduated therefrom in 1873. He then practiced for one year at Holmesville, Pike County, Miss., and in the spring of 1874 came to Texas, and until 1884 practiced his profession at Elgin, Bastrop County, at the end of which time he took up his abode in Kyle. He has been successful in building up a large practice here, which is increasing all the time, and is among the best people of the section. He is a member of the Texas State Medical Association, the Austin District Medical Association, and is an ex-President of the latter. He is railroad surgeon of this place, and is chief examiner for all the old line insurance companies of this section. In January, 1877, he was married to Miss Mary Alice Davis, a native of Texas and a daughter of G. R. Davis (deceased), of Elgin. They have seven children: William C., Elmer L., Mary Eura, Lora E., Frankie R., Alie D., and Monroe T. The doctor and his wife are members of the Baptist Church, and he has always been quite active in politics, and was a delegate to the State Convention at Dallas in 1894. He is Past Chancellor Commander of Invincible Lodge of Kyle of the Knights of Pythias, and is the medical examiner for the Endowment Rank, and he is also a member of the Knights of Honor. He is a scholarly gentleman, agreeable in manners, and has been very successful in curing the ills to which suffering humanity is heir. He has a handsome residence, which he erected in 1884, and there he and his amiable wife dispense a refined yet generous hospitality to the many friends whom they have gathered about them. His grandfather, William Martin, came to Mississippi at an early day and in this State was called from life at an advanced age. He was a minister of the Baptist Church, a well known and useful citizen and was universally respected. He was born in Dublin, Ireland, and when an infant he was brought by his parents to the United States, and with them located in the Palmetto State.

CALVIN M. LANE. From the biography of every man may be gleaned some lessons of genuine worth, for it is here that we discover the secret of his success or failure. The life of him whose name heads this sketch has been characterized by noble impulses, successfully carried out; by faithfulness to every duty, no matter how trivial, and by the most honest methods of conducting his affairs. At the present time he is filling the responsible position of Treasurer of Caldwell County, Texas, to which office he was elected November 2, 1880, and his long tenure indicates his efficiency and trustworthiness. He is a Tennessean by birth, born November 2, 1828, the eldest son of John and Elizabeth (West) Lane, also Tennesseeans, the father being a successful farmer by occupation. He died in 1890 and his wife in 1849. In the State of his birth the subject of this sketch attained manhood and received his education. In 1850 he came to Texas and located in Lockhart, Caldwell County, and up to 1852 was engaged in farming. He then began working at the carpenter's trade, continuing for six years, after which he began making saddle trees, and was thus employed by the Confederate Government during the war. After the war was over he erected a large saddle tree factory and shipped his goods to many adjoining States. While following this occupation he also conducted a large undertaking establishment, which he is still engaged in. He was at one time one of the Directors of the School Board, and was its Secretary for some time. He was married in 1856 to Miss Dora M. Sullivan, a native of Tennessee, and the daughter of Blackstone B. Sullivan, who came to Texas in 1848. To the union of Mr. and Mrs. Lane twelve children were born, seven of whom are now living. He and his wife are members of the Christian Church, and socially he belongs to the A. F. & A. M., the I. O. O. F., the K. of H., and A. L. of H. He is an able official and his friends, both political and otherwise, are many.

JUDGE JOSEPH O'CONNOR. The bar of Gonzales County, Texas, has won an enviable name throughout the State for the erudition, success and courtesy of its members, many of whom have achieved a wide reputation for their ability and a correct apprehension of what pertains to the profession. Among those who stand deservedly high as a member of this bar, with his brother lawyers and with the courts, is Judge Joseph O'Connor, who has been successfully engaged in the practice of his profession since 1847. He has always been a close student of law and has won the confidence and esteem of the community and the profession as a careful and efficient lawyer. He is a Virginian by birth, born in 1823 to Dennis and Elizabeth (Hesser) O'Connor, who were born in the Isle of Erin and the State of Pennsylvania respectively. In his youth Dennis O'Connor came to the United States with his father, and with him located in the Old Dominion, where he followed the calling of a mechanic throughout the remainder of his life. He died there in 1837, and his widow in Missouri in 1860, whither she had moved in the fall of 1837, after the father's death. Up to 1837 Judge Joseph O'Connor had been a regular attendant of the schools of Virginia, and he also attended the district schools of Missouri for some time after his removal to that State. Later he entered Marion College, Mo., and in 1844 the Miami University of Oxford, Ohio, from which he was graduated in 1845. Immediately following this he began the study of law in Palmyra in the office of Stanton Buckner, and in 1847 was admitted to the Palmyra bar. In 1852 he came to the Lone Star State and for five years practiced his profession at Bastrop, after which he moved to Corpus Christi and there remained until the opening of the Civil War. In the spring of 1863 he was appointed Clerk of the District Court of the Confederate States of Brownsville, later at Corpus Christi, and upon that place being threatened by the enemy the place of justice was removed to Gonzales. As soon as the courts were reopened in 1867 Mr. O'Conner resumed the practice of his profession, and in a short time had built up a clientele which spoke eloquently as to his standing as a lawyer and his popularity with the masses. In 1860 he had been elected District Judge of the Twelfth Judicial District, from Corpus Christi, but soon thereafter the Civil War closed the courts in the State, thus verifying the adage, *Non silent leges inter arma.* In 1875 he erected a pleasant and commodious residence on the outskirts of Gonzales, where he lives in semi-retirement, his practice now being mostly confined to land cases, in which he has shown remarkable foresight and judgment. In 1864 he was married to Miss Sarah Buchanan, a native of Texas and a granddaughter of Arthur Burns, who was a member of De Witt's colony, that settled Gonzales. The union of Mr. and Mrs. O'Connor has been blessed in the birth of four children: Birdie, wife of W. L. Clark; Lillie, wife of William Campbell, of San Antonio; Etta and Fred J.

JAMES W. NOLAN. Among those who have built up the agricultural interests of this section and have become prominent in that calling is James W. Nolan, a native of Texas, born in Harrison County in 1845. His father, John Nolan, was born in South Carolina, but at an early date moved to North Carolina where he married Miss Nancy Montgomery, a native of the Old North State. Afterwards the father moved to Mississippi and thence to Texas, settling in Harrison County at an early date. In February, 1852, he came to Lavaca County and settled on the Lavaca River, about five miles from Hallettsville, where he made a settlement of 1,107 acres, all wild land. He made many improvements and became an extensive farmer for those days. There he and wife passed the remainder of their days, he dying in February, 1878, and she in 1881. Both were members of the M. E. Church. From his seventh year, James W. Nolan was reared in Lavaca County and here received his education. He spent much of his time in youth in assisting his father clear the home place and is now the owner of the same. At the present time it consists of 850 acres in one tract and he has 240 acres under cultivation. He also owns other tracts of land. In 1863. Mr. Nolan enlisted in a company commanded by Bill Tate, and served on the Rio Grande for some time. Later he joined Capt. Patrick's Company and served in Texas with him until the close of the war. On the 14th of August, 1866, he was married to Miss Fannie Lemons, who was born in Mississippi and who was a daughter of James Lemons of Mississippi. Born to this union were nine children, four of whom are living: Nannie W., Wiley B., James D. and Willie C. Four died in infancy and one, John K., was killed when twenty-one years of age. Mr. Nolan is a good citizen of the county and a man interested in all worthy movements.

M. M. FITZGERALD. The poet who found "his warrant welcome at an inn" must have had in mind one of those hostelries in which the convenience of a home are forever present without the disagreeable and exacting duties that make home life domestic slavery. Such a house is that of which M. M. Fitzgerald is the proprietor at Gonzales, Texas, and this fact has come to be recognized by all, but is especially appreciated by traveling men, who find its home-like comforts and freedom particularly agreeable. Another particularly pleasing thing about the house is that one can be housed and fed according to the length of his purse, and at the same time have excellent accommodations. Mr. Fitzgerald is a model host, for he is agreeable and courteous and makes the welfare of his guests one of his personal interests. He is a native of Liberty, Liberty County, Texas, born in 1844, the eldest child of T. R. and Martha (Whitlock) Fitzgerald, who were born in Georgia and Texas respectively. T. R. Fitzgerald was for many years a resident of Mississippi, but finally drifted to Texas with his parents, when he was a young man, (about 1838 or 1839) and settled in Polk County, where his father died. The maternal grandfather settled on the San Jacinto River at a very early day and there he was engaged in tilling the soil. After the marriage of T. R. Fitzgerald and Martha Whitlock, they moved to Liberty County, and there Mr. Fitzgerald became quite prominent in public affairs, and for several terms served as Sheriff of the county. He died in 1873, but his widow still survives him. Up to the age of seventeen years M. M. Fitzgerald made his home in his native county, then left home to take up arms in defense of the Confederate cause, becoming in February, 1861, a member of a company of militia, which was soon ordered to the Island of Brazos Santiago on the Gulf, a few months later to Houston and a few days later to Virginia. Upon the arrival of the Company at Richmond it became a part of the Fifth Texas Regiment, Hood's Brigade, and became Company F. He served in the Virginia wing of the Confederate army until the war closed, participating in all the battles of importance, and almost miraculously escaped wounds or capture. The last eighteen months of his army life were spent as a courier, and for a time, just before the close, he was Commissary Agent, buying stock for the brigade. At the close of the war he started home and almost the entire distance from Virginia to Texas was made on foot. He reached home in the summer of 1865 and soon after secured the position of express messenger on the Houston & New Orleans Railroad, which position he held for some time. After then clerking for a short time in Houston, one year was spent in farming on the San Jacinto River, and a like period was spent as a clerk in Galveston. He then came to Gonzales County, became a resident of the town of Gonzales in 1881, and in 1888 opened the hotel of which he is now proprietor, and is doing a deservedly profitable business. From 1870 to 1887 he was mainly engaged in cattle dealing and during this time made about sixteen trips over the trail to Kansas, each trip occupying about three months, and were enlivened by many thrilling incidents. He was married in 1872 to Miss Augusta Kokernot, a native of Texas, and a daughter of D. L. Kokernot, a Texas veteran, and to this union six children have been given: Blanche, Maud, Edna, who died October 28, 1892 at the age of fourteen years; Sam Max, Mattie and David Crockett. Mr. Fitzgerald has been a member of the I. O. O. F. since 1872, and is now a member of Gonzales Lodge No. 38, in which he has filled all the chairs. He is also a member of the Royal Goodfellows, has been City Secretary four years and at the present time, is also discharging the duties of City Treasurer. Mr. Fitzgerald is a good business man, and, being a " royal good-fellow" has many friends among the best citizens of the county.

CAPT. FERG. KYLE. This gentleman, the founder of the town of Kyle, Texas, owes his nativity to the State of Mississippi, where his eyes first opened on the light of day in 1833. He was the third of eight children born to Claiborne and Lucy (Bugg) Kyle, who were Tennesseeans by birth. The father came to Texas in the winter of 1844, made his home for one year at Gonzales, then moved to Austin where he remained until 1849. He then settled on the Blanco River, two miles west of the present site of Kyle, and became one of the early settlers of this section. He became very prominent while residing in Mississippi, was active in political matters, served his section as a member of the State Senate, and made an able and incorruptible legislator. At one time he was prominently spoken of for Governor of that State. After coming to the Lone Star State he served as a member of the State Senate one term, and for three terms was a member of the House, and while a member of the Legislative body, did some effective work for his section and for the State in general. He became a political leader in this part of Texas and as widely and very favorably known, as a shrewd politican, a man of excellent morals, a useful and worthy citizen and a prosperous business man. He was the owner of a very large and valuable farm at the opening of the

Civil War. After a useful and well spent life, he was called upon to pay the last debt of Nature in 1868, and his death was a source of much regret to all who knew him. He was a member of the A. F. & A. M. His wife died in 1863. He was a son of John Kyle, who was of Scotch-Irish descent and one of the early settlers of Tennessee. The Buggs were prominent Tennesseeans and one of Mrs. Kyle's uncles was a member of Congress from that State during President Pierce's administration. Capt. Ferg. Kyle accompanied his parents to this State, received a practical education in the schools of Austin, and remained under the shelter of the parental roof until the opening of the great Civil War, when he donned a suit of gray and became a private in the Eighth Texas Cavalry, Terry's Rangers, and was at once sent east of the Mississippi River and after the first battle in which they participated, he was made First Lieutenant of his company. After the battle of Shiloh he was advanced to a Captaincy and was in all the engagements in the Army of the Tennessee, and acted as Volunteer Aid to Gen. Cheatham on the 22nd of July, 1864. After the fall of Atlanta an order came from Richmond to send two officers from each regiment from the trans-Mississippi to return and collect absentees, and Capt. Kyle was one of the officers chosen. He collected a number in Texas, and reported to Gen. Hays on the day that they heard of Lee's surrender. He was then ordered back to Austin by Gen. Hays, and by the time he had reached that city the war had ended. His brothers William, Polk, Curran and Andrew Jackson were all privates in his company. After his return home Capt. Kyle engaged in farming and stock raising and was following this occupation very successfully when he was elected to the Twelfth General Assembly of the State, and while a member of that body served on several committees. He was Sergeant-at-arms of the Seventeenth and Eighteenth General Assemblys and he has always been quite active in politics. In 1860 he was married to Miss Anna Moore, a native of Alabama and a daughter of Judge David E. Moore, who came to Texas in the early '50's. He eventually became a resident of Hays County and was County Judge of Hays County at one time. He died in the '70's. In 1867 Capt. Kyle moved to his present farm, which was formerly the old Moore Homestead, and on this the town of Kyle was founded and named in honor of the captain, in 1882. The union of Captain and Mrs. Kyle has resulted in the birth of nine children, the eldest of whom died in infancy. The others are: Mary, Sidney Johnson, Albert Johnson, Ailene, Josephine, Edward Johnson, Rosa and Ellen. Capt. and Mrs. Kyle are members of the Baptist Church and are widely known and have many warm personal friends throughout Hays County.

WILLIAM WILEY CARPENTER. One of the most positive truths taught by modern science is that mental and physical qualities are hereditary in man, and this statement of fact is as old as Moses, who declared that the generations to come should feel the influence of the fathers' actions. The subject of this sketch is descended from a worthy ancestry, and owes his vigor of body and his strong mentality to his parents and his parents' parents. He was born in Alabama in 1835, the sixth of nine children born to William S. and Mary (Long) Carpenter, who were natives of Ohio and Tennessee, respectively. William S. Carpenter came to Texas in 1852 and settled on a farm in Caldwell County, where he tilled the soil for several years, and died in 1875, his wife's death occurring in the year 1674. The subject of this sketch was seventeen years old when he came to Texas with his parents, and for a number of years thereafter he aided his father in tilling the soil. Upon the opening of the great Civil War he enlisted in Capt. McDade's Company for six months, and at the end of that time was discharged at Galveston. He at once re-enlisted in the service, becoming a member of Company K, Seventeenth Texas Infantry (in which two of his brothers also served), and was in the trans-Mississippi Department, and was a participant in the battle of Milliken's Bend on the Mississippi River, the battles of Mansfield and Pleasant Hill in the Banks' Campaign and the Saline River fight in Arkansas, as well as various skirmishes and engagements of less note. He was at home when the war closed. He at once re-engaged in farming, but two years later became a clerk in a mercantile establishment, and after some time had elapsed opened a mercantile establishment of his own in Lockhart, which he ably conducted for about sixteen years. One year thereafter was spent on his farm, and in 1884 he was elected to the office of County Clerk and, after filling the position with great credit for six years, returned to his farm. In 1893 he was appointed to this office to fill a vacancy, and at present is discharging the duties of this position. His estate comprises about 100 acres of fine land, nearly all of which is under cultivation. He was married in 1868 to Miss Mary J. Kelley, a native of Gonzales, Texas, and daughter of Charles Kelley, who came from Arkansas to Texas in the '40's. To this union six children have been born: Elizabeth, who died in 1886 at the age of seventeen years; Vida, Etta, Willie, Marvin and Albert. Mr. and Mrs. Carpenter are members of the Methodist Church, and socially he is a Mason and a member of Lockhart Lodge No. 690, of which he is at the present time the Master. He has been High Priest of Luling Chapter, and is also a member of the Knights of Honor and the American Legion of Honor. He is an able official, a genial gentleman and his honorable business methods and correct principles have been the means of winning him many friends.

DR. JAMES W. NIXON. The old saying that "a prophet is not without honor save in his own country," which has come to be applied not only to prophets but to men in nearly every profession, trade and walk of life, is most completely controverted in every community in the country by the manifestation of high esteem on the part of the people for the able and honorable members of the medical profession. The physician, more generally, perhaps, than even the pastor, endears himself to the family circle, and while he may not be strictly of it, he is at all times very near to it, and his relations are so confidential that his welcome is more spontaneous and hearty than that of many connected to it by the ties of blood. Among the most honored family physicians of Gonzales County, Texas, is Dr. James W. Nixon, who enjoys a large and lucrative practice and numbers among his patrons many prominent and influential citizens. He was born in Guadalupe County, Texas, in 1855, the eldest of seven children born to Robert T. and Laura N. (Wood) Nixon, who were born, reared and married in the Old North State, and about 1852, immediately after their marriage, they came to Texas, purchased a large tract of land, on which they made many improvements and on which the father still resides, she having died in 1872. He was Captain of a company in the Confederate army during the war, and served principally in Texas. Dr. James W. Nixon received his initiatory training in the common schools of his native county, after which he was for some time an attendant of the Academy of

Seguin. In 1878 he began the study of medicine in the University of Virginia, and one year later entered Tulane Medical College, of New Orleans, from which he graduated in March, 1880, and for ten years thereafter practiced his profession in Guadalupe County. Since that time he has been a very successful practitioner of Gonzales County, being located at Wrightsborough the first three years, and the last year at Gonzales. In 1893–94 he took a post graduate course, to further fit him for his noble calling, and, although his residence here has been of short duration, he has already impressed the people with the fact that he thoroughly understands his business and that they may safely trust the lives of their loved ones in his hands. He is a close student, is constantly endeavoring to promote and discover new remedies for prevailing diseases, and has recently been experimenting with the Mexican shrub "Choparo armargoso," (not Ord. Sinarubacæ Texanum) a small, thorny bush which grows throughout southwest Texas and Mexico, its property being to check and cure chronic cases of dysentery, and has met with the best success in its use. It has been known and used by the Mexicans for many years, and it was said to have been used by Gen. Taylor's soldiers in 1846, with great success. Dr. Nixon was married in 1890 to Miss Mary King, a native of Georgia, by whom he has two children: Robert Leroy and James William, Jr. Mrs. Nixon is a member of the Methodist Church, is an intelligent and amiable lady, and Dr. Nixon is a member of the Knights of Pythias. They are well known in the best social circles of Gonzales, and their home is a tasteful and hospitable one.

JAMES VALLENTINE. The agricultural part of the community is its bone and sinew, from which come the strength and vigor necessary to carry on the affairs of manufacture, commerce and the State. Among the prosperous farmers of Lavaca County stands the name of James Vallentine, who was born in Nacogdoches County, Texas, December 7, 1836, while his parents, Henry and Mary (May) Vallentine, were fleeing from the Mexicans during the Texas Revolution. Henry Vallentine was a native of Virginia, and came to Texas in 1833, with De Leon's colony. He first settled in Jackson County, and was here married to Miss May, a native of Maryland, who came with her father, John May, to Texas at the same time. For some time after their marriage Mr. and Mrs. Vallentine resided near the present town of Yoakum, and then they located where our subject now resides. Mr. Vallentine opened up a small farm, but which at that time was the largest in the section, and on the organization of the county he was made County Commissioner, which position he held for a term or two. He died in 1881, after spending a long and useful life. Mrs. Valentine died when our subject was a child. James Vallentine was reared on this home place and received but limited educational advantages. In 1861 and 1862 he was a member of a ranging company and operated in western Texas. In 1863 he was married to Miss Emma Goodson, a native of Mississippi, and daughter of Arthur Goodson who came to Texas about 1850. He is engaged quite extensively in the stock business, and has followed this very successfully for about thirty years. Of his magnificent farm of 1,400 acres he has 600 acres under cultivation, and has made most of the improvements himself. This land represents much hard labor and enterprise, and is the visible result of the work of Mr. Vallentine and his worthy wife who has been his able assistant throughout the years of their union. The social circles of this section recognize in this worthy couple an element of great value and influential helpers in the promotion of intelligence and true sociability. To their union has been born an interesting family of ten children, nine of whom are living: Alice, wife of S. J. Guthrie; Willie, Eva, wife of S. Hinds; Henry Arthur, Fannie, Susie, James, Una May, Earle and Arthur Henry, who died in infancy. Mr. Vallentine has a fine place and a beautiful home, the improvements being excellent and the house a model of convenience.

DR. G. W. McCALEB. It has come to be a recognized fact with the medical fraternity and with the general public, that owing to the advance of science and the multiplication of facilities for acquiring knowledge and practice, many of the younger physicians of to-day are better informed and more skillful practitioners than were many of the old physicians of a couple of generations ago. In every large city of the United States, as well as in many of the better of the country towns, the young doctor is the more popular of the two classes mentioned, and has the larger practice. Among the successful young physicians of Gonzales County, Texas, Dr. G.W. McCaleb is worthy of mention. He was born in Montgomery County, Texas, being the sixth of ten children born to Jesse and Dorcas McCaleb, who were natives of Tennessee and Texas, respectively. The paternal grandfather, Zill McCaleb, immigrated to this State from Tennessee, was in the Texas Revolution, and was a participant in the battle of San Jacinto. He afterward settled at Linnville, but fled from that place during the noted Indian raid of 1840, when the town was burned, and took refuge in Montgomery County, and later moved to Falls County, where he was called upon to pay the last debt of nature, in 1869.

Jesse McCaleb was a farmer and merchant, a man of unusual intelligence and one whose reputation was above reproach. He ably filled the office of Justice of the Peace, County Commissioner and State Representative, being elected to the last mentioned honorable position from Montgomery, Trinity, Harris and Walker counties. While discharging his duties as legislator of the Twentieth General Assembly, he was cut down by the hand of death, in 1888. His wife's death occurred in 1871. Dr. G. W. McCaleb received a good literary education in the Academy of Thornton and the Southwestern University of Georgetown, 1874, and in 1880 began the study of medicine under the direction of a competent medical practitioner, and at the same time was engaged in teaching school. He attended lectures in Tulane University, of New Orleans, and graduated from the same. He began the practice of his profession in Caldwell County, and there he continued to reside for several years. In 1889-90 he took a post-graduate course at New Orleans, including the study of the eye, ear, nose and throat. In 1890 he took a post-graduate course in the New York Polyclinic, and this time devoted almost his whole attention to surgery, and diseases of women and children. Upon his return from New York City he located in Gonzales, where he has built up a practice of which many older physicians might well be proud. He is making a name for himself, and will, without doubt, rise to a still higher position in his profession. He is a member of the State Medical Society, belongs to Gonzales Lodge of the A. F. & A. M., and is also a member of Gonzales Lodge No. 105 of the Knights of Pythias.

OTTO GROOS. A banker and one of the early merchants of Kyle, Texas, is Otto Groos, who first saw the light in New Braunfels, Texas, in 1847, a son of J. J. and Catherine Groos, who came thither from Germany with the colony of 1845, and settled at New Braunfels. The father was a civil engineer and surveyor, and after locating in Texas, became Surveyor of Comal County, and afterward was Clerk of the same for several years. During the war he served as Captain of a company of militia. Later he conducted the Guadalupe Hotel for three years, and then in 1872, was elected to the office of Land Commissioner of the State of Texas, in which capacity he ably served until his death in 1878. He was an intelligent and well posted man, and his ability was recognized by the people of the section in which he resided, and he was one of the leading men of that time. His wife died in 1876. In New Braunfels the subject of this sketch was given a practical education, and after working under his father for some time, he began life as a surveyer, and during 1871 and 1872 he was County Surveyor of Comal County. He then went to Austin, and was clerk in the land office there for eight years, but in the fall of 1881, at the founding of the town of Kyle, he came to this place, and erected the first business house in the town and at once engaged in general merchandising, a business he followed with reasonable success for two years. He then sold out and engaged in the real estate business and surveying, and was finally elected Surveyor of Hays County, which office he ably filled three terms, and at the same time did a successful real estate and insurance business. In the spring of 1894, he established the bank at this place, and in May the style of the firm became the Kyle Bank, with a paid up capital of $24,000. Mr. Groos owns a fine farm near the town of Kyle, comprising 175 acres of well improved land, and all the improvements on this place have been made by himself, and are of a most substantial and valuable character, besides adding much to the appearance of the farm. Mr. Groos' attentions have by no means been confined to the above mentioned interests, for he also owns a share in a drug store, in fact, he is wideawake and pushing, and is quick to see and grasp at opportunities for bettering his financial condition. He was one of the organizers of the Kyle Oil Company, is Treasurer of the company, and was also one of the organizers of the Kyle Water Company, and is President and Treasurer of that company. He is a shrewd and far-seeing man of business, is enterprising and ambitious, but withal is upright and honorable, in every way worthy, particular, and, in fact, is a most agreeable gentleman to meet and with whom to have business dealings. He was first married in 1871 to Miss Alice Mather, a native of Texas, who died in 1885, leaving four children: William, Adolph, Sarah, and Maggie. His second marriage was celebrated in 1888, with Miss Mattie Barber, a native of Texas, and a daughter of Dr. J. G. Barber, who was a pioneer of this section, a noted physician, who died July 4, 1894. Mr. Groos' second union has resulted in the birth of three children: Mary, John and Jasper.

HON. EDWARD H. RAGAN. He whose name heads this sketch is regarded as one of the leading lawyers of his section of the State, and commands the respect as well as the admiration of his brother practitioners, and is a living refutation of the popular idea that "there is no honest lawyer." He was born in Grainger County, Tennessee, February 4, 1834, the eldest of nine children born to Daniel and Catherine (Webb) Ragan, the former of whom was born in Virginia, and the latter in Tennessee. The paternal grandfather, Daniel Ragan, was born in Ireland, and upon coming to the United States, located in Virginia, where he followed the calling of a merchant, and later, but at a still early period, located in Sullivan County, Tennessee, and was eventually called from life at Kingsport. The maternal grandfather, John Webb, was one of the very early settlers of Knoxville, Tenn., and there his home continued to be until his death in 1843. He was a leather manufacturer on a large scale for that day, and in this branch of human endeavor became wealthy. Daniel Ragan, the father of the subject of this sketch, was a minister of the Presbyterian Church, and spent his life in Sullivan County, Tennessee, dying in 1869. Until eighteen years of age Edward H. Ragan spent his life in his native State, and his literary education was obtained in the schools of Knoxville, and at Bakersfield, Vt. In 1852 he took up his residence in Texas, at Lockhart, Caldwell County, and brought with him a daguerreotype outfit, and finished the first picture ever taken in the town. He soon after sold out, however, and engaged in teaching school, and at the same time studied law, and in 1854 was admitted to the bar, and at once entered upon the practice of his profession at Lockhart. Unlike many who first enter professional life, it did not take him long to obtain his first brief, and so ably did he handle the cases that were placed in his charge, that he soon had all the legal work that he could attend to. In 1856 he was married to Miss Sarah N. Barrow, a native of Mississippi, who was brought to Texas when a child by her father, Samuel Barrow, who was for a long time Sheriff of Gonzales County. In 1859 Mr. Ragan was elected to the office of Justice of the Peace, and was holding that office when the great Civil War opened. He at once resigned and enlisted in Company K, Seventeenth Texas Infantry, which command operated in Louisiana and Arkansas, and he was a participant in the battles of Milliken's Bend, Mansfield, Pleasant Hill, and Jenkins' Ferry. He then returned to Louisiana, thence to Texas, and was in this State when the war closed. He soon after went to Galveston and was salesman in a large clothing store there for one year, at the end of which time he returned to Lockhart, and resumed the practice of law, and also became connected with newspaper work once more. In 1855 he started the *Watchman*, which was the second paper of Lockhart, and he continued its publication until he entered the army in 1861, when he stored his material and machinery away, but it was all destroyed during that period. In 1869, in connection with N. C. Raymond, of Austin, he began the publication of the *Texas Plowboy*, for there had been no paper published in Lockhart since the *Watchman*, but he sold his interest in this paper in 1871, to Mr. Raymond, who removed it to Austin, but on his way to that city died very suddenly. In the same year 1871, Mr. Ragan established the *News Echo*, which he conducted for about one year, when the office was destroyed by fire. The *Plowboy* was devoted to agricultural matters, and the others were published in the interests of the Democratic party. At one time Mr. Ragan was appointed to the office of County Clerk to fill a vacancy, was later elected County Attorney, a position he held four years, and, after being out of office for two years, was elected to the same position for another two years. In 1875 he was elected County Judge, the first under the new constitution of 1875, and held the office for three years. In 1890 he was again honored by his party by being elected to the Twenty-second General Assembly from the Ninety-first District, composed of Guadalupe, Caldwell and Hays counties, was re-elected in 1892, from the Fifty-first District, composed of the county of Caldwell. During his first term he served on Judiciary Committee No. 2, Agricultural Affairs, Insurance Statistics and History, and Constitutional Amendments. He introduced the following bills: One for extending the time in holding the District Court of Caldwell County, one for amending the attachment laws of the State, and a bill relating to official business, all of which became laws.   He was also the author of an amendment to the Constitution, reducing the rate of interest of the State to 6 and 8 per cent.   While a member of the Twenty-third Assembly he introduced a bill to amend the law in regard to taking depositions in civil suits, which was the first bill passed and signed by the Governor. A bill establishing a special road law for Caldwell County; and in connection with Harry Golden of Dallas, he was the author of a bill to establish a State Board of Arbitration to settle difficulties between employes and employers. The bill passed the house, but did not get through the Senate.   Another bill. which he introduced was for making an appropriation for the maintenance of the Confederate Home. He served on the following committees: As second on Judiciary Committee No. 1, Chairman of the Committee on Judicial Districts, Committee on International Affairs, Committee on Privileges and Elections and was a member of the special committee which preferred impeachment charges against Land Commissioner McGaughey, and was appointed Speaker of the Committee to conduct the trial before the Senate.   In his practice he has made criminal law a specialty, and has been very successful. Possessing decided literary taste he has written much on many subjects, and composed a beautiful poem on the death of Jefferson Davis, which was read in his speech in the House of Representatives on that occasion.   His first wife died in 1870, having borne him five children, two of whom died before their mother.   In 1874 he was married to Mrs. Martha (Rickenbaugh) Gutheridge, of Fulton, Mo., who only lived about a year after marriage.   He married his present wife in 1877—Miss Ellen Runkle, a native of Missouri, and to them four children have been born, three of whom are living.   Mr. and Mrs. Ragan are members of the Presbyterian Church, he is Superintendent of the Sunday School, and socially he is a member of the I. O. O. F.

JOHN FRANKLIN LAIRD.   The calling of the merchant is one of the utmost importance to any community and one of its most successful followers at Wrightsboro is John Franklin Laird, who also has charge of "Uncle Sam's" business at that place.   He is a product of Upshur County, Texas, where his eyes first opened on the light of day January 25, 1851, his parents being Andrew J. and Elvira (McKain) Laird, the former of whom was born in Buckingham County, Virginia.   At an early day he pushed westward, and eventually found himself in the "Lone Star State," and here he became the owner of a large tract of land and began devoting his attention to planting, a calling which has since received his attention.   He has resided on his present place ever since coming to the State—a period of forty years—and by his many improvements has made it one of the valuable pieces of property in his section.   He has always supported the principles of the Democratic party, and has held the offices of County Commissioner and Justice of the Peace, and in both capacities showed intelligence and capability.   He has been a widower since 1876.   John Franklin Laird, his son, was educated in the common schools of Upshur County, and on his father's extensive plantation he acquired a thorough knowledge of agriculture, and after starting out in life for himself he followed that line of human endeavor for years.   In December, 1874, he located in Wrightsboro, opened here a general mercantile establishment and has conducted it successfully ever since.   Like his sire before him, he has always been a Democrat in politics, and since he first located in Wrightsboro he has held the position of Postmaster, and has filled the office with ability and faithfulness. He has shown his approval of secret societies by joining the A. F. & A. M., and is a member of Shuler Lodge. In 1881 he led to the altar Miss Ella T., daughter of Abner Avant, who is a well known planter of this county, and a substantial citizen. He has been a widower since 1875. To Mr. and Mrs. Laird three children have been given: Frank Leslie, Lula E., and Esther, all of whom are bright and promising children.

DR. MATTHEW T. HENDRICKS. Health is the most precious gift of nature, and how to retain it and how to regain it when lost are matters of vital moment. Some obtain health in travel, others in physical recreation, and both are beneficial, but they do not always accomplish the object in view. Medical science must be resorted to and a good physician employed. Caldwell County, Texas, is especially favored in this respect, for she numbers many excellent physicians among her professional men, prominent among whom is Dr. M. T. Hendricks, who was born in Franklin County, Tenn., in 1845, the twelfth of thirteen children born to Frederick F. and Rebecca E. B. (Campbell) Hendricks, natives of Virginia; the father a farmer and stock raiser by occupation. The paternal grandfather, Thomas Aaron Hendricks, was a Virginian also, and at a very early period became a resident of Franklin County, Tenn., where he followed the occupations of farming and stock raising until his death. The maternal grandfather, John Buchanan Campbell, was a Virginian, a lawyer by profession, and was one of the early settlers of Lexington, Ky. He was commissioned a Colonel in the Eleventh United States Infantry, under General Scott, for the War of 1812; was in a number of battles, and was killed in the battle of Chippewa, in 1813. His father was a Colonel in the Revolutionary War, and was in all the southern battles, while his mother's brother, William Campbell, was the commander at King's Mountain, and became a General in the same war. Two members of the family have become State Governors, one of Virginia and the other of Tennessee. Frederick F. Hendricks died of cholera, in Tennessee, in 1851, at the age of fifty-one years, and two years later his widow and children came to Texas and settled in Caldwell County, where they purchased a farm on which Mrs. Hendricks made her home until her death in 1872, when seventy-two years of age. She was a finely educated woman, and did much to train and educate her children at home, and from her Dr. M. T. Hendricks received his early training. He was attending school in Lockhart when the war opened, and when a call was made for volunteers he at once dropped his books and responded, becoming a member of Sibley's Brigade for the New Mexican campaign, participating in the battles of Val Verde and Glorietta. At the end of one year he became a member of Company B, Greene's Brigade, and became Second Sergeant. He was then in Texas, Louisiana and Arkansas, and participated in thirty-six engagements, the principal ones being Galveston, Brasier City, Franklin. Bisland, Mansfield, Pleasant Hill, Blair's Landing, Yellow Bayou and others. He was wounded in the head at Val Verde, and when the war closed was in Texas. He then returned home, and at odd times, while tilling the soil, he read medicine. In 1867–68 he attended lectures in Galveston, and after graduating in 1870 began practicing the "healing art" in Caldwell County, and in 1878 moved to Lockhart. In 1890 he took a post-graduate course at the Policlinic Medical College at New York City, and took a special course in surgery. He was one of the organizers of the Caldwell Medical Society, in 1874, and at that time he was appointed a member of the Medical Examining Board, a position he held for about five years. He is now Vice-president of the Caldwell County Medical Society. He has a very large and lucrative practice, and is very favorably known to the profession.

WINSTON JONES DAVIE, M. D. Although the calling of the physician is one of great importance, it is even more so when combined with that of the druggist, and to these two most important of human callings the attention of Dr. Winston Jones Davie is given. He is one of the foremost residents of Wrightsboro, but is a native of Clarksville, Tenn., where he was born September 10, 1860. His parents, Montgomery D. and Cornelia (Leavell) Davie, were born on Blue Grass soil, and the former became quite a prominent politician. About 1850 he removed with his family to Tennessee, and there he became President of the Bank of America at Clarksville, with branches at Dresden and Memphis. When the war came up he was the owner of a large flouring mill at Clarksville, but at the approach of the Union army he retired south, as did many others, with his negroes, and the property which he left behind him was subjected to spoliation at the hands of both armies. He held large possessions in Louisiana, Mississippi and Arkansas, and after the war was over he returned to Kentucky, and has since been a resident of Hopkinsville. He has taken an active part in the new movement of Patrons of Husbandry, and has been Master of the State and National Grange. While a resident of Tennessee he served several years as a member of the State Legislature, during which time he labored faithfully for the interests of his own immediate section and for the State at large. Wherever he has resided he has been a citizen of prominence, his brilliant mind, public spirit and courteous ways winning him the respect and liking of his fellows. The immediate subject of this sketch was educated in the schools near Hopkinsville, Ky., and in Fox Place Academy, where he finished his literary education, but he later pursued a medical course at Atlanta, graduating there with high honors. He finished his medical education in St. Louis, graduating from an institution of that city in 1885. He at once located in the vicinity of Hopkinsville, but about a year from that time moved to Missouri, where he spent several years. In 1889 he came to Texas, and first located at Cistern, in Fayette County, but for about a year and a half past has been a resident of Wrightsboro, where he has already gained an enviable reputation as a medical practitioner, and where he has a well-appointed and popular drug store. He was married in 1888 to Miss Agatha, daughter of William and Mary Brewer, of Council Grove, Kansas. Dr. Davie and his wife have two interesting children: Cornelia Frances and Flora. Another child, Montgomery Winston, died in early childhood. Dr. Davie is descended from Scotch ancestors, and is possessed of many of the most worthy traits of character of that race. His great-great-grandfather, William Davie, was a delegate from South Carolina to the Constitutional Convention, and aided in the framing of that instrument.

REV. WILLIAM JASPER JOYCE. This gentleman is one of the pioneer circuit riders of the Lone Star State, and during the long term of years that he has labored in the vineyard of the Master his efforts have been well rewarded. He is a product of Georgia, born in 1828, the eldest child born to Henry and Sarah (Posey) Joyce, who were born in Georgia and South

W. R. Richardson

Carolina respectively, the former being a farmer and stock-raiser of considerable prominence. The paternal grandfather, Henry Joyce, was a Virginian, while his father was a native of Ireland, and came to America in colonial times. The grandfather was a soldier of the Revolution, and fought principally in the Southern States. In 1836 Henry and Sarah Joyce moved to Alabama, thence to Texas in 1849, and in Red River County the father was called from life in 1855, his widow surviving him until 1893, when she, too, passed away at the age of ninety-three years. In the State of Alabama the subject of this sketch was reared, but he unfortunately received a limited education, although he possessed a naturally fine mind. He came with his parents to Texas in 1849, and when he had attained his majority he left home, and for one year thereafter was engaged in farming in Arkansas. He then went to Ouachita County, same State, and for some time served as Deputy Clerk of the courts. In the fall of 1852 he again came to Texas, and in 1857 began his labors as a minister of the Methodist Episcopal Church South, and has continued in that work ever since. He was ordained a deacon in Tyler and an elder in Jefferson, Texas. He began his work in Harrison County, and for four years remained in the eastern part of the State doing station and circuit work. In 1861 he was stationed at Palestine, but when the war opened he joined the Confederate army, Company A of the Second Texas Mounted Rifles, and served ten months as a private in New Mexico, and was a participant in the battle of Cottonwoods, in which his horse was shot near where he stood. He was then made Chaplain of his regiment, but at the end of 1863 resigned this position and resumed his ministerial labors in the West Texas Conference, and was following this occupation on the frontier when he had to carry firearms to protect himself against the Indians. At one time his horse was stolen by them when he was eighty miles from home, and he was often exposed to hostile and marauding bands of savages. After preaching for twenty-eight years in western Texas he is now superannuated. About 1874 he came to San Marcos and has since made his home here. He was presiding elder for ten years, eight of which in the San Marcos district. He has been agent for the American Bible Society, but since being superannuated in 1893 he has been associated with Mr. Steele in the real estate business, as a member of the firm of Steele & Joyce, and has done comparatively well financially. He has had some success as a revivalist, has done some effective work at camp meetings, and his experiences on his way to fill appointments on the frontier were many times thrilling. He was married in 1863 to Miss Laura Mitchell, of San Antonio, a daughter of Asa Mitchell, a native of Pennsylvania, who came to Texas about 1824. Nine children have been born to Mr. and Mrs. Joyce: Emily, wife of Prof. S. W. Stanfield, of Coronal Institute; May, wife of Judge W. Kelso, of Eagle Pass; William H., special fire insurance agent at Dallas; Harvey W., book-keeper American National Bank, Dallas; Albert G., financial clerk in the postoffice at Dallas; Martin O., cashier of the Mexican International R. R., at Pedris Negris, Mexico; Laura Lee, Robert D. and Dora A. Mr. Joyce is a Mason, and he and his family are well known and highly honored citizens of the Lone Star State.

MRS. SARAH ANN BRACHES. Sarah Ann Ashby, now the Widow Braches, was born in Shelby County, Ky., in the town of Shelbyville, March 12, 1811, the daughter of John M. and Mary (Garnett) Ashby, the former of whom

17

removed to Kentucky from Ashby's Gap, Va. In 1831 he located at Old Petersburg, Lavaca County, Texas, and while returning to his home in this State, after a visit to Kentucky, died at Matagorda, Texas, his wife's death having occurred a few years earlier. In 1829 Sarah Ann Ashby was married to Bartholomew A. McClure, of Kentucky, with whom she came to Texas in 1831 as one of DeWitt's colonists, and located on a large tract of land on Peach Creek, in Gonzales County, nine miles from the town of Gonzales. Mr. McClure became very prominent in the affairs of this section, and was a participant in the Texas Revolution of 1835–36, but was not a participant in the battle of San Jacinto, owing to the fact that he had been sent as a special messenger for Gen. Houston to eastern Texas for recruits. Upon the retreat of Gen. Houston from Gonzales in 1836, he camped one night at the McClure homestead, and in the morning he made a speech to the people beneath a live-oak tree that is still standing in front of the house, warning the citizens of the danger of remaining in the locality, which eventually resulted in the "run away" before the army of Santa Anna. Mrs. McClure (now Mrs. Braches) started in an ox cart, with two young sons, and followed the army so that she was within hearing of the guns in the battle of San Jacinto, at a place called Grigby's Bluff. She and some other women visited the battlefield a few days after the battle, and found all the Mexicans who had been slain still lying on the ground unburied. Mr. McClure was with Gen. Sid Johnston for about one year after this before he rejoined his family, who were then living near the present city of Houston. Mrs. McClure saw the site of that place surveyed, at which time it consisted of one house—a mere hut— and many tents. In the spring of 1838 they returned to their home, and when the county of Gonzales was organized Mr. McClure became the first County Judge, an office he held four years. During this time he had begun the arduous work of improving his place, but died in 1841, before he had made much headway in this respect. He was in what was called the Blanco Valley Indian fight, a number of years before his death, and it is to such men as him that the present state of advanced civilization was made possible. He and his wife became the parents of three sons, but two of them died while they were residing in the eastern part of the State. In 1843 Mrs. McClure and her son returned to Kentucky, where she inherited seven negro slaves, with whom she returned to Texas and began farming and stock-raising. After remaining a widow for two years she married Charles Braches, who came to Texas from Mississippi about four years prior. He was a participant in the Mexican War, and was also in several bloody Indian battles. After his marriage he turned his attention to agricultural pursuits, became an extensive stock-raiser, and also became prominent in the political affairs of Gonzales County. Prior to his marriage he had been elected to the State Legislature, and he was always interested in and had a comprehensive knowledge of the current issues of the day. His career was closed by death in 1889, after a useful and well-spent life. He left one child, Mrs. H. K. Jones, of Dilworth, who has one daughter who is married and resides in Gonzales—Mrs. J. B. Kennard—and had three children that died in infancy. Joel B. McClure, Mrs. Braches' eldest child, was a soldier of the Civil War, and was one of Terry's Rangers. He was wounded at the battle of Shiloh, which compelled him to leave the service, and he returned home very much broken in health, and never fully recovered, and died a few years later. John M. Ashby, Mrs.

Braches' father, had six children who came to Texas, and one daughter who was born in Gonzales. There are now four daughters living, of whom Mrs. Braches is the eldest. The others are: Isabella, wife of Gen. Henry E. McCulloch, of Seguin; Fannie, wife of Major Roderick Gellhorn, of Big Hill, Gonzales County, and Euphemia, wife of Major William King, of Seguin, all prominent and esteemed people. Mrs. Braches has a pleasant and comfortable home which was erected forty years ago, of material brought overland from Port Lavaca and other places. She owns about two leagues of land, and the most of her fine farm is under cultivation. This farm is located on the old stage road from Columbus to San Antonio, and for over twenty years she kept a stage stand. In 1839, while she and Mr. McClure were returning home from Columbus on horseback, and had reached a point a few miles from home, they encountered a band of hostile Indians, and they at once began a race for their lives, the better speed of their horses alone saving them. While Mrs. McClure was attempting to make a short cut to the timber, she encountered a gully which seemed almost an impassable barrier, but her noble horse made the leap safely and carried its mistress to safety. When the Indians arrived at the gully they all halted and looked with wonder on such a feat, which none of them dared attempt. Mrs. McClure halted at a hill beyond and hurled back a shout of triumph at the Comanches. In all the country no one has seen more of frontier life than has she, and her reminiscences of old-time incidents are of thrilling interest. She has managed her large estate successfully, and is known for miles and miles around, not only for her many charities, but for her knowledge of frontier life and the bravery she displayed during many trying periods. Although somewhat feeble from her many years of toil, she still takes a great interest in current affairs, and being a great reader is well posted on nearly all topics. Her friends are legion, and she is a noble example of those women who braved dangers, hardships and privations that she might secure a home and the comforts and blessings of civilization for her descendants.

WILLIAM H. STEELE. To her noble, pushing, hard-working business men is due the great prosperity, wealth and advancement of Hays County, Texas. To their zeal, energy and integrity will its future greatness be indebted, as it has been to a great degree in the past, and among the names prominent in the real estate interests of this section, is that of William H. Steele, whose home is in San Marcos. He first saw the light of day in Tennessee in 1837, being the fifth of nine children born to James T. and Mary (Harralson) Steele, who were born in Kentucky and Tennessee respectively. They were married in the latter State, but afterwards lived in Kentucky, where the father followed the occupation of merchandising. In 1836 the father came to Texas, accompanied by his brother, William H. Steele, and they were engaged in the mercantile business at old Washington for about three years and were quite successful. At the end of that time the father returned to Kentucky, and there he was called from life about 1846. In 1850 his widow with her family came to Texas, locating first at Washington and then at Seguin, and in the latter place she taught in a female educational institution for some time. She was also in Goliad for some time, and after a short visit in Kentucky she returned to Texas and died in Fayette County in 1871. She was an able and well known educator, and was an active and earnest worker in and a strict member of the Methodist Church. Her father, Herndon

Harralson, was a Virginian, who removed to Tennessee in an early day and spent the rest of his life in Haywood County. He was Captain of a military organization to protect the settlers against Indian depredations, and was prominent in .the affairs of Tennessee in that early day. The subject of this sketch was nine years of age when he was brought to this State, and in the schools of Goliad he received a good practical education. As soon as old enough he engaged in stock trading and continued this occupation up to the opening of the war, when he enlisted in Company E, Twenty-sixth Texas Cavalry, C. S. A., served in the trans-Mississippi Department, and was in the battles of Mansfield, Pleasant Hill and Yellow Bayou. After the war he settled in Fayette County, Texas. and at Fayetteville engaged in merchandising for about six years. During this time he was married to Henrietta Thomas, a native of Texas, and a daughter of Rev. C. W. Thomas a pioneer Methodist preacher of the Lone Star State. In 1875 he came to San Marcos and engaged in land speculation, in which he was very successful and he made a large amount of money. He operated the first ice factory of San Marcos, but has for some years done a real estate business as a member of the firm of Steele & Joyce. To the union of Mr. and Mrs. Steele four children have been born: Charles H., who is a dentist of Laredo; James S., who is a physician of Dripping Springs; Mary S., wife of L. Blachaller, and Mattie W., who died at the age of sixteen years. All the family are members of the Methodist Episcopal Church, and Mr. Steele is a member of the A. F. & A. M. Rev. Charles W. Thomas, father of Mrs. Steele, was born in the Nutmeg State in 1816, a son of Charles and Susan (Warner) Thomas. Rev. Charles Thomas was educated in the noted Yale College, after which he went to Georgia, and was engaged in teaching in that State. He came to Texas in 1840, located at Rutersville, Fayette County, and at once began teaching in the college at that place, continuing there for four years, when he went to Independence and taught one year. He then spent several years in La Grange, and in 1841 was licensed to preach, and did so during the time that he was teaching up to 1856, when he gave up teaching and began devoting himself solely to the ministry, being a member of the Bastrop Circuit. At the end of one year he was changed to the Washington Circuit, and in 1858 was appointed Presiding Elder of the La Grange District, in which capacity he served two years. In 1860-61 he preached on the Navadad Circuit, in the Colorado River Valley, and this occupation he continued to follow throughout the war, in various counties, mostly in the Austin District. In 1851 he traveled on horseback 4,500 miles, and preached about fifteen times each month. He resided in Colorado County until 1887, when he came to San Marcos, soon after which he was taken ill, and his health has not been of the best since. He was married in 1841 to Miss Susan Hill, a native of Georgia and a cousin of Ben H. Hill. She was a daughter of Asa Hill, who came to Texas in 1834 or '35. She died in August in 1886, leaving four children, seven having died. Henrietta, is the wife of William H. Steele; Mary is the wife of a Mr. Chapman; Asa A., is President of the Coronal Institute; and Eugene L., who is the Cashier of the Glover National Bank. Mr. Thomas has been a Mason since 1846.

WILBUR FISK KING. Farming is the primitive occupation of man, and its votaries have usually been men of integrity, public spirit and extremely law abiding. A progressive tiller of the soil in Gonzales County, Texas, is

Wilbur Fisk King, who, in addition to his agricultural duties, ably fills the office of County Surveyor. He was born September 22, 1840, to John A. and Mary (Davidson) King, the former of whom was born in Tennessee and the latter in North Carolina, of English-Irish descent. The father was an experienced Civil Engineer, and his son now has in his possession a compass which his father carried and which bears the marks of a seven days' Indian fight, in which his father was engaged. The latter was a stanch supporter of Gen. Sam. Houston, and often entertained the "First President" at his hospitable home. After the close of the great conflict between the North and South, he spent some years in Mexico engaged in his calling, but upon returning to the States, became a stanch Democrat. He was a member of the Masonic fraternity and belonged to Lone Star Blue Lodge No. 450, at Smiley, and Gonzales Chapter. A Methodist in his religious views, he died in that faith September 9, 1881, while his wife, who also belonged to that church, passed away in 1863. In the schools of Yorktown and Gonzales the subject of this sketch received his education, and when the great Civil War came up was the first to volunteer from DeWitt County, and became a member of the First Texas Mounted Rifles. When his regiment was disbanded twelve months later, he joined Waul's Legion, which was immediately sent across the Mississippi River and became a part of Forrest's Command. He was at Vicksburg, was wounded at Coffeyville by a spent ball, though not seriously, and was in various other minor engagements. He was at home on a furlough, and was just preparing to rejoin his command when news reached him of Lee's surrender. At that time he was totally without means, and he commenced to farm and raise stock in DeWitt County, near Yorktown, but at the end of two years came to Gonzales County and to his present home. He has interested himself in the political affairs of his section, is a Populist in his views, and has clear and well defined reasons for his political convictions. He is now serving his third term as County Surveyor, being first elected on the Independent ticket, next on the Democratic ticket and lastly by the Populists, who have again nominated him for the position, without solicitation on his part. He was married in 1865 to Miss Josephine Walker, a daughter of George H. and Susannah (King) Walker, who were natives respectively of Georgia and Tennessee. After their marriage they removed to Mississippi, and in Marshall County, of that State, Mrs. King was born. Her father was a successful planter and died in 1878, while her mother was called from life in Mississippi in 1873. To Mr. and Mrs. King the following children have been born: Carrie L., John A., Selina H., Mary D., Dora Lee and Cora B. (twins), and Walker W. Mr. and Mrs. King are members of the Methodist Church and he is a worthy member of Lone Star Lodge of Smiley of the A. F. & A. M.

WILLIAM PRESTON WITHERS. This intelligent and substantial citizen and early settler of Lockhart, Texas, is the product of Scott County, Kentucky, where he was born in 1823, the eldest of seven children born to Hugh and Fannie (West) Withers, who were also natives of the Blue Grass State. The paternal grandfather, John Withers, was a Virginian, a farmer by occupation, and about 1800 became a resident of Kentucky. In that State he was married to Mary Emerson, a native of the same State as himself, and there reared his family. He was in the War of 1812 and was also in many Indian battles. In 1829 he with his family moved to Missouri, and until his death he resided in Marion County. He was called from life at the age of sixty-four years and his wife when ninety-four years old. They took many slaves with them to Missouri and he was the most extensive farmer in Marion County. The maternal grandfather, James West, was reared at Fredericksburg, Va., and he also became a resident of Kentucky about the year 1800, and for a long time thereafter he took part in many fights with the Indians. He was married to a Virginia lady, Elizabeth Snell, and about 1824 they removed to Boone County, Missouri, where Mr. West followed farming and the calling of a mechanic. He was a skillful gunmaker, and made firearms for a large community, and the subject of this sketch has in his possession a rifle which was made by his grandfather, which shows skillful workmanship. The latter died in Missouri about 1835. Hugh Withers and Fannie West were married in Kentucky, removed from that State to Missouri in 1828, and followed farming in Marion and Monroe counties. In 1853 he took up his residence in Caldwell County, Texas, and here passed from life in 1868, his wife's death occurring in 1840. They were members of the Christian Church. The subject of this sketch was five years old when taken to Missouri, and in that State he was reared and educated. In 1849 he was one of the first to cross the plains to California, and went thither in a train of twenty wagons and sixty men. He crossed the Rocky Mountains at the South Pass, being 104 days on the journey with ox teams. Thousands of buffaloes were then on the plains, as well as antelope and black-tailed deer, the deer being in the mountains and elk in the Sacramento Valley. He crossed Utah, and at Georgetown, in California, was successfully engaged in mining for a time. He then engaged in trading in beef cattle and mules, but at the end of two years returned home by water to New York, thence to Missouri, where he arrived in 1851. In 1852 he came to Texas and at once bought a ranch in Caldwell County, consisting of 1,000 acres, eight miles north of Lockhart, and he at once stocked his place with 100 mares and engaged in the raising of horses and mules. During the war he served in the Quartermaster's Department at San Antonio, and was engaged in buying stock for the Government. He was mainly engaged in the raising of mules up to 1875, at which time he was the owner of about 2,000 acres of land. He then purchased 200 acres more adjoining Lockhart (part of it now within the corporation) and on this place he made many improvements and has a very comfortable and pleasant home. His land yields about thirty bushels of corn to the acre and an average of one-half bale of cotton. He was first married in 1851 to Miss Sarah E. Berry of Virginia, who died in that State just one month after their marriage, while they were on their wedding tour, and in 1853 he took for his second wife Amanda M. Shropshire, a native of Missouri, but at the time of their marriage a resident of Yazoo City, Miss. She died in 1872, leaving seven children: John Shropshire, Gustavus Bower, Bayford, Fannie, wife of William Randall; Paulina, Madison and Katie. Mr. Wither's third marriage took place in 1876, Josie Virginia Coleman, of Versailles, Mo., but a native of Kentucky, becoming his wife. Mr. and Mrs. Withers are members of the Christian and Baptist churches respectively and are highly respected throughout Caldwell County.

ANTHONY WAYNE POUNCEY. Among the many productive and extensive farms in Gonzales County Texas, the one of which Anthony W. Pouncey is the owner is one of the most valuable, and under his intelligent care and energy his plantation yields abundant harvests. He was born in Twiggs County,

South Carolina, in 1812 to John and Polly (Holmes) Pouncey, natives of North Carolina and South Carolina, respectively. The father was a mechanic by trade and in 1818 removed to Montgomery, Ala., where he built the first frame building ever put up in that place. He was an old line Whig in politics, a member of the A. F. & A. M., and in his religious views was a Hardshell Baptist. He died in Butler County, Alabama, at the age of sixty-six years, and his wife in Florida from an accident at the age of fifty-six years. The immediate subject of this sketch received a limited education in Alabama, but realizing that a good education was of the utmost necessity to a successful business career, he did much private reading after he had reached man's estate, and as a result is well posted on all the current topics of the day and a man of unusual intelligence. In his youth he served an apprenticeship as a mechanic, but abandoned that occupation after a few years. For about four years after his removal to the Lone Star State, which occurred about 1844, he labored as a carpenter in Austin, but at the end of that time he came to Gonzales County, and was in a number of engagements with the Indians and Mexicans, with whom the settlers were having considerable trouble. Since that time his attention has been devoted to tilling the soil and as a result of his labors he has a good farm, a comfortable home, and the respect and esteem of those with whom he has come in contact, and especially is this the case with those with whom he has had business relations, for he is the soul of honor in all his transactions, and believes in " doing as he would be done by." He was elected by the Democratic party to the office of County Sheriff, a position he held four years, and also held the position of Justice of the Peace a like length of time. He was the Democratic nominee for the State Legislature at one time, and would undoubtedly have been elected had he not been prostrated by sickness and unable to look after his interests. For half a century he has been connected with the Hardshell Baptist Church, and is in every respect a true Christian and a worthy man. During the Civil War he served in the Confederate army for nearly four years on the border. He was married to Martha Lane, of South Carolina, in 1836, and their union has resulted in the birth of two children: William F. and Mary Adaline. The mother of these children died in Austin in 1847, and in 1851 he married his second wife, Mary Ann Morrow, a native of Tennessee, by whom he has four boys and two girls: John M., Anthony Wayne, William D., Mary E., wife of J. E. Withers; Joseph E. J., and Sarah E., wife of Stephen I. Cantley.

EDWARD NORTHCRAFT. Architecture is one of the most difficult of all the arts, as it requires a highly cultivated taste, a subtle knowledge of the harmonies of form and proportion and an observation sufficently artistic to catch the spirit of a facade or an entire and complicated structure. When a thorough knowledge of this is combined with that of the builder, one cannot fail of success, and among those who have made a reputation for themselves along these lines is Edward Northcraft, who was born in Indiana in 1833, a son of Edward and Mary Elizabeth (Leath) Northcraft, Virginians by birth, who moved to Indiana in 1821, in which State they resided until 1841, when the State of Missouri became their home. The father was a contractor by occupation, but also followed farming, and died in that State in 1862, the mother's death occurring in 1868. The subject of this sketch was reared and educated in Missouri, and in 1852 crossed the plains to California and was engaged in mining in that State for four years.   He then made a trip to Central America, just in advance of Gen. Walker, and after passing through that country returned to Missouri.   He located at Canton, Lewis County, and engaged in building, stock raising and the livery business, and there continued to follow these occupations until 1867, when he came to San Marcos, Texas, and engaged in contracting, building and farming.   While Governor Ross was in office he held the position of Superintendent of Public Buildings for the State, and during this time superintended the erection of the Reform School at Gatesville, the Orphan Asylum at Corsicana and the State Normal School at Huntsville.   He has also erected court houses in the following counties: Presidio and Upsher.   He has also built about forty jails throughout Texas and has made this line of work a specialty for many years.   He is an able draughtsman, but he is also skilled and experienced in the designing and erecting of all kinds of buildings.   He was one of a quota to secure the Government investigation as to the advisability of erecting a fish hatchery at San Marcos, and in 1892 it was adopted by the Government.   Mr. Northcraft furnished plans and specifications for the dam, which were adopted by the Government, and the contract for its erection and completion were given to him for $7,000, and he fulfilled his contract to the letter.   The dam is most firmly constructed of fine material, and this excellent work is a great credit to the contractor.   Mr. Northcraft's residence, comprising thirty acres, is on the edge of the town.   He has a fine herd of Jersey cattle, owns some of the best thoroughbreds in the State, and is the only breeder of this stock in the immediate vicinity.   He has a handsome residence of his own designing and construction and his home has become known for the hospitality which is extended to all who enter there.   He was married in 1862 to Miss Mary Eliza Donaldson, a native of Illinois and a daughter of Maj. Donaldson (see sketch).   Mr. and Mrs. Northcraft have four children.

HARTWELL KING JONES.   To the person who closely applies himself to any occupation which he has chosen as his calling in life, there can come only one result—that of success—and by the exercise of brain and brawn Hartwell K. Jones has become one of the wealthy farmers of Gonzales County.   He was born in Decatur, Ala., in 1840, the third son born to Signal and Susan (King) Jones, who were natives of the Old North State.   The paternal grandfather, Redding Jones, was a North Carolinian, and died in Wake County, that State, while the maternal grandfather, Hartwell King, died in Alabama, whither he moved from his native State of North Carolina.   The father of the subject of this sketch was a merchant of Decatur, Ala., but became a resident of Texas in 1855, settling near San Antonio.   His wife died in Gonzales, in 1866, and he afterwards returned to Alabama, where he married his deceased wife's sister, and died in 1890.   Hartwell King Jones was a student at Oxford University, Mississippi, but when war was declared in 1861 he returned home and enlisted in Company K, Twenty-fourth Texas Dismounted Cavalry, and was sent to Arkansas and attached to Churchill's Brigade, and was captured at Arkansas Post, at which time he held the rank of Third Lieutenant.   After his capture he was sent to Camp Chase, near Columbus, Ohio, where he was kept a prisoner for five months, after which he was taken to Fort Delaware on the Delaware River, and one month later, in April, 1863, was exchanged at City Point, Va.   His brigade was then attached to Gen. Pat Cleburne's Division of the Army of the Tennessee, was wounded severely in the battle of New Hope Church, near Kenesaw Mountain, and was there captured. At the end of five months he was exchanged and joined Gen. Hood at Decatur, Ala., and was a participant in the Tennessee campaigns. He was in command of the skirmish line the night he joined Hood's army at Decatur, and all that night fought at his old birthplace. He was made Adjutant at the time of his first exchange, was later made Quartermaster. At the New Hope Church fight he went into that battle as a volunteer, as his office exempted him from battle. In the latter part of the war he was made Adjutant General and surrendered with Gen. Johnston as Jonesboro, N. C. He at once returned to his home in Texas and joined his father in merchandising in Gonzales, and was unsuccessful, but soon after turned his attention to farming. In 1871 he located on his present estate, ten miles east of Gonzales, and is now the owner of about 2,600 acres of fine farming land, on which the station of Delworth was located when the railroad was built, and has a fine tract of about 500 acres under cultivation. In 1890 he erected his present handsome residence, which is of modern architecture and very conveniently arranged, and has without doubt one of the finest places in the county. Everything about his place indicates that he is a man of thrift and judgment, and he has the great satisfaction of knowing that the greater bulk of his magnificent property has been acquired through his own far-seeing judgment and determined efforts. October 29, 1867, he was married to Miss Mary F. Braches, a daughter of Mr. and Mrs. Chas. Braches, a sketch of whom appears elsewhere in this work, and to their union one child has been given: Anna Ashby, now the wife of J. B. Kennard, of Gonzales. Mr. and Mrs. Jones are members of the Methodist Church, and he is a member of the A. F. & A. M., Gonzales Lodge No. 30 and Chapter No. 51. He is one of the substantial men of the county, and an upright and highly honored citizen.

JAMES L. MALONE. He whose name heads this sketch is one of the early settlers of Texas, was born in Georgia in 1825, and was the youngest of seven children born to Robert and Agnes (Nichols) Malone, the former of whom was born in Virginia and the latter in Georgia. The paternal ancestors came from Ireland to this country and settled in Virginia, and from this State Robert Malone removed to Georgia in his early youth, in which State he eventually married. In 1846 he became a resident of Texas, and in Hays County of this State he was called from life in 1864, having been a stanch Democrat in his political views throughout life. His wife died in Georgia, of which State her people were prominent residents. James L. Malone was reared on a farm in Georgia, and after coming to Texas, in 1846, made his home in Austin for several years, in the vicinity of which place he was engaged in farming. In 1852 he moved to Hays County and purchased a farm of 1,000 acres near San Marcos, on which he erected a substantial residence and made his home for over forty years. During that time he made many very valuable improvements on the place, and had about 500 acres under cultivation. In 1892 he disposed of his farm and moved to San Marcos, in which place he erected him a handsome home. When he first came to the State the Indians were very troublesome, and the family was compelled to undergo many hardships during these early times. In 1850 he led to the altar Miss Eliza P. Pitts, a native of Georgia and a daughter of Gen. John D. Pitts, who was born on the ocean while his parents were en route from London, England, to this country in 1798. His parents located in South Carolina, and later in Washington County, Georgia, where his father, who was a sea captain prior to coming to this country, died. John Pitts was his eldest son, and he was reared in Georgia, and upon reaching manhood represented Stewart County in the State Legislature for one term. He married Eliza Daves, a native of South Carolina, and in 1841 came to Texas and settled in Austin County, where he was engaged in farming the following year. He afterwards resided four years in Grimes County, and in 1847 came to Hays County and erected about the first residence in San Marcos. The next year he was appointed Adjutant General by Governor Woods, and during the two years that he filled that office his family lived in Austin. He then returned to Hays County and made the first settlement at Stringtown, near San Marcos. He became an extensive farmer and stock raiser, and for years was very active in the political affairs of his section and a delegate to numerous conventions. He was a member of the secession convention at Austin in 1861, but was taken sick there and died on his way home, his wife having previously died in 1851. They were members of the Methodist Episcopal Church, which was the first church organized in San Marcos, and was organized in the home of Gen. Pitts, with seven members enrolled, four of whom were members of his family. Mrs. Malone is the only one of the original seven who is now living. To Mr. and Mrs. Malone the following children have been born: Mrs. E. P. Duggan, Mrs. Laura McKie, Robert Malone, Mrs. Glenn Rylander, Mrs. Pitts Hunter, William Malone, John Malone, dead; Samuel Malone, dead; Davis Malone, Ward Malone, Nina Malone, dead; B. Malone, Wilsie Malone, dead; Alma Malone, Zoe Malone.

DeWitt Clinton Evans. The farming class of America, and especially the southern tier of States, is noted for the degree of intelligence that is possesses among its representatives. Mr. Evans is a most progressive agriculturist, and in this, as well as in other respects, he has endeavored to keep out of old grooves, and has always favored the adoption of new and improved methods in conducting his operations. He is a product of Washington County, Arkansas, where he was born in 1835, a son of Lewis and Eliza (Palmer) Evans, who were born in South Carolina and Tennessee respectively, their marriage occurring in the mother's native State. They later moved to Washington County, Arkansas, where the father eventually held the office of County Sheriff, and for a number of years he was successfully engaged in merchandising at Evansville, a town which was named in his honor. In 1849, like so many others, he was taken with the "gold fever," and made his way across the plains to California, having charge of a wagon train. Besides mining he followed other pursuits in that State up to 1853, when he returned to Arkansas, and almost immediately came with his family to Texas, and for a few years was a resident of DeWitt County. He then came to Gonzales County and purchased a farm of 640 acres, sixteen miles north of Gonzales, on which he made his home for a number of years. He died at the home of his son, DeWitt C., December 20, 1879, and his wife in 1888, both having been earnest members of the Cumberland Presbyterian Church. DeWitt C. Evans received his initiatory education in the public schools of Arkansas, and when the family came to Texas, in 1853, he came with them and for some time made his home with his parents. He later began dealing in horses and cattle, and afterwards turned his attention to stock raising, but in 1861 cast aside all personal considerations to enlist in the service of the Confederacy and became a member of Norris' Regiment, with which he served throughout Texas. Three of his brothers were also in the Confederate army. Mark L. Evans raised a company at Gonzales, of which he became Captain, and which formed a part of Terry's Rangers. He was killed at the battle of Perryville. H. Clay, the other brother, was a private in his brother Mark's company, served throughout the war, and is now a resident of Kansas. Albert G. served in the Commissary Department of Wall's Legion until the termination of hostilities, and is now a prominent commission merchant of St. Louis. Upon his return home after the war had closed DeWitt C. Evans opened a mercantile establishment at Sweet Home, Lavaca County, Texas, but one year later came to Gonzales County, and for three years followed the same occupation in Gonzales. At the end of this time he sold his property there and bought a farm on the Guadalupe River, seven miles north of town, where he now has a fine estate of 1,400 acres, mostly rich river bottom land, 450 acres of which are under cultivation. His land will readily yield twenty-five bushels of corn to the acre, and one-half bale of cotton, and other products of the temperate zone can be raised as well. He has a fine herd of Durham cattle, headed by a fine registered male, but formerly gave much attention to the raising of horses. He is one of the thrifty farmers of the county, and the upright life he has led has won him numerous friends, whom he has the faculty of keeping. August 9, 1866, he led to the altar Miss Georgia Patton, a native of Mississippi, who was brought to Texas in her infancy by her parents, Dr. A. G. Patton and wife, who located at Sweet Home. To Mr. and Mrs. Evans the following children have been born: Ola, who died in infancy; Mark P., Samuel Cicero, Alfred Foster, Albert L., Mattie B., Nellie, and an infant daughter that died unnamed. Mr. Evans is a worthy member of the Baptist Church, while he has been a Mason for a number of years, having become a member of that order in Gonzales.

ROBERT H. FITZGERALD. The subject of this notice is one of the prominent farmers of Gonzales County, Texas, and as his entire life has been passed in ceaseless activity, it has not been without substantial evidences of success, as will be seen by looking over his extensive, productive and well-kept farm. He was born in Polk County in 1852, the eldest of seven children born to William and Nancy Elizabeth (Hubert) Fitzgerald, natives respectively of Tennessee and Mississippi. The father was taken to Georgia by his parents when a boy, was reared and educated (such education as could be had at that time) there. About 1845 he came to Texas and located in the eastern part of the State, afterwards locating in Polk County, and finally in Gonzales County in 1854. He at once energetically engaged in farming and stock-raising, and prior to his death, which occurred in 1863, he had accumulated a large share of this world's goods. His widow, whom he married in eastern Texas, still survives him. She was the daughter of Robert Hubert, who came to Texas from Mississippi, during the early history of this region, and spent the rest of his life as a citizen of the Lone Star State. Robert H. Fitzgerald attended the common schools of the vicinity in which he now lives during his youth, and upon starting out in life for himself he gave his attention to the raising of stock on the open range, an occupation he followed profitably for a number of years. His estate now comprises 4,000 acres, over a considerable portion of which roam large herds of cattle, the most of which are well graded. Being a man of thrift and energy he has 1,200 acres of land under cultivation, and his place is one of the most valuable in the county. The land is extremely productive, and Mr. Fitzgerald spares no pains to increase its productiveness and improvement, with the result that it is increasing in value all the time. He has a handsome and commodious residence, recently completed, pleasantly located, and in every way a most desirable place of abode. On his most productive land corn averages 40 bushels to the acre, while cotton yields three-fourths of a bale. In November, 1871, he was married to Miss Emma Littlefield, a daughter of H. B. Littlefield, a native of Maine, who came to Texas in 1836. He served in the Texas Rebellion, and afterwards devoted his attention to farming, and also successfully conducted a country store for about fifteen years. He died in 1888, leaving two children. To the union of Mr. and Mrs. Fitzgerald seven children have been born: Cora, wife of W. P. Fischer, of Gonzales; Walter Hubert, Archer Hutson, Nettie, Raymond, Gerald and Ethel. Mrs. Fitzgerald is a member of the Methodist church and has in every way proved a helpmeet to her husband.

CHARLES H. WORD. The exhaustless pages of history fail to disclose an older or more honorable calling than that of the agriculturist, and one of its thriftiest and most enterprising exponents is Charles H. Word, of Hays County, Texas. He was born in northern Alabama, in 1840, to Charles and Jane (Bailey) Word, who were natives of the Palmetto State. The father eventually died in Madison County, Alabama, after having followed successfully the life of a farmer. The paternal grandfather, William Word, was born in South Carolina, but became an early settler of Madison County, Alabama. He was a soldier of the Revolutionary War, was an officer of a South Carolina regiment, and died in Alabama. The maternal grandfather, James Bailey, was also a South Carolinian, became a resident of Alabama in 1812, and was eventually called from life in Madison County. In the State of his birth Charles H. Word was reared and received fair educational advantages, and early in 1861 his sympathy for the South led him to enlist in the State Troops of Alabama at Fort Morgan, which was afterwards organized in the regular Confederate service as the seventh Alabama Infantry, and Mr. Word formed a part of Company B, Army of the Tennessee. He was in many battles, was captured in 1863 and was kept a prisoner at Rock Island, Ill., until Aug. 19, 1865. He was in all the engagements in which his command participated from Shiloh to Missionary Ridge, with the exception of the battle of Murfreesboro. After his release from prison he returned to his old home only to find it had been laid waste by the Federal army, and his mother was occupying one of the negro cabins on the old plantation. His brother, William H., was Captain in a Mississippi regiment (the Thirty-second) and was killed at Perryville, while a brother-in-law was killed at Franklin, Tenn., and another at Shiloh. His two widowed sisters were with his mother when he returned. They had a large estate at the beginning of the war, but were practically ruined at the close of hostilities. Charles H. at once rebuilt a home, re-fenced his land and once more began the work of improvement, and the first year made an excellent crop. In 1866 he sold the place and came to Texas, settling in Guadalupe County, where his mother died in 1876, on a farm on the San Marcos River. In 1867, Mr. Word was united in marriage with Sarah V. McGehee, a native of Alabama, and a daughter of Charles L.

McGehee, the latter of whom came to Texas in an early day and built the first sawmill in Bastrop County. He at one time owned large landed interests and many negroes, and was decidedly wealthy before the war. He had the contract to erect the first Capitol building at Austin, Texas, but died, in 1855, before he could fill the same. Mr. Word made his home Guadalupe County until 1885, when he came to Kyle, erected him a comfortable home in this place, and soon after bought a plantation of 600 acres, with 400 acres under cultivation, the entire tract being fertile and valuable. He has been quite active in political matters, has been a worker for his party, and has been a member of several State conventions. He has been a member of Live Oak Lodge No. 304, of the A. F. & A. M. for the past six years, and also belongs to the K. of H. He is a self-made man in every respect, is one of the substantial and valued citizens of Hays County, and he and his family are worthy members of the Methodist Church. He and his wife are the parents of the following children: William A., Mary B., Carl, Vance, Iva, Harry and McGehee.

VIRGIL BENJAMIN COLLEY. He whose name heads this sketch has been successfully engaged in following the primitive occupation of man the greater part of his life, and was initiated into the mysteries of this most worthy of callings on his father's plantation in the State of Georgia. He is a product of Calhoun County, Georgia, where he was born August 10, 1856, the sixth in a family of ten children born to George W. and Rachel (Griffin) Colley, both of whom were also Georgians by birth. George W. Colley devoted his attention to planting throughout life, in which he was very successful, and he also became prominent in the political affairs of his section, and represented his county in the State legislature several terms, and was also a member of the Constitutional Convention that was held in his State. He was elected to the position of County Judge on the Democratic ticket, a position which he ably filled, and to which he added much dignity, and in various other ways he showed that he was a man of intelligence and public spirit. He was a soldier of the Confederacy during the great Civil War. In 1879 he took up his residence in Gonzales County, Texas, and is still living in this section, an honored citizen. His wife was called from this life in the Lone Star State in 1889. The subject of this sketch was reared in his native State, and there received a practical education in the common schools. Like his father before him, he became prominent in the political affairs of his section, and for some time filled the office of Deputy Sheriff and Tax Collector. In 1880 he moved to Texas, where he joined his father and brother in the management of a public cotton gin, and at the same time purchased a ranch and began tilling the soil and raising stock. He made his way almost unaided, and has every reason to be proud of the success that has attended his efforts, for he is now in good financial circumstances, and, what is even better, has the respect and high regard of all who know him. He is a man of marked enterprise, and was one of the chief movers and directors in building the San Antonio & Gulf Co. Shore R. R., which is now in process of construction and which will be a great factor in developing this section of the State. In his political views Mr. Colley is a Populist, has held the position of School Trustee, and in his religious views is a Baptist. He was married in 1888 to Miss Medora Beach, of Gonzales County, and to them two children have been given: Virgil Beach and Mary Brown.

DAVID L. KOKERNOT (deceased). The long life that was granted to him whose name heads this sketch was usefully spent, and his memory will long remain green in the hearts of those who knew and loved him in life. He was born in Holland, December 12, 1805, and was a small lad when brought by his parents to the United States, and in the city of New Orleans he was reared and educated, and there he was left fatherless and motherless. He began life for himself as a merchant, but upon his removal to Nacogdoches County, Texas, in 1835, he for some years gave his attention solely to farming and stockraising. During the trouble between Texas and Mexico he participated in the Rebellion, and was a participant in a number of noteworthy engagements, the most important of which was the battle of San Jacinto. From Nacogdoches County he removed to San Jacinto Bay, where he was for several years successfully engaged in the lumber business, and his next change of location was to Columbus, on the Colorado River. In 1855 he came to Gonzales County, settling in the Big Hill neighborhood, where he bought land and became a stockraiser and farmer, occupations to which his attention was devoted up to the time of his death in 1892, at which time he was in full communion with the Methodist Episcopal Church, of which his widow is also a member. Her maiden name was Caroline Maley, and to them eight children were given, seven of whom are living: Elizabeth, widow of a Mr. Barber; Julia, widow of a Mr. Lang; Lee M.; Amanda, wife of a Mr. St. John; Augusta, wife of M. M. Fitzgerald; Mary, wife of H. B. Littlefield and John William, who is a stockman of Brewster County. Lee M. Kokernot was born June 6, 1836. During the Civil War he became a member of Company I, Eighth Texas Cavalry (Terry's Rangers), and took part in the battle of Stone River and many others of importance, remaining in the service until the war closed, and surrendering with Gen. Johnston at the close, in North Carolina. He then returned to Texas, and was very extensively engaged in stockraising for a number of years. He now owns one of the finest tracts of land in Gonzales County—over 10,000 acres—of which about 450 acres are in cultivation. In 1883 he erected one of the most beautiful private residences in the county, and he and his family are enjoying all the luxuries and advantages that wealth can give them. He was married in 1866 to Miss Sarah Littlefield, who died in 1874, leaving five children, four of whom are now living. In 1876 he wedded his present wife, Miss Hilda Carnes, a native of Louisiana, by whom he has three children. This family is one of the most prominent and highly respected of the county, and the name alone is a passport to popular favor.

WILLIAM SPRAIN. A very extensive farmer and stockman of Austin County, Texas, is William Sprain, who owes his nativity to Prussia, Germany, where he first opened his eyes on the light of day July 16, 1846. In 1850 he was brought by his parents, F. F. and Henrietta Sprain, to America, the voyage thither being made as steerage passengers on a sailing vessel, and which occupied nearly nine weeks. They landed at Galveston, and from there went to Houston, where they rented a blacksmith's shop for their residence while he made preparations for moving further West. He brought the wheels for a wagon with him from Germany, but the remaining portion of the wagon he was compelled to make himself after coming here. As soon as this vehicle was completed he purchased a yoke of oxen and, together with other families, moved to Independence, Washington County, which trip consumed about two weeks. After raising a crop on rented land one season, he purchased a farm of 150 acres near Brenham, but after six years' residence there he purchased 275 acres of prairie land four miles south of Brenham, at $5.00 per acre, and there his home has since continued to be. When he first came to this country he had some means, and consequently fared better than many another "new comer." He now has one of the finest homes in that section of Washington County, and his farm is admirably cared for. By his wife, who died in 1891, he became the father of the following children: Henrietta, widow of J. F. Winkelmann; William, Henry and Betty, twins, the former of whom is dead; Adolph, who resides with his father in Washington County, and J. F., who is book-keeper and secretary for the Smith Bile-Beans Company of New York City. Eleven children were born to them, but the others died young. William Sprain was educated in the public schools of Washington County, and at the age of twenty-two years commenced life independent of his father, but staid with him until January 4, 1871, when he came to Austin County. Here his father presented him with a portion of his present farm, which consists of 660 acres, which was purchased at an average cost of $3.37 per acre. He now has fifty acres of the same under cultivation, and all under fence. He gives considerable attention to the raising of cattle, and it is his intention to improve his breed of stock, mixing them with Herefords and Durhams. He also breeds some very good horses. He was married in 1868 to Miss Dora Tesch, daughter of Louis J. Tesch (see sketch), and to them two children have been born, but both are dead. Mr. and Mrs. Sprain are members of the Lutheran Church, and have many friends throughout this section. During the war Mr. Sprain was detailed to remain at home and operate the grist mill owned by his father for the benefit of the public and the Confederate army. He has said that he ground grain day and night with a guard standing over him to see that he did so. This mill was built in the fall of 1860, and was one of the first steam mills in the county. In 1869 Mr. Sprain's father returned to his old home in Germany, but found things much changed, and said that trees that had been planted by him thirty years before, and were then no larger than bean stalks, had been used for saw logs. The old log house in which the family first located in Washington County had only a dirt floor and a stick and mud chimney, but this state of affairs afterward changed for the better, and the present home is a modern, beautiful and comfortable one. He is now in his eightieth year, is a Lutheran in his religious belief, and in politics has always been a Republican, although his boys are all Democrats.

J. T. DUNCAN. Among the leading attorneys of La Grange, Texas, is J. T. Duncan, a man of unquestioned integrity, and competent in his profession. To a thorough knowledge of the legal science, he joins the general culture derived from a varied and extended course of reading, and is skillful in the presentation of the most involved or intricate facts, and forcible in his manner of dealing with difficult and entangled subjects. He was born in Washington County, Texas, in 1854, and is the son of George J. and Elizabeth (Dallas) Duncan, natives of Kentucky. This family was one of the earliest and most prominent ones of Virginia. The grandmother of our subject on the paternal side was a native of North Carolina, but the maternal grandparents were natives of Pennsylvania. The latter came to the Lone Star State in 1833, and settled near Independence, Washington County. In 1839 the father of our subject came to Washington County, and engaged in farming. He was a single man then, but married Miss Dallas in 1851, afterward residing in Washington County until 1880, when he moved to Milam County, where he died in 1893. He was in Summersville's campaign against the Mexicans in 1840, and proceeded as far as Laredo. This expedition was for the purpose of forever settling the boundary line between Mexico and Texas, and this body of hardy Texans suffered many hardships on this trip. At one time Mr. Duncan got lost from his command, and before reaching the main army suffered greatly. To his marriage were born five children. J. T. Duncan was educated in Baylor University, of Independence, graduating from that institution in 1877, and immediately afterward he came to La Grange, Texas, where he entered the law office of Timmons & Brown. In June, 1878, he was admitted to the practice of law in this State, and subsequently formed a partnership with R. J. Andrews, the same continuing until 1881, when Mr. Andrews died. He was appointed Mayor of this town in 1878, and was then elected to the office, his term expiring in 1882. Since that time he has not aspired to public positions. Mr. Duncan is attorney for the San Antonio & Aransas Pass Railway Company, a position he fills to the entire satisfaction of all the people interested. January 1, 1885, Mr. Duncan formed a partnership with Judge L. W. Moore, the style of the firm being Moore & Duncan. Judge Moore is one of the oldest and best known attorneys in the State, being ex-Member of Congress and ex-Judge of this judicial district. Mr. Duncan confines himself strictly to the practice of his profession, and is remarkably well adapted to the requirements of the same, and his strength lies in his great fairness and liberality, coupled with a keen discernment of motives behind actions.

DR. DANIEL M. REAGAN. In addition to curing the ills to which poor humanity is heir, Dr. D. M. Reagan is also quite extensively engaged in tilling the soil, and in both these useful and honorable callings he has met with a more than average degree of success. He is a product of Gadsden County, Florida, where he was born in 1828, the fourth of seven children born to William and Minnie (McLean) Reagan, who were North Carolinians. The paternal grandfather was John Reagan and at an early date his ancestors settled in the Old North State, coming thither from Ireland. The maternal grandfather was a native of Scotland. After the marriage of William Reagan, he moved with his family to Florida, at a time when the Indians were very hostile, and on one occasion while he was from home hunting the Indians, he, with several others, was besieged in a block-house. During this time the Indians attacked his home, which was defended by Mrs. Reagan and several negro women, and though numerous attempts were made to burn the house down they were unsuccessful and the women managed to keep the Indians at bay, by shooting at them through the loop-holes, until morning. The Indians then left and the next night Mrs. Reagan, with her several children and the negro women, sought refuge in the timber in an adjoining creek bottom where they remained all night. The next day the men returned. Such troubles, and others more or less dangerous, extended over the period of Dr. Reagan's youth, and, as was to have been expected, he received limited educational advantages. He was left an orphan in early childhood, also, for his father died in 1836, at the age of thirty-six years, and his mother prior to that time. In 1847 he entered the service of the

J. H. McElroy.

United States for the Mexican War as a member of a Florida Battalion, and upon his arrival in Mexico was promoted to the rank of Major. He went by water to Tampico, then to Vera Cruz, and was at anchor in the bay when Gen. Scott bombarded that city. He then marched inland to the City of Mexico, and after the battle of Jallapa, the Florida battalion was attached to a Massachusetts regiment and then participated in numerous engagements. He was honorably discharged at Vera Cruz and was paid off on his arrival in New Orleans, and he also at this time sold a land warrant. With this money he took a four years' course of literary training at Geneva, Ala., then returned to Euchana, Fla., and began reading medicine with Dr. W. D. McCranie, after which he attended a course of lectures at New Orleans. In 1853 he came to Texas, located at Lockhart, continued his studies with Dr. D. Port Smith, the pioneer physician of that place, and the next year went to Millican, where he practiced his profession for one year. In 1857 he was married to Miss Elizabeth Buttrell, a native of Georgia, and a daughter of William Buttrell, who was an early settler of Leon County, Texas. Soon after this event Dr. Reagan purchased a farm of 640 acres, of which 200 acres are under cultivation, at once settled on this place and practiced medicine and tilled the soil until 1862, at which time he became Assistant Surgeon in the Twelfth Texas Cavalry, commanded by Col. William Parsons. He was soon after made Surgeon of this regiment, in which capacity he served until the war closed, participating in all the engagements of the Red River campaign. During the war, while stationed at Houston, he was appointed Medical Purveyor to go to Mexico to purchase medical supplies, by Gen. Kirby Smith, and after purchasing a large supply at Brownsville, returned to his command, with which he remained until the war closed. In 1860 he had entered the Graffenburg Medical Institute and after taking a course of lectures graduated therefrom. In 1866-67 he was in Galveston by invitation and attended a course of lectures at the college there. In the last mentioned year he located in Limestone County where he practiced until the winter of 1868, then went to Red Rock, Bastrop County, where he made his home until 1874. In that year he married Mary F. Meredith, for his first wife had been called from life December 19, 1865, and soon after his second marriage he moved to Manchaca, in 1880 to Mountain City and in 1881 came to Kyle, of which place he was the first resident physician. Here he remained until 1888 when his residence, office, entire stock of medicines, instruments, library, etc. were destroyed by fire, and he then came to Buda where his home has since been and where he has built up a lucrative practice. He is a member of the Bastrop County Medical Society and was formerly a member of the Texas State Medical Society. He is the owner of a good farm near Manchaca, Texas, of which fifty acres are under cultivation. By his present wife he has one child—Minnie, wife of W. H. Birdwell, a merchant of Buda. The doctor and his wife are members of the Baptist Church, politically he is quite active, and socially he is an agreeable and pleasant gentleman to meet.

JEFFERSON DAVIS PATTESON. Although many men in Gonzales County, Texas, are successfully engaged in tilling the soil and in raising stock, none of them all deserve more honorable mention than Jefferson Davis Patteson, for he is thrifty, progressive, industrious and as a natural sequence—successful. He is a product of the county in which he now resides, for here he first saw the light of day on the 27th of March, 1857, his parents being George

18

and Martha (Verhein) Patteson, the former of whom was a native of Tennessee, in which State he engaged in planting until his removal to Texas several years prior to the birth of the subject of this sketch.   Mr. Patteson was a lifelong Democrat, and at the time of his death, in 1870, was a consistent member of the Methodist Church.   His widow, who still survives him, is a member of the same church.   The immediate subject of this sketch is essentially a self-made man and self-educated, for his father was called from life when he was small, and at an early age he was compelled to fight life's battle for himself.   By dint of conscientious toil, judicious economy, and keen business foresight, he managed to obtain a start, and after this had been made, the rest came much easier.   He now devotes his attention to the raising of Devon cattle, Cleveland Bay horses, the pacers having his most undivided attention, and Berkshire hogs and has met with flattering success in this branch of agriculture.   He is an extensive land owner, and is one of the wealthiest men in his county, and his land is especially well adapted for grazing, being abundantly supplied with water and pasturage.   Mr. Patteson has done much to raise the grade of stock in his section, and his stock animals are especially well bred and valuable.   A man of practical good sense and sagacity, he has bent the force of circumstances to his will and is in the enjoyment of a competency which is the result of his own honest toil, and therefore fully merited.   Politically he has always supported the men and principles of the Democratic party, but aside from some minor positions, such as Road Supervisor and School Trustee, he has never sought, or desired to hold, public office.   He was married in 1883 to Miss Mary Ann Webb, by whom he is the father of six children: Walter L., Jesse W., Arthur L., Ethel M., Jeff B. and Mary E.   Mr. and Mrs. Patteson are worthy members of the Methodist Episcopal Church.

JOHN FOSTER BEASLEY, M.D.   He whose name heads this sketch has been familiar from earliest boyhood with the occupation of farming, for his father was a planter, and by him he was initiated into its mysteries.   In addition to this his humanity, natural kindness of heart, and earnest desire to benefit his fellows, has found expression in the field of medicine, for he has been a practitioner of the "healing art" for many years, and has won a reputation for skill and knowledge of his profession which is by no means local.   He is a native of Assumption Parish, La., where his eyes first opened on the light of day February 14, 1829, his father being a planter by occupation and a mail contractor.   In the schools of his natal State the subject was initiated in the mysteries of the "world of books," and being a youth of discernment and possessing a fine intellect, spiced with sufficient spirit to prevent him from being what is termed a "molly coddle," he made good progress in his studies, and, after making up his mind to study medicine, was sent to Charleston, S. C., where he attended medical lectures for some time, afterwards graduating from the Philadelphia College of Medicine in 1852.   After successfully practicing his profession for several years in northern Louisiana, he came to Gonzales County, Texas, in 1855, and here his home has been ever since.   Immediately upon his arrival in this section he made a purchase of a considerable tract of land, which he at once began improving and upon which his home has since been.   He has added greatly to the value of his property in various ways, has a comfortable and hospitable home, and has successfully conducted his place in conjunction with his large practice.   He has always supported the measures of the Democratic party, and his reasons for his political convictions are clear and well defined. In 1863 he was a member of Waul's famous legion, the campaigns of which are matters of history. Socially he is a member of Lone Star Lodge No. 450 of the A. F. & A. M. He was married March 15, 1860, to Miss Mary J., daughter of W. M. Mangum and D. C. Dennis, and to their union five children have been given: Leslie, Henry A. W., Pierre, Lela, wife of C. D. Dixon, and Corinne. On September 27, 1894, he was called upon to mourn the death of his beloved wife, who now lies buried in the cemetery of Lone Star Lodge No. 450 A. F. & A. M.

CHRISTIAN H. VICK. The calling which occupies the time and attention of this gentleman is as old as the world, and the majority of those who have followed it have been noted for their honesty and many other worthy traits of character. Christian H. Vick is no exception to this rule, for he is a useful, law-abiding citizen, and in pursuing the calling of agriculture he has been successful. He was born in Mecklenburg, Germany, February, 1837, a son of Christian and Dora Vick, also natives of that country. The father was a shipbuilder by trade, and died in Europe when the subject of this sketch was a small boy, after which his widow with her eight children came to America in 1852 and settled in Austin County, Texas, where the mother resided until her death in 1892, at the age of eighty-eight years. Five of her eight children survive. She was twice married, and by her first husband, Mr. Slabourn, became the mother of three children: Mary, wife of John Slenze, John, and Sophia, wife of Fritz Forth. Mr. Vick's children are as follows: Henry, who was killed at Richmond, Va.; Mena, widow of August Kruser; Dora, wife of Adolph Miburn and Christian H., Joseph, who was killed in one of the battles around Richmond, Va. When Mrs. Vick brought her family to this country, she arrived in straitened circumstances, but lived to see her children in good circumstances and well respected. Christian H. Vick was fifteen years old upon his arrival in this country, and the first day that he was in the Crescent City, while listening to the negroes count staves, learned to count one hundred in English, which shows his aptitude for learning. The acquirement of the language was comparatively easy for him, and in all respects he has shown himself to be apt and intelligent. He came to Austin County with his mother and with her and his brothers rented land for several years. He remained with his mother until 1856, when he left home and became a cowboy, and one of the longest drives of beef cattle ever made was made by Mr. Vick in 1858, while in the employ of Kyle & Terry, driving from where the village of Sealy now stands to Chicago, going via Fort Leavenworth, Fort Scott, and to Tipton, Mo., the terminus of the Missouri Pacific, and from there on to Chicago. This trip consumed eight months and the journey to that city was made on horseback. He returned by the Illinois Central Railroad to Cairo, up the river to St. Louis, where he spent two or three days, then to New Orleans, from there to Galveston, thence to Richmond, and from there home, a distance of thirty miles, during which time they did not see a house. In 1862 he joined an independent battery of light artillery, was attached to Col. Bates' Regiment, and was in the trans-Mississippi Department until the war closed, not participating in any particular engagement. He was a teamster and at Berwick City, La., captured a commissary team, which he was allowed to drive until the close of the war, and two of the mules were presented to him, the other four being taken by the officers of the company. The company of which he was a member stood guard all one night to save this team for Mr. Vick, in appreciation of his uniform kindness to them in relieving them of heavy loads, which he placed in the munition wagon which he always drove. On his way home after the war he met an old comrade on foot who had left Shreveport before he did and Mr. Vick presented him with one of his mules, which that gentleman afterwards sold in San Felipe for $150. He at once returned to his former occupation, continuing until December 20, 1866, when he was married to Miss Mary Bushwall, a native of Austria, whose parents died soon after reaching this country. After his marriage Mr. Vick engaged in farming and stock raising, and after renting land for two years, purchased 160 acres of improved land for $5 per acre. This he sold in 1871 for $8.25 per acre, and then bought his present farm of 632 acres, which at that time was unimproved, paying for the same $1.05 per acre. He now has 150 acres in a fine state of cultivation, and well improved with all necessary farm buildings, which are sightly and substantial. All this land is under fence. Mr. Vick raises a superior breed of horses and mules, and some graded cattle. He has taken little interest in politics, although he is a stanch Democrat. His family consists of the following children: Chessie, wife of James T. Boyd; Fannie, wife of C. L. Corey; Jennie, John, Daisy, Dora, Christian, and Frank (deceased). Mr. and Mrs. Vick are members of the Missionary Baptist Church, and socially he belongs to Sealy Lodge of the K. of H. He is an upright and worthy citizen and numbers his friends by the score.

CAPT. WILLIAM DE WOLF PECK. In few branches of trade has the march of progress wrought such a veritable revolution as in the hardware and agricultural implements and kindred lines of business. What with inventions, improvement and the development of skill something closely akin to perfection has been reached in this department of industrial activity. A popular house is that owned and operated by Capt. William De Wolf Peck at Gonzales. He was born in Bristol, Rhode Island, February 21, 1832, a son of Nicholas and Amy (Bradford) Peck, who were also born in "Little Rhody," the former being a merchant and sea captain. In 1835 he came to Texas and lived in Gonzales, and joined the Texas army, and was a resident of that place at the opening of the Texas Rebellion, and was there, when the town was burned by order of General Sam Houston in 1836, and retreated with the army to San Jacinto and was a participant in the battle of that name. After the battle, in 1836, he returned to the State of his birth, and returned to Texas in 1837, bringing his eldest son, Benjamin B. Peck, with him, and lived in Gonzales a short time, and then settled on his "headright league of land," near Texana, where he died in December, 1838. His widow and the remaining members of his family, with the exception of the subject of this sketch, remained in Rhode Island, and there Mrs. Peck breathed her last in 1889. Benjamin B. Peck took an active part in the Indian campaigns in Texas, and was in many fights, but being in bad health at the commencement of the Civil War, and not able to take the field, he was appointed Provost Marshal for the Confederate Government during the Civil War, but died at Gonzales in May, 1863, where he had resided for many years, having engaged in the mercantile business at that place in 1845. The subject of this sketch was sixteen years of age when he came to Texas in January, 1849, and here he clerked for some time in his brother's store in Gonzales, continuing until January, 1855, when he became a partner in the business, the firm taking the name of B. B. Peck

& Co. They continued to do business together until the commencement of the war, when they gave their services to the Confederacy. William joined a volunteer company that marched to San Antonio, under command of Gen. Ben McCulloch, and captured the government property there, and then marched to Indianola and captured the property there. On October 28, 1861, he enlisted at Galveston in Capt. B. Shropshire's Company F, Nichol's Infantry Regiment, Texas Volunteers, and on April 12, 1862, re-enlisted in the cavalry battalion of Waul's Texas Legion, and helped to organize Company D, of which he was elected First Lieutenant, which became a part of Waul's Legion, and was at once sent across the Mississippi River to Vicksburg. After remaining there a short time the cavalry was detached from the Legion, and ordered to Corinth, Miss., but on arriving at Lumkins Mills, below Holly Springs, met Gen. S. Price's army after their retreat from Corinth. Soon after crossing the Mississippi River he was made Captain of his company, and he was with Gen. Van Dorn on his raid and capture of Holly Springs, and operated in Mississippi, Tenessee, Alabama, and a short time in Florida, at different times under commands of Gens. N. B. Forrest, Stephen D. Lee, J. R. Chalmers, and a short time under Gen. Wort Adams. His command participated in the attact on Fort Pillow under Gen. Forrest, and was in many hotly contested battles. In the spring of 1865 he returned to Texas on a leave of absence and recruiting expedition, and while there the war closed. In 1865 Capt. Peck resumed business at Gonzales, and soon had all the debts which he and his brother had contracted before the war, paid in full. He then took in Capt. A. G. Evans as partner, under the firm name of Peck & Evans, and for a time operated extensively in the cattle and mercantile business. In 1875 that firm was dissolved, and since that time he has been doing business in his own name and has devoted the most of his attention to the mercantile business, and now carries a fine stock of hardware, crockery, glassware, woodenware and agricultural implements. His stock is well chosen, and as he sells at reasonable prices, he has a large patronage. He is looked upon as one of the pioneers of the place, and he has a warm place in the esteem of all whom he knows, for his many worthy qualities as a citizen and business man have won the respect of all. The headright league of land his father entered after coming to this State is still owned by him and the other heirs. Capt. Peck was married September 4, 1866, to Mrs. Mary E. (Jeffries) Peck, a native of Kentucky, and a resident of Texas since 1853. They have two children living: John C., and Callie L. Baron. Mrs. Peck is a member of, and an earnest hard worker in, the Christian Church, and he has been a member of the I. O. O. F. since 1851, and a member of the Grand Lodge of Texas.

EDWARD G. MAGRUDER, M.D. This practitioner of the "healing art" has been very successful in pursuing his calling, a state of affairs which is clearly shown by the large practice which he commands. He was born in Giles County, Virginia, February 12, 1857, being the youngest of ten children born to Patrick H. and Evelinah (Dulaney) Magruder, natives of old Virginia. The former was born in Washington, D. C., in 1803, was taken to Virginia when a lad and was there living at the time of the Civil War, engaged in milling, being too old for service. In 1882 he came to Texas, and here breathed his last about one year later, at the age of eighty years. His father was a brother of the celebrated Gen. Magruder, and was with Patrick Henry in the early sessions of Congress, and doubtless took an active part in the War of Independence. The wife of P. H. Magruder, died in Texas in 1887. Their children were named as follows: Mary, widow of A. G. Rider, of Virginia, now of Sealy, Texas; William H., of New Orleans; Addie, the deceased wife of Robert Green, of Virginia; Fortunatus B., M.D., resides in San Angelo, Texas; Robert (deceased); Olivia, is the wife of W. G. Pratt, of Virginia; Marshall (deceased); Lucy A, wife of W. A. Sanders, of Sealy; Emma L., wife of James Phillips, of Sealy, and Edward G. The latter was educated in the schools of his native State, and at the age of seventeen years commenced the study of medicine, taking his first course of lectures in the medical department of the University of Louisville, Ky., when twenty-two years of age, where he graduated in the class of 1879–80, and immediately after located in Sealy, where he was not compelled to wait long for patronage, and is now the oldest physician of the village. He does a general practice, but is especially skilled in surgery and makes a specialty of that branch of his profession. He was married in 1889 to Miss Bettie G. Ward, a native of Austin County, Texas, and a daughter of Nathan P. and A. C. Ward, a sketch of whom appears in this work. Dr. and Mrs. Magruder are the parents of two children: Hazel and Henry W. Dr. Magruder is the local surgeon for the G. C. & S. F., and the M. K. & T. R. R'ys, and is the medical examiner for several insurance companies. His practice extends over a wide territory, and when he first engaged in the practice of his profession it covered many miles. He is a member of S. F. Austin Lodge No. 1952, of the K. of H., Sealy Lodge No. 665 of the K. and L. of H., and the J. R. Castleton Lodge of the K. of P., and is medical examiner for all three lodges. Politically he is a Democrat and on all occasions supports its men and measures. He and his wife are members of the Missionary Baptist Church, in which he is one of the deacons and he has always taken a deep interest in religious matters. The doctor had four brothers who served in the Civil War, under Stonewall Jackson. Their names were: William H., Fortunatus B., Robert and Marshall. Fortunatus B. was wounded four times, and he and William H. were both captured, were imprisoned in New York, were finally exchanged and were with Lee at the time of the surrender. The doctor's success in healing the sick and afflicted has been remarkable, and he will without doubt rise to eminence in his profession, for he has the talent and the ambition to do so.

GEORGE C. WILLRICH (deceased). The prudent ways and careful methods of German settlers are conspicuous in Fayette County, Texas, where many representatives of that race have settled, and George C. Willrich was no exception to the rule. Honest, upright and persevering, no man held a higher place in the estimation of the people of the county than he. He was born in Germany, January 19, 1798, son of William W. Willrich, who occupied a prominent position under the French Government. The latter's wife was a Miss York, of English parentage. George C. Willrich was attending school at Magdeburg during the time that Napoleon was at the height of his glory, and he and a number of other boys ran away from school and joined Blucher's portion of the army. At that time he was between fifteen and sixteen years of age. During the battle of Waterloo Mr. Willrich, although but sixteen years of age, commanded a regiment and was the youngest officer in that historical battle. Afterwards he returned to Goettingen and graduated at the university there while still quite young. After finishing his education he married Miss Gertrude E. Bostleman, and subsequently secured a government position. Later still he received the appointment of Judge of the District Lüneburg. His wife died and he was married again. In 1846 he came to America, bringing with him his second wife and the children of both unions. The children of the first marriage were named as follows: George W., deceased; Margaret, Charles, Paulina, deceased; Martha, deceased; Charlotte, deceased, and Franciska. To the second union were born these children: Julius, Anna, Otto and Louisa. After coming to this country Mr. Willrich purchased a number of slaves, a large portion of land, and engaged actively in farming and stock-raising. The results were very satisfactory, and at his death, which occurred April 30, 1876, when seventy-eight years old, he left his family in very comfortable circumstances. His eldest son, George W. Willrich, was born in the old country July 6, 1823, and there received a thorough education. Later he began the study of law, graduated, and came to the United States with his father in 1846. In 1848, during the revolution in his country, he went back to take part in the war, but on landing found it practically over. He wrote a number of articles on the matter, was apprehended before he could return to America, and kept a prisoner for six months before he could make his escape. He hid in the house of a friend in Hamburg, and remained secreted for a year before he made his final escape. Returning to America in 1853, after an absence of five years, he began teaching at Rutersville, Fayette County, Texas, a military school, and, being a man of superior literary attainments, became professor of languages. Later he taught at Baylor University, Independence, Washington County, this being the first university established in the State, and was professor of languages in that institution also. On the 3d of June, 1860, he was married to Miss Liane DeLassaulx, a native of Alsace, and the daughter of Otto DeLassaulx (see sketch). Prof. Willrich died April 28, 1861, soon after marriage, leaving a son, George. Mrs. Willrich afterwards married George Tuttle, of Flatonia. Young George Willrich was educated in the schools of St. Mary's College, San Antonio, and Jesuit College, Seguin, and finished in St. Mary's College, Galveston, where he graduated with considerable honor, taking first place in nearly all his studies. He then studied law under Gen. Felix Robertson, of Waco, from 1882 to 1884, and was admitted to practice in the courts of the State in the latter year. Since then Mr. Willrich has confined himself to the practice of law, and has met with more than ordinary success. He is a man of positive character, strong intellect, and one who has won the respect and admiration of all. In politics he has ever been interested in the welfare of the Democratic party, and in May, 1886, he was appointed County Attorney. In 1888 he was re-elected to that position without opposition. His practice in the civil and criminal courts of the county increased so rapidly that in May, 1890, he resigned the office of Prosecuting Attorney to take charge of his extensive law practice. For some time he has been in partnership with Capt. R. H. Phelps, who is one of the pioneer attorneys of LaGrange. The law practice of this firm is second to none in the city, and for a lawyer of his years Mr. Willrich has a reputation which few enjoy, and which older practitioners might well envy. He has made his way in life unaided, and has been more than ordinarily successful. He owns considerable real estate, and has a good farm in a fine state of cultivation. He selected his wife in the person of Miss Olivia Tuttle, a native of this county, and daughter of G. W.

and Mary A. (Karnes) Tuttle, early settlers of this county. George Will-rich's grandparents on both sides of the house were of very prominent families in their native country, and brought with them to the United States their coat of arms. Both families espoused the cause of the South during the Civil War, but, though the secession of the Southern States was a failure, no more loyal subjects resided in the State of Texas than they.

DR. ROBERT J. JAMESON. The standing of every profession is marked by the character of the man who represents it. Deplorable as it is, it is never-theless true that the inducements offered by the medical profession for the gratification of personal ambition and the accomplishment of selfish ends have drawn into it men whose influence has been only to degrade the profes-sion. When, therefore, we find a man of true worth and genuine ability giving his energies to the elevation of the profession, it is but just that he should receive the eulogies of men. Such an one is Dr. Robert J. Jameson, who was born in Georgia in 1858, the fifth of eight children born to Wesley and Mary (Jordan) Jameson, who were natives of South Carolina and North Carolina, respectively. The father was a successful tiller of the soil, and dur-ing the Civil War was killed in the battle of Kenesaw Mountain. His father was a native Virginian, an early emigrant to South Carolina, in which State his declining years were spent. His father was a native of Ireland. The subject of this sketch was educated in the State of his birth, and in 1877 began the study of medicine. After a time he began attending lectures in the Medical Department of the University of Georgia, at Augusta, and in 1881 was graduated from the same as an M. D. He at once began practicing his profession at Red Clay, Ga., being there associated for two years with Dr. W. B. Wells. From that time until 1885 he was a practitioner of Apison, Tenn., then came to Texas, located at Buda, of which place he is the eldest medical practitioner. He has taken a post-graduate course at the Policlinic College of New Orleans, and has given special study to diseases of the ear, nose and throat, in the treatment of which he has been very successful, as he has also been in general practice. He keeps in constant touch with his pro-fession, and has already become well known as a skillful medical practitioner. He has made many friends in the Lone Star State, and has a large and con-tinually increasing practice. The doctor is a great lover of fine horses, and has some fast travelers in his stud. He engaged in the breeding of racing stock in 1892, and he has some fine thorough and standard bred animals. He has a fine male horse—"Hal"—which he brought to this State from Georgia, and he has some exceptionally fine thoroughbred mares, and is endeavoring to breed a cross with standard males. He is also the owner of a Tennessee jack, which is without doubt the finest animal of the kind in the State. His stable is well fitted up for his stock, and he has a private race track over which he trains and speeds his animals. The doctor is a member of the Southwestern Association of Railway Surgeons and State Medical Societies of Tennessee, and is local surgeon of the I. & G. N. R. R. at Buda. His brother, Dr. G. M. Jameson, is a graduate of the Medical College of Mem-phis, Tenn., and is now located at Kyle, where he has a finely fitted up drug store.

WILLIAM MONTGOMERY PHILLIPS. This intelligent and thoroughly wide-awake man of affairs is successfully engaged in the mercantile business at Smiley Lake, Gonzales County, Texas, but is a product of Caroline County,

Virginia, where he was born January 4, 1814, his parents being Thomas and Elizabeth (White) Phillips, who were also natives of the Old Dominion, the former being of Dutch, and the latter of Irish descent. The maternal grandfather was a Captain in the American Army under Gen. Jackson and was a participant in the famous battle of New Orleans during the War of 1812. Thomas and Elizabeth (White) Phillips, died in Virginia when the subject of this sketch was quite young, and he was left to fight life's battles as best he could. With a determination and a desire to rise in the world, he wisely made the most of every opportunity that presented itself, and through his own efforts he acquired a good practical education, amply sufficient for all the ordinary duties of life. From his native State he removed to Fayette County, Tennessee, in 1835, and there was engaged in agricultural pursuits until 1839, when he took up his residence in Sabine County, Texas, where he was engaged in following his former pursuit until he dropped his farming implements to join Hayes' Texas Rangers, under Capt. Benton, and was a participant in the Salado fight near San Antonio. He was also under Summerville in the Mier expedition, but was of that larger portion of the forces that turned back when the countermand came from Gen. Sam. Houston, just before the engagement and capture of the 170 adventurous spirits at Mier. He received a headright claim upon coming to Texas for 640 acres on the head of the Brazos River, and for several years after the close of the Mexican War was engaged in farming this land. In 1859 he opened a mercantile establishment in the town of Gonzales, but when the great Civil War opened, the yard measure was thrown aside for the army musket, and donning a suit of gray he enlisted in Company B, of the Cavalry Department of Wall's Legion, and served in the Army of the Tennessee, being under Gen. Forrest at the Siege of Vicksburg. He was also at Holly Springs and other engagements, and during the entire war he served in the Army of the Tennessee as Forage Master. A short time before the close of the conflict he became disabled and at the time of Gen. Lee's surrender he was at home on furlough. He at once resumed farming, which he followed for about one year after the war, then opened a mercantile establishment at Rancho, but in 1883 removed his stock of goods to Smiley Lake, and here has conducted a successful business ever since, his patronage being large and continually increasing. He is a highly honored business man of his section, straightforward and thoroughly reliable, and although he has been successful from a pecuniary standpoint, he has received his best reward in the respect which is accorded him by all. In politics he has always been a Democrat, and has held the office of County Commissioner two terms. He is a Royal Arch Mason, and is a worthy member of Gonzales Lodge. He was married in the State of Virginia to Miss Catherine Partlow, who died after having borne her husband three children, Elizabeth, Minerva and Sarah, all of whom are dead. In 1840 he wedded Miss Mary Brown, of Sabine County, Texas, who is also deceased. The last union resulted in the birth of an interesting family of children.

G. N. DILWORTH. A noteworthy business man of Gonzales, Texas, is he whose name heads this sketch, and the welfare and progress of the town and county in which he resides, has always been of paramount interest to him. His walk through life has been attended with success, for he not only commands the respect of his fellows, but has accumulated a comfortable fortune, the result of his own shrewdness and far-sightedness. He owes his nativity to Georgia where his eyes first opened on the light of day in 1837. He was the eldest of three children born to James C. and Elizabeth F. (Norwood) Dilworth, who were natives, respectively of Florida and Georgia. The father was a planter throughout life, and was following this occupation at the time of his death in 1842. In 1850 the widow with her children came to Texas, and on a farm in Gonzales County they made their home for some time, the mother dying there in 1884. The early education of G. N. Dilworth was acquired in the public schools of Gonzales, and upon starting out in life for himself it was as a tiller of the soil. In 1858 he came to the conclusion that "it is not good for man to live alone," and accordingly wooed and won for his wife Miss Martha E. Huff, after which he continued farming until 1873, when he came to Gonzales and engaged in the banking business. The bank with which he was connected had been established in 1866 by Lewis & Dilworth. Hugh Lewis, James C. Dilworth and himself comprising the firm, and James C. Dilworth, being a brother of our subject. He died in 1878. G. N. Dilworth took active charge of the business in 1873, and has continued at its head ever since. The banking business is a clean and honorable one and the most astute and able minds of the country find in that line the most congenial work, and this has been the case with Mr. Dilworth, and the bank of which he is the head merits special mention, because intelligent and practical business men control it, and because it is substantially founded. The bank has been located in its present building since 1885, and is well furnished and equipped. In addition to his interest in this institution Mr. Dilworth is the owner of a large ranche and raises, buys and sells cattle which he ships extensively to northern markets. Besides this property he is the owner of two fine farms, and considerable unimproved land in the county, a considerable portion of each being under cultivation, and well improved. He is also owner of the Battle Grounds where the first battle for the Independence of Texas was fought. Mr. Dilworth was largely instrumental in securing the branch of the Southern Pacific Railroad in 1881, and again in 1889 was a hard and earnest worker for the establishment of the branch of the San Antonio & Aransas Pass Railroad, his efforts being successful in each case. He was extremely liberal in the use of his means to complete these enterprises, and as a slight recognition of the inestimable services rendered by him the people of the Aransas Pass Railroad named the station of Dilworth, in this county, in his honor. His union has resulted in the birth of eight children, six of whom are now living. Mr. Dilworth and his wife are members of the Baptist Church.

JOHN M. HARRISON. This leading merchant and banker of Flatonia, Texas, is a man whose earnest and sincere efforts to make life a success are well worth the imitation of all. His industry, sobriety, and economy as well as his honesty, have served to place him among the most prominent men in this section, and by all he is highly esteemed. He first saw the light of day in Quincy, Ill., May 11, 1830, and of the five children born to his parents, Robert P. and Elmira C. (Wilcox) Harrison, he was second in order of birth. His parents were natives of Virginia and Kentucky, respectively. They moved from Quincy to Washington County, Missouri, when our subject was an infant, and there resided for some time. Later they moved to Christian County, Kentucky, and there made their home until 1849, when Dr. Harrison moved to Russellville, Logan County, Ky., from there to Texas, in 1851, settling for one year in Washington County. He then moved to Fayette County, and there died in 1878, after a long and useful life. His wife died in Kentucky. Their children were named as follows: J. P., John M., Mary E., wife of J. B. Hill, of Gonzales County; Ellen A., wife of E. H. Ibey, of Bosque County, and R. R., of this city, Flatonia. John M. Harrison received his education in the schools of Christian County, Kentucky, and remained with his father until his fifteenth year, when he began clerking in a dry-goods store in that State, remaining thus employed for three years. In 1851 he came to Texas with his father and immediately began merchandising in Columbus, Colorado County. Columbus was at that time a village of over 1,500 inhabitants and our subject remained there for four years when he sold his stock of goods, and in 1857 moved to Fayetteville. In the latter city he carried on business until 1862, when he sold out and joined the Confederate service. After the war he engaged in merchandising at La Grange, carried it on for four years, and then moved to Flatonia, where he established his present business. At the close of the war Mr. Harrison was considerably in debt to his New York merchants, and this had to be paid as soon as he could make it. As he was left a financial wreck it was some time before he could make any headway, but he persevered, and his business for fifteen years has been about $125,000 annually, carrying a general stock of goods noted for its excellence. Besides his mercantile interests, Mr. Harrison is the owner of farming lands in this and Colorado counties, and he is the owner of a private bank which has done a large share of the exchange business of the section. The banking business was established in 1884. In the year 1853 Mr. Harrison celebrated his marriage with Miss Margaret W. Hall, a native of Christian County, Kentucky, and daughter of Alexander Hall. Eight children blessed this union, two of whom died in infancy: Nettie, wife of W. H. Kerr, of Flatonia; Alma, wife of Jonathan Lane, of La Grange; Kate, wife of C. Foster, of Flatonia; Martha, wife of W. H. Nash, of Alvin, Brazoria County; H. H. and C. P., of Flatonia. Both Mr. and Mrs. Harrison take quite an active interest in church and church work, and he is a teacher in the Sunday School. Mr. Harrison is a member of the A. F. & A. M. Flatonia Lodge No. 436, and in politics is a stanch Democrat, being quite deeply interested in political matters. Mr. Harrison is one of the most successful business men in the county, and has the satisfaction of knowing that all his property is the result of his own exertions.

DR. HENRY HATCH BEVERLY. He whose name heads this sketch is following two occupations which are of the utmost importance to mankind, for, viewed from the standpoint of man's physical inequalities, there are none who carry out the roll of good Samaritan so thoroughly as the druggist and medical practitioner. He it is to whom every one goes for everything, from a wash for a dangerous wound to a lotion for the complexion; he is supposed to be thoroughly posted on all the ills to which the human flesh is heir, in fact is expected to be an epitome of human knowledge, and in nearly every instance is an exceptionally well informed and intelligent man, at least such are the facts in the case regarding Henry Hatch Beverly, of Smiley, Texas. He was born in Shiloh, Alabama, May 2, 1853, the younger of two children born to Thomas A. and Paulina (Townsend) Beverly, the former of whom was born in North Carolina and removed to Alabama in his young manhood, where the greater portion of his life was spent as a merchant. Upon the opening of the

"Irrepressible conflict" he entered the Confederate service, and in 1862 died near Chatanooga, Tenn. He was a Master Mason, and was a worthy member of the Methodist Church, of which his widow, who makes her home with Dr. H. H. Beverly, is also a member. In the schools of Alabama the subject of this sketch was given a thorough education, and he wisely made the most of his opportunities. After deciding upon the profession he wished to follow through life, he set about accomplishing his object by attending lectures in the New Orleans Medical College, and was graduated from this institution in 1883. His first practice was done at Pilgrim's Lake, Texas, but after a short time he removed to Smiley Lake, Texas, where he now holds forth. Although his residence here has covered but a short period, he has built up a reputation for ability, thoroughness and conscientious effort as a medical practitioner and knowledge of his profession, and great accuracy as a druggist that has made him very popular with all classes. He has always given his support to the Democratic party, and for a number of years has been a worthy member of the Cumberland Presbyterian Church.

DAVY CROCKET BURLESON. He who heads this sketch is the only living child of General Edward and Sarah G. Owen (Burleson), who were born in North Carolina and Kentucky, respectively. In 1848 General Edward Burleson moved to Hays County, Texas, and located at the head of the San Marcos River, where he made his home until death closed his early career, January 1, 1851, at which time he was holding the office of State Senator. The subject of this sketch was reared in San Marcos, and was educated there and at Baylor University. He began life for himself as a tiller of the soil, on a farm of his own near San Marcos, and was following this occupation at the opening of the Civil War. In March, 1862, he assisted in raising and organized a company for the Confederate service at Seguin, of which he was elected to the office of Second Lieutenant. Upon the organization of the regiment to which it belonged, he was elected First Lieutenant of Company B, Thirty-Second Texas Cavalry, and saw the most of his service in Texas and Louisiana. The first battle in which he participated was at Blair's Landing, Louisiana, where he was in the thickest of the fight, and after that he was in daily service and followed up General Banks on the latters retreat down Red River to Yellow Bayou, where was fought one of the hardest battles of the war. In the winter of 1864 his command came to Texas, and in the spring of 1865 it was disbanded at Houston. Prior to the Civil War he had seen some military service for he, in 1855, went out with Captain James H. Callihan, as a ranger, to protect the frontier against the Indians. While they were stationed in Kerr County, the captain suggested the plan to invade Mexico, and at Santa Rosa captured many escaped negro slaves, but this expedition was opposed by Lieutenant Edward Burleson and some others, who withdrew from the service, but Callihan and many others crossed the Rio Grande and had a battle on the San Fernando River and were defeated, losing several men, although the majority of them escaped and made their way back to the United States. In 1856, the brother of the subject of this sketch—Edward Burleson, was commissioned by several to go to Mexico and secure title to lands about San Marcos, and in this expedition he was accompanied by Davy Crocket Burleson and four others. They visited Saltilio, but could come to no satisfactory terms, and it was then proposed that with the funds on hand they should buy stock which they could drive back to Texas. They were captured by a Mexican mob, were imprisoned at Hascienda Potosi and were kept in captivity, in divided parties, for some two weeks. The Alcalde at that place then told them that it had been decided to shoot them, but fortunately for the prisoners the Mexicans afterwards changed their minds, and they were eventually released and returned to Texas. In 1857 the subject of this sketch completed his education in a well-conducted college of the Lone Star State, and in 1858–59 he held the position of Sergeant-at-arms in the State Senate at Austin. In 1860 he again entered the service of the State as a member of his brother Ed's rangers, and while thus occupied had some thrilling experiences. In 1861 he led to the altar Miss Louisa Ware a native of Mississippi, and a daughter of Colonel A. G. Ware, a prominent official of Mississippi at one time, who came to Texas in 1850, settling at Manchaca Springs, where he acquired large land interests and was very prominent in public affairs. He was for some time Sheriff of Travis County, and there passed from life in 1859. In 1865 Mr. Burleson removed from San Marcos to the mountains, and took up his residence on a horse ranche, but two years later he moved to the vicinity of the town of Buda, and here his home has since continued to be. He has an excellent farm of 236 acres, of which 140 are under cultivation. In 1893 he lost his estimable wife. She was a worthy member of the Christian Church, and had borne him eight children. The subject of this sketch is a sterling and useful citizen, and is a member of one of the oldest and most highly honored families of Texas. His father, General Burleson, was a conspicuous figure in Texas, and was an active soldier from the firing of the first gun at Gonzales to the battle of San Jacinto, throughout the history of the Republic of Texas and during the Mexican War.

JAMES BLAKE KENNARD. The rapid growth of Gonzales and Gonzales County, Texas, has called for extensive work on the part of lumber yards to meet the demands made upon them in the past few years. Very prominent among those engaged in the lumber business is James Blake Kennard, whose hustling abilities are well recognized in this county, in which he ranks as one of the most worthy representative people engaged in industrial life. He was born in Grimes County, Texas, in 1861, the second of four children born to Nathaniel William and Jane (Bradbury) Kennard, the former of whom was born in Alabama. He was a wholesale merchant of Mobile until about 1855, when he came to Grimes County, Texas. In 1861 he enlisted in the Confederate army, serving until the termination of hostilities, then returned to his home in Texas, and was engaged in farming until his death in 1869. His widow still resides in Grimes County. In the Plantersville High School of Grimes County the subject of this sketch received his early education, and began life for himself as a book-keeper. Later he became a traveling salesman and has for the past several years represented the firm of William D. Cleveland & Co., of Houston, a position he filled with marked credit to himself and to the unbounded satisfaction of his employers. In March, 1894, he bought his present business at Gonzales, and carries a stock valued at about $6,000 to $8,000, comprising sash, doors, blinds, builders' hardware, fencing material, etc., his place of business being conveniently located on Water street in the business portion of the town and on a joint switch of the two railroads. In every respect Mr. Kennard is a wideawake business man, and, being of pleasing address and affable and cordial manners, he is making many friends and building up a patronage that is in every way satisfactory. He has already greatly extended his business connections, in fact, is proving himself a live man of affairs, and one well able to look after his own interests, although to his credit be it said that he never does so at the expense of others or of his good name. He was first married in 1883 to Miss Mary G. Fore, of Anderson, Grimes County, Texas, but was called upon to mourn her death in 1888, she leaving him with one daughter to care for: Eloise J.; Mary, another daughter, died in infancy. His second marriage took place August 16, 1893, Anna Ashby Jones, a native of Gonzales County, becoming his wife. She is a daughter of Hartwell K. Jones, and granddaughter of the venerable Mrs. Braches. Mr. Kennard is a member of the Methodist Church and socially he is a member of the A. F. & A. M.

MARCUS LAFAYETTE HOPE HARRY. This prominent old settler of Austin County, Texas, owes his nativity to Lincoln County, N. C., where he was born January 5, 1830. His parents, John H. and Sophia (Tucker) Harry, were born in North Carolina, but the Harry family first settled in Virginia upon coming to this country. The paternal grandfather, John B. Harry, took quite an active interest in the political affairs of his day and represented his county in the State Legislature. His children were Elizabeth (Bridges); John H.; David, who was in the Texas and Mexican War, and George Washington. John H. Harry came to Texas in 1836, bringing with him a company of men for the purpose of joining the Texas force against the Mexican government, and served under Gen. Houston as Quartermaster. He was deputized to transport the archives and State arms from Port Lavaca to Austin just previous to the burning of Port Lavaca by the Indians, and had with him only the teamsters on this trip. As he was leaving Port Lavaca he passed by the Indian camp, and as a matter of precaution he took some of the guns he had in his charge and braced them in the wagon box with the muzzles protruding, as a warning to the Indians. He returned to North Carolina in the spring of 1838, and brought his family to this State in the fall of that year, and after a short stay in San Augustine County he moved to Houston, where he opened an hotel, which was one of the very first to be established in the place. Congress convened at Houston in those days and its members boarded with Mr. Harry. He was quite a politician himself and admired as the greatest men in the world, Gen. Washington, Gen. Jackson and Gen. Houston, being an intimate friend of the latter. While never holding any civil office under the Republic of Texas, yet he took an active interest in all political matters. He left Houston in the spring of 1839 and moved to Austin when it contained only a few board houses and one log house, the latter containing one room, and was the hotel of the place. While there he was engaged in the jewelry business in connection with a general store, and besides this did considerable trading with the Indians, who were usually hostile, but would occasionally come to settlements with peaceful intent. After the State Capitol had been removed to Washington Mr. Harry purchased a one-fourth league of land in the southern portion of the county, on which he established a small store and started three wagons to peddling between Austin and Houston. This was a very dangerous business, for Indians were plentiful and always on the warpath, but Mr. Harry continued this business until his death in 1844, having died of yellow fever on the 12th of October. He was twice married, first to the mother of the subject of this sketch, and by her became the father of four children, three of whom died when small. Mrs. Harry died in Lincoln, N. C., in 1835, and after Mr. Harry's return to that State, was married there to Sarah McCullough, whom he brought back with him to Texas. They had one child that died of yellow fever, and the mother died February 13, 1839. Marcus L. H. Harry, after the death of his father, was the only survivor of the family and at the age of thirteen was left to shift for himself. While his father was ill he was nursed by an Irishman who guarded the famous Napoleon on the Island of St. Helena. Mr. Harry was just preparing to send his son, Marcus, to North Carolina to be educated, but died before his plans could be matured, but left his son with a one-fourth league of land, the greater part of which he afterwards lost, and owing to false surveys sold his land for $500. He commenced life for himself at the age of fourteen with two horses, two cows and calves and five head of hogs and a certificate for 640 acres of land in Hill County. This he afterwards sold and purchased land in Austin County and engaged in the stock business. By the time he was twenty-one years old he had fifty or sixty head of cattle. When in his eighteenth year he hired out for a year's schooling, which he took when in his nineteenth year. When twenty-two years old he was married to Mrs. Elizabeth (Pryor) Roberts, a native of Alabama, who came with her father, William Pryor, to this country in 1824. Mrs. Harry was one of the few women who visited the battle-ground of San Jacinto and viewed the dead Mexicans, who never found a burial. The first year after his marriage he and his wife raised ten bales of cotton and 400 bushels of corn, and by energy and good management prospered. At the opening of the war he had sufficient land and stock to exempt him from military service. He finally joined a company of scouts and couriers on the coast, and got permission to haul cotton from this place to Matamoras. At the close of the war he owned a good home and 1,000 head of cattle, and in 1870 he owned about 4,000 head. In 1873 his stock died very rapidly, but two years later was offered $23,000 in gold for his cattle and $2,000 for his horses. He now owns 2,400 acres of land, lying on both sides of the Brazos River, and has 400 acres under cultivation. Mr. and Mrs. Harry have four children: David (deceased); Harriet C., wife of A. J. May; Amanda E., wife of D. A. Horn; and Sarah Sophia, wife of W. E. Belt. Mrs. Harry died in 1884, at the age of sixty-five years. She was for many years a member of the Methodist Episcopal Church, but at the time of her death was a member of the Missionary Baptist Church. Politically Mr. Harry has always been a Democrat.

JOE MILTON LOWRY. Although it has been said that a "Jack of all trades" is master of none, yet it has been proven time and again that a man may engage in a variety of occupations and succeed in them all if he has the requisite mental abilities and the determination and energy to push his enterprises to a successful termination. The worthy subject of this sketch is not only a prosperous merchant of Smiley, but he is also a successful miller and farmer, a fact which speaks plainly as to his intelligence, push and enterprise. He was born in the county in which he is now residing, February 14, 1860, and is a son of Wedon S. and Frances (Pritchett) Lowry, the former of whom was born on Blue Grass soil, and during life followed the calling of a mechanic and farmer. At the age of eighteen years he ran away from home and enlisted in the Mexican War, and after that struggle was over he settled in Gonzales County, Texas. When the great

war between the North and the South commenced, he joined the Confederate
army and served the Southern cause faithfully until Gen. Lee's surrender,
having had charge of the Commissary Department at Gonzales for some time
prior to the close.   He became a member of Gonzales Lodge of the A. F. &
A. M., and at the time of his death in 1891, was a worthy member of the
Methodist Church, of which his wife, who was called from this life in 1861,
was also a member.   The early educational advantages of Joe Milton Lowry
were such as the schools of his native county afforded, which were by no
means of the best, but, being naturally intelligent, he made fair progress
in his studies notwithstanding his limited opportunities, and is now one
of the well informed men of his section, progressive, wideawake and public
spirited.   He is deeply interested in the progress and welfare of the section
in which his home has so long been, and is one of her most progressive
and useful citizens.   On the 22nd of February, 1893, he was united in
marriage with Miss Mattie, daughter of Robertus R. and Adaline (Wright)
Hinton, both of whom were born in the State of Mississippi and are now
substantial citizens of the Lone Star State.   Mr. Lowry has always been
a Democrat in politics, and he and his wife are members of the Baptist
Church.

WILLIAM GUYLER.   This old settler of Austin County, Texas, was born
in Hopkins County, Kentucky, October 1, 1823, a son of Samuel and Quintina
(Bailey) Guyler, the paternal ancestors having come to this country previous to the Revolutionary War and settled in Virginia.   The paternal
grandfather removed to Kentucky in 1803 or 1804 and there reared a family.   His farm was on a branch of Deer Creek, now called Guyler's Creek,
and there Samuel Guyler grew to manhood and was married.   The Baileys
came to this country from England prior to the Revolution, and were
known as Huguenots, but were not French.   They also settled in Virginia,
and about 1800 the family of Mrs. Guyler removed to Kentucky, where
a large family reached maturity.   Mr. and Mrs. Guyler both died when
the subject of this sketch was quite young, and he was left without brothers
or sisters, being an only child.   He received a limited education and commenced to do for himself at the age of nineteen years almost totally without
means.   After doing farm work for some time he engaged in keeping school,
and before coming to Texas in 1859, he had married and had become the
owner of some good property in Hardin County, Kentucky.   Soon after his
arrival here he purchased about 3,000 acres of land, for the most of which he
paid from $2.50 to $2.75 and for a 400 acre tract of bottom land he paid $4.00
per acre.   Like nearly all who came to Texas during that time he engaged
in the stock business, and one time he was the most extensive sheep raiser
in this portion of the State.   He also raised large numbers of horses and
cattle without really intending to do so, but food was so abundant that
stock required little or no care.   In 1860 Mr. Guyler erected the first
steam mill ever put up in this portion of the county, and purchased his
mill stones and machinery in the city of New Orleans.   When the Civil
War came up Mr. Guyler naturally espoused the cause of the South, and early
in 1861 he offered his services to the Confederacy, but being a miller, and the
only one in the county, he was detailed to attend to his mill for the benefit
of the families left behind.   During the years 1864-65 Mr. Guyler became a
member of Capt. Tauman's company and was attached to the Fourth Texas

BATTLE OF

FORT DONELSON,

Feb. 13-16, 1862.

0   ¼   ½   1 Mile

Road to Ft. Henry

Impossible except by Boats

GEN. GRANT'S HEAD Q'RS

SMITH'S DIV.

Bridge

Hickman

CONFEDERATE

30TH TENN. REG.

BUCKNER'S DIVISION

WALLACE'S DIVISION

McCLERNAND'S DIVISION

RIFLE

Indian

DOVER

FORT DONELSON

Landing

Transports

Gunboats

Guns

Water Battery

Guns

Guns

3 Guns

Guns

N

N

CUMBERLAND RIVER

Cavalry which operated in the southern portion of the State, and was mainly engaged in guarding prisoners. At the opening of the war he had some twenty-five negroes and at the close of the war had none, a financial loss which he could not help feeling severely. He, however, owned quite a large body of land along the Brazos River, containing about 300 acres, and a like amount of prairie land. He was the first Postmaster of Wallis, and filled this position for seventeen years successively, having been appointed to the position in 1869 by Gen. Grant, the place at that time being known by a different name. He was married in 1845 to Miss Lydia A. English, a daughter of Hiram and Elizabeth (Yeager) English (see sketch of H. B. English,) who came here in poor health in 1857, the father's death occurring in 1874. He left one child, Lydia A. (Mrs. Guyler) who has borne her husband the following children: Elizabeth R., wife of Dr. C. J. Hester of Brook Haven, Miss.; Ada C., wife of Nathan P. Ward of this place; Lydia E., who first married George Hester and after his death Sidney Poindexter of Jackson County, Texas; Mallie, wife of Dr. F. B. Magruder of San Angelo, Texas; Sara J., the deceased wife of S. D. Groouver; Robert W., a merchant and the present Postmaster of Wallis, and four children that died in early childhood. Mr. and Mrs. Guyler are members of the Missionary Baptist Church, and he is a member of San Felipe Lodge of the A. F. & A. M. He has been a life-long Democrat and was one of the strong supporters of the action taken by Texas in 1861.

CARROLL C. COX. He whose name heads this sketch is an energetic and enlightened farmer of Gonzales County, Texas, and his many broad acres are tilled and cared for in a manner which shows him to be progressive, thrifty and energetic. He was born in Seguin, Texas, in 1868, the eldest of five children born to Dr. James M. and Eliza B. (Anderson) Cox, who were natives of Virginia and Georgia respectively. The father was principally self-educated, and in his youthful days was quite an extensive traveler. He studied medicine in Arkansas under a preceptor, and about 1840 became a resident of Texas. He remained in the northern part of the State for some time, then came to Seguin, Gaudalupe County and from there to Gonzales County, where his home continued to be until his death, which occurred in March, 1883. He was engaged in merchandising also for some time, in addition to following his profession, and was for some time Postmaster at a place called Oak Forest. His medical education was finished by a course in Tulane University, New Orleans, and later in the city of New York, and he became the leading physician of Seguin and the surrounding country. He became the owner of a large tract of land in Gonzales County, on which he farmed and raised stock, the latter occupation being carried on quite extensively. His wife was the Widow Anderson when he married her, and she was a daughter of Carroll, who was a native of South Carolina, and after residing in several States, became a resident of Texas about 1840, coming thither from Arkansas. He bought and located large tracts of land, about 100,000 acres, a considerable portion of which was on and about the present town of Yoakum, and on this property he lived and labored until his death. He was one of the most extensive farmers of his time, and was one of the law abiding and public spirited citizens of the county. His career was closed in 1879 when quite advanced in years, and his wife also lived to a ripe old age. Owing to the fact that his father died when he was but a lad, Carroll C. Cox received but limited educational advantages, for the burden and management of the farm then fell upon his youthful shoulders, thus debarring him from attending school. He, however, possesses a naturally fine mind, and besides being thoroughly up in his calling, he is well posted on the general issues of the day and has original and intelligent views regarding them.   December 20, 1892, he was married to Miss Mary Holmes, a native of Texas and a daughter of William Edward Holmes of Gonzales County.

H. C. WALLACE.   An extensive and deservedly successful business man of Kyle, Texas, is H. C. Wallace, who is the owner and manager of a large lumber yard at that place. He owes his nativity to Missouri, where he was born in 1841, the eldest child born to William J. and Mary J. (Burch) Wallace, who were natives of Kentucky and Missouri respectively. The paternal grandfather, Samuel Wallace, took up his residence in Howard County, Missouri, at an early day, and there devoted his attention to farming. The maternal grandfather, also, was one of the first settlers of Missouri. William J. Wallace attained manhood in Howard County, then went to Livingston County, and there spent the rest of his life, dying in 1888. His wife's death occurred in 1858, and both were members of the Methodist Episcopal Church South. H. C. Wallace was reared in Livingston County, and in August, 1861, entered the Confederate service, first as a member of Hughes' Regiment, Missouri State Guards, then of Clark's, and later King's Battery, and was a participant in the engagements at Lexington and of Elk Horn.   In 1862 he crossed the Mississippi River at Memphis, and until the close of the war was with Johnson's Tennessee Army, and Van Dorn's and Jackson's Division Cavalry. He was wounded in an engagement in Tennessee, and during the last year of the war was in Mississippi and Alabama, and was in Gainesville, Ala., at the time of Lee's surrender. He then returned to his old home in Missouri, after a time engaged in farming and carpenter's work alternately, then came to Texas, and in 1867 located at Columbus, where he was engaged in contracting and building for some time.   In 1873 he engaged in the lumber business at Columbus, but one year later went to Schulenburg, where he was in this business for six years. Following this he was at Rockdale one year, and in 1881, when the new town of Kyle was founded, he located here, and here he has been successfully engaged in business ever since. He has an excellent and complete stock of lumber, and in addition handles builders' hardware, paints, oils, sash, glass, etc., his stock being valued at from $6,000 to $8,000, and his annual sales about $25,000.   He was one of the organizers of the oil mills, has served as Alderman five terms and has also been active in school work, and somewhat active in politics of a local character.   He was married in 1874 to Miss Julia Friarson, by whom he has eight children: William P., Ada, Keith, Charles, Cornelia, Carl, John and James.   The family are attendants of the Methodist Episcopal Church, and Mr. Wallace is a trustee and steward of the same. He is a public-spirited citizen, and a useful and valued citizen of the town.

WALTER T. BROWN, M.D.   During the few years our subject has been a practitioner of the healing art he has made many friends, his ability has become well known, and as a consequence he has built up a large practice.   He is progressive in his practice, a close student, keeping himself well up in American literature of the day, and an excellent citizen.   His birth occurred in this county July 7, 1867, and he is a son of William W. and Mary (Clements) Brown, (see sketch of W. W. Brown).   Dr. Walter T. Brown received his scholastic training in the schools of this county. In 1887 he matriculated at Louisville Medical College and in the following year attended the Kentucky School of Medicine, and was graduated from the Louisville Medical College in the class of 1889. Immediately after this he located in Wallis, Texas, and has here built up a most flattering practice within the past five years. Few young physicians in the State have a larger or more extensive practice than Dr. Brown, and few have won the confidence of the public to a greater degree. He was married in March, 1893, to Miss Jodie Pennington, daughter of E. L. Pennington (see sketch). Dr. Brown is Physician and Surgeon for the Aransas Pass Railway for the Houston Division, and holds other responsible positions. He is a member of the K. & L. of H., and a member of the Methodist Episcopal Church. Mrs. Brown holds membership in the Christian Church. Both are highly esteemed in their community. Politically, Dr. Brown is a Democrat. In connection with his practice he is interested to some extent in agricultural pursuits.

ALGERNON SIDNEY BILLINGS. A most important calling is that to which A. S. Billings is devoting his attention, and it is one for which he seems to have a decided liking and a natural aptitude, a secret, without doubt, of his success in this line of human endeavor. He acquired a knowledge of and liking for the business on his father's plantation, for he was a small planter and stock-raiser, and upon starting out in life for himself it was his determination to eventually engage in the business. He is a product of De Kalb County, Tennessee, where he first saw the light of day March 2, 1849, his parents being Gibson and Mary (Alcorn) Billings, who were native Tennesseeans. They emigrated to Gonzales County, Texas, when the subject of this sketch was five years of age, and here Mr. Billings devoted his attention to planting and stock-raising. He was a member of the Home Guards under Capt. Kelly for some time, always supported the principles of the Democratic party, and in 1882 was called from this life, his wife passing away in 1866. In the common schools of his native county A. S. Billings was educated, and when he started out to fight life's battles for himself it was totally without means, but he possessed an abundant amount of pluck and determination, together with a goodly amount of energy, and, by dint of much persistent labor, in time succeeded in obtaining a foothold on the ladder of success. From that lowly position he climbed rapidly upward, and is now one of the wealthy farmers and stockmen of Gonzales County. He is now the owner of a ranche of 9,000 acres, finely stocked and well improved, indeed a valuable and desirable property, and he has the unbounded satisfaction of knowing that it has been earned by honest efforts on his part. Like his father before him he is a Democrat in politics, but he has never been an office seeker, and has never held nor aspired to any official position with the exception of the minor one of School Trustee. He was united in marriage with Miss Lucy C. Alley in 1874, and from whom he was divorced in 1883. Their union resulted in the birth of three children, all of whom are now dead. His second union took place in 1883 to Lucy A. Wheat, who bore him two children: Algernon S. and William C. He married his third and present wife, Ella O'Neal, in 1888, and this union has resulted in the birth of four children: John, Frank, Alice and Etta. Mr. Billings is a Knight Templar Mason, Gonzales Lodge No. 11, and also belongs to Smiley Lodge of the I. O. O. F. Mr. and Mrs. Billings are members of the Baptist Church, he being a deacon, and are highly honored citizens of the section in which they reside.

WALTER REEVES HOKE. A widewake citizen and upright and enterprising business man of Gonzales County, Texas, is W. R. Hoke, who is successfully engaged in milling and ginning at Slayden. He was born in Caldwell County, of the Lone Star State, on the 25th of June, 1859, and is a son of Burrell and Jane (Hubbard) Hoke, the former of whom was born in the Old North State, and the latter in Georgia. In early manhood Burrell Hoke removed to Texas and took up his residence in Caldwell County, where he turned his attention to farming and the mechanical arts until the opening of the great Civil War, when he joined the Confederate forces, and faithfully and bravely supported the cause of the South until he was killed in the battle at Atlanta, Ga. His widow still survives him. He was a Democrat politically, and being an intelligent, energetic and honorable man, would undoubtedly have become an eminent citizen had he lived. The subject of this sketch was the elder of two children born to his parents, and his early educational advantages were limited to the common schools of Guadalupe County, and were by no means of the best. Owing to the early death of the husband and father, he was obliged to depend upon his own resources at an early day, and in the rough but thorough school of experience, he gained a practical knowledge of men and things, and the lessons thus learned have been of the greatest benefit to him. He began farming in Guadalupe County, where he continued to till the soil until 1886 when he came to Gonzales County, and in the vicinity of Slayden purchased a farm on which he resided until 1890 when he sold out and erected a public gin, which is an exceptionally fine one, is fitted up with modern and improved machinery and is liberally patronized. It has a capacity of twenty-five bales, ginned and compressed, in a day, his press being of the Winship make. His gin averages about 800 bales per year, but this year he expects to exceed this by several hundred bales. He is a man of excellent reputation, has many friends, and is in every way deserving the success that has attended his efforts. He is a Democrat of pronounced type, and has held the office of Deputy Sheriff. He was married in 1880 to Lena, daughter of William and Emma Appling, residents of Guadalupe County, the former of whom was born in Georgia and the latter in North Carolina. To Mr. and Mrs. Hoke the following children have been born: Burrell, Cora (deceased), Oliver, Mollie, Basil and Pierce. Mr. and Mrs. Hoke are members of the Primitive Baptist Church.

ISAAC W. PITTS. Alabama has contributed her share toward the advancement and progress of the " Lone Star State," in the number of excellent citizens she has sent here. Among the number may be mentioned Isaac W. Pitts, who came here at an early date, and has ever been an influential, law abiding citizen, and a man whose intelligence and integrity are well known. He was born in Pike County, Alabama, October 17, 1833, son of Jesse and Millie J. (Duncan) Pitts, natives of Georgia. While still single the parents moved to Alabama, and in that State their nuptials were celebrated. There Mr. Pitts tilled the soil until 1849, and then moved to Texas, first stopping in Washington County. In the fall of 1850 he came to this county, and located five miles south of San Felipe, where he reared his family, and devoted his attention to the management of his farm. He purchased a large tract of land in this State and continued to reside in this section until 1860, when he moved to Bell County, where he made his home for ten years. Later he moved to Coryell County, and resided there for some time, or until his children were married, when he and wife broke up housekeeping and made their home with their children and grandchildren until death claimed them. Mrs. Pitts died at the home of our subject in 1882. After this Mr. Pitts returned to Coryell County, and died at the home of his grand-daughter, Mrs. Tankfera. His remains were brought to this county, and placed besides those of his wife. Mr. and Mrs. Pitts' children were named, as follows: Isaac W., Silas T., died in Galveston, in 1863, while in the Confederate service; Erasmus, deceased; Lee P., deceased; John M., resides in Bosque County; Emily, deceased, was the wife of William Hensley, also deceased; L. M., an attorney, resides at McGregor, in Coryell County, and one child deceased. When a boy, Isaac W. Pitts received his education at Orion, Pike County, Alabama, a fine English education for his day, and came to Texas with his father in 1849, landing at Houston, December 16th, coming to this county with his father in 1850 when in his seventeenth year and remained with his parents until in his twenty-second year. After that he engaged in farming and stock-raising, and although he started with small capital he purchased 177 acres of unimproved land in 1856, for which he paid $2,000. On this land he settled, and began at once improving. Like the majority of early Texans, he gave most of his attention, however, to the stock business in which he was largely interested, but in 1883 he sold 800 head of cattle, the proceeds of which he invested in land on the Brazos River, bottom and prairie land, 2,000 acres in all, 500 of which is now under cultivation. Besides he has his homestead in the town of San Felipe, consisting of a small lot of land (six acres), on which stands a handsome residence, one of those old-fashioned rambling southern homes, so dear to the hearts of its people. In 1862 Mr. Pitts joined the Confederate Army, light artillery, but saw considerable cavalry service. For some time he was in the trans-Mississippi Department, and was stationed at the mouth of the Brazos River. He was never in any battles. Soon after joining, Mr. Pitts hired a substitute, and came home, but immediately afterward he was forced out with the militia and became a member of Captain Munien's company, being stationed at Hempstead to guard prisoners. After six months' service he was exempted, as was every man who owned 500 head of cattle or fifteen negroes, according to the law. Since 1883 Mr. Pitts has devoted his time to farming and stock-raising and is raising some improved cattle and horses. For several years Mr. Pitts was Justice of the Peace, and in politics has always been a strict Democrat. In the year 1856 he was married to Miss Elizabeth Hill, a native of Arkansas, and daughter of John Hill (see sketch of Jacob Hill.) To Mr. and Mrs. Pitts were born seven children: Mary J. (deceased), John B., (deceased); Emily, (deceased); one died unnamed; Annie Elizabeth, George W., of Kerr County; and J. T. (deceased.) Mrs. Pitts died in 1873. Mr. Pitts selected his second wife in the person of Miss Katie Bollinger, a native of this State, their marriage taking place in 1873. Her father, John Bollinger, came to Texas as early as 1833 and settled in this county. Two children were born to our subject's last union: Henry A., of this county, and Jesse J. Mr. and Mrs. Pitts are earnest members of the Methodist Episcopal Church.

Louis Brenner. This wideawake young business man is engaged in both farming and merchandising at Oak Forest, Texas, and, being shrewd, pushing and energetic, he is prospering financially. He owes his nativity to Prussia, Germany, where he was born in 1863, a son of Louis and Jane (Berger)

Brenner, the former of whom was a blacksmith by trade, but is now retired from the active duties of life, and is enjoying the fruits of his early industry in the Fatherland. The mother died in 1863, soon after the birth of the subject of this sketch. The latter not only attended the public schools of his native land, as all able-bodied German lads are required to do, but in addition was placed in the University of Karlsruhe, graduating from this institution by the time he had attained his twenty-first year. He made a specialty of the study of chemistry, was a faithful and persevering scholar, and made rapid progress in his studies. After leaving school he came at once to the United States, and upon landing in the city of New York started at once for San Antonio, Texas, where his brother Henry had preceded him a few years. After remaining in that city about one year he went to New Orleans, where he clerked in a drug store for some twelve months, then returned to New York City. From that city he went to Baltimore, and from there embarked for his native land, where he served one year in the German army. The opportunities afforded a young man in this country for attaining a fortune had greatly impressed him, however, and in December, 1888, he returned to New York, and soon after joined a brother in Seguin, Texas, at which place he followed clerical duties for about one year. Belmont, Gonzales County, then became his home, at which point he opened a drug store, the first one in the place. After about a year he combined his business with that of C. T. Rather, whom he later bought out, and then continued business on his own responsibility for a year longer. Soon after this he came to Oak Forest, where he has since been located, and where he is recognized as an active, energetic and successful business man. He is the owner of 800 acres of fine farming land, of which 450 are under cultivation, and many of the improvements that have been made thereon are the result of his own efforts. His place is one of the finest in that section, and everything about it indicates that the owner is a man of thrift, push and enterprise. He has a comfortable and pretty home, has a number of tenant houses on his place, besides a good blacksmith shop and his store building. He keeps a general line of goods, and under his capable management the business has prospered financially. February 10, 1891, he was married to Miss Ida Cox, a native of Texas and daughter of Dr. Cox. Their union has resulted in the birth of one child, Milton. Mr. and Mrs. Brenner are members of the Methodist Church, and he has for some time been stewart in the church at Oak Forest.

JOEL W. ROBISON (deceased). One of the earliest settlers of Fayette County, Texas, as well as one of the first of the State, Joel W. Robison, was born in Washington County, Ga., October 5, 1815. He came to Texas with his parents and one sister in 1832, and settled first in Brazoria County. He found the country new and most of the people Mexicans there. The political condition of the country was in a turmoil, there being two factions of Mexicans struggling for supremacy. Santa Anna, the leader of the government faction, had declared in favor of the constitutional government. Mr. Robison and his father, J. G. Robison, enlisted in Capt. Henry S. Brown's company, and under command of Capt. John Austin marched to Valasco, June 26, 1832, and engaged in that desperate struggle, which, after eleven hours' conflict, resulted in the surrender of the garrison to the Texan army. In 1833 Mr. Robison, with his father and the remainder of the family, moved up to the border settlements between the Colorado and Brazos rivers. He, as a boy soldier, joined Capt. York's company in an expedition against the Indians in the territory, and continued to do service in defense of the advancing frontier settlements. In 1835 he joined the expedition against the Indians on the Upper Trinity, and soon after his return from the last-named expedition the Texans assembled in consultation at San Felipe. They proclaimed a declaration of rights and advocated measures of resistance to the quartering of Mexican troops in the State, in violation of the Colonization Contract, when it was decided to raise an army for this resistance. Young Robison was among the first to respond. He went at once to San Antonio, engaged under Col. Bowie, and was in that splendid victory, the battle of Conception, October 28, 1835. In November of the same year he was one of the number under Col. Bowie in the Grass fight before San Antonio, where another splendid victory for the Texan army was achieved. Mr. Robison continued with the army as a private until the battle of San Jacinto, April 21, 1836, and he was one of a party of six with Sylvester when Santa Anna was captured. They surrounded him in a small tract of timber, and Sylvester, not knowing who he was, proposed shooting him. Mr. Robison opposed doing so. The soldiers started Santa Anna toward the headquarters of Gen. Sam Houston, on foot, and as his feet were sore he said he could not walk, and that the soldiers might kill him if they wished to. They prodded him with their guns, but it had no effect. Santa Anna had made up his mind not to walk. Mr. Robison took compassion on him and had him mount behind himself, and they thus proceeded to Gen. Houston's tent. There for the first time Sylvester and his men found out the true value of their prisoner. No doubt had they found it out before, the "Little Napoleon" would never have reached camp. After returning home (at the close of the war), Mr. Robison's father, J. G. Robison, was elected from a county to the first Texas Congress which assembled at Columbia. In the latter part of 1836, immediately after the adjournment of Congress, the father returned home, his family then residing in the territory of which this county was afterwards composed, between Round Top and Warrenton, within one mile of the latter place. Afterwards Mr. Robison, together with his brother Walter, and a faithful old negro servant, took an ox team and went to Columbus for a sack of salt (twenty miles). On their return home at the close of the second day, and when within a half mile of that place, they were surrounded, captured, killed and scalped by the Indians. Joel W. Robison, his son and the subject of this sketch, looking over the trail leading toward Columbus next day, saw at no great distance his father's oxen with the wagon, and at once went to investigate. His horror can be imagined. He carried his father and uncle, as well as the negro, to a place of safety from the wolves, etc., until he could get help to give them Christian burial. In 1837 Joel W. Robison married Miss E. A. Alexander, a native of Kentucky. From 1837 to 1845 he was in nearly all the expeditions against the Comanches, and other Indians in Texas. He was a private while in the army, although appointed Lieutenant by Gen. Houston. His wife was born in Kentucky, June 25, 1821, and emigrated with her father, Samuel Alexander, to this county in 1832, settling in what is known as the Block House Settlement, five years before the organization of Fayette County, making her one of the earliest settlers in the county—a period of fifty-four years—from 1832 to 1887. While Col. Robison performed his duties as a soldier for his country, Mrs. Robison was ever mindful of hers, faithfully discharging the onerous duties of pioneer life with a cheerfulness that was remarkable. She had but one brother, Jerome Alexander, who fell with Dawson on the Salado, near San Antonio, in 1842. In 1858 Mrs. Robison professed religion and joined the Methodist Church, with which she remained until her death in 1887. Mr. and Mrs. Robison were the parents of seven children, three sons and four daughters, five of whom survive: Almeida, wife of T. A. Ledbetter; Samuel A. (deceased); Neal, of this city; Lucy, wife of J. F. McClatchy; Fannie, wife of Dr. J. W. Smith; J. G., of Williamson County, and one died young. Mr. Robison chose the occupation of farming as his life's work, and became a wealthy citizen. He represented Fayette County in the State Legislature from 1860 to 1862, and advocated secession. Mr. Robison was always a very pronounced Democrat, and was a leader of his party in the county, attending all the State and county conventions, and was Chairman of the County Democratic Committee for several years. For many years prior to his death Joel W. Robison was one of the leading men in his section, or in the State. In 1874 he was a member of the convention that formed the present constitution of Texas. Prominent men of Texas, in passing through his section, always made his house their home. He was an old-school gentleman, courteous, kind and pleasant to all, and was much honored and respected throughout the county and State. His son, Neal W. Robison, the present County Collector, was born in Fayette County, Texas, July 16, 1848, and was educated in this county during 1867, '68 and '69, when he attended the University of Virginia. There he made law a specialty, but never entered into the practice of the profession. In 1870 he formed a partnership with his father in the mercantile business in the village of Warrenton, and was thus engaged until 1879. At that date he was married to Miss Halley P. Carter, a native of Texas, and daughter of John H. and Nunly Carter, natives of Virginia, where their ancestors were among the pioneers. Mr. Carter came to the Lone Star State in 1845 and engaged in merchandising, in which occupation he met with substantial results. His death occurred in 1894, when seventy-eight years old, regretted by many friends. Of the nine children born to his marriage seven now survive: Bettie, now Mrs. Davis, of Houston; America, married S. C. Olive, of Waco; Judith, now Mrs. Horwell, of this city; John B., of this place; F. C., of this county; Mrs. James Farquhar, of this city, and Hallie P., wife of subject. Directly after his marriage Mr. Robison engaged in the cotton brokerage business for a number of years, or until 1882. He was then elected Tax Collector of this county, an office which he has filled up to the present time—twelve years—to the entire satisfaction of all concerned. He is a member of the A. F. & A. M., and his father was a Royal Arch Mason of Fayette. Like his father he has been a life-long Democrat, and is a public spirited and progressive citizen. This family is one of the best known and most highly respected in the county, and the male members have taken a deep interest in the welfare and upbuilding of the same.

ABRAHAM O. HAMON. Although the subject of this sketch was reared to the occupation of planting and has followed that occupation the greater portion of his life, he has for some time been successfully engaged in merchandising also, at Hamon. He was born in Columbia, Tenn., March 30, 1830, a son of John E. and Ruth (Brooks) Hamon, both of whom were born and reared in Maury County, Tennessee, and were of Welsh extraction. In his early manhood John E. Hamon removed to Carroll County, Mississippi, and in 1854 took up his residence in Gonzales County, Texas, where he was engaged in planting in the vicinity of his son's present place of abode until his death, which occurred in 1880. His wife was a devoted member of the Methodist church, and died in Mississippi in 1854, just prior to her husband's removal to Texas. In Carroll County, Mississippi, Abraham O. Hamon received his educational training, and was for some time an attendant at Jackson College, Columbia, Tenn., in which well-known institution he acquired an exceptionally good education. Several years prior to his father's removal to the Lone Star State he came thither, and he very shortly after engaged in merchandising in the town of Gonzales, but for some time past has followed this occupation at Hamon. The principles of the Democratic party receive in him a stanch supporter, and at different times the members of this party have elected him County Commissioner and Justice of the Peace. Before he left the State of Mississippi he had filled the positions of Deputy Sheriff and Deputy Clerk. After the passage of the Conscript act he enlisted with Col. Ashby Smith in the Confederate service, but was taken ill several months later and was sent home on a furlough. He then joined Mann's Battalion and was stationed on Galveston Island until the close of the war. He was married, in 1855, to Miss Sarah Withers, and to their union six children have been given: Emma, wife of John Dubose Lea; Mollie, wife of Serre Dubose; William E., Harry A., and May, who died at the age of seven years. Mr. Hamon's second marriage took place in April, 1883, Miss Annie Box becoming his wife. She was reared in London, and is the mother of four children: Horace Hugh, Ruth, William J. and George Abraham.

BERNARD BROWN. Many of the most active and enterprising residents of Lavaca County, Texas, are natives of the county and have here spent the greater part of their lives. In them we find men of true loyalty to the interests of this part of the State, who understand, as it were, by instinct, the needs, social and industrial, of this vicinity, and who have a thorough knowledge of its resources. Prominent among these men is Bernard Brown, who was born on his present farm near Hallettsville in 1847. He is the youngest of ten children born to James and Ann Manning, both natives of Missouri. The parents came to Texas in 1832, resided for about a year in the eastern part of the State, and then came to this locality. They settled on land five miles from the present site of Hallettsville, and there passed the remainder of their lives, the father dying in January 1853, and the mother in April 1880. Both held membership in the Catholic Church. Mr. Brown made many improvements on his fine farm and took a deep interest in public affairs. His father, Bernard Brown, was a native of the Blue Grass State, but at an early date moved to Missouri, and thence to Texas. He settled on land on the Lavaca River, and part of Hallettsville stands on the old place. Our subject, Bernard Brown, passed his youth and received his education in Texas and when starting out in life for himself, engaged in the stock business, which he has followed for the most part ever since. He has a handsome place, with 350 acres under cultivation, and 1,200 acres in the home place. Mr. Brown also owns 1,920 acres in Frio County. In the year 1869 he was married to Miss Margaret A. Blackburn, also a native of Texas, and a daughter of Gideon Blackburn, a native of Tennessee. Mr. Blackburn came to Texas about 1840 or '41, and located on the Mustang Creek, now in Lavaca County. To

Mr. and Mrs. Brown have been born these children: James Gideon, Ida Ann, Rebecca Alice, Ada, Charles Andrew, Mary Viola and Bernard Milton. The parents are members of the Catholic Church.

JOHN V. DE POYSTER. He whose name heads this sketch is engaged in a diversity of employment, and he has been equally successful in each. In McNairy County, Tennessee, he first saw the light of day, on the 25th of January, 1861, and in that State his parents, Samuel B. and Mary (Walker) De Poyster, were also born, the former being of French lineage. In 1869 the parents moved to Gonzales County, Texas, and there the father was engaged in planting until death called him to his long home in 1881. He was a Democrat politically and as a citizen was always public spirited and law abiding. His widow survives him and is a member of the Cumberland Presbyterian Church. John V. De Poyster was taken from the State of his birth at the age of eight years, and has ever since resided in Texas, with the interests of which State he has identified himself. He has been an especially useful and enterprising citizen of Gonzales County, and is deservedly classed among her most intelligent and worthy citizens. After commencing his knowledge of the world of books in the public schools of Gonzales County, he finished his education and graduated with honors from the Sam Houston Normal School at Huntsville, but prior to this from the Boulton High School. Since that time the greater portion of his time has been devoted to teaching the "young idea," and in this has met with marked success and has acquired the reputation of a thorough eductor and able disciplinarian. He is a partner with his brother, Thomas J., in a public gin at Hamon, which is well equipped with two 60-saw Hill gins and a Reynolds press. This gin has a capacity of about fifteen bales per day, and will this year gin about six hundred bales. These wideawake young men are also the proprietors of a grist mill, which is remarkably well conducted, and for miles around supplies the citizens with an excellent grade of flour. Mr. De Poyster's enterprise and push have done much to improve Gonzales County in many ways, and in the capacity of an educator he has done not a little to raise the standard of the schools of the county. He is a Democrat politically, is a member of the County Board of Examiners, a position he has held for four years, and socially he is a member of the K. of P. Thomas Jackson De Poyster, his brother, and partner in business, was born in McNairy County, Tennessee, also, his birth occurring July 15, 1848. He is the active manager of the gin, mill and farm which he and his brother own, and is a remarkably active, pushing and enterprising man of business. Another brother of John V. De Poyster, is also an active man of affairs, and a worthy and useful citizen of the county.

JAMES BAILEY WELLS. The stock-raising and planting interests of Gonzales County, Texas, are ably represented by the honored subject of this notice, who owes his nativity to Panola County, Mississippi, where he was born on the 11th of March, 1847. His parents, Walker T. B. and Sarah (Wright) Wells, were both born in Georgia, but the former removed to Alabama, when quite young, thence to Mississippi, and at the age of thirty-five years emigrated to Gonzales County, Texas, this being in 1852. He was very fond of hunting in his youth, and this taste was abundantly gratified when he first came to this section, for there was an abundance of big game here. He was engaged in tilling the soil for a livelihood, in politics was a Whig, but never held any official position. He died in 1879, and was survived one year by his widow, who was a worthy member of the Baptist Church. James Bailey Wells was reared and educated in Gonzales County, but owing to the fact that his father was a poor man with a large family of eight daughters and four sons to provide for, all of whom survived him and his wife, his sons were not given the benefit of a collegiate education, therefore, the subject of this sketch is the architect of his own fortune. He laid the foundation of his present worldly possessions by breaking wild horses at five dollars each, and with the money thus obtained invested in cattle, which he found exceedingly profitable. He has been a sagacious trader in land and cattle, and at one time owned 9,000 acres in Gonzales County, but from time to time has made sales of his real estate and now owns 3,000 acres, and is leasing 20,000 acres for the accommodation of his herds of cattle. He makes dealing in these animals a specialty and matures and markets 1,500 steers each year. He has a beautiful home in Gonzales, but gives active and personal management to his varied interests in the country. His youth prevented him taking part in the struggle between the North and South during the war, but before the war closed he served one year and eight days in Watson's Company, Benivedes Regiment, on the Rio Grande, and while there acquired a limited knowledge of Spanish and since, from controlling and working many Mexicans on his ranche, has become proficient in that language. He is a Knight Templar in the A. F. & A. M., and in his political views is a Democrat, and for five years past has been a member of the City Council, and for many years was Inspector of Animals for the county. In 1873 he led to the altar Miss Josephine Henry, daughter of Garner and Emeline (Hodges) Henry, and to their union the following children have been given: Charles Monroe, Effie, Martha Edna (deceased); Bailey W. (deceased); Audra (deceased); and James Bailey, Jr.

WILLIAM L. STEPHENSON. It is an indisputable fact that the United States stands alone in the pre-eminence of having an array of citizens, who, without adventitious aid or accident of birth, have attained to wealth and distinction in the localities in which they reside, and this is eminently true in the case of William L. Stephenson, who is one of the leading farmers of Hays County. He was born in the Blue Grass State in 1844, November 2d, the seventh of eleven children born to James and Mary Ann (Aplin) Stephenson, who were natives of the State of Kentucky also. The paternal grandparents were early settlers of Kentucky, and from that State moved to Missouri at an early day, where the rest of their lives was spent, the grandfather, John Stephenson, dying at a ripe old age. James Stephenson came to Texas from Kentucky in 1852, and after residing in Bastrop County for three years came to Hays County, and settled at Mountain City, which was before that place had received a name. He became an extensive farmer and stock-raiser, and was following these occupations at the time of his death, in 1866. The mother lived until 1892, and died at the age of eighty-two years. Both were worthy members of the Methodist Church. The subject of this sketch was eight years old when brought to Texas, and here he grew to mature years. In 1862 he entered the Confederate army as a member of Company A, Thirty-second Texas Cavalry, Wood's Regiment, and was in all the engagements in which his regiment participated, from Blair's Landing to Yellow Bayou, La., and did much hard riding and picket duty. Four of his brothers were in the Confederate army also: John Y., was in Company A, Thirty-second Texas Cavalry, and now resides in Kyle; Joel, was in Capt. Fisher's Company, Garland's Regiment of Infantry; A. B., was in the same company and regiment (Sixth Texas Infantry), and was captured with his regiment at Arkansas Post. Joel soon after made his escape, but A. B. was taken to Camp Chase and was there kept in captivity for a long time. He was then exchanged at City Point, Va., and from that time until the close of war was in about thirty-two regular engagements. He now lives in San Antonio, Texas. Joel served in Arkansas and for a short time on the Rio Grande River in Texas, and was in the last battle of the war in that section, at Point Isabel, and is now a resident of Blanco County, Texas. Taylor, the other brother, entered the Confederate service in the fall of 1864, as a member of Capt. Carrington's Company, and served on the Rio Grande River under Col. Rip Ford, and was also at Point Isabel. After the war was ended, William L. Stephenson came home and engaged in stock-raising as a means of livelihood. In 1868 he was married to Miss Sallie Allen, a native of Bastrop County, Texas, daughter of P. J. Allen, who came to this State from Alabama in 1835, and died in Hays County in 1860. His wife was Miss Jane Walker, and two of her brothers became residents of Texas in 1836, Martin Walker being a participant in the battle of San Jacinto, where he was very severely wounded in one of his shoulders. He resided in Bastrop County all his life, dying March 5, 1889. The other brother, W. W. Walker, was a Texas ranger for a time, and in one engagement with the Redskins was wounded by an arrow. He served in Company A, Thirty-second Texas Cavalry, Confederate States army, during the Civil War, and died in 1888, leaving a widow and children. Since 1880 Mr. Stephenson has resided on his present fine farm of 640 acres, and has 400 acres under cultivation, but the entire tract is capable of a high state of cultivation and, accordingly, remarkably valuable. He has a handsome, modern residence and everything about him to make life enjoyable and comfortable. He has a good general herd of Durham and Jersey cattle, and a few special Durhams and Jerseys for milk.

WALTER LITTLE. This retired farmer and worthy citizen of Fayette County, Texas, was born in Fort Bend County (that county being then a portion of Mexico), Texas, October 31, 1828, son of William Little, a native of the Keystone State, and Jane (Edwards) Little, who was born in Tennessee. When a young man Mr. Little went from his native State to what is now Missouri, and was for a time a resident of St. Louis, which was then a frontier post. Leaving St. Louis in 1821 he came to Texas with Stephen F. Austin and assisted in the erection of a fort, this being the first settlement of whites aside from a small settlement made at St. Augustine, near the Louisiana line, in the State. The company that first settled at Fort Bend consisted of five men, though seventeen came with Austin. However, twelve returned to the States. Those remaining and completing the fort for the protection of future settlers, as well as for themselves, were James or Charles Beard, William Smithers, Joseph Polly, William Little and another not remembered. In 1822 a number of families arrived from the States, among them that of William Morton, the grandfather of our subject. These early settlers had very little trouble with the Indians during 1824, and as new settlers came pouring in the Indians moved farther out. In 1836 Texas had a population of 20,000, though a large number were slaves. Very little farming was done, most of the land being used for pasturage, and large droves of horses and cattle covered the immense prairies. As early as 1828 considerable trouble occurred with the Indians, who began to grow jealous of the many settlers now pouring in. Mr. Little, father of our subject, was never in but one Indian fight previous to 1836, and that was at Jones Creek. In the fall of 1835 Mr. Little was serving in the Texan army, and consequently was not in the battle of San Jacinto. Having been sent by Gen. Sam Houston to remove his family with others, Mr. Little took them into the bottoms of the Brazos River, among the immense canebrakes, and as the river was very high at that time he could not get them across the bayous. Later, when the trouble was over, they returned to their homes. Mr. Little remained on his farm until his death, in 1841, when fifty years old. He left seven children: John, William, Walter, Martha, James, Robert and George, all deceased except our subject and the last named, who resides in Columbus, Colorado County, this State. The Edwards and Morton families came to Texas about 1822, and Mrs. Little was the step-daughter of William Morton. The latter was the first white man who ever navigated the Brazos River, as he came with his family from the mouth up to where the town of Richmond now stands, in Fort Bend County. Mr. and Mrs. Little were the first white couple married west of Trinity River, their union taking place April 2, 1824, and although not Catholics, they were married by a priest, on account the laws of Mexico, which made marriage not legal nor children lawful unless the ceremony was performed by one. John Little, the paternal grandfather of our subject, came from Pennsylvania in 1823 with his wife, and when quite an old man served in several Indian wars in the East. He was also in the Revolutionary War. William Little was his only child. The latter's wife, and the mother of our subject, was the step-daughter of William Morton, as before stated. Mr. Morton made the first brick in the State, and was one of the wealthiest men in this section of the State. He died in 1833, leaving a family of four children: John, Louisa, Mary and William. Walter had but little chance for an education. In 1836 a young man came from Kentucky and taught school in the neighborhood, and young Little and his brothers attended for six months. This was all the schooling he ever received, but being of an inquiring and investigating turn of mind, with a thirst for knowledge, he secured a very good business education and became a competent surveyor. Having been reared to farming and stock raising he chose that as his life's occupation, and followed it successfully from 1848 to 1860, being the owner of a number of slaves when the Civil War broke out. Mr. Little served in the Quartermaster Department during those troublesome times, and afterwards speculated in land until 1879, when he returned to his former occupation of farming, and continued this until 1890. He then sold out, and in 1893 moved to town. He was married first in 1858 to Miss Sarah Wilson, daughter of Dr. Hugh Wilson, of Rock Bridge County, Va., and by that union became the father of two children: Hugh, of Winchester, and Mary, wife of Edward McRee, of Colorado County. Mrs. Little died in January, 1870, and in November of that year Mr. Little married Miss Maggie Laird, daughter of Thomas and Ann (Carter) Laird, natives of Pennsylvania and Virginia respectively. Mr. Little's second union resulted in the birth of three children: Nellie, Walter and Sam. On the 1st of February, 1861, Mr. Little moved to Fayette County, this State, and here served four years as County Commissioner. He was never an office seeker, takes but very little interest in politics and is independent in his views. Socially he is a member of the A. F. & A. M.—Morton Lodge No. 72, and is also a K. of H. of this place.

CHRISTOPHER COLUMBUS LITTLEFIELD. A noble class of men have built up the agricultural and stock-raising interests of Gonzales County, Texas, and have made it a garden spot in the great commonwealth of the State. Among those who have been active and efficient in this work is he whose name stands at the head of this sketch. He has been identified with the farming interests of the county for many years, and in every walk of life has conducted himself in an honorable, upright manner. He owes his nativity to Gibson County, Tennessee, where he was born October 5, 1838, a son of Zachariah N. and Mary A. B. (McGarity) Littlefield, both of whom were born in the Palmetto State. During his early manhood the father removed to Gibson County, West Tennessee, and in 1838 removed to Panola County, Miss., and from there, in 1853, to Gonzales County, Texas, and was engaged in planting near Belmont, on the Guadalupe River, until his death in 1866. He was a Whig in politics. His wife survived him until 1874, when she, too, passed away. In the State of Mississippi the immediate subject of this sketch was reared until about fifteen years of age. He came to Texas with his parents, arriving in January, 1854. His father's possessions consisted principally of negroes; he, of course, lost nearly all he possessed by the war, and therefore Christopher Columbus was left with a very small patrimony with which to commence the battle of life. At the opening of the war he enlisted in the Eighth Texas Cavalry, "Terry's Texas Rangers," and served with the Army of the Tennessee in every engagement from Bowling Green, Ky., to its final surrender and parole at Charlotte, N. C. He returned home with the rank of Second Lieutenant, and with the consciousness of having performed every duty assigned him to the best of his ability. For seven years after his return home he was engaged in farming and stock driving on the Guadalupe River, near Belmont. In 1873 he removed to Landis Creek, near Leesville, where he continued the pursuits of farming and stock-raising to some degree of pecuniary success. Politically he is a Democrat, but the conflict and strife of the political arena has no charms for him, hence has never been an office seeker, his time being completely occupied by his private business. He is a Master Mason of Leesville Lodge No. 334, of the A. F. & A. M., and he and his wife are members of the Baptist Church. He was married in 1866 to Miss Lucy A. Bratton, a daughter of John and Louisa Bratton, residents of Gonzales County, Texas. To the above union of Mr. and Mrs. Littlefield the following children were born: Zachariah, Jr., Braxton B., who died in 1885, at the age of sixteen years; Virgil C. and Rayburn A. In 1873 his wife Lucy A. died. In 1874 he married the second time, Miss Sarah Elizabeth Bratton, a younger sister of his first wife, and to this union the following children were born: Lucy Lina, Edgar W., who died in 1877; Mary Louisa, Oran Ireland, Cleveland Rass, and an infant that died unnamed at a few hours of age.

MORGAN DENMAN. Nowhere within the limits of Gonzales County, Texas, is there a man who takes greater interest in its agricultural affairs than Morgan Denman, or who strives more continually to promote and advance these interests. Every life has a history of its own, and although in appearance it may possess little to distinguish it from others, yet the connection of Mr. Denman with the agricultural interests of this region has contributed to give him a wide and popular acquaintance with many of the citizens of the county, if not personally, then by name. He was born in Guadalupe County, Texas, in 1864, the eldest of three children born to Morgan and Annie (McCahaen) Denman, the former of whom was either born in or came to this State when a very small child. He died at the age of eighty-two years, after having followed the useful and honorable calling of the farmer. His widow still survives him. In the county in which he was born, Morgan Denman, the subject of this sketch, was reared and educated, obtaining such education as the common schools of that day afforded. Upon starting out in life for himself it was as a tiller of the soil, and the fine property of which he is now the owner shows that he is well adapted to the calling. Since December, 1893, he has been a resident of Gonzales County, and now lives on and owns the old Dr. Cox homestead at Oak Forest, which comprises a very fine tract of 300 acres, the most of which is fertile river bottom land. Besides this valuable property he also owns a good farm of 150 acres in Guadalupe County, and both of his places are well improved and in an excellent state of cultivation. Several years ago he came to the conclusion that the raising of mules would be a profitable business, and to this much of his attention has since been given, and as a monetary venture it has fulfilled his expectations. He has now a herd of twenty-six brood mares and a fine blooded Kentucky jack. In 1893 Mr. Denman was married to Miss Adella Cox, a daughter of Dr. Cox, of Gonzales County, and their union has resulted in the birth of one daughter, Grace. Mr. and Mrs. Denman are worthy members of the Methodist Episcopal Church.

VIRGIL S. RABB. The life of any man is of great benefit to the community in which he resides when all his efforts are directed toward its advancement, and when he is honest, upright and progressive. Such a man is Virgil S. Rabb, a native of Fayette County, Texas, born February 15, 1839, the son of John and Mary (Crownover) Rabb, and the grandson of William and Mary (Smalley) Rabb, and John and Mary (Chesney) Crownover. William Rabb was born in the Keystone State, in Fayette County. At an early date he moved with his family to near St. Louis, Mo., on the Illinois side of the river, where he erected a water mill for grinding flour, ran it successfully, sold out and moved to Washington, Ark., and there resided until 1819. He then came to Texas, but did not bring his family until 1822, coming with Austin's colony. However, he himself was here in 1821 and raised his first crop on Rabb's Prairie that year. This was the first crop made by an American in this section. His son, Capt. Thomas J. Rabb, accompanied him on both his early trips, and they assisted in building one of the first forts, or block-houses, of Austin's settlement. Early in 1822 William Rabb crossed the Colorado River where La Grange now stands, and one of the first block-houses in the county was erected four miles east of West Point and close to the Colorado River, at a bluff called Indian Hill, the entire neighborhood taking part in the building. William Rabb first located on the west side of the river. In 1831 he built a water mill on the Colorado River, on Rabb's Prairie, getting the stones from Scotland, but the rest of the material from New Orleans. This was the first mill built in the county. In getting the stones from the coast Mr. Rabb made a wooden axle and used the stones for wheels, attaching the tongue to them, wagons not having yet come into fashion in Texas. In that way he brought them from Matagorda, a distance of over 200 miles. For this Mr. Rabb received from the Mexican Government three leagues of land, which he selected on Rabb's Prairie. In 1833 occurred the big overflow of the Colorado River and the mill was destroyed, this being the second overflow of the river after the settlement. Previous to this, in 1823, an Indian scare occurred, but the settlers had gathered in the fort, and although kept there for three days by the Indians, they escaped with no loss greater than having some of their stock killed. After the Indians had left, Mr. Rabb and his friends moved to Wharton County, where his sons, Thomas and Andrew, had previously located, and resided there until 1829. He then returned to this county and settled for the first time on Rabb's Prairie, where he was actively and extensively engaged in raising stock. During the building of the mill before mentioned, or in 1832, he passed away when about sixty years of age. For some time during his life he resided in Illinois, and became the owner of fifty or sixty negroes, but later he lost them all when that State passed a law freeing them, except one called Frank, who came with him to Texas. Mr. and Mrs. Rabb reared a family of five children: Rachel, wife of A. M. Newman; Andrew, John, Thomas (called Captain Rabb), and Ulysses. John Rabb, father of our subject, came to Texas in 1822, and located on the west side of Colorado River, nine miles north of La Grange. He immediately went into the Colorado bottom and commenced to clear land, but subsequently, on account of Indians stealing his stock, moved to Fort Bend County. From there he moved to Wharton County, Texas, where he improved a good farm and where he resided until 1829, when he located on Rabb's Prairie, this county, on the place now known as the Dr. McKinney place. On the mill mentioned as being built by William Rabb, John Rabb did most of the work and took charge of it until it was washed away. After this he turned his attention to farming and stock-raising and continued this until 1848. Previous to this, in 1835, he joined the Texas army and was in the fight at Gonzales, Conception and others, and when the army had fallen back to Burnham's block house on Colorado River and began again to retreat, Mr. Rabb came home and took his family, with others, as far as Robin's Ferry on the Trinity. He then returned to the army, but was not in the battle of San Jacinto. Returning home afterwards he devoted his energies to building up his fallen fortune, for he was a heavy loser during the war. Later he was in many Indian fights, but did not take part in the War of 1848, but was represented by his son Montgomery, who was a member of Hays' Regiment. In that year Mr. Rabb built the first steam saw mill in the county, located on Rabb's Creek in the northern portion of this county, and he operated this mill until 1859. He then sold to Alexander McDow for $45,000, this being the largest transaction made in the county up to that time, and bought Barton's Springs, near the city of Austin, which embraced a track of land of thirty acres. The remainder of his days were passed in retirement and he died June 5, 1861, after spending one of the most active lives of the early settlers. His wife survived him until October 13, 1882, dying when in her seventy seventh year. Both were earnest members of the Methodist Episcopal Church and the first Methodist sermon ever preached west of the Brazos River was preached in his house. The nine children born to this worthy couple were named as follows: Montgomery, George W., Melissa, Marion, J. W., L. D., V. S., Mary, wife of David Croft of this county, and G. T. of Austin. All these children are deceased except our subject, Mary and G. T. Our subject's maternal grandfather, John Crownover, was a native of one of the Carolinas. V. S. Rabb was educated at Rutersville, and branched out for himself in 1862 by joining

Sincerely yours

Edwin H. Terrell

the Confederate army, Company I, Sixteenth Texas Infantry. He was made Third Lieutenant and served in the trans-Mississippi Department, and was in all the battles of Louisiana, except those that occurred while on "leave of absence." Later he was made Captain of his company by general promotion, and was honorably discharged from the army at Hempstead, Texas. After his return home he erected a saw mill, but only followed this for six years, when he engaged in farming, continuing this until 1884. He then moved to La Grange to educate his children, and while there was in the lumber business. In 1891 he moved to West Point, this county, and in connection with the lumber business here has been engaged in merchandising since 1890. In the latter occupation he has been successful, and has opened stores at Winchester and Smithville. Mr. Rabb was married in 1869 to Miss Dulcie Kenedy, a daughter of A. S. and Mary (Earthman) Kenedy. Mr. Kenedy came to Texas in 1837 from Alabama, his native State. Mr. and Mrs. Rabb are the parents of six living children: V. S., Jr., Gussie, David P., Dulcie, Jr., George F. and Sallie L. Two children are deceased. Mrs. Rabb is a member of the Christian Church. Like his father, Mr. Rabb is a strong Democrat in politics, and takes a deep interest in the welfare of his party. He is a prominent and influential citizen and a man who has done his share towards the county's advancement. His brother, J. W. Rabb, was a member of Captain Jarmon's Company of the Terry Rangers, known as the Eighth Texas Cavalry, and served through Tennessee, Kentucky, Mississippi and Georgia, and participated in all the battles fought by that noted regiment, except during a short period when he was disabled by a wound, from which he never fully recovered. His death occurred in 1885.

LOUIS TURNER. This well known pioneer, who is everywhere respected for his sterling worth, is now retired from the active duties of life and enjoys the ease secured by a well-spent and active career. He was born in Prussia, Germany, November 26, 1834, and of the nine children born to his parents, Christian and Mary (Buttermann) Turner, he was seventh in order of birth. The parents were both natives of the old country, and there the father died when our subject was about eight years of age. The latter remained in his native country until grown, received a fair education, and served an apprenticeship at the locksmith and gunsmith trades. He then took passage for the United States, landed at Baltimore, and went from there to Cincinnati, Ohio, where he joined an elder brother. He then worked in a machine shop for several months, after which he traveled for a time, looking for a location. After this he was on a steamboat on the Mississippi River a few months, and then located in New Orleans, where he worked in a gunsmith shop for nearly two years. On account of his health he came to Texas, and spent one year in Victoria, after which, in 1856, he located in Hallettsville, where he engaged with a gunsmith. After remaining with him eleven months, Mr. Turner bought the business out, and carried it on successfully until the spring of 1862. He then enlisted in the Confederate army, Whitfield Legion, and left Hallettsville with Company A, as chief bugler of the legion. He first went to Arkansas, was afterward sent to Mississippi, thence to Corinth, where he was in the battle fought at that place in October, and then went to Iuka. While in the battle at the latter place, and when he had the bugle at his mouth to blow a charge, a bullet from the enemy struck the bugle and made a hole through it, but he kept on blowing until the charge was made. In this battle he was

20

slightly wounded in the side, and five bullets perforated his coat. He was captured on the Hatchie River at the second battle of Corinth and taken to Bolivar, Tenn. The second day in prison some of the boys asked him to play the reveille, and being always full of sport, he complied, and afterward blew a charge. Soon after an officer came and asked for the man who blew the calls. Mr. Turner came forward, and after a little conversation the bugle was taken by the officer and never returned. Mr. Turner was kept in confinement for ten days, after which he was paroled and came to Texas. After being exchanged, he joined Hardeman's Regiment and at once went to Arkansas, where he was in the battle of Poison Springs, etc. His command made a raid on Fort Smith, Ark., and he was one of 300 volunteers to attack a regiment of Federals on the prairie of Des Arc, Ark., six miles from Fort Smith. Before the line was fully formed he was shot in the leg, the bone broken, and the horse on which he was riding killed. From the time he was wounded, 9 o'clock in the morning, until 5 o'clock P. M., he remained on the battlefield, and while lying there wounded, two Indians came on the field and shot a wounded man. Mr. Turner only preserved his life by feigning death. A little later two men came on the field and robbed him of money and all valuables, and then a guard came, who remained until an ambulance made its appearance. In this three dead men were placed, with our subject on top of them, and in this manner he rode to Fort Smith, a distance of six miles. Mr. Turner became feverish in the hospital, and got so bad that he was placed in the dead ward, where he remained over a week, after which he began to improve. He was then returned to the hospital, where he remained a long time, and was then sent to Little Rock. There he remained an invalid until the war closed. After leaving prison, and when he began to get a little better, he made rings from buttons, and selling these got sufficient money to buy a mule and saddle and bridle. Thus equipped, he made his way to Hallettsville, Texas, from Little Rock, and arrived there July 27, 1865. When he fell from his horse on the battlefield near Fort Smith a friend saw him fall and wrote home to his people that he had been killed. Now, when he made his appearance at home, a most exciting and pathetic scene ensued, for his friends thought he had been dead for a year. After recovering, Mr. Turner resumed business as a gunsmith in Hallettsville, and continued this until 1874. Being a superior workman, he had more work than he could do, and trade came from a long distance. About the year 1872 he began to erect an hotel, and two years later this was completed, and was the first stone building in the town, as well as the best one at that time. Mr. Turner conducted this hotel until about 1884, and it was most popular and well patronized. He is now retired from active pursuits and is enjoying a comfortable and happy existence. He has been quite active in political matters, has served as Alderman and Mayor, and was Deputy Sheriff under Smothers. Mr. Turner has also been Trustee of the School Board, and has held other local positions. In 1861, previous to entering the army, our subject was married to Mrs. Josephine (Bragger) Dubois, a daughter of Jasper Bragger, a native of Germany. Mr. Bragger came to the United States and settled in Texas in 1846. There he died the next year. Miss Josephine was first married to John Dubois, by whom she had two children: Leola, wife of Dr. Shelley, and Mary, who died when thirteen years of age. Her union to our subject resulted in the birth of three children: Ida, wife of Dr. Eidson, of Shiner; Louis, died when about fourteen years of age, and Lena. Aside from his property in the city, Mr. Turner has a fine tract of 200 acres adjoining the town. He is a natural musician, and has done much toward maintaining a band in Hallettsville. He joined the band before the war, soon became its leader, and after reorganizing it after the war, was at its head for many years. He was the main organizer of the Hallettsville Shooting Club, and for years its President and main director, building it up to a noted association. He is one of the most prominent men of the county and is well liked.

EDWARD DICKINSON. This prominent farmer of Oak Forest, Gonzales County, Texas, was born in the vicinity of where he now lives in 1845, the second of five children born to Edward and Rachel (Heminger) Dickinson, who were natives of England and Germany respectively. The father, accompanied by an elder brother, John Dickinson, came to the United States near the close of the '20s, and to Texas with Austin's colony about 1830 or 1831. He made a settlement, and located his headright eleven and a half miles above Gonzales, on the Guadalupe River, and on that place made his home the remainder of his life. He was a participant in the Texas Revolution, was in all the engagements in this section, the most noted of which was the famous battle of San Jacinto. For services which he rendered his country he was given a land bounty which, however, was not located until after his death. It comprises 960 acres in Taylor and Jones counties, and is owned by the subject of this sketch. The father's death occurred in 1848, while on a visit to New Braunfels. His widow afterward married a Mr. Booth, and is still living. John Dickinson, uncle of the subject of this sketch, was killed by Indians not long after he had come to this State, while boating on the San Antonio River near San Antonio. Edward Dickinson, the subject of this sketch, was reared in the county in which he now resides, and was educated in the common schools, where he made fair progress in his studies. Immediately after attaining his majority he engaged in farming. Previous to this, however, in March, 1862, when but seventeen years of age, he enlisted in the Confederate service, becoming a member of the Second Battalion of Wall's Legion. After being drilled in camp for three months, he was sent east of the Mississippi River, which he crossed at Vicksburg, and his command joined the army of Gen. Price at Holly Springs, Miss., after which he participated in the battle of Fort Pemberton. They then moved back to Vicksburg, and were invested in that city until its fall, July 4, 1863. Mr. Dickinson then returned home and joined his mother in Lavaca County, but in 1864 once more entered the Confederate service, at Galveston, and was on the coast of Texas until the close of the war. He made his home in Lavaca County with his mother until the spring of 1867, and was married there in 1866 to Miss Kate N. Vancil, a native of the Lone Star State, and a daughter of Peter Vancil, an early settler of that county from Illinois, coming thither in 1837, at the age of fifteen years. He was a farmer. In 1867 Mr. Dickinson came with his wife to Gonzales County, and until 1883 lived on the old homestead, then bought his present farm, a fine tract containing 312 acres, of which 120 are under cultivation, and well improved with substantial and commodious buildings. He has a small herd of horses and cattle in Runnels County, but the principal part of his attention is given to his fertile farm, which yields about forty bushels of corn to the acre, and one-half bale of cotton. He has been quite actively interested in politics, has been a delegate to various conventions, and has held the office of County Commissioner to the entire satisfaction of his constituents. He is popular with all classes, and in a business way commands the respect of all. He and his wife have three children: Edward Conrad, William Calvin and Olive. Mrs. Dickinson is a member of the Christian Church and Mr. Dickinson is a-member of the honorable order of Masons.

JOHN B. LEWIS. In Clark County, Alabama, April 1st, 1845 there was born a child who grew to sturdy manhood, not in that county, but in this, whither his parents moved the same year. The parents, W. W. and Sophia (Bell) Lewis, first located near where Industry now stands and found the country sparsely settled, not more than half a dozen families within ten miles. All their marketing was done at Houston, sixty-five miles distant, but there was a tread-mill in the vicinity where all their milling was sent. Mr. Lewis was an extensive stockman and farmer. Up to 1861 he was engaged in farming and stock-raising, but when his services were needed in the South he enlisted in Company F, Green's Regiment, and served on the Western border of Texas, and also in Arizona and New Mexico. While fighting in the battle of Val Verde he fell mortally wounded and died in a temporary hospital. He left a wife and five children, our subject being the youngest. The children were named as follows: Mary E., widow of Matthew Hosea; Sophronia J., widow of Henry Chatham; Lavonia, deceased, was the wife of Charles B. Syme; James M., served in the Confederate army in the same company with his father, but was principally in Louisiana, Arkansas and Texas; and John B. In 1862 Mrs. Lewis was married to G. W. Wilson and by him became the mother of two children, Josephine V., wife of John Kaiser, and C. H., of Fisher County. Mr. and Mrs. Wilson resided in Washington County, Texas, for many years, and there his death occurred. She died in Lee County while on a visit. During his boyhood days our subject attended the common schools, but for the most part his education has been received by his own individual efforts. When in his sixteenth year he enlisted in Company E, Second Texas Cavalry, of Waul's Legion, and served under Generals Forrest, Van Dorn and Wheeler. He was in the latter part of the battle at Corinth, Second Holly Springs, Boliver, Jackson, and in the engagements in and around Tupelo, Miss. From there he went to North Alabama, fought in and around Tuscumbia, but subsequently returned to Mississippi, where the Confederates attacked Grant's forces around Vicksburg. He was in the vicinity of that city at the time of the surrender. After this he was in numerous engagements, but the most serious one was on Wolf River, Tennessee, and at Fort Pillow. He served from the fall of 1862 until the close of the spring, 1865, his last engagement being in southern Alabama near Mobile. Arriving home in June, 1865, he engaged actively in farming and stock-raising, and continued this up to 1878, when he was elected Sheriff. This position he filled in such a capable and satisfactory manner that he was re-elected and remained in that office for twelve years. After the first race for that position he had no opposition. From 1890 to 1892 he served as County Commissioner, but since then he has given his attention strictly to farming and stock-raising, and has some fine graded Jersey cattle on his farm. In the year 1879 he was married to Miss Mary J. Bell, a native of this county and daughter of Jasper and Elizabeth (Brewer) Bell. Mr. Bell was one of the early settlers of this section and was a soldier in the Confederate army. He died when Mrs. Lewis was a small girl, and Mrs. Bell afterwards married Thomas H.

Burns, another early settler of the county. To Mr. and Mrs. Lewis have been born three children; Birdie, Nora and Edna. Mr. Lewis is a Mason, Bellville Lodge No. 223 and Bellville Chapter, R. A. M.

JOHN MITCHELL FLY, M. D. It would be a difficult matter to name a branch of business more important to the welfare of a community than that devoted to the sale and importation of drugs and chemicals, or one demanding more ability and scientific knowledge on the part of those engaged; and this is doubly important when the proprietor of such an establishment is also a successful medical practitioner, for the good done by him is twice as great. Both these occupations are followed by John Mitchell Fly, who, in addition to his professional duties, is quite extensively engaged in planting in Gonzales County. He was born near Camden, Madison County, Miss., May 30, 1849, a son of John Dalton and Julia (Stokes) Fly, the former of whom was born in Maury County, Tennessee, and the latter in North Carolina. John D. Fly was a planter and stock-raiser, and while still in his early manhood came to Mississippi, but in 1851 removed to Texas, and settled near the town of Gonzales on the Guadalupe River, where he devoted his attention to farming. He is still living with his second wife, and is spending his old age with relatives in Mississippi. He is a Master Mason and in his religious views is a Methodist. The immediate subject of this sketch was reared in Gonzales County, Texas, and received his education in the private schools of that place, after which he finished his education in Stonewall Institute, of which his uncle, G. W. L. Fly, was Master. Upon reaching a suitable age, twenty-two years, he began the practice of medicine, and after two years returned to the University at New Orleans, where he graduated in medicine from this well-known institution in 1874. He began the practice in the town of Leesville, where he has continued with the best results for the past twenty-three years. His name is almost a household word throughout the section in which he lives, for he has entered nearly every home in his professional capacity, and as a druggist and planter he by no means occupies an unimportant place. In politics he is a Democrat of the Jeffersonian school, and socially is a Master Mason of Leesville Lodge, No. 334, and a Royal Arch Mason of the Chapter of Gonzales, Texas. He was first married October 15, 1877, to Miss Ella J. Matthews, to which union two children have been born: Clara M. and Hattie B. The mother of these children died March 23, 1886, and Dr. Fly's second marriage was celebrated December 16, 1891, Miss Annie Brown becoming his wife. They have one child, Roger Q.

CURRAN KYLE. Among the representative farmers of Hays County, Texas, it is a pleasure to present a sketch of the gentleman whose name appears at the head of this article, and whose pleasant home and excellent farm attest the thrift and enterprise of the owner. He was born in Holly Springs, Miss., in 1841, a son of Claiborne and Lucy (Bugg) Kyle, who were natives of the State of Tennessee. The paternal grandfather, William Kyle, was born in the State of Virginia, but his father was a product of the Isle of Erin. The mother's people were of Scotch lineage. Claiborne and Lucy Kyle came to Texas at an early day, and a further notice of them will be found in the sketch of Capt. Ferg Kyle. Curran Kyle was but twelve years of age at the time he accompanied his parents to the Lone Star State, and owing to the unsettled condition of the country at that time, his advantages, so far as an education was concerned, were limited. He made his home with his parents until the bursting of the war cloud which had so long hovered over the country, at which time he enlisted in Company D, Eighth Texas Cavalry (Terry's Rangers), and was a participant in all the engagements in which his regiment took part. He saw some hard service, but bore the privations and dangers of war well, and was one of the most faithful soldiers that ever donned the gray. While in battle he had four horses killed under him, and during his service was wounded five times. After the war he came home and engaged in stock-raising and made a specialty of the breeding of blooded horses, and this has always been one of his favorite and most paying occupations. He has resided in Hays County ever since coming to the State, and in 1887 became the owner of a fine farm of 420 acres near Kyle, all of which is exceptionally fertile land, well adapted for general farming. Two hundred acres are under culti-vation and well improved with good farm buildings, and all the improvements that are on this place nave been made by Mr. Kyle, and are of a substantial and valuable kind. Mr. Kyle has always supported the principles of the Democratic party, and he has been quite active in the political affairs of his section. He is a member of the Baptist Church, a thorough gentleman, is agreeable in manners and of a kind and generous disposition, ready to aid those in distress. He was married in 1865 to Miss Emma Breedlove, a native of Kentucky, and a daughter of Ira Breedlove, an early settler of Texas. Mrs. Kyle is also a member of the Baptist Church.

JOHN L. DICKINSON. Among the reliable and substantial farmers of Gon-zales County, Texas, may be mentioned John L. Dickinson, who has done a good deal to bring the county to its present admirable state of cultivation, for he was reared to the calling of a farmer, and this occupa-tion has received his attention to a greater or less extent up to the pres-ent time. He was born on the farm on which he now resides, March 2, 1843, the eldest child born to Edward and Rachel (Heminger) Dickinson. The father came from England with his brother, John, and located a head-right on the Guadalupe River, three miles from the present town of Bel-mont. He was a participant in many battles with the Indians from the time he located here (1824) almost up to the day of his death, and was also in the Texas Revolution. He died while on a trip to New Braunfels, July 27, 1848, and was buried there, but being a prominent Mason, his body was exhumed by the members of that order in 1850, and was brought for burial to Gonzales. His wife came from Germany to Texas with her people at the age of ten years, but all of the family died soon after with the exception of herself and her sister Christine. She was reared by a family who bore the name of Cravens, and her sister by a family named Hill. She married Mr. Dickinson in 1841 and was taken by him to his headright on the Guadalupe River, but left a widow seven years later. She then married Josiah Randolph who died six month later, and in 1854 she was married to James Booth. John L. Dickinson was brought up in Gonzales County, but in 1860 moved to Lavaca County with his mother. In 1861 he offered his services to the Confederacy and for six months thereafter was located at Galveston. April 8, 1862, he re-enlisted in Waul's Texas Legion and was at once sent to Vicksburg, Miss., thence to the northern part of the State, and took part in the engagement there. His command was then returned to Vicksburg and he was in that city during the memorable siege. After its fall, July 4, 1863, he started home on the 12th of that month and there remained until November of that year, when he once more entered the service, his operations being confined to Texas until the close of the war in May, 1865. On Christmas day, 1866, he led to the altar Miss Elizabeth A. Fitzgerald, a native of Texas, and in 1873 he came to his present home, his old birthplace and his father's old homestead. His estate comprises 1,107 acres, of which 135 are under cultivation and which yield forty bushels of corn and one-half bale of cotton to the acre. The most of this farm is rich river valley land, and as Mr. Dickinson is intelligent and practical in its cultivation, the income he derives therefrom is in every way satisfactory. He and his wife have eight children: William Edward, John L. jr., Nettie May, Mary Estelle, Otis Alphonso, Holly Clio, and two others that died in early childhood. Mr. and Mrs. Dickinson are members of the Missionary Baptist Church and move in the best social circles of their section.

PETER L. HABERMACHER. Agricultural pursuits have occupied the attention of this gentleman the greater portion of his life and he has proved himself one of its most worthy exponents, being thrifty, progressive and pushing. He was born in Harris County, Texas, April 17, 1854, a son of Casper J. and Eliza J. (Coots) Habermacher, natives of Germany and Missouri respectively. The maternal ancestors came from England, but the father's people came from Germany to America in 1832 and settled near where the town of Harrisburg, Texas, now stands. Casper J. was a small lad at the time he accompanied his parents to this county, and for a number of years after coming here the family were in very straitened circumstances, and the family labored at anything they could find to do, such as picking cotton, corn, etc. Frequently Casper would labor at cotton picking, obtain a little corn in this way and carry it on his back ten miles to the mill to have it ground into meal. Thus the family existed for some time, but through their energy and perseverance, better times soon came to them and they began farming on their own account. The family were in the "run away" from the Mexicans in 1834. Mr. Habermacher harnessed a yoke of oxen to a slife on which he placed their beds and bedding and such of the children that could not walk, and the remainder of the family made their way on foot to a place of safety. In 1856 Mr. Habermacher came to Austin County, and here his father lived for a number of years, the mother outliving him one year. They experienced more than the average share of trials and privations incident to pioneer life, but their efforts and their results teach a lesson to the thoughtful, and are worthy of emulation. All their clothing was homespun, and their table was always supplied with an abundance of wild game, such as venison, turkey, beef, etc., for droves of wild cattle were numerous, and herds of wild horses were also numerous on the prairie and along the river bottoms. When Casper J. was married he had little to commence housekeeping on, but he had abundance of health and energy which was in itself a goodly capital. He began dealing in cattle, the money for the purchase of which was made by making saddle-trees. After a time he started a tan yard also in connection with his saddle-tree business and, as above stated, eventually drifted into the cattle business, at which he made a handsome fortune. After coming to Austin County he turned his attention to stock exchange and had a permit from the Confederate Government to furnish cattle to the Confederate soldiers, thus he was not in active service. He died in this county in 1883, his widow surviving him one year. They reared a family of four children: Susan, wife of Austin Cole, Peter L., John S. and James C. At the time of his death Mr. Habermacher owned about 1,250 acres of land, with 450 under cultivation, and about 1,000 head of cattle. Peter L. Habermacher, the immediate subject, of this sketch, received the principal part of his education in this county, but for a short time attended school in Harris County. At the age of twenty-seven years he commenced doing for himself, having given his services to his father up to this time, and was married to Miss Susan Allen of this county, a daughter of James and Penelope (Johnson) Allen (see sketch). At the time of his marriage his father gave him 700 acres of land, slightly improved, and he has since added to this until he now owns 2,000 acres of fine prairie and bottom lands, and has under cultivation some 350 acres. Like his father he is considerably interested in stock and owns some 300 head of cattle and quite a fine drove of horses. He was married in 1881 and his union has resulted in the birth of five children: Miles A., Clintie, Mary E., Susan C. and Hermon G. Both Mr. and Mrs. Habermacher are members of the Christian Church, and politically he has always supported the principles of the Democratic party.

ANTON SCHNABEL. This worthy business man is a member of the firm of A. Schnabel & Co., of Belmont, Texas, and in the conduct of his affairs has shown himself to be shrewd, practical and far-seeing. He owes his nativity to Gaudalupe County, Texas, where he first saw the light in 1863, his parents being John and Eliza Schnabel, the latter of whom came to Texas in 1847 and the father a few years later. The maternal grandfather, Anton Troeste, upon his arrival in this State with his family, settled near the town of New Braunfels where he became the owner of a tract of land which he greatly improved and on which he resided until his death in 1891. Upon his arrival in Texas (about 1849) John Schnabel at once became a Texas Ranger and was in a number of fights with the Indians. He was married to Miss Troeste in 1859, and at once began devoting his attention to tilling the soil, but his labors were interrupted by the opening of the Civil War, and he enlisted in the Confederate service. He afterwards became very extensively engaged in farming, and with two other men purchased a tract of land containing 8,000 acres in Gonzales County, six miles northeast of Belmont, which has since been mostly sold out to small farmers. Mr. Schnabel is now the owner of the old homestead of Anton Troeste, comprising 225 acres, all of which is in a high state of cultivation, and under Mr. Schnabel's thrifty and practical management yields larger crops than many larger and less carefully tilled places. He was left a widower in 1886, his wife having been, as he is, an earnest member of the Catholic Church. Anton Schnabel, the immediate subject of this sketch was reared in New Braunfels, and was educated in the schools of that place and of Austin. After finishing his education he worked for a time on the ranch of his father, then came to Belmont, and, with W. J. Grubbs, founded his present business. In 1893 he erected his present store building, which is 36x72, and he carries a well selected stock of general merchandise valued about at $6,000, his annual sales amounting to about $25,000. He is one of the leading merchants of the place and deserves the success with which his efforts have been attended, for he is courteous, accommodating and honorable in his methods of dealing with his customers, and disposes of his goods at prices within the reach of all. His establishment is tastefully arranged, is well stocked and his patronage is rapidly on the increase. He may be called a "hustler" and is prospering accordingly. He has been Postmaster of Belmont since 1891, has been a member of numerous conventions and served on various committees. He and family are active Republicans and are public spirited and law abiding citizens. In 1888 he was married to Miss Annie Rinehard, a native of Texas, a step-daughter of August Ebert, and to their union two children have been given: Malinda and Eugene.

MAJOR A. W. HILLIARD. The calling of the farmer is as old as the world, and the majority of men who have followed it have led upright and blameless lives, and the career of Major A. W. Hilliard is no exception to this rule. He was born in Greensburg, Ky., in 1841, the sixth of eight children born to Micagah and Catherine O. (Hutchinson) Hilliard, who were also Kentuckians. The paternal grandparents were of Scotch-Irish descent and were from South Carolina, while the maternal grandparents were Virginians of English descent. Micagah Hilliard died when the subject of this sketch was a child, but his wife survived him until the 6th of February, 1892, when she, too, passed away. The subject of this sketch remained in the State of his birth until 1854, when he accompanied his mother to Lexington, Mo., where his home continued to be up to 1861. He then enlisted in the Confederate army with which he served until the war closed, and then went to Colorado, and was there engaged in mining until 1868, when he began assisting in the construction of the Union Pacific Railroad, a portion of the time being on the road with a construction train. He then returned to his old home in Missouri, and after remaining there for a few months came to Texas, and in various parts of the State became largely interested in the stock business. After a time he also engaged in merchandising at Sweetwater, Pecos and Midland, but since 1891 has resided on his present estate, which is situated two and a half miles west of Kyle, and comprises 1,200 acres of excellent land in the Blanco River valley. Two hundred acres of this land are under cultivation and much of Mr. Hilliard's time is spent in beautifying and improving his handsome farm. He has a very valuable herd of Jersey cattle, headed by "Live Oak," one of the most valuable male Jerseys in the State, with a magnificent pedigree, and is quite extensively engaged in the dairy business, and has separators for separating cream from new milk. He was a successful merchant and banker, and was one of the organizers and President of the First National Bank of Midland, Texas, until he resigned in 1894. He was largely interested in and was one of the stockholders of the oil mill at Dublin, Texas, and in his agricultural operations he has been no less successful than as a business man. He is now enjoying a little relaxation from years of active toil, yet he always seems to be busy, and his fine place is plainly showing the attention which he bestows upon it. He has always taken an active interest in political matters, and although he works for the success of his party, he is by no means an office seeker. January 15, 1891, he was married to Mrs. Julia Mitchell, a daughter of Major Nance. She was born in Arkansas and is an intelligent and amiable lady.

THEODORE WOLTERS. Some lessons of genuine worth may be gleaned from the life of every man, and the history of Theodore Wolters has been marked by all that goes to make up useful and noble manhood, and in him is the material of which useful citizens are made. He possesses in a marked degree the push, industry and determination necessary to a successful career in any occupation, and his high reputation and upright, honorable career, in the various official positions he has been called upon to fill, have served to place him in the foremost ranks of the representative citizens of Fayette County. He is now the most efficient Mayor of Schulenburg, and discharges the duties of that position in a very satisfactory manner. Mr. Wolters was born in the village of Industry, Austin County, Texas, April 15, 1846, and is the son of Jacob and Louisa (Marks) Wolters, natives of Germany. Mr. Wolters came to this country in 1835 and located first in the city of New Orleans. Later he located in Colorado County, Texas, and then sent back to the old country for his wife (first wife) and five children. This family experienced many hardships in those early days, being entirely ignorant of the requirements of Western life, and not able to converse very fluently in English. Indians, too, were quite numerous and hostile. Mr. Wolters erected a double log and block house, a very strong one, for the purpose of protecting his family from the Indians, and his neighbors often came and remained with them nights. For three years they pounded or ground their corn with a pestle, and used either a hollowed rock or stump for this purpose. The latter part of the year 1835 Mr. Wolters joined the Texas army and was stationed at Victoria. He with others, whose families were in an exposed settlement, were ordered home to see to the welfare of their families, and Mr. Wolters, with his own and his neighbor's family, went east of the Brazos River, in what is now Waller County. He made this trip in a truck wagon of two wheels, the same being made by sawing a couple of rounds off the end of an oak log, and later he was offered a league of land for his cart and oxen. Mr. Walters said the State of Texas could not have bought the outfit at that time. The family remained on the Brazos until after the battle of San Jacinto and then came back to Colorado County. Here they found most of the houses burned, but they immediately began to rebuild and to make other improvements. Indians continued to bother them, stealing horses and cattle, until about 1839 or '40. Mr. Wolters traded one-half league of land for an improved place in the town now called Industry, and moved to that section. He was a baker by trade, but had learned the chair maker's trade of his father in Germany, and when the country began to settle up he engaged in chair making, turning his rounds with the old fashioned hand lathe. By an accident Mr. Wolters lost one of his fingers about this time. He came to Texas with limited means, but by industry and good management became the owner of a handsome property before his death, which occurred in 1865. He was in a buggy drawn by a fiery team of horses which took fright, ran away, and threw Mr. Wolters out, killing him instantly. A friend who was with him in the buggy was killed at the same time. The children born to Mr. Wolters' first union were named: Robert, of this city; August, was in the Mexican War and is now deceased; Mina, deceased, was the wife of George Herder; and Ferdinand, deceased. The mother of these children was killed by a fall from a mustang pony. Mr. Wolters was married to Miss Marks, mother of our subject, in Houston, Texas, and the bridal trip was a horseback ride from that city to his home, ninety miles distant. Four children were the fruits of this union: Edward, deceased; Theodore, our subject; Herman, deceased; and Franklin, deceased. Mrs. Wolters died in 1862. The following year Mr. Wolters married Mrs. Romary, who died shortly afterward. Amid pioneer surroundings our subject grew to mature years, and the Civil War breaking out hurt his chances for an education to some extent. In 1863 he enlisted in the Confederate army and was stationed at Brownsville on the Rio Grande River. He participated in a land and naval battle close to Sabine, where the Confederates captured two gunboats and about 400 prisoners, together with arms, amunition, etc. The remainder of the time Mr. Wolters was stationed at Galveston, and surrendered there in May, 1865. For two years after the war Mr. Wolters was engaged in farming, but since 1881 he has been in business in the town of Schulenburg. In the year 1889 he was elected Mayor, and has been re-elected at each succeeding election. He was married at New Ulm in 1870, to Miss Margaret Wink, a native of Texas and daughter of Louie and Catherine (Meyer) Wink, natives of Germany, who came to this country in 1840. Mr. Wink was a blacksmith by trade and died in 1861. He was the father of the following children: Margaret, William, Henry, Mary and Lizzie. Mr. and Mrs. Wolters are the parents of six living children: Jacob (see sketch), Edmond, Ottlie, Katie, Agnes and Wallace. Mrs. Wolters is a member of the Catholic Church. Mr. Wolters was reared a Lutheran. He is a member of the A. F. & A. M., Lyons Lodge No. 105, and takes considerable interest in the political issues of the day, being an old line Democrat.

WILLIAM HENRY BROWN. This substantial citizen is successfully engaged in planting, merchandising and public ginning at Leesville, Texas, and from the fact that he is one of the most intelligent and progressive men of his section, strictly honorable in all his business transactions, he is held in high esteem by all, and has numerous warm personal friends. He is a native of Eaton, Ohio, where he was born October 6, 1830, a son of Daniel and Mary (Hubbel) Brown, the former of whom was born in New Jersey and the latter in Ohio. They emigrated to Texas in 1836, and although he much desired to do so, he was not permitted to enter the service of the Mexican War, owing to the fact that his health was extremely delicate, but one of his sons was in that war and was a participant in a number of battles. The father was a planter, and became the owner of a considerable amount of land in Sabine County. He was a Democrat in politics, a Methodist in his religious views, and in 1858 was called from life, his wife having passed to that bourne whence no traveler returns in 1848. The subject of this sketch was reared, and in a limited sense educated, in Sabine County, and from a mere lad has made his own way in the world. He now relates that after his marriage and upon his arrival in Gonzales County, his capital was one little skillet and $10 in money. For some time he ran a grist mill for William Means, then farmed for himself for two years, at the end of which time the war came up and he enlisted in Foster's Company and served in Texas and Louisiana. After the war he returned to Gonzales County, and for one year thereafter farmed in the vicinity of Leesville, then for four years conducted a mill and gin for others. In due course of time, by good management and judicious economy, he had amassed sufficient capital to start a mill of his own, and after some years also added farming and merchandising to his former occupation. His success in the accumulation of worldly goods has been marked, and he is now one of the wealthiest men in the section in which he resides, which fact is due to his own determined and persistent efforts. His son, S. A. Brown, is a partner in the mercantile business, and is a capable, intelligent and honorable business man. Mr. Brown is a Democrat in politics, is active in Church and Sunday School work, and for the past twelve years has been Sunday School Superintendent. He was married in 1854 to Miss Rachel Long, daughter of John and Eliza Long, residents of Louisiana. The father is still living, but the mother died in 1880. To the union of Mr. and Mrs. Brown nine children have been given: Daniel, John, Jacob, Sampson A., Jesse (deceased), Mary, married Alexander Smith, and died in 1890; Alice (deceased), George and Lela.

JUDGE GEORGE W. KYSER. The judges of the Caldwell County Court have always been noted for their character and ability, and one of the most popular of the many worthy men elevated to the bench in the history of Caldwell County jurisprudence is Judge George W. Kyser. He was born in Lafayette County, Mississippi, in 1845, the fifth of ten children born to William Marion and Elizabeth J. (Rogers) Kyser, the former of whom was born in Alabama, and the latter in Virginia. The paternal grandfather, George W. Kyser, was born in South Carolina, moved to Alabama at an early day, followed the calling of a planter and there died. The maternal grandfather, George W. Rogers, was a Virginia planter, but afterwards became a resident of Mississippi, and was there called from life. William M. Kyser was reared in the State of his birth, but was married in Mississippi, in 1852 came to Texas, and for two years resided in Bastrop County. From that time until 1881 he lived in Hays County, and is now a resident of Luling. He has devoted his attention to farming and stock-raising throughout life, and since 1889 has been a widower. The subject of this sketch grew up in Hays County, Texas, left the school room at the age of seventeen years, and enlisted in Company A, Wood's Regiment, Thirty-second Texas Cavalry, and served in the trans-Mississippi Department, participating in the battle of Blair's Landing, and in all the engagements of Banks' retreat down the Red River, being also in the Yellow Bayou battle. His command was disbanded at Houston in the spring of 1865. For six months succeeding this he went to school, then began farming and stock-raising, and followed the former occupation principally until 1881, when he went to Luling. Here he engaged in the livery business and in 1886–87 was Mayor of the town, and at the same time held the office of Justice. In 1888 he was elected County Judge, and people have shown their appreciation of his ability in this office by re-electing him ever since. He has always been quite active in politics and has been a delegate to various conventions. He was married in 1882 to Miss Emma J. Kirtley, a native of Kentucky, and a daughter of John Kirtley, who came to this State from Kentucky. To them five children were born, three of whom are dead. Those living are: Elizabeth Julia and Bruce. Mrs. Kyser is a member of the Methodist Episcopal Church, and socially Judge Kyser is a member of the A. F. & A. M. and the K. of P. and the A. O. U. W., over all of which lodges he has been presiding officer. He is a Master Workman of the latter organization and has represented this lodge in the Grand Lodge. He is also a member of the Luling Chapter in the A. F. & A. M. When the question of a new Court House for Caldwell County was discussed, the Commissioners were equally divided, and Judge Kyser seeing the need of a new building, as well as having been advised that the old building was unsafe, after due deliberation cast the deciding vote in favor of a new building. It was erected under careful supervision, and is said to be the finest building of the kind for the money in the State. It is a credit to the architect and builders, and is the pride of the county. The walls are of Muldoon gray sandstone, from Fayette County, trimmed with red sandstone, surmounted by a clock tower. Its size is 96 x 72 feet, three stories in height, the floors are tiled, and the interior finish is of pine. The house is practically fire proof, with absolute fire proof vault, and occupies the center of the public square and is a great ornament to the town. The judge is proud of the distinction of being a Southern gentleman, a rebel during the late war, and since that time a Collar Democrat.

ROBERT F. SELLERS. Among the prominent farmers and stock feeders of Gonzales County, Texas, none deserve more prominent recognition than Robert F. Sellers, who was born in Fayette County, Texas, in 1849, the third of four children born to Robert and Nancy (Sellers) Sellers, who were natives of the State of Tennessee, where they were also reared, educated and married. In December, 1835, they came to Texas and after a short residence in St. Augustine they came to La Grange, where they erected one of the first cabins of that place. There he located his headright—a league of land—in the southwestern part of Gonzales County, but very soon after the Texas Rebellion broke out, and he at once joined Gen. Houston's army, but at the time of the battle of San Jacinto was on detached duty, so did not participate in that engagement. He later purchased land in Fayette County, which he greatly improved by the most persistent labor, but gave up this calling for a time to take part in the Mexican War. In 1852 he moved to Colorado County, where he opened up a remarkably fertile farm, but in 1882 moved to Luling, where he died in August, 1893, his wife having passed from life in 1883. They both had been church members from their early youth, and he had for many years been connected with the Masonic fraternity. He was first married to Miss Margaret Miller, by whom he became the father of two children: Martha, who died in 1864, was married to Rev. Green Andrews, by whom she became the mother of three sons and two daughters,—Frank, an eminent attorney of Benton, is the present Attorney General of Texas and is a popular and prominent man, and W. T., of Throckmorton, is also a lawyer and prosperous; and Elizabeth. His second union resulted in the birth of four children: Isaac, now a Baptist Minister, located at Georgeton; Nannie, Robert F., and Annie. These children were all reared in Colorado County, and were educated principally in the schools of La Grange. The paternal grandfather of the subject of this sketch, Robert Sellers, was one of the earliest settlers of Gibson County, Tennessee, to which section he removed from South Carolina. The maternal grandfather, Lard Sellers, was also born in that State, and was a pioneer of Maury County, Tennessee. He was a very prominent farmer, and after the war moved to Missouri, in which State he died. The Sellers family are of Irish descent, and the present members of the family are all descended from three brothers who came from Ireland to this country during colonial times. The immediate subject of this sketch began life for himself by taking charge of his father's farm in 1870, and continued so to do until 1882 when he went to Lampasas County and engaged in the sheep and cattle business. A few years later he went to Bell County, and there remained for three years engaged in farming and feeding cattle, and driving herds to Colorado. In February, 1889, he came to Gonzales County and bought his present farm of 502 acres, and now has 200 acres under cultivation and improved with good buildings, fences, etc., the result mainly of his own efforts. He is well posted and up with the times, farms on scientific principles, and never fails to have good crops, if the season is at all favorable. He is very thorough in all his work, and his estate is considered one of the best in the county. In 1877 he engaged in feeding stock, and as he feeds nothing but a good grade, he sells them for the highest price in the spring, after he has fed them during the winter. He is said to feed the best cattle in the county. He was married in 1874 to Miss Nolie Roberts, a native of Louisiana, and a daughter of Capt. William T. Roberts, who came from that State to Texas, and is now engaged in farming in Fayette County. To Mr. and Mrs. Sellers four sons have been given: Steward, Richard, and Isaac and Robert (twins). Mr. and Mrs. Sellers are members of the Baptist and Presbyterian churches, respectively, and he is quite prominent in politics. Col. Harvey Sellers (deceased), was a prominent and wealthy merchant of Galveston, Texas, and New York, and was a soldier of the Confederate army during the war. He enlisted as First Lieutenant of the Bayou City Guards, Fifth Texas Regiment, of Hood's Brigade, and upon the organization of the regiment he became Adjutant, and subsequently Adjutant General. On Hood's promotion he followed him successively in rank on the staff until Hood became Major General, and was one of his constant advisers. Col. Sellers was without doubt one of the ablest soldiers ever sent from Texas. He served as Lieutenant in one of the companies of Col. Jeff Davis' Regiment, the First Mississippi, in the Mexican War.

CHAUNCEY B. DONALSON. No name is more familiarly known is Hays County, Texas, than that of Donalson, and therefore it is proper that some mention of the family should be made herein. He whose name heads this sketch came from Kentucky, for on Blue Grass soil he first saw the light in 1835, he being the third of the seven living children born to Major Donalson, a sketch of whom appears in this work. Chauncey B. Donalson was taken to Illinois in 1840, in which State he acquired a practical common school education, and finished his scholastic education in Christian College at Canton, Mo., which institution he attended for one year. At the time his father was appointed Marshal of Kansas he was made his father's deputy, in 1854, his father returning to Illinois and leaving him in charge, and his first official act was to arrest a man by the name of Kibbe for murder. In the spring of 1855 he summoned the jury for the court at the city of Leavenworth, and he opened it, Judge Lecompton presiding, which was the first court ever convened in that territory. A little later he did the same thing for Judge Bush Elmore in another district in that territory, and was compelled to ride over two hundred miles to summon his jury. During the first session of the first Legislature in 1855, at Shawnee Mission, he was a frequent attendant of that body. He was in charge of the posse that attempted to make the arrests at Lawrence just previous to the battle at that place in 1856. In the fall of 1857 he was married at Canton, Mo., and there was engaged in merchandising until 1862, when he sold out and went to Montana in the spring of 1863, and was in business at Virginia City for about five years, one of which was with Gen. George P. Dorris. A portion of his time was also spent in the mercantile business at Helena, of which place he was one of the very first merchants. While in that section he made five trips across the plains to St. Louis for goods, the whole trip being made by stage coach, and did quite a lucrative business while in the West. While in business in Montana Mr. Donalson made four trips from St. Louis to Fort Benton, a place on the Missouri River, about three thousand miles above St. Louis, by steamboat, each trip taking from forty-five to ninety days, on one of which the Indians attacked the boat several times, killing two of the hands and wounding several others. On his arrival in Virginia City he saw five men hanged by the Vigilance Committee, and during his stay in that country saw a number of others treated likewise. In 1870 he came to Texas, and for a time resided in San Marcos, but in 1874 located on his present ranch of 738 acres, known as "Live Oak Springs," on the Blanco River and near the I. & G. N. Railroad, of which fine tract 450 acres are in an admirable state of cultivation. All the improvements on this fine place have been made by Mr. Donalson, and the farm takes its name from some springs which were in early times a favorite and well-known camping place, and the land surrounding them was owned and named by Major Johnes. Mr. Donalson is engaged in the raising of cotton and corn, and he also raises a good grade of stock. He is an agreeable and intelligent gentleman, is a moving spirit in the community in which he resides, and has always been quite an active worker for the Democratic party. He was married in 1857 to Miss Ella C. Grant, of Canton, Mo., daughter of Gen. Thomas D. Grant of that State. She died in 1867, in Virginia City, M. T., leaving two daughters: Fannie, wife of R. M. Yarington of this county, and Jennie. In the spring of 1875 Mr. Donalson wedded Miss Cora Jackman, a daughter of Col. S. D. Jackman, a pioneer of Texas from Missouri, who was then a member of the State Legislature of Texas from Hays County. Mr. Donalson's second union has resulted in the birth of five children: Carroll, Lee, Sidney, I. B., and Laura Bell. Mrs. Donalson is a member of the Christian Church.

CAPT. JAMES PINCKNEY WARD. A well-kept hostlery is an institution of the utmost benefit and convenience to any community, and is especially appreciated by the traveling public who are compelled to make their homes in the different hotels of the towns in which their duties call them. The establishment of which J. P. Ward is the proprietor is conducted very efficiently, and many home comforts and conveniences can be had there. In addition to this business he is also engaged in farming in the vicinity of Leesville. He is a product of the Old North State, and first saw the light on the 17th of March, 1830, his parents being David and Samantha (Barnes) Ward, the former of whom was born in the Palmetto State. The mother is descended from the famous Pinckney family of South Carolina. David Ward removed to North Carolina in his early manhood, thence to Mississippi, where he engaged in planting. He was a Democrat in politics, and was chosen by his party to fill the office of Judge of Smith County. After residing in Mississippi he removed to Erath County, Texas, where he was called from this life in 1892 at the extreme old age of 91 years. His wife died in 1863. The subject of this sketch was reared and educated in Smith County, Miss., and until the opening of the great Civil War was engaged in planting, the details of which occupation he had learned from his father while growing up. In 1861 he dropped his farming implements to take up arms in defense of the Southern cause, and he became a member of Company G, Thirty-seventh Mississippi Infantry, and held the rank of Captain of the same for three years. He was for four years in the trans-Mississippi Department, and was a participant in the siege of Vicksburg, and for eleven months was imprisoned on Johnson's Island. After being paroled he returned home to Mississippi, and as every vestige of his property had been swept away he decided to locate in Texas, and for about eighteen years he was a resident of Lavaca County. During this time he was engaged in farming, and much attention was also given to raising and buying live stock.   In 1884 he located in Leesville, Gonzales County, and here put up a substantial hotel, which he has conducted with marked ability ever since. The measures of the Democratic party have always seemed good in his eyes, and he has at all times given that party his hearty support.   He is a member of Leesville Lodge No. 334, of the A. F. & A. M., in which he has attained to the Blue Lodge.   He was married in 1853 to Celia, daughter of Daniel and Charity Rhode, natives of South Carolina, and to their union the following children have been given: Zipparah, wife of L. C. Rankin; Leah, wife of T. W. Rucker; Laura, wife of C. A. Ryan; David, Lula, wife of B. G. Meyers; Ida, wife of John L. Allen; Sterling, Edna, deceased; Carrie, wife of Rayburn Littlefield, and James.   A fact worthy of note in connection with the war record of Captain Ward is, that he was in fights covering 113 days, was wounded several times, but returned home in comparatively good health.

H. H. RUSSELL, a prominent farmer and County Surveyor of Lavaca County, Texas, is a man whose intelligence, enterprise and energy, with many other estimable qualities, have secured for him a popularity not derived from any factitious circumstance, but a permanent and spontaneous tribute to his merit. Born in Mississippi in 1846, he was the third child of R. C. and Elizabeth (Bibbs) Russell, natives of Tennessee and Mississippi respectively.   The parents came to the Lone Star State in 1851 and made a settlement on the Lavaca River, two miles from Hallettsville, where the father became the owner of about eight hundred acres of land.   He made many improvements, cleared much of the land, and resided there until after the war, when he moved to Bosque County.   There he resides at the present time.   His wife is deceased. As our subject was about five years of age when he came with his parents to this county he remembers very little of any other place of residence.   He attended school until the breaking out of war, and in 1861 entered the Confederate army, at the age of 14 years, Patten's Company, Border's Regiment, and Fulcrods' Battalion, and served in Texas, usually as guard for prisoners. After the war he attended school at Waco for a year, and afterward at Hallettsville under Gen. A. P. Bagby.   Later he was appointed Sheriff and afterward elected County Surveyor, which position he has held for the most part since.   To some extent he has also been engaged in farming, and owns, in partnership with James Ballard, eight or ten thousand acres in various parts of the State.   In 1891 he erected his fine residence in the suburbs of Hallettsville, and this is presided over by his excellent wife, who was formerly Miss Anna Hemphill, a native of Mississippi, and daughter of John B. Hemphill, who came to Texas in 1878 and died here in 1885.   Mr. and Mrs. Russell's union resulted in the birth of nine children, three of whom are deceased.   This family holds membership in the Baptist Church, and it is one of the representative ones in this section.   Mr. Russell is a thoroughly experienced surveyor, and a most competent official.   He has a pleasant home and is a cordial, pleasant and agreeable gentleman.   On his fine farm in this county he has a small herd of Jersey cattle, and is something of a stock man.

MRS. PENELOPE ALLEN.   This estimable lady is the widow of the late James W. Allen, and is the daughter of J. L. and Eliza (McGee) Johnson, who, like herself, were born in Alabama, her birth occurring in Mobile, Feb. 1, 1829.   The father, John L. Johnson, was a man of superior education, and after his removal to Austin County, Texas, in 1843, he became widely and favorably known.   He settled on the farm now owned by M. L. H.

J. H. Moore.

Harry, but did not live a great while to enjoy his new home. At that time different members of the Allen family lived to the north of him, and south there resided Judge Barnett, and there were a few other scattered settlers. He succeeded in putting under cultivation a small strip of land, and shortly after coming here established a ferry opposite his house on the Brazos River, but it was two years before Mrs. Allen's mother got to see the face of a white woman. Their milling was done with a pestle and mortar, but a few years later they had their grists ground at Houston, until mills were erected nearer home. After Mr. Johnson's death Mrs. Johnson moved on the prairie and purchased the farm on which Miles Allen is now residing, and there she reared her family, consisting of the following children: Elizabeth (deceased), first married James Henry, and after his death George Gaylord; Lemuel (deceased), Penelope, Margaret, the deceased wife of James Cole, William (deceased), Harriet, the deceased wife of Austin Cole; John, who resides in Wise County, Texas; James (deceased) and Daniel. When Mr. Johnson first began the improvement of his place, he put in his house a puncheon floor, there was a dirt and stick chimney, and the house was covered with boards fastened or weighted down with poles. He had to go to Houston for all supplies, but as the country improved this state of affairs changed. Mr. Johnson had studied medicine during the early part of his career, and as doctors were very distant, Mr. Johnson cared for his own family in time of sickness. Mrs. Johnson died in Coryell County, in 1885, at the age of seventy-three years. James W. Allen was born in Texas, in 1832. His grandfather, Martin Allen, and two sons, James and Benjamin, were early settlers of Texas, and in this section James reared his family, as did also Benjamin and another son, Miles, the father of James W. The latter was principally reared in this county, and was here married to Miss Johnson, in 1853. He died in 1871, at the age of thirty-nine years, having been a successful stockman of this county. He was successful in the conduct of his affairs and left his family well provided for. The children born to himself and wife are as follows: Winnie, wife of O. G. Cannon (see sketch); Miles J., whose sketch appears in this work; Susan, wife of Peter Habermacher, of this county; Mary E., wife of B. F. Davis; James (deceased), and S. N., who is married to Edna Tomlinson and lives in this county. The latter's wife was born in Alabama, a daughter of Newton and Martha J. (Frazier) Tomlinson, who came to this State in 1876 and settled in the northern portion of Austin County. His wife died in 1880, after having borne him the following children: Madison, Levi (deceased), Edna, James (deceased), John, Delia, wife of Arthur Pennington, William, Luther and one child that is dead. Mr. Tomlinson married a second time, but his wife died soon after their marriage. S. N. Allen and his wife have three children: James W. (deceased), Robert N. and Penelope. The youngest child born to James W. Allen and wife is John L., who married Miss Lottie Bell of this county, a daughter of Mike Bell. He has three children: Susan, Audley and Mike. Miles J. Allen, another son of Mr. and Mrs. James W. Allen, was born in this county Nov. 10, 1856, and in the common schools of this county he received a practical education. After the death of his father, he being the eldest son, the most of the management of the home farm fell on his shoulders, and tilling the soil and the raising of stock has since occupied his attention. He remained with and aided his mother until he was twenty-three years old, and he was then married, August, 1878, and moved to a home of his own. At that time he owned

21

some stock, and soon after purchased 177 acres of land, paying for the same $2,500, about seventy-five of which are under cultivation. He was married to Nora, daughter of J. N. and Elizabeth (Blagrave) Weaver, natives of Indiana. Mr. Weaver came to Texas before his marriage and died in Austin County about 1884, having been a Confederate soldier. Mr. and Mrs. Allen are the parents of six children: Daisy, Peter, Lottie, Newton, Winnie and Ader. Mr. Allen and his wife are members of the Christian Church, and politically he is a Democrat, and socially is a member of San Felipe Lodge No. 231, of the A. F. & A. M., and is also a demitted member of the R. A. M., of Bellville. He has never been deeply interested in politics, but has filled several minor official positions creditably.

ROBERT C. BOTTS. The County of Gonzales, Texas, affords excellent opportunities for the agriculturist, and in following this calling Robert C. Botts has become well known, and in the conduct of his affairs has shown good judgment and business foresight. He is a Kentuckian by birth, for on Blue Grass soil he first saw the light of day in 1848. He was the third of five children born to Benjamin and Frances (McIlvain) Botts, who were also natives of Kentucky, the father being a farmer by occupation. He came with his family to Texas in 1851, and located on a small tract of land near Gonzales, where he engaged in farming and stock-raising, and where he eventually passed from life in 1891, at the age of eighty-two years. His widow is still living. Robert C. Botts was reared in Gonzales County and was educated in the town of Gonzales. After remaining at home and assisting his parents until he had attained his majority, he began farming and stock-raising on his own responsibility, and in 1875 also opened a mercantile establishment at Gonzales, and soon after a store and mill and cotton gin at Wrightsboro, all of which he successfully conducted at the same time, but in 1883 disposed of his mercantile interests. He now owns a valuable farm of 1,500 acres on the San Marcos River, near his father's old homestead, 500 acres of which are under cultivation and are improved with buildings of an excellent character and substantial fences. Besides this admirable farm he also owns some valuable property in Gonzales. For a number of years he has taken much interest in grading his stock and now has some excellent animals on his place, a fact which is well worth the emulation of others. He has been an active worker for the good of his section, and is ever ready to assist in the advancement of the best interests of his State and county. In 1879 he wooed and won for his wife Miss Cornelia Lovett, a native of Texas, who came to Texas in her youth, her mother being a native of Scotland. To her union with Mr. Botts three children were born: Frances, Lovett and Ashton. The latter died in early boyhood. Mr. Botts was left a widower in January, 1887, and since then has remained unmarried. He is a member of Gonzales Lodge of the A. F. & A. M., and was one of the organizers, and is still a stockholder in the Gonzales Electric Light Company.

MRS. TOBITHA KILLOUGH. This estimable lady, the widow of I. G. Killough, and daughter of Col. John H. and Eliza (Cummins) Moore, is a lady of much more than ordinary ability, as she received a moderate education in her youth, and has since, year by year, added to her stock of knowledge. Her maternal grandfather, James Cummins, was a member of Austin's first colony, coming here in 1821 or '22. He followed farming the first year, but, while he went back East for his family, the Indians destroyed his crop of corn, and for three months after returning the family lived without bread. His home was on the opposite side of the river from where Columbus now stands, in Colorado County, and his great grand-daughter now owns the farm. A few years later he moved on what was later known as Cummins Creek, and began tilling the soil there. He was the first man to settle on that creek and it received his name. While living there he held the position of Judge of what is now Colorado County, and was a prominent man in his time and day. He was too old to take part in the war with Mexico and died in 1849, leaving five children: Eliza, mother of subject; Nancy, married Jesse Burnham; Sarah, widow of a Mr. Strong; Harriet, wife of Abram Bairer, and Wiley. Several of Mr. Cummins' children died young, but one of them, Mariah, was the wife of a Mr. Cook. Col. John H. Moore came from Tennessee to Fayette County, Texas, in 1819, when about nineteen years of age, with a trading party by way of Santa Fe, New Mexico. He followed trading through the States for two years, and in 1826 was married to Miss Cummins, with whom he settled on Cummins Creek. He was married by bond by the Alcalde or political chief, and this was afterwards sanctioned by the priest in order to be lawful. About 1828 Colonel Moore received his headright from the Mexican Government, and located where the town of La Grange is now standing. He built the first house in that place, a block house, close to where the magnificent court house now stands. Indians were troublesome in those days, but the residents of La Grange were not molested, although about six miles north of that place many citizens were massacred. Colonel Moore was in nearly all the wars with the Indians, and took part in nearly all the principal engagements. At the battle of Red Fork, on Colorado River, he followed the Indians to their homes, destroyed their wigwams, and took prisoners their women and children, holding them at LaGrange and Austin until they could exchange them for whites. Captain Moore kept an Indian boy for two or three years. The latter was but seven years old when captured, and when ten years of age he could talk the English language quite fluently. He became much attached to Colonel Moore and family, and did not wish to be exchanged, as his mother and father had been killed during the fight. Colonel Moore commanded a company of men in the war with Mexico in 1835 and '36, and fought at San Antonio and other engagements, but was not in the battle of San Jacinto, but was in hearing distance of it, being on the other side of the Bayou, which was past fording or swimming. He was not in the war with Mexico in 1848. When not scouting for Indians he was engaged in farming and stock-raising, and occasionally went out on hunting expeditions. He always kept a pack of hounds for bear hunting, a sport of which he was particularly fond, and not infrequently had narrow escapes, often being obliged to carry his disabled dogs home. About 1832 Colonel Moore presented the city of LaGrange with the land on which it is situated. This place and Austin were competing points for the capitol and Austin secured it by one vote. Mr. Moore was quite an active politician, and he was public-spirited and progressive. His death occurred in 1883, April 12th. Mrs. Moore died in 1875. They left six children: William, deceased; Tobitha, Eliza, deceased, was the wife of R. V. Cook of Columbus; John H., deceased; Robert, deceased, and Mary, wife of Mr. Hunt. Mrs. Killough was educated in Rutersville, Texas, and after finishing went to Tennessee to visit her relations, going by way of New Orleans and returning with two of her uncles, who brought their families and slaves by the overland route. They were about six weeks in making the trip. Mrs. Killough was married in 1854 to I. G. Killough, a native of Tennessee, of the town of Bolivar. He came to Texas in 1851 and engaged in farming and stock-raising, and also speculated in real estate. A strong Democrat, he took an active interest in political matters, and was elected to the Thirteenth General Assembly, serving one year. About this time he moved to Austin, resided there for a number of years, and then returned to LaGrange, where his interests were centered. He was a farmer, and at the time of his death, which occurred October 2, 1878, was one of its most popular ones. He left a family of eight children: Eliza M., wife of R. O. Foris of Flatonia; Lucy, wife of W. H. Saunders of LaGrange; Maggie E., wife of W. T. Burns of Houston; Annie, wife of J. M. Moon of this State; David M., of this county; John H., Robert E. Lee, at home, and Ira G., at home. Mr. Killough was a member of the A. F. & A. M., and was an elder in the Cumberland Presbyterian Church for a number of years, and an active worker in the same. He was a man of generous impulses and a warm heart, and was noted for his liberality to the friendless and forsaken. In 1861 Mr. Killough raised a company known as Company I, Green's Brigade, and first went to New Mexico, where he participated in three fights. Later he was in the battle of Galveston, and went from there to Louisiana, where he was in the fight with Gen. Banks from the 13th of April to the close of the campaign, Mansfield, Yellow Bayou and all the other engagements of that campaign. Mr. Killough was noted for bravery, and at the taking of Fort Donelson was hit on the head with a brick bat, being in too close quarters for a gun to be used. He continued in the army until cessation of hostilities and then surrendered. He was home but three times from 1861 to 1865, and was in active service all the time.

JERRY M. NANCE. As a progressive tiller of the soil and intelligent and successful stock-raiser, Jerry M. Nance ranks with the foremost of Hays County. He was born in Arkansas in 1850, the sixth child born to Major Ezekiel and Louany (Pate) Nance, who resided in Hempstead County, Arkansas, in which State they made their home until 1850, when he came to Texas and located on the Blanco River on a farm which he soon purchased, but the mother died before moving to Texas in 1850. During the war the father held a civil office, and during that time he lost quite heavily, and many of the excellent improvements which he had made on his farm were destroyed. He early erected a cotton gin on his place and afterwards put up a fine grist mill and beef packing establishment on the Blanco River, which was very widely patronized in those days. He eventually became the owner of 6,500 acres of land, of which 400 were in a fine state of cultivation, and on this place he passed from life in September, 1885. After the death of his first wife he married again, and his second wife, with five boys and one girl, still survives him and resides on the old homestead. Jerry M. Nance was reared and educated in the Lone Star State, and was here married in 1877 to Miss Bassie Haupt, a daughter of Col. William W. Haupt, an early settler of Mountain City, Hays County. In 1877 he drove a herd of cattle to Wyoming Territory; also in 1880 he drove a herd to Kansas. In the year 1877 the plains of Texas were covered with buffalo. In 1878 he moved to the farm on which he now resides on Plum Creek, one mile east of the present town of

Kyle, where he has a fine estate of 545 acres, of which 250 acres are under cultivation, and this acreage he is continually increasing. His land yields abundant harvests; has a fine herd of Holstein cattle, and he is about the only stockman in the county that raises this breed. He has a valuable place and a handsome and comfortable home, which has become widely known for the hospitality which is freely extended to all. His wife is a member of the Episcopal Church, and their union has resulted in the birth of ten children: Elmo, Albert, Lola, Jerry, Jr., Flora, Sallie, Winnie, Mattie and two that died in infancy.

HIRAM FRANKLIN HALL. This thrifty agriculturist and stockman of Rancho, Gonzales County, Texas, is a worthy example of what can be accomplished when the spirit of determination is in one, for he began life for himself in limited circumstances, but is now a prominent citizen, and owes his good luck to his own persistent efforts rather than to outside influence or factitious circumstances. He was born on the 9th of January, 1831, in Matagorda County, while Texas was still under the dominion of Mexico, and his intimates still humorously term him "a Mexican." His parents, Elisha and Jemimah (Thompson) Hall, originally came from South Carolina and Florida respectively, and the father was about thirty years of age at the time of the removal of the family to the Lone Star State. The subject of this sketch was born in a tent, before his father had had time to build a house; but this state of affairs was soon remedied, and Mr. Hall energetically engaged in planting. During the trouble with Mexico he was a member of the Home Guards. He has always been a Democrat, politically, and was also a worthy member of the Masonic fraternity. He breathed his last in Matagorda County in December, 1836. His wife, who was born in Florida, was also called from life in Matagorda County, her death occurring in 1841. The youthful days of Hiram F. Hall were spent in his native county, but after the death of his parents he moved to Wharton County, where his grandparents resided. Upon attaining his majority he fell heir to a very small patrimony, but with intelligence and wisdom he carved out his own way in life, and decided to follow that occupation to which he had been reared—tilling the soil—and he has made a success of this branch of human endeavor, and he has also found the raising of stock a profitable source of revenue. He has been a resident of Gonzales County since 1854, and since that time has been the owner of the ranche on which he lives, which consists of over 300 acres of valuable and exceptionally fertile farming land. He has liberally aided his children in establishing themselves in life, and still has a comfortable competency. He is a pronounced Democrat in politics, and socially is a member of Lone Star Lodge at Bundick School House of the A. F. & A. M. He was married in 1854 to Miss Caroline Elizabeth, daughter of William and Leacy Mangum, residents of Gonzales County. Their union has resulted in the birth of the following children: Fannie became the wife of Dr. J. B. King and died January 10, 1885; William M. died in July, 1860; Fred H. died in June, 1891; D. Cory, and Ralph Edgar.

JOE L. O'BANION. The calling of the cotton-ginner is one of the utmost importance in the South, and he who devotes his attention to it usually finds that his time is fully and profitably occupied. At least, such has been the case with Mr. Joe L. O'Banion, who is the successful manager of the Gonzales Gin Company. This wideawake and enterprising man of affairs was born in Washington County, Texas, in 1857, the eldest and now the only living child born to Benjamin and Mary E. (Copenhaver) O'Banion, who were born in Georgia and Tennessee respectively. From the State of his birth Benjamin O'Banion came to Texas with his parents when he was but 12 years of age, and grew up and was educated in Washington County. He was in the ranger service through the '50s, was married in 1857, and in 1861 entered the Confederate service. While fighting for the cause of the South he was prostrated by illness and returned home to die in 1862, but his widow survives him and resides in San Antonio. His wife came to Texas with her parents, and with them settled in Caldwell County. Her father, Milton Copenhaver, was murdered in Lockhart in 1857. Joe L. O'Banion was reared in Caldwell County, and is wholly self-educated. He learned the printer's trade on the *News Echo* in Lockhart, on which he worked for three years, but his health then failed him, and he gave up the business to learn the trade of a machinist in that city. Until 1885 he worked in various portions of that county, then came to Gonzales County and located at Oak Forest, and at once reopened and rebuilt the Oak Forest gin, which he greatly improved by putting in new machinery and increased its output thereby from 100 to 1,500 bales per year. In 1893, with the firm of Miller & Sayers of Gonzales, he bought the De Witt gin of that place, and these gentlemen put in entirely new machinery and remodeled the whole plant. It now has a capacity of seventy bales per day, and is kept running continually. They have the Winship ginning system complete, and the steam machinery of W. T. Adams, which makes it one of the finest and most complete plants in the State of Texas. During the dull months Mr. O'Banion travels and sells machinery and gins for the W. T. Adams Machine Company of Corinth, Miss., and being agreeable in manners, intelligent and courteous, he has been successful in this line of human endeavor also. All the machinery of the Gonzales plant was put in under his direction and supervision, and was by no means an easy thing to do. They have an engine of 150-horse power, eight 70-saw gin stands, all of which are neat, tasteful and well protected against fire by hose throughout the building, complete and in perfect working order. Although Mr. O'Banion is a thoroughly self-educated and self-made man, he is a shrewd and far-seeing man of business; has made a success of his life, and numbers his friends by the score. He was married in 1880 to Miss Lou Alice Johnson, a native of Texas and daughter of Albert C. Johnson, a native of Indiana, who came to the Lone Star State at an early day and served in the Confederate army during the Civil War. He now resides in San Marcos. To Mr. and Mrs. O'Banion the following children have been born: Ada Cecil, Eugene Carroll, Madison Monroe, Lucile Fenton, Lela May, and Vesta Adams. Mr. O'Banion is a member of Gonzales Lodge of the A. F. & A. M. He is one of the substantial men of the county, and is highly respected.

ALBERT F. FIELD. A livery stable is a most essential institution, both for pleasure and convenience. To be able to command at any moment a horse and rig for a drive in the country or for business or other purposes is a privilege the value of which cannot be too highly estimated. Foremost among the liveries of Caldwell County, Texas, is the well-known resort of Albert F. Field. This stable, from the large business it does, not only exemplifies the importance of the city, but reflects credit upon its management. Mr. Field was born in the county in which he now resides, six miles south of Lockhart, June

5, 1856, the youngest of eight children born to Henry Hill and Mary Russell (Calvin) Field, who were born in Virginia, and at an early day became residents of Caldwell County, Texas. The father was a worthy and successful tiller of the soil, and died in 1858, while the mother died in 1885. In the county of his birth the subject of this sketch was reared and educated, and for a time in his early manhood followed various occupations, such as clerking, etc., and for about one year was one of the famous Texas Rangers, under Capt. Hall. In 1878 he received the appointment of Deputy Sheriff, a position he filled until 1882, after which he was elected to the office of County Sheriff, and after serving ten successive years he declined further election. He was an extremely popular official, and at each succeeding election the citizens of the county showed their appreciation of his ability by giving him an increased majority. He has ever taken an active interest in politics and is a prominent, active and influential Democrat, and without doubt further political honors are in store for him. He is at present the Democratic nominee for Sheriff of Caldwell County. In January, 1887, he became the proprietor of his present livery stable, and has a remarkably well equipped establishment, with about twenty-four head of horses at all times ready for use, and a fine line of buggies and carriages. He is also quite extensively engaged in buying and selling stock; in fact, is a wideawake and pushing business man, quick to see and grasp at opportunities for bettering his financial condition, but never at the expense of others or of his own fair name. November 22, 1882, he was married to Miss Kate W. McDowell, a native of Tennessee and daughter of Tillerton McDowell, and to their union the following children have been born: Mary Virginia, Katie Rankin, Albert Steele, Thomas Creigh, who died at the age of ten months; Henry Hill, and Warwick Francis. Mr. Field is a member of the K. of P., is an agreeable and social gentleman, has a handsome and comfortable home in Lockhart, and a very interesting family.

WILLIAM J. FISHER, who is engaged in the mercantile business at Waelder, Gonzales County, Texas, was born in Colorado County, Texas, 1843, a son of Thomas D. and Martha E. (Blackwell) Fisher, who were Virginians by birth, and first removed to Tennessee, thence to Vicksburg, Miss., and there engaged in the mercantile business for a while, which proved to be unsuccessful, parting with the most of his means. Thence they moved to Texas in 1839, stopping for a short time in the then village of Houston, from thence to a small settlement at Rutersville, Fayette County, where the Methodists had established a good school, of which denomination they were adherents. This was in the days of the Republic of Texas. After some two years they returned to Colorado County, Texas, and engaged in stock-raising and farming, settling the place where the subject of this sketch first saw the light. From this place they moved back in Fayette County, where soon after both parents died, in the year 1853. At this time William J. Fisher was ten years old, and he continued to make his home in Fayette County, living with his only sister, who married shortly after the death of his parents. His school opportunities were not good, at least he did not avail himself of the opportunities he then had, preferring to ride after stock and the freighting of goods and lumber from Houston and the pine regions in east Texas to the west. At the opening of the great Civil War he was in school at Fayetteville, Texas, and following after the custom of the times, with more patriotism than discretion, in 1861 enlisted in a volunteer company which with other companies rendezvoused at Camp Clark, on the head waters of the San Marcos River, and after being in camp there for some thirty days the Confederate authorities concluded that they would discontinue the receiving of six month volunteers, and he, for one, with the little experience of the thirty days before him in camp life, concluded if the Confederacy could dispense with his services for the six months he would gracefully retire to the civic pursuits from which he came, a wiser boy by having experienced something of camp life preparatory for war. But in 1862 he re-enlisted in Willis' Battalion Mounted Volunteers, and destined for the cis-Mississippi Department, arriving at Vicksburg, Miss., at about the time of the battle of Corinth, thence north to Cold Water, where Van Dorn and Price had retreated after their disaster at Corinth. He was with Van Dorn in his raid around Grant's army, in his surprise and capture of Holly Springs, the base of Grant's supplies, which caused the latter to reverse his position and face back and change the programme of his advance on to Vicksburg by the river way. He was in several engagements of minor import, was courier for Gen. Lloyd Tillman for a short while, and was with Gen. N. B. Forrest in his running fight with Gen. A. J. Smith, which from start to finish covered some forty miles. He was in the fight at old Harrisburg or Tupelo, under Gen. Stephen D. Lee, and in a great many small skirmishes, and was with Gen. Forrest at Fort Pillow. After the fall of Vicksburg he was despondent and was satisfied that the Confederacy was a failure, and was glad when the war terminated by the surrender of Lee, Johnston and Kirby Smith. Adapting himself to the surroundings and the altered conditions of affairs, he set energetically to work to till the soil and to the occupation of freighting goods from the railroad terminus inland, after which he engaged in business in Fayetteville, Texas, where he continued to make his home for three years. In 1875 he bought a farm in the western part of the county, containing about 500 acres, and up to 1881 was engaged in tilling the soil, then came to Waelder and opened a general mercantile store, and was engaged in the purchase and sale of cotton. His real estate now comprises about 900 acres, of which about 150 acres are under cultivation. The land is productive and yields about twenty bushels of corn to the acre and one-half bale of cotton. In 1870 he led to the altar Miss Evelyn Dycus, a native of Texas, and daughter of Dr. F. A. Dycus, who came to Texas from Kentucky about 1848, and settled in Caldwell County, where he became well known as a skillful physician, also in Fayette County, where he lived a great many years. To the union of Mr. and Mrs. Fisher twelve children were born, nine of whom are living: Leila, Belle, Frances Preston, James T. H. Corinne, Junius, Bomar, Roy and Jennie. Those deceased are Carroll, Lloyd and Eva. Mr. and Mrs. Fisher are members of the Missionary Baptist Church, and he is a deacon in the same and a teacher in the Sunday School. In politics he is of the Democratic faith.

WILLIAM W. LOCK. Among the progressive and extensive farmers and stock-raisers of Hays County, Texas, is William W. Lock, whose place of residence is in the vicinity of Kyle. He is a product of Southwest Missouri, where he first saw the light in 1835, being the only child born to William W. and Elizabeth (Gibson) Lock, native Tennesseeans. The grandparents of William W. Lock, with their families, removed from Giles County, Tenn., to Southwest Missouri, of which section they were among the pioneers, and in early times were considerably annoyed by the depredations of Indians. The parents of our subject were married in Missouri, and there the father was engaged in tilling the soil up to the time of his death, which occurred shortly before the subject of this sketch was born. The widow afterwards married again, and in 1868, with her husband and family, moved to Texas, and in Hays county, this State, she passed from life about 1891. The subject of this sketch was reared in the State of his birth, and about 1855 came to Texas and took up his residence in Hays County. He at once secured employment at tending stock, which he continued for about four years, then engaged in farming and stock-raising for himself. In 1861 he married Miss Lavina Hall, a native of Mississippi, and daughter of Jesse M. Hall, who was an early settler of Guadalupe County, and is now an extensive farmer of that county. In November, 1861, Mr. Lock joined the Confederate army, as a member of the Eighth Texas Cavalry (Terry's Rangers), Company E, with which he served until the close of hostilities. He had three horses shot from under him in battle and was in many perilous places, as were all the members of this famous regiment. He was serving on detail duty in Georgia when the war closed, and he at once returned home. He had lost all his stock, so turned his attention to farming, and soon after purchased a farm near Mountain City, where he spent about twelve years, during which time he purchased another fine tract on the prairie, now near the town of Kyle. He was for a long time engaged in raising blooded stock, and was the first man in Hays County to import blooded Durham cattle, which he brought from Kentucky about 1868. He has bred some of the best racing stock in the county, many of his animals winning races and selling for big money. He now has a thoroughbred stud of ten mares and one fine male animal, and in cattle he is now handling the Holstein breed, in which he is very successful. Besides his large home farm of 400 acres he has other valuable tracts and is remarkably well fixed financially. He has a family of thirteen children, and socially is a member of the A. F. & A. M.

JAMES C. ODOM. This leading stockman of Austin County, Texas, was born in De Witt County, this State, February 9, 1854, a son of Albert and Louisa (Cole) Odom, natives of the State of Louisiana. The parents came to this State prior to their marriage, in the early '40s, and settled in Harris County when Houston was only a trading village. They were married soon after coming to the State, after which they moved to De Witt County, thence to Atascosa County, and in 1862 returned to De Witt County, where he entered the Confederate army as a private. He died shortly after enlisting, in Wharton County, of fever. While residing in Atascosa County the Indians were very troublesome, and on one occasion, while tending his herd of horses, Mr. Odom discovered in the vicinity of his home and stock some twenty-five or thirty Indians of hostile intent, but he got between them and his house and stock and managed to keep them at bay until his man went to Pleasanton for assistance. During this time the family were barricaded in the house, but when reinforcements arrived the Indians retired. On nearly every moonlight night the redskins were to be seen prowling about the homes of the settlers, stealing horses and cattle and sometimes exterminating whole families whose homes were at all isolated. At that time, Mr. Odom states, that Big Foot Wallis was in the country and the settlers felt comparatively secure, for his knowledge of Indian nature was thorough and he knew not the meaning of fear, and consequently was a great protection. Mr. Odom was successfully engaged in the stock business for many years, but confined his attention chiefly to the raising of horses, which were of an excellent breed of Texas stock. At his death he left a wife and five sons, all of whom were too small to look after the stock properly, and by the time the war had closed the stock was scattered over four or five counties and numbers of them had become wild. Of the sons left, Oliver was the eldest and he was killed in Wilson County in 1884; James C.; Milam M.; Frank D. and A. M. In 1868 Mrs. Odom was married to A. C. White, and now resides in San Antonio. Her second union resulted in the birth of the following children: Raymond G., J. H., William and Maggie. James C. Odom was left fatherless at the age of seven years, and thus his opportunities for acquiring an education were exceedingly limited, but by attending school for two or three months out of the year, obtained a fair education. He commenced life for himself at the age of fifteen years as a herder, and continued this work until 1875. From 1869 to that time he was in the saddle and in camp, and in 1871 took a herd of 800 big steers from near Fort Mason, Texas, to Solomon City, Kan., and made the entire trip on horseback. During this time he says he was thirty-six hours in the saddle without anything to eat or drink and without changing horses. During 1866 he was employed by some ex-Confederate soldiers, who were desirous of keeping out of the hands of the Federal soldiers, and after he had shielded them on several occasions, Uncle Sam's boys became suspicious of him and young Odom was arrested, and after they had made him believe that his days on earth were numbered they finally let him go, and this episode finished his scouting days. Mr. Odom was in De Witt County in 1870, when that section was stirred up by civil strife, or a vendetta between the Peace and Jacobs families. He was in the employ of the Peace brothers, and on one occasion, while herding their horses, some fifteen men rode up and forced him at the muzzles of their guns to lead them where the Peace brothers were supposed to be stopping, but fortunately they were not at that place, and thus bloodshed was averted. Mr. Odom says that he felt decidedly queer, and no doubt looked even worse than he felt. This vendetta grew to an immense magnitude, in which some forty men eventually lost their lives. In 1875 Mr. Odom was married in Wharton County to Mrs. Mary (Beeks) Copeland a daughter of William and Jane V. (Cavanaugh) Beeks, who were early Texans, the Cavanaughs experiencing considerable trouble with the Indians, Mrs. Beeks being at one time quite severely wounded by them. At that time her father was from home, and the savages made a raid on three families that lived outside the settlement, and although Mrs. Cavanaugh tried to make her escape with her children, she was overtaken by the Indians and all the family were killed except Mrs. Beeks, who was shot in the left breast and left for dead. An old Indian placed his foot on her body and pulled out the arrow with which he had shot her, and she realizing that her only chance of her escape lay in making them believe she was really dead, she lay very still and never flinched as he rudely drew out his murderous weapon. She was twelve or thirteen years of age at this time and suffered from this wound all her life. She was in this country before the war of 1836 and was in what was called the "run-away." When Mr. Odom was married he was quite a poor boy, but his wife had some cattle and he continued in this business. In 1873 they came to Austin County, and since that time have lived in this and Wharton counties. He owns a fine farm of 330 acres, with 115 under cultivation, and he has a beautiful and well appointed home in Wallis. He is a member of the Cattle Syndicate composed of J. S. Dobney, J. A. Stone, J. S. Jarrol and J. C. Odom, owning some four or five thousand head of cattle in this and Wharton counties. He and his wife are the parents of one child: Hettie H. They are members of the Christian Church, and the K. & L. of H., and politically he has always been a Democrat.

CORNELIUS JAMES HANSON, merchant and hotel keeper at Rancho, Gonzales County, Texas, is a native of England, born in Halifax, Yorkshire, March 7, 1831, and the fourth of nine children born to Joseph and Rachel (Rathall) Hanson, both natives of Yorkshire and both of old families of that part of England. The father followed the occupation of a weaver, and was a member of the Independent Presbyterian Church. His death occurred in 1874. He was a member of the Ancient Order of Foresters. The mother, who was also an Independent Presbyterian in her religious views, died in England in 1885. Cornelius James Hanson was reared and educated in England, and when but a lad was apprenticed to an iron molder. Growing weary of this, and being of an adventurous disposition, he resolved to seek his fortune in America, and reached these shores without money or friends, when twenty-one years of age. Landing in New York City he worked his way to Cleveland, Ohio, where he worked some time in an iron foundry, and went from there to Philadelphia. He arrived in that city without a cent, and immediately enlisted in the United States army for the First Infantry Band. He was sent to Corpus Christi, and continued in his capacity as musician for many years. When the Civil War broke out his sympathies were with the South, and he went out of one army into the other. The first years he was with Edgar's Battery, which, at the end of one year, was assigned to Wall's Legion. He was in many of the engagements in Mississippi—Holly Springs, Fort Pemberton, siege of Vicksburg, etc. After the siege of Vicksburg and after being paroled, he went to Virginia with General Wall, and served in Walker's Division in Louisiana and Arkansas. Mr. Hanson then came to Texas with General Wall, and was on his plantation at the time of the surrender. Afterward he determined to roam no more, but marry and settle down. He rented a farm near what is now called Rancho, and pursued the occupation of farming for fourteen years, when he embarked in the mercantile business. Later he began keeping hotel, but has not neglected his farming and stock-raising interests, as a glance over his place will show. His land will average one-half bale of cotton and twenty-five bushels of corn to the acre. Mr. Hanson is a man of enterprise, and is one of the leading spirits in constructing the Gulf Shore & San Antonio R. R., which will do much to develop this section. He has taken $500 worth of its stock. His son, William Mangum Hanson, was one of the first to urge the building of such a road, and has been one of its chief promotors. He is now one of its directors. With Dr. J. B. King and J. S. McNeall he has taken the contract for the entire line to supply the road with commissaries. For years he has been connected with his father in the store, and for two years was Deputy Sheriff and United States Marshal. He has quite a record for activity for a young man twenty-eight years of age. Politically our subject is a Democrat. For seven years he was a Justice of the Peace, and he is a Mason and an Odd Fellow. In his religious views he is a Methodist, and is a leader in musical work. In June, 1865, he was married to Miss Susan L. Mangum, daughter of William R. and Leacy Mangum, the father a native of North Carolina and the mother of Georgia. Both parents died in this State, the father in Matagorda County, of which he was an old settler, in 1852, and the mother in Gonzales County in 1876. Only one child has been born to this union, William Mangum Hanson, who is married and has three children.

MAJOR EDWARD BURLESON. This distinguished old Texas ranger came of a numerous and distinguished family, many members of which became prominent in the sections in which they resided and a number of whom were early settlers of the Lone Star State. His father, Edward Burleson, became an early resident of Hays County, and was a leader of the pioneers who settled on and near the Colorado River, while Texas was a part of Mexico. He was recognized as a man of great bravery and coolness in times of danger, and although a man of ordinary education, he possessed a naturally good mind, and was well posted and up with the times. He was of a social disposition, was an accommodating and kind neighbor, was a faithful and devoted friend, was peaceable in disposition, and seldom had any quarrels. It was said of him that if goaded to a certain point his rule was to fight, unless the other party apologized. After the acceptance of a mission to the United States by Gen. Stephen F. Austin, Edward Burleson was made General of the Texas Army, then besieging San Antonio. The party which went to that city under the celebrated Milam, and after he fell were led by Col. Frank Johnson, were really under Edward Burleson's orders. The town of San Antonio was surrendered to Gen. Burleson, December 10, 1835. He then raised a regiment and joined Gen. Sam Houston's army, and bore a distinguished part in the battle of San Jacinto. He was afterwards a member of the Senate of the Republic of Texas, and was later elected Vice-president of that Republic. On December 26, 1851, Gen. Burleson died in the City of Austin, at which time he was a member of the Senate of the State of Texas, and was buried on the plat of ground which had been set apart as the final resting place of distinguished Texans. He was one of the naturally great men of the State, and was distinguished by the clearness of his views, his adaptability to the interests and welfare of the land of his adoption, for his practical bent of mind and for the excellence and wisdom of his councils, which when given could always be relied upon. He could never advocate any measure, which in his opinion, was a violation of the law, or which might be injurious to the future well-being of the country, in fact, he made a model citizen. He was born in Buncombe County, North Carolina, in 1798, and his wife, who was Miss Sarah G. Owens, was born in 1796, in Kentucky. The children born to them were: John, April 6, 1824; Edward (subject), November 30, 1826; Grace B., July 4, 1832; Joseph R., David Crockett, September 6, 1837; Elizabeth T., October 14, 1841, and several that died in infancy. Gen. Burleson became a resident of the municipality of Bastrop, now Bastrop County, and became the owner of the fine old plantation known as Baron de Bastrop's, on the Colorado River. At that time the settlers were frequently subjected to hostile invasions from the Indians, and security against their outrages was scarcely obtainable in any part of Texas. Gen. Burleson was possessed of the qualifications to lead the people in their defense of their firesides and families, and in the course of time the Toncahuas Indians became the allies of the Texans. On one Sunday a Toncahua Indian went to the home of Gen. Burleson to consult him. The General was attending divine services in a school house near, and on reaching the place of worship the Indian called out "Burleson!" The General looked at the Indian and shook his head. This was repeated several times. The Indian then lost patience, and called out distinctly: "Burleson, white man talk heap, must lie some." Gen. Burleson was a farmer and taught his sons to work. When quite young they were permitted to accompany their father on his scouting expeditions. Edward Burleson, the immediate subject of this sketch, was sent to school when opportunity permitted, and he was known to be a rather precocious youth in many respects, yet he never appeared to appreciate books. He had a decided taste for out-door sports, and was fond of hunting. Fortune favored him, and when the question of annexing Texas to the United States arose, he entered the service of the United States Government, and was under the command of Major Benjamin McCulloch, with whom he was in the battle of Monterey, his father, Gen. Burleson, being also a participant in that engagement. He was also at Buena Vista, and his company performed able and efficient service on that memorable occasion. He is also entitled to a share of the credit attached to a company, acting the part of spies for Gen. Taylor's army. They penetrated the lines of Gen. Santa Anna's army and carried to their General a correct estimate of the enemy's numbers. Major Burleson was married to Miss Emma Kyle, a native of Mississippi, and daughter of Col. Claiborne Kyle, of Hays County, Texas. They were well suited, and it was a match based on mutual love and esteem. He settled a mile from San Marcos, became a model farmer, acquired property and became very popular with all. He appeared not to covet office, yet he could have been elected to any position within the gift of the people of the State. He was to a great extent absorbed by his devotion to his family, and was a kind and indulgent father to his children, who were named as follows: Edward C., John William, James G., Ford McCulloch, Albert Sidney, Kyle, who died in 1856; Edward, Jr., was drowned while bathing in the Rio Blanco in 1873; Emma K., Lily K., Mary K. Mrs. Burleson died March 12, 1877. Ford Burleson became a prominent physician of San Marcos, but died in the prime of life, May 21, 1887, leaving a widow, who was formerly Miss Northcraft, and a young daughter. James G. Burleson, son of Maj. Edward Burleson, is one of the most prominent business men of Caldwell County, and is the efficient President of the First National Bank of Lockhart. He was born in Hays County, Texas, August 1, 1859. His maternal ancestors, the Kyles, came to Texas during its early history and settled on the Blanco River. Col. Claiborne Kyle, the maternal grandfather of James G. Burleson, was a very popular man in Mississippi, and at one time was a prominent candidate for Governor of that State. James' father, Edward Burleson, in addition to his other affairs, was a member of the Constitutional Convention of Texas in 1879, and was also a member of the committee to locate the state penitentiary at Rusk. The early education of James G. Burleson was acquired in the Coronal Institute at San Marcos, and in 1876–77 he entered Georgetown College, D. C., but, owing to the death of his father in 1877, he left school shortly after, and entered the County Clerk's office of Hays County as Deputy, and there remained until 1880, when he was elected Clerk of the District and County Court, and was successively re-elected to that office for six years. Retiring from office, in 1886, he came to Lockhart and organized the banking house of James G. Burleson & Co., which establishment existed and prospered until 1889, when it was succeeded by the First National Bank of Lockhart, which was organized May 20, 1889, with a capital of $50,000, and Mr. Burleson was made its President. The bank has now a surplus and undivided profits of $13,000, and is in a very prosperous condition. It occupies a handsome building on the public square, and is fitted and furnished with all modern appliances and conveniences in the way of fire and burglar proof safe and vaults. The present officials are among the strong financial men of this section: James G. Burleson, President; L. J. Story, Vice-President; Ed. J. L. Green, Second Vice-President; J. M. Jolly, Cashier, and A. R. Chew, Assistant Cashier. Mr. Burleson still owns the old family homestead near San Marcos, which comprises 1,000 acres of fine farming land, of which 250 are under cultivation. He is also a stockholder and one of the directors in the First National Bank of San Marcos, and was one of the organizers of that institution. He also assisted in organizing the Lockhart Oil Mill & Power Co., a valuable corporation of Lockhart. He has always been an active worker for the Democratic party, and has been a delegate to several State Conventions. He was married February 15, 1883, to Miss Mary D. Green, a native of Texas and daughter of Ed. J. L. Green, of San Marcos, by Rev. Thomas A. Lancastar, the same divine who on February 15, 1854, officiated at the marriage of his father and mother. They have four children: Mary, Edward, James G., Jr., and Eliza. Mrs. Burleson is a member of the Christian Church. Mr. Burleson devotes his entire time and attention to the interests of his bank and his other financial interests, and has but little time to give to political matters, although he is a stanch Democrat. While at College at Georgetown, D. C., he was appointed to the United States Naval Academy, at Annapolis, Md. It was a life he had for some time been anxious to adopt, but at the same time his elder brother, J. W. Burleson, was appointed to the Military Academy at West Point, and as two members of the same family could not enter the service, James G. withdrew. He is a pleasant and courteous gentleman, an exceedingly shrewd and practical business man, and is in every way worthy the honored ancestry from which he sprung. He is a member of San Marcos Lodge No. 342 and of San Marcos Chapter No. 129, Royal Arch Masons, also a member of Lockhart Lodge No. 115, K. of P., and while not a member of any Church he is a firm believer in the Roman Catholic religion.

ADOLPH G. WANGEMANN is a gentleman who has been steadily growing in popularity during the seven years he has been engaged in business here, and is now one of the leading merchants of Shiner. He was born in Austin County, Texas, in 1854, and is a descendant of an old German family. The openings of the fields of commerce and finance of the United States offer to the natives of the old world opportunities which can hardly be said to exist in those countries, and among those who availed themselves of those advantages was Henry W. Wangemann, grandfather of our subject. He came to Texas with his family in 1845, and settled at Industry, Austin County, where he followed merchandising until killed by being thrown from a buggy. There his son, Ernst Wangemann, father of our subject, also a native of Germany, grew to manhood. He and his brother, Adam, served in the Mexican War, and later he was engaged in merchandising at New Ulm.

There he died about the year 1882. He married Miss Louisa Scham, also a native of Germany, who came with her parents to this country at an early day and settled with them in Washington County. She is still living. To their union were born eleven children, of whom our subject was the eldest. The latter was reared in Austin County, but was educated at St. Joseph Institute, Colorado County, Texas. After this for some time, he clerked for his father, and then embarked in business for himself at Schulenburg, where he remained from 1877 to 1887, when he came to Shiner. He was among the first to settle in this place, and here began business in the old Post Office building. Soon he completed his present large business building, thirty by ninety feet, and carries a stock valued at about $25,000, and does an annual business of about $60,000. Mr. Wangemann was married in 1877 to Miss Annie Kessler, a native of Austin County, Texas, and the daughter of Charles A. Kessler, of Fayette County. Five children have blessed this union: Charles, Freda, Adele, Hilda and Adolph. Mr. Wangemann is member of the K. of P., K. of H., the Sons of Hermann and the Yorktown Association. He was a member of the first Board of City Council, and is School Trustee of this district. Wideawake, thorough and reliable, Mr. Wangemann does a good business, and is one of the prominent men of Shiner.

REV. SAMUEL JOHNSON (deceased). This prominent old pioneer of Texas, who has long since passed to his reward, was born in Alabama, where he studied for and became a minister of the Methodist Church. He was a public spirited citizen, well posted and up to the times, and he was always quite actively interested in political matters, and for some time was a member of the State Senate of Alabama, but resigned that office on account of ill health, and in 1838 came to Washington County, Texas. Here he became a successful planter, but he also continued to preach the gospel gratuitously throughout the State, but as the climate of Washington County did not agree with his health, he sold his plantation there and organized an emigrating party to push west over two hundred miles, and they located in Comal County. The population was sufficient then to perfect the organization of a new county, which was done mainly by Mr. Johnson, at the town which became known as Blanco City, and Mr. Johnson became the first County and District Clerk, while his son-in-law, A. V. Gates, was the first County Judge. After holding his office for several years, Rev. Johnson resigned at the opening of the great Civil War, and entered the army as Chaplain in Johnson's army, and, although over age, he continued to fill this position for two years, when he was appointed by Jefferson Davis as District Tax Collector for this section, an office he filled until the war closed. His subsequent life was spent at Blanco in the stock business, but he also preached whenever called upon to do so, and, although not a nember of any conference, nor engaged in any regular work, he did much good, and both by precept and example showed the proper way to live. He died in 1882, and is buried in the old Johnson Cemetery near Blanco. He was married to Miss Harrison in Alabama, and in 1877 celebrated his golden wedding, and the following year his wife died. Ten children had been born to them, only two of whom survive: Mrs. John M. Watson, a resident of Troy, Bell County, Texas, and Mary K., now Mrs. M. K. McPherson, of Kyle. The latter was the youngest child born to her parents, and she was first married in 1868 to Thomas P. Rountree, Jr., a native of

Louisiana, whose father was a Colonel in the Confederate army, and served in the trans-Mississippi Department until the war closed. He is now living in Gillespie County, Texas. Thomas P. Rountree came to Texas in 1866, and located in Travis County, where he married, after which he moved to Hays County. To him and his wife the following children were born: Leonidas Johnson, Emma Lucile, wife of Walter J. Sweeney of Columbia, Emmett, Deputy Collector of Customs at Eagle Pass, Texas, and Oscar. In 1870 his widow married Capt. McPherson, a native of Arkansas, who obtained his title during the Civil War. He was sent to the Indian Territory to assist in preserving order there, under Gen. Maxey, and after the war closed he was stationed there and engaged in merchandising, and also founded a paper. In 1887 his career was closed by death, and his widow and three sons survive him, the names of the latter being, Granville, Melville and Wallace. In 1891 Mrs. McPherson received the appointment as Matron of the Southwestern Texas Insane Asylum, but after holding this position capably for one year she was compelled to resign on account of ill health, and has since been a resident of Kyle. Her son, Leonidas Johnson Rountree, is now the able editor of the *Star Vindicator*, of Kyle. He was born near Dripping Springs, Hays County, Texas, July 15, 1869, but unfortunately his school days only lasted for about ten months. At the age of eleven years he entered the newspaper office of the *Star Vindicator*, published at Blanco by his stepfather, the latter of whom was soon taken sick, and young Lee was soon compelled to assume charge of the same, and after the death of Capt. McPherson, in 1887, the paper was conducted for some time by young Lee and his mother. The *Star Vindicator* was first established at Caddo, Indian Territory, in 1872, by Granville McPherson and Dr. D. M. Hailey, and it was conducted on independent principles, but supported Gov. Boudinot in his famous campaign to open the territory to settlement. In 1878 the paper was moved to Blanco, and published by Capt. Granville McPherson until his death, after which the paper was moved by his widow to Kyle, and it has since been under the management of her son, Lee J. Rountree, who espouses the principles of the Democratic party through its columns. Mr. Rountree is a member of the State Press Association, and is Secretary of the Southwest Press Association. He is President of the Hope Hook and Ladder Company of Kyle, the pioneer company of the city, and in many other ways he has manifested an interest in the affairs of his section. For the past four years he has been quite active in political matters, and has had the honor to represent his county in every convention held in the last four years. In 1890 at the age of twenty-one he was appointed Assessor and Collector of Taxes of the town of Kyle, and in 1891 was elected without opposition, but resigned on account of business relations before his term expired.

R. L. MILLER. He whose name heads this sketch was the first merchant of Waelder, Texas, and has ever since done a prosperous business there. He has been successful in the accumulation of worldly goods, and by his energy, undoubted honesty and desire to please his patrons, he has built up a wide connection that is continually increasing. He was born in Tennessee, January 7, 1833, a son of Isaac and Susan (Swan) Miller, who were born in South Carolina and came to Texas in 1842 from Tennessee, settling at Salem, near the Sabine River. There they remained until 1845, then moved to New Braunfels, and in 1847–48 went to San Antonio, thence to Lockhart for a year or

A. B. KERR.

two, then located in Belton, where Mr. Miller erected the first hotel of the place. After residing in two or three other places he located in Hopkinsville, Gonzales County, where he died in 1863, and the mother in 1892, at the age of eighty-five years. The subject of this sketch received his education in the public schools of the various localities in which his parents resided, and being intelligent and persevering, he was well fitted to begin teaching school at the age of eighteen years, an occupation which he followed successfully for ten years. During this time he also served as Justice of the Peace. In 1866 he was appointed by Governor Hamilton as Clerk of the District Court, an office he held one year, and in 1870 he was elected County and District Clerk of Gonzales County, in which capacity he served one term of four years. In 1867 he engaged in merchandising at Hopkinsville, where he continued to do business until 1873, then moved to Waelder and bought the first lot sold in the place, and erected the first building and did the first mercantile business ever done there. In 1874 he erected his present building, in which he carries a stock of goods worth about $6,000 or $7,000, his annual sales amounting to about $20,000. He is the owner of farming land to the amount of 7,000 acres, and has 800 acres adjoining the town of Waelder, 100 of which are under cultivation. He is a brother of ex-Congressman J. F. Miller, of Gonzales. He was married January 1, 1865, to Miss Sarah E. Hopkins, a native of Mississippi, who came to Texas in her childhood with her father, D. S. Hopkins, after whom the town of Hopkinsville was named. Mr. Miller's union has resulted in the birth of twelve children, all of whom are living. He is a member of Hopkinsville Lodge No. 113 of the A. F. & A. M., is the oldest member of the lodge, and has passed through all the chairs. He is also a member of the Chapter and Commandery, the latter at Gonzales. His wife is a member of the Baptist Church, and they are deservedly classed among the most substantial citizens of the county, and through their own efforts have become possessed of the liberal means that are now at their disposal.

JOSEPH MARION MANGUM. The present age is undoubtedly the one of greatest progress in every way, and every year witnesses new triumphs in the world of racing horses. Mr. Mangum, who is one of the stirring, substantial and prosperous farmers and stock-raisers of Rancho, Gonzales County, Texas, is deeply interested in the raising of fine horses, and is the owner of the noted racing stallion " Cold Deck," of the "Steel Dust" strain. From his ranche have gone out such fine animals as " Billie," who makes his quarter of a mile in twenty-two and a half seconds; "Little Joe," time twenty-one and three-fourths seconds, and sold for $2,000 in the City of Mexico, where he is at the present time; "Blue Eyes," time twenty-two seconds. This horse ran at Dallas, Texas, fair in 1893, and beat the Texas record for four and a half furlongs. "Yellow Wolf" made the time in twenty-two seconds. Mr. Mangum has made his way from modest beginnings to his present substantial condition, and it is all owing to his industry and good management. He is now the owner of about 2,200 acres of land, and has every reason to be proud of the result of his industry. He was born in Talapoosa County, Ala., January 31, 1839, son of William R. and Leacy (Dennis) Mangum, the father a native of North Carolina, and the mother of Georgia. William R. Mangum was a successful planter, and emigrated to Texas as early as 1840, settling in Matagorda County, where he bought land and engaged in farming and stock-raising.

There he passed the remainder of his days. He was a Democrat in politics.
The mother passed away in 1876. Joseph Marion Mangum received the rudiments of an education in Matagorda County, and finished in Gonzales County,
Texas, where his mother moved when he was fourteen years of age. In 1862
he enlisted in Terry's Rangers, cavalry, and was discharged on account of
sickness the same year. After that he served in Duff's Regiment, on the border, until the end of the war. When he returned home he had very little
means to start with, but by industry and perseverance he has become one of
the prosperous men of his section. He was married in 1876 to Miss Mattie
Gillespie, daughter of James C. and Nancy (Yeary) Gillespie, and seven
children were born to this union, six of whom are living: Edna, Joseph D.,
Mattie Lee, Maud, Eugene, Mamie, and Brown, who died in infancy.

LEANDER C. CUNNINGHAM. The name of Cunningham has been known in
Texas for nearly three-score years, for in 1833 Leander C. Cunningham came
to the State, and here has since resided. He was born in East Tennessee in
1810, the youngest of nine children born to James and Margaret (Cunningham) Cunningham, and when five years old was taken by his parents to Alabama and there took up their abode, the mother's death occurring very shortly
after. In 1837 his father, James Cunningham, came to Texas, and after following the useful and honorable calling of the farmer, died in 1844. Leander
C. Cunningham was educated in the common schools, and upon reaching a
suitable age began the study of law, and in 1832 was licensed to practice his
profession at Hanceville, Ala. In April, 1833, he came to Texas and became
the first law practitioner of Bastrop, at which place he continued to make his
home for about twenty-six years. He was a soldier in the Texas Revolution,
and was a participant in the noted battle of San Jacinto. About 1845 he
turned his attention to mercantile pursuits, which he continued to follow without interruption until 1860, and did a very large and successful business.
When the railroad was completed in that section he moved to Alleyton, where
he continued business until 1872. While in Bastrop he was quite active in
politics, and held the responsible office of County Judge for three terms, and
while on the bench his decisions were made with impartial fairness, and to
the satisfaction of all concerned. In January, 1874, he came to the new town
of Waelder, and was the first railroad agent of the place, and here opened the
first lumber yard, in which business he continued until 1892, when he
embarked in his present business. He keeps an excellent assortment of furniture of all kinds, besides paints and oils, and also deals in coffins. He carries
a stock of goods worth about $2,000, and is doing a fair annual business. He
was married in 1838 in Bastrop, to Mrs. Ann Slaughter, a native of Kentucky,
her maiden name having been Sloan. To their union six children were given,
five of whom are now living: James L., a druggist of Houston; Andrew D.,
a telegraph operator; Caroline, widow of Doctor J. G. Walker; Harriet J.,
wife of I. W. Middlebrook, of Columbus, Texas; Virginia, wife of B. M. Baker,
of Columbus; their first daughter, named Ann, died at the age of eight years.
Mr. Cunningham and his wife are members of the Methodist Church, and he
is a pronounced Prohibitionist. He is a fine old gentleman, well preserved
and hale, and all who have the honor of his acquaintance are his friends. His
married life has extended over a period of fifty-four years, and has been an
unusually prosperous, long, and happy one.

EZEKIEL W. WALKER. The entire life of Mr. Walker has been passed in
ceaseless activity, and has not been without substantial evidences of success,

as will be seen from a glance over the following facts in his life. His career is an example of industry, perseverance and good management, rewarded by substantial results, well worthy the imitation of all who start out in life as he did, with no capital except a good constitution and a liberal supply of pluck and energy. He was born in Simpson County, Miss., July 2, 1828, the only child born to Ezekiel and Frances (Lee) Walker, who removed from their native state of South Carolina to Mississippi at an early day. The father was a successful planter of Simpson County until his death, which occurred in the year of our subject's birth in 1828. In the State of Mississippi Ezekiel W. Walker was reared and educated, and began life as a planter. In 1850 he came to Texas and located in the northeastern part of Gonzales County, where he bought a farm of 300 acres in 1852, which he successfully tilled until 1862, when he cast aside personal considerations to enlist in the cause of the Confederacy, becoming a member of Company B, Seventeenth Texas Infantry, under Col. Allen, and served in the trans-Mississippi Department in Texas, Louisiana and Arkansas. He was in many important battles, and when the war terminated was located at Hempstead. He at once returned to his farm in Gonzales County, and in addition to tilling his land was engaged in teaching school for a year or so. He has always been quite active in political matters, and in 1866 was appointed to the office of County Sheriff, but for good reasons declined to accept the position, but when elected to the office of Justice of his precinct, No. 3, accepted the same, and has been re-elected ever since, a fact which speaks eloquently as to his intelligence and popularity. He made his home on his farm until about 1878, when he moved to Waelder, where he now has his office. He is the owner of a good farm of 200 acres, about four miles from town, 100 acres of which are under cultivation, and, as the land is productive, large crops are raised each year. December 7, 1848, Mr. Walker was married to Miss Mary E. Hopkins, a native of Georgia and daughter of Samuel Hopkins, and, of a family of nine children born to them, three are now living: Ezekiel Dennis, Frances Elizabeth, wife of John Anderson, of Gonzales County, and Johanna Louise. Those dead are: Needham W., Benjamin Francis, James Eli, George Washington, Mary Jane, and John S. Mr. Walker and his wife are members of the Baptist Church, and socially he is a member of Hopkinsville Lodge No. 183 of the A. F. & A. M. Mr. Walker is a man of noble traits of character, is highly esteemed and popular in the section in which he resides, and is one of the pioneers of the Waelder neighborhood.

JACOB F. WOLTERS. La Grange, noted for the ability of its bench and bar, may be counted particularly fortunate in including in the latter some of the ablest distinctly young lawyers in the country. A visit to the courts shows them conspicuous in important cases, appearing with or in competition with the veterans whose names are perhaps better known than these, but who find it necessary to brush up their knowledge of old practice and keep an eye out for new practice if they are not to be outgeneraled by the sharp and shrewd young men, whose self-reliance has made them develop much more rapidly than did the young lawyers of the generation of the veterans. Among the most popular of this younger circle of practitioners stands the name of Jacob F. Wolters, who was born in Austin County in 1871, and is the son of Theodore H. and Margaret (Wink) Wolters, natives of Austin County, but of German parentage. The father of Theodore H. Wolters, Jacob Wolters, came from the Fatherland with his wife, and, with other early German emigrants, settled at Industry, Austin County, Texas, in 1839. Farming was his occupation in life. He was twice married, his first wife dying shortly after coming here, and he then wedded his second wife. His first union resulted in the birth of two sons and two daughters, and his second marriage was blessed by the birth of four sons. (For further particulars see sketch of Theodore H. Wolters, of Schulenburg.) Jacob F. Wolters, our subject, was educated in the public schools of Schulenburg, and finished at the Add-Ran College, Hood County. Returning home when nineteen years of age he commenced the study of law in the office of Phelps & Willrich in 1890, was admitted to the bar in 1892, and the same year was elected County Attorney. He announced for re-election in 1894 and had no opponent; but in August the firm of Phelps & Willrich dissolved partnership, and he immediately withdrew from the race and formed a partnership with that able lawyer and jurist, his old preceptor, Judge R. H. Phelps. He selected his life companion in the person of Miss Sallie Drane, of Columbus, Colorado County, and their nuptials were solemnized in 1893. Her parents, Robert and Eliza (Hargrove) Drane, were early settlers of Texas, and Mr. Drane was a successful farmer of that State. After his death, in 1878, his widow married A. C. Hereford, and is now living. Mr. and Mrs. Wolters' marriage resulted in the birth of one son, Theodore Drane, whose birth occurred June 27, 1894. Politically, Mr. Wolters advocates the principles of the Democratic party, and takes a decided interest in the political issues of the day. His father is a stanch Democrat. He is the only one of his family who has adopted a professional life, and his success in that direction has been quite phenomenal. Mrs. Wolters is a graduate of Hamilton College, Lexington, Ky., and is a lady of excellent judgment and good taste, and is a worthy member of the Christian Church.

WILLIAM ARCHIBALD WILLIAMS. Activity and enterprise are in no direction more lucidly marked than in farming and stock-raising. This calling is the pulse of the country's progress and development. Among those engaged in this occupation, who have met with more than ordinary success, stands the name of William A. Williams, whose fine place attests by its thriving appearance the spirit and enterprise that marks its owner. His parents, John and Mary (McAdams) Williams, were natives of Kentucky, and of Scotch and Irish origin respectively. When but a boy the father went to Boston, Mass., and there learned the house-painter's trade. Later he moved to Tuscaloosa, Ala., and there received his final summons in 1838. The mother, who was a Methodist, died in 1857. William A. Williams was born in Tuscaloosa, Ala., June 4, 1854, and when about 10 years of age left home suddenly, without giving his parents previous warning. This he did rather than go to school, fear of the teacher being the main cause. He went to Montgomery and remained there two years, making his own living. He then returned home to see his parents, and afterward, in 1849, came, with a cousin, to the Lone Star State. Possessed of an unlimited amount of push and energy he has made and lost two or three fortunes, going security, and in the war; but he still owns 1,200 acres of valuable land near Rancho, where he farms and raises stock. During the Civil War he enlisted in Davis' Company, McCord's Regiment, and served four years and four months. He participated in the battle of Fort Donnelson, and the balance of the time was in Texas, scouting on the border, following Indians, etc. Mr. Williams is a First Degree Mason, a member of

Leesville Lodge, and an Odd Fellow, No. 214, Rancho Lodge. Politically he is a Populist, and held the office of County Commissioner four years. In religion he is a Methodist. Mr. Williams was married in 1854 to Miss Margaret Scott, daughter of Jonathan and Nancy (Maiden) Scott, and twelve children have been the result of this union, nine of whom are still living: Frances, deceased; Mollie, wife of Boone Glover; Thomas W., Elder, deceased; Collie, deceased; Sebel, wife of George McDonald; Cornelia, wife of James Churcher; Ora, wife of Milton McGee; Dosia, wife of Sam Wiley; Hampton W., Tilton, and Adeline, widow of Chesley Elkins.

COLONEL JOHN JACOB MYERS, (deceased.) The life narrative of the head of a family is interesting, not only to posterity, but also to the citizens of the section in which he has resided, and this truth is doubly true when such a man has established for himself and his children a reputation for integrity, character and ability, and has been of value in the development of that portion of the country which has been his home.

Such a narrative do we have in this sketch of the life of Col. John Jacob Myers, who was born in Lincoln County, Missouri, October 25, 1821, a son of Elijah Myers, who was an early settler of that State from Kentucky. In the State of Missouri the subject of this sketch was reared on a farm, and much of his education was obtained at home, under the instruction of his father. He was with Gen. John C. Fremont in his expedition across the plains to the Pacific coast, and thence to Mexico with the famous pathfinder. After the close of the Mexican War, Mr. Myers returned to Missouri, and married Miss Sarah E. Hudspeth, of Jackson County, Missouri, October 3, 1848. The only child of this union, Samuel Myers, aged ten months, died in 1850. He was engaged in gold mining in California, 1849 to 1851. He then returned by water to New York City, thence by rail to Missouri. After a short stay at his old home he came to Texas, where his wife died, March 14, 1852. He purchased lands, began farming and stock-raising in Caldwell County. November 6, 1856, he was married to Miss Eliza Jane Skaggs, of Warren County, Kentucky, a daughter of Abram Moredock and Rhoda Boone (Smith) Skaggs, who were also Kentuckians by birth, their parents being among the very first settlers of the Blue Grass State from Virginia. The mother was a relative of Daniel Boone, and the father was a soldier of the war of 1812, and fought on the frontier with Gen. W. H. Harrison, being one of the famous "Hunters of Kentucky;" of which poem the opening verse reads, as follows:

> "Ye gentlemen and ladies fair
> Who grace this famous city;
> Just listen while you've time to spare,
> While I repeat a ditty.
> And for this opportunity
> Just think yourselves quite lucky,
> For 'tis not often that you hear
> A hunter from Kentucky."

Mr. and Mrs. Skaggs removed to Caldwell County, Texas, in 1854, and the mother was called from life in the following year. In 1856 the father returned to Kentucky, and died in that State, in the fall of 1861. He was a Master Mason. He was always interested in military affairs, mustered a company, and was Captain of the local militia. After the marriage of Mr. Myers, he and his family resided on a farm near Lockhart, until the opening of the Civil War, and when a company was raised in June, 1861, Mr. Myers was at once chosen its Captain, and his commission as Captain of the Lone Star Mounted Rifles is dated July 1, 1861. He was ordered to report to Colonel Moore, at Galveston, and started with his company September 6, 1861, and was mustered into the Confederate States army, September 1861, for during the war. He was advanced in rank from Captain to Major, then to Lieutenant Colonel, while at Galveston. He was in many engagements at the head of his company, and later while serving in Louisiana was promoted to the rank of Colonel. He was in the Red River Campaign in Louisiana, against Banks' army, and at the battle of Mansfield on April 8, 1867, was promoted to Colonel of his regiment, the Twenty-sixth Texas Cavalry, and commanded the same until the close of the war. He was in many severe encounters in the swamps of Louisiana, and saw some hard service, but faithfully, ably and bravely performed every duty as a Confederate soldier. He was home on a short furlough, just before the close of the war, and was on his way to join his command, when met by the news that the Confederates were overpowered, and the war ended. He at once returned home, resumed farming and stock-raising, also buying and driving stock, and, in the latter occupation, soon became one of the most extensive in that section of the country. He was one of the first to drive cattle to the northern States, and later he drove large herds to Kansas and Utah. He was taken sick in Kansas, while on a trip there with cattle, and returned home, and died December 10, 1874. He left a widow and seven children: Hettie Virginia, wife of Jas. F. Cahill, an attorney-at-law of San Antonio; George, married, and living at Batesville, Texas; John Jacob, Abram Elijah, Robert E. Lee, Eliza Jane, married J. H. Williams, a stockman, and lives at Marfa, Presidio County, Texas; Eva Boone; Carrie Ellen, and Lafayette, who died in infancy, preceding their father to the better land. Colonel Myers was an enthusiastic member of the A. F. & A. M., (was a Royal Arch Mason) was a member of the I. O. O. F., and he and his wife were worthy and consistent members of the Presbyterian Church. He removed with his family to Lockhart in 1870, and there, before death claimed him, he made numerous friends, and his life was one of usefulness and honor. He was a member of the United States Army in California and throughout the Mexican War till 1847, and was advanced from a private to a Lieutenant in rank, which fact speaks highly of his military ability and popularity, because advancement then in the United States service to a commission was rarely granted to other than trained soldiers, and even then only to those of high courage and military power. He left a goodly property, as well as the heritage of an honest name to his children, and on the old homestead the widow still resides.

THOMAS B. BUDD. In writing a review of the industries of Gonzales County, Texas, there is no subject more worthy of attention than the lumber business, and this is especially the case at Waelder, for the town has built up so rapidly that it has been necessary that large quantities of building material should be handled to supply the demand. One of the most prominent engaged in this line of business is Thomas B. Budd, who is a sensible man, possessed of a practical knowledge of his business. His stock of lumber is always selected with the utmost care, and customers may be assured that his goods are always what he represents them to be. He was born in Fayetteville, Fayette County, Texas, February 21, 1857, the son of John and Isabella

(Fisher) Budd, who were born in Louisiana and Tennessee, respectively, and were married in Texas, to which State the mother came when a child, with her parents. The father came here after reaching manhood, and engaged in teaching school in Fayette County, and also gave much attention to preaching the gospel of the Missionary Baptist Church. He continued his ministerial labors during his lifetime, and was known far and wide as a man of more than average intellect, and of the most upright morals. In the fall of 1872 he became a resident of Lee County, and there was called from life in 1876. He was compelled to ride long distances to fill his appointments, and, while laboring for the Master, organized many churches, and was the means of saving many souls. He was very popular and well liked, had a host of friends, and was always kind and considerate in the home circle. His wife died in Lee County, November 13, 1872. They left six children, four of whom are now living, the subject of this sketch being the second in order of birth. He was reared in Fayette County, obtained a fair education in the common schools, and after the death of his father, began driving stock, making trips North. In 1886 he came to Waelder and opened a lumber yard, in connection with which he conducts a well appointed furniture store, the first business of that kind to be established in the place. He also carries a stock of builders' hardware. He is in the prime of life and in the full vigor of mental and physical manhood, and his success in life is the reward of honest effort applied to legitimate business; and his friends rejoice that his lines are cast in pleasant places. He has in process of erection a handsome residence, and now expects to make Waelder his home indefinitely. Miss Maggie Kirtley, a native of Minnesota, became his wife in 1889. She was brought to Texas by her parents when a child, and with them located in Colorado County, then came to Gonzales County, but the father's death occurred in Bell County. Mr. and Mrs. Budd have two children: John and Eunice. Mrs. Budd is a member of the Baptist Church.

WILLIAM BURKE. Many of the best known farmers of Texas have been born outside its confines, and this is the case with William Burke, whose birth occurred in Union County, Arkansas, January 14, 1836. His parents, James and Martha (Ogden) Burke, were natives of Kentucky and North Carolina, respectively, but when both were young they came with their parents to Arkansas. James Burke, like his father, followed farming, and in the fall of 1845 he came to Texas, and settled in Tyler County, where he remained for five years. In 1850 he came to Fayette County, and the following year settled on the prairie about five miles east of Flatonia, where he followed farming and stock-raising. He was too old to participate in the War of the Rebellion, but he enrolled for the War of 1812, and was in Louisiana during the battle of New Orleans. His death occurred in 1873, when seventy-six years old. His wife still survives and finds a comfortable and pleasant home with her son, our subject. She was born June 5, 1805. Eleven children were born to their marriage, six of whom are now living: Mariah L., widow of James T. Burke; William, Benjamin F., resides in Lavaca County, Texas; P. P., of Williamson County; I. R., of this county, and Arminta J., wife of B. W. Cocke, of Williamson County, Texas. William Burke received but a common school education, but during his youth was favored with some educational advantages not given to the boys growing up with him. When twenty-three years of age he began life as a farmer, and when in his twenty-fourth year, May, 1861, he and T. S. Menefee organized a company known as Fayette County State Rights Guards, of which he was made First Lieutenant and Mr. Menefee, Captain. This company was never called for, and in the month of October, 1861, he and the captain went to Galveston and joined Capt. Fred. Tates' company, at Galveston. This was attached to Col. E. B. Nicholas' regiment of infantry, and he remained with this for six months, being mustered out at Galveston in May, 1862. In the latter part of that month he joined Capt. Frank Weeks' Company, for three years, or during the war, and in July, 1862, his command crossed the river at Vicksburg, and the first battle he participated in was at Coffeeville, Miss. He was with Gen. Forrest in many of his numerous fights, among them the following: Harrisburg, Fort Pillow, Holly Springs, where Mrs. U. S. Grant was captured, and our subject was on guard duty over her for some time. He says Mrs. Grant was very pleasant to her captors. At this place the Confederates captured about three thousand wagons and mules, all the provisions, and a large amount of amunition, etc. From there Mr. Burke's command went to La Grange, captured seventy-five men, and then went to Grand Junction, and tore up the railroads. At Middleburg, Tenn., the command attacked a stockade and lost quite heavily, as five thousand United States cavalry made their appearance. Mr. Burke was at the fall of Vicksburg and Jackson, and after the fall of those places he was engaged on picket duty on Big Black for one month. From there he went to meet Gen. Frank P. Blair, and was in a battle at Tuscumbia, Ala. His command returned to Mississippi to meet Gen. Sturgis who came in with a command of negroes, and in the battle that followed many were killed and the remainder captured. Two thousand of the negroes were sent to Mobile, Ala. Mr. Burke was captured on the Tallahatchie River and kept a prisoner at Memphis for six weeks. He was then exchanged and returned to the army in September, joining his company at Mobile, Ala. After this he served as a scout on Pearl River, Mississippi, and was chased by E. J. Davis' force, and was in many skirmishes. On the 2d of March, 1865, one-half of the Battalion was furloughed home, and Mr. Burke was appointed Quartermaster of the boys as they returned. Our subject arrived at home March 28, and his furlough expired in June, 1865, but war was over by that time. This was Mr. Burke's first furlough. While serving the latter part of the war he held the rank of Second Sergeant, and was a brave and faithful soldier. After reaching home he remained with his father and engaged in farming and stock-raising, meeting with good success in this occupation. In the year 1865 he was married to Miss Mary M. Hunter (see sketch of Robert H. Hunter), and their union was blessed by the birth of three children, Robert J., a physician of this county; W. P., of Louisiana, and Edward M., a farmer, of Jackson County, Texas, who married Miss Pearl Pharr of Fort Bend County, Texas. Since the war, Mr. Burke has followed farming and stock-raising and owns two valuable farms. He is interested in political matters, but has never but once been before the people for an office. He is a member of the Farmer's Alliance and is President of the same in his county.

G. R. SMITH. This wideawake man of affairs and substantial intelligent, citizen has for some time devoted his attention to the occupations of ginning and milling at Waelder, Gonzales County, Texas, and in pursuing this branch of human endeavor has met with a more than ordinary degree of success. He was born in Tennessee in 1859, and was a son of Calvin M. and Nancy

(Spears) Smith, who were also Tennesseeans by birth. The father was a soldier of the Confederate army and was killed at the siege of Morristown, Tenn. His son, W. S. Smith, came to Texas and took up his residence in Waelder just prior to the completion of the railroad to this place. He soon began working at the carpenter's trade, became a contractor, and erected many of the first buildings put up in the place. He erected and operated the second cotton gin ever built in Waelder, and this gin he sold to his brother, the subject of this sketch, and it has since been under the control of the latter who has operated it intelligently and therefore profitably. He has been a resident of Waelder since 1880, having previous to that time been a resident of Tennessee, where he was reared, educated, and, until his removal to Texas, engaged in farming. He has been the sole proprietor of the gin and cotton mill since 1888, and later purchased a fine residence and other property in the town. His plant is fitted up with a 40 horse-power boiler and engine, and his gin is of the Van Winkle & Carver make, and has a capacity of twenty-four bales per day, the average number of bales per season amounting to 1,000. In February, 1893, Mr. Smith was married to Miss Lillie Brown, a native of Texas.

Dr. WILLIAM H. LANCASTER is an exceptionally popular and successful physician. He is scholarly and well informed in every branch of his profession, is intelligent and well posted on all matters of public interest, and stands well in the community, both as a citizen and as a professional man. Although he has been a resident of this town only since 1887, he has already given abundant evidence of the ability which qualifies him for a high place in the medical profession. He is a native of Jackson County, Alabama, born in May, 1849, and was the eldest of seven children born to John Nathaniel and Mary A. (Jones) Lancaster, natives respectively of Tennessee and Alabama. The maternal grandfather, Moses Jones, was an early settler of Alabama, and an active man in the various walks of life. He settled in Bellefonte, that State, purchased a large tract of land, and in connection, carried on merchandising. For some time he was Probate Judge, and he was an early editor, conducting a paper during the war. The Federal soldiers then came and destroyed all his property. One of his sons, Henry, was in the Confederate army, and was Major of the Eleventh Alabama Regiment during the siege of Atlanta. There he lost his life. Mr. Jones died about 1873 or 1874. He was a very active and prominent man in his community. The paternal grandfather of our subject married in Tennessee and moved to North Alabama, where he purchased a large estate, but died soon after. His wife was a Miss Hudson, of a wealthy and influential family. After her husband's death she married Judge T. M. Rector, a prominent lawyer of North Alabama. She and her husband came to Texas in 1853, located east of Austin, and he farmed the rest of his life, dying in 1893. Many of his relatives reside in this section. The grandmother died in February, 1867. The father of Dr. Lancaster was reared in Alabama, and there married Miss Jones. He followed farming there until 1856, when he came to Texas and settled in Travis County. He served four years in the Confederate Army. About 1884 he moved to Lockhart, and now resides in that town. Dr. W. H. Lancaster was seven years of age when he came with his parents to Texas, and he was educated at Manor, Texas. In 1873 he began the study of medicine in New Orleans, Tulane University, and during the years 1875 and '76, attended Louisville Medical College, where he took his degree in the latter year. He then began practicing at Lockhart, remained there about ten years and one year at Red Rock, and in 1887, came to Moulton, where he was among the first to locate. He assisted in surveying the town and bought the first lot sold in the place. Since then he has been in constant practice here, and he also opened the first drugstore at this place. Dr. Lancaster is quite active in politics, and is a frequent contributor to the paper in the vicinity. He took a post graduate course at Tulane University during the winter of 1881 and '82, and is now a member of the State Medical Association of which he is Third Vice-president. The doctor is a pleasant, genial gentleman and his large practice is constantly increasing. He is greatly interested in the development and growth of this part of Texas, and besides his pleasant place in Moulton, owns property in Jackson County. He is a Mason and Master of Moulton Lodge No. 298. Dr. Lancaster was married June 10, 1880, to Miss Linda Ella Williamson, a native of Alabama and daughter of John H. Williamson of Lockhart. Four sons and one daughter are the fruits of this union: Moore, Lewis, Lifford Williamson, Bessie Edna and Frank Houston. Dr, Lancaster is a member of the Christian and his wife a member of the M. E. Church.

FREDERICK W. TURNER. One of those business men whose probity is well known and whose career has been distinguished for enterprise is Frederick W. Turner, a successful and leading liveryman of Schulenburg, Texas. He was born in Westphalia, Prussia, May 10, 1838, and is the son of Christian and Mary Turner. Christian Turner was twice married, and became the father of four children to the first and nine to the second union. His death occurred when our subject was four years old. The latter was reared in his native country, learned the blacksmith trade there and then came to America with his mother. The older members of the family had preceded them and settled in various sections. They were named as follows: Charles, Edward, Sophia, Lewis and Albert. Three, Lena, Theodore and Henry died in the old country. Our subject and his mother landed in Baltimore in 1856, October 27th, and proceeded at once to Cincinnati, where they remained three months. From there they went to Indiana and located at Batesville, Ripley County, where they remained until March, 1858, then our subject came to Texas. Locating first at Hallettsville, he worked at any honest employment he could find, overseeing, etc., and made Hallettsville his home until 1861. At that date he joined Company D, Second Texas Cavalry under Capt. James Walker of Hallettsville, and his company with three others, was under immediate command of Lieut. Col. John R. Baylor (the celebrated Indian Fighter), and did service in Arizona and New Mexico for nearly two years. During this time he was in several engagements with the United States troops stationed on the frontier, the following being the most prominent: Fort Fillmore, and Fort Craig, the former being a prominent engagement for the number taking part, and a complete victory for the Confederates. During the two years Mr. Turner served with his company in the west, twelve members of his company were killed by the Indians, eight at Fort Davis and four in New Mexico. Returning from this trip in the fall of 1862, Mr. Turner went with his company to Louisiana and during this time was in a number of skirmishes. In 1863 he returned to Texas and, shortly afterwards, was transferred to the city of Galveston and was in the battle of Galveston on New Year's night, 1863.

Later Mr. Turner got transferred from Company D, Second Texas Cavalry to Company C, Second Texas Infantry, and was stationed at Galveston for eight or nine months. Still later he was transferred to the Confederate States navy on board the Missouri, an iron-clad steamer built at Shreveport, La., and in March, 1865, was transferred to the General Webb. During the remainder of the war he was engaged in running the blockade from Shreveport to New Orleans, which was not successfully accomplished. They went about twenty-eight miles below the city of New Orleans, but could go no further on account of the United States vessels. Capt. Reed commanding the Confederates, ordered his men to set fire to the vessel, jump overboard and swim ashore. This order was promptly obeyed. Our subject, being the Second Engineer, was in the engine room when the order was given. Coming up from that room, covered with perspiration, he plunged into the river. This was a very dangerous thing to do, and Mr. Turner says he would never attempt such a feat again under similar circumstances. He reached the shore in safety, but was captured the next day and sent to New Orleans, where he was kept a prisoner until the close of the war. He was exchanged at the mouth of the Red River, about two thousand soldiers of each side, and after being paroled both Federal and Confederates ate and slept together for two or three days, and enjoyed themselves most thoroughly. Our subject did not go back to Texas right away, but stopped in Natchez, Miss., where he secured employment. Finding that he could not get a start, he secured transportation to New Orleans, and from there went to Galveston and thence to Columbus, the end of the railroad. From there he walked to Hallettsville, remained there a short time and then returned to Galveston, where he worked at the carpenter trade. There he remained until 1867 and then came to Hallettsville, where he was engaged in carpentering and paper hanging for five or six years. Later he held the position of Deputy Sheriff for four years, and for another year was variously employed. On the 1st of March, 1874, he purchased his present business, which he has been engaged in up to the present time. He has met with well deserved success in this occupation and has one of the leading establishments of the kind in the county. He owns a fine residence in Schulenburg, and this is presided over by his excellent wife, formerly Miss Sisley A. Pace, a native of Virginia, whom he married in the year 1866. Her parents, highly respected people, were among the early settlers of Texas. Mr. and Mrs. Turner have reared a family of thirteen children: Albert, of Yokum, this State; Charley, of this city; Robert, of this city; Edward, of Karnes County; Lillie, of this city; William F., of this city; Carrie, of this city; Joseph, of Lavaca County; Corene, Louis, Estella, Katie and Selma, the last five also of this city. Mr. Turner was reared in the Lutheran faith and Mrs. Turner holds membership in the Christian Church. In the year 1869 Mr. Turner became a member of the Masonic Fraternity at Hallettsville, and he is now a member of Lyons Lodge. He was appointed Marshal of Schulenburg a portion of one term, and accepted the position for the benefit of the town. He takes but little interest in political matters, but votes for the most part with the Democratic party.

NATHAN EASON. He whose name heads this sketch is the junior member of the well known mercantile firm of Eason & Company, of Waelder, dealers in general merchandise. He was born in Colorado County, Texas, in 1858, the youngest child born to Needham W. and Clarissa Ann (Ward) Eason, who were born, reared and married in the Old North State, and about 1857 took up their abode in Texas. They settled in Colorado County, near Prairie Point (now Oakland), and there purchased a large tract of land and engaged very extensively in planting with a large force of negroes whom he brought with him from the Old North State. He did not live long to enjoy his home in the West, for he was called from life in 1858, after which his widow ably conducted the place until the opening of the Civil War, and also during that time, although on not so extensive a scale. After the war she conducted the place with the aid of hired help, and showed, in her management of business affairs, that she was a woman of marked business ability and keen discernment. She was called from life in 1871, a worthy member of the M. E. Church, as was also her husband, who was a Royal Arch Mason, and a prominent man. The subject of this sketch was educated in Concrete College, of Concrete, Texas, and upon entering business life became associated with his brothers in merchandising at Oakland. With an elder brother, Warren K., he came to Waelder in 1881, and established their present flourishing business, and now occupy a commodious building on the Square and carry a stock of goods valued at from $5,000 to $6,000, their annual sales amounting to $25,000. Their stock includes dry goods, clothing, groceries, hardware, etc., and their establishment is handsome and well appointed. These wideawake business men are large cotton buyers, and they are justly considered among the enterprising business men of the county. Warren K., the senior member of the firm, was born in 1855, was educated at Concrete, De Witt County, and was married in 1883 to Miss Maggie Bell, a native of Texas, by whom he has had two children, both of whom are dead. He is a member of the Baptist Church. Jacob Andrew Eason, another brother, was born in 1850 and received a good practical education in the country schools. He was associated with his brothers in the mercantile and stock business in Oakland, but sold his interests to them, and engaged in teaching school and now resides in Waelder. He is married and has two children.

JUDGE JOHN P. BELL. It seems to have been the ambition of Mr. Bell, one of the foremost lawyers of this county, to make the best use of his native and acquired powers, and to develop in himself a true manhood, and the large clientage he has gathered around him, as well as the large circle of friends he has won, abundantly testifies as to the success of his efforts. He was born in Austin County, December 22, 1844, whither his parents, Andrew J. and Calpernia (Shellbourne) Bell, came in 1832 or 1833. They were natives respectively of Tennessee and Alabama, and were married in the State of Texas. After coming to this county they located near where New Ulm now stands, in this county, and Mr. Bell's first service for Texas was in the Blue Grass fight with the Indians, west of this place. He was also a member of the Texas army against Mexico in 1846–48, and participated in many engagements with the Mexicans and Indians. His career was a remarkable one. A fine specimen of the frontiersman, Mr. Bell was ever ready to serve his country, and, enjoying excellent health, no one ever found him missing when duty called. The first office he held in the county was that of Sheriff, to which he was elected in 1850. As this office did not pay him he resigned at the close of the first year, and in 1853 was elected to represent Austin County in the Legislature, with but slight opposition. So satisfied were his constituents at the close of the term, that he was re-elected in 1855. He favored the "Know

Nothing" wing of the Democratic party. Mr. Bell was a true and chivalrous son of the South, and during the Civil War devoted his energies to the Southern cause. At the election for President in 1860 he supported Breckinridge, of Kentucky, and although, when the war broke out, his health would not permit his serving on the field, he became provost in his county and rendered essential aid to his cause. When the cause was lost he submitted with heroic fortitude, but remained unchanged in faith and principle until the day of his death, dying a true Jeffersonian Democrat. It may be truly said that perhaps no individual has ever resided in Austin County, whose career has been more indelibly stamped upon its history, and whose memory has been more revered by his numerous friends and associates, than that of Andrew J. Bell. His love for his friends was one of his ruling passions, and his great fidelity, reliability, sincerity and devotion to them were well known. He came to this country when a boy, and as a boy he trod the broad plains of the Lone Star State when deer, buffalo and other animals were to be seen in vast numbers. His wife survived until April, 1887. They reared four children, viz.: Mrs. R. Minturn, of this place; John P., George C., also of Austin County and Mrs. C. H. Bethany, of this county. John P. Bell, ex-County Judge and generally known as Judge Bell, received the rudiments of an education in the common schools of this county, and later attended Williams' Academy, at Fayetteville, Fayette County, for a short time. When but sixteen years of age, he joined Capt. Hargroves' company of scouts, which afterwards became a part of Col. Reuben Brown's regiment of cavalry. Serving in the trans-Mississippi Department for some time, he was then promoted to Sergeant, and participated in a few skirmishes. After the war he engaged in farming, and followed this with varying success until 1868, when he began the study of law, being admitted to the bar in January, 1869, Judge McFarland presiding. The same year he was elected Presiding Justice of the county, and held that position until 1876, and was then elected County Judge, which office he held until 1881. Since that time he has held no office, but devotes his time to his profession, and has all the legal work he can possibly attend to. In 1881 he formed a partnership with James H. Shellbourne under the title of Bell & Shellbourne, and this firm is one of the best known in the county and enjoys an enviable reputation. Judge Bell was married in 1872 to Miss L. A. Bethany, daughter of J. W. and M. A. (Woods) Bethany, who were married in Alabama in 1843, and came to Texas in 1847. In this State Mr. Bethany passed away, leaving a wife and nine children. He was a prominent Mason and a successful farmer. Mr. and Mrs. Bell became the parents of four children: Lucy, James J., Anna and Bessie. The judge is a member of the A. F. & A. M. Bellville Lodge No. 223, of which he is Past Master, and he is a member of Bellville Chapter, R. A. M., No. 151, of which he is High Priest and Past High Priest. He is a charter member of the chapter, and is the Past Grand High Priest of the R. A. M., of Texas. He is also a member of the Knights Templar Lodge, of Brenham, No. 15. Both he and wife are consistent members of the M. E. Church.

WILLIAM BUCKNER HOUSTON, who is prominently connected with the farming and stock-raising industry of Gonzales County, Texas, is progressive in his ideas and tendencies, and favors all reforms and enterprises that tend to build up the locality in which he resides, or that will benefit his fellowman. He was born in DeWitt County, Texas, May 6, 1852, and is a son of

James A. and Julia A. (Harris) Houston, the father being of the same parentage as John N. Houston. James A. Houston was born in Mecklenburgh, N. C., in 1827, and in the early settling of Mississippi, his father, Robert B. Houston, immigrated to that State with James and four other children. There he became an extensive planter and large slave owner. In 1846 he came to Texas and settled in DeWitt County, where he followed farming and stock-raising until his death, in 1854. He left four children. James A. was educated in Oxford University, Mississippi, and just after completing his course his father decided to move to Texas. He became a farmer and stock-raiser in his new home, and in 1848 married Miss Julia A. Harris, daughter of Hon. Buckner and Nina (Steele) Harris. Judge Harris was prominent in the early days of Mississippi as a lawyer and jurist, and was closely related to Hon. Wiley P. Harris, Chief Justice of the Supreme Court of that State. Mr. Houston bought a home in Gonzales County in 1863, but died before he could take possession. He had enlisted in the army, but was prevented by ill-health from active service. Although not a member of any church, he was a believer. He left a wife and six children, the latter being named as follows: Robert A., deceased; James Dunn, William Buckner, Dora, wife of John W. Tinsley; Merry Harris and Minnie James. In 1869 Mrs. Houston married William P. Matthews, of Gonzales County, and was widowed the second time in 1873. She now finds a comfortable and happy home with her son, William Buckner Houston. The latter was educated in Gonzales County, and when nineteen years of age branched out for himself, without means, in the cattle business, living chiefly on a range in Gonzales County. He was interested with his brother, J. D. Houston, in a large ranch in the Pan Handle, which they sold for $525,000, the second largest deal ever consummated in Texas. He is now interested with his brother in a large ranch on the Pecos River, and in his own right owns about 6,000 acres in Gonzales County. He has about 5,000 head of cattle. In politics he is Democratic, and held the office of City Councilman for four years. Mr. Houston was married in 1884 to Miss Ada Lewis, daughter of Judge Everett Lewis, of Gonzales. One child, Ada Lewis Houston, was born to this union. Mrs. Houston died January 5, 1889, and Mr. Houston selected his second wife in the person of Miss Sue L. Jones, their nuptials being celebrated in 1892. Her parents, Capt. Augustus H. and Minerva (Lewis) Jones, are residents of Gonzales County, of which they were early settlers.

ROBERT AUGUSTIN HOUSTON, brother, of W. B., was one of the most successful farmers and stock-raisers of Gonzales County, was born in De Witt County, this State, April 25, 1849, and died in Gonzales County February 1, 1894. Owing to the devastating effects of the Civil War, which swept away their property, and the death of the father at that time, Robt. A., while yet a mere boy, left school to assist his widowed mother support her growing family. Thus he was deprived of the advantages of an education. When twenty years of age he married Miss Sallie J. Broadus, who survives him, and started out to take up the burden of life on his own account. He met with most wonderful success, for, without education, without means or influential friends, with but his strong arms and indomitable will, he carved out a fortune far beyond his greatest expectations. He directed his energies toward the up-building of the cattle industry, then in its infancy, and soon became recognized as an expert in the business in all its details. He was considered one of the safest, though most liberal traders in the Southwest, and at his death was one of the largest and most influential stockmen of the country. Though connected with some of the best and proudest families of the South, Mr. Houston was plain of speech and simple and unaffected in manner. Hospitable and generous to prodigality, he never allowed any worthy movement to fail for want of support on his part. Steadfast and faithful in his friendship, loving and tender in his home, charitable and attentive to the poor, few men of the county were more loved and honored than he. Eight children survive him.

JAMES DUNN HOUSTON. A remarkably successful stockman of Gonzales County, Texas, is James Dunn Houston, who was born in De Witt County, this State, in 1850, the second of four children born to James Andrew Dunn and Julia A. (Harris) Houston, native Mississippians. The paternal grandfather, Robert Houston, was also born in Mississippi, but was one of the very early settlers of De Witt County, Texas, and there became an extensive farmer and stock-raiser. While living in that county he was assassinated. The maternal grandfather, William Buckner Harris, was a Mississippian also and was one of the first to take up his residence in De Witt County, coming to this State with Mr. Houston, and settling in the same vicinity. While a resident of Mississippi he was elected to the office of District Judge, and upon retiring from the bench came to Texas, bringing with him a large amount of property in the shape of negroes, whom he at once put to work on his extensive plantation here. He eventually died in Gonzales County. J. A. D. Houston was brought to the Lone Star State when a child, was educated here, and in this State was married at the youthful age of twenty years. Immediately after the celebration of his nuptials he engaged in farming in Caldwell County, and at the untimely age of thirty-six years he was called from life there, in 1863. His widow still survives him. James Dunn Houston, the immediate subject of this sketch, came to Gonzales County the year of his father's death, and for some time he attended the public schools of this place. At about the age of eighteen years he engaged in the stock business, and would drive his herds north to Kansas for pasturage. When twenty-three years of age he went on the frontier in the Pan Handle and located a ranche, his brother, Robert A., being his partner in this venture, but he was the business manager for four years. In 1882 he and his brother sold their interest in the business for $525,000, which was one of the largest sales ever made in the State, only one exceeding it. He then began an extensive purchase of ranche property in Gonzales and Wilson counties, and in 1883 located a ranche on the Pecos River, which comprised about 6,000 acres of well watered land, and his pasture in this and Wilson counties contains over 22,000 acres, over which roam at will about 12,000 head of stock. He has his stock well graded with fine Short-horn males, imported from the North. He has been universally successful, is a self-made man, and is one of the most important stock-raisers of the State, and in this industry has become very wealthy, although he is still young in years. He has had the discernment to see and grasp at all opportunities that have presented themselves, has made the most of his chances, and as a result he has amassed a grand fortune. In 1881 he erected his handsome home in Gonzales, and in addition to the property above mentioned he has about 300 acres of river bottom land in cultivation, which land is exceptionally fine and productive. He was married in December, 1875, to Miss Dora Chenault, a daughter of Felix Chenault, an early settler of Gonzales, and to their union two children have been given: Gussie and George Littlefield.

JEFFREY BARKSDALE HILL. This family originated in England and came to America in colonial days. Isaac Hill, the paternal grandfather of our subject was born in Georgia and came to Tennessee with his seven sons, locating in the Cumberland Mountain region, where he was among the pioneers, and where his death occurred. The father of our subject, Asa Hill, did not go to Tennessee with his father, but he and his brother John remained in Georgia, the former for some time, and the latter all his life. Benjamin Harvy Hill, deceased, son of John, was the noted statesman of Georgia. Asa Hill was married in his native State to Miss Elizabeth Barksdale, a native of Georgia, and daughter of Jeffrey Barksdale, for whom our subject was named. Mr. Barksdale was born in Georgia, fought on the bloody fields of the Revolutionary War, also in many wars previous to that, and died in his native State, leaving many descendants. Asa Hill made a trip to Texas in 1834, secured a headright of land in Washington County, and the next year brought out his family. This family was one of seventeen that chartered a schooner and came by sea to Matagorda, arriving on the last day of May, 1835. Settling in Washington County with his family, Mr. Hill began improving and developing his place, but unfortunately lost his headright by bad title. At the outbreak of the Texas Revolution Mr. Hill, our subject, and a younger bother of the latter, James Monroe, at once entered the Texas army. Jeffrey was taken ill on the way to Gonzales to organize with the troops, and was compelled to return home. Mr. Hill was at the burning of Gonzales, and then returned home to move his family to a place of safety. James Monroe Hill continued with the army and was in the battle of San Jacinto. Afterwards he was in the Woll campaign, and in the Texas service for several years. At the present time he is Vice-president of the Texas Veteran Association and resides at Austin. In 1842 Mr. Hill and his two sons, our subject and John C. C., were members of the Somerville expedition, and at the division of that expedition, when Somerville returned to Texas, Mr. Hill and his two sons continued and were members of what became known as the Mier expedition, and so became captives of that disastrous campaign. Our subject was one of the twenty-three wounded at Mier, and so remained in the hospital at that place. Mr. Hill and his son, John C. C., were taken to Matamoras the next day, and the latter was favored by General Ampudia, the Mexican commander. The father was one of the 170 to make a drawing for his life a few days after at Saltillo, and drew a white bean, thus being saved. John C. C., then fourteen years of age, was now taken in friendly charge by General Ampudia, and sent to school at the City of Mexico. Through the latter's influence his father was liberated and able to return home. Our subject was kept a prisoner about twelve months, and was then also liberated by his brother's influence, leaving the prison of Perote Castle, City of Mexico, and returning home. The bother, John C. C., remained in Mexico, was adopted by General Ampudia, and for many years was sent to school by that general. He now resides in Monterey, Mexico. The father died in Fayette County, 1844, and the mother in Waelder, in 1891, when eighty-nine years of age. Both were members of the Methodist Church. Our subject was born in Georgia in 1814, and was third in order of birth of the children born

E. Mullen

to his parents. He was living on the home place at Rutersville when his father died, and he continued farming for a number of years. In 1856 he married Miss Mary E. Harrison, daughter of Dr. R. P. Harrison, who moved to Texas from Kentucky in 1855. After his marriage Mr. Hill moved to his farm near Fayetteville, Fayette County, where he resided until he moved to Gonzales County in about 1860. Two years later he entered the Confederate army, was in C. J. Catchings' Company, Heavy Artillery, and served mainly at Galveston for three years. Owning a farm in Gonzales County Mr. Hill resided on that until 1882, when he moved to Waelder, and is now retired from the active duties of life. This Texas veteran and pioneer of the State is one of the representative men of his section. His career has been a remarkable one, and so it is considered by all acquainted with him. Although now in his eighty-first year, time has dealt very leniently with him and he has the appearance of a man much younger. To his marriage with Miss Harrison were born nine children: John R., a loan and exchange dealer in Waelder; William Thompson, railroad agent in Mexico; Jeffrey Barksdale, Jr., a lawyer in Waelder; Green Washington, Preston, Elizabeth (Bettie), wife of W. H. Hill; Lula V., wife of Lee Chaddock, of Cuero; Martha, deceased, and Thomas Jefferson, deceased.

JOHN WILLIAM AUGUST KLEINE, merchant of Gonzales, Texas, was born in Ziesar, near Brandenburg, Prussia, March 16, 1831; was second in a family of five children born to August and Fredrika Kleine, both natives of Brandenburg, Prussia. The father was manager of a large plantation and sheep ranch. He remembered when Napoleon's army marched on its way to Prussia, and was eight years old when the battle of Waterloo was fought. His death occurred in 1867, and his wife's in 1863. Both were members of the Lutheran Church. Our subject, J. W. A. Kleine, was educated in his native country, and on September 27, 1854, he, with a younger brother, sailed from Braham for America, and after being seven weeks on the ocean arrived at Galveston November 20. On the 5th of December he arrived in Gonzales, after traveling two weeks in an ox wagon over an open and muddy country in the middle of a very cold winter. Later his brother set out for California and Nevada, the then newly discovered gold fields, and while there he contracted sickness and, returning to Texas, died there in 1870. Our subject worked at his trade of cabinet maker until the war opened, when he enlisted in Cook's Heavy Artillery, and for three years and two months gave his services to the Confederacy, chiefly on Galveston Island. Returning to Gonzales he resumed his trade, and in 1875 had accumulated enough capital to add a stock of furniture to his cabinet business, and in 1877 he erected "Kleine's Hall," and later he added to his business that of undertaking. For years now he has had the leading business in his line for the section, and is held in high esteem by his customers and friends. For twenty-five years he has been a member of the I. O. O. F., and received his veteran "jewel" this year. He is a Lutheran in religion, has a pleasant home in Gonzales, and is still surrounded by his children. His wife was formerly Miss Babette U. Pfeuffer, a native of Bavaria. Their nuptials were celebrated April 25, 1867, in New Braunfels, Texas, whither her father had moved. Six boys were born to this union, four of whom are now living—George, August, William Christoff and Walter Daniel—the twins died when infants. His wife, Babette Kleine, died September 18, 1886. His large business house looks very imposing, and the hall above is large and roomy.

SAMUEL B. MOORE. The country around Moulton, Texas, is as desirable as any in all the State, and that is saying a great deal. On every hand may be seen rich rolling prairies intersected here and there with running streams, and the value of living in such a fertile section has become known, for it is rapidly settling up. It might well be called the farmer's and stockman's paradise. Samuel B. Moore, an early settler of this section, and one of the largest stockmen in the State, has found this a fruitful field for his operations. He has resided in this county since 1853, and has made a large fortune in cattle and the advance in the value of his land. He came originally from Alabama, where his birth occurred in 1835, and of the four children born to his parents, William J. and Mary (O'Daniel) Moore, he was the eldest. The father was a planter in Alabama, his native State, and there made his home until 1845, when he came to Texas, settling in Fayette County. Later he moved to Lavaca County, 1853, and bought 500 acres, on which the town of Moulton has since been built. Here he became a very extensive farmer and stock-raiser and an influential citizen. For some time he held the office of County Commissioner, and he also held other positions of trust. His death occurred October 10, 1858. His wife, who was a native of South Carolina, died in this county March 26, 1880. John Moore, our subject's paternal grandfather, was a native of Mississippi and an early settler of Alabama. Until about ten years of age Samuel B. Moore remained in Alabama, and he then came with his parents to Texas. In the schools of Fayette County he received the remainder of his education, and when starting out for himself, followed in the footsteps of his father and became a farmer and stock-raiser. On the 4th of November, 1857, he was married to Miss Lydia Crouch, who was the daughter of Jackson Crouch, one of the early settlers of Texas, and now a resident in the vicinity of Moulton. In 1862 Mr. Moore enlisted in the Confederate army, Company D, of Col. Wood's Regiment, and went down on the coast. Later he was transferred to Company D, Twelfth Regiment, and served in Texas, Missouri and Indian Territory, being on scout duty most of the time. After he had returned home he resumed farming and stock-raising, and with his brother, William J. Moore, drove several herds to Kansas. He and his brother bought about 12,000 acres of land, now lying between the towns of Moulton and Shiner, and in 1887, when the Aransas Pass Railroad was laid out, they gave the right of way for ten miles through their ranch. The town of Moulton was located on their property. This has now a population of about 500, is on an elevation surrounded by a magnificent country, and is a flourishing little place. In 1888 Mr. Moore erected a large hotel. After this, in 1892, he erected his fine residence, and has one of the handsomest places in the State. In 1881, as the country was becoming quite thickly settled, Mr. Moore and his brother moved their stock, 6,000 head, to Fort Bend County. The company of Moore & Allen was then formed, and about 50,000 acres of land was bought for pasture. This land soon advanced in value from $5 to $25 per acre, and the town of Alvin has grown up on it. They own much land yet, but have sold some to a great advantage. They bought a ranch of 80,000 acres in Uvalde and King counties, and have 20,000 head of cattle on both places. Mr. Moore has mainly graded cattle, and on his place at home has a small herd of blooded Jersey cattle. He has made the breeding and handling of cattle a systematic business, and drove herds North for years. He now breeds mainly on the Fort Bend County ranches, and ships the steers to the western ranches to feed and grow for market. He has been eminently successful, but understands his business to such an extent that success is certain. To Mr. Moore's marriage were born eight children: William J., Gazie, Lula, Frank, Lillie, Ella, Allie, and one deceased. Mr. Moore is a Mason, having become a member of that order during the war, is a Methodist in religion and a stanch Democrat in politics.

HENRY W. SPECKELS, Mayor of La Grange, Texas, and book-keeper for Speckels & Shaw, one of the leading dry goods merchants of the city, is a citizen who has developed a high order of ability in connection with the material interests of Fayette County, and whose rare personal and social qualities have given him a deserved and added prominence. Mr. Speckels was born in this county in 1864 and is a son of John and Marguerite (Imken) Speckels, natives of Germany. In the year 1847 this worthy couple came to America and settled at Frayersburg, where they remained for one year. In 1849 they came to this county and settled on a farm near Warrenton, where they followed agricultural pursuits until 1891. They then moved to La Grange. Their finances were at a low ebb when they came to this country, and for a year or two, or until they could open up land and build a log house, they lived in a tent. Mr. Speckels made most of the household furniture in those days, and although rude and uncouth in appearance, it answered the purpose. They experienced many hardships and were wholly without flour the first year. They finally got a start and Mr. Speckels became a prominent stockman of his section, owning large herds of sheep, cattle and horses. He had managed to buy two or three negroes previous to the war, and although he was too old for service, his eldest son, Garrett Speckels, served throughout the war. Neither did Mr. Speckels take part in the Mexican War. He has been the architect of his own fortune, and at one time owned 950 acres on the prairie. He and his estimable wife have a comfortable home in La Grange, and there expect to pass the remainder of their days. They have reached the ripe age of seventy-seven and seventy-two years respectively, and bid fair to live many years longer. Both are members of the Lutheran Church. Their family, consisting of eleven children, five sons and six daughters, three of whom died young, are named as follows: Garrett, a farmer; John, of the firm of Speckels & Shaw; George, of the firm of Letzerich & Speckels; Johanna, now Mrs. A. Heintze; Meta, wife of Louis Walter, of this city; Mary, wife of William Neese, a farmer of this county; Annie (deceased) was the wife of R. Aschen, Jr., and H. W., our subject. The last named was educated in the country schools of Fayette County, and when eighteen years of age started out for himself, although during a portion of each year he was with his parents. He followed clerking and book-keeping until 1889, when he came to La Grange and accepted the management of Mr. Heintze's business, which consisted of dry goods and groceries: Mr. Heintze was also a large cotton buyer or cotton broker, and of this Mr. Speckels was general manager. In 1891 Mr. Heintze sold his business to Speckels & Shaw, and our subject assumed the management of their immense business, which, during the years 1891, '92 and '93, amounted to from $90,000 to $100,000 annually. In 1894 this firm sold the grocery department, and now does an annual business of about $65,000, employing four new men as clerks. In 1893 Mr. Speckels was elected Mayor of La Grange, an office which he holds to the general satisfaction of all. While he does not take a very active interest in political matters, he is nevertheless outspoken in his convictions, and a strong Democrat. In 1894 Mr. Speckels was elected by the ice and soda water manufacturers as manager of their large trade in the town, and this firm also handles extensively the celebrated beer manufactured by W. J. Lemps. Since March, 1894, ice is only sold by this company in the city, they having a monopoly of the ice and soda water trade both in the city and surrounding country. Mr. Speckels was married in 1890 to Miss Annie Meerscheidt, a native of this town and daughter of Arthur and Lena (Von Rosenberg) Meerscheidt, both of whom were born in Germany. Mr. and Mrs. Meerscheidt came to Texas in an early day, and like others of the early settlers, experienced many hardships. He was a poor man, but by persistent effort he overcame all difficulties and amassed considerable property in mercantile pursuits. However, during the latter part of his life he met with reverses. His death occurred in 1888, but his wife survives him and resides in San Antonio. Mr. and Mrs. Speckels have two children, Lilian and Gilbert. Mr. Speckels is a member of the Knights of Pythias, Dawson Lodge No. 131, Uniform Rank, and also belongs to the K. & L. of H., and Hermann's Soehne, a German Lodge.

DENNIS SHEFFIELD HOPKINS, who has retired from the active duties of life and is now spending a happy and contented old age in the thriving town of Waelder, Gonzales County, Texas, was born in Georgia in December, 1819; son of Samuel and Elizabeth Hopkins, both natives of the Blue Grass State and of Scotch-Irish descent. Our subject was reared and educated in his native State, and there learned the tanner trade. When thirty-one years of age he came to Texas and settled in Gonzales County, where he has since resided, engaged in farming and stock-raising until within the past few years. He was married in Georgia in 1840 to Miss Sarah J. Motley, and fifteen children were the result of this union, eight sons and seven daughters, thirteen of whom are now living and all married, as follows: Nancy J., wife of W. J. Steubing; James F., the present Tax Assessor of the county; Coleman P., Sarah E., wife of R. L. Miller; Mary J., wife of Fred Steubing; John P., William A., Cicero L., was accidentally drowned; Henry T., Christopher C., Martha A., wife of M. Harrell; Texana M., wife of John M. Crozier; Kate L., wife of D. A. Petty; Samuel Houston, deceased, and Alice, wife of J. J. Johnson. Mr. Hopkins has over 100 grandchildren. Coleman P. Hopkins, the third child, now resides in Waelder. He is a prominent farmer and stock-raiser, and a useful and influential citizen. He first saw the light in Harris County, Georgia, February 13, 1844, and was brought to Texas by his father when but seven years of age. Here he received the rudiments of an education, attending school only twelve months in his life, but he became a good reader and in that way has stored his mind with much useful knowledge and thus largely corrected his early deficiency. He takes many papers, and no man in the county is better posted on current topics. The father being poor and having a large family to support, Coleman was obliged to make his own way in life, and he started out as a farmer and stock-raiser, and in a few years added a store to his interests. He has always been a great and successful trader, and has met with more than ordinary success. At the present time he has 4,000 acres in pasture and arable lands, and is one of the foremost men of his section. In the year 1862 he enlisted in the Confederate army, Company B, Twenty-sixth Texas Cavalry, and this was kept on the

Texas coast until 1864. Later the regiment was sent to Louisiana and there Mr. Hopkins took part in twenty-seven engagements, notably Mansfield, Pleasant Hill, Marksville and Prairie and Yellow Bayou. In politics he has ever been a Republican, but has never held any office except that of Town Councilman and School Trustee. In religion he is a Baptist, and has given freely to the church and to charity. In the year 1867 he was married to Miss Mary A. Fry, daughter of Ludwig and Lavina Fry, pioneers of Texas. Mrs. Hopkins died in 1880 leaving one child, Samuel Houston Hopkins, now a prominent young lawyer of Gonzales, who graduated at the College at Bryan and at the University at Austin, where he delivered the valedictory. Mr. Hopkins was married in 1884 to Miss Alice B. Shotwell, a native of Caldwell County, whose parents died when she was an infant. She was reared by an aunt, Mrs. Butler. Her father's name was Cicero Shotwell. To Mr. and Mrs. Hopkins have been born four children: Mary M., Coleman P., Jr., Dora A., deceased, and Cicero, deceased.

CLAY NICHOLS, M. D. The aim of the modern physician is high and it is no longer possible for a person to pick up a smattering of medicine here and there, nail up his shingle and strike out, hit or miss, when called upon to prescribe in cases of illness. The demand of the age is for gentlemen of culture, refinement and scholastic finish, who shall add to literary education a thorough course of professional education in some established institution of recognized authority. Dr. Clay Nichols, of Sweet Home, Texas, has met these requirements most fully, and beyond what is even expected or fulfilled in most cases. Being thoroughly equipped for the successful practice of this most noble of callings, he has the confidence and esteem of his brethren, and is building up a desirable practice as a result of his superior attainments. He was born in Austin County, Texas, in 1868, the eldest child born to the marriage of William A. and Helen (Woolsey) Nichols, who were natives respectively of Alabama and Georgia. About 1860 William A. Nichols located in Austin County, Texas, and later was married in Colorado County of this State to Miss Woolsey. While the great and lamentable Civil War was in progress he was a soldier in Parsons' Brigade, and was First Lieutenant in one of its companies. Notwithstanding the changed condition of affairs after the war was over, he energetically returned to the pursuits of civil life, and in 1879 removed to Lavaca County, and with his family resides in the town of Sweet Home. Much of his attention, especially in later years, has been given to land speculation, and he is an intelligent and well-posted man on all matters of general interest, and his business particularly. Dr. Clay Nichols was educated in the public schools of Lavaca County, and completed his literary knowledge in the Normal Institute of Huntsville, Texas, becoming a thoroughly well informed and accomplished young man. In 1888 he determined to make the practice of medicine his life work, and began fitting himself for this noble calling in Tulane University, New Orleans, from which he was graduated as an M. D. in 1890. Immediately thereafter he located at Thomaston for a short time, after which he opened an office at Sweet Home, where he has since built up a paying practice. His intimate knowledge of his profession, together with genial, pleasant and agreeable manners, a nature that is full of sympathy with his fellows, and a spirit of broad and liberal charity, have made him one of the most popular practitioners of the county, notwithstanding his youth and the short time that he has followed his profession. Upon becoming a resident of Sweet Home he opened a drug store, which is the only establishment of the kind in the place, and in December, 1893, he became a member of the firm of Palmer & Co., at Yoakum, druggists, the business at Sweet Home being conducted under the firm name of W. A. Nichols & Co. In each establishment a large stock of drugs of all kinds is carried, as well as a full line of stationery, school books, toilet articles; in fact, everything usually found in a well-appointed drug store. Since 1891 Dr. Nichols has held the position of Postmaster at Sweet Home, and he is the surgeon for the railroad at that place.

JONATHAN RAMSEY KEITH, farmer and stock-raiser of Gonzales County, Texas, has been a resident of this county for the past twenty-six years, but was born in Anderson County, Tennessee, May 1, 1843. Of the thirteen children born to his parents, Austin and Melinda (Adkins) Keith, our subject was fourth in order of birth. The parents were also born in Tennessee, and the father was a planter there. About 1874 he came to Texas, and made his home with his sons until his death in 1893. He was a member of the Baptist Church and in his early days was a zealous worker in the same. The mother died January 29, 1892. She was also a member of that church. Jonathan Ramsey Keith came to the Lone Star State when twenty-five years of age, and settled near his present home. When he reached this State he had the modest sum of $25, but he was full of ambition, push and energy, and entered actively upon his career as a farmer and stock-raiser. As the years passed along he bought land and added to it from time to time, until he is now the owner of 2,300 acres of fertile land near Bellmont. This he has well stocked and equipped, and 300 acres are under cultivation, averaging one-half bale of cotton or thirty bushels of corn to the acre. He is raising horses and cattle, and is improving the blood of each by the use of pure strains. Mr. Keith is a Mason, third degree, Leesville Lodge, and is a member of the Methodist Church. He has no political aspirations and is independent. In the year 1892, on the 7th of September, he was united in marriage to Mrs. Annie Meyer, widow of A. Meyer and daughter of Mr. Zumberg. One child, Jonathan Ramsey, Jr., has blessed this union. During the war Mr. Keith enlisted in Company K, Third Tennessee Regiment, Confederate service, cavalry, and was at Chickamauga, Shelbyville and other fights, but was scouting chiefly. He served all through the war.

F. M. TAYLOR (deceased). It is with true interest that the biographer takes up his pen to speak of those worthy citizens whose active lives have ceased on earth, but whose influence extends still, and will continue to extend, among all who knew them. F. M. Taylor was born in the Old North State in 1819, of English or Scotch descent, is descended from a highly honored family of this country, and at the age of twelve years was left an orphan by the death of his mother, his father having been cut down by the reaper, Death, several years earlier. His youth and early manhood were spent in the State of his birth, and he eventually became Clerk of Nash County. He was married there in 1837 to Miss Emma King of Virginia, and came to Texas in 1851 and settled in De Witt County on the Guadalupe River, where he bought a large tract of land and at once set about the work of improving the same. In 1860 he completed his handsome residence, a typical Southern mansion, and being active in the affairs of his section he was chosen a member of the

State Legislature in 1860–61. He prospered financially, notwithstanding the devastation made throughout the South during the war and the changed condition of affairs afterwards, and he eventually purchased another large tract of land, which he had considerably improved and would, in time, have made it a magnificent place had not death closed his career in 1877, his demise being the result of an accident. His widow still survives him, and is an earnest member of the Baptist Church. To their union four sons and a daughter were given: Benjamin B., Thomas R., Samuel, Emma, now the wife of M. K. Shiner, of San Antonio, and F. M. Thomas R. Taylor at the opening of the Civil War enlisted in Company C, Sixth Texas Infantry, was Second Sergeant of his company and was captured at Arkansas Post, exchanged at City Point, Va.; after that served in the Eastern army on detached duty, owing to an injury to one of his eyes. He surrendered with Johnston's army in North Carolina, and has since resided on the old home place, and has considerably interested himself in politics. He and his father were quite extensively engaged in mercantile pursuits at Concrete for about fifteen years, then retired from business. Thomas R. owns some 1,000 acres of valuable farming land, about 250 of which are under cultivation, and he is widely known as a thrifty and enterprising farmer. The old Taylor estate lies on the hills and in the rich valley along the Guadalupe River, all of which land is rich, productive and highly valuable, and has about 350 acres in cultivation. The old homestead erected by F. M. Taylor is on a sightly hill, and commands a magnificent view of the surrounding country. The place has been greatly increased in value by additional purchases of land, and is occupied by the widow Taylor and two of her sons. Azariah King, the father of Mrs. Taylor, was born in Virginia in 1796, and was of English descent. He was a tinker by trade, and was quite extensively engaged in the manufacture of distillery machinery, at which he made a fortune. His father was wealthy, but at his death one of his daughters took their negroes to Illinois and freed them. He had a family of three children, one of whom died in North Carolina and two came with him to Texas; Dr. James E. King, who practiced his profession here, and Mrs. Taylor. He settled on a large tract of land near the Taylor homestead, on which he died in 1873, his wife's death having occurred in 1852. Dr. James E. King married a Miss Lucy Harrison, and died in 1872, leaving a son and five daughters, all of whom are married and settled in life.

COL. ANDREW G. PICKET. The hustling towns, thriving villages and cultivated farms of Wilson County, Texas, have so long been common objects to our sight that it seems almost beyond belief that we have in our midst an honored citizen who was one of those hardy pioneers who saw this country when it was a primeval wilderness. No theme is more agreeable to the biographer than that of the early days, and the life story of one who has passed through that trying period and has made his way to comfort and prosperity through hardships and privations is of interest to every reader. Such a story do we have in the life of one, the gentleman whose name we now give. Col. Andrew G. Picket was born in middle Tennessee, October 12, 1821, and is a son of Darlton Picket, a native of Virginia, who, with his father, moved to Kentucky with Daniel Boone and was a frontiersman and Indian fighter. Later he moved to Tennessee. For many years he was Clerk of a County Court in Middle Tennessee. In 1855 our subject came to the Lone Star State and settled at Sutherland Springs, where he engaged in merchandising, farming, etc. Wilson County was organized in 1860, and our subject was elected County Clerk and Justice. Soon after he issued the first license of marriage as Clerk of the county, and as Justice married the couple. This is now recorded on the books as License No. 1. He was in the army two years in Louisiana and Arkansas, and after returning home he was re-elected County Clerk, serving until ousted by military authority in 1866. In the year 1872 he was again elected County and District Clerk, and served in that capacity two terms. The year 1884 saw him elected to the office of County Judge, and during that time he erected the present handsome court house. A few years later he was again elected to the same office, thus showing his popularity with the people. In 1872 he came to Floresville, and was the first American to take residence in the new county seat. He was then County Clerk, and was appointed by the proper authority, to have the town laid out and sell the lots. He laid the town out with wide and regular streets, so that it is now a handsome place. At the present time Mr. Picket is conducting the hotel of the place, the Picket House, and is a popular and agreeable landlord. For some time he ran the mail route from Helena to San Antonio, daily trips each way. Judge Picket is a Mason, a member of Floresville, Lodge No. 515. He became a Mason in Cumberland Lodge No. 8, in Tennessee, the same to which General Jackson belonged. He is a member of the Baptist Church. The colonel has been three times married, first in 1842, again in 1857, and the third time in 1877 to Miss Adelia Polley, a native of Texas. His first wife was a Miss Hughes, of Tennessee, and his second a Miss Walker, of Virginia, a sister of Judge Alexander Walker, of New Orleans, and cousin of the well known Dr. Stone. Our subject reared and educated Simon P. Hughes, ex-Governor of Arkansas, and William P. Hughes, now Colonel in the United States army, both brothers of his first wife. Col. Picket is a landmark of Floresville, the father of the town, and has been prominently identified with county affairs for nearly forty years. A sound, substantial and prosperous citizen, he has decided literary tastes, has a large library and is a well informed man.

J. S. ALLEN. He whose name heads this sketch, comes of historic stock for he is the second cousin of the famous General Ethan Allen of Revolutionary fame, and consequently is a descendant of a good old New England family whose settlement in this country antedates the War of Independence by a number of years. James S. Allen was born in Kentucky in 1815, a son of Samuel and Mary (Lamme) Allen, natives of Virginia and Kentucky, respectively, and grandson of the Virginian, Richard Allen, and great-grandson of Rev. John Allen, who was a native of Massachusetts, and an own cousin of Gen. Ethan Allen. Rev. John Allen moved to Virginia, and began operating a mill, but during the great American Revolution he and two of his sons were in the colonial army under General Washington, the two latter of whom were killed in battle. Another son, Richard, was too young to enter the service of his country, so was detailed to run the mill, and furnish flour to the colonial troops. Years afterward he moved to Kentucky with quite a party of his wife's relations—the Gatewoods—and made a location in the vicinity of Lexington, where he lived to the ripe old age of 106 years. Samuel Allen, his son, and father of the subject of this sketch, resided in the Blue Grass State all his life, was in the Indian Wars with Gen. W. H. Harrison, and was in the battle of the River Thames, when the great Chief Tecumseh was killed, and always said that one Whitaker did the deed. The latter and the great chief were lying about fifteen feet apart, and fired at each other at the same time, both being killed. Samuel Allen died in 1838 and his wife in 1833, having become the parents of seven children, several of whom are still living in Missouri, the subject of this sketch being the eldest of the family. J. S. Allen, the subject of this sketch, received a good collegiate education in Missouri, his alma mater being Marion College but, his initiatory education was received in his own home. He began life for himself by coming to Texas with the other students of Marion College, for the purpose of entering the army in 1835, and upon their arrival at Houston were mounted by General McKinney, and Mr. Allen selected a valuable race-horse as his mount. As he was young and slight he was detailed as courier, and on this work he was sent to San Antonio and was in the Alamo with Travis, at the beginning of the siege. He was sent out by Travis to try and get word to the people at Gonzales in the hope of relief. In this desperate endeavor his race horse was his salvation, for he charged through the Mexican lines and was a target for a thousand guns, but miraculously escaped in safety, and in about two days reached Gonzales, but there no relief could be obtained. He was later in operation as scout with "Deaf" Smith, and burned bridges behind the Mexicans, on the advance to San Jacinto, and before they could reach the field the battle had been fought. In a few months Mr. Allen returned to his home in Missouri, but two years later returned to the "Lone Star State," and became a ranger in Captain Bell's company, and was in battle with the Indians at Corpus Christi. Later he made a settlement at Indianola, gave his attention to the stock business, and eventually became Mayor of the city and Justice of the Peace. At the opening of the Civil War he was Assessor and Collector of the county, and was captured and taken to the fort at Pass Cavallo, from which he made his escape and went to Port Lavaca, and in 1865 came to the place where he now resides. He is the owner of a fine farm of 260 acres, with 100 acres under cultivation, is a substantial and progressive citizen, and has taken quite an active part in the affairs of his adopted State, is a citizen of integrity and is highly esteemed. He has a pleasant and comfortable home, which has become widely known for the hospitality which is extended to all. Mr. Allen was married in 1849 to an estimable lady who died in 1869, having become the mother of seven children, four of whom are living: Mary Louisa, wife of Joseph Cunningham; Cora, wife of a Mr. Everhardt (both of whom are dead), their two daughters being reared by Mr. Allen; Amelia, (deceased); Julia, (deceased); W. J., who is married and has three children; Sterling Price, who is married and has two children, and Robert Lee. Mr. Allen is a worthy member of the Baptist Church, and socially is a Mason.

JOSEPH JEFFERSON MANSFIELD. The various county attorneys of Colorado County, Texas, have always been noted for their character and ability, and one of the most popular of the many worthy men who have filled this position is Joseph Jefferson Mansfield, who is a lawyer of far more than ordinary ability, a thorough student of his profession, and being an excellent judge of human nature, is admirably fitted for the office he is filling. He is a product of Wayne County, West Virginia, where his eyes first opened on the 9th of February, 1861, his parents being Joseph J., and Amanda (Smith) Mansfield, his mother, a native of Chesterfield County, Virginia, and his father of Bedford County. He was an exceptionally well educated man for his days, and was a graduate of Virginia College, and afterwards became a very successful legal practitioner, and ably filled the office of Commonwealth's Attorney. He at one time made the race for Congress, but was defeated, but the simple fact that he ran for the office shows that he was a man of more than ordinary ability. He was a Colonel in the State Militia, and at the opening of the great struggle between the North and South he entered the Confederate service with that rank and was killed early in 1861 while trying to reach his home, where he was going with the intention of raising a brigade. After his death his widow married Dr. H. Walker, and is yet living in West Virginia. The immediate subject of this sketch grew to manhood in the county that gave him birth, and took one course at Bethany College, Wheeling, W.Va., and attended the high school afterward. In 1881 he came to Texas, and worked at the fruit tree business for some time, then up to 1885 clerked in a railroad office at Rosenberg. He then decided to make the law his profession, and began his studies at Alleyton, and in the latter part of the same year was admitted to the bar. He at once entered upon the practice of his profession at Alleyton, then Eagle Lake, and finally came to Columbus, where his legal ability received almost immediate recognition, and he at once entered upon a successful practice. While a resident of Eagle Lake he held the position of Mayor, and there received his nomination for County Judge, but was defeated by Judge Riley. In 1892 he was elected to the office of County Attorney, and at this election had no opponent. He was married in Eagle Lake to Miss Anna Scott Bruce, a daughter of Dr. J. S. Bruce, of a fine old Virginia family. Mr. Mansfield is a member of the K. of P., the A. O. U. W., and is a prominent Mason, having represented his lodge in the Grand Lodge of the state a number of times, and now and for four years has held the office of District Deputy Grand Master. In politics he has always been a Democrat, and on two different occasions he has held the office of Notary Public. He has been Lieutenant of two military companies and Captain of one. He is a useful citizen of the county, and has many friends throughout this section.

DR. ISAAC H. BREWTON. Dr. Brewton claims South Carolina as his native State, and his parents, Jonas and Mary (Snoddy) Brewton, were born in that State also. The ancestors of this family came to America from France, and landed in Charleston, S. C., in colonial days. The father of our subject was a planter, and passed his entire life in his native State. The original of this memoir received his scholastic training in Woodruff, S. C., and subsequently began studying medicine at Spartanburg Court House, S. C., with Lionell C. Kennedy. During the years 1855 and 1856 he attended Charleston Medical College, and graduated from that institution in the latter year. He then began practicing at Woodruff, S. C., in 1856, and in 1858 took a post-graduate course at Richmond, Va. When Civil War broke out he entered the army as private in the First South Carolina Cavalry, and after two years' service was appointed Assistant Surgeon, serving in the Medical Department from that time on until the war closed. He was in the Army of Virginia, and participated in the battles of Rapidan and Brandy Station. At the close of the war he came to North Texas and remained there until 1885, when he came to South Texas and located in Kernville. Soon after he came to Wilson County, and is now County Physician and medical examiner for the Twenty-fifth Judicial District. He is also medical examiner for the Equitable, New York Life and Mutual insurance companies. Socially he is a member of the A. F. & A. M., the I. O. O. F. and the K. of H. He selected his wife in the person of Miss Eva Williams, daughter of Bucknor Williams, who was a prominent man of North Texas, and their union was celebrated June 15, 1868. To this marriage four children have been born, two sons and two daughters.

WILLIAM ARMSTRONG. This gentleman is one of the early settlers of Texas and a veteran of the Mexican War, but is a product of the Buckeye State, his birth occurring in the vicinity of Cincinnati in 1823. His parents, George and Theresa (Rice) Armstrong, were worthy people, and he was well reared, but he left home when very young and with a friend, Jim Luka, went to the head waters of the Mississippi River, and there hunted, trapped and traded in furs and skins on Lake Pippin for one winter. They dealt principally with the Indians, trading them whisky for furs and skins, but this was dangerous business, for at one time, after imbibing too much "fire water," they took possession of the place, and Mr. Armstrong and his companion were glad to escape with their lives. They made their way to the mouth of the St. Croix River by water, and during this voyage Mr. Armstrong lost overboard a fine silver-mounted gun. Worn out and without a dollar, all his winter's work in the hands of the Indians, he worked his way down, four hundred miles, to Dubuque, Iowa, in the mining region, where he met with another loss—his fine watch and his friend disappeared simultaneously. Being still of an adventurous spirit, he and five companions started overland for California, and with the expectation of joining a wagon train went to Independence, Mo., but the train had passed several days before, and he and his companions decided to come to Texas. During this journey of more than two thousand miles he rode a horse, "Iowa Jim," which he afterwards sold in Austin, Texas, for $120. There he joined the ranging service, becoming a member of Capt. Katy's Company, and served three months, at the end of which time he joined Capt. Ross' Company for six months. While stationed at Waco a treaty was made with the Indians, in which the whites were to take charge and destroy all whisky. Mr. Armstrong was put in command of fifty men to perform this duty, and, as Mr. Armstrong says, "of course our canteens were full all the time in those days." A short time afterward the Mexican War broke out, and all the rangers of each company of Texas volunteers enlisted, except ten men in each company. Mr. Armstrong was put under command of Gen. Harney, and started for Mexico. In crossing the Rio Grande River several men were drowned. Pushing on through Carmargo a part of the command of eight hundred men was left in that vicinity, and the remainder went on to Monterey, where Mr. Armstrong had his horse shot from under him in the storming of the city. Afterwards he was sent back on the Rio Grande, and made a few raids up and down that river. He was finally retired and paid off at San Marcos, after which he lived in different parts of the State. From that time on, as no settlers were on the frontier but the rangers for many years, he met with many thrilling adventures and narrow escapes. In 1848 he married in Burleson County Miss Zaruah Fulcher, a native of Arkansas, after which he removed to Lavaca County and engaged in farming and stock-raising to a considerable extent, annually driving large herds of animals inland. While in the ranging service he took out a land warrant for pay, and had he held it would at this time have been one of the largest land owners of the State, as he had the offer of many acres of land where Waco now stands for ten cents per acre. In 1864 Mr. Armstrong's wife died, leaving him with five sons and one daughter, and in the fall of that year he was married to Miss Nancy Ryan, also from Arkansas. In 1868 he moved to Bee County and bought a large ranch below Beeville, in the conduct of which he was very successful and on which he resided until he came to Frio County in 1882. He made a specialty of raising good horses, and had some of the finest animals in the State at that time. Upon coming to Frio County he purchased a ranch on McGill Creek, twelve miles from Pearsall, and has 6,000 acres under fence. This is the best ranch of its size in the county, and over its broad acres roam a large herd of good graded cattle, horses, mules, etc. Mr. Armstrong's home is in Pearsall, and is commodious and comfortable. He has seen much of Texas, but thinks that Frio County is destined to be the most desirable portion of this great State, and here expects to spend the remainder of his days. He has many friends and is a very desirable and useful citizen.

A. B. BRISCOE. The pursuits of life are as varied as are the tastes and capacities of men, and it is an interesting and useful study to observe the degree of their assimilation. Mr. Briscoe is now a prominent banker of Floresville and a member of the firm of A. B. Briscoe & Co., of that place. He was born in the Republic of Texas, Harris County, in 1842, and was second in order of birth of the family born to the union of Andrew and Mary Jane (Harris) Briscoe, natives of Mississippi and New York, respectively. Harris County was named after Mrs. Briscoe's father, John Harris, who was one of the first settlers. As early as 1829 the father of our subject came to Texas to look at the country, and in 1832 he made a permanent settlement here. He was a prominent lawyer and the first Judge of Harrisburg District before the county was organized. He was a man of prominence, of much intelligence, force of character and determination. He served in the Texas Revolution, was Captain of Company A, and participated in the battles of San Antonio and San Jacinto. He was one of the signers of the Declaration of Independence of Texas. Later he moved to New Orleans and engaged in the banking and brokerage business, making his home there until his death in 1850. The original of this notice was educated in Texas, and later attended the college at Russelville, Ky., where he was pursuing his studies when Civil War broke out. Returning to Texas, whither the family had removed after the father's death, our subject enlisted in Terry's Texas Rangers, with whom he remained during the entire war, participating in all the battles of the Tennessee army, and being with Generals Johnston and Bragg. When the war closed he returned to the Lone Star State and located at Indianola, where he engaged in the cattle shipping business for about five years. After that he was in the mercantile business at Harrisburg for five years, and then went to Goliad County, where he was in the cattle business again and where he, in connection with his partner, J. Payne, had a pasture of about 10,000 acres. He was about the first in that section to fence a ranch. He had a good grade of stock, and continued in business there until 1890, when his wife died and he sold out and went to San Antonio. In May, 1892, he came to Floresville and started his present bank, which has been very successful. In the year 1871 he was married to Miss Annie F. Payne, a native of Indiana and the daughter of

Hon. J. Payne, who came to Texas in 1859, and who has been associated with our subject in business for the most part since. Four children have been given Mr. and Mrs. Briscoe: Carrie, wife of T. P. West, of San Antonio; Mary, Birdsall and Payne. Mr. Briscoe is a member of the A. F. & A. M. Lodge of Goliad.

SAMUEL B. PIER. This gentleman is one of the leading farmers of Austin County, and what he now has in the way of worldly possessions, has been obtained through his own good business qualities, his ability to turn everything to a good account and his push and energy. Born in Travis, Austin County, Texas, July 22, 1844, he is the eldest son to arrive at mature years of James B. and Lucy (Merry) Pier, natives of the Buckeye State. The Pier family came originally from France, and our subject's paternal grandparents were Ira and Sarah (Bradford) Pier. The Bradfords came to America in the Mayflower and settled in Massachusetts, but subsequently scattered all over the Union. Our subject's immediate ancestors on that side of the house came to Ohio in an early day, and Sarah (Bradford) Pier was the first white child born in that State. James B. Pier came with his family to Texas in 1835, but the following year, during the trouble between Texas and Mexico, the family left this county and went East to Sabine River. Mr. Pier served in the Texas Army, but was on detail duty at the time of the battle of San Jacinto. When he first settled in this county he had very little of this world's goods, but after the war he received a large tract of land for his services. Also, by being an early settler, he received a certificate for land from the Republic of Texas. Part of the land was in this county and part in Hays. This worthy pioneer and veteran served also in the war with Mexico in 1846 and 1848. After settling in this county he first engaged in merchandising and was one of the first business men as well as one of the first settlers of Travis. He merchandised at Travis until his death in 1888, after a long and useful career. His death occurred near the first place he purchased in Texas, after a residence of fifty-two years and when seventy-four years, two months and twelve days old. This worthy citizen was the father of six children, three of whom died young. The others were named: Lucy E. (deceased), was the wife of W. W. Cochran; Sarah C., wife of H. P. Wiley, of Travis, and Samuel B., our subject. The last named attended the schools of his neighborhood, received a fair education, and, when seventeen years of age, or in 1861, joined Col. Nicholas' Regiment and served at Galveston for six months. After that he joined Capt. McDade Wallers' Battalion, Company C, which formed a part of Gen. Green's Brigade, and served in the trans-Mississippi Department, participating in the battles of Camp Bisland, Yellow Bayou, and numerous others. He served as a scout for some time, and was in many dangerous places. After cessation of hostilities Mr. Pier attended school for six months, and then for a short time engaged in merchandising. Stock business next attracted his attention, and this he continued until lately, buying and selling many animals, and meeting with good results. Lately he has practically gone out of the stock business, and devotes his time and attention to farming, cultivating about 400 acres of his land. Mr. Pier's wedding occurred in 1868 with Miss Emma Cochran, a native of this State and county and daughter of Thomas and Betsie (Walker) Cochran, natives of New Hampshire. (See sketch of N. Cochran.) Mr. and Mrs. Pier are the parents of seven children, as follows: Thomas J., a physician of Fayette County; Emma L. (deceased), Anna B.,

Leila M., Ira O. (deceased), Norris G. and Kinchen C.   Mrs. Pier is a member of the Methodist Episcopal Church, and Mr. Pier is an ardent supporter of the Democratic party.

A. W. MURRAY.   For the past thirty-six years Mr. A. W. Murray has been a resident of Wilson County, Texas, during which time he has identified himself with the interests of his section, has won numerous friends, and has built up a reputation for honesty and fair dealing that is in every way merited. His birth occurred in Wilmington, N. C., in 1833, and there his parents, Owen and Margaret (Ormsby) Murray, who were of Scotch origin, were also born. The father was a farmer all his life, and in 1849 he left his native State and went overland to Nashville, Tenn., thence by river to Cape Girardeau, Mo., and then overland again to Morgan County, where he located near Versailles. He followed farming there until 1858, when he came to Texas and settled in Cibolo Creek, then Guadalupe County, where he tilled the soil until his death in 1887.   The mother passed away the same year.   Both were members of the Presbyterian Church for over fifty years, and were well respected whereever they made their home.   Until sixteen years of age our subject attended the schools of South Carolina, and then went with his parents to Missouri, remaining with them until he had attained his majority.   After this he managed a stock farm for a man one year, after which he engaged in merchandising, buying and handling stock, etc.   In 1858 he embarked in business for himself, general merchandising, and continued this in Missouri until 1859, when he closed out and came to Texas, arriving in December of that year and locating on Cibolo Creek, where his father had settled.   There he bought land and entered actively upon his career as a planter.   In 1861 he enlisted in the Eighth Texas Infantry, and later was transferred to the Engineer's Corps, operating in Texas and Louisiana.   He was in Shreveport of the latter State when the war closed.   He had three brothers, John D., Robert W., and James C., who were in the Fourth Texas Infantry, Hood's Regiment, and served through the war in the Virginia army.   Robert W. was badly wounded and lost a leg, and James C., who was a corporal, but was in charge of a company at Gettysburg where he was killed.   Returning to his home our subject engaged in farming and continued this for some time.   In 1882 he was elected Sheriff, served two years, and in 1886 he located permanently in Floresville, where he operated an hotel for a time.   In 1891 he embarked in his present business, furniture and undertaking, under the firm name of A. W. Murray & Co., and carries a stock of goods valued at $1,200.   He does an annual business of $3,000, and is very popular with his numerous patrons.   Mr. Murray was married in 1856 to Miss Anna Mobley, a daughter of Rev. William Mobley, who was born in Missouri.   Eight children were born to this union, seven of whom survive.   Mr. Murray lost his most estimable wife in 1891.   She was a member of the Presbyterian Church, and our subject and children hold membership in the same.   For a number of years Mr. Murray has been an elder, and is one of the most active workers of this church.

FRANK O. NORRIS, M.D.   This worthy and skillful practitioner of the "healing art" has been a resident of Eagle Lake, Texas, since 1877, being the second longest resident physician located in the place.   He was born in Dallas County, Alabama, November 11, 1850, to J. E. Norris, a native of Georgia, who removed to Alabama when a young man, married Miss M. A. Seawell there, and there spent the rest of his life.   His attention was devoted to farming, and at the opening of the Civil War he was too advanced in years to enter the service. Dr. Frank O. Norris was educated in Wilcox County, Alabama, and when quite young, at about the age of eighteen years, he began the study of medicine, attended lectures at Mobile, Ala., and graduated in 1876. The following year, as above stated, he came to Eagle Lake, at once seemed to win the confidence of the citizens, and entered upon a practice that has constantly grown and increased, until it now completely occupies his time, and is satisfactory from a monetary point of view. He is cheerful and hopeful in the sick room, is quick and accurate in diagnosing a case, has a happy faculty of inspiring his patients with courage and hope, and has therefore always been remarkably successful. In 1876 he was united in marriage with Miss de Aughdrille, of Alabama, but her death occurred in this State soon after they had located here. In 1879 Dr. Norris married again, Miss Alice Williamson becoming his wife, and they are worthy members of the Baptist Church, in which the doctor is a Deacon. He is a Royal Arch Mason, belongs to the Blue Lodge, and has represented his lodge in the Grand Lodge of the State, is a member also of the K. of H., the A. O. U. W., which he has also represented in the Grand Lodge of Texas, and the American Legion of Honor. He has been President of the Colorado County Medical Association, and was a member of the American Medical Society and the State Medical Association. He is a general practitioner and stands high in the profession. He has also attended the New Orleans Policlinic.

Dr. GEORGE W. BEAKLEY is an exceptionally popular and successful physician of Floresville. He is scholarly and well-informed in every branch of his profession, is intelligent and well posted on all matters of public interest, and stands well in the community, both as a citizen and as a professional man. He came originally from Missouri, where his birth occurred in 1858, and was the third child born to the marriage of Dr. W. B. and America (Scantlen) Beakley, natives respectively of Tennessee and Arkansas. The father was a soldier in the Civil War, was in the engagements of Gen. Price's army around Springfield, and on the retreat of that general he came to Texas; being then over age he did not again enter the army. He was one of seventeen who started with dispatches from the field, and was the only one to get through all right. After coming to the Lone Star State he located in Bell County and engaged in farming and stock-raising, but was greatly bothered by the Indians. In 1865 he sold out and went to Lavaca County, but the health of his family not being very good there, he moved to Gonzales County in 1866, and made his home there for two years. From there he moved to Travis County and settled on a tract of land on which the town of Manchaca was subsequently built. From there he moved to Coleman County in 1885, and there he now resides. In nearly all the places that he located he practiced his profession, and was very popular with all. Our subject grew to mature years in Texas, received a fair education in the common schools, and in 1883 began the study of medicine, entering the Louisville Medical College, from which he was graduated in 1885. Soon afterward he began practicing at his home in Manchaca with Dr. W. A. Ellison, his former preceptor, but subsequently moved from there to Fairview, in Wilson County, where he carried on a successful practice for two years. After that he was in San Antonio for two years trading horses. In the year 1890 he went to St. Louis and attended a full course of medical lectures, graduating from the Missouri Medical College the following year.

From there he came to Floresville and resumed his practice. In 1893 he went to Cincinnati and took a course in the Eclectic Medical Institute, after which he returned to Floresville, and has since had a good practice. Dr. Beakley was married on his 28th birthday, August 31, 1886, in Fairview, Wilson County, to Miss Louvenia J. McIntyre, a native of Mississippi. Two children have been born to this union: Venie Ruby, died at the age of nine months, and Mary Elsie. The doctor is a member of the Masonic order, Floresville Lodge No. 515, and he and wife hold membership in the Baptist Church. He has sold out his farming and stock-raising interests, and has since devoted himself exclusively to his profession. Although the doctor is still young in years, he has built up a reputation for skill and efficiency for which many older physicians might envy him. He graduated with distinction from the Louisville Medical College, and won one of the medals of his class. Two of the doctor's brothers are practicing physicians—Joe F. and Ben B. Beakley.

WILLIAM C. KROEGER. Among those whose career in business has been rendered conspicuous by the honorable methods and careful attention shown throughout is William C. Kroeger, owner of a steam gin and grist mill at Floresville, Texas. An inspection of his establishment will find him busy meeting the large demand of his patronage. Mr. Kroeger is a native of Germany, born in 1839, and the son of Andrew and Christine Kroeger, natives also of the old country. Our subject was partially educated in Germany, and in 1856, when about 17 years of age, he decided to seek his fortune in America. He settled in Guadalupe County the same year, but soon after moved to San Antonio, where he made his home for twenty-five years, following clerking in a mercantile establishment for a short time. Following this he was on the frontier for some time, and in 1861 joined a company of Texas Rangers from San Antonio and started for Virginia. As they could not get through they were attached to Gen. Johnson's army in Tennessee. Mr. Kroeger participated in the battles of Shiloh, Perryville, Murfreesboro, Chickamauga, and in the battles from Dalton to Atlanta, 104 days in almost constant engagements; fought Sherman's army all the way to the coast, then up to North Carolina, where he was in the last battle of the war, at Bentonville. He was in every engagement of the Army of Tennessee, except the East Tennessee campaign, for he was wounded at Farmington, Tenn., October 4, 1863, captured and taken to Alton, Ill. From that place he made his escape February 8, 1864; after many hardships reached his regiment April 20, near Dalton, Ga. He subsequently returned to San Antonio, making the distance from North Carolina to that place on horseback, and later became Deputy Sheriff of Bexar County, serving in that capacity three years. Following that he engaged in merchandising, and also acted as Government contractor for some time. In 1867 he was married to Miss Ophelia G. Fisk, daughter of Capt. James F. Fisk and granddaughter of Deaf Smith, noted in history. In 1875 Mr. Kroeger moved to Wilson County and engaged in farming, merchandising and ginning. He was Postmaster of Fairview, County Commissioner, and Justice. In 1889 he came to Floresville, and was elected the first Mayor of the place. When he came here he bought a gin, which was burned in 1889, but he immediately built his present large establishment. It has a capacity of twenty-five bales, is well equipped with all modern improvements; and he also owns the gin at Fairview and the gin and mill at Calaveras, these having

James B. Wells.

a capacity of fifteen and eight bales daily, respectively. To. Mr. and Mrs. Kroeger have been born seven children: Ernstine, Laura A., I. Simpson, Walker Barry, Susan, William C., and Carl F.

HENRY VANDERHIDER. Among the worthy residents of De Witt County, Texas, it is but just to say that Henry Vanderhider occupies a conspicuous and honorable place, for he has always been honest, industrious and enterprising, and as a result has met with more than ordinary success. He is a man well known in agricultural circles, and is recognized as a careful, energetic farmer, who, by his advanced ideas and progressive habits, has done much to improve the farming interests of his section. No man takes a greater interest in the agricultural and stock affairs of this section than Mr. Vanderhider, and no one strives more actively to promote and advance these interests to a higher plane. He is a product of Missouri, born in 1840, a son of Henry Casper and Lavina (Langton) Vanderhider, who were born in Germany and Kentucky respectively. The father came to the United States in his early youth, and after following the occupation of blacksmithing in Missouri for some time, he engaged in merchandising at Perryville, Perry County, Mo., an occupation to which his attention was successfully given until his death in 1841 or 1842. The maternal grandfather, Walter Langton, came to Missouri from Kentucky at an early day, settled in Perry County, and there passed from life about 1845. In 1850 Mrs. Vanderhider, with her mother and brothers and sisters, came to Texas and settled in Lavaca County, and here they purchased a goodly tract of land, on which she died in 1888. From the time he was 10 years old Henry Vanderhider has been a resident of Texas. In 1861 he enlisted in Sibley's Brigade, Company C; was at once sent to New Mexico, and was in the battles of Val Verde and Glorietta. This brigade was afterward disbanded at San Antonio for a month or so in order to obtain horses, and upon being fully reorganized went to Louisiana, and was in several engagements in that State, after which it was ordered back to Texas, and was in the battle of Galveston, when that city was taken from the Federals. After a few weeks it was sent back to Louisiana, and Mr. Vanderhider was in the engagement at Pleasant Hill, in the Red River campaign after Gen. Banks. After the war was over he returned home, engaged in carpentering, and in 1866 was married to Miss Mary Ryan, a native of Texas and the daughter of James Ryan, a Pennsylvanian, who came to this State at an early day, and was a participant in the Texas Revolution. He died at the home of Mr. Vanderhider in Lavaca County. In the fall of 1874 Mr. Vanderhider bought his present farm near Yoakum, but is the owner of two farms, which comprise in all 815 acres, of which 150 acres are under cultivation. To the union of Mr. and Mrs. Vanderhider eleven children have been given, nine of whom are living: Agnes, wife of L. C. Knox; James Henry, who married a Miss Manning; Walter Patrick, Augustus, who married a Miss Hart; Viola, died at the age of 14 years; Emma, Guy, Henry Leo, died at the age of 3 years; Edmond, Julius, and Annie. The family are members of the Catholic Church.

RUDOLPH KLATT. He whose name heads this sketch is possessed of those qualifications that go to make up a successful man of business, and being intelligent, active and reliable, he is better fitted than the average man for official position, and this fact was recognized by his election to the office of County Clerk of Fayette County, in 1892. He was born in Posen, Prussia, in 1853. His father, A. Klatt, was also born there. In 1856 the latter came to

24

the United States with his family, landed at Galveston on the 25th of December, and almost immediately took out his naturalization papers, for he had determined to make this country his future home, and had come here for protection and liberty.   He had been an active soldier in the Prussian army and in the Reserve.   When he was thirty-two years of age he married, and thereafter devoted his attention to farming, and upon coming to this State located in the settlement known as Welcome, in Austin County, where he made his home until his death in 1859.   His wife was Anna Krause, who was also born in Prussia, and died in this country in 1862.   The subject of this sketch was the youngest of ten children born to his parents.   The eldest son, August, died at Holly Springs, Miss., during the war, at which time he was a soldier of Wall's Legion.   Rudolph was but a lad at the time his mother died, and for sometime thereafter he made his home with an elder sister, and attended school for a short time in the neighborhood of Brenham.   He then lived in different places, consequently his schooling was very irregular, and he attended about twenty-four months in all, three of which were spent in a private school and two at Parson's Bend, in Austin County.   He was naturally fond of his books, made the most of his opportunities and, having read a great deal, he is one of the well-informed men of the county.   During the season he was engaged in farm work, then began clerking in a store in Brenham, continuing from March until August, 1876, when he went to High Hill and took charge of a cotton gin and sawmill at that place for his father-in-law, where he continued to successfully labor until the latter part of 1878.   He then unfortunately lost one of his hands in the mill, and in 1879 began teaching school in Sedan, where he remained until 1881; went from there to High Hill and taught the Middle Creek School four years, then went to La Grange and taught in the High School from 1885 to 1887.   From that time until 1892 he was at Round Top and there had charge of the graded school, and was then elected to his present official position, which he has filled with marked ability up to the present time.   He has served as a member of the Board of School Examiners, and for a number of years was President of the County Institute, having previously served as Secretery of the same for a number of years.   He was married in 1876 to Miss Mary Hillje, daughter of J. F. Hillje, who was born in Frelsburg, Colorado County, Texas.   They have two sons and three daughters, and Mr. Klatt proudly tells that when his eldest daughter was but thirteen years old she passed an examination and assisted her father as a teacher in the school.   Mr. Klatt, is a member of the A. O. U. W., Robert Blume Lodge No. 54, of High Hill, the Sons of Hermann and the I. O. O. F.

HARRIS T. GREEN.   The great natural resouces of Fayette County, Texas, have been developed by the practical and intelligent toil of such men as Harris T. Green, who is recognized as a man full of spirit and business enterprise.   He is an old settler of this section and one of its leaders in agriculture.   Born in Mississippi in 1849, he is the son of Jesse and Mary (Spencer) Green, natives of Alabama.   This worthy couple came with their parents to Mississippi at an early date, and there celebrated their nuptials.   In 1850 Mr. Green moved to Texas, and the first year rented land in Washington County, near the town of Brenham.   Later he purchased the Black Jack Springs and the land surrounding it for some distance, and soon after erected a horse gin. There he resided until 1855, when he purchased six hundred acres where his son now resides, and there died the same year.   His wife, with the assistance of her sons, improved the place. Mr. Green served his township as Justice of the Peace while residing at Black Jack Springs, and was a man whose industry and perseverance, as well as his honesty and uprightness, won the respect and esteem of all. He left five children as follows: William W., (deceased), Jesse C. (deceased), Harris T., James A., of Karnes County, where he follows farming, and Sarah J., wife of George M. Williams. Mrs. Green was married in 1857 or '58 to John S. Black, and they resided in this county until her death, which occurred April 1, 1874, leaving by her second marriage one child, Frances E., wife of Louis C. Potter, of Temple, Texas. Harris T. Green was educated in this county, in the common schools, and in Baylor University, Independence, Washington County, Texas, where he remained two years, and during the last year assisted in the schools there, having a class in English grammar and arithmetic. When twenty-three years of age he left that place and returned home, where he at once engaged in farming and stock-raising, meeting with more than usual success. At the present time he is the owner of seven hundred acres of fine land, a good rural residence and sufficient outhouses. He is a genial, pleasant man to meet and has many friends in his section. In carrying on his farming interests he does not lose sight of the stock-raising industry, and has a nice herd of Jersey cattle. Mr. Green was married first on Dec. 18, 1873, to Miss Mary M. Black, daughter of J. S. Black (stepfather to our subject), and a native of this county. Mrs. Green, who was born Dec. 6, 1850, died Sept. 1, 1883, when thirty-three years of age. She was a member of the Baptist Church, and a most estimable lady. Three children were born to this union: Jessie T., born Oct. 12, 1874, Annie A. (deceased), born July 28, 1878, and Milton A., born Sept, 21, 1881. In 1884 Mr. Green married Miss Mary E. Morrow, a native of this county and daughter of James and Mary V. (Armstrong) Morrow, natives of Alabama, who came from Mississippi to this State at an early date, and were married here about 1852 or '53. Mr. Morrow came to Texas and settled on the Navadad, in this county, when Indians and wild game abounded. He was one of the Indian fighters of his day and had many narrow escapes from them. He made a trip to California overland during the gold fever, and was of an adventuresome spirit. Mr. Morrow was twice married, his first union resulting in the birth of one child, William, who is now deceased. By the mother of Mrs. Green he became the father of six children: Frances S., wife of W. J. Black, resides in Colorado County, Texas; James I. A., resides in this State, Martin A., of Reynolds County; J. T., deceased; Mary E., wife of subject, and Carrie, deceased. Mr. Morrow died in 1865. Mrs. Morrow afterwards married August Koltermann, and had two children, Frederick W. and August. To Mr. and Mrs. Green were born six children: Sallie E. and Fannie V. (twins) were born Dec. 2, 1884; H. T., born June 24, 1886; James M., born Nov. 19, 1887; Lee M., born Nov. 11, 1891, and Ruth, born August 22, 1893. Mrs. Green was born March 2, 1861. The first year Mr. Green, father of subject, resided in the neighborhood he lived in a log house, and died there the same year, his wife improving the plantation. Books were very scarce in those days, and "reading, 'riting and 'rithmetic" were the only branches taught for many years, and then grammar was introduced. In 1860 a splendid school building was erected, close to Mrs. Green's residence. Here the boys of the surrounding country received most of their education thereafter.

BOUGH & HOUSTON. A pleasing feature presents itself in the preparation of an eventful history of this kind, and that is the encouraging outlook which

Floresville, Texas, has for the future. This promising aspect is made apparent to the observer through the business tact and enterprise as manifested by the young men who stand at the helm of the great commercial and industrial establishments of to-day. Floresville is credited as being the leading lumber distributing center of this section. Holding a prominent position in this connection, is S. V. Houston, a member of the firm of Bough & Houston, and a young man of marked business ability. Like many of the prominent residents of the county he is a native of Alabama, born in 1861, although his parents were really residents of Texas. The paternal grandfather, Ross Houston, came to Texas in 1854, and settled on the Cibolo Creek, where he engaged in farming and stock-raising. The father of our subject, Dr. John P. Houston, was a native of Alabama, and at an early age began the study of medicine at Louisville, Ky. He began practicing in Florence, Alabama, and was there married to Miss Jennie Vaughan, also a native of that State. Soon after he returned to Texas, where he had formerly resided, practiced for a year or two in Cibolo Creek, and then moved to Waco, where he resided until his death in 1871. The mother died there in 1880. Dr. Houston and his partner, Dr. Caldwell, were the leading physicians of the section, and were well and favorably known. The principal part of our subject's education was received in Waco, and his first occupation as a boy was in a lumber yard. After this he farmed for a time in McLennan County, and in 1880 came to Floresville, where he clerked in the County Assessor's office for a few years. He left that position to engage with Martin & Schryver, who owned a lumber yard here, and for several years acted as manager and agent. In January, 1890, he formed a partnership with W. P. Bough, who had previously bought out Martin & Schryver, and the present business was founded. Their extensive business is located on the railroad near the depot, and they occupy a large office. They carry builder supplies, hardware, etc,, as well as lumber, lime, cement and brick, and a stock of goods valued at about $15,000, and do a large annual business. In 1892 the firm erected the Opera House, a large building 50 x 90 feet, two stories, and well equipped with stage scenery, etc. They also own a large ranch of 7,000 acres in Live Oak County, and have 650 head of beef cattle. Mr. Houston is a member of the Masonic Fraternity, Floresville Lodge No. 515, and he is also a Knight of Pythias.

QUINCY DAVIDSON, an old and respected citizen of the county, whose influence and judgment are second to that of no man here, is a native of the Old North State, born in 1812, and the fourth in order of birth of ten children born to George Washington and Mary (Randall) Davidson, the former a Virginian and the latter a native of North Carolina. The father moved to North Carolina at an early date, and was there married to Miss Randall. Later he represented his county in the Legislature and the Senate, and was one of the influential and valuable citizens of that part of the State. About 1827 he moved to Tennessee, and settled in Henry County, near Paris, where he followed planting. In the fall of 1846 he came to Texas, and located in Mission Valley, where he passed the remainder of his days, dying soon after the Civil War, when ninety years of age. His excellent wife passed away in 1852 or 1853. The Davidson family is of Scoth-Irish descent, and the ancestors came to America in colonial times. Quincy Davidson attended school at Lawrence, North Carolina, and continued his scholastic training after reaching Tennessee. From there he went to Mississippi, and engaged as clerk in Tillatoba, Tallahatchie County, of the Northern part of the State, and in 1836 was in business for himself a short time. From there he went to Carroll County and followed clerking for six or seven years, and then went to Wilkinson County, that State, where his brother, Truxton, an eminent lawyer, was located. There he engaged in cotton planting, remained four years, but seeking a larger field, came to Texas in 1846. He settled in Mission Valley, bought a quarter league of good land, for which he paid one dollar per acre, and resided on it for about seven years, making many improvements. He then sold it for ten dollars per acre, and he now resides in Victoria County. During the Civil War he was too old to enlist, but he contributed to the support of the soldiers' wives and widows by proceeds from his farm. After the death of a Mr. W. T. Mitchell, in 1867, who was executor of the will of the late J. O. Wheeler, Mr. Davidson was appointed administrator, and through his judicious business qualifications that vast estate was liquidated, and distribution made, during possibly a crisis never exceeded for the "demonitization of property," that then prevailed. In 1870, in company with W. L. and L. C. Wheeler, he secured a charter from the city of Victoria to erect a toll bridge across the Guadalupe River, and did so at a cost of $16,500. This he continued for many years at great profit. In 1875, he bought his present estate of 1,500 acres in Mission Valley, and he now has it well improved, all fenced and subdivided into pastures, and also has 200 acres under cultivation. On this he has erected a good residence and he has a most desirable property. Mr. Davidson has ever been quite active in political matters, but usually declined office, though prior and since the war he has held the office of County Commissioner for sixteen years. In the year 1867 Mr. Davidson lost his wife, who left six children, all now living: Truxton, Quincy, Jr., Green, Geo. Washington, Kate, and Clara Cornelia, wife of A. R. McNees, of Memphis, Tenn. Mr. Davidson's brother, Truxton, came to Texas from Mississippi in 1850, and died at our subject's home a few months later. Their sister, Lucy Randall, resides with our subject, and is eighty-five years of age. The youngest brother, Green, came to Texas with his father in 1846, and after marrying settled in Bell County, where he remained until 1861, when on an expedition against hostile Indians, he was killed by them near the headwaters of the Colorado River. Mr. Davidson comes of a long lived stock and, although over eighty years of age, time has dealt kindly with him and he is still active and hearty.

JAMES A. HARBERT. This gentleman has been successfully engaged in merchandising and planting at Eagle Lake, Texas, since 1866, but owes his nativity to Madison County, Tennessee, where he was born in 1839. His father, William Harbert, came from Tennessee to this State in 1855, and located in Columbus, where he was called from life during the last year of the war in Clinton, Texas, while on his way home from Mexico, at which time he was eighty years of age, or more. He was quite successful as a planter and merchant, and he and his brother John accumulated fortunes valued at a million dollars, but lost very heavily during the war, as a great deal of their money was in slaves. His mercantile establishment was located at Denmark, Tenn. It is supposed that he was a soldier of the War of 1812. He was married to Elizabeth Waddell, whose death occurred prior to his own, and both were worthy church members. He was a Democrat in his political views. Of a family of eight children born to them, the subject of this sketch was the fifth in order of birth, and but four are living at the present time The school days of James A. Harbert were spent in Independence, Texas, at Baylor University, of which Dr. Burleson was the head, but he completed his education in 1859, after which he assisted his father, and was with his uncle Stephen in the store at Columbus up to 1861, when he joined Bates' Regiment, after which he was transferred to Brown's Regiment, in which he served until the close of the war, being stationed on the coast all the time, a portion of time at Galveston and other points on the coast. In 1866 he began working on the farm near Columbus, and remained there until the latter part of that year when he came to the farm of 500 acres near Eagle Lake, where his home continued to be up to 1881. Since that time he has resided in Eagle Lake and was associated in business with Capt. William Dunovant until 1890, but since that time he has carried on his affairs alone. His business operations have met with success, and he has enough of this world's goods to keep him from hard labor. In 1868 he was married to Olivia Putney, who was born in Hardeman County, Tennessee, and died January 2, 1891, without issue. She was an earnest member of the Methodist Church, of which Mr. Harbert is also a member, and politically he is a Democrat.

GILBERT ONDERDONK. It was once accepted as an axiomatic fact that fruit could not be grown in Southern Texas, and all theories offered in rebuttal were ridiculed; but Mr. Gilbert Onderdonk has effectually silenced the scoffers by practically demonstrating the fact that fruit can be grown here. Having gained this victory, the realization of his hopes is but a question of time, involving more studious investigation, more labor and expenditure of money —that "open sesame" in the estimation of mankind, and key to many of the hidden mysteries of nature's occult self. Mr. Onderdonk, who is one of the early settlers of Mission Valley, Victoria County, Texas, and the well known proprietor of the justly celebrated "Mission Valley Nurseries," as well as the pioneer pomologist of Southwestern Texas, was born in Schoharie County, New York, September 30, 1829. He was third in order of birth of nine children born to the marriage of John and Harriet (Ward) Onderdonk, both natives of the Empire State. The Onderdonk family is of Dutch extraction, and the first member to make his advent into this country came here as early as 1620, settling in New York State. John Onderdonk, father of subject, was a real estate man. He moved to Niagara County, New York, at an early date, and there passed away in 1870. The mother died when our subject was an infant. Gilbert Onderdonk was educated in Homer, New York, and graduated at the State Normal School at Albany in 1849. Even when but a small boy, Mr. Onderdonk took a great interest in horticulture, and when but eleven years of age he began to originate new varieties of Irish potatoes. He was so successful in these boyhood enterprises that, at the age of fifteen, he took eleven premiums at the New York State Fair upon varieties of potatoes originated by himself. After graduating, as above stated, he thought of teaching, but on account of ill health left home in the fall of 1850, and with his own horse and buggy made his way to Washington, D. C., where he spent the winter. In the spring he went to Richmond, from there by canal to Lynchburg, Va., and spent the summer in the mountains of that State, still traveling for health. He afterward returned home and remained there until the fall of 1851, when he started for Texas, reaching Indianola on the 14th of November, just one month after starting. The first winter he spent at Green Lake, hunting, and game was so abundant that he has never cared to hunt since. In the spring his health was so improved that he taught school for a few months, after which he found employment with the late Rev. S. F. Cocke, and had charge of his cattle ranch on Green Lake. Here he secured an insight into the stock business and soon after he commenced the business of raising horses, on a ranch purchased on the San Antonio River, continuing the same until the spring of 1856. Previous to this, in 1855, he was married to Miss Martha Benham, daughter of Col. S. A. Benham, of Kentucky. In 1856 Mr. Onderdonk bought a tract of 360 acres in Mission Valley, and removed there the year following, as above stated. The same year he drove his horses to Booneville, Mo., and realized a handsome profit from the sales. Later he began to experiment in horticultural pursuits here and was assured that certain kinds of fruit would thrive. He is now realizing the dream of his lifetime in having made a collection of fruits, flowers, and material for landscape work for southwest Texas. Mr. Onderdonk is as much of a devotee of science as those who pursue their occult investigations of nature's hidden truths with the aid of retorts and crucibles; indeed horticulture may not inappropriately be called the poesy of science, contributing as much to the material wants as to the mental enjoyment of its votaries. Like others who invent, discover or develop ideas, machinery, or resources calculated to ameliorate the condition of their kind, Mr. Onderdonk does not hope to see his labors fully appreciated in his lifetime, though thoroughly confident that time and experience will eventually lead men to acknowledge the invaluable nature of the study which has so engrossed his time, attention and pecuniary resources. The nursery business of Mr. Onderdonk has developed into quite titanic proportions, as he furnishes the whole of southwestern Texas and western Louisiana with fruit trees; a fact that points conclusively to his appreciation as a competent and reliable pomologist on the part of the people who have tested his many varieties of acclimated trees and shrubs. His gardens are a scene of constant activity during the short winters, in which all the packing, shipping, etc., are necessarily done. He published his first catalogue in 1872, and now has about seventy acres devoted to nursery stock. In 1883 he located a branch on the railroad, a station which he named Nursery, made the first improvements and became the first Postmaster, a position he still holds. To his marriage have been born five children: John Austin, Mary, wife of Geo. W. Eason, of Tyler; Frank S., a Methodist preacher of San Diego; and Gilbert S. and Lillie, twins. Mr. Onderdonk has been quite active in politics, formerly holding several county offices, and held the following offices all at one time: County Commissioner, Justice, Assessor of Precinct, member of Board of Appeals and Revision, and member of the County Board of Education. All these he resigned. During the war he was in Co. E., Eighth Texas Infantry, and was in the battles of Corpus Christi and Fort Esperanza, and at the close of these battles was ordered back by Col. Ireland to blow up the works. He was captured and severely wounded in the foot by an accident while in prison. For eight months he was held in New Orleans and then exchanged, after which he rejoined his command near Galveston, serving until the close. Socially Mr. Onderdonk is an Odd Fellow, and he and family are members of the Methodist Church.

JACOB HILL. This old settler and worthy citizen, now living at San Felipe, Texas, has been a resident of this State since his thirteenth year, and during all that time his career has been above reproach, and by judicious and honorable management his affairs have developed to a gratifying magnitude. Mr. Hill owes his nativity to St. Francis County, Arkansas, born September 15, 1827, and his parents, John and Mary M. (Bollinger) Hill, are natives of Kentucky and Missouri, respectively. When a young man, John Hill went to Arkansas and was married in St. Francis County of that State, in 1825. There his death occurred in 1841, at which time he was living in Pope County. The Bollinger family came from Pope County, Arkansas, to Texas in 1833, and settled in Jefferson County, remaining there until after the war with Mexico. This family furnished its full quota of men for Texas service, and two of them, our subject's uncles, served in the battle of San Jacinto, Ephraim and Peter, both of whom were privates. Afterwards the family moved to Austin County, and there John Bollinger, grandfather of subject, died full of years and honors. He and wife reared a family of eleven children: Ephraim, was killed by the Mexicans or Indians about 1839; Conrad, died in this county; Elizabeth, died in Fort Bend County, was the wife of William I. Allbright; Mary M. (mother of subject); Peter, deceased; Sarah, wife, of H. B. Littlefield, died in Fort Bend County; Hiram, died in this county; Caroline, married Benjamin Allen and died in this county; Catherine, deceased, was the wife of Mr. Hillyard, who was County Clerk of the county for many years; John, Jr., died in this State, and Louie, died in this county. Mrs. Hill left Arkansas and came to Texas in 1842, and, as she found most of her relatives located in this county, decided to settle here too. She made the trip from Pope County, Arkansas, in wagons, brought her family with her, also her household effects, and although the trip was fraught with danger, she arrived in safety. Here her death occurred in this county in 1855. She was the mother of five children, four of whom reached mature years: Jacob, John, of this county; Elizabeth, deceased, was the wife of William Pitts, of this county, and George W. died in the Confederate service. Jacob Hill received only a limited education, and most of that after he became a man, and came with his mother to Texas in 1842. When twenty-one years of age he started out for himself as a stockman, and at this made a decided success. During the Civil War he served for a short time in the Confederate army, but hired a substitute and gave his time and attention to stock-raising. Since the war, however, he has given much of his attention to farming, and in 1881 sold off his cattle, 1,800 head, and put the proceeds in land. He now owns 250 acres of land, after giving each of his children a 400-acre tract. Mr. Hill was married in 1854 to Miss Sarah A. Allbright, a native of Arkansas, and daughter of William I. Allbright. Seven children were born to this marriage, one of whom died in infancy: Annie, deceased, was the wife of Arthur Gray; James H., Georgie E., wife of R. S. Hinsly, of this county; George B., William I., Jacob W., and John, deceased. Mrs. Hill died in 1889. For many years she was an earnest member of the Methodist Episcopal Church. In 1893 Mr. Hill married Miss Lorena Davidson, of Belton, Texas, and daughter of W. T. and Callie (Smith) Davidson, early settlers of Bell County. She is a member of the Methodist Episcopal Church. Mr. Hill takes very little interest in political matters, but votes with the Democratic party. When Mr. Hill first came to the Lone Star State game abounded, and he participated in many exciting bear hunts, and had many narrow escapes. He still keeps as a relic of those exciting times the old smooth bore rifle with which he did all his hunting. He has killed hundreds of deer and other animals, bear, panthers, etc., and many of them at where the town of Sealy now stands.

HENRY W. ONCKEN. This substantial, enterprising and useful citizen was born in the Grand Duchy of Oldenburg, Germany, March 27, 1835, to Gerhard and Helen (Bollenhagen) Oncken, both of whom were also born in Oldenburg, Germany, where both were called from life. The father was quite a successful farmer, and he was, as were all the members of his family, an educated and influential citizen and a worthy member of the Lutheran Church. One of his brothers was a Supreme Judge in the old country, and died in 1865, when sixty-five years of age. The immediate subject of this sketch was one of a large family, and was given good educational advantages, which he wisely improved. When eighteen years of age he determined to seek his fortune in the new world, and after a voyage of several weeks he landed in the city of New Orleans. After a time he came by water to Galveston, thence to Houston by ox team, and from their to Frelsburg. He had considerable means upon his arrival here. He came thither with a number of young men from the same neighborhood in Germany as himself, nearly, if not quite, all of whom have become substantial citizens. Mr. Oncken at once began working for other people, but at the end of six months went to Roos Prairie, and for a short time was in the employ of Gen. Baylor, after which he went to Columbus, and there was sick with the cholera for some time. He had commenced farming for himself in Fayette County, seven miles south of La Grange, and on the 15th of January, 1861, was married to Miss Knipscher, who, like himself, was born in Germany. Her people came to Texas when she was a child, and here made a comfortable home. She died about 1883, having become the mother of two sons and two daughters. For his second wife Mr. Oncken was married January 7, 1886, to Mrs. Steinbonner, who has borne him two sons and a daughter. In the summer of 1863 he joined the Second Texas Infantry, Company C, stationed at Galveston, and was there when the war closed. Before entering active service he had been hauling cotton to Mexico for the Confederate Government, and in 1862 he came to near Weimar and bought 1,120 acres of land, of which he has since sold 470 acres of prairie and 220 acres of timber land. He has been very successful in his agricultural operations, and has also been quite prominently connected with public affairs, and during the thirty-three years that he has resided in this place he has held a number of positions of honor and trust. For a great portion of this time there was no such town as Weimar, and he can now look from his post office and see quite a thriving and populous place. He has given valuable aid to the building up of the town, and is considered one of the leading citizens. He is a member of the Lutheran Church, is a Democrat in politics, and socially is a member of the A. O. U. W.

COL. L. B. CAMP, deceased. Man does not come into the world with matured thoughts and ideas. He learns a few isolated facts, and from these he evolves related truths, and only at the time of saying "vale" to the world is he a man in stature and intellect. His life is but a preparatory school for the life to come. It is so with every one and not less so to the man whose name is above. He developed, he acquired, he struggled, he died, when to the finite mind he was only ready to live well, but a nobler life is continued above. Col. L. B. Camp was a product of Georgia, born in 1806, and as early as 1840, came to Texas, settling in Upshur County, where he remained for some time. He then moved to West Texas in 1859, where he became an extensive farmer and stock-raiser. He was first married to a Miss Stephens, of Georgia, who died in the early '40s, leaving six children, all of whom came to Texas with him. In 1853, the colonel was married to Mrs. Nancy Phillips, a native of Alabama, who bore him ten children, four of whom are deceased. In August, 1880, Col. L. B. Camp passed away, but his wife is still living and makes her home in Wilson County. He was very prominent in politics and was a member of the Thirteenth General Assembly. At the breaking out of war he was a member of the Secession Committee of Texas, but voted against it, remaining a Union man until cessation of hostilities. His son, L. B. Camp, was the youngest child born to his second marriage. The latter's birth occurred in Refugio County, Texas, in 1867, and he received a thorough education in St. Mary's College, San Antonio, Bryant, Texas, and in the University of Virginia, where he studied law, being admitted to the bar in that State in 1890. The same year he was admitted to the bar in San Antonio, and in September he formed a partnership with Judge Lawhon, under the firm name of Lawhon & Camp. Soon after he began practicing Mr. Camp acquired a high reputation as a practitioner of unusual ability, persistence, force and adroitness, and as a result has risen rapidly to the top of his profession, enjoying a large practice and the unbounded confidence of his fellow lawyers and the people. He is calm, dispassionate, eloquent, and all his arguments are firmly grounded upon legal and equitable principle. Socially he is a Mason, a member of Floresville Lodge No. 515. In the year 1891 he was married to Miss Orie Lee Lawhon, daughter of Judge Lawhon (see sketch), and a conscientious member of the Baptist Church. Many members of the Camp family are living in San Antonio and vicinity, and are prominent and prosperous people.

JESSE L. GONZALES. Strange as it may appear, the instances are rare in which men who are born in this county fail in business. This is, of course, owing to the fact that they are in exact touch with the vim and live spirit of enterprise that manifests itself in this section. When to this credit of nativity is added the advantage of youth, the success is certain to become all the greater, as proven by the business record of Jesse L. Gonzales, a prosperous merchant of Nursery, Texas. He was born in Victoria County, Texas, in 1869, and his parents, J. M. and Magdelina (Lopez) Gonzales, were natives of Mexico and San Antonio, Texas, respectively. The father, a prominent stockman, came to Victoria County, Texas, in 1859, and located at the head of Spring Creek, where he became the owner of the largest farm in the county, having 1,000 acres under cultivation, and raising principally corn and cotton, forty to fifty bushels of the former, and a bale of the latter to the acre. He raised a good grade of cattle and many fine draft horses. His death occurred November 7, 1893, and the mother's previous to this, December 12, 1876. Our subject received good educational advantages, attending St. Joseph's College, Victoria, and the Alamo business college in San Antonio, graduating from the latter in 1885. After this, he began clerking for D H. Ragan in Victoria, and was book-keeper for the firm of Gonzales, Oliver & Coleman, a prominent concern of Victoria. In 1891 Mr. Gonzales started in business at Nursery, eleven miles West of Victoria, and on the South Pacific Railroad, erected his large store house, and now carries a stock of goods valued at $2,000. He does an annual business of $15,000, general merchandising, and is a wideawake, pushing young business man. He bought property in Nursery, and has a handsome orchard of pears, peaches and grapes.

He also owns a farm of fifty acres under cultivation and an interest in his father's large estate as yet undivided. On the 11th of December, 1893, he was married at Mission Valley to Miss Guadalupe L. Lozano, daughter of Crisoforo Lazano, a native of Mexico, who came to Victoria County, about 1863, and there followed farming until his death, October 11, 1893. Mrs. Lozano is still living. Mr. Gonzales and family are members of the Catholic Church. The Gonzales are of Spanish origin.

JAMES S. DABNEY. This enterprising young man of affairs was born near Hopkinsville, Ky., March 28, 1852, a son of Cornelius I. and Susan (Garnett) Dabney, who were born on Blue Grass soil, and came to Texas in the fall of 1853, settling in what is known as Kentucky Ridge, in the northern portion of Austin County. For the first year they rented land, but the next year purchased and began the improvement of a place of their own, on which they remained until the father's death in 1882. Mr. Dabney was active in the affairs of this section, and for some time served in the capacity of County Commissioner. Although a member of the Confederate army during the Civil War, he was not in active service, being on special detail. His widow still survives him and resides in Hood County, Texas. Besides his widow he left nine children: A. G., of Hood County; J. S., C. I., of Austin County; Mary F., wife of Peter Harvey, of Jones County; E. M., Dr. T. H., Susan O., Annie, of Hood County, and Eustacia, wife of Leonidas C. Hill, of Beeville, Bee County. James S. Dabney received most of his education on Kentucky Ridge, attending college but one term. He began life for himself at the foot of the ladder at the age of twenty-one years, and after a time he purchased a farm in the northern part of Austin County, for which he paid the sum of $30 per acre. After residing on the same for eight years he sold it for about the same that he gave for it, and purchased a larger place, paying $6,000 for 200 acres. Two years later he sold this and moved to the farm on which he now resides, purchasing 600 acres for $2,000. He has since made other purchases, and is now the owner of 3,000 acres, of which 200 acres are under cultivation. He has also been in the stock business since coming to this place, and is now a member of a cattle company composed of some of the most thrifty farmers of the county, and handles some 4,000 or 5,000 cattle annually. On the 4th of December, 1871, Miss Lottie Harvey, of Austin County, and daughter of G. W. and Marcia (Cameron) Harvey, became his wife, and the following children have been given them: Austin E., a druggist; Mollie, Marcia, Henry and Plem. Mr. and Mrs. Dabney are both members of the Christian Church, and he is a member of the K. & L. of H. He has always been interested in local politics, and has always supported the Democratic party. His wife's mother was born in the State of New York, and her father in Alabama; but both were raised in Austin County, Texas. Mr. Harvey has been a minister of the Christian Church for quite a number of years, and has been instrumental in bringing many souls to Christ. Mrs. Harvey departed this life November 23, 1893. Mr. and Mrs. Harvey reared three children: Peter, of Jones County; Lottie, wife of J. S. Dabney, and Phœbe, wife of Dr. L. B. Creath, of Beeville, Texas, who is President of the Commercial National Bank in that city.

JAQUELIN SMITH BRUCE, M.D. This successful medicine man of Colorado County, Texas, has practiced the art of healing the sick since 1859, during which long term of years he has met with a more than average degree of success, and his name is a familiar household word throughout this section. He was born in Winchester, Va., in 1836, his father being John Bruce, who was born in Perth, Scotland. He was finely educated and was a graduate of the College of St. Andrews. When a young man of nineteen he came to the United States and located in Virginia, and for many years thereafter was engaged in teaching in Winchester Academy, Va. During the latter part of his life he devoted his attention to farming, and was following this occupation at the time of his death, which occurred in 1857, at the age of sixty years. He was married to Miss Sidney Smith, whose people came to this country from England, and by her reared four sons, of whom the subject of this sketch is the youngest; Edward is a portrait painter and magazine writer of Winchester, Texas; George is a physician at Moundsville, West Va., and Douglas is a farmer of Clarke County, Va. The mother of these children is dead. Dr. Jaquelin S. Bruce was educated in Winchester Academy and at the University of Virginia, after which he commenced fitting himself for the practice of medicine at Winchester, Va., and in 1857 graduated as an M. D. from this institution. His alma mater was destroyed by fire during the war. He at once commenced practicing his profession in Stafford County, Va., but in 1859 came to Texas and located on the west side of the Colorado River, in this county, in the vicinity of Eagle Lake. In the spring of 1862 he became a recruit in Hood's Brigade, Company B, Fifth Texas Infantry, and remained with that regiment until after the second battle of Manasses, when he was appointed Assistant Surgeon in the Forty-seventh Virginia Infantry, Richmond Medical Department, and held this position until the close of the war. He was wounded at the battle of Manassas, was at Seven Pines, Gaines Mill, Malvern Hill, Second Manassas, besides participating in other bloody battles in Maryland and Virginia, and in numerous skirmishes. He surrendered at Appomattox at once returned home and embarked in the cotton business, but after a time gave up that occupation and resumed his medical practice, to which his attention has since been devoted. In 1866 he was married to Miss Minna Rivers, a daughter of Jones Rivers, and was called upon to mourn her death in 1869. She became the mother of one child, who is now the wife of J. J. Mansfield, County Attorney of Colorado County. In 1872 the doctor married Miss Susie Rivers, a sister of his former wife, and they have two children: Jennie and Jaqueline, both at home. The doctor and his wife are members of the Episcopal Church, and he is a member of the Blue Lodge of the A. F. & A. M. at Eagle Lake. The doctor was in the mercantile business for a few years with L. B. Lake, but of late years has been in the drug business.

H. MYLIUS. He whose name heads this sketch, although now quietly engaged in pursuing the calling of a merchant at Yaokum, Texas, has been engaged in various occupations and has led quite a checkered career, notwithstanding which fact he has accumulated a competency, and has refuted the old saw that "a rolling stone gathers no moss." He owes his nativity to Germany, where he was born April 19, 1839, a son of Dr. Adolph T. and Amelia (Stearn) Mylius, who came to the United States in the beginning of the year 1846 as a member of the Fischer and Miller Colony, and landed at Indianola, Texas. Dr. Adolph T. Mylius had been a prominent surgeon in the German Army for about eight years, and was a successful general practitioner, being located for some time in the vicinity of the city of Berlin.

He continued his practice after coming to this country, but after the death of his wife from cholera at Indianola in the summer of 1846, Dr. Mylius removed to Gillespie County, with some members of the colony, but returned to Indianola at the end of two years, where he made a name for himself as a medical practitioner, and was successfully engaged in pursuing the arduous duties of his profession until his death, which occurred about 1858. He practiced through the yellow fever epidemic of 1852, gave valuable aid to the sufferers of that dreaded scourge, and won the highest praise for his ability, his energy, his kindness of heart and his sympathy. His family consisted of three children: the subject of this sketch; Annie, who after the death of her mother was reared by H. Bunge and now resides in San Antonio, and Albert who was reared by G. W. Volt, is married and is a resident of San Antonio, also. The subject of this sketch was a regular attendant of the public schools up to the death of his father, when he became a sailor, which calling he followed for sixteen years, in the coasting trade. He was Captain of a boat that carried mail from Matagorda to Indianola and to Salura and back twice a week for five years. At the end of this time he purchased a sloop, which he ran independently from Indianola to Matagorda and Corpus Christi. In 1861 he espoused the cause of the section in which he resided and became a member of Company G, Sixth Texas Infantry and went to Houston, where he was detailed to the marine department and put on a gunboat in Matagorda Bay. He was thus engaged for two years, at the end of which time he was detailed to the steamer Camargo to run the blockade and make his way to Matamoras, at which place he was when news came of Lee's surrender. He then returned to Indianola and bought a sloop, and also became the owner of a sloop called the Anna Mary at the beginning of the war, which was captured by the Federals in Matagorda Bay, used by them for a time and was then burned. Mr. Mylius called his new sloop the Parasto, which he used in the coast trade, regularly, to Corpus Christi. This vessel he sold in 1874, and then built another which he ran in the oyster trade for about four years, at the end of which time he sold out to engage in the grocery and ship chandlery business at Indianola. There he was successfully engaged in business until the great storm of 1886, when his property was destroyed. For one year thereafter he was engaged in general merchandising in Galveston, at the end of which time, for the benefit of his health, he moved to Cuero, where he was in business for seven months. In 1887 he came to Yoakum and opened the second dry goods store in the place, but after a time sold his stock of goods and now has a stock of china, crockery, tin, wooden and hollow ware, his being the third business house erected on Grand Avenue. He is doing well financially and has a paying patronage. In 1871 he was married to Miss Antinono Cloudt, a native of Texas and a daughter of George Cloudt, who came to Texas about 1846 and at once became a soldier in the Mexican War under Gen. Taylor. While in the service he had a horse killed under him, for which the Government paid him eighty-five dollars in 1886. He was a farmer and stock-raiser at Long Mott, Texas, and there died in 1888, leaving six daughters and one son to mourn their loss. The union of Mr. and Mrs. Mylius has resulted in the birth of ten children: Albert, Henry, Annie, Emma, Bettie, Clarence, Pearl, Herman, Frank, and a child that died in infancy.

WILLIAM TRIGG MCLEARY, M. D.   To heal the sick and cure the ills to which the human body is heir is noble but arduous labor, and is the most trying on brain and body of any in the field of science.   He whose name heads this sketch was a very successful practitioner of the healing art, but for some years has been retired and in every respect has earned his rest.   He was born in Tipton County, Tennessee, in 1828, and received his literary education in Mountain Academy, after leaving which he at once commenced the study of medicine, and later graduated from the Jefferson Medical College of Philadelphia.   Upon completing his medical education, he located for the practice of his profession at Salisbury, Hardeman County, Tenn., and there continued in the practice of his profession until 1866, when he came to Columbus, Texas, where he was a successful practitioner until 1867 and then moved on a farm fourteen miles west of Columbus till 1880, then to Weimar in the same year   Upon his arrival here he purchased a tract of land near Weimar, and located in this place and here his home has since continued to be, although he has been retired for some time.   During the Civil War he was a surgeon in Polk's Division, Twenty-third Tennessee Regiment, and was at the battle of Shiloh, and in other important engagements.   He is a member of the Colorado County Medical Association, and is connected with that society in the capacity of President, a position which he ably and faithfully fills.   He has been quite an extensive writer of medical literature and has furnished a number of articles to medical journals, that have received extended and favorable notice.   He is widely known all over the State as a skillful surgeon and stands high with the medical fraternity.   He is a Royal Arch Mason, a member of the I. O. O. F., and the K. of H.   He was married to Miss Amanda Elizabeth Pugh, who died June 11, 1890, having become the mother of six children.   Samuel B. McLeary is their only son, and his school days were spent in Osage and Weimer Academies and in Bingham School, finishing his literary education in 1885.   In very early boyhood he began the study of medicine and spent the years of 1887-8-9 at the Jefferson School of Medicine in Philadelphia, graduating in the last mentioned year.   He then graduated from the New York Policlinic Surgical School, but had practiced his profession since 1889. Like his worthy sire before him he has been quite successful as a practitioner and has the confidence and respect of his patrons and an extended practice.

G. T. ROSS, M. D.   The pioneer physician of this place, Dr. G. T. Ross, was born in the State of Alabama in 1830, and no doubt inherited his taste for the medical profession from his father, William Ross, who was also a successful and prominent physician.   The latter married Miss Carrie Bond, who bore him thirteen children, three of whom came to Texas, William, James and our subject.   These children were named in the order of their births as follows: T. J., who now resides in Brunswick, Tenn.; Mary, married Rev. Nathan Sullivan; Dr. J. A., W. B., Harriet, deceased; Sarah, deceased, G. T., Martha, married T. P. Slater; R. N., a physician, resides at Lone Oak, Ark.; Fredonia, deceased; James A., deceased, and one died in infancy.   Twelve of these children grew to mature years and married.   The Ross family came originally from England previous to the Revolutionary war, and three brothers of this family fought for independence.   They settled in South Carolina, but subsequently moved westward, and an ancestor of our subject, John Ross, located in Kentucky at a very early period.   His son, John, grandfather of our subject, reared a large family there, and William Ross, father of subject, was born in that State and there grew to mature years. He went to Alabama from Kentucky and thence to Tennessee, where he died. Dr. G. T. Ross received a fair common school education in his youth, and later entered Worcester Medical College, Massachusetts, and was graduated from that institution in 1854. He practiced for two years in Shelby County, Tennessee, moved to Round Top, Texas, and practiced one year, but from there he moved to San Felipe, Texas, in 1858, and has been in active practice here since, with the exception of the years since 1890. Though he still continues to do considerable office practice, the doctor was paralyzed in his left side in 1890, and does not do any work that would bring on a second attack. When Dr. Ross first came to Texas his practice covered miles in every direction, and he was for many years kept busy almost night and day. When not thus employed, much of his time was given to hunting and fishing, and being an expert in both, he derived much pleasure from these pursuits. He has killed many deer, bear, etc., in his day and had many exciting adventures. Dr. Ross did not serve in the Civil War, but practiced his profession among the people, he and Dr. Gibson being the only physicians in that section. After the war the doctor became deeply interested in agricultural pursuits, and owns a fine farm in the Brazos bottoms, 1,000 acres under cultivation, raising from four to six hundred bales of cotton per year. In connection with farming the doctor has been deeply interested in raising fine stock and has some excellent animals on his place. He was married in 1859 to Miss Lenora Daugherty, a native of this county, and daughter of Bryant and Anna (Roberts) Daugherty, pioneer settlers of Texas. Dr. and Mrs. Ross are the parents of eight children: G. T., deceased; Fredonia, deceased; Maggie, deceased; Mary, wife of Dr. J. S. Davidson of this place; Anna, deceased; Daisy, deceased; Annett, deceased, and Mittie. Dr. Ross has served San Felipe as Mayor and Alderman, and for many years as Notary Public. For twenty years he was a member of the Board of Medical Examiners and all the medical associations throughout the county. Since 1858 the doctor has been a member of the Masonic Fraternity at Round Top, Fayette County, and of the San Felipe Lodge No. 239, since 1860, and also Bellville Lodge of R. A. M., since 1889. He served the Masonic Fraternity as Past Master for twenty years, but retired about 1888. Dr. Ross has always taken quite an active interest in Masonry, and for over twenty years attended every meeting of the Grand Lodge of the State. Politically he is a Democrat.

WILLIAM OWEN MURRAY. Another evidence of what perseverance, hard work and pluck can do is illustrated in the life of William O. Murray, senior member of the firm of Murray & King, general merchants of Floresville, Texas. In him is found a man whose business career is a decidedly interesting one, showing the competency which can soon be attained when energy and industry are brought to bear. Mr. Murray was born in Versailles, Mo., in 1857, and he is a son of Asa W. and N. A. Murray, the parents natives of North Carolina and Missouri respectively. The father, who had been a dealer in general merchandise, came to the Lone Star State in 1859 and settled on a farm on the Cibolo River, where he made his home until 1882, when he was elected Sheriff and Collector of Wilson County, and then he came to Floresville, and is now engaged in business in this city. William Owen Murray was reared in this State and received his scholastic training in the common schools and by his own exertions. When twenty-one years of age he branched out for himself as a clerk, and later was Deputy County Clerk for County Clerk Hughes for several years. He then resigned. In 1883 he engaged in business for himself with Mr. Foster, under the firm name of Murray & Foster, general merchants, and that partnership lasted one year. Then Mr. Murray bought out his partner's interest and conducted the business alone until September 22, 1890, when his store was burned and he lost nearly all his stock of goods. All the business buildings owned by him were destroyed by the fire at that date. Following this Mr. Murray made arrangements to immediately rebuild, also to admit Mr. Henry C. King as partner. The building is brick, 31x70 feet, two stories high, both floors being used by the firm in their retail business, and there are two warehouses for storage. These enterprising young business men carry a stock valued at $13,000, and they do an annual business of about $40,000. Their stock is composed of dry goods, groceries, farm implements, farming tools, wagons, etc., and, in fact, all goods for a general store. Mr. Murray bought the first car-load of wagons in 1886, and in 1887 the first cultivator that was ever brought to Wilson County. This firm has one of the best arranged and tastiest stores in the place, and both are pleasant, agreeable business men. In October, 1883, Mr. Murray was married to Miss Ella Peacock, a native of Texas, and the daughter of Thomas Peacock, an early settler of this State. Five children are the fruits of this union: Mattie, Ida May, Laura, William O., Jr., and DeWitt. The family hold membership in the Presbyterian Church, in which our subject is deacon. He is a member of the Masonic Fraternity, Floresville Lodge No. 515, and was Secretary of the same for several years.

B. F. ROSSER. Among the sons of Kentucky who brought with them to this State the sturdy habits of independence, integrity and industry, which have ever marked those of that nativity, we are gratified to be able to name Mr. B. F. Rosser, whose fine farm of 8,000 acres is among the best of the Lone Star State. He possesses those advanced ideas and progressive principles regarding agricultural life, which seem to be among the chief characteristics of the average native Kentuckian, and in every walk of life he has conducted himself in an honorable and upright manner. Mr. Rosser was born in 1839 to the union of John and Mahala (Wyth) Rosser, both natives of that grand old State, Virginia. About the time of our subject's birth he was left fatherless and he grew to mature years in his native State. From there he went to Missouri and later to Arkansas, where he made his home for nine years. In 1859 he came to Texas and located in Wilson County, where he was actively engaged in stock-raising until the breaking out of the Rebellion. In 1861 he enlisted in Company K, Second Texas Regiment, cavalry, and served in that State until cessation of hostilities. Returning to Wilson County, he has since been extensively engaged in stock-raising. Industrious, enterprising and thorough-going, he has made a complete success of life, and of the 8,000 acres he resides upon, 350 are under cultivation. He owns other tracts, portions of which are under a good state of cultivation. He owns about thirteen acres in the town of Floresville. He raises a fine grade of cattle, Durham and Holstein, and is progressive and advanced in his ideas. The intelligence and ability shown by Mr. Rosser in conducting his large ranch, and the interest he has taken in the advancement of measures for the good of Wilson County, caused him long since to be classed as one of the leading

M. B. BENNETT.

citizens of his section. Before he erected his late residence he was burned out, his losses amounting to about $5,000. In 1871 he celebrated his nuptials with Miss Texanna Martin, a native of Tennessee, and seven children were given them, four of whom are now living: Lee, Ben, Kate and Frank. About 1882 Mr. Rosser and family moved to Floresville, and here he has since resided. In 1890 he erected his present handsome residence.

DR. O. D. COPPEDGE. In giving a history of the prominent citizens of De Witt County, Texas, this work would be incomplete were not mention made of Dr. Coppedge, for he is deservedly ranked among its prominent planters and stockbreeders. His estate comprises about 1,000 acres, of which 350 acres are under cultivation, and he has devoted much attention to raising a good grade of stock, being one of the first to introduce graded Jersey cattle in this section, and has raised many fine animals. His property comprises the site of the first building erected in the village, which was made of concrete material, and from that fact gave the place its name, which it has since maintained. He has also devoted considerable attention to the raising of fruit, and has large orchards. In 1868 he erected a pleasant residence in Concrete, and is possessed of sufficient philosophy to enjoy the comforts of life. His lands stretch across the rich bottom of the beautiful Guadalupe River, and are very productive and valuable. Dr. Coppedge was born in North Carolina April 15, 1835, and was the eldest of six children born to William D. and Henrietta (Drake) Coppedge, who were also natives of the Old North State, the father being of English descent, his ancestors having come to this country during colonial times. The maternal grandfather, William Drake, was a Virginian, and was a soldier of the Revolution. William D. Coppedge died in North Carolina in 1890, and his wife in 1892, both having been worthy members of the Baptist Church. Dr. O. D. Coppedge was educated in Wake Forest College, and in 1854 began the study of medicine, graduating from the University of Pennsylvania two years later. He at once began the practice of his profession in the State of his birth, but six months later moved to Texas, locating at Concrete, where he once more began his labors of healing the sick and afflicted. In 1861 he went to Gonzales and joined Smith's Company, Wall's Legion, C. S. A., but before the force could leave the State Dr. Coppedge was taken seriously ill and was compelled to give up all idea of entering the service, but sent a substitute in his place. He returned home, and upon his recovery, about one year later, he joined the State troops, with which he served until the war was over in the capacity of Lieutenant. Since that time he has practiced his profession but very little, his farming and stock-raising interests fully occupying his time. In 1859 he was married to Miss Mary Stevens, a native of Mississippi and daughter of Joseph Stevens, who came to Texas in 1846 and located near the present site of Concrete, locating on a large tract of land. The family was accompanied by Mrs. Coppedge's maternal grandfather, William Steen, who died at Natchitoches, La., on the way thither. Joseph Stevens died in 1861, and his wife May 1, 1860, both worthy members of the Baptist Church. To the union of Dr. and Mrs. Coppedge the following children have been born: William, Mitchie, wife of Claud N. Blackwell; Ettie and Lawrence. Dr. Coppedge has long been connected with the A. F. & A. M., and he and his wife are members of the Baptist Church.

25

HENRY BOEDEKER. To successfully fill the office of County Treasurer it is absolutely necessary that a man should possess certain requirements, the most important of which are honesty, accuracy and reliability, and these are found in ample measure in Henry Boedeker, who is the efficient Treasurer of Colorado County, Texas. He is a product of that country that has given to the United States some of her most progressive and reliable citizens—Germany—and there he first saw the light of day August 4, 1830. His father, Frederick Boedeker, who was an official in the employ of the German government, died in 1892, at the extreme old age of ninety-three years, and his principles and views were quite democratic. He insisted on five of his sons coming to America, for which country he had a deep admiration, and gave as his reasons that they would find good homes, with less labor, than in the old country, and free institutions. Four of these sons are now living, and are well-to-do citizens of the Lone Star State, which proves the wisdom of their father's views. August is a wealthy citizen of Milan County, Texas; Otto resides in Burleson County, Theodore in Washington County, and Henry in Colorado County. The latter received good educational advantages in his native land, and, like all German youths, learned a trade, his being the harness and saddle maker's business. August had been a resident of the United States for some time when he, in 1852, was followed to this country by Henry, Otto and Theodore, who reached this country after a nine-weeks ocean voyage, landing at Galveston. As Otto and Theodore had but little means, they worked their passage to this country, and even then, upon their arrival in Galveston, their means were very limited. They went to Houston, where they were met by their brother August, with several ox teams and some ponies, and they at once entered upon an active and industrious life. Very soon, however, Henry came to Columbus and opened a harness and saddle shop, and during the war was detailed by the Confederate Government to make harness and saddles for the army, and was thus employed until the war closed. His intelligence, and interest in the progress and development of Colorado County led to his election to the office of County Treasurer in 1876, and this office he has filled by re-election ever since, which is an eloquent tribute to his intellect and ability to discharge the responsible duties of this office. He, for some time past, has had no opposition for the office, for it seems to be well understood that no more efficient official could be secured. During these long eighteen years he has continued his business until 1880, since which time he has given his entire attention to his official duties, and other interests which are quite extensive and valuable. Mr. Boedeker is a free hearted, jovial and witty German-American, who numbers his friends by the score and who has the unbounded confidence of, and is popular with, all classes. In 1882 he visited the home of his boyhood, in company with his son Charles, and viewed the scenes of earlier days with much interest. He was married to Louisa Thulemeyer, a native of Germany, who is now deceased. She bore him five children: William H., a successful business man of Laredo, Texas; Charles, who is a railroad agent on the Southern Pacific, with headquarters at Eagle Lake, Texas; Lena, who is the wife of Robert E. Farmer, Deputy County Clerk of Colorado County. These are the living members of the family. In 1876 Mr. Boedeker was a second time married, Mrs. Mary Thulemeyer becoming his wife. Mr. Boedeker is a member of the I. O. O. F., and is Past Grand of Columbus Lodge, No. 51, and is also a member of the Encampment.

ALVAH CHESLEY. The American Bar can show an array of eminent talent, of profound erudition and of judicial ability equal to that of England, France and Germany. Alvah Chesley, the oldest attorney of Bellville, is one of the brightest members of the bar of the county, and ranks among the foremost lawyers of the State. He brings to the profession a most intimate knowledge of law, together with the qualities of pleader and advocate in a high degree of excellence. He is a product of the Granite State, born September 27, 1831, and is a son of Benjamin F. and Sarah (McDuffie) Chesley, both natives of New Hampshire, where their ancestors were early settlers. During his youth Alvah Chesley had good educational advantages, and was graduated from New Hampton Institute, New Hampshire. In the year 1859 he came to Texas, and for one year wielded the ferule in the schools of that State. When Civil War opened he immediately enlisted in the Confederate Army, Company F, Sixteenth Infantry Regiment, and served through Louisiana and Arkansas. At the close of hostilities he was discharged at Hempstead and returned home to Bellville. As he had been admitted to the bar before entering the army in 1861, he immediately entered upon the practice of his profession, and has continued this up to the present time. While devoted to his profession, which he pursues unremittingly, Mr. Chesley finds time for the cultivation of a taste for politics which he has. The principles and teachings of Thomas Jefferson are in full harmony with his own views, and he gives an unqualified support to his party's candidates. In the year 1876 he was elected a member of the Legislature, and in 1883 and 1884 he was in the Senate. In the year 1869 he was united in marriage to Miss Margaret E. Haggerty, a native of Georgia, who came, with her parents, Mr. and Mrs. James J. Haggerty, to De Witt County, Texas, in 1854. Mrs. Haggerty yet survives. To Mr. and Mrs. Chesley have been born two children: Josephine and Alvah. Socially Mr. Chesley is a Mason, having joined that order in his native State, and he now holds membership in Bellville Lodge, No. 223. He is also a member of Bellville Chapter No. 151., R. A. M.

JOHN HOCKER. As a prosperous tiller of the soil and stock-raiser, no one in this section deserves more honorable mention than John Hooker, whose career has been marked by honest effort, sound judgment, and, consequently, by success. He was born in Howard County, Missouri, September 16, 1834, a son of James A. and Polly (Todd) Hocker, the former of whom was born on Blue Grass soil, but removed to Missouri in 1807, where he bought a farm, and grew tobacco extensively. He was a large slave owner and used them profitably on his extensive tobacco plantation. He was originally an old line Whig, but became a Democrat, and was an active worker for the success of this party. He held several minor offices, and was frequently urged to run for the Legislature, but always declined to do so, as he preferred to devote his time and attention to other pursuits rather than to the strife and turmoil of the political arena. He was a progressive and successful farmer, who left his impress upon the community in which he resided. He died in the spring of 1865, and his wife in 1840. The subject of this sketch was reared in Howard County, Missouri, and after attending the common schools for some time, he finished his education in Central College, Missouri. At the age of twenty-one years he went to Kansas and pre-empted 160 acres of land, but about eighteen months later returned to Howard County, and for two years was engaged in farming there. In the fall of 1860 he was married to Miss Amanda E. Alexander, and in 1863 he left his home to enlist in the service of the Confederacy as a member of the force commanded by General Sterling Price, and was in active service until the close of hostilities, participating in many skirmishes and at the battle of Lexington. He was in the midst of the fray when General Marmaduke was captured. Upon his return to his home in Missouri, he was engaged in farming until 1878, on land which he had obtained by his own unaided efforts (the war having swept away his father's property), but after a time removed to Martindale, Texas, in the vicinity of which place he farmed for three years, then purchased and moved on the farm on which he is now living. His union has resulted in the birth of four sons: John B., who died in Kansas; William Lee, James R., and Paul B.

JAMES A. STONE. This gentleman is one of the esteemed residents of Austin County, where in various capacities he has proved his claim to upright and meritorious citizenship. For many years he has followed farming and stock-raising, and is one of the leaders in those occupations in his section. He was born in Washington County, Texas, November 28, 1860, and is the son of Samuel and Bettie V. (Stone) Stone. (For further particulars of parents, see sketch of Samuel Stone.) James A. Stone was educated at Bryant (A. & M. College) South Western University, at Georgetown Texas, and after finishing his schooling remained with his father on the farm until his twenty-first year, when he purchased a farm of 120 acres and a cotton gin in Washington County. There he resided for two years and then moved to Sealy, where he was actively engaged in the stock business. Four years later he came to this place, Wallace, and has since continued the stock business on an extensive scale, being one of the syndicate of cattlemen, J. S. Dobney, J. A. Stone, J. S. Jerrell and J. C. Odom. This is one of the largest stock firms in the country. Mr. Stone was married in 1860 to Miss Addie V. Stone of Virginia, and the daughter of F. and A. V. (Knight) Stone, both parents being dead. Of the five children born to her parents, Mrs. Stone and S. L. of Virginia, are the only ones now living. Our subject's union has been blessed by the birth of three sons: Luther L., Samuel V., and J. Vernon. Mr. Stone is little interested in real estate his principal occupation being buying and selling stock at which he has been unusually successful. On his twenty-first birthday his father presented him with one thousand dollars, and from this beginning his accumulation of property has been made. Besides his farm and stock Mr. Stone owns a beautiful residence in Wallis. He is one of the progressive men of the county, and a leader in his section. Although but little interested in political matters he always votes the straight Democratic ticket. He is a member of the Knights of Honor, and Mrs. Stone holds a membership in the Methodist Episcopal Church.

J. J. HOLLOWAY, the subject of this sketch, was born December 11, 1837, in Person County, North Carolina. He being the oldest child born to the marriage of John A. Holloway of Person County, North Carolina, and Mary A. Bass, of Halifax County, Virginia. In 1844 his father, John A. Holloway, represented Person County, in the State Legislature, on the same ticket with James K. Polk, who ran for President. In 1845 his father and family, consisting of wife, four children, and nine negroes landed at Houston, Texas, in the month of April, whence they were conveyed on ox wagons to the town of LaGrange, Fayette County, and soon thereafter located on a farm eight miles below LaGrange, on the Colorado River, where his father died, in June, 1846. His mother then removed to Rutersville, and in 1847 married P. J. Shaver, who soon after located the town of Fayetteville in the year 1848. Our subject remained at Fayetteville with his step-father and family until 1860, being absent ten months at school in 1859, under the tutorage of Prof. Wm. Halsey at Chappell Hill and Rufus C. Burleson, at Independence, Mo., known as Baylor University. In 1860 he visited relatives in Virginia and returning in 1861, joined the Confederate army as volunteer in the first company from Fayette County. Having served six months in Capt. Ben Shropshire's Company, Nichols Regiment, he again volunteered in Waul's Legion, Willis' Battalion of Cavalry, and on the 2d day of September, 1862, crossed the Mississippi River at Vicksburg, after which time, in Company D. Willis' Battalion, he fought under Gen. Chalmers, Gen. Van Dorn, Gen. S. D. Lee and Gen. Bedford Forrest. In April, after the close of the war, he returned to his home in Fayette County, Texas, and worked on the farm and labored as a wagoner on the road, hauling cotton and pine lumber, until February 8, 1866, at which time he was married to Lizzie A. Nicholson, in the town of La Grange. In the fall of 1866 he engaged in the general merchandise business with his father-in-law, James Nicholson, under the firm name of Nicholson & Holloway. In 1867 his partner died in La Grange of yellow fever, and in 1868 he formed a co-partnership with John A. Trousdale, under the firm name of Trousdale & Holloway, and remained with him until after the disastrous overflow of the Colorado River in 1869. After settling his affairs in LaGrange, he removed to his farm in Fayette County, in the year 1871, and remained there until the extension of the G. H. & S. A. R. R., and in 1873 removed to Weimar, in Colorado County, Texas, it then being the terminus of the railroad. In 1873 he built the first business house in Weimar, and for twelve years was a partner with T. A. Hill, under the firm name of Hill & Halloway, engaged in wholesale and retail groceries, commission, and forwarding business in connection with banking. In 1885 the firm of Hill & Holloway was dissolved by mutual consent, and J. J. Holloway, with his son, J. B. Holloway, as cashier, opened a private bank and general grocery business. In 1893 J. J. Holloway retired from the banking business and turned over the grocery business to his son, J. B. Holloway, and son-in-law, S. P. Smith, who married his eldest daughter, C. A. Holloway, and they are now engaged in the wholesale and retail grocery business. Many cities of larger pretensions than Weimar might be proud of their trade, which amounts to from $60,000 to $75,000 per annum. The style of their firm is Holloway & Smith. Mr. Holloway has, by his wife, six children, four boys and two girls, all living and in fine health. They have three grandchildren, two by his son and one by his daughter, Mrs. C. A. Smith. His mother, Mary A. Shaver, at the ripe age of seventy-five years is still living at this place, surrounded by her children and grandchildren, and bids fair to be with them for many years yet. The subject of this sketch having been for nearly twenty-five years in business, and having had some hard times to contend with, can say truthfully that he has never paid a debt with less than 100 cents to the dollar. He has been very successful as a business man, and says his success he attributes to energy, perseverance and close attention to business. Coupled with courtesy, his manner is distinguished by kindness, charity, and a kind regard and respect for his fellow man. Mr. Holloway has always been in the lead in all enterprises calculated to build up a town and forward the happiness and prosperity of the people. Though he will soon be fifty-seven years old he can tell a joke and enjoy a laugh with the boys as if he was himself a youngster of eighteen years. May he live long and prosper.

WILLIAM J. GLASS. This gentleman is a prominent citizen of De Witt County, Texas, and one whose constancy to the business in hand, and whose thrift, has added so greatly to the value of the agricultural regions of the section. Everything about his large estate, which comprises 1,400 acres, indicates that he is an agriculturist of advanced ideas and progressive principles, and his farm is one of the most productive and best kept in the community. He has 300 acres in a fine state of cultivation, and devotes a considerable portion of the rest to the raising of good graded stock. He has also given considerable land to his children. He was born in the Keystone State, February 7, 1818, to John and Mary (Johnson) Glass, who were born in Maryland and Pennsylvania, respectively, the former of whom died in 1850, and the latter in 1823. The paternal grandfather was a native of the Emerald Isle, while the maternal ancestors were of English descent. William J. Glass was reared in the State of his birth, and was educated at Washington College, Washington County, Pennsylvania, from which institution he graduated in 1846, and in this class also graduated James G. Blaine, of Maine. He began life as a school teacher in his native State, but in 1848 came to Texas, arriving at Galveston in the fall of that year, on election day, and voted for Henry Clay. In 1850 he became President of the College of Seguin; a position he filled with distinguished ability for six years, winning golden opinions as an educator and disciplinarian. The attendance greatly increased under his rule, and it was acknowledged by all that the institution was more prosperous under his management than it had ever been before. On account of failing health he was compelled to give up this occupation for some time, and came to Concrete, and here was occupied in "teaching the young idea" until the opening of the Civil War, and built up an excellent school at this place. At the end of that time he began raising stock on his present estate, which is one of the finest and most valuable in the county, and is situated about four miles east of Hochheim. The land is slightly rolling prairie, the soil is rich and productive, and all is susceptible of cultivation. In 1850 Mr. Glass led to the altar Miss Fidelia Stevens, a native of Ohio, and a daughter of Obediah Stevens, who came to the Lone Star State about 1849, and by her is the father of eight living children: Glendora, wife of John Hankins, resides at Kerrville; John A. is married and is a stockman of Brown County, Texas; William J., Jr., is a minister of the Methodist Episcopal Church, is married and resides in Coke County; Mary F. is the wife of Dr. Davis of Mitchell County; M. H. is married and resides near his parents; Barney graduated from the Medical Department of Jefferson College, Philadelphia in 1885, and later from a New York institution and became a successful practitioner of Cuero, where he died in 1890, leaving a widow; Kate is the wife of J. B. North; Edward, and Maggie, live at home. Mr. Glass is a member of the A. F. & A. M., is a man of worthy principles, is a useful citizen and very highly respected.

COL. SAM STONE. From the earliest ages agricultural pursuits have received attention, and it is not to be wondered at that it has become the art that it is at the present time. Among those who have become well known in their calling stands the name of Col. Sam Stone, whose fine farm in ·Washington County, Texas, which he owned until 1882, is one of the best in the section. Colonel Stone is a native Virginian, born in Mecklenburg County November 12, 1831, and his parents, Samuel and P. F. (Bridgeforth) Stone, were natives of the same State, where their ancestors were among the first settlers. The paternal grandfather fought in the War for Independence. Both families were large slave owners and wealthy and influential people. The father of our subject passed his entire life in Virginia, dying there in 1852. His children, seven in number, were named as follows: William, Fortunatus, Abner, Alexander, came to Texas in 1852 and died here in 1857; Sam (our subject), J. L., a physician of Roanoke, Va., and Martha, wife of Charles May. Col. Sam Stone went to Mississippi in his twentieth year, and two years later to Texas, settling in Washington County. He brought with him three negroes and immediately began farming, and when the war closed he lost about twenty slaves. He purchased his first land in 1859 and immediately began improving. In the year 1862 he joined Company C, Twentieth Texas Infantry, but later was discharged on account of ill health. He was on the invalid list for two years, and at the close of the war his financial condition was anything but good, his health was still poor and the outlook was rather dreary. Yet he went to work, and by his untiring energy and perseverance soon tided himself safely over the shoals and into the clear water beyond. In 1872 he moved from near the town of Washington, Washington County, to near Brenham, in same county, where he followed farming and stock-raising until 1882, and then moved to this section. Here he has engaged in the stock business for a time, but for the last three years he has speculated in land. At this he has met with a fair degree of success, and is classed among the successful business men of the community. At the time Colonel Stone settled in Washington County there were but few inhabitants, and most of them foreigners. Vast herds of horses and cattle covered the prairies, and an occasional Indian was to be seen. Land was very cheap. The colonel selected his wife in the person of Miss Bettie V. Lockett, a native of Virginia, and daughter of Steven and Bettie (Vaughan) Lockett, also of that State. Mr. Lockett and family came to Texas in December, 1854, and settled in Washington County, where he followed farming. He died in 1855. He and his wife reared a family of eight children, five of whom survive: H. E., John M., C. C., Katie and Bettie V. Colonel Stone has never sought office, but lately he has taken a decided interest in the race for Governor, having been an active Clark man in 1892. He was also deeply interested in the Congressional race in 1894, and was an earnest worker for the Democratic party. His marriage has resulted in the birth of four children, as follows: Steven L., stockman of this county; J. A., of Wallace, this county, is also in the stock business; Thomas W., of this place, and Robert A., at home. Mrs. Stone is a member of the Missionary Baptist Church.

JAMES HENRY GARY. The calling of the agriculturist is one of the most important to which a man can devote his attention, and is also, without doubt, one of the most honorable. It has been made the theme of story and song for ages, and about it has been woven a veil of romance that will remain as long as time endures. One of the noble followers of this calling is James Henry Gary, who was born in Perry County, Ala., in 1836, a son of William and Jane (Ferguson) Gary, the former of whom was born in South Carolina, and removed when a young man to Alabama, from which State he went to Noxubee County, Miss., where he became quite an extensive land owner. He next took up his residence in Choctaw County, Miss., where he also owned a considerable extent of land, and there he was called to that "bourne whence no traveler returns" in January, 1863. His wife was born in South Carolina also, and died in Choctaw County, Miss., in 1860. The boyhood days of James Henry Gary were mainly passed in Noxubee County, where his home continued to be until he was about twenty-one years of age. Later he emigrated to Texas, and when the war opened enlisted from that State in Company C, Capt. Alexander Brown's regiment, and was in the coast and border service of Texas. After hostilities had ceased he returned to Wharton County, and after farming there for some years returned to Hays County in 1868, and in 1880 bought the property on which he now resides in Guadalupe County, which consists of about 5,000 acres in this and Guadalupe County; 1,500 are under cultivation and are capable of producing one-half bale of cotton or twenty-five bushels of corn to the acre. He is paying some attention to the raising of horses and mules, but the most of his attention is devoted to other branches of his calling. He has held a number of minor official positions, such as School Trustee, etc., and in every instance discharged his duties with marked ability and faithfulness. In 1865 he led to the altar Miss Mollie Roberts, a daughter of Isaac and Barbara Roberts, both of whom where born in Georgia, but from that State removed to Florida and later to Texas. Mrs. Gary was born in Florida, and was reared there on her father's plantation in Bee County, where her mother died July 17, 1890, but her father's death occurred at her home in Guadalupe County, Texas, April 20, 1894. To the marriage of Mr. and Mrs. Gary ten children have been given: Charles F., William I., James W., John H., Mary E., Emma G., Barbara A., Osceola, Martha J. and Arthur E.

JAMES D. MONTGOMERY. A man's life-work is the measure of his success, and he is truly the most successful man who, turning his powers into the channel of an honorable purpose, accomplishes the object of his endeavor. It seems to have been the ambition of James D. Montgomery to make the best use of his native and acquired powers, and as a lawyer, politician and citizen he has been a success, and the friends whom he has gathered about him are legion. He is a product of Dardanelle, Ark., where he was born in 1850, the fourth of a family of seven born to James R. and Jerusha (Mason) Montgomery, who were born in Mississippi and Indiana respectively. The paternal grandfather died in Mississippi, when James R. was an infant, and the maternal grandfather, D. D. Mason, was a native of Indiana, removed to Arkansas at an early day, and until his death resided in Yell County. James R. Montgomery was reared by Gen. William Montgomery, of Mississippi and Arkansas, with whom he moved to Arkansas about 1820. He came to Texas in 1835 with his brother-in-law and three sisters, and in the troubles of 1836 his brother-in-law was killed, he and his sisters returning to Arkansas. He was married in 1840 to Miss Mason, and for a time was engaged in merchandising at Gaines' Landing, Ark., where he also conducted a wood yard. In the spring of 1851 he returned to Texas, and was a resident of Grimes County until 1857, when he went to what is now Waller County, and erected the first house in Hempstead. There he lived until his death in 1867. He erected the Old Planters' Exchange Hotel, which he conducted for a time, but during the progress of the great Civil War, was engaged in farming and stock-raising. His wife was born in 1822, is still living and makes her home with her son, the subject of this sketch. James D. Montgomery received his education in the common schools of Texas, and at the early age of eighteen was elected Deputy Sheriff of Waller (then Austin) County, a position he held a long time. In the city of Hempstead he held all the offices of the city, with the exception of Treasurer, and there made his home until March 10, 1890, when he came to Yoakum and started in the real estate business and insurance. He was soon elected Justice of the Peace, in 1892 was elected Mayor of the town, and in 1894 was re-elected. In 1877 he was admitted to the bar, but did not actively engage in the practice of his profession until after he came to Yoakum. He is a well posted man in his profession, as well as on the current topics of the day, and has already made himself an invaluable citizen of Lavaca County. Socially he is a member of Yoakum Lodge No. 348 of the I. O. O. F., and is now District Deputy Grand Master and District Deputy Grand Patriarch of the Grand Encampment. He has held all the offices in the K. of H., is Grand Guide in the Grand Lodge of the K. & L. of H., being a member of Watson Lodge No. 100 at Hempstead, and is Sovereign Commander of Yoakum Lodge of the Woodmen of the World. He has always been active in politics and has been a delegate to the last three Democratic State conventions of Texas. In 1877 he led to the altar Miss Lizzie Hooper of Texas, a native of Corpus Christi, and daughter of Thomas E. Hooper, an early settler of the section, and for a long time District Clerk of Nueces County, and to them six children were given: James R., Eula, Cleveland, Mary E., Alexander Henry, and Adlai. Mrs. Montgomery is a member of the Episcopal Church.

MAJOR JOHN S. SHROPSHIRE. Although he whose name heads this sketch has long since passed to that bourne whence no traveler returns, he still lives in the hearts of the many who knew and loved him in life. A native Kentuckian, he came to Texas prior to the opening of the late Civil War, and located in Colorado County, where he at once entered upon the practice of law, for which he had a decided taste, and in which he was remarkably successful. He was a man of more than ordinary talent, was finely educated, and had not death closed his career at an untimely age, would without doubt have made a name for himself in the profession. Being an enthusiastic Southerner, he joined the Confederate forces at the opening of the Civil War, became a member of Sibley's Brigade, Green's Regiment, and was killed in the battle at Glorietta, in New Mexico, in 1862, at which time he was Major of his regiment, and had the name of being a fearless and intrepid soldier. After his death his widow married Judge W. S. Delany, whose sketch appears in another part of this volume. The son of Major John and Mrs. Shropshire, C. T. Shropshire, was born in Colorado County, Texas, in 1861, grew up here and while growing up he obtained a good education in the schools of Columbus. When but a lad he commenced farming in this county, at the same time engaged in the stock business, and to the latter occupation his attention has been devoted almost exclusively for the last eleven years, and he is regarded as one of the most extensive stockmen of this section. His judgment is excellent, and as he is of an energetic and ambitious disposition, his operations have prospered. Mr. Shropshire had the exclusive management of Judge Delany's ranch in Wharton County for a number of years, and it was his home, but recently he returned to Columbus, where he is at present. He was married on the 29th of November, 1893, to Miss Nellie Hahn, of this place, a daughter of Christian Hahn, and they have a comfortable and pleasant home, where they dispense a generous, yet by no means ostentatious, hospitality to their many friends. Mr. Shropshire is a Democrat politically, and socially belongs to the Knights of Pythias.

DR. ISAAC EDGAR CLARK. The profession of the physician and surgeon is one that has drawn to it at all periods of its history the brightest and most upright of men, and prominent in this respect is Dr. Isaac Edgar Clark, whose cheerful confidence in the sick room is often as potent as his medicines, and he is at all times a student in his profession, ever grasping after new truths in science. He keeps himself thoroughly posted in his profession, his diagnoses being almost instantaneous and very seldom incorrect. He was born December 23, 1860, in Polk County, Texas, and of the five children born to his parents, Harvey S. and Cleo (Robertson) Clark, he is third in order of birth. The parents were natives of Tennessee, and the father was a physician also, a graduate of Jefferson Medical College of Pennsylvania, of the class of 1854. Immediately after graduating the elder Clark came to Texas and settled in Polk County, where he resided until 1863. During the war he served as Surgeon of a Confederate regiment, principally on the Rio Grande. In 1863 he moved to Gonzales County and located about seven or eight miles from Gonzales, purchasing a large plantation in Peach Creek Bottoms, and becoming the owner of a large number of negroes. On this place he resided until 1866, when he removed to Lavaca County, near Hallettsville, and there he has since been engaged quite extensively in farming and stock-raising. He introduced the first thoroughbred and standard bred horses in the county, and is the owner of one of the finest stock farms in this section of the State. His first wife died in 1875. They were the parents of the following children: Willie M., became the wife of W. E. Meyers; Lula, deceased; I. E., our subject; Cally F., and Marietta, wife of M. H. Nennel. In 1876 Dr. Clark was married to Miss Mollie Edds. Dr. I. E. Clark received his education in Covington, Tenn., and subsequently began the study of medicine under his father. When eighteen years of age he attended Jefferson Medical College, and graduated from that well-known institution when twenty-one years old, receiving honorary mention in materia medica. This was twenty-eight years after his father graduated from the same school. Our subject located at Moravia, Lavaca County, Texas, and almost immediately entered upon a large and successful practice. Both as a physician and surgeon he takes a prominent place, and is well known in this and adjoining counties. In 1887 he located in Schulenburg, and here he has since remained, engaged in the active practice of his profession, principally with Bohemians and Germans. In 1888 the doctor purchased 200 acres of land situated on Navidad River. This is known as the Bermuda Valley Stock Farm, one hundred acres of which is Bermuda grasses, and is situated only one-half mile west of Schulenburg, where is located the Schulenburg Live Stock and Fair Association, of which Dr. Clark is the organizer and one of the directors. In 1889 the doctor introduced his first thoroughbred horses, and since then he has placed on his farm many standard bred horses and mares. He has some fine animals. One, a two-year-old, makes its quarter of a mile in thirty-five seconds, and another, a yearling, makes that distance in forty seconds. They are of the "Lexington," "Getaways," "Sam Harpers," "Keen Richards" (standard bred),

"Wilks Sidney" and Almont Jr. Semi-annually a fair is held on the doctor's grounds, and animals from this and adjoining counties are exhibited. The doctor has won several premiums. In 1894 five races were run on these tracks, and our subject won three of them. Dr. Clark was married in 1888 to Miss Ella Walters, a native of this county, and the daughter of Robert and Adolphine (Welhansen) Walters, and niece of Theodore Walters (see sketch). Mr. and Mrs. Clark have two children: Cleo A. and Harvey R. Socially the doctor is a member of the I. O. O. F., Western Star Lodge No. 174. He is also a member of the A. F. & A. M., A. O. U. W., K. of H., all of this town. In his political views the doctor is a Democrat, and is deeply interested in political matters, working for the interests of his party.

CAPT. ROBERT THOMAS NIXON. In the capacity of farmer, stock-raiser and public ginner, Capt. R. T. Nixon has met with a good degree of success, and this success is in a great measure owing to his own persistent efforts and the exercise of sound judgment for which he has always been noted. He owes his nativity to Ashborough, Randolph County, N. C., where he was born on the 13th day of April, 1827, the eldest of eight children born to Zachariah and Sarah (Thomas) Nixon, both of whom were natives of the Old North State, the former being of Scotch and the latter of English extraction. Zachariah Nixon was engaged in farming and merchandising all his life, but met with reverses in business during the latter part of his career, and his son, Capt. Robert Thomas Nixon, who had emigrated to Texas and established a humble home, wrote for him to come and make his home with him, but while on board ship on his way thither, was taken sick and died, in 1855. His wife was a very estimable lady. On account of the serious financial reverses which his father experienced, the subject of this sketch received poor educational advantages, and after his marriage in his twenty-fifth year (1852) to Miss Laura Ann Wood, he emigrated to Texas in a two-horse wagon, and after a three months' overland journey reached the State of Texas with $300 in his pocket, but this was soon spent in settling doctor's bills. He soon located on his present plantation, and the little log cabin which he erected there is a part of his present residence. He bought his land on time, at two dollars per acre, sold his watch and one mule, and with this and the product of one year's work paid for 400 acres. He now controls 14,000 acres of fine arable and pasture land, over whose broad acres roam about 1,000 head of cattle; good graded Jerseys and Durhams, and 300 head of horses and mules. Fifteen hundred acres are under cultivation, and will average one-half bale of cotton or twenty-five bushels of corn to the acre. When the Civil War opened in 1861, he organized a company and served in the Home Guards as Captain for three years. By his first wife he became the father of nine children: James W., John P., Stephen D., Margaret, wife of W. B. Stevens; Elmyra, wife of Dr. N. Champion; Viola, wife of Garret Wilson; Robert Lee, Sam Houston and Alexander Stevens. The mother of these children died in 1872, and one year later Mr. Nixon married Miss Fannie Andrews, a native of North Carolina, and daughter of Eleazer and Mary (Hicks) Andrews, also of the Old North State. The father died in the State of his birth during the war, and the mother in Texas. To this last union six children have been given: Beulah, Corinna, Myrtle, Alta, Patrick Ireland and Zebulon Vance. He is a Free Mason of Belmont Lodge, is a Democrat politically, and for years he has successfully filled the office of County Commissioner. He has been a markedly successful man in everything that he has undertaken, and is strictly self-made. He was at one time a candidate for the State Legislature, and only missed being elected by seventeen votes. When a boy he worked for eight dollars per month, and with his earnings supported himself, his brothers and his sisters, for which he deserves much credit.

CHARLES F. WOODS. To omit the name of Mr. Charles F. Woods from this volume would be to leave out one of the prominent and successful farmers and stock-raisers of this section, who has not only made himself thoroughly identified with the farming and stock-raising interests here, but by his pleasant and genial manner has won a host of warm friends. His father, John Woods, a native of Tennessee, and his mother, Elizabeth (Foley) Woods, a native of Alabama, came to Texas in 1853 and settled in Lavaca County, where the father followed farming until his death in 1863. His wife survived him until 1875. They had a family of twelve children, eight of whom lived to mature years: Washington, Ann, Fremont, Willie, Louisa, Maggie, James, Arthur, Mary, wife of Buck Harris; John, is a banker of Del Rio; Octavio, wife of Frank Farley, and C. F., all now deceased but the four last mentioned. Washington Foley, our subject's maternal grandfather, was one of the pioneers of Texas before it became a republic, and experienced much trouble with the Indians, being often attacked by them. He reared seven sons and two daughters, and these children settled in Lavaca County early in the settlement of the same. One of his sons, Arthur, was killed in Lavaca County. He was out scouting for Indians when he was attacked by a band, and in trying to make his escape his horse sank in a quagmire. He dismounted and sought the timber, but the Indians surrounded him, and he saw his chances for escape were cut off. The Indians promised him protection if he would surrender, but no sooner had he given up his gun than they tied his hands and feet and proceeded to flay the bottom of his feet and torture him in a dozen different ways, until death put a stop to their fiendish doings. Another son, Grimes, was killed in one of the numerous Indian and Mexican skirmishes in an early day. The Foley family at one time owned more slaves than any other family in the Republic and several hundred of these were set free at the close of the war. Mr. Foley's sons-in-law were also large slave owners and planters. None of the older members of this family cared to hold office. On the other side, John Woods, banker, and brother of our subject, represented his section of the State in the House and Senate of the Legislature, but he is the only member of the family with any political aspirations. Charles W. Woods received his scholastic training in Lavaca County, and for a short time attended school at Concrete, DeWitt County. He grew to manhood on the farm, and early learned the arduous duties of the same, and since growing up he has given this occupation his undivided attention. He gives much of his time to the stock business, both raising and buying, and handles annually from 700 to 1,000 head of cattle. In the year 1875 he married Miss Belle Jones, of this State, daughter of William and Emma (Crain) Jones. Mr. Jones has held several positions in the county, serving as Sheriff of Val Verde County, Texas, where he is now engaged in stock-raising in addition to the duties of his office. Mr. and Mrs. Woods have no children of their own, but they are educating his brother Arthur's children, the latter's wife, now deceased, being a sister of our subject's wife. These children, three in number, are named as follows: Hix, Daisy and

Hattie. The two last named are in the Galveston schools, and during the coming year Hix will attend school at Georgetown, Texas. Both Mr. and Mrs. Woods are members of the Methodist Episcopal Church South, and Mr. Woods is a member of the I. O. O. F., Flatonia Lodge No. 336. Mr. Woods is one of the most progressive and pushing young men in the county. He gives his hearty support to all worthy enterprises, and is well liked in his section.

JOE R. LANE. Prominent among the successful business men of Flatonia, Texas, stands the name of Joe R. Lane, who is a member of the firm of Armin & Lane, extensive merchants of this place. Mr. Lane is a native of this county, born in 1859, and the son of Rev. C. J. and E. E. (Crockett) Lane, natives of Alabama. C. J. Lane came to the Lone Star State in 1851 or '52 and settled in Fayette County. In connection with his ministerial duties he also carried on farming, and resided on his estate until 1874, when he moved to Flatonia. Soon after coming here he had charge of the Pine Springs Circuit, and after that he filled most of the churches in the different circuits. He served for two years as Presiding Elder of Austin District, and soon after, in 1874, embarked in merchandising in Flatonia in company with J. M. Harrison, under the firm name of Harrison & Lane, in a general supply trade. Later he sold his interest to Mr. Harrison; and then engaged in business under the firm name of C. J. Lane & Co., continuing with the same until his death in 1881, when sixty-three years old. He had ministered to the spiritual wants of his fellow-man for thirty years and over. Mr. Lane was twice married, his first wife being Miss Sallie Mosley, and by that union one son was born, H. A., of Kansas. By his last marriage he became the father of nine children: Jonathan, a prominent attorney of La Grange, and at one time State Senator from this county; C. E., attorney at La Grange; Sallie, now Mrs. C. M. Shipman, of Plank, Texas; Mariah P., now Mrs. A. S. Mann, of La Grange; T. W., a La Grange attorney; E. E. (deceased), was the wife of W. M. Lawley; Amelia, and W. G. Joe R. Lane, the second in order of birth of these children, was educated for the most part in this county, in the common schools, and for a short time in his youth was in the store of Vaughan & Bunting, in Flatonia. When twenty years of age he started out to carve his own way in life, and has worked for this and other firms in this village up to the present time. In 1889 the firm of Armin & Lane was established, and our subject became general manager of the dry goods department of the business. This firm does an annual business of about $100,000, and carries everything to be found in a first-class village store. Mr. Lane is agent for several fire insurance companies throughout this section, and is a wideawake, pushing, enterprising business man. He is passive in political matters, although he takes a deep interest in the welfare of his political friends. He is a member of the K. of P., Flatonia Lodge No. 208, K. of H., Flatonia, of which he is an officer, and he is also an active member of the former lodge. He is one of the most progressive young men in the county and deserves the success that has fallen to his lot.

HENRY HILLMANN. There is no more important business in which a man can engage in the South than that of cotton ginning, for that is a product universally raised, and for shipment it is a prime necessity that it should be properly prepared for the market. He has been engaged in the business of cotton ginning in Yoakum since 1893, and is one of the prominent and well known men of the place, notwithstanding his brief residence here. He was born in Fayette County, Texas, in 1853, a son of Charles and Dora (Myer) Hillmann, who were native Germans, but came to this country in their youth, their parents locating in the Lone Star State. Charles Hillmann was a tiller of the soil and died in 1872, his wife's death occurring a few years before. Henry was brought up on his father's farm, and such education as he has, which is sufficient to fit him for the practical duties of life, has been learned in the hard school of experience. He also learned the details of ginning, at Bluff, Fayette County, and was there in business until 1893, when he sold out and came to Yoakum, and here has since been successfully engaged in business. He is also the proprietor of a planing mill, and is prepared to manufacture all kinds of tanks and all kinds of woodwork on short notice. Mr. Hillmann is a man of good business qualifications, is public spirited and enterprising and his genial manners have won him numerous personal friends. He was married in 1877 to Miss Emma Sauer, a native of Texas, and to their union four children have been given: Charley, Ida, Ella and Dora. Mr. Hillman has in his possession a madstone, which at one time belonged to Dr. Evens, of Flatonia, and was used by him twenty years ago. After the death of the doctor it came into the possession of his son-in-law, Dr. Allen, and in 1893 Mr. Hillmann purchased it of the doctor, having contracted for it years before. Dr. Evens used the stone in his practice for many years, and worked many cures from the bites of mad dogs and snakes. Mr. Hillmann has used it on ten people who have been bitten by mad dogs, and in every case worked an immediate cure, also on several who had been bitten by snakes. This is without doubt a valuable stone, and is the only one in the entire county. It is one of the largest ever found, and weighs about one pound. It is about three inches in diameter, is very nicely marked in a peculiar way, and shows what must have been wrinkles in the stomach of the animal in which it was found.

JUSTUS S. DAVIDSON, M. D. In practicing the calling of medicine, Dr. J. S. Davidson has not only shown that he is well posted in his profession, but that he can practically apply his knowledge, and as a very natural consequence he has already won a large practice. He has met with a degree of success flattering in the extreme, and, being patriotic, progressive and public spirited, he is all that could be desired as a citizen. He was born March 23, 1861, in Bell County, Texas, the son of Wilson T. and Caroline, or Callie, (Smith) Davidson. Wilson Davidson is now a resident of Belton, Texas, but at one time was one of the leading farmers of Bell County, as well as one of its pioneers, and his father was killed there by the Indians as early as 1832. This family was one of the earliest in that county. When a boy, Justus S. Davidson attended the schools of Belton and the old College at Salado, thus receiving a good, practical education as a foundation for his medical studies. When in his twenty-fifth year, he entered the medical school at Louisville, and was graduated from the same in the class of 1888. Locating at San Felipe the same year, he has since been practicing in partnership with his father-in-law, Dr. G. T. Ross, a prominent physician of this county. (See sketch.) Our subject was married in 1891 to Miss Mary F. Ross, and they have one bright little child, Ross Wilson Davidson. The doctor and wife are members of the Methodist Episcopal Church South, and the doctor takes a great deal of interest in politics and always votes with the Democratic party.

THOMAS STERNE. In recounting the forces that have combined to make Victoria County, Texas, what it is, more than a passing reference must be made to the life and labors of Thomas Sterne, of whom it may be truthfully said that no one has done more to lay the foundations of the county's prosperity deep, and to build upon them surely and well. He is a product of Bedford, Pa., born February, 1817, and was the son of Thomas and Jane (Guthrie) Sterne, the father a native of England, and the mother of Scotch descent, but born in Pennsylvania. The father was Sheriff of the county in which he lived in Pennsylvania for some time, also followed teaching, and there died in 1817, when our subject was but two weeks old. The mother received her final summons in Pennsylvania in 1867. Owing to circumstances over which he had no control, our subject received but a limited education in youth, and when fourteen years of age he entered a printing office, serving as an apprentice for seven years, in " the art preservative of arts," in the office of the *Bedford Gazette*, where, while learning a trade which might secure for him a living in the future, he stocked his mind with much and varied information. A bright young man attends a pretty good school when he works in a newspaper office at the case. This, we think, Mr. Sterne will admit is true. In 1840, young, in excellent health, and willing to work for the fruition of his hopes, Mr. Sterne removed to the city of Louisville, Ky., where he worked as a journeyman printer on the *Louisville City Gazette*. Previous to that he was in the Buckeye State for some time. From Kentucky he went to Arkansas in 1842, and established the *Arkansas Intelligencer* in the town of Van Buren, this being the first paper of the town. He was near Indian Territory, and his paper had a large circulation among the Indians. In 1845 he made a trip on horseback throughout Texas, and was over most of the southwestern part of the State. He passed from San Antonio through the then desert to the Gulf, at Corpus Christi, and over much of the intervening country. Visiting Victoria he thought it the best place to launch a new enterprise, and soon had the press, cases, type, and other fixtures of his office moved to that city. There the first number of the *Texan Advocate* was issued, May 2, 1846, and it was the first paper published West of the Colorado River. Mr. Sterne published this paper until 1853, when, on account of failing health, he sold out and engaged in stock-raising. The paper is still published here. He bought the present place, three miles from Victoria, in 1859, and now has a very lovely home. Mr. Sterne is the owner of about 3,000 acres of good land, all capable of cultivation. He has about 200 acres under cultivation, and can raise thirty-five bushels of corn to the acre. Since 1860 he has only known one failure of crops in this section. He has graded stock, Durham, Holstein and Hereford cattle, and good blooded hogs. He has held a number of prominent positions in the county—County Commissioner, Alderman of Victoria, etc., and is prominently identified with every enterprise of note. In the year 1841 he was married to Miss Mary E. Jones, of Louisville, Ky., who accompanied him to Texas, and here died in 1853. His second marriage occurred in 1854, to Miss Araminta Cunningham, a daughter of Judge John A. Cunningham. To this union eight children were born, all living: Thomas J., resides in Victoria; May, became the wife of H. D. Sullivan, Sheriff of the county, and makes her home in Victoria; Ida, became the wife of F. E. Sibley, of Victoria; Wilson C., of Port Lavaca; Minnie, married Eugene Sibley, banker, of Victoria; Andrew

G., a lawyer, living in Rio Grande City, Texas; Sadie and Ford still living with the parents. In the year 1839 Mr. Sterne was made a Mason at Flemmingburg, Ky., and in 1846 he was made an Odd Fellow at Newport, Ky. He was one of the charter members of the first Masonic Lodge established in Southwest Texas, founded in 1846, Victoria Lodge No. 9, and from this lodge all the lodges of the surrounding counties were founded. Mr. Sterne commenced his apprenticeship in 1831, and is probably the oldest printer in the Lone Star State, and is enjoying the sunset of life surrounded by a loving family, and many warm personal friends. The members of this family hold membership in the Presbyterian Church.

JUDGE CHARLES RILEY. This prominent man and able Judge of Colorado County, Texas, was born in Princeton, Ky., July 14, 1849, and is a son of Philip Riley, who was born and reared in Madison County, Mississippi. The father, Prof. Phillip Riley, from his native county went to Princeton, Ky., and entered Cumberland College, and after graduating from this institution, he filled a professorship in his alma mater for some time, then went to Bethel College, Tennessee, where he remained for about six years. In 1856 he came to Texas and located at Columbus, and took charge of what was known as Columbus Female Academy, which school he conducted with marked ability up to the first year of the war, when he entered the Confederate service. For two years he was on detailed duty at Columbus, Texas, as clerk and bookkeeper in the Commissary Department, but after hostilities had ceased he again turned his attention to teaching, first in Colorado College and then in Columbus. Following this he became book-keeper for the firm of Young & Allen, and continued to fill this position up to the day of his death, in November, 1872, when about fifty-four or fifty-five years of age. He was married to Rose Frazier, who bore him six children and is still living. The immediate subject of this sketch is the eldest of the five now living. Lucy, wife of Robert Ennis, manager of the Aransas Pass Railroad, lives in San Antonio; Ida, wife of Robert Wolters, resides in Columbus, Texas; Edward E. is Secretary and Treasurer of the Keith & Perry Coal Company, of Kansas City, Mo.; Philip M. is in Jefferson, Texas, and is a Cumberland Presbyterian Minister, and Estelle, died in Columbus, the wife of George Atkinson. Judge Charles Riley received his education in the High School of Columbus and in Colorado College, and he also went to school a short time after the war had closed. He then entered the printing office of the *Columbus Times* and later of the *Colorado Citizen*, continuing thus occupied for four or five years, or until 1871, at which time he entered the office of the District Clerk, and after a time became Deputy District Clerk of the county. He continued as Deputy until February, 1874, when the Clerk resigned his office and Mr. Riley was appointed to his place, and continued thus to serve until the present State Constitution was adopted, when he made the race for the office, but was defeated by a small majority. Following this he was Deputy in the County Clerk's office for two years, and in November, 1878, was elected to the office of County Judge, and has held this position ever since, with the exception of the years 1891–92, being again elected to the office in 1892. He has worn the judicial ermine with dignity and ability, has shown the utmost fairness and intelligence in his decisions, and has proven a popular and very efficient officer. In May, 1872, he was married to Miss Sallie M. Grigsby, who was born in Wharton County, Texas, a daughter of William Grigsby,

John M. Fly, M. D.

who became a very extensive planter of that county. She died June 18, 1894, having become the mother of three sons and one daughter: Cora, who is a prominent and talented music teacher in Columbus, Texas; Marion E., Charles and Joseph. Judge Riley is a member of the I. O. O. F., Columbus Lodge No. 51; politically is a stanch Democrat, and in his religious views is a Methodist.

DR. MILTON J. BLIEM. The profession of medicine affords to the student of that science a never ending source of investigation and experiment. New remedies are constantly being discovered, steady progress is being made in surgery, and new diseases are presenting themselves under varying forms of civilization. This most important science bearing upon our happiness, comfort and welfare, is making great strides toward a comprehensive grasp of the whole subject of man, in relation to health and disease—the prevention and the cure of ills that flesh is heir to. In the noble army of workers in this great field the name of Dr. Milton J. Bliem takes a prominent place, and although young in years, he has already won an enviable reputation, being now one of the leading physicians of San Antonio, Texas. Dr. Bliem was born in Northampton County, Pennsylvania, December 18, 1860, and was the only surviving son born to Rev. J. C. and Selinda C. (Swartz) Bliem, both of whom are natives of that State and of German origin. The father inherited a taste for farming, his ancestors in the main being engaged in that peaceful pursuit, but during the war he was Collector of Internal Revenue, and in 1864, he became a minister of the Evangelical Association. Since that time he has been actively and constantly at work in church matters. He and wife are still living and reside on the old home place. Dr. Milton J. Bliem is the eighth generation of the Bliem family in America, his ancestors coming from Germany and settling in eastern Pennsylvania in the year 1735. He was educated at Lafayette College, Easton, Penn., graduating in 1882, as one of the seven honor men of his class. He also won three prizes for proficiency in various branches, and left that institution bearing with him the respect and esteem of his preceptors and fellow students. From there he went to Chicago and began the study of medicine at the Chicago Homeopathic Medical College, where he graduated in 1884, at the head of his class. He at once secured, by competitive examination, an appointment as Resident Surgeon in Cook County Hospital, that city, and held that position for eighteen months, after which he began practicing in that city. Later he was appointed to the Chair of Pathology in his alma mater, and soon after to the Chair of Physiology. He also served as surgeon for the County Hospital, and was building up a large practice and quite an enviable reputation when, on account of failing health of his wife, he came to San Antonio in 1889. Here he soon entered on a large practice, which has since been constantly increasing, and the best effort of his skill is being employed in alleviating the distress of humanity. In the year 1885 he was married to Miss Emma Louise Yost, a daughter of Rev. Wm. Yost, of Cleveland, Ohio, but of an old Pennsylvania family. Two children have been born to this union: Marion Louise and Howard Milton. This family holds membership in the Madison Square Presbyterian Church in which the doctor is an active worker, an elder, and a member of the board of trustees. He is Treasurer of the Y. M. C. A., has been President, and has also been President of the State Association. Aside from this he is President of the Society of Christian Endeavor, one of the charter members

26

of the San Antonio Scientific Society, and a member of the Illinois and Texas State Homeopathic Medical Association, of which he is President, and the American Institute of Homeopathy. He often contributes to the medical literature of his school, and, although he has been a member of the Chamber of Commerce, he is mainly active in the medical and religious lines of work.

WILLIAM L. BARNETT. In mentioning the prominent and successful farmers and stock-raisers of Gonzales County, Texas, it would be an oversight, indeed, were not mention made of William L. Barnett, whose fine farm and excellent buildings convince the observer that the owner is a man of progress and ambition. He came originally from Purdy, Tenn., where his birth occurred January 3, 1830; son of George W. Barnett, a physician and Eliza (Patton) Barnett, whose father lived to be ninety years old. The Pattons were a long lived family. Dr. George W. Barnett came to Burleson County, Texas, in 1833, where he stopped one year, and then moved to Washington County, where he bought a farm near Brenham, and practiced medicine. When what is known as the "run-away scrape" occurred, (occasioned by the advance of Gen. Santa Anna,) Dr. Barnett made an effort to join Gen. Sam. Houston's forces, but the battle of San Jacinto was fought just before he could reach him. However he was at the retaking of San Antonio and at the celebrated Grass fight. His heirs now hold the letter patent to 640 acres, in recognition of three days' service at the battle or seige of San Antonio. Dr. Barnett always took a prominent part in politics, and was a warm friend and supporter of Sam. Houston. He was a delegate to every Congress held under the Republic of Texas, and he was one of three commissioners appointed to select a site for the capital, making their choice in Austin. He moved to Gonzales County in 1846, and soon after was made County Judge of the same. Two of his sons came with him, but returning for the remainder of his family in 1847, he was ambushed and killed by Indians in 1848. An elder in the Cumberland Presbyterian Church he organized the first church of that denomination west of the Colorado River. William L. Barnett was but three years of age when his father came to Texas, and he was educated in Washington County, this State, under Hugh Wilson, a Presbyterian minister. After the death of the father he and his brother, James A., carried on the work their father had begun toward developing a new home in Gonzales County. In 1855 he led to the altar Miss Elizabeth, daughter of George H. and Celina Walker of Marshall County, Mississippi. She came out on a visit to a brother and met Mr. Barnett. Politically Mr. Walker was a Democrat, and in religion a Cumberland Presbyterian. Planting was his principal occupation in life. His people were Cumberland Presbyterians and her grandfather, Samuel King, was one of the five to organize the church on the Cumberland River in 1810. Her father died in 1877 and the mother in 1873, the latter just ten days after celebrating their golden wedding. In politics Mr. Barnett is a Democrat, and socially a Third Degree Mason, a member of Shuler Lodge No. 317. To his marriage were born four children, all living, Ella, George W., John G. and Robert Lee.

JUDGE WILLIAM S. DELANY. Generally age and experience are essentials to success in whatever branch of human endeavor a man may see fit to devote his life, and it is an indisputable fact that public men seldom rise to distinction suddenly. In the example before us we have a man who without any special fortuitous circumstances, rose by his own force of character, energy and good judgment, to the position of Judge of the Commission of Appeals of the State of Texas. He was born in Union County, Kentucky, September 18, 1825, to Henry F. Delany, who was a native of Virginia, and was taken to Kentucky by his parents, and after residing for some time at what became known as Delany's Ferry, they removed to Union County, and their spent the rest of their days. He was graduated at Lexington, Ky, and after practicing his profession for some time at Salem, Ky,, he went back to Morganfield and there died in 1831 at the age of forty-four years. He became a minister of the Cumberland Presbyterian Church, and was instrumental in establishing a college of that denomination in Princeton, Ky. He was a very prominent church worker, and the last years of his life were devoted to ministerial labors in Kentucky, Indiana and Illinois. Delany College, Indiana, was named in his honor. His wife was Miss Rhoda Prince, whose father came to Kentucky from Georgia, and for him the town of Princeton, Ky., was named. Mrs. Delany died in 1861, the mother of nine children, of whom the subject of this sketch was the eighth, all of whom were educated at Princeton, and from Cumberland College, located there. The subject of this sketch graduated in 1847, after which he was appointed Professor of Greek and Latin in his alma mater, continuing as such until 1853, when he went to Memphis, Tenn., where he remained until April, 1860, when he came to Texas and commenced the practice of law in Colorado County. He served for several years as District Attorney. He was afterward appointed a member of the Commission of Appeals, a position he held from 1881 to 1885 with Judge R. S. Walker and Judge A. T. Watts. In 1874 he had been elected to the State Legislature, and was Chairman on the Committee on Finance. In 1850 Miss Gabriella Shropshire, of Bourbon County, Kentucky, became his wife. She died in 1861, having become the mother of five children, all daughters, and all living. In 1863 Mrs. Carrie (Tait) Shropshire, widow of Major John T. Shropshire, who was killed at the battle of Glorietta, became his second wife. Her father was a wealthy Alabamian, and gave each of his eight children 100 slaves. To Judge Delany's second union two sons were given. Judge Delany owns large bodies of land in Wharton and other counties, and during all his active professional life he has given considerable attention to planting interests and stock-raising. The judge is a member of the Episcopal Church, is a Royal Arch Mason and was a member of the Grand Chapter in Kentucky. His life has been a useful one, and as a result he has many friends throughout the State.

JUDGE DON EGBERT ERASTUS BRAMAN. Nearly eighty years have passed over the head of the venerable man who is the subject of this sketch, leaving their impress in the whitening hair and lined features, but while the outward garments of the soul show the wear and tear of years, the man himself is richer and nobler and grander for the experience that each successive decade has brought him. He is an early settler of Matagorda County, Texas, Ex-County Judge of the same, and is now a resident of Victoria. His birth occurred September 21, 1814, at Norton, Bristol County, Massachusetts, and he is the son of Andrews and Nancy (Hawes) Braman. In tracing the genealogy of the family, we find that he is the grandson of Sylvanus and Sarah (Andrews) Braman, great-grandson of Sylvanus and Experience (Blanchard) Braman, great-great grandson of Daniel and Rachel (Campbell) Braman, and great-great-great grandson of Thomas Braman, who came from England about 1635 and settled in Northern Massachusetts. Andrew Braman, father of our subject, graduated from one of the New England colleges, and although he studied for the bar, did not practice. Instead, he followed agricultural pursuits, and subsequently moved to Providence, R. I., where his death occurred about 1833. The mother followed him to the grave about two years later. The ancestors on both sides were among the Pilgrims. Judge Braman was educated in Providence, R. I., and in 1833 went to Georgia, where he remained until 1835. He then went to what is now Eufallan, and participated in a raid against the Cherokee Indians. In 1836 he went to New Orleans, and the following year came to Texas with a lot of volunteers for the Texan army. Landing at Matagorda, he soon went out and joined the army at Camp Johnson, in Jackson County, and was in service twelve months. From there he went to Matagorda and became a custom officer for about a year. In 1847 he was appointed Clerk of the First Judicial District Court, and, studying law while he held that office, was admitted to the bar of that court in 1853. Afterwards he practiced his profession for years. For several years he was Mayor of Matagorda, and was appointed County Judge by Governor Pease. He was greatly opposed to the war, and wrote articles against it during the time. Judge Braman is the owner of large tracts of land in the county, thousands of acres of the most fertile portions, and to some extent has been engaged in stock-raising. On the 28th of April, 1841, he was married to Miss Mary Elizabeth, daughter of George Burkhart, a native of Philadelphia, who came to Texas in 1839. The following children were born to this union: Nancy, died in childhood; Erastus, died in manhood; George, died in 1852; Daniel Hawes, died in 1861; Alexander, educated and became a lawyer; William Cheever, resides in Matagorda, was educated at Andover and at home, studied law with his father, was admitted to the bar in 1877, and owns land in Matagorda County, and a large number of cattle; Mary Elizabeth, Nancy Hawes, Catherine Burkhart, died in 1892; Daniel Hawes and Julia. Daniel Hawes was educated at Victoria and New Orleans, studied medicine at Tulane University, New Orleans, and is now practicing in Victoria. Our subject is a member of the Catholic Church, but Mrs. Braman and most of the children hold membership in the Episcopal Church. Formerly Judge Braman had a large law practice, but he has now retired from the active duties of life, and makes his home partly in Victoria, where he has a handsome residence, and partly in Matagorda.

JAMES G. BLANKS. For many years the name of Mr. Blanks has been inseparably linked with the business history of De Witt County, Texas, whose annals bear testimony to the integrity of his character and the brilliancy of his intellect, and is the synonym of honesty, industry and business integrity. At the present time he is occupied in discharging the duties of President of the Yoakum Improvement Company, the Yoakum Oil Mill and Manufacturing Company, at Yoakum, Texas, and has thoroughly illustrated the fact that he is the "right man in the right place." He is a thorough Texan by birth and bringing up, his natal place and day being Lockhart, Caldwell County, September 15, 1862. His parents, John G. and Martha (Montgomery) Blanks were born in Kentucky and Missouri, respectively, but about 1857 the father located in the Lone Star State, and has since given the most of his time and attention to real estate and mercantile interests, proving himself an enterprising and progressive citizen. His father-in-law, John W. Montgomery, came from Pike County, Missouri, at an early day, and here followed the occupations of farming and stock-raising. James G. Blanks was educated in the Missouri State University, and began life for himself by becoming associated in business with his father at Lockhart, with whom he continued from June, 1882 to 1890. Since the last mentioned year he has been in business at Yoakum and assisted in completing the organization of the First National Bank, being soon promoted to the position of Cashier, which he filled two years. During this time he conceived the idea of starting a water-works, electric light company and an ice factory, and in his usual energetic manner he put these enterprises on foot, in 1892, by organizing the Blanks Ice, Water & Power Company, and erecting the present plant, which cost $42,000, the capital stock amounting to $50,000. Nothing but machinery of the most modern make is used, and the plant is a valuable one and a great boon to the citizens of the town. It was sold during the same year that it was organized to the Yoakum Improvement Company, and was consolidated under that name. Mr. Blanks first held the responsible position of President, and has so continued since it has been connected with the electric light plant, the entire cost of both amounting to $55,000. Mr. Blanks is also a director of the bank, and he is also connected with the oil mill, which will be put in operation during the fall of 1894. Mr. Blanks has been at the head of nearly every enterprise that has been started in the place, in fact, has proven himself an ideal public citizen, progressive, public spirited, law abiding, and, since locating in Yoakum, has been of inestimable value to the place, a fact which the citizens are not slow to recognize and acknowledge. Mr. Blanks is the owner of considerable individual town property, and is one of the well-to-do men of the place. He has the satisfaction of knowing that his possessions have been acquired through his own efforts, and that he does not owe any man a dollar. He was first married in 1883 to Miss Annie Hollingsworth, who died in 1884, and in 1886 he wedded Miss Mamie Jordan, of Lockhart, Texas, by whom he has one child—May. He and his wife are members of the Christian Church, and socially he is a member of the K. of P. and the I. O. O. F.

BENJAMIN WAYNE HUMPHREYS was born near Nashville, Tenn., in 1816. His parents moved to Madison County in 1825, near Jackson. His health and activity are perfect. Although his eyesight is impaired, he refuses surgical assistance. His father, Daniel Jones Humphreys, was born in North Carolina, as was his father, Capt. Benjamin Humphreys, who led his company through the Revolutionary War, and was in many battles with General Wayne's Division. He had camp fever at Valley Forge, which left his hearing badly damaged. His mother was born near Nashville, and was educated there. Her name was Margaret E. Seat. The Humphreys family was founded in this country by Humphrey Jones (with a handle to it), who left Wales on account of some political trouble in the time of Cromwell and the Charleses. For some reason he had his name reversed. The Southern branch has added the letter "s." His father, at seventeen years of age, went with his neighbor, Gen. Andrew Jackson, through the Creek and Florida wars. He was given the office of Ensign, and planted the flag on many Indian fortifications. He served as Sheriff of Williamson County, and Tobacco Inspector in his district. B. W. Humphreys got a fair education in English, but higher schools were out of his reach. He studied on without a teacher, and in 1840 entered the State University, junior class. He graduated 1842, A. B. The Master of Arts degree was tendered him by the faculty in 1845, He studied medicine with Dr. Thos. Newbern, took a course of lectures in Louisville in 1846, and entered practice with Dr. Newbern. In 1847 he entered Jefferson College and graduated next year. Four years practice on big plantations broke his health, and in 1853 he came to Texas and settled on a nice farm on the San Marcos. He was soon in a large practice. In 1869 he moved to Seguin for schools and succeeded well.

GEORGE HERDER. Of all the many men that Germany has given to the United States, and their name is legion, no one has proven a more substantial, law abiding and public spirited citizen than George Herder. He was born in Oldenburg in 1818, was educated in the land that gave him birth, but being of a pushing and ambitious disposition, he determined to woo the fickle goddess, Fortune, in the New World, and accordingly, in 1834, came to the United States on a sailing vessel, landing in the city of Galveston. He at once took up his residence in the vicinity of Frelsburg, but in 1858 moved to High Hill, Fayette County, where he continued to reside until 1884, when he moved to Shiner, Lavaca County, and died three years later at Schulenburg, while there on a visit. While living in his native land he was successfully engaged in tilling the soil, and after coming to this country he continued to follow this occupation for some time, then engaged in the mercantile business at High Hill, and during the few years he remained in the business he succeeded admirably. In course of time he led to the altar Miss Minna Wolters, who was born in the old country, and was called from life in Texas in 1878. Mr. Herder was a soldier in the Texas Rebellion, and was a participant in the famous battle of San Jacinto, and was later a participant in the Mexican War, but during his service was not out of the State. He was a man of more than ordinary business capacity, upright and honorable in every worthy particular, and numbered his friends by the score. To himself and wife twelve children were born, eight of whom are still living, and are residents of Fayette, Lavaca and Colorado counties. George Herder, the youngest of these children, was born in 1863, and spent his school days at High Hill. When a lad of sixteen he entered the general mercantile establishment of Russek, at Schulenburg, with whom he remained one year, following which he was with Heyer Bros. one year, and in 1882 commenced business for himself and on his own responsibility, but in a very humble manner. He commenced with a small general line of goods, but has increased his stock from time to time, as his means permitted and the demands of his patrons increased. He has built up a surprisingly large business by his energy, foresight and desire to please, and of those who have been in business as long as he has is one of but three merchants in that place who has not failed. He has handled 35,000 or 40,000 bales of cotton, and in this, as in his mercantile business, his trade has covered a wide territory. In 1885 he was united in marriage with Miss Mary Hefner, of Weimar, and they are worthy members of the Christian Church, while socially he is a member of the K. of P. and the A. O. U. W. Politically he, as well as his father before him, is a stanch Democrat, believing in no high tariff, nor in an unsound dollar.

BISHOP ALEXANDER GREGG (deceased.) Alexander Gregg, First Episcopal Bishop of Texas, was born in the Darlington District of South Carolina,

October 8, 1819, at Society Hill. He was a descendant of the famous High-land Clan, the McGregors, whose heroic deeds have been told in song and story. Not long after the time of Cromwell, a fragment of this clan moved from the North of Scotland to Londonderry, Ireland, whence the immigration to America took place. The name underwent a gradual and easy transforma-tion from McGregor to Gregg, and in 1752 the name under this last form first appeared on the Pedee River. From the brothers, John and Joseph, de-scended the large connection of the name. From Joseph came David, the father of our subject. The Greggs of that early day in America were men of force and enterprise, and became locally famous in the Indian wars, and in the War of the Revolution. Rev. B. A. Rogers knew Bishop Gregg long and closely, and from the memorial sermon delivered by him we gather the follow-ing facts, best told in his graceful and gracious words: "At the age of nineteen, the young Alexander, a stalwart youngster, straight as an arrow, without the taint of a single bad habit, and inheriting in a marked degree much of the mental, moral and physical structure peculiar to his Scotch an-cestors, graduated with first honors at South Carolina College, was soon after admitted to the bar, and commenced the study of law at Cheraw. As a lawyer his practice was not long, but said to have been successful. Up to the age of twenty-four years he seemed to have no special religious tendencies, but at that time, while upon a visit to relatives, his attention being unexpectedly and pointedly called to the claims of both religion and the church, he returned home, gave himself for some days to solitude, thought, prayer and study, and then announced his determination to renounce the profession of law and enter the ministry. This was in 1843, and the same year he was baptized and con-firmed, and at once became a candidate for holy orders. In 1846, at St. David's Church, Cheraw, he was ordained Deacon, and at St. Phillip's Church, Charleston, on the 10th of December, 1847, he was ordained to the priest-hood, both by Bishop Gadsden of South Carolina. During the convention of 1859, though he was personally unknown to any member of that body, upon the high recommendation of Bishops Elliott, of Georgia, and Davis of South Carolina, Mr. Gregg was put in nomination, and, upon the first ballot, every clerical vote but two was given to him, and he was unani-mously confirmed by that body. Yet he himself knew nothing of such an effort being in contemplation until after his election; and then, according to the Bishop of Tennessee, first learned from the lips of one who was sitting behind him in the convention of the Diocese of South Carolina, that was then in session, who whispered over his shoulder the news just received, that, to him, was so bewildering and so fateful. With those who knew him best, there was no question as to what he would do. It was not his first trial. Though his parish was the oldest field of legal labor, it was the seat of his early friendships, the home of his friends. His family was around him there, and always with him, and his heart was in Cheraw. Texas was far away, almost boundless, almost trackless; with little to offer but endless work, limitless fatigue, and constant sepa-ration from his wife and children. And he came, having been consecrated in Memorial Church, Richmond, during the session of the general conven-tion there in 1859. The election of a stranger, utterly unknown to any-body in the Diocese, had naturally given occasion to some little adverse comment, and it is not strange that his arrival should have been anticipated with some anxiety. But when he came, his very appearance set all hearts at rest. Of good size and fine form, erect, open-browed, clear-eyed, of manly and dignified bearing, speaking according to his own convictions, yet guarded in form and manner of expression; cool and collected, but decided and self-confident; claiming no infallibility, but tenacious of the right and dignity of his position, he was everywhere accepted at his true value, as every inch a man, every ounce a Bishop. Before the meeting of the Diocesan Convention in 1860, the Bishop, with his family had settled in Austin, and began his work by the publication of a pastoral letter in the newspapers, in which he invited correspondence with every member of the Church throughout the State. And in reply to the great number of answers received, he sent back letters filling each particular case, and all written with his own hand, and eventually he visited every place and nearly every family from which those letters had been received. And what he did then was but the beginning of a work that ended only with his life, and up to 1874, when the Diocese was divided, with no curtailment of limits either in territory or hardships; for, though railroads and stage lines had multiplied, so had country parishes, missions and families. So that still his visitations were made by every type of conveyance known to our frontier life, and a large proportion of the nights, as well as the days, of each year were spent upon the road. During his whole official life his visitations were not simply from parish to parish, but literally from house to house. He was not content to know the leading persons of the church, but he knew them all, could call them by name, and was familiar with their personal affairs, hopes and anxieties. In every family his coming was a pleasure; the father honored, the mother revered and the children loved him. Even his Sunday School catechisms were so seasoned with something unexpected and pleasurable that the children looked forward to them from year to year as times of especial enjoyment Of the outcome of his long labors here, I can do no better than to compare the beginning with the end. At the convention of 1860 (his first), the statistical showing of the Diocese was: Number of communicants, so gathered as to be capable of tabulation, 456; clergy, 14. At that convention, in his first address, the Bishop showed a clear comprehension of the work he had undertaken. He adverted to the salient points of duty, put himself into the van, sounded a bugle call for advance, and unfalteringly led the missionary work for the thirty-three years. When, at last, literally worn out in the work, he fell by the way, and from the middle of his last visitation, he went home to die, he could count within the limits of his old Diocese more than sixty clergymen. In preaching Christ he never forget his Church, and his giant shoulders carried such weight as no other man in the American Church ever bore. But there was no shrinking or turning back, no repinings, no regrets for the choice that had placed them upon him. His heart was larger than his load, and he loved every ounce of its weight, and rejoiced in every effort that it demanded. At his home in Austin, surrounded by his children, he passed away July 10, 1893." Bishop Gregg married Miss Charlotte Wilson, daughter of Oliver H. and Sarah (Wilson) Kollock. Oliver H. Kollock was a native of Massachusetts, who in his young manhood emigrated to South Carolina. In early life he was a lawyer, but later a farmer. His ancestors came over on the Mayflower. Of ten children born to Bishop Gregg, only five survive him: David, a prosperous merchant of Luling; Wilson, a lawyer of Fort Worth; two widowed daughters, Mrs. Wilmerding and Mrs. Cochran, residing at Sewanee; and Oliver Hawes Gregg, a farmer and stock-raiser of Guadalupe County, who was born in Cheraw, S. C., September 12, 1845, where his boyhood was spent and his education received. At the age of seventeen (after removal to Texas a short time prior to the breaking out of Civil War) the last named entered the Confederate service as First Lieutenant, with a recruiting commission. He was soon transferred to Baylor's Texas Rangers, and saw duty on the frontier. He was in the last battle of the war, at Brownsville. At that time he was serving in Carrington's Company, Ford's Regiment. After the war he clerked in San Antonio some time, and in December, 1866, he was placed in charge of a branch house at Prairie Lea, established by his San Antonio house. In 1871 he bought the place upon which he now resides, and, with an interval of seven years, during which he was associated with his brother, David, in the mercantile business in Luling, has led the life of a planter. He married November 7, 1867, Miss Margaret Amelia Rector, a daughter of Pendleton Rector, a native of Alabama, who emigrated to Brazoria County in 1831, and was conspicuous in all the Mexican and Indian troubles during the Confederation and the Republic. He was at the battle of San Jacinto, and served as courier to Sam Houston, when the duties of the position were equivalent to running the gauntlet. He was the owner of a letter patent from his Government for services rendered, and was a man of great bravery. He died in Guadalupe County in March, 1888. Two gentle and cultured daughters and a promising son grace the hospitable home of Mr. and Mrs. O. H. Gregg: Mary E., Charlotte W. and Alexander Pendleton.

ROBERT WILLIAM PEIRCE. In tilling the soil and in raising stock he whose name heads this sketch has shown excellent judgment, and being also persevering and progressive he has made the most of every opportunity that has presented itself, which tended to benefit him financially, the result being that he has accumulated a good property. He was born in Tuscaloosa, Ala., January 25, 1827, the fourth of nine children born to John King and Sarah Oldham (Finch) Peirce, the former of whom was born in Cork, Ireland. He came to America in his young manhood. In 1821 he settled in Tuscaloosa, Ala., where he conducted an oyster saloon and restaurant. After accumulating sufficient funds he opened a confectionery and notion store. In 1838 he removed to Columbus, Miss., where he continued the same business until reverses in fortune overtook him. His friends elected him Magistrate, and he obtained prominence in this capacity. He was a member of the I. O. O. F. and of the A. F. & A. M. In the former order he was a member of the Encampment. He was very active and prominent in Masonic circles. He was reared a Roman Catholic, but while in Columbus, under the preaching of Dr. Daniel Baker, he was converted, and joined the Cumberland Presbyterian Church. He died in March, 1855, and was buried by the Masons and Odd Fellows in Columbus. His wife was born in Newport, R. I., but she met Mr. Peirce in Baltimore, and married him there. She died in 1869, and was buried by her husband's side. The boyhood days of Robert William Peirce were chiefly spent in Columbus, and his education was received principally at the old Franklin Academy there. After leaving school he entered the printing office in Columbus; after three years he went into the drug business. In the fall of 1848 he removed to Mobile, Ala., where he continued in the same business, pursuing it with reasonable financial results until the spring of 1853, when he came to Texas, landing in Galveston. From thence, after a short stay there, to Indianola; thence to Lavaca, Petersburg, Gonzales, and up the beautiful San Marcos River to Prairie Lea, to Lockhart, and finally settling in Austin. His brother, John K., a daguerreotypist, accompanied him to Texas. At the places above named they took pictures with good success. His object in thus traveling was to find a suitable location and enter the drug business again, but becoming convinced that it was his duty to preach the gospel he applied to the Quarterly Conference of Austin Station, Texas Conference, March, 1855, and was licensed, Rev. Daniel Morse, P. Elder, and Rev. James Wesson, preacher in charge, as Secretary, signing the license. In the interim, before the session of the Texas Annual Conference in December of the same year, he was employed to preach on the Fayetteville circuit by Rev. Homer S. Thrall, D.D. He made his home with Dr. Thrall and his estimable lady. Besides the study of theology, he studied moral and intellectual philosophy, rhetoric, and composition; reciting lessons in these last to the wife of Dr. Halsey, at Rutersville College. She was a most accomplished teacher. Mr. Peirce had received instructions from her twenty years before this, in Tuscaloosa, Ala. Before the meeting of the Annual Conference at Galveston, in December, same year, his Quarterly Conference recommended him as a suitable candidate for membership. He was received. His first appointment was on both sides of Galveston Bay; second, Kerrville circuit; third, Perdinales circuit; fourth, Oakville circuit; a part of this last year, 1859, he had charge of Corpus Christi station. Although not an eminent preacher, he was a good pastor, and revivals resulted from his zeal for the salvation of souls. The two years that he traveled in the mountains—1857 and 1858—he had not only to put his trust in God, but "keep his powder dry." It was an Indian country. Roving bands of them made frequent forays on the frontier settlements for the purpose of theft. Coming down their wonted trails during the full of the moon they would carry off the horses of the settlers, sometimes sneaking up very near the house where a horse had been tethered, cutting the rope, thus securing him for their own use. They were very cunning. It is customary on the frontier for the "cowboys" to take with them, on their hunt for stock, a number of cow ponies. When in camp these are generally herded, and if discovered by these *diablos*—as the Mexicans call them—they tie to the tail of one of their horses a dry cow's hide and dash through the herd, stampeding them. Then they are almost sure to get some of them. Exposed as he was among them, it was prudent that he should be prepared to defend himself. One good man, a Methodist local preacher, on his circuit in 1858, thought he ought not to carry a gun, but put his "trust in God." In a few months after this advice was given this same good man, Rev. Jonas Dancer, was killed by the Indians. They are cowardly. If they are discovered while on their forays they invariably try to kill the person; if not, they do not molest them. This conduct is for the purpose of evading pursuit. He did not get sight of an Indian during the two years, but on several occasions saw fresh signs of them. In 1857 he was on two scouts after them; once with Mr. Alonzo Reese, who had been out early in the morning to look for his oxen. About one mile from his home—where Mr. Peirce had spent the night—he discovered moccasin tracks. He came back hurriedly. Mr. Peirce, being the only man at hand, went back with him. They discovered the tracks, which led toward a high mountain, and they climbed it, where they saw the two moccasin tracks, one very large, the other very small. These were noted tracks; had often been seen on the frontier, but could never be overtaken. Another time he accompanied a party of eight others to the head waters of the Guadalupe. The main object was to find the bones of two young men who had been killed by the Indians, a few months before, in order to give them decent sepulture. At the same time they kept a close watch for Indians. They did not see any recent signs, nor did they find the bones of the unfortunate young men. At the time of this sad affair above spoken of, Mr. Spencer Goss, who was one of the party, was severely wounded, his thigh being broken by the Indian's bullet, and thought by his family and friends to be dead; but after nineteen days, crawling through the Cedar mountains, he reached Kerrville, twenty-five miles from the scene of conflict. He subsisted during this time on wild grapes. This party of young men had become careless, and had placed most of their guns out of reach. While eating their breakfast the Indians crawled up and secured their guns and opened fire on them. Mr. Goss met with one thrilling adventure while on his arduous trip. He was confronted by a large black bear, and for some time the menacing attitude of bruin was such that he despaired of life; but he was unharmed, and left to pursue his painful journey. On an occasion that Mr. Peirce accompanied his presiding elder, Dr. H. S. Thrall, to a quarterly and camp meeting, near San Saba, the wife of Dr. Thrall, who was with him, thought she discovered an Indian dodge into a cedar thicket, about one hundred yards ahead of them. They halted and consulted what was best to do. The conclusion was, as they had only one six-shooter between them, to return a few miles to get a gun, which they did, and, returning, Mr. Peirce suggested, and they placed a long stick, having the appearance of a gun, in the front part of the vehicle, while he carried the borrowed gun on his horse. They reached their destination without molestation. Mrs. Thrall seemed as little frightened as either of the trio.

Once, as Mr. Peirce was going to Bandera to preach, near by the Bandera Pass, he thought he discovered an Indian attempting to cut him off; the person was too far off to be distinguished. His first impulse was to put spurs to his fine mare and make his escape; a second thought, there is only one, and having a Sharp's rifle, he could make a good fight. It was only a cowboy wishing to make inquiries. Only a short time before this Indians had attacked a citizen in the suburbs of Bandera, killing a man with a spear. At the Annual Conference held in Goliad, in the latter part of 1859, Mr. Peirce located, with the intention of returning on a visit to his mother in Columbus, Miss.; but on account of the *Goliad Messenger* being left without printers (they having volunteered to go to the Rio Grande to join Col. John S. Ford's command to help subdue Cortinas, the notorious Mexican bandit), the proprietor, Rev. A. F. Fox, prevailed on Rev. H. S. Horton and Mr. R. W. Peirce, to remain a short time with him till he could procure printers. It was almost impossible to get them, and he made a reasonable offer to sell a half interest to Mr. Peirce, which he accepted, deferring the contemplated visit till the fall of 1860. His connection with the paper as publisher, then editor, continued till 1866. He then itinerated three years more, and taught school two years. When the great Civil War opened, he entered the Confederate service as Chaplain in Col. Tom Green's Regiment, Sibley Brigade. On their way to Arizona near the Rio Grande River, it was reported to Col. Green that Indians were seen on a mountain to the left. The colonel sent a scout of men under command of St. Clough to attend to them. This was a false alarm. Before reaching Fort Thorn, he was preaching to the soldiers one night, and when about half through the sermon, tattoo was sounded for roll call, when he dismissed them with the benediction. Next morning he informed the Colonel that he would resign his office as Chaplain as soon as the expected fight at Fort Thorn took place. Col. Green was a kind, genial, generous hearted man, and why he permitted Divine service to be interrupted has always been a mystery to Mr. Peirce. The colonel thought that he ought to remain with them, but Mr. Peirce thought it too personal. After the fight at Val Verde—one mile above Fort Thorn—in which Mr. Peirce connected himself with Capt. Campbell's Company to participate in the battle, he returned to Texas. A short time after this Gen. H. A. McCulloch left with a body guard for Arkansas, where he took command of a division of troops. Jesse Boring, M.D. and D.D., was appointed Chief Surgeon of the division. Mr. Peirce was employed to purchase medicine, and act as druggist for Dr. Boring temporarily, expecting to get a chaplaincy when there was a vacancy. When encamped on the waters of White River, in Arkansas, the death rate was large in the division. Mr. Peirce contracted rheumatism, and was failing in health, when Dr. Boring advised him to return to Texas. The doctor and Mr. Peirce were intimate friends, and he assured him that men were dying in camps, whose pulse indicated no disease. Mr. Peirce himself felt that he would die, if he remained in Arkansas. And he says that the atmosphere at times, during his stay there, had to him a putrid odor. He returned to Goliad, Texas, where in a short time a company of cadets was formed. These were youths from sixteen to eighteen years of age, the commanding officers being older men. Some of the parents of these youths were solicitous for Mr. Peirce to accompany them, to look after their morals, etc. Lieut. Col. Fulcrod was anxious for his presence with them. He went, and acted as Chaplain for the battalion, without a commission. But it was not long, victory perching on the banner of the stars and stripes, they were disbanded to return home. These young soldiers were called "the seed corn of the Confederacy." Mr. Peirce became a member of the Masonic fraternity at the age of twenty-one, in Columbus, Miss., and is now a member of Hardeman Lodge No. 179, Luling, Texas. He also joined the "Temple of Honor" at the age of seventeen in Columbus, Miss., and is yet a teetotaler. Politically he is a Populist, believing that a reform in our government is essential to its prosperity. He was married, December 18, 1871, to Mrs. Fannie Appling, widow of Mr. Frank M. Appling, daughter of Mastin and Sarah Gane (Martin) Ussery. She is a native of Tennessee. They emigrated to Texas in 1852. The father died in 1883, but the mother still survives. Mrs. Peirce became the mother of one child by her first husband, whom she named Collie Frank. Her last union has resulted in the birth of four children: John Mastin, Sarah Fannie, Mary Roberta, and Annie Louisa Finch. He still preaches as a local preacher when his health permits. His home is in Guadalupe County, five miles west of Luling, Texas. His wife, by her frugality and industry, assisted much in his prosperity.

H. S. TOM. There is an obscurity in the game of life that, to the robust mind, is always attractive. The important uncertainty of the final outcome, its value to all, serves as an incentive to great deeds. To push forward and win the battle is the common impulse and ambition of humanity. But in this vast concourse of struggling warriors, the number who achieve success is comparatively small, and in the majority of cases is confined to those who, by reason of family inheritance or extended learning, have a far better start than their fellows. Without these qualifications success is rarely attained, but when it is, the fortunate being is invariably the possessor of an indomitable will, untiring energy and an unusual amount of native shrewdness and ability. Such a man is H. S. Tom, the subject of this sketch and a prominent rancher of Wilson County, Texas. Mr. Tom is a native of the Lone Star State, born in Washington County in 1839, and was the youngest of the family of children born to Joseph and Ellen (Whiteside) Tom, natives of Tennessee. In 1838 the parents moved to Texas and settled in Washington County, where the father followed farming until his death in 1844. His wife passed away in that year also. After the death of his parents our subject was reared by an elder brother until thirteen years of age. In 1853 he came to an uncle living in Guadalupe County and made his home with him until 1855. Two years later he went to Atascosa County, where he remained until after the breaking out of hostilities. In 1862 he enlisted in a company of State troops and served on the frontier until 1864, when the regiment was transferred to the Confederate service, operating in the State of Texas until the war closed. Afterwards Mr. Tom returned to Atascosa County, where he engaged in the stock business and where he has had stock interests since, owning a ranch of about 12,000 acres. In 1877 he moved to Wilson County and in 1889 located in Floresville, where he erected a fine residence which is presided over in a charming manner by his wife, who was formerly Miss Hannah Campbell, a native of Ireland and a daughter of Peter Campbell, who was an early settler of Texas, locating in Guadalupe County in 1852. Mr. and Mrs. Tom's nuptials were celebrated in 1865 and ten children were born to this union, four of whom are now living: Lillie, Gertrude, Nora and Campbell. The family holds membership in the Catholic Church.

GEN. WILLIAM HUGH YOUNG. One of the professions of life which seem to require a particular adaptability and natural gift is that of the lawyer. It is one of the most highly honored as well as most exacting ones. It requires an abundance of legal lore to gain the plane of success, but when that plane is once reached, the reward of patient study and work is a goodly and honorable one. A gentleman particularly gifted in this way, who has chosen San Antonio, Texas, as the favored place wherein to practice his profession, is Gen. William H. Young, an old soldier and a prominent real estate man. He is a native of Missouri, born January 1, 1838, to the union of Hugh F. and Fannie Hampton (Gibson) Young, both natives of Virginia, the former born in Augusta and the latter in Montague County. Hugh F. Young followed merchandising and farming in his native State until 1834, and then moved to Yazoo County, Mississippi. There he married Miss Gibson and subsequently went to Missouri, but only remained there a short time when he came to Texas via Arkansas, and in 1841 settled at Clarksville, Red River County. There he followed farming and business enterprises and became a prominent politician, holding the office of Chief Justice of Red River County. In 1853 he moved to Grayson County, where he held the same position, and was one of the representative men. When the Civil War broke out he was commissioned Brigadier General of the reserved force by the Governor. In 1863 he moved to Palestine and from there to San Antonio in the fall of 1864,

making his home there until his death in 1888.   His wife, the mother of
our subject, died in 1842 and his second union was with Miss Electa Alexander, who bore him one child, Newton Alexander, and who died at the time
of this child's birth.   Mr. Young's third union occurred in 1849 with Miss
Sarah E. Rainey.   One son was born to this union, Frank E., who is now
deceased.   The original of this notice was educated in Texas and at Nashville,
Washington College, being in the latter three years.   For two years after this
he was in Mackenzie College, Clarksville, Texas, and then entered the University of Virginia for a five year's course.   However, two years later he was
compelled to leave on account of the Civil War, and he returned to Texas,
where he enlisted on the first call of the government for infantry troops.   He
was at once elected Captain of Company C, Ninth Texas Infantry, and started
for Bowling Green, Ky.   At Memphis he received orders to go to North
Mississippi, where he participated in the battle of Shiloh.   Immediately after
this terrible engagement he was elected Colonel of the regiment and participated in the battle of Chickamauga, and was afterwards in all the battles of
that campaign.   During the battle of Murfreesboro the regiment was ordered
to join the army of Joseph E. Johnston in Mississippi, where he was wounded.
For a time he was in the hospital at Columbus, but joined his regiment before
the battle of Chickamauga, where he was badly wounded in the chest.
After this he was unfit for duty until the middle of December when he
joined the army at Meridian, Miss.   In March, 1864, he went to Richmond
on military business, but later rejoined the army and was all through the
Atlanta campaign in all the battles.   At Atlanta, Ga., Gen. M. D. Etor
in command of subject's brigade, was wounded and Col. Young was promoted to Brigadier General, August 15, 1864, and was in command of the
brigade until the surrender of Atlanta.   He was with Gen. Hood in his
campaign northward, and was with Gen. French in his battle at Altoona
Heights on the Georgia Railroad, on October 5th and 6th.   At that place
he was wounded and left on the battle-field for some time.   Two days later
he was captured and placed in a hospital, and still later sent to Johnston
Island where he was released July 25, 1865.   He then came to Texas and
joined his father at San Antonio.   Immediately he began the study of law
and was admitted to the bar April, 1866, soon after beginning to practice
with his father-in-law.   They were also engaged in the real estate business
and have shown themselves gentlemen of prime ability, honor and conserv-
atism.   On the 3d of November, 1869, he was married to Miss Fannie M.
Kemper of Virginia, and one son, Hugh Hampton, has been born to this
union.   This son is now a student of the University, where he ranks high.

  JESSE J. HARRISON.   Prominent among the people of Colorado County,
Texas, who have made for themselves honorable names, and who have acquired
a competency of this world's goods largely through their own unaided efforts,
is the gentleman whose name forms the heading of this sketch.   He has
always interested himself in the political affairs of this section, and has for
some time ably filled the office of District Clerk of the county.   He was born
in Obion County, Tenn., September 7, 1850, and is a son of Dr. Jesse Harrison, for a sketch of whom see the biography of Dr. R. H. Harrison.   Jesse
J. Harrison spent his school days in his native county and in Leake County,
Miss., and at the age of twenty years became a salesman in a general store in
Dunklin County, Mo., and was there married to Miss Abbie Sheets, and as a

wedding trip started from southeast Missouri for Texas in a wagon. After reaching the Lone Star State he farmed in Grayson County for four years, then came to Columbus, Colorado County, and after remaining in his father's office for some time was elected to the position of City Marshal, and filled this position with marked ability for six years, at the end of which time he was elected District Clerk, and since then has attended to the duties of that office with efficiency and to the entire satisfaction of all concerned. Mr. Harrison is personally very popular, for he is not only cordial and sincere in manners, but he endeavors to do his duty at all times; is an honorable, upright gentleman and a true and devoted friend. Mrs. Harrison's people were residing in Clarkston, Mo., at the time of her birth. To her marriage with Mr. Harrison five children have been given: Maggie, Robert H., William and Ed. living, and Lily, who died when quite young. Mrs. Harrison and her daughter Maggie are earnest and active members of the Baptist Church, and the entire family move in the best social circles of the place, and their home is a pretty and hospitable one. Mr. Harrison has always been noted for his social disposition, and socially is a member of the I. O. O. F. and the K. of P.

E. MULLEN. He whose name heads this sketch has charge of the interests of "Uncle Sam" at Yoakum, Tex., and has proved himself in every way worthy the trust reposed in him. He was born on the Isle of Erin, and like his countrymen he possesses much natural mother wit and versatility, and that he is a substantial and useful citizen is a self-evident fact. In 1849, when he was but one year old, he was brought by his parents, Barney and Mary (Murray) Mullen, to the United States, and in the "Hoosier State" they settled and engaged in farming in Martin County. There the father died in 1867 and the mother in 1856. E. Mullen was reared to the honorable and useful calling of the farmer, and while pursuing his laborious duties he learned many useful lessons, chief among which was energy and perseverance, but, unfortunately, was denied the privilege of obtaining a scholastic education, with the exception of about twelve months. He was engaged in farm labor until he was about twenty-eight years of age, when he turned his attention to coal mining in Indiana, a calling which occupied his attention for about two years. He was very anxious to give his services to the Union cause in 1862, enlisted in the service and went to Indianapolis, but owing to his extreme youth he was rejected by the officials. In 1868 he began the study of telegraphy, and soon after secured work on the Cairo & Vincennes R. R., with which he was connected for eight years at station and telegraph work. He was then for some time stationed at Columbia, Ill., as employe on the Cairo & St. Louis R. R., but after a short time returned to the Cairo & Vincennes R. R., with which he remained two years more. In 1882 he came to Austin, Texas, as operator for the T. & G. N. R. R. for four months, was then located at San Diego for six months, was twelve months with the Mexican National R. R. at Santa Catarina, Mexico, was then at Lampazos, Mexico, with the same road two years, was with the F. C. I. M. Ry. twelve months at Sabinas, Mexico, at the end of which time he went to San Antonio, Texas. He was the agent, operator and train despatcher for the S. A. & A. P. there, the first agent that road had at any point. For the same road he went to Kennedy Junction as agent and operator, but after a short time returned to Mexico and for four months was the operator at Monterey. He was next connected with the G. C. & S. F. R. R. at Ballinger, Texas, for about a year and a

half, and in 1889 went to Lexington, Texas, and was for some time with the
S. A. & A. P. again, where he filled the position of station agent and operator.
While there, and during the administration of General Harrison, he was
appointed Postmaster of Yoakum, receiving his commission July 1, 1890.
He has greatly advanced the revenue of the office by placing boxes on the
street to secure the mail that was usually posted on the train, and in six
months' time the office was raised in grade to a Presidential office, and in
other ways has greatly advanced in importance owing to Mr. Mullen's labor
and push. Mr. Mullen has been quite active in political matters, and in 1892
was a delegate to the Fort Worth Republican convention. He was a candidate for Mayor of Yoakum and received a majority of the votes, but by a
typographical error in the printing of four tickets lost the office. He has
shown the greatest interest in the prosperity of Yoakum, owns considerable
real estate in and about the place, and is one of the most substantial and
highly respected citizens of the town. He is an efficient Postmaster, and
higher honors await him in the way of political preferment. He has made
an enviable reputation for himself in all locations where his lot has been cast,
and as a railroad man was efficient, trustworthy and intelligent, and a favorite
with the officials of the different roads with which he was connected. He was
married to Miss Mary Fonkhauser, of Illinois, in 1880, and by her became the
father of four children, all of whom are deceased. Mr. Mullen is a member
of the Catholic Church, while his wife is a Lutheran. Socially Mr. Mullen is
a member of the A. F. & A. M., and is a charter member of Yoakum Lodge
No. 348 of the I. O. O. F.

HON. R. N. WEISIGER. No name is more familiarly known in Anderson
County than that of Weisiger, and it is so thoroughly interwoven with its
history and progress that a work of this character would be incomplete without
frequent reference to some member of the family. The man from Kentucky
has always been a potential element in the civilization and development of
Texas. No better blood ever infused pioneer life; no sturdier arm ever set
about the task of subduing the wilderness, and no less vigorous mental activity
could have raised a great commonwealth. Mr. Weisiger was born in Danville,
Ky., in 1838, and was the eldest child born to the marriage of Dr. Joseph and
Mrs. Clay (nee LaShelle Reed) Weisiger, natives of the Blue Grass State. The
paternal ancestors came from Prussia to Virginia about 1741 or '42, and Joseph
Weisiger was the progenitor of this family in America. Daniel Weisiger, our
subject's grandfather, was born in Virginia, but at an early date came to Kentucky and located where Lexington now stands. He participated in the Indian
troubles, and after a few years moved to where Frankford now stands, being
one of the first settlers of that region. His son, our subject's father, was the
first white child born there. Our subject's maternal ancestors were of Scotch-
Irish origin, and came to Virginia about 1740 or '50. His grandfather, John
Reed, was a native of the Old Dominion, and came to Kentucky in the pioneer days, located in what is now Boyle County, and raised the first crop of
corn there. He became a prominent man in that section, was the first County
Clerk of Lincoln County, and was well liked for his many estimable qualities.
His death occurred in Washington County, Penn. The father of our subject
was an able physician, and practiced medicine in Kentucky until 1852, when
he came to Texas. He located in Mission Valley, Victoria County, and
became one of the largest planters of that time, following that until his

death. During the war he was made Director of this district. The mother died in Kentucky in 1851. The original of this notice came to Texas in 1852 with his father, but subsequently returned to Danville, where he entered Central College, graduating in 1858. In his class were many men who have since become prominent. After leaving college he came to Texas and engaged in planting and stock-raising. He brought blooded animals from Kentucky, and was the first to advance the grade of Texas stock. About this time the war cloud hung darkly over the nation, and in 1862 Mr. Weisiger enlisted in Company A, Watter's Battalion of Green's Brigade, and served mainly in Louisiana and Arkansas, being in all the engagements of that department. Soon after enlisting he was made First Lieutenant, and in 1863 he became Captain of his company, commanding the same in all its engagements except one. During the war he was on the frontier of Texas, capturing bushwhackers, and was returning south, near Waco, when word was received of the final surrender. Mr. Weisiger then returned to his home and engaged in his previous occupation, farming and stock-raising, six miles above Victoria. He had three brothers in the Confederate army. William held the rank of Captain, and was in the last battle of the war. Evan was Surgeon of the Second Texas Infantry, and served with Bragg, and Robert, the youngest, entered the army as a private and became a Major. His death occurred soon after the war. Our subject continued stock-raising for many years, and during this time introduced some of the best bred stock of Texas. He owned the race horse "Incomode," and the descendants of this stallion have won many races. In politics Mr. Weisiger has been an earnest worker and a prominent factor for years. He was elected to the State Senate in 1890, and during the regular and called sessions was a member of the following committees, judiciary No. 2, finance, penitentiary, internal improvements, public lands, state affairs, claims and accounts, stock and stock raising, agricultural affairs, labor, and mines and mining. He was elected chairman of the four committees last mentioned.

He was made permanent Chairman of the sub-committee of the Confederate Home, has been a delegate to conventions innumerable, and was a delegate to the first Democratic State Convention, held at Austin, in 1869, and to nearly all since. Mr. Weisiger is pronounced and fearless in his political views, a strong advocate of measures he approves, and in all things conscientious and honest. In the month of June, 1875, he was married to Miss Annie Callinder, a native of Kentucky, and the daughter of W. L. Callinder. Eight children were born to this union: Robert, Reed, Isabella, Lucy, Sallie and William. Two sons died in infancy. In 1890 Mr Weisiger moved to his residence in Victoria in order to educate his children. He is a member of the Presbyterian and Mrs. Weisiger is a member of the Methodist Episcopal Church. Socially he is a Mason. As Senator, when the branch of the Legislature differed so as to the re-districting the State, he was the only man appointed on the joint committee, outside of the members from a small section of North Texas, but he succeeded in securing a re-districting that suited the people of the southern part of the State. In the distributing question, the alien land law, which raised such a fight, Mr. Weisiger was selected on the joint conference committee, which drafted the present law as a substitute, and arranged it to the general satisfaction of all, these two being the most important questions coming before the extra session, and our subject having a potent voice in settling both. He cast the sixth and last vote against the passage of the celebrated alien land law, which has had such an effect in the affairs of Texas. Although an active worker in politics, he has always refused office, except the one term in the Senate as stated. He was made Commander of the William R. Scurry Camp of United Confederate Veterans, No. 136, at its organization in 1890, and has continued in that capacity since. Mr. Weisiger's ancestors on both sides were among the prominent people of Kentucky. His natural inclinations were for constant advancement in all things, so that whatever he undertook he strove to elevate and improve. Impulsive, but strong-minded, of superior qualities and high character, he has given the world an ornate life, well worth the emulation of youth. His course in the Senate showed the power of the statesman, the impress of the scholar and a general knowledge of the country's good.

JOHN RABON APPLING. The occupation of farming and stock-raising has no more able follower than John Rabon Appling, whose shrewd, intelligent and far seeing ideas have placed him in a sound financial position and have won him the respect of a large circle of friends. He was born in Tuscaloosa County, Alabama, June 15, 1844, the sixth of eleven children born to Burwell and Calthy C. (Peteet) Appling, both of whom were born, reared and married in Georgia. They resided in Alabama for some years, and in the fall of 1854 emigrated to Guadalupe County, Texas, their farm being near the present town of Luling, on the Guadalupe River. They were worthy members of the Methodist Church, were upright and law abiding citizens, and in the conduct of his business affairs the father was very successful and accumulated a good property. He was called from this life in 1862, and the mother breathed her last in 1881. The early life of John Rabon Appling was spent in Guadalupe County, Texas, but the opening of the great Civil War, when he had just entered school, prevented him from obtaining the education he so much desired and needed. He enlisted in McDowell's Company, Seventeenth Infantry, and served in Arkansas and Louisiana, participating in the battles of Mansfield, Pleasant Hill and Yellow Bayou, and was also in the thirty days' skirmishing attending the retreat of Gen. Banks. He was in active service for over three years, and after the surrender of Gen. Lee he returned home with the consciousness of having performed every duty faithfully and to the best of his ability. He was then given a slight start by his father, but the bulk of his property he accumulated through his own thrift and energy. His real estate now amounts to 700 acres, of which 120 acres are under cultivation and yield abundant harvests. He has also given considerable attention to the raising of horses and cattle, in fact is a pushing and enterprising man, well posted in all the different branches of his calling. A stanch Democrat, politically, he has never held office, nor desired to do so, for his time and attention have been fully occupied otherwise. He was married in January, 1885, to Miss Jesse Johnson, a daughter of Addison and Frances (Wright) Johnson who came from Alabama to this State at an early day. The father died in 1873, but the mother is still living (1894). To Mr. and Mrs. Appling four children have been given: Frank, Gus, John and Claude.

SHADRICK MARION GUTHRIE. Since the days of Adam, agriculture has been an honorable, useful and most necessary occupation, and the great majority of the men who have followed this calling have been useful and law-abiding citizens. S. M. Guthrie is no exception to this rule, and is possessed of those qualities of energy and thrift which could not fall short of success in whatever section he might locate, for he has the spirit and determination to bend the force of circumstances to his will and receive benefit therefrom. He is a Kentuckian by birth, where he first saw the light in 1835, being the second in a family of twelve children, born to William E. and Etheldra (Brasley) Guthrie, who were also born on Blue Grass soil. The father was a farmer, mill man and mechanic, and about 1837 located in Pontotoc County, Mississippi, where he began operating a grist mill, which he successfully conducted until 1851, when he took up his abode in Lavaca County, Texas, and here erected the second mill ever put up in the county, which was quite centrally located. After a time he moved to Falls County, Texas, where he put up a mill and gin, and later moved to Bell County, where he erected a flouring mill, cotton gin, and saw mill on the Lampasas River, dying there on the 2d of March, 1882, at which point his widow still resides. He was a member of the Baptist Church the greater portion of his life, and his wife is also of this denomination. In 1851 S. M. Guthrie came to Texas with his father, attended school a short time in Lavaca County, and was married in 1862 to Miss Martha E. Culpepper, a daughter of F. G. Culpepper, the oldest citizen of the county. In 1863 he enlisted in the Confederate army, and served in Louisiana, Arkansas, and on the Kansas border. During his service he participated in the battles of Mansfield, Pleasant Hill, Camden, Jenkins Ferry, and was with Price on his Missouri campaign. After the war was over he went to Houston, Texas, and then returned to his family near Old Sweet Home, where he owned a good farm. On this land he made his home until 1880, when he bought his present farm of 564 acres, about five miles from Yoakum. He has 200 acres under cultivation, all of which is good arable land, and which yields abundant crops of the products of that region. He has for many years been the proprietor of cotton gins and owned the second one in Yoakum. He and his wife have six children: William F., Shadrick Marion, Jr., Jackson, Ed., Nannie Irene and Lemie. Mr. Guthrie is a member of Yoakum Lodge of the A. F. & A. M., and is a popular man and highly respected in the locality in which he resides. His paternal grandfather, Shadrick Guthrie, was a pioneer of Kentucky, as was also his maternal grandfather.

GEN. SAMUEL HOUSTON. In early days there drifted within the borders of Texas men of splendid talents and marked genius, who sought new scenes, far removed from those of earlier days. One of those who bravely fought for the freedom of Texas, and was one of the most striking types of her early men, was Gen. Samuel Houston, whose life is inseparably linked with the early history of the Lone Star State. He came of Virginia stock, and was himself a native of Rockbridge County, that State, his birth occurring March 2, 1793, and from his ancestors he inherited Scotch and Irish blood. After the death of his father the family removed to near the Cherokee Territory, in the State of Tennessee, and there much of his time was spent among the Indians, by one of whom he was adopted. He grew up with but little education, and in 1813 enlisted in the Seventh United States Infantry, and soon attained the rank of Sergeant. He took part in the battle of Horseshoe Bend, where his great courage attracted the attention of Gen. Jackson, and he continued fighting, although he was wounded several times. He soon rose to the rank of Second Lieutenant, and for a time acted as sub-Agent for the Cherokees, at Jackson's request. He became First Lieutenant in March, 1818, but resigned the following May, owing to criticism which emanated from the War Department, which accused him of complicity in smuggling negroes from Florida into the United States; but he demanded an investigation and was fully exonerated. In June, 1818, he began studying law in Nashville, and in a few months was admitted to the bar, and his first practice was done in Lebanon. The following year he was elected Attorney of Davidson District, moved to Nashville and was also appointed Adjutant-General of the State. In 1821 he was elected Major-General, and within a year resigned the office of District Attorney. In 1823 he was elected to Congress, was re-elected in 1825, and in the last year of his term he fought a duel with Gen. White, whom he wounded. In 1827 he became a candidate for Governor, and so great was his popularity that he was elected by an overwhelming majority. In January, 1829, he married a Miss Allen, of Sumner County, Tenn., but after a few weeks of wedded life Houston suddenly left his wife without a word of explanation, but always protested that the cause of separation in no way affected his wife's character. He was very strongly condemned for his action in this matter, and amid a storm of vituperation, made his way up Arkansas River to the mouth of the Illinois River, where for three years he made his home with his Cherokee father by adoption. In 1832 he made a trip to Washington in the interests of the Indians, wore the Indian garb, and was warmly welcomed by President Jackson. While there he was accused by William Stansberry, an Ohio Congressman, of attempting to obtain a fraudulent contract for furnishing the Indian supplies, and to retaliate, he attacked Stansberry and gave him a beating. For this he was fined $500 and mildly reprimanded, but Jackson remitted the fine. He then made a trip to Texas and became a member of the convention that met at San Felipe de Austin, April 1, 1833, at which a constitution was adopted in which Houston inserted a clause prohibiting the establishment of banks; was shortly after elected General of Texas east of the Trinity River, and was a member of what was called the "General Consultation," that met in October, 1835, for the purpose of establishing a provisional government, and successfully opposed a declaration of independence as premature. At this time he was elected Commander-in-Chief of the Army of Texas, but was deprived of his office through jealousy, before he could perfect a military organization. He was a member of the convention that met at New Washington, and adopted a declaration of complete independence March 2, 1836, and he was re-elected Commander-in-Chief. After the battle of the Alamo and of Goliad, Houston, with 700 men, met the main body of the Mexicans, 1,800 men, on the banks of the San Jacinto, during which engagement the American battle cry was, "Remember the Alamo!" The battle lasted less than an hour, during which time the Mexicans were totally defeated, their loss in killed being 630, and in captured 730, Santa Anna being among the latter. Houston, who was slightly wounded in the ankle, was treated with great injustice by the civil authorities, and retired to New Orleans, but in the autumn of 1836 returned to Nacogdoches. An election for President of the Republic had been announced, and twelve days before the election Houston announced himself as a candidate for the office, and out of 5,104 votes polled, he received 4,374, and became the first President of the Republic of Texas. Upon the expiration of his term, December 12, 1838, he left the country in a healthy condition, at peace with the Indians, on a friendly footing with Mexico, and with its treasury notes at par. For the two terms of 1839-1841 he was a member of the Texas Congress and did effective service for the State. In 1840 he was married to Miss Margaret Moffette, having secured a divorce from his first wife, and his second wife exercised a most wholesome and restraining influence over him. At the close of his second term in Congress he was again elected to the Presidency of the Republic, and labored faithfully from December 12, 1841, to December 9, 1844, to remedy the mistakes made by his predecessor, Lamar. Congress in June, 1842, passed a bill making him Dictator, and 10,000,000 acres of land were voted to resist the Mexican invasion that threatened. These measures were vetoed by Mr. Houston, and in time the danger passed away. In 1838 he took the first steps toward securing the annexation of Texas to the United States, and in 1845 Texas was admitted to the Union, and in March of the following year Mr. Houston became a United States Senator and served until 1859. He was a stanch Union man, strongly opposed the repeal of the Missouri compromise, and voted for all measures of compromise during the slavery agitation. He also opposed the Kansas and Nebraska bill, refused to sign the Southern address, and, during his entire term of service, he earnestly advocated the cause of the Indians, whom he always maintained had never violated a treaty. He was widely spoken of as a Presidential candidate, but Franklin Pierce received the nomination. At Concord, N. H., he was again brought forward by the Democrats in 1854, as the people's candidate, and in the convention that met in 1856 Millard Fillmore was nominated in his stead. In the convention that met in Baltimore, in 1860, John Bell, of Tennessee, received the nomination, although Houston stood next. In 1857 Mr. Houston had been defeated for Governor of Texas by Harrison B. Runnels, but in 1859 he entered the lists as an independent candidate, and defeated Runnels. He greatly deplored Lincoln's election to the Presidency in 1860, but maintained that this was no grounds for secession. When Texas declared for secession in 1861, and all State officials were required to take the oath of allegiance, Mr. Houston refused to do so, and was deposed on the 18th of March. He likewise refused United States troops that were offered him, and on the 10th of May, 1861, he made a speech at Independence, Texas, in which he defined the position of the Southern Unionists, but took no part in public life thereafter.

WILLIAM E. SINGLETON. It often happens that the most valuable guides which example furnishes in the rush of the nineteenth century life are available in circles limited by personal association. It is true, furthermore, that the qualities most worthy of emulation are usually combined, in a successful man, with a shrinking from personal fame or notoriety, which discourages even friendly attempts to uncover the secrets of success in a successful career. Among the substantial and distinguished men of the County of Wharton, Texas, stands the name of William E. Singleton, cotton weigher at that place, and nominee of the White Men's Association, which is equivalent to an election. He was born in Chicot County, Ark., in 1856, and is the son of James A. Singleton, M.D., a native of North Carolina, who came from Chicot County, Ark., to Texas, and located in DeWitt County, where he passed the closing scenes of his life, dying in 1868, when sixty-eight years of age. Mrs. Singleton died in 1882. William E. Singleton, the youngest child born to his parents, secured a good practical education in Concrete College, and when nineteen years of age turned his attention to farming, carrying this on for one year in DeWitt County, and one year in Gonzales County. From there he went to the western part of the State, resided at Uvalde and Eagle Pass two years, and later came to Wharton, where he immediately engaged in business. His unusual ability and thorough good judgment drew at once a most satisfactory patronage, and he continued in business until the year 1892, when he was elected to the position of cotton weigher. This position he fills in a most efficient and satisfactory manner, and his popularity is well deserved. Mr. Singleton has shown his appreciation of secret organizations by joining the Knights of Pythias and the Knights of Honor, holding the office of Master-at-Arms of the former, and Dictator and Past Dictator of the latter. In politics he is an ardent supporter of Democratic principles.

JOSEPH EHLINGER. This gentleman is a successful attorney-at-law of Fayette County, Texas, and from his ancestors inherits many of the sterling characteristics of the French people. His grandfather, Joseph Ehlinger, was a soldier of Napoleon's Army, and was with him in all his latter campaigns, participating in many battles, and in the famous march to Moscow. After the battle of Waterloo and the fall of the great general, Mr. Ehlinger came to America, landing in the City of Baltimore, Md., after which he went to New Orleans, where he became a contractor and builder, and when Texas was fighting for independence, he came to this State and joined issues with Gen. Sam Houston, becoming a member of Company F. He took part in the famous battle of San Jacinto, at which time he captured a Mexican, Lopez, who remained with Mr. Ehlinger as long as he lived, and when released he refused to return to Mexico. An old powder-horn which he carried is now in possession of the subject of this sketch, as was also his old flint-lock rifle, but one of the younger boys, while endeavoring to appropriately celebrate the 4th of July, loaded the gun to the muzzle, pulled the trigger by means of a fishing line and at a safe distance, and it is perhaps needless to remark that the valuable old relic is not now in the possession of the family. After peace was declared, Joseph Ehlinger returned to his native country, France, and upon his return was accompanied by his family, with whom he located in Houston. He obtained a headright in Fayette County, now known as Ehlinger's League, and went there to improve the place before removing his family thither. While returning to Houston he had to cross Buffalo Bayou, which was much swollen, and in endeavoring to swim across he was drowned. During his lifetime he built the first hotel at Columbus for Colonel Robison, and erected many other buildings throughout the country. He was much troubled with the Indians when he first came here, and, with several others, was in a number of fights with them. His son, Charles Ehlinger, was born in France in 1826, and accompanied his father to Texas in 1840, and after the father's untimely taking off, on him devolved the care of the balance of the family. He built the first house at Ehlinger, also a steam saw and grist mill there, which were the first institutions of the kind in the county. At the commencement of the war he raised a company of 104 men, for Cook's Regiment, and after being in the field service for nine months, he was detailed as Government agent to collect provisions, etc. He then began the operation of his mill in the interests of the Confederacy, and was thus actively employed until the war closed. In 1866 he opened a store at Ehlinger, and for a long time had a very extensive trade, in all probability the largest in the county.

He was a shrewd and successful business man, and became a very extensive land owner. Before the war he was Justice of the Peace for many years. His wife, Minnie Miller, was born in Westphalia, Germany, and was brought to this country when about twelve years old by her father, Christopher Miller. While Charles Ehlinger was in Galveston in 1872, for the double purpose of buying goods and meeting his son Joseph, who was on his way home from the University of Virginia, he met with accidental death. His widow survived him until 1883, having become the mother of ten children, nine of whom are now living: Morris, who is in Shiner, Lavaca County, Texas; Elizabeth, who is the wife of C. J. H. Meyer, who represented Fayette County in the last session of the State Legislature; Caroline, who is the wife of Fred Meyer, also of this county; Elo Frank is a merchant at Goliad in Goliad County, Texas; John P., is the Postmaster at La Grange; Charles W., is a merchant at Ehlinger; Otto is a druggist at La Grange; Minnie, is the wife of Charles Gerndt, who farms near Ehlinger. Joseph, the immediate subject of this sketch, graduated from the Law Department of the University of Virginia in 1872, and after his father's death he assumed charge of his estate, continuing to look after the same for about ten years. He then moved to La Grange, and commenced the practice of law in 1882, was elected to the position of County Clerk, continuing in that office four terms, or until 1890, when he resumed the practice of his profession. He has been identified with all the important enterprises that have been started here for years, and was the prime mover in the building of the new Catholic Church here, and was also interested in the building of the Opera House and the Bridge here. He is a progressive citizen, and has been of material benefit to the place since taking up his residence here. In 1873 he was united in marriage with Miss Minnie Frels, a daughter of Capt. William Frels, the founder of Frelsburg of this county. They have three sons and a daughter.

BENJAMIN F. BUCKNER, M. D. The profession of medicine, while a very inviting field for the student and humanitarian, is one that demands much self denial and the exercise of repression, and the sacrifice of the ordinary methods of advancing one's interests. Austin County is peculiarly fortunate in the personnel of its practitioners, the ethical code being maintained at the highest possible standard, and the individual members being gentlemen of culture and refinement, and physicians of repute and eminence. In this number the name of Dr. Benjamin F. Buckner holds a prominent place, and his attainments in his profession, his courteous treatment of his brethren, the success he has attained in the practice, and his broad, considerate and devoted care of those who require his professional services, all combine to give him an enviable distinction among physicians, and a deserved popularity with the public. The doctor was born in Rusk County, Texas, January 27, 1867, a son of Arthur W. and Murtis (Kilgore) Buckner, natives of Georgia, but removed to Louisiana when quite young, in which State they were married. The Buckners and Kilgores started West at the same time, and while the Kilgores stopped in Louisiana the Buckners came on to Texas, Arthur W. being a small lad at that time. John S. Buckner, the paternal grandfather, located in Rusk County, and on the old homestead on which they first settled Arthur W. made his home until his death in 1894, at the age of sixty-nine years. At the time of his death he was one of the oldest settlers in the county, as well as in the State. His father, John S. Buckner, was a tiller of the soil, and was a soldier of the Mexican war. He reared two children only, Arthur W., and Mumford. Arthur W. was a Democrat in politics, and although a very active worker for the success of that party, he would never allow his name to go before a convention. He was ever true to his convictions, and was a firm believer in the future of the Lone Star State. His life was singularly pure and upright, no duty was ever neglected, and the esteem in which he was held by all who knew him was but a natural sequence of right living. His wife was a daughter of Allen Kilgore, and a Miss Bush, who spent their lives in Louisiana, where the father had devoted his time to planting. They reared a family of eight children: Mrs. Baugh, of Louisiana; Susan (Taylor), Adelia (Rogersmore), Bettie (Hester), Murtis (Mrs. Buckner), Benjamin, Wade (deceased), and Jasper. Arthur W. Buckner was a soldier of the Confederate Army, which he joined in 1861, serving until the close in the armies of Virginia and Tennessee under General Hood, with the rank of Captain. He received a wound in his left leg from which he suffered the balance of his life. He was in numerous battles, and surrendered with General Hood. When the war opened he was very wealthy, and owned a fine plantation and many negroes, besides a large amount of stock, yet he left everything to battle for the cause in which he believed, and at the close of the war returned home to find his plantation laid waste and his negroes and stock gone. Under these adverse circumstances he labored patiently, and in time found himself as well fixed as before the war, and much more independent in other ways than he was then. Considerable money was due Mr. Buckner before the war, and this was paid him during that time in Confederate money, and Mrs. Buckner has fire screens made of Confederate $50 bills for all the fire places in the old home, which are among the most unique fire screens now to be seen either North or South.

Soon after the war Mr. Buckner erected a steam cotton gin and saw mill, which he operated for many years, and he was also engaged in merchandising for some time. In 1893 he disposed of his mercantile interests to two of his sons and retired from active life, but did not live long to enjoy his wealth and cessation from labor. He left a widow and seven children to mourn their loss, the names of the latter being: John E., Allen, A., C., Fannie, wife of B. M. Adams; Benjamin F., Mary, wife of T. J. Hillin, and Thomas J. Dr. Benjamin F. Buckner was educated in Alexander Institute at Kilgore, Texas, and in the University of Texas at Austin, and took his first medical lectures in 1886–87 at Tulane University of Louisiana, from which he graduated in the class of 1887–88. For a short time he practiced his profession in Monroe, Texas, after which he spent one year in the Cherokee Nation, and was then for a short time in Tampa, Florida. Not liking the country he returned to Texas, since which time he has been a successful medical practitioner of Austin County, and a resident of Sealy since June, 1894. He was married in 1893 to Miss Kate E. Swearingen, a daughter of Lemuel and Sallie (Clark) Swearingen, both early settlers of this county, having come here in the ' 20's. They had five children: Kate, Mary, Richard, Cora, and Lawrence. Dr. Buckner is an exceptionally successful practitioner, is a member of the State Eclectic Association, and the Eclectic Association of Cincinnati. Besides graduating from the Regular school he, in 1892, attended the Eclectic Medical School of Cincinnati, from which he graduated in the spring of 1893.

CLARENCE W. McNEIL. The *Daily News*, of Laredo, Webb County, Texas, is ably edited and successfully managed by Clarence W. McNeil, and the paper finds a warm welcome in all the best homes of this section. Mr. McNeil owes his nativity to Woodville, Tyler County, Texas, where he first saw the light on the 31st of December, 1859, the youngest of four children born to Dr. William L. and Victoria (McNeil) McNeil, natives of Ohio and Florida, respectively. The father was a graduate of the Medical Department of Yale University, and began the practice of his noble and useful calling in the State of his birth, but in 1853 left his old home to come to Texas, and took up his residence in Colorado County. Here he was eventually united in marriage with Miss McNeil, who had come to this State with her parents in 1846. Later they removed to Wharton County, and after residing there for some time came to Tyler County, and here Dr. McNeil successfully practiced his profession, and also conducted a drug and commercial business in the town of Tyler, his career in these lines being closed only by the hand of death in 1873. During the great struggle between the North and South he served in the Confederate army as a surgeon, and was always a strong Southern sympathizer, although Northern born. His wife was called from life February, 1860, when the subject of this sketch was but six weeks old, after which Dr. McNeil married a second time, his wife being a Miss Moir. When the subject of this sketch was one year old he was placed in charge of his maternal grandmother at St. Mary's, Refugio County, but shortly after the family removed to San Antonio, and there resided until 1865, at which time Live Oak County became their home, and continued such up to 1868, when they once more made a change, this time taking up their abode in Rockport, the county seat of Aransas County. After Clarence McNeil had attended school for about eight years he was sent to Gonzales and became an apprentice on the *Gonzales Enquirer*, under editor S. W. Smith, but about one year later he went to Galveston and worked on the *Galveston News* for several years. He then returned to Live Oak County and established the *Lagarto Echo*, which he sold out after conducting it for one year, and since 1883 has resided in Laredo. He worked on the *Times* as a printer for some time, and subsequently as editor. From 1885 to 1887 he was engaged in "teaching the young idea" in Webb County, after which he engaged in merchandising in Laredo, which occupation he successfully followed for five years. Following this he became the editor of the *Laredo News*, which position he has since very acceptably, faithfully and ably filled. He has been constantly in the newspaper business, as editor, reporter or correspondent, since his early boyhood, and at various times has represented the *New York Herald*, the *St. Louis Globe-Democrat* and *Republic*, the *Chicago Times*, the *New Orleans Picayune*, the *Galveston News*, the *Houston Post*, and *San Antonio Express*. He is an honorary member of the San Antonio International Typographical Association. In his political views he has always been a stanch Democrat, an active worker for the party, and has been delegate to many conventions. On the 4th of March, 1888, he was married to Miss Pinkie Taylor, of Laredo, to which union three children have been given: Edna Victoria, Clarence Wallace, and Brewer Taylor. Mrs. McNeil is a member of the Episcopal Church.

CLARENCE D. KEMP. The average citizen, interested as he may be in the progress and development of the section in which his interests are centered, pursues the even tenor of his way with little thought of the wonderful improvements that are going on about him in the way of beautiful farms, thriving villages, etc. Not so with Mr. Clarence D. Kemp, who is a live, progressive and most highly esteemed citizen. He has witnessed with pride the rapid progress made in Wharton County in the last quarter of a century, and though by no means advanced in years, being now only about forty-two years of age, has contributed his share towards its advancement, during that time. He is one of the prominent planters of the county and has a fine home twelve miles southeast of Wharton, on Caney Creek. Mr. Kemp was born at Monroe, La., in 1852, and is a son of Thomas and Eliza (Scott) Kemp, the former a native of Jackson Parish, La., and the latter of Alabama. When a young man the father moved to Texas, and first located on Caney Creek, in the neighborhood where our subject now resides, and was here married to Miss Scott, the daughter of Jonathan Scott. She came here in 1829, with almost the first colony, and is still living on Bay Prairie with her son, our subject. Mr. Kemp died in this county in 1854, when but thirty-five years of age. He had served in the Mexican War, was at Vera Cruz and other battles of that war. He did not own any land. To his marriage were born two children, of whom our subject is the elder. The other, Telitha, now deceased, was the wife of John McMahon. Our subject was reared in this county, had no education, and when old enough commenced driving cattle, continuing this for twenty-five years. He gathered together and brought in many a herd that had wandered away and crossed the border into Kansas, and worked for John Kokernott and others during this time. When thirteen years of age he commenced working for himself, and has since taken care of his mother. He has had a great deal of experience in the stock business, and is engaged in that at the present time, feeding and shipping a large number. In the year 1875 he was married to Miss Jane Crawford, who was born in Wharton County, and they have two interesting children: Hattie and Taylor. At the time of his marriage Mr. Kemp bought the land he now owns, 100 acres of bay prairie, and afterwards over 406 acres of excellent land, in fact, as fine as there is in the State. Although he has had to fight his own way in life, his earnest and persistent efforts have been rewarded and he has met with substantial results. For eight years he was Postmaster at Waterville, and during that time formed a partnership with Hamilton B. Dickson (who was recently Sheriff of the county, and who was killed in the performance of his duty). They had a gin which had a capacity of 600 bales yearly. In politics Mr. Kemp is a Democrat.

DOLPH P. MOORE. The original of this notice is a man whose pleasing manner and accommodating spirit have gathered around him many friends. In this day, when the strife for place breeds so much selfishness, the virtue of these qualities is the more apparent. Dolph P. Moore, a man widely and popularly known, is now filling the office of County Treasurer, with credit to himself and to the satisfaction of his constituents. He was born in Indianola, Texas, in 1852, and is the son of Robert Baxter Moore, a native of the State of New Jersey, who came to Texas about 1846 or '47, and located first at Victoria and afterwards at Indianola. There he met his death by drowning during the storm of 1875. He was born in the year 1807, and when a young man learned the carpenter trade, following building for the most part during the remainder of his life. He was married in the State of New York to Miss

Mary C. Layton, who still survives and makes her home with her son, Capt. W. E. Moore. She is a member of the Baptist Church, and her husband held membership in the same. Of their seven children four are now living. Dolph P. Moore attended the high schools of Indianola, and when seventeen years of age began his career as a merchant with the firm of Price Bros. at Deming's Bridge, and a few years later at Elliott, for himself. At one time he was the owner of land where Bay City stands, and had other interests in the county. In the month of November, 1892, Mr. Moore was elected County Treasurer, and is the present incumbent of that office. So wisely and well has he discharged the duties of that position that he has received warm praise from political friend and foe alike. Although he started with limited means to fight his way in life, he has made a good battle, and is now in very comfortable circumstances. In the year 1879 he married Miss Louisa Wendel, daughter of John Wendel, of this county. Six children blessed this union, three sons and three daughters. In his political views Mr. Moore is a Democrat, but liberal in his opinions.

JUDGE HENRY MANEY. This honored citizen of Frio County, Texas, was born in Rutherford County, Tennessee, November 5, 1829, the third of five children born to Henry and Mary W. (Browne) Maney, who were born in North Carolina and Virginia, respectively. The father was a farmer, and in 1826 removed with his family to Rutherford County, Tennessee, but in 1854 or 1855 came to Texas and settled in Guadalupe County, where the father died in 1865 and the mother in 1877, both being members of the Presbyterian Church. The paternal grandfather, James Maney, was born in France and came to America during colonial times, at which time he was a child, and the rest of his life was spent in North Carolina, while the maternal grandfather, Samuel Browne, was of English birth and one of the early settlers of Virginia, where he died when Mrs. Maney, his daughter, was a child. Judge Henry Maney was reared in Tennessee, and he was the first student to enter Union University at Murfreesboro, which institution he attended four years, and at the age of fifteen he entered the University of Nashville, from which he graduated in 1847. He then began the study of law in Manchester, Tenn., with William K. Wilson, but after a time he returned home to continue his studies there, and was admitted to the bar by Chancellor Bromfield Ridley and Judge Thomas Maney (an uncle), after which he began practicing his profession at Woodbury. He was a partner of Edwin A. Keeble for about nine months, but came to Texas in 1851, and began practicing at Seguin. In February, 1852, he married Mary Malinda Erskine, a native of Virginia, and daughter of Michael Erskine, who came to Texas from Mississippi about 1842. In 1854 Judge Maney and his father-in-law started for California with a herd of 1,000 cattle, and with thirty-five men made the trip via El Paso, up the Rio Grande River to Fort Thorn, thence westward to within about forty-five miles of San Diego, and here the cattle were wintered. The loss on the trip was only about fifty head. In the canyon, in which Fort Davis is now situated, they camped in August, and the Indians came at night and attempted to stampede their herd, and failing to do that they secured three work oxen and drove to a place in a deep canyon about twelve miles from camp. Capt. Callahan, the foreman, with a company of about twelve men followed the Indians, and after a sharp brush with them they secured a dozen head of horses, and lost not a man. They were then troubled by the Indians no more until they neared

Santa Cruz, Mexico (then thought to be in Arizona), when, uniting their forces with some other drovers, they started on the trail of the Redmen, and the next day at about three o'clock had a fight with them at the San Pedro River. The Indians gave way, but fought as they retreated, and twenty-one of their number were slain. Our travelers then continued their journey. Judge Maney and Capt. Callahan returned to Texas by water in 1855, and in 1856 the judge resumed the practice of his profession in Seguin, and in 1857 was elected Chief Justice of Guadalupe County, and served two years. In 1861 he enlisted in the Confederate army, Company A, First Regiment of Sibley's Brigade, and was on the frontier and in the battle of Val Verde. He was there wounded, and for three months was confined to the hospital, and about August 15, returned to San Antonio, where he was honorably discharged. In 1864 he was elected to the Tenth Legislature of Texas. He was appointed Judge of the Twenty-second Judicial District in 1870 by Governor Davis, but was removed in 1873 by the change of administration. In 1876 he was elected to the office of County Judge, under the new constitution, and served three years. In 1883 he moved to Pearsall, and though long an active legal practitioner, is now in semi-retirement. Of a family of fourteen children born to himself and wife, eleven are now living. The judge is a Mason, and he and wife and seven children are members of the New Church. His life has been a somewhat remarkable and checkered one, but always a strictly honorable and upright one.

GUSTAVE A. HEILIG. A faithful and painstaking and accurate official is Gustave A. Heilig, Assessor of Fayette County, Texas, and the people of the county have not been slow to recognize and acknowledge his fitness for his present office. He owes his nativity to Posen, Prussia, where he was born November 2, 1855, a son of Ferdinand J. Heilig, who was also a Prussian and a highly educated gentleman. After teaching in his native land for some time he came to America with his family, and located in New Braunfels, in Comal County, Texas, and in the New Braunfels Academy he was a successful teacher for about twenty-eight years. He is now living in retirement in New Braunfels. He was born July 3, 1826, and his wife, who was formerly Miss U. F. Habermann, was born in Prussia, August 26, 1828, and is also living. Their union resulted in the birth of nine children, of whom the subject of this sketch was the second in order of birth. He attended the school taught by his father until he was fourteen years of age, at which time he became a salesman in a store in New Braunfels for a term of two years, and when not yet seventeen years old, he passed the required examination, and commenced teaching in Guadalupe Valley, in Comal County, where he remained one term. He then taught two years in Mission Valley, then for five years taught the Bluff School in Fayette County, after which he taught in the German-English Academy at Austin for one year. He was then appointed Deputy Sheriff of Fayette County, but he soon after became Deputy Assessor, and after filling this position for two years, was elected to the office of Assessor, which position he has since filled with marked efficiency. In 1890 he engaged also in the lumber business with John T. Harwell, and remained associated with this gentleman until his interest was recently purchased by Mr. G. A. Hall. In the early part of 1894 he became a member of the mercantile firm of H. C. Heilig & Co., which firm does a very extensive business in hardware, farming implements and groceries. The prospects for a successful business future for Mr. Heilig are excellent, and any good fortune that may befall him, is well merited. His operations have not been confined merely to these enterprises, but he is also interested in the La Grange Compress Company, as well as other important enterprises. In 1888 he was united in marriage with Miss Rosie Alexandria, daughter of Capt. Alexandria. He has attained to the Royal Arch degree in the A. F. & A. M., and he has represented the Knights of Pythias and Legion of Honor in the Grand Lodges of the State, and also belongs to the I. O. O. F. and Hermann's Soehne. He has seen much of the development of this section, and well remembers when the early settlers were greatly troubled by the Indians, who would drive off their stock and steal anything else that they could get their hands on.

JAMES UNDERWOOD FRAZAR. This prominent citizen of Eagle Lake, Texas, is a member of the well-known firm of Frazar Bros., who are among the most extensive planters of this section of the State. He was born in Holmes County, Mississippi, in 1856, to Micajah Frazar, who was a product of the Old North State, and who removed from there to Mississippi in 1869, and the following year purchased the land on which the subject of this sketch is now living, consisting of 2,000 acres. He was an attorney-at-law, and took an active part in the political affairs of his day, laboring for the success of the Democratic party, but never for the purpose of holding office. While in the Lone Star State he devoted the most of his attention to planting, and was a very useful and highly esteemed citizen. He died in 1873 at the age of sixty-nine years, his death being a source of much regret to all who knew him. The school days of James Underwood Frazar were spent in his native State of Mississippi, and, owing to the death of his elder brother, Algernon S., soon after the death of the father, James U. had to take the management of affairs into his own hands, and has had control of them ever since. He has two sisters, who are married, and two that are single, who live with him, and by subsequent purchases they have become the owners of about 3,000 acres of excellent farming land, all in one body, and another tract of about 1,000 acres. This property has been acquired by the Frazar brothers through the exercise of much industry and perseverance. In addition to their extensive farming operations, they have also conducted a general mercantile store for the past five years and, although they were burned out about three years ago, they resumed business and have carried it on successfully ever since. Mr. Frazar raises large quantities of cotton annually, and was one of the first men in this section of the country to engage in the sugar business; and Capt. Dunovant, an extensive sugar raiser, secured his start in this enterprise, from Mr. Frazar. He has always been wideawake, pushing and active, and therefore successful.

CRISTOBAL BENAVIDES. Various have been the occupations that have occupied the time and attention of this most worthy citizen during his walk through life, but for a number of years past his time and attention have been given to the occupations of merchandising and the raising of stock. He was born in the town in which he now lives in 1839, the third child of Jose and Tomasa (Cameros) Benavides, who were born in Laredo, Texas, and Mexico, respectively. The paternal grandfather, Jose Maria Benavides, was a Captain of the Mexican army, and came to Laredo with his company. He was married to Dona Petra Sanchez, a granddaughter of Tomaz Sanchez, the founder of the town of Laredo. The father was an extensive ranchman and resided in Laredo during his life. His first marriage was to Dona Ramon, to which union two sons were given, Refugio and Santos. The father died in 1846. The subject of this sketch was reared in Laredo, and was educated in the schools of this place and at Corpus Christi. In his early youth he engaged in speculating in stock, and also before the war he had contracts for carrying the mail. In 1861 he entered the State service as a Sergeant, in a company commanded by his brother Santos, and remained in the service on the Rio Grande River for about one year. During this time he was advanced in rank to Lieutenant. The regiment to which he belonged was finally reorganized, and was mustered into the Confederate service under Col. Duffe, and in the meantime Refugio was commanding a company, Santos being a Major, and he himself became a Captain of Santos' company, who was then eventually raised to the rank of Colonel, and the regiment was thereafter known as Benavides' Regiment. This command served mainly on the Rio Grande River, and was in many engagements. Col. Santos Benavides was ill at about the close of the war, and Cristobal was with him at Laredo when the last battle of the war was fought under Col. Ford, near Brownsville, in which engagement Refugio Benavides commanded a company. At the close of the war the subject of this sketch was united in marriage with Dona Lamar Bee, and immediately thereafter engaged in business with his brother Santos, and his present mercantile business was founded under the firm name of S. Benavides & Bro. They did a wholesale and retail business for several years; were among the leading merchants of the place, and also conducted a branch establishment at Nuevo Laredo. Santos Benavides died in 1891, but since about 1875 the firm has been known as C. Benavides. He carries a stock valued at about $10,000, and by good management a large annual business is done. In 1866 the subject of this sketch engaged in the raising of sheep, and although he started with a small herd, he, in time, became the owner of 20,000 head. He owns land in Webb County to the extent of 45,000 acres, and for some time past has made a specialty of graded Durham cattle. He is a wideawake and enterprising man of business, and being strictly upright in his business he is highly honored. His union has resulted in the birth of the following children: Carlota (Valdez), Maria (Sanchez), Santos, a lawyer; Lamar, Lilla, Cristobal, Jr., Eulalio, Louis, Melitona, and Elvira. The oldest members of this family were educated in Austin, and all the family are attendants of the Catholic Church. The life of Mr. Benavides has been singularly pure and upright, and he is extremely proud of his children, who have every attribute of worthy citizenship, qualities which they have without doubt inherited from their worthy progenitors. He was a brave and gallant officer during the great Civil War, and his brother Santos deserves especial mention in this connection, for he knew not the meaning of fear, and was an able and skillful commander. He did much to preserve peace on the Texas frontier, and in the record of the brave officers of Texas his name will always hold an honorable place. He was commissioned a General, but the war ended before he assumed his rank. He was a good business man also, and a law-abiding, public-spirited citizen, whose usefulness was only closed by his death.

GEORGE A. HALL. To succeed in any calling one must be energetic, up with the times, and quick to grasp at all opportunities for bettering one's financial condition. Such a man is George A. Hall, whose name heads this sketch. He is a son of Alfred C. Hall, who was a native of Illinois, and who came to Texas about 1830 with his father, James Hall, the third. There was a James

Hall who was of Scotch-Irish lineage, who came to the United States and located in Kentucky, of which State he was a pioneer settler, and he afterward located in what became Nashville, Tenn., of which place he was the first resident. He went from there to Illinois, where he spent the rest of his life. He had a son James, who was the grandfather of Alfred C., and in Jackson County, Ill., his home continued to be until his death. James Hall, his son and father of Alfred C., came to Austin County, Texas, located in Bear District, of which he was Judge before Texas became independent. He was a farmer and trader, and died in 1854, after having taken part in the Texas Rebellion as a private. Alfred C. Hall entered the service of the Lone Star State when but 14 years of age, and he and his father took part in numerous battles. The family had a great deal of trouble with the Indians when they first located in the State, and one member of the family was killed by the Redskins. Alfred C. Hall, father of the subject of this sketch, lived in Bastrop County for a time, then resided for a number of years in Fayette County, and is now a resident of Washington County, Texas. He has been very successful as a farmer and business man, and has accumulated a fair share of this world's goods. He was married to Elizabeth Hunt, who was born in this State, and by her became the father of three children: Clara, who died in Indianapolis, Ind., in 1876; Thomas A., who resides in La Grange, Texas, and George A., who was born November 27, 1847. The latter secured an excellent education in Baylor University, but left this institution to enter the army, becoming one of McNally's scouts. At the close of the war he commenced farming in this (Fayette) county, and here he has since resided. He has extensive farming interests, and is also connected with John T. Harwell in the lumber business, the firm being known as Harwell & Hall, and also has a lumber yard of his own at New Ulm, in Austin County. He is, besides, connected with the extensive grocery interests of La Grange, besides various other enterprises, in all of which he has been active and successful. In 1886 he was united in marriage with Mrs. Moore, a daughter of Col. W. W. Ligon. Mr. Hall is a member of the K. of H., the A. O. U. W., and the K. of P., and is a member of the Christian Church.

GEORGE AUSTIN. He who is careful of small things, and who earns a reputation for honesty and reliability by observing the promises he has made, is already on the high road to a consummation of his hopes. Such a one is Mr. George Austin, the most efficient County and District Clerk of Matagorda County, who was born here in 1857. His father, William H. Austin, who was born in Catskill, Greene County, New York, left there when a young man and came to Matagorda County, where he was engaged as a pilot on Matagorda Bay. In after years he became a merchant and followed that successfully for many years. During the Civil War he ran a mail boat between that town and Indianola for the Confederate Government, was captured at the latter place and taken to New Orleans, where he was retained for a number of months. He was married in Lavaca, Calhoun County, Texas, May 30, 1854, to Miss Mary Elizabeth Ives, daughter of Charles Ives, who came originally from England, and settled in Galveston, Texas, at an early day. That city then consisted of a few fishermen's huts. Mr. Ives did not remain there long, but went to Lavaca, Calhoun County, where he followed the trade of builder. The father of our subject was born in the year 1827, and died September 28, 1878, in the State of New York, whither he had gone on a visit. He was buried at Catskill. For many years he had been a faithful member of the Episcopal Church, and in politics supported the principles of the Democratic party. He was a member of the I. O. O. F., a charter member of Matagorda Lodge No. 47, and represented his lodge in the Grand Lodge. Mrs. Austin was a member of the Baptist Church. They reared four children, who were named as follows: William E., a prominent attorney of this county; George, our subject; Nettie E., wife of Charles J. Hatch, a merchant of San Antonio, and Charles S., residing in San Antonio, is Secretary and Treasurer of F. F. Collins Manufacturing Company and General Manager of the same. Our subject attended the private schools of this town, but in 1873 he went on his father's schooner, plying between this place and Indianola. From 1878 to 1886 he was in the Clerk's office, and at the latter date was elected to the office of County and District Clerk, which position he now holds. He succeeded his brother to that position. On the 25th of January, 1887, he was married to Miss Anna M. Serrill, of this place, daughter of Richard and Sophia Serrill. Mr. and Mrs. Austin are members of the Episcopal Church and liberal contributors to the same. He is an Odd Fellow, holds the office of Noble Grand, and represented his lodge at Fort Worth in 1884. He is also a member of the K. of H., Rising Sun Lodge No. 2570, and is Financial Recorder.

HON. ALBERT C. HORTON was a native of Georgia, born in 1798. His father was a man of position and affluence, but died while young Horton was yet a boy. The care of the estates fell upon his son's shoulders, the subject of our sketch, who had received from nature a strong understanding and a hardy constitution, and early in life developed those traits of character which in after time made him one of our grandest patriots. He moved from his native State to LaGrange, Franklin County, Alabama. There he met and married the handsome Eliza Holliday, of the family long prominent in the annals of that State, at the residence of her brother-in-law and guardian, W. J. Croom, father of Col. John L. Croom, of Matagorda. This was in about the year 1823. There he was initiated into the secrets of Masonry, and continued a member throughout his long life. Later he made his home in Greensboro, where he was elected and served one term in the State Senate, about the year 1832. It was at this juncture that he resolved to come to Texas. Giving up position, honor and fame, he turned his face Westward, and cast his wealth and fortunes with the young empire. He chose Matagorda County as his home. This was in 1835. After purchasing several leagues of land and making provision for his family's comfort, he offered the patriots his purse and services for the good of the just and holy struggle that liberty was making against the oppressor, Santa Anna, then at the head of the Mexican Government. Santa Anna, seeing the necessity of early action on his part if he expected his policy to be dominant in Texas, in October, 1835, he sent General Cos, his brother-in-law, with a well-equipped force to Texas to subdue the revolutionary spirit. How they were met and routed at Gonzales by the patriots, under the gallant Moore, driven and forced to take refuge within the walls of the Alamo, at San Antonio; how later his concentrated forces surrendered to the Texans and were allowed to depart for Mexico, are among the brightest achievements of the patriots, and are parts of Texan history narrated elsewhere in this volume. Santa Anna, after the defeat of his General, set about with his usual celerity to come in person at the head of an army that would crush the revolution out of existence. Early in the year 1836 he was in Texas with 8,000 men, furnished and provisioned for his campaign of destruction. And now Mr. Horton comes out prominently, and ever after was one of Texas' leading men. He raised, mounted and armed a cavalry force at his own expense, and joined the brave, but afterwards the ill-fated, Fannin, then stationed as Colonel commanding the Southern army at the fort at La Bahia (Goliad). Fannin's force was made up of volunteers from Georgia and Alabama, many of whom Horton had known in their homes. After some slight fighting, in which Horton and his troops succeeded in beating off the Mexican advance forces sent to attack the fort, the news of the fall of the Alamo and the treacherous butchery of its brave defenders fell like a clap of thunder upon the hearts of the Texan patriots. The certain knowledge of what they had to expect if beaten drew them together and nerved each heart for a struggle to conquer or die. It was then that Fannin received positive orders from Houston as Commander-in-Chief, to retreat, fall back and form a junction with the main army somewhere in the East. Here the clear-sightedness of Horton was displayed. He urged Fannin to immediately obey the order, seeing that with the small force then at his disposal what would inevitably follow; but alas, Fannin, rash, reckless and brave to a fault in his daring, with but 350 effective men, imagined himself secure and counted upon his ability to carry his army and supplies safely through, without loss, back East. In vain did Horton urge and plead against his Commander's waste of time, until too late. In a few days Urrea and his forces were upon them, when Fannin began his retreat. He dispatched Horton and his cavalry to skirmish in front, and with his forces moved on in the direction of Victoria. When about ten miles on his journey his progress was interrupted by the approach of the Mexican forces, numbering in all above 1,000. Upon Horton's return he found them surrounded and cut off, and with his troops he was fortunate in making good his escape to Victoria. Their subsequent fate, how in violation of a treaty and formal guarantee that their lives and liberty would be spared them, they were taken back to Goliad and by the orders of the tyrant, Santa Anna, murdered, is part of the history of this State. It is only sufficient to say, had Horton's advice been followed this noble band would have been saved to Texas. The subject of our sketch, after the disaster, arrived safely and joined the army in the East. The battle of San Jacinto followed soon after, and in the fearful onslaught on that glorious day, ended with the annihilation of Santa Anna's power in Texas. This victory gave birth to the liberty for which the patriots had expended treasures, and which they consecrated by the blood of the heroes of the Alamo and La Bahia. With the rout of Santa Anna's army, his capture following, hostilities ceased, peace and quiet for a time were restored to the people of the country. Now came the real labor of the patriots, that of bringing order and good government out of chaos and ruin from the demoralized condition of affairs following the splendid victories won by the colonists. To quiet contending factions and inaugurate a unison of thought and feeling between the settlers, taxed the wisdom of the leading men of the day to the utmost. Colonel Horton had retired to his home, but as he had served the people in the field, he was called to lend his talents to her councils. He was elected to the first Congress and served as one of its best members, and helped frame the constitution of the Republic.

28

He was afterwards appointed by President Lamar one of the Commissioners to select and locate the city of Austin. When the question of annexation came about he was one of its warmest advocates and served as one of the annexation committee. When Texas assumed State government he was elected Lieutenant Governor; J. Pinckney Henderson being the first Chief Executive. War against the United States being declared by Mexico consequent to Texas' admission into the Union, Henderson taking the field at the head of the Texas troops, Colonel Horton was called to the executive chair, and acquitted himself in the discharge of the onerous duties to the satisfaction of the entire people. His term of office over, he followed his inclinations and returned to devote his energies to the management of his vast estates. Sometime in the early '40s he had moved into the upper part of Matagorda County, but when this county was organized in 1846, became a part of Wharton. Here he went into planting on a scale never before witnessed in this portion of the Union. Considering the sparsely settled condition of the country then, and lack of transportation, the output of his farms was on a vast scale. He would send to market 650 to 700 bales of cotton, but it was the product of sugar and molasses which engrossed his time—450 to 500 hogsheads of sugar and 1,600 barrels of syrup was considered a fair estimate of the yearly output of his cane crop. He had always been a faithful member of the Baptist Church, and was first a Trustee and afterwards President of the Baylor University, making that institution a present of $5,000 and a magnificent bell, and it was his intention ultimately, to endow a professorship of not less than $50,000. But the specter of war loomed up above the horizon and changed the outlook and hopes of a people. The war wrecked his once princely fortune, and the failure of the Southern cause told heavily upon Governor Horton, and he did but survive it. He passed away peacefully at his summer home on Matagorda's coast in October, 1865, with the love and esteem of a people and State whom he had helped make great and prosperous.

JAMES H. HILDEBRAND. For many years, or since boyhood, Mr. Hildebrand has given the occupation of farming his principal attention, and as a result has met with substantial returns. He is also one of the old settlers of this section, but is a native Kentuckian, born June 20, 1835, to the union of David and Mary M. (Crawford) Hildebrand, natives of Pennsylvania and North Carolina, respectively. Grandfather Hildebrand came from Germany, his native country, and settled in Pennsylvania. From there he moved to North Carolina, and thence to Kentucky, dying in Lyons County in the latter State. There his wife also passed the closing scenes of her life. They reared a family of six children: George, of Illinois, near Springfield; Isaac, of the same part of Illinois; Mary, married Eden Lawrence, of Illinois; Jennie (deceased), Mary (deceased) and David. On the 11th of January, 1851, Mr. Hildebrand moved to Texas and located in Washington County, ten miles north of Brenham, where he purchased land in the then northwestern part of the county, but what was then Lee County. There he passed the remainder of his life, dying November 7, 1893, leaving two children. His wife had passed away in 1889. Both were members of the Methodist Episcopal Church. Mr. Hildebrand was a member in good standing of the Masonic fraternity, Salem Lodge, at the time of his death, having joined that order at McClellan Lodge, of which he was a charter member. He was a man of unquestioned integrity, and was a representative citizen. Of the six children born to his marriage only two are now living: James H., William (deceased), Mary M. (deceased), George R., of Lee County; David S. (deceased), served four years in the Confederate army, and Lizzie (deceased). Like most boys reared on a farm, our subject received his education in the country schools of Washington County, and when twenty-one years old began life for himself as a farmer and stock-raiser. He first began tilling the soil on his father's farm, and remained under the home roof until his thirty-first year. During the years 1864 and 1865 he served in Capt. Dowles' Company, and was in service in the States. Later he became a member of Capt. Roland's Company, Wall's Legion, of which he was a member when the war came to an end. Being a cripple, he was not in the regular service, but his brothers were members of Capt. Whitehead's Company, De Bray's Regiment, and served throughout the war. Our subject was married August 6, 1865, to Miss Melissa Wittenburg (see sketch of W. J. Hildebrand), and afterward resided in Washington County until 1873. He and wife then moved on their present place of residence, and are now the owners of 454 acres of fine land, with 100 acres under cultivation; 310 acres are under fence. Mr. and Mrs. Hildebrand's union resulted in the birth of three children: Mary E., died in May, 1893; Narcissa F. and Jane. Mrs. Hildebrand is a member of the Baptist Church and Mr. Hildebrand holds membership in Lyons Lodge, No. 195, of the A. F. and A. M. Politically he is a Democrat.

JOHN MATTHEWS. It is unnecessary to speak in words of colored praise of business men, who, on account of their long tenure and extensive operations, comprise almost a history of the business in which they are engaged. Their very existence is emphatic evidence of the honorable position that they occupy, and the long course of just dealing that they have pursued. John Matthews, the oldest merchant of Caney, and of Matagorda County, Texas, six miles east of Bay City, the new county seat of Matagorda County, is a native Virginian, born in Loudoun County, six miles south of Harper's Ferry, sixty-nine years ago, or on the 23d of February, 1834. His father, Simon Matthews, was a very successful farmer, but died at the early age of thirty-five years. Of the six children born to his marriage, our subject is the eldest, and spent his school days in the Academy at Hillsboro. When a boy of only sixteen years he went to Baltimore and spent a few years selling goods. In 1856 he came to Texas, and remained in San Antonio for one year, after which he came to Caney and bought out a store kept by P. C. Evans, who is now a resident of Virginia, but who had opened a store there in 1852. This was the only store at that time between the towns of Matagorda and Wharton, and Mr. Matthews soon had a very extensive trade. However, he lost the most of this during the Rebellion, for at the close of the war he had many outstanding debts, and many thousand dollars in Confederate money and bonds. These are still in his possession. He did not enter the army, but was appointed receiver of cotton, and kept that appointment until the war closed. He was also engaged in transporting cotton to Mexico, etc. After the war he resumed business in a very small way, but is now one of the foremost business men of the county. In connection with his business interests he is also engaged in planting, and has met with a fair degree of success in that calling, as in all other enterprises to which he has turned his hand. Mr. Matthews was married in Texas in 1861 to Miss Van Dorn, daughter of Isaac Van Dorn, who was an early settler of this county, the first Sheriff, and a successful stockman. Six children were born to Mr. and Mrs. Matthews, four sons and two daughters, five of whom are now living. In his religious views he is a Methodist, and in politics a stanch Democrat.

AUGUST FAHRENTHOLD. Among those to whom success has come early is the original of this notice, who inherits from his Teutonic ancestors much of their industry, perseverance and energy. He was born in this county in the year 1866, and was second in order of birth of twelve children born to his parents, L. and ———— Fahrenthold, natives of Germany. L. Fahrenthold was born in the year 1842, and came to the United States a boy with his parents, who located at Frelsburgh, in Colorado County. For some time he followed farming, but subsequently ran wagons between Texas and Mexico, hauling cotton. Still later he started a gin at High Hill, in Fayette County, which he operated until five years ago, and then associated himself with George Herder, Fred Hillje and D. W. Jackson, under the firm name of Fahrenthold & Co., and started to settle up the West Ranch, which they had purchased. They decided to build a town there, and this they have done, with a good prospect for a city. Lumber yards, stores, gins and fine residences have been erected, and the place is in a thriving condition. It is called El Campo. Five years ago this was a station on the G., H. & S. A. Railroad consisting of a section-house on the prairie, with not another house in sight. Mr. Fahrenthold erected the first gin in the place, and by his untiring efforts and excellent executive ability has done much to improve and develop the place. He has resided near El Campo for the past two years, and no man in the county stands higher in the estimation of the people than he. August Fahrenthold received his schooling at High Hill, but when fourteen years of age he left the school room and assisted his father on the farm until eighteen years of age. After that he engaged in business in Weimar as salesman until 1888, after which he opened a store and carried on business for himself there until January, 1894. At that time he and Fred Hillje started a store at El Campo, on an extensive scale, and they are doing a flattering business, having thus far (October, 1894) sold $50,000 worth of goods. Our subject is the manager of the business and takes charge of everything. In the choice of a wife he selected Miss Ida Ramthune, and they have one bright little daughter. Both he and wife are members of the Lutheran Church, and he is a member of Hermann-Soehne, a German order.

WILLIAM J. HILDEBRAND. Prominent among the people of Fayette County, Texas, who have made for themselves honorable names, and who have acquired a competency largely through their unaided efforts, is the gentleman whose name forms the heading for this sketch. A native of Robertson County, Tennessee, born May 22, 1832, Mr. Hildebrand was the eldest of three children, all sons, born to the union of Absolom and Sarah (Smith) Hildebrand, natives of Tennessee and North Carolina, the former being of German and the latter of English parentage. The Hildebrand family came to Tennessee at quite an early day, but the Smith family was one of the first in Robertson County, that State. Our subject's maternal grandfather was Capt. John Williams of Revolutionary fame. His commission was issued by George Washington. He came from Wake County, North Carolina, to Tennessee, and settled in Robertson County, here he married and reared seven children, six daughters and one son: John W., Margaret, Sarah, mother of our subject, Elizabeth, Wilmoth B., Nancy and Rachel. Absolom Hildebrand's parents,

Henry and———(Traughber) Hildebrand were natives of North Carolina, and came to Tennessee when Absolom was a small boy, locating in Robertson County, where they reared five children, Michael, Absolom, William, Enoch, and Sarah. In the year 1831 Absolom Hildebrand and Miss Sarah Smith were married. For some time after this they resided in Robertson County, in all, about six years, and then removed to Hancock County, Illinois, Mr. Hildebrand dying there within three days after his arrival. Later Mrs. Hildebrand returned to Robertson County, Tennessee, and she was there married in 1841 to J. M. Shelton, by whom she had two children. Mrs. Shelton died on the 16th of July, 1844. The children to her first union were named as follows: William J., our subject; Henry I., resides in McCulloch County, Texas; Elbert W., died in 1879 in Kingman County, Kansas; and John M., who resides in Erath County, Texas. William J. Hildebrand received the principal part of his education in the "Lone Star State," and is mainly self-educated. In 1851, or when nineteen years of age he left Tennessee for Texas, and for one year after reaching this State resided in Travis County. After this he drifted around in different counties until 1857, when he came to this neighborhood. For two years he taught school, his first term being three miles east of Schulenburg and composed of all American children. In the year 1858 Mr. Hildebrand was married, and when the Civil War broke out he was engaged in stock-raising. During the winter of 1861 and '62 he again wielded the birch, but on the 3d of March, 1862, he left home as a member of Capt. Preston's Company (M), Whitfield's First Texas Legion of Cavalry, and proceeded immediately to Des Arc, Ark. There he was dismounted and sent to Corinth, Mississippi, but did not reach that place in time for the battle. However his company did some skirmishing. He was first engaged in a battle at Iuka, Miss., afterwards at Davis' Bridge, Miss., and was with Van Dorn and Price during the second battle of Corinth, but was left with the wagons. Later the army fell back to Holly Springs, and from there to Water Valley, where the company and legion were mounted and made a portion of "The Texas Brigade," commanded first by Gen. Z. S. Ross, of Texas, and under him much hard fighting was done. From there the command was sent to Tennessee to the assistance of Gen. Bragg, and soon after this Mr. Hildebrand was detailed as scout, and was with Gen. Van Dorn until the latter's death. After that he was attached to the staff of Gen. Forrest until W. J. Jackson gathered an army to go to Pemberton's assistance at Vicksburg, when he was with Jackson until that General was ordered to Louisiana, April 8, 1864. Then he got a furlough for sixty days. On the 28th of April, 1864, he arrived home, this being his first visit after enlisting. In July, 1864, he joined the army at Atlanta, Ga., and accompanied Hood's army to Columbia, Franklin and Nashville. The first was fought in Lawrence County, between Jackson's cavalry on the Confederate side and a division of United States cavalry. This Mr. Hildebrand thinks was the prettiest fight he saw during the war. The Confederate forces were victorious and drove the Federal forces to Columbia, or near there. Our subject's last skirmish was at Pulaski, Tenn., and here he was cut off from the remainder of the army. To prevent capture he went to Robertson County, where he remained with relatives until the war closed. He surrendered by special permit of Gen. Rosecrans, at Nashville, Tenn., and as soon as possible reached home. Here he found everything in fair shape and with a team of

well-broken oxen he began hauling lumber from near Houston, making from
five to six dollars per day. He continued hauling and freighting until 1873,
when the Sunset Railroad was a certainty, after which he followed farming
and stock-raising. He cultivates from four to six hundred acres, mostly
cotton, and is breeding some fine horses. Mr. Hildebrand was married in
1858 to Miss Narcissa Wittenburg, a native of Missouri, and daughter of John
and Jane (Crawford) Wittenburg, natives of Crawford County, Missouri.
Mr. and Mrs. Hildebrand's union was blessed by the birth of six children,
who were named as follows: John W., deceased; one died in infancy; H. E.
is Clerk of the Court of Civil Appeals, of San Antonio; Olive, at home;
Walter J., attending Jefferson Medical College; and Ira P., in college. Mr.
and Mrs. Hildebrand are earnest and consistent members of the Christian
Church, and Mr. Hildebrand is a member of Lyon Lodge No. 195, A. F. & A.M.
He has served as Justice of the Peace for a number of years, and in 1886,
was elected County Commissioner, serving two years. Politically he is a
Democrat. His son, John W., one of the leading young attorneys of the
State, held an enviable position, both as a lawyer and as a citizen. He was
in partnership with an attorney of San Antonio, who was one of the most eminent jurists in the State, at the time of his death. He was killed in the village of Castroville, Texas, June 2, 1887, by the Sheriff of Medinia County, that
State. The eulogy passed upon the life and character of this gifted young
man, shows the great respect in which he was held by his many friends.
The resolutions of respect formed by these friends, and presented to the District Court were as follows:

Resolutions on the untimely death of the late J. W. Hildebrand, Esq.:

Having been informed of the untimely taking off of our brother, J. W. Hildebrand,
believing that thereby the bar has lost a faithful and industrious member, always true to the
profession, and therefore true to his clients, that the State has lost a patriotic citizen, that our
community has lost a genial and warm-hearted gentleman, that his wife has lost an affectionate husband, and his children a thoughtful, attentive, provident and indulgent father.
Now for the purpose of making known our views and expressing our sympathy with his
bereaved family, be it resolved; that these resolutions be presented to the honorable District Court, and spread upon the minutes, and the Secretary of this meeting of his brethren
of the bar be directed to furnish a copy of this memorial to his widow, and also copies to the
journals of this city with request that they publish it.

OSCAR BERGSTROM (Chairman.)
L. W. WALTHALL.
T. F. SHIELDS.

In connection with above, a lengthy article was written and presented by
a Mr. Franklin (an attorney) who was an intimate, personal friend of the
deceased. Mr. Hildebrand left a wife and two children to mourn his untimely
death.

THOMAS JOHNSON. A well-kept hostelry is an indispensable institution in
any town of any pretensions, and is a great convenience to the traveling public. Thomas Johnson, proprietor of the Hotel Johnson at Sealy, has all the
requisites of a host, for he is attentive to the wants of his patrons, courteous
and accommodating at all times, keeps a clean and comfortable house, sets a
well appointed table and is reasonable in his charges. In addition to this
business he is also engaged in farming, and his energy and push have been
the means of placing him in an independent financial position. He was born
in Marion County, Mississippi, February 19, 1854, the eldest of three children born to Henry W. T. and Emily (Rankin) Johnson, natives of New
York, and Marion County, Mississippi, respectively. Henry W. Johnson first

came South when quite a young man, as a civil engineer, and for some time remained in the employ of a Railway Company, after which he returned to the City of New York, where he pursued a medical course and graduated from an institution of that city. He then returned South and entered the Army as assistant surgeon for the Mexican War, but prior to this had also graduated from the Louisiana Medical School. After the close of the war he married and immediately engaged in the practice of his profession. He came to Texas with his family in 1859, and after one year's residence in Harris County, went to Polk County, where he made his home until 1874. He came to Austin County in 1890, and here is now residing, being in his seventy-second year. His wife is also living, and is about sixty years of age. Dr. Johnson was for a time in the Confederate Army, being in the Commissary Department, and during his service was in the trans-Mississippi Department and in the State of Texas. His children are Thomas, C. R., of this county, and Mattie (Anderson) who resides in Kansas. Thomas Johnson was educated in Walker County, Texas, and at the age of twenty-one engaged in farming for himself. He came to Austin County in 1886, and here he and his brother engaged quite extensively in agricultural pursuits, besides which they own and operate a large steam cotton gin. A great deal of their attention at present is devoted to the cultivation of the Louisiana sugar cane, and expect, and have every reason to do so, to make a success of this enterprise. Mr. Johnson was married November 18, 1875, to Miss Mary R. Warren, of Mississippi, whose parents, Jesse and Rebecca (Ball) Warren were both members of prominent old families of Mississippi, the Warrens having been first New England colonists, a branch of the family finally drifting southward. Mr. and Mrs. Johnson were united in marriage in the Indian Territory, where both families resided for several years. They have four children: Rufus A., W. Eva, C. Rebecca, and Lou Emma. In 1874 Mr. Johnson entered the Texas State service, and was stationed on the frontier, and for nearly one year did a great deal of scouting, but was in no regular engagement. Mr. Johnson has resided in Sealy since 1893, this change being made that his children might have the advantages of better schools. He is a Democrat politically, and socially is a member of Bellville Lodge No. 195 of the K. of P. His wife is a worthy and consistent member of the Methodist Episcopal Church.

JAMES MERIWETHER. This gentleman is successfully and profitably engaged in looking after the interests of "Uncle Sam" at Pearsall, Texas, and as a citizen, is public spirited, law-abiding and useful. He was born in Dyer County, Tennessee, in 1847, the youngest of eleven children born to George W. and Martha (Williams) Meriwether, who were natives of Georgia, but were among the early settlers of that part of Tennessee, in which section the father was called from life in 1847, when the subject of this sketch was an infant. His widow was called from life in Seguin, Texas, in 1878 or 1879. In 1854 she came to this State with her family and located in Gaudalupe County, near the San Marcos River. In 1863 the subject of this sketch enlisted in the Confederate army, and was first in Fullcrod's, which later consolidated with Bordus' Battalion. He served mainly in Texas on detail duty and was at Galveston at the close of the war. He then rejoined his mother in Guadalupe County, and afterwards moved to Goliad, and for some time thereafter he pursued the paths of learning at a well-conducted educational institution. He then engaged in farming and the raising of cattle, and when the town of Luling was started, about 1871 or 1872, he moved to that place and erected about the second dwelling there. Very shortly after, he embarked in the livery business, but about 1875 purchased a mill on the San Marcos River, near town, and operated the same successfully until about 1882, then removed to Helena, Karnes County, where he was in the mercantile business for some time. About one year later he moved his stock of goods to Pearsall, but did not continue in this business here. He located on a one-quarter section of land near the town, and later became the owner of a ranch of 640 acres, but this he sold and moved to the town in 1890, and for some time was profitably engaged in the real estate business, and was in time appointed to the office of Justice of the Peace and made an excellent official. In January, 1894, he was appointed to the position of Postmaster of the town, and he is very competent in this position. He was married in 1870 to Miss Allie Hill, a native of Goliad County, Texas, and daughter of Rev. Robert Hill, an early Methodist preacher from Alabama, who became well known throughout this State, especially on the frontier. He died about 1860. Mr. and Mrs. Meriwether have six children: George B., Claud Hill, who died at the age of seventeen years; Eugene T., Clarence C., James and Fannie. Mr. Meriwether and his family are members of the Methodist Episcopal Church, and socially he belongs to the K. of H. He owns some city property and has many friends.

DR. JOHN PHILLIPS. Dr. John Phillips is recognized as one of the leading authorities in the surgical and medical profession in Wharton County, and has attained a degree of eminence that is well merited. He is an indefatigable worker and enthusiast in his profession, devoting to it his ripe experience, his untiring energy and his great skill. His birth occurred at Jones' Bluff, Sumpter County, Ala., December 21, 1839, and he is the son of Jack Phillips, who was an extensive planter for those times. During the time the Cherokee Indians were the principal inhabitants of his part of Alabama, Mr. Phillips had a government contract for forwarding mail, and held that for some time. His death occurred in 1845, and his wife died in 1851. One child, besides our subject, was born to this union, George M., who is a resident of Idaho. In Jackson College, Columbia, our subject received a thorough education, and while still quite young began the study of medicine, attending lectures at Nashville, Tenn., and several courses of lectures in Philadelphia, where he pursued his studies until a few years before the war. Not wishing to remain in the North he, with several other students, went South to New Orleans, and there he was graduated from the University of Louisiana in March, 1860. Immediately after he went to Sumpterville, Sumpter County, Ala., and was in practice there until 1861, when he went with Bragg to Pensacola and joined the Fifth Alabama Infantry, Confederate Army, under Col. Rhodes, serving in the surgical department most of the time. He was First Assistant Surgeon, and after the battle of Manassas joined Jeff. Davis' Legion and held the same position until detailed and sent to Richmond, where he was engaged in hospital duty. At the close of the war he was with Wade Hampton in South Carolina. He lost his horse and was obliged to walk home to Alabama. Dr. Phillips was in many prominent engagements, viz.: Manassas, Winchester, Yellow Tavern, Martinsburg, Wilderness, Spottsylvania, Petersburg and others. After reaching his native State the doctor was engaged in rafting cotton on flatboats to New Orleans, and in this way made considerable money. On the 29th of December, 1865, he came to the Lone Star State and located at Wharton, where he has remained since. His practice extends over a wide scope of country, and he has numerous patrons all over the State. On the 1st of October, 1868, he was married to Miss M. T. Galbraith, daughter of Col. E. D. Galbraith, an extensive planter of the county, and an early settler of the same. Their only son, Philoman Jack, recently graduated from the Kentucky School of Medicine at Louisville, and is connected with his father in the practice of medicine, and has met with flattering success. He has never lost a case of pneumonia, although he has had many, and his skill and ability as a physician are thoroughly established. For some time previous to studying medicine this young man was engaged in planting, carried this on very extensively, and he was also in the drug business for some time. At present he is giving his entire attention to his practice, as is also our subject. The latter is a member of the Baptist Church, as are also his wife and son, and he is a Master Mason and a Knight of Honor. He is a member of the Medical Association, and contributes liberally to the circulation of medical journals.

CHRISTIAN BUMGARTEN. Among those who have inherited the thrift and energy of their German ancestors is the gentleman mentioned above, Christian Bumgarten, who was born in the Province of Saxony, Germany, March 13, 1836, and who is now President of the oil mill of Schulenburg, and one of the large farmers of this section. No better citizens have come to Texas than those who emigrated from Germany, for they brought as their inheritance the traits of character which have ever distinguished that race. His parents, Christian and Mary (Bararmaester) Bumgarten, were born in Germany also. Our subject was educated in Germany, and in 1855, when nineteen years of age, he determined to cross the ocean to America. While in the old country he learned the trade of ship carpenter, and after reaching the United States located in Galveston, which at that time had but 1,000 inhabitants. There he followed his trade for nine months, and then made a tour of inspection throughout eastern Texas. Returning to Galveston he remained there but a short time, and then, in the spring of 1857, came to Fayette County, Texas, locating first in LaGrange, where he worked at his trade. In the spring of 1857 he was married, and soon afterwards he purchased sixty-eight acres of improved land, for which he paid ten dollars per acre. He still resides on that place. For some time, in connection with farming, he engaged in contracting and building, and many of the frame houses in this section are the monuments of his work. In the year 1862 he joined the Third Infantry, and soon afterwards was detailed as civil engineer, in which capacity he served until cessation of hostilities. After the war Mr. Bumgarten was without means, his buildings were destroyed and his stock stolen. He was obliged to start from the beginning again. He branched out as a civil engineer, and in 1873 the town of Schulenburg was laid out, he owning a portion of that land. After this Mr. Bumgarten was engaged largely in contracting, and started the first lumber yard, cotton gin, planing mill, sash and door factory, etc., in the place. These enterprises he carried on for a number of years. As early as 1869 he erected his first cotton oil mill, and this was the first one known in this section of the State. This mill had a capacity of only eight tons, and did not prove a financial success, as everything had to be transported by team for thirty miles, and cotton seed oil was not very well known at that

time. Mr. Bumgarten erected the first buildings in Schulenburg, both brick,
frame and stone. About the year 1883 he first engaged in the building of
oil mills, and in the improvement of oil mill machinery. His first mill was
erected for himself at this place. Since then he has erected one at Hempstead,
another at Rockdale, one at Caldwell, Taylor, Kyle, Luling, Hallettsville, and
owns a controlling interest in all of them. He alone owns the one at Schulenburg. Mr. Bumgarten has made considerable improvement in the oil
press, one being a perforated plate known as the Bumgarten plate, and which
is now generally in use and manufactured in Dayton, Ohio. Of this patent
Mr. Bumgarten is justly proud. He has other patents on oil machinery which
he has never placed before the public, and one of these will require an entire
change in the mechanical construction of most of the machinery. They will
doubtless be in general use in the future. Mr. Bumgarten is also the owner
of a large farm, and has 700 acres under cultivation. This farm is worth
from thirty to forty dollars per acre. When Mr. Bumgarten first settled in this
section there were only about twelve or fifteen families here, game was plentiful, and Indians did not trouble them to any great extent. Mr. Bumgarten
was married in June, 1859, to Miss Anestenia Paundswartz, a native of the
Kingdom of Saxony, who came to this country with her aunt and uncle in
1856. She was born March 16, 1841, and was the daughter of Gustave and
————— (Schulze) Paundswartz. Mr. and Mrs. Bumgarten are the parents
of fourteen children, five of whom are deceased: Ernst, Gust, Anna, wife of
Knox Walters; Christian, Elizabeth, Charley, Willie and Fritz. Mr. Bumgarten has never sought office, but he takes quite an active interest in the
political issues of the day. He is democratic in his views, and public-spirited
and progressive. He and wife are members of the Lutheran Church.

DR. RALPH REDDITT. The arduous, yet most noble calling, that of the
physician, has been successfully followed by Dr. Ralph Redditt for nearly
fourteen years, and during this time his labors have been Herculean in relieving the pains and ailments to which suffering humanity is heir. He is the
oldest physician in point of practice in Pearsall, Texas, but owes his nativity
to Holmes County, Mississippi, where he first saw the light in 1860. In order
of birth he was the second of seven children born to Dr. T. H. and Martha B.
(Hardin) Redditt, the former of whom was born in the Old North State and
the latter in Arkansas. The paternal grandfather, Joseph Redditt, was also
a North Carolinian by birth, but became one of the very early settlers of
Carrollton, Miss., in the vicinity of which he became extensively and successfully engaged in the raising of cotton. He died in the State of his adoption.
The maternal grandfather, Joseph Hardin, was a Tennessean and moved from
there to Arkansas, thence to Hill County, Texas, where he was called from
this life in 1863. In the State of Mississippi Dr. T. H. Redditt received his
literary education, and afterwards began the study of medicine. He then
entered the medical department of the University of New Orleans, from which
he graduated in 1843, and he immediately began practicing his profession in
Louisiana. After a very short period he came to Hill County, Texas, and
while residing there met, wooed and won for his wife Miss Hardin, after
which he returned to Mississippi and practiced his profession in Yazoo County
until his death in 1866, his widow still being a resident of that State.
Dr. Ralph Redditt received his early literary training in Yazoo County and
also at the State University at Oxford, Miss., after which he began the study

of medicine at New Orleans and later pursued his researches in Louisville, Ky., graduating in 1880 from a medical institution of the latter place. He at once began the practice of his profession in Holmes County, and continued in this line of human endeavor until February, 1891, when he came to Pearsall, mainly owing to poor health, and has recovered his old-time vigor fully and has built up a practice which is the just reward of honest merit and conscientious work. He is one of the most active physicians of the County, owns considerable property in this section and expects to here make his future home. He was married in September, 1893, to Miss Ella Loggins, a native of Texas, and a daughter of J. A. Loggins of Pearsall. The doctor and his wife are worthy members of the Methodist and Baptist churches respectively and move in the best society circles of their city.

JOHN D. BUNTING is a man of much intelligence, energy and ability, and his success in his chosen occupation has served to place him among the leading farmers and stock-raisers in his section. Like many other citizens of the county, Mr. Bunting is a native of North Carolina, born in Nash County, March 11, 1840, the eldest son and seventh child of eight children born to the marriage of David and Martha (Bowden) Bunting, natives also of the Old North State, and of English parentage. Both the Bunting and Bowden families came to America at a rather early day and settled in North Carolina, where most of the members engaged in agricultural pursuits. Several of our subject's uncles, on his mother's side, served in the War of 1812. David Bunting came to Texas in 1846 and settled in Gonzales County, fifteen miles south of the Guadalupe River, where he engaged in farming and stock-raising. About 1853 he moved from there to the valley of the Guadalupe, resided on this farm for four years and then moved near Moulton, where he still followed farming, until his death. His wife had died previously. They reared a family of nine children: Mary, deceased, was the wife of John Wood; Nancy, wife of H. L. Neely; Catherine, wife of N. B. Burkett; Nicy, wife of J. H. White; Martha, deceased, was the wife of N. Freeman; Atha, wife of A. L. Willisford; John D., Jefferson L., deceased, and Alonzo S., a minister of the Baptist Church resides in Weatherford. The original of this notice received but a limited education in his youth, attending for a short time the schools of Gonzales, and started out to fight life's battles for himself. He enlisted in Company I, Eighth Texas Cavalry, or Terry's Rangers in September, 1861. He was mustered into service at Houston, Texas, and joined the main Confederate forces at Bowling Green, Ky., participating in the following battles and skirmishes: Woodsonville, Shiloh, Perryville, Chickamauga, Knoxville, etc. He was captured near Mossy Creek, Tenn., January 29, 1863, and was sent to Rock Island, where he was retained until the close of the war, being exchanged the day of the final surrender of the trans-Mississippi Department of the Confederate forces. He was furnished transportation to Alexandria, La., and from there to the town of Beaumont, Texas, in company with some of his friends, and walked from the latter place to Alleyton, and thence home, arriving there foot-sore, and completely tired out but in good health, June 8, 1865. He at once engaged in farming, but later gave that up and began merchandising in connection with that occupation. At the present time he is engaged in the stock business in connection with farming. He came to this county in 1887, located in Flatonia, and here he has made his home up to the present. While a resident of Gonzales County, in 1886, he was elected a member of the County Commissioners, but he has never cared for office, preferring to attend strictly to his various enterprises, thereby making a success of them. He has never taken a very active interest in political matters. On the 5th of November, 1865, Mr. Bunting was married to Miss Mary Vaham, a native of Texas and the daughter of A. N. and Margaret (Gerwin) Vaham, natives of Germany, and early settlers of Gonzales County. Mr. and Mrs. Bunting are the parents of eight children: Mamie, Maggie, William D., Walter, Salome, Henry, Elulah and Jefferson. Mr. and Mrs. Bunting are worthy members of the Missionary Baptist Church, and Mr. Bunting is a member of Moulton Lodge No. 298, of the A. F. & A. M., and Moulton Chapter No. 134. Nowhere in the county will we find a more extensive stock dealer than Mr. Bunting, who is the owner of several large tracts of land and who is wide and favorably known.

JOHN MATTHEWS. This prominent and successful cotton-raiser is part owner and manager of a large plantation on the Colorado River, six miles below Eagle Lake, belonging to his father's estate, where he has devoted his attention to agricultural pursuits ever since 1871. He was born in Henrico County, Virginia in 1852, a son of Nathaniel Matthews, who also devoted his attention to planting throughout life, and owned large interests in Texas, where he came annually to spend the winter. He was born April 2, 1809 and died November 2, 1877, at the age of sixty-eight years. A brother of his, John Matthews, settled in Jackson County as early as 1828, where he went with some fifty slaves, established a cotton plantation on Mustang Creek, but not meeting with success in the farming operations on account of extreme drouths and consequent failures in crops, he abandoned the farm and moved over on the Colorado River, where he bought a half league of land and developed the present plantation, and farmed with great success until 1861 when, failing in health, he retired from business, deeding his brother, Nathaniel Matthews, his vast estates and returning to Virginia, where he died the latter part of the same year at his brother's home. The school days of the subject of this sketch were spent in Virginia, and in 1871 he graduated from the Virginia Military Institute, after which he at once came to Texas, and has ever since had charge of the plantation. This estate consists of half a league of land, situated on the Colorado River and the soil of the same is as fertile as any in the State, being of a rich alluvial nature, and the annual agricultural yield is enormous. He also owns some sugar interests, is wideawake, pushing and energetic, and he raises from 500 to 600 bales of cotton annually. Besides giving much of his time and attention to these occupations, he is also the manager and part owner of an excellent mercantile establishment, which brings him in a good sum annually, for it is liberally patronized. Mr. Matthews possesses excellent business qualifications, is shrewd, practical and far-seeing, has made a success of all his undertakings, but has never deeply interested himself in politics and is not a member of any secret order. A younger brother, Luke Matthews, has been associated with him in business ever since coming to the State in 1878. He also graduated from the University of Virginia, afterwards studied law and for some time after coming to the Lone Star State practiced his profession in Taylor County, but for some time past has been successfully engaged in tilling the soil and in mercantile pursuits.

WILLIAM H. WHEELER, liveryman, who ranks among the leading business men of Flatonia, Texas, is a native of the "Old North State," born in Wilkes County, August 16, 1840. His parents, Richard and Katie (Church) Wheeler, were also born in North Carolina, and there resided for many years From there they moved to Georgia, where the mother died in Gilmore County, and then, when our subject was still but a small boy, he was brought by his father to Alabama. There the father died in Jackson County soon after. Their family consisted of eight children, as follows: James, of Randolph County, Arkansas; Sarah A., widow of Robert Garen, of Texas; Martha, of North Carolina; A. L., of Benningham, Ala., William H.; John, of Jackson County, Alabama; Amanda, deceased, and Bethel, of Jackson County. His parents dying when he was but a small boy prevented our subject from getting anything but a limited education, and he was thrown on his own resources at an early age. When sixteen years of age he began the struggle of life for himself, and in 1857 came to Texas by way of New Orleans and Galveston, the latter being a small place at that time. From Galveston he went to San Saba County, engaged in wagoning for J. H. Gay during the winter season, and in summer attended school. In 1861 he joined Company D, Second Texas Cavalry, was in service in New Mexico, where he was engaged in the battle of Valverde. From there he returned to San Antonio, thence to Galveston and was engaged in the recapture of that city. From there he went to his command in Louisiana, and was engaged in but one battle, La Fouche Crossing. Following this his command was at various points in Texas and was stationed at Corpus Christi at the close of the war. He was discharged in June 1865, and came at once to Hallettsville, Lavaca County, where he remained for ten years. During the first three years he was engaged in clerking in a general store, but in 1868 he established a general mercantile business there and for seven years conducted this business. However, during the years 1869 and 1871 he traveled for J. B. Woodyard & Co., from Galveston, and in 1876 or '77 he moved to that place. There he embarked in the hotel and livery business, and this he has since followed with more than ordinary success. After the war he started out with limited means, and after coming to Flatonia met with good success and is now the owner of a nice property in town. He also owns some fine farming land and a large interest in a stone quarry which, when properly developed, will be a fortune in itself. On the 8th of January, 1873, Mr. Wheeler married Miss Emma A. Arnim, a native of Texas, and daughter of Albert and Louisa Arnim, who were born in Germany. Mr. and Mrs. Arnim came to America in 1851, and were one of the early German families of Texas. Mr. Arnim was a prosperous merchant for many years, but, feeling the infirmities of age coming on him, retired from business recently. He makes his home at Hallettsville. Mr. and Mrs. Wheeler have six children: Ella, Richard, Katie, William, Leslie and Margaret. Mrs. Wheeler is a member of the Methodist Episcopal Church, and with her husband is a member of the Royal Society of Goodfellows, of Flatonia, Lodge No. 333. Mr. Wheeler joined the Odd Fellows Lodge at Galveston in 1868, and is a member of Clark Lodge, No. 336, of Flatonia. Politically he is a strong supporter of Democratic principles.

RAFAEL VIDAURRI. The position of Secretary and Treasurer of the city of Laredo, Texas, is ably filled by the gentleman whose name heads this sketch, and here it may be said that no more fitting person for the position could be found. Not only is he intelligent and capable, but he is also industrious, conscientious and faithful in the discharge of his duties, and his efforts are thoroughly appreciated by the townspeople. He is a native of the place, born in 1859, and is the eldest of ten children of Atanacio and Ignacia (Farias) Vidaurri, natives respectively of Laredo, Texas, and the State of Coahuila, Mexico. The father was an extensive ranchman, and raised an excellent grade of horses, cattle and sheep on his ranch of 20,000 acres. He was a public spirited citizen, and was active in many ways; became a Lieutenant in the Confederate army, and was a faithful and useful soldier. Was Mayor of Laredo in 1877, having served before as Alderman of the city and Commissioner of Webb County. He died in 1885, at the age of fifty-two years, but his widow still survives him. The paternal grandfather, Rafael Vidaurri, was also born in Laredo, and was robbed and killed by the Indians while en route to Chihuahua, Mexico. The subject of this sketch was educated at Monterey, Mexico, and San Antonio, Texas, and at the conclusion of his studies began life as a clerk in the store of Raymond Martin. In 1879 he was appointed Deputy Secretary and Treasurer of Laredo by its City Council, and in 1880, by the vote of the people, was elected City Secretary and Treasurer, which position he has since filled, with the exception of one term, up to the present time. He has always been active in local politics, is a well educated gentleman, and is a genial and sociable companion, a valued and trusted friend and a most capable and trustworthy public official. He has charge of the undivided estate of his father, on which he gives much attention to the raising of horses and cattle. He was married in 1891, to Miss Constancia, a daughter of Hon. Rafael Varrios, Consul of the Republic of Mexico, and their union has resulted in the birth of a daughter whom they have named Hortensia. Mr. and Mrs. Vidaurri are members of the Catholic Church, and are upright and useful citizens.

JUDGE WILLIAM J. PHILLIPS. Judge William J. Phillips is one of Wharton County's most respected citizens; his private character is one to be admired and loved, his public record is without a blemish. Throughout his career he has been actuated by pure motives and manly principles, and by following a fixed purpose to make the most and best of himself he has overcome many difficulties and risen step by step to a place of influence and honor among public-spirited and high-minded men. He came to Texas in 1837 with Lieutenant-governor Albert C. Horton, and this State has continued to be his home up to the present. Judge Phillips is a native Virginian, born in Fredericksburg in 1828, and when but a child was left fatherless, his father, William J. Phillips, dying in Alabama, whither he had moved to get a start after losing all his means on security debts. Young Phillips received the principal part of his education in Alabama, and after his parents died was adopted by Governor Horton, who subsequently moved to Texas, accompanied by our subject. Here the latter attended school as opportunity offered, first at Columbia and later at Matagorda. He was associated with Governor Horton in all his expeditions against the Indians and Mexicans on the frontier during the Mexican War, and went with the latter to Austin, where he was in the Attorney-General's office; later he joined the company of spies or scouts in the army of Ben McCulloch under General Taylor, and in that capacity furnished the army much valuable information. Bold and determined, with a courage that never failed, he entered upon his career as a spy, and although placed in many trying and hair-raising positions, knew no such word as fail. He and Gen. Ben McCulloch, with much coolness, entered Gen. Santa Anna's lines and became possessed of such information that General Taylor was enabled to conquer the enemy. This was a very dangerous undertaking for Mr. Phillips, for certain death awaited him if captured, and at one time he was chased by the Mexicans, but succeeded in getting back in time to notify General Taylor that the whole army was coming. Mr. Phillips was Orderly Sergeant of McCulloch's spy company, and as he had for many years been fighting Mexicans and Indians he was used to their ways and wonderfully successful as a spy. This all happened before our subject was of age, and he is the only member of the company now living. At one time, while riding along, he had his saddle perforated with bullets, but he himself escaped uninjured. Mr. Phillips received his discharge in 1847, and soon after, when General Taylor was elected President of the United States, our subject was appointed Collector of Customs at the port of Matagorda, which position he held during Taylor's and Fillmore's administrations, and was re-appointed by Pierce. Later he began his career as a merchant at Matagorda, on a very extensive scale, shipping sugar and cotton to New York City. After the storm of 1854, when Matagorda was destroyed, Mr. Phillips moved to Wharton, where he was about the first merchant. He received the contract from the State to clean Colorado River from the mouth, and this he did, making it navigable to Wharton. Next he received the contract to grade a railroad, with Col. D. Hardeman, to Columbia, and finished that contract just before the war, but the rails were not laid on account of the war. During this trying time Mr. Phillips opposed secession. He held the office of County Judge for a time, and when the war cloud was the darkest he went to Matamoras, Mexico, and remained there until peace was declared. He and Governor Horton differed in but two particulars—secession and the railroad. Mr. Phillips not favoring disunion voted against secession, but as his was the only vote of the kind it was not counted, those having charge of the election wanting theirs to be the banner county of the State. After the war Judge Phillips went to Washington City, and after remaining there a short time returned to Texas, where he was appointed Assessor of Internal Revenue of his district. He took the qualified oath (not the iron-clad oath, as he had held office during the war), and served eighteen months. The Senate would not confirm him, because he had failed to take the oath, and he afterwards went to Washington where, by hard work, he had a bill passed for the purpose of paying himself and other officials in the same condition. In the year 1876 General Grant appointed him United States Marshal for the East District of Texas, with headquarters at Galveston, without solicitation, and he held that position three terms, under Grant, Hayes and Garfield. He was burned out during the big fire at Galveston, but soon retrieved his fortune. Planting has been his principal occupation in life—cotton exclusively, and he has met with substantial returns. In the month of December, 1858, he was married to Miss Sarah A. Boone, of La Grange, La., and she died in Galveston in 1882. Three sons born to this union are also deceased: David S. was thrown from a horse and killed when thirteen years of age, June, 1872; William J. died in 1866 when four years of age, and Ben McCulloch, named for Mr. Phillips' old comrade, was born in June, 1861, and died in 1887. He was with his father in the Marshal's office. On the 23d of October, 1889,

Mr. Phillips married Miss Evans, of a well-connected family of Texas, and daughter of Joseph L. Evans, who died in San Antonio. Judge Phillips has been a member of the Baptist Church since 1852, but he is not associated with any secret organization.

JOHN FRANCIS HOLT. One of the prominent stockmen of Matagorda County, Texas, who left a home of comfort in the East to brave the hardships and privations of the early settlers of this section, is John Francis Holt, whose success in his chosen calling has been well merited. He was born in Andover, Mass., in 1838, and in 1850 came to Matagorda County to live with an uncle, John Plunkett, who was a native of the Emerald Isle. In 1830 Mr. Plunkett landed in Matagorda County, and there passed the remainder of his life engaged actively and extensively in the stock business until his death in 1886, when seventy years of age. He was a soldier in the war with Mexico, and participated in the battle of San Jacinto. His sister, the mother of our subject, came to make her home with him, and here she, too, passed away. Our subject, who was but twelve years of age when he came to Matagorda County, received most of his education here and here grew to mature years. In 1861, when a few years over twenty-one years of age, Mr. Holt joined the first company from this county, Sixth Texas Infantry, and participated in the battles of Chickamauga, Missionary Ridge and Arkansas Post, where he was taken prisoner. He remained five months at Camp Butler, after which he was exchanged and joined his command at Petersburg, Va. After this he was in the Atlanta campaign, and was wounded at Atlanta and disabled from further duty. Returning to Texas he commenced raising stock, and this has continued to be his chosen calling since. His life has been passed in ceaseless activity, and has not been without substantial evidences of success, as will be seen from a glance over his broad acres. His career is an example of industry, perseverance and good management worthy the imitation of all. Mr. Holt now resides on Bay Prairie, near Caney, where he owns 10,000 acres of land, a beautiful residence and seemingly everything to render him happy and contented. This pleasant home is presided over by his wife, formerly Miss Wilkinson, whom he married in 1866. Her father, John Wilkinson, was a prominent old settler here, too, and fought in the battle of San Jacinto. To the marriage of Mr. and Mrs. Holt have been born two children, both daughters: Anna E. Kilbride, wife of Edward Kilbride, and Louisa W. Religiously Mr. Holt is an Episcopalian, and socially an Odd Fellow and a K. of H.

ABNUS B. KERR. A noted writer has said: "The present is the child of all the past, the mother of all the future." If this be true, where will the generations of the future find a more impressive lesson or faithful guide than in the study of the lives of those men who have achieved a successful prominence in the busy walks of life? There is in the intensified energy of the business man, fighting the everyday battle of life, but little to attract the attention of the idle observer; but to the mind fully awake to the stern realities of life there are noble and immortal lessons in the life of the man who, without other aid than a clear head, a strong arm and a true heart, conquers adversity and wins for himself honor and distinction among his fellow men. Among such men we may mention Abnus B. Kerr, who is one of the leading business men of the county. He was born March 4, 1832, in Augusta County, Virginia, of which State his parents, Robert G. and

Cassandra C. (McCutchen) Kerr were also natives. Robert G. Kerr was born in 1803 and died in Fayette County in 1893, at the ripe old age of ninety years. His father, William Kerr, was one of the first settlers of Virginia, and was in the war for independence. He came from either Scotland or Ireland, and his wife was a native of Holland. William Kerr and wife reared a family of eight children: David Samuel X., William, Jr., Robert G., Betsie, wife of John Wallace; Sallie, married Peter C. Hogue, an eminent Baptist minister; Peggie, married Elijah Hogshead, of Virginia; and Jane, who married Dr. William T. Anderson, a prominent surgeon of White Sulphur Springs for many years, is still living. Our subject's maternal grandparents, Downey McCutchen, commonly known as Capt. McCutchen, was also in the Revolutionary War and held the rank of Captain in the Army of Patriots of Virginia. Both the Kerrs and McCutchens were large property owners and very influential families. Mr. McCutchen reared a family of seven children: Robert, Chapman, Cyrus, a physician; Amanda, married Colonel Emonson, of Lexington, Va., and became the mother of three daughters; Cassandra C., Rebecca and Temperance, who married William Suddeth and became the mother of one son, James, who is now an eminent physician of Washington, D. C. Robert G. Kerr, a farmer and planter, was the son of wealthy parents, and remained in Virginia until 1874. He met with many reverses on account of security debts, and our subject cared for him and the remainder of the family until the death of both parents, the mother dying in 1880, when seventy-five years of age. This worthy couple reared four children: A. B., Mary C. A., Jerusha E., wife of J. E. Gillespie, and Robert O., of Bell County. Abnus B. Kerr, the oldest of the above mentioned children, secured a fair education in the common schools of Augusta County, Virginia, and in 1852, when twenty years of age he started out to fight the battle of life for himself. He went to Charleston, W. Va., and from there down the Ohio and Mississippi rivers to New Orleans. Many were taken sick with cholera on the boat, and died at the rate of five a day, and of the eighteen who started with our subject, two died of that dread disease. Boats were not allowed to stop in the towns, but would land at wood yards, and other places, and dig pits in the sand for the corpses of their unfortunate comrades. About fifty persons were thus buried. On this boat was a lady who was going South with her little child to join her husband, who was a merchant in Louisiana. The lady promenaded the deck with Mr. Kerr, seemingly in the best of health, but before morning she was a corpse. Her body was placed in a casket and conveyed to New Orleans. The child clung to Mr. Kerr, and would not go with any of the ladies, and he took charge of the forlorn little creature until it reached its father in New Orleans. From New Orleans Mr. Kerr went to Indianola, and thence made his way to Gonzales by ox team, landing in that town with little money November 1, 1852. He at once succeeded in getting work, and was book-keeper for a Mr. Gishard, a Frenchman, with a salary of $51 per month. He remained with that gentleman but one month, for he had to keep the books and clerk as well. As he could not do both at once, he was obliged to take care of the books at night, in a little house open to the weather. There Mr. Kerr contracted pleurisy, came very near dying, and when he recovered paid all his money to the doctor. He was without money, out of a position, had no friends, and was too proud to write home for money. As he could not get work at his business,—book-keeping,—he decided to turn his hand at anything; and as the first brick

20

house of Gonzales was under construction at that time, he accepted a position as hod-carrier for the masons, at seventy cents a day and board himself, paying forty cents per day for board. This building was known as the Kiser Hotel, and on it our subject worked as hod-carrier until March, 1853. At that time Major Neighbors was raising a company of rangers to guard the surveyors going north to survey land in Peters Colony. This land was to be surveyed from where Dallas now stands, north. Mr. Kerr wished very much to go, but had no horse or outfit, which all rangers were required to furnish. He had shown such spirit and grit after his sickness, in taking up the hod, that he won the respect and esteem of all, and one citizen, a Mr. R. Saddler, said he would furnish the saddle, a countryman furnished the horse, another a gun and thus Mr. Kerr was equipped, with the understanding that he was to pay for the outfit should he ever get able. The company was organized at Austin and started in March, with a company of surveyors under Col. Hitchcock. This land was to be surveyed for the Texas Emigration & Land Company of Peters Colony. Seventeen hundred square miles were surveyed in nine months, and many very interesting experiences had our subject during that time. At one time a chief of the Wichita tribe had stolen a number of Government horses from Fort Crogan, or near Burnett, and Major Sibley, who was in command, followed with horses and men, and overtook him and his wife and followers near the Indian agency, on the Clear Fork of the Brazos, where the company of rangers were camped. The latter assisted in capturing the chief and his wife, and he was kept closely confined in a tent. While there he stabbed his wife and started for Major Sibley's tent to assassinate him, but was stopped by a guard, whom he shot. Other guards came up and the chief was shot through the breast. Finding the wound mortal, the latter plunged the knife in his own breast. On the 2d of July, 1853, Mr. Kerr and a friend, a Mr. Gibbons, of Arkansas, decided to go to Fort Belknap, a distance of twenty-five miles from the camp of the rangers, to get their guns repaired. While hunting a suitable place to cross the Brazos River, they came suddenly on a camp of 150 Indians on the war path. Mr. Kerr and his friend lost no time in getting away from there, but were pursued by Indians on foot and on horseback. The friend was on a fine mare, and this left our subject's little pony far in the rear. Mr. Kerr called to his companion to wait, but the latter seemed to be deaf. The race continued until within sight of Fort Belknap, and the horses of the boys were almost exhausted. They reached that place in safety, and a party of soldiers started back after the Indians, but did not succeed in capturing any. After remaining a week at the fort the boys returned by a different route, and with an escort of dragoons. On the 31st of November Mr. Kerr was transferred from the ranger service to the surveying corps, where he received sixty dollars per month, thirty dollars more than he had received previously. Still later he was transferred to the transcribing department, where he received $75.50 per month. In that capacity he served until he reached Austin, November 1, 1853. He then clerked for some time, and was offered a salary of seventy-five dollars per month to work in the land office. About this time Mr. Kerr and his companions were paid off for their trip with the surveyors, and Mr. Kerr received $440. Returning to Gonzales, he paid off his debts, spent a short time with his friends, and on the last of January, 1854, he went to Cibolo, near Selma, Bexar County, and purchased a small herd of cattle and a tract of land from J. M. Hill. He made considerable money out of this. During the fall of 1854 he met his first wife, Miss May Murcer, and while she was attending school, they were married, Aug. 2nd, 1855, Mrs. Kerr was the daughter of Levi and Sarah (Munifee) Murcer, the father, a large sugar merchant, and a wealthy and influential citizen at Egypt. During the fall of 1855 Mr. and Mrs. Kerr loaded their household goods in an ox wagon and moved to Fayette County, on a tract of 200 acres of land that her grandfather, Judge Munifee, had given her. This land was unimproved, and Mr. Kerr built his own house with lumber brought from Higgins' mill at Bastrop. He also fenced in some land and engaged in farming and improving his place up to the outbreak of war. During that eventful period he took charge of his father-in-law's stock, and, together with his own, moved them to Colorado County, where he remained for two years. Returning to Fayette County in 1866, he began surveying, and soon became familiar with the land of the county. He engaged largely in land speculations, buying and selling large tracts of land, and accumulated considerable property. Since then he has been engaged for the most part in farming, stock-raising and merchandising. By his first union Mr. Kerr became the father of four children, as follows: Thomas O., a merchant of Muldoon; James L., manager of a rock quarry; William B., of San Antonio, manager of the coal and wood business at that place; and R. L. Kerr (deceased). Mrs. Kerr, who was a most estimable lady, and an earnest member of the Baptist Church, died in 1868. In 1870 Mr. Kerr married Miss Bettie Ragsdale, a native of Texas and daughter of Charles C. and Sarah (Sealorn) Ragsdale, early settlers of Texas. Four children were born to his second union: John A., a graduate of the Law School of Texas, at Austin, prior to his twenty-first year (something that had never happened in Texas before), is now practicing his profession in Fayette; Mary, died in 1882; Charles G., a student; and Alice L. Mr. Kerr and sons own a large business in Muldoon, this county, and a large stone quarry at that place, the finest in the State. He has a $300,000 contract with the city of Galveston to furnish rock for the city, and sends out from thirty-five to forty car loads per day. Mr. Kerr also owns one-half interest in coal mines at Rockdale, Milam County, shipping twelve car loads per day. The company has leased this mine to the Brickett & Egget Plant Co., and on this they get a royalty of thirty cents per ton. The company with which Mr. Kerr is connected have other mines they will open soon, and sell in the crude state as now. The mercantile business is in charge of one of his sons, and is the most successful enterprise of the kind in the county. Mr. Kerr owns in Texas 50,000 acres of land, and has under cultivation about 4,000 acres, which makes about seventy-five farms, occupied by about seventy-five renters. Mr. Kerr also owns 50,000 acres of land in Mexico, on which there is quite a village. This ranch is worth at least $300,000. The Southern Pacific is planning a road through it, and Mr. Kerr has given the right of way. Our subject has taken little interest in political matters for a number of years, but during middle life he served fourteen years as Justice of the Peace, Tax Collector, School Director, Notary Public, and County Commissioner. Finding nothing in politics, he quit. He was sent by the county to Denver, Col., to devise a means of getting deep water at Galveston. This was the convention that gave that enterprise a start. He is a strong advocate for deep water on the Texas coast. Socially he is a member of the A. F. & A. M., a Royal Arch and demitted member. Few men in the State are at the head of as many enterprises as Mr. Kerr. Charitable and generous, he gives freely to all worthy enterprises, and takes the lead in all good work. From the year 1870 to 1880 Mr. Kerr was prominently identified with the organization of the Texas State Grange, and for eight years was a member of the first executive committee. He undoubtedly possesses a mind the equal of which few men can boast. He controls to-day, more different financial enterprises than any other man in the State and is known and recognized far and near as the "Millionaire Rock King of Texas."

DR. JOSHUA P. ARTHUR. The man who rises to an enviable place in the medical profession, rises by his own individuality, and is never pushed up on the wave of a growing and general movement, like the rising tide of commerce —often the success of the merchant is but a part of the success of the branch in which he has invested, and is referable only slightly to his individual efforts. The physician's advance to prominence is more often the just reward of personal merit and professional learning, efficiency and success. This thought has been suggested by a brief consideration of the professional career of Dr. Joshua P. Arthur, who may be regarded as a representative, both worthy and conspicuous, of the better element in this profession of self-made men. He is the oldest physician, in point of practice, in Laredo. He was born in the city of Philadelphia, Penn., in 1840, the eleventh of twelve children born to Enoch and Margaret (Yonker) Arthur, who were also natives of Philadelphia. The paternal grandfather, John Arthur, was of German and English descent, but was born in Germany. He came to America when young, and fought for American independence in the Revolutionary War, and was with Gen. Washington at the time he crossed the Delaware River at Trenton. The maternal grandfather, Abraham Yonker, was born in Pennsylvania, there was engaged in tilling the soil; but his people were of Holland Dutch stock, and on coming to this country first settled in the State of New York, and the town of Yonkers, N. Y., was named in honor of this family. The wife of Abraham Yonkers was a Miss Leech, a direct descendant of Tobias Leech, who came to America with William Penn in 1682. Enoch Arthur, father of the doctor, was a successful lumber merchant of Philadelphia, in which city he died in 1870, at the age of 74 years, his wife dying in 1889 at the age of 89 years. Tobias Leech sought a home in the wilds of America with one hundred other emigrants, the voyage thither being made in the good ship "Welcome." He was born in Chittenham, England, and he and his wife, who was a Miss Heather, died in 1726. He built the first brick house ever erected in the city of Philadelphia. To him and his wife eight children were born, and their great-granddaughter, Sarah, married Yost Yonkers, whose daughter Margaret married Enoch Arthur in 1816. Dr. Joshua P. Arthur was educated in Philadelphia, and began life for himself as a clerk in a drug store belonging to his brother, and at the same time began to read medicine, but his studies were interrupted by the opening of the Civil War. In 1862 he passed the military examination, and entered the Federal army as a medical cadet on transport duty on the James River, in which capacity he served several months. He then attended his second course of lectures, after which he entered the army as contract surgeon, serving in his professional capacity until the spring of 1865, when he was commissioned Assistant Surgeon in the Thirty-sixth United States Colored Troops. At the close of the war he was ordered to Texas with his regiment, and during the balance of 1865–66 was at Brazos Santiago, Texas. In November, 1866, he was mustered out of the service, but soon after took another contract as Acting Assistant Surgeon in the United States army, and was on duty at Brownsville and other places. In May, 1867, he returned to Philadelphia, Pa., and took his third course of lectures in the medical department of the University of Pennsylvania, and was graduated therefrom in the spring of 1868. In October of the same year he took another contract with the United States army, and was located at Brownsville, Texas. In 1870 he was ordered to Laredo as Post Surgeon at Fort McIntosh, and there remained until 1879, at which time he resigned, and has since practiced his profession among the people of this city and county with very satisfactory results. He ranks high in his profession, and is President of the Medical Examining Board of this district. In 1889 he engaged in the drug business as a member of the firm of A. M. Slack & Co., but the firm is now known as the Malinche Drug Company, with Ed. D. Sisk as partner and manager. They are doing an extensive business, and have a large jobbing trade. In 1869 Dr. Arthur was married to Miss Amanda T. Arrison, a native of Pennsylvania, and to their union two daughters have been given: Helen, wife of Henry Deutz, and Florence Marion, wife of Ed. D. Sisk. Dr. Arthur has been quite active in Masonic circles, and is a member of the Blue Lodge, Chapter and Commandery of Laredo, and holds the office of Treasurer in each. He is a public-spirited citizen in all ways, and has many friends in Webb County.

Q. T. LANE. It has been said that the profession of law is one of the most momentous and important of human callings, and that the man who takes upon himself the practice assumes the weightiest responsibilities that the confidence and trust of his fellowmen can put upon his shoulders. As a branch of human endeavor it brings into play the most brilliant talents, the most extensive knowledge, the strongest sentiment, moral, spiritual, material, and its power for good or evil is vast and invincible. As a man whose honor is above criticism, and whose ability places him in a most enviable position as an attorney, may be mentioned Q. T. Lane, one of the leading members of the legal fraternity in Flatonia. He is also one of the old settlers of the town, for he came here at a very early date. Mr. Lane was born in North Alabama in 1838, and with his father, Jonathan Lane, came to Texas in 1853, settling in Fayette County. The elder Lane tilled the soil successfully here until his death, in 1876. His wife was Mariah Gillespie, was of same State, and they reared a family of six children: C. J., deceased, was a minister; Fannie M.; John, Q. T., Eliza, deceased, was the wife of J. R. Crockett, and Henrietta, wife of J. R. Birch. In the schools of Alabama Q. T. Lane received his education, and after coming with his parents to Texas assisted them in the work on the farm. Previous to the war he hauled stock principally, and in 1861 he joined Company C, Eighth Texas Cavalry, or Terry's Rangers. He was on the east side of the river during the first year of the war, and participated in several battles of note and several skirmishes in the latter part of 1863. On account of ill-health he was discharged from service, but after remaining home a short time he joined Col. Bates' Regiment, and was soon transferred to Capt. Dun's Company, Gen. Green's Brigade, and was mostly in service along the coast. Mr. Lane was discharged at Brenham, July 1, 1865, and, coming home, immediately engaged in the stock business, which he followed until 1872, when he came to Flatonia. Here he followed clerking; but during the time studied law, and was admitted to the bar in 1887. Since then he has followed his profession with marked success. He was married in the year 1867 to Miss Elizabeth M. Sullivan, a native of Texas and daughter of John and Lucy (Morton) Sullivan, natives of Mississippi. Mr. Sullivan came to Texas in 1855, and settled in Fayette County, where he followed farming until his death. His wife still survives him. Mr. and Mrs. Lane are the parents of three children: Lucy, Fannie, and Sue. In politics our subject is a Democrat, and he and wife are worthy members of the Methodist Episcopal Church.

CAPTAIN WILLIAM DUNOVANT. This gentleman has long been successfully engaged in sugar and cotton planting, and has also been a prosperous general merchant at Eagle Lake. He was born in Chester District, S. C., March 20, 1844, a son of A. Q. and Mary (Lowry) Dunovant, natives or Chester and York Districts, S. C., respectively. The father was a planter and merchant, and was active in politics, and for some time was a Member of the State Legislature and a member of the convention that voted for secession. During the great Civil War he was a member of Governor McGraw's staff. He died November 6, 1868, at the age of fifty-three years, and his widow in 1875, when fifty-one years old. They were members of the Episcopal Church, and he was a Democrat of pronounced type in his political views, and was a member of the I. O. O. F. The paternal grandfather, John Dunovant, was a member of the State Senate of South Carolina, and other members of the family were also prominent, R. G. Dunovant being Inspector-general of the State of South Carolina at the time it seceded from the Union, and was in command of Fort Moultrie when it was bombarded by the Federals. Capt. William Dunovant was one of a family of nine children, four of whom reached maturity, and he is the only son who is living at the present time. He spent his school days at Mount Zion College in Chester District, and at Winnsboro, in Fairfield District. He left school at the age of sixteen, but was quite well advanced in the higher branches and the classics. In December, after the State had seceded from the Union, he joined the Seventeenth South Carolina Infantry, commanded by ex-Governor Means, and was a member of Company F, in the Seventeenth, until the close of the war. After a time he was promoted to the rank of Captain of the Flag Company, which he commanded until the participating in the second battle of Bull Run. When Grant attempted to blow up Petersburg, Capt. Dunovant lost his right arm, and although he was in the battles of Kingston, N. C., Jackson, Miss., and others, he missed several battles in which his command took part, owing to the fact that he had been wounded on two different occasions. In August, 1865, he came via New York to Texas and located near Eagle Lake, in Colorado County. At that time he was a comparatively poor man, and in debt, but he bought land on credit and commenced raising cotton. The land was a very productive tract, on the bend of Old Caney, and he accordingly prospered. He now owns 1,000 acres of valuable land in the Lone Star State, and up to the present time he has been engaged in planting, stock-raising and merchandising, and has followed each successfully. The captain has never married, but two of his sisters live with and keep house for him. When he first embarked on the mercantile sea, J. A. Harbert was his partner, and continued so to be for a number of years, but he is now alone. He raises annually about 1,500 bales of cotton, and is now the only sugar planter on Caney, and will this year probably make a large amount of sugar. He has recently built a sugar house, and has it well fitted up to successfully carry on this work. He has always been too busy as a business man to accept honors at the hands of his friends, although he has always been an active and faithful Democrat.

JAMES J. HAYNES. The life of this gentleman has been one of usefulness and profit to the section in which he has so long made his home, and he is one of her most honored and honorable citizens. He owes his nativity to Rio Grande City, Texas, where he first saw the light of day in 1853, being the eldest born of John L. and Angelica I. (Wells) Haynes, who were natives of Virginia and New York respectively. The early life of John L. Haynes was spent in the State of his birth and in Mississippi, during which time he received an excellent education, mainly, however, from his own personal study. He was a Lieutenant of volunteers, in a company from Mississippi, to the Mexican War, and served until the close of that conflict, being in the northern part of Mexico, with Taylor's army. After the war was over he remained in that country and engaged in business at Camargo, and also at Rio Grande City, Texas, his business associates being N. Mitchell and Rafael Aldrete. Their commercial interests grew and increased rapidly, and after being elected to a county office, Mr. Haynes retired from business. In 1857 he was elected to the State Legislature, and until 1861, ably represented Starr County in that body. On the secession of the State from the Union he resigned and went to headquarters, where he secured a commission as Colonel, then returned to Texas, raised a regiment and became Colonel of the Second Texas Regiment of Cavalry. In 1864 the First and Second regiments were consolidated, and he was made Colonel of the First Texas Cavalry, in which capacity he served in Texas, Louisiana and Mississippi. He was at Baton Rouge when the war closed, and was ordered to San Antonio, Texas, where his regiment was disbanded. Soon after this he was appointed Collector of Internal Revenue, in which capacity he served for about four years. In 1870 he made the race for Congress, on the Hamilton ticket in the Austin District, but was defeated. The following year he was appointed Collector of Customs at Galveston, and in 1882 was appointed to the same office in Brownsville, whither he removed with his family, and there he continued to reside and hold the office until 1884. In 1885 he came to Laredo and made his home with his son, the subject of this sketch, until his death, in 1887. He was editor of the *Daily Republican* at Austin, and his native ability and excellent education ably fitted him for literary work, and he was a valued correspondent of the *New York Tribune*, as well as other periodicals. While a member of the Legislature he secured the confirmation of many Spanish land grants, which were of great value to the people of this part of the Lone Star State. He was in public life the greater part of his career, and was one of the best known and most highly esteemed citizens of Southwest Texas. He was considered an authority on all matters of Texas history, after the time he located in the State, for he was very observing, and an active participant in all the principal events on the Rio Grande border. His first military service was in Texas, and he was afterwards sent East. He was always very active in sustaining the Republican party, and was one of the leaders of the same until his death. His literary work was very extensive, and his writings always breathed a loyal spirit, and great faith in the future of

Texas. As was almost inevitable, he had some political enemies, but he was widely known for his sterling qualities of honor and manhood, and was loved by many. In 1885 he came to Laredo and made his home with the subject of this sketch until his death in 1887, at which time he was an active member of the Episcopal Church and a member of the A. F. & A. M. His widow now lives in New York City with her daughter. The subject of this sketch was an attendant of the public schools of Austin until he was about sixteen years of age. In 1871 he accompanied his father, whom he assisted in the investigation of the titles of many land claims. In the winter of 1871, at Austin, and in 1872, he went to Brownsville with his father and was Inspector of Customs there until 1873, when he was appointed United States Commercial Agent at Mier. In 1874 he was appointed to the same position at New Laredo, and in that capacity served until the winter of 1880, since which time he has been in business at Laredo as Custom House Broker. Like his worthy sire before him, he is an active Republican in politics, and is a delegate to all the conventions of his party. He has been a member of the Board of Aldermen for two terms, and has always manifested great interest in the welfare of his section. He was married in 1881 to Miss Angela M. Arrizola, a native of Mexico. Socially he is a member of the A. F. & A. M. His maternal grandfather, Dr. James Wells, was born in New York City, and in 1836 became a resident of Fayette County, Texas. During the Mexican War he went to that country as a surgeon in the United States army, and after the close of hostilities returned to Texas and practiced his profession in Fayette County until a short time before his death, which occurred in Austin in 1866. The paternal grandfather was a merchant of Bedford County, Va.

MARION DE CAUSSEY, M.D. There are men, and the number is by no means small, who drift into what we are accustomed to look upon as the learned profession, in the same way that thousands of other men in the lower walks of life drift into the ordinary bread-winning occupations, and it is fortunate for him and for all concerned if the occupations to which he devotes his attention is to his liking. That Dr. De Caussey has been wise in choosing his life occupation can not be doubted when his large patronage is taken into consideration, and the success which has attended his efforts is known. He was born in Leon County, Florida, April 6, 1841, a son of Andrew and Catherine (Boyle) De Caussey, who were natives of the Palmetto State. The De Causseys were among the early French settlers of this country, and the founder of the family in this country belonged to that persecuted band of Hugenots, who sought an asylum and religious freedom in this country. A. De Caussey was a farmer by occupation, and soon after his marriage he moved with his wife to Florida, where he lived until his death, his widow surviving him several years. They reared the following children: Charles, who resides in Guthrie, Indian Territory; Henry, of Florida; Ard (deceased); Sarah, widow of W. W. Whidden, of Florida, and Marion. The maternal grandfather, Charles Boyle, was a soldier of the Revolution, and participated in the battle of Cowpens. Dr. De Caussey was educated in Waukunah Academy, Florida, and in 1869 he entered the Medical Department of Tulane University, Louisiana, where he spent one term, later graduating in the class of 1871–72 from a medical institution of Galveston, Texas. Very soon after he came to Austin County, and after making a few changes, came to his present location in 1889, since which time his practice has been confined to this county. When the Civil War opened his home was still in Florida, and from there he enlisted in 1862, in Company A, Fifteenth Confederate Regiment, commanded by Col. Harry Maury, which regiment was formed of men from different States, hence the name. The doctor was at Mount Pleasant, the siege of Mobile, and was in numerous minor engagements, and, although his regiment was for a time with the Army of Tennessee, it was principally on detached duty, and was in Alabama, Mississippi, Tennessee and the eastern part of Louisiana. His command under Gen. N. B. Forrest surrendered at Wetumpka, Ala., a short time after the surrender of Gen. Joseph E. Johnston. After the close of the war up to 1869, Dr. De Caussey followed mercantile pursuits, then came West as above stated. He was married in 1886 to Mrs. E. V. Clift (*nee* Guess), daughter of Isaac Guess, a farmer of Mississippi, and their marriage has been a happy one. Mrs. De Caussey is a member of the M. E. Church, while the doctor is a member of the A. F. & A. M. and the Knights of Pythias, being Prelate of John R. Castelton Lodge No. 188. He has never taken any active part in political matters, but has been a life-long Democrat. He is a member of the Texas Medical Association, the Austin County Medical Association, and has always taken much interest in local medical societies. He is one of the most successful general practitioners of the county, and at the same time is one of the oldest and best known. He is prepossessing in personal appearance, and in disposition is genial, social and kindly.

NATT HOLMAN. This gentleman is classed among the oldest farmers and much esteemed citizens of his section of the State and, although Fayette County has her full quota of vigorous, thorough-going, prosperous men, whose popularity is based upon both their social qualities and their well known integrity, none among them is better liked than the gentleman whose name is mentioned above. Mr. Natt Holman was born in Austin County, Texas, June 24, 1842, and is a son of John T. Holman, Sr. (see sketch). For the most part our subject received his education in this county, but for about five months he attended Baylor University at Independence, Texas. Leaving that institution in 1861, he joined Company A, E. B. Nichols' Regiment, with which he remained for six months, stationed at Galveston. After being discharged at the expiration of enlistment, he came home and joined Gen. Waul's Legion, with which he went to Mississippi. There he was transferred to Company F, Eighth Texas, or "Terry's Rangers," and participated in all the engagements of this noted regiment, from the time he joined until cessation of hostilities. At Raleigh, N. C., our subject, with about twenty-five or thirty others, left the command to surrender, and went to find Gen. Kirby Smith, who was operating in Louisiana, Texas and Arkansas. Getting as far as Tuscaloosa, Ala., they learned of Gen. Smith's surrender. Mr. Holman and three friends remained with an aunt of the former's until they could have some clothing made, when they started for home (Texas). Arriving at Natches, the Federal authorities furnished them transportation and provisions to Shreveport, La., and filled their canteens, not with water, but with Kentucky corn juice, and haversacks with hardtack and bacon. On the 4th of July, 1865, Mr. Holman found himself at his father's house in Fayette County, on the Colorado River. Here he found affairs in a sad condition. His stepmother had died, and left the father with a family of small children to care for. This he proceeded to do while our subject took charge of the farming and stock-raising interests. With the forces on hand, most of the slaves having left his father, our subject gathered the crop of 1865, and in the following year put in another crop. In 1867 he went East for farm help, traveling through Mississippi, Alabama, Georgia, and the Carolinas, without success until he reached Newburn, N. C., where he found about seven thousand contrabands, negroes, being fed by Uncle Sam, under charge of Gen. Stubbs. After stating to the General the aim and object of his visit (the securing of negroes for his farm), the latter entered into the spirit of the enterprise; partially it is true to get the negroes off his hands, and to place them where they could be self supporting, thus adding to the wealth of the country; and secured for Mr. Holman all the help he needed. By and with the aid of Gen. Stubbs, whom he considered one of the most polished gentleman he had ever met, Mr. Holman secured United States transportation for his people to Texas, *via* New Orleans. In that city the Government gave him bacon and hardtack for the negroes, and this they cooked themselves. On the 20th of February, 1868, Mr. Holman reached his plantation rather late for farming in Texas, as most of his neighbors had their corn up. With the help he brought with him he made excellent crops in 1868–69. Many of the negroes remained with him for a number of years and one is with him at the present time, and is now fairly well off. Mr. Holman is one of the most prominent farmers in the county, owning 1,650 acres of land on Colorado River, all inclosed, with 825 acres in a fine state of cultivation, for which he receives from $4.50 to $5.00, per acre, rent. For quite a number of years he was one of the extensive dealers in cattle, but has now gone out of that business, except winter feeding for the market, which he still follows. Mr. Holman was married in La Grange, January 22, 1868, to Miss Mary L. Lewis, daughter of Dr. R. H. and S. A. (Minter) Lewis. For many years Dr. Lewis was one of the leading physicians of his town, locating here in 1857. His death occurred in 1877, and he left a wife and several children, five of whom still survive: Robert H., of this place; B. P., of Beaumont; Mary L., Roberta, wife of J. N. Hall, and Rosa, wife of D. N. Pope, of Falls County. Mr. and Mrs. Holman are the parents of seven children, as follows: W. S., an attorney of this place; Anna M., Natt, Jr., Virginia, Lou M., Emma H., and John T., Jr. A lifelong Democrat, Mr. Holman takes a deep interest in political affairs, but does not care for office. He is a non-affiliating member of the I. O. O. F., a member of the A. O. U. W., and the K. of H., and for many years a member of the Cumberland Presbyterian Church. He conducts his affairs upon a basis of sterling integrity, and is adjudged a most worthy and honored citizen. Mrs. Holman and daughters are members of the Episcopal Church.

COLONEL CALVIN G. BREWSTER. This gentleman is most successfully engaged in the brokerage and commission business at Laredo, Texas, but was born in Tiskilwa, Bureau County, Illinois, in 1844, the fourth of six children born to Dwight W. and Emily C. (Kinney) Brewster, the former of whom was born in Maryland, and the latter in Pennsylvania. In 1847 the parents came to Texas, and located Corpus Christi, and Mr. Brewster became associated in business there with Col. H. L. Kinney, but in 1852 his career was closed by death. Soon after this sad event the widow and fatherless children returned to Illinois, and in Peru, Ill., the subject of this sketch resided, until the opening of the Civil War in 1861. He then enlisted in the Union service as a member of Company H., Nineteenth Illinois Infantry (Chicago

Zouaves), and was with the Department of Missouri until July of that year, when with his command he was transferred to the Army of the Cumberland in Kentucky, and was a participant in the battles of Murfreesboro, Chickamauga, and many other engagements in that State, and surrounding States. He was made a prisoner at the battle of Chickamauga, was in several different prisons in Richmond and Danville, Va., and placed in a dungeon under Libby Prison, where he was confined for eight months, and was one of the very last of the prisoners to be paroled and sent to Patterson Park Hospital at Annapolis, Md., where he was exchanged and returned to his regiment at Chattanooga. By this time his term of enlistment had expired, but he remained on special service in Chattanooga for a time, and then returned to Illinois. He then entered Lombard University at Galesburg, and after pursuing his studies in that institution for about a year and a half, he went to St. Louis, and from 1866 to 1867 was in the commercial business in that city. In 1868 he came to Texas and joined his brother at Corpus Christi, and was soon appointed storekeeper under Collector of Customs W. W. Ward, an office he held for three years. He was then made Inspector under Collector Kearney, was in 1874 appointed Deputy Collector of Customs at Laredo, under Collector Plato, and held this office under various officials until the election of Cleveland to the Presidency. He then came to Laredo under appointment of Deputy Collector, and in November, 1889, was appointed Collector of Customs of this district, and discharged the duties of this office until December 16, 1893. He has been very active in the affairs of the Republican party, and on two different occasions was a candidate for Congress on that ticket; in 1888 against Crain, and again in 1892. He received the largest vote ever given a Republican in this district, but, as was to be expected, was defeated. In 1871 he was a candidate for the State Legislature, but was defeated by only a few votes thus forcibly illustrating the esteem in which he is held in his district and his ability to poll a large vote. He has been a delegate to all various State Conventions, and was the one to propose the name of Mr. Davis for the Governorship at the Dallas convention in 1873. He was for many years extensively engaged in the stock business, and found it a profitable and congenial employment. He was married in January, 1869, to Miss Lydia A. Barnard, a native of Texas, and daughter of James R. Barnard and Mary J. (Mohoney) Barnard, the former of whom was born in the State of New York. He went to Mexico as a newspaper correspondent in the United States army in 1846, and after the war was over, remained in that country and edited an American paper in the City of Mexico. He afterwards engaged in newspaper work in Texas, and eventually passed from life in Corpus Christi. The union of Mr. Brewster resulted in the birth six daughters: M. Emily, Vivia A, Alma K., Fredrica F. (deceased), Mabel F. (deceased), and Lamar F. The Brewsters settled in New England during colonial days and have ever since figured prominently in its history. They came to this country in the famous old ship the "Mayflower," and finally members of the family drifted into Maryland from Connecticut. Colonel Brewster is of an extremely social disposition, is a gentleman in every sense of the word, and his walk throughout life has been characterized by the most honorable business methods and by "enmity towards none and charity for all." His conduct as a soldier was courageous and fearless, and at the battle of Stone River he was complimented by special order of Division Commander General Negley, for gallant conduct on the field of battle. He is now a member of the G. A. R., of which he has been Post Commander for several years. Socially he belongs to the A. F. & A. M., and he has long been a worthy member of the Episcopal Church. His maternal grandfather, Simon Kinney, was a Pennsylvania lawyer, and like the Brewsters are colonial and revolutionary stock.

JOHN LAFAYETTE CROOM. The subject of this sketch forms an appropriate place in the history of those men whose sterling integrity, force of character, and whose ability and good sense in the management of complicated affairs, have contributed so much to the advancement of this section. He is a native of Alabama, born in La Grange, November 26, 1826, and is of a prominent old North Carolina family, the grandfather, Richard Croom, being a native of that State, and a representative citizen there. He was married in 1786, and was a soldier in the Revolutionary War. The parents of our subject, W. J, and Elizabeth (Holliday) Croom, were also natives of the Old North State, the father's birth occurring there December 10, 1795. The Holliday family was also represented in the Revolutionary War by our subject's grandfather, who fought bravely for independence. John LaFayette Croom was married November 5, 1846, to Miss Ellen R. Davis, daughter of Elisha Davis and a cousin of the late Gen. B. F. Cheatham of Tennessee. Her father came to Texas in 1833, settled on Caney, and opened a plantation there when settlers were few and far between. He was born in North Carolina, but went from there to Tennessee when twelve years of age. His father, Frederick Davis, was an old Revolutionary soldier. The latter at an early date moved from that State to Nashville, thence to Franklin. Seven miles from Franklin he opened a plantation where he lived till his death in 1831, aged eighty-four.

ELISHA DAVIS became a very successful and extensive planter, and died in Natchez, Miss., while returning to Tennessee from Texas. After the death of her husband Mrs. Davis married Judge Seth Ingram, one of Austin's 300. For some time he served as surveyor, and received as compensation two or three leagues of land extra. Mrs. Ingram died in Matagorda in 1873. W. J. Croom was an influential and well respected citizen. He named the town La Grange in honor of the home of LaFayette. Mrs. Croom, subject's wife, had two cousins who were members of the Board of Lady Managers of the World's Fair. John L. Croom was the father of the following children: Mrs. C. L. Bruner, of Georgetown, Texas; Judge Wiley J., Ex-County Judge of Wharton County; and John L. Croom, Jr., (deceased), was an attorney. Mr. Croom spent his school days at La Grange, Ala., and at St. Joseph College, Bardstown, Ky. In June, 1846, he joined Captain Picken's Company, First Regiment Alabama Infantry, commanded by Col. John R. Coffee and was made First Sergeant. Our subject received honorable discharge from service, and on his way from Mexico he stopped to see his aunt, Mrs. Governor Horton, who was residing in Matagorda, Texas, and this State has continued to be his home for the most part since. He did, however, return to Alabama for a short time, but the State of Texas had a great attraction for him and he subsequently made his home within its borders. In 1851 he returned to Texas, and turned his attention to planting in Matagorda County, until 1865. In 1872 he was elected County Clerk and held this position eight years when he resigned, and in 1880 embarked in the real estate business. In 1887 he came to Wharton, and has done a great deal to advance the interests of the town and county.

Felix G. Mahon was born near Columbus, Ky., in 1839, his parents being Pressley B. and Mary (Hancock) Mahon, both of whom were born in western Kentucky, and in 1841 came to Houston, Texas, the journey thither being partly made by water. Shortly after they came to Colorado County, located in the northern part of the county, and here the parents spent the rest of their lives. The Indians were at first very troublesome in the upper counties, and they were compelled to put up with many hardships and other unpleasant things, but with true philosophy they made the best of everything, and in due course of time there was a better state of affairs. Pressley B. Mahon died in Colorado County at the age of thirty-four years, after which his widow married Clem Allen, a planter of this county, and here she passed from life in 1878. Her father, Samuel Hancock, was a Kentuckian, was a soldier of the War of 1812, and is also supposed to have participated in a number of early Indian wars. Felix G. Mahon grew up on the farm owned by his father, and secured a good education at Soule University at Chapel Hill, leaving that institution in 1881, and afterwards joined the Confederate army, becoming a member of Carter's Brigade, which joined the army at Arkansas Post. After being captured at that place he was taken to Camp Butler, near Springfield, Ill., and was there exchanged three months later, after which he became a member of Granberry's Texas Brigade in the Army of Tennessee. He was in the engagements at Missionary Ridge, Chickamauga, Ringald Gap and Dalton, and from there in all the engagements to Atlanta, and on the 22d of July was wounded by a gunshot. This disabled him for further duty. At the close of the war he returned to Texas and began raising cattle, and for several years was in the Kansas trade. In 1878 he was elected to his present position of County Assessor, and has since continuously filled that position, a fact that speaks eloquently as to his ability and popularity. He was married in 1872 to Miss Fannie Arnold of this county, a descendant of the old and noted Henning and Meriwether families of Tennessee, and to their marriage a son and three daughters have been given. Mr. Mahon is a member of the I. O. O. F., the K. of P., is public spirited and enterprising, and has proven himself a valuable and useful citizen.

G. C. Thomas, merchant, and son of one of the oldest and most prominent settlers of Winchester, Texas, is a wideawake, systematic business man of that thriving city, where he now makes his home. He was born in Austin County, Texas, April 12, 1846, to the union of Nathan and Mary Harris (Phelps) Thomas. Nathan Thomas made his first trip from Tennessee to Texas in 1837, and in 1838 brought his family. He first settled in Austin County, and secured a headright of 1,280 acres, though he did not locate on it. He purchased considerable land from private individuals, part timber and part prairie land, and located in Austin County when the settlers were few and far between. There being no lumber mills in that section, Mr. Thomas' house was made of hewn logs and floored with whipsawed lumber. As there were no churches there in those days, preaching was held at the homes of the few settlers, and Mr. Thomas' house was the headquarters for the ministers as they passed through the country. Trading was done at Houston, Texas, eighty or ninety miles distant, and the goods were brought to this section in wagons. Mr. Thomas was a Colonel in the militia of Tennessee, and was in several expeditions against the Indians. He engaged in merchandising long before the war, and after that eventful period, or in 1868, he embarked in merchandising in this place with his two sons, W. H. and G. C. This firm continued to do business until 1884, but previous to that, in 1880, Mr. Thomas moved to Waxahachie, and there died in 1883. He had been twice married, his first wife bearing him eight children, as follows: Mary, deceased; Sarah, deceased; Susan, deceased, was the wife of William A. Williams; W. H., G. C., Louise, deceased, was the wife of J. H. Moore; Ellen, deceased, was the wife of Dr. T. W. Moore, and one died young. Mr. Thomas' second marriage was with Miss Olivia Ledbetter, of this county (see sketch of W. H. Ledbetter). She now resides in this county. G. C. Thomas attended the schools of Winchester in his youth, and in 1863 joined Capt. Grady's Company, but was afterwards attached to Company H, of a Regiment, and stationed mostly at Galveston. He was not in any battles, and was discharged at Harrisburg in June, 1865, his being about the last regiment discharged in the Confederate service. This regiment was composed of boys from sixteen to eighteen years of age, and old men from forty-five upward. Upon his return home he assisted in gathering the crop of 1865, and in 1866 attended school. The following year he attended the commercial school at New Orleans, and in 1868 engaged in the mercantile business, which he has continued up to the present time. He also engaged in farming, and is the owner of 300 or 400 acres of excellent land on Colorado River. Besides this Mr. Thomas owns quite large tracts of land in the hill section. He has been one of the most industrious, thorough-going and popular business men of this section, and for many years had an immense trade. Miss Anna Gates, who became his wife in 1875, was born in Alabama, daughter of A. R. and Elizabeth (Thompson) Gates, natives of Alabama, from which State they came to Texas in 1852. Mr. Gates was a prominent attorney of this county, and was also an extensive farmer. To Mr. and Mr. Thomas have been born three children: Alexander G., William H. and Fannie P. Fraternally Mr. Thomas is a member of the K. & L. of H., and politically he is an ardent Democrat, being Chairman of the Democratic Committee of his section. His father was a member of the Congress of the Republic of Texas in 1841, and was a member of the State Legislature from this and Washington County in 1866. This was the first legislative body after the war, and the last Democratic legislative body until Hon. Richard Cook, in 1874, was elected Governor. Mrs. Thomas is a member of the old school Presbyterian Church.

MICHAEL O'CONNELL. This gentleman inherits the energy and perseverence of his Irish ancestors, and the practical value of shrewdness and discrimination combined with strict probity is exemplified in his present prosperous condition. He was born in County Limerick, Ireland, in 1821, and his father, Edmund O'Connell, who was a farmer, was also a native of that country. Michael, when a boy of eighteen, left the land of his birth and crossed the Atlantic to America. For some time he was engaged in farming near Troy, New York, but later went to Grand River, Mich., and thence to Refugio County, Texas, where he commenced dealing in mules. The first year after reaching this country he worked for wages, but since then he has been in business for himself. For some time after coming to this State he drove mules from Texas, but after locating in Matagorda County he turned his attention to the cattle business. His first purchase of land in Texas was 1,200 acres from Judge Due, in Refugio County. At the present time he is the owner of 20,000 or more acres of the finest land to be found anywhere in

Matagorda, Refugio and San Patricio counties, and he also owns valuable real estate in Michigan. Many years ago he braved the dangers, trials and privations of pioneer life in Texas, and is a splendid type of the enterprise, industry and self-reliance of those early settlers. During the Rebellion Mr. O'Connell belonged to the Confederate Cotton Bureau, and was supervisor of the supply train between Texas and Mexico. This was a very dangerous position to hold in those stirring times, but Mr. O'Connell was possessed of much courage, and discharged its duties in a manner satisfactory to all. He is now one of the heaviest dealers in cattle, mules and horses in the county, and usually handles from 2,000 to 3,000 annually. His duties in this relation have been so pressing that he has had no time to accept office at the hands of his friends, and in politics votes for the best man. Twenty-nine years ago, or in 1865, he was married to Miss Mary Dickson, a native of Ireland, who has borne him three children: Michael, Jr., Daniel, and one deceased. Mr. and Mrs. O'Connell are members of the Catholic Church. Although he received some little schooling in his native country, most of Mr. O'Connell's education was received after coming to America, for he attended school both in the Empire State and in Michigan. He is a man well respected for his push and energy, as well as his many other estimable qualities, and owes his success to his own individual efforts.

O. G. CANNON. One of the old settlers and extensive stockmen of Austin County, Texas, is O. G. Cannon, who has proven a progressive, public-spirited and useful citizen of this section. He owes his nativity to Montgomery County, Alabama, where he was born in 1847, to Henry and Elizabeth (Duncan) Cannon, natives also of Alabama. The family came to Texas in 1849, and settled in Austin County, five miles south of San Felipe, where the father tilled a large plantation for three years. In 1853 he moved to what is now Fort Bend County, and was there engaged in the stock business until his death in 1870. In 1862 or 1863 he joined the Confederate army, with which he served until the close of the war, his services being confined to the State of Texas. He brought three slaves with him to this State, but while coming thither by water from Mobile, Alabama, the cholera got among their slaves and Mr. Cannon lost thirteen negroes, whom they buried in the Gulf. Mr. Cannon was very successful as a stockman, became the purchaser and owner of the Cole Bros. claim and over his broad acres large herds of cattle roamed, but he never drove but one herd of fat cattle to New Orleans. To himself and wife four sons and four daughters were given, of whom the subject of this sketch is the only one living member, all dying young except Newton, who lived to be twenty-two years of age. At the time the family came here the country was very sparsely settled, the region was wild and unbroken, and Indians, at that time quite hostile, were numerous. Cattle and wild horses roamed the prairies, and on the edges of both the Brazos and Colorado rivers herds of wild cattle were numerous, and Mr. Cannon handled stock for a number of years. The wild horses of this region were the descendants of the horses left by Santa Anna's men on their retreat after the battle of San Jacinto. The herds thus started were not all captured until 1866, when Mr. Cannon and several others started out on a big horse drive and gathered up all stock that had been lost during the war and that was not branded. They captured two mares that had been left by the Mexicans in 1836. At this time Mr. Cannon caught a fine male animal that had belonged to his father, but had wandered away, and he was the last un-branded wild horse captured since the war. This country was for many years the stockman's paradise, five or ten miles being as close as a man wanted his nearest neighbor to be. O. G. Cannon grew to manhood on his father's ranch and naturally became familiar with the stock business at an early day, and has ever since devoted his attention to this calling, and, like his father before him, he is the most extensive stockman of the county. He handles of his own raising about 1,500 head and otherwise as high as 2,500 head. The horses of his own breeding are about 500 head, and now has 100 fine animals. He has made a specialty of raising fine cattle for thirteen or fourteen years of the Durham, Hereford and Burmah breed, for beef, and since 1868 has been improving the breed of his horses, being the first man in the county to import thoroughbred horses. Although his horses are not graded, they are fine animals, and some of the stock that he now has are thoroughbreds. He has also been raising some excellent mules, and sold his last jack for $700. He has 300 acres of land under cultivation, and 3,500 acres in all, some of which is along the Brazos bottom and the rest prairie land. He is one of the old-time hunters of Texas, and the happiest periods of his life are when he is out on a hunt for bear or other game, or out on a "drive" with his cattle, rounding up for branding. He is a wideawake and enterprising man, keenly alive to his own interests, but strictly honorable withal, and he has been an extremely useful citizen. He was married June 21, 1871, to Miss Winnie N. Allen, a native of this county and daughter of J. W. and V. (Johnson) Allen, and their union has been blessed in the birth of seven children: W. G., J. H., Rosa, Nettie, Edna, May, and Oliver G. Mrs. Cannon is a member of the Missionary Baptist Church, and politically he has always supported the Democratic party. He is a member of the A. F. & A. M. and the K. of P., and is quite active in both orders.

WILLIAM A. GILES. William A. Giles, senior member of the firm of Drake & Giles, dry goods merchants of Winchester, Fayette County, Texas, is a gentleman whose walk through life has been characterized by a sturdy independence, uncompromising honesty, great energy, and the utmost loyalty to his family, his friends, and his country, and he may truly be said to be a man among men. He is a native of Georgia, born in Houston County, August 18, 1855, and his parents, John F. and Fannie A. (Jenkins) Giles, were natives of North Carolina and Georgia respectively. John F. Giles and family came overland from Georgia at an early date and settled in Fayette County, where Mr. Giles purchased timber land and began making a home. He resided on his farm until the breaking out of the Civil War, when he enlisted as a private in the Confederate army and was in the trans-Mississippi Department. He participated in several battles, among them Pleasant Hill, Yellow Bayou, and Mansfield, La., and died in the latter State in 1863. He left a wife and five children, of whom our subject was the eldest son. The others were named as follows: Emma (deceased), was the wife of L. Turman; Addie and Albert (twins). The former married Prof. J. R. Goodwin of Winchester; Albert (deceased), and Fannie, wife of J. D. Green, of Jones County, Texas. Mrs. Giles was a lady of superior educational abilities for Texas in her day and time, and taught school for many years. She gave to each of her children a good education. William A. Giles commenced life early for himself, received a good common school education, and when fourteen years of age began clerking in Eastern Texas, the Village of Putnam, for Conger & Giles, the latter an uncle of our subject, for three years. When eighteen years of age he engaged in farming in this county, and continued this until 1888, when he embarked in merchandising at this place, with the before-mentioned partner, S. F. Drake, a native of LaGrange and son of one of the early settlers of this county. Messrs. Drake & Giles do a general mercantile business, and have a large and constantly increasing trade. They commenced with small capital, but by judicious handling they have now a business of $35,000, and are wideawake, experienced men of business. Besides his mercantile interests Mr. Giles has a farm of 175 acres. Although he commenced life with little or no means, he had the push and perseverance necessary for a successful career, and has met with his reward. Early in life he learned self-reliance from his mother, and to that noble woman he is greatly indebted for his success. Mr. Giles has been twice married, first in 1878, to Miss Sarah T. Hall, a native of this county and daughter of T. P. Hall, who is one of the early settlers. To this marriage two daughters were born, one died in infancy, and Emma is now living. Mrs. Giles, who was a devoted member of the Methodist Episcopal Church South, died in 1882. In 1893 Mr. Giles was married to Miss Mattie Wilks, also a native of this county and daughter of J. E. and M. E. Wilks, early settlers of this county. Mr. Giles is a member of the K. of P., Smithville Lodge No. 92, and the K. of H., Winchester Lodge No. 2069. While not an office seeker Mr. Giles takes considerable interest in political matters, and since attaining his majority has been a leading Democrat in his locality.

HON. GREEN C. DUNCAN. There is such uniformity in the great body of men, that but little profit could result from the study of most of them. Occasionally an unusual character is developed, either physically, morally or intellectually, and so impresses itself upon the people within the reach of its influence that it deserves to be noted and studied. The subject of this sketch is such a character. He is a native Kentuckian, born near Bardstown, October 10, 1841, and the son of Green Duncan, whose father went to Kentucky from Virginia many years ago, cleared up land and became an extensive planter. Green Duncan, also a native of the Blue Grass State, was three times married, and one son, Henry C., born to the first union, is a resident of Kentucky, near Bardstown. Nancy Wilson, the second wife, was our subject's mother. A son and daughter was born to Mr. Duncan's third marriage, and they now reside on the old homestead. Mr. Duncan held many positions of trust and honor in his native State, serving in the Legislature for some time, and especially made his influence felt when matters of moment were under consideration. His death occurred in 1869, when seventy-two years of age. He was a Clay Whig in politics and from the first was opposed to secession. In Center College, Danville, Ky., our subject received his schooling, and left his books to enlist in the Confederate army in 1861, a company going from Kentucky to Memphis in August or September of that year. At first he was in Col. Marshall Walker's Tennessee Regiment, and later in the Eighth Kentucky Mounted Infantry, joining General Forrest's Cavalry. He was promoted to the rank of First Lieutenant, and was captured at Island No. 10 and sent North, where he remained a prisoner from May 16 until September at Camp Chase and Johnson's Island. After being released he joined his command, and was with General Waul at Coffeesville, Miss., Champion Hill, Jackson, Guntown, Brice's Cross Roads, Franklin, Nashville, and then went to North Carolina, but left the Confederate army at Columbia, Miss., after the battle of Selma, Ala.   During his service he had five horses shot from under him, but was never wounded.   He rode horseback to Memphis, sold the horse there and went home to Kentucky.   Soon after, coming to Texas to look after some landed interests that belonged to a member of the family, he was so favorably impressed with the appearance of the country, that he decided to make his home here.   He resided on Caney Creek, in the lower part of Wharton County, for a few years, and then sold out and came to his present property.   In 1872 he purchased 1,200 acres of land, now his home planta-tion, and he now has one of the loveliest homes in the section.   He has been trading in stock ever since locating here, and has driven and traded stock all over Texas and Mexico.   In 1881 he formed a partnership with George H. Northington, and since then has done an extensive mercantile business.   They own a ranch of 7,200 acres in Bernard, and another of 4,100 acres in Burnet County.   This is one of the most substantial firms in the county.   Mr. Dun-can was elected to represent his county in the Twenty-second Session of the Legislature, and served on the Committees of Stock and Stock-raising, Roads and Bridges, Towns, Cities and Corporations, Statistics, Claims and Accounts, etc.   July 11, 1872, he married Miss Mamie J. Bowie, a daughter of George Bowie, and five children have been given them: Matie, Harris, Vance, Bowie and Donald.   Mrs. Duncan is a member of the Episcopal Church.

CAPT. E. R. TARVER.   He whose name heads this sketch is an early set-tler of the town of Laredo, and owes his nativity to Lowndes County, Ala-bama, where his eyes first opened on the light of day in 1840, he being the fifth of nine children born to the marriage of John Andrew Tarver and Mary Fields, the former of whom was born in Georgia and the latter in Alabama. John A. Tarver was engaged in planting throughout life, was always active and industrious, was prominent in the political affairs of his section, and represented his county in both branches of the State Legislature.   He died in Alabama in 1850 and the same year the mother passed away in Texas.   Her people were Virginians, while Mr. Tarver's ancestors were residents of Georgia.   When twelve years of age the subject of this sketch came to Texas, and in this State received the principal part of his education, being an at-tendant of the Military Institute at Rutersville, from which he graduated in 1859, after which he was engaged in farm labor until the opening of the great Civil War.   He at once enlisted in the Eighth Texas Cavalry (Terry's Rangers) and served in Company G, until after the bloody battle of Shiloh, when he was transferred to the trans-Mississippi Department and was ap-pointed Aid-de-camp of General Bee, and served with him until the close of the war.   He then returned home to resume the occupation of tilling the soil, and, after considerable time spent in preparation, he was admitted to the bar at Floresville, Wilson County, Texas, in 1874, and there his maiden work as a legal practitioner was done.   Since 1881 he has been a resident of Laredo, and from 1882 to 1886 he was Superintendent of the schools of this place. The four following years he discharged the duties of County Attorney, and at the present time is a City Alderman and Mayor *pro tem.*   He is the Dem-ocratic nominee for the Legislature from this district, and as he is a capable and worthy man in every respect, he will doubtless poll a large vote.   He has been a delegate to many county and State conventions since the war, and was appointed receiver for the Laredo Improvement Company in 1892, and the duties of this position he is still ably discharging. He is one of the enterprising and active citizens of southwest Texas, is a very useful and highly valued citizen of Webb County, is a competent and trustworthy official and is an excellent all-round man. In 1867 his marriage with Miss Julia Legette, a native of South Carolina, was celebrated, and to their union the following named children have been given: Kate, Ellen, Edward R., Bee and Lizette. Captain and Mrs. Tarver are members of the Episcopal Church and are highly valued members of society.

GABRIEL FRIEDBERGER. Like many other parts of the State, Fayette County, Texas, has been benefited by an influx into it of a better class of German emigrants, who have helped to build up the prosperity of this section. Gabriel Friedberger, of the firm of Friedberger & Johnson, dry goods merchants of LaGrange, was born in the Kingdom of Wurtemberg, Germany, in 1835, and his parents, Simon and Leo Friedberger were natives of the same place. When thirteen years of age our subject went to Paris, France, learned the trade of designing, and became so proficient that after one month he was designing for about 200 girls. When fourteen years of age he ran away from Paris and crossed the ocean to America. He borrowed ninety-five francs from a friend, just the amount to pay his passage, and landed in the city of New York without a cent. Going to an hotel he told the landlord his condition, but told him he had a trunk full of clothes. For one week Mr. Friedberger sought employment without success, and became very despondent, so much so that he shed tears. A gentleman from Philadelphia seeing him in that condition questioned him, learned his story and paid his way to the City of Brotherly Love. He also purchased him a cheap suit of clothes and paid his hotel bill. When young Friedberger reached Philadelphia he was told that he must peddle goods among the farmers, and although he had not bargained on this, he could do nothing better at the time and started out with a pack of $35 worth of goods. It was not until the second day of his travels that he plucked up courage to ask anyone to buy his goods. Finally before noon of that day he met a Mr. Moser, a German, who made him go to his house, gave him his dinner and insisted on his staying all night. It was during harvest and Mr. Moser had eleven cradles in the field, and in the morning Mr. Friedberger asked for and received a job of binding wheat for twenty-five cents per day. The next day he received fifty cents, and the following day $1.50 for cradling. He worked until he had made forty-five dollars and then returned to Philadelphia with his pack, paid the man there all he owed him, and then started out with another pack, so heavy that when he came to a hill he was obliged to go on his hands and knees. For one year he followed peddling and farming, making $200. About six months after, coming to Pennsylvania, he met his brother, Samuel, on the road, but after parting from him did not see him again for six months. They then, with a cousin, went to Florida where they sold goods by wholesale. They had three teams and hacks going, made considerable money in the year they remained there, and with $3,000 went from there to Georgia, where they peddled for six months. There they met with still better success, but subsequently all three came to Texas, making the trip overland from Georgia to New Orleans, and were engaged in peddling, wholesale, lots of $40 per lot for six months.

They then sold two teams in the fall of 1851, and returned to New Orleans with $40,000 in gold. The first bank of that city refused to take their money and sell them New York drafts, fearing the boys had stolen it. However the second bank did not refuse, although Mr. Friedberger says he and his companions were a tough looking set, and after getting their money they went to New York City, where they purchased goods with the intention of settling in Texas. They opened their first stores in Austin and LaGrange in 1851, and in Bastrop in 1853. Our subject remained in Austin until 1853, when his cousin came to that city and he went to Bastrop, where he remained in business until 1857. He then returned to his native country, spent one year with his parents, and while there purchased a tannery and learned the business. Returning to his adopted country, he and his brother and cousin returned to Texas, and engaged in business in Bastrop, LaGrange and Columbus, where they sold goods until 1861. Then the cousin went to Europe, the brother went to New York, and in 1862 our subject was burned out in Bastrop, losing $22,000. In 1864 he quit the mercantile business, bought cotton and shipped to Mexico, and the next year went into the wholesale cotton business at Matamoras. There he made considerable money, but left that city in 1865 and decided to locate in Galveston. He placed in a warehouse $155,000 worth of goods, intending to smuggle them to the American side of the river, and although he had considerable trouble in doing this, he was finally successful. The difficulties and troubles that beset his path, during this time, would have discouraged any other man, but he had been trained in a severe school, and bore his misfortunes with the greatest fortitude. He sold about $50,000 worth of goods in Galveston, and shipped the remainder to LaGrange, where for the third time he commenced business. Since then he has carried on business in that city, and during the first eight or ten years of his last venture had the principal business of the country. In 1870 he and his brother Simon went into business exclusively in the city of Austin, remained there for four years when the brother sold out and went to New York, where his death occurred in 1888. Our subject has been engaged in business for forty-four years, and during that time has won a reputation for honesty and reliability that any one might envy. He purchased his first farm in 1861, 436 acres, and now has 235 acres under a good state of cultivation. At the present time he owns 1,200 acres, although at one time he owned 7,000 or 8,000 acres. During the war he owned several hundred horses, but at one time 300 head were stolen, although Mr. Friedberger recovered sixteen head. In November, 1863, he was married to Miss Libbie Diamond, a daughter of M. O. and Eliza (Hemphill) Diamond, two very old families of Texas. Mr. Diamond erected the first house in the city of Galveston. The Hemphill family came to Bastrop County about 1834 and its members were in the Indian wars and in the War of 1848. The former family came from Connecticut and the latter from Georgia. Mr. Friedberger is of Jewish origin and all are of the Jewish faith. Mrs. Friedberger was born in America, and is a descendant of English ancestors. Mr. Friedberger's father was a farmer as well as a merchant, and a wealthy and influential citizen. He and wife reared a family of seven children: Matilda, wife of Soloman Landaurr, of Germany; Joseph (deceased), Henrietta, deceased, was the wife of C. Klein, of Paris; Jacob, Helena, Samuel (deceased), and Gabriel, our subject. Our subject and wife have no children. He is a Mason,

LaGrange Lodge No. 34, of which he is Treasurer, and was formerly an officer in the I. O. O. F. Mr. Friedberger has never been an office seeker, but served his ward for many years as Alderman, and takes a deep interest in every advancement and progress made in his section. He is a stock-holder in the compress company, and is also a Director in the same.

DR. THOMAS JEFFERSON TURPIN. The successful physician must be a man of patient research, capable of sustaining study, and of large sympathies. Free and broad should be his mind, to seek in all departments of human knowledge some truth to guide his hand; keen and delicate the well trained sense, to draw from nature her most treasured secrets, and unlock the doors where ignorance and doubt have stood sentinel for ages. How fine his fiber who hears the querulous murmur of the sick man only to soothe the fretful brain with loving kindness, to meet impatience with cheerful patience, and bring back the troubled heart to peace by tender sympathy. The above paragraph is but an attempt to sketch one who is highly respected in Webb County, Texas, and who in his own person approaches closely the ideal physician— Dr. Thomas Jefferson Turpin. He was born in Gallatin County, Ky., in 1847 to Philip Osborn and Mary Ellen (Butler) Turpin, who were natives of Virginia and Kentucky respectively. The paternal grandfather, Horatio Turpin, was born in Virginia in 1755, and was married to Mary Bancroft, a daughter of Dr. Bancroft, a Surgeon of the British navy. He moved to Kentucky in 1820, and died in that State in 1826. He had been an Ensign in "Light Horse Harry's" Brigade during the Revolutionary War, and afterward became a planter and the owner of a large tract of land in Kentucky and numerous slaves. His father, Thomas Turpin, married Mary Jefferson, an aunt of President Thomas Jefferson. He was a Colonel in the Virginia Militia under the Colonial Government, and his commission was signed by Governor Dinwiddie in 1754. The Turpins are of English descent, and Philip Turpin, who was the first of the family to come to America, settled in Virginia about 1650. The maternal grandfather, Maj. Thomas Butler, was a Lieutenant and Aid to Gen. Jackson in the War of 1812, and he was in charge of the city of New Orleans at the time of that battle. His father was Gen. Percival Butler, of the Revolutionary War. He removed to Kentucky from Pennsylvania about 1780, and was intimately associated with Daniel Boone and other famous pioneers and Indian fighters. The Butlers are of Irish descent, and came to America about 1750, owing to political troubles in their native land. The original settler in this country was Thomas Butler, an Irish gentleman. The Butlers lived in Carroll County, Ky., from remote times, and the grandfather of the subject of this sketch, Thomas Butler, was several times elected to the State Legislature, and was Collector of the Port at New Orleans while Jackson was President. Philip Osborn Turpin was a successful planter, served in the State Legislature at the same time as Thomas Butler, and was Major of the State Militia. He died in 1881 and his wife in 1860, both being worthy members of the Presbyterian Church. The subject of this sketch received his literary training in Carrollton, Ky., and in 1867 began the study of medicine, graduating from the School of Medicine of Louisville, Ky., in 1869. He then spent that year as a resident interne at the hospital at Louisville, and then went to Philadelphia and entered the Jefferson Medical College, graduating therefrom in 1870. In 1871 he came to Texas, and after several years' residence at Corpus Christi, returned to Kentucky, where he married in 1878. In 1880 he returned to the Lone Star State, and up to 1889 made his home in Corpus Christi, after which he spent one year in California for the benefit of his health. Upon his return here he located at Laredo, where he has since been in the active practice of his profession. In 1871–72 he was State Quarantine Officer, was appointed to the same office in 1890, and in 1892 was reappointed. He is a member of the California Medical Association, was a member of the Kentucky Medical Association, and now is a member of the Board of Medical Examiners for this (the Forty-ninth District). He was also a member of the same board at Corpus Christi, was City Physician there also, and was County Physician of Nueces County. In 1893, while filling the position of State Quarantine Officer, he also held the office of Inspector M. H. S. His wife, Miss Fidie Buckner, is a daughter of the late William Buckner, a native of Kenton County, Ky. The doctor and his wife have one child, Catherine. The doctor has been in the active practice of his profession for twenty-five years, and in his efforts to heal the sick and afflicted he has met with a more than ordinary degree of success, and is an accomplished and skillful practitioner, whose name is a familiar and loved household word.

GEORGE H. NORTHINGTON. It has been said that the study of biography yields to no other subject in point of interest and profit; and while it is true that all biographies, and more especially those of successful men, have much in common, yet the life sketches of no two individuals are alike. Each has its distinctions and various points of interest, and each is accordingly complete in itself. Among the well-known business men and extensive cotton planters of Wharton County, Texas, is George H. Northington, a member of the mercantile firm of Duncan & Northington. His paternal grandfather, Andrew Northington, was a product of the Old North State and an early settler of Texas, settling in this State in 1831, Brazoria County. He had left his family in Kentucky, and later he brought them here and settled at Bernard. This family experienced all the hardships usual to new settlers, and Mr. Northington helped to fight the Mexicans and Indians, as well as subdue the wilderness. Mentor Northington, his son and the father of our subject, was born in Triggs County, Ky., whither his father had moved from North Carolina, and later came with the family to Texas. When only fourteen years of age he was in service against the Indians under Gen. Green, and for his service received a headright in Jones County, Texas. There his death occurred in 1889. He also served in Scott's Company, organized in Washington County, and was at Sabine Pass and other engagements during the Civil War. He married Miss Elizabeth E. Heard, daughter of Capt. J. E. Heard, who was a native of Mississippi, but who subsequently moved to Alabama, and thence to Jackson County, Texas, with an Alabama colony. Soon after Col. Heard came to Wharton County and located at Caney, at a place now widely known as Egypt, where he made his home until after the war. From there he moved to Washington County, Texas, and died there when quite an aged man. He was Captain of troops in Texas during the war for independence, and participated in the battle of San Jacinto, as well as in a number of desperate Indian fights. As a planter he was unusually successful, and his Egypt place was one of the best improved in the State, with fine brick residence, brick barns, and quarters for his negroes. He raised annually immense quantities of cotton and considerable sugar. His daughter,

Elizabeth, was born in Alabama in 1827, and died in 1892. Her marriage with Mentor Northington resulted in the birth of two sons, William A., who is a planter and merchant of Egypt, and our subject. The latter's birth occurred in Wharton County, Texas, in 1854, and his schooling was obtained in the university at Chapel Hill and Randolph Mason College in Virginia. In his choice of an occupation in life he chose planting and trading in stock, and has followed this for the most part since. He owns 1,900 acres of land here, a large tract in Jones County, and is interested with his father in extensive tracts of grazing land. In the year 1881 he formed a partnership with Mr. Duncan in the mercantile business, carries an extensive stock of goods, and is doing a good business. He also owns a gin near the store. In the year 1875 he married Miss Josie Simmons, of Chapel Hill, and eight children have been given them, three sons and five daughters. Mr. Northington has served as County Commissioner, and is a reliable and worthy citizen.

. JOHN T. HARWELL. This prominent old settler of Fayette County, Texas, has resided here for many years and during that time has earned the well deserved reputation of being not only an esteemed and highly respected citizen, but a man of more than ordinary learning. He was born in Georgia in 1840, to the union of F. E. and Mary A. (Ware) Harwell, who were also natives of that State. About the year 1841, the parents decided to move to the Lone Star State, and in February of that year settled in Fayette County. At that time there were probably not over seventy-five voters in the county. Mr. Harwell followed farming and bought land in that section, and became a prominent and worthy citizen. Indians bothered the settlers greatly, but Mr. Harwell had no trouble with them. He served in the Seminole War in Florida, but afterwards returned to the peaceful pursuits of farming and stock-raising, which he followed up to the time of his death, 1875, when fifty-seven years of age. His wife survived him until 1880, and died when sixty years of age. They left a family of seven children, five sons and two daughters: John T., subject; J. C., of Bell County; Samuel, of the same county; Louisa, now Mrs. Robert J. Talley of Bell County; Carrie, now Mrs. Ligon of the same county; Dan and Nicholas both residing there. The father of these children took very little interest in politics, but was a man well liked by all. John T. Harwell was educated in the college at LaGrange, Texas. As he was but an infant when brought by his parents to this section, all of his recollections are of this State, and here his interests are centered. In 1861, when twenty-one years of age, Harwell joined Company A, Fifth Texas Cavalry under Capt. John Shropshire and Col. Tom Green, and served on the west side of the Mississippi River, participating in the battles of New Mexico, in 1862, Glorietta, New Mexico, Donley's Ranch, New Mexico, and was in the re-taking of Galveston, January 1, 1863. Mr. Harwell was in the navy at that time, and assisted in capturing the gunboat, Harriet Lane. He also participated in the battles of Pleasant Hill, Mansfield and Yellow Bayou, besides numerous skirmishes, and in another engagement where 250 Confederates captured 1,700 Union soldiers. When the war closed Mr. Harwell returned to his home, and without any capital, started out to fight his own way in life. He decided to follow in the footsteps of his father, and engaged in farming on land he purchased soon after the war. His first crop was in 1866. Until 1881 Mr. Harwell cultivated the soil, but he then sold out and moved to LaGrange, where he followed the lumber business. This he has continued up to the present time, and has met with fair success. He now owns the only lumber yard in the city, and has associated with him in business George A. Hall, of this place. In the year 1865 he married Mrs. Bettie Ligon, daughter of A. R. Jones, one of the old settlers of this county. One child was born to this union, Bessie, who became the wife of N. M. Williams of LaGrange. Mrs. Harwell died in 1882. She was a worthy member of the old school Presbyterian Church. In 1883 Mr. Harwell married Mrs. Judith McKennon, *nee* Carter, another of the first settlers of the county, and one of the oldest merchants in LaGrange. Mr. and Mrs. Harwell have one son, John F. In his political views, Mr. Harwell is a stanch Democrat and takes a deep interest in its welfare. He has been Chairman of several Democratic conventions in the county, and is an active worker for the success of his party. All his time is devoted to the lumber trade, which is increasing as the county improves, and success has rewarded his efforts. He witnessed the country grow from a wilderness to its present prosperous condition and contributed his share towards its advancement. He says he often stood in his door and shot deer and turkey in those good old days.

CHRISTOPHER MARMION MACDONELL, upon his arrival here in 1852 from Newry, Down County, Ireland, of which place he was a native, settled down to commercial pursuits. After two years of that work, being of an adventurous nature and a direct decendant of the Glengarry chiefs of the Macdonell Clan, from Inverness-shire, Scotland, he moved to San Patricio County, southwest Texas. One of them said that "a Macdonell who was not a soldier must be a priest." At this time a company of rangers was being organized to protect the frontier. Young Macdonell was one of the first to join, under Capt. Nolan. They went to the Rio Grande, where they had many skirmishes with the Comanches and fierce Apaches, then infesting that country. After four years of scouting, fighting and hard riding, he settled down to stock-raising, and when the tocsin of war sounded in 1861, he had accumulated a comfortable fortune. Not being married, he left his stock and lands and joined Company I, Eighth Texas Cavalry, better known as the famous "Terry's Texas Rangers," in which command he fought through the whole four years of the great Civil War between the States, never once coming back to look after his material interests until the end of the strife. While Gen. Hood was moving into Tennessee from Atlanta, Lieut. Macdonell was appointed Chief of Scouts by that eminent commander, with whom he was a great favorite, and he was ordered to keep in the rear as far as possible, in order to better observe the enemy's movements. After Hood's failure at Franklin, our subject retreated with his command through north Alabama and middle Georgia, and rejoined Gen. Johnston in South Carolina, with whom he staid until the surrender at Greensboro, N. C., in 1865. He remarked to the writer of this sketch years afterwards that he succeeded in retaining an old mule which he rode to Montgomery, Ala., when he sold it and with the proceeds succeeded in making his way to New Orleans and Galveston, Texas, when, learning that an old friend of his, Col. E. J. Davis, of the Union forces, was in command, he went to his headquarters to see him. When the negro soldier who was on guard saw his tattered old Confederate jacket, with the buttons still on, he cursed him and deliberately cut the buttons off with his knife. His fight had ended and he swallowed the insult in order to see Col. Davis. In a few minutes he reached his quarters. The Colonel was glad to see him and gave him the necessary permit and other assistance to proceed to San Patrico County, which he did overland, on horseback. On arriving at old "San Pat.," as it is called by the natives, he was met by Captains Robert Dougherty and Chas. Callaghan, old friends and ex-Confederate officers, who were then in a position to aid him materially, which they did. After resting a month, he proceeded to Laredo, accompanied by Capt. Callaghan. After gathering together the few remains of his former ventures, he and Capt. Callaghan became partners in what is now known as the famous Callaghan sheep ranch, the largest in Texas. At that date, the winter of 1865, there were six resident Americans in Laredo. Not satisfied with one venture, he opened and started a large commission house, trading with the neighboring republic. In the 70's the house of C. M. Macdonell was the largest on the frontier, doing an annual business of $2,000,000. He became rich beyond his most sanguine expectation, but lived more plainly than any of his many employes. He spent thousands in aiding his friends or any worthy man or cause that applied to him, seeming to take a pleasure in doing it, appearing utterly oblivious of self. In politics he was a consistent Democrat, opening his purse freely for all party needs; never sought office for himself, but did for his friends. He often mentioned an incident that happened in Reconstruction days: A negro regiment was stationed here. Many of the officers and the "old rebel," as they pleasantly called him, were very friendly, more particularly as he always kept a barrel of whiskey on tap in his office for his friends to help themselves. One day two officers came in, and, after helping themselves pretty freely, became pugnacious over a lithograph of Gen. R. E. Lee, which was hung up in the office. One of them went so far as to draw his sword and strike Mr. Macdonell, who bowed and told them they could have the office and its contents, as he did not feel in the humor of again taking up arms against the United States. The next day the offending officer came down and apologized for the affront, which was freely granted. As was learned, the young man never was in an engagement where there was any need to draw his sword during the unpleasantness. Mr. Macdonell lived here until the fall of 1888, when after a short illness of three days, he quietly and peacefully departed this life, regretted by the whole population, many of whom are his beneficiaries. He left an estate, valued at $1,000,000, to a brother and sister who survive him. His brother, Allan Macdonell, who spent his early life in Russia, a civil and military engineer by profession, and a member of the Imperial Polytechnique, of St. Petersburg, Russia, is here settling up the estate, aided by P. J. Macmahon, a native of Sligo County, Ireland, and a leading real estate and insurance agent, who came here in 1882, armed with a letter from his relative, Capt. Robert Dougherty, to his old friend, Macdonell.

HIRAM B. ENGLISH. One of the early settlers and leading stockmen of Austin County, Texas, is Hiram B. English, who was born in Hardin County, Ky., January 21, 1849, to R. B. and Melvina (Fousher) English, both of whom were born on Blue Grass soil. The paternal ancestors came from England not later than 1727, and settled in Bloomfield Parish, Va., and the maternal ancestors belonged to the French Huguenots, and also settled in that parish. After the English family had settled in Virginia they were all killed by the Indians, with the exception of two sons, Robert and John, the subject of this sketch being descended from the former. Both brothers served in the colonial army during the Revolutionary War. In 1811 Robert moved to Kentucky with his wife and family, consisting of ten children, and settled in the then sparsely settled Hardin County. ' Here he eventually died, as did also his wife, who was Sarah Smith, of Bloomfield Parish, Va. Their children were: Noah, Weeden, Silas, Lemuel, Samuel, Hiram B., Jane, who married James Dellard; Matilda, who married Thomas Shackelford; Mahala, who married James Howard, and Sallie. Hiram B., the grandfather of the subject of this sketch, moved with his family to Texas in 1857, and settled near Wallis, but about 1868 moved to San Felipe, where he later passed away. He brought a number of slaves with him to this State, and settled on unimproved land, at which time there were but few families in the neighborhood, and only about four families between Wallis and Bellville, a distance of twenty-six miles. Their nearest neighbor was three miles away, and their milling was done twelve miles from home, at a mill owned by David Randon, a half-breed Indian. His wife, Elizabeth Yeagor, was born in Springfield, Ky., a daughter of Josiah and Lydia A. (Horden) Yeagor, both of whom were among the early settlers of the Blue Grass State. The Yeagors came to Kentucky from Virginia, and the Hardens direct from Old England. An uncle of Mrs. English was Gen. John Hardin, the great Indian fighter of Kentucky, who was deputized by the people of Kentucky to make a treaty with the Indians, but he was so much dreaded by them that when they found him in their power they put him to death by means unknown to his family. The Hardins became famous in the early troubles with the Indians. Mrs. English, the grandmother, now lives with the subject of this sketch at the age of 88 years, and says that during the Indian outbreaks in Indiana the people of Springfield, Ky., became very much excited, and the men went to Indiana to make war upon the Red man, while the women who were left at home fortified themselves in a large, strong log hotel, being told that Indians were seen lurking in the neighborhood. Josiah Yeagor's parents were Cornelius and Elizabeth (Fisher) Yeagor, of Virginia, the former of whom was of German descent. His wife was a daughter of Stephen Fisher and granddaughter of Lewis Fisher, who came to Virginia, when quite a young man, from Germany. The wife of Lewis Fisher was Barbara Blakenbecker, whose father came to America in 1717. Stephen Fisher's wife was Magdaline Garr, of Virginia. Hiram B. English and wife reared three children: Robert B., Lydia A., wife of William Guyler, and Josiah Y. Robert B. English was born in Hardin County, Ky., January 26, 1825, and came with his father to Texas in 1857, and he at once engaged in farming, residing on the land on which he first settled, December 25, 1864. He was a physician, and a graduate of the Louisville Medical School, and when first he came to this State he was the only regular physician between San Felipe and Richmond, a distance of thirty-five miles. The territory over which he practiced covered forty miles, and he had many thrilling experiences while on his nightly rides. He died in 1864. Although he was never much interested in politics in Texas, he represented Hardin County, Ky., in the State Legislature one term. He was a Democrat of the old school. To his marriage, which occurred in 1848, the following children were born: Hiram B., Martha E., deceased, became the wife of F, G. Eidman, and left one child, who is studying medicine in Galveston; Josephine Y., is the deceased wife of W. C. Cliett, and left six children—Bertie, Louis, Martha, Thomas, Henry, and Annabel; Lucy A., was twice married, first to W. H. Josey, and after his death to S. J. Franklin. Mrs. English is still living, and resides in Sealey. She is now 65 years of age. Hiram B. English, the subject of this sketch, was an attendant of Baylor University in 1863–64–66–67, and attended several other good schools at San Felipe and other places. He commenced doing for himself at the age of sixteen years, and after the death of his father, being the only son, he had to assume charge of the family. Owing to the changed condition of affairs after the war, the family was left in bad circumstances financially, for their slaves were all freed and only fifty acres of their land was in cultivation. He at once set energetically to work to improve the place, and wisely put what money he earned in cattle (oxen), and at the close of the war owned ten yoke, for which he received $50 per yoke. When he married he divided his earnings equally among his mother, himself and his three sisters, and had left as his share, in 1873, $1,000. He has since devoted his attention to farming and stock-raising, and now owns 1,200 acres, with 100 under cultivation, and handles about 3,500 head of stock. His wife, Miss Annie Blacknall, formerly, was born in North Carolina, a daughter of William and Mary N. (Ward) Blacknall, also of the Old North State, the latter of whom came to Texas in the spring of 1857, the father having died in North Carolina. She has resided here ever since, with the exception of during the war and a few years after. Mr. and Mrs. Blacknall had but two children, Sophia, wife of Dr. J. J. Josey, and Mrs. English. The latter has borne her husband the following children: Mary B., Ada, Mittie, Mollie, Sophia, Lucy J., deceased, and Lenora J. Mr. English is one of the old-time Democrats of the State, and held one important appointment under Governor Ireland, that of Inspector of Hides for his county; was re-elected by a big majority, and held that office until the county was exempted from that tax. He is Chancellor Commander of J. R. Castleton Lodge No. 188, of the K. of P., S. F. Austin Lodge No. 1952, of the K. of H., and is Deputy Grand Commander of Sealy Lodge No. 665, of the K. and L. of H., of which he is a charter member, and has held nearly all of the important offices. His wife is a member of the Methodist Episcopal Church. Mr. English has in his possession a tree of the Fisher family which dates back to 1717, and furnishes the names of over 5,000 of the descendants of the first one of the family to settle in this country. Mr. English's grandmother English resides with him, and is a great-great-grandmother, having nursed the fourth generation of her own direct descendants.

WILLIAM O. VICTOR. By a thorough knowledge of his business, gained step by step, and through his own experience, Mr. William O. Victor has become one of the most successful apiarists in Southeast Texas. He is a native of Wilcox County, Ala., born in the town of Camden, June 10, 1861, and the son of Octavius and Amanda M. (Armstrong) Victor. Octavius Victor was born in the State of Virginia, but when a young man made his way to Alabama, where he joined the Confederate army early in the war. Like many another brave soldier, he fell at Malvern Hill, and left a wife and child in Alabama. In 1869 or '70 his widow married J. C. Watts, a planter, who subsequently came to Texas, where he died in 1878, while on a trip looking for a location. In 1879 Mrs. Watts came to this State, and soon entered the postoffice as deputy. In 1880 she received the appointment of Postmaster at Wharton, which position she has held in a very satisfactory manner since. For some time our subject was in the postoffice, and later he embarked in merchandising with W. O. Victor, under the firm name of

W. O. Victor & Co., on a rather limited scale, In 1883 he quit that business and started out as an agriculturist, but was engaged in various other enterprises at the same time. While on a business trip one day he discovered a swarm of bees, and this gave him the idea that bee-farming would be profitable. That year (1884) he collected twenty-five colonies in hollow logs, nail-kegs, etc., and during the season he increased this to forty-five. However, he had not had the necessary experience yet, and the following season lost all but seven. This did not discourage him, and he gradually added to his colony, and has ever since met with the best success. He now owns about 450 colonies, seventy of them on the River apiary, some on the Lee and Home apiaries, and about 200 a short distance east of Wharton, where he has his extracting outfit, and carries on his operations for extracting honey. He has made the business a very profitable one, and it has grown to such a degree that, although he had just ordinary supplies at first, he now ships by the carload. This season he has handled 40,000 pounds of honey, and will have from 10,000 to 20,000 more. However, this has been an extra season for him. He has all the latest appliances for extracting, and ships to Galveston, Houston, etc., and makes an effort to concentrate his business near home, but annually ships to New York, St. Louis and other markets. In 1888 he was appointed Official Weigher of the county, which position he filled very capably and satisfactorily. Seven years ago, or in 1887, he was married to Miss Hope E. Gillespie, of this county. Both are members of the Baptist Church, and he was Clerk in the same for some time. In politics he is an ardent supporter of Democratic principles.

JOHN A. HALL. The business in which John A. Hall is engaged is one of the utmost importance in any community, and especially in a growing community, for his product enters more or less into the construction of all buildings, and is consequently in constant demand. He owns an extensive lumber yard at Weimar, and ever since embarking in the business here he has commanded a paying patronage. He was born in Logan County, Ky., in 1844, and is a son of Alexander Hall, who lived and died on Blue Grass soil. He was a farmer by occupation, and was also quite extensively engaged in trading, and, after an active life, died when the subject of this sketch was but a small child. His widow, who was formerly Miss Jennie Gibson, afterwards married Robert P. Harrison, whom she accompanied to Texas, and after one year's residence in Washington County they lived for a time in Fayette County, and finally settled in Colorado County. In Fayette and Colorado counties the subject of this sketch grew up, and he acquired a practical education in the neighboring common schools. Early in 1862 he joined Wall's Legion, Col. Willis' Regiment, with which he participated in many battles, but during the last two years of the war he was with Gen. Forrest's Tennessee Cavalry, and was fighting all the time. His command surrendered in Mississippi, but Mr. Hall was at home on furlough at that time. During his entire service he was never wounded or taken prisoner, but had two horses killed under him and numerous bullets passed through his clothes, but left him unharmed. After the cessation of hostilities he turned his attention to the peaceful pursuit of farming, but has since been connected with various kinds of enterprises, and for a number of years was a salesman in the lumber yards of W. B. McCormick. In 1883 he came to Weimar and established himself in business, but also had a yard at Waelder, in Gonzales County, and did a

did a successful business at both places, being associated with another gentleman. Since the death of his partner in 1890, he has been engaged in business on his own responsibility, and has succeeded remarkably well. At the close of the war he was absolutely penniless, and the first dollar he ever made was in buying sugar, which he traded for wheat at Waco, and ground into flour, which he sold. He has also dealt quite heavily in stock, and made one trip to Kansas, and he has also been quite an extensive dealer in cotton. He has always been quite enterprising and pushing, and is in every sense of the word a self-made man, who would make his way, no matter where his lot might be cast. In 1872 he was married to Miss Sallie Gafford, who was born in Mississippi, and died in 1875. His second marriage took place in 1882, to Miss Annie, the daughter of W. B. McCormick, and they have one daughter living. Mr. Hall is a member of the Methodist Church, in which he is trustee and steward, and socially he belongs to the A. F. & A. M., the I. O. O. F. and the A. O. U. W.

JOHN W. BROWN, M. D. The name of this successful and prominent physician is well and favorably known throughout the county, and through his ability and well-merited success he has built up a practice that is eminently satisfactory. He owes his nativity to the Palmetto State, Marion District, born in 1832, and is the son of John and Elizabeth (Fulmore) Brown, the parents having been born right on the line in Robinson County, N. C. There they married and resided until 1838, when they made their way to Hinds County, Miss., settled below Raymond, and there died the same year, 1838. Mr. Brown followed planting, and was a prominent man wherever he made his home. He held the office of Sheriff in North Carolina, and was also in the Legislature for some time. He and wife were members of the Episcopal Church. She died in Texas in 1846. They reared a family of three sons and two daughters, three of whom are now living: Peter R., a planter of Alvin, Texas; Mrs. Jesse Vick, who was born in Franklin Parish, La. Our subject spent his early days in the old home in South Carolina, attended the academy in Marion District, and then commenced the study of medicine, attending lectures first in Charles County, S. C., and then at the Old University of New York, graduating from the same in 1851. He first located and began the practice of medicine in Tensas Parish, and remained there one year. He purchased large tracts of land, but the same year suffered an overflow from the Mississippi River, and the following year came to Texas. Dr. Brown bought land near the line of Matagorda and Wharton counties, and had to cut a roadway through to get his place. He came with eight negroes, and made such extensive crops that he soon became the owner of many more negroes, owning about one hundred at the breaking out of the Civil War. These were, of course, all freed, but about six have remained with him ever since. His old home place, called "Pledger Place," consisting of 3,180 acres, Mr. Brown has recently sold. He also owned a place of 300 acres above the old home place, and 250 acres below that place. He is the most extensive cotton planter in Matagorda County, usually having 2,000 acres in cotton, and is a wideawake, thorough-going citizen. Recently he moved to his present place, "Hardeman Place," thirty miles north of Matagorda. In connection with numerous other industries, the doctor still carries on his practice, and his time is fully employed. He selected his wife in the person of Narcissa D. Pledge, of Matagorda County, and their marriage took place March 4, 1862. A few days after his marriage, the doctor enlisted in the Texas Rangers as private post-surgeon, and in April took part in the battle of Shiloh. He remained in the medical department, and afterwards joined Brown's Regiment of Cavalry, medical department, as post-surgeon, and remained with the same until the close of the war. Two children were born to our subject's marriage, but one child, a son, named John, died in infancy. The daughter, India, resides in Galveston. Dr. Brown was never very deeply interested in political matters, but attends strictly to his practice and planting, especially the latter.

J. WALTER DURBIN. The office of Sheriff is one that has been filled by the illustrious head of this Government, and is a position that demands the exercise of great circumspection, great personal courage and a general and apt intelligence. The county of Frio, Texas, is fortunate in its choice of its present incumbent, J. Walter Durbin, the subject of this sketch, who adds to strict integrity the other qualities essential to thorough discharge of the responsibilities connected with the station, and is well known in the Southwest. He is a native of Carroll County, Mississippi, born in 1860, and was the eldest child born to Warren' and Narcissa (Criel) Durbin, who were natives of Mississippi. The father was a Confederate soldier and served in Hood's Brigade of the Army of Virginia. He was successfully engaged in tilling the soil in Mississippi, came to Texas in 1893, and now resides in Denton County, where he owns some property. J. Walter Durbin was reared and educated in Mississippi, and in 1879 came to Dallas, Texas, but after a short time removed to Collin County, and then entered the ranging service in the northwest part of the State, but during this time was sent to all parts of the State. He was first in Company C, with Capt. George H. Smith, with whom he served in the Pan Handle until 1885, when he was sent with his company to Frio County. In 1887, owing to the disbanding of Company C, he joined Company D, under Capt. Frank Jones, and with this patrolled the frontier of the Rio Grande from Brownsville to El Paso. He retired from the service at Alpine, Texas, in 1889. In February, 1887, he captured the bandit, Bud Crenshaw, and secured the large reward of $1,500 for his capture, and while in the service had some very stirring and exciting adventures. At the same time he also held the commission of Deputy Marshal. In 1889 he went to Old Mexico, and was engaged by the Fronterzia Mining Company, to guard silver bullion from the mines to the railroad, a distance of 160 miles, and was thus employed for about eight months. He then came to Pearsall, and soon after his arrival, in December, 1889, engaged in business for himself, continuing for a short time. In 1892 he was elected to the office of Sheriff, and has since ably filled this office up to the present time. He has been a very active and capable official, and during this time has captured and brought back to the scene of their crimes many criminals, in fact more than any other officer in the same length of time. He has captured men in Mexico and Arizona and Indian Territory, and on one occasion captured a man who had been at large ten years. He had been convicted and sentenced to prison, but broke jail and made his escape. Mr. Durbin is a member of the Sheriff's Association, and socially is a member of the A. F. & A. M. He has a handsome home in Pearsall, and an excellent farm in the country, containing 100 acres, all of which is under cultivation. It is well improved and is one of the most valuable places of its size in the county. He lost heavily by the great fire of 1890, but none the less is in good financial circumstances. He has always been active in politics, has been a delegate to many conventions, and as a public spirited citizen, as well as in his official capacity, he has ever labored for the cause of law and order. He is a born detective, and has been the means of bringing many of the worst criminals of the country to justice. In 1890 he married Miss Mollie Burden, a native of this county, and a daughter of J. L. Burden, an early settler here, and they have two children: Julia Hays and Walter Cook.

ROBERT W. KOLLMANN. It is almost invariably the case that reliable, intelligent and capable men are chosen to fill responsible official positions, and the case of Robert W. Kollmann, who is the Clerk of Colorado County, is no exception to this rule. He was born in this county, February 13, 1864, and has resided here all his life, therefore the people have had every opportunity to judge of his character and qualifications, and nothing but words of praise have been bestowed upon him. His education was obtained in Herman Seminary, where he pursued his studies until 1879 or 1880, when he went to Galveston, and worked for the firm of J. P. Lalor & Co., for a few months, at the end of which time he went to Houston, where he spent two years. He then located in Weimar, and embarked in business with Thomas Fisher, but after a time Mr. Fisher withdrew, and Mr. Kollmann then conducted his establishment alone until he was elected to the office of County Clerk in 1892, which is the only public position he has ever held, and to which he was elected on the Republican ticket, notwithstanding the fact that he had three opponents, and polled as many votes as the other three put together. He is an intelligent young man, energetic and pushing, and counts his friends by the score, a fact which is in direct refutation of the old saw that "a man is not without honor save in his own country." He is of a genial disposition, and socially he is a member of the K. of P. He was married in 1885.

THOMAS A. LEDBETTER. The cultivated farms, bustling towns and thriving villages of Fayette County, Texas, have so long been common objects to our sight that it seems almost beyond belief, that we have in our midst an honored citizen who was here when the country was a wilderness, when Indians and wild animals abounded, and when the settlers were few and far between. Thomas A. Ledbetter, who has witnessed the growth and development of the country, and has contributed his share towards its advancement and progress, was born in Perry County, Tennessee, November 24, 1832, and was the second child born to the marriage of Hamilton and Jane (Peacock) Ledbetter, natives of North Carolina. Hamilton Ledbetter entered the Lone Star State in 1838 or 1839 with a large number of slaves, and in 1840 brought his family here. He settled on the Guadalupe River in Victoria County, engaged in farming and stock-raising, and there made his home until 1844, when he moved to Fayette County. He purchased land in this county, although he did not intend to locate, but thought of staying here until trouble with the Indians had ceased. He served in the Texas army but a short time, and during that time went on an expedition against Gen. Wall. During the Civil War he was a strong Union man, and at the beginning of the war no man stood higher in the estimation of his neighbors than he did. He withstood the tide of popular disfavor better than any other public man of his views in the county, and when he was solicited to run for the State Senate, it was at the request of the entire people of the county, regardless of politics. The people of Fayette

County (especially those advanced in years), well remember the true friend they had in Hamilton Ledbetter (see sketch of W. H. Ledbetter for further particulars of parents). Thomas A. Ledbetter received the rudiments of an education in La Grange, but failing health prevented him from attending college. In 1860 he engaged in farming, and the following year joined a company in the regiment of Col. Nichols, and was stationed at Galveston. He was never in any battles, and was honorably discharged from this command in May, 1862. The same year he joined a company, raised by Col. Webb, of Fayette County, and served in the cavalry along the coast and around Valasco. He was in the Quartermaster Department for two months, but the rest of the time he was in active service. Following the war he engaged in farming and stock-raising, but since 1886 he has resided in La Grange, where he has a comfortable and pleasant home, presided over by his excellent wife, who was formerly Miss Almeda Robison (see sketch of J. W. and Neal Robison). Mrs. Ledbetter was born in the year 1844, and is a lady of charming personality. Mr. Ledbetter is the owner of 457 acres of fine land on the Colorado River, and has 220 acres under cultivation. On his prairie farm he has 125 acres cultivated. The ten children born to his marriage are named, as follows: W. A., of the Chocktaw Nation, and an attorney of considerable note; Ada B., who became the wife of R. E. Dortch; H. C., of La Grange; Annie O., Lena J., Seth I. S., Guy T., of the Nation; Hugh A., Anna and Alberta. Politically Mr. Ledbetter is independent. During his youth Mr. Ledbetter had many thrilling experiences with the Indians, and at one time came very near being captured by them. In 1840, while residing with his parents in Valasco, about 500 thieving Indians came down among the stockmen of that section, with the purpose of carrying off horses, cattle, etc. Mr. Ledbetter with his brother and several negro boys were on the river bank, eating black haws one day, while a negro woman was washing clothes in the river near by, when they saw several Indians approaching. They dropped from the haw tree as quickly as possible, but unfortunately our subject's hat caught on a limb and remained in the tree. He could not leave that, he thought, and Indian or no Indian, he returned to the tree, secured the coveted hat and, although the Indians were very near, saying "howdy," he made off with great speed, and made his escape in the underbrush. He soon joined his brother and the negro boys, and they together with the negro woman returned to the house. The next day the Indians came to massacre the family, but were driven away by several men who had gathered at the house in the meantime. Amid such rude and dangerous surroundings Mr. Ledbetter's youthful days were spent.

THOMAS W. DODD. Among the well known lawyers of Webb County, Texas, is Thomas W. Dodd, a man of unquestioned integrity and competent in his profession. To a thorough knowledge of the legal science he joins the general culture derived from a varied and extended course of reading. Skillful in the presentation of the most involved and intricate facts, forcible in his manner of dealing with difficult and entangling subjects, accurate in his perceptions of the true bearing of a case, he takes an enviable position among the more prominent practitioners of his section. He was born in Bartow County, Ga., in May, 1840, the eldest child born to Christopher and Sarah (Lowry) Dodd, who were born in South Carolina and Georgia respectively. The paternal grandfather, William Dodd, was a South Carolinian, and his father, Charles Dodd, was a native of Ireland, and came to this country in

1754, settling in South Carolina, where he was called from this life at the age
of one hundred and five years. He was a member of the State Senate from
the Spartanburg District, S. C., for fifty-six consecutive years, and during the
Revolutionary War was a Captain in the colonial service, and in the engagement at Cowpens was wounded in a personal combat with a British officer.
He was a leading man of his day, and by occupation was a tiller of the soil.
The maternal grandfather, David Lowry, was born in the Palmetto State, and
was a participant in a number of Indian wars and later in the War of 1812.
He came to Texas in 1872, and died in Smith County three years later in his
eighty-seventh year, a planter by occupation and of English descent. Christopher Dodd was reared in the State of his birth, and at the age of eighteen
years went to Georgia, where he married and lived the balance of his life,
dying in 1893 in his seventy-seventh year. His widow still survives him and
lives in Georgia. The subject of this sketch first received a high-school
education and was, at the breaking out of the war between the States, attending college at Cassville, Ga., in the Cherokee Baptist College, from which he
entered the Confederate service as a member of the Eighteenth Georgia
Infantry, Company F, Hood's Brigade, but in 1862 was transferred to the
Fortieth Regiment, and was promoted from the ranks to Sergeant, then Lieutenant, and then Captain of Company I, in 1863, which he commanded until
July 22, 1864, when he lost his arm at Atlanta. He participated in twenty-
eight battles, besides many minor engagements, until he was wounded. After
that he worked his way home, and during 1865 taught school for about six
months, after which he began reading law and was admitted to the bar in
September, 1866. In October of the same year he was elected County
Attorney of Bartow County, but in 1867 entered the University of Georgia,
from which he graduated in August, 1868, after which he settled in Polk
County and was engaged in the practice of his profession until 1875, as a
partner of Maj. Joseph A. Blance. He then came to Texas, and until November 8, 1884, was a resident and practitioner of Tyler, Smith County, where
he continued to make his home until November 8, 1884, since which time he
has resided in Laredo. During his residence in Tyler he held the positions
of Alderman and Mayor for nine years, and has been a very public-spirited
citizen also of Laredo. He has always taken an active interest in politics, and
has attended every State convention, with one exception, since coming to Texas,
and has been an active worker in each. He came to Laredo to take charge of
the land business and local litigation for the Texas-Mexican R. R., and has
since been the General Attorney of the Mexican National and the Texas-
Mexican R. R's. in Texas for the past five years, and has been Vice-president
of the Texas-Mexican R. R. Company for the last five years. He has been
an advocate of railroad commissions since 1873, and believes it to be a possible way of solving the railroad problem in so far as government control can
accomplish it. He is a keen and far-sighted lawyer and a well-posted and
intelligent railroad man. He was first married in February, 1864, to Miss
Mattie E. Dodd, of Union District, S. C., but she died November 28, 1865,
leaving an infant daughter, Mattie E., wife of William H. Sweetman, of
Laredo. June 15, 1871, Mr. Dodd wedded Miss Ada Josephine Pearce, a
native of Polk County, Ga., and to their union nine children have been given,
three only now living, to-wit: Sallie May, Georgie S. and Ida Herf. He and
his wife are members of the Baptist Church, and in politics he is a Democrat.

31

W. H. Ledbetter. W. H. Ledbetter is one of the most notable attorneys of Fayette County, and in the practice of his profession has acquired both prominence and success. As this profession is one of the highly honored as well as most exacting ones, it requires an abundance of legal lore to gain the plane of success, but when that plane is once reached the reward of patient study and work is a goodly and honorable one. Mr. Ledbetter is a native of the Lone Star State, born in 1834, and is the third son of Hamilton and Jane (Peacock) Ledbetter, natives of Tennessee. Hamilton Ledbetter came to this State first in 1838 or 1839, with a large number of slaves, and in 1840 he brought his family to the then new section of the State, where Victoria now stands. In 1844 he moved to this county and settled on the farm where he was engaged quite extensively in planting. At that time there were not over 400 voters in the county. Indians seldom came into this section of the State on mischief bent, but while Mr. Ledbetter was residing in Victoria County, Indians made a raid on the outlying settlements and forced their owners to flee to the village of Victoria for protection. In August, 1840, while Mr. Ledbetter was away from home, the Indians made a raid, and finding no one at home but Mrs. Ledbetter they contented themselves with driving off horses and cattle, but did no other damage on this occasion. On the following morning, however, they came with war paint on and with the intention of murdering the whole family. Mrs. Ledbetter had called in several men and they repulsed the savages. After the Indians had left, the family made their way to Victoria through the cornfields, and this probably saved their lives, for the Indians continued to prowl around for several days and killed quite a number of men. Mr. Ledbetter was too old for service during the Civil War, but he was a conservative man and old line Whig previous to the war. Afterwards he took quite an active interest in the political affairs of the day. In 1872 he was chosen by the people to represent them in the Thirteenth General Assembly as State Senator. He served until 1874. In the year 1888 he passed away after a long and useful life of eighty years, honored and respected by all acquainted with him. Mrs. Ledbetter died in 1884 when seventy years old. They reared a family of nine children: J. A. was killed at the battle of Vicksburg, Miss., in 1863. He was Captain of a company in Wall's Legion; T. A. resides in this city; W. H., our subject; A. G. (died in 1883). He was also a soldier in the Confederate army, and was severely wounded two or three times; Olivia, wife of Walter Kirkum, of Waxahachie, Texas; Cecelia, at home; Ada, wife of S. R. Caureathers; James P., a prominent attorney of Coleman County, Texas, and Jennie, now Mrs. W. J. Ewing, of Texas. W. H. Ledbetter received his scholastic training in the schools of Fayette County, though he finished at Independence, Washington County, Texas. He commenced the study of law when twenty-one years of age, under the celebrated General Webb, now a resident of La Grange, and was admitted to practice in the courts of the State in 1857, Judge Duville presiding. He located in this place, La Grange, and practiced his chosen profession until 1862, when he enlisted in Company I of Colonel Flournoy's Regiment, called the Sixteenth Texas Infantry. He was elected Lieutenant, and was in the following battles: Perkins' Landing, Milliken's Bend, Mansfield and Pleasant Hill. At the latter place he was taken prisoner, but exchanged soon afterward and returned to his command, with which he remained until the war closed. In June, 1865, he came home, and finding himself almost bankrupted he engaged in the practice of law. He had been the owner of nearly twenty slaves, and his father had owned nearly one hundred when the war broke out. In 1876 Mr. Ledbetter was elected to represent the people in the Fifteenth General Assembly, State Senate, and in 1878 was re-elected to serve in the Sixteenth Assembly. Since then he has confined himself to the practice of his profession. Mr. Ledbetter has been twice married, his first wife being Miss Bettie Pope, who was born in North Carolina. She died in 1864, leaving two children, William, now of Panama, S. A., graduated at Annapolis in 1885, and later entered the employ of individuals in South America, and Olivia is now the wife of J. M. Smith, of Houston. Mr. Ledbetter's second marriage occurred in 1868 to Miss Tennie Hill, a native of Tennessee, and daughter of John G. and Fannie (Griffin) Hill. Her parents came to Texas prior to the rebellion. Mr. and Mrs. Ledbetter's union resulted in the birth of two children, Emmett and Aline, both of whom are at home. Mrs. Ledbetter is a member of the Episcopal Church, and Mr. Ledbetter is a Democrat in politics.

TERRELL J. WHITTEN. When this representative citizen first came to Wharton County, April, 1849, there were but a limited number of people here, and of these only one man besides our subject is now living, Judge W. T. Hall, who was one of the first to settle in this county. Terrell J. Whitten was born in Franklin County, Georgia, in 1832, and the son of Alvin E. Whitten, a native of South Carolina, and Catherine W. (Jones) Whitten, of Georgia. The parents were married in the latter State, but later moved from there to Holmes County, Mississippi, where they remained until 1847, and then started for Texas. They spent the first winter in Matagorda, and in 1849 came to Wharton, where Mr. Whitten followed planting, and later merchandising. His wife died in 1850 and he in 1853. Both were for many years earnest members of the Baptist Church. They reared a family of nine children, only two besides our subject now living: Charles H., a farmer and merchant of Alabama, and William S., who resides in this State. Young Terrell J. Whitten received his education in this State, and at the time of his father's death was a salesman in a store. Later he was elected Justice of the Peace and Clerk of the County, and discharged the duties of those positions in a very creditable manner. When the Civil War opened he joined Brown's Regiment and remained with it until the close of the war, serving most of the time in Texas. He held a position of deputy in the office of Dr. J. B. Collinsworth, who was Surgeon at the time. Following the war Mr. Whitten engaged in merchandising, and was also engaged quite extensively in the stock business. For five years he acted as salesman and was then made Hide Inspector, being the first to hold that position in the county. Later he was made Deputy Clerk and Justice of the Peace, and held those positions for some time, and ever to the satisfaction of the people. He also engaged in planting and has followed that successfully since. So satisfactory were his services as an official that he was again elected to the position of Justice of the Peace. He is one of the county's most worthy citizens, and his reputation for integrity and honorable methods is of the highest. He was Deputy Sheriff during the Reconstruction period, a time when it was a very dangerous position to hold, but his courage and intrepid spirit never flagged, and he was ever to be found at the post of danger. In the year 1881 he was married to Mrs. L. F. Still, daughter of Lemuel Calloway, of an old Texan family.

One daughter was born to this union, Fannie Eugenia. Socially Mr. Whitten is a member of the Blue Lodge in Masonry.

FREDERICK HILLJE. This gentleman who is the operator of the Weimar Oil Works at Weimar, Texas, comes of sturdy German parents, J. F., and Wilhelmina (Farenthold) Hillje, and first saw the light in Frelsburg, Texas, in 1854. His father was born in Germany in 1821, and there continued to make his home until 1852, at which time he took passage on a sailing vessel for the United States, landed at Galveston, and at once made his way to Frelsburg, where he was married, soon after which he moved to High Hill, Fayette County. In 1892 he came to Weimar, and was here called from life in June, 1893. He had learned the wheelwright's trade in his native land, and at this he worked after coming to this country. He erected a cotton gin at High Hill which he operated by horse-power for a time, then erected a steam cotton gin and mill, and later built the oil mill at High Hill, but in 1880 moved the works to Weimar on account of better transportation facilities. He was a shrewd and successful business man, and possessed in a large degree the German characteristic of acquiring property. His widow was also born in Germany, and at an early day was brought to this country by her father.

Frederick Hillje, the eldest child born to his parents of a family of four sons and three daughters, spent his school days at High Hill, and from 1868 to 1874 was attending school at New Orleans, after which he was, for four years, employed by a cotton commission house. In 1874 he returned to High Hill and embarked on the mercantile sea with his father, the firm being known as J. F. Hillje & Son, but after a time they removed their place of business to Schulenburg. In 1879 he embarked in the cotton seed oil business, and brought the works to Weimar in 1880, and here has very successfully operated them ever since. He was married at High Hill, to Miss Eliza Herder, a daughter of Col. George Herder, and by her is the father of three children: Anna, Emil and George. Mr. Hillje, like his worthy sire, is a shrewd man of business, and is a partner in the extensive business house of A. Fahrenthold & Co., at El Campo. He has been one or the aldermen of Weimar for four years, and socially is a member of the A. O. U. W., and the Hermann Soehne.

A. JAMES MATHERNE. The American public schools are the safety of the Republic, and nothing approaching them in extent, influence and cost of maintenance is to be found upon the face of the earth. This country is the only one where the children of the poorest may receive a fair education free, and where provision is made for sparsely settled sections as well as for those living in cities. Webb County, Texas, is especially favored in having for its County Superintendent of Schools a man of progressive ideas, of practical purpose, an organizer of great ability and one interested in the cause of education. A. James Matherne, the subject of this sketch, is eminently qualified to fill the position he holds, and during his administration, whatever its duration, the best possible results may be sanguinely expected. He was born in Lafourche Parish, Louisiana, in 1854, the only child born to James and Eliza (McClentic) Matherne, who were natives of Louisiana and Indiana, respectively. The paternal grandfather, Matthew Matherne, was a native of Louisiana, and planter by occupation. His ancestors were Acadians, and were transported to Louisiana during one of the early French and Indian Wars in America. The maternal grandfather, Andrew McClentic, was born on the Isle of Erin, and on coming to America first settled in Indiana, but in 1838 removed to Louisiana. James Matherne was a farmer by occupation, and when in the prime of life in 1853, his career was closed by death, a few months before the birth of the subject of this sketch. A. James Matherne was educated in the schools of Cape Girardeau, Mo., from which he was graduated in 1872. He then became a teacher in St. Vincent College in the grammar grade, but the next year returned to Louisiana, and continued his pedagogic labors in Lafourche parish. In 1875 he came to Brownsville, Texas, and taught in St. Joseph's College, but the next year again returned to Louisiana, and continued teaching there. He was married there to Miss Leah Le Blanc, a native of Louisiana, and a member of one of the old Acadian families, and continued the occupation of teaching in his native State until 1884, when he came to Laredo, and taught in the city schools one year. At the end of that time he moved to the town of Palafax, where he opened the first school ever established in the place. Three years later he returned to Laredo, and after teaching in the Northern part of the town for three years, he was nominated for the position of County Superintendent, and at the following election was elected to the office. Under his able and painstaking management great improvement has been made in the schools of the county, and his administration has shown the wisdom of the people in placing him in this responsible position. He is a practical and proficient teacher, has been engaged in that pursuit all the active years of his life, and is very popular with all classes. He is the father of two children: James and Antoinette, and he and his family are members of the Catholic Church. His mother, who is a most intelligent and active lady, is teaching in Louisiana and Texas, and makes her home with her son. She was born in 1832, a daughter of Andrew and Louisa (Hobbs) McClentic, natives of Ohio, but her paternal grandfather was a native of Ireland, and the mother's people were of Dutch stock. Her parents were married in Indiana, and there the father died of cholera in 1834, after which, in 1837, the mother married Benjamin Barker, and the new family at once started for Texas, via the Mississippi River. They stopped to visit friends on the Bayou La Fourche in Louisiana, and there hearing of the great financial crashes throughout the land, and Mr. Barker, meeting with severe losses, they were compelled to remain in Louisiana, locating on the beautiful Bayou La Fourche, where its banks were an almost unbroken wilderness. Here Mrs. Matherne's mother died in 1862, and Mr. Barker in 1865. Eliza, at the age of sixteen years, began teaching school, and was the first public school teacher in the parish of La Fourche. Her first school room was an abandoned cooper shop with a dirt floor, and here she "wielded the birch" until twenty years of age, when she married James Matherne, who only lived five months. After the birth of her son, the subject of this sketch, the young widow once more resumed the occupation of teaching and followed it without interruption for fourteen years, when she was again married, this time to Gilbert Davenport, a native of Kentucky, who served in the Georgia militia during the war, and died in 1866. His widow once more resumed her former profession of teaching, continuing the occupation in Louisiana until 1887, when she came to Texas, and has been teaching constantly here ever since, and has passed the greater part of her life in school work. She has been very successful in this line of human endeavor, and bears an excellent reputation as an instructor of the young. She is a pleasant and intelligent conversationalist, and a woman of many noble traits of character.

JUDGE AUGUSTINE HAIDUSEK. A man is a monument to the industry and progress of his race when by strength of character and mental powers he rises to prominence in the enterprises in which he engages. Texas has within her borders many men toward whom she may point the finger of pride, and whose names are synonymous with her advancement morally, intellectually and financially. Such a man is ex-County Judge Augustine Haidusek, who is now the editor and proprietor of The *Svoboda*, a paper well known throughout this section. He was born in Moravia, Europe, September 19, 1846 or 1847, and his parents, Valentine and V. (Kladiva) Haidusek, were natives of that country also. Valentine Haidusek was a farmer in his native country and the owner of considerable land. About the year 1856 he came to America and settled first in this county, where he immediately purchased unimproved land, made a home, and there resided until the close of the war. He then sold out, but purchased in the county where he resided until his death, December 22, 1867. He was too old for service in the Civil War. The family consisted of three children by his first wife, who died in Moravia. They were named Theresa, wife of Joseph Lebeda, of this county; John, deceased, served in the Confederate army, as did also Augustine, our subject. To Mr. Haidusek's second union were born six children, five daughters and one son, only two of whom survive: Ignac, resides on the old homestead, and Mary, wife of Frank Krouskopp, of Lavaca County. Augustine Haidusek was educated by his father in Bohemia, but up to 1866 his schooling was of a desultory character. He secured his English education under difficulties, much of it while splitting rails, but the word failure was unknown to him, and he carried on his studies up to 1864, when he enlisted in Company F, Bates' Regiment, stationed at the mouth of Brazos River, in charge of Fort Valasco, where he remained until the close of hostilities. Returning home, he assisted his father during 1866 and 1867, and after the death of the latter he attended school for six months, the first part of 1868. While in school he studied English exclusively, was assisted in every way by the students, and progressed rapidly. During the summer of 1867 he engaged in clerking in a dry goods store in La Grange, Texas, and was thus engaged when yellow fever broke out in 1867. Many people died in the town, and Mr. Haidusek returned home. It was during this fall that he studied the English language by firelight, and in 1868 he taught school for three months, both in the Bohemian and English languages. During the early part of 1869 he engaged in almost any enterprise to make an honest living, but carried on his studies whenever he could find time, having obtained possession of a few law books, which he read most industriously. Finding his English still too imperfect to understand that language, as presented by Blackstone, Capt. A. H. Croro, a member of the firm in whose office he studied law, taught him English. Later Mr. Haidusek read law with the firm of Jarman & Croro, leading attorneys of this place at that time, and on the 22d day of December, 1870, he was admitted to the bar. He immediately entered upon the practice of his chosen profession and was, beyond doubt, the first Bohemian ever admitted to practice in the courts of the United States. Immediately after being admitted to the bar Mr. Haidusek took an active part in political matters, and in 1874 was elected Chairman of the Democratic Executive Committee of the county. In 1875 he was elected Mayor of the city of La Grange, which position he filled so ably that he was re-elected in 1877. The following year he resigned. He was the first Bohemian Mayor of any city in the United States. He resigned that position to make the race for County Judge against J. C. Steel, and was defeated in 1880. He was nominated from this and Lee County as floater to represent them in the Legislature, and was elected by a handsome majority. He served one term. In 1884 he made his second race for County Judge against J. C. Steel, and this time was successful. He was re-elected twice, and served six years in succession. During his term in office country roads were much improved, many bridges were built, and the condition of the free schools was improved. His highest aim was to improve the methods of teaching, as well as to try and improve on the standing (morally and otherwise) of the teachers. It was during Judge Haidusek's administration that the contract was made for the building of the new and magnificent court house of Fayette County. This building is three stories high, of gray sandstone, with trimmings of white and red sandstone and marble, and is one of the handsomest court houses in the State. In 1890 Judge Haidusek became the owner of The *Svoboda*, a Bohemian paper, published in the interests of the Democratic party. It is published every Thursday, and has a circulation of 3,000 actual paying subscribers in Texas, besides a fair circulation in other States, and in Moravia, Bohemia, and other parts of Europe. Its circulation in Europe has induced a great number of emigrants to Texas. At the time he first took charge of the paper, in 1888, its circulation was 450, with a debt of $2,400. Under Judge Haidusek's able management, for two years previous to the purchase of the paper by him, this debt was paid off, and the circulation was greatly increased. Mr. Haidusek has always taken an active part in politics. During the split in the Democratic ranks in Texas, in 1892, he was with the Clark faction at Houston, and on his return he was made Chairman of that faction for Fayette County. That position he resigned after the meeting of both factions in convention at the city of Dallas, in the spring of 1894, where both parties agreed to harmonize their differences. Later he was again made Chairman of the Democratic Executive Committee of the county. Judge Haidusek was married May 22, 1872, in this county, to Miss Anna Becka, a native of Austin County, Texas, born near Bellville, June 27, 1856, and the daughter of John and Catherine (Zgabay) Becka, natives of Moravia. They came to this country in 1825, settled in Austin County, and, as Mr. Becka had tilled the soil in the old country, he followed the same occupation after settling in Texas. His death occurred March 18, 1891. His wife survives him and makes her home with her children. They reared a family of six children, as follows: Veronica, wife of Ignac Baca; John, Anna, Charley, of this county; Louis, of Lavaca County, and Agnes, wife of J. F. Zapalac, of this county. Judge and Mrs. Haidusek became the parents of five interesting children, two of whom, the eldest, V. H., and the second, are deceased. The others are Jerome L., at home; George L. and Vlasta. Mr. Haidusek and wife and children hold membership in the Catholic Church. He is a member of the K. of H., A. O. U. W., and is also a member of the C. S. P. S., a Bohemian order. The parents of our subject were among the first Bohemians who purchased land on the west side of the Colorado River; but there were others who purchased land at the same time, viz., Joseph Peter, Valentine Holeeb, Joseph Sramek, Joseph Kalig, Ignac Muzny and Frank Marak. The father of our subject, as well as the subject himself, was born in the northeast portion of Moravia, near the Carpathian

Mountains, at a village called Mist. When Valentine Haidusek first settled in this county there was no house between his farm and the town of La Grange, a distance of fifteen miles.

RAYMOND MARTIN. This successful and far-seeing business man of Laredo, Texas, was born in France in 1828, the youngest son of Jean Marie, who was a merchant of France, and died in that country in 1856, his wife's death occurring two years later. Paul and Joseph Martin, brothers of Raymond, came to the United States in 1852, and located in New Orleans, but in 1853 Paul came to Texas and spent the rest of his life in San Antonio, while Joseph went to Cuba and was killed in that country. In the month of December, 1849, Raymond Martin took passage on board a vessel bound from France to New Orleans, and after remaining in that city until 1854 came to Laredo, Texas, and at once engaged in the mercantile business, at which time there were only two stores in the place. He became one of the leading merchants of the town, but owing to the changed condition of affairs during the war, this business was almost completely given up. When hostilities had ceased he resumed merchandising with renewed vigor, and did a very prosperous and extensive business. In 1879 he erected the Commercial Hotel, at that time the best building in Laredo, and with shrewd business foresight and much public spirit he has erected other fine buildings and business blocks. Since 1861 he has also been engaged in sheep-raising, being the second man to engage in this business in this section, and for years he was very extensively engaged in this occupation. He has a ranch of 95,000 acres, all of which is fenced, he being the first to fence his land in all this region, and in various other ways he has shown that he has views and opinions of his own, and the will and determination to carry out his ideas. At times 50,000 head of sheep have grazed over his broad acres, and many thousand head of cattle. In 1887 he retired from the retail mercantile business and is now engaged in conducting the affairs of his estate and other private interests. He was one of the organizers of the Laredo Bank, and has been a leader in local politics and has served in the capacity of city Alderman for three years. He was also one of the organizers of the City Water Works, and has been intimately associated with all enterprises that promise good to Laredo or Webb County. He was one of the earliest foreign settlers of the town, and he enjoys the highest social distinction and respect of the citizens in the section in which he has so long made his home, and where the best energies of his life have been expended. He was married January 10, 1870, to Miss Tirza Garcia, a native of Laredo, and daughter of Borthelo Garcia, an old and prominent citizen of this county. To Mr. and Mrs. Martin ten children have been given, all of whom are living. The family are members and attendants of the Catholic Church, and have a commodious and comfortable home in Laredo.

JOHN P. DAVIS. This worthy citizen of LaSalle County, Texas, and resident of Cotulla, is a Texan by birth, and first opened his eyes on the light of day in Gonzales County, in 1858, being the third in a family of five children born to James and Sarah (Wilburn) Davis, the former of whom was a Georgian, but the latter a Texan by birth. About 1850 James Davis came to the Lone Star State and settled in Gonzales County, where he became an extensive stockman and died about 1860, in which year his wife also passed from life. The maternal grandfather of the subject of this sketch, C. H. Wilburn, was one of the very early settlers of this State, and was always a public spirited and law abiding citizen. John P. Davis was reared by his grandmother, who resided at Waelder, Texas, and when still quite young in years he engaged in the stock business on a ranch owned by the family, in the pursuit of which calling he showed good judgment and consequently made money. In 1882 he came to Cotulla, LaSalle County, bought a ranch of his own and has since been actively engaged in following that occupation at which he first started out. Being a public spirited and intelligent and well posted citizen, he has also been quite active in politics and was elected by his party in 1890 to the office of County Sheriff of LaSalle County, which capacity he served ably for one term. He was for a time in the mercantile business in Cotulla, but gave this up to engage in other pursuits. He has proven himself an able, and shrewd business man, and is now the owner of a comfortable competency, the result of his own efforts. He was also a conscientious and capable official, in fact, is a model citizen, and as such is highly honored by all who know him. He was married in 1880 to Miss Annie Hunt, a native of the State of Texas, and daughter of Benjamin F. Hunt, who came to this State from Mississippi.

JAMES W. TOWELL. This prominent and influential citizen of Columbus, Texas, owes his nativity to Sumner County, Texas, where he was born in 1847 to Isaac and Mary (Whitworth) Towell, who were married in that county. They afterwards moved to Illinois and settled on the Wabash River, and there he devoted his attention to farming for some time. Unfortunately during his youth he had received no educational advantages, but after his marriage, with the efficient assistance of his wife, he acquired a practical education and after a time took up the study of medicine, with the intention of making that his profession, and finally began attending a medical college of Cincinnati, Ohio, from which institution he graduated. In 1846 he and his family moved to near Benton, Yazoo County, Mississippi, where he successfully practiced his profession until 1854, when he located in Covington, Tenn., and was at this place when the war opened. He at once joined Company I, Seventh Tennessee Cavalry, under Gen. Forrest, was wounded at Lamar, Miss., and discharged from the service. After the war he took up his residence in Leake County, Mississippi, and in 1866 came to Colorado County, Texas, where he died in 1888 at the age of seventy-six years. His wife, who died in 1855, bore him ten children, of whom the immediate subject of this sketch was the seventh. After her death, Dr. Towell married Miss Glass of Covington, who survives him. James W. Towell was educated in the schools of Tennessee, and in the early part of 1865 joined Company I, Seventh Tennessee Cavalry, with which he served until the close of the war, participating in but one skirmish, which was his only opportunity of shooting the detested "Yanks." He surrendered at Selma, Ala., April 16, 1865, after which he accompanied his father to Texas, and after one year spent in Texas, he came to Colorado County and located at about six miles from Columbus, where James W. entered a tract of river bottom land. On this place he remained until 1872, when we went to Harris County, twenty-five miles north of Houston, where he was engaged in helping to operate a tram railroad for a saw mill company. After spending three years there he returned to Colorado County, and up to 1891 lived on a farm ten miles northwest of Columbus, where he and Mr. Carey Shaw operated a cotton gin in partnership. In 1892 they built a gin at Columbus, which is a model in every respect, and is fitted up with all kinds of modern appliances and machinery. They built another gin at Alleyton, a year later, which they also operate, and in connection with their plant they have an electric-light plant, by which the town of Columbus is illuminated. Mr. Towell is the manager of the gins and the electric light plant, and the success with which his enterprises have been attended, shows that he is wideawake and a live and progressive business man. In 1879 he was united in marriage with Miss Laura Shaw, a daughter of Col. Shaw, and to their union four children have been born. Socially Mr. Towell is a member of the Knights of Honor, the A. O. U. W., and the Maccabees. His father was a surgeon in Harrison's well known hospital for a time, and was widely and favorably known in his professional capacity.

COL. ISAAC N. DENNIS. It is a well attested maxim that the greatness of a State lies not in its machinery of government, not even in its institutions, but in the sterling qualities of its individual citizens, in their capacity for high and unselfish effort, and their devotion to the public good. Among those who are entitled to due recognition is Col. Isaac N. Dennis, one of the prominent attorneys of Wharton, Texas. He was born in Dallas County, Alabama, June 25, 1829, and received his literary training in Richmond College of his native county. Later he began the study of law in Alabama, but subsequently continued his law studies at Cambridge, Mass., and was admitted to the bar in 1850. In 1852 he came to Wharton, Texas, to get married, and being favorably impressed with the appearance of the country, settled at Wharton. There he began practicing his profession in partnership with the late Judge Quinan, an eminent attorney and jurist, and continued with him for a number of years. In 1855 he represented Wharton and Matagorda counties in the Legislature, and continued a member of that body for three terms in succession. He was Chairman of the Committee on State Affairs, also Chairman of the Committee on Engrossed Bills, and served until the ratification of the secession ordinance. When Civil War opened he joined the staff of Gen. P. O. Hebert, and during the entire war served in Texas, Arkansas and Louisiana. In the year 1865 he began planting very extensively on Caney Creek, and continued this with an unusual degree of failures, caused by destruction of cotton by cotton worms, until a few years ago when he resumed the practice of law. He still has planting interests though. Col. Dennis was a member of the Eighteenth Legislature, representing Matagorda, Galveston, Brazoria, and Wharton counties, and served in the term of 1879, until after the Revised Statutes adopted, etc., as Chairman of the Committee on Federal Relations, as well as a member of the Committee on Public Health, History of Texas, Private Land Claims, State Asylums, etc. In January, 1853, Miss P. L. T. Horton, a daughter of Governor Horton, became his wife. She died in 1863, while Col. Dennis was in the army. The one daughter, Lida, born to this union has also passed away, but she grew to mature years and became the wife of Judge W. J. Croom of Wharton. In 1865 Col. Dennis married Miss Sadie Hinton, who died soon after marriage. His third marriage occurred in 1869, when Miss Maggie Knox, of Galveston, became his wife. Her death occurred in May, 1889. This last union resulted in the birth of four children: John H. H., who is a graduate of the law department of the University of Texas, and at present in partnership with his father; Mills commenced the study of Medicine at Galveston Medical College; Nancy, Jack and Newton. Col. Dennis has been a member of the Baptist

Church since boyhood, and since the age of twenty-one has been a member of the Masonic Fraternity and the Independent Order of Odd Fellows. He has always been an advocate of Democracy.

GEORGE R. PAGE. In the capacity of County Clerk of Webb County, Texas, George R. Page is conscientious, faithful and energetic, in fact, is the right man in the right place, as his friends, as well as those who differ with him politically, are not slow to recognize. He was born in Vernon County, Missouri, in 1862, the second of three children born to Maurice A. and Mamie (Caulkins) Page, who were born in New York and Pennsylvania respectively. The parents met while attending school, were eventually married, in Hamilton, N. Y., afterwards moved to Ohio, and the father was placed in charge of Maumee College, now South Toledo, afterward becoming a professor in Kalamazoo College, Michigan. About 1858 or 1859 he moved to Missouri on account of ill health, from there to Kansas in 1864, in which State the father still resides, but the mother died in 1880. Maurice A. Page was admitted to the bar in New York, and practiced his profession in Missouri and Kansas, and is now following that occupation in Garnett. The subject of this sketch was reared and educated in the Sunflower State, and when quite young was placed in a printing establishment to learn the trade, and continued working at this occupation in Kansas for years. When he was nineteen years of age he came to Texas, and in 1882 located in Laredo and secured employment on the *Laredo Times* as foreman, afterward becoming local reporter, and was connected with that paper eight years. In 1888 he was elected County Commissioner of the Third Precinct, in which capacity he served one term. In November, 1890, he was chosen as a suitable candidate for the office of County Clerk, was elected to the position, and in 1892 was re-elected, and is now ably discharging the duties of this office. He has been quite active in the political affairs of Webb County ever since 1886, and for several years has been a delegate to various conventions, and in 1894 was a delegate to the State Democratic Convention at Dallas. Socially he is a member of Laredo Lodge No. 283 of the I. O. O. F. and Laredo Lodge No. 120 of the A. O. U. W. He is an intelligent young man, an efficient official, and a public spirited and law abiding citizen. He was married in 1890 to Miss Ella Bell, a native of Illinois, but at the time of their marriage a resident of Garnett, Kansas.

ROBERT HENRY HARRISON, M. D. The inscription on the old Grecian temples, " know thyself," is written in the hearts of men of this generation, who devote their lives to the healing of the sick and the prevention of disease. So earnestly, so persistently and so scientifically have they imparted their knowledge each to the other, that it now really seems as though the power of life and death were in the hands of the live and progressive physicians of to-day. Their operations in surgery, their discovery of inoculation for the prevention of certain maladies and their general success in practice, combine to give to the profession the distinction of "greatest among the great." In the number of those who have labored patiently and earnestly for this knowledge is Dr. R. H. Harrison, of Columbus, Texas, whose life is a record of steady seeking after that which would give him power over the enemy of the physical man. He was born in Gainesville, Ga., November 13, 1826, a son of Jesse and Margaret (Hulce) Harrison, the former of whom was born in Fairfax, Va. The mother is living with her son Dr. Harrison in Columbus, Texas, and has reached the advanced age of eighty-seven years. Her father was an officer in the War of 1812, and was a participant in the famous battle of Horseshoe Bend. Jesse Harrison was a son of Robert Harrison, who was an American soldier of the Revolution and was a second cousin of General Harrison of Virginia. The first of the Harrisons to go to Virginia was a seafaring man, and from first to last the family have been great lovers of liberty. Jesse Harrison in his younger days was a planter, and upon his removal from his native State to South Carolina he followed that occupation. He was married in the Palmetto State, but this wife lived only long enough to bear him two children: Isaac and Mary. After her death he wedded Miss Hulce and moved to Gainesville, Ga., where he gave his attention to gold mining for some time. He then began studying medicine in Columbus, Ohio, and after having attended medical lectures at Philadelphia, Penn., he began practicing the profession at Saundersville, Tenn., a small place near Gallatin, and later pursued this calling at Clarksville, Nashville and Troy, and was living in the latter place at the time of his death in 1855, at the age of sixty-seven years. He was a Calhoun Democrat, and was always an active politician. His wife was born in Georgia, and ever since 1842, has been a worthy and consistent member of the Baptist Church. She became the mother of eight children: Dr. R. H., Dr. John B. of Union City, Tenn.; Margaret is the deceased wife of Walter McDaniel of Columbus; Van Houton is a physician of Clarkston, Mo.; Nancy is the wife of Frederick Fleming of Cameron, Texas; Betty P. is the wife of Robert T. Bond of Union City, Tenn.; Jesse J. is the District Clerk of Colorado County, Texas, and Tennessee who died young. Dr. Harrison attended the schools of Clarksville, Tenn., and the John Tyler High School in Kentucky, but near Clarksville, Tenn., and bore off the honors of his class at the age of seventeen. He at once commenced the study of medicine, and took advantage of a private hospital of which his father was the head in Nashville, during his preparation for this profession. He then entered the Physio Medical College of Cincinnati, Ohio, from which he later graduated, then entered the Medical Department of the University of Alabama at Mobile, from which he was also graduated, and still later finished the medical course in the Medical College at Cincinnati at the age of twenty. He then commenced the active practice of his profession in partnership with his father at Troy, with whom he was connected from 1846 to 1850, and for three years thereafter he practiced in Clarksville. He then went to Memphis, Tenn., and in addition to practicing his profession, he became an instructor in the Reformed Medical College of that city, as Professor of Materia Medica and Therapeutics. After remaining there three years he went to Holly Springs, Miss., and after spending a like time there bought property in Shelby County, Tennessee, and retired from the practice of his profession to a certain extent, opened a mill and engaged in the mercantile business, at the same time giving some attention to planting. He was in Shelby County at the opening of the great Civil War and there organized a heavy artillery company for duty at Fort Pillow, which he commanded, and which, immediately after the battle of Shiloh, was attached to the Ninth Tennessee Infantry, and became the color bearing company, or Company E. He was Captain of his company, and at the battle of Perryville, his company went in forty men strong and in fifteen minutes only fifteen men were left to tell the tale, and of his regiment Dr. Harrison was ranking officer, all the others having been killed. He was recommended for promotion and was in the battle of Murfreesboro, and was then ordered by Gen. J. E. Johnston to report to General Pemberton at Vicksburg, and took command of a company of conscripts, which he was to recruit. He was taken prisoner in Shelby County while on this duty, and was first taken to Columbus, Ky., thence to Alton, Ill., and finally to Johnson's Island, and after twenty-one months of imprisonment was sent to Richmond, Va., where he was exchanged. He had been promoted to Colonel of cavalry, and was ordered by Secretary of War Breckinridge to report to General Forrest, then in Mississippi, for duty, but never reached that command. He was placed in command, instead, of a reserve brigade at Montgomery, Ala., and then returned to Columbus, Ga., where he, with 2,000 men, fought with great credit 20,000 of the enemy. This was the last battle of the Confederacy east of the Mississippi River, after which he went to Macon, Ga., and was paroled. He was never wounded but once during his long, hard service, and that was but slightly by a spent ball at Perryville. He was in the service from April, 1861 until June, 1865, at which time he returned to his home at Harrison's Mills, named in his honor, but during the time that he was in prison, his mill and other property including a very fine library and a large amount of excellent stock were destroyed. During the war he had sent his officer's pay to a non-combatant relative in Mississippi who had invested it in cotton, and he at once went to that State and located on the V. S. P. R. R. in Newton County, there engaged in the mercantile business and became quite an extensive dealer and trader in cotton. He was quite successful, and during this time he purchased a steamboat and cleaned out the Pearl River to Jackson, Miss., and then, on account of a railroad bridge, could get no further. He had intended going as high as Carthage, with the intention of carrying supplies and cotton. He sued the railroad on account of the bridge, but was defeated in the suit and lost heavily in other respects. In 1869 he came to Columbus, Texas, and once more turned his attention to the practice of medicine, and in 1874-5-6 was Chairman of the editing committee of the State Medical Association. In 1877 he became President of the State Association, and he is justly proud of his record in this respect, as the association grew and became, under his administration, a magnificent institution. In 1880 he organized a Medical and Surgical service for the Galveston, Harrisburg & San Antonio Railroad, with a hospital at Columbus, and he was placed in charge and had control of the same until 1887. During these seven years the railroad became a part of the Southern Pacific road, and the Sabine Pass and Eastern Texas Railroad were added to it and extended to El Paso, in all 1,240 miles. Dr. Harrison had charge of this entire road, and while discharging his duties treated 11,657 patients, with a mortality of 35. No hospital in America can show a better record, and he has just reason to be proud of his success. The doctor has always been a stanch Democrat, and socially is a member of the K. of H. and the K. and L. of H., besides the I. O. O. F., in which he has been the presiding officer of his lodge, and he is an active and influential member of the District and County Medical Societies. On the 5th day of May, 1855, he was married to Martha V. Towell of Covington, Tipton County, Tenn., and by her has six children: Martha V., wife of E. J. Sandmeyer, cashier and attorney of the Stafford Bank of Columbus; R. H., jr., a graduate of the Medical College of Cincinnati, Ohio, and is practicing his profession with his father; Helen, wife of R. T. Knox, M. D., of Hallettsville, Texas; Maggie, wife of Wilson Littlefield, a local agent on the S. P. R. R. at Columbus; Mary and John W., at home. Dr. Harrison is a well preserved man of sixty-eight years, is active and public spirited, and it may with truth be said that very few medical practitioners have met with greater success.

FRANK LIDIAK. Among the sons of Moravia who have brought with them to the United States the enterprise and thrift which have ever distinguished those of that nationality, we are gratified to name Frank Lidiak, who is now the proprietor of the *Deutsche Zeitung*, a well known and popular paper. He was born in Moravia, in the empire of Austria, September 23, 1853, and is the second son, now living, born to Joseph and Anna (Pohrabac) Lidiak, also of Moravia. Joseph Lidiak came to America in 1860, just prior to the Civil War, and located in La Fayette County, Texas, at what is known as the Bluff Settlement, where he immediately engaged in agricultural pursuits. This he continued until 1863, when he became a member of Martindale's Company, Confederate service, and was made Corporal of that company. For the most part his service was confined to the State. Mr. Lidiak afterward returned to the peaceful pursuits of farming, and continued this up to the time of his death, in 1889, when sixty-six years of age. He had been quite successful in his financial operations, and, although he came to this country a poor man, his energy and ambition carried him to the front. Mrs. Lidiak passed away in 1884, when sixty-five years old. They left a family of four children: John, a farmer of this county, served in the United States army during the war. He had gone to Brownsville with cotton for his neighbor, and the latter, selling the cotton and team, left John Lidiak 365 miles from home. He met a number of his friends who were enlisting in the Union army, and he was persuaded by them to join. Thus it was that only after a two years' residence in Texas, father and son were arrayed against each other in this great struggle. The latter was a member of Hammett's Company, First Texas Cavalry, United States army. Frank, the second son born to Joseph Lidiak, is our subject; Annie, and Joseph, a farmer. Frank Lidiak attended his first school when sixteen years of age, a country school in La Fayette County. After that he entered a private school taught by a German named Cremer, and in this night school learned English and German. Having always talked Bohemian at home, he became quite familiar with all three languages, and taught school at the Bluff school-house for three years—1873–74–75. Following that, he served as Deputy County Clerk for three and a half years under T. Q. Mullen, and then established the first Bohemian paper in the State, at La Grange. This paper was called the *Slovan*, and continued for five years, when Mr. Lidiak sold out. Afterward he was appointed to a Deputy Collectorship in this, the third district, under President Cleveland's first administration, and served in that capacity until September 10, 1888. On the 19th of August, 1890, in company with other citizens of this county, Mr. Lidiak established a paper called the *Fayette County Democrat*, and was connected with this paper, of which he was the managing editor, until January 17, 1891. In 1892, in the month of February, he purchased the German paper of this county, the same having been established September 1, 1890, and being the second German paper ever published here. Although the first was short-lived, it has become one of the leading papers of the county. It is Democratic in its principles, and had a circulation of 600 when Mr. Lidiak made his first publication, February 11, 1892. Since then Mr. Lidiak has increased the circulation to over

3,000, and it is sent out weekly. It is the only German paper in the county. Mr. Lidiak commenced the publication of an Almanac in the Bohemian language, called " The Slovan," after the style of an American magazine—given to nice stories, the laws of the country, custom of the people in early days, and other important matter, besides the different calendars. On the 19th of June, 1877, he was wedded to Miss Pauline Adamcik, a native of Moravia and daughter of Frank and Rosella (Janda) Adamcik, both of whom came to America in 1860, where Mr. Adamcik engaged in farming. Mr. and Mrs. Lidiak are the parents of seven children: Sophia, Lillie, Edna, Frank, Jr., Anna and Martha (twins), and George J. Mr. and Mrs. Lidiak hold membership in the Roman Catholic Church, and in politics he is a Democrat and one of the leaders of that party.

JOHN HARRISON McCROSKY. For the past twenty years Mr. McCrosky has been engaged in the stock business in this community, and he has shown much wisdom in the management of his affairs, for he is now one of the substantial and well-respected citizens of the county. He is possessed of those advanced ideas and progressive principles so characteristic of the native Kentuckian, and is one of the extensive dealers in stock and land in the Lone Star State. His birth occurred at Woodville, Ky., in 1854, but he spent his boyhood days in Louisville, where he engaged in any honest employment he could find. In the year 1870 he first entered the State of Texas, and for about four years was engaged in various enterprises which netted him substantial results. After that he engaged in business with a Mr. Pierce, a relative, and for the past ten years he has managed the old Capt. Duncan ranch, handling stock, planting and ginning. His home is on Bay Prairie, and is presided over by his wife, who was formerly Miss Mattie Kuykendall, daughter of Thomas Kuykendall, who is an old and prominent citizen of Matagorda County. Previous to this union Mr. McCrosky had married Miss Minnie Murdock, whose death occurred a short time afterward. Mr. McCrosky is socially a very companionable man and an excellent citizen, for he is enterprising, public-spirited, and law-abiding. In this brief summary of points in his career it should be said, as excuse for any omission, that a biography of more pretension could best convey the lessons of his life of industry and intelligent management, which is full of instruction to all. His career, though only fairly begun, shows that honesty, capacity and power " to hustle," receive their reward at last, and in good measure.

SAMUEL WORTH THOMAS. Among the most capable and energetic officials of Frio County, Texas, is Samuel Worth Thomas, who was born in Newton County, Texas, in October, 1847, the seventh of eight children born to John W. and Paulina (Joslin) Thomas, who were natives of the Old North State and Tennessee respectively. The father's people moved from North Carolina to Alabama, thence to Mississippi, where the grandfather died. John W. Thomas was reared in Alabama and Mississippi, was married in the latter State, and in 1839 or 1840 took up his residence in the Lone Star State, near the county seat of Newton County, where he engaged in tilling the soil. He resided in various counties, and in September, 1865, settled in Atascosa County, where he died in 1868, his wife having died in 1859, in Caldwell County. Samuel Worth Thomas was principally reared in Caldwell and Hays counties, but accompanied his father to Atascosa County in 1865, attending school in the various locations in which his parents lived. When in his eighteenth year, his father died, and he then began making his own way in the world, and for a time he was engaged in driving stock and in the stock business. In 1870 he engaged in the breeding of horses, and after settling in Frio County, Texas, he continued that occupation, in connection with farming, until the fall of 1880, when he was elected to the office of Assessor of Taxes of Frio County, an office he filled with satisfaction for two years. At the next election he was chosen to his present office, and has filled the office by re-election ever since—County and District Clerk. Although of late years he has given much attention to political and official matters, he has found time to look after his landed interests, and owns two good farms, containing in all about 490 acres, of which ninety acres are under cultivation. February 2, 1872, he was united in marriage with Miss Mary E. MacMahon, a native of Tennessee, born near the city of Nashville, and to their union eight children have been given: Llewellyn, Frederick Alexander, Bessie Jane, Irvin McHenry, Samuel Wynn, Myrtle Alice, Leslie Ernest, and John. Mrs. Thomes and two daughters are members of the Christian Church.

SAMUEL V. EDWARDS. This early and honored settler of LaSalle County, Texas, was born in Erath County, this State, in 1859, and was the youngest son born to Samuel V. and Elizabeth (Salmon) Edwards, who came to Texas at an early day, and were among the first settlers of Erath County. He is supposed to have come to Texas with Captain Ross, and with him settled Waco, and he was afterwards in the Ranger service and was a Lieutenant in Ross' company. He was married in Waco, and then moved to Erath County, where his home continued until his death in 1870. During the Civil War he served on the Texas frontier, and was an active and well-known citizen of the Lone Star State. His wife died in 1869. Samuel V. Edwards left home soon after the death of his father and took up his residence near what is now the town of Cotulla, and became a cowboy in the employ of D. G. Franks, Joe Cotulla, Jim Lowe, and others who were leading ranchmen of this county. In 1882 he joined the Texas Rangers under Capt. Joe Shelly, and operated on the border in many expeditions against horse and cattle thieves and the dangerous characters of that time. In 1884 he became Deputy Sheriff under C. B. McKinney, an ex-Captain of the Rangers, and in 1886, while with the Sheriff to make an arrest at Twohig in this county, he and the Sheriff were both shot, the latter fatally, and he suffered a severe gunshot wound through the body. He fell from his horse and his would-be murderers, Bud Crinshaw and James McCoy, made their escape. A large reward was offered for their capture by the State and county, and eventually Crinshaw was killed by officers who were attempting his arrest, and McCoy was caught and eventually hanged in San Antonio. In 1882 Mr. Edwards was appointed Deputy United States Marshal, and has held that office up to the present time. In 1884 he was elected Hide and Animal Inspector of LaSalle County, and has been successively elected to that office since. When Mr. Edwards first came to this county the Indians were very troublesome, and he took part in many expeditions against them. He arrested Greene McCullough in Cotulla soon after he had killed Charley Bragg, and the next morning McCullough was hanged by a mob. These are only an incident or two in the many exciting events in Mr. Edwards' life. He made a brave and fearless officer, and discharged his duties at a time when he frequently took his life in his hand in trying to arrest the desperadoes that infested Texas. He has done much for the cause of law and order on the Texas frontier, and his usefulness can therefore hardly be estimated. In 1885, with Captain Shelly and Captain McKinney, they started out to search for some murderers who had shortly before killed three Mexicans about eighteen miles west of Cotulla. They trailed them for three days, from the place where the deed was committed to a cabin several miles away, and, taking them by surprise, captured them easily. They were John Laxon, Felix Taylor, Simps De Spain and one other, all noted desperadoes. He is now the engaged detective for the Cattle Raisers' Association of Texas, and also buys and sells fat cattle, shipping them to Northern markets, and is a very extensive operator. He is a shrewd business man, is doing remarkably well financially, and is well and favorably known over a large territory, both professionally and in a business way. He has been a terror to evil-doers, and his career has been quite a remarkable one. He was a delegate to the State Convention at Dallas in 1894, and has been a member of every convention held in LaSalle County. In 1882 he was married to Mrs. Jane M. Huff, a native of DeSoto, Mo., by whom he has two sons, Lane, and an infant unnamed. Mr. Edwards' two brothers, Tom and Joe, came to Erath County, Texas, and both were foully murdered one night at their home in that county. He has one sister, Susan E., wife of Charles Hubbard, of Erath County.

HON. FRANK BURTIS EARNEST. He whose name heads this sketch is one of the trusted servants of Uncle Sam, for he held the position of United States Custom Officer of the Corpus Christi District. He is a product of Washington County, Tennessee, born in 1858, the second of five children born to Felix W. and Eva (Burtis) Earnest, who were also Tennesseeans by birth. The father was a successful lawyer of Jonesboro, but gave up his practice at the opening of the Civil War to accept the position of Major in Vaughn's Regiment, Army of the Tennessee, and was in Vicksburg during the siege, but managed to make his escape from the city just before its fall, and worked his way with a small detachment to Virginia, after which he participated in the engagements in that State and in Tennessee until the war closed. He had been elected to the State Senate just prior to the opening of the war, but joined the army instead, and after returning home and resuming the practice of his profession, he was again elected to this office and served with marked ability for one term. He has always been remarkably active in the politics of his section, and during Cleveland's first administration he was appointed Postmaster of Jonesboro, in which place he is still living. His father, Henry Earnest, was a North Carolinian, and became one of the pioneers of Greene County, Tennessee. He was in numerous Indian wars in early days, and held the commission of Colonel. He did not marry until he was fifty-one years of age, then spent the rest of his life in Tennessee, dying at the age of ninety-six years. He was an active and useful citizen and served his county as a member of the State Legislature. Two of his brothers were in the battles of King's Mountain, and also assisted in quelling many early Indian outbreaks. The maternal grandfather of the subject of this sketch, Joseph L. Burtis, was a Virginian, born near Lexington, and was by profession an architect. He was also engaged in planting, and during the latter years of his life followed this occupation in Washington County, Tennessee, where he eventually passed from life. Hon. Frank B. Earnest was educated in William and Mary College, Virginia, after which he became editor of the *Daily Tribune*

at Knoxville, which position he occupied for two years. In 1879 he went to
Cincinnati, where he was engaged in newspaper work for a short time, but in
December, 1879, he came to Austin, Texas, joining his uncle James H. Burtis,
a lawyer, who was soon after appointed Assistant Attorney General and served
through Governor Ireland's two terms. Mr. Earnest began the study of law
under his uncle, but soon after went to the unorganized county of LaSalle,
and there in the fall of that year located on a ranch. The county was organized in 1880, and on the selection of Cotulla as the county seat Mr. Earnest
removed to that place, and having been admitted to the bar prior to that time,
was consequently the first lawyer of the town, as well as one of the first settlers of the place. After a short time he was elected to the position of County
Judge, in which capacity he served four years, and during his term of service
the county court house was erected as well as a new jail building, and Mr.
Earnest also strongly advocated other improvements. He continued the
practice of law there until 1888, then came to Laredo and engaged in the
practice of his profession here, and built up an exceptionally extended and
lucrative practice. He has always been interested in politics, and in November, 1893, he was elected to his present office, Collector of Customs of the
district. He is one of the brilliant and promising young men of southwestern Texas, is a forcible and fluent stump speaker, has done much to
further the interests of the Democratic party, of which he is a member, and
was a Cleveland Elector in 1888. He is Past Chancellor of Aztec Lodge
No. 111, K. of P., of Laredo, and in disposition is jovial and generous,
honorable and upright in character, and his keen intellect and sturdy
common sense make him a man of mark. In 1884 he was united in marriage
with Miss Josephine Waugh, a native of LaSalle County, and daughter of
William A. Waugh. Mr. and Mrs. Earnest have two children, Frank
and Ida.

ALEXANDER H. MEYER. A more worthy and exemplary citizen never
lived within the borders of the State of Texas, and it is to such men as Alexander H. Meyer, that the State owes its rapid advancement and enlightened
development. He came at that fortunate period when everything was in the
formative state, and although his life has been one of almost ceaseless toil
and labor, his success has been commensurate with his labors. Mr. Meyers is
one of the oldest settlers of Austin County, and was born in Prussia, Jan.
20, 1846, to the marriage of Henry and Christina (Brandenberger) Meyer,
natives also of the old country. Henry Meyer and family left Prussia for
America in 1846, with other families of that nationality, and on the way the
mother of our subject died with cholera. These families landed in the city
of Galveston, and formed the Fisher and Miller Colony, after which they
settled near New Braunfels, Comal County. Mr. Meyer soon removed to
Columbia, in Brazoria County, and for one year resided there. From that
section he removed to San Felipe, at that time the State capital, and being
a carpenter and cabinet maker, followed his trade there until 1865. In
the fall of that year he removed to Hempstead, Waller County, Texas, and
there died in 1884. His second marriage was with Miss Henrietta Rickson,
a native of Hamburg, Germany, and three children were given them: Ida,
wife of Peter Kissel; Louise, wife of P. C. Duer, of Hempstead, and Charley
A., of Hempstead. To his first marriage were born these children: Julius
A., residing in Hempstead, Texas, and A. H., our subject. In 1857 Mr.

Meyer engaged in merchandising at San Felipe, and in connection with his trade, was thus engaged until the war closed. He came to America a poor man and died worth about six or eight thousand dollars, after losing about ten or fifteen thousand. He held the office of County Commissioner two terms, when Austin and Waller were one, and was an exemplary and most worthy citizen. His father was a soldier under Napoleon, and fought in the battle of Waterloo. He was a Frenchman. Alexander H. Meyer received only a common school education, attending only about eighteen months, but subsequent years of study and observation has fitted him in an admirable manner to fill all the duties that have devolved upon him. He did not serve in the regular Confederate army, but served in the State Militia for twelve months, and scouted through the country, principally. In November, 1866, Mr. Meyer was working for wages at fifty cents per day, but he also owned a small herd of cattle, about seventy-five head, and took much interest in stock-raising. In 1866 he turned his attention to that industry with greater earnestness, on a small scale at first, to be sure, but he met with excellent success, and is now as wealthy a man as there is in the county, in point of land and cattle, owning about 1,700 acres of land and 1,200 head of cattle. He was married in 1877 to Miss Emma Laura Cook, who was born in this county, and whose parents, William and Mary (Bowlinger) Cook, were early settlers of this section. Mr. and Mrs. Meyer are the parents of five children: Ana L., Vada E., Herman A., Willie F. and Kate E. Mr. Meyer is a member of the Knights and Ladies of Honor and Sons of Hermann, all of Sealy. Politically Mr. Meyer is a Democrat, and has always been a leader of his party in his section.

WILLIAM DE RYEE. This skillful and well-known chemist of Corpus Christi, Texas, was born in Werzburg, Bavaria, in 1825, the son of Nicholas and Augusta De Ryee, the former of whom was born in France, the latter in Saxony. He pursued his studies in Munich, paying special attention to chemistry, geology and natural philosophy, and pursued his studies for the military service, and became a member of the geological survey. In 1848 he participated in the revolution of that country, joining the people against the King at Munich, and in 1848, immediately at the close of the troubles, he went to Holland, where he embarked for the New World, and in due course of time landed in New York. After a time he made his way to Tennessee, and, after following mining for a period, he erected a cotton seed oil mill in 1849, the first in the United States, and also invented the first machine to hull cotton seed. The works eventually burned down, but fortunately not until the success of the venture had been assured. Succeeding this, he once more engaged in mining, in Tennessee and Virginia, and, in 1856, came to Texas on his way to the mines of Arizona, and stopped at San Antonio, where he began his work as a chemist, and in connection with this engaged in photography, and invented the transparancies, which he used in giving exhibitions in St. Louis and other large places. He also invented a new printing process called homeography used by the Confederacy for its cotton bonds. In 1861 he was appointed by the Military Board of this State as Chemist. He was given complete charge of the works at Austin, and was engaged in the manufacture of gun caps. The enterprise, under the able and faithful management of Mr. De Ryee, proved a decided success and the machinery was so improved as to increase the production of caps to an almost unlimited extent. After a time he was appointed

by the Confederate Government as chemist of the Trans-Mississippi Department, when he resigned from the State service for the Confederate service.
In 1863 Mr. De Ryee went to New York, purchased a stock of drugs, and in
January, 1866, opened a drug store in Corpus Christi, which business is now
under the capable management of his son. Mr. De Ryee has been engaged
in geological surveying in southwest Texas, and also in assaying, and his
knowledge of this science eminently fitted him for the office of Commissioner
from Texas to the Exposition at New Orleans, where he had charge of the
geological exhibit. He has a handsome residence on the bluff of the Rio
Grande above Laredo, and "from turret to foundation stone" nature and
science can everywhere be found. His home is filled with valuable collections
of minerals and curios of all kinds, the detailed description of which would
occupy far too much space. All has been said when it is stated that the collection is very valuable and varied, and must be seen to be appreciated. Mr.
De Ryee was married in 1849, in the State of Tennessee, and his union resulted in the birth of three children. He has held the office of District Surveyor of a large part of southern Texas for several years and then resigned.
He is active and vigorous, both mentally and physically, and is still the leader
of his family as well as its patriarch.

THOMAS O. HOWARD. In the front rank of his calling stands Mr. Thomas
O. Howard, farmer and stockman, whose excellent farm and pleasant home
is one of the ornaments of Sealy, Austin County. The wideawake manner in
which he has taken advantage of every method and idea which tended to
enhance the value of his property has had much to do with his success in
life. Mr. Thomas O. Howard is a native Kentuckian, born May 20, 1839,
and a son of Logan and Mary (King) Howard, natives of North Carolina
and Kentucky respectively. Both the Howard and King families were early
settlers of the Blue Grass State, and the Howard family came overland to
Texas in the fall of 1853, settling near the Village of Travis, eight miles west
of Bellville, where the father, our subject, purchased a farm. There was
passed the remainder of his days, his death occurring in 1855 or 1856. His
wife survived him until 1890. They were the parents of the following
children, all of whom were boys and lived to be men: Ireason, of this place;
Sidney G. (deceased), died in the Confederate army; Silas G., resides in
this city; Thomas O., subject; Wayne, of this county; William R., of Waller County; Logan, of this county; King R. and Zenas F., both of this county.
Thomas O. Howard was educated partly in Kentucky and partly in the
Lone Star State, attending only the common schools. In 1862 he joined
Company A, Elmoe's Regiment, Harrison's Brigade, and participated in the
recapture of Galveston, where he and his regiment were stationed. This
regiment was disbanded at Richmond, Fort Bend County, the soldiers returning
home. Our subject, like many others of that early period in the West
immediately started out as an agriculturist on rented land. For twenty
years he farmed on fertile land and in 1884 purchased the place in
Sealy where he now resides, consisting of 250 acres unimproved land, for
which he paid $12 per acre. He has only fifty acres now under cultivation,
but has one of the finest residences in the county. He handles for the most
part horses, mules, jacks and jennetts, and breeds a splendid lot of horses.
Mr. Howard was married in 1862 to Miss Anna Wills, of Washington
County, near Brenham. She was the daughter of Reuben and Jane (Buster)

Wills, early settlers of Washington County. Both families came here in the days when Texas formed a part of Mexico, and one of Mrs. Wills' brothers was one of the Mier prisoners, but fortunately did not draw a black bean. To Mr. and Mrs. Howard have been born ten children: Mary J., wife of Joseph Lux, Jr.; Silas and Marshall (twins), William, Nettie, Lillian, Anna (deceased), Emma, Alma and Zada. Mrs. Howard is a member of the Christian church, and the family is respected and liked in the community.

SAMUEL H. SMITH. This substantial citizen of Rockport, Texas, owes his nativity to Brazoria, Brazoria County, where he was born in 1839, the eldest of four children born to John and Catherine (Gillette) Smith, natives of Virginia and Missouri respectively. The father was one of the 300 of Austin's first colony, and he located his headright on the Nueces River near Rockport. He served throughout the Texas Revolution, was in nearly all the Mexican expeditions and was a participant in the famous battle of San Jacinto. After living in Montgomery County for a long time he moved to Grimes County, where he was called from life. He was an especial friend of Gen. Sam Houston, and was the first Sheriff of Montgomery County, dying about 1848. He was successfully engaged in tilling the soil, and erected the first cotton gin in Montgomery County. Samuel H. Smith was reared in Montgomery, Grimes and Guadalupe counties, but in 1857 moved to Bee County and engaged in stock-raising. In 1861 he espoused the Confederate cause, and in Donnelly's Company joined the First Texas Cavalry. His first duty was as forage master, but he was afterwards promoted to the rank of Lieutenant, then to Assistant Quartermaster, and finally to Captain and Commissary of his regiment. Succeeding this he was made Major, and was then made Commissary of Buschell's Brigade, with which he served on numerous campaigns. He was at Corsicana at the close of the war. He then returned to Bee County, where he engaged in buying, raising and shipping cattle, and he was instrumental in having a packing-house established in the coast country, which was of great benefit to the country. In 1857 he came to Aransas County to furnish cattle for the factories, and has since that time resided at his present home at Rockport. He has always been extensively engaged in stock dealing, and he has a magnificent ranch of 44,640 acres in Mullin County, all of which is fenced and well watered. He was one of the early members of the Aransas Pass Harbor Company, is an active worker in the enterprise, and everything to which he devotes his attention prospers. He supports all causes for the good of the community, is one of the leading citizens of the county, has a pleasant, comfortable home, and is prospering financially. September 15, 1874, he was married to Miss Clara Hynes, a native of Texas, and a daughter of John Hynes, who came to this State from Ohio at a very early day, and took an active part in many engagements with the Indians. He held many civil offices in Refugio County, and was at one time County Judge of Aransas County. He died in 1887, at the age of sixty-three years. To Mr. and Mrs. Smith have been born the following children: Clara Frances, John and James (twins), William and Samuel (twins), Grace Catherine and Matthew Hynes. The family are attendants of the Catholic Church.

HON. PERRY J. LEWIS. This gentleman seems to have a natural adaptability to the honorable profession of law, for in its practice he has shown a high degree of learning and proficiency. His reputation and record are first-class for integrity and trustworthiness in all matters intrusted to him. He is careful and painstaking in all pleadings and court proceedings, and for clearness and accuracy of all legal instruments drawn by him ranks high in his profession. He was born at Mason, Mason County, Texas, in December, 1864, the third of four children born to William C. and Celia (Peters) Lewis, who were natives of Maryland and Louisiana respectively. The father came to Texas in 1851 and settled in Mason County, where he became a merchant and stock-raiser. During the war he occupied an office under the Confederate Government and was stationed at Fort Mason. He was married in Mason County to Miss Peters, who came to Texas with her father at a very early day. The Indians at that time were exceedingly hostile and troublesome and caused them considerable annoyance even for a number of years after the war. In 1865 Mrs. G. W. Todd, an aunt of Mr. Lewis, was killed by them. In 1866 the father, with his family, moved to Fredericksburg, Gillespie County, and there he became a very extensive stockman. In 1889 he moved to San Antonio, where he now resides, and is the live-stock agent for the Santa Fe railway. Hon. Perry J. Lewis was reared in and educated in Gillespie County, and until 1880 was an attendant of the public schools. At that time he was appointed Deputy County and District Clerk of Mason County, and was engaged in those duties for one year. In 1881, at the early age of sixteen years, he was admitted to the law department of the Washington University at St. Louis, and graduated from that institution in 1883, being one of the very youngest graduates and persons to be admitted to the bar. He was admitted to practice from that school in the courts of Missouri, and those papers admitted him to practice in Texas without having the disabilities of minority removed. In the same year he came to San Antonio, and has since, by earnest work and study, and the closest attention to the details of his profession, built up one of the largest practices in the city. He worked alone for four years, but in 1887 formed a partnership with Joseph S. Carr that continued until the spring of 1891, but since that time has been alone. His practice is mainly civil, and is carried on in all the courts of Texas. In 1892 he was elected State Senator from the Twenty-fourth District, composed of the counties of Bexar, Bandera, Kendall, Kerr, Gillespie and Medina. He was appointed to and served on more committees than is usual with members in their first session, and his committee work placed him in a deservedly high position among the members, and showed the State at large that he had special aptitude for legislative duties. In the Judiciary Committee No. 1 he did most efficient service, and helped to shape and frame many valuable laws and resolutions. On the Committee of County and County Boundaries he did much exceptionally good work. He was chairman of the Committee of Frontier Protection, and was made chairman of the committee to form the rules and regulations for the impeachment trial of Hon. W. T. McGaughey, the Land Commissioner. Besides the above he served and was an active worker on the following committees: Constititutional Amendments, Town and City Corporations, Education, State Affairs, Penitentiaries, Public Lands, State Asylum, Commerce and Manufacturing, and General Land Office. He secured the passage of a bill to form five courts of civil appeals, with one to be located at San Antonio, and also that of an act to provide for determining the rights of non-residents and unknown persons to property in Texas, and also secured the passage of a bill in the Senate to appropriate $5,000 to repair the Alamo, but this was defeated in the lower house. This record shows but imperfectly his work in the Senate, but is abundant proof that he was a working member. He was a member of the Chamber of Commerce of San Antonio, and quite involuntarily has been prominently brought forward in politics. He is a consistent Democrat, and is chairman of the Democratic Executive Committee for the Fourth Supreme Judicial District. Robust and hearty, in the prime and vigor of full manhood, he is still unmarried, and devotes his entire time to his profession.

ROBERT REES PORTER, M. D. During the time that Dr. Porter has been a medical practitioner of Brazoria County, Texas, he has made many friends, his ability has become well known, and as a consequence he has gained a large practice. He was born in Giles County, Tennessee, in 1832, and is the son of Rees Whitsett and Elizabeth (McLaurine) Porter, the father a native of Christian County, Kentucky, and the mother of Powhatan County, Virginia. Both were taken by their parents to Tennessee when young, and there grew up and were married. Mr. Porter followed planting in Tennessee until 1879, when he came to Texas and made his home with our subject until his death, October 31, 1892, when eighty-three years old. Mrs. Porter, who was considerably younger than her husband, died in 1873. For many years they were members of the Methodist Church, and he was steward of that Church in Columbia. Their family consisted of five children, and our subject, the eldest, spent his school days at Beach Grove Academy under Professor Peebles. In 1850 he commenced the study of medicine under Dr. Rufus G. White of Pulaski, and then entered the University of Pennsylvania, the oldest medical college in the United States, where he remained three years. In January, of the following year, he came to this county from Nashville, whither his people had moved, and in the fall of the year commenced the practice of his profession which he continued until the fall of 1861. He then entered the Confederate army as Assistant Surgeon of Bates' Regiment, afterwards served in the same capacity with Brown's Battalion, and remained with the latter until 1864 when he resigned and came home. He then resumed the practice of medicine, and has continued it up to the present time. He had a very extensive practice when he first came to this county, traveling many thousand miles and treating many cases, and he still enjoys a large patronage. Dr. Porter was married in Tennessee in 1854, and later graduated from the Medical Department of the University of Nashville, after leaving the college in Pennsylvania. He selected his wife in the person of Miss Elizabeth C. Lytle of Williamson County, Tennessee. They have had no children. Dr. Porter was made a Mason in Nashville, Cumberland Lodge No. 8, and has since taken a deep interest in the affairs of the order. He has advanced to the following positions: Royal Arch Mason, Royal and Select Council, Past High Priest, and is a member of the order of High Priesthood. The doctor has never held any official positions in the county from the fact that he does not care for them.

COLONEL PHILIP EDWARD PEARESON. The gentleman whose name heads this article is widely known as an able lawyer, a brave and gallant soldier, and a man who has achieved success by his own excellence, ability and energy. Col. Philip E. Peareson has been a resident of Richmond, Texas, since the year 1867, and for a time has been senior member of the law firm of Peareson & Ballowe. He is a native of Alabama, born in Talladega, October 24, 1841, and the son of Dr. Edward A. and Margaret C. (Shortridge) Peareson, the father a native of Fairfield District, South Carolina, and the mother, of Mount Vernon County, Kentucky. The parents were married in Talladega, Ala., whither Edward A. had gone when a young physician, and where he met with great success. He had acquired his literary training at Charleston, S. C., at Citadel College, and his medical training in a college there, graduating from the same. From there he went to Paris, graduated again in medicine, and became one of the most successful and accomplished physicians in the South. In 1846 he located in Victoria, Texas, but two years later went to Matagorda, where he passed the remainder of his days, dying December, 1865, when fifty-two years of age. The mother is still living, and finds a comfortable home with her son, our subject. Dr. Peareson was a Calhoun Democrat. In 1861 he took out the first troops from Matagorda, and this company (Company D), which he had organized was attached to the Sixth Texas Infantry. He was discharged about the middle of the war on account of ill health, and afterwards was on special duty in the Medical Department as well as the Provost Department. For many years he was a prominent Mason, master of the Lodge, and High Priest of the Chapter for many years. He was a member of the Episcopal Church, and his wife held membership in the same. They reared a family of four sons and one daughter, as follows: John B., a planter of Sealy, Austin County; Mrs. Doctor T. C. Thompson, of Galveston, and two deceased, Adolphus Butler, who was a physician, died in Richmond, Texas, when twenty-five years of age. He served in the Confederate Army during the war; and Sidney F., who died when a child. Our subject, the eldest of these children, spent his school days in the University of Virginia, and later in the University of Alabama, but left the latter a few months before graduating to enter the army. However, he received his diploma the same as though he had graduated. Joining his father's regiment as junior Second Lieutenant, he remained with the Sixth Texas Infantry until it was transferred to the Army of Tennessee, becoming part of Granbury's Brigade of Cleburne's Division. He served as Inspector General on General Granbury's staff with the rank of Captain, and was captured at the battle of Franklin, Tenn., taken to Johnson's Island, where he was confined until July, 1865. He participated in the battles of Arkansas Post, Chickamauga, Missionary Ridge, Ringold, Ga., and the Georgia campaign, battles around Atlanta, Jonesboro, Springfield and Franklin, where he was captured. He had commanded his company through the Georgia campaign. The whole regiment was captured at Arkansas Post and Col. Peareson was sent to Camp Chase, Ohio. He was soon exchanged, however. He never had a furlough after joining the Army of Tennessee, and although he was in all the engagements of his company he was, perhaps, the only member of the same who was never struck by a bullet. After the war he commenced the study of law at Matagorda, and was admitted to practice at Columbus in March, 1867. He at once located here, and since then has been active in his profession. Colonel Peareson is a man of broad culture and elevated tastes, and possesses a knowledge of the law and a command of language that gives him unusual power as an advocate. All his time is employed, on one side or the other, in all important cases, etc. In 1866 he was elected District Clerk of Matagorda County, and in 1879 was made District Attorney of Wharton, Matagorda, Fort Bend, Brazoria and Waller counties, having been appointed by Governor O. M. Roberts. He gave up the latter office, however. He takes a deep interest in the success of the Democratic party, and attends District and State conventions. In September, 1865, he was married to Miss Minnie Rugeley, a daughter of Alexander Rugeley of Matagorda County, and these children have been born to the union: Edward A., a planter; D. Rugeley, an attorney, and our subject's partner; Mrs. Kate Andrews, of this place; Thomas B,, and Parthenia E. The two last named are in school at the present time. Captain Pearson is a Mason, has been High Priest of the Chapter, and representative in the Grand Lodge of the State. He is also a member of the I. O. O. F., and the K. of H. In religion he is an Episcopalian. He derives the title of Colonel from having been elected at one time as Colonel of the Third Regiment of the Texas Volunteer Guard. Colonel Pearson is the present Commander of Frank Terry Camp No. 227, U. C. V.

DR. BYRON F. KINGSLEY. The most important science bearing upon man's happiness, comfort and welfare, is that of medicine, and one of its most able, experienced and successful followers is Dr. Byron F. Kingsley, of San Antonio, Texas. He was born in New York, in 1852, a son of Chester and Susan D. (Meade) Kingsley, natives, respectively, of New York and Pennsylvania. Four years after the death of the mother, which occurred in New York in 1864, Mr. Kingsley moved to Coldwater, Mich., but did not live long to enjoy western life. He devoted his attention to tilling the soil till toward the close of his life, and was a man of excellent principles, kindly disposition and good judgment. The subject of this sketch was reared and educated in his natal State, and for some time also, was an attendant of the University of Michigan. In 1870 he began the study of medicine under a preceptor, and a year later entered the pharmaceutical department of the State University of Michigan. The next year he entered the Medical Department of that Institution, where he spent two years in fitting himself for the practice of the profession. In 1874 he entered the Detroit Medical College, from which he was graduated, and later in the same year was graduated from the Long Island College Hospital, of Brooklyn, N. Y. His first practice was done in the city of St. Louis, but at the end of one year he removed to Illinois, and for two years thereafter was County Physician of Green County. In February, 1877, he came to Texas, and entered the city of St. Antonio on the first passenger train that arrived in the place. In June, 1879, he became an Acting Assistant Surgeon of the United States army at San Antonio, which position he held until July, 1883, during which time he was Assistant and Post Surgeon at Fort Davis and other posts in Texas, Indian Territory and Colorado. In July, 1883, he returned to San Antonio, and here he has since successfully practiced the "healing art." In 1890 he started the Kingsley Sanitarium at 108 Elm street, which has a capacity of some fifteen beds. His sister Josephine graduated from the Medical Department of the University of Michigan in 1873, a member of the second class of women that ever graduated from that college. She practiced the profession of medicine in Detroit, Mich., until 1878, where she organized a women's hospital, of which she became house physician. In 1878 she came to San Antonio, and has secured a large practice among women and children, their diseases occupying the most of her attention. In 1890, with her brother, Dr. B. F. Kingsley, she started a sanitarium, and expects to convert it into a hospital some time in the future. Their sanitarium is devoted to the treatment of surgical, abdominal and women's diseases, and those requiring the use of electricity. The subject of this sketch is a member of the West Texas Medical Association, of the Texas State Medical Association, of which he has been, respectively, President and Vice-president, of the American Medical Association, of the Association of the Acting Assistant Surgeons of the United States army, of the American Health Resort Association, and of the American Public Health Association. The doctor was married April 26, 1892, to Miss Nellie A. Glennon, of Chicago, Ill., and to them was born a son that died in infancy. Dr. Kingsley is a member of the Knights of Pythias and the Elks. In the social circles of San Antonio, Texas, the doctor and his wife are favorites, and their home is a very comfortable, refined and hospitable one.

WILLIAM M. BRISCOE. Prominent among the energetic, far-seeing and successful farmers and stockmen of Ford Bend County, Texas, is the subject of this sketch, whose birth occurred in this county in 1851. It has been said, and with truth, that success in any calling is an indication of close application, industry and faithfulness. Such has been the case with our subject who is not only one of the substantial men of the county, but a man who has won and will hold the esteem of all. His parents, James M. and Susan (Mason) Briscoe, died at the Capital Hotel in Houston, in 1852. Mr. Briscoe had gone on a visit to his old home in Mississippi, and was returning when he was taken sick in Houston, and died there. His wife had gone from Fort Bend County, to attend him in his sickness, and being in ill health herself, died the following day. He was born in Claiborne County, Mississippi, and came to Fort Bend County, Texas, in 1838, becoming a very extensive planter. He was once Probate Judge of the county. His father, Parmenus Briscoe, came to Texas in 1835, and purchased the William Andrus League (now partly owned by our subject). He had been United States Marshal in the State of Mississippi, and while serving in that capacity arrested Aaron Burr at the mouth of Coles Creek in Mississippi, while he was endeavoring to make his escape after his alleged treasonable schemes. Mr. Briscoe afterward went to California, and on the return voyage died and was buried at sea. One of his sons, Andrew Briscoe, was one of the signers of the Declaration of Independence of Texas, and was the first Judge of Harris County, after Texas became a Republic. He commanded the only company of regular troops that participated in the battle of San Jacinto. He came to Texas in 1834 or 1835, was a man of means, and after a few years went to New Orleans, where he engaged in the commission business and where he died in 1849. Of the four children born to the parents of our subject, the latter and Mrs. T. W. Mitchell of Houston, are the only ones now living. One son, Mason Briscoe, recently died leaving a large estate which our subject is settling up. He served in the Confederate Army, throughout the war, but was in Texas all the time. Wm. M. Briscoe received his schooling at Dinwiddie College, Virginia, and after leaving school in 1868 or '69, commenced planting for himself. Possessing a strong character and an ambitious nature, he has met with nothing but success and is now the owner of three plantations of 1,500 acres, all connecting and in good condition. Mr. Briscoe has always handled stock. His union with Miss Nora Smith occurred in 1878 and resulted in the birth of five children, one son and four daughters. Mrs. Briscoe's father, T. J. Smith, was in Texas during the Texas-Mexican War, took a prominent part in it, and was captured by the Mexicans. As he was a blacksmith by trade he was not killed, but put to work.

COL. JAMES B. HAWKINS. Matagorda County, Texas, has still the honor of numbering among its inhabitants the pioneer settler, Col. James B. Hawkins, who is now a venerable and venerated citizen of eighty-one years. It is the lot of but few men to attain the high position of honor and distinction which he has attained; with him success in life has been reached by his sterling qualities of mind and a heart true to every manly principle. To such men as he the people of the present are indebted for the improvements, well cultivated farms and thriving villages which they now enjoy. Col. Hawkins was born in Franklin County, North Carolina, in 1813, and now resides on lower Caney, at Hopkinville, which thriving town was named in his honor. His primary education was received in the schools of Raleigh, and when seventeen years of age he was sent to West Point where he remained two years. His father gave him a plantation in North Carolina, and he carried this on for eight years. In 1834 he was married to Miss Ariella Alston, a native of North Carolina, and daughter of Wellis Alston, a Congressman of note. Sometime after his marriage, Col. Hawkins went to Mississippi, remained there a short time and then in 1845 made his way to this State with a number of negroes. He immediately began clearing his plantation of the heavy timber with which it was covered, planted sugar cane, and was one of the first to commence that kind of planting, meeting with good success. He continued this business on an extensive scale and shipped to New York City, having a line of steamers to carry his produce there. There were 2,400 acres in his first purchase, and he raised enormous cotton crops aside from his other industries. He continued the sugar business for eight years after the war, handling convict labor, but since then the colonel has given much of his time and attention to the stock business. He now owns between 40,000 and 50,000 acres of land, the finest in the world. He and his most estimable wife have passed together sixty years of married life, and now in the sunset of their career are surrounded by every comfort. They reared eight children, but only two now survive, Virginia, Mrs. Brodie, resides in North Carolina, and Frank, who manages the Lake Austin Stock Ranch. The others were James, who died before the war; Edgar, Willis was all through the war, and died in the Old North State during that distressing period; John D. was all through the war, and died soon afterward; Sallie was the wife of Ferdinand Stitch, of Tennessee, at the time of her death, and Ella, died in childhood. The colonel and his excellent wife are worthy members of the Episcopal Church, and liberal contributers to the same. While a resident of North Carolina, our subject was Colonel of the militia in Warren County. His father John D., represented his county in both the House of Representatives and Senate, and was not only a brilliant young lawyer, but an influential and successful planter.

FRANK HAWKINS. It is somewhat embarrassing to write of the career of a living man standing at the meridian of his manhood whose life, so far, has been one complete success. Mr. Frank Hawkins commands the admiration and respect of the community at large, and for many years his name has been synonymous for integrity and good judgment, and he has proven himself a most capable and practical citizen. Since his boyhood days he has been Manager of Lake Austin Stock Ranch, which is on Bay Prairie, where his father, Col. Hawkins, is located. Our subject is a native of Matagorda County, born in 1849, and here all his interests are centered. The ranch of which he has the entire management is one of the finest in the State, and the residence, a magnificent one, is built on the shore of Lake Austin, from which the ranch takes its name, and commands a beautiful view of the lake and the surrounding country. It is an ideal home. Our subject has received good educational advantages, attending school at Austin College for some time, and later in a preparatory school at Frankfort-on-the-Main in Germany, finishing at Ashley College in England. Since leaving school he has had charge of the ranch, which he carries on in a systematic and business-like manner, and which is looked upon with pride by every citizen of the county, showing as it does the energy and industry of its owners. In the year 1887 he was married to Miss Elma Rugely, a native of this county, and the daughter of Dr. H. L. Rugely, a successful and skillful physician. Mr. and Mrs. Hawkins are prominent members of the Episcopal Church.

MARTIN McHENRY KENNEY. Martin McHenry Kenney has been so long and so prominently connected with the interests of Austin County that he is most widely known as one of its prominent citizens, and his reputation as such is of the highest character. He is at present County Surveyor of Austin County, and has held other positions of like importance. Mr. Kenney was born in Rock Island, Ill., December 11, 1831, and is a son of Rev. John W. Kenney, a native of the Keystone State, and of Irish parentage. The latter's father, James Kenney, came to this country from the Emerald Isle, and settled near Philadelphia. Later, but still at an early date, he moved to Ohio among the frontier settlers there. In that State he reared his family and there passed the remainder of his days. He was implicated in the rebellion of Ireland in 1798. His son, John W., father of our subject, was born in 1799, and moved with his father to Ohio in 1810, when that State was in its infancy, and grew to manhood amid noble surroundings. He became a minister of the Methodist Episcopal Church, and was stationed in various States, Virginia, Tennessee and Kentucky, and carried on his ministerial duties nearly all his life. In the year 1824 he was married in Kentucky to Miss Mariah E. McHenry, daughter of Barnabas McHenry, a pioneer settler of the Blue Grass State. From the latter State Mr. McHenry moved to Ohio, and thence to Rock Island in the latter part of the '20s, while the garrison was under command of Gen. Gaines. While Rev. Kenney was not in charge of any church at Rock Island, he was the first, or one of the first, Methodist Episcopal ministers of that place, and preached at the garrison. He participated in the battle of Stillman's Defeat, was captain in the Black Hawk war, and was crippled for life by his horse falling on him. He served the war through as Captain of his company, participated in quite a number of skirmishes, and was mustered out in the spring of 1833, while the cholera was raging. His house was burned by the Indians, but his family and other families escaped and sought safety in the fort. To the fort Mr. Kenney went also, but soon after an epidemic of cholera broke out in its most malignant form. He then moved his family to the mountains, but not until he had lost one daughter by that disease. In the fall of 1833, in company with his family and his wife's sister, Miss L. A. McHenry, he started in a two-horse wagon for Texas. Crossing the Ohio River at Shawneetown, the Mississippi River at Cape Girardeau, and the Arkansas River at Little Rock, he found at the latter place many Indians who were going West. He and family remained several days as guests of the garrison, and Mr. Kenney had to expostulate with the soldiers to prevent them from filling his wagon to overflowing with things they considered necessary for the family's future comfort. At Nacogdoches, Texas, he met a gentleman well dressed, with a wide-brimmed hat, who was very polite and agreeable in manner. Later he found out that this gentleman was ex-Governor Sam Houston. Mr. Kenney located on the west bank of the Brazos River, where a town had been laid off by a Capt. J. W. Hall and called Washington; in February, 1834, he erected the first house in that old town. He here made a canoe, and as his leading object was to explore the Brazos River and see if it was navigable, after some time spent in this endeavor decided that it was not. From there he moved to Austin County, settled on Caney Creek, and after residing with a man called "Big-foot" Stephenson, built a house on his headright league, now in Austin County, eight or ten miles north of Bellville. There Mr. Kenney passed the closing scenes of a long and useful life. In 1834 the first camp-meeting was held in the county, and the following year another meeting was held, and here the son, Martin McHenry, was baptized the same year. In 1835 Mr. Kenney was a member of the Advisory Committee, and in 1836 he made the motion to close the land office. The same year he was appointed to organize the militia, and later, with J. B. Pier, joined the Texas army at Gonzales, but later they met Nathaniel Reed, who told them that Houston's Army had met and whipped the Mexicans, and had captured Santa Anna. Afterwards Mr. Kenney returned to his ministerial duties. He never aspired to any political position, and died January 9, 1865, when sixty-six years of age. His wife survived him until 1875, and died at the age of seventy-four years, her birth having occurred in 1801. They reared six of the seven children born to their marriage: James H., was killed by the Indians at Corpus Christi in 1845; Sarah (deceased); Ann J., widow of Abram Lee; M. M. (subject); Emily, wife of Joseph McCampbell, of Beeville; John, died in 1861, and Susanna, wife of W. T. Campbell. Martin McHenry Kenney was educated in the common schools of this county, and his first movement in starting out for himself was to join the Rangers, with whom he remained for several years. From 1852 to 1853 he engaged in merchandising, and in 1854 he went to Colorado in company with Dr. Graham, under Capt. A. B. Gray, to seek a route for what was then called the Pacific Railroad, the object being to explore the thirty-second parallel across the country. This took them about six months, and he remained in Colorado for two years, engaged in mining, principally at Snow Point, on the Eagle River. He also spent some time in exploring, and returned from Colorado in 1856. Locating at Goliad he studied law and was admitted to the bar. In 1857 he was elected Deputy Surveyor, and held that position until 1859. Until 1861 he then practiced law and in February, 1862, he enlisted in Company K, Twenty-first Regiment of Texas Cavalry, joining the army at Hempstead, and serving in the Trans-Mississippi Department. In the City of Helena he was on the Marmaduke Raid to Cape Girardeau, Missouri, in 1863, and in a severe engagement on the 10th of May, 1863, in which he took active part, he was severely wounded. After the battle of Helena, he went to Missouri, to get some horses left there by the army, and joined the same in Louisiana. After the battles of Mansfield, Pleasant Hill, etc., had command of his company, fought Banks down in Alexandria, and then had command of the pickets for some time. His command disbanded in May, 1865, and he soon after returned to his home, but not to remain there long. He went to Mexico, remained there one year, and then went to Argentine Republic, South America, to explore the country. Returning to his home in Texas, in 1869, he remained there until 1874, when he joined the State forces of Texas, under Major J. B. Jones, and was Quartermaster of his company for one year.   In 1876 he began his career as a surveyor in the western portion of the State.   Mr. Kenney was married in February, 1877, and settled in Bellville, where he resumed the practice of law and surveying, and has continued this ever since.   His wife was Miss Anna Matthews, of Chapel Hill, and daughter of the Rev. Matthews, of Mississippi. Mr. and Mrs. Kenney had three children: John W. (deceased), Maggie E., and Mary M.   Both daughters are attending the College of Chapel Hill. Mrs. Kenney is a member of the M. E. Church.   Mr. Kenney is a member of Graham Lodge No. 20, A. F. & A. M. at Brenham, and he is also a demitted member of the R. A. M., Brenham Chapter No. 151.   In 1878 Mr. Kenney was elected County Surveyor for two years, and in 1892 he was elected a member of the Legislature from this district.

DR. FRANK D. BOYD.   To cure the ills and relieve the pain to which suffering humanity is heir is a most noble and worthy calling, and he who practices it successfully deserves the thanks of all mankind.   Dr. Frank D. Boyd is one of the successful medical practitioners of San Antonio, Texas, and is absorbed day and night in the anxieties and duties of his profession, which is perhaps the most trying on brain and body of any in the field of science.   He was born in Rusk, Texas, in 1867, and was the only child born to John A. and Amy E. (Harrison) Boyd, natives of Tennessee and Alabama, respectively. The paternal grandfather, William Boyd, was born in Tennessee, and as a calling followed the occupation of merchandising.   He came to Texas in 1850, located at Rusk, and became one of the prominent business men of that place, died in 1894, one of its oldest citizens.   The Boyds are of Scotch-Irish lineage, and settled in this country during colonial days, in old Virginia.   The maternal grandfather, Samuel T. Harrison, was born in Virginia, but afterwards became a resident of Alabama, where he married and reared his family and became quite widely known in public affairs.   He was for quite a number of years a member of the State Legislature, and was with that body when the great Civil War opened, and was a strong advocate of secession.   He was an extensive and wealthy planter, and died at his comfortable home in 1883.   He was a third cousin of President William Henry Harrison.   From 1854 up to the day of his death he was a resident of Texas, his home being in what is now Cherokee County.   John A. Boyd came to Texas with his parents in 1850, and all the active part of his life has been devoted to mercantile pursuits, with the exception of four years during the war, when he was Commissary of the Third Texas Regiment.   Dr. Frank D. Boyd made his home in the town of Rusk until 1885, attending the public schools, and then entered the A. and M. College at Bryan, Texas, but on account of sickness left that institution in 1886 and went to Pecos City for his health and remained there for one year.   Upon his return, in 1887, he began studying medicine at Waxahatchie, Texas, with Dr. Gracye, and in September, 1888, entered the University of Louisville, Ky., from which he was graduated with honors in 1890, after which he went to New York City and took a thorough course in the Post-Graduate School, and then spent several months in the various hospitals of that city, making a special study of diseases of the eye, ear, nose and throat.   He then returned to Louisville, Ky., where he was appointed Assistant Professor of Diseases of the Eye, Ear, Nose and Throat, which position he filled with marked ability for two years.   He then came to San Antonio and began the practice of his profession, and has become a successful and popular physician. He was married in 1892 to Miss Mattie Callahan, a native of Louisville, and both are worthy members of the Baptist Church. The doctor is an active worker in the Sunday-school and Church. Is a director of the Young Men's Christian Association, and is a Christian gentleman in every sense of the term. He is a member of the Cherokee Medical Association and also the Texas State and the Western Texas Medical associations. He is active in these bodies, for he is a close and faithful student in his profession, keeps thoroughly in touch with the progress made in it, and without doubt a bright professional future is before him. Socially he is a member of the Elks and the K. of P., and in his political views is a Democrat, which party he has represented in various county and State conventions.

HENRY P. WILEY. The career of Henry P. Wiley fairly illustrates what one may accomplish who is actuated by an honest, manly purpose, and a determination to make the most of his opportunities and ability. Mr. Wiley is one of the foremost farmers and stock-raisers of Austin County, Texas, and a man whose career has ever been above reproach. He is a native of Roane County, Tennessee, born May 13, 1836, and son of H. H. and Mary B. B. (Boyd) Wiley, the former a native of Tennessee and the latter of Virginia. The Wiley family came originally from Scotland, and settled in what was then North Carolina, now Tennessee, while the Boyds settled in Virginia. The parents of both Mr. and Mrs. Wiley came to Tennessee in a very early day, and H. H. Wiley, who was born in 1799, died in that State in 1881. His wife passed away in the same State in 1877, when seventy-three years of age. Mr. Wiley was Quartermaster of Colonel Shelley's Regiment of United States troops from Tennessee, but at the close of the war was with the army of General Schofield. For many years Mr. Wiley served as County Clerk of Roane County, previous to the war, and was a speculator of considerable magnitude in the coal business, being at one time proprietor of the Coal Creek mines in Tennessee. He and wife reared a family of ten children: Eliza J., widow of J. G. Mitchell; Andrew C., deceased, was killed in middle Tennessee; Martha E., wife of W. S. Geers; Mary E., Thomas A., deceased; Angeline M., wife of W. J. Hornsby; Henry P., Edwin F., William B. H. and Howard H., all of whom reside in Tennessee except our subject, and all the sons being prominent business men. Henry P. Wiley received his education in the common schools, with the addition of one term in the Academy of Kingston, Roane County, Tennessee. Mr. Wiley came to Texas in 1859, was at Goliad until 1861, when he joined the First Lone Star Rifles of Galveston for six months. When his term expired Mr. Wiley joined McDade's Company, Waller's Battalion and Green's Brigade, and participated in the battle of Camp Bisland and several skirmishes. He was wounded in the fight at Bisland, a minie ball entering his left ear and passing through the cheek bone on the opposite side, just missing the brain. The officers and comrades in the fight supposed that he was dead, and left him on the field of battle. Recovering consciousness he made his way to the camp, and the wound never laid him up a single day. On the day following he was captured, and paroled from the hospital at Franklin, La. After recovering, in January of the following year he rejoined his command and served until the close of the war as a private. Afterwards, in 1865, he returned to this county. In the first part of that year, January, he married Miss Sarah C. Pier, a native of this county and daughter of James B. Pier. (See sketch of S. B. Pier.) For some time after his marriage Mr. Wiley worked at the carpenter trade, but subsequently gave that up and turned his attention to farming, becoming the owner of 175 acres of well improved land, besides 400 acres of prairie land in Waller County. His marriage resulted in the birth of eight living children: Lillian M., wife of Loundes Cuny; Sarah A., wife of Dr. D. H. Brewer; Henry P., Atta H., Waller C., Julia B., Floyd B., and Donald H. Both Mr. and Mrs. Wiley are members of the Methodist Episcopal Church, and in politics the former is a Democrat.

MRS. LUCY PIER. Mrs. Lucy Pier, widow of James B. Pier, an early settler of this county, was born in what is now Lake County, Ohio, January 17, 1814. Her husband was born in the same State, November 23, 1813, and came of an old Massachusetts family, his father, Dr. Ira W. Pier, having been born there May 19, 1784. The latter's wife was Sarah Bradford, a native of Ohio, and daughter of Robert Bradford, who came of English stock, and who was a lineal descendant of Sir William Bradford, who came over in the Mayflower, and who was Governor of Massachusetts. Robert Bradford, after the War of Independence, came to Ohio in company with Israel Putnam's brother, and established a fort at Point Hammer, Ohio, and here Mrs. Pier was born, January 9, 1794. Robert Bradford's wife was Kesiah Little, also of an old English family. Dr. Ira W. Pier's mother was a Webster, of the Daniel Webster family. Mr. Pier, himself, was of French extraction. Dr. Pier reared a family of eight children, who grew to mature years. They were named as follows: Eliza, James B., Wealthy H., Sarah A., Robert O., Mary J., Ira O. and Lucy M. James B. Pier was a merchant and druggist and came to Texas on the 14th of February, 1835, and landed at the mouth of the Brazos River. With a prairie schooner, drawn by three yoke of oxen, it took him from the 15th of February, 1835, to the 31st of March of that year to move his family and household goods to the mouth of Mill Creek. He then moved to the Travis neighborhood, reaching there February 15th as a settler of the Mexican government. Mr. Pier secured a league of land in Hays County. He had a limited supply of money, and they lived very economically until they had made a start. Game peculiar to that section abounded, and the table always had a liberal supply of meat. On the 1st of March, 1836, Mr. Pier started for the relief of the Alamo, but learning that it had fallen he returned and removed his family to a place of safety. His family and Rev. McKinney's of this section were the last to leave their homes in the scare of March and April of that year.

After he had got his family settled in a place of safety, Mr. Pier promptly returned to the battlefield of San Jacinto. His company was there detailed to guard a bridge at the time of the bloody San Jacinto fight. Afterwards Mr. Pier returned to his home, but found nothing left but a little bacon and salt. Their beds were gone, ditto the dishes, etc., and they commenced again in a very primitive manner. In the year 1837, Mr. Pier met with a misfortune, breaking his collar bone, and taught school during the year. In the winter he returned to the place where he had first settled, and the family reside there at the present time. He engaged in farming and stock-raising, and about 1840 embarked in the mercantile business on his place. The latter occupation he continued up to 1860, and for many years was Postmaster at Travis, being the first one to hold that position there. He was

Confederate Postmaster during the Civil War, and was not in any actual service but once when he guarded prisoners at Hempstead, as he was a member of the home guards. After the war, Mr. Pier again engaged in merchandising and continued this up to his old days, his greatest delight being in carrying on this occupation. He died on the 5th of February, 1888, when seventy-four years of age. (See sketch of S. B. Pier.) Lucy Pier is the daughter of Ebeneezer and Charlotte (Adams) Merry, the former a native of West Hartford, Conn., born July 21, 1773, and the latter of Rutland County, Vermont, born August 17, 1780. Both the Merry and Adams families came to America about the beginning of the year 1700, and many members of both served in the Revolution. During the War of 1812, Mr. Merry carried the express, mail, etc., from Sandusky to Buffalo, N. Y., and had many narrow escapes. Mr. Merry reared a family of eight of the nine children born to his marriage: Sarah, Mary, Julia, Martin, Samuel, Lucy, Elizabeth, and Ebeneezer. Mrs. Pier's parents were married in the city of Avon.

JAMES WAHRENBERGER. There are few men who show such fitness for their avocation, in that they possess decidedly artistic tendencies and are in love with their profession, as James Wahrenberger, who is one of the most successful architects of San Antonio. He owes his nativity, however, to Austin, Texas, where he was born August 9, 1855, the eldest child born to John and Caroline (Klein) Wahrenberger, natives of Switzerland, in which country, the maternal grandfather, Charles Klein, was also born. He came to Texas in the early 40's, and has since resided in Austin. The father came to Texas as a young man, settled in Austin in 1836, and while residing near there was attacked by Indians on the present site of the State Capitol, during which fray he was wounded in the arm. He was commissioned to take word to Gen. Houston during Gen. Wall's invasion of Texas, carried the message safely and returned with the army. He was well known in Texas as "Dutch John," and became prosperous as the proprietor of an hotel, his fine cafe being liberally patronized, and was a fine confectioner. He was an ardent Confederate sympathizer, but ill health prevented him from joining the army, and he died in 1864, after having spent a useful life. His wife still lives in Austin. James Wahrenberger resided in Austin until he attained his fourteenth year, when he was sent to Philadelphia and spent two years at West Pennsylvania Academy. In 1872 he went to Europe and pursued his mathematical studies while attending lectures at the Politechnic College at Zurich, where he remained one and one-half years. He then went to Carlsruhe, Baden, and became a student at the oldest and one of the best politechnic institutions of Europe, where he spent three years and completed his course of studies, making a specialty of architecture. He graduated in 1876, after which about a year was spent at Stuttgart. He then made a trip to Italy and other countries, after which he returned to his home in America, having spent six years in foreign study and travel. Following his return five years were spent at his home in Austin, during which time he was intrusted with much professional work, both of a public and private nature, and acquitted himself with ability. In 1882 he came to San Antonio, and among many others, designed and superintended the building of the Turners' Hall, St. Louis College, many of the prominent commercial buildings and some of the handsomest private residences in the State. In 1880 he was one of the contestants, and was one of only two from Texas to compete for the State

Capitol, and secured second place, an honor which was fully merited. He is a member of the American Institute of Architects, was President of the State Association of Architects for two years and is one of the charter members of that organization. While in Europe he was married to Miss Johanna Sequin, a native of Switzerland, and to their union two children have been given: Frank and Hedwig. Mr. Wahrenberger is a member of the Catholic Church and is an honorable Christian in every worthy particular. He is an educated, polished gentleman, an able architect and a student and artist in his profession, destined to make his mark in the world.

PROF. ALEXANDER A. BROOKS, A. M., PH. D. While the life of an educator is generally barren of incidents for popular biography, it is still true that the work of a protracted life in this sphere must have many points of interest to practical thinkers, to philosophical speculators on education, and to the great work of educational progress. Years employed in any department of human labor cannot be without its fruits and its lessons. Professor Alexander A. Brooks was born at Waverly, N. Y., in 1827, the sixth of twelve children born to Alexander and Sarah (Holgate) Brooks, who were born in Pennsylvania and Connecticut, respectively. The paternal grandfather, John Brooks, was of English descent, and was born in Massachusetts, while the maternal grandfather was a Pennsylvanian. Alexander Brooks, the father of Prof. Brooks, was a woolen manufacturer, and built a large manufactory in Tioga County, New York, and founded the village of Factoryville, but his establishment was destroyed by fire in 1852. He was called from life in 1876, and his wife in 1842. The subject of this sketch was educated in the University of Michigan and in the University of Rochester, N. Y., and graduated in 1851 as a member of the first graduating class of that institution. In 1853 he received the degree of A. M. in course, and in 1874 he was awarded by his alma mater the degree of Ph. D., only one other being given this honor. In 1851 he removed to Marion, Ala., and accepted the chair of Latin in the Howard College, now at Birmingham, and after remaining there one year was placed in charge of the Quitman Institute, at Quitman, Mississippi, where he remained four years. He then came to Gonzales, Texas, and up to the opening of the Civil War had charge of Gonzales College. He spent one year in the service of the Confederacy, then re-opened the college at Gonzales, and was at the head of that institution until 1873. At that time he went to Goliad and took charge of Goliad College. Having purchased the college buildings he successfully conducted the institution up to 1885, when he sold out the property to the Methodist Conference. After a short residence in San Antonio, he came to Corpus Christi, and in this place has since continued to make his home. The Goliad College was conducted under military discipline, and there were connected with it literary, commercial, music and art departments. There was a full college curriculum, and Prof. Brooks graduated many students from this institution, who afterwards became leading people of Texas. This school was a very flourishing one, the buildings were excellent, and it was well patronized. Prof. Brooks was married in 1853 to Miss Clara Laurette Brown, daughter of Daniel B. Brown, of Ann Arbor, Mich., and to their union three children have been given: Frank A., who married Miss Bessie A. Wright, and died in 1894; William H., who married Miss Susie Gussett, a daughter of N. Gussett, of Corpus Christi, and Anna M. Prof. Brooks is a member of the Blue Lodge and Chapter of the A. F. & A. M., and he is a communicant of the Episcopal Church. Dr. Brooks has been a successful teacher for thirty-seven years and has achieved a reputation as an educator second to none in his adopted State.

MASON LOCKE WEEMS, M. D. Nothing strange or singular clings about the fact that health is the paramount topic of interest in all parts of the world. It is but reasonable that this should be so. Health is capital, comfort, happiness, life, everything, and how to retain it, and how to regain it when lost, is of vital interest to all. As a successful physician, Dr. Mason Locke Weems has done much for the cause of suffering humanity, and won honor and the evidence of deserved success for himself. Dr. Weems comes of prominent Virginia stock, and is a native of that State, born in Prince William County. His grandfather, Dr. Mason Locke Weems, graduated in medicine in Edinburgh, Scotland; was eminent in his profession, and was a personal friend of George Washington. During the latter part of his life he turned his attention to the ministry, and was an earnest and conscientious Episcopal. He was a resident of Virginia nearly all his life, but died in Charleston, S. C., while there on a business trip. He received his literary education in his native country, and was a D. D. as well as an M. D. His son, Dr. Mason Locke Weems, the father of our subject, was also a physician, and graduated in medicine from the University of Pennsylvania. For some time he practiced medicine in Washington city, but left there on account of his health, in 1837, and went to the Lone Star State, settling on Bay Prairie, Matagorda County, where he resided two years. From there he moved to a point six miles below Wharton, and was the first Probate Judge of the county, serving in that capacity several terms. He also became an extensive planter, as well as a successful one, and, although he experienced many hardships when first settling here, he entered upon his career as an early settler earnestly and persistently, and came to the front, both as a physician and planter. He had adventures with the Indians, and assisted in defending the settlers against them. Socially he was a Master Mason, and in religion a Unitarian. He married Miss Asenath Otis Slade, of Prince William County, Va., who now makes her home with her children, and, although eighty-four years of age, she still retains her faculties in a remarkable degree. Seven children were born to the above-mentioned union, of whom our subject is the oldest and the only one now living. The father of the immediate subject of this sketch died in February, 1856. Mason Locke Weems, subject, was born June 28, 1831, and no doubt inherited a taste for medicine from his ancestors. He studied medicine under his father, and then entered the University of Louisiana, medical department, from which he graduated in March, 1852. The following year he commenced the practice of medicine in Wharton County, below Wharton, and in 1855 came with his father to Columbia. He at once entered upon his career as a physician, and after the death of the father settled up the estate. From 1857 to 1880 he was engaged in merchandising, but during that time, in 1862, he was made Surgeon of Gibson's Battery, holding that position until peace was declared. On the 11th of June, 1857, he married Miss Anna Eliza Smith, of Matthews County, Va., and the fruits of this union were seven children, of whom Mason Locke Weems was the eldest, he dying when only one year of age. Dr. Weems named another son Mason Locke Weems, who graduated in medicine at Tulane University in 1890. Susan V. died when seven years of age; Annie Laurie is the wife of John H. Craig, of this county; Marcus Aurileus third son, is a graduate of the University of Pennsylvania, medical department, class of 1890, and is practicing with his father; Zuleika, at home, and Sands Smith, the fourth son, aged twenty-one, is in an express office in Velasco. Dr. Weems is a Royal Arch Mason, and has been a member of the order since 1856. In religion he is an Agnostic.

THOMAS S. BIGGS. This prominent farmer, ginner, and mill man is well and favorably known throughout his section, and by his perseverance and industry has become one of the substantial men of his section. He was born in Holmes County, Ohio, November 19, 1833, and is a son of Samuel and Margaret (Stephenson) Biggs, natives of Pennsylvania, and of English and Scotch parentage respectively. The Biggs family trace their American ancestry back to a period antedating the Revolution, and our subject's grandfather, Samuel Biggs, as well as his great-grandfather, William Biggs, served throughout the war for independence, and were present at the surrender of Lord Cornwallis. The father of our subject was a farmer, and had moved to Iowa at an early date. He came to Texas in 1880, and here died in 1887 at the ripe old age of eighty-nine years. He was twice married, two children having been born to the first union, Susan, widow of James Smith, and Margaret, who is now deceased. Mr. Biggs' second union, with Miss Stephenson, resulted in the birth of five sons: Andrew, deceased; David, of Iowa; Thomas S., Hezekiah, engaged in the milling business in New Mexico, and Samuel H., of Nebraska. The mother of these children died in Iowa in 1877, when eighty-two years of age. The Buckeye State furnished our subject with his education, and later he went with his parents to Iowa, where he learned the machinist's trade. After coming to Texas he was engaged in building mills in different sections of the country for some time. In 1861 he joined Waller's Battalion for six months, and was stationed at Galveston. Upon being discharged at the close of his term he soon joined Capt. Stephens' Company, of Elmoe's Regiment, and soon after was detailed to work in the shops, principally at Hempstead, where he manufactured wagons and superintended a sawmill. He was manager of the Government shops. At the retaking of Galveston, Mr. Biggs was one day late, and although very anxious to get there in time, failed to do so. He was in only one small engagement on the coast, and was in the artillery department at this time. Mr. Biggs was on board a Confederate boat during one cruise. When the war closed he was working in the shops at Hempstead, and he remained there for two years, running a wagon shop. In 1867 he came to this locality, and at once engaged in the manufacture of wagons. In 1876 he built his first grist and second saw mill in this section of the county, if not in the country, and has since added cotton ginning. Mr. Biggs has had an extensive business in his line, both in milling and in the manufacture of wagons, and, being an honorable business man, deserves the success to which he has attained. He located on fifty-seven acres of slightly improved land, and his house was among the early frame buildings erected in this part of the county. Mr. Biggs selected his wife in the person of Miss Sarah Miller, of Austin County, and daughter of John and Diser (Tubbs) Miller, early settlers of this county from Alabama. Mr. Miller died rather young, and Mrs. Miller passed away in 1887. They had three children: Berry, who died in the Confederate army; Sarah, wife of our subject, and Texanna, deceased, who was the wife of J. M. Jackson, left two children. To Mr. and Mrs. Biggs have been born four children, as follows: A. B., a successful physician of this place, who graduated from Louisville Medical College in the class of 1889; Thomas I., a dentist of this place; Jennie A., and John P. Mr. Biggs is a member of the Masonic order, Bellville Lodge No. 223, and R. A. M. of Bellville Chapter No. 151. He was made a Mason at Hempstead Lodge No. 67 in 1863, and while there filled all the chairs in the Blue Lodge and Chapter. He is now a charter member of Bellville Chapter. Both Mr. and Mrs. Biggs are members of the Methodist Episcopal Church South.

JUDGE W. B. HOPKINS. The responsible position which this gentleman is filling, that of Judge of Nueces County, Texas, is one demanding the utmost good judgment, keen insight into men and their motives, and the ability to "make the punishment fit the crime." No more able official could be found than Judge W. B. Hopkins, and the citizens of the county realize this fact and appreciate the services he has rendered. He was born at Cumberland Court House, Va., March 8, 1866, the second of seven children born to A. C. and Anna P. (Atkinson) Hopkins, who were also born in the Old Dominion, of which State the paternal grandfather, Henry L. Hopkins, was also a native. The latter was a very active man of his day, and for some time was a member of the State Legislature. His brother, George, was a lawyer by profession, became a Circuit Judge, afterward a member of Congress, and was then appointed by President Buchanan as Minister to Spain. The maternal grandfather, William Atkinson, was a member of a prominent Virginia family, which had among its numbers many prominent men. He was a lawyer during the early part of his career, then became a minister of the Presbyterian Church. Both branches of the family were of Scotch-Irish descent. A. C. Hopkins, father of Judge W. B. Hopkins, was a minister of the Presbyterian Church also, and during the great strife between the North and South he served throughout the entire struggle as Chaplain in Jackson's command. In 1866 he moved to West Virginia, and still resides in that State engaged in ministerial labors. Judge W. B. Hopkins was educated in Charlestown Academy and at Hampden-Sidney college, after which he took a law course in the University of Virginia, and was admitted to the bar in the fall of 1890 at San Diego, Texas, having come to this section in the summer of 1886. For one year thereafter he had charge of the male department of the Deaf and Dumb Institute at Austin, as Monitor, then was one year with Stayton & Kleberg, lawyers, of Victoria, but since that time has resided in Corpus Christi, where he has built up a large practice. He has been active in political affairs of the county, has labored faithfully and earnestly for the success of the Democratic party, has been a delegate to numerous county conventions and to two State conventions. In 1892 he was elected to the office of County Judge of Nueces County, and has filled the same with marked ability. He was married in 1893 to Miss Ola L. Wright, a native of Texas and a daughter of George W. Wright, of Live Oak County, and their home has become well known for the generous hospitality that is extended to all. Mr. Hopkins is a member of the K. of P.

GEORGE H. BUSH. As a farmer and stockman George H. Bush takes a prominent place among the foremost men of the county, and in every walk of life he has won respect and esteem. He was born in this county August 12, 1852, to the marriage of N. W. and Julia (Thacker) Bush, natives of Kentucky. In 1836 the father left his native State, and made his way to Texas by way of

New Orleans, Galveston, Houston and San Felipe, just as soon as the Independence of Texas was acknowledged. Mr. Bush came in company with his brother-in-law, John W. Collins, and settled on a piece of land seven miles north of Bellville, when but a few families were living in that section. The McNutt and Marshall families were the pioneer settlers of this immediate section. One of them had five sons, and the other four, so that there were eleven men in all to fight the Indians who were hostile then. They had secured their land from the Mexican Government. At that time wild horses and wild cattle were numerous, and a grove near the present town of Buckhorn is called Jackson Grove, although at one time it was called Mustang Point. Mr. Bush served in the War of 1848, and did good service for his country. During the latter part of the Rebellion he served in the Confederate State Militia. Previous to the war he had served for a number of years as County Assessor and Collector, and during the late war was elected to the Second Legislature of the State under the Confederate Government. He was a most worthy and intelligent citizen, and his death, which occurred in 1882, when sixty-nine years of age, was a severe blow to all. His wife had died in 1861, when forty-eight years of age. Their six children were named as follows: James H., was in the Confederate army, and died at Bowling Green, Ky., November 25, 1861; Martha (deceased), was the wife of W. O. G. Wilson, who surveyed the first line on the H. & T. C. R. R.; William T., of Louisiana, now in railroad and telegraphic employ, served all through the war in the Confederate army; Sarah E., wife of R. P. Falldis, of Minneapolis, Minn.; George H. and Zenas, died in 1865. George H. Bush attended the schools of Hempstead, Waller County, in his youth, and for a short time was in school at Chapel Hill, where he received good instruction. For the most part our subject was reared in Waller County, although he had moved with his father to Galveston, where the latter was in the commission business there, but remained only for a short time. When fourteen years of age he commenced life for himself, first as a hired hand in the stock business, driving a herd from Starr County to Lower California. However, he did not get quite as far as that, stopping at Lower Rio Grande. When he came back he went to San Antonio, and there hired himself to Uncle Sam as assistant wagon master, and held that position for two years, making many trips among the Indians. Teamsters were obliged to act as soldiers, and the first trip was made to Jacksboro with supplies to the Indians, and thence to Fort Griffin, Fort Consh and Fort Clark. He then returned to Hempstead, and for two years clerked there for a relative. In 1872 he made a trip to Kansas with cattle. Two years later, or in 1874, he married Mrs. Taglionia Collins, daughter of Thomas Cochran (see sketch of N. Cochran), and eight children were given to them: William C., Julia P., Anna M., Zollie E., Talonia, Samuel P., George and Eula. Mrs. Bush has one daughter by her first marriage, Johanna, now the wife of James H. Foster. Mrs. Bush is a member of the Methodist Episcopal Church. While residing at Hempstead Mr. Bush was a member of the Masonic Fraternity.

CHIEF JUSTICE JOHN W. STAYTON (deceased). In the death of the honored gentleman whose name heads this sketch, not only the bar, of which he was the brightest ornament while in the practice of his profession; not only on the bench, where he occupied the highest place, but the entire people of the State of Texas, of which he was for over forty years a most exemplary citizen, mourn the loss of one whose every thought was for the good of his section. He was born in Washington County, Kentucky, December 24, 1831, and was bereft of his father, who was a farmer, before he was five years old. He was taken by his mother to Paducah, Ky., and was there given all the educational advantages which a mother's love and means could furnish, but, at the early age of thirteen, death also deprived him of his mother, and he was left to fight life's battles as best he could. For four years thereafter he resided with his grandfather on a Kentucky farm, and while he was occupied with the pursuits incidental to the life of a farmer's boy, he eagerly perused such books, periodicals and newspapers as came in his way, and in this manner stored up a valuable and varied fund of information, which was of material use to him in later years. He was very desirous of obtaining a thorough collegiate education, and instead of devoting his small income to this purpose, he yielded to the wishes of his guardian. His out-door life strengthened and improved his constitution, and at the age of seventeen he was a well-informed and sturdy youth, with excellent principles, such as the Kentucky of that day turned out. He had always been desirous of becoming a lawyer, but owing to adverse circumstances could not do so until he had earned some money with which to defray his expenses and as a means to this end he began working in a blacksmith's shop, and continued that honorable and useful occupation for four years. In time he gathered together sufficient means to enable him to continue his studies, and at the age of twenty-one he became assistant in a large country school. During this time much of his spare time was devoted to the study of the higher mathematics and the ancient languages, and at the same time he pursued the study of law under the direction of his uncle, Judge Henry Pirtle, of Louisville. In 1855 he entered the law department of the University of Louisville, and in March, 1856, was graduated therefrom with distinction. He was married about a month later to Miss Jennie Weldon, and in November, 1856, he, with his young wife, immigrated to Texas, and located at LaGrange, but failing health and pecuniary losses caused him to make another change, and he took up his abode in Atascosa County, and shortly after the organization of Pleasanton, he moved to the place, established a blacksmith shop, and at the same time began the practice of law. In the fall of 1858 he was elected District Attorney, was re-elected in 1860, and at the expiration of his second term enlisted in the Confederate army as a private, after which he was commissioned to raise a company of cavalry, which he did, and served through the war as commander, and in war as in peace he was faithful to every trust reposed in him, and if military honors were not bestowed upon him, it was because he labored in a field where they could not be won. After the cause for which he fought was lost, he rejoined his family in Sutherland Springs, Wilson County, but later removed his family to DeWitt County, where he resumed the occupation of teaching for about one year. In 1866 he formed a law partnership with Samuel C. Lackey, at that time the leading lawyer of that county, and they opened an office in Clinton, and in 1871 were joined by Maj. A. H. Phillips, and the firm took the name of Phillips, Lackey & Stayton, after which he removed with his family to Victoria. Major Phillips retired from the firm in 1878, but in March, 1880, R. J. Kleberg and R. W. Stayton were admitted as partners, and the firm became Stayton, Lackey & Kleberg. Mr. Stayton's practice brought him not only fame, but friends and property; the reward of his unremitting industry, his kind heart and his comprehensive knowledge of the law. While pursuing the even tenor of his way as a country lawyer he was, in 1881, appointed by the Governor as Associate Justice of the Supreme Court of Texas, to fill a vacancy, but hesitated to accept the office for several days. In 1882 he was selected by the Democratic Convention as a candidate for Associate Justice of the Supreme Court, and to this position was elected by a good majority, and served in that capacity until the resignation of Chief Justice Willie, when he was appointed by Governor Ross to fill the vacancy. He rendered efficient and faithful service on the Supreme bench until 1888, when he was elected by the people of Texas as the Chief Justice of this honorable court, and held the scales of justice with an impartial hand until called before a higher tribunal in July, 1894. He was a man of strong physique, compactly built and muscular, and his naturally strong constitution was further improved by labor on the farm and at the forge. He was quick tempered, but it was held under excellent control, and he was always frank and generous. Although a man of thrifty habits, he never stooped to acquire wealth by questionable means. He was a member of the A. F. & A. M., was an humble and consistent member of the Presbyterian Church, and was the kindest and most considerate of husbands and fathers. He left a widow and three children, besides grandchildren, to mourn his untimely death. His son, Robert W., is a lawyer of San Antonio; his eldest daughter is the widow of Fielding Breeden, and his youngest daughter is the wife of John T. Bonner, of Tyler, Texas. He was known far and near as a man whose watchword was duty; he was always actuated by the principles of justice, and bearing no malice he was universally beloved. He was entirely free from anything approaching austerity; he was pure in conversation and life, and was at all times a gentleman. He was a patriotic and enterprising citizen, and was remarkably successful as a legal practitioner. His clear and logical mind, his calm, deliberate style of manner, and his profound learning, well fitted him for the high official position which he so ably filled. Very few of his decisions were overruled, and many of them stand forth prominently in the jurisprudence of Texas, for the guidance of the profession in this and coming generations. October 20, 1894, the Supreme Court convened in special session, and passed resolutions of sorrow and regret over his untimely death, as did also the Texas Bar Association.

ROBERT W. STAYTON. This able legal practitioner, of San Antonio, Texas, has inherited much of his father's ability, intelligence and acumen as a lawyer. He is a member of the law firm of McLeary & Stayton, and is a successful attorney of large practice. He was born at Pleasanton, Atascosa County, Texas, December, 8, 1858, the eldest child and only son born to Judge John W. and Jennie (Weldon) Stayton, both of whom were born in Kentucky. Robert W. Stayton attended school in Virginia from fifteen to twenty-one years of age in Hampden and Sidney College and in the University of Virginia, graduating in special courses in each. He finished the law course in the latter institution, after which he was admitted to practice at Cuero, in March, 1880, and entered upon the practice of his profession at Victoria, Texas, at the same time. He continued in that place until 1888, when he removed to Corpus Christi, which city continued to be his home until October, 1893, when he came to San Antonio and formed a partnership with General McLeary. They do an extensive general practice in the courts of Texas, are able, well posted and intelligent lawyers, and the cases which are given to their care are carefully and laboriously studied and considered, so that when their cases are called they are prepared to meet every argument of their opponents. Mr. Stayton has always been quite active in politics, but the political arena, so far as he himself is concerned, has had no charms for him. In 1892 he was a Presidential Elector from the Eleventh Congressional District of Texas. For a number of years he has been an active member and officer of the State militia, becoming a member of the Victoria Rifles, at Victoria, in 1885. On his removal to Corpus Christi he soon became Captain of the Corpus Christi Light Guards, and is now Judge Advocate-General with the rank of Major. He was married in December 1881, to Miss Annie Vineyard, of Texas, daughter of John W. Vineyard, who removed from Kentucky to Missouri and thence to Texas in 1857. To Mr. and Mrs. Stayton two children have been given: John W. and Robert W., Jr. Mr. Stayton became a member of the Masonic Fraternity at Victoria, and has since advanced to the higher branches and degrees of that order through the Chapter, Commandery, etc., and is now a member of the Mystic Shrine. He has been Master of the Blue Lodge, and ever since joining has been an active worker in the order. He was also made an Odd Fellow at Victoria, and went through all the chairs of the lodge there. He is a finished and scholarly gentleman, has built up the largest practice in the city of San Antonio, and is looked upon as one of the legal lights of the State.

SAMUEL A. SHELBURNE. The life history of him whose name heads this sketch most happily illustrates what may be attained by faithful and continued effort in carrying out an honest purpose. It is a story of a life whose success is measured by its usefulness—a life that has made the world brighter and better. Samuel A Shelburne, one of the oldest and most highly esteemed citizens of Austin County, is a native of Tenn., born July 26, 1817, the son of John P. and Nancy (Dunkin) Shelburne, natives of Virginia. James Shelburne, the great grandfather of our subject, was born in England, as was also his son, Samuel, the grandfather of our subject. The latter came to America at a period antedating the Revolution and settled in the Old Dominion, where he passed the remainder of his days. When a young man, John P. Shelburne came to Tennessee, then almost a wilderness with but few settlers, and was soon after elected Sheriff of Williamson County. About 1838 he came to Texas, settled in the county near where Industry now stands, and found himself almost without neighbors, as but few were living here at that time. In February, 1839, an election took place and the voters for twenty miles around gathered at Industria. They numbered twenty-one in all. For groceries, etc., the pioneers at that time went to Houston, but soon a little store was started at Industry and some trading was done at San Felipe. Mrs. Shelburne died in 1858, and Mr. Shelburne in 1882, when eighty-two years of age. These children were the fruits of their union: Jane, Samuel A., Sarah P., William H., deceased; William L., deceased; Calpernia H., deceased; James H., deceased; George F. deceased; Elizabeth, deceased; Virginia A. and Tennessee. Samuel W. Shelburne was educated principally in Williamson County, Tenn., although he attended for a time the country schools of Lauderdale County, Ala., where his father moved when Samuel was but a boy. He came to Texas with his father in 1838 and made his home under the parental roof until his marriage, January 8, 1845, to Miss Adeline Bell. Her father, William Bell, came to the county as early as 1834. In 1863 Mr. Shelburne joined the State militia, Captain Shyman's company, and was mostly stationed along the coast.

He was in but one engagement, and that was when they captured a transfer boat loaded with provisions, which, after capturing, they sent to the mouth of Brazos River. He was at home when the war closed. Like most of the planters in the South, he lost heavily during the war, and especially by the Emancipation Act, being the owner of a good many slaves. However, he was not at all discouraged, but engaged actively as a farmer and stock-raiser, and has met with a reasonable degree of success. He has never taken an active interest in political affairs, but for fourteen years was Justice of the Peace and Notary Public for some time. He and wife are the parents of thirteen children: James H., Julia A., wife of George B. Dixon, of Huntsville; Sarah J., John P., of this county; Nancy, deceased; Callie, deceased, wife of Dr. C. C. McCloud; William, deceased; Samuel A., Jr., of Fayette County; Ida, wife of T. D. Mackett, of Temple, Texas; Ernst, deceased; Mollie L., Georgie, deceased, and one died in infancy. Mr. Shelburne was made a Mason in Belleville Lodge No. 223, in 1858. Although, as before stated, he is not active in political affairs, he has been a life-long Democrat and expects to continue in its ranks. Mrs. Shelburne came to Texas in 1834, from Shelby County, Tenn., and settled in Fayette County, living for one year on Cummings Creek, near where Fayetteville now stands. At that time there were but six or seven families living in the section where they settled, and the Indians troubled them very much. Mr. Bell settled in that section in April, 1834, and died in July of the same year. The following autumn Mrs. Bell moved her family where New Ulm now stands, and remained there until 1836, when she with numerous other families left on account of the Mexican invasion, coming as far east as San Augustine. When the war closed Mrs. Bell moved back to New Ulm and she and her sons began improving the home place and gathered the crop that they had put in before moving. Mr. and Mrs. Bell were the parents of eight sons and one daughter: William, deceased; Thomas H. (deceased) was in the War of 1836 and participated in the battle of San Jacinto; James N., deceased, also fought in that battle and was afterwards killed by the Indians and Mexicans in 1848; A. J. was in the same war; John P., James J., Granville, deceased, and Francis. Mrs. Bell died in 1845. Adaline, the seventh in order of birth of the above mentioned children, and the only daughter, was born October 24, 1824. When her parents first came to Texas they took their corn to a neighbor's and ground it in a crude mill. The first house erected by them was of logs, with puncheon floor, and the first lumber used by them was sawed by the boys with a whipsaw. The first mill for grinding was a horse mill erected by a Mr. Daugherty, whose sons still live in the county. Game was abundant, and the early settlers did not lack for meat on their tables. Indians, too, were quite numerous, and many interesting adventures could be related by the old settlers.

GEN. T. J. RUSK. This unfortunate Texan soldier and statesman was born in South Carolina December 5, 1808, and died by his own hand in Texas in 1857. His father was an immigrant from Ireland, and was by trade a stonemason. It is possible that but for the fact that the Rusks lived on the land of the Hon. John C. Calhoun, the General might have followed in his father's footsteps. Mr. Calhoun, impressed by the boy's brightness and intellectual promise, secured him a place in the law office of William Grisham, clerk of Pendleton District, where he made himself familiar with the law. In due time he was admitted to the bar, and soon afterward located at Clarksville,

Georgia, where he married the daughter of Colonel Cleveland and acquired a lucrative practice. He was swindled, however, in a mining speculation by which he lost his entire savings, and followed the men who had wronged him to Texas, only to find that they had spent or put beyond his reach all his money. Locating at Nacogdoches he practiced law, and afterward became conspicuous as a Texan patriot. He distinguished himself in the War of Independence, and subsequently commanded various expeditions against the Indians. In 1839 he was appointed Chief Justice of the Republic, but soon resigned and retired to practice law at Nacogdoches. In 1845 he was president of the annexation convention, and was one of the first two Senators to the United States Congress, and this position he held until his suicide in 1857, brought about by a fit of mental aberration induced by a malignant disease and the loss of his wife. He was a man of rare qualities, and held in the highest esteem by all who knew him. On account of his death Congress wore the usual badge of mourning for thirty days.

HON. JAMES H. SHELBURNE. The subject of this sketch, one of Texas' "favorite sons," and a most honored citizen, now State Senator of the Sixteenth Senatorial District, is a man of progressive ideas, rich attainments, high minded and clean handed—in a word a leader worthy the name. He was born a pioneer, and is himself a product of civilization, his birth occurring in this county December 2, 1845. The family to which he belongs is of English origin. His father, Samuel A. Shelburne, was a native of Tennessee, and came to the "Lone Star State" in 1838. (See sketch.) Like many of the influential and prominent men of this section Mr. Shelburne received his education in the common schools, and in 1861, when Civil War opened, he enlisted in Company F, Brown's Regiment, Texas Cavalry, and served in the trans-Mississippi Department. He participated in the battle on Matagorda Bay, and in a number of minor engagements, serving as a non-commissioned officer during the latter part of the war. Col. Beard's regiment had mutinied or rebelled, and Mr. Shelburne and his command were sent to quell them. On the way there they received information that the war was over, and subsequently disbanded on the Brazos River. Returning home he at once engaged in freighting from Houston and eastern Texas to this section of the county, and continued this until 1870. He then began teaching in this county, and at the same time studied law with the result that he was admitted to the bar in 1872, Judge L. Lindsey presiding. Mr. Shelburne at once commenced practicing his profession in this county, and in 1882, previous to moving to Bellville he had served as Justice of the Peace for a number of years. In 1881 he formed a partnership with Judge Bell, and in 1887 was elected to the Legislature of the State, serving two years. He was a member of that body when the capitol was built, and was one of the committee delegated to receive the capitol when finished. During the same year he was one of the committee who was appointed to examine the Comptroller's report and count the money at that time in the Comptroller's office. During the time he served in the House he was a member of most of the important committees of the same, and ever took a prominent part. After 1889 he remained quietly at home until 1892, when he was elected Senator of the Sixteenth Senatorial District, embracing Austin, Fort Bend, Harris and Waller counties. During that time he was second on Judiciary and first on Towns and City Corporations, Education, Public Lands, Roads and Buildings, Claims and Accounts,

General Land Office.   He was also Chairman of Committee on Federal Relation, member of the Committee on Public Buildings and Grounds, and will
hold his present position until 1896.   On the 5th of March, 1867, he was
married to Miss Mollie A. Perkins, a native of Mississippi and daughter of
L. P. and L. A. (Spence) Perkins.   Mr. Perkins came to this State and
county in 1860, and here served in the trans-Mississippi Department of the
Confederate Army.   He was a farmer, and now resides in Georgetown,
Williamson County, retired from all manual labor.   He and wife are the
parents of seven children who reached manhood and womanhood.   Mr. and
Mrs. Shelburne are the parents of six children: Lulu, wife of Silas Howard
of Sealy.   Mrs. Howard now resides in Austin, and is one of the most noted
musicians in the county; Aubrey, of this city; Mamie, a music teacher of
considerable reputation in this and other counties of Texas; Nona, Georgia.
and Callie.   The first and fourth children are graduates of Bellville College,
Mr. Shelburne is a Mason, a member of Bellville Lodge No. 223, and is an
R. A. M. of Bellville Chapter No. 151.   Mr. Shelburne has held all the
offices in the Masonic Order, and for many years was Master of his lodge.
In the Chapter he has held all the chairs except that of H. P.   He is also a
member of the K. of H.

    HON. HENRY C. KING.   It is a pleasure to chronicle the history of a man
whose life has been one of honor and usefulness, and although he has considerably passed the zenith of his career, Hon. Henry C. King enjoys to the
fullest extent the comforts of a home that is made beautiful by the sweet spirit
of kindliness and mutual appreciation among the members of the family.
He comes of good old Georgia stock, and was born in that State in 1830, the
fourth of eight children born to Stephen Clay and Mary Eleanor (Fort) King,
who were born in Massachusetts and Georgia respectively.   The paternal
grandfather, Daniel King, born in Kingston, (now Palmer) Mass., September
2, 1749, was an officer in the Revolutionary War, attaining the rank of Captain, and was a participant in the famous battle of Bunker Hill.   After the
war he resided for some time in Connecticut, then moved to Wilbesbarre, Penn.,
and died March 5, 1815, after having devoted his attention to farming.   His
father, Thomas King, was born at Kingston, Mass., in 1879, and died in 1801.
His father was John King, of Edwardston, England, born in 1681; was an
officer of the British navy; came to America with a grant of lands and settled in
Massachusetts in 1710, and founded Kingston in that colony.   He died in
1744.   The maternal grandfather, James Fort, was a native of North Carolina,
and became a Lieutenant in the Revolutionary War, and participated in the
siege of Yorktown.   He was married to Martha Gibson, of North Carolina,
after which he removed to Georgia, about the beginning of this century.   He
was a member of the Legislature of Georgia, and a Major in the State
Militia.   He died in that State in 1848.   He was also of Scottish descent,
and of an old and prominent family.   His wife was a daughter of Stephen
Gibson, a wealthy planter.   Stephen Clay King, father of the subject of this
sketch followed the occupation of planting, was married in the State of
Georgia, and there spent his life.   He died while visiting his son at San
Antonio, Texas, in 1860.   He had always taken much interest in public affairs,
and was a member of the convention of 1858, which postponed secession.   He
was often solicited to make the race for some official position, but always
declined.   His wife died in 1852.   The subject of this sketch was reared

and educated in Georgia, and graduated at Oglethorpe University in 1849, after which he at once began studying law under James L. Pettigrew, of Charleston, S. C., the foremost lawyer of his day. Owing to failing health the law course was not completed, and the winter of 1851–52 was spent in the Rocky Mountains for sport and health. In the summer of 1852 he made another trip to the Rockies, the journey being made up the Arkansas and down the Platte rivers, and during this time his health was greatly benefited. In 1854 he began planting in Georgia, but the life in the West had still its attractions for him, and in 1856 he made a trip to the base of Pike's Peak and spent one summer in that hunter's paradise, accompanied by a younger brother and a hired guide and camp servants. In 1860 he made a trip to Colorado, visiting Denver; its site on his former visits was a wilderness, then a city of 4,000 souls. The summer of 1859 had been spent in Texas, mainly in San Antonio, on a visit to George W. Kendall, of New Braunfels, and in 1860 he returned here, to permanently locate, and took up his residence in San Antonio. His health again failing him in 1861, he bought a ranch north of the city and retired there to reside until 1869, during which time he was engaged in the raising of cattle. In 1869 he went to Boerne, Texas, and there, in 1870, began practicing law, but seven years later located in San Antonio, where he has since resided, and for some time past has been retired. He has always been quite active in politics, and in 1872 was honored by an election to the State Senate, and was Chairman of the Committee on Indian Affairs, and a member of the Judiciary and other committees. He introduced a number of bills, and did able and effective work while a Senator, but after serving one term declined re-election. He was a member of the State Constitutional Convention of 1875, served on various important committees, and was Chairman of the Committee on Public Lands. He was appointed by Governor Coke, and also Governor Hubbard, a Commissioner of canal and ditches for navigation and irrigation, and has been Commissioner of the State for the sale and lease of school lands. He was appointed by President Harrison as a Democratic World's Fair Commissioner at Large from Texas, and as such did valuable work in that State. He was married in 1856 to Miss Jean Adams Parland, a native of Georgia, who died in 1891, having become the mother of seven children: Mary Parland, Martha Gibson, wife of W. W. King, of Georgia; Jean Parland, wife of J. Mastella Clarke, of Mexico, the proprietor and publisher of *The Two Republics;* Cornelia, Henry C., Jr., with *The Express;* and Sophia and Frances, twins, the latter of whom died in 1891. Mr. King is a member of the Presbyterian Church, is a Mason socially, and is a polished, courteous and scholarly gentleman, and is universally esteemed.

STEPHEN FULLER AUSTIN, born at Austinville, Wythe County, Virginia, November 3, 1793, entered the Colchester Academy in Connecticut, in 1804, the Academy at New London in 1805 and the Transylvania University in Kentucky in 1808. At the age of twenty-one years he was chosen a member of the Missouri Legislature and served in that body until 1819, when he moved to Little Rock, Arkansas, where he was appointed Circuit Judge. Shortly after, he became a resident of New Orleans, where he was to co-operate with his father, Moses Austin, in the colonization of Texas. In the pages devoted to the history of the English speaking colonies and the wars of Texas his name occurs often. As a military commander he had no ambition. As to his temper, he himself published that he was hasty and impetuous, and that he had forced upon himself a stringent discipline to prevent a fit of passion that might destroy his influence. In his disposition he was open-hearted, unsuspecting and accommodating almost to a fault. He was therefore often imposed upon, especially in the minor demands of benevolence and justice in social life. He excelled in a sense of equity, constancy, perseverance, fortitude, sagacity, prudence, patience under persecution, benevolence and forgiveness. He was never married. During the first years of his residence in Texas his home was at the house of S. Castleman, on the Colorado. Later, when his brother-in-law, James F. Perry, removed to the colony, he lived, when in Texas, with his sister at Peach Point plantation, in Brazoria county. Besides this sister he had a younger brother, named James Brown Austin, who was well known in Texas.

PAT. WHELAN. The official position which this gentleman is filling is one for which he seems to have a natural adaptability, for he is courageous, energetic, intelligent and wideawake—qualities which are most essential in the make-up of a good sheriff and collector. He owes his nativity to the Isle of Erin, where he was born in 1843, the eldest child of M. and Margaret (Murphy) Whelan, the latter of whom died in Ireland. Since 1870 the father has resided in America, in the city of Corpus Christi. Pat Whelan, in 1861, when but eighteen years of age, decided to seek his fortune in free America, and after landing in New York made his home in that city until 1865, when he came direct to Corpus Christi, and in the vicinity of that place worked on a ranch for a few years. In 1870 he was appointed to the position of City Marshal, then became Deputy Sheriff, and so efficiently did he discharge the duties of this position that in 1880 he was elected to the office of Sheriff, and has been re-elected at each successive election ever since, a fact which speaks eloquently as to his efficiency and popularity. For the past ten years he has been a member of the Sheriffs' Association of Texas, and in every way in his power strives to preserve order and lodge the law-breaker where he belongs, and to his credit be it said that he usually accomplishes his purpose. He has always been actively interested in politics and has served as a delegate to various State conventions. He was married in 1863 to Miss Joanna Whelan, a native of Ireland, and some of her relatives were among the very first settlers of Refugio county. To Mr. and Mrs. Whelan one daughter has been given, Margaret, wife of S. J. Ross, of Brooklyn, N. Y. Mr. and Mrs. Whelan are members of the Catholic Church.

JOHN S. MAYES. In the year 1852, John S. Mayes, who had grown up in Wilkinson County, Mississippi, and was possessed of the ambition, courage and sturdy manhood which have ever been distinguishing characteristics of American pioneers, made his way to Fort Bend County, Texas, and settled in this section, two miles west of Foster. He was born in Wilkinson county, Mississippi, in 1829 and is a son of John and Ann D. (Foster) Mayes, the latter a sister of Randolph Foster, now deceased, but who at one time was a very prominent citizen. John Mayes was one of the first settlers of Mississippi, participated in the war with the Indians, and was in the battle of New Orleans. He died in East Baton Rouge, La., when our subject was about eighteen years of age. Mrs. Mayes died in Texas, whither she had come with our subject in 1852, in the year 1872 when over seventy years of age. Both parents were members of the Baptist church. They reared a family of six children, of whom our subject is fourth in order of birth. The latter received his schooling in Woodville, Miss., but left his books when nineteen years of age and commenced trading in stock. About this time he came to Texas, and he drove stock from this State to Louisiana and Mississippi. In 1852 he came to his present property, as before stated, and now owns about 1,000 acres of as fine land as can be found in the county. In 1862 he joined Wilke's 24th Texas Cavalry, but was dismounted by Tom Hindman and afterwards was under Gen. Pat. Cleburne. He participated in many battles in Gen. Hardy's army corps and while at St. Louis was taken a prisoner and confined in McDowell's College, which was confiscated for the purpose. For three months he was kept a prisoner and was then detailed to help gather up conscripts in Texas. Although in a number of prominent engagments he was never severely wounded. At the close of the war he still kept on planting on his place in this county and made most of the improvements, although his older brother, Gordon Mayes, had improved the place to some extent. Our subject cleared up most of the land, but aside from this he was engaged in freighting and dealing in hides, etc., running a wagon to Houston once a week for three years. In the year 1870 Mr. Mayes married Miss Lucretia Foster, a daughter of Randolph Foster, who came to Texas with the Austin colony. Mr. Foster was in Houston's army and it is thought took part in the battle of San Jacinto. He has been dead quite a number of years. By this union three children were born to Mr. and Mrs. Mayes: John G., is now in business in Fulsher; Juliet, at home and Mitchell, at Fulsher engaged in business with his brother under the firm name of Mayes & Foster.

JAMES BOWIE, born in Georgia about the year 1790, settled in Catahoula parish, Louisiana, in 1802, with his parents, and in the "Twenties," became notorious in connection with a duel, fought on the sand-bar opposite Natchez by Dr. Maddox and Samuel Wells, which resulted in the wounding of fifteen and the death of six of the persons interested. Bowie's knife, made from a blacksmith's rasp by his brother Rezin, and used by him in the killing of Major Norris Wright, was sent to Philadelphia, fashioned into the form of a knife and named after the desperate character who used the steel first with such deadly effect. At Galveston, James, Rezin P. and John Bowie engaged in buying negroes from Lafitte's pirates and conducting them through the swamps of Louisiana; in 1819, James was attached to Long's expedition; in 1830, he became a naturalized citizen of Saltillo and by specious promises and exact life won the love of Señorita Veramendi of San Antonia de Bejar. On November 2, 1831, with nine other Americans and two negroes, he defeated 164 Tehuacan and Caddo Indians with the loss of one killed and three wounded, while eighty at least of the Indians lost their lives. In 1835, he broke away from all marital engagements, and in the battles of Nacogdoches and Conception, fought in 1835, opposed Mexican interests and continued so to do until killed at the Alamo, March 6, 1836.

LORENZO DE GAVALA, born at Merida, Yucatan, in 1781, was a physician of his native place down to 1820, when he was elected deputy to the Spanish Cortes. On returning from Spain, he was elected deputy and subsequently chosen Senator in the Mexican Congress. From 1827 to the outbreak of the Jalapa revolution in 1830, he was Governor of the State of Mexico; but then had to relinquish the office. In 1833, however, he was re-elected deputy and commissioned Governor of the old State; a joint resolution of Congress permitting him to hold both offices. In 1834, he was appointed Minister to

France; but resigned the portfolio and was appointed one of the commmissioners from Texas and Coahuila in 1834; was one of the signers of the Texan Declaration that year and the second Vice-president of the Texan Republic. He hoped with the aid of his English speaking friends and of the natives of the Republic to establish a dictatorship, not only over Texas, but also over Mexico, and might have carried out his plans had not death claimed him on November 15, 1836—eight months and nine days after his friends perished at the Alamo.

DAVID CROCKETT, born on the banks of the Nola Chucky River, Tennessee, August 17, 1786, was the son of John Crockett, one of the Irish soldiers of the American Revolution. His grandparents were massacred by the Indians, one uncle was wounded by them, and another captured. In 1798 his father apprenticed him to a Dutchman, who had settled in Virginia, but the youth did not appreciate his new position and soon set out for his distant home at the mouth of Limestone Creek, in Tennessee. A little later he started for Baltimore, with the object of becoming a sailor; but the man, on whose wagon he traveled, held his clothing and seven dollars in money, and may be said to have returned the prodigal to his parents. For some years he worked on the farm, when not engaged in hunting or making love to the two girls who jilted him. About the age of nineteen years, he met a girl who did marry him, and moved with him to Lincoln County, Tenn. In 1813 he enlisted in Capt. Jones' Company for the Creek War, and subsequently was commissioned Colonel in Jackson's Army during the campaign in Florida. The death of his wife shortly after his return made the way clear for his marriage with a soldier's widow, and with her he moved to Shoal Creek, where he served as Justice of the Peace, and in which district he was elected to the Legislature. Then he removed further into the wilderness, settling at Obion, Tenn., where he made hunting a profession. Re-elected to the State Legislature, he opposed Gen. Jackson for United States Senator, and offered himself as a candidate. Of course, the State would not spoil an uneducated, unpolished hunter, by sending him to the Senate; so that after adjournment he is found getting out a raft of lumber for the New Orleans market. In driving the Mississippi the lumber was lost, and Crockett returned to Obion to re-establish himself as a statesman. In 1827 he was elected a member of Congress, and re-elected in 1829. In 1831 he was defeated; in 1833 was re-elected, and in 1835 defeated. Vexed with Tennessee, he directed his steps towards Texas, where he enlisted a few adventurers like himself; beat a party of fifteen Texans who opposed him, and chased them to the Alamo, then commanded by Col. W. B. Travis. On March 6, 1836, he died within that fortress, pierced by the swords of the victors.

W. W. COCHRAN. This prominent merchant and farmer of Austin County, with postoffice at Cochran, has ever been interested in the growth and progress of Austin county, for he was born there December 7, 1836. His parents, James and Emeline (Foster) Cochran, were natives of New Hampshire and Louisiana respectively. James Cochran came here when single and immediately engaged in merchandising at San Felipe. He was one of the early settlers of the State, settling here in 1825, and merchandising continued to be his principal occupation until the War of 1836, when he became one of Houston's soldiers. He was on detail duty when the battle of San Jacinto was fought, and assisted in getting different families to places of safety. During his absence from San Felipe his store, with residence and contents, was burned, and when he returned home at the end of the war he had to build a new store and buy a new stock of goods, for all he had left was his land. In 1837 he moved close to where his son, W. W., is now living, and was here engaged in raising stock and farming on a small scale. At that time Houston was the principal trading point; milling was done at Chapel Hill, thirteen miles distant, and our subject remembers the time when he went there on horseback, bent under his two bushels of corn. Later on, Mr. Cochran erected the first mill and cotton gin in this section of the State. He was a prominent man in that section, and in 1840 was elected a member of the Congress of the Republic of Texas, having for his opponent Col. I. L. Hill, brother of Ben. Hill, of Georgia. He served one term and died in 1847. Mr. Cochran was a man much admired, not alone for his bright intellect and superior abilities, but for his admirable qualities as a citizen and neighbor. He taught school in other portions of the South before living in Texas, for he was but eighteen years of age when he left his native State. The Cochran's family was among the pioneer ones of the Granite State and Mr. Cochran was the first one of his family who came South. After residing here for some time and accumulating considerable property, he sent for two brothers, Thomas and Jeremiah, and one sister, Lucy A. Jeremiah participated in the battle of San Jacinto; Lucy A. married twice, first McHenry Winburn, by whom she had four children, only one of whom is now living, McHenry Winburn, who is warrant clerk in the Comptroller's office at Austin. Mrs. Winburn's second union was with Joseph Robison, a nephew of Joel Robison, and six children were born of this union. Mrs. Cochran's parents came to Texas in 1833 and settled near Hempstead, in Austin County. Mr. Foster was a farmer by occupation. He participated in the battle of San Jacinto, and was detailed to assist the families out of danger. He reared six children: Permelia, married Maclin Bracy; James was in the War of 1836; B. F., also a soldier in that war, residing in this county; Emeline, mother of subject; Evantha, married Judge Richardson Scurry, who was District Judge of this section, and a member of Congress from eastern Texas before the Civil War. He died during that time; Josiah, deceased, was in the War of 1848; Mr. Foster was also a soldier in that war. Of the thirteen children born to the parents of our subject, all grew to mature years and eleven married and reared families. All but four, as stated, remained in the East. James Cochran and wife were the parents of five children, three of whom grew up: W. W., our subject; J. D., resides in Cochran, where he is engaged in merchandising; James, deceased, was in the Confederate army. Mr. Cochran died in 1847, and Mrs. Cochran in 1870. About 1849 Mrs. Cochran was married to William S. Day, of Alabama. He was an attorney of Brenham, Washington County. This union resulted in the birth of seven children, three of whom reached mature years: Elish L., physician of Brenham; Evantha, wife of R. C. Wood, of Dallas, and J. H., a farmer of this State. The original of this notice was educated in Chapel Hill, and when nineteen years of age engaged in farming and stock-raising in this county. This he followed until 1862, when he enlisted in Company E., Twenty-first Texas Infantry, and served in the trans-Mississippi Department. In 1863 Mr. Cochran was dangerously ill and pronounced by physicians to be beyond their aid. At the end of six months he had recovered sufficiently to join Col. Ford's command in the western portion of Texas, and was placed on detail duty, serving in that capacity until

the war closed.   He never participated in any battles, and while on his way
home the war closed.   Farming and stock-raising were again resumed, but he
found that his property had been considerable damaged by the war.   In 1882
he engaged in merchandising, and about this time the Postoffice of Cochran
was established and named in honor of the family.   Since then Mr. Cochran
has been engaged in merchandising in connection with his farming, and has
met with success.   He has under cultivation 325 acres.   Mr. Cochran has
held a number of minor offices, County Commissioner, Justice of the Peace,
etc., and takes only passing interest in political affairs.   He was married in
the year 1858 to Miss Lucy Pier, sister of S. P. Pier, (see sketch), and they
are parents of one child: W. D., attorney of San Antonio, who was a member
of the Nineteenth Legislature from this county.   Mrs. Cochran died in 1880, and
in 1882 Mr. Cochran married Miss Mary S. Hucoby, a native of Alabama, and
daughter of Rev. John Hucoby, of that State, who came to Texas after the Rebellion.   Three children have been born to Mr. and Mrs. Cochran: Eva,
W. W. Jr., and Lillian.   Mr. and Mrs. Cochran hold membership in the M. E.
Church, and he is a Mason, a member of Bellville Lodge No. 223.   Politically he is a Democrat.

BURIENNE F. STEWART.   This successful and thriving agriculturist came
originally from Mississippi, his birth occurring in Wilkinson County, June
26, 1842, and for many years now he has been a resident of this county, where
all his interests are now centered.   He is far seeing, industrious and perse-
vering-characteristics which he has no doubt inherited from his Scottish ancestors, for his grandfather was a native of that country.   The latter came to
the United States and made Georgia his home, and when his son, B. C.
Stewart, the father of our subject, was a fair sized boy, moved to Wilkinson
County, Miss., where the remainder of his days were passed.   He was a
planter, and his son, B. C., also adopted that occupation and carried it on
successfully all his life.   He held the office of Supervisor of Wilkinson County
and was also Magistrate of same for some time.   Burienne F. Stewart spent
his school days in Wilkinson County, Miss., and at Centenary College, at Jackson, La., where he remained until June, 1861.   He then abandoned his books
and joined the Twenty-first Mississippi Regiment, under Col. Humphreys and
Gen. Barksdale, and continued in the same until the battle of Chickamauga, when
a bomb-shell took of his left arm.   Before that, he had participated in the
battle of Yorktown, Seven Pines, Richmond, Sharpsburg, Fredericksburg,
Chancellorsville and Harper's Ferry when the last surrendered.   His command took a prominent part in the battle of Gettysburg, and there Gen. Barksdale met his death.   Our subject, however, was sick at the time, and did not
participate in the engagement.   Upon his return to Mississippi, after the war,
Mr. Stewart commenced farming in Adams County, that State, below Natchez,
on the Mississippi River, and continued there until 1876, when he moved to
the Lone Star State and to his present farm.   He is now the owner of 1,000
acres of land, partly in the bottom of the Brazos, and the balance prairie, and
has experimented in fruit, small farming, etc., but makes a specialty of cotton
and stock-raising.   He is public-spirited and interested in the welfare of the
county, and gives his hearty support to all worthy measures.   He held the office
of County Commissioner for four years, at a time when it was a difficult
position to hold, and discharged the duties of the same in a very satisfactory
manner.   The year 1876 witnessed his marriage to Miss Margaret Ward, of

Wilkinson County, Miss., and to this union have been born eight children, three sons and two daughters now living and two sons and one daughter dead. Mr. and Mrs. Stewart are members of the Methodist Church and earnest workers in the same.

GEN. BEN MCCULLOCH. The family from which General McCulloch sprung was doubtless of Scotch-Irish origin, and in the distinguished general above named were the best qualities of both races. His great-grandfather came to this country prior to the Revolution, and in direct descent from him is Ben, Alexander and Ben, the latter being the subject of this sketch. His father married a Miss Frances Le Noir and settled in Nashville, Tenn., from which State he served with General Jackson in the War of 1812. He was a graduate of Yale College, of decided character and of generous disposition. He died in Dyer County, Tennessee, August 4, 1846, at nearly sixty-nine years of age, his birth having occurred in Virginia. He was a member of the Methodist Episcopal Church. His son Ben was born in Rutherford County, Tennessee, November 11, 1811, and at home he received a fair knowledge of the rudiments, but through much reading in later years he became an educated gentleman. During his youth he was engaged in farm work and found much diversion in hunting, for deer, turkey, bear and other game abounded. He was for a time engaged in flatboating and rafting, and in 1820 moved to Alabama with his parents. To follow his career through boyhood would be of the utmost interest. Suffice it to say that he was an industrious youth faithful to all his duties, and the promise he gave of rising to eminence was amply fulfilled. He was an intimate friend, notwithstanding the difference in their years, of the famous Davy Crockett and his son "Bill." About 1835 his career in Tennessee drew to a close and Texas became the scene of his activity, and his love for her grew and strengthened with the number of blows he gave and received in her service. He took an active part in the Texas Rebellion and commanded a piece of artillery at the battle of San Jacinto, and for bravery, of which Gen. Sam Houston was a witness, he was promoted to a First Lieutenancy. In 1836 he raised a company in Tennessee, but was not called into action, and in 1837 he returned to the State of his birth and fitted himself for surveying, and in February, 1838, began his work there, and at the same time participated in many engagements with the Indians after the battle of San Jacinto, the number of which will never be known. In 1839 he was influenced to become a candidate for Congress and was elected. About three weeks after this the Indians went on the war path and Mr. McCulloch again took the trail, and off and on for a number of years thereafter he was on the war path, the engagements with the Comanches being especially bloody and trying. He was chosen as Representative of the first Texas Legislature, served faithfully in that capacity, and showed his interest in the land of his adoption to be as deep and earnest as he had while fighting for her liberty with the Mexicans, during which he distinguished himself for bravery and had won a national reputation as a skillful and daring soldier. In 1849 he was seized with the "gold fever," and made the overland trip through Mexico to the port of Mazatpan, and thence by ship to San Francisco, and was afterwards elected Sheriff of Sacramento, and it is needless to say made an efficient officer. He returned to his Texas home in 1852, and the following year was appointed by President Pierce as Marshal for the District of Texas, a position he filled for eight years, during which

period he spent much time in the libraries of the national capital, studying the
text books upon the art of war.   During the Mormon troubles he accepted
the post of Commissioner, and through his wise and prudent measures a col-
lision was averted and the trouble with that turbulent people composed.   At
the opening of the Civil War he was tendered a Colonel's commission by Jefferson Davis, with authority to raise a Texas regiment for the Confederate
service, but declined for good reason, and in May of the same year was commissioned a Brigadier-General in the service of the Confederate States and
assigned to the command of the military district embracing the Indian Territory west of Arkansas, and discharged his duties with distinguished military
ability.   He afterward took conspicuous part in numerous battles in Missouri,
and in various hotly contested engagements brought order out of confusion,
when the chief commander was uncertain what to do, and so calm, cool and
collected was he at all times that he inspired all with confidence, and wherever he appeared, Louisians, Arkansans, Texans and Missourians greeted him
with enthusiastic cheers that spoke, in a manner impossible to be misunderstood, the confidence the men had in their General.   In that field in the west
General McCulloch was one of the towers of Southern strength, and it was to
his individual efforts on various occasions and his powers of generalship that
resulted in Confederate victories.   Very few men acquitted themselves of a
more delicate trust, imposing the very weightiest responsibilities, with greater
credit to themselves than General McCulloch did on the field of Oak Hills,
with which victory his name and fame are indissolubly wedded.   His reports
of the battle were modest and manly, and on all other occasions he showed
himself to be straightforward and accurate.   After the evacuation of Springfield the Texas regiment entered the place and was comfortably established
for the winter, through the good management and forethought of their gallant
commander.   Although he was often maligned and had many enemies, it cannot be denied that he possessed executive ability of the highest order and
was loved and respected by his men, who hesitated not to follow where he led,
and that was always in the hottest part of the engagement, although he wisely
did not uselessly expose his men to danger.   At the battle of Pea Ridge he
commanded a corps of Arkansas, Louisiana and Texas troops, and while riding forward to reconnoitre was killed by the bullet of a sharpshooter.   Thus
closed a gallant and useful career, in the prime of manhood.   Perhaps the
character of no public man was more misunderstood than that of General
McCulloch, for although he was called a ruffian, desperado, unpolished back-
woodsman, etc., he was, on the contrary, genial and kindly in disposition, the
idol of his men, a bold, graceful rider, a desperate fighter, a reckless charger,
and a courageous ranger, and Indian fighter of the highest type.   Had he
lived in the days of chivalry he would have been a knight of the superior
class, but having lived in the present day he was what may be truly termed a
great civilian and a distinguished soldier.

JUDGE EDWARD S. RUGELEY, SR.   Texas is known as a progressive State,
and contains many able and brainy professional men, among whom Judge
Edward S. Rugeley takes prominent rank.   His capacity, sound judgment,
and persevering industry are well known in Matagorda County, where he has
made his home for many years, and where he is classed among the representative citizens.   His father, John Rugeley, was born in South Carolina, and died
in Matagorda County in June, 1878, when eighty-four years of age.   The

father was educated in his native State, and after growing up moved to Alabama. This was in 1824. In 1840 he came to Texas, located on Caney Creek, about thirty miles above the town of Matagorda, and settled in the canebrake, where he improved an extensive plantation, and there passed the closing scenes of his life. He was a member of Congress in the Texas Republic, and was a member of the State Legislature in Alabama. Although very wealthy at one time, he lost heavily during the war, but retrieved his fallen fortune to some extent afterward. He married Miss Parthenia Irvin, who died in Alabama, leaving eight children, five sons and three daughters, our subject and Mary B. Rochelle, who is now a resident of DeSoto Parish, La., being the only survivors of the family. Mr. Rugeley was married again in Alabama, to Miss Eliza Colgin, now deceased, who bore him these children: H. L., a physician of Matagorda; Frank, a speculator of this county; Edgar, also residing here; Irvin, in this county, and Sarah, of Hays County, Texas. Judge Edward S. Rugeley received his early education in Alabama, and finished in Columbia College, in South Carolina, in 1841. Later he commenced the study of law, and was admitted to the bar in 1845, when twenty-three years of age, his birth occurring in South Carolina September 12, 1822. Immediately after being admitted he located at Matagorda, and had a flattering practice for several years. His professional career is a credit to the county, while his prosperity is well deserved, notable, and permanent. Many years ago he gave up his practice and commenced planting on Caney River, and continued this until about six years ago, when he was elected County Judge and rented his plantation. During the great storm of 1875 he was a member of the Constitutional Convention sitting at Austin, Texas, but resigned that position to come home. In 1861 he was in the State service, and in November he joined Bates' Regiment and held the rank of Captain. Most of the time he was in the State of Texas guarding the State line to repel invasion, and at one time commanded the post at Matagorda. In May, 1865, he left the service with limited means, and had to commence from the start again. Gradually ascending upon the plane of success, he is now one of the substantial men of the county, and is surrounded by every comfort. Judge Rugeley was married in Alabama, in 1845, to Miss Mary E. Smith, and to them were given four sons and three daughters, as follows: Smith, a planter of Caney River; Frank, a merchant in Matagorda; Edward, is a planter; Caroline D., is now Mrs. Blair of this place; Lelia, is Mrs. Elmore, of Caney River, and Mary B., is Mrs. Brooks, of Wharton. Mrs. Rugeley is a member of the Methodist Church. In his early life Judge Rugely was a Whig, and for many, many years now he has been an ardent supporter of Democratic principles. For forty years he has been advocating the removal of the county seat, and in the recent movement for that purpose took an active part.

JOHN G. PHILLIPS. The nature of man is so complex, his individuality so pronounced, his process of reasoning so varied and peculiar, that no two human beings are ever found to be nearly alike. Some men snatch success from the very jaws of failure, some are alternately prosperous and unfortunate, while a few are so evenly balanced that their lives appear to be utterly free from friction. Their course is steadily onward, and from youth to maturity there is no indication of a single backward step. Thus it has been with John G. Phillips, a prominent rancher of Brazoria County, and a man who has slowly and surely made his way to the front in his chosen occupation.

The father of our subject, James R. Phillips, with a brother, Sidney, moved to Texas at a very early date, and there passed the remainder of his days. Sidney, his brother, fought bravely in the battle of San Jacinto. James R. married Mrs. Mary (Pentecost) Rector, the widow of Mr. Rector, who was a farmer and a prominent stockman west of Columbia for many years. Of the four children born to Mr. and Mrs. Phillips, our subject was the youngest. At the early age of nine years he started out to fight his own way in life, and his first venture was in the stock business. He was first with Cornelius Davis, but subsequently engaged in business for himself, eight miles north of Columbia, and success has smiled upon his efforts. He is well known throughout the county, and is highly esteemed, not alone for his industry and perseverance, but for his estimable qualities as a citizen and neighbor. Mr. Phillips selected his wife in the person of Miss Jennie D. Price, daughter of Dr. Jacob Price, who is now engaged in the milling business at Beaumont, Texas.

JUDGE WESLEY OGDEN. After the burden and heat of the day this able judge and enterprising citizen has retired from the active duties of life, and is in the enjoyment of a competency which his early industry brought him. He is a product of Monroe County, N. Y., born in 1817, the fifth child of Benjamin and Lucy (Johnson) Ogden, who were natives of the Keystone State. The paternal grandfather, William Ogden, was a Pennsylvanian, and his father was one of two brothers who came to this country from England, one settling in Pennsylvania and the other in New York. William was a soldier of the Revolution, and afterward settled on a large tract of land at the head of the Ohio River. The maternal ancestors were of German descent, but the maternal grandfather, Moses Johnson, was born in Pennsylvania. Benjamin Ogden and Lucy Johnson were married in Pennsylvania, and moved to Monroe County, N. Y., about the beginning of the present century, settling in the wilderness as a farmer. He was an officer of the War of 1812, and was a participant in the battle of Lundy's Lane under Gen. Scott. He died in 1833, his wife having passed from life during the infancy of the subject of this sketch. Although Judge Wesley Ogden was reared in a wild country, he was fairly well educated, and spent several years in an academy and a year at Brockport College. He began life for himself as a teacher in Summit County, Ohio, after which he began the study of law at Akron, Ohio, and was admitted to the bar there in 1845. He then returned to Rochester, N. Y., and taught school in that city from 1845 to 1849, but during this time his physician ordered him South, owing to his failing health, and in the last-mentioned year he arrived in Port Lavaca, Texas. He had been seriously afflicted with lung trouble, but in six months' time he had almost fully recovered. He at once began the practice of law at Port Lavaca, and in 1866 was appointed District Attorney for the old Tenth District by the Federal authorities, and held that office for about a year, and was then appointed District Judge of the same, the duties of which office he ably discharged until the fall of 1870. In that year he was appointed by Governor Davis one of the Judges of the Supreme Court of Texas, and held that office about four years, the last year being Presiding Justice, in which capacity he served until the close of Gov. Davis' administration.

In 1874 he began practicing at San Antonio, continuing to 1888, since which time he has lived in retirement, remote from the strife and turmoil of political and professional life. He was married in 1845 to Miss Church, but she died in Texas in 1853, leaving three children: Helen, wife of Sam M. Johnson; Henry, who died in 1865, and Charles W. a lawyer of San Antonio. In the latter part of 1858, Judge Ogden married again, his wife being Miss Elizabeth H. Chichester, of New York, and five children have been given them: Lilian, wife of Edward F. Glaze; Mary S., Alma, wife of William Brooke, son of Gen. Brooke; William B., of Eagle Pass, and Ida. Judge Ogden has been an active Republican all the days of his life in Texas, and is a grand old man, highly esteemed and respected. His life has been useful and well spent, and at the close of his career it can with truth be said of him, " well done, thou good and faithful servant."

JOSE ANTONIO NAVARRO. Jose Antonio Navarro, in whose honor Navarro County was named, was born in San Antonio de Bejar, February 27, 1795, his father having been a native of Corsica and an officer in the Spanish army. He was a stanch Federalist and a foe to military despotism. In 1834–35 Navarro was a land commissioner for Bejar District; a member of the Convention in 1836, and a member of the Congress in 1838–39. He was condemned by Santa Anna to imprisonment for life, though during his captivity he was several times offered pardon, liberty, and high office if he would abjure his native country, Texas, forever. These propositions were rejected with scorn. In December, 1844, just before the fall of Santa Anna, he was removed from San Juan de Uloa and allowed to remain a prisonor at large in Vera Cruz, whence he escaped January 2, arriving at Galveston February 3, 1845, after an absence of more than three years and a half. On his return he was elected delegate to the convention held that year to decide upon the question of annexation, and was afterward Senator from Bejar District in the State Congress. He died in his native city in 1870.

JUDGE ISAAC BARTON McFARLAND. This prominent old citizen of Rockford, Texas, is a product of Tennessee, where he was born in 1819, the oldest child of Robert and Hannah (Barton) McFarland, who were Virginians by birth. The paternal grandfather, Robert McFarland, Sr., was descended from a Scotch family that settled in the Old Dominion during colonial times, and he became a soldier of the Revolutionary War, and was afterwards a Colonel in some of the engagements against the Creek Indians, and also the Cherokees, in Alabama. He became Sheriff of the county in which he lived in Tennessee, and served also as a member of the State Legislature. He became a pioneer settler to Tennessee, and there was called from life. The maternal grandfather, Rev. Isaac Barton, was also born in Virginia, and when very young became a minister of the Baptist Church. He went to Tennessee when that State was a wilderness, and located in the same part of the State as Mr. McFarland, where he became well known in his ministerial capacity. He died in 1832 when nearly ninety years old, and seventy years of this time were spent in expounding the gospel, which he continued almost up to the day of his death. He was of English descent. Robert McFarland, Jr., (father of I. B.), was a tanner by occupation (and the son worked in the yard when a boy), and the father, up to the day of his death in 1844, kept a yard. He was Lieutenant in the regular army of a rifle company on the Northwest frontier in 1812–13, at Ft. Erie and other places, and was commanding a company at the battle of Sandy Creek, as well as at other places. For over twenty years he held the office of Justice of the Peace in Jefferson County, his home in Tennessee. His first wife died when the subject of this sketch was an infant, and Mr. McFarland afterwards married again and reared two sons, William, an ex-member of Congress from Tennessee, and Robert, a Major in the Confederate service, and after the war one of the Supreme Judges of Tennessee, now deceased; and five daughters. The subject of this sketch was born in Dandridge, the county seat of Jefferson County, Tennessee, and raised in that county. He received very limited educational advantages for some time, then attended a good private school, conducted by the Rev. Mr. Doak, near Greenville, Tenn. At the age of twenty-two years he began the study of law at Boonville, Mo., in the office of Stuart & Miller, and was admitted to practice there in 1845. The same year he came to Texas, located at LaGrange, entered upon the practice of his profession and met with marked success in his efforts to adjust the difficulties of his neighbors. He for a long time held the position of County Judge, and while on the bench discharged his duties with marked ability; also served one term in the Legislature. In 1865 he moved to Austin, and the same year was appointed District Judge of that district, an office held one year, at the end of which time he was appointed District Judge on the Gulf Coast, and remained on that circuit for about two years. In 1870 he, under a new constitution, was appointed Judge of another district, moved to Brenham and held that office, with the exception of one term, until 1890. The judge, in all, has served twenty-four years on the bench (district and county) in several districts, during which time he showed impartial fairness, an earnest and laudable desire to adjust the wrongs of the oppressed and punish crime, and in the discharge of his duties showed that he was a keen judge of human nature. His practice as a lawyer began with the new constitution, after the annexation of the State, in the spring of 1846, but since 1890 he has been retired and is enjoying a comfortable home in Rockport. He was married in 1845 in Missouri to Adaline, daughter of William George, a prosperous farmer of Missouri, who died about 1850. Mrs. McFarland was born in Tennessee, and is still living, and has borne her husband five children: William Robert, now in California; Julian, a resident of Brenham; Bates, a lawyer of Rockport, was admitted to practice at Austin in 1874; Frederick, who died Sept. 19, 1873, at the age of eighteen years; and Martha, who died in infancy. Judge and Mrs. McFarland are members of the Cumberland Presbyterian Church, and socially he belongs to the F. & A. M., in which he is a Knight Templar. He is a member of the Blue Lodge, Chapter and Commandery of Brenham, and is well known in Masonic and professional circles.

CAPT. PEYTON RANDOLPH MITCHELL. This prominent citizen of Nueces County, Texas, was born in Harrodsburg, Mercer County, Kentucky, in 1827, the eldest son born to William and Annie (Bohon) Mitchell, natives respectively of Virginia and Kentucky. The paternal grandfather, William Mitchell, was born in Ireland, but came to this country during colonial days, and settled in Virginia, from which State he enlisted in the Colonial army during the Revolution, serving under Gen. Washington throughout the entire war. He moved to Indiana during the territorial days, and there several of his sons became prominent in public affairs, Robert holding the position of District Judge for some time. The grandfather reached the patriarchal age of 110 years. The maternal grandfather, John Bohon, was a French Hugenot, who took refuge on the Island of San Domingo, and afterwards settled in South Carolina during the early settlement of the country. He attached himself to Gen. Marion's staff during the Revolution, and served with him until the war closed, when he went to Virginia, and was there married to Ann Ransdale, of Scotch descent, and with his young wife joined Daniel Boone and went to Kentucky and became one of the founders of Harrodsburg. He and his family at first lived in a blockhouse, to protect themselves from the Indians, and in that State he and his wife eventually died, leaving a large family. William Mitchell, father of the subject of this sketch, was reared in Indianapolis, Ind., and after attaining his majority went to Kentucky and was there married and made his home until 1833, when he moved to Pettis County, Mo., where he became a wealthy farmer. He died in Pettis County, Mo., at the age of ninety-four years, in 1867, and his wife died in 1856. Peyton R. Mitchell was six years old when he accompanied his parents to Missouri, and as the country was very new and unsettled at that time, he grew up with limited advantages. At the age of eighteen years he desired to enlist in the Mexican War, but was prevented from so doing by his father, so he ran away from home, went to Fort Leavenworth, joined Gen. Price, and became a teamster in his regiment, in which capacity he served in New Mexico, assisting in the capture of Fernando de Yaos, in which engagement he was slightly wounded. After serving as a teamster in Mexico for some time he fought as a volunteer teamster, and was in the battle of Sacramento, Mexico. He did not return to Missouri after the war was over, but joined a. friend, Jim Hickman, and clerked in a store at Chihuahua, where he remained one year, then joined a trader and came to San Antonio, then to his home in Missouri. He soon entered Pleasant Ridge College, which he attended four years, after which he was engaged in teaching for about two years in the same institution. For some time thereafter he was engaged in the border warfare in Kansas and Missouri, and was at the burning of Lawrence and Ossawattomie, during which time he held the rank of Lieutenant. In the fall of 1857 he came to Goliad, Texas, and began trading in horses and cattle, and in 1859 drove a herd of one thousand beeves to the city of Chicago. Upon his return he opened a livery stable at Goliad, which he conducted until the opening of the Civil War, when he assisted, in raising a company, and upon the organization of the regiment was elected Lieutenant of Company E, 8th Texas Infantry. He was afterwards appointed Adjutant General, and served on the Texas frontier on the Gulf Coast, and was at the battle of Corpus Christi. After the battle of Galveston, in which he took part, he, in 1864, was promoted to Captain, and defended Padre Island with his company until the war terminated. In 1861 he was married to Miss Ellen Uzenia Steen, a native of Louisiana, and a daughter of Major John C. Steen, an early and prominent settler of Texas. He soon after the war bought a ranch in Bee County, and engaged in the stock business, and in 1870 began driving cattle on the trail to Kansas, continuing until 1874. At that time he bought stock and became one of the business managers of the Colman-Fulton Pasture Co., with which organization he was connected for eight years, it being one of the largest ranches in the State. They shipped largely to New Orleans and Cuba, but in 1884 he sold his interest, came to Corpus Christi and engaged in merchandising, a business that occupied his time and attention up to 1890, since which he has been devoting his attention to the real estate business. In 1865–66 he served as Surveyor of Bee County, but he has by no means been an office-seeker. He and his wife have two daughters: Mrs. A. E. Aikman, of San

Antonio, and Celeste, a student of that place. Mr. Mitchell and his wife
are members of the Christian Church, and he is a Mason and Odd Fellow.

  NEHEMIAH COCHRAN. Exchange and barter are two of the world's most
important factors, and without these the public would indeed find themselves
in a sad plight. The calling of the merchant as well as that of the farmer,
is one of the oldest, as well as one of the most honorable, of all lines of industry. Nehemiah Cochran, a prominent merchant and farmer of Austin
County, was born here June 28, 1836, the son of Thomas and Betsie P.
(Walker) Cochran, natives of the Granite State. His father came to this
State in 1834 in company with Amber Underwood and Robert Cochran, the
latter of whom was killed at the battle of the Alamo. Thomas Cochran was a
brickmason by trade, but after moving to Texas he engaged in farming and
stock-raising, like the majority of the citizens there. In 1836 he joined his
fortune with the Republic of Texas, but was not in the battle of San Jacinto,
he being on detail to see after the safety of the women and children. When
Mr. Cochran first came to the State he did not bring his wife and children,
but in the fall of 1835 he returned to New Hampshire for her and also was
accompanied by his brother, Jeremiah, and sister, Lucy Ann (see sketch of
W. W. Cochran), when he returned to the Lone Star State. Jeremiah fought
in the battle of San Jacinto. Thus, like the women of Carthage, though
they did not cut off their hair for bow strings, yet they exposed themselves to the
cruelty of Mexicans, who were more relentless than the Roman soldiers under the relentless General Scipio. Mr. Cochran offered his services to the
United States in the war with Mexico, but was not accepted, as the war closed
about this time. Thomas Cochran died in 1877, when sixty-five years of age,
and his wife passed away in 1887, when she had passed her seventy-first
birthday. They were the parents of eight children: Sarah, deceased, was
born in New Hampshire; Nehemiah, subject; Ann, widow of Matt Henson;
Milan, deceased; Thomas M., died and was buried in Louisiana while serving in the Confederate army; Mary, deceased, was the wife of K. Collins;
Emily, wife of S. B. Pier, and Talconia, the wife of G. H. Buch, of this
county. Nehemiah Cochran was educated in this county, attending the common schools, and when twenty-one years of age very naturally selected the
occupation to which he had been reared, farming and stock-raising, as his
occupation in life. That he continued until 1861, when he joined the Confederate army, Company C, Waller's Battalion, of which he was subsequently made
Third Lieutenant. He was attached to Green's brigade and served in the trans-
Mississippi Department, principally through Arkansas and Louisiana, and participated in the battles of Pleasant Hill, Mansfield and all the engagements fought
with Banks clear to Alexandria. Following the battle of Pleasant Hill, Mr.
Cochran acted as Assistant Quartermaster for Waller's Battalion. Mr. Cochran
was home on a furlough when the war closed. In 1860 he had purchased a
stock of merchandise, for which he had given a mortgage on his place to secure the payments, so that at the close of the war he was in a worse condition
by far than if he had never engaged in the mercantile business. He had to
at once devise means for paying off the mortgage, and he began raising cotton, and also engaged in the stock business, in which he was very successful.
In 1872 he again returned to merchandising, in Buckhorn, and continued
without intermission until 1893, since which time he has followed farming and stock-raising. Mr. Cochran has now about 300 acres, besides large

tracts of pasture land, all of which he has accumulated by industry and good management since the war. In 1866 Mr. Cochran was elected to the lower House of Representatives of Texas, during the time that Throckmorton was Governor. In 1878 Mr. Cochran was again elected to the same office, Governor Roberts being elected Governor the same year. During the last term Mr. Cochran was Chairman of the Committee on Roads and Bridges and other public improvements. He was married in 1865 to Miss Malinda Collins, a native of Texas and daughter of John W. and Malinda (Bush) Collins, early settlers of Texas. Mr. and Mrs. Cochran had but one daughter, Laura A., wife of J. W. Foster. Mrs. Cochran died in 1869. In 1871 Mr. Cochran married Miss Florence Montgomery, a native of Indiana, and the daughter of McGrady and Minerva (Lucas) Montgomery, who came from Indiana to Texas in 1852. Though Mr. Montgomery was in Texas in 1836 and served in the war against Mexico, he returned to Indiana, but later again returned to this State. To Mr. and Mrs. Cochran were born seven children: Thomas N., a merchant and farmer; Carrie E., John F., Elizabeth, Sarah, deceased; Mary, and Irad. Mr. and Mrs. Cochran are active members of the Methodist Episcopal Church South, in which Mr. Cochran is Steward, and he is also one of the trustees of the property of the church for this district. Politically he is a Democrat.

DANIEL J. DEWALT. Living on the celebrated Oyster Creek, Fort Bend County, Texas, on the plantation where he was born in 1861, is the subject of this sketch, who is the son of T. W. and Charlotte DeWalt. The father was born in the Palmetto State, and when a young man went to Brazoria County, Texas, where he met and married Miss Brown. When the gold excitement in California was intense, he had a severe attack of the gold fever, and, like many others, made his way to the Pacific coast. One year later, on his return through Mexico, he brought horses to the prairies of Texas, where his son, Daniel J., now lives, and subsequently brought his family there. On that farm his death occurred in 1874, when about fifty-two years of age. His wife died soon after. During the Civil War he served as Captain of a company in the Confederate army, and was stationed at Galveston and on the coast most of the time. He was an attorney, and for some time held the office of Justice of the Peace, and had a fine law library. After settling in Texas, he was engaged in raising cane and cotton, and was preparing to engage in the former on an extensive scale at the time of his death. He was a Mason, and in politics supported the Democracy. Mr. DeWalt was a very successful business man, and became the owner of 4,672 acres of rich bottom land, 1,000 head of horses, 500 head of cows, and made a specialty of raising fine horses. Mrs. DeWalt was a church member and an excellent woman. One child besides our subject was born to their marriage, Thomas W., who died August 24, 1894, had been County Clerk of Fort Bend County, but at the time of his death was selling goods at Planter's store. Daniel J. DeWalt spent his school days in different parts of the country. For two years he was at De LaSalle Institute, Toronto, Canada, two years in Pampapike College, near Richmond, two years in Roanoke College, Virginia, and passed high examinations in mathematics and philosophy. When nineteen years of age he left the school-room and was authorized by the court to settle up his father's estate. He found that it was in debt, and he went to work, stock-raising and cotton-planting, paid it off, and last year engaged in the sugar culture, erecting a large sugar-house. Mr. DeWalt has been engaged in various enterprises, selling goods, raising vegetables for Northern markets, and has never known what failure was. Full of energy and good sound sense, he has made his way to the front in every enterprise he has undertaken, and now owns a plantation on the Brazos river consisting of 1,200 acres, another of about 1,200 acres on Oyster Creek, and a residence plantation of 1,100 acres, on the prairie. He has an orchard consisting of ten acres of Lecompte pear trees. He is also engaged in various other enterprises that net him big returns. When he first left school he was obliged to go to work and earn part of the money that had been spent for his education. He has put all the improvements on his fine place, and has made it pay from the start. In the year 1889 he was married to Miss Lou Cessna, who was probably born in Fort Bend or Brazoria County, and who is a daughter of C. K. Cessna. He is a member of the Executive Committee of the Democratic party, and has never had time to accept official honors at the hands of the same.

TRAVIS L. SMITH. The unusual success of him whose name heads this sketch, is the result of persevering and well-directed effort in the line of his native talent. He has a purpose in life, and works with all will for its attainment. He and his brother, John G. Smith, are classed among the most successful business men of the county, having first branched out for themselves on a limited scale in Columbus. Since then their business has increased to such proportions that they now have branch stores at ·Brazoria, Chenango, Wharton, West Columbia and Valasco. Both of the Messrs. Smith brothers are gentlemen of more than ordinary executive ability and refinement. The geniality and courtesy with which their business relations are marked, cause them to also be favorites in society as well. Travis L. Smith was also born in Matthew County, Va., in 1852, and is a son of Thomas Smith, a Virginian, whose death occurred in that State when he reached his sixtieth year. Young Smith attended the schools of his native county, secured a fair education, and came to Texas in 1871 to join his brother, John G. Smith, who was then a salesman for Dr. Weems. For a few months after this he was employed in a hide house in Galveston, and his brother, in 1872, opened a general mercantile store at Columbia, first on a very modest scale, but our subject joined him, and, as business increased, opened stores in different cities of the county. They met with success from the first, and all their stores are stocked with a superior grade of goods. Aside from this the brothers own about 20,000 acres of the finest land in Texas, or in the world, and also have several steamboats on the river between Columbia and Galveston. They have not been so taken up with their various enterprises that they have neglected their duties as citizens, on the contrary, they are interested in all worthy movements, and give liberally of their means to further the same. They are interested in the development of this county, and have contributed their share towards its advancement. Their steamboats are the Hiawatha and Alice Blair, and they own the ferry at Columbia and other places. Our subject has charge of the Columbia business, and thoroughly understands every detail of merchandising. He was married in 1873, to Miss Nettie Masterson, daughter of Judge T. G. Masterson, who was an old and prominent citizen of this county. Socially Mr. Smith is a K. of H. and Mrs. Smith is a member of the Episcopal Church.

ROBERT H. WILLIAMS (deceased). All may glean from the life of this citizen much that will be of benefit to them in their future career, for he was not only recognized as a man of superior ability, but one whose honesty and upright-ness were never questioned. Self-made and self-educated, all his success in life was due to his great industry, preseverance and progressiveness. Born in Caswell County, N. C., October 10, 1796, he continued to make his home there until about twelve years of age, when he went to Shelbyville, Tenn., and there obtained employment. When grown he went from there to Mississippi, and thence in 1823 to Texas, being one of the original Austin Three Hundred. Later he came to Madagorda County, and located on the Robert H. Williams' grant, where he opened his land in 1824. He resided there and in Matagorda until his death. In 1825 he was appointed by Stephen F. Austin, Alcade of the district embracing Wharton and Matagorda counties. He held that position for seven years, and was then elected as a delegate to the Convention that sent Austin to Mexico, where that gentleman was imprisoned. Our subject was in many engagements with the Indians, took part in the battle of Velasco, May 17, 1832, and there lost one of his eyes by a gunshot. He furnished provisions for the soldiers during the Revolution, and was very useful in other ways. Mr. Williams was married in Jackson County, Texas, to Miss Mary Lawson White, daughter of B. J. White, one of the signers of the Dec-laration of Texas' Independence. Mrs. Williams was born in Alabama, and died in 1886, when seventy eight years of age. Mr. Williams met with unus-ual success as a planter, became unusually well off, but lost very heavily dur-ing the war. In fact, he lost all but his land; his son, Dr. Williams, of this county, now has $40,000 in Confederate bonds and money that belonged to his father. The latter believed thoroughly in the ultimate success of the Con-federacy, and just before the emancipation bought twenty-seven slaves. He never sought political honor, but gave his entire time to planting, which brought in good returns. To his marriage were born five children, two sons and three daughters: Christopher H., Lydia E., wife of Geo. W. Caldwell, who is now deceased. She resided in San Antonio; Mary L. wife of Dr. J. T. Fry, is now deceased; Laura R., wife of George P. Bass, and Robert H., Jr., who was accidently killed when sixteen years of age. Dr. Williams was born February 28, 1838, in the stockade built on R. H. Williams' place on Caney Creek. He spent his school days in the University of Nashville, and later attended medical college at the old Louisiana School of Medicine. In 1859 he left school and returned to planting, which he continued up to the breaking out of the war. In 1861 he received an appointment from Jeff. Davis as First Lieutenant of Infantry, and he reported to Gen. Hebert, at Houston. For five months he was in the latter place drilling soldiers, and was then sent to Louisiana, but a short time afterwards was sent back to Texas, and stationed at the mouth of the Brazos River. He had charge of the fort at the mouth of Bernard and here had some trouble with an ironclad, only three shots being exchanged at first, however. The vessel then moved back for repairs, and afterwards shelled the fort all day. Dr. Williams now has two shells ornamenting his gate posts. From there he was ordered to Brownville, on the Rio Grande, under Gen. Slaughter, and while there our subject was pro-moted to the rank of Captain. At the close of the Civil War he took charge of his father's place, which he carried on until the death of the latter. During the year 1867 he went to Galveston, and remained there for three years, but since that time he has resided in this county. His place, "Rotherwood", is on Caney Creek, and Rotherwood Lake is on the place. Dr. Williams is Justice of the Peace and Notary Public, and only accepted the position to keep incompetent people out. Recently he was nominated County Commissioner, for which office he is eminently fitted. In 1861 he was married to Miss Theresa Herbert, daughter of Dr. Herbert, and a native of this county. Four children blessed this union: Mrs. Jane Spillman, of Galveston, and Mrs. John Rugeley, of this county. Mrs. Williams died in 1873. Two died young. The doctor's second union occurred May 30, 1881, and Mrs. Alice B. Heidt, a grand-daughter of Dickson H. Lewis, of Alabama, and sister of Judge Rugeley, became his wife. Five children were given to them: Christopher H., Jr.; Jessie M., Ada C., Robert H., and Carlisle H., who is now ten years of age, and is attending the San Antonio schools. Mrs. Williams is a member of the Methodist Church, and both the worthy doctor and his wife are highly esteemed.

JOHN W. THORNTON, one of the early settlers of Austin County, was born in Oglethorpe County, Ga., April 19, 1832, a son of Carlton Crawford and Mary (Wise) Crawford, natives, respectively, of Georgia and Virginia. The Wise family removed to Georgia when Mrs. Thornton was a child, and there she married Mr. Thornton. In 1836 they removed to Hinds County, Miss., and there they both died, Mr. Thornton in 1872. The Thornton family were well-to-do people of social prominence in Hinds County, Miss. Mr. Thornton was not an office-seeker, but was influential politically. After the death of his first wife, in 1845, he married again. By his first marriage he had the following named children: Judith, who married O. Flowers, and is now deceased; John W., the immediate subject of this sketch; Sophronia, who married James Porter, of Texas, and is deceased; Elizabeth, the wife of Samuel Carroll, of Utica, Hinds County, Miss.; Sarah, the wife of Anthony Crockett, of Tyler, Texas; Nancy, who married William Brown, of Victoria, Texas; Mary Fleming, who married James Porter after the death of Sophronia; Thomas H., of Tyler, Texas, a well-known wholesale and retail grocery merchant. By his second marriage Mr. Thornton had one son, who lives in Mississippi. John W. Thornton received his education in the township schools of Hinds County, Miss. Leaving school at seventeen, he was for two years in charge of his father's plantation in Hinds County, Miss. In 1853 he came to Texas, and located in Fort Bend County, and engaged in stock-raising, bringing with him a capital of some $3,000. By the time the war began he had accumulated considerable property, mostly in cattle. His patriotism impelled him then to join Company F, of the Twenty-fourth Texas Cavalry, a famous regiment of horse (afterwards dismounted), which was under command of Colonel Wilkes. He served in the trans-Mississippi campaign, and on the 12th of January, 1863, was taken prisoner at Arkansas Post. After being held a prisoner of war at City Point, Va., and at Springfield, and Camp Douglas, Ill., he was exchanged in May, 1863, and joined the First Consolidated Texas Regiment, temporarily commanded by General Whitfield. He served mostly on garrison duty, in the Army of Virginia, until the fall of 1863, when he was transferred to the Army of Tennessee, and served under General Bragg, participating in the battles of Chickamauga, Lookout Mountain, Missionary Ridge, Ringold, Atlanta, Resaca and Peach Tree Creek, and numerous other engagements. After the fall of Atlanta he served under Hood in the Tennessee campaign, and participated in the battles of Franklin and Nashville. After the retreat into North Carolina by way of Mobile, he fought under Gen. Joseph E. Johnston, at Benton, N. C., and surrendered with Johnston at Hillsboro, N. C., in April, 1865. He was paroled a month later, and came home, the United States Government furnishing him transportation so far as practicable. The journey from Hillsboro, N. C., to Nashville, Tenn., was made mostly on foot. From that place, by means of Government transportation, he made his way more easily to Texas, arriving at home in June, 1865. He now found himself stripped of most of his earthly possessions, and had to begin life anew, and it was not until about 1871, that he may be said to have recovered from the effects of the war. It was about this time that he removed from Fort Bend County to San Felipe, Austin County, where he lived until 1887, when he removed to Sealy, Austin County, where he has since lived. Since locating here he has served most of the time as Deputy Sheriff. He was married in March, 1853, to Miss Mary J. Silliman, a native of Mississippi, daughter of Abram and Mary (Frisby) Silliman, who had removed to Texas in 1852. Of their eight children three died young, and the following survive, another, Oliver C., having died: Lelia O., wife of Frank B. Chilton, of Austin; Mary, wife of George E. Morse, of Houston; Florence, who has been for ten years a teacher at El Paso; Nancy, also a teacher. Mrs. Thornton died in 1871, and in November, 1872, Mr. Thornton married Mrs. Sarah J. Pratt, *nee* Munger, whose parents, Albert and Sarah (Earl) Munger, came early to Texas, where her father became interested in the patriot movement, and fought at San Jacinto, and later was known as one of the oldest settlers in central and southern Texas. They have one daughter, Mattie, who is a teacher at Carlton College, Bonham, Texas.

DR. A. B. GARDNER. To form an estimate of a man's success in life it is necessary to know what he has accomplished. In studying his life and character we are naturally led to inquire into the secret of his success, and the motives that prompted his action. The following is a brief sketch of the oldest resident physician of Bellville as well as one of its most successful ones. Dr. A. B. Gardner is a native of the Blue Grass State, born in Warren County, November 7, 1852, and the second child born to the marriage of A. B. and Rebecca (Elam) Gardner, natives of Virginia and Tennessee. A. B. Gardner, Sr., was one of the pioneer settlers of Warren County, Kentucky, going there in 1818, from Virginia, when a young man, and he there followed farming for many years. He served his country in the War of 1812 and was Lieutenant-colonel of a regiment of Virginia, participating in the battle of New Orleans where was wounded. He was three times married, his first union taking place just before emigrating to Kentucky. Mr. Gardner was ever interested in political affairs, and was a great admirer of Henry Clay. In the year 1848 he represented his county in the Kentucky Legislature on the Whig ticket, and remained a member of the same for two terms. Although opposed to secession he was a son of Virginia, and of course his sympathies were with the South, and he identified himself with her interests as much as his age would permit. For about ten years he held the office of Justice of the Peace after the Civil War, and possessing rare qualities, both personal and social, he enjoys the esteem of all who know him. With a record unsullied and to the regret of all he passed away in 1876, when eighty-six years of age. As before stated he was three times married and the father of fourteen children, two by his first union, seven by the second, and five by the third. Ten of these children lived to be grown, and a son of the second wife served in the Confederate army. Of the five children born to the third marriage, four reached mature years, as follows: Minerva, wife of T. J. Carter, of Bonham, Texas; A. B., subject; Rachel, wife of J. M. Williams, of Oakland, Ky., and Ella. The mother of these children, a most excellent woman, passed away in 1884, when seventy years of age. At her hands our subject received the most of his educational training during his youthful days, the war interfering with his schooling, and to her he attributes much of his success in life. In 1869 he entered the University of Kentucky, at Lexington, and after remaining there one session, 1871, commenced the study of medicine at Smith Grove, Ky. In the fall of the latter year he entered the University of Louisville, and graduated in the class of 1874. The same year he came to Texas and located at McDade, Bastrop County, where he practiced his profession for six years. In 1880 he went to the city of New York, and graduated at Bellevue Hospital Medical College, after which he located at Bellville, Austin County, Texas, and has here remained up to the present time. His practice, large from the first, has been steadily increasing, and he is to-day one of the most successful and influential physicians in the county. In the year 1876 he was married to Miss Hattie Campbell, of Bastrop County, and daughter of Duncan Campbell, who was born in Scotland, and who was an early settler of Bastrop County. Two interesting children have been born to Dr. and Mrs. Gardner, as follows: Lulu and Claud. Dr. Gardner is a member of the Masonic Fraternity, Bellville Lodge No. 223, a Royal Arch Mason, and a member of the Chapter 151. He has filled most of the offices of the order, twice Master of the same and is interested in its welfare. In politics he is a Democrat, but is not active. The doctor is a member of both the County and State Medical associations, and of the latter is Chairman of the Committee on Diseases of Women and Children.

ARTHUR EDWARD SPOHN, physician and surgeon, living in the city of Corpus Christi, Texas, was born in Ancaster, Canada, in 1845. His parents, Philip and Elizabeth (Bowman) Spohn, were natives of Albany County, New York, and Canada respectively. He is the seventh son in a family of eleven children. His paternal grandfather, Jacob Spohn, of Dutch descent, was born in Albany County, New York, but his people first came to this country with the early Dutch settlers of New York. His maternal great-great-grandfather came from Germany in 1706, and settled near the Mohawk River, at a creek which still bears his name (Bowman's Creek). His great-grandfather, Jacob Bowman, joined the British army during the French and Indian War of 1753-54, serving with Washington, and was awarded for his services lands near Wyoming, in the great bend of the Susquehanna River. He remained loyal to Great Britain, and these lands were confiscated after the Revolutionary War; but the British crown gave the family another grant of land near the City of Hamilton, Canada, which still remains in their possession. His paternal ancestors took sides with the States of the Union; on the maternal side they were United Empire Loyalists. His grandfather, Peter Bowman, was a Captain in the British service. Philip Spohn, the doctor's father, was a farmer, and on his homestead in Ancaster, Canada, the subject of this sketch was reared, and received his preliminary education in the schools of Ancaster, Barrie, and McGill University, Montreal. He commenced his medical studies in the Medical Department of McGill University, receiving in 1865 the senior prize in practical anatomy from that college. He entered the Medical Department of the University of Michigan, in 1866, and passed the final examinations required by that University in medicine and surgery, etc. He then went to the Long Island Hospital College, graduating there in 1867, and was appointed Resident Physician and Surgeon of the Hospital, and Assistant Professor of Surgical Anatomy in the Long Island Hospital College, Session 1867 and '68. He came to New Orleans with the First United States Artillery in 1868, as an assistant army surgeon, thence to Texas, serving on the lower Rio Grande about two years, a part of which time he was in charge of the military quarantine. In 1870 he went to Mexico, where he did considerable surgical work during the Diez revolution, and at the end of two years came to Corpus Christi, Texas, and in 1876 was united in marriage to Miss Sarah Josephine, daughter of Captain Mifflin Kenedy. They remained in New York one year after their marriage, and while there the doctor graduated at the Bellevue Hospital Medical College. In 1888 he made a trip to Europe accompanying a patient who had been bitten by a rabid wolf, to consult Pasteur, and while there attended the hospitals of Paris. He spent 1892 and '93 in Philadelphia and New York, devoting most of his time to hospital attendance. During the past fifteen years has been in the United States Marine Hospital Service at Corpus Christi. The doctor's practice is specially surgical and gynecological, and extends all over the State of Texas, and a part of Mexico. He has been remarkably successful in these branches of his profession, and on the 20th of November, 1891, performed the first Porro-Caesarean delivery in a case of Osteo Malacia ever performed in the United States, saving both mother and child. In 1870 he invented a tourniquet for bloodless operations, which has been adopted as a field instrument for army use. His surgical work is done in his private infirmary, called Bay View, at Corpus Christi, supplied with all modern appliances, and trained nurses. He is a member of King County Medical Society, New York, Central and Western Texas Medical associations, is a regular correspondent of several medical journals, and in June, 1894, was elected a member of the Board of Censors of the Medico-Chirurgical College of Philadelphia.

HON. JAMES HARVEY MCLEARY. In order to become distinguished at the bar, it is necessary that a man should possess excellent judgment, a thorough education, an intimate knowledge of his profession, and a decided liking for its arduous labors. Such a man is Judge J. H. McLeary, a prominent lawyer of San Antonio, Texas, where he has resided for more than twenty-four years. Judge McLeary is of Scotch-Irish extraction; his ancestors having come to America from the north of Ireland in the early years of the seventeenth century. One of the family, who then spelled their name "McCleary," was killed at the battle of Bunker Hill, and his name was mentioned by Daniel Webster in his great oration at the laying of the corner-stone of the Bunker Hill Monument. Himself a soldier of the Civil War, in the army of the Confederacy, he is descended from Revolutionary sires by more than one branch of his family. His father's maternal grandfather, Samuel Moore, was a captain in Morgan's Riflemen; and his maternal grandmother's grandfather, Michael Hogg, belonged to Morgan's Riflemen, and participated in the battles of Cowpens and Ryefield. The first member of the family in this country was called Thomas McCleary. His son, Michael, settled in Pennsylvania,

35

where his son, John, was born in 1765. John McCleary was the great-grandfather of the subject of this sketch. His eldest son, James Allen McCleary, was born on the 28th of April, 1788, in Virginia, where his father resided until he was four years old. John McCleary then removed to Oglethorpe County, Georgia, where he resided until about the breaking out of the War of 1812, in which his son, James Allen, participated. James Allen McLeary was married to Miss Eliza Allen Moore, daughter of Capt. Samuel Moore, in Lincoln County, Kentucky, on the 6th of August, 1809, and shortly after removed with his father, John McLeary, and his father-in-law, Capt. Moore, to middle Tennessee. Here, in Bedford County, Samuel Davies McLeary was born, on the 9th of February, 1816. He was one of a large family of children. Samuel D. McLeary, after acquiring a classical education in the common schools of west Tennessee, where his father had removed while he was yet a boy, graduated with the degree of M.D., at Transylvania University, at Lexington, Ky., in 1841, and shortly thereafter married Sarah Ann Weller, at Randolph, Tenn., and began the practice of his profession in the neighborhood of Randolph. His health failing, he removed to middle Tennessee, and settled in Smith County, near Carthage, where James Harvey McLeary was born on the 27th of July, 1845. Dr. Samuel D. McLeary lived for several years at LaFayette, Macon County, and in 1854 removed to Tipton County, where he resided for two years, and in January, 1856, he with his father, James Allen McLeary, immigrated to Texas, bringing his little family, which consisted of his wife, his son and a daughter, and settled in Colorado County near Weimar, on Harvey's Creek, where his son Harvey was partially educated in the country schools. In 1859, Harvey was sent to Soule University at Chappell Hill, Texas, where he remained until June, 1861, when he joined the Confederate army, and was mustered into the service of the Confederate States at San Antonio, Texas, on the 28th of August, 1861, becoming a member of Company "A," of the Fifth Texas Cavalry, a regiment at that time commanded by Colonel Tom Green, afterwards so famous as a cavalry leader in the campaigns of the trans-Mississippi Department. The lad served as a private soldier for four years, participating in numerous battles and skirmishes, and receiving four wounds, two of them very serious, which left him at the close of the war a cripple, hobbling around on crutches. His discharge states all this, and adds, "None deserve more credit than the above soldier." He returned from the war, and in September, 1865, resumed his studies at Soule University. In September, 1866, he went to Lexington, Va., to attend the Washington College—now Washington & Lee University—then presided over by Gen. Robert E. Lee. He remained at Washington College for three years, graduating in June, 1868, with the degree of Bachelor of Arts, and in June, 1869, with the degree of Bachelor of Laws. During the last year of his college course, he was Assistant Professor of History and English Literature; the professor of the above branches being Col. Wm. Preston Johnston, son of Gen. Albert Sidney Johnston, now President of the Tulane University of Louisiana. While in the intermediate class at college, he received the gold medal of the "Graham Philanthropic Society," for oratory; the medal was presented to him by the Hon. Geo. B. Peters, then the President of the Society, who was afterwards Attorney-general of Shelby County, Tennessee. Gen. Peters, from that day to the present, has been a stanch friend of McLeary; and during the celebrated trial of H. Clay

King, Peters was for the prosecution, while McLeary was for the defense. On his graduation, in June, 1868, he stood first in his class, and received the highest honor in the gift of the college, which was the Cincinnati Oration, "Awarded to that student who attains the highest standard of general scholarship." At this time there were over four hundred young men at the Washington College, many of them over twenty-one years of age, who had been officers in the Confederate army from the rank of Brigadier-general down. With such honors as these, why should not this Texas boy feel proud, after competing with young men much older than himself, and many who had received the advantages of good schools in their younger days. In June, 1869, he returned to Texas, and in the District Court of Colorado County, at Columbus, was admitted to the bar, and at once began the practice of law. During these years at college, he was engaged to be married to Miss Emily Mitchell, of San Antonio, Texas, and in December, 1869, they were married and shortly afterwards settled in San Antonio. Three years after his young wife died, leaving him two children, one of whom survived her mother only a few weeks. In August, 1875, he married Miss Mary King, his present wife, daughter of Hon. V. O. King, afterwards the Commissioner of Insurance, Statistics and History for the State. Immediately on his arrival in San Antonio, he formed a law partnership with Judge C. L. Wurzbach, with whom he continued in business for five years. In 1873, he was elected to the lower branch of the Texas Legislature, and served in that capacity until he was elected to the State Senate two years later. In 1880, he was elected Attorney-general of the State, and served in that capacity for two years, declining the nomination for the same office two years later.

While in the Legislature, Judge McLeary served in the House as Chairman of the Committee on Education, and in the Senate as Chairman of the Committee on Privileges and Elections and State Affairs. From his position he took a leading part in shaping legislation, and was the author of the law giving to towns and cities the right to control their own public schools. He also had the honor of being godfather to the fifty-six new counties, comprising the Panhandle of Texas, since he named each one of them after some prominent historical character, among others, the heroes who perished at the Alamo. It was the prominent part he took in legislative affairs which brought him forward as a candidate for Attorney-general. While Attorney-general he recovered from the International and Great Northern Railroad Company 4,680 square miles of land, which that company claimed for that portion of its line constructed between Austin and Laredo.

During all these years McLeary has been an ardent and devout Mason, having taken his first degree the night of his twenty-first birthday. He was promoted step by step until he was elected Grand Master of Masons in Texas, and served in that exalted position during the year 1881. To the literature of Masonry he has contributed a little work upon which he might be satisfied to rest his reputation as a scholar in this branch of learning. The publication embraces 156 pages of closely printed correspondence, with domestic and foreign representatives of the order, and contains an instructive review of the progress and achievements of Masonry in every part of the civilized world.

After retiring from the office of Attorney-general he returned to private life, and resumed the practice of law in San Antonio. In 1884 he was elected an Elector from the State at large on the Cleveland ticket, and had the honor of casting an electoral vote for President for the first winning Democrat in twenty-five years. In May, 1886, without any solicitation whatever on his part, he was appointed Associate Justice of the Supreme Court of Montana, being the first Democrat ever appointed to that bench. He held this office until March, 1888, when he resigned on account of the severity of the climate and the deficient salary. He then returned to Texas and formed a partnership with Judge W. W. King in the practice of law. Their partnership was particularly agreeable and profitable, and was only dissolved when Judge King was appointed to the district bench in 1889. In 1888 he was again an elector on the Democratic ticket, and for the second time had the honor of casting an electoral vote for Grover Cleveland for President. This time he was Chairman of the Electoral College. From his course in politics it can readily be inferred that Judge McLeary is, and always has been, a stanch friend of Grover Cleveland. Every one in Texas has always known where to find him politically—a stanch and true Democrat, "without variableness or shadow of turning."

When the trial of H. Clay King came off at Memphis, Tenn., Judge W.W. King, McLeary's former partner—being Col. H. Clay King's half-brother—requested him to go to Memphis and assist in the defense of the case. Judge McLeary readily consented, and reached Memphis shortly after the trial had begun, and made an argument before the jury which took up three days and consumed eight hours in actual delivery. The courtroom was crowded during the entire time of McLeary's speech, many men and women being moved to tears. 'Twas said by many of the old people present, that "the speech was the grandest and most eloquent ever delivered in Memphis since the days of Sargeant S. Prentiss." In June, 1890, he formed a law partnership with Hon. J. R. Fleming, under the firm name of McLeary & Fleming. This partnership continued for over three years, Judge Fleming retiring in September, 1893. On the invitation of Judge McLeary, Col. R. W. Stayton, then assumed the place in the firm made vacant by the retirement of Judge Fleming, and since that time the partnership has been continued under the name of McLeary & Stayton. It is considered the ablest law firm in the city of San Antonio, and the peer of any in the State. Its members are so well known and popular that when any important question arises in Southwest Texas they are always consulted. Although devoted to his profession, Judge McLeary deems it the duty of every patriot to take a becoming interest in politics. He attended the State convention in Lampasas in 1892, and was sent as delegate to Chicago. As might have been expected, he was an enthusiastic supporter of Mr. Cleveland, and being personally acquainted with the nominee, he was appointed on the committee of notification to inform the candidates of the action of the convention. Chairman Wilson, recognizing the sound judgment and literary culture of Judge McLeary, made him a member of the sub-committee to prepare the address to Cleveland and Stevenson, which duty he performed to the entire satisfaction of all concerned. After the grand ceremonies of notification at Madison Square Garden, in New York City, on the 20th of July, in which Judge McLeary took a prominent part, he spent a month or two with his wife and son on the New England coast, from which pleasant recreation he returned to resume his arduous labors at the bar. Since his retirement from the

Supreme Bench in Montana, Judge McLeary has devoted himself unremittingly to the duties of his profession. For the last few years he has been quite in demand as an orator on public occasions, delivering addresses at the reunion of Green's Brigade, and before the faculty and students of Tulane University of Louisiana, before the University of Texas, the Italian Society of San Antonio, and other addresses, which may be considered models of correct style and elegant oratory. Doubtless, if the demands of his profession would permit, he could become quite a successful man in purely literary pursuits, and some of his friends venture the prediction that when he retires from the duties of his profession on the laurels and the fortune already acquired, and hereafter to be achieved by him, that he will devote his later years to the pleasures and profits of authorship.

James Harvey McLeary is a man of fine physique, having a well-shaped, massive head, with broad forehead, indicating well developed intellectual powers, depth of learning, firmness and zeal; those requisites so necessary to make a brilliant, talented and successful lawyer. He is now in the height of his prosperity, with such a law practice that he is often compelled to refer clients to other firms. He is blessed with a comfortable home, made happy by an accomplished and Christian woman for a wife; his eldest daughter, Mary, having been recently married to a wealthy young planter, Noah R. Cotton, of Louisiana; and three other beautiful daughters, Helen, Sarah and Bonnie, and one son, Samuel, to comfort him as he grows older. A good and true husband, a kind and affectionate father, a devoted friend, a stanch Democrat, an able lawyer and unflinching patriot, are words most fit to describe James Harvey McLeary, who is already known as a worthy son of Texas throughout the limits of the nation.

> "Statesman, yet friend to truth; of soul sincere,
> In action faithful, and in honor clear;
> Who broke no promise, served no private end,
> Who gained no title, and who lost no friend;
> Ennobled by himself, by all approved,
> And praised unenvied by the men he lov'd."

ANDREW C. McJUNKIN. Mr. Andrew C. McJunkin is perhaps as fair an example of a self-made man as is to be found in Fort Bend County. His success is largely due to his inflexible integrity, marvelous foresight and his habits of thoroughness, perseverance and honesty. He is now a prominent planter of Fort Bend County, residing near Fulshear, and is greatly esteemed by a wide circle of loyal friends. Mr. McJunkin was born in Wilkes County, Georgia and is a son of Dr. D. W. McJunkin of Union District, South Carolina. Dr. McJunkin practiced medicine for a great number of years in Georgia and died in Greene County, that State in 1874 or '75, when about seventy-five years of age. He was twice married, and Andrew C., our subject, is the only one of the first children now living. Young McJunkin spent his school days in his native county, and walked four miles to school, not that he wished to attend, but his father used a persuader that was quite effectual. He left the school when eighteen years of age, but remained on the farm until in 1851 when he commenced farming for himself. In 1853 he made a trip to Texas by way of Galveston and Houston where he loaded his belongings on an ox wagon and then walked to Bastrop, 150 miles. Soon after he went to Austin, the State Capital then consisting of a log cabin or two, and split rails in the cedar brake for two months to secure money enough to return to Georgia. In December, 1854, he again started to Texas with some slaves, in the capacity of overseer. He came on a steamer to Brazos River, and then made his first visit to Richmond. From the latter place he went overland to Egypt in Wharton County and cleared up the place now belonging to Mrs. Hearne for Col. O. L. Battle. After two years he commenced for himself in Fort Bend County in Hodges Bend, and was there when Civil War broke out. May, 1862 he joined Brown's Regiment and was stationed at Galveston and along the coast during the remainder of the war. Afterwards renting land on the Perry plantation and then on the McNeal place he became possessed of sufficient means to buy a large tract of land in 1869. In 1870 he commenced cultivating it, and to the original track which consisted of 270 acres he added to from time to time until he now owns 1,327 acres of prairie and bottom land. He made most of the improvements on the place and has one of the finest homes in the section. In connection with planting he is engaged quite extensively in the stock business. In the year 1867 he wedded Miss Mary J. Hudspeth, daughter of Henry Hudspeth, an old timer in Texas. Six children have blessed this union, four daughters and two sons, and they have grown up in this county. Mr. McJunkin is a whole-souled, genial and most agreeable gentleman and is universally liked. He and Mrs. McJunkin hold membership in the Methodist Church.

PRESLEY WARD, one of the leading farmers and stockmen of Austin County, was born July 12, 1838, in Franklin County, North Carolina. His parents, Richard and Elizabeth J. Ward, were of old North Carolina families, members of which served in the Revolution. Presley Ward was educated at Lewisburg, N. C., came with his brother, Nathan P. Ward, to Texas in January, 1860, and invested in a large tract of Brazos lands. Mr. Ward was excused from military service from 1861 to 1864, when he was called out with the militia; but beyond service in the camp of instruction at Houston, did not make an acquaintance with the horrors of civil war. At the close of the struggle he found his negroes no longer slaves and himself in debt. Though he paid about $5,000 on 1,000 acres of land and had considerable cotton, he was yet in debt about $5,000 or $6,000. He remained in Fort Bend County until 1869, when he removed to this county, where he worked with his brother until 1871, when he purchased the 400 acre tract, then slightly improved, for $3,500. To this he has since added 800 acres, of which he has now under cultivation 350 acres, together with 200 acres of his 660-acre tract of black lands on the prairie and in the bottoms. He owns large herds of graded stock, the only stock which he raises. Though the results of the Civil War compelled him to begin life anew, he is now one of the wealthiest citizens of this county, and actually the architect of his own fortune. On February 22, 1871, he married Miss Fanny L. Staggers, of Alabama, whose parents moved from South Carolina to Alabama at an early day, where they died in 1870. Mrs. Ward then visited her sister, Mrs. Whitney, in Texas. She was formerly Mrs. Murry, and the mother of two children, namely, Mary, who married a Mr. Cowling, and Margaret, who married a Mr. Ruff, of Alabama. To her marriage with Mr. Ward two children were born: Richard M. and Morrison F., the latter a student of Georgetown College, Texas. Mr. and Mrs. Ward are members of the Methodist Episcopal Church. Mr. Ward, like his ancestors, is a Democrat, and one of the ablest counselors of his party in this county.

ELLIS P. BEAN, born at Bean's Station, Tenn., in 1782, moved to Natchez in 1800, and there joined Philip Nolan's company of filibusters, being No. 22 in the command. In the adventure between the Brazos and Trinity rivers with the Spanish troops, Bean was one of the nine men captured and held at Chihuahua for three years, when they were allowed a measure of liberty and given a permit to labor for their support. The fourth year Bean (being a hatter) worked at his trade, and then with two others attempted to escape. At El Paso they were arrested, flogged, ironed and imprisoned, but the friends of Bean at Chihuahua obtained for him his liberty. A second attempt to escape being frustrated, he was sent to a point south of Mexico City, and thence to Acapulco, where he was placed in a dungeon. Neglecting to close the look-out one night, a monster reptile found its way in and awakened the sleeping prisoner. Knowing the character of his visitor, he stealthtly withdrew a knife which he had concealed in his clothes and pierced the serpent's head. When the keeper reported this exploit, the Commandant permitted him to join the chain gang, which was indeed a measure of relief. Another attempt to escape was marked by the murder of three guards by him. He was pursued, subjected to repeated punishments; but at the close of a year was permitted to walk in the prison yard. This time he thanked the authorities by killing several soldiers and escaping; but he was recaptured in California, 300 miles away, taken to the old prison, chained down and left to the mercy of the vermin. In 1810, when the Royalists were called upon to defend the crown, Bean was tendered the oath and allowed to serve as a soldier. A few days later he was one of a scouting party sent to reconnoitre the Republican position. When close to the camp of the Revolutionists, he proposed to his fellow soldiers the propriety of casting their fortunes with Morelos, and they acquiescing, reported for service. Soon after, the conquering Republicans reached Acapulco, where the guards of the prison and government officers begged their lives of the man they had so cruelly treated. For thirty-six months he was the ablest Lieutenant of Morelos. Two years later he was dispatched to New Orleans to seek aid for the Morelos party, and while *en route* married a woman at Jalapa. On January 6, 1815, he arrived at New Orleans, fought in the battle of January 8th, attached some friends to his cause, and returning, lived with his Jalapan wife until 1827, when he took part in the Fredonia or Nacogdoches War. He commanded at Nacogdoches until 1835, when he returned to Jalapa as an officer on the retired list of the Mexican army. His death is said to have taken place prior to 1860.

DR. JOHN DOUGLAS WESTERVELT. Among the many who have practiced the "healing art" in this portion of Texas, Dr. John W. Westervelt stands among the foremost. He owes his nativity to the Palmetto State, where he was born in 1840, the third in a family of twelve children born to John Irving and Sarah (Leak) Douglas Westervelt, natives respectively of New York and South Carolina. The paternal grandfather, Harmon Westervelt, was a successful lawyer of New York City, and was descended from worthy Dutch ancestors, his father having come from Holland to this country and made a settlement in New York, and the name of the family in the old country was Van Westervelt. The maternal grandfather was a successful physician of Virginia, and became one of the most celebrated physicians and surgeons of his day. He belonged to one of the F. F. V.'s, and was a man of far more than average intellect. John Irving Westervelt was a chemist and druggist in business for many years at Cheraw, S. C., where he made his home until the war. After a time he joined his son at Corpus Christi, but eventually returned to South Carolina, and died at the residence of his youngest daughter in 1893, at the age of eighty-two years. His wife died in 1862, a worthy member of the Episcopal Church. The subject of this sketch was educated in South Carolina, at Cheraw, and other places of that State, and spent one year in the military academy at Columbia. He then studied telegraphy for some time, and upon the opening of the Civil War entered the Confederate service and was on General Beauregard's staff as his chief operator, and received the message announcing General Lee's surrender. He had acquired a taste for the study of medicine and decided to practice it, while clerking in his father's drug store in Cheraw, prior to the war, and by the advice of Dr. Cornelius Kollock entered his office as a student in 1858. At the same time he began the study of telegraphy, and later became an operator at Marion, S. C. At the close of the war he taught school for two years, at the end of which time he again engaged in telegraphy, but this time in the city of Philadelphia, where he resumed the study of medicine, having by no means lost sight of his desire to follow that profession. After the lapse of some time he returned to South Carolina and took a course at the Atlanta Medical College, and from that time until 1874 practiced the medical profession in Georgia, when he finished his medical studies in the above named institution, graduating with credit. He practiced for one year in Clarksville, Ga., then in Spartanburg County until 1881, and in 1882 came to Corpus Christi, Texas. After one year spent in this place he returned to Spartanburg County, Ga., but six years later came back to Corpus Christi, where he has since been very successfully engaged in the practice of his profession. He is a general practitioner, has built up a large practice through merit, and is now City Health Officer and County Quarantine Physician. He was married in 1866 to Miss Eliza W. Styron, a native of the Old North State, and their union has resulted in the birth of eight children: Luolo Virginia, wife of William I. Smith of Charleston; Harmon, John W. Jr., a physician and surgeon at Alice, Texas, was a student of the College of Baltimore and the Barnes' Medical College, of St. Louis, and is at present Surgeon of the Texas-Mexican Railroad; Jennie Louise, William De Ryee, Eau Claire; Richard Sidney and George Conrad. The doctor is a stanch Democrat, is a public-spirited citizen, and is highly honored throughout the section in which he lives.

JOHN GEORGE SMITH. There is nothing more interesting to a student of human nature than to trace the career of a man who, endowed with energy and ambition, enters boldly into the struggle of life, and makes for himself a high place in the busy world. John George Smith, of the well-known firm of Smith Bros., of Columbia, Brazoria, West Columbia, Wharton, Velasco, etc., was born in Matthews County, Va., February 9, 1850, and is a son of Thomas and Ann F. (Brooks) Smith, also natives of Matthews County, Va. The parents were married in that State and died there, the father when sixty years of age and the mother a few years later. Early in life Thomas Smith was a merchant, but later he became a farmer, and followed that the remainder of his life. During the Civil War he was taken prisoner, carried to Fortress Monroe, and confined for some time. A brother of his was killed in the war. Mr. and Mrs. Smith were members of the Methodist Church and active workers in the same. Their family consisted of twelve children, five now living: Miss E. A. Smith, now in Virginia, on the old Smith plantation; Mrs. Mary A. Borum, of Columbia; J. G., Mrs. J. A. Borum, in Matthews County, Va., and T. L. (See sketch.) Our subject's education was received in his native county, and when thirteen or fourteen years of age he left school. In 1868 he went to Brazoria County, Texas, where he had an uncle, J. W. Brooks, living, and clerked for Captain Tyler and A. A. Metcalf, at Quintana, in this county. Later he started in business with his brother, T. L. Smith, at Columbia, on a limited scale, and they have since increased the business to its present proportions. They have excellently arranged and attractive places of business, with fine show windows and an unrivaled variety of choice goods. Their patronage comes from the best people, and their business policy is one that enables them to retain the confidence of the most fastidious customer. They opened a branch store, first at Chenango, afterwards at Brazoria, then Wharton, Quintana and West Columbia. Our subject took charge of the store at Brazoria, and as time passed he began buying land, first seventy-five acres, but he now owns and controls many thousand acres in Brazoria and Wharton counties principally. In the year 1888 he was married to Miss Willie Weisiger, a native of Fort Bend County, Texas, and daughter of Dr. E. S. Weisiger, who is Health Officer at Quintana. Two children have been born to this union, Evan S. and Eunice G. Mr. Smith is a member of the K. of H., and Mrs. Smith affiliates with the Presbyterian Church.

WALDO G. THOMPSON. In the occupation of farming, Waldo G. Thompson has attained a degree of success that can only be accounted for in the facts that he has ever been industrious and persevering, and that to it he has devoted the greater portion of his life. His beautiful home and excellent farm attest the thrift and enterprise of the owner, who has been a resident of this section for many years. Mr. Thompson is a native of that grand old State, Virginia, his birth occurring in Clarksburg, Harrison County, March 4, 1827, and the son of Amos Thompson, who was also a native of the Old Dominion. The latter was married there to Miss Kittie Hughes, and later, with a number of other families, viz.: Frank Wallman, Louis Liedstrand, Jack Sutherland, John Stillwell, Dave Patterson, John Dowling, who is still living, and old man Webster. Mr. W. G. Thompson's father and his family came to Texas, making the journey down the Mississippi to New Orleans, and thence in a sailing vessel to old San Jacinto, and from there to Matagorda. The father of our subject was a butcher by trade, but died within six months after coming to this county, and after locating at the head of Bay Prairie. His wife followed him to the grave about five years after settling here, when forty-five years of age. He was fifty-four at the time of his death. Both were faithful members of the Baptist Church. Of the eight children born to them only one besides our subject, who was the seventh child, is now living, Robert S. Waldo G. Thompson's first recollections were of the boundless prairies of the Lone Star State and the privations the family were obliged to stand. At that early date flour was twenty-five dollars per barrel, and he remembers that hounds brought fifty dollars per pair. During the war between the United States and Mexico he was engaged as teamster and remained with the army all the time. Later he teamed all over the country, principally from Matagorda to Austin, and continued this until the breaking out of Civil War. In connection, however, he was engaged in the stock business on the Colorado River, and carried on old Jack Smith's plantation. In the spring of 1861 he joined Brown's regiment of cavalry, afterwards Captain Mosley's battery of artillery, and was in Louisiana for the most part, participating in the battles of Mansfield, Pleasant Hill, Yellow Bayou, Chaneyville, etc. For three years he was in the service, and during that time he was never wounded nor taken prisoner. With limited means after the war he came to this county and settled in Elliott, where he now lives. He is the owner of 2,300 acres of land, and is engaged in the stock business quite extensively. He has made all the improvements on his place, trees, fences, etc., and has one of the finest residences in this section. This is kept in admirable order by his wife, who was formerly Miss Hannah Elliott, daughter of John Elliott. The Elliott family came originally from England. To Mr. and Mrs. Thompson were born eight children, four now living: R. C., at Davis, Indian Territory, where he deals in stock; Annie Z., wife of James Higgins, of Crystal Falls, this State; Ida, at home, and John E., at home. Those deceased are: Kittie E., wife of John K. Johnson; Fannie, William, and Walter C. Mr. Thompson and wife are united with the Methodist Church, and are earnest and consistent workers in the same. He is a member of the A. F. & A. M.

REV. WALTER R. RICHARDSON. The church over which this able and distinguished divine has presided for the past twenty-six years—St. Mark's of San Antonio—was organized by Rev. J. F. Fish, Chaplain of the United States army, under the name of Trinity Church, in July, 1850, and he was succeeded to the rectorship by Rev. Charles F. Rottenstein, then Rev. Lucius H. Jones, who gave the church the title of St. Mark's. His successors were as follows: Rev. J. Hamilton Quinby, Rev. H. G. Batterson, Rev. W. T. D. Dalzell, Rev. R. H. Murphy, Rev. Joseph J. Nicholson Richt, Rev. Alexander Gregg, Rev. C. A. Wagner, Rev. Melville C. Keith, and Rev. W. R. Richardson. This last mentioned gentleman is a son of Texas, born in 1837, and was the third child of Stephen and Lucinda (Hodge) Richardson, natives of Mount Desert Island, Me., and Kentucky, respectively. The paternal grandfather, Stephen R. Richardson, was a seafaring man, and came of worthy Irish stock. The first of the family to locate in this country were Stephen and Hugh Richardson, who settled in Maine during colonial times, and Rev. Walter R. Richardson's grandfather's house was a rallying point for the famous "Minute Men," in the beginning of the great struggle with the mother country. The maternal grandfather, Alexander Hodge, was one of Austin's colony to Texas. He was a member of a Georgia family, and removed from there to Kentucky, thence to Arkansas, and from there to Texas, in which State they arrived in January, 1825, locating in Hodge's Bend on the Brazos River, where he reared a large family, and is supposed to have died prior to the Revolution. Stephen Richardson secured a good English education, although his opportunities were limited. He enlisted in the War of 1812, and served for one year on the Northern frontier. In the enthusiasm of enlisting he had a dream one night, in which the incidents were so marked that they impressed themselves indelibly upon his memory. The dream was of being in a battle, and although he passed through the War of 1812, he did not participate in any engagement, but the battle of his dream took place twenty-three years later—the Grass fight of San Antonio—during the Texas Revolution. After the War of 1812 was over, in company with his brother Richard, he conducted some glass works at Middlebury, Vt., but the plant was burned two years later, and he and his brother returned to their home via Canada, and in 1816 he engaged in teaching school at Shawneetown, Ill. After a time he came down the river on a flatboat, and located in New Orleans, from which place he made business trips to Campeachy and Tampico, and on his second trip to the latter place he was shipwrecked in the Gulf of Mexico, near the mouth of the Brazos River, in December, 1822. Now being in Texas he joined Austin's colony, and located in San Felipe on his league of land about 1828, and here married in the latter part of that, or the first of the following year. His nearest neighbor was eleven miles away, and Indians were hostile and numerous, but they bore the hardships, privations and dangers of frontier life with fortitude, and their efforts to secure a competency were rewarded. After a time they moved to Brazoria County, and established a sawmill on Chocolate Bayou, near the town of Liverpool, and there the subject of this sketch was born. In 1833 the father joined the Texas Army, and was Aid-de-camp to Gen. Stephen F. Austin, who was one of the 301 men who stormed and captured Bexar from the Mexicans in 1836, but shortly before this he was in the Grass fight, and realized his dream of long before. In the Bexar fight he was with Colonel Johnston in Veramendi House in Goliad, and when Colonel Milam fell Mr. Richardson was the last person to speak to him before his death. Mr. Richardson then retired with Austin, leaving a force of men in the Alamo, and in 1836 was compelled to move his family in the "runaway," and located in Galveston, but was within hearing of the guns at the battle of San Jacinto. After placing his family in safety he returned to his home, and from his sawmill supplied the Republic with much lumber. He was a great admirer of General Austin, and the latter was his groomsman at his wedding, and sponsor at the baptism of him and his wife, and also at the baptism of their eldest children. In 1838 they moved to Harrisburg, and established a sawmill on the east side of the Bayou there, and he became part owner of the Yellowstone, the first steamer to run to Houston. He moved to Houston in 1849, and there lived in retirement until his death in 1860. His widow survived him until 1880, when she died at the home of the subject of this sketch in San Antonio. The father was a Mason, and both were Episcopalians. The father, a sturdy pioneer, was a strong, practical, but most sympathetic and kind hearted man, and was well and favorably known in the business life of those early days. Rev. Walter R. Richardson was educated in the common schools of Texas, and in St. Paul's College at Anderson, where he was also a tutor for some time. Upon leaving this institution he began teaching in a private school in Harrisburg, after which he went to Austin and began the study of theology, and at the same time taught in the school conducted by Rev. Charles Gillette. From there he went to and finished his studies in the Berkely School of Divinity at Middletown, Conn., but his studies there were brought to a sudden close by the opening of the Civil War in 1861. In November of that year he returned to Houston, and in 1862 was ordained deacon, and began his first labors as a minister of the gospel, his field being Goliad and Victoria. In 1864 he was called to the church in Huntsville, and the following year he was ordained a priest, and was called to St. Mark's Church in San Antonio in 1868, at which time the congregation was worshiping in St. Mary's Hall, the unfinished school building of the Diocesan school, which was established by Bishop Gregg but two years before, but which was broken up by the dreadful epidemic of cholera in 1866. The walls were unplastered, the second story was without a floor, rough school benches served as seats, and a canvas screen served as a vestry room. Improvements were made through the generosity of members, and the building was finished, after which another step was made in the purchase of the whole property for $2,000, with condition annexed that it must not be alienated from the church. In the fifth year of Mr. Richardson's rectorship, 1873, work was begun on the present church building, which had been begun in 1859, but was interrupted by the war, and it was sufficiently completed to enable them to hold their first services on Easter, 1875, and it is regarded as one of the handsomest churches in the State. Slowly, but surely, the spiritual temple also grew, owing chiefly to the fluctuating character of the frontier town, but patient labor for the Master resulted in ultimate success, and the membership is now large, and among the thinking classes. Dr. Richardson has devoted his entire time and energies to the interests of the church and her people, and his success in building up the church, clearing it of debt, and in the saving of souls has been of the most flattering character, and he has met with a portion of his reward in this life in the affection and esteem of his flock, and in the universal esteem in which he is held. His brother, Alfred S., is a lawyer of Houston, and has been quite active politically, and is now City Secretary. His first wife was Miss A. E. B. Bowen, a niece of Gen. J. W. Barnes, of Grimes County. After her death he married Miss Elizabeth Brooks, of Ohio.

WILLIAM R. NASH. William R. Nash, the subject of this sketch, is a man who, whatever he undertakes, develops regularly to its fitting consummation. He is ever reliable when demands are made upon his services, and is weak in no particular, and under no circumstances. Mr. Nash is at present in charge of the Brown-Weeks stock ranch in Brazoria and Fort Bend counties, and is thoroughly familiar with this occupation in its every detail. He was born in the Empire State in 1860, and is a son of Edward D., and Catharine (Cook) Nash, the father of St. Lawrence County, N. Y., and the mother of Brooklyn, N. Y. Edward D. Nash came to Texas about 1848, and engaged in mercantile pursuits, and met with more than ordinary success. He died in 1860, when about forty-two years of age, and his widow afterwards married John Adriance, who is now a retired merchant, and who has resided in this county for nearly sixty years. (See sketch.) Our subject, in 1874, took the advice of a physician, and commenced stock driving, first with Cornelius Davis, with whom he remained until 1885, in partnership, part of the time, and later with the firm of Davis, Brown & Co. Later still he became connected with the Brown-Weeks ranch, and with that he has remained up to the present time. This ranch is very extensive, but Mr. Nash grew up in the business, and has had a very wide experience. He has control of about 70,000 acres of land, etc., and is one of the most thorough-going, wideawake young men of the county. In the year 1884 he married Miss Ina Young, a daughter of Col. Overton Young, a prominent planter before the war. Mr. Nash is an influential member of the Episcopal Church, and is a Royal Arch Mason.

COL. STERLING C. ROBERTSON. From the campaign of the War of 1812–14 down to 1842, this daring and patriotic man was a participant in every struggle of his countrymen. He was born in Nashville, Tenn., about 1785, and died in Robertson County, March 4, 1842. He was educated, and brought up a planter in Giles County, Tenn. In the War of 1812 he served as Major of Tennessee troops. In 1823, having plenty of means, he gratified his love of adventure and enterprise by forming a company at Nashville to explore the then "wild country" of Texas. When he had arrived at the Brazos, he formed a permanent camp at the mouth of Little River. All the party returned to Tennessee, however, except Robertson. He visited the settlements that had been made, and conceived the idea of planting a colony in Texas. Filled with enthusiasm over this plan, he went to his home in Tennessee, where he purchased a contract which the Mexican Government had made with Robert Leftwick for the settlement of 800 families. The colony embraced a large tract of land, and Robertson was to receive forty leagues and forty *labors* for his services. In 1829, at his own expense, he introduced 100 families, who were driven out by the military in consequence of false representations made to the government. The matter was finally adjusted, and in the spring of 1834 the colony was restored. In the summer of the same year he laid out the town of Sarahville de Viesca. A land office was opened about October 1, and the settlements were rapidly made. In the summer of 1835 he made a tour of Tennessee, Mississippi, Louisiana and Kentucky, making inducements to immigration. He had been authorized by the Mexican Government to offer to settlers who were heads of families one league and one *labor* of land, and lesser proportions to others. At the outbreak of the Revolution he had introduced more than 600 families into the colonies, fully one-half of the whole number at his own expense. Colonel Robertson was a Delegate to the General Convention of 1836, was one of the signers of the Declaration of Independence, and of the Constitution of the Republic of Texas. In the spring of 1836 he commanded a military company, and for bravery at San Jacinto received a donation of 640 acres of land. He was a member of the Senate of the First Congress of the Republic of Texas. He died in Robertson County, March 4, 1842, in the fifty-seventh year of his age.

TITO P. RIVERA. This substantial citizen of Corpus Christi, Texas, was born on the Pacific Coast, in Mexico, in 1844, the eldest son born to Julian and Josefa (Herrera) Rivera, both of whom were born in Spain, the former being an extensive silver miner, and a man of considerable wealth. He and his wife died in Mexico. The subject of this sketch was educated in a private school up to the age of nine years, and in March, 1852, was permitted by his father to accompany a party of men over the mountains to procure food for his miners, and on the way back the party were attacked by Comanche Indians, who secured all the pack mules, sixty in number, and captured the subject of this sketch, who was then a boy of nine years. The Indians then started for their home, which was in northwestern Texas, and many were the adventures that they had on the long and tiresome journey thither. After a time they reached a point in Texas, now near Ola, on the Brazos River, and during this entire time he did not see a white face, but was kept in captivity about three years, at the Comanche Agency, near Camp Cooper, Texas, on the Clear Fork of the Brazos. In December, 1855, he was surrendered to the United States troops on payment of $125, at which time Gen. John R. Baylor had charge of the Agency, and Robert S. Neighbors was Superintendent of Indian affairs. Chief Govaro-choo-koospy, (meaning an old bear's head), was in communication with Mr. Neighbors while the Indians were in a wild condition, and as Mr. Rivera could read and write in Spanish, he acted an interpreter and did all the writing, and after a time, when he dared do so, added a postscript which resulted in his release. At that time he was about twelve years of age, and was taken by Major Neighbors to his home, near San Antonio, and remained with him until the fall of 1859, when the Major was killed, and Mr. Rivera then made his home with William Albert Wallace, who treated him kindly and considerately, and with whom he had an excellent home until he entered the Confederate army, in April, 1861, becoming a member of Company B., under Captain William A. Pitts, First Regiment Texas Mounted Riflemen, in which he served on the frontier of Texas for one year, at which time his command was disbanded. At the end of that time he enlisted in Company E, of the Thirty-third Texas Cavalry, and served in that State, Louisiana, Arkansas and the Indian Territory. Mr. Rivera became Orderly Sergeant of his Company, but was soon detailed to clerical duty in the Adjutant General's office, but was finally mustered out at Nashville, Texas, and was paroled by General Canby. Soon after the war Mr. Rivera engaged in the cattle business, and went with William H. Gasley with a drove of horses North, spending eighteen months on the trip. He continued in the cattle business until February, 1868, then went to Victoria, Texas, as a clerk in a commission house, thence to Port Lavaca, where he was married October 12, 1870, to Miss Mollie H. Holloway, a native of Mississippi, and a daughter of William P. Holloway, who came to Texas in 1867. In 1870 he went to Galveston, where he remained as book-keeper until June, 1873, for B. L. Mason & Co., but since that time has been a resident of Corpus Christi. He soon after became associated with Dodridge, Lott & Co., bankers and commission merchants, and was with them and their successors until the failure of the firm in February, 1891. He has been quite prominent in the affairs of this section, has been an active and industrious business man, and while connected with the bank served faithfully and intelligently in the capacity of Cashier. He has been a member of the City Council, and socially belongs to the K. of P., the K. of H., of which he is Deputy Grand Dictator, being Past Chancellor Commander of the first mentioned organization, the A. O. U. W., and is a charter member of the lodge in each case. He is a communicant of the Episcopal Church, and is a highly esteemed and thoroughly respected, genial gentleman.

DR. ROBERT E. MOSS. To win both a reputation and a fortune as a practitioner of the healing art, requires that a man shall have a thorough knowledge of his profession, keep thoroughly posted and up with the times in the advance made in the science, and that he shall at all times be ready to brave, the elements, and use his knowledge and skill in behalf of suffering humanity. Dr. Robert E. Moss has fulfilled these requirements, and is a popular and prominent physician of San Antonio, Texas, and at the present time is confining his attention to diseases of the eye, ear, nose and throat. He was born in Spartanburg District, S. C., April 3, 1858, the third of six children born to Oliver Harrison and Mary (Snoddy) Moss, who were natives of the same State and district. The paternal grandfather, James Moss, was a native of Virginia, and in that State was educated, but during early manhood he settled in South Carolina and engaged in teaching school. At the opening of the War of 1812, his patriotism found expression in enlisting in the service of the United States, and he was on active duty until the war closed, after which he engaged in planting, an occupation that occupied his attention until his death, which occurred at his old plantation home in Spartanburg District in 1858. His father came to America in colonial times, and he took up his residence in Virginia. One of his ancestors in England was an officer of the army of King George III, and was knighted for bravery on the battlefield. The maternal grandfather, John Snoddy, was born in Spartanburg District, and his father was born in Dublin, Ireland, and settled in South Carolina prior to the Revolutionary War, through which he served as a soldier of the Colonial army. One of his brothers was killed by the Tories. John Snoddy's mother was a Scotch lady, so the descent of Dr. Robert E. Moss is English on his paternal side, and Irish-Scotch on the maternal. All his ancestors were stanch Presbyterians, and were members of the famous old Nazareth Presbyterian Church at Spartanburg District, now over 120 years old. Oliver Harrison Moss was farming at the opening of the Civil War, and was unanimously elected Captain of a Company which served for a year as part of the Home Guards, and was then attached to Lucas' battalion and located on James Island till near the close of the war, and constantly refused promotion in rank, preferring to remain as Captain. In 1874 he moved to North Carolina, near Asheville, and bought a handsome place on the French Broad River, but he and his wife have recently moved to Texas, and make there home with the subject of this sketch. The latter received a good education in Reidville, S. C., and in 1878 began the study of medicine by entering the medical college at Charleston, S. C., and in 1880 he entered the Jefferson Medical College of Philadelphia, and remained there until he graduated in 1883. He came to Texas and began practicing in Hill County, from whence he moved to Mexia, Texas, in December, 1883, and did an extensive practice. In March, 1891 he went to New York City and took a three months post graduate course at the Polyclinic College and at the Manhattan Eye and Ear Hospital. In 1892 he returned to New York and spent six months in study with the celebrated and famous specialist, Doctor Knapp. His special studies have eminently fitted him for his present practice, which is rapidly on the increase. He is a member of the Southwest Texas Medical Association, and of the State Medical Association, of which he is Chairman of the Section of Ophthalmology. In 1886 the doctor was married to Miss Mattie Blake, a daughter of Gen. T. W. Blake, of Plantersville, Texas. The latter came to Texas from the Old North State at an early date, and was a well known lawyer there for years. Mrs. Moss' grandmother was a member of the family of Dursts, who were the pioneers of that part of Texas, and their home was used as a fort to protect them against the Indians in early times. To the doctor and his wife one child has been given, Wilbur B. The family attend the Presbyterian Church, and are highly respected in the community in which they reside. The doctor is a pleasant, scholarly and courteous gentleman, and has a beautiful and comfortable home, and his offices are among the handsomest in San Antonio.

ROBERT L. NEELEY, one of the young business men of Sealy, was born in Brazos County, Texas, November 17, 1861. His parents, Andrew G. and Louisa W. (Hodges) Neeley, were natives of Tennessee and Alabama respectively, who came to Texas in 1861 and settled in Brazos County. Mr. Neeley, Sr., brought with him 150 slaves, all of which property he lost soon after through the fortunes of war. He was a preacher of the Cumberland Presbyterian denomination, a great believer in the inviolable character of personal as well as real property, and a man of industry and foresight. The war inflicted business disasters on him, as well as upon others, and he died in May, 1869. His widow survived him many years, and died leaving eight children, namely: George A. and Jessie M., deceased; John B., a stockman of Brazos County; Ada R., wife of G. A. Parker, of this county; Joel H., deceased; Robert L., of Sealy; Lula H., married and residing at Columbia, Tenn., and Mollie E., wife of Henry Hodges, of Brazos County, this State. The father of this large family was a prominent Mason, the best educated Cumberland Presbyterian in all Texas, and a practical business man. His neighbors were his dearest friends, and to them his death was an irreparable loss. His wife, like himself, was a practical woman, who, while aiding in the advancement of the family interests, did not lose sight of what she owed to the unfortunate and distressed of the community. The son, of whom this sketch is given, was educated at Bryant, Texas, in the public school and college. At the age of thirteen years he began life on his own account, and at fifteen years of age was employed as a stockman. During the erection of the capitol at Austin he was foreman of a gang; later entered railroading in the transportation department; then began business at Sealy, in partnership with J. B. Rice, under the firm name of Neeley & Rice. On March 15, 1894, he married Miss Ida Beyer, a native of Austin County, whose father was a German and mother of German descent. Mr. Neeley, like his forefathers, belongs to that great political party, the feathers of which were clipped so closely in November, 1894, but which grows stronger with each clipping, and comes to the front at intervals with a full fleece.

ERNEST JOSEY, a farmer and stock-grower of Sealy, Austin County, was born at San Felipe, in this county, August 8, 1872. His parents, J. J. and Sophia Josey, natives of the Carolinas, came to Texas with their parents, and were married in this State. Mr. Josey, Sr., brought to his new home strong arms and a sense of industry as his only capital, but through agriculture and trade in the old town of San Felipe, accumulated a snug fortune, so that at his death, in 1893, his wealth was accounted at $60,000 or $70,000. His wife died in 1890, leaving three children, namely: Anna, now Mrs. Henry Pitts, of San Felipe; Carrie, now Mrs. George Hill, of that town, and the subject of this sketch. Ernest Josey received a practical education in the school of San Felipe, in a business college of Houston, and in the Georgetown (Texas) college. In 1890 he married Miss Addie Bostick, a daughter of Dr. J. W. and Rebecca (Taylor) Bostick, early settlers of Austin County, and to this marriage one child, James J. Josey, was born. Mr. Josey has now in cultivation 200 acres of Brazos bottom lands, of his estate of 1,000 acres, the greater part of which is on the Brazos bottoms. As a stock-grower he is well known, for to that branch of his business he gives close attention. Like the great majority of Texans he belongs to the Democratic party, and is no silent member of that old political organization. To the material interests of Sealy (where is his handsome residence) and of Austin County in general, he devotes consideration, and to all projects which promise benefits to the people he lends a helping hand. His wife, a member of one of the old families of the county, is a lady possessed of knowledge and tact—a fit partner for the young planter.

ROBERT W. THOMPSON, M. D. One of the most prominent citizens of Austin County, socially and politically, is Dr. Robert W. Thompson, who is even more eminent as a physician and surgeon. His strong, practical common sense and solidity of character mark him as one to be trusted under any and all circumstances. In every relation of life he has promptly and conscientiously met every just demand upon him. Mr. Thompson was born in Dallas County, Ala., December 12, 1842, to the marriage of James A. and Jane (Bethany) Thompson, natives of North Carolina or South Carolina. The parents were married in Alabama, and came to Texas (via Galveston and Houston) in 1848 and settled in this county, nine miles west of Bellville. Previous to coming to the Lone Star State, Dr. Thompson taught school in Alabama, but afterward was actively engaged in farming. Here he held the office of County Commissioner, and died in this county in 1854. His wife only survived him two years, dying in 1856. Of the nine children born to them, two died when small. The seven who grew to mature years were named as follows: Margaret, deceased, was the wife of J. F. Willis, deceased; Isabella, deceased, was the wife of James Daugherty; William A., of Hamilton County, Texas; F. M., of Lavaca County; Robert W., Hillyard J., deceased, and Elizabeth, deceased, was the wife of Dr. G. W. Forster, of Georgetown, Texas. Our subject, Robert W. Thompson, secured a fair education in the common schools of the county, and in March, 1862, when twenty years of age, he joined Company A, Twentieth Infantry of Texas, and served in the transMississippi Department, participating in but one battle, the retaking of Galveston in 1863. For the most part during the remainder of the war he was stationed at Galveston, and worked hard for the Confederacy as a special detail. His command was disbanded at Richmond, Fort Bend County, in June, 1865. While in camp Dr. Thompson's spare time was not spent in idleness, but most of it in the study of medicine. Afterward he applied himself diligently to the study of his chosen calling, and in 1866 attended his first course of lectures in the medical department in the University of Louisiana (now Tulane University), and was graduated from the same in the class of 1867 and 1868. Returning home he located at Nelsonville, Austin County, and there continued to practice until 1891, when he moved to this place. This was in the fall, and since that time he has had a large and steadily increasing practice. From the first his success was assured, in this most important science bearing upon man's comfort, happiness and welfare, and he has shown himself eminently worthy the trust reposed in him by all classes. Miss Virginia Minton, a native of this county and daughter of Alfred Minton (see sketch of Robert Minton), became his wife in 1872, and of the three children born to this union two survive, John H., at home, and James R. Dr. Thompson is a dimitted member of the A. F. & A. M., G. W. Foster Lodge No. 306, and he is a dimitted member of Robert E. Lee Chapter No. 109, of Nelsonville. Dr. Thompson has always been interested in politics, is a stanch Democrat, and in 1868 was elected to represent his county in the Legislature. He has also served as County Commissioner, and held other important offices. Both the doctor and wife are members of the Methodist Episcopal Church.

ANDREW JACKSON ADAMS. Andrew Jackson Adams is one of Fort Bend County's substantial farmers and soldier-citizens, and has always sustained a high reputation in his community. He owes his nativity to Perry County, Ala., born January 8, 1832, on the day the battle of New Orleans was fought, and his father, who was a great lover of "Old Hickory," gave him the name of Andrew Jackson. The father, Gen. James C. Adams, was a native of Georgia, as was also the mother, Caroline (Bohannan) Adams. About the year 1817 this estimable couple moved to Alabama, and thence, in 1858, to Texas, locating first at Huntsville. Later they moved to Harris County, and died in Lynchburg. Mr. Adams owned the ground on which the battle of San Jacinto was fought, and was always a planter. While a resident of Alabama he was Brigadier General of the State Militia, and held other prominent positions. His wife died in 1842, and he afterward married Miss Margaret Campbell, who is also deceased. Mr. Adams died in 1869 when seventy-one years of age. To his first union were born ten children, two now living—subject and J. Y. Adams, who is a planter in this county. Four of the sons born to this marriage were in the Confederate army, Eighth Texas Cavalry, known as the Texas Rangers. J. Y. Adams was in the Fourth Alabama Infantry, and served in Virginia. Gen. Adams stood very high in Masonry in Texas, and was a man who had the interests of the order at heart. Of the two children born to his second marriage, both are now deceased. Our subject attended the schools of Perry County, and finished at Howard College, Marion, that county. He later engaged in planting in Marengo County, Ala., and continued this successfully until March, 1859, when he came to this county. Settling on the Brazos River, seven miles below there, Mr. Adams continued to make his home there until 1868, when he bought the Stafford place, moved here the following year, and has 820 acres in town tract, and 640 acres on the prairie. Mr. Adams put on the improvements and cleared up two-thirds of the land. Early in the year 1862 he joined the Eighth Cavalry, Company H, and remained in that company, holding the rank of private, until the close. He participated in the battle of Perryville, Ky., to the Gulf, and was at Greensboro, N. C., on detail duty. He also took part in the battles around Atlanta, Ga., Chickamauga and Knoxville. He was wounded once, but never taken prisoner. When he left the army he had no money, and was in debt. In the year 1872 he married Miss Columbia Ballard, while she was on a visit from Mississippi, and eight children were given them, three of whom are now living, all sons. Mrs. Adams is a member of the Methodist Church, and he is a Mason, taking almost as much interest in the order as did his father.

WILEY C. MUNN. As a merchant the gentleman whose name heads this sketch has been more than ordinarily successful, and has pursued his calling with energy and persistence, a secret, no doubt, of his success. He was born near the town of Jefferson, Texas, in 1861, his father, John H. Munn, having been born in Alabama. He came to Fayette County, Texas, many years ago, but since that time has resided in many different localities of the Lone Star State, although he has been a resident of Colorado County since the subject of this sketch was a young boy. His attention, during the active period of his life, was devoted to farming and stock-raising, but he is now retired from business and is living in Weimar. During the Civil War, or from 1861 to 1864, he was a soldier, and was stationed at Galveston the greater part of the time. His marriage resulted in the birth of eight sons and one daughter, three sons and the daughter having died quite young, four of whom are now living: N. C., who is a sheep-raiser of Coleman County, Texas; Richard, who is in business in Tyler, Texas; John, is associated in business with his brothers, N. C., and Wiley C. George is dead. The immediate subject of this biography spent his school days in Waco, and in 1884 started in business for himself on a limited scale, which has since broadened and branched out until it reached its present proportions. He has handled a great deal of cotton, amounting to 3,000 or 4,000 bales annually, and now continually carries an enormous stock of goods, and does considerable jobbing also. In 1884 he was married to Miss Georgia Jackson, a daughter of D. W. Jackson, the present representative of Colorado County in the State Legislature, and an old, well known and honorable citizen. Mrs. Munn is a worthy member of the Baptist Church, and socially Mr. Munn is a member of the K. of H. and the A. O. U. W. He and his wife are favorites in the social circles of Weimar, and their pleasant home has become well known for the free-hearted hospitality that is extended to all.

Rees P. Sweeny. Among the residents of Brazoria County, Texas, Mr. Rees P. Sweeny has made, through his upright and honorable record, many sincere friends, and there is no man at present residing in his locality who holds a higher position among its residents, or is more highly esteemed than he is. Mr. Sweeny, the present Collector of Taxes in Brazoria County, was born in Nashville, Tenn., November, 1856, son of Dr. Franklin Sweeny. The latter was a boy when his father, John Sweeny, left Tennessee in 1832 and landed in Brazoria County, Texas, early the following year. John Sweeny located on choice prairie land, and was one of the first men to start sugar culture in Brazoria County. He and J. P. Caldwell started in that business the same year. He was the father of ten children. Two of his sons served in the Texas army, and participated in the battle of San Jacinto, but all the children are now deceased, with the exception of one, John Sweeny, who now resides on Chance's Prairie, this county. Franklin Sweeny studied medicine under old Dr. Chinn, a noted physician in that section many years ago, and he also studied in Nashville, Tenn., and graduated from a medical college there. His death occurred in 1861. His wife, whose maiden name was Sarah E. Porter, was also born in Tennessee, and is now a resident of Galveston. Our subject, one of four children, spent his school days in Nashville, Tenn., and in 1871 he returned to Brazoria County, where he worked at a little of everything almost, to earn a living. For two years he ran a schooner on Brazos River, but later commenced farming on Chance's Prairie. In 1880 he was appointed Deputy Sheriff and Collector of this county, and in 1888 he was elected Sheriff and Collector, which position he held until 1890, when the office was divided. After that he held the position of Collector, was re-elected in 1892 and in the recent election. "That the man deserves the office and the office the man" has been demonstrated by the reforms that have been inaugurated in all departments of the office. He has the confidence of all, and was one of the few elected on the Republican ticket, but was endorsed by both parties. In March, 1892, he married Miss Betty R. Patton, a daughter of Matthew Patton, who is an old and prominent citizen of this county. Mr. Sweeny is a Royal Arch Mason.

Hon. John Henry Brown was born in the wilds of Missouri Territory, Pike County, October 29, 1820, and both his parents were Kentuckians, and at the time of his birth owned a fine farm and numerous slaves and live stock. The father, Capt. Henry S. Brown, was a man of great courage, possessed a love for adventure, and where danger was the thickest was always to be found, and was a fearless leader in conflicts with the Indians, and as skilled in woodcraft as the Red man himself. After a well-spent life, full of adventure, he died suddenly in Brazoria, July 26, 1834. Brown County, Texas, was named in his honor. His father, Caleb Brown, was a native of Maryland, born in 1759, and was a soldier of the Revolution. John Henry Brown, until was twelve years of age, was engaged in such farm labor as his strength enabled him to perform, and he then worked on a newspaper in his native town, which was then edited by A. B. Chambers, afterwards of the St. Louis *Republican.* After making his home for some time with Dr. James Kerr, on the Lavaca River, he moved to Austin in 1839 and obtained employment on the first issue of the *Texas Sentinel,* with which he was connected until the summer of 1840. After participating in a raid against the Indians, he returned to his uncle's, and was afterwards in the "Archer Campaign" and a number of other expeditions in defense of the raider frontier of Texas, and at Plum Creek a battle was fought in which the Indians were totally defeated. Mr. Brown killed an Indian chief in a single handed chase, and captured his cap surmounted with buffalo horns, which a friend soon afterward sent to the Cincinnati museum. In 1842, in obedience to a call for aid by a courier who arrived at midnight from San Antonio, Mr. Brown started for that place, and on reaching Cibolo a company was formed and he was made Lieutenant, after which he joined Capt. John C. Hayes in San Antonio, but the campaign did not result in anything decisive, and the volunteers were dispersed, and Lieutenant Brown attached himself to the spy company of John C. Hayes, after which several months were spent west of San Antonio, acting as pickets against both Mexicans and Indians. Upon his return home in the summer he found that he had been made Major of a regiment destined for service against Mexico, but was never called into service. After the capture of San Antonio by the Mexicans in 1842 Mr. Brown was made Lieutenant of a company, and a battle was fought at Salado; and in a sharp skirmish near that place Mr. Brown was wounded in the hip, which has proven more or less troublesome ever since. He took part in an engagement on the Honda, then returned home and was elected Lieutenant of a company for the Somerville expedition, but the expedition was a failure. Lieutenant Brown reached his mother's home at night, barefooted and nearly naked, and that winter and spring were the darkest days of Texas. June 9, 1843, Mr. Brown married Miss Mary F. Mitchell, of Groton, Conn., in Missouri, and the following winter was spent in Missouri, where Mr. Brown was very ill for some time. He then returned to Texas, and his first child, Julius Rufus, was born at his mother's home February 1, 1846. Later was employed on the Victoria *Advocate,* and was on the editorial department while the Mexican War was in progress, during which time he began writing historical pioneer sketches, and has at intervals continued to do so to the present. Many of his articles have been used in historical works, and he has preserved many interesting facts of Texas pioneer history from oblivion. When the State Militia was formed in 1846 he was made Brigadier-Major, and held the position four years, with the rank of Colonel. From 1848 to 1854 he resided in Indianola, during which time he founded the Indianola *Bulletin,* and was a contributor to De Bow's *Review.* After thorough and exhaustive reading he became a disciple to States' rights. In 1854 he purchased an interest in and became co-editor of the Galveston *Civilian,* but the chief editorial work fell upon his shoulders, and through some bitter political times he conducted his paper with such ability and wisdom that he was unanimously nominated for the Legislature, and then began his first work as a public speaker, which resulted in his triumphant election. He was an active and conscientious worker in the legislative body, and his course was eminently satisfactory to his constituency, and he was re-elected to the position. During this time he greatly improved Galveston in many ways, and numbers of abuses were corrected. He continued his editorial labors during this time, published numerous chapters on the Indian wars and pioneer history of Texas, and advocated the building of a railway from Galveston to Kansas City, Mo. He served his third term in the Legislature and introduced many important bills. Owing to declining health he in March, 1858, sold his interest in the *Civilian* and his home in Galveston, and removed to Belton, where in July he was appointed Commissioner by the Governor. The following year the Indians became very hostile, and Colonel Brown was at once placed in command of a company, and was very active for some time thereafter in quelling the Redmen. In the autumn of 1859 Colonel Brown became editor of the Belton *Democrat*, which wielded a wide influence in the political affairs of that stirring period. When the war opened he became a member of Gen. Ben McCulloch's staff, and after the latter's death at Elkshorn he was appointed Adjutant-general on the staff of Gen. Henry E. McCilloch. Owing to ill health he returned to his home in Texas in 1863, and after he had recovered from a surgical operation which had been performed by Drs. Parish and Herndon, he was placed in command of the Third Frontier District to protect it from Indians and bushwhackers. After Lee's surrender he moved with his family and resided in Mexico, and during the four years that he resided there he filled some important offices under the Mexican government. He was an extensive writer to various Texas papers during this time. In 1870 he arrived in New Orleans with his family, and for some time thereafter he delivered a series of lectures in different cities in the North. He rejoined his family in Texas in 1871. Julius, who served with distinction in the Confederate army, died in Dallas, Texas, in 1873; Pierre Mitchell, who also served in the war, married, and died May 19, 1876; Clara (Mrs. T. B. Mitchell), Lizzie and Marion Taylor constitute the family. In 1872 he was elected to the State Legislature once more, and as of yore he was an active worker. At various times he has filled honorable and responsible positions, and, to his credit be it said, always with marked ability. Although ill health has been his portion the greater part of his life, he has been one of the foremost citizens of Texas in all ways, and is now one of the honored citizens of the State and a resident of Dallas. He has published several volumes on the history of Texas.

COL. FRANCIS MARION HICKS. This prominent old settler of Texas was born in Georgia, Nov. 16, 1826, being the fourth of five children born to William A. and Margaret (Moon) Hicks, who were married near Raleigh, N. C., and were born in Tennessee and North Carolina, respectively. The paternal grandfather, John Hicks, was born in Virginia, and was a soldier of the Revolution. After that great strife was over he moved to Tennessee, of which State he was among the first settlers. He came of English ancestors, who settled in Virginia during colonial days. William A. Hicks settled in Georgia when a young man, and engaged in planting and trading, but afterwards moved to Alabama and then to Mississippi, thence to Arkansas, and finally to Texas in 1849. Here he settled in Cherokee County and became one of the settlers of Rusk. He was an old line Whig politically, and was elected to the Legislature from Cherokee County, which was strongly Democratic. He was also a County Clerk in Georgia, and was quite a party leader of the Whigs there, and a strong Henry Clay man. He became a prominent planter of Cherokee County, and there made his home until death closed his career. His wife died when the subject of this sketch was a boy, in Hickstown, Ga., which place was named in his honor. It was a gold mining town, and his early days were spent as a miner. He was a Royal Arch Mason, and was an active and enterprising citizen. Francis M. Hicks was educated in Mississippi, was married at Paulding, Jasper County, and began life as a merchant. In 1852 he came to Cherokee County, Texas, but shortly after removed to Corsicana, Navaro County, Texas, and began business as one of the early merchants of the place. Shortly after he sold out and returned to Rusk, where he was engaged in business until the outbreak of the war. In 1861 he entered a company and went to Galveston, where he was detailed to act as Commissary at Rusk, and served in that capacity about one year. He was then detailed by Gen. Kirby Smith as the financial agent of the Government iron works at Rusk, and served in that capacity until the war closed, his assistance being almost invaluable to the Government. The war left Mr. Hicks almost destitute, but he at once embarked in business at Rusk, where he continued until 1868, when he went to Shreveport and opened a commission house, which is known as the Hicks Company, Limited. In 1872 he associated with him Mr. Robert H. Howell, under the firm name of Hicks & Howell, dealers in groceries and the cotton factorage business. They were very fortunate in their operations and prospered from the very beginning, and on the solid foundation which was then laid there had been builded the stanchest commercial organization in the State of Louisana, outside of the city of New Orleans. After sixteen years of lucrative business, the firm of Hicks & Howell was dissolved, and Mr. Howell took from the establishment a fortune without the least affecting its standing or credit. Mr. Hicks then took into partnership his son, S. B. Hicks, a young gentleman whose education, training and natural business ability peculiarly fitted him for the responsible position to which he was called. The firm name was then changed to F. M. & S. B. Hicks, and continued in existence for four years, during which time the failing condition of Col. Hicks' health caused him to throw the burden of the extensive business, in all its multitudinous details, on the shoulders of his son, who proved equal to the occasion, and won his spurs in an arena where many older and more experienced had failed. In 1892 the present incorporation was formed under the name of the Hicks Company, Limited, whose business is exclusively wholesale grocers and cotton factors, their place of business is admirably located where the house has for many years been established. Col. Hicks' name is justly at the head of this establishment, though he is no longer able, on account of his health, to take an active part in its affairs. He was compelled to seek a change of climate, came to San Antonio, and has been greatly benefited thereby. The active management of the business now devolves upon his son, S. B. Hicks, Vice-President, who is ably assisted by Capt. W. T. Crawford, Secretary and Treasurer. Mr. W. F. Chase is the cashier and book-keeper, T. H. Scovell is head salesman, and F. H. Gosman has charge of the cotton department. All these gentlemen have been long connected with the business, and are by experience and special adaptability thoroughly equipped for their several responsible and exacting positions. To give an idea of the immense business transacted by this house, it is but necessary to state that its storeroom, merchandise and cotton warehouses, have a floor space, under roof, exceeding by 16,000 square feet, an acre of floor space, and the annual sales aggregate considerably over a million dollars. Col. Hicks' kindly face and genial manners endears him to all with whom he comes in contact, and socially or otherwise makes him popular with all classes. He is a man of rare business qualifications and indomitable energy, and to him is due full credit for the decided success achieved by the firm, whose name will always adorn the best pages of Shreveport's commercial history. He was made a Mason in Mississippi, and in April, 1851, was married to Miss Ann E. McDugald, a daughter of James McDugald, of Scotland, who became a prominent lawyer of Mississippi at Paulding, where he was an active citizen and served as State Senator. To Col. Hicks and his wife four sons and four daughters were given: Emma L., Lelia, wife of Dr. Lawrence, of Longview, Texas; Francis Marion, Jr.; Clara, wife of Callie McArthur Walke, who is a business man of Shreveport; Samuel B., who was educated in Shreveport and graduated at Soule College, New Orleans, in which educational institution he won a medal. He is now General Manager and Vice-president of the Hicks Co. of Shreveport; Marshal was educated at Shreveport and graduated at the Southwestern University of Clarksville, Tenn. He studied law for two years at the State University, Austin, Texas, from which he graduated and began practicing at Minneola, Texas, with Capt. Giles, a prominent lawyer. He came to San Antonio and was appointed District Attorney of Laredo District, by Gov. Hogg, after which he was elected to that office and served four years. He is now a practitioner of San Antonio, but was married in Clarksville. Richard Yale is also a lawyer of San Antonio. Annie McD.; and one that died early. Francis Marion was educated at Rusk and Shreveport, La., studying medicine in the later place also, after which he attended lectures at Bellevue College Hospital, New York, from which he graduated. He began practicing at Rusk, but in a short time went to Tyler, Texas, where he built up a large practice, but labored so incessantly that he injured his health, to improve which he went to California, and in 1890 returned to San Antonio, where he has built up a large practice. His attention is given to all branches of his profession, but he makes something of a specialty of surgery and surgical cases, and is a member of the Texas State Medical Society; and is also a member and First Vice-president of the Southwest Texas Medical Association. He is surgeon of the International & Great Northern Railway at San Antonio, and while at Tyler he was chief, and later, consulting surgeon of the Cotton Belt Railroad, but resigned from the former office on account of ill health. While at Tyler he was medical examiner for nearly all the old line life insurance companies. The doctor is a student in his profession, and in 1882 spent six months studying at the Jefferson Medical College, and the Medical department of the University of Pennsylvania, at Philadelphia. In 1885 he went to New York and took a post graduate course at New York Polyclinic Medical College, and made extensive special study of surgery and diseases of the eye, ear and nose, to aid him in his office of Chief Surgeon of the Cotton Belt Railroad. In 1887 he made a trip to California in search of health, but since coming to San Antonio he has enjoyed comparatively good health. He was married in 1887 to Miss Margaret R. Spence, a native of Texas, and a daughter of John Spence, one of the early settlers of the Lone Star State from Maryland. He belongs to an old Scotch family that came to this country during colonial times, that assisted in founding and became members of the first Presbyterian Church in America, at Snow Hill, Md., and from that time down to the present day some member of the family has been an elder in that historic church. Mrs. Hicks is a highly educated lady, of decided literary and musical taste and talent. She graduated from the Augusta Female Institute at Staunton, Va., the finest young ladies' college in the South. There she won a medal for scholarship and music. Her union with Dr. Hicks has resulted in the birth of two children. The doctor and his wife are members of the First Presbyterian church, and he is an elder in the same. Politically he has always been in sympathy with the Democratic party, and has served as delegate to various conventions.

COL. STEPHEN M. BLOUNT. This historic name will live while Texas has a history, as one of the signers of the Texas Declaration of Independence. In 1888 he was the oldest surviving one of the signers. He was born in Georgia, February 13, 1808, and became prominent there as an official, and especially in connection with military affairs. He was colonel of the Eighth Regiment of Georgia militia, and was Aid-de-camp to military generals in 1832–34. In 1835 he emigrated to Texas, and there conceived a warm personal friendship for General Houston. In 1836 he was elected a member of the convention that declared the independence of Texas and nominated General Houston for Commander-in-chief of the Texan forces. In 1837 he was elected Clerk of San Augustine County, and held that position four years. His life was a most active one, and he never ceased to recall with pride the part he took in the achievement of independence for Texas, or to regard Houston as one of the grandest of men.

PROKOP HOFFMAN. This is one of the very oldest, and most assuredly one of the most highly esteemed citizens of Corpus Christi. He is a product, however, of Bohemia, where he was born in 1820, the fifth of seven children born to Edward Hoffman, who lived and died in the old country. In 1849 Prokop Hoffman came to the United States, and after a short residence in New Orleans, came direct to Corpus Christi. His brother, Alexander, had preceded him to this country in 1846, and in the same year he enlisted in the army for the Mexican War, becoming a member of Company A, First Missouri Regiment. After that war was over he came to Texas and became extensively engaged in the cattle and sheep business, but was killed by the Indians in 1861. Another brother came to America in 1856, came at once to Corpus Christi and here spent his life, dying at San Diego in 1890. Prokop Hoffman began his life in Corpus Christi as a barber, and continued that occupation up to the opening of the Civil War, when he assisted in raising a company, but did not enter the service. He began running a line of hacks and wagons at Brownsville, and did quite an extensive trading business until Brownsville fell into the hands of the Federals. At the close of the war Mr. Hoffman brought a stock of provisions from Indianola, and until a few years ago was quite extensively engaged in merchandising. He became the owner of a ranch of 6,000 acres, engaged in the cattle business, but disposed of the property in 1889 for $40,000. In 1865 he was appointed County Treasurer, and the following year was elected to the same office, including the present limits of Duval County, and was re-elected at the expiration of his first term. He has been Alderman of Corpus Christi for a long time, and has also ably filled the office of Justice of the Peace. He was married in New Orleans in 1849 to Miss Adelaide Rennar, a native also of Bohemia, and to their union five children have been given: William, who married Miss Roscher, has been associated with his father in business for years; Alexander, born in 1853, was drowned in Corpus Christi Bay in 1890, and the other children died in infancy.

WILLIAM I. GLENN. The name of this gentleman, who is now County Attorney of Austin County, is by the great mass of the people of this section regarded as synonymous with good citizenship and unselfish devotion to the public weal. There is no cloud upon it, and it is brightened by use like rare gold. There has been no sphere in which its owner has been called to labor in which he has not acted with wisdom and in the most shining good faith. As citizen, lawyer, etc., he has won the respect and esteem of all. Mr. Glenn was born in this county October 16, 1842, and is a son of Alexander and Sarah P. (Shelburn) Glenn, natives respectively of Georgia and Tennessee. The Glenn family came to Texas in 1840, and the following year Mr. Glenn married Miss Shelburn. Later, he taught school, also followed farming, and for thirteen years previous to the war held the office of Surveyor. After the war he held that position for eight years, making twenty-one years in all. During the Civil War he did not enter the service, but remained at home, and being a man of considerable means, gave freely of it to the widows and orphans of the brave soldiers who had fallen. He also gave liberally of his means to those in service. Mr. Glenn commenced life a poor man, and remained in Alabama with his parents until twenty-eight years of age. He then came to this State, as before mentioned, gathered around him considerable wealth, and, like a dutiful son, returned to Alabama for his parents, and then brought them with him to his adopted State. Few men were better or more favorably known in this portion of the State than Mr. Glenn, whose charitable acts and noble deeds were well known. In 1887 he became a member of the Missionary Baptist Church, as did also the partner of his joys and sorrows, his most excellent wife. She still survives him. Their happy married life extended over a period of fifty-three years, and they reared eight children: W. I., Sinia E. J., wife of William H. Francis, of this place; Calpernia T., wife of John W. Good, District Clerk of this county; Sarah A., John P., Eliza S., wife of George S. Cummings, Clerk of Austin County; James A., of Galveston, Texas, where he holds the position of chief clerk in the postoffice, and Lucy, wife of S. P. Cummings, of this county. At the time Mr. Glenn came to the county, San Felipe was the county seat. He took quite an active part and assisted in surveying and laying out the present city site, and subsequently moved to the place, being one of its oldest settlers, having resided here for forty years. While living in Alabama Mr. Glenn first commenced surveying, and followed this for some time before coming to Texas. He was also engaged in steamboating on the Tennessee River for some time. William I. Glenn received his early education in the common schools of Austin county, and in the school in Industry. In the year 1868 he commenced reading law under A. Chesley of this place, and was admitted to the bar in December of that year, Judge James McFarland presiding. Mr. Glenn then located in this county, where a flattering practice awaited him, and a few years afterwards was appointed County Attorney, serving two years. From that time until 1886 he was out of office, but in the fall of that year he was again elected County Attorney, and has been successively chosen to that office at each election since. In 1861 he joined Capt. M. Dade's Company of Kirby's Battery, and was stationed at Dickinson's Bayou and Galveston for six months. His term of enlistment expiring, he at once joined Company F, Sixteenth Infantry, and participated in Gaines' Landing, Mansfield, Pleasant Hill, Jenkins' Ferry, etc. From here he was transferred to Company G, Third Regiment, Green's Brigade, cavalry, but did not take part in any more battles. He was discharged at Crockett, Houston County, and returned home some time in June, 1865. The remainder of that year and in 1866 he was engaged in freighting from Houston, and in 1867 he farmed his father's land, working negroes, and meeting with unusual success. This life did not suit him, however, and as before stated, he began the study of law. In the year 1872 he was married to Miss Mary E. Pilley, a native of this county and daughter of M. R. and Alice (Bradbury) Pilley, very early settlers of Texas. Mr. Pilley was born in England, and after coming to this country served in the war with Mexico. He was one of the Mier prisoners, had to draw a bean for his life, and although he drew a white bean and was saved, he suffered such untold hardships that he almost wished he had drawn a black one. The Bradbury family was first represented in Texas by William Bradbury, who came to the Empire State in 1828, and was one of the brave soldiers who fell during the Civil War. He was Chief Justice of Austin County for several years, and subsequently served as County Clerk. Mr. and Mrs. Glenn are the parents of eight children, four of whom survive: Robert P., Fred I., Richard C. and Elenor. In religion, Mr. and Mrs. Glenn are members of the Episcopal Church, and in politics he has ever affiliated with the Democratic party. He is a member of the Masonic Fraternity, Bellville Lodge No. 223; the Knights of Honor, Bellville Lodge No 2105, and also Woodmen of the World.

MAJOR JOHN S. McCAMPBELL. For a man to become distinguished at the bar requires that he should be possessed of more than average intelligence and be ambitious to excel, and if these qualities are possessed by him, he will, without doubt, rise to eminence in his profession. Major John S. McCampbell has been more than usually successful in pursuing the legal profession, and has built up a clientele that is large and lucrative. He was born in Knox County, Tenn., in 1827, the youngest of nine children born to William B. and Patsy (McReynolds) McCampbell, who were also natives of Tennessee. The paternal grandfather, Solomon McCampbell, was born in Scotland and came to America in colonial times, being accompanied by his two brothers. They settled in Tennessee, Kentucky and Virginia, respectively, and all served during the Revolutionary War. William B. McCampbell was a merchant and farmer, and followed these occupations in Alabama after his removal to that State in 1832. He was a soldier in the War of 1812, and became a very substantial citizen of Alabama. From that State the family removed to Texas in 1837, and for a time resided in Washington County, where the mother was called from life. The remainder of the family then went to Austin County, and in 1845 to Goliad, where the father resided until his death in 1863. In 1837, when the family were en-route to Texas and had crossed the Gulf from New Orleans to Texas on the schooner Flash, it was chased by a Mexican war vessel, and the Flash was wrecked on the west end of Galveston Island. The people were saved by Parry Humphries, and all were compelled to walk to Galveston, about forty-five miles distant. Mr. McCampbell had a large stock of goods on board with which to go into business, but all was lost.

Major John S. McCampbell was ten years of age at the time he came to the Lone Star State, and in 1845 he was placed in school at Jacksonville, Ala., where he remained one year, then joined the army for the Mexican war, Coffee's regiment, and during the one year that he was in the service he took part in the capture of Vera Cruz. At the cessation of hostilities he returned to Alabama to school, and remained there until 1849, when he went to Knoxville University, completing his studies there. Upon his return to Jacksonville, he began studying law and was admitted to the bar, after which he at once came to Texas, and in 1851 began practicing at Goliad. In 1852 he was united in marriage with Miss Anna E. Atlee, a native of Pennsylvania. In 1861 he was appointed by Judge Devine as Confederate States Receiver of his district, a position he held until 1864. He then raised a company for the Confederate service, and was elected First Lieutenant of a company belonging to Mann's battalion, but the war ended soon after. In 1868 he came to Corpus Christi, Texas, where he has since been in the active practice of his profession, and is well known to his brother practitioners and to the citizens of the section in which he lives. He has a handsome home near town, a good farm and other valuable property, the result of his own persistent efforts and determination to make a success of his life. He is a member of the A. F. & A. M., Council Degree of Goliad, and he and his wife have long been connected with the Presbyterian Church. To Major and Mrs. McCampbell five children have been given: Elizabeth, wife of E. H. Wheeler, of New Orleans; Edwin Atlee is a lawyer, and is associated with his father in the practice of his profession; Ada G., wife of J. S. Henderson; William B., a lawyer of Corpus Christi, and Eva.

JAMES H. FRENCH (deceased). Although called to that bourne whence no traveler returns, this gentleman so lived, while here on earth, as to win him the universal respect and confidence of his fellow mortals, and is especially deserving of mention in this volume, devoted to the history of prominent and useful citizens. He was born in the Old Dominion March 26, 1835, in Warrenton, Fauquier County. His paternal grandfather, Stephen French, was born in the north of Ireland, but emigrated from that country with two brothers, William and James, in colonial times, and settled in Prince William County, Va. At the age of eighteen years Stephen enlisted in the patriot army, endured the hardships of Valley Forge, and took part in the battle of Yorktown. James French, his son, and father of the subject of this sketch, was born in Prince William County, Va., March 18, 1801, and became a farmer of enterprise and intelligence, and for three years was a member of the House of Delegates from Fauquier County, Va., and after a well-spent life died May 7, 1850. The maternal grandmother, Martha Williams, was a member of the distinguished Williams and Lanier families, of North Carolina and Tennessee, respectively. The subject of this sketch had two sisters and two brothers, Marcellus, Junius B., Matilda and Rosalie. Marcellus French moved to Texas in 1852, and in 1857 he commanded an expedition for the relief of Gen. Walker, in Nicaragua, and in August of the same year he was elected to the Legislature from Bexar and Atascosa counties. He returned to Virginia in July, 1861, and was in the Confederate army of Northern Virginia, which he joined in October, 1861, ranking as Captain in Lamb's brigade of cavalry, and since the war has resided in Virginia. Junius B. was also an officer in the Confederate army, being Adjutant of the Forty-third

North Carolina Regiment, and was killed at Gettysburg July 1, 1863. Matilda became the wife of David Hewes, of Oakland, Cal., and is now deceased, while Rosalie married Arthur Brown, whose father was British Consul at Hawaii, Sandwich Island, in 1861. James H. French received a liberal education at the academy of his native town, which was supplemented by a course in the preparatory school of Columbia College, Washington, D. C. An enterprising spirit led him to emigrate to the new State of Texas. He located at San Antonio in 1851, and made that city his home mainly until his death, and having inherited considerable property from his father, he employed it with such prudence and sagacity as to accumulate quite a handsome estate. When the Civil War broke out he entered the Confederate army, in May, 1861, and served in the Adjutant-General's office until the 19th of October, 1861, when he was appointed Captain, and was assigned to the Commissary Department of the army under Gen. Herbert, on the Rio Grande River. In January, 1863, he was transferred to the purchasing department, where he remained until March, 1865, when he took charge of the reserve department of supplies located at San Diego, for the forces operating under Col. John S. Ford. At the close of the war he found that his fortune had been swept away, leaving him little more than his energy, enterprise and push, with which to retrieve what he had lost, and place his young family again in comfortable circumstances. At the close of the war he was thirty years of age, and possessed the qualities that rarely fail to win success. He inspired confidence in those with whom he came in contact, and won many warm friends by his manly conduct and honorable bearing, and he was admirably adapted to discharge the duties which he was afterwards called upon to perform. The city of San Antonio had been wretchedly misgoverned, its credit had fallen to a low ebb; its treasury was depleted; its bonds were hawked in public at a heavy discount; its script was looked upon as of little worth; its public school system had been abandoned; debt rested like a nightmare upon the city, paralyzing its business energies and clogging the channels of commerce; bankruptcy stood like a gaunt and hungry wolf at the door; recklessness and negligence had marked previous administrations of public affairs, and ruin or repudiation seemed the only alternatives. It was at such a time that the people of this city began to disregard party lines in local affairs, and to look about for some good man of business tact, who would be able to reconstruct the municipal government out of the chaotic mass. Capt. French, though voting with the Democrats, was by no means a partisan. At city affairs he looked with a business and not a party eye. He longed to see badly kept books overhauled and the balance sheet struck, so that property holders might know how heavily their property was mortgaged. He desired to see schools revived, improvements begun, and new enterprises projected and carried out. His fellow-citizens had confidence in his judgment and integrity, and therefore, in 1875, he was brought forward without distinction of party as a candidate for city Mayor, in opposition to the regular Democratic nominee, and after a spirited contest he was elected by a majority of 104 votes. Had the board of aldermen the progressive ideas that characterized him, there would have been an immediate and healthful revolution, but he found himself confronted by a hostile and stubborn opposition, and could make but slow headway. He familiarized himself with the details of municipal affairs, looked into the public debt, made himself acquainted with the cause of former failures, and projected and advocated plans to relieve the city of its burdens, and pointed out the nicety of certain improvements, and suggested the means by which they might be accomplished. In short, he addressed himself heart and soul to the task of redeeming San Antonio, and street contracts were carried out and paid for in money, confidence was again restored to the people, the doors of the public schools were thrown open, the amount and character of the city debt was ascertained and classified, and public business was conducted on such principles only as a strict business man would adopt. At the end of the first year of his service he was able to present an intelligent view of the solution, and to show tax payers how their city business had been conducted. At the end of two years he had fully ingratiated himself in the favor of the conservative class, and when he was nominated in 1877 for a second term, he was triumphantly elected, and received a largely increased majority. Although he was again confronted with difficulties, and was compelled to fight his way inch by inch, yet he succeeded in introducing many needed reforms and improvements. The credit of the city was partially restored, and all felt the influence of his wise and patriotic measure. In 1879 he was again nominated for Mayor, and elected by a majority of 803 votes. He endeared himself to the citizens by bringing order out of chaos, lifting the city out of the mire and placing it upon solid rock. He was re-elected in 1881, again for the fifth term in 1883, but in 1885 declined to become a candidate for the office, but was nominated Alderman, and for the following two years fulfilled the duties of this position, which ended his career as a public man; twelve of the best years of his life having been given to the service of his city, the home of his adoption. Capt. French was married in San Antonio, Texas, October 15, 1856, to Miss Sarah L. Webb, who was born at Detroit, Mich., October 6, 1836, a daughter of Henry Webb, who was Cashier of the Bank at Ithaca, N. Y. Mrs. French, through her father, is descended from the Webb family who came from England and settled in New England in 1640, and intermarried with the Adams and Bradford families, of Revolutionary and Plymouth Rock fame. Her mother was Olive Ann Sellsrigg, whose grandfather, Jeremiah Sellsrigg (formerly Sellkirk), enlisted at the age of sixteen and served through the Revolution. His wife was a sister of Matthew Vassar, the founder of Vassar College. Mrs. French is a scholarly and eminently talented lady. She was appointed Regent for Texas of the General Society of the Daughters of the Revolution, and has been very active in enrolling members, the membership in Texas being quite large. She was also recently made a member of the Historical Society of the State of Virginia. To the union of Mr. and Mrs. French five children were given: Junius B., born January 29, 1858, graduated from Roanoke College, Virginia, in 1879, and afterwards, in 1883, at Hampton-Sidney College, where he studied theology, and is now pastor of the Broadway Presbyterian Church in Fort Worth. He married Miss Annie Dial, of San Marcos, and has three children. Olive Ann was born February 25, 1860, and was educated at Vassar College. She married Joseph P. Devine, of San Antonio, and they have had six children, one of whom is now dead. James Vassar, born June 25, 1864, attended Hampton-Sidney College, and married Miss Augusta Hirshfield, of Fort Worth; Sarah L., born February 21, 1867, and Franklin G., born July 25, 1872. Mr. French was reared under Presbyterian influence, and was regarded as orthodox in his religious views. His personal appearance was attractive and pleasing. His features were clear cut and expressive, his eyes were deep blue, his hair gray, and in height he was six feet and one inch tall, and weighed 240 pounds. He was a distinguished figure in any assembly, and his talents would cause him to be recognized as a gentleman of fine ability and distinction. His death occurred in San Antonio September 6, 1893. The following article is taken from the editorial of the San Antonio *Express* of September 8, 1893: "James H. French is dead, an Apollo with silver hair, a Chesterfieldian gentleman under any circumstances, to all a monitor, to man an example, to age a staff, to youth a guide, philosopher and friend. All knew him, and to know him was to love him, for his heart was a well-spring of courtesy and kindness, pure as a child's, broad and deep as humanity. He was brave as Cæsar, generous as Macenas, tender as Guaetemu, and true as the stars to their appointed courses. He looked quite through the outward show of things into the things themselves, and none, however poor their lot or lowly their condition, were passed by without a graceful, cheery recognition that added a new significance to life. The market woman and the leader of society shared alike his cordial salutation, and the honest toiler in his working blouse received the same courtly consideration as the distinguished citizen. It is strange that all, without distinction, should feel that death had dispoiled them of one near and dear—that the entire city should mingle its tears with those of the stricken family. For ten years Mayor of the city, for more than four years Alderman, he left an unblemished reputation. His hands were ever clean and his character above reproach. He possessed great administrative and executive ability, and considering the limited means at his command left many enduring monuments of his progressive spirit. In public and private life his counsel was eagerly sought, and to him the poor and helpless turned as instinctively as the helianthus turns its face to the rising sun. Honored as a citizen, esteemed as a neighbor, beloved as a friend, idolized as a husband and father, such was he whom death has claimed, who now lies before us, the pathetic ruin of his former self, the strong hand irresponding to our convulsive pressure, the warm heart chilled at last, the cheery voice which scattered bowers of sunshine shimmering like purest gold down many a desolate path now hushed forever. The heart sinks low in anguish, and beneath the dark shadow, and the hand still tingling with his cordial salute, trembles and hesitates at the task so unexpectedly forced upon it, that of recording that James H. French has passed from time to eternity. Our loss is irreparable. We only unite in tendering our sympathy to those nearer and dearer to him than all others, so suddenly called upon to yield to God their greatest treasure. Mr. French was buried at the City Cemetery on Powder House Hill, September 8, and the funeral services were conducted by Rev. D. Hanson Irwin, whose text was 'Thou shalt be missed, because thy seat will be empty.' The sermon was a touching and appropriate tribute to the dead. The City Hall remained closed that day, and business was suspended in many of the leading commercial houses of the city, as a token of respect and affection to him who had passed from among them."

CONRAD FRANZ. It is almost invariably the case that natives of Germany prove themselves in every respect industrious, progressive, law-abiding citizens, and the United States may well be proud of her Teutonic element. One who is considered an exceptionally successful man is Conrad Franz, who came from Germany with his father, John Franz, and landed in Galveston October 11, 1845. The latter was born in the Kingdom of Nassau, and while living in Germany had been in the state mines. He was a wheelwright by trade, and after coming to this country stopped at Indianola with the German colony for three months. From there he went to Matagorda and thence to the Peninsula, where he has made his home for fifteen years, dying there in 1858, when fifty-seven years of age. His wife, whose given-name was Elizabeth, died on the Peninsula in 1873, when fifty-three or fifty-four years of age. They were members of the Lutheran Church. While residing on the Peninsula the father followed the wheelwright trade, and there reared his family, eight children, four of whom died young. Those living are: Catherine Williams, of Big Hill, this county; Conrad, our subject; Mrs. E. Berg, and Mrs. Zipprian, of Big Hill. In his native country Conrad Franz received a fair education in his native language, but did not learn to speak the English language until after coming to the United States. He learned the wheelwright and ship carpenter trade under his brother-in-law, but subsequently turned his attention principally to ship building, and had a shipyard on the Peninsula. During the war he had a yard at Matagorda and quite a number of men at work, partly for himself and partly for the government. He made a number of ships that went to Mexican ports, and kept on building until the war closed. Mr. Franz then moved to the plantation, twelve miles north of town on the Colorado River, 3,400 acres, and turned his attention to farming and stock-raising, but still followed carpentering to some extent. He built bridges on all streams in the county with exception of Colorado River. From 1869 to 1873 he held the office of Sheriff, but previous to this held the position of County Commissioner. He was married in this county in 1856 to Miss Baxter, daughter of William Baxter, and a native of this county. Fifteen children were born to this union, twelve of whom are now living, and all in this county but two. These children are: Mary, deceased, was the wife of Henry Eidlebach; William R., is in Matagorda County; Martha A., wife of William C. Williams, at Big Hill; Manda Jane, wife of Greenbury Savage, of this county; John C., in Matagorda County; Charles P., at home; Joseph Samuel, James H., deceased; Silas E., in Matagorda; Paul Franklin, on a farm; Marie T., wife of Emanuel Sexton, at this place; Eliza Lorena, Maggie F., wife of J. C. McGehee; Arthur G., deceased, and Myrtle E., at home. Our subject was born February 17, 1831. He is a member of the K. of H. at Matagorda, and he and his wife are members of the M. E. Church.

OSCAR C. LOVENSKIOLD. This successful merchant and Mayor of Corpus Christi, Texas, was born in the city of New Orleans, La., in 1850, being the oldest in a family of seven children born to Baron Charles G. and Sophia F. (Clark) Lovenskiold, the paternal ancestors being of illustrious Icelandic-Danish descent. The paternal grandparents were Baron Frederick Stephanus Lovenskiold and Charlotte Elizabeth de Tuxen, the former of whom was born in Copenhagen, Denmark, October, 24, 1794, and married on the 24th of November, 1821. To this worthy couple but one child was born, Baron Charles G. Lovenskiold. Baron Frederick Stephanus Lovenskiold was the Attorney-general to His Royal Highness the King of Denmark, and was Commander of the Order of Knights of Donnebrog, and resided in a castle there. He was a man of decided literary tastes and wrote many books, mainly of Icelandic history. His father, the founder of this branch of the family, was born in Iceland October 6, 1752, and was in the government service. He moved to Copenhagen and was married there to Grunild Cecilia Dybe in 1792, and there continued to make his home until his death March 4, 1829. Baron Charles G. Lovenskiold was the only member of the family that ever came to the United States, and his arrival in Florida dates from about 1847. He removed from there to New Orleans, La., and was married there in 1849 to Miss Clark, a daughter of Capt. Joseph Clark, of Newton Center, Mass., and Sarah (McLain) Clark, of New London, Conn. Baron Charles G. Lovenskiold came to Corpus Christi with his family in 1855 and became one of the most brilliant lawyers in western Texas. He was an impressive and forcible speaker, clear and concise in his statements, a man of keen discernment, a finished scholar and a fine Spanish, Danish, French and English scholar. He was of dominating literary taste and genius, was a contributor to papers, periodicals, etc., before he was twenty years of age. During the Civil War he served as a Colonel in the Confederate army, and was active and prominent in political matters. He was elected Alderman of the city of Corpus Christi, and died in that office in 1875, a prominent member of the A. F. & A. M. The subject of this sketch was born November 28, 1850, in New Orleans, but the most of his school days were spent in Corpus Christi, and during the war he was under the tuition of Father Gonard, a Catholic priest, and at the close of the war he entered the College of Christian Brothers at New Orleans, and was an earnest, studious and dutiful student, and still retains his instructors in kindly remembrance. In 1868 he entered the commercial house of Edey, Kirstein & Wallace in Corpus Christi, at first without salary, but was soon paid twenty dollars per month for his services, and that was frequently advanced thereafter. The members of the firm changed occasionally, but Mr. Lovenskiold was always retained and usually with advanced salary until about 1874, until he was receiving a salary of seventy-five dollars per month. He had always, from early boyhood, had a desire to become a merchant and a ranchman, so at the time he concluded to start in business for himself, although without capital but with many friends, he bought a stock of groceries on credit, and on the 4th of May, 1874, embarked on the mercantile sea. At about the same time he bought a piece of land, purchased some sheep to stock it, and at the same time bought some city property, all on credit. His natural and acquired business ability, with the practice of judicious economy, caused all these enterprises to thrive and prosper, so that he met all payments promptly, and was soon out of debt. He now owns a handsome store on the bluff, carries a stock of goods valued at about $2,000 and does an annual business of about $4,000. He has excellent ranch property in the county, amounting to 10,000 acres of the best land, all which is fenced and stocked with improved breeds of cattle, horses and sheep. He has also been active in politics, and in 1886 was elected Alderman for the Fifth Ward for two years by a large majority, and in 1888 was re-elected without opposition. In 1890 it was the desire of his many friends that he run for Mayor, and he reluctantly consented and was defeated. Soon after there was a vacancy in the Board of Aldermen and he was elected to fill the position for one year, and in 1891 was re-elected for two years. At the expiration of his term he was again nominated for Mayor, and on the 5th of April, 1892, defeated his former opponent at the polls, and in April, 1894, was honored with a re-election. He has been a very useful citizen, and the way he has surmounted the many difficulties that have strewn his pathway reflects the greatest credit upon his good judgment. He has been a member of the A. F. & A. M. at Corpus Christi since about 1877.

Col. James W. Fannin. This brave and unfortunate hero occupies a warm place in the memory of old Texans. He participated in the battle of Conception in October, 1835. Directly afterward he was stationed at Velasco in command of the force there. Early in 1836 he was appointed military agent to raise and concentrate all volunteers who were willing to take part in an expedition against Matamoras. A year later he assisted in the defense of Goliad, but made a fatal mistake which precipitated his defeat. He and his entire command were made prisoners and massacred. No less than 300 thus fell victims to Mexican inhumanity and barbarism. A dashing and intrepid officer, Colonel Fannin was yet lacking in caution, and it is believed that he might have prevented the awful butchery by which he and his brave followers died had he properly estimated the strength of the enemy.

R. J. Ransom. This gentleman, who is the manager of the Harlem sugar plantation, owned and operated by the State of Texas, was born in Carroll County, Miss., November 7, 1835. His father, William Ransom, was a native of Georgia, but at an early date moved from that State to Mississippi, where he died. He was a saddler by trade, but after moving to Mississippi became a planter. For eight years he served as Sheriff of Carroll County, held other responsible positions, and was a prominent man. His death occurred in 1845, when forty-five years of age. A large family was born to his marriage, only four of whom are now living in Texas. One son is manager of Capt. Dunovant's sugar plantation at Pugh Lake, one daughter is in Houston, and another in Dallas. R. J. Ransom, on growing up, turned his attention to farming, and after a time went to the Yazoo River in Mississippi, where he made his home until 1859, when he came to Texas. His mother had come to this State in 1857, and his first trip was on a visit to see her. While here he was persuaded by Jefferson Kyle and Col. B. F. Terry to take charge of their sugar plantation, which is the one now owned by Col. E. H. Cunningham. After a few months on this place he went to Bazoria County for the same firm, Kyle & Terry, to take charge of a sugar plantation for them there. This was the Chenango plantation. In 1862 he joined the Confederate Army in a minute company up and down the coast in Texas, and with D. S. Terry's scouts on Gen. Wharton's staff was then in Louisiana. After the war he resumed charge of Terry's two plantations until, in 1869, he came back to Fort Bend County, and again took charge of Kyle & Terry's place, Sugarland. In 1876 he was managing convicts for Mr. Dunlavy, and for Mr. Freman in 1877, remaining with these gentlemen until 1880, when Col. Ellis bought out Mr. Freman. After this Mr. Ransom was with first one and then the other, Col. Ellis and E. H. Cunningham, until 1885, when he purchased a place of his own on the railroad and farmed for a time. Under his supervision these mammoth sugar places have been cleared up and ditched, and his reputation as a farmer and manager had become so well known that when the State bought the Harlem place he was selected as manager. This was in October, 1886. In four years under his management the farm has paid for itself. The sugar house has all the latest improvements, and there are now $2,000 to the credit of the State besides. He is a most scientific farmer, and as a manager none better can be found. They have the State convicts on the place, and they are so well treated and well managed that it seems a pleasure on their part to work hard. Mr. Ransom believes in humane treatment, and is well liked by all under him. In 1869 he married Miss Mary Ella Bertrand, a daughter of Thomas Bertrand,

and a native of Fort Bend County. Four sons and three daughters have blessed this union. Mrs. Ransom and her eldest daughter are members of the Methodist Church. A son, Reel F., is a merchant at Richmond, and with his father, holds membership in the Episcopal Church. Mr. Ransom has been a Mason for many years.

JOHN HOCKBORTH. The above mentioned gentleman is one of the wide-awake, pushing and progressive business men of this county, where he has resided all his life, and where his interests are centered. He was born January 9, 1852, and of German parentage, his father, Frederick W. Hockborth, with his family, having emigrated from that country to this in 1845. Leaving his family in Galveston, he walked to Houston, and from there to this section, with but fifteen dollars in his pocket. Three months later he brought his family here in an ox wagon, and was then obliged to hunt for a living for two years, on account of raising small crops. The fourth year after settling here he farmed on a much larger scale and purchased a tract of unimproved land ten miles west of Bellville, where he made his home for about forty years. Success crowned his persistent efforts, and he became one of the substantial men of his neighborhood. Not long ago he moved to Sealy, and has been engaged in the brokerage business since. His children, consisting of four sons and two daughters, were named as follows: Gustave died in the Confederate service; Albert (deceased); Frederick W., of this city; John, Emily, married Adolph Haedge; and Ida, deceased, was the wife of F. M. Lockwood. John Hockborth attended the common schools of Austin County in his boyhood, principally during the Civil War, and remained with his father, assisting in the farm work, until his nineteenth year. Desiring a change, he went to Industry, clerked there for a short time, and then went to Cat Springs, where he continued that occupation. In the fall of 1879 he came to Sealy, opened the third store of the place and the first general store, with a capital of $1,600. Since that time he has been favored with a good patronage, and now does an annual business of from fifty to seventy-five thousand dollars. Besides, he has improved and cultivated one hundred and fifty acres of land, and makes a specialty of raising Holstein and Jersey cattle, owning a fine herd of each. The year 1879 saw him married to Miss Lina Baade, of this county, and daughter of John and Lina Baade, natives of Germany. Two children were born to this union: Henry and Lina. Mrs. Hockborth died in 1883, and in 1887 Mr. Hochborth was wedded to Miss Louisa Rebenstein, also a native of this county. Three children have blessed this union: Ella, Fred and George. Both Mr. and Mrs. Hochborth worship in the Lutheran Church. Politically Mr. Hockborth is a Democrat, and in 1892 he was elected by that party to the office of County Commissioner. He is a member of the Sons of Hermann (a German order), Lessing Lodge, No. 12.

CAPT. WILLIAM E. MOORE. Enterprising methods, when combined with industry and shrewdness, will place any man on a prominent road to success and gain for him an enviable reputation. In this connection few men have engaged in the merchandising business who have acquired a higher position than Capt. William E. Moore, one of Ashby's most prominent citizens. He is a product of Newark, N. J., born in 1837; and the son of Robert Baxter Moore, also of that State. The mother of our subject was Mary (Layton) Moore, who was born in 1812. She now makes her home with her son, the captain. Mr. Moore was born in the year 1807. This worthy couple were married in 1831, and eight years later moved to Mobile, Ala. During his early life the father was a cabinetmaker, but after settling in Mobile he embarked in merchandising, and was also interested in the William Fry, a steamboat on the Alabama river. In 1845 Mr. Moore moved from Alabama to Texas, and settled in Victoria County. Later he located in Indianola and became a planter, but also carried on contracting in the last named city. He became quite prosperous, but lost heavily during the war. He and his wife were both earnest members of the Baptist Church, and she still attends the same and is hale and hearty for her years. Of their seven children, four are now living: Joseph W., the eldest, enlisted in the First Texas Cavalry as Orderly Sergeant, and was killed, or died, at Mansfield, La.; Spencer is deceased; Dolph P. is a merchant of Matagorda, and Treasurer of the county; and H. E. is a merchant at Deming's Bridge; Miss E. J. Moore is living at Ashby. Capt. William E. Moore received his schooling in Indianola, and his boyhood days were spent there in assisting his father on the farm. In September, 1861, he went to Houston, and was in the first regiment of cavalry that crossed the river. He was in Company K from July, 1864, until April, 1865, and was with Alex. Shannon, now Postmaster at Galveston, on scouting duty. The captain participated in the battles of Wootsonville, Shiloh, Murfreesboro, etc. On the 16th of July, 1862, he was shot through the body and told that he would die, but it is hardly necessary to add that he did not, but recovered rapidly, and by the following November joined his regiment and was in the battle of Stone River. There he was when the war closed, and he came home without surrendering, and in company with three others came back to Texas, arriving there in August, 1865. He came through New Orleans and pawned a gold watch to get to Galveston, and borrowed money there to get home. Following the war he drove stock to New Orleans until 1870 for old Jim Foster and Sam Allen, of Houston. From 1870 to 1886 he ran a boat to Indianola. In 1882 he opened a store in partnership with H. E. Moore, his brother, at Deming Bridge, and carried it on with success until 1891, when he came to Ashby. He has owned a ranch there for some time, and although he has sold considerable of his land, still has 1,300 acres left. The captain has held the office of County Commissioner for the precinct for five consecutive years, and is prominently identified with every laudable enterprise in the county. In the year 1867 he led to the altar Miss Gussie Butterfield, a native of Kentucky, who died in 1868. In 1869 he married Miss Mary Swift, a native of Seguin, Texas, who died in 1878. Four children were born to this union, two of whom are living: Maggie, wife of Gill Kuykendall, and Inez, at home. The deceased were Ella and an infant. In 1881 Capt. Moore married Miss Kate Moore, a native of Bolixi, Miss., who bore him four children: Hamilton, Vera, Ashby and Gladys. Capt. Moore and wife are members of the Methodist Church, and he is Recording Steward in the same. This church stands on Capt. Moore's land, and he was instrumental in its building. He is a Mason, and is Postmaster at Ashby, which office he established in August, 1890.

JAMES W. JOHNSTON. This gentleman, who is one of the leading stock men of Austin County, Texas, has qualifications for managing his own business so that he is not dependent on others to manage it for him. Though young, he is full of energy, business qualifications, and thoroughly fitted for the calling he has undertaken. Born on the 27th of May, 1861, in Cat Springs, Austin County, this State, he is a typical Texan, warm hearted, liberal and progressive. He is a son of L. L. and Susan P. (Everts) Johnston, natives respectively, of Mississippi and Texas, and the grandson of Dr. Johnston, (see sketch.) L. L. Johnston came to the Lone Star State at a very early period, and afterwards contributed his share towards its progress and development. In the year 1849 he went overland to California, and suffered untold hardships, going without water for three days. He remained on the Pacific coast for two or three years, engaged for the most part in freighting, and was quite successful, carrying back to Texas quite a large sum of money. This he invested in cattle and horses, and for many years was a very prominent stockman. In 1866 he sold his horses for a large tract of land in Coryell County, and continued to handle cattle until his death, in 1877. At that time he owned about four thousand head of cattle, besides a vast amount of real estate. His wife died about 1869. Their family consisted of the following children: Eliza, wife of C. L. Osman, of Coryell County; James W., L. L., of Wharton County; Jack, (deceased); Sam, (deceased); and Thomas F., of Wharton County. After the death of the mother of these children, Mr. Johnston, in 1872, married Miss Kate Northington, of Wharton County. She still survives, and resides in a neighboring county. Mr. Johnston served in the Confederate army, and was statoned on the frontier of Mexico. James W. Johnston received merely a common school education, and at the early age of seventeen years began life for himself in the cattle business, that being the main calling he had followed up to that time. After the death of the father the property was divided up, and since then Mr. Johnston has been actively engaged in the cattle business. Like his father, he has met with excellent success in this pursuit, and handles from five hundred to one thousand yearly. He also owns 2,137 acres in Wharton County, Texas, and 1,600 acres in this and Austin County, Brazos bottom, and a small black land farm on the prairie, besides his homestead place of 107 acres. Mr. Johnston was married in 1878 to Miss Annie F. Whitley, a native of Alabama, and daughter of James and Sue (Stagers) Whitley, who came to this State after the war. Mr. Whitley was an earnest sympathizer with the Confederate cause, and was through the entire war from 1861 to 1865, and was with General Lee at the surrender, participating in most of the battles fought in that general's army. He died about 1876, but his wife still survives and resides in this county. To Mr. and Mrs. Johnston have been born four children: Walter (deceased), Dallas, Annie L., and James W., Jr. Mr. Johnston is a Mason, San Felipe Lodge No. 239, and Royal Arch Mason of Bellville Chapter, No. 151. Mr. Johnston is a stanch Democrat. Our subject's maternal grandfather, Samuel Everts, came to Texas before the War of 1836, and participated in that memorable struggle and many of its principal engagements with both the Indians and Mexicans. For this he secured much land in the State of Texas. He reared seven children: Samuel, killed while in the Confederate services during the ' 60's; Frank, killed by an infuriated ox; Susan (mother of subject); Mary, wife of Jack Johnston; William, Thomas, and Mariah, (deceased.)

JOHN ELLIOTT. This widely known and very popular citizen now residing on Wilson's Creek, in Matagorda County, was born in Melton Mobrey, England, February 18, 1832, and in company with his brother, William, came to the United States in 1848. The latter was eighteen years of age, and our subject sixteen at that time. They landed in Galveston after a short tarry in New York City, where the elder brother followed his trade, mechanic, and then made their way to Matagorda County, where an uncle, George Elliott, a blacksmith, was residing. There the uncle worked at his trade, but during the latter part of his life ran the ferry across Colorado River for many years, and still later was pilot at the mouth of the Brazos, and kept hotel there, too He died at Columbus in 1862, when sixty-two years of age. He came from England to Virginia, and at an early date was married in that State, and then in the '30's came to Texas. The father and mother of our subject came to this State in 1849, and located in the town of Matagorda, where the father followed the shoemaker's trade a short time. Later he became a prominent stockman, following that occupation until his death in November, 1885, when eighty-four years of age. His wife died in 1852. He was a member of the Christian, and she of the Presbyterian Church. While residing in England the father was a member of the I. O. O. F. Of the eight children born to this estimable couple, four are now living, and all in this county. William is the eldest, John, our subject, next, Elizabeth, wife of John Wendell, and Anna, who is the wife of Walso G. Thompson, (see sketch.) The early education of our subject was received in England, and he attended school for three months after coming here. When grown he embarked in the stock business, and since then has shipped many cattle to New Orleans, on Morgan Line Steamer, and has driven cattle all over the State of Texas. He and his brother William bought 500 acres of land where Elliott Ferry now is, and remained there until driven out by the river. Twenty-one years ago, or in 1873, John came to his present property, then wild prairies, built his handsome residence, and commenced at once to improve. In 1862 he commenced furnishing beef for the Confederate army, went from this county to Vicksburg with a drove of cattle, and butchered every day of the trip for a division of men. After the siege of Vicksburg Mr. Elliott returned to Texas, and was at Prairie Landing from that time until the war ceased. He lost nearly all his property, but has since been quite successful, and is now the owner of 3,000 acres. The first vote he ever cast was in the recent election for the removal of the county seat to Bay City. This was on his sixty-third birthday, his vote was the sixty-third cast, and there was sixty-three majority for removal. In the year 1852 he was married to Miss Ellen Trimble, a native of Indiana, whose father died a prisoner in Mexico. She passed away in 1864 leaving three children: Annie, wife of William Johnson of this county; Fanny, wife of George Byrd, of Waco; and Ellen, wife of Pleasant Dowdy, of this county. In 1867 Mr. Elliott married Mrs. Butterfield who died in 1871. The only child born to this union, Susan, died with yellow fever while attending school. In 1873 Mrs. Mary Gamble, daughter of William A. Dowdy, became his wife. Her father, was one of the first settlers in Matagorda County. He served in the Seminole war and in the Mexican war, being wagon-master in the latter. His home was in New Orleans for many years, but later he came to Matagorda where he became a stock dealer and contractor. After the storm of 1854 he rebuilt the town of Matagorda. He was born in Bedford County, Tennessee, in 1810, and died in 1887. Socially Mr. Elliott is a Mason, and his wife holds membership in the Methodist Church.

Gus. R. Scott. Although still in the dawn of a successful career, that has attended his efforts in a professional way, our subject has already given abundant evidence of the ability which qualifies him for a high place in the legal profession. Truly ambitious, and with an ambition whose aim is pure and unsullied, there seems no reason why his unquestioned ability should not find full scope in adjusting the difficulties of those around him. He was born in Madison County, Mississippi, in 1853, the third of five children born to C. W. and Margaret (Russell) Scott, natives of North and South Carolina, respectively. The paternal grandfather died in North Carolina, where the greater portion of his life was spent. The maternal grandfather, Fergus Russell, was born in the Isle of Erin, and after coming to the United States, located in South Carolina, from which State he moved to Mississippi, where he engaged in planting, and there spent the rest of his life, dying about 1876. C. W. Scott left the Old North State when about twenty years of age, and for about six years thereafter labored as a clerk in Yazoo City, Miss. He was married in Madison County, Miss., and about 1848 came to Texas, and having made thorough preparation, practiced medicine here until 1852 when he returned to Mississippi, and turned his attention to planting. During the Civil War he served for a time in the Confederate army, but left the service after a time, on account of poor health. He died at Oxford, Miss., in 1881, and his wife in 1888. Up to 1869 the subject of this sketch resided in Madison County, Mississippi, and in 1870 entered the State University, where he remained for five years, at the end of which he came to Texas for his health. In May, of the following year, he went to Austin and at once began reading law in the office of Judge E. P. Hamblen, and was admitted to the Bar in 1877—after which he formed a partnership with the Judge, which continued for one year. His pulmonary trouble again returning he left Houston to seek a more favorable clime, and after touring the State, finally settled in Corpus Christi. Gradually his health was recovered, and he again resumed his profession, and has since practiced in the Supreme and other State courts. He was married in Houston on April 21, 1881, to Miss Ella R. Dickinson, of that city, by whom he has one child, Lucile, born in 1883. He and his wife are highly honored people of the community in which they reside.

J. R. Josey. The bulk of the men who have legitimately achieved success have been men of courage, honesty of purpose, integrity and energy. The United States have given rare opportunities to men with those characteristics, and Mr. J. R. Josey certainly possesses them in a marked degree. He is at present the well-known and popular proprietor of Josey Hotel and is a success as a business man. He owes his nativity to Walker County, Texas, born March 22, 1857, and is seventh in order of birth of ten children born to T. J. and Mary (Wilson) Josey, natives of South Carolina and Alabama, respectively. The father and mother were married in Alabama and came to Texas in 1855, settling in Walker County, where he tilled the soil very successfully for some time. In the year 1862 he raised a company and joined the Confederate army, serving through the entire war. Like most men who fought in the Southern army, Mr. Josey found his finances at a low ebb after the war, much of his property having been destroyed, and paid off his indebtedness during that time and afterwards, dollar for dollar. Thus at the time of his death he was one of the men who did not take advantage of the law then in force, to relieve them of their indebtedness. He always followed farming and freighting, and kept a train of wagons running from Huntsville to Brownsville, and from Huntsville to Lynchburg. Most of his property was made after the war, and as he was unusually successful, he left much valuable real estate. His widow still survives and makes her home in Alvin. Although in her seventieth year, she still enjoys fairly good health. Of the ten children born to this worthy couple all but one grew to mature years: E. T., E. M., H., Mollie, John, R. P., J. R., J. W., W. H. and Albert. When a boy J. R. Josey attended the schools of Walker County, and when it became necessary for him to choose some occupation in life, he very naturally (for he had been reared to the same) selected agricultural pursuits. For two years he carried on this industry in Walker County and then moved to Dodge, that county, and followed merchandising for five years. Not meeting with a fair degree of success he moved to Groveton, Trinity County, where he engaged in the hotel business. In 1884 he came to this place, when only one railroad was here and few residents, and for a few years tilled the soil. In 1887, at the building of the Aransas Pass Railway through this place, engaged in the hotel business for the second time. This venture proved successful, and Mr. Josey has been in the business since. He has a well furnished, two-story building of many rooms, and his table is supplied with all that can be obtained in a country town. Mr. Josey is also engaged in farming and is the owner of two farms of 263 acres in all, with 130 acres under a fine state of cultivation. He with his brother owns 640 acres of good prairie land which cost them $5 per acre in 1894. Mr. Josey is a great manager and a man of excellent judgment, being now one of the town's most influential citizens. He has been twice married, first to Miss Sarah A. Roark, of Walker County, Texas, and daughter of R. and Sarah (Palmer) Roark, early settlers of Texas. One child, John Russell, was born to this marriage. Mrs. Josey died in 1879, and in 1883 Mr. Josey was married to Miss Laura A. Dupuy, of Walker County, and daughter of J. A. Dupuy, of the same county (see sketch of J. A. Dupuy). Mr. and Mrs. Josey are the parents of four children: Rena A., Blanche A., John D. and Mattie L. Mrs. Josey is a member of the Baptist Church. Socially our subject is a K. of H., and politically a Democrat.

REV. ROBERT A. PARTAIN. John C. Partain, the father of our subject, was born in Tennessee, February 17, 1802, and as early as 1825 came to Texas, in which State he passed the remainder of his life, dying there when comparatively a young man. He married Miss Nancy Smalley, a native of Kentucky, born in 1803, and subsequently moved to Matagorda County, on Live Oak Bayou, where he experienced much trouble with the Indians. Mrs. Partain's sister, who was the wife of Elisha Flowers, had been visiting a neighbor, and on the way home was attacked and killed by the Indians. Mrs. Flowers had a little child with her, but it escaped uninjured. Mr. Partain moved to Tres Palacios, on the west side of the Colorado River, but later settled where our subject now lives, in a little log house, and began clearing and improving. He joined the Texas army and participated in the battle of San Jacinto. Previous to entering the army he was detailed to take his family with others to New Orleans for protection, and he also drove his stock to what he considered was a safe place, but lost all of them. After the war his family returned to Matagorda County, and soon afterward he passed away. Afterwards Mrs. Partain made her home with her son, Robert

Abner Partain, until her death, August 12, 1888. Her father, Andrew Smalley, left his native State, Kentucky, about 1825, and came to Texas by way of the Mississippi and Brazos rivers. Here he died soon after. He followed the hatter trade in his native State, and was an industrious, well respected citizen. Mrs. Partain was a member of the Methodist Church for many years. To her marriage were born four children, of whom Robert A. is the only one now living. Eliza J., died when a small child in New Orleans; Alfred, died when about twenty-four years of age; John C., died in 1856, when grown; R. A. Partain was born in this State August 1, 1837, and here spent his boyhood, receiving his education in the common schools. His mother managed the ranch until her sons were old enough to help her, and our subject's early life, when not in the school-room, was spent on horseback handling immense herds of stock. That business he has continued up to the present time, and he has made his fortune in it. During the Civil War he enlisted in a company of cavalry and was elected Lieutenant. Later he enlisted in Company D, Buschell's Cavalry Regiment, and served all his time in this State, on the Rio Grande River for the most part. Mr. Partain served as County Commissioner one term, and also held the position of Justice of the Peace for some time. When a boy of fifteen years he joined the Baptist Church, and in 1889 commenced preaching, having been licensed at that time, and was ordained to the full work of the gospel ministry the first Sunday of December, 1889. Since then he has carried on his ministerial duties successfully, and organized a church with the assistance of other brethren, of which he was elected pastor, in Jackson County On the 24th of December, 1857, he was married to Miss Jeanette Perham O'Neal, who was probably born in Mississippi, and who died in 1889, on the 28th of April, when forty-six years of age. Her people came originally from Alabama, and after residing for some time in Mississippi and Louisiana finally located here. To Mr. and Mrs. Partain were born these children: Robert A., Jr., a merchant of Bellville; Zachariah, Sarah Emma, wife of Mr. B. F. Keeling, of this neighborhood; John A., a planter here; Anna Laura, wife of James Smith, and Charles N. In 1891 Mr. Partain married Miss Ella Burns, of DeWitt County, and the following children were born to them: Jennie Ella and Delia Roberta. Mr. Partain is a member of the Masonic Order, Deming's Bridge.

JOSE ACEBO. This substantial and law-abiding citizen of Corpus Christi, Texas, was born in Spain in 1855, the eldest child of J. Antonio and Tomasa Acebo, also natives of Spain, in which country the father died and the mother is still living. In his native land the subject of this sketch was educated and reared, and in 1869 he sought a home in the New World, and for one year was a resident of New Orleans, La. He then came to Texas and located at Brownsville, where he remained as a clerk for three years, at the end of which time he came to Corpus Christi. He began laboring here as a clerk, but in 1876 embarked in business for himself and in 1879 began business in his present store on the bluff, where he has a fine establishment, fitted up with an excellent stock of general merchandise. He is reasonable in his prices, is attentive and polite, and makes a point of pleasing his customers in every way in his power. He has been somewhat active in politics, was elected an Alderman for the Fifth Ward, and is now serving his fourth term, of two years each. He has been quite prosperous in his business ventures and is the owner of a stock ranch of 12,000 acres in this county, which is well improved and stocked with horses and cattle. In 1878 Acebo was united in marriage with Miss Annie Kelly, who was born in the Lone Star State, and is a daughter of Martin Kelly, an early settler of this State. To Mr. Acebo's union the following children have been given: Mary, John, Joseph, Dimas, Rosa, Lenora, Alphonso, Raymond, and Victoria, who died in infancy. The family are members and attendants of the Catholic Church.

MIRABEAU BUONAPARTE LAMAR was born at Louisville, Ga., August 16, 1798, and died at Richmond, Texas, December 19, 1859. He was prominent in the movement which resulted in the independence of Texas. In 1836 he was appointed Secretary of War of the new Republic, and as such was strongly opposed to entering into negotiations with Santa Anna. He was in the same year appointed Major-general of the Texan army, but his hasty advice caused him to be unpopular among his men and he was induced to retire. He was that year elected Vice-president of the Republic, and was left in charge of the general government when Gen. Houston, as Commander-in-Chief of the Texan forces, departed for the seat of war. In 1838 Mr. Lamar was elected President of the Republic for the term 1838-40. In his inaugural address he advised the "extermination or extinction" of the Indians, and encouraged the Santa Fe expedition which proved so disastrous, and on the whole he proved himself if not a very unwise, certainly a very unfortunate statesman. His administration was, from first to last, extravagant financially and many of his measures were demoralizing.

JUDGE THOMAS G. MASTERSON. There are perhaps few among those who were at one time prominent and respected citizens of this part of Texas whose memory is more respected, and whose genuine worth more widely recognized, than that of the late Judge Thomas G. Masterson. His birth occurred in Tennessee, and he remained there until 1832, when he decided to move to Texas, in which State he purchased large tracts of land, principally at Velasco, or at the mouth of the Brazos. He predicted that Velasco would be the seaport town of Texas, if not that, then a very important place. He was fifty years ahead of the time, for Velasco is now rapidly becoming one of the foremost cities of the State. Judge Masterson engaged in business in partnership with Judge Edwin Waller, under the firm name of Waller & Co. He was an attorney and a graduate of a law school in Nashville, but after making Texas his home he turned his attention to merchandising. After purchasing land in Texas in 1832, Judge Masterson returned to his native State and settled up a large estate, remaining there until 1837 after which he made Brazoria County his home until his death in 1884, when about sixty-nine years of age. Thus terminated the life of a man whose honesty, uprightness and general ability, gained the esteem of all who knew him. He held the office of Chief Justice of Brazoria County and County Clerk for a number of years, and during the Civil War was enrolling officer. He had five sons in the Confederate Army, but his family, born to his union with Miss Christianie I. Roane, daughter of Doctor Roane of Tennessee and a niece of Governor Roane, consisted of William, Judge James R., ex-District Judge of Houston and Montgomery counties for over twenty years, was Judge Advocate in the Confederate service; T. W., deceased, was the commander of the first company leaving Austin to join the Confederate army, and was in Virginia until the latter part of the war, when he was on Gen. Wharton's staff; Judge

Arch, the present County Judge of Brazoria County, was a boy of seventeen on entering the service. The principal part of the time he served in Texas, but he was transferred east of the river, where he participated in many battles in Virginia and was present at the surrender of Gen. Lee; Branch T., now of Galveston, was on his way to join the army when the war closed; Harry, the youngest son, has been County Judge of this county and is a prominent citizen of the same, and Mrs. T. L. Smith, who is the only daughter. The mother of these children is still living. William Masterson, the eldest child, was born in the year 1835 and received his schooling under his mother's tuition. When fifteen years of age he became a clerk in Brazoria, and later was in the District Clerk's office for a time. Following that he opened a store and was appointed Deputy United States Marshal under Col. Young. He took the census in 1860, went to Washington, and while there heard the firing on Fort Sumpter. Early in 1862 he joined the Twenty-second Texas Infantry, Confederate army, and was appointed by Col. Hubbard to the office of Adjutant. Later he was made Lieutenant, and on the battlefield of Mansfield was promoted to the rank of Captain, which position he held but one day as he lost his left arm in that battle. After the war Mr. Masterson became a planter, rented Gen. Wharton's plantation, and after five years was appointed Public Weigher at Galveston by Governor Hubbard, without solicitation on his part. That position he held for ten years, through three administrations, and during that time bought the plantation he now owns. Socially he is a Mason.

JAMES A. DUPUY. There is no calling that has been dignified and graced in modern poetry more than that which in practical life is most prosaic. Burns, Whittier and others have thrown a veil of romance about the sturdy form of the farmer as well as the calling which he follows and have made it honored by all men. James A. Dupuy has been very successful as a tiller of the soil and has a comfortable home, which his industry has brought him. He was born in De Soto County, Mississippi, August 18, 1840, and is the son of J. L. and Tabitha (Evans) Dupuy, natives of Alabama, who removed to Mississippi after their marriage, where the father became actively engaged as a practitioner of the healing art. The doctor graduated from two medical colleges, and during the war with Mexico, was a member of the Texas army and served as Surgeon in General Houston's command. After the war was over he located in Walker County, Texas, and was here joined by his wife. She resided with her father, Jesse Evans, for some time but herself became the owner of land. She died, having become the mother of two children: Martha Bell, who first married J. L. Owens and after his death Edward Wilkerson, and is again a widow, and James A. After the death of the mother of these children Mr. Dupuy married a second time and became the father of the following children: D. C., Mary C., wife of J. D. Hibbett; Matilda, wife of Joe Hunter; Susan S., and Edward. Mr. Dupuy died near Waco in McLennan County, Texas in 1884. James A. Dupuy was educated in Walker County, Texas, and in early life became familiar with the duties and intricacies of farming and stock-raising. When he first went to Huntsville, there were three stores, hotel, and a livery stable, but at that time there was no penitentiary. One of his slaves moulded most of the brick that entered into the construction of the first penitentiary. Mr. Dupuy was married in 1861, but immediately after joined Company I, Twenty-sixth Texas Cavalry, served in the trans-Mississsippi Department and was in all the battles with Gen. Banks including Mansfield, Pleasant Hill and Yellow Bayou. During this time Mr. Dupuy was under fire for forty-two days, and on one occasion, had his horse shot from under him. This was the nearest he ever came to being wounded. At Yellow Bayou he captured several small squads of famished soldiers whom he sent to the rear and never saw again. He was appointed body guard for Gen. Bee and was with him at the fight at the mouth of Red River, where Lee had Banks' army at his mercy for a time, killing them in platoons as they would try to cross the river. Mr. Dupuy was sent with Gen. Bee with eight or ten men up Red River, for the purpose of ascertaining if any Federal troops were crossing the river. When they returned to Bee's headquarters Bee was not there, but Gen. Banks was resting on the ground with his entire army. Mr. Dupuy and his men dismounted and walked from near the Federal lines for two miles, but upon reaching Alexandria road, were accosted by about eighty United States troopers. The Confederate boys halted and demanded to know "What in —— they were doing out at that time of night," and Uncle Sam's boys answered in kind. The parties then held a consultation and agreed that they had had enough fighting for that day and Mr. Dupuy and his companions were allowed to go on their way. In 1865 he returned to his old home in Texas, and made Walker County his home until a few years ago, when he came to Austin County and purchased a small farm. His wife was Miss Cynthia Melard, of Walker County, Texas and a daughter of J. T. and Mintora (Jones) Melard, of Mississippi. Of eleven children born to them, the following are living: Laura, wife of J. R. Josey; James E., a merchant; Robert L., a merchant: Bell, Joe L., Alva C., Holla D., Howard E., Miniretab and Celia K. Mrs. Dupuy is a member of the Missionary Baptist Church and politically Mr. Dupuy is a Democrat.

W. S. K. MUSSETT. This early and prominent citizen of Corpus Christi, Texas, owes his nativity to the State of Missouri, where he first saw the light in 1833. He was the second of nine children born to Tyre and Eliza Ann (Hargrave) Mussett, the former of whom was born in Virginia and the latter in Missouri. When a young man Tyre Mussett removed westward to Missouri, was married in that State, and about 1834 removed to Van Buren, Ark. Very shortly afterward they moved to Texas, and were in the famous "runaway," returning to Van Buren, Ark. There the father engaged in merchandising for several years, and at the same time owned a store in the Indian Nation. In 1848 he came with his family to Corpus Christi, and here the father resided until his death, which resulted from an accident in 1872. At that time he was residing on a large tract of land near the town of Corpus Christi, and he was the first man in the entire community to improve a place outside of the town limits. He was quite extensively engaged in the stock business and was a thrifty and progressive farmer. His widow still resides on the home place, and through his good management and far sightedness, was left in comfortable circumstances. While a resident of Arkansas, Mr. Mussett was a member of the State Legislature. The immediate subject of this sketch was educated in Arkansas, and upon attaining his majority, he began trading in mustangs. In 1862 he was appointed Deputy Marshal for the Confederate Government, a position he held until the close of the war. He had two brothers, Thomas B. and Elias T., who were soldiers of the Confederate Army, the former of whom is still a resident of Corpus Christi, but the latter was shot and killed in this city in 1892 while City Marshal. After the war the subject of this sketch engaged in stock-raising and farming, and in 1882 erected his fine residence on the site of his lifelong home near the town. He has been a shrewd and successful manager and is very comfortably fixed financially. He was married in 1858 to Miss Sarah Fore, who died in Austin in 1859, leaving one child, James H., who died in Colorado in 1887. Mr. Mussett was again married in 1860, Mrs. Salina E. (Clymer) Cook becoming his wife. She was born in Ohio, a daughter of Samuel T. and Diantha M. (Van Amburgh) Clymer, who moved to Indiana and from there to Texas in 1854, locating at Gatesville first, then at Corpus Christi in 1859. The father's death occurred here two years later, the mother passing from life in 1890 at the age of eighty-six years. Their daughter, Mrs. Mussett, first married in 1854 and after the death of Mr. Cook in 1856, she came to Texas and joined her parents, bringing with her her son, Robert Owen Cook. To Mr. and Mrs. Mussett six children have been given: John Williams, who was married in 1884 to Miss Seana M. Wright. He has been very active in politics, and in 1875, was Deputy Postmaster under James W. Ward, has served as Alderman of Corpus Christi for three years, served as cashier of the Mexican Railroad from 1882 until the fall of 1885, and also served as Inspector and Clerk of Customs from November 1885 to 1888. He then returned to his former position with the railroad company, and after a short time was appointed agent for the S. A. & A. P. R. R. of this place, a position he filled until August, 1890. In November of that year he was appointed County Assessor and in 1892, was re-elected to the office. He is a member of the K. of H. and is a promising and representative young man, well advanced to higher honors. Lee Clymer, the second child, died in December, 1887; Ida Minerva, is the wife of O. B. House of Corpus Christi; Tyre H.; Perry W. and Anna M. The family attend the Presbyterian Church and Mr. and Mrs. Mussett have a very comfortable home.

LOUIS TESCH. This gentleman owes his nativity to Prussia, Germany, where he was born July 6, 1844, a son of Louis and Anna E. (Mengel) Tesch, also of Prussia, who came to America in 1850, and for one year resided in Austin County, Texas, near San Felipe, then took up their residence near Brenham in Washington County. Mr. Tesch came to this country a steerage passenger on a sailing vessel, and was eight weeks only in making the passage from Hamburg to Galveston. He rented land for some time in this and Washington counties, and died in 1859, leaving a wife and six children, the eldest son of whom, the subject of this sketch, was but fifteen years of age. The eldest child, a daughter, was nineteen years of age. Her name was Miner and she eventually married W. W. Hoffmann, and is now deceased. Louis, Charles (deceased); Dora, wife of William Sprain of this county. Texana is the wife of H. Ehlart, of Washington County, and Ida, who is the wife of F. A. Sprain. After the death of Mr. Tesch, his widow married August Keicke, of Brenham, and they have one son, Theodore. Mrs. Keicke died in 1870. Louis Tesch remained with his mother until her second marriage. In 1864 he joined Captain Carr's company for the Confederate service, and was in several of the last battles of the Red River Campaign. He received his discharge at Brownsville, and after returning home at once engaged in farming with his step-father, with whom he remained until 1868, when he purchased a small tract of improved land in Washington County, for which he paid the sum of $16 per acre. Four years later he sold the land for $30 an acre, and moved to his present location near Wallis, where he paid $4,000 for a 350-acre farm. He has since added sixty-seven acres, which has greatly increased in value since he became its owner, owing to the many improvements that he has made thereon. Besides this fine farm he has 497 acres of unimproved land west of Wallis, for which he paid $12.75 per acre. Of this he has since put seventy-five acres under cultivation, and has erected a good tenant's house on it. He also owns property in the town of Brenham, all of which has been gathered together through his own energy and shrewdness. He has also about 200 head of cattle besides a number of horses and mules. In 1869 he led to the altar Miss Bettie Sprain, a native of Washington County, and daughter of F. F. and Henrietta (Peeper) Sprain, and their union has resulted in the birth of two children: Fred L., Deputy County Clerk, and Hannah, wife of H. F. Wehmeyer, of Brenham. Both Mr. and Mrs. Tesch are members of the Lutheran Church, and politically he is a Democrat. He is one of the most successful men in the county, and his good fortune is due to his persistent efforts.

NOLAN KELLER. Francis Keller, the grandfather of our subject, was probably born in Germany, and came to this country to make a home and a reputation. He settled in Woodville, Miss., kept hotel for a number of years, and then in 1828 or 1829 entered the "Lone Star State" to buy land. His grandson, our subject, is now living on land purchased by him at that time. He purchased about ten leagues of land scattered all over that part of the State, from the Mexican Government, but the records having been burned prevents the family from proving their claim. He settled in Matagorda, but subsequently started to return to Mississippi, and while camping out was robbed and murdered. His wife and family were then living in Woodville, Mississippi, at that time, and they moved to this county. His son, James W., father of our subject, with the three other children, a son and two daughters, were quite well grown when they came to this county, becoming residents of the same about 1838 or 1839. James W. was married in this State to Miss Martha Wheeler, who was born in Tennessee, where her people were old settlers. She is still living, and although about seventy years of age, is fairly well preserved. James W. did not take part in the Texas war, but had trouble with the Indians, who would steal everything they cared for. He became quite an extensive stockman for that time, for there were but few in the business then. For many years he held the office of Justice of the Peace, and our subject remembers when he sentenced a man to be whipped. He was progressive and public spirited, and was alive to all enterprises for developing and improving his section. His death occurred in 1854 when a comparatively young man. For many years the mother was a member of the Methodist Church. Of their six children, five now survive: Nolan, our subject, the eldest; Crittenden is a resident of New Berlin, Texas; James is a resident of this county; Mrs. McSparran of this county, and Mrs. Pybus; Wilbur died in the army, when about eighteen years of age. Nolan Keller was born on the place near where he now lives in 1843, attended the schools of this county and finished at San Antonio. In 1862 he joined Waller's Battalion, went east to the Mississippi River, and was in many battles and skirmishes, being in Louisiana most of the time. He was taken prisoner near New Orleans, and sometime afterwards, when he had but partially recovered from the measles, he and several companions tried to escape by wading the swamps back of the city. This brought on a relapse, and he nearly died. For the most part he was on scouting duty. After the war, he commenced driving stock all over the western and southern portions of the State. He is still engaged in the stock business, and is the owner of 2,000 acres. Recently he was nominated for the office of County Commissioner. In the year 1865 he was married to Miss Susan Reed, who died in 1875. Six children were the fruits of this union, three sons and three daughters. His second marriage, with Miss Mary Wheeler, occurred in 1881. She was born in this county, and is a member of the Baptist Church. Two children were born to this marriage, a daughter and a son.

ELIJAH L. PENNINGTON. This old settler of Texas was born in McDonald County, Illinois, February 5, 1826, the sixth of twelve children born to the union of Riggs and Johanna (Orsborne) Pennington, Virginians. The Penningtons originally came from England, and four brothers of that name settled in Virginia, but after a time their descendants became scattered, and after his marriage Riggs Pennington moved to Illinois, and in 1817 settled in McDonough County, but after a few years moved to Knox County, and settled within one mile of where Galesburg now stands, where his home continued to be until 1837, when he brought his family overland to Texas, and located near Brenham in January, 1838. He purchased a one-fourth league of land on which a log house had been erected, paying for his land $3.50 per acre. Here he died some thirty-five years later, at the age of eighty-six years, his wife also dying at that age some three years earlier. Their children are as follows: Wesley (deceased), Stephen (deceased), Lydia, the deceased wife of John Whittaker; Matilda, widow of John B. Dupuy; Elijah, Eliza J., widow of W. W. Hackworth; Elihu (deceased), E. L., William (deceased), Hansford, (deceased), Julia (deceased), and Acey. Elijah L. Pennington was eleven years of age when he accompanied his parents to this country, and on his father's farm here he attained his majority, and engaged in farming and stock-raising. In 1885 he came to Austin County, and settled at Wallis, in the vicinity of which place he bought 400 acres of unimproved land for $4.00 per acre, and he now has 100 acres in excellent cultivation. At different times he has followed various occupations, but has invariably returned to his first love —the farm, in which calling he has met with good success. He was married in 1846 to Miss Martha Trunmier, a native of Alabama, who came with her parents, Thomas and Martha Trunmier, to Washington County. Their marriage resulted in the birth of the following children: Elihu, William, Jane, wife of Ed Holt; and Mary, wife of Charles Graham. Mrs. Pennington died in 1855, and the following year Mr. Pennington espoused Miss Rebecca J., daughter of John W. and Melisa (Gray) Bowers, all of Alabama, who located in Washington County, Texas, in 1853. To Mr. Pennington's last marriage the following children were born: Wesley, Robert, Martha, wife of B. Lester; Frank, Arthur, Joannah, Albert and Alberta (twins), Isabel and Matilda. In 1862 Mr. Pennington joined Company F, of Carter's Regiment, and served in the trans-Mississippi Department, participating in no regular engagement, but in numerous skirmishes. At the close of the war he found himself minus his negroes, his stock, and considerably in debt, but he immediately adapted himself to the changed condition of affairs, energetically engaged in farming and soon had paid off all his indebtedness. He is thoroughly in love with his calling, a secret, no doubt, of his success, makes a study of his business, and is correspondingly successful. Like his worthy sire before him he is a strong Democrat in politics, but has never sought office. He and his wife are members of the Christian Church, and are active workers in the same.

PAUL COALSON. In our country's earliest history the name of Coalson is well known, for our subject can trace his ancestry back to a period far before the Revolutionary War, in which one of his ancestors served as a General in the American army. Other members of his family held high positions of trust and responsibility, and all were respected and influential citizens. Mr. Coalson's grandfather, who resided at Thomasville, Ga., was a noted attorney well known all over the State. Such is the noble record and proud heritage in the family which for many years has been so worthily represented in this State by Paul Coalson. The latter was born near Thomasville, Thomas County, Ga., in 1849, and his parents, E. B. and Hattie A. (Young) Coalson, were natives of the same State. Both are now deceased, the former dying in 1872, when forty-eight years of age, and the latter in 1891, at the residence of our subject in Fort Bend County, Texas, when over sixty years old. Mr. Coalson was a farmer. During the Civil War he served in Hood's Battalion of Georgia Cavalry, and participated in the Georgia Campaign. He was never wounded, but had his horse shot from under him. Both he and wife were strict members of the Baptist Church, and he was a Deacon in the same. Ten children were born to them, and nine are now living. Paul Coalson, the second child, received a fair education in the schools of his native county, assisted his father on the farm, and when a young man began the study of medicine, attending Tulane Medical College in New Orleans. He followed farming in the State of Georgia until 1883, when Miss Jemison Wyche, of Thomas County, Georgia, became his wife. Their bridal trip was to Texas, where they made their home, and their happy domestic life was made complete by the birth of six children, two sons and four daughters. Mr. Coalson settled in the bottoms, twelve miles from Richmond, where he owns 800 acres of very fine, fertile land. This land at that time was a wilderness, but under our subject's supervision most of this has been cleared up and put under cultivation. Industrious and persevering, Mr. Coalson has made his way to the front among the representative farmers and stock men of his county, and is a public spirited and influential citizen. Mrs. Coalson is a member of the Baptist Church. Her father, Henry Wyche, who came to the United States from Germany with his family, makes his home with Mr. and Mrs. Coalson.

NATHAN P. WARD. This successful farmer and ginner, of Austin County, Texas, owes his nativity to Franklin County, New York, where he was born June 11, 1833, a son of Richard and Elizabeth (McGena) Ward, natives of Virginia and Franklin County, North Carolina, respectively. The former removed to the Old North State and there met and married his wife. The Ward family came from England at an early day, and first settled in New Jersey, but from there the father of Richard Ward, John Ward, moved to the Old Dominion, where he reared his family. The paternal great-grandfather, Benjamin Ward, was a soldier of the Revolution. Richard Ward was a carpenter in early life, but in his latter days became a farmer. He and his wife became the parents of fifteen children, eight of whom reached maturity: Mary, married William Blackmall; Seth, Benjamin, married a Miss Ward, of Work County, North Carolina, and reared four children; Abraham, Atkin,

N. P., Sarah, who married George T. Gray, of this State; and Presley, of Austin County, Texas. Both Mr. and Mrs. Ward died in the Old North State, the former having taken quite an active interest in the political affairs of that State at an early day, and represented Franklin County in the State Legislature. Nathan P. Ward fortunately received an excellent education in his youth, and in 1857 graduated from Chapel Hill College, North Carolina, and for his future work engaged in the study of law. He was admitted to the bar the same year that he graduated from school, but after practicing for one year his health gave way, and, following the advice of his doctors, he came West in 1859 by public conveyance. He landed at Houston in January, 1860, but located at San Felipe, where he remained for one year, after which he removed to Fort Bend County, where he engaged in farming and stock-raising. There he continued to make his home until 1867, when he again settled in San Felipe, and after a residence of ten years there once more returned to Fort Bend County. In 1880 he moved to Willis, Austin County. When Mr. Ward and his brother Presley came to this State they purchased 2,400 acres of land in this and Fort Bend County, and, having brought with them sixty negroes, they set energetically to work to farm this land. Their sister accompanied them thither and shared equally with them in everything. They purchased their land for fifteen dollars per acre, all located on the Brazos River, and under the able management of the brothers it became one of the finest bodies of land in the two counties. They paid cash down $15,000, and this left them with a debt of $30,000 on their shoulders, and as the war came up soon after they had located here, their negroes were freed, and they found themselves deeply involved. After a time Mr. Ward purchased 1,200 acres of land, of which 300 were improved, and here Mr. Ward lived and tilled the soil for ten years, when he sold out and purchased 300 acres of land in Fort Bend County, for which he paid $3,500. This place he sold in 1884 and bought 1,800 acres of land in this county, for which he paid eight dollars per acre. He has since sold 600 acres, and of the amount of land left him he has 350 acres under cultivation, on which he has resided since 1893. In 1884 he erected the first steam cotton gin in Wallis, which is fitted up with fine modern machinery and three stands. Mr. Ward was married in 1869 to Miss Ada C. Guyler, a daughter of William and Lydia A. (English) Guyler. (See sketch of William Guyler and H. B. English.) Of ten children born to Mr. and Mrs. Ward nine are living: Bettie, wife of Dr. E. G. Magruder, of Sealy; Nathan P., Jr., Lydia, Kate, Maggie, Myrtle, Ethel, William and Benjamin R. Mr. Ward joined the Confederate army as a private in 1862, was in the trans-Mississippi Department, and in 1863 was made Quartermaster. During his service he was in the battles of Mansfield, Pleasant Hill, Jenkin's Ferry and Salem. The army of which he was a member was disbanded at Hempstead in May, 1865, and he returned home. Mr. Ward was on detached service for some time in the northern part of Texas buying horses for the army. He has never been an office seeker, and only filled the office of Justice of the Peace at the earnest solicitation of his many friends. He served four terms in his precinct, and at the present time is Justice of the Peace of Precinct No. 8. He has always been a pronounced Democrat.

ROBERT HANCOCK HUNTER. This old and much respected citizen of Fayette County, Texas, was born May 1, 1813, in Circleville, Ohio, a State which has contributed so much of wealth and population to other parts of the

Union. Of an old fashioned family of fourteen children born to Dr. Johnson and Mary Martha (Harbert) Hunter, he was fourth in order of birth. The parents were natives of South Carolina, the father born May 22, 1787, and the mother August 29, 1792. Immediately after their marriage, which occurred in their native State, they moved to Ohio, making the journey on horseback with all their household goods, and settling in Circleville, where the doctor practiced his profession for a number of years. From there the father moved to Missouri, and thence in 1821 to Texas, going by way of Nocogdoches to San Antonio, and taking with him a large quantity of medicine. The Beramendis agreed to sell his medicine for him, and later he returned to Missouri. In March, 1822, he moved to Texas with his family, and made the journey by water, in a small boat, called a scow. When he reached the mouth of the River by which he traveled he found a small schooner wrecked on the beach, with its mast broken and rigging rotted, and the remains of three human beings lying near. They had been dead for some time, as their bones were bleached by wind and weather. Dr. Hunter and a man he had with him, Jack, a sailor, fastened up the cracks in the schooner, got her in fair shape, and pushed her out in the river. Later he conveyed a small portion of the cargo that he had had on the scow to the schooner, and towing the latter, started down the river. A strong southeast wind separated the schooner and scow, and the latter went ashore. Later they went back for the scow, for there was much of value on it yet, but on arriving where it had washed ashore, they found about forty men, wreckers, under a man by the name of Yoakum, who declared that he had seen nothing of the scow. The men had been drinking heavily, and Dr. Hunter was sure that they had got hold of his rum. He could do nothing, however. This was a severe loss to the family, for all, or most of their clothing was gone, a barrel of sugar, two barrels of pickled pork, a big box of bacon and hams, a barrel of sea bread, bedding, cooking utensils, farming implements, etc., etc. After this the family lived on what they could find, and for three days suffered very much for food. About that time the man Jack, killed a small alligator, roasted its tail, and this helped them out. They reached Galveston in safety, met a friend there, and were given something to eat. This friend, Capt. Rochs, gave the doctor half a barrel of flour, one of pickled pork, a cask of rice, and another of sea-bread. He said "It is a wonder that Yoakum did not kill you all, he is a highway-robber." Later Dr. Hunter took his family and several others, up Trinity River, and landed at San Jacinto Bay. There he left them, and went to San Antonio for the drugs and money he had left with the Beramendis. He there got $1,300 in Mexican gold, and fifty head of horses and ten head of mules. He then hired two Mexicans to help him drive his stock home to San Jacinto Bay, and while camping out the first night, the Mexicans robbed him of his money. Although one of the Mexicans was captured and whipped, he would tell nothing about the money. The doctor then returned to his family, and there found a letter awaiting him from a Mr. Scott, to whom he had loaned the schooner, to go to New Orleans. This gentleman wanted the doctor to prove how he came by the schooner. This he did, but as it was a revenue cutter with the name on it, he had to give it up. Later Dr. Hunter took the ten mules he had brought home, went to another point, and bought a small sloop. After that he commenced trading, getting a cargo of corn, and taking it to market. In this business he made considerable money. At

38

one time, when he had on board a large cargo of cotton and was near the mouth of the Brazos River, his sloop was wrecked, but he managed to reach an island in that river. There he remained for twenty-one days, suffering greatly from hunger, but was finally rescued. On the 7th of April, 1829, Dr. Hunter moved his family to Fort Bend County, and continued practicing his profession for about four years. After that he gave his time to farming and stock-raising, which he followed until his death in 1855. Although he met with much misfortune he became a prosperous man, and left his family in comfortable circumstances. His children were named as follows: Robert H., born May 1, 1813; John C., born May 5, 1817, was in the war with Mexico in 1835-36; Harriet, born November 15, 1818, first married E. G. Head, and after his death wedded Col. J. M. Frost; Thomas J., born March 1820; Thaddeus W., born September 29, 1823, was the first white male child born in Austin's Colony, Texas, and is now the oldest living Texan in the State; Messenia, a twin of Thaddeus W., married Alex. McCloy, and left one son, J. F. McCloy. She died February 26, 1853; Martha, born December 21, 1825, married three times; Letitia, born July 28, 1828, died young; William, born July 13, 1830, now resides in Houston; Amanda W. C., born November 21, 1833, married Dr. J. Kirkendall; and Walter C., born September 21, 1836, was killed in Colorado County in 1885. The mother of these children died in December, 1860. Robert Hancock Hunter's education was received for the most part under the parental roof, but the first real schooling he obtained was when he had reached his twenty-seventh year, and then only for about six weeks. In 1835 he joined Capt. James Perry's company, went to San Antonio, and his first battle was at the taking of that city. Later he went back to Fort Bend County, and as Col. Travis was calling for troops, Mr. Hunter joined Capt. John Bird's company, and started for San Antonio. Later this company joined forces with Gen. Houston at Peach Creek. Mr. Hunter was sick and did not participate in the battle of San Jacinto, but he assisted in guarding the baggage at Harrisburg under Major McNutt. About this time what is known as the "runaway scrape" was in full progress. This was the families leaving the State. The father of our subject drove about a thousand head of cattle to San Jacinto to cross over the river, but the ferry was so thronged with people that he could not cross, and was obliged to leave them at the mercy of both armies. Those that were not killed were stolen. After Texas became a republic, Mr. Hunter turned his attention to farming and stock-raising, and made his home in Fort Bend County until January, 1845, when he moved to Guadalupe County. Previous to this, however, in 1841, Mr. Hunter was married to Miss Samirah M. Beard, in Brazoria County, and then after that, until he moved to Guadalupe County, was engaged as overseer. After moving to Guadalupe County he settled two miles below Seguin. Mr. Hunter and party had a narrow escape from Indians while moving to Guadalupe County, and after reaching that section never went to the woods to chop without carrying his gun with him. Some of his neighbors had considerable trouble with them. Mr. Hunter and his father-in-law, Mr. Beard, built a water-mill on San Geronimo Creek, two miles below Seguin, and hired six men to get out the timber, he and Mr. Beard keeping guard while this work was going on, and giving warning if Indians were to be seen. When the men went to church, they invariably carried their guns with them, stacked them in a corner in the church, and in going there and back kept a sharp outlook for

the wily Indians.   One night an Indian got into Mr. Hunter's stable to steal
his horse, but could not unfasten the door from the inside, and dug his way in
and out under the foundation.   Other settlers had similar experiences with
them.   In 1848 Mr. Hunter took his family down to the Brazos in Fort Bend
County, and on his way back with his wife and children stopped under three
large live oak trees not far from where Flatonia now stands.   There were no
settlers then, the grass was quite high, and Mr. Hunter gathered a big arm-
ful of grass and touched a match to it.   Soon he saw signs of fire in other
directions, and was sure that Indians were in the vicinity, and that they thought
his smoke a signal and were answering it.   He did not tarry there very long,
and the next day heard that a man was killed in that section, by the Indians.
In 1857 he moved to Victoria, on account of the drought and grasshoppers in
Guadalupe County, and in 1880 moved up near Flatonia, Fayette County.
There he lost his estimable wife in April, 1888.   Their union was blessed by
the birth of seven children, four of whom are now living: Mary M., married
William Burke; Joryna, married Dr. M. F. Walker; John C., married Miss
Kate Briem, and is living in Edna, Jackson County, and the youngest son, F.
F., is unmarried, and resides in Galveston, with his brother-in-law, William
Burke.   Those deceased are: Marcus W., who died while serving in the Confederate army; Messenia, and G. Ann.   Mr. Hunter and his brother, T. J.,
are the oldest living Texans in the State, that is of Austin's Colony, and
although now in his eighty-second year, is well preserved both physically and
mentally.   He has spent his entire life in subduing the wilderness, and has
contributed his share towards its advancement.   He is a member of the M. E.
Church South, and until within a few years has always voted the Democratic
ticket.   He has lost faith in that party, and now votes with the People's or
Populists' party.

MAJOR N. H. COOK, farmer and stockman, Sealy, Austin County, was born
in Somersetshire, England, November 23, 1844, son of William Cook, who
came to America in 1846, and settled within ten miles of San Felipe.   Mr.
Cook came to Texas comparatively poor, and found the country sparsely settled, and agriculture neglected in favor of stock-raising.   There was much
uncleared land and the people were mostly living in log houses.   He was
quite successful in a financial way, and became influential in the community.
He was many years a Justice of the Peace.   At the time of the war he was
too old for service, but his sympathies were for the Southern cause.   He died
in 1866, aged fifty-five.   His wife died in 1861, aged sixty-one.   They reared
a family of four children: William J., deceased; A. E., wife J. W. Greer;
Mary, wife of D. J. Parker; N. H., the immediate subject of this sketch.   N. H.
Cook received his education mostly in the public schools of Austin County,
but was for a time a student at a school in La Grange County.   In 1862 he
enlisted in the Confederate service and served gallantly as a private during
the war.   He was mustered out of the service at Shreveport, La., and, with
several friends, immediately returned home.   In order to avoid being taken
as prisoners of war to New Orleans, they left Shreveport on the evening
before the surrender.   He engaged in stock-raising after the war, a business
in which he has since continued with much success, and since 1868 he has
never, in any year, missed being on the ranges during the driving and range
season.   Considering the condition of the country, his operations have been
extensive.   He was married December 2, 1869, to Miss Mary E. Kidd,

daughter of Robert Kidd. They are the parents of six children: William R., of Austin County; Mrs. Marshall Howard, of Austin County; Mary J., N. H., Jr., Marion E., Emma L. Major Cook cultivates only about 100 acres of land, but owns about 1,000 acres, besides 500 head of cattle. This fine property he has amassed entirely by his own exertions. In some years he has handled several thousand head of cattle, and is regarded as a leading man in this interest. He is a member of the Knights of Pythias, and he and his wife are members of the Methodist Episcopal Church. William Cook, his father, was prominent in Masonic circles. The Cooks, father and son, may be called life-long Democrats.

FRANCIS MARION KIDD, one of the leading citizens of Austin County, was born in North Carolina, September 1, 1844, a son of Robert and Rebecca (Hitchcock) Kidd, natives, respectively, of Virginia and North Carolina. Mr. and Mrs. Kidd were married in North Carolina and came to Texas in 1849, locating in Jefferson County. Mr. Kidd was born in 1778, and died at the remarkable age of one hundred and sixteen years, three months and two days. He was a temperate man in every way, though he was a moderate user of alcoholic stimulants and tobacco. He was of English descent. Mr. and Mrs. Kidd had seven children: H. S., who, as a Confederate soldier, disappeared at the second battle of Atlanta; Sarah, deceased; F. M., George W., Treasurer of Jefferson County; Annie E., wife of C. C. Caswell; Martha, deceased; Mary E., wife of Major N. H. Cook, of Austin County. Francis Marion Kidd was educated in the common schools of Jefferson County. At the age of seventeen he enlisted in the Confederate service, and was on active duty until the close of the war in the artillery and afterward in the navy, making a most brilliant record as a soldier, and passing into history as one who refused to surrender, even when commanded to do so by his superior officer. He returned home in June, 1865, and for a few years was engaged in farming. For fifteen years he dealt extensively in stock. For two years he resided at Sealy, then returned to his farm. In 1892 he went to Mexico, and until the spring of 1894 made his headquarters in the City of Mexico. He began his business career with a limited capital, but by the exercise of those qualities common to self-made men, has prospered satisfactorily, and now occupies a leading position in the community. Until 1875 he was employed by his father. He now owns several hundred acres of land, has considerable land under cultivation, has a good number of cows, and pays particular attention to dairy interests, owns a handsome residence and other good improvements. Mr. Kidd was married January 1, 1885, to Mrs. Vada Hackney, daughter of John W. and Elizabeth (Cook) Greer, formerly the wife of K. C. Hackney, deceased. Mr. and Mrs. Kidd are members of the Methodist Episcopal Church. Mr. Kidd is a prominent member of the Knights of Honor and is a leading Democrat, though he has never been an office seeker.

DR. WILLIAM DE RYEE. This skillful and well known chemist of Corpus Christi, Texas, was born in Wurzburg, Bavaria, in 1825, the son of Nicholas and Augusta De Ryee, the former of whom was born in France and the latter in Saxony. He pursued his professional studies in Munich, paying special attention to chemistry, geology and natural philosophy. In March, 1848, he participated in the revolution of that country, joining the people against the King. After the election of the Archduke Johan, of Austria, as administrator of the German Commonwealth, by the People's Parliament in Frankfurt, he went to Holland, where he embarked for the New World. After a stormy voyage of fifty-six days he landed in the city of New York. With a German colony he then came to Tennessee, and there erected a cotton-seed oil mill, the first in the United States, in the year 1849, also invented a machine to hull cotton-seed. The works eventually burned down, but not until the success of the invention had been assured. Succeeding this he prospected for copper in the Alleghenies, traced the Ducktown copper belt into Virginia, and discovered in North Carolina the mica, asbestos and graphite deposits, which at the present time are so successfully worked. In 1856 he came to Texas, on his way to the mines in Arizona, but being struck with the salubrious climate and the resources of Southwest Texas, he stopped at San Antonio, where he began his work as a chemist, and in connection with this he engaged in photography, and invented "Photographic Transparencies," which he exhibited in St. Louis, Cincinnati and other large cities. In 1857 he invented a new photo printing process, which he called homeography, by which process the Texas Cotton Bonds were printed during the war. In 1859 he had an illustrated and biographical album of the members of the Eighth Legislature and the heads of the departments printed, a richly ornamented copy of which was presented by the citizens of Austin to President Buchanan. In 1860 he made a prospecting tour into Mexico, discovered the copper veins near Candela and the Sabine coal fields, returning at the outbreak of the war. The military board of Texas, to supply an indispensable article of which the troops and people were destitute, contracted with him to erect a percussion cap factory. He was given complete charge of the works and the enterprise under his able and faithful management proved a decided success. In connection with this factory he erected a copper-refining furnace and steam copper rolling machinery, both of new designs, also manufactured explosion balls, smokeless powder and torpedo igniters. The rocks of the furnace he had quarried from the soapstone deposits in Leona County. Towards the end of the war he resigned his State position and accepted appointment as Chemist of the Confederate Nitre and Mining Bureau. His reports upon the nitre caves in Texas and their proposed utilization were highly complimented by the Chief of Bureau in Richmond, and he was ordered to organize a prospecting party for the discovery of copper and lead ores. While preparing for said expedition the war came to a close. In 1865 Dr. De Ryee went to New York, purchased a stock of goods, and in January, 1866, opened a drug store in Corpus Christi, which business is now under the capable control of his son, Mr. Charles H. De Ryee. In 1867 he opened a copper-mine in Archer County, and reported the discovery of the permean formation in said and adjoining counties. A United States and State Geologist disagreed with this report, but the fossils found there are now in the collection of the celebrated Paleonthologist, Prof. Cape, in Philadelphia, and prove the correctness of Dr. De Ryee's statement upon this important discovery. Returning home he found Corpus Christi in the midst of a yellow fever epidemic. After the death of all resident physicians and druggists, among them a son, Emil De Ryee, and failures of the usual remedies in an atmosphere putrefied from the remains of a badly managed beef packery, he introduced an antiseptic treatment—solution of chlorine and solution of creosote alternately every hour, and one of the incoming physicians also adopting it, over 200 patients, so treated, recovered. During the year 1878 he convinced the county authorities that the yellow fever existed in New Orleans, was appointed one of the health officers, and strict quarantine enforced. The New Orleans authorities denied the existence of yellow fever. However, a terrible epidemic followed, and Corpus Christi, through timely precaution, escaped. Sometime afterwards he again prospected in Mexico and invested in real estate in Monterey and in Tapa Chica, where he practiced medicine, and acted as volunteer Signal Officer, reporting to Gen. Greeley in Washington. Under contract with the Laredo Improvement Co. he made a geological survey of the counties of Webb and Encinal, showing in his report how some valuable mineral deposits in the prevailing Eocene formations may be profitably utilized. His scientific attainments eminently fitted him for the office as Commissioner of his district to the exposition at New Orleans, where he had charge of the geological exhibit. He has a handsome residence on the bluff of the Rio Grande above Laredo, and "from turret to foundation stone" nature and science can everywhere be found. His home is filled with valuable collections of science and curios of all kinds—specially representing the resources of the country through which the Mexican National Railway passes, the detailed description of which would occupy too much space. All has not been said when it is stated that the collection is very valuable and varied, but it must be seen to be appreciated. Dr. De Ryee was married in 1849, and his union resulted in the birth of five children. He has held the office of District Surveyor of a large part of Southern Texas for several years, and then, under the Reconstruction, not being willing to take the "iron-clad oath," he resigned. He is a man of fine intellect, cultured and refined and he is an original thinker. He is active and vigorous, both mentally and physically, and is still the leader of his family, as well as its patriarch.

GEORGE H. NORTHINGTON. It has been said that the study of biography yields to no other subject in point of interest and profit, and while it is true that all biographies, and more especially those of successful men, have much in common, yet the life sketches of no two individuals are alike. Each has its distinctions and various points of interest, and each is accordingly complete in itself. In biographies of the older Texans this is intensified, and perhaps it is not too much to say that in the field of sketches of interest and reminiscences the State of Texas affords the reaper a mine unequaled and unsurpassed. Among the well-known successful men of business and planters of Wharton County, Texas, is George H. Northington, a member of the mercantile firm of Duncan & Northington. His paternal grandfather, Andrew Northington, was a product of the Old North State and an early settler of Texas, settling in this State in 1831, Brazoria County. He had left his family in Kentucky, and later he brought them here and settled on the Bernard River. This family experienced all the hardships usual to new settlers, and Mr. Northington helped to fight the Mexicans and Indians, as well as subdue the wilderness. Andrew Northington married Priscilla Dawson, of Kentucky, in the year 1819. From this union two children were born: first, Rachel Ann, who married Joel Hudgins, a member of an extensive family whose descendants yet live in Texas; second, Mentor Northington, the father of the subject of this sketch. Mentor Northington, his son and the father of our subject, was born in Trigg County, Ky., whither his father had moved from

North Carolina, and later came with the family to Texas. When only fourteen years of age he served in the field under the command of General Green against the Indians, and was rewarded for his services with the grant of a headright in Jones County, Texas. The same ancestral acres are now in possession of his descendants. There his death occurred in 1888. He also served in Scott's company, organized in Washington County, and fought with his command at Sabine Pass and other engagements during the Civil War. He married Miss Elizabeth E. Heard, daughter of Capt. W. J. E. Heard and America Morton, who was a native of Tennessee, but subsequently emigrated to Alabama, and from that State came to Jackson County, Texas, with an Alabama colony. They were the parents of Quinn and Susan Ann Heard. Soon after Captain Heard removed to Caney, then in Colorado County, latterly made a portion of Wharton County, when organized in 1846 by an act of the first Legislature. The site of his new home gained the name of Egypt, owing to an occurrence which took place in its early history, brought about by the scarcity of grain in the land while Captain Heard's settlement teemed with plenty. Here he lived and prospered until after the late Civil War, moving thence to Washington County, Texas, and died there ripe in years, a true patriot who had served Texas long and well. This Captain Heard was a man of note in his day, a bold, hardy pioneer, who offered up his fortune for his adopted county and threw aside all for the independence of his beloved Texas when the dark war cloud burst upon the colonies and the tyrant Santa Anna, with his black angels of death, gathered like the swoop of a whirlwind around the defenseless people. It was then Captain Heard drew about him kindred spirits, formed them into a company and joined the patriot army under General Houston before the field of San Jacinto. With his company (Company F) forming part of the First Regiment, commanded by Col. Edward Burleson, he fought upon that fated day. It was his company that first reached the Mexican cannoneers, and with the cry, "Remember the Alamo!" brained the gunners at their pieces. When, in 1842, Texas was threatened by Mexican invasion, we find, from an address to the people of Texas, issued and signed by Andrew Northington and Thomas Thatcher, urging the patriots to arm for resistance, Captain Heard already in the field with his company, stationed at Victoria. He participated with the early settlers in opposing the ravages of the Indians, and was in several bloody and desperate engagements. As a planter he was unusually successful, and his Egypt place was one of the best improved in the State, with a substantial brick residence, brick barns and quarters for his negroes. He raised annually immense quantities of cotton and heavy outputs of sugar. His daughter Elizabeth was born in Alabama, in 1827, and died in 1892. As a child she, in 1836, suffered the hardships consequent to the flight of the settlers before the ravages of invading Mexicans. Her marriage with Mentor Northington resulted in the birth of two sons: William A., who is a planter and merchant of Egypt, and our subject. The latter's birth occurred in Wharton County, Texas, in 1854, and his schooling was gained in the University at Chapel Hill and Randolph Macon College in Virginia. In his choice of an occupation in life he took planting and trading in stock, and has followed this constantly since. In the year 1881 he formed a co-partnership in business as merchants with Hon. Green C. Duncan. The business has prospered under the firm's methods, and to-day they number among the largest dealers in Wharton County. Their storehouse and ginhouse establishments, farm houses and shops comprise a miniature city, bustling with thrift and business activity. In 1875 Mr. Northington espoused in marriage Miss Jessie Simmons, of Chapel Hill, formerly of Greensborough, Ala., and daughter of J. S. and Sarah E. Logan. Eight children have blessed this union, three sons and five daughters, as follows: Mentor, Jessie Josephine, Nettie Elizabeth, Sadie Francis, Mamie Duncan, George Heard, Ruth Virginia and William Andrew. Of Mr. George Northington himself, he can fairly be called a representative citizen of Texas, descended of hardy and thoroughgoing stock. He is proud of his native State, of her wealth and prosperity, and points back with pride five generations to the manner born. The elemental forces, which were strong points in his ancestors, are strongly outlined in his character. Upright and honest, he has served his people in public trusts, and has their confidence as a worthy citizen.

EDWIN HOLLAND TERRELL, LL.B., was born at Berksville, Indiana, November 21, 1848, the youngest of the eleven children of Rev. Williamson and Martha (Jerrell) Terrell. His father who was a prominent and efficient minister of the gospel, long well known in central and southern Indiana, died in 1873. When his mother died, in 1849, Edwin, who was scarcely a year old, was taken into the family and reared under the care of George Holland, an eminent jurist, at Richmond, Ind. He entered De Pauw University (then Asbury University) in 1867, and was graduated in 1871 with the valedictory honors of a class of thirty-three members. In his freshman year he was initiated into Delta Chapter of the Beta Theta Pi, was corresponding secretary of the Chapter for three years, and represented it at the conventions held at Columbus in 1869, and at Chicago in 1870. He was Vice-president of one of the later conventions held at Chicago, and President of the first convention which was held at Wooglin. He has always taken an active interest in matters of this fraternity, having been one of the three founders of the Wooglin Club, and one of the associate editors of the last catalogue.

In 1871, soon after his graduation from De Pauw University, Mr. Terrell came to Texas as an attache of the United States army, his brother, Col. C. M. Terrell, being stationed here. After spending about ten months at San Antonio, and in the State, he accompanied Col. Terrell to Omaha, Neb., and was on the western frontier until the fall of 1872, when he resigned his position to enter the senior class at Harvard Law School. He was graduated with the degree of LL.B. in 1873, and subsequently became a member of the Harvard Chapter on its reorganization. Mr. Terrell pursued his studies in Europe in 1873 and 1874, incidental to which he attended the lectures of the Sorbonne, Paris. Returning in 1874 he began the practice of his profession in Indianapolis, Ind., where he was admitted to the bar. He soon associated himself with Messrs. Barber and Jacobs, two prominent and successful attorneys, under the firm name of Barber, Jacobs & Terrell. In the summer of 1877 he removed to San Antonio, where he has since resided. He practiced law for about a year after taking up his residence in San Antonio, and then retired to give his attention to other important interests. He soon became identified with several prominent enterprises, as Vice-president of the San Antonio Gas Company, as one of the promoters and constructors of the San Antonio & Aransas Pass Railroad, as Vice-president of the San Antonio Board of Trade, and otherwise. His activity in these important concerns was of the greatest benefit to San Antonio, and won him the esteem and admiration of the best citizens.

In 1887, although a Republican, Mr. Terrell was nominated by the Citizen's Committee of One Hundred for Mayor of San Antonio, and at the election came within a few hundred votes of defeating the regular Democratic nominee. Since casting in his lot with the Texans Mr. Terrell has taken a leading part in the counsels of the Republican party of that State. He was a delegate to the Republican National Conventions held in Chicago in 1880 and in 1888. Of the last National Convention he was one of the honorary secretaries, and he was selected as a member of its committee on notification. In 1889, when President Harrison nominated Mr. Terrell to be United States Minister to Belgium, the San Antonio *Daily Express* (Dem.) said editorially: "In appointing Mr. Terrell to the Belgian ministry President Harrison secured the services of a gentleman, and a sober, reliable, competent, painstaking business man—one who has been a Northerner, and was never a carpetbagger; who has been a Republican, and was never a 'radical;' who has lived in the South, and was never spit upon because of his nativity; who has exercised his political rights, and was never bulldozed or shotgunned; who is able to give a good account of himself and the people among whom he has resided. His selection reflects credit upon him and upon the administration which knew enough to choose him."

Mr. Terrell's diplomatic experience has been varied and extensive, he having taken part in a number of noted conferences during his four years' official residence abroad. He was Plenipotentiary on the part of the United States in the International Congress on the Slave Trade, which was in session at Brussels from November, 1889, to July, 1890, and which drew up the slave trade treaty, or what is known as the "General Act of Brussels," the effect of which has been to bring ruin to the Arab slave-traders and man-hunters in Central Africa. In January, 1892, Secretary Blaine summoned Mr. Terrell to Washington to assist him in the ratification of this treaty, then pending in the Senate and subsequently ratified.

In July, 1890, Mr. Terrell was Special Plenipotentiary for the United States in the International Conference, which met at Brussels, and drafted the treaty for the publication of the Customs Tariffs of most of the countries of the world, which treaty was afterwards ratified by our Government. In November and December, 1890, he represented the United States on what is known as the "Commission Technique," an outgrowth of the Anti-Slavery Conference, which elaborated a tariff system for the Conventional Basin of the Congo, as defined in the treaty of Berlin of 1885. In this special commission the United States had important commercial interests at stake, and, during its session, Mr. Terrell obtained a formal declaration, agreed to by all the interested powers having possessions in the Congo Basin and by all the ratifying powers of the Berlin treaty, guaranteeing to the United States and its citizens all the commercial rights, privileges and immunities in the entire Conventional Basin of the Congo possessed by the signatory powers to the treaty of Berlin. In 1891 Mr. Terrell obtained the removal by the Belgian Government of the onerous and discriminating quarantine regulations which had been applied to live stock shipped from the United States to Belgium, and which had practically destroyed that industry in the latter country. During that year he negotiated with King Leopold a treaty of "Amity, Commerce and Navigation" between the United States and the Congo State, which was subsequently ratified by the President and Senate. In November, 1893, Mr. Terrell was appointed one of the delegates on the part of the United States to the International Monetary Conference at Brussels, and on its assembling, was selected as its Vice-president. He delivered, on the part of the Conference, the reply in French to the address of welcome pronounced by Prime Minister Beernaert. His ready command of the French language and his surpassing powers as an entertainer greatly contributed to the social success of the American Legation during his ministry at Brussels. October 1, 1893, after his return to private life, Mr. Terrell received by Royal decree of King Leopold II, the decoration of "Grand Officer of the Order of Leopold" an honor rarely conferred and one which indicated the highest personal esteem of the King and the successful character of Mr. Terrell's mission.

In 1892, De Pauw University conferred upon Mr. Terrell the honorary degree of LL. B. He is a thirty-second degree Mason and belongs to all the divisions of the order represented at Indianapolis. He is prominent also in Knights of Pythias circles and is a member of the Military Order of the Loyal Legion. Mr. Terrell was married in the summer of 1874 to Miss Mary Maverick, only daughter of Hon. Samuel A. Maverick, a pioneer and long a well known citizen of San Antonio. Mrs. Terrell died at the United States Legation at Brussels in January, 1891. Six children survived her: Maverick L., a student at De Pauw University; George Holland, Martha, Luvis, Mary and Dorothy. Mr. Terrell has recently erected one of the most elegant residences in San Antonio.

HON. JOHN ADRIANCE. The name Adriance has been identified with the growth and progress of this country for many generations, and this family trace their ancestry in America back to the settling of New Amsterdam. The Adriance and Brinkerhoff families were closely connected, and were prominent and influential in the section in which they lived. Among those who are justly entitled to be enrolled among the makers of the great common-wealth of Texas is John Adriance, who has been a resident of the State for nearly sixty years. He was born at Troy, N. Y., November 10, 1818, and when but a child, was left fatherless. His father, George C. Adriance, was a hatter and fur dealer, and a man of excellent business ability. He resided at Troy, N. Y., and although heavily insured, lost heavily by the great fire there. Socially a Mason, he was a very prominent member of that order. John Adriance secured a good education in his native town, and later attended a select school at Truxton, N. Y. After the death of his father he lived with an uncle, Hon. John Miller, who was an eminent physician and a member of the United States Congress. In the stores of Truxton our subject received an excellent business training and later went to Berlin, Chenango County, N. Y., where he was in the employ of the Farmers and Mechanics' Cotton Manufacturing Co. Still later he entered the employ of John Haggerty & Sons, the largest house in New York City, an auction house dealing in package goods. At the suggestion of his uncle he made up his mind to come to Texas for his health, and left there on the 25th day of October, 1835, on the schooner Julius Cæsar and engaged as a clerk for Townsend & Jones. He did not expect to remain, but settled at Bell's Landing, Texas, subsequently named Marion, and for many years past known as Columbia, and has since made his home there. He is truly a Texas veteran, having served in Capt. Jacob Eberly's

Volunteer Company of thirty-five mounted men, detailed by Gen. Sam Houston before he crossed the Brazos at Groce's, to remain at Marion until all the families fleeing before the enemy had crossed the river. Being cut off from reaching the army across the country, they thus made their way to San Luis, where they crossed the Pass with the aid of a yawl from the steamer Yellowstone, and by a night march reached the east end of Galveston Island. The following morning, the steamboat Laura started with provisions and volunteers with the hope of reaching the army, when Capt. Eberly and fifteen of his men (including the subject of this sketch) volunteered as part of the guard on the steamer, and the balance remained as a corps of observation on the island. At Redfish Bar they met the steamer "Cayuga" with Mexican prisoners and the glad tidings of the battle of San Jacinto. Returning to the island, they embarked for the battleground on the steamer Yellowstone. When Santa Anna and his officers were placed aboard the Yellowstone, he was one of the volunteer guard while lying in the stream, thence to Galveston Island, where they were transferred to the steamer Laura and accompanied them to Velasco. Mr. Adriance is one of the oldest merchants of Texas, now living, having commenced business with Mr. C. Beardslee at West Columbia during the first session of Texas Congress in 1836 and 1837, under the firm name of Beardslee & Adriance. This firm was dissolved in the spring of 1839. In the fall of 1839 in connection with Col. Morgan L. Smith, formerly of the City of New York, an ex-Alderman of that city, and the first Colonel of the celebrated Seventh Regiment of that city, he took the first regular stock of goods to the present Capital of Texas, Austin, under the firm name of John Adriance & Co. Disposing of this stock, he returned to Columbia on the 1st of January, 1840, and entered into business with Colonel Smith under the firm name of Smith & Adriance, which continued for several years. Columbia, at that period, was the trading point for a good portion of the State. At the close of this co-partnership, Mr. Adriance continued in mercantile pursuits until the close of the war, when he retired. He was the first to volunteer to enter the Confederate service during the Civil War, but on account of his age was not accepted. He built the war house here. At one time he owned most of the land on which Columbia now stands and still owns quite extensive interests. Merchandising has been his principal business in life, and as he is a man thoroughly trustworthy and reliable, and possesses a true appreciation of all the requirements of his line, he amassed quite a fortune previous to the war. Mr. Adriance was one of the incorporators of the Galveston & Brazos Canal, and, through his influence, New York merchants contributed many thousands of dollars towards the completion of the enterprise. He and Col. M. L. Smith were the first owners of the Waldeck plantation, where they started the manufacture of sugar, but later he sold out his interest. Mr. Adriance was one of the most earnest workers and contributors in building the Houston Tap and Brazoria railroad and its extension to Wharton, and for three years was in charge of the Immigration Department of the International & Great Northern Railway, at Palestine. He was a member of the Thirteenth Legislature of Texas, nominated at Galveston without his knowledge until two days after it was made, and has often been solicited to run for the same office, which he has declined, preferring the quiet paths of life. He has taken a deep interest in the welfare of the Agricultural and Mechanical College of Texas since its first establishment, also of the

Prairie View State Normal School, and a member of the Board of Directors at this time. He is a prominent Mason and Past Grand High Priest of the Grand Royal Arch Chapter of Texas, and well known throughout the state. He joined this order in 1851. For twenty-five years he was a member of the committee of work in Grand Chapter. In the A. & M. College, he was a member of the Finance Committee for five years, first with L. L. Foster and now J. E. Hollingsworth. Mr. Adriance was married in Watertown, N. Y., to Miss Lydia A. Cook, daughter of Dr. Cook, a surgeon in the United States navy. She died in 1871, leaving one son, Duncan, who is Associate Professor of Chemistry in the A. & M. College, and a daughter who is now Mrs. George C. Munson of this county, and an unmarried daughter at his home. After her death Mr. Adriance married Mrs. D. E. Nash, a sister of his former wife. He is a member of the Episcopal Church, and has been a Lay Reader many years. Time has dealt leniently with him and he bids fair to enjoy many years more of usefulness.

HON. GREEN C. DUNCAN, of Wharton County. There is such uniformity in the great body of men that but little profit could result from the study of most of them. Occasionally an unusual character is developed, either physically, morally, or intellectually, and so impresses itself upon the people, within the reach of its influence, that it deserves to be noted and studied. The subject of this sketch is such a character. He is a native Kentuckian, born near Bloomfield, Ky., October 10, 1841, and the son of Green Duncan, whose father went to Kentucky from Virginia many years ago. He is of Scotch blood. His paternal grandparents were Thomas Duncan and Mary Green. The latter's parents, Levin Green and Mary Ellis. Thomas Duncan's parents were Coleman Duncan and Mary Lyne. His grand father, Henry Duncan, whose father was Henry Duncan, Sr., came from Scotland to Virginia. The mother of the subject of our sketch was Nancy C. Wilson, whose father was Isaac Wilson (whose parents were Robert Wilson and Mary Vance) and mother, Jannette Sutherland, whose parents were John Sutherland and Annie Cameron, sister of Archibald Cameron, the Presbyterian preacher.

Green Duncan, the father of the subject of our sketch held many positions of trust and honor in his native State. When a young man was Sheriff of his county for several years, and also was a member of the Legislature, and especially made his influence felt when matters of moment were under consideration. He was a Clay Whig in politics. His death occurred in 1869, when seventy-two years old. In Center College, Danville, Ky., our subject received some education, but left his books to enlist in the Confederate army in 1861 in a company going from Kentucky to Memphis, Tenn., in August or September of that year. At first he was in Col. Marsh Walker's Tennessee Regiment, and was made Sergeant and promoted to Lieutenant. When General Macall surrendered Island No. 10, the subject of our sketch with his command was captured and sent North where he remained a prisoner from May until September. After being exchanged he was transferred to the Eighth Kentucky Infantry, which regiment was afterwards mounted and placed under the command of General Forrest. He was in the battles of Coffeeville, Champion's Hill, Baker's Creek, Harrisburg, Franklin, Nashville, and Murfreesboro, and the different engagements from Montevallo to Selma, Ala. He surrendered with the Confederate army at Columbus, Miss., after the battle of Selma, Ala. During his service he had four horses shot under him, and one shot after dismounting and while standing beside him, but was never wounded. After the surrender he rode horseback to Memphis, Tenn., and then took steamer for Kentucky. After a few months stay at his home in Kentucky, he came to Texas to look after a track of land he inherited, and was so favorably impressed with the country that he decided to make it his home. In 1872, he purchased the land which is now his home, and he now has one of the lovliest homes in the section. He has been trading in stock ever since locating here and has driven stock from Mexico. In 1881, he formed a partnership with George H. Northington in the mercantile and stock business. In 1890, Mr. Duncan was elected to the Legislature from the sixty-six Floatorial districts (composed of the counties of Wharton, Matagorda, Brazoria and Galveston.) He served on several very important committees. He made a fine record and was an efficient, working member. Though solicited by his friends to again become a candidate, he positively refused, saying that politics had no charms for him and that his business required his whole attention. July 11, 1872, he married Miss Mamie J. Bowie, of Matagorda County, a daughter of George Bowie (whose parents were John Bowie and Sarah Harwell) and Francis Millhouse (whose parents were Philip Millhouse and Rebecca Vasser.) They have five children, Nantie, Harris, Vance, Bowie, and Donald. Mrs. Duncan is a member of the Episcopal Church.

DR. RUDOLPH MENGER, City Physician of San Antonio, is a native of Texas, and was born in that city in 1851. He is the son of Simon M. and Augusta M. Menger, both parents being natives of Thuringia, Germany, who came to Texas in 1846, landing at old Indianola. Mr. Menger had been well educated in Germany, was a thorough musician, and had there taught school and music. From Indianola he pushed inland to Comal County, and located on a farm near New Braunfels; at the same time he began teaching vocal music. He moved to Bexar County, and located on a farm a few miles from San Antonio, and from his home he rode into San Antonio and gave singing lessons. Some of the people of San Antonio remember how he rode in from the country, horseback, to teach music. About 1850 or a little earlier, he moved to the city, and probably continued teaching music incidentally for several years. About 1858 he started a soap factory, the first every conducted in all the southwest. The business was conducted in a small way at first, and the proprietor of the new enterprise saw many discouraging days, but it was always advancing toward success, and in later times he had the satisfaction of seeing his business flourish, and the trade was extended to many points in Mexico. Several of his sons were associated with him in business, as they grew to manhood, and his son Erick conducts the business still. August went to Houston and started in business there for himself, and established a flourishing house which he conducted till his death in 1893. Two sons, Oscar and August, served in the Confederate army; August served till the close, but Oscar was twice severely wounded and, disabled from his wounds, was compelled to return home. The father died in 1892 at the ripe age of eighty-five years; he was a prominent Mason. The mother had died some years prior. Our subject's primary education was secured in San Antonio, and he began life as a clerk in Kalteyer's drug store, and then under the able instruction of the proprietor, he also began the study of pharmacy. He was thus engaged from 1866 to 1869, when he went to Germany, and entered the University of Leipsic, in Saxony, where he began the study of medicine. He spent five years in study there, and graduated in November, 1874. He returned at once to San Antonio, and became assistant surgeon in the United States army till the close of 1875, when he was appointed city physician, and served till 1881; then for several years he devoted his time to his private practice, which became quite extended. In 1892, he was again appointed to the office of City Physician, and is now serving in that office to the satisfaction of all. In fact he has greatly improved the appointment of the city hospital, and that institution under his direction is almost perfect in its operation and utility. He also has a large general practice; is an active member of the West Texas Medical Society, and does some occasional contributing for various medical journals. He was for a long time medical examiner for the New York Medical Life Insurance Company, and many other old line companies. He was married, in 1879, to Miss Barbara C. Menger, a native of San Antonio, and daughter of William L. Menger of the same family name, but no kin. Her father was an old and well known pioneer to San Antonio, from Germany. He erected the Menger Hotel, one of the finest hotels in all the United States, and a popular resort to all visitors to the Alamo City. He was a very prominent and active citizen of San Antonio, and started the first brewery in the city. To the union of our subject and wife, seven children have been born: Minnie, born July 4, 1880; Eddie, August, Louis, Gustave, Rudolph, Jr., and an infant son, unnamed.

ENOCH JONES (deceased), of San Antonio, Texas, was one of the early and most successful merchants of that city for years. He was born at Worcester, Ohio, in 1802, son of the Rev. Thomas Griffith Jones, of Wales, who immigrated to the United States from that country first to Pennsylvania, and soon pushed on further west to or near Massillon, Ohio. He was the first Baptist minister west of the Alleghany Mountains. He became very prominent in many ways, and must have been a most active and able man. He became a member of the Ohio State Legislature and a banker, besides being engaged in other business. Enoch Jones was principally self-educated, and at about the age of twelve years entered the grocery store of Mr. Alexander, and at that early age began his long, successful and honorable business career. Before his majority he secured the contract to construct the locks and the western division of the Pennsylvania Canal, and in his younger years constructed the dam at Johnstown, one of the first large reservoir dams ever erected in this country. From Massillon he moved to Detroit, and began a most extensive business for that time, starting a store in the city and engaging, on a large scale, in lumber manufacturing in that thickly wooded country. He married, in 1838, Mrs. Olive Ann Selkrig Hoyt (see sketch of James H. French). The business in Detroit not proving successful, he came in 1839 to Texas, and in partnership with Mr. Smith began the extensive purchase of wild land. After a short time he returned North, settling in St. Louis, and again starting a most extensive commercial business, and founded a trade that extended throughout all the Southwest. In this enterprise he was associated with several other gentlemen, and the business was pushed to inconvenient extents for the means of transportation and communication in that early day. At the same time Mr. Smith, in Texas, was making large land purchases, but dying about 1845 it prompted Mr. Jones to close out his interest in St. Louis and again return to Texas. He now located for a short time in the country, but soon erected a one-story building on Military Plaza and started one of the first large businesses of San Antonio. This building is still standing, but the business was removed to a two-story building erected at the corner of Market street on Main Plaza, and was there conducted till the outbreak of the Civil War. It was then suspended. For years this house, which was composed of our subject and Mr. J. Ulrich, was one of the largest in all the South. During all this time he was a large stock-raiser and one of the largest land owners in Texas. He had a most excellent mind for business, as his success shows. His most excellent wife died in 1848, leaving two daughters, Olive Ann—Mrs. T. A. Washington, and Flora Kate—Mrs. H. B. Adams. Mr. Jones was married again to Miss Charlotte Thompkins, a native of New York, where she was well educated. She came to Texas in the early '50s, locating as a school teacher at Nachatoches. She soon came to San Antonio and became a successful teacher, till her marriage to Mr. Jones. To this union there were several children. One son, Enoch Griffith, is Justice of Precinct No. 1 of Bexar County. He was educated at the University of the South at Sewanee, Tenn., and at Washington and Lee College, Lexington, Va. Mr. Enoch Jones was an extensive and successful merchant, stock-raiser and land owner. He acquired through foresight, good judgment and sound business methods a landed estate of forty Spanish leagues, equal to nearly 175,-000 acres. All his personal estate, which was very large, consisting of merchandise, horses, sheep, cattle, implements, etc., and nearly the whole of this princely domain was lost to his heirs, partly through vicissitudes consequent upon the Civil War, but mainly through mismanagement and "vile indirection." We copy a description of Mr. Jones' country home: "The Jones mansion was built by Mr. Enoch Jones before the war as a family residence, and we doubt that there is a building in San Antonio to-day that compares with it in its substantial character and convenience. It is a two-story square building, with a half-basement story. It contains fourteen large rooms and three wide halls, facing the south, with galleries running the full length of the building. The stone used in the building is a grayish sandstone, almost equal to granite, and certainly superior to any limestone used in our city. So substantial is the work that after twenty years no crack or flaw is found in the walls. Mr. Jones was a gentleman of wealth and possessed excellent taste. He built the mansion for the enjoyment of his family and the entertainment of his friends. An immense cistern catches the water from the roof for the use of the family, and a drain takes from the premises all slops and refuse material. The mansion stands on a natural plateau, commanding a magnificent sweep of country. The bright, murmuring Medina meanders at the foot of the plateau, and standing on the galleries you have a view of wood, of valley and of distant hills which, even in winter nakedness, is entrancingly lovely. The lines of two railroads—International and Sunset—are discernable less than a mile away. Mr. Jones had a large flock of sheep here twenty-one years ago, and the mansion, stables, sheds and stone walls attest the permancy of the improvements made."

THORNTON AUGUSTIN WASHINGTON (deceased), the eighth child of John Thornton Augustin and Elizabeth Conrad (Bedinger) Washington, was a descendant of Col. Samuel Washington, the full brother of the first President of the United States. He was born at "Berry Hill," afterwards "Cedar Lawn," near Charleston, Jefferson County, Virginia (now West Virginia), January 22, 1826. He was educated at the old Charleston Academy and at home under a private tutor, and then finished his education at Princeton College, where he graduated. He was then appointed, by the Hon. William Lucus, a cadet at West Point, and entered that Military Academy in June, 1845. He graduated in June, 1849.

"Statement of the military service of T. A. Washington, late of the United States army, compiled from this office:

"He was a cadet at the United States Military Academy from June 1st, 1845, to July 1st, 1849, when he graduated and was appointed a Brevet Second Lieutenant, Sixth United States Infantry; June 26, 1850, was promoted to Second Lieutenant, and to First Lieutenant December 8, 1855.

"He joined his regiment November 8, 1849, and served with it in Nebraska to August, 1850; in Texas to September 8, 1853; on leave to April 8, 1854; with regiment in Texas to May 20, 1854, and recruiting service to June 30, 1855; on duty at United States Military Academy to November 1, 1856; with regiment in Texas to May 29, 1859; Acting Assistant Adjutant General, Headquarters Department of Texas, to February, 1860; at San Antonio, Texas, in charge of regimental records, to May 26, 1860; with regiment in Texas to December 24, 1860; Aid-de-camp to Gen. David E. Twiggs, commanding the Department of Texas, to March 6, 1861; Acting Assistant Quartermaster and Acting Assistant Commissary of Subsistence at Indianola, Texas, to April 8, 1861, upon which date he resigned.

(Signed)   "CHAUNCY MCKEEVER,
                                      "*Asst. Adj't General.*"

He was selected, October 13, 1851, by the regimental commander, under orders of Gen. Persifer F. Smith, to command a mounted escort to Maj. Wm. H. Emory, United States Topographical Engineer, Astronomer and Surveyor, United States and Mexican boundary commission, and outfit, from Fort Merrill, on the Rio Sico, sixty miles west of San Antonio, Texas, to Frontera, New Mexico, a few miles above El Paso, Texas. He then returned with his party of surveyors to Fort Duncan, Eagle Pass, Texas, reaching there about the middle of January, 1852, making a total march of about 1,500 miles in about six weeks' time. Nearly his whole time in the United States military service was spent on the extreme frontier till he resigned in 1861. He at once joined the Confederacy, and was commissioned by President Jefferson Davis Captain in the regular army of the Confederate States. He went from Texas to Richmond, Va., in August, 1861, and entered the Adjutant General's office, and was acting Adjutant General and Chief of Staff to Gen. Robert E. Lee in his organization of the Southern Atlantic States. He returned with him to Richmond in May, 1862, and was promoted to Major and Quartermaster in the regular army, and detached from General Lee's staff by President Davis on special service to the trans-Mississippi Department, where he operated in a wholly independent capacity till the close of the war. He returned to his home in San Antonio, and followed the profession of civil engineering for many years. He was appointed an examiner of the returns of the public surveys in the United States General Land Office, Department of the Interior, Washington, and died in that office at Washington, D. C., July 10, 1894. He was married in San Antonio, Texas, March 8, 1860, by the Rev. R. F. Bunting, to Miss Olive Ann, daughter of Enoch and Olive Ann Jones, of San Antonio, Texas. (See sketch of Enoch Jones). To the union of our subject and wife were born seven children: Flora May, George Thornton, Lee Washington (daughter), Sally, Lawrence Berry, Olive Ann, Elizabeth. Our subject's widow, Olive Ann (Jones) Washington, still survives him and resides in San Antonio. She was born in Detroit, Mich., September 8, 1839, and removed with her father's family, when a small child, first to St. Louis, Mo., thence to Brazos River, Texas, thence to San Antonio, where she found a permanent home. She was educated at the Moravian Female Seminary, Bethlehem, Pa., and is a refined and educated lady. Mrs. Jones' great-great-great-grandfather on her mother's side came from Glasgow, Scotland, to this country in 1730; he could only speak the Erse and Latin. His name, as he pronounced it, was William Selkriggs, but it is supposed that it was *Selkirk*, although his descendants have always written the name Selkrig. He settled in Waterbury, Conn., and was in the King's service from 1752 to 1759, and was in the battle of Abercrombie. Mrs. Jones' great-grandfather was born at Derby Narrows, May 25, 1756, and served in the War of the Revolution from 1775 to 1783, and was in Colonel Baldwin's regiment in Gen. Israel Putnam's command. He was in the battles of Long Island and New York, and was with the troop that crossed with General Washington over the East River after the battle of Long Island. He often saw General Washington. Once, as he and other soldiers were returning to their homes on sick leave, the General asked them, "Where are you going, boys?" They told him, and he said, "Go, and don't forget to come back." He was also with General Putnam at Burgoyne's surrender, in 1778, and was twenty-five years old at the close of the war. Mrs. Jones' grandfather, Lorrin Selkrig, was born December 25, 1786. He married Jemima Vassar, of Poughkeepsie, N. Y., a sister of Matthew Vassar, the founder of Vassar Female College, of that place. Their daughter, Olive Ann Selkrig, who married for her second husband Enoch Jones, was her mother. She was born November 20, 1810, and died in San Antonio, Texas, August, 1848.

JOHN HERMAN KAMPMANN (deceased), of San Antonio, stands as one of the most conspicuous examples of self-made man that this State can present. He came to San Antonio in the robust health of youth, competent in his profession and line of trade, but with scarcely money enough to pay for a day's entertainment. At the close of his long life, he died leaving monuments of wealth and hosts of friends, and no man to say that by him he had lost a dollar, but rather that in many cases great good had come to him by the aid and friendship of Mr. Kampmann. San Antonio points to him with pride. Our subject was born in Waltrop, Kreis Reibinghausen, Munster, Westphalia, Prussia, December 25, 1818, a son of John Peter and Elizabeth Selingshof. His father died when our subject was fourteen years of age, but the mother lived to old age. Our subject was educated in the elementary school, but in early youth went to Cologne, and there worked in summer and attended the university during winter. He early had a taste for all mechanical pursuits, with a strong preference for architecture and building; so to fit himself for that profession he served successively as an apprentice to the trades of carpenter, blacksmith, stone mason, plasterer, etc. About his first work while still a youth, was as a stone cutter on the great dome of the Cologne Cathedral. He was next associated with a Mr. Heiden, a builder, and with him they erected many buildings along the river Rhine. They were the builders of the Apollinaris Church, under the direction of Count Fürstenberg. He now became the Count's superintendent of construction and architecture, with whom he was on the most friendly terms. He served in the military service for three years, and was appointed to an office in the service at the expiration of the time. He again joined Mr. Heiden and Count Fürstenberg, and was the superintendent of many buildings erected by the count. Another effort was made to press him into the army, but through the influence of Count Fürstenberg he was granted a furlough to go to England, and on his departure the count said: "I am afraid Herman, you will never return." This proved true, for he did not. On reaching England, he soon sailed for America. Arriving at New Orleans, he went to Galveston, Texas, thence to Indianola, and thence in ox carts, taking two weeks to make the trip, to New Braunfels. After sojourning there a short time, he came to San Antonio, in 1848. Absolutely without means, as a friend (?) in New Braunfels had borrowed his money, he began life as a mechanic, on such building work as he could secure. After a short time he joined Mr. John Fries, an early builder in San Antonio. They soon secured several contracts, among them to erect the land office at Austin and the courthouse at Bastrop. The latter building was several years in construction, and during that time he resided in Bastrop, but returned to San Antonio in 1852. In 1850 he married Miss Caroline Bonnet, a native of Charlottenberg, Prussia, near Coblentz on the Rhine. She came to Texas with her parents, Henry Daniel and Maria Hennig, in 1845, landing at Galveston January 1. They were of the colonists for New Braunfels, and went at once to that place, but in three months came to San Antonio. Here Mr. Bonnet bought teams and did carting, also engaged in stock-raising, but had his home in the city during the remainder of his life. During the latter twenty-five years he lived retired, and died November 22, 1883, eighty-four years of age. His wife, to whom he had been married fifty-five years, survived him eleven months, she dying October, 1884. About 1852 the partnership of our subject and John Fries was dissolved, and subject from that time on continued alone, erecting the best of such buildings as were built in San Antonio before the war. At the outbreak of war, subject raised a company of Germans, becoming Captain of a company that was attached to the Third Texas Infantry. They were stationed at Camp Verde for some time, and then ordered to Brownsville, where they served on frontier defense for about one year, then went to Galveston. Here subject was promoted to Major, but his health was greatly impaired by rheumatism, and he was detailed to start a hat factory at La Grange, to make hats for the soldiers. Nearly every thing in the way of facilities and appropriate tools, etc., was lacking, but by employing mechanics from Mexico, he soon had the factory in good working order, and made thousands of hats which were turned over to Gen. Kirby Smith. He continued at that post till the end of the war. At once he resumed building in San Antonio, soon erected a large factory and planing mill for himself, to make doors, sash, blinds, etc., and for this establishment brought the first steam engine to San Antonio. Its advent was a great day for the city then. It was a most successful venture, and for a long time it afforded employment for many men, often 150. Mr. Kampmann did the work on the Menger Hotel, which later became his by purchase, when he completed this fine building to its present design; it still belongs to the estate, and has long been known as one of the best hotels in the United States. The following is quoted from a newspaper article on the completion of the Kampmann Block.

"The style of architecture in San Antonio, when Mr. Kampmann came to this city, was almost entirely Mexican. This soon changed, however, with the buildings designed and planned by Mr. Kampmann. While the contractor he often worked upon them himself. His first house was built on Alamo Plaza, and was the Bitter house, and is still standing. The next, the Stomberg house, had to make way for the Menger Hotel, and from that time dates the development of San Antonio, and with it the building of more substantial houses; so much so that Mr. Kampmann found it advisable to lay aside the pick and trowel, and go into that business as a contractor and builder. * * * He later built many houses for himself, and his last work was the erection of a large four story block on the corner of Main Plaza, West Commerce Street and Solidad Street. The only fact connected with it is that owing to the narrow street the beautiful facades do not come to that prominence which they so richly deserve. Nevertheless Mr. Kampmann has built himself a monument that will remind future generations of its projector and builder, and also recall to them the first and most successful contractor and builder of San Antonio."

In 1883 he with Mr. Edward Hoppe formed a stock company to erect a brewery. From this the Lone Star Brewery was constructed in 1884, at a cost of $150,000. He was the first President of this institution. He was also one of the projectors and organizers of the San Antonio Gas Company, and was President of this company till his death. He was the first to introduce electric bells in San Antonio. He began the erection of his handsome home, where his widow still resides, in 1854, but it was not completed till after the war. It now stands as one of the handsome homes in San Antonio. He was most sympathetic with all workmen, and he often started some work to give the needy ones work, when there was no regular employment. He erected St. Mark's Episcopal Church. This work was long delayed, but the present handsome church was at length completed. He became a member of the Masonic order, Alamo Lodge No. 44, in 1855, was quite an active Mason during all the succeeding years. Resolutions of condolence and sympathy, passed by the lodge and presented to his widow, bear this high tribute to his worth:

"His business life was successful, and he was highly esteemed for probity and upright dealing. By energy, prudence and foresight he attained a position among the business men of Texas, second to none. Socially he was urbane, courteous and polite; respected by all who knew him. As a Mason he was zealous and true, and as a husband and father he was affectionate, kind and indulgent."

In the latter years of his life he lived retired, and devoted some time to raising high grade Jersey cattle. He bought a tract of land adjoining the town, where he erected a summer home, and where he seemed to delight to spend quiet days attending to his stock. Since our subject's death his son Herman, drilled an artesian well on this place, which has a strong flow of highly impregnated sulphur water; it has proved to be most valuable for many ailments, and is destined to become much more popular as it becomes better known. Mrs. Kampmann, who has visited many noted springs in the United States and Europe for her health, has found a nearly total cure, for a long and deep-seated affliction. He died at Colorado Springs, Col., while on a visit to that resort for Mrs. Kampmann's health, September 6, 1888, and was buried at San Antonio, September 13. He left a widow and three children: Ida, was educated in Europe, in 1875 married Dr. John Herf, a brilliant young physician. He died, leaving one child, John Herf. After seven years

of widowhood, she again married to Theodore Meyer, vice-president, and one
of the partners of Meyer Bros. Drug Company, of St. Louis. To this union
there are two children: Theo and Elizabeth. Herman, who was educated at
Philadelphia, Pa., and Troy, N. Y. He is married to a most estimable
lady, Elizabeth Simpson. They have four children: Herman, Jr., Isaac, Ida and
Robert. Since his father's death he has managed the Kampmann estate,
and is besides interested in several individual enterprises, has been the
promoter of many things for San Antonio's benefit and is one of the leading
business men of the city. Gustav, was educated in Virginia and Tennessee.
Mrs. Kampmann is an active member of St. Mark's Episcopal Church, and a
worker ; is a member of the German Ladies Aid Society, and greatly interested in works of charity.

HENRY B. SHINER, of San Antonio, one of the most successful stockmen of
southwest Texas, was born in Victoria in 1848, and was the second in a family of
five children born to Peter and Emma (Hemmez) Shiner, parents, natives of Lux-
emburg, Belgium. They came to the United States in their youth, and settled in
Victoria, Texas, where they were married in 1846, the father having settled there
in 1842. He was an early merchant there, and also at an early day engaged in
stock raising. In 1858 he moved to a ranch in DeWitt County, but probably resided there no more than a year when he returned to Victoria, and
resumed the mercantile business, though he continued to conduct the ranch in
DeWitt County. In 1861 he removed with his family to San Antonio, arriving July 16. He made his future home in this city taking no active part in business. He was a strong Union man during the war, and always outspoken
when to speak one's mind on that side was often dangerous. He was quite
active in public affairs. After the war he served as County Commissioner for
some time, and was Alderman of San Antonio for a time as well. He died
October 20, 1861, at the age of sixty-five years up. His excellent wife survived
him till January 25, 1892. Our subject was educated at San Antonio and
New Orleans, but during the trying war times had little chance to attend school
or think of study. He began life for himself as a stockman, when the
State was an open range, and all things free. He was successful from the
start, and drove cattle on the trail to Abilene, Kan. Seeing that a change
was soon to occur in the method of handling and raising stock, he began
to buy land making purchases in Lavaca County, in 1875. This was a magnificent stretch of country, though the wild lands. On the construction
of the Aransas Pass Railroad, it passed for a long distance through his
property, and he donated land for a town site which was named Shiner in his
honor. This town now has a population of about 1500 people, and all the
surrounding country is a vast farm, the land proving to be very rich for
farming purposes, and is now all highly improved. Our subject still owns
town property there, and a highly improved and valuable farm of 500
acres adjoining the town, nearly all under cultivation, and all improved by
him. He also has an excellent and valuable ranch of 40,000 acres in Mc-
Mullen County, on which he has some of the best improved and graded
stock, horses and cattle, in southwestern Texas. Early in his cattle experience
in 1873, he brought improved stock to Texas—Durham cattle from Missouri,
also fine breeding horses, among the first in Lavaca County. His ranch is
well watered, lying on the Neuces River. He is a practical stock man,
has been in the business since its start almost in Texas, and has seen it

through all its changes. He has been quick to advance and improve, grasping each opportunity as it was presented. So now in the full success of the past, he can look forward to a still more prosperous future. He was married in 1874 to Miss Louie West, a native of Texas, and daughter of Washington West, who settled at Sweet Home, Lavaca County, in 1854, and was a prominent citizen of that place till his death in old age. He was an earnest supporter of the Methodist Episcopal Church. To our subject and wife, five children were born: E. May, Henry B., Jr., Lulu, Iva and Annie. Subject is a member of the Blue Lodge, Chapter and Commandry of San Antonio, in Masonry. In 1893 he erected one of the most handsome residences in San Antonio, where he now resides in comfort on Garden Street. It is a lovely home. He is a very pleasant and progressive man. In politics he is outspoken for the right as he conceives it, but not a hide bound party man—good of country first, party second.